Medieval Drama

Blackwell Anthologies

Editorial Advisers

Rosemary Ashton, University of London; Gillian Beer, University of Cambridge; Gordon Campbell, University of Leicester; Terry Castle, Stanford University; Margaret Ann Doody, Vanderbilt University; Richard Gray, University of Essex; Joseph Harris, Harvard University; Karen L. Kilcup, University of North Carolina, Greensboro; Jerome J. McGann, University of Virginia; David Norbrook, University of Oxford; Tom Paulin, University of Oxford; Michael Payne, Bucknell University; Elaine Showalter, Princeton University; John Sutherland, University of London; Jonathan Wordsworth, University of Oxford.

Blackwell Anthologies are a series of extensive and comprehensive volumes designed to address the numerous issues raised by recent debates regarding the literary canon, value, text, context, gender, genre, and period. While providing the reader with key canonical writings in their entirety, the series is also ambitious in its coverage of hitherto marginalized texts, and flexible in the overall variety of its approaches to periods and movements. Each volume has been thoroughly researched to meet the current needs of teachers and students.

Old and Middle English *c.*890–*c.*1400: An Anthology. Second edition
edited by Elaine Treharne

Medieval Drama: An Anthology
edited by Greg Walker

Chaucer to Spenser: An Anthology of English Writing 1375–1575
edited by Derek Pearsall

Renaissance Drama: An Anthology of Plays and Entertainments. Second edition
edited by Arthur F. Kinney

Renaissance Literature: An Anthology
edited by Michael Payne and John Hunter

Restoration Drama: An Anthology
edited by David Womersley

British Literature 1640–1789: An Anthology. Second edition
edited by Robert DeMaria, Jr

Romanticism: An Anthology. Third edition
edited by Duncan Wu

Children's Literature: An Anthology 1801–1902
edited by Peter Hunt

Victorian Women Poets: An Anthology
edited by Angela Leighton and Margaret Reynolds

The Victorians: An Anthology of Poetry and Poetics
edited by Valentine Cunningham

Modernism: An Anthology
edited by Lawrence Rainey

American Gothic: An Anthology 1787–1916
edited by Charles L. Crow

The Literatures of Colonial America: An Anthology
edited by Susan Castillo and Ivy T. Schweitzer

Nineteenth-Century American Women Writers: An Anthology
edited by Karen L. Kilcup

Nineteenth-Century American Women Poets: An Anthology
edited by Paula Bernat Bennett

Native American Women's Writing: An Anthology of Works *c.*1800–1924
edited by Karen L. Kilcup

MEDIEVAL DRAMA

AN ANTHOLOGY

EDITED BY **GREG WALKER**

Blackwell Publishing

BLACKWELL PUBLISHING
350 Main Street, Malden, MA 02148-5020, USA
9600 Garsington Road, Oxford OX4 2DQ, UK
550 Swanston Street, Carlton, Victoria 3053, Australia

First published 2000

6 2009

Library of Congress Cataloging-in-Publication Data

Medieval drama : an anthology / edited by Greg Walker.
p. cm. — (Blackwell anthologies)
Includes bibliographical references and index.
ISBN 978-0-631-21726-8 (alk. paper)—ISBN 978-0-631-21727-5 (pbk. : alk. paper)
1. English drama—To 1500. 2. English drama—Early modern and Elizabethan, 1500–1600. 3. Mysteries and miracle-plays, English. 4. Moralities, English. 5. Interludes. English. I. Walker, Greg. II. Series.

PR1260.M43 2000
822'.108—dc21

00-023101

A catalogue record for this title is available from the British Library.

Typeset in 9 on 10½ pt Garamond 3
by Ace Filmsetting Ltd, Frome, Somerset
Printed and bound in Singapore
by Ho Printing Singapore Pte Ltd

The publisher's policy is to use permanent paper from mills that operate a sustainable forestry policy, and which has been manufactured from pulp processed using acid-free and elementary chlorine-free practices. Furthermore, the publisher ensures that the text paper and cover board used have met acceptable environmental accreditation standards.

For further information on
Blackwell Publishing, visit our website:
www.blackwellpublishing.com

SP - small presentation
BP - big presentation
E - essay

Contents

★ Chester, The Post-Reformation Banns	201
━ Matthew Hutton's Letter to the Mayor and Council of York (1567)	206

PART II RELIGION AND CONSCIENCE: THE MORAL PLAYS   207
   Introduction   209
   Croxton, *The Play of the Sacrament*   213
   Wisdom   235
   Mankind   258
   Everyman   281

PART III POLITICS AND MORALITY: THE INTERLUDES   299
   Introduction   301
   Henry Medwall, *Fulgens and Lucres*   305
   John Skelton, *Magnyfycence*   349
   The Enterlude of Godly Queene Hester   409
   John Heywood, *The Four PP*   433
   John Heywood, *The Play of the Weather*   456
   John Bale, *Johan Baptystes Preachynge*   480
   John Bale, *The Three Laws*   493
   Sir David Lindsay, *Ane Satyre of the Thrie Estaitis*   535
     The Description of the 1540 Interlude   538
     Ane Satyre of the Thrie Estaitis (the 1552–4 text)   541

Textual Variants   624
Glossary of Common Hard Words   627

Introduction

The period from the mid-fourteenth century to the 1550s was one of the most turbulent and formative in British history, and the startling changes in religion, politics, and culture which it experienced are fully reflected in its dramatic literature. I have tried to reflect that intimate relationship between drama and its cultural context in the selection of texts for inclusion here, focusing on plays which combine dramatic quality and playability with a strong engagement with social, political, and spiritual issues. This anthology brings together for the first time generous selections from all the major dramatic genres to provide readers with a sense of the breadth and depth of dramatic activity in Britain in these years. It prints material from the narrative Cycle Plays of York and N-Town, with supporting pageants from Chester and Wakefield, demonstrating how the drama of the towns and cities of East Anglia and the North of England mediated religious culture to a heterodox urban audience, and explored biblical events in an intensely contemporary setting. Rather than selecting individual pageants from the various towns to form a synthetic cycle, as has been the case with previous anthologies, this volume contains coherent sequences of Plays from York (the Cycle from which the earliest texts survive), representing the major events in Christian history, supplemented by important material from Chester and Wakefield, and the extended *Mary Play* from the N-Town manuscript. This both allows a clear narrative line to develop and permits the comparison of the treatment of the key stories of the Creation and Fall and the Shepherds' visit to the infant Jesus between the Cycles. As a result, both the continuities between the Cycles and their distinct qualities of tone, dramaturgy, and theological emphasis can be suggested and something of that power to address and convey religious sensibilities that made them a central element in popular culture throughout the period can be felt.

In the second and third sections, the attention turns to the secular drama, the Moral Plays and Interludes performed in great halls and domestic and religious spaces throughout Britain in the late fifteenth and sixteenth centuries. The texts included demonstrate the range of themes and issues covered by these plays, from the salvation of the individual human soul to the renovation of the political nation, and the range of settings and audiences for which they were designed, from the royal courts of Henry VIII and James V to the towns and villages of East Anglia, or the playing fields of Edinburgh and Fife. The flexibility of the Interlude form is explored, as are the ways in which it was utilized by playwrights and their patrons to address issues of direct political and social concern to them and their audiences.

The title and chronology of the volume call for comment. I have deliberately named this anthology *Medieval Drama*, even though there is much within it that does not seem at first glance to be very medieval, and I would, had there been space available, have included still later material, notably the English Interludes *Respublica* and *Gorboduc*, which would have taken the volume into the reign of Elizabeth I. I chose this broad chronology chiefly because it makes most sense to set the material in its widest possible cultural context, but also in order to draw attention to the term 'medieval' itself in all its awkward glory. It, more perhaps than any other period denomination, provokes immediate and often misleading reactions. One of the greatest strengths, and weaknesses, of the term is its chronological vagueness. The limits of the medieval period are a complex and much debated issue. At one end it is bounded by the ragged frontiers of the late classical age, at the other by the much-vaunted splendours of the Renaissance. Neither boundary is clear-cut, but from either perspective 'the medieval' is, almost by definition, characterized by what has been lost, or is yet to be rediscovered. It is seen as an homogenous dark backward and abysm of time in which naiveté, superstition, and formulaic repetition replace insight and innovation, and the collective culture of the church obscures and devalues individual experience. Such prejudices are frequently encountered outside the privileged circle of the academic specialist (and not infrequently within it too), and are nowhere more prevalent than in discussions of the drama. Nowhere are they more inappropriate, either, but it is hard to counter such views in the absence of widely available and affordable editions of the plays which would refute them on every count. By making good the lack of readily accessible texts, this collection will, I hope, contribute to the ongoing rehabilitation of medieval drama that has been spearheaded by scholars, directors, and actors since the mid-1970s, and which has revealed how sophisticated, vital, and often extraordinarily idiosyncratic the plays of the period could be.

I have opted for a late terminus for this volume both to demonstrate the longevity of medieval dramatic techniques and preoccupations and in order to reflect the transitional nature of drama generally throughout this period. There was no immediate and dramatic break with the past in the later sixteenth century, albeit the building of the professional playhouses after 1567 had a crucial impact upon the culture and economics of 'playing'. But even here the boundaries were porous. The Renaissance playwrights reaped the dividends of earlier innovations, the plays designed for the playhouses were also performed in the great halls of manor houses, royal palaces, and the Inns of Court, and the forms and characters of the Moralities and Interludes were effectively revisited in archetypally 'Renaissance' plays such as Marlowe's *Faustus* and Shakespeare's *Richard III* and *1 Henry IV*.

If I have been deliberately liberal in allowing the collection to stray forward into the later sixteenth century, however, I have been brutal in my suppression of any tendency on its part to wander back beyond 1400. I have omitted all the rudimentary and fragmentary texts of the earlier period, partly on aesthetic grounds, out of a desire to provide readers and actors with whole plays to consider and perform, but partly also because they inevitably give a misleading sense of development. When set against the complete texts from a later period, they might suggest support for the now discredited evolutionary model, moving from the early liturgical experiments through the ever more sophisticated Cycles and Moralities to the Interludes, in which drama left the church for the streets and ultimately parted company with religion altogether to head off on the secular high road to the playhouses and Shakespeare. There *is* an apparent chronology to the arrangement of texts here, as the York material in the first section was in existence by the early fifteenth century, and the Interludes in the third section were all written after 1485. But any suggestion that this makes the Interludes more modern or representative of drama in the sixteenth century should be wholeheartedly resisted. The Cycle Plays were being performed (and revised and adapted) throughout the period covered by this volume (and beyond), and probably to larger audiences than any of the other plays collected here.[1] And they did not, as was once thought, die out or dwindle away through lack of interest. As the letter from Matthew Hutton to the Council of York demonstrates, they had to be actively suppressed by those who found their religious values – and their evident popularity – dangerous. Similarly, the Moralities were being copied (and in the case of *Everyman* and *Hester*, printed) well beyond the advent of the playhouses. There was no progression from simple religious plays to sophisticated secular ones. The differences in the levels of characterization between the Cycles and the Interludes have more to do with the differing conditions of indoor and outdoor drama, and the skills of the available actors, than with any supposed inferiority of the Cycle playwrights. What changed fundamentally in this period, of course, was not the drama but the culture which produced it and which it was designed to

[1] The surviving texts for Chester all date from the late sixteenth century, those from Wakefield from the mid-sixteenth.

serve. The onset of the Reformation prompted a profound rethinking of the purposes and effects of dramatic playing, and the results of that reappraisal can be seen in what follows, both in Bale and Lindsay's experiments with 'reformed drama' and in the documents printed at the end of the first section, the letter from Matthew Hutton to the Mayor and Council of York (1567), expressive of one reformer's doubts about the validity of the city's Creed play, and the Post-Reformation Banns from Chester, which sought to address such doubts and reformulate the nature and content of the Chester Cycle in a way more accessible to the new order. Although, here again, as the extracts from the late fourteenth-/early fifteenth-century *Tretise of Miraclis Pleyinge* demonstrate, such questions were not new; the reformers had simply made explicit a number of issues which had always adhered to the performance of religious drama.

Ultimately, the volume has been designed upon the principal that the plays will speak for themselves, advertising their own intellectual and theatrical qualities. Within the broad chronological sweep, and the limitations of space, the selection of texts has been as wide-ranging as possible, although I have deliberately concentrated on material from York in the biblical section, for the reasons cited above. The chance to bring together so many of these plays, and especially to set Lindsay's magnificent *Satyre of the Thrie Estaitis* in its entirety alongside the English religious and political plays of the same period, more than justifies the venture. The opportunities which the volume provides for the drawing of comparisons and contrasts, both chronologically and between genres (and, in Lindsay's case, geo-politically and linguistically too) will enable readers new to the material to gain a true sense of the riches contained in the surviving texts from the period (which are themselves, of course, only a small proportion of the works actually produced and performed), and those already familiar with it to make new connections and set favourite works alongside less familiar material.

Readers are thus faced with an *à la carte* menu from which to construct a diet after their own tastes. I have tried to convey some of what I see as the drama's greatest strengths in the choices that I have made. First and foremost I have given pride of place to plays which demonstrate theatrical vitality and playability, but I have also given room to those plays which reveal the drama's social and political concerns; its focus (bordering at times on an obsession) with social fragmentation and disorder, debate, dispute, conspiracy, and rebellion, and the attempt to resolve those fractures through the agency of the law and the exercise of authority (whether divine, royal, or domestic); its engagement with the real concerns and conditions of its audience, even when it is addressing the most refined of theological mysteries, its self-reflexive interest in the power and purposes of play and game, ritual and spectacle, and its reflection of the popular spiritualities of the period, encompassing both the desire to have access to the 'authentic' narratives of the biblical text and the potentially contradictory impulses of affective piety and Marian devotion with their focus on apocryphal materials and non-textual sources of inspiration. But I have tried to avoid too great a degree of prescriptivity in the selection and arrangement of material. Ultimately readers may follow their own way through the volume. Those interested in following the representation of gender and the issues it aroused on the medieval stage can pursue the depictions of female virtue in the York *Nativity* plays, the N-Town *Mary Play*, and the *Enterlude of Godly Queen Hester*, and of female culpability in *The Fall of Man*, *Adam and Eve*, and *Christ Before Pilate I*, and the deep vein of misogyny mined in Lindsay's *Satyre of the Thrie Estaitis* (which also explores, in its own exuberant fashion, those anxieties about male sexuality – and impotence – which are broached in the York Pageant of *Joseph's Trouble* and the depiction of Mary's spouse in the Nativity sequence). Readers concerned with political and social issues can turn to the expression of social protest and evidence of regional and class conflict in the Towneley and Chester *Shepherds' Plays*, the treatment of social abuses in *Wisdom*, and Lindsay's powerful evocation of rural poverty and the oppression and exclusion of the underclass in *The Thrie Estaitis*. The last also reveals, in an unusually frank and explicit form, the obsession with issues of good and bad government, and of the responsibilities and characteristic weaknesses of kingship which run through the Interlude drama, most notably in Skelton's *Magnyfycence*, and the anonymous *Hester*, and which colour the treatment of Christ's inquisitors in the York Cycle. The religious Cycles also reveal the anxious, and at times complex and conflicted, attitudes towards racial and religious difference in the period. The depiction of the Jews in the York Passion sequence raises issues which are taken up with greater vehemence in the Croxton *Play of the Sacrament*, and in a different vein in *Hester*, where racial persecution is itself one of the themes discussed. Issues of personal morality and spirituality are never far from the forefront in these plays, either, and readers interested in pursuing late medieval notions of public and private piety, personal conduct, and attitudes towards crime and social responsibility will find much to catch their attention in all of these plays.

The texts also reveal much about the conditions of performance and the principles of playing in the period. Whether it is the techniques developed to meet the demands of acting in the crowded streets of York or Chester, the different strategies for directing audiences and creating meanings in place-and-scaffold production, or the uses to which the peculiar conditions of the late medieval great hall were put in the Interludes, these plays show how intimately – and how fundamentally – medieval drama was a creature of its physical and cultural environment, of the communities which produced it and the spaces in which they lived and worked. The texts demonstrate how effectively the audiences were drawn into the dramatic action, and how their reception of the plays was conditioned by their involvement in them. The techniques developed for depicting sin and vice in dramatic form demonstrate the dramatists' sophisticated appreciation of the nature and limitations of dramatic play, and the dangers (both pragmatic and intellectual) posed by acting in the service of religious truth. Far from being the products of a naive and primitive dramatic culture, the plays demonstrate the vibrant energies and complex religious, cultural, and theatrical sensibilities that went into their writing and performance. As such they deserve to be read – and, better still, performed – not merely as precursors of later glories, but as works in their own right, rich in significance and resonance, with their own important place in literary and cultural history.

Editorial practice

All of the plays have been newly edited from original sources or photographic facsimiles. I have retained the Middle English characters thorn 'þ' (pronounced 'th') and yogh 'ʒ' (which has a similar range to the modern 'gh' or 'y'), but have standardized the use of i/j, u/v, and u/w to conform with modern practice, and have capitalized proper nouns such as Heaven, Hell, and Earth on those occasions when they are not capitalized in the originals. In the interests of clarity, and as a further indication of a character's allegiance, I have capitalized the pronouns relating to God and the Trinity where they are spoken by believers, but left them uncapitalized in speeches by unbelievers. Thus the Jewish Priests speak of God as 'He' but Christ as 'he'. The punctuation employed is editorial, as is the division of the text into stanzas where that is not already evident in the originals. In all other matters I have tried to stay as close to the originals as possible, to provide readers with as authentic a sense of the manuscripts and early printed editions as is possible in a modern anthology.

All references to the Bible in the footnotes and glosses are to the Authorized (King James) Version. All references to Chaucer's works are to *The Riverside Chaucer*, edited by Larry D. Benson (3rd edn, Boston, 1987).

Acknowledgements

This volume draws upon a long-lasting love for and fascination with medieval drama, and so my greatest debt is to those who first aroused my interest in the early theatre, to my school teachers Ruth Kirby and Angela Wallin, and to my university tutors John J. McGavin and Bella Millett, both of whom have remained friends and mentors ever since. I am particularly grateful to John McGavin for his consistent encouragement throughout this project, even when I pestered him with arcane queries about Lindsay's terminology and prosody. His generosity in agreeing to read the volume in its entirety prior to publication saved me from numerous errors of commission and omission and added many invaluable improvements and new readings.

I am also extremely grateful to those scholars and friends who have helped me with information and advice as I wrestled with the challenges that the play texts threw up. In particular I should like to thank my colleagues at Leicester: Vincent Newey, Gordon Campbell, David Salter, Andrew and Michael Hagiioannu, Michael Davies, Pip Willcox, Roger Warren, and especially Elaine M. Treharne, who initially suggested the idea of an anthology of Medieval Drama to Andrew McNeillie at Blackwell Publishers. I am also grateful for the help and support in this and my earlier work on drama of Michel Bitot, Marie-Héléne Besnault, André Lascombes, and Jean-Paul Pittion of the Université François Rabelais, Tours, Claire Jowitt of the University of Wales, Aberystwyth, Peter Smith of Nottingham Trent University, Bob Godfrey of University College, Northampton, Kevin Sharpe and George Bernard of the University of Southampton, and Tony Kushner of the Parkes Centre at Southampton and the Cavaliers, not least for his continued faith in my slip-fielding abilities. Thanks are also due to Fiona Sewell for her exemplary copy-editing and to Andrew McNeillie for his unfailing enthusiasm and professional guidance at all stages of the project, which I could not have completed with sanity intact had it not been for help at vital stages from my wife, Sharon, and the IT skills of Patricia Joynt, paragon of mothers-in-law.

Chronological Table

Historical events	Literary and dramatic landmarks
	1376 Earliest surviving reference to the York Cycle.
1377 Death of Edward III. Accession of Richard II.	*c.*1377 William Langland, *Piers Plowman*, the B-Text.
	*c.*1380–1400 *Sir Gawain and the Green Knight*, *Pearl*.
1381 The Peasants' Revolt.	
	*c.*1382–5 Geoffrey Chaucer, *Troilus and Criseyde*.
	*c.*1386 John Gower, *Confessio Amantis*.
	*c.*1387 Chaucer, *The Canterbury Tales* begun.
*c.*1395 Second version of the Wycliffite Bible in English.	
1399 Deposition of Richard II. Accession of Henry IV.	
	*c.*1400 Death of Chaucer.
1401 Statute permitting the burning of Lollard heretics.	
	1408 Death of Gower.
1413 Death of Henry IV. Accession of Henry V.	
	1415 The York *Ordo Paginarum*.
1422 Death of Henry V. Accession of infant Henry VI.	1422 Earliest surviving reference to the Chester Cycle.
1453 End of Hundred Years' War. Beginning of Wars of the Roses.	
1461 Henry VI deposed. Edward IV proclaimed king.	
	1463–77 Earliest surviving text of the York Cycle.
1470 Henry VI reinstated.	
1471 Henry deposed and murdered. Edward IV restored.	1471 Death of Sir Thomas Malory.
1476 First printing press in England established by William Caxton.	
1483 Death of Edward IV. Richard III succeeds after death of the Princes in the Tower.	
1485 Richard III killed at Bosworth. Accession of Henry VII.	1485 Caxton prints Malory's *Morte D'Arthur*.
1488 James IV becomes King of Scotland.	

	c.1490 Production in Antwerp of *Elkerlijc*, the Dutch precursor of *Everyman*.
	c.1490–c.1510 Approximate date of the Towneley Cycle manuscript.
	c.1495 *Everyman* and Henry Medwall's *Nature* and *Fulgens*.
	c.1500 Approximate date of the N-Town manuscript.
1502 Death of Henry VII's eldest son and heir Prince Arthur.	
1509 Death of Henry VII. Accession of Henry VIII. Henry marries Katherine of Aragon, Arthur's widow.	
	c.1510 *Everyman* printed.
1513 Battle of Flodden. James IV killed. Accession of the infant James V.	
1514 Thomas Wolsey becomes archbishop of York and Henry VIII's chief minister.	c.1514 The anonymous interlude *Hickscorner* printed.
1515 Wolsey becomes a cardinal.	
	1516 Thomas More's *Utopia* (Latin version) printed.
1517 Martin Luther publishes his 'Theses' in Wittenburg.	
1519 Expulsion of 'the minions' from Henry VIII's privy chamber.	1519 John Skelton's *Magnyfycence* written.
1520 Henry VIII proclaimed 'Defender of the Faith' by Pope Leo X.	c.1520 Date of surviving manuscript of the Croxton *Play of the Sacrament*.
1521 Luther officially banned by the Pope. Publishes a (Protestant) translation of the New Testament.	1521–2 Skelton's anti-Wolsey satires written.
1526 William Tyndale prints the first (Protestant) New Testament in English in Worms.	
1527 Henry VIII's 'Great Matter', his dissatisfaction with his marriage to Katherine of Aragon, begins to be discussed.	
	1528–30 *Godly Queene Hester* written (not printed until 1561).
1529 Fall of Cardinal Wolsey. Thomas More becomes lord chancellor.	1529 Death of Skelton.
	c.1530 Skelton's *Magnyfycence* printed.
	1533–4 John Heywood's Interludes printed by William Rastell.
1533 Thomas Cranmer becomes archbishop of Canterbury. Coronation of Anne Boleyn. Henry VIII excommunicated.	
1535 The royal supremacy of the Church in England made law. Execution of Thomas More.	
1536 Execution of Anne Boleyn.	
1536 Beginning of the Dissolution of the English Monasteries.	
1536–7 The Pilgrimage of Grace (a popular rising against religious change in the north of England).	
1538 English Bible ordered to be placed in all English churches. Arrival in Scotland of Mary of Guise, James V's second wife.	1538 John Bale's *Three Laws, Johan Baptystes Preachyng, God's Promises* printed.
	1538–9 Bale's *King Johan* performed at Archbishop Cranmer's house.

1539 Act of Six Articles limits religious change.
1540 Thomas Cromwell executed.

1542 Death of James V. Accession of infant Mary Queen of Scots.
1543 Unauthorized translations of the English Bible banned, and access to the authorized texts restricted by law.
1546 Murder of Cardinal Beaton.
1547 Death of Henry VIII. Accession of infant Edward VI. Somerset becomes protector.
1547 Dissolution of the Chantries in England. Belief in Purgatory is proscribed.
1548 Mary Queen of Scots removed to France.
1549 Act of Uniformity. Book of Common Prayer promulgated.
1552 Execution of Somerset.
1553 Death of Edward VI. Accession of (Catholic) Mary I in England after abortive attempt to have Lady Jane Grey made Queen.
1554 Reginald Pole becomes cardinal legate in England. John Knox meets Jean Calvin in Geneva. Mary of Guise becomes regent in Scotland.

1558 Death of Mary I. Accession of Elizabeth I.
1559 Knox returns to Scotland. Onset of new phase of reform in Scotland.

1540 Original version of Sir David Lindsay's *Thrie Estaitis* performed in Linlithgow.
1542 First edition of Edward Hall's *Chronicle* printed.

1552 Lindsay's *Thrie Estaitis* performed in Cupar, Fife.
1553 *Gammer Gurton's Needle* and Nicholas Udall's *Respublica* performed.

1554 Lindsay's *Thrie Estaitis* performed in Edinburgh.

1555 Death of Lindsay.

1564 Birth of William Shakespeare and Christopher Marlowe.
1567 Moves begin to suppress the York Cycle.
1575 Last performance of the Chester Cycle.
1576 Suppression of the Wakefield Cycle.
1580 Last attempt to stage the York Cycle fails.
1591 Earliest extant text of the Chester Cycle.

Places mentioned in the text

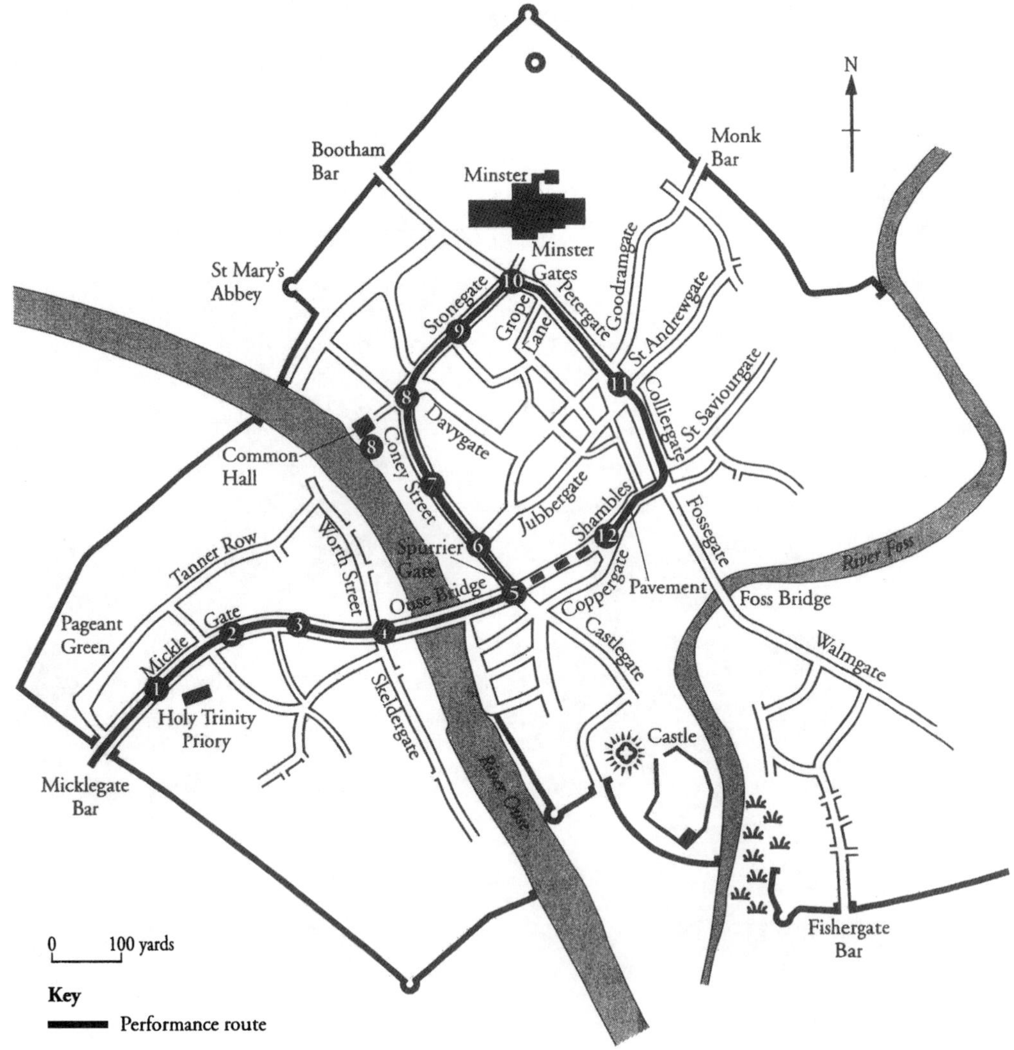

The York performance sites

Part I

Religious Narrative: The Biblical Plays

Religious Narrative: The Biblical Plays

Introduction

Medieval drama took many forms, but the most spectacular of all was the civic religious drama of towns such as York, Chester, Coventry, and Wakefield, referred to most commonly in modern times as the Mystery Plays or the Corpus Christi plays. For perhaps three hundred years before the building of the London playhouses, these plays held sway as the most popular and enduring form of drama in England, and were performed annually – or at least in most years – in many of the largest towns and cities in the country. Their popularity, and their importance to medieval culture, lay at least in part in their ambition. They aimed to show, in the course of a day (or over three days as became the case in Chester), the whole history of the universe from the creation of Heaven and Earth to Doomsday (the Last Judgement), when God would judge the living and the dead, and time and history themselves would cease in the end of all things mortal and temporal.

An index of the popularity of these plays can be found in the references to them in other sources. Their chief characters, and the styles in which they were performed, were so well known that they became proverbial. Chaucer's *Canterbury Tales* contain a number of allusions to the Cycle plays. His Miller, for example, is said to shout 'in Pilate's voice' (*The Miller's Prologue, Canterbury Tales* I l. 3123) when he demands to tell a tale: a reference to the way Pontius Pilate was depicted in many of the Cycle plays, as a loud, ranting braggart. And a character in the Miller's own tale, the parish clerk Absolon, plays Herod – another bragging tyrant – on a high scaffold in order to win more popularity with the women of Oxford (ibid. l. 3384). Over two hundred years later Shakespeare famously had Hamlet tell the actors who come to Elsinore not to 'Out-Herod Herod' by acting in a melodramatic and histrionic way. The plays could also have a profound effect upon their audiences. An old man in Cartmel, Lancashire, in the seventeenth century, for example, when questioned by a zealous reforming cleric about his religious beliefs, could remember nothing he had heard in sermons or homilies, but, on hearing the name of Jesus mentioned, recalled having seen 'that man you spake of once in a play at Kendal [Lancashire], called Corpus Christi play, where there was a man on a tree and blood ran down'. This witness may not have been typical, but it seems clear that, for over two centuries, the Cycle plays offered people a ready access to religious narrative and the articles of the faith, were a watchword for certain kinds of acting and certain dramatic effects, and their reputation spanned the nation.

The civic drama has, as we have seen, been known by a number of names. Each is in one way or another inadequate to describe the variety of forms and auspices of the surviving plays. They are often called Mystery Plays, partly because they deal with religious mysteries (making known the ways of God – and the central principles of the Christian faith – to their audiences), and partly also because (at York, Chester, and probably Wakefield) they were put on by the craft guilds: the organizations (part trade-regulating body, part religious confraternity) responsible for administering the crafts or 'mysteries' that dominated the medieval urban economy. To make their subject matter manageable in economic and dramatic terms, the Cycles divided universal Christian history into separate playlets or pageants. At York and Chester these pageants were performed on large wagons, akin to modern carnival floats, which would be manhandled around the city by men hired for the purpose. And each pageant was assigned to a separate trade guild which had to pay for and maintain their wagon, build or purchase props and costumes, and generally make sure that their part of the wider Cycle was performed smoothly and effectively on the day of the production. In York, for example, the enterprise was financed by the levy of 'pageant silver', a tax on guild members collected and administered through the year by 'pageant masters' elected by each guild, whose job was to produce or 'bring forth' their play. This division of labour had the practical advantage of spreading the financial burden of this huge enterprise across the civic community, but also meant that large theological and moral issues could be played out in small-scale human dramas with a limited cast of characters. The processional performance of individual pageants at separate locations thus managed to combine universality of theme with intimacy of performance. The entire history of humankind was played to the populace of a major city, yet no individual performance would have been to more than about 200 people, creating an intimate relationship between actors and audience that, as we shall see, was central to the nature of these plays.

The craft guilds were often allocated pageants with a special link to their own trades. Thus in York the Pinners, the makers of nails, produced the Crucifixion play, and the Tilethatchers put on the play of the Nativity – the central prop of which was a stable roof with a hole in it through which the light of the star of Bethlehem was made to shine at the moment of Christ's birth. This association of trade to play was not intended chiefly as an advertisement for the traders involved, although in some cases this may well have been a welcome by-product (as when the Goldsmiths were able to show off their finest cups and basins in the *Herod and the Magi* pageant, as the vessels in which the gifts of gold, frankincense, and myrrh were presented). It was chiefly a means of getting the actors, and the audience, to identify with the religious content of the play. If Christ was shown being crucified by local people using the tools that they themselves had made, then the religious message that we are all in a real sense responsible for crucifying Christ – because we are all sinners – would be all the more effectively presented. More positively, the collective endeavour of the craftsmen in the production of the plays served to sacralize their trades, investing their labour itself with a role in God's salvific plan.

As well as a communal affirmation and confirmation of religious belief, the plays were a celebration and a promotion of the fortunes and welfare of the city which produced them. The proclamation moving the Chester Cycle from Corpus Christi Day to Whitsunday, for example, tellingly declared the Cycle to be 'not only for the augmentation and increase of the Holy Catholic faith of our saviour Jesus Christ to exhort the minds of the Common people to good devotion and wholesome doctrine thereof, but also for the commonwealth and prosperity of this city'. The alternative name, 'Corpus Christi plays', is still popular among some scholars nowadays, although it too has its advantages and drawbacks. In the case of York (and Chester before the move to Whitsunday) it points to the occasion and the subject matter of the plays more effectively than 'Mystery Plays' does. Some of the Cycles (but by no means all, hence the drawback) were indeed put on at Corpus Christi (literally 'The Body of Christ'), the feast which celebrated the miracle of the Mass, whereby – according to Catholic theology – the bread and wine of the Eucharist miraculously became the body and blood of Christ (through a process known as transubstantiation) when the priest said the words of consecration. Transubstantiation became an established part of Christian dogma in 1215, as a result of the fourth Lateran Council, but it was not until 1264 that the feast of Corpus Christi, at which the consecrated Host was paraded around the town or village in celebration, was proclaimed. And it was not until 1311 that it was formally instituted into the Church Calendar on the first Thursday after Trinity Sunday (i.e. at some point between the 21 May and 24 June), at which time cities in the North of England could be relatively sure of up to seventeen hours of daylight in which to perform the plays which soon became an important part of the celebrations.

In this selection of material from the Cycles, the focus is on the Creation of the world, the Fall of humankind, and the life and Passion of Christ, as these are the primary foci of the bulk of the surviving texts. In these plays human history is presented as a vast universal comedy, charting the Fall and Adam and Eve's expulsion from Paradise, and humanity's eventual redemption through the Incarnation and sacrifice of Jesus. The bulk of the pageants selected are from the York Cycle, as this is the earliest of the surviving plays, with supplementary pageants taken from Chester and the Towneley manuscript where they add a new element to the treatment of these themes, or provide useful points of contrast or comparison to the York material. In addition, an independent segment of the so-called N-Town Play, constituting the early life of the Virgin Mary, is also included (see the section on N-Town, below).

The end of the Corpus Christi plays came in the late sixteenth century. It was once thought that, with the coming of the Reformation, they simply declined in popularity to the point where they could no longer be sustained. But it is now clear that, rather than simply withering away, they remained popular and had to be actively suppressed by their opponents. Because the Cycles were so fundamentally Catholic in their interpretation of Christian history, they inevitably attracted criticism from the more zealous advocates of Protestantism. But such theological opposition was not new. At some point in the late fourteenth or early fifteenth century a critic of the plays drew up a detailed assault upon the whole notion of religious drama entitled *The Tretise of Miraclis Pleyinge* (the central portion of which is printed in the selection of documents at pp. 196–200). A number of the points raised in the *Tretise* foreshadow the objections of the Protestant reformers. What distinguishes the latter, however, is that by the mid-sixteenth century, the Protestant critics were in positions of power and thus able to put their prejudices into practice.

It was not always a case of central government interference in local politics which brought about the plays' demise. In some cases the initiative was taken at the local level, with Protestants within the city hierarchies taking steps to pre-empt what they thought the Crown and Privy Council would require. This is what happened at York, where the city authorities, clearly anxious about the acceptability of their religious drama to the new Elizabethan regime, submitted the text of their (now lost) Creed Play to the Dean of York, the reformer Matthew Hutton, for his opinion. His formal response (see p. 206) indicates both his own distaste for the material, and his disquiet about the possibly more serious objections of the Privy Council in London. In the end the Creed and Corpus Christi plays were suppressed by the simple expedient of the ecclesiastical authorities calling in the sole composite texts for scrutiny and then never returning them. Similar attempts were made to censor, or perhaps suppress outright, the Wakefield Cycle in 1576, although the outcome of the intervention is unclear from the surviving evidence.

The civic communities did make serious efforts to adapt their plays to meet the objections of the reformers. At York the pageants dealing with the life of the Virgin Mary were removed from the Cycle. At Chester a new set of banns was written (see pp. 201–5) defending the play as a reformist work, and a number of the more contentious elements in the pageants were removed. But a combination of moves by reformers within the city and pressure from the Privy Council in London resulted in the eventual suppression of the Chester play as a whole. The last full performance came in 1575.

York

The earliest evidence of the existence of a Cycle at York dates to 1376, when the city was at the height of its commercial success, although it is likely that the play was being performed considerably earlier than this. In 1415 the Town Clerk drew up the *Ordo Paginarum* ('The Order of the Pageants', see pp. 10–11), a description of each pageant and its theme, which shows that the cycle was by this time in roughly the form that would endure until the late sixteenth century (see Johnston and Rogerson, *REED: York*, for subsequent references to the content of the Cycle).

At York each pageant was played on a different wagon. The wagons varied in cost and complexity from the simple flat cart probably used for the *Crucifixion* pageant to the ingeniously designed multi-level structure used for the Mercers' *Last Judgement*, and each would be stored for the remainder of the year in warehouses known as pageant houses adjacent to Pageant Green (see the map of York on p. xvi). On Corpus Christi day the wagons stopped at various pre-selected sites or stations along the way, at which the play was performed before moving on to the next station where it would be performed again. So on the day of the production, a long crocodile of pageant wagons would develop, winding its way around the streets of York, playing the pageants at between twelve and sixteen different stations, each of which was marked with the banners of the city, and some at least of which had scaffolds erected from which those willing and able to pay for a seat could watch the performance in relative comfort. Each station had its own character and particular local significance, which would have given the pageants played there their own distinct resonances. The first (number 1 on the map) was Holy Trinity Priory, just inside Micklegate Bar, at which the performance would begin, with the first appearance of the Barkers' guild's pageant of *The Fall of the Angels* at *c.*4.30 a.m. Other significant stations included the Common Hall gates (station 8), where the mayor and civic officers were obliged to view the play each year, the Minster (station 10), where the cathedral clergy would be gathered, and the final station (station 12), the Pavement, where the last performance of the day would take place late into the night, and the Mercers' *Last Judgement* would consign the sinful souls to eternal damnation, symbolically at the site in York where official proclamations were read out, and public executions conducted.

Chester

The Chester play was probably also a product of the late fourteenth century. Certainly it seems to have been well established by the time of the earliest extant record of its existence, dating from 1422. Originally, like York, a Corpus Christi play, the Chester play was moved to Whitsun (the feast celebrating the descent of the Holy Spirit on the disciples at Pentecost, held on the seventh Sunday after Easter) and expanded from one to three days in duration. As at York, the Whitsun version of the play was performed processionally on wagons at five stations located around the city. As the production was spread over three days, however, wagons could be shared between those guilds performing on different days, and the logistics of the performance kept simpler. Of the Chester pageants, the *Fall of the Angels*, *Adam and Eve*, and the *Shepherds* pageants are printed here.

The Towneley/Wakefield Cycle

The single manuscript record of the plays generally associated with Wakefield was once owned by the Towneley family of Towneley Hall, near Burnley in Lancashire, hence the play's alternative title 'The Towneley Cycle'. The Cycle as it survives is made up of several elements, some of the pageants having been adopted and adapted from the York Cycle, and others being the work of a gifted dramatist now referred to as the Wakefield Master. Evidence for the method of performance and the precise auspices of the play is lacking (even the ascription to Wakefield has to be treated with some caution, see Mills, *Recycling the Cycle*, p. 17), but, as in York and Chester, the individual pageants seem to have been produced by craft guilds. *The Second Shepherds' Play*, probably the best known of all the medieval religious pageants, represents Towneley in this anthology.

N-Town

Once erroneously known as the *Ludus Coventriae* ('The Play of Coventry'), the text now known as the N-Town Play probably originates from East Anglia. Like the Holy Roman Empire, however, which was famously neither holy, Roman, nor an empire, it did not come from a town whose name began with an 'N', and it is strictly speaking not a single play but an amalgamation of originally diverse material loosely compiled into a Creation-to-Doom sequence. The name itself comes from the banns attached to the manuscript, which conclude with the statement 'At vi of þe belle we gynne [begin] oure play / In .N. town' (ll. 526–7), where 'N' probably stands for the Latin word '*nomen*' (name), and indicates that the speaker should insert the name of the town in which they were playing at that point. This suggests that at least some of the material contained in the manuscript was intended for touring rather than for regular performance in a single town. Which material that might have been is slightly less clear. Within the manuscript as it stands there are traces of several distinct 'plays': a fragmentary Creation-to-Doom cycle of pageants, two distinct Passion plays, and plays on the early life and the Assumption of the Virgin Mary (for a helpful account of the manuscript and its possible genesis, see Alan J. Fletcher, 'N-Town', in Beadle, *Cambridge Companion*). Of these I have selected the *Mary Play* for inclusion in this anthology, both as it is a distinctive and powerful play in its own right, evocative of the important role played by Mary in popular religious devotion in the period, and because it offers a valuable prelude to and parallel of the material on the life of Christ which forms the bulk of the material selected from York.

The texts

York

The copy text used is the only surviving complete manuscript, British Library Additional MS 35290. In addition I have consulted the following editions:

R. Beadle, ed., *The York Plays* (London, 1982).

R. Beadle and P. King, eds, *York Mystery Plays: A Selection in Modern Spelling* (Oxford, 1984).

R. Beadle and P. Meredith, eds, *The York Play: A Facsimile of British Library Additional MS 35290, Together with a Facsimile of the Ordo Paginarum Section of the A/Y Memorandum Book* (Leeds, 1983).

P. Happé, ed., *English Mystery Plays* (Harmondsworth, 1975).
L. T. Smith, ed., *York Plays* (Oxford, 1885).

Towneley

The text is based upon Huntington Library MS HM1, consulted in photographic facsimile in A.C. Cawley and Martin Stevens, eds, *The Towneley Cycle: A Facsimile of Huntington MS HM1* (Leeds, 1976).

In addition I have consulted the following modern editions:

D. Bevington, ed., *Medieval Drama* (Boston, 1975).
A.C. Cawley and M. Stevens, eds, *The Towneley Plays*, EETS ss 13 and 14 (2 vols, Oxford, 1994).
J. Coldeway, ed., *Early English Drama: An Anthology* (New York, 1993).
P. Happé, ed., *English Mystery Plays* (Harmondsworth, 1975).

Chester

There are five surviving complete manuscripts, all dating from the period 1591–1607, roughly a generation after the last performance of the cycle. As a base text I have used the (1591) Huntington Library MS 2, consulted in photographic facsimile in R.M. Lumiansky and D. Mills, eds, *The Chester Mystery Cycle: A Reduced Facsimile of Huntington Library MS 2* (Leeds, 1980).

In addition I have consulted the following modern editions:

R.M. Lumiansky and D. Mills, eds, *The Chester Mystery Cycle*, EETS, ss 3 (London, 1974).
D. Mills, ed., *The Chester Mystery Cycle: A New Edition with Modernised Spelling* (E. Lansing, 1992).

N-Town

The base text is British Library MS Cotton Vespasian D VIII. In addition I have consulted the following printed editions:

P. Meredith, ed., *The Mary Play from the N-Town Manuscript* (London, 1987).
P. Meredith and S. J. Kahrl, eds, *The N-Town Plays: A Facsimile of British Library MS Cotton Vespasian D VIII* (Leeds, 1977).
S. Spector, ed., *The N-Town Play: Cotton Vespasian D8*, EETS ss 11 and 12 (2 vols, Oxford, 1991).

Documentary sources

The documentary records relating to the cycle plays, and much else besides, are collected in the relevant volumes of the Records of Early English Drama (REED) Series:

L. M. Clopper, ed., *REED: Chester* (Toronto, 1979).
A.F. Johnston and M. Rogerson, eds, *REED: York* (2 vols, Toronto, 1979).
P. Meredith and J. E. Tailby, eds, *The Staging of Religious Drama in Europe in the Later Middle Ages: Texts and Documents in English Translation* (Kalamazoo, 1982) also contains valuable material.

Further reading

R. Beadle, ed., *The Cambridge Companion to Medieval Theatre* (Cambridge, 1994).
M. G. Briscoe and J. C. Coldeway, eds, *Contexts for Early English Drama* (Bloomington, 1989).
E.K. Chambers, *The Medieval Stage* (2 vols, Oxford, 1903).
R.J. Collier, *Poetry and Drama in the York Corpus Christi Play* (Hamden, Conn., 1977).
J. D. Cox and D.S. Kastan, eds, *A New History of Early English Drama* (New York, 1997).
C. Davidson, *From Creation to Doom: The York Cycle of Mystery Plays* (New York, 1984).
P. Happé, *English Drama Before Shakespeare* (Harlow, 1999).
S. Kahrl, *Traditions of Medieval English Drama* (London, 1974).
V.A. Kolve, *The Play Called Corpus Christi* (Stanford, 1966).

D. Mills, ed., *Staging the Chester Cycle* (Leeds, 1985).
D. Mills, *Recycling the Cycle: The City of Chester and its Whitsun Play* (Toronto, 1998).
D.M. Palliser, *Tudor York* (Oxford, 1979).
L. Potter, ed., *The Revels History of English Drama: Volume I: Medieval Drama* (London, 1983).
E. Prosser, *Drama and Religion in the English Mystery Plays: A Re-evaluation* (Stanford, 1961).
R. Rastall, *The Heaven Singing: Music in Early English Drama* (Cambridge, 1996).
C. Richardson and J. Johnston, *Medieval Drama* (London, 1991).
J.W. Robinson, 'The Art of the York Realist', *Modern Philology* 60 (1963), pp. 241–51.
F.M. Salter, *Medieval Drama in Chester* (Toronto, 1955).
M. Stevens, *Four Middle English Mystery Cycles* (Princeton, N.J., 1987).
J. Taylor and A. H. Nelson, eds, *Medieval English Drama: Essays Critical and Contextual* (Chicago, 1972).
P. Travis, *Dramatic Design in the Chester Cycle* (Chicago, 1982).
G. Wickham, *The Medieval English Theatre* (London, 1974).
R. Woolf, *The English Mystery Plays* (London, 1972).

In addition to the above, useful articles are regularly published in a number of journals. Especially useful are *Comparative Drama*, *Early Theatre*, *Leeds Studies in English*, and *Medieval English Theatre*.

Useful Internet addresses

http://etext.lib.virginia.edu/mideng.browse.html
The University of Virginia's Electronic Text Centre's Middle English Collection, from where texts of the York and Towneley Cycles and *Everyman* can be accessed.

http://www.chass.utoronto.ca:8080/~medieval/www/pls/
The site of the Poculi Ludique Societas, who sponsor early drama productions at the University of Toronto (the major location for work on early drama in North America). A good site for downloadable images of modern productions.

http://www.chass.utoronto.ca/~reed/reed.html
http://www.chass.utoronto.ca/~reed/stage.html
The homepage and theatre resource page of the Records of Early English Drama organization, a good source of material on medieval drama and links to other relevant sites.

http://www.comp.lancs.ac.uk/medstud/yorkdoom/index.html
The homepage of the York Doomsday project, organized by Professors Meg Twycross and Pamela King, leading exponents of early drama performances in the UK.

http://www.humanities.mcmaster.ca/~reed/early/index.html
Gives abstracts of current articles and lists the content of articles in back numbers of the journal *Early Theatre*, which developed out of *Records of Early English Drama Newsletter*.

http://www.leeds.ac.uk/theatre/emd.htm
The homepage of a new journal, *European Medieval Drama*, edited from Italy by Professor Sydney Higgins of the University of Camerino. The site is a good source of links to other medieval sites, information and comment on medieval drama and other related topics.

http://www.byu.edu/~hurlbut/fmddp/corpus.html
A good site for those interested in medieval French drama.

http://www.acad.cua.edu/as/engl/toronto/york98.htm
The York Plays in Toronto website, an excellent source of information, maps, and downloadable images related to a recent modern production of the York Cycle.

York, *The Ordo Paginarum*

The *Ordo Paginarum* ('Order of the Pageants'), written by the Common Clerk of York, Roger Burton, in 1415, contains a brief description of the contents of each of the pageants. It offers a valuable early insight into the scope and nature of the Cycle as well as a useful guide to what one articulate citizen of York thought was most striking or significant about each section of his city's play. Interestingly Burton focuses on the numbers of actors, the major properties used, and the iconography of the actors' movements and poses, suggesting that, while the purpose of the text may have been to provide a pragmatic checklist of the resources, human and material, needed for each pageant, the author was also engaging in a sophisticated theological and psychological interpretation of the pageants as he wrote. As such it is a valuable account of the impact and reception of the Cycle as well as a useful source of practical information about its contents. The text of the *Ordo* is printed in volume I of Johnston and Rogerson, *REED: York*, along with an alternative translation from the original Latin text (in volume II, pp. 702–9). Pageants printed in this anthology are marked with an asterisk.

The Order of the Pageants of the Play of Corpus Christi . . . compiled in the year of Our Lord 1415 by Roger Burton, Common Clerk

*1. *The Tanners [later the Barkers]*: God the Father Almighty creating and forming the heavens. Angels and Archangels: Lucifer, and the Angels who fell with him into Hell.

2. *The Plasterers*: God the Father in His own Person creating the Earth and all that is in it in the space of five days.

3. *The Cardmakers*: God the Father forming Adam from the dust of the earth, and making Eve from Adam's rib, and breathing into them the breath of life.

4. *The Fullers*: God forbidding Adam and Eve to eat of the Tree of Life.

*5. *The Coopers*: Adam and Eve and the Tree between them, the Serpent deceiving them with fruit. God speaking to them and cursing the Serpent: and the Angel with a sword driving them out of Paradise.

6. *The Armourers*: Adam and Eve and the Angel with a spade and distaff assigning tasks to them.

7. *The Gaunters {Glovemakers}*: Abel and Cain making their sacrificial offerings.

8. *The Shipwrights*: God forewarning Noah to make an Ark of smoothed wood.

9. *The Pessoners [Fishmongers] and Mariners*: Noah in the Ark, and his Wife, the three sons of Noah with their Wives, with animals of different kinds.

10. *The Parcheminers [Parchment-makers] and Bookbinders*: Abraham offering his son Isaac on an altar, a Servant Boy with wood, and the Angel.

11. *The Hosiers*: Moses raising up the Serpent in the desert, King Pharaoh, and eight Jews marvelling and waiting.

12. *The Spicers*: A learned Doctor declaring the prophet's words concerning the birth of Christ. Mary, the Angel greeting her, Mary greeting Elizabeth.

*13. *The Pewterers and Founders*: Mary, Joseph wishing to put her away secretly, the Angel telling them to go to Bethlehem.

*14. *The Tilers*: Mary, Joseph, the Midwife, the Child born and lying in a manger between the ox and the ass. The Angel speaking to the Shepherds, players in the following pageant.

15. *The Chandlers*: The Shepherds speaking to each other, the star in the East, the Angel announcing the joy of the new-born boy-child to the Shepherds.

16. *The Orfevers [Goldsmiths], Goldbeaters, Moneymakers*: The three Kings coming from the East, Herod interrogating them about the child Jesus, the Son of Herod, the two Counsellors and a Messenger. Mary with the Child, and the star above, and the three Kings offering gifts.

17. *Formerly the House [Hospital] of St Leonard, now the Masons*: Mary with the child, Joseph, Anna, the Midwife with doves, Simeon receiving the Child in his arms, and the two Sons of Simeon.

18. *The Marshals*: Mary with the Child and Joseph fleeing to Egypt: the Angel announcing the message.

19. *The Girdlers, Nailers*: Herod ordering the children to be slain, four Soldiers with spears, two Counsellors of the King, and four Mothers weeping over the slaughter of their children.

20. *The Spurriers [Spurmakers], Lorimers [Bridlemakers]*: The Doctors, Jesus as a boy sitting in the Temple in their midst, asking them questions and answering their questions. Four Jews, Mary and Joseph looking for him, and finding him in the Temple.

21. *The Barbers*: Jesus, John the Baptist baptising him, and two Angels attending.

22. *The Vintners [Wine-merchants]*: Jesus, Mary, the Bridegroom and the Bride, the Steward with his Servant, with six jars of water when the water turns into wine.

23. *The Fevers [Smiths]*: Jesus on the pinnacle of the Temple, and the Devil tempting him with stones, and two Angels, attending, etc.

24. *The Curriers [Leatherworkers]*: Peter, James, and John,

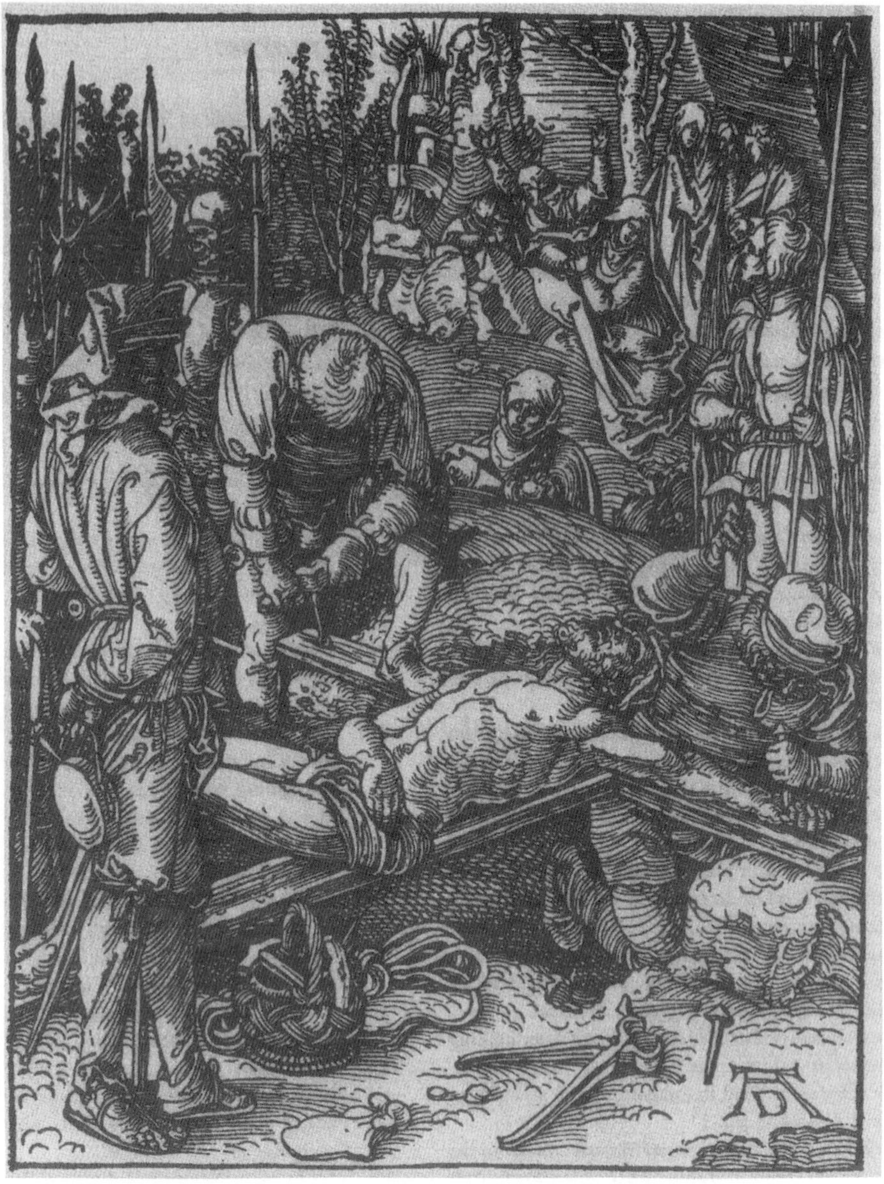

Albrecht Dürer, *Nailing to the Cross*, 1511, woodcut. Reproduced courtesy of Dover Publications.

Jesus going up into a mountain and transfiguring himself before them. Moses and Elias [Elijah] appearing, and a voice speaking in a cloud.

25. *The Ironmongers*: Jesus and Simon the Leper asking Jesus to eat with him. The two Disciples, Mary Magdalene washing the feet of Jesus with her tears and drying them with her hair.

26. *The Plumbers [Lead workers], Pattenmakers [Makers of wooden shoes]*: Jesus, two Apostles, the Woman taken in adultery, four Jews accusing her.

27. *The Pouchmakers, Bottlers, and Capmakers*: Jesus, two Apostles, Lazarus in the tomb, Mary Magdalene, Martha, and two Jews, marvelling.

*28. *The Skinners, Vestmentmakers*: Jesus on the ass with its foal, twelve Apostles following Jesus, six Rich Men and six Poor Men, eight Children with palm branches, singing *Benedictus*, etc., and Zaccheus climbing the sycamore tree.

*29. *The Cutlers, Bladesmiths, Sheathers, Scalers [Scale makers], Bucklermakers [Shield-makers]*: Pilate, Caiaphas, two Soldiers, three Jews, Judas selling Jesus.

30. *The Bakers*: The Paschal Lamb, the Lord's Supper, the twelve Apostles, Jesus girt with a linen cloth washing their feet. The institution of the Sacrament of the Body of Christ according to the New Law, the Communion of the Apostles.

31. *The Cordwainers [Shoemakers]*: Pilate, Caiaphas, Annas, fourteen armed Soldiers, Malchus, Peter, James, John, Jesus, and Judas kissing Jesus and betraying him.

*32. *The Bowyers and Fletchers [Arrowmakers]*: Jesus, Annas, Caiaphas, and four Jews striking and mocking Jesus. Peter, the Woman accusing Peter, and Malchus.

*33. *The Tapissers [Carpet and Tapestry-makers], Couchers [Upholsterers]*: Jesus, Pilate, Annas, Caiaphas, two Counsellors, and four Jews accusing Jesus.

*34. *The Litsters [Dyers]*: Herod, two Counsellors, four Soldiers, Jesus and three Jews.

35. *The Cooks, Waterleaders*: Pilate, Annas, Caiaphas, two Jews, and Judas bringing back to them the thirty pieces of silver.

*36. *The Tilemakers, Milners [Millers], Turners, Hairsters, Bollers [Makers of Wooden Bowls]*: Jesus, Pilate, Caiaphas, Annas, six Soldiers holding poles with banners, and four others leading Jesus to Herod, asking for Barabus to be released and Jesus to be crucified, and then in the same place binding and flogging him, putting the crown of thorns on his head. Three Soldiers casting lots over the garments of Jesus.

37. *[The Shearmen]*: Jesus covered with blood, carrying the Cross towards Calvary. Simon of Cyrene, Jews forcing him to carry the Cross. Mary the mother of Jesus, then John the Apostle telling her that her son has been condemned to death and is going to Calvary. Veronica wiping the blood and sweat from the face of Jesus with a veil on which the face of Jesus is imprinted, and other Women lamenting Jesus.

*38. *The Pinners, Lateners [Founders of brass alloy], Painters*: The Cross, Jesus stretched out on it on the ground, four Jews scourging and dragging him with ropes, and then raising the Cross and the body of Jesus nailed to the Cross on the Mount of Calvary.

39. *The Butchers, Poulterers*: The Cross, two Thieves crucified, Jesus hanging from the Cross between them. Mary, the mother of Jesus, John, Mary the mother of James, and Mary Salome, Longinus with his spear, a Slave with a sponge, Pilate, Annas, Caiaphas, the Centurion; Joseph of Arimathea and Nicodemus taking him down and laying him in the tomb.

*40. *The Sellers [Saddlers], Verrours [Glaziers], Fuystours [Saddletree-makers]*: Jesus harrowing Hell, twelve Spirits, six Good and six Bad.

*41. *The Carpenters*: Jesus rising from the tomb, four armed Soldiers, and three Marys lamenting. Pilate, Caiaphas, and Annas. A young Child sitting at the tomb, dressed in white, talking to the women.

42. *The Winedrawers*: Jesus, Mary Magdalene with spices.

43. *The Boggours [Brokers?], Sledmen [Woolpackers?]*: Jesus, Luke, and Cleophas in pilgrims' clothes.

44. *The Scriveners [Scribes], Limners [Illuminators], Questors [Pardoners], and Dubbers [Booktrimmers?]*: Jesus, Peter, John, James, Philip, and the other Apostles, with a piece of roasted fish and a honeycomb, and the Apostle Thomas touching the wounds of Christ.

45. *The Taillyours [Tailors]*: Mary, John the Evangelist, eleven Apostles, two Angels, Jesus ascending from among them, and four Angels holding a cloud.

46. *The Potters*: Mary, two Angels, eleven Apostles, and the Holy Spirit descending upon them, and four Jews, marvelling.

47. *The Drapers*: Jesus, Mary, Gabriel with two Angels, two Virgins and three Jews of Mary's kin, eight Apostles and two Devils.

48. *The Lynwevers [Linen-weavers]*: Four Apostles carrying the bier of Mary, and Fergus hanging from the bier, with two other Jews and an Angel.

49. *The Wool-We[a]vers*: Mary ascending with a crowd of Angels, eight Apostles, and St Thomas the Apostle preaching in the desert.

50. *The Hostilers [Innkeepers]*: Mary, Jesus crowning her, and a crowd of Angels singing.

*51. *The Mercers [Merchants]*: Jesus, Mary, twelve Apostles, four Angels with trumpets, four with a crown, spear, and two whips. Four Good Spirits and four Bad Spirits, and six Devils.[1]

[1] Compare this brief description of the pageant with the detailed account of the properties in the Mercers' Indenture of 1433, p. 159, below.

York (The Barkers/Tanners), *The Fall of the Angels*

Played at the first station at dawn (4.30 a.m.) on Corpus Christi Day, the pageant might make powerful use of the natural effects available to the playwright, enacting the Creation of the world and the division of light and dark as the sun rises over York. The pageant effectively counterpoints harmony and discord. Heavenly harmony is represented by the hymns of praise directed by the Good Angels towards their creator, God; discord enters the universe in the speeches of self-regard spoken by Lucifer and the other Fallen Angels. The rebellion of the latter is literally a thought-crime; no sooner do they voice their pride than they fall into Hell to be transformed into devils (significantly interrupting the eight-line stanza characteristic of the pageant with their stichomythic cries): as Lucifer subsequently complains at l. 116, 'I sayde but a thoghte.' As Lucifer's crime is also an act with meta-dramatic force – an attempt to impersonate or resemble God – the episode begins a self-conscious exploration of the nature and aims of acting and pretence which runs through this and other civic Cycle Plays. In practical terms, the fall was probably engineered via a trapdoor from the platform of the pageant wagon to a Hell-mouth at a lower level, and the transformation of angels to devils achieved by either a swift change of costume or the substitution of other actors, already costumed, concealed in Hell.

The Barkers (or Tanners) prepared the animal hides which were the raw material for leather goods, and could equally furnish the costumes and masks employed in this pageant.

[*Dramatis Personae*: *Deus* (God the Father), *II Angelus* (two Good Angels, Cherubim and Seraphim), *II Angelus Deficiens/Diabolus* (two Fallen Angels/Devils, the first of whom is Lucifer).]

DEUS
Ego sum Alpha et O: vita,
Via, veritas, primus et novissimus.[1]

I am gracyus and grete, God withoutyn begynnyng;
I am maker unmade, all mighte es in Me;
I am lyfe and way unto welth-wynnyng;
I am formaste and fyrste, als I byd sall it be.
My blyssyng o ble sall be blendyng,[2]
And heldand, fro harme to be hydande,
My body in blys ay abydande,
Unendande, withoutyn any endyng.

Sen I am maker unmade and most es of mighte,
And ay sall be endeles and noghte es but I,
Unto My dygnyte dere sall diewly be dyghte
A place full of plente to My plesyng at ply;
And therewith als wyll I have wroght
Many dyvers doynges bedene,
Whilke warke sall mekely contene,
And all sall be made even of noghte.

But onely þe worthely warke of My wyll
In my sprete sall enspyre þe mighte of Me;[3]
And in þe fyrste, faythely, My thoughts to fullfyll,
Baynely in My blyssyng I byd at here be
A blys al-beledande abowte Me,[4]
In þe whilke blys I byde at be here
Nyen ordres of aungels full clere,
In lovyng ay-lastande at lowte Me.

Tunc cantant angeli, 'Te deum laudamus, te dominum confitemur.'[5]

Here undernethe Me nowe a nexile I neven,
Whilke ile sall be Erthe. Now all be at ones
Erthe haly, and Helle, þis hegheste be Heven,
And that welthth sall welde sall won in þis wones.[6]
This graunte I ȝowe, mynysters myne,

3 gracious 5 gaining of happiness 6 order, [so] shall 8 radiating, shielding from harm 9 continuing 10 Unending 13 duly, ordained 14 to shape to my pleasing 16 deeds (i.e. the Creation) 17 continue 18 from nothing 24 to 25 Nine 26 to 27 separate place/island 28 isle 29 complete 31 my servants

1 'I am Alpha and Omega [i.e. the beginning and end], the life, the way, the truth, first and last.' Revelation 22:13.

2 'The blessing of My face will be shining'.

3 'But only the precious labour of My will will be inspired in My spirit by My power'.

4 'I order here to be about Me an all-protecting bliss [i.e. Heaven itself]'.

5 'Then the angels sing "We praise Thee, God, we acknowledge Thee lord."'

6 'And all who shall experience happiness shall live in these places.'

To-whils ȝhe ar stabill in thoghte,
And also to þaime þat ar noghte[7]
Be put to My presone at pyne.

Of all þe mightes I have made, moste nexte after Me
I make þe[e] als master and morour of my Mighte;
I beelde þe[e] here baynely in blys for to be.
I name þe[e] for Lucifer, als berar of lyghte.
Nothyng here sall þe[e] be derand;
In þis blis sall be ȝhour beeldyng,
And have all welth in ȝoure weledyng
Ay-whils ȝhe ar buxumly berande.

Tunc cantant angeli, 'Sanctus, sanctus, sanctus, dominus deus sabaoth.'[8]

PRIMUS ANGELUS, SERAPHYN
A, mercyfull maker, full mekill es Þi mighte,
Þat all this warke at a worde worthely has wroghte.
Ay loved be þat lufly lorde of His lighte,
That us thus mighty has made þat nowe was righte
 noghte,
In blys for to byde in His blyssyng.
Ay-lastande in luf lat us lowte Hym,
At beelde us thus baynely abowete Hym,
Of myrthe nevermore to have myssyng.

PRIMUS ANGELUS DEFICIENS, LUCIFER
All the myrth þat es made es markide in me!
Þe bemes of my brighthode ar byrnande so bryghte,
And I so semely in syghte myselfe now I se,
For lyke a lorde am I lefte to lende in his lighte,
More fayrear be far þan my feres.
In me is no poynte þat may payre;
I fele me fetys and fayre,
My powar es passande my peres

ANGELUS CHERABYN
Lorde, with a lastande luf we love Þe[e] allone,
Þou mightefull maker þat markid us and made us,
And wroghte us thus worthely to wone in this wone,
Ther never felyng of fylth may full us nor fade us.
All blys es here beeldande aboute us.
To-whyls we are stabyll in thoughte
In þe worschipp of Hym þat us wroght,
Of dere never thar us more dowte us.

SECUNDUS ANGELUS DEFICIENS
O, what, I am fetys and fayre and fygured full fytt!
Þe forme of all fayrehede apon me es feste;
All welth in my weelde es, I wote be my wytte;
Þe bemes of my brighthede are bygged with þe
 beste.
My schewyng es schemerande and schynande,
So bygly to blys am I broghte;
Me nedes for to noy me righte noghte,
Here sall never payne me be pynande.

ANGELUS SERAPHYN
With all þe wytt [þ]at we welde we woyrschip Þi
 wyll,
Þou, gloryus God þat es grunde of all grace;
Ay with stedefaste steven lat us stande styll,
Lorde, to be fede with þe fode of Thi fayre face.
In lyfe that es lely ay-lastande,
Thi dale, lorde, es ay daynetethly delande,
And whoso þat fode may be felande,
To se Thi fayre face, es noght fastande.

PRIMUS ANGELUS DEFICIENS, LUCIFER
Owe, certes, what I am worthely wroghte with
 wyrschip, iwys!
For in a glorius gle my gleteryng it glemes;
I am so mightyly made my mirth may noghte mys,
Ay sall I byde in this blys thorowe brightnes of
 bemes.
Me nedes noghte of noy for to neven,[9]
All welth in my welde have I weledande;
Abowne ȝhit sall I be beeldand,
On heghte in þe hyeste of Hewven.

Ther sall I set myselfe full semely to seyghte,
To ressayve my reverence thorowe righte of o
 renowne;
Owe, what I am derworth and defte . . .

[*The rebel angels fall.*]

32 Whilst 34 in punishment 35 second only to 36 mirror/reflection 39 harming 40 dwelling 41 control 42 all the time you are obedient 47 abide 49 To prosper 50 lack 51 revealed 52 brightness, burning 54 live 55 Fairer by far, fellows 56 feature, decay 57 beautiful 58 surpassing 59 worship 60 created 62 defiling of filth, corrupt 66 harm, we need never fear 67 very finely shaped 68 shape, beauty, fixed 69 control 70 as great as 71 appearance, shimmering 72 greatly 73 I do not need to worry at all 74 torment me 76 the basis 77 voice 79 truly everlasting 80 gift, generously given 81 tasting 82 to go hungry 84 glow, glittering 85 fail 88 [in my] wielding 89 higher yet, placed 90 On high 91 in sight 92 of 93 worthy and noble

7 '[I promise] to those who are evil that they shall . . . '

8 'Then the angels sing "Holy, holy, holy, lord God of Hosts."'

9 'It is not necessary for me to talk about harm'.

Owe! Dewes! All goes downe!
My mighte and my mayne es all marrande.
Helpe, felawes! In faythe I am fallande.

II ANGELUS DEFICIENS
Fra Heven are we heledande on all hande,
To wo are we weendande, I warande.

LUCIFER, DIABOLUS IN INFERNO
Owte! Owte! Harrowe![10] Helples, slyke hote at es here;
This es a dongon of dole þat I am to dyghte.
Whare es my kynde become, so cumly and clere?[11]
Nowe am I laytheste, allas, þat are was lighte.
My bryghtnes es blakkeste and blo nowe,
My bale es ay betande and brynande,
That gares ane go gowlande and gyrnande.
Owte! Ay walaway! I well even in wo nowe.

II DIABOLUS
Owte! Owte! I go wode for wo, my wytte es all wente nowe,
All oure fode es but filth we fynde us beforn.
We þat ware beelded in blys, in bale are we brent nowe.
Owte on þe[e] Lucifer, lurdan, oure lyghte has þou lorne!
Þi dedes to þis dole nowe has dyghte us,
To spill us þou was oure spedar,
For thow was oure lyghte and oure ledar,
Þe hegheste of Heven hade þou hyght us.

LUCIFER IN INFERNO
Walaway! Wa es me now, nowe es it war thane it was.
Unthryvandely threpe ȝhe; I sayde but a thoghte.[12]

II DIABOLUS
We! Lurdane, þou lost us.

LUCIFER IN INFERNO
ȝhe ly! Owte, allas!
I wyste noghte þis wo sculde be wroghte.
Owte on ȝhow, lurdans! ȝhe smore me in smoke.

II DIABOLUS
This wo has þou wroghte us.

LUCIFER IN INFERNO
ȝhe ly, ȝhe ly!

II DIABOLUS
Thou lyes, and þat sall þou by!
We! Lurdans, have at ȝowe, lat loke!

ANGELUS CHERUBYN
A, lorde, lovid be Thi name þat us þis lyghte lente,
Sen Lucifer oure ledar es lighted so lawe,
For hys unbuxumnes in bale to be brente.
Thi rightewysnes to rewarde on rowe
Ilke warke eftyr is wroghte,[13]
Thorowe grace of Þi mercyfull myghte.
The cause I se itt in syghte,
Wharefore to bale he es broghte.

DEUS
Those foles for þaire fayrehede in fantasyes fell,
And hade mayne of migh mighte þat marked þam and made þam.
Forthi efter þaire warkes were, in wo sall þai well,
For sum ar fallen into fylthe þat evermore sall fade þam,
And never sall have grace for to gyrth þam.
So passande of power tham thoght þam,
Thai wolde noght Me worschip þat wroghte þam;
Forþi sall My wreth ever go with þam.

Ande all that Me wyrschippe sall wone here, iwys;
Forthi more forthe of My warke wyrke nowe I will.
Syn than þer mighte es for-marryde þat mente all omys,
Even to Myne awne fygure þis blys to fulfyll,
Mankynde of moulde will I make.[14]
But fyrste wille I fourme hym before

94 Oh! Deus! 95 failing 96 falling 97 tumbling on all sides 98 heading 98+ in the fire (of Hell) 99 it's so hot here 100 misery, appointed 102 loathliest, before 103 dark 104 kindling and burning 105 one, howling, grimacing 106 alas 110 curse thee, villain 111 have brought 112 ruin, furtherer 114 promised 115 worse 117 lie! 118 should 119 smother 121 pay for! 122 look here! 124 fallen, low 125 disobedience 131 beauty 132 power from 133 according to 135 shield 136 superior 138 wrath 140 even more

10 'Alas! Help!': traditional cries associated with evil or fallen characters.

11 'What has become of my nature, that was once so comely and beautiful?'

12 'You chide [me] unhelpfully/unfairly'.

13 'Your justice [is] to reward each deed as it deserves'.

14 'Since the strength of these who intended evil is destroyed, in order to complete this bliss [i.e. to repopulate Heaven] I shall make mankind from the dust in My own image.'

All thyng that sall hym restore,
To whilke þat his talente will take.

Ande in my fyrste makyng, to mustyr my mighte,
Sen Erthe es vayne and voyde and myrknes emel,[15]
I byd in my blyssyng ȝhe aungels gyf lyghte
To þe Erthe, for it faded when þe fendes fell.
In Hell sall never myrknes by myssande.
Þe myrknes thus name I for nighte;
The day, þat call I this lyghte,
My after-warkes sall þai by wyssande.[16]
Ande nowe in my blyssyng I twyne tham in two,
The nighte even fro þe day, so þat thai mete never,
But ather in a kynde courese þaire gates for to go.
Bothe þe nighte and þe day, does dewly ȝhour deyver,
To all I sall wirke be ȝhe wysshyng.
This day warke es done ilke a dele,
And all þis warke lykes Me ryght wele,
And baynely I gyf it My blyssyng.

145 sustain **146** his nature will lead **147** demonstrate **151** be missing **152** I name this darkness, 'night' **155** divide **157** natural, paths **158** do your duty **159** you shall be a witness **160** every part

[15] 'Since the Earth is empty and void, and everywhere in darkness'.

[16] 'By which they will know my later works'.

Chester (The Tanners), *The Fall of Lucifer*

The Chester pageant of *The Fall of Lucifer* may have been a late addition to the Cycle, and thus post-dates the York *Fall of the Angels* by up to a century. The two pageants have many features in common, however, despite their chronological distance. Like the York pageant, the Chester play treats material from the first day of Creation. Deus majestically expounds His own omnipotence and the doctrine of the Trinity, and creates Heaven and the nine orders of angels in a highly Latinate, 'learned' vocabulary appropriate to His status. As at York, the Chester wagon probably had a Hell-mouth at ground level into which Lucifer and his companion Lightborne (whose name is a variant of 'Lucifer', the fallen angel mentioned in Isaiah 14:12) descend at their fall, perhaps to be replaced by other actors already costumed as the demons into which they transform. Unlike York, however, the Chester pageant allows Lucifer an overt act of rebellion, the usurpation of God's authority by sitting in His throne; although here too the rebellion is overtly an act of impersonation, a point emphasized by the verbal echoes of God's words in Lucifer's boasts. Order, hierarchy, and harmony are again the central concerns of the pageant, manifested in God's creation, and momentarily disrupted by Lucifer's rebellion. These concepts were probably reflected in performance by rows of seats around the central throne, upon which the angels sat as they were brought into being. The various orders of angels are traditionally ranked from the highest, Seraphim, through Cherubim, Thrones, Dominations, Virtues, Powers, Principalities, and Archangels, to Angels, the lowest order. Even if only one of each is present on the pageant wagon, this would give a minimum cast size of twelve or thirteen (depending upon whether the third Demon, Ruffian, called to by Lucifer, is represented onstage), making the Chester play a far more impressive spectacle than its York counterpart.

The Tanners prepared animal hides, some of which might have been used for the costumes of the devils.

[*Dramatis Personae*: *Deus* (God the Father), *Lucifer* (later *Primus Demon*), *Angeli* (Angels), *Arcke Angelis* (Archangels), *Lightborne* (later *Secundus Demon*), *Virtues*, *Cherubim*, *Dominations*, *Seraphim*, *Principalities*, *Thrones*, *Powers*, *Ruffian* (a third Demon).]

DEUS

Ego sum alpha et oo,
Primus et novissimus.[1]
It is my will it shoulde be soe;
Hit is, yt was, it shalbe thus.

I ame greate God gracious,
Which never had begyninge;
The wholl foode of parente is sett
In My essention.
I ame the tryall of the Trenitye
Which never shalbe twyninge,
Pearles patron ymperiall,
And *Patris sapiencia.*
My beames be all beawtitude
All bliss is in My buyldinge.
All meirth lyeth in mansuetude,
Cum Dei potentia,
Bouth viscible and inviscible.
As God greatest and glorious,
All is in *Mea licencia.*

For all the meirth of the majestye
Is magnifyed in Me.
Prince principall, proved
In My perpetuall provydence,
I was never but one
And ever one in three,
Set in substanciall southnes
Within selestiall sapience.
The three tryalls in a throne
And true Trenitie
Be grounded in My godhead,
Exalted by My exelencie.
The might of My makeinge
Is marked in Mee,

7 ancestry, parentage 8 essential nature 9 three parts 10 separated 12 Paternal wisdom 13 blessedness 14 creation 15 happiness, humility 16 with the power of God 17 visible 19 my dominion 24 (anything) other than one 26 solid truth 27 wisdom 30 divinity 32 creativity

[1] 'I am Alpha and Omega, [the beginning and the end,] first and last.' Revelation 22:13.

Dissolved under a deadem
By My devyne experience.

Nowe sithe I am soe soeleme
And set in My solatacion,
A biglie blesse here will I builde,
A Heaven without endinge,
And cast a comely compasse
By comely creation.
Nyne orders of angells,
Be ever at onsce defendinge.
Doe your indevoure and doubte you not
Under My dominacion
To sytt in celestiall saftye.
All solace to your sending.
For all the likeinge in this lordshipp
Be laude to My laudacion.
Though might of My most majestie
Your meirth shall ever be mendinge.

LUCIFFER
Lorde, through Thy mighte Thou hast us wrought,
Nine orders here that we may see:
Cherubyn and Seraphin through Thy thought;
Thrones and Dominations in blisse to bee;

With Principates, that order brighte,
And Potestates in blisfull lighte;
Also Vertutes, through Thy greate mighte,
Angell and also Arke Angelle.

Nine orders here bene witterlye,
That Thou hast made here full right.
In Thy blisse full brighte the bee,
And I the principall, Lorde, here in Thy sighte.

DEUS
Here have I you wrought with heavenly mighte,
Of angells nine orders of greate beautye,
Iech one with others, as it is righte,
To walke aboute the Trenite

Nowe, Luciffer and Lightborne, loke lowely you bee,
The blessings of my begyninge I gave to my first operacion.
For crafte nor for cuninge, cast never comprehension;
Exsalte you not to exelente into high exaltation.[2]
Loke that you tende righte wisely, for hence I wilbe wendinge.
The worlde, that is bouth voyde and vayne, I forme in the formacion,
With a dongion of darknes, which never shall have endinge.
This work is nowe well wrought by My devyne formacion.
This worke is well donne, that is soe cleane and cleare.
As I you made of naughte, my blessings I geve you here.

ANGELIE
Wee thanke Thee, lorde, full soveraignely,
That us hath formed soe cleane and cleare,
Ever in this blesse to byde Thee bye.
Graunte us Thy grace ever to byde here.

ARCKE ANGELIS
Here for to byde God grante us grace
To please this prince withouten peare;
Him for to thanke with some solace,
A songe now let us singe here.

[*The angels sing*] '*Dignus Dei*'.[3]

DEUS
Now, seeinge I have formed you soe fayer
And exalted you so exelente;
And here I set you nexte My cheare,
My love to you is soe fervente:
Loke you fall not in noe dispaier.
Touch not My throne by non assente.
All your beautie I shall appaier,
And pride fall oughte in your intent.

LUCIFFER
Ney, lorde, that will we not in deed,
For nothinge tresspasse unto Thee.
Thy greate godhead we ever dreade,
And never exsaulte ourselves soe hie.

34 United under (My) crown 36 majestic 37 happiness 38 great (place of) bliss 40 circle/circuit 43 once 44 duty 47 endeavours 48 pleasure, realm 49 (should) be worship of My glory 50 Through, supreme 51 increasing 61 fittingly 62 they 66 Each 67 (go in) procession 68 humble 69 benignity, action 72 act, going 73 create 74 dungeon 78 royally 86 fair 88 chair (i.e. throne) 90 Ensure 91 in no circumstances 92 ruin 93 If, comes in any way 96 fear

[2] 'Do not try to comprehend [more than you should] either for power or for knowledge; do not exalt yourself too high in your pride.'

[3] 'Worthy God'. Mills (*Chester Mystery Cycle*, pp. 17–18) suggests this may have been the Benedictus anthem for the second Sunday after Easter, '*dignus es domine*' ('Thou, O Lord, art worthy to receive glory and honour and power because Thou created all things').

Thou has us marked with greate might and mayne
In Thy blesse evermore to byde and bee,
In lastinge life our life to leade.
And bearer of lighte Thou has made me.

LIGHTEBORNE
And I ame marked of that same moulde.
Loveinge be to our creator
That us hase made gayer than goulde,
Under His dieadem ever to indure.

DEUS
I have for-byd that ye neare shoulde;
But keepe you well in that stature.
The same covenante I charge you houlde,
In paine of Heaven your forfeyture.

For I will wende and take My trace
And see this blesse in every tower.
Iche one of you kepe well his place;
And, Lucifer, I make thee governour.
Nowe I charge the grounde of grace
That yt be set with My order.
Behoulde the beames of My brighte face,
Which ever was and shall indewer.

This is your health in every case
To behoulde your creator.
Was never non so like Me, soe full of grace,
Nor never shall as My fygure.
Here will I bide nowe in this place
To be angells comforture.
To be revisible in shorte space
It is My will in this same houre.

LUCIFFER
Aha! that I ame wounderous brighte,
Amongest you all shininge full cleare!
Of all Heaven I beare the lighte,
Though God Hymselfe and He were here.
All in this throne yf that I were,
Then shoulde I be as wise as Hee.
What saye ye, angells all that bene here?
Some comforte soone now let me see.

VERTUTES
Wee will not assente unto your pride
Nor in our hartes take such a thoughte;
But that Our Lorde shalbe our guyde,
And keepe that He to us hath wroughte.

CHERUBYN
Our Lorde comaunded all that bene here
To keepe there seates, bouth more and lesse.
Therfore I warne the[e], Luciffer,
This pride will torne to great distresse.

LUCIFFER
Destresse? I commaunde you for to cease
And see the beautie that I beare.
All heaven shines though my brightnes
For God Him Selfe shines not so cleare.

DOMINACIONES
Of all angells yee beare the price
And most beautie is you befall
My counsell is that you be wise,
That you bringe not yourselves in thrall.

PRINCIPATES
Yf that ye in thrall you bringe,
Then shall you have a wicked fall;
And alsoe your ofspringe,
A way with you they shall all.

CHERUBYN
Our brethers counsell is good to here,
To you I saye, Lucifer and Lightborne.
Wherfore, be ware you of this cheere,
Least that you have a fowle spurne.

LIGHTEBORNE
In fayth, brother, yet you shall
Sitt in this throne: arte cleane and cleare,
That yee may be as wise with all
As God Him Selfe, yf He were heare.
Therfore you shalbe set here,
That all Heaven maye ye behoulde.
The brightnes of your bodie cleare
Is brighter then God a thousand foulde.

THRONES
Alas, that beautie will you spill
Yf you keepe it all in your thought;
Then will pride have all his will
And bringe your brightnes all to naughte.

98 created 99 bliss 100 (ever)lasting 102 made from 103 worship 104 brighter, gold 105 crown, endure 106 approach 107 statute (i.e. obey that rule) 108 hold (i.e. keep) 109 of forfeiting Heaven 110 make My way 113 (My) deputy 114 graceful place (i.e. Heaven) 116 radiance 117 endure 118 happiness 121 person 124 seen again 129 Even if . . . 136 Rather 137 has made for us 138 are 140 thee 141 turn 146 are the best 147 fallen to you 149 slavery 150 yourselves 153 Away, all (fall) 154 hear 156 behaviour/attitude 157 downfall 159 (you) are . . . 160 as well 166 ruin

Let yt passe out of your thought,
And caste awaye all wicked pride;
And keepe your brightnes to you is wrought,
And let Our Lorde be all our guyde.

Potestates
Alas, that pride is the wall of beautye
That tornes your thought to greate offence.[4]
The brightnes of your fayer bodyes
Will make yee to goe hense.

Luciffer
Goe hense? Behoulde, sennyors one every syde,
And unto me you caste your eyen.
I charge you, angells, in this tyde
Behoulde and see now what I meane.
Above greate God I will me guyde
And set myselfe here. As I wene,
I ame pearlesse and prince of pride,
For God Him Selfe shines not so sheene.

Here will I sitt nowe in His steade,
To exsaulte my selfe in this same see.
Behoulde my bodye, handes, and head:
The mighte of God is marked in mee.
All angells, torne to me, I read,
And to your soveraigne kneele one your knee.
I ame your comforte, bouth lorde and head,
The meirth and might of the majestye.

Lighteborne
And I ame nexte of the same degree,
Repleth by all experience.
Me thinkes yf I mighte sit him bye
All Heaven shoulde doe us reverence.
All orders maye assente to thee and me;
Thou hast them torned by eloquence.
And here were nowe the Trenitie,
We shulde Him passe by our fullgens.

Dominationes
Alas, why make yee this greate offence?
Bouth Luciffer and Lighteborne, to you I saye,
Our Soveraigne Lorde will have you hense
And He fynde you in this araye.
Goe too your seates and wynde you hense.
You have begone a parlous playe.
Ye shall well witt the subsequence:
This daunce will torne to teene and traye.

Lucifer
I redd you all doe me reverence,
That ame repleth with heavenly grace.
Though God come, I will not hense,
But sitt righte here before His face.

[*As God returns, the angels sing*] *'Gloria tibi Trinitas'*.[5]

Deus
Saye, what arraye doe ye make here?
Who is your prince and principall?
I made thee angell, and Lucifer,
And here thou woulde be lorde over all!
Therefore I charge this order cleare,
Faste from this place looke that yee fall.
Full soone I shall chaunge your cheare:
For your fowle pride, to Hell you shall.

Lucifer, who set thee here when I was goe?
What have I offended unto thee?
I made thee My frende; thou arte My foe.
Why haste thou tresspassed thus to Me?
Above all angells there were no moe
That sitt so nighe My majestye.
I charge you to fall till I byd 'Whoo',
Into the deepe pitt of Hell ever to bee.

Nowe Luciffer and Lighteborne fall.

I Demon [Lucifer]
Alas, that ever we were wroughte,
That we shoulde come into this place!
Wee were in joye; nowe we be naughte.
Alas, we have forfayted our grace!

II Demon [Lightborne]
And even heither thou hast us broughte
Into dungeon to take our trace.

172 (that) is made for you 178 seignours on . . . 179 eyes 180 command 182 advance myself 185 brightly 187 seat 191 on 192 both, commander 195 Perfect 196 It seems to me 199 won over 200 Even if 201 surpass, brilliance 205 If, manner 206 get 207 begun, perilous 208 consequence 209 dance, grief 210 command/advise 212 (move) away 214 business 218 pure order (of angels) 219 Immediately 220 mood/appearance 222 gone? 223 How 228 say 'Stop' 233 forfeited 235 make our way

4 An enigmatic phrase, meaning, perhaps, 'Alas that pride walls beauty around, and turns your thoughts (away from God and) towards great offence.'

5 'Glory to Thee, O Trinity', the vespers antiphon for Trinity Sunday (Mills, *Chester Mystery Cycle*, p. 21).

All this sorrowe thou hast us soughte:
The Devill maye speede thy stinckinge face!

I DEMON
My face? False feature, for thy fare!
Thou hast us broughte to teene and treay.
I cumber, I congere, I kindle in care,
I sincke in sorrowe; what shall I saye?

II DEMON
Thou haste us broughte this wicked waye
Through thy mighte and thy pryde,
Out of the blesse that lasteth aye,
In sorowe ever more to abyde.

II DEMON
Thy witt yt was as well as myne,
Of that pryde that we did shewe.
And nowe bene here in Hell fier
Till the Day of Dome that beames shall bloo.

II DEMON
Then shall we never care for woo,
But lye here like two feeyndes blacke.
Alas, that ever we did forgett soe,
That Lordes love to lose that did us make.[6]

I DEMON
And therfore I shall for His sake
Shewe mankynde greate envye.
As soone as ever He can hym make,
I shall sende, hym to destroye,
One (of myne order shall he bee),
To make mankinde to doe amisse.
Ruffyn, my frende fayer and free,
Loke that thou keepe mankinde from blesse

That I and my fellowes fell downe for aye.
He will ordeyne mankinde againe
In blesse to be in great arraye,
And wee ever more in Hell paine.

II DEMON
Out, harrowe! Where is our mighte
That we were wonte to shewe,
And in Heaven bare soe greate lighte,
And nowe we be in Hell full lowe?

I DEMON
Out, alas! For woo and wickednesse
I ame so fast bounde in this cheare
And never awaye hense shall passe,
But lye in Hell all waye heare.

DEUS
A, wicked pryde! A, woo worth thee, woo!
My meirth thou hast made amisse.
I maye well suffer: My will is not soe,
That they should parte this from My blesse.
A, pryde! Why mighte thou not braste in two?
Why did the[e] that? Why did they thus?
Behoulde, My angells, pride is your foe.
All sorrowe shall shewe where soever yt is.

And though they have broken My commaundement,
Me ruse yt sore full sufferently.
Never the lesse, I will have Myne intente:
That I first thought, yet soe will I.
I and two persons be at one assente[7]
A sollempne matter for to trye.
A full fayer image We have imente,
That the same stydd shall multiplye.

In My blessinge here I begyne,
The first that shalbe to My paye.
Lightenes and darkenes, I byde you twene:
The darke to the nighte, the lighte to the day.
Keep your course for more or myne,
And suffer not, to you I saye;
But save yourselfe, bouth out and in.
That is My will, and will allwaye.

As I have made you all of noughte
At Myne owne wisheinge,
My first day heare have I wroughte.
I geve yt here My blessinge.

236 sought (out) for us 237 favour 238 faitor (i.e. deceiver), deeds 239 anger, grief 240 cower, beg, burn, woe 244 (for) ever 248 (we) are 249 Judgement (Day), trumpets, blow 250 escape from 251 fiends 256 creates him (i.e. Man) 259 sin (and fall) 260 Ruffian (another devil) 261 Heaven 262 From which . . . for ever 263 (God) will arrange for mankind 264 ceremony 271 chair 274 curse you, woe! 277 thus 278 break 279 thee 281 appear 282 (Even) though 283 I suffer it, patiently 287 begin 288 fair, likeness, conceived 289 will repopulate that place 291 first (deed), pleasure 292 divide 293 to (be) 294 less 295 do not deviate 296 retain your own nature, both 297 (be) always 298 from nothing 299 desire

6 'To lose the love of that Lord who made us.'

7 'I and the other two Persons [of the Trinity, i.e. Christ and the Holy Spirit] are of one mind'.

York (The Coopers), *The Fall of Man*

In Christian terms human history begins with the Fall of Adam and Eve, represented in this intimate and subtly characterized pageant. It is the Fall which condemns all humanity to damnation, a fate from which they are redeemed only by Christ's Incarnation and sacrifice of Himself on the Cross. As well as introducing Adam and Eve, with their human emotions and weaknesses, the pageant also offers us the first sight of Satan in his role as tempter, which he will reprise in the York *Temptation of Christ* (not anthologized here), and *Christ Before Pilate I*. Satan's malice and envy are motivated by his knowledge that God will choose to be incarnated in human rather than angelic form, which he takes as a slight on his own angelic nature.

Precisely how Satan transformed himself 'in[to] serpent's likeness' is not clear from the text, although a costume or mime are equally effective possibilities. One potent iconographic tradition which might have influenced the pageant shows the serpent with a woman's face (see the Chester *Adam and Eve*, following), thus adding a further misogynistic element to that implicit in the emphasis upon Eve as the 're[a]dy way' to bring about human corruption. The characterization of Adam is, however, not wholly heroic either. Unlike Milton's character, Adam here falls, not for love of Eve, but for the same self-seeking reasons as his spouse.

The Coopers made barrels, tubs, and other wooden vessels.

[*Dramatis Personae*: *Satanas* (Satan), *Eva* (Eve), *Adam*, *Dominus* ('Lord': God the Father), *Angelus* (Angel, traditionally the Archangel Michael).]

SATANAS *incipit, dicens:*

For woo my witte es in a were
That moffes me mykill in my mynde;
The Godhede þat I sawe so cleere,
And parsayved þat He shuld take kynde
Of a degree
That He had wrought, and I denyed
Þat aungell kynde shuld it noȝt be.
And we wer faire and bright,
Þerfore me thoght þat He
The kynde of us tane myght,
And þerat dedeyned me.

The kynde of man He thoght to take
And theratt hadde I grete envye.
But He has made to hym a make,
And harde to her I wol me hye,
That redy way,
That purpose prove to putte it by,
And fande to pike fro hym þat pray.[1]
And travayle were wele sette
Myght Y hym so betraye,
His likyng for to lette,
And sone I schalle assaye.

In a worme liknes wille Y wende,
And founde to feyne a lowde lesynge.[2]
Eve, Eve!

EVA

Wha es þare?

SATANAS

I, a frende.
And for thy gude es þe comynge
I hydir sought.[3]
Of all þe fruyt that ye se hynge
In Paradise, why ete ye noght?

EVA

We may of tham ilkane
Take al þat us goode þought
Save a tree outt is tane,
Wolde do harme to neyghe it ought.

0+ Satin begins, saying: 1 whirl 2 moves 4 perceived, take [on the] nature 5 species/rank 6 opposed/objected 10 might take 11 offended 13 at that 14 mate/partner 15 straight, go 19 effort would be well spent 21 pleasure, prevent 22 immediately, try 23 serpent's likeness 25 Who is there? 31 seem good to us 32 one is excluded 33 go anywhere near it

1 'To forestall that plan and attempt to steal that prey from him.'
2 'And attempt a blatant deception.'
3 'And I have sought to come here for your good.'

SATANAS
And why þat tree, þat wolde I witte,
Any more þan all othir by?

EVA
For oure lord God forbeedis us itt,
The frute þerof, Adam nor I
To neghe it nere;
And yf we dide we both shuld dye,
He saide, and sese our solace sere.

SATANAS
Yha, Eve, to me take tente;
Take hede and þou shalte here
What þat the matere mente
He moved on þat manere.

To ete þerof He you defende
I knawe it wele, þis was His skylle:
Bycause He wolde non othir kende
Thes grete vertues þat longes þertill.
For will þou see,
Who etis the frute of good and ille
Shalle have knowyng as wele as Hee.

EVA
Why, what-kynne thyng art þou
Þat telles þis tale to me?

SATANAS
A worme, þat wotith wele how
Þat yhe may wirshipped be.

EVA
What wirshippe shulde we wynne therby?
To ete þerof us nedith it nought,
We have lordshippe to make maistrie
Of alle þynge þat in erthe is wrought.

SATANAS
Woman, do way!
To gretter state ye may be broughte
And ye will do as I schall saye.

EVA
To do is us full lothe
Þat shuld oure God myspaye

SATANAS
Nay, certis it is no wrathe,
Ete it saffley ye maye.

For perille ryght þer none in lyes,
Bot worshippe and a grete wynnynge,
For right als God yhe shalle be wyse
And þere to Hym in all-kyn thynge.
Ay, goddis shalle ye be,
Of ille and gode to have knawyng,
For to be als wise as He.

EVA
Is þis soth þat þou sais?

SATANAS
Yhe, why trowes þou noȝt me?
I wolde be no-kynnes wayes
Telle noȝt but trouthe to þe[e].

EVA
Than wille I to thy techyng traste
And fange þis frute unto oure foode.

Et tunc debet accipere pomum.[4]

SATANAS
Byte on boldly, be nought abasshed,
And bere Adam to amende his mode
And eke his blisse.

Tunc Satanas recedet.[5]

EVA
Adam, have here of frute full goode.

ADAM
Alas woman, why toke þou þis?
Owre Lorde comaunded us bothe
To tente þe tree of His.

35 nearby 36 forbids 38 approach it 40 many happinesses 41 pay attention 42 hear 43 reason was 44 expressed himself in that way 45 forbad 46 know, reason 47 wanted no one else [to] know 48 properties belonging to it 52 what kind of . . . 54 knows 56 gain 57 we do not need 58 have authority 59 on earth is made 60 do not be foolish! 61 greater 62 If 63 We would hate to do [anything] 64 offend 65 risk/(cause of) anger 66 safely 67 peril 68 gain 69 just as 70 equal, every 72 evil, good, knowledge 76 by no means 79 take/seize 81 take [some to], change his mood 82 improve his happiness 84 took 86 pay attention to

4 'Then she should bite the apple.'

5 'Then Satan goes away.'

Thy werke wille make Hym wrothe,
Allas, þou hast done amys.

Eva
Nay Adam, greve þe[e] nought at it,
And I shal saie þe reasonne why.
A worme has done me for to witte
We shalle be as goddis, þou and I,
Yf þat we ete
Here of this tree; Adam, forthy
Lette noght þat worshippe for to gete.
For we shalle be als wise
Als God þat is so grete,
And als mekill of prise.
Forthy ete of þis mete.

Adam
To ete it wolde Y nought eschewe
Myght I me sure in thy saying.

Eva
Byte on boldely, for it is trewe,
We shalle be goddis and knawe al thyng.

Adam
To wynne þat name
I schalle it taste at thy techyng.

Et accipit et comedit.[6]

Allas, what have I done, for shame!
Ille counsaille, woo worthe the[e]!
A, Eve, þou art to blame,
To þis entysed þou me.
Me shames with my lyghame,

For I am naked as methynke.

Eva
Allas Adam, right so am I.

Adam
And for sorowe sere why ne myght we synke,
For we have greved God Almyghty
Þat made me man,
Brokyn His bidyng bittirly.
Allas þat ever we it began!
Þis werke, Eve, hast þou wrought,
And made þis bad bargayne.

Eva
Nay Adam, wite me nought.

Adam
Do wey, lefe Eve, whame þan?

Eva
The worme to wite wele worthy were.
With tales untrewe he me betrayed.

Adam
Allas, þat I lete at thy lare
Or trowed þe trufuls þat þou me saide.
So may I byde,
For I may banne þat bittir brayde
And drery dede, þat I it dyde.
Oure shappe for doole me defes,
Wherewith þay shalle be hydde?

Eva
Late us take there fygge-leves,
Sythen it is þus betydde.

Adam
Ryght as þou sais so shalle it bee,
For we are naked and all bare.
Full wondyr fayne I wolde hyde me
Fro my Lordis sight, and I wiste whare.
Where I ne roght!

Dominus
Adam, Adam!

Adam
Lorde?

Dominus
Where art thou yhare?

Adam
I here Þe[e] Lorde and seys The[e] noʒt.

87 action, angry 88 wrong 91 let me know 95 Do not prevent us from getting 98 of as great value/esteem 99 food 100 not decline 101 be certain of 105 prompting 107 evil advice, curse you! 109 enticed 110 I am ashamed of my body 113 many sorrows 116 orders 120 do not blame me 121 dear, who else? 122 is well worthy of blame 124 listened to, advice 125 trifles (foolishness) 127 curse, bitter choice/instinct 128 evil deed 129 Our bodies stun me with horror 130 With what shall they . . . 131 fig-leaves 132 Since it has turned out thus. 135 very gladly 136 From, if I knew where 137 I wish I were unborn/uncreated! 139 but do not see you

[6] 'And he accepts and eats.'

Dominus
Say, wheron is it longe,
Þis werke why hast þou wrought?

Adam
Lorde, Eve garte me do wronge
And to þat bryg me brought.

Dominus
Say, Eve, why hast þou garte thy make
Ete frute I bad þe[e] shuld hynge stille,
And comaunded none of it to take?

Eva
A worme, Lord, entysed me therto;
So welaway,
That ever I did þat dede so dill!

Dominus
A, wikkid worme, woo worthe þe[e] ay,
For þou on þis maner
Hast made þam swilke affraye.
My malysoune have þou here
With all þe myght Y may.

And on thy wombe þan shall þou glyde,
And be ay full of enmyte
To al mankynde on ilke a side,
And erthe it shalle thy sustynaunce be
To ete and drynke.
Adam and Eve alsoo, yhe
In erthe þan shalle ye swete and swynke,
And travayle for youre foode.

Adam
Allas, whanne myght we synke?
We that haves alle worldis goode
Ful defly may us thynke.

Dominus
Now Cherubyn, Myn aungell bryght,
To Middilerth tyte go dryve these twoo.

Angelus
Alle redy Lorde, as it is right,
Syn Thy wille is þat it be soo,
And Thy lykyng.
Adam and Eve, do you to goo,
For here may ȝe make no dwellyng;
Goo yhe forthe faste to fare,
Of sorowe may yhe synge.

Adam
Allas, for sorowe and care
Oure handis may we wryng.

140 How has this come about? 142 made 143 this state 144 mate 145 be left to hang 149 stupid 150 woe be with you always 151 in this way 152 trouble 153 curse 155 belly, glide 157 every side 161 sweat and labour 165 cursedly 167 Middle-Earth 169 Since your wish 170 pleasure 173 Go, travel

Chester (The Drapers), *Adam and Eve*

As was the case with the York *Fall of Man*, the Chester *Adam and Eve* dramatizes events from the first three books of Genesis. The pageant wagon would have been dressed in much the same way to represent Paradise, with an emblematic Tree of Knowledge set in the middle. The Serpent's entrance would probably have been made through a trapdoor, and God may well have descended from an upper level to create Adam and Eve on the wagon's main stage. Thus movement in three dimensions is an important feature of this play, suggesting humanity's potential either to ascend or to descend from their position in Paradise, depending on the exercise of their free will and God's mercy. The most striking features of the pageant would, however, have been the costumes rather than the set. Adam and Eve's nakedness was probably represented by undyed or skin-coloured body-suits, to which fig-leaves and, later, animal skins could be attached. The angels would also have been sumptuously dressed and, like God, would have either worn golden masks or had gilded faces to symbolize their heavenly natures. The most spectacular costume would undoubtedly have been that of the Serpent, with its woman's face, snake's tail, and feathered body. The Drapers made cloth for clothing and decorative purposes, and so would be well placed to produce such varied and impressive costumes. It is also possible that the Creation of Heaven and Earth would have been enacted using painted cloths depicting the various elements and creatures mentioned by God, adding a greater degree of spectacle to events than was evident in the York pageant.

[*Dramatis Personae*: *Deus* (God the Father), *Adam*,
Demon (later *Serpens*, the Serpent), *Eva* (Eve),
IV Angelus (four Angels).]

DEUS
Ego sum alpha et omega,
Primus et novissimus.[1]

I, God, moste of majestye,
In whom begininge none may bee;
Enlesse alsoe, moste of postee,
I am and have binne ever.
Now Heaven and Earth is made through Mee,
The Earth is voyd ondly, I see;
Therfore light for more lee
Through My might I will liever.

At My byddynge made be light.
Light is good, I see in sight.
Twynned shalbe through My might
The light from the stearnes.
Light 'day' wilbe called aye,
And the stearnes 'night', as I saye.
This morne and evene, the first day,
Is made full and expresse.

Now will I make the firmament
In myddeste the water to bee lent,
For to bee a divident
To twynne the waters aye;
Above the welkyn, beneath alsoe,
And 'Heaven' hit shalbe called thoo.
This commen is morne and even also
Of the seoconde daye.

Now will I waters every chone
That under Heaven bine great one,
That the gather into one,
And drynesse sone them shewe.
That dryenesse 'yearth' men shall call.
The gatheringe of the waters all,
'Seeyes' to [name] have the[y] shall;
Therby men shall them knowe.

I will one yearth yerbes springe,
Ichon in kinde seed-gevinge;
Trees diverse fruite forth bringe
After ther kynde eachone;
The seede of which aye shalbe
Within the fruite of each tree.

4 there is no beginning 5 Endless, greatest of power 6 been (for) 8 merely empty 9 greater pleasure 10 prefer 13 Divided 14 darkness 18 completely and openly 19 sky 20 (the) middle (of), placed 21 partition 23 sky 24 then 25 Thus come the 26 second 27 I will (into being), one 28 there are many 29 they 30 soon, appear 31 'the earth' 33 'seas' 35 on, herbs (to) grow 36 by nature seed-bearing 38 According to their nature

[1] 'I am Alpha and Omega, [the beginning and the end,] first and last.' Revelation 22:13.

This morne and even of dayes three
Is both commen and gonne.

Now will I make through My might
Lightninges in the welkyn bright,
To twyne the daye from the night
And lighten the earth with lee.
Great lightes I will too:
The sonne and eke the moone also;
The sonne for day to serve for oo,
The moone for night to bee.

Starres also through Myne entente
I will make one the firmamente,
The yearth to lighten there the be lent;
And knowne may be thereby
Courses of planets, nothinge amisse.
Now see I this worke good iwisse.
This morninge and evon both made is,
The fourthe day, fullye.

Now will I in waters fishe forth bringe,
Fowles in the firmament flyinge,
Great whalles in the sea swiminge;
All make I with a thoughte.
Beastes, fowles, fruit, stone, and tree:
These workes are good, well I see.
Therfore to blesse all well liketh Me,
This worke that I have wrought.

All beastes, I byd you multyplye
In yearth and water, by and by,
And fowles in the ayre to flye,
The yearth to fulfill.
This morne and evon through My might
Of the fiveth day and the night
Is made and ended well aright,
All at My owne will.

Now will I one earth bringe forth anon
All helpely beastes, every chone
That crepon, flyen, or gone,
Each on in this kynde.
Now is this donne at My byddinge:
Beastes goinge, flyinge, and crepinge;
And all My worke at My likinge
Fully now I fynde.

Then, goinge from the place where He was, {God} commeth to the place where He createth Adam.

Now Heaven and Earth is made expresse,
Make wee man to our likenesse.
Fishe, fowle, beast, more and lesse,
To mayster he shall have might.
To our shape now make I thee;
Man and woman I will there bee,
Grow and multyplye shall yee,
And fulfill the Earth on hight.

To helpe thee thou shalt have here
Herbes, trees, fruit, seede in fere.
All shalbe put in thy power,
And beastes eke alsoe;
All that in yearth bine livinge,
Fowles in the ayre flyinge,
And all that gost hath and likinge,
To sustayne you from woe.

Now this is donne, I see, aright,
And all thinge made through My might.
The sixt day heare in My sight
Ys made all of the best.
Heaven and Earth ys wrought all within
And all that needes to be therin.
Tomorrowe, the seaventh day, I will blinne
And of workes take My rest.

But this man that I have made,
With goste of lief I will him gladde.

Adam rysinge.

DEUS
Rise up, Adam, rise up, ryse,
A man full of sowle and liefe,
And come with Mee to Paradice,
A place of deyntee and delite.
But it is good that thou be wise;
Bringe not thyselfe in striefe.

(minstrelles playe.)

Then the Creatour bringeth Adam into Paradice, before the tree of knowledge, and saith:

44 lights 45 divide 46 pleasantly 47 two 48 sun 49 ever 51 My will 52 in 53 where they are placed 55 nothing imperfect 61 whales 65 it pleases Me well 67 order you (to) 69 air 70 populate 71 evening 72 fifth 75 on, at once 76 helpful 77 creep, walk 78 according to their 81 to 83 openly 84 in 86 He shall have power to command 87 image 90 populate, fully 92 in abundance 94 as well 95 are 97 spirit, desire 101 here 103 (i.e. within six days) 105 stop 108 spirit, life 110 soul 112 pleasure 114 trouble

DEUS

Here, Adam, I give thee this place,
Thee to comforte and solace,
To keepe it well while thou hit hasse,
And donne as I thee bydd.
Of all trees that bine herein
Thou shalt eate, and nothinge sinne;
But of this tree, for weale nor wynne,
Thou eate by no way.

What tyme thou eates of this tree,
Death thee behoves, leave thow Mee.
Therfore this fruit I will thee flee,
And be thou not too bould.
Beastes and fowles that thou may see
To thee obedyent shall they bee.
What name they bee given by thee,
That name they shall hould.

Then God taketh Adam by the hande and causeth him to lye downe, and taketh a ribbe out of his syde, and saith:

DEUS

Hit is not good man only to bee;
Helpe to him now make Wee.
But excice sleepe behoves Mee
Anon in this man heare.
One sleepe thou arte, well I see.
Heare a bone I take of thee,
And fleshe alsoe with harte free
To make thee a feere.

Then God doth make the woman of the ribbe of Adam. Wakinge [Adam] sayth to God:

ADAM

A, Lorde, where have I longe bine?
For sythence I slepte much have I seene;
Wonder that withouten weene
Hereafter shalbe wiste.

DEUS

Ryse, Adam, and awake.
Heare have I formed the[e] a make;
Hir to thee thou shalt take,
And name hir as thee liste.

Adam, rysing up, saith:

ADAM

I see well, Lord, through Thy grace
Bonne of my bones Thou hir mase;
And fleshe of my fleshe shee hase,
And my shape through Thy saw.
Therfore shee shalbe called, I wisse,
'Viragoo', nothinge amisse;[2]
For out of man taken shee is,
And to man shee shall drawe.

Of earth Thou madest first mee,
Both bone and fleshe; now I see
Thou hast her given through Thy postee
Of that I in me had.
Therfore, man kyndely shall forsake
Father and mother, and to wife take;
Too in one fleshe, as Thou can make,
Eyther other for to glad.

Then Adam and Eve shall stand naked and shall not bee ashamed. Then the Serpente shall come up out of a hole, and the Dyvell walkinge shall say:

DEMON

Owt, owt! What sorrowe is this,
That I have loste soe much blysse?
For onste I thought to doe amysse,
Out of Heaven I fell.
The bryghtest angell I was or this,
That ever was or yet is;
But pryde cast me downe, I wisse,
From Heaven right into Hell.

Gostlye Paradice I was in,
But thence I fell through sinne.
Of yeart[h]ly Paradice now, as I weene,
A man is given masterye.
By Belsabubb, I will never blynne
Till I may make him by some gynne
From that place for to twyne
And trespasse as did I.

Should such a caytiffe made of claye
Have such blisse? Nay, by my laye!

116 delight 117 you have it 118 do 119 are 120 not 121 profit or pleasure 123 If at any time . . . 124 you will deserve, believe Me 125 want you (to) avoid 126 bold 131 It, alone 133 I should prompt sleep 135 Asleep 137 happy heart 138 companion 139 been? 141 Wonders, doubt 144 mate 146 you like 148 made 149 has 150 command 154 cleave 155 From 157 power 158 of my substance 159 by nature 161 Two 162 Each, please 165 once 167 before 171 Spiritual Paradise (Heaven) 173 Earthly Paradise (Eden) 176 plot/trick 177 separate 178 sin 180 law

2 '*Virago*', Latin: 'woman', from *vir*: 'man'.

For I shall teach his wiffe a playe
And I may have a whyle.
For her to disceave I hoppe I may,
And through her brynge them both awaye.
For shee will doe as I her saye,
Hir hoppe I will begylle.

That woman is forbydden to doe
For any thinge she will therto.[3]
Therfore, that tree shee shall come to
And assaye which it is.
Dight me I will anone tyte
And profer her of that ylke fruite;
Soe shall they both for her delyte
Bee banyshed from that blysse.

A maner of an edder is in this place
That wynges like a bryde shee hase,
Feete as an edder, a maydens face:
Hir kynde I will take.
And of the Tree of Paradice
Shee shall eate through my contyse:
For wemen they be full licourouse:
That will shee not forsake.

And eate shee of hyt, full witterlye
They shall fare both as dyd I:
Be banyshed both of that valley
And hir osprynge for aye.
Therfore, as brooke I my panne,
The edders coate I will take one;
And into Paradice I will gonne
As faste as ever I maye.

Supremus volucris penna, serpens pede forma, forma puella.[4]

SERPENS
Woman, why was God soe nyce
To byd you leave for your delice
And of each tree in Paradice
To forsake the meate?

EVA
Nay, of the fruite of yche tree
For to eate good leave have wee,
Save the fruite of one wee muste flee;
Of hyt wee may not eate.

This tree heare that in the middest is,
Eate wee of hit, wee doe amysse.
God sayde we should dye I wys
And if we touch that tree.

SERPENS
Woman, I saye, leave not this,
For hyt shall yee not loose the[e] blysse[5]
Nor noe joy that is His,
But be as wyse as Hee.

God is subtyle and wisse of witte
And wotteth well when ye eate it
That your eyne shalbe unknyt.
Like godes yee shalbe
And knowe both good and evill alsoe.
Therfore Hee warned you therfroe.
Yee may well wotte Hee was your foe;
Therfore, doe after mee.

Take of this fruite and assaye;
Yt is good meate, I dare laye.
And, but thou finde yt to thy paye,
Say that I am false.
And yee shall knowe bothe welle and woe
And been like godes both too,
Thou and thy husband alsoe.
Take thou one apple and noe moo.

EVA
A, lord, this tree is fayre and bryght,
Greene and seemely to my sight,
The fruite sweete and much of myght,
That godes it may us make.
One apple of yt I will eate
To assaye which is the meate
And my husbande I will gett
One morsell for to take.

182 If 183 deceive, expect 184 out (of Paradise) 186 hope, beguile 190 test what it is like 191 quickly prepare myself 192 offer, same 193 through her 195 kind of snake 196 has 198 nature, adopt 200 cunning 201 eager for pleasure 202 That (characteristic) 203 (If) she eats from it 204 both suffer 206 their offspring, ever 207 I suffer my pain 209 go 211 strict 212 forestall, delight 214 fruit 216 permission 217 Except, avoid 220 (and) we do wrong 221 die 223 believe 227 cunning 229 eyes, opened 232 forbad, from it 234 do as I do 235 try (it) 236 bet 237 unless, liking 239 happiness 240 the two (of you) 242 more 245 very powerful 248 try (of) what sort 250 small portion

3 'Whatever a woman is forbidden to do, that thing she will want to do above anything else.'

4 'Upper part with a bird's feather(s); serpent-shaped in the foot, in figure a girl': a description of the Serpent.

5 'You shall not lose Heaven because of it'.

Then Eve shall take of the fruite of the Serpente, and shall eate therof and say to Adam;

EVA
Adam, husbande, liffe and deare,
Eate some of this apple here.
Yt is fayre, my leeffe feare;
Hit may thou not forsake.

ADAM
That is soothe, Eve, withouten were;
The fruite is sweete and passinge feare.
Therfore I will doe thy prayer;
One morsell I will take.

Then Adam shall take the fruite and eate therof, and in weepinge manner shall saye:

Out, alas! What ayleth mee?
I am naked, well I see.
Woman, cursed mote thou bee,
For wee bothe nowe shente.
I wotte not for shame whyther to flee,
For this fruite was forbydden mee.
Now have I brooken, through reade of thee,
My Lordes commandemente.

EVA
Alas, this edder hathe done mee nye!
Alas, hir reade why did I?
Naked wee bine bothe forthy,
And of our shappe ashamed.

ADAM
Yea, sooth sayde I in prophecye
When thou was taken of my bodye:
Mans woe thou would bee witterlye;
Therfore thou was soe named.

EVA
Adam, husbande, I reade we take
This figge-leaves for shames sake,
And to our members an hillinge make
Of them for thee and mee.

ADAM
And therwith my members I will hide,
And under this tree I will abyde;
For surely, come God us besyde,
Owt of this place shall wee.

(minstrelles playe.)

Then Adam and Eve shall cover ther members with leaves, hydinge themselves under the trees. Then God shall speake:

DEUS
Adam, Adam, where arte thou?

ADAM
A, Lorde, I harde Thy voyce nowe,
For I naked am, I make a vowe,
Therfore now I hyd mee.

DEUS
Whoe tould thee, Adam, thou naked was,
Save only thy trespasse,
That of the tree thou eaten hasse
That I forbydd thee?

ADAM
Lord, this woman that is here,
That Thou gave to my feare,
Gave mee parte at hir prayer,
And of hyt I did eate.

DEUS
Woman, why has thou donne soo?

EVA
This edder, Lorde, shee was my foe
And sothly mee disceaved alsoe,
And made mee to eate that meate.

DEUS
Edder, for that thou haste donne this anye,
Amongste all beasts on Earth thee by
Cursed thou shalt bee forthy,
For this womans sake.
Upon thy brest thou shalt goo,
And eate the yearth to and froo;
And emnytie betweene you too
I insure thee I shall make.

Betweene thy seed and hirs alsoe
I shall excyte thy sorrowe and woe;
To breake thy head and be thy foe,
Shee shall have masterye aye.

251 loved one 253 dear husband 255 doubt 256 fair 257 as you ask 259 afflicts 261 must 262 are ruined 263 where 265 broken, your advice 267 harm 268 why did I follow her advice? 269 are 270 bodies 273 man's woe (i.e. 'wo-man') 277 for, covering 278 from 281 when God comes . . . 282 we (go) 284 heard 285 I swear (it) 287 told 288 Unless (it was), sin 289 have 292 companion 293 request 298 food 299 because you, harm 300 near you 303 belly 306 ensure 308 provoke

Noe beast one Earth, I thee behett,
That man soe little shall of seett;
And troden bee full under foote
For thy mysdeede todaye.

DEUS (*ad Evam*)
And, woman, I warne thee witterlye,
Thy much payne I shall multyplye.
With paynes, sorrowe, and great anye
Thy children thou shall beare.
And for that thou haste done soe to daye,
Man shall master thee alwaye:
And under his power thou shalte bee aye,
Thee for to dryve and deare.

DEUS (*ad Adam*)
And, man, alsoe I saye to thee,
For thou haste not donne after Mee,
Thy wyves counsell for to flee,
But donne doe hir byddinge
To eate the fruite of thys tree,
In thy worke warryed the earthe shalbe;
And with greate travell behoves thee
One earth to gett thy livinge.

When thou one Earth traveled hasse,
Fruite shall not growe in that place;
But thornes, brears for thy trespasse
To thee one earth shall springe.
Herbes, rootes thou shalte eate
And for thy sustenance sore sweate
With great mischeyfe to wynne thy meate,
Nothinge to thy likinge.

Thus shall thou live, soothe to sayen,
For thou haste byne to Mee unbayen,
Ever tyll the tyme thou turne agayne
To yearth there thou came fro.
For earth thou arte, as well is seene;
And after this worke, woe and teene,
To earth there thou shalt, withouten weene,
And all thy kynde alsoe.

Adam shall speake mourninglye.

ADAM
Alas, now in longer I am ilente!
Alas, nowe shamely am I shente!
For I was unobedyente,
Of weale now am I wayved.
Nowe all my kynde by mee ys kente
To flee womens intycemente.
Whoe trusteth them in any intente,
Truly hee is disceaved.

My licourouse wyfe hath bynne my foe;
The devylls envye shente mee alsoe.
These too together well may goe,
The suster and the brother!
His wrathe hathe donne me muche woe;
Hir glotonye greved mee alsoe.
God lett never man trust you too,
The one more then the other.

DEUS
Nowe wee shall parte from this lee.
Hilled behoveth you to to bee.
Dead beaste skynes, as thinketh Mee,
Ys best you one you beare.
For deadly nowe both bine yee
And death noe way may you flee.
Such clothes are best for your degree
And such shall yee weare.

Then God, puttynge garmentes of skynnes upon them {, says}:

DEUS
Adam, nowe hast thou thy wyllynge,
For thou desyred above all thinge
Of good and evell to have knowinge;
Now wrought is all thy will.
Thou wouldeste knowe both weelle and woe;
Nowe is it fallen to thee soe.
Therfore hence thou muste goo,
And thy desyre fullfilled.

Now lest thou [covett]este more
And doe as thou haste donne before,
Eate of this fruite to live evermore,
Heare may thou not bee.
To yearth thyder thou muste gonne;
With travell leade thy liefe thereone.
For syccere, there is noe other wonne.
Goe forthe; take Eve with thee.

311 on, promise 312 esteem 314+ (to Eve) 315 certainly 317 suffering 319 because 322 direct, punish 322+ (to Adam) 324 as I said 328 cursed 329 labour 330 On 331 have laboured 333 (and) briars, sin 336 sorely sweat 337 hardship, produce, food 338 In no way 339 truly to tell 340 been, disobedient 342 (i.e. until you die) 345 shall (return) 347 languor, thrown 348 shamefully 350 From happiness, excluded 351 taught 352 enticement(s) 353 Whoever, matter 355 been 357 two 358 sister 361 two 363 depart, bliss 364 It suits you to be covered 365 skins 366 on 367 mortal, you both are 371 what you wanted 373 knowledge 378 With 379 desire 383 go 384 labour 385 surely, place

(minstrelles playe.)

Then God shall dryve Adam and Eve out of Paradice, and sayth to the Angell:

Deus
Nowe will I that there lenge within
The angelle order Cherubynn,
To keepe this place of weale and wynne
That Adam lost thus hathe,
With sharpe swordes one everye syde
And flame of fyer here to abyde,
That never a yearthly man in glyde;
For given the[e] bynne that grace.[6]

Primus Angelus
Lorde, that order that is righte
Is readye seett heare in Thy syghte,
With flame of fyer, readye to fyght
Agaynst mankynde, Thy foe,
To whom noe grace is claymed by righte.
Shall none of them byde in Thy sighte
Tyll Wysdome, Right, Mercye, and Mighte[7]
Shall buy them and other moe.

Secundus Angelus
I, Cherubyn, muste here bee chyce
To keepe this place of great pryce.
Sythenn man was soe unwyse,
This wyninge I muste weare;
That hee by crafte or countyce,
Shall not come in that was hise,
But deprived bee of Paradyce,
Noe more for to come there.

Tercius Angelus
And in this herytage[8] I wilbe,
Still for to ever see
That noe man come in this cyttye
As God hath me beheight.
Swordes of fyer have all wee
To make mann from this place to flee,
From this dwellinge of greate dayntee
That to him first was dighte.

Quartus Angelus
And of this order I am made one,
From mankynde to weare this wone
That through his gilte hath forgone
This wonninge full of grace.
Therfore departe the[e] must eycheone.
Our swordes of fyer shall bee there bonne
And myselfe there verye fonne,
To flame them in the face.

Minstrelles playe.

[*The play goes on to relate the story of Cain and Abel, Adam and Eve's offspring.*]

387 stay within (Paradise) **393** can sneak in **403** careful **404** value **406** dwelling place, defend **407** skill, cunning **408** his **409** But (must) **413** city **414** instructed **417** delight **418** for him, originally prepared **420** guard, dwelling **421** lost **423** each one **424** their reward **425** their true foe

6 'For you (the Cherubim) have been given that privilege.'

7 The four chief attributes of God mentioned in Psalm 85:10–11, often personified as the 'Daughters of God' in the medieval period.

8 '[Humanity's original] inheritance'.

York (The Pewterers and Founders), *Joseph's Trouble About Mary*

The basic plot of this pageant – Joseph's doubts about Mary's chastity, his decision to disown her, the visitation by an angel while he was sleeping, and his eventual reconciliation with his wife – are contained in Matthew 1:18–25. The details of treatment and characterization are, however, more innovative, based upon apocryphal material such as the Gospel of Pseudo-Matthew, and medieval theological and literary traditions. The dramatist makes considerable comic use of the scenario of a husband's doubts about his wife's sexual honesty, drawing upon fabliau material such as that used by Chaucer in *The Miller's Tale* and *The Merchant's Tale*, in which old husbands are cuckolded by their younger, more sexually active wives. Joseph's eagerness to avoid playing the role of the aged cuckold provides his motivation in the pageant, just as the audience's knowledge of Mary's honesty provides the comic irony which both disarms his anger and maintains Mary's integrity.

There are, however, more serious dimensions to Joseph's portrayal. He is a man whose view of the world has been conditioned by prosaic common sense (and some rather misogynistic ideas about the nature of women), who has to come to terms with the intrusion of the miraculous into his everyday life. In this he is an Everyman figure, representative of humankind's difficulties coping with the nature of divine mysteries, a facet of his role emphasized by the sympathy which his comic exasperation usually elicits from audiences in performance. He begins the pageant 'making his moan'; complaining about the conditions of his life in a fallen world in a way characteristic of representatives of 'natural man' in other pageants (note the portrayal of the Shepherds in the York and Chester *Shepherds'* pageants). Behind the comedy it is also possible to detect theological anxieties concerning Christ's paternity and Mary's perpetual virginity (which, despite the lack of clear biblical support, had become an article of faith by this period). Joseph's great age and physical and sexual impotence are repeatedly alluded to (here and in the Nativity pageant following) in order to rule out any possible doubts concerning his role in Christ's conception, or any possible sexual relationship with Mary after Christ's birth. Central to the portrayal of Joseph here, however, is his capacity for redemption. Like natural man, once he is presented with divine revelation, he is capable of reconciling himself with both his spouse and his God, and so of achieving salvation.

The Pewterers and Founders made jugs, pans, and other vessels out of pewter and other metals.

[*Dramatis Personae*: *Joseph*, *I & II Puella* (two maidservants of Mary), *Maria* (the Virgin Mary), *Angelus* (the Angel Gabriel).]

JOSEPH
Of grete mornyng may I me mene
And walke full werily be þis way,
For nowe þan wende I best hafe bene
Att ease and reste by reasoune ay.[1]
For I am of grete elde,
Wayke and al unwelde,
Als ilke man se it maye;
I may nowder buske ne belde,
But owther in frith or felde
For shame what sall I saie,

That þus-gates nowe on myne alde dase
Has wedded a yonge wenche to my wife,
And may noȝt wele tryne over two strase?
Nowe, Lorde, how lange sall I lede þis liff?
My banes er hevy als lede
And may noȝt stande in stede,
Als kende it is full ryfe.
Now, Lorde, Þou me wisse and rede
Or sone me dryve to dede,
Þou may best stynte þis striffe.

1 mourning/grief, complain 2 wearily by 5 age 6 weak, infirm 8 can neither sprint nor stand 9 wood, field 11 thus, old age 12 girl 13 [I] may not easily step over two straws 14 lead this life 15 bones, as lead 16 stand upright in (my) place 17 it is known everywhere 18 guide 19 towards death 20 end

[1] 'For now, [rather] than walking, I [should] more reasonably have been at ease and rest.'

For bittirly þan may I banne
The way I in þe temple wente,
Itt was to me a bad barganne,
For reuthe I may it ay repente.
For þarein was ordande
Unwedded men sulde stande,
Al sembled at asent,
And ilke ane a drye wande
On heght helde in his hand,
And I ne wist what it ment.[2]

In-mange al othir ane bare I;
Itt florisshed faire, and floures on sprede,
And thay saide to me forthy
Þat with a wiffe I sulde be wedde.
Þe bargayne I made þare,
Þat rewes me nowe full sare,
So am I straytely sted.
Now castes itt me in care,
For wele I myght everemare
Anlepy life have led.

Hir werkis me wyrkis my wonges to wete;[3]
I am begiled; how, wate I noȝt.
My ȝonge wiffe is with childe full grete.
Þat makes me nowe sorowe unsoght
Þat reproffe nere has slayne me.
Forthy giff any man frayne me
How þis þing m[i]ȝt be wroght,
To gabbe yf I wolde payne me,
Þe lawe standis harde agayns me:
To dede I mon be broght.

And lathe methinkeþ, on þe todir syde,
My wiff with any man to defame,
And whethir of there twa þat I bide
I mon noȝt scape withouten schame.
Þe childe certis is noght myne;
Þat reproffe dose me pyne
And gars me flee fra hame.
My liff gif I shuld tyne,[4]
Sho is a clene virgine
For me, withouten blame.

But wele I wate thurgh prophicie
A maiden clene suld bere a childe,
But it is nought sho, sekirly,
Forthy I wate I am begiled.
And why ne walde som yonge man take her?
For certis I thynke over-ga hir
Into som wodes wilde,
Thus thynke I to stele fra hir.
God childe ther wilde bestes sla hir,
She is so meke and mylde.

Of my wendyng wil I non warne,
Nevere þe lees it is myne entente
To aske hir who gate hir þat barne,
Ȝitt wolde I witte fayne or I wente.

All hayle, God be hereinne.

I Puella
Welcome, by Goddis dere myght.

Joseph
Whare is þat ȝonge virgine
Marie, my berde so bright?

I Puella
Certis Joseph, ȝe sall undirstande
Þat sho is not full farre you fra,
Sho sittis at hir boke full faste prayand
For ȝou and us, and for all þa
Þat oght has nede.
But for to telle hir will I ga
Of youre comyng, withouten drede.
Have done and rise uppe, dame,
And to me take gud hede.
Joseph, he is comen hame.

Maria
Welcome, als God me spede.

21 curse 23 a bad deal/arrangement 24 sadness, always 25 therein, commanded 27 gathered by arrangement 28 a dry/barren stick 29 held high 30 did not know 31 I carried one among the others 32 blossomed, spread on it 36 regrets, greatly 37 greatly troubled 38 it throws me into sorrow 40 A solitary (bachelor's) 42 I do not know how 44 brings, unlooked for 45 dishonour, almost 46 if, asks 47 might have happened 48 Even if I tried to lie 50 I would be put to death 51 It seems hateful to me, other hand 53 whichever, the two I put up with 54 may 56 pains me 60 As far as I am concerned 61 know 62 shall bear 63 not her (she), truly 65 why would not 66 to sneak away from 67 woods 68 sneak away 69 God forbid that, slay 71 going, I won't change my mind 72 intention 73 gave, baby 74 I want to know before 78 bird/maiden 80 not far from you 81 book, earnestly praying 82 all those 83 Who have any need 84 go 89 as God will help me (a blessing)

[2] For these events, see the N-Town *Mary Play* ll. 735–947.

[3] 'Her deeds make me wet my cheeks (i.e. cry)'.

[4] 'I would stake my life that . . . '

Dredles to me he is full dere;
Joseph my spouse, welcome er yhe.

Joseph
Gramercy Marie, saie what chere,
Telle me þe soth, how est with þe[e]?
Wha has ben there?
Thy wombe is waxen grete, thynke me,
Þou arte with barne, allas for care.
A, maidens, wa worthe ȝou,
Þat lete hir lere swilke lare.

II Puella
Joseph, ȝe sall noȝt trowe
In hir no febill fare.

Joseph
Trowe it noght arme? Lefe wenche, do way![5]
Hir sidis shewes she is with childe.
Whose ist Marie?

Maria
Sir, Goddis and youres.

Joseph
Nay, nay, now wate I wele I am begiled,
And reasoune why?
With me flesshely was þou nevere fylid,
And I forsake it here forthy.
Say maidens, how es þis?
Tels me þe soþe, rede I;
And but ȝe do, iwisse,
Þe bargayne sall ȝe aby.

II Puella
If ȝe threte als faste as yhe can
Þare is noght to saie þeretill,
For trulye her come never no man
To waite her body with non ill
Of this swete wight,
For we have dwelt ay with hir still
And was nevere fro hir day nor nyght.
Hir kepars have we bene
And sho ay in oure sight;
Come here no man bytwene
To touche þat berde so bright.

I Puella
Na, here come no man in þere wanes
And þat evere witnesse will we;
Save an aungell ilke a day anes
With bodily foode hir fedde has he,
Othir come nane.
Wharfore we ne wate how it shulde be
But thurgh þe Haly Gaste allane.
For trewly we trowe þis,
Is grace with hir is gane,
For sho wroght nevere no mys,
We witnesse evere ilkane.

Joseph
Þanne se I wele youre menyng is
Þe aungell has made hir with childe!
Nay, som man in aungellis liknesse
With somkyn gawde has hir begiled,
And þat trow I.
Forthy nedes noght swilke wordis wilde
At carpe to me dissayvandly.
We! Why gab ye me swa
And feynes swilk fantassy?
Allas, me is full wa,
For dule why ne myght I dy.

To me þis is a carefull cas;
Rekkeles I raffe, refte is my rede.[6]
I dare loke no man in þe face,
Derfely for dole why ne were I dede;
Me lathis my liff.
In temple and in othir stede
Ilke man till hethyng will me dryff.
Was never wight sa wa,
For ruthe I all to-ryff;
Allas, why wroght þou swa
Marie, my weddid wiffe?

Maria
To my witnesse grete God I call,
Þat in mynde wroght nevere na mysse.[7]

90 Doubtless 91 are 92 God-have-mercy (a blessing) 93 how is it? 95 belly, large 96 with child 97 curse you 98 let her learn such ways 100 such evil deeds of her 102 stomach (lit. sides) 103 Whose is it? 104 I know well 106 you were never physically defiled by me 107 reject (paternity) 110 unless 111 You will take the consequences. 112 Even if you threaten your worst 113 nothing, about it 114 she's never been with any man 115 harm 119 keepers 121 meanwhile 123 this house 124 swear 125 Except, once each day 127 No one else came 128 do not know 129 Except, Holy Ghost alone 131 His, goes with her 132 no sin 134 clearly 137 some trick 139 absurd claims 140 To tell, deceivingly 141 lie to, so 142 feign 143 woeful 144 sorrow 145 sorrowful situation 148 miserably 149 I hate 150 place(s) 151 will drive me to shame 152 so sorrowful 153 I am destroyed by sadness

5 'Believe it not harmful? Dear woman, do not be foolish!'
6 'I rave fruitlessly, my reason is destroyed.'
7 'The thought of doing wrong never entered my mind.'

JOSEPH
Whose is þe childe þou arte withall?

MARIA
Youres sir, and þe Kyngis of Blisse.

JOSEPH
Ye, and hoo þan?
Na, selcouthe tythandis than is þis,
Excuse þam wele these women can.
But Marie, all þat sese þe[e]
May witte þi werkis ere wan,
Thy wombe allway it wreyes þe[e]
Þat þou has mette with man.

Whose is it, als faire mot þe[e] befall?

MARIA
Sir, it is youres, and Goddis will.

JOSEPH
Nay, I ne have noght ado withall,
Neme it na more to me, be still!
Þou wate als wele as I,
Þat we two same flesshly
Wroght never swilk werkis with ill.[8]
Loke þou dide no folye
Before me prevely
Thy faire maydenhede to spill.

But who is þe fader? Telle me his name.

MARIA
None but youreselfe.

JOSEPH
Late be, for shame!
I did it nevere; þou dotist dame, by bukes and belles![9]
Full sakles shulde I bere þis blame aftir þou telles,[10]
For I wroght nevere in worde nor dede
Thyng þat shulde marre thy maydenhede,
To touche me till.
For of slyk note war litill nede,
Yhitt for myn awne I wolde it fede,
Might all be still;

Þarfore þe fadir tell me, Marie.

MARIA
But God and yhow, I knawe right nane.

JOSEPH
A, slike sawes mase me full sarye,
With grete mornyng to make my mane.
Therfore be noȝt so balde,
Þat no slike tales be talde,
But halde þe[e] stille als stane.
Þou art yonge and I am alde,
Slike werkis yf I do walde,
Þase games fra me are gane.

Therfore, telle me in privite,
Whos is þe childe þou is with nowe?
Sertis, þer sall non witte but we,
I drede þe law als wele as þou.

MARIA
Nowe grete God of Hys myght
Þat all may dresse and dight,
Mekely to þe[e] I bowe.
Rewe on þis wery wight,
Þat in his herte myght light
Þe soth to ken and trowe.

JOSEPH
Who had thy maydenhede Marie? Has hou oght mynde?

MARIA
Forsuth, I am a mayden clene.

JOSEPH
Nay, þou spekis now agayne kynde,

158 carrying (lit. with) 160 how? 161 It's a miracle! (ironic) 162 Women can always excuse themselves 163 see you 164 can see, are shameful 165 betrays 166 had sex with 167 as you hope for good fortune 169 nothing to do with it 170 Discuss it no more 174 folly 175 secretly 176 lose 178 Stop that! 182 anything, defile 183 To accuse me of 184 There is little need for this problem 185 my own, raise it 186 If everything could be settled quietly 188 Other than, no one 189 makes, sorry 190 moan 191 bold 192 told 193 stone 194 old 195 even if I wanted to 196 These, are beyond me 197 privately 199 no one, but us 200 as much as you (do) 202 order and achieve 204 Have pity, weary 205 come (lit. alight) 207 any knowledge 209 against nature

[8] 'We two never did such evil physical acts.'
[9] 'You are mad, woman, by books and bells!' (the ceremonial paraphernalia of the Mass).
[10] 'For, according to you, I should bear the blame for this, even though I am completely innocent'.

Slike þing myght nevere na man of mene.
A maiden to be with childe?
Þase werkis fra þe[e] ar wilde,
Sho is not borne I wene.

Maria
Joseph yhe ar begiled,
With synne was I never filid,
Goddis sande is on me sene.

Joseph
Goddis sande? Yha Marie, God helpe!
Bot certis þat childe was nevere oures twa.
But woman-kynde gif þat list yhelpe,
Yhitt walde þei na man wiste þer wa.[11]

Maria
Sertis it is Goddis sande;
Þat sall I never ga fra.

Joseph
Yha, Marie, drawe thyn hande,
For forther ȝitt will I fande,
I trowe not it be swa.

Þe soth fra me gif þat þou layne,
Þe childe-bering may þou noȝt hyde;[12]
But sitte stille here tille I come agayne,
Me bus an erand here beside.

Maria
Now grete God He you wisse,
And mende you of your mysse
Of me, what so betyde.
Als He is Kyng of Blisse,
Sende you som seand of þis,
In truth þat ye might bide.

Joseph
Nowe lord God þat all þing may
At Thyne awne will bothe do and dresse,
Wisse me now som redy way
To walke here in his wildirnesse.
Bot or I passe þis hill,
Do with me what God will,
Owther more or lesse,
Here bus me bide full stille
Till I have slepid my fille,
Myn hert so hevy it is.

Angelus
Waken, Joseph, and take bettir kepe
To Marie, þat is þi felawe fest.

Joseph
A, I am full werie, lefe, late me slepe,
Forwandered and walked in þis forest.

Angelus
Rise uppe, and slepe na mare,
Þou makist her herte full sare
Þat loves þe[e] alther best.

Joseph
We! Now es þis a farly fare
For to be cached bathe here and þare,
And nowhere may have rest.

Say, what arte þou? Telle me this thyng.

Angelus
I, Gabriell, Goddis aungell full even,
Þat has tane Marie to my kepyng,
And sente es þe[e] to say with steven
In lele wedlak þou lede þe[e].
Leffe hir noȝt, I forbid þe[e];
Na syn of hir þou neven,
But tille hir fast þou spede þe[e]
And of hir noght þou drede be,
It is Goddis sande of heven.

The childe þat sall be borne of her,
Itt is consayved of þe Haly Gast.
Alle joie and blisse þan sall be aftir,
And to al mankynde nowe althir mast.
Jesus His name þou calle,
For slike happe sall Hym fall
Als þou sall se in haste.

210 No one could ever claim such a thing 212 these are mad words 213 She (i.e. such a woman) 215 defiled 216 blessing 222 never depart from (that claim) 223 withdraw . . . (i.e. stop, be quiet) 224 further yet, ask 225 so 229 (go on) an errand nearby 231 correct, mistake 232 concerning me, whatever happens 234 word about 235 live 238 easy 240 ere (i.e. before) 243 I stay 244 slept sufficiently 246 be more attentive 247 loyal partner 248 dear 249 Having wandered 250 no more 251 sore 252 best of all 253 marvellous business 254 pursued (lit. caught), both 257 truly 258 taken, into 259 am sent to you, openly 260 loyal wedlock, continue 261 Leave 262 Nor speak ill of her 263 hurry to her 265 will 268 then shall follow 269 most of all 271 (a) fate, befall him 272 soon

11 'Women! Even if they want help, they do not want anyone to know the cause of their sorrow.'

12 'Even if you hide the truth from me, you will not be able to hide the pregnancy [from everyone]'.

His pepull saffe He sall
Of evyllis and angris all,
Þat þei ar nowe enbraste.

Joseph
And is this soth, aungell, þou saise?

Angelus
Yha, and þis to taken right:
Wende forthe to Marie, thy wiffe alwayse,
Brynge hir to Bedlem þis ilke nyght.
Ther sall a childe borne be,
Goddis Sone of Heven is Hee
And man ay mast of myght.

Joseph
Nowe lorde God full wele is me
That evyr þat I þis sight suld see,
I was never ar so light.

For for I walde have hir þus refused,
And sakles blame þat ay was clere,[13]
Me bus pray hir halde me excused,
Als som men dose with full gud chere.
Saie Marie, wiffe, how fares þou?

Maria
Þe bettir sir, for yhou.
Why stande yhe þare? Come nere.

Joseph
My bakke fayne wolde I bowe,
And aske fo[r]gifnesse nowe,
Wiste I þou wolde me here.

Maria
Forgiffnesse sir? Late be, for shame!
Slike wordis suld all gud women lakke.[14]

Joseph
Yha, Marie, I am to blame
For wordis lang-are I to þe[e] spak.
But gadir same nowe all oure gere,
Slike poure wede as we were,
And prike þam in a pak.
Till Bedlem bus me it bere,
For litill thyng will women dere;[15]
Helpe up nowe on my bak.

273 save 274 From all evils and troubles 275 Which now embrace them 277 and to understand me correctly 279 Bethlehem, same 282 greatest 283 I am so happy 286 For because 288 I must beg her to forgive me 289 do with good cheer 290 how are you? 291 because you are here 293 I should 295 If I thought you would hear me 296 Leave that 299 long ago 300 gather together, possessions 301 such poor clothes, wear 302 gather 303 I must carry it to Bethlehem

13 'And blamed the innocent who was always pure'.

14 'There should be no need for any good woman to offer those words.' (lit. 'such words should all good women lack').

15 'Because [I know] women will be distressed by minor things' (or, reading 'bere' for 'dere', 'Women can only carry small amounts').

York (The Tilethatchers), *The Nativity*

Although simple in narrative terms, this short pageant resonates with symbolic and theological significance. As the central event in Christian history, the Nativity, the beginning of the Incarnation of God as man in the form of Jesus, is the focus of universal forces. The cold and darkness into which Christ will be born, and the dilapidated state of the stable in which this will take place, effectively symbolize the corrupted state of the fallen world which He will ultimately redeem. Significantly, it is Joseph, representative of 'natural humanity', who stresses – and feels most pointedly – the harsh conditions of life in a world which is literally as well as metaphorically a thoroughfare of woe (ll. 7–13). His absence at the moment of birth, significantly on an ultimately redundant errand for light to illuminate the Light of the World, continues the theme of his marginalization noted in *Joseph's Trouble*. The redemptive significance of events is symbolized both by the repeated reference to the realization of prophecy in the pageant, and by the simplicity and serenity of the birth itself, free from the painful labour which has been woman's lot since the Fall. In performance Mary may simply have knelt to pray and then risen to reveal the 'child' from beneath her skirts. As Beadle and King note (*York Mystery Plays*) the paradoxes inherent in the Incarnation are suggested by Mary's worship of the infant who is simultaneously her child, spouse, and father. Thus the mother prays to her baby for comfort at the same time as she seeks to provide for his well-being.

The Tilethatchers were responsible for roof-building, and their work was probably displayed prominently in the representation of the stable on the pageant-wagon to which Joseph draws attention at ll. 17–18.

[*Dramatis Personae*: *Joseph*, *Mary*.]

JOSEPH

All-weldand God in Trinite,
I praye Þe[e] lord, for Thy grete myght,
Unto Thy symple servand see,
Here in þis place wher are pight,
Ourselfe allone.
Lord, graunt us gode herberow þis nyght
Within þis wone.

For we have sought bothe uppe and doune
Thurgh diverse stretis in þis cite.
So mekill pepull is comen to towne
Þat we can nowhare herbered be,
Þer is slike prees.
Forsuthe, I can no soccoure see,
But belde us with þere bestes.

And yf we here all nyght abide
We schall be stormed in þis steede:
Þe walles are doune on ilke side,
Þe ruffe is rayved aboven oure hede,
Als have I roo.
Say Marie, doughtir, what is thy rede,
How sall we doo?

For in grete nede nowe are we stedde
As þou thyselffe the soth may see,
For here is nowthir cloth ne bedde,
And we are weyke and all werie
And fayne wolde rest.
Now gracious God, for Thy mercie,
Wisse us þe best.

MARIA

God will us wisse, full wele witt ȝe,
Þerfore Joseph be of gud chere,
For in þis place borne will He be
Þat sall us save fro sorowes sere,
Boþe even and morne.
Sir, witte ȝe wele þe tyme is nere
He will be borne.

JOSEPH

Þan behoves us bide here stille,
Here in þis same place all þis nyght.

1 All-controlling (lit. wielding) 4 placed 5 Ourselves 6 good shelter 10 people 11 sheltered 12 such (a) crowd 13 Truly, comfort 14 Other than to shelter, these beasts 16 exposed to the storm, place 18 roof is holed 19 As I regret 22 placed 24 (bed)clothes nor . . . 25 weak, weary 26 happily would 27 through 28 Teach us (what is) best 29 as you well know 30 be happy 31 born 32 Who, every sorrow 33 evening and morning (i.e. all the time) 36 we had best stay

Maria
ȝa sir, forsuth it is Goddis will.

Joseph
Þan wolde I fayne we had sum light,
What so befall.
It waxis right myrke unto my sight,
And colde withall.

I will go gete us light forthy
And fewell fande with me to bring.

Maria
All-weldand God yow governe and gy,
As He is sufferayne of all thyng
For His grete myght,
And lende me grace to His lovyng
Þat I me dight.[1]

Nowe in my sawle grete joie have I,
I am all cladde in comforte clere.
Now will be borne of my body
Both God and man togedir in feere,
Blist mott He be.
Jesu, my sone þat is so dere,
Nowe borne is He.

[*Jesus is born.*]

Hayle, my lorde God, hayle, Prince of Pees,
Hayle, my fadir, and hayle, my sone;
Hayle, soverayne sege all synnes to sesse,
Hayle, God and man in erthe to wonne.
Hayle, thurgh whos myht
All þis worlde was first begonne,
Merknes and light.

Sone, as I am sympill sugett of thyne,
Vowchesaffe, swete sone, I pray Þe[e],
That I myght Þe[e] take in þe armys of myne
And in þis poure wede to arraie Þe[e].
Graunte me Þi blisse,
As I am Thy modir chosen to be,
In sothfastnesse.

Joseph
A, lorde God, what þe wedir is colde,
Þe fellest freese þat evere I felyd.
I praye God helpe þam þat is alde
And namely þam þat is unwelde,
So may I saie.
Now, gud God, Þou be my bilde,
As Þou best may.

A, lord God, what light is þis
Þat come shynyng þus sodenly?
I can not saie als have I blisse.
When I come home unto Marie
Þan sall I spirre.
A, here be God, for nowe come I.

Maria
ȝe are welcum sirre.

Joseph
Say Marie, doghtir, what chere with þe[e]?

Maria
Right goode Joseph, as has ben ay.

Joseph
O Marie, what swete thyng is þat on thy kne?

Maria
It is my sone, þe soth to saye,
Þat is so gud.

Joseph
Wele is me I bade þis day
To se þis foode.

Me merveles mekill of þis light
Þat þus-gate shynes in þis place,
Forsuth it is a selcouth sight.

Maria
Þis hase He ordand of His grace,
My sone so ȝing,

39 wish 40 Whatever happens 41 very dark 42 as well 43 go and get 44 try (to find) fuel 45 guide 46 sovereign, everything 50 soul, great joy 51 covered in pure happiness 53 in unity 54 Blessed may 57 Hail! 59 man, who'll end 61 (He) through whose power 63 Darkness 64 simple subject 65 Allow 66 arms 67 these poor clothes 70 truth 71 how, weather 72 worst freeze, felt 73 those who are old 74 especially, who are infirm 76 protection 79 suddenly 82 ask 83 may God be here (a blessing) 85 how are you? 86 as always 90 I am happy I lived long enough 91 this child 92 greatly marvel about 93 thus 95 ordained 96 young

[1] 'And bestow on me the grace that I might be able to worship Him.'

A starne to be schynyng a space
At His bering.

For Balam tolde ful longe beforne
How þat a sterne shulde rise full hye,
And of a maiden shulde be borne
A sonne þat sall oure saffyng be
Fro caris kene.[2]
Forsuth, it is my sone so free
Be whame Balam gon meene.

Joseph
Nowe welcome, floure fairest of hewe,
I shall Þe[e] menske with mayne and myght.
Hayle, my Maker, hayle, Crist Jesu,
Hayle, riall Kyng, roote of all right,
Hayle, Saveour.
Hayle, My Lorde, lemer of light,
Hayle, blessid floure.

Maria
Nowe Lord þat all þis worlde schall wynne,
(To Þe[e] my sone is þat I saye),
Here is no bedde to laye The[e] inne,
Þerfore, my dere sone, I Þe[e] praye,
Sen it is soo,
Here in þis cribbe I myght Þe[e] lay
Betwene þer bestis two.

And I sall happe Þe[e], myn owne dere childe,
With such clothes as we have here.

Joseph
O Marie, beholde þe beestis mylde,
They make lovyng in ther manere
As þei wer men.
Forsothe it semes wele be ther chere
Þare lord þei ken.

Maria
Ther lorde þai kenne, þat wate I wele,
They worshippe Hym with myght and mayne;
The wedir is colde as ye may feele,
To halde Hym warme þei are full fayne
With þare warme breth,
And oondis on Hym, is noght to layne,
To warme Hym with.

O, nowe slepis my sone, blist mot He be,
And lyes full warme þer bestis bytwene.

Joseph
O, nowe is fulfillid, forsuth I see,
Þat Abacuc in mynde gon mene
And prechid by prophicie.
He saide oure sayvoure shall be sene
Betwene bestis lye,

And nowe I see þe same in sight

Maria
Ȝa sir, forsuth þe same is He.

Joseph
Honnoure and worshippe both day and nyght,
Ay-lastand lorde, be done to Þe[e]
Allway, as is worthy;
And lord, to Thy service I oblisshe me
With all myn herte, holy.

Maria
Þou mercyfull maker, most myghty,
My God, my Lorde, my sone so free,
Thy handemayden forsuth am I,
And to Thi service I oblissh me,
With all myn herte entere.
Thy blissing, beseke I Thee,
Þou graunte us all in feere.

97 star, for a time 98 birth 99 Balaam foretold long ago 102 saviour 103 From painful troubles 104 noble/generous 105 whom Balaam meant 106 flower of most beautiful colour 109 royal, source of all justice 111 giver 114 that is to say 115 thee in 119 these two beasts 120 wrap 122 gentle beasts 123 worship, their own way 124 As (if) 125 seems clear from their behaviour 126 They know their lord 130 They are trying to warm him 131 breath 132 breathe, it is clear to see 134 blessed 137 What Habakkuk foretold 140 Lying between beasts 142 He (Jesus) is the one (foretold) 145 proper 146 dedicate myself 147 wholly 152 my entire heart 154 in fellowship (i.e. together)

2 See Numbers 24:17. The prophecy of the virgin birth is in Isaiah 7:4.

Albrecht Dürer, *The Nativity*, 1509, woodcut. Reproduced courtesy of Dover Publications.

Towneley, *The Second Shepherds' Play*

The Second Shepherds' Play, so called because it was the second of two pageants on this theme in the Towneley/Wakefield Cycle, written by an anonymous dramatist now referred to as the Wakefield Master, continues the exploration of the effects and implications of the Incarnation begun in *Joseph's Trouble* and *The Nativity*. Like Joseph in the latter, the Shepherds enter lamenting the harsh conditions of life in a fallen, mortal world in desperate need of redemption. In so doing they both recapitulate the terms of God's curse on humanity issued as a result of the Fall, and touch upon a number of very specific and sensitive contemporary issues for late medieval English society. These range from the oppression of poor husbandmen by powerful landowners and their retainers to the misogynist complaints of hen-pecked husbands against their wives. Unlike the *Nativity* pageant, however, this play introduces a new and startling element into the treatment of the biblical material in the form of Mak the Sheepstealer and his wife Gyll, and the broad comedy associated with their attempt to steal a sheep and disguise it as their baby. This original material is deftly woven into a series of striking parallels between the human and the divine, the false and the real Nativity, which run through the pageant, and in which material that might have been in other hands a blasphemous mockery of the biblical story is turned by the Wakefield Master into a powerful prefiguration of it. Most obvious among the parallels are the Shepherds' successive visits, first to Mak and Gyll's house in search of their stolen sheep (where they discover the animal trussed up in a cradle to look like a baby), then to the Bethlehem stable where they find the true Lamb of God, Jesus, sharing the bedding of animals in the stall. In dramatic terms the parallel would have been all the more obvious if, as seems likely, the same crib and set had been used for both locations, with the Shepherds merely circling the stage to indicate their journey from hovel to stable.

In making the short journey from one nominal location to another, however, the Shepherds symbolically enact a far more significant movement, that of humankind from the Old Law of Judaism to the New Law of Christianity, a move reflected in the pageant's shift from a fundamentally realistic dramaturgy to one based upon symbolism. The first movement, from an Old Law dominated by justice, to a New characterized by mercy, is revealed in the Shepherds' decision not to harm Mak for his deception and assault upon their already precarious livelihoods, but merely to toss him in a blanket. This ritualistic, gamesome punishment is in keeping with the mood of the play, and with the Shepherds' own essentially generous natures. It is, after all, through an act of spontaneous generosity (implicitly of Christian charity) – the decision to return and offer a gift to Mak and Gyll's 'baby' – that they discover the deception and recover their sheep. The move from realism to symbolism reaches its climax in the gifts offered by the Shepherds to the infant Christ, the cherries (implausibly produced in a harsh Yorkshire winter) suggesting the miraculous nature of Christ's birth, and also (in their blood-red colour) his future sacrifice; the bird symbolizing the Holy Spirit (often represented as a dove) and thus Christ's divinity; and the ball suggesting His kingship (it being round, like an orb, and also taken from the 'royal' game of tennis). There are also implicit parallels between these gifts and those offered by the Magi, myrrh (symbolic of death and suffering), frankincense (divinity), and gold (kingship).

[*Dramatis Personae*: *III Pastors* (three Shepherds; Coll, Gib, and Daw respectively), *Mak*, *Uxor Eius* ('His Wife'; Mak's wife Gyll), *Angelus* (Angel), *Maria* (the Virgin Mary).]

I Pastor

Lord, what these weders ar cold! And I am yll happyd.
I am nere hande dold, so long have I nappyd;
My legys thay fold, my fyngers ar chappyd.
It is not as I wold, for I am al lappyd
In sorow.
In stormes and tempest,
Now in the eest, now in the west,
Wo is hym has never rest
Myd day nor morow.

Bot we sely shepardes, that walkys on the moore,
In fayth we ar nere handys outt of the doore.
No wonder, as it standys, if we be poore,

1 this weather is, clothed 2 almost numb, slept 3 sore 4 I (would) wish, wrapped 8 (who) has 11 homeless

For the tylthe of oure landys lyys falow as the floore,
As ye ken.
We are so hamyd,
For-taxed, and ramyd,
We are mayde hand tamyd
With thys gentlery men.

Thus thay refe us oure rest, Oure Lady theym wary!
These men that ar lord-fest, thay cause the ploghe tary.
That men say is for the best, we fynde it contrary.
Thus ar husbandys opprest, in pointe to myscary
On lyfe.
Thus hold thay us hunder;
Thus thay bryng us in blonder;
It were greatte wonder
And ever shuld we thryfe.

For may he gett a paynt slefe or a broche now on dayes,
Wo is hym that hym grefe or onys agane says![1]
Dar no-man hym reprefe, what mastry he mays,[2]
And yit may no-man lefe oone word that he says,
No letter.
He can make purveance[3]
With boste and bragance,
And all is thrugh mantenance[4]
Of men that are gretter.

Ther shall com a swane as prowde as a po,
He must borow my wane, my ploghe also,
Then I am full fane to graunt or he go.
Thus lyf we in payne, anger, and wo,
By nyght and day.
He must have if he langyd,
If I shuld forgang it;
I were better be hangyd
Then oones say hym nay.

It dos me good, as I walk thus by myn oone,
Of this warld for to talk in maner of mone.
To my shepe wyll I stalk, and herkyn anone,
Ther abyde on a balk, or sytt on a stone,
Full soyne.
For I trowe, perde,
Trew men if thay be,
We gett more compane
Or it be noyne.

II PASTOR

Benste[5] and Dominus! What may this bemeyne?
Why fares this warld thus? Oft have we not sene.
Lord, thyse weders ar spytus, and the [wyndes] full kene,
And the frostys so hydus thay water myn eeyne,
No ly.
Now in dry, now in wete,
Now in snaw, now in slete;
When my shone freys to my fete,
It is not all esy.

Bot as far as I ken, or yit as I go,
We sely wedmen dre mekyll wo;
We have sorow then and then: it fallys oft so.
Sely Copyle, oure hen, both to and fro
She kakyls;
Bot begyn she to crok,
To groyne or [to cluc]k,
Wo is hym is of oure cok,
For he is in the shakyls.

These men that ar wed have not all thare wyll;
When thay ar full hard sted, thay sygh full styll;
God wayte thay ar led full hard and full yll;
In bower nor in bed thay say noght ther tyll,
This tyde.
My parte have I fun;

13 cultivation 15 hamstrung, 16 over-taxed, oppressed 17 subservient 18 By, gentry 19 rob us (of), curse! 20 bound to a lord, hinder 22 labourers, to the point of death 24 under 25 strife 26 would be 27 If we should ever prosper 31 believe 34 bragging 36 greater 37 fellow, peacock 38 wagon, plough 40 live 42 wants (it) 43 (Even) if, go without 45 (even) once 46 myself 47 moan 48 walk, listen 49 ridge 50 soon 51 by God! 53 We (shall), company 54 Ere, noon 55 mean? 56 goes, we've not seen this often 57 weathers, spiteful 58 hideous, eyes 61 sleet 62 shoes freeze 63 easy 65 married men, endure 66 happens 68 cackles 69 croak 70 groan 71 him (who) is 72 shackles 73 their 74 pressed, continually 75 knows 76 nothing about it 77 Nowadays 78 found/played

[1] 'For, if [anyone] gets himself a painted sleeve or a brooch nowadays, woe betide anyone who upsets or contradicts him!' Such tokens, bearing the emblems of a lord or gentleman, were worn by his retainers as badges of their loyalty, and used as marks of authority in the community.

[2] 'No man dares to reprimand him, whatever oppressive acts he commits'.

[3] Purveyance was the process whereby noble or royal servants could force producers to sell to them at a fixed (and usually low) price, ostensibly for their master's use.

[4] Maintenance was the use of a noble or gentleman's power and influence to protect or assist his retainers, not always within the law.

[5] 'Bless us!' (*Benedicité*).

I know my lesson.
Wo is hym that is bun,
For he must abyde.

Bot now late in oure lyfys, a mervell to me,
That I thynk my hart ryfys sich wonders to see.
What that destany dryfys, it shuld so be;
Som men wyll have two wyfys, and som men thre,
In store.
Som ar wo that has any,
Bot so far can I:
Wo is hym that has many,
For he felys sore.

Bot yong men of wowyng, for God that you boght,
Be well war of wedyng, and thynk in youre thoght,
'Had I wyst' is a thyng it servys of noght;
Mekyll styll mowmyng has wedyng home broght,
And grefys,
With many a sharp showre;
For thou may cach in an owre
That shall sow the fulle sowre
As long as thou lyffys.

For as ever rede I pystyll I have oone to my fere
As sharp as a thystyll, as rugh as a brere;
She is browyd lyke a brystyll with a sowre loten
chere;
Had she oones wett hyr whystyll she couth syng full
clere
Hyr Paternoster.[6]
She is as greatt as a whall;
She has a galon of gall.
By Hym that dyed for us all,
I wald I had ryn to I had lost hir.

I Pastor
God looke over the raw![7] Full defly ye stand.

II Pastor
Yee, the Dewill in thi maw, so tariand!
Sagh thou awre of Daw?

I Pastor
Yee, on a ley land
Hard I hym blaw. He commys here at hand,
Not far.
Stand styll.

II Pastor
Qwhy?

I Pastor
For he commys, hope I.

II Pastor
He wyll make us both a ly
Bot if we be war.

III Pastor
Crystys Crosse me spede, and Sant Nycholas!
Ther of had I nede; it is wars then it was.
Whoso couthe take hede and lett the warld pas,
It is ever in drede and brekyll as glas,
And slythys.
This warld fowre never so,
With mervels mo and mo,
Now in weyll, now in wo,
And all thyng wrythys.

Was never syn Noe floode sich floodys seyn;
Wyndys and ranys so rude, and stormes so keyn.
Som stamerd, som stod in dowte, as I weyn;
Now God turne all to good! I say as I mene:
For ponder.
These floodys so thay drowne,
Both in feyldys and in towne,
And berys all downe,
And that is a wonder.

We that walk on the nyghtys, oure catell to kepe,
We se sodan syghtes when othere men slepys.
Yit me thynk my hart lyghtes; I se shrewys pepe!
Ye ar two all-wyghtys. I wyll gyf my shepe
A turne.

80 bound (to a wife) 81 endure 83 breaks, such 84 destiny commands 87 woeful 88 This much I know 91 wooing, bought 92 wary, marriage 93 'Had I known . . .' is no good 94 continual lamentation 95 griefs 97 hour 98 bring, bitterly 99 lives 100 Epistle, as, companion 101 rough, briar 102 bristle, sour face 105 whale 107 died . . . (i.e. Christ) 108 wish, run until 109 deafly 110 mouth, (for) so dallying! 111 saw, anything, fallow 112 heard, blow, comes 114 Why? 117 Unless we are wary 118 bless me 119 worse (now) than 120 Whoever could 121 fear, brittle 122 slips (away) 123 fared 125 weal/well-being 126 shifts (and decays) 127 Noah's, seen 128 rains, violent 129 staggered 130 believe 131 Think about it 133 fields 134 carries everything away 136 in, cattle (i.e. sheep), tend 137 unexpected 138 lightens, villains looking 139 ghosts 140 (I will) turn (them away)

6 'Once she has wet her whistle [had a drink], she can sing the Lord's Prayer very loudly!'

7 'God bless the lot of you!': addressed to the audience.

Bot full yll have I ment;
As I walk on this bent,
I may lyghtly repent,
My toes if I spurne.

A, syr, God you save, and master myne!
A drynk fayn wold I have, and somwhat to dyne.

I Pastor
Crystys curs, my knave, thou art a ledyr hyne!

II Pastor
What, the boy lyst rave! Abyde unto syne
We have mayde it.
Yll thryft on thy pate!
Though the shrew cam late,
Yit is he in state
To dyne, if he had it.

III Pastor
Sich servandes as I, that swettys and swynkys,
Etys oure brede full dry, and that me forthynkys;
We ar oft weytt and wery when master men wynkys;
Yit commys full lately both dyners and drynkys.
Bot nately,
Both oure dame and oure syre,
When we have ryn in the myre,
Thay can nyp at oure hyre,
And pay us full lately.

Bot here my trouth, master: for the fayr that ye make,
I shall do therafter, wyrk as I take;
I shall do a lytyll, syr, and emang ever lake,
For yit lay my soper never on my stomake
In feyldys.
Wherto shuld I threpe?
With my staf can I lepe,
And men say 'Lyght chepe
Letherly for-yeldys.'[8]

I Pastor
Thou were an yll lad to ryde on wowyng
With a man that had bot lytyll of spendyng.

II Pastor
Peasse, boy, I bad! No more janglyng,
Or I shall make the[e] full rad, by the Hevens Kyng
With thy gawdys!
Wher ar oure shepe, boy? We! Skorne!

III Pastor
Sir, this same day at morne
I thaym left in the corne,
When they rang lawdys.[9]

Thay have pasture good, thay can not go wrong.

I Pastor
That is right, by the Roode! Thyse nyghtes ar long,
Yit I wold, or we yode, oone gaf us a song.

II Pastor
So I thoght as I stode, to myrth us emong.

III Pastor
I grauntt.

I Pastor
Lett me syng the tenory.

II Pastor
And I the tryble so hye.

III Pastor
Then the meyne fallys to me:
Lett se how ye chauntt.

[*They sing.*]

Tunc intrat Mak in clamide se super togam vestitus.[10]

Mak
Now, Lord, for Thy naymes vij,[11] that made both moyn and starnes
Well mo then I can neven, Thi will, Lorde, of me tharnys;[12]

141 spoken 142 heath 144 stub 145 my master! 146 eat 147 curse, lazy servant! 148 likes to, until after 150 luck, head 151 came 152 ready 153 it (i.e. some food) 154 servants, sweat, labour 155 Eat, displeases me 156 wet, weary, sleep 157 very slowly 158 certainly 159 mistress, master 160 run 161 cut our wages 163 pledge, food, provide 164 work according to what I receive 165 always play about in between 166 I've never had too much to eat 168 why, complain? 169 leap 172 ride with when wooing 173 money 174 prattling 175 swiftly 176 tricks 177 scorn (you)! 183 someone gave 184 cheer us up 185 agree 186 tenor part 187 treble, high 188 mean/middle 189 sing 190 moon, stars

8 '[A] cheap [i.e. poor] bargain is repaid badly.'
9 'Lauds': the first canonical hour of the day.
10 'Then shall Mak enter with a cloak [hung] over his tunic.'
11 By rabbinical tradition, God had seven names.
12 'Many more than I can name, Your will regarding me, is unclear (to me)'.

I am all uneven, that moves oft my harnes.
Now wold God I were in Heven, for the[re] wepe no barnes
So styll.[13]

I PASTOR
Who is that pypys so poore?

MAK
Wold God ye wyst how I foore.
Lo, a man that walkes on the moore,
And has not all his wyll.

II PASTOR
Mak, where has thou gone? Tell us tythyng.

III PASTOR
Is he commen? Then ylkon take hede to his thyng![14]

Et accipit clamidem ab ipso.[15]

MAK
What! Ich be a yoman, I tell you, of the kyng;
The self and the some, sond from a greatt lordyng,
And sich.
Fy on you! Goyth hence,
Out of my presence!
I must have reverence;
Why, who be ich?[16]

I PASTOR
Why make ye it so qwaynt? Mak, ye do wrang.

II PASTOR
Bot, Mak, lyst ye saynt? I trow that ye lang.

III PASTOR
I trow the shrew can paynt, the Dewyll myght hym hang!

MAK
Ich shall make complaynt, and make you all to thwang
At a worde,
And tell evyn how ye doth.

I PASTOR
Bot, Mak, is that sothe?
Now take outt that sothren tothe,
And sett in a torde!

II PASTOR
Mak, the Dewill in youre ee! A stroke wold I leyne you.

III PASTOR
Mak, know ye not me? By God, I couthe teyn you.

MAK [*deciding to recognize them*]
God looke you all thre! Me thoght I had sene you.
Ye ar a fare compane.

I PASTOR
Can ye now mene you?

II PASTOR
Shrew, pepe!
Thus late as thou goys,
What wyll men suppos?
And thou has an yll noys
Of stelyng of shepe.

MAK
And I am trew as steyll, all men waytt,
Bot a sekenes I feyll that haldes me full haytt;
My belly farys not weyll; it is out of astate.

III PASTOR
Seldom lyys the Dewyll dede by the gate.[17]

MAK
Therfor
Full sore am I and yll.
If I stande stone styll;
I ete not an nedyll
Thys moneth and more.

192 uncertain, brains 195 cries, poorly 196 knew, fared 198 he desires 201 I am, yeoman (retainer) 202 self-same, messenger 208 behave so strangely? 209 appear saintly?, long (to) 210 villain, feign 211 (be) beaten 215 cut out, southern speech 216 turd! 217 eye, give 218 hurt 219 watch over, recognized 220 company, remember yourself? 221 look! 222 go 224 bad reputation 225 For 226 steel 227 sickness, feel, grabs, hotly 228 fares, order 229 dead, road 232 As I stand here 233 ate (a tiny amount)

[13] 'I wish to God that I was in Heaven, as there are no babies crying all the time there.'

[14] 'Is he here? Then everyone keep close watch on their possessions.' Mak has a reputation as a thief.

[15] 'And he [III Pastor] shall take the cloak from him [Mak].'

[16] 'Who am I?' As well as adopting lordly manners, Mak employs an affected southern accent and dialect, using forms such as 'ich', 'goeth', and 'doth'.

[17] i.e. the Devil rarely truly suffers. Like Mak, he only pretends to do so in order to catch out the unwary.

I Pastor
How farys thi wyff? By my hoode, how farys sho?

Mak
Lyys walteryng, by the Roode, by the fyere, lo.
And a howse full of brude. She drynkys well, to;
Yll spede othere good that she wyll do![18]
Bot s[h]o
Etys as fast as she can,
And ilk yere that commys to man
She brynges furth a lakan,
And som yeres two.

Bot were I not more gracyus and rychere befar,
I were eten outt of howse and of harbar;[19]
Yit is she a fowll dowse, if ye com nar;
Ther is none that trowse nor knowys a war
Then ken I.
Now wyll ye se what I profer,
To gyf all in my cofer
To morne at next to offer
Hyr hed mas-penny.[20]

II Pastor
I wote so forwakyd is none in this shyre:
I wold slepe if I takyd les to my hyere.[21]

III Pastor
I am cold and nakyd, and wold have a fyere.

I Pastor
I am wery, for-rakyd, and run in the myre.
Wake thou!

II Pastor
Nay, I wyll lyg downe by,
For I must slepe truly.

III Pastor
As good a mans son was I
As any of you.

Bot, Mak, com heder. Betwene shall thou lyg downe.

Mak
Then myght I lett you bedene of that ye wold rowne,
No drede.
Fro my top to my too,
Manus tuas commendo,
Poncio Pilato;[22]
Cryst Crosse me spede!

Tunc surgit, pastoribus dormientibus et dicet:[23]

Now were tyme for a man that lakkys what he wold
To stalk prevely than unto a fold,
And neemly to wyrk than, and be not to bold,
For he might aby the bargan, if it were told
At the endyng.
Now were tyme for to reyll;
Bot he nedes good counsell
That fayn wold fare weyll,
And has bot lytyll spendyng.

[*Mak begins to cast a spell.*]

Bot abowte you a serkyll, as rownde as a moyn,
To I have done that I wyll, tyll that it be noyn,
That ye lyg stone styll to that I have doyne,
And I shall say thertyll of good wordes a foyne.
'On hight
Over youre hedes my hand I lyft;
Outt go youre een. I fordo your syght.'
Bot yit I must make better shyft,
And it be right.

Lord, what thay slepe hard! That may ye all here;
Was I never a shephard, bot now wyll I lere.
If the flok be skard, yit shall I nyp nere.
How, drawes hederward! Now mendys oure chere
From sorow:[24]

235 fares she? 236 sprawling 237 children, too 241 each year 242 baby 246 foul slut, (knew the truth) 247 knows a worse (one) 256 exhausted 257 *You* stay awake! 258 next to you 260 am 263 hinder, whisper 264 doubt 265 toe 268 bless me! 269 lacks, desires 270 then, sheepfold 271 nimbly, too 272 pay dearly, reckoned up 274 act swiftly 277 money 278 circle, moon 279 until noon 280 until 281 few 284 eyes, forestall 285 preparation 286 If it is to go well 287 how, hear [they are snoring] 288 learn 289 scared, sneak close

18 'The Devil take anything else she does!'

19 'Even if I were more gracious and richer by far, I would still be eaten out of house and shelter'.

20 'I'd give everything in my coffer tomorrow morning as my offering at her funeral mass [i.e. to see her dead].'

21 'I believe there's no one so tired in this county [as me]: I would sleep, [even] if I will earn less money.'

22 'Into your hands I commend . . . [my spirit], Pontius Pilate': a corruption of Christ's last words on the Cross (see Luke 13:46), here blasphemously directed not towards God but to Pontius Pilate.

23 'Then, while the shepherds sleep, he shall rise, and say:'

24 'Hey! It comes this way! Now my [sorrowful] mood improves'.

A fatt shepe, I dar say,
A good flese, dar I lay,
Eft whyte when I may,
Bot this will I borow.

[*Mak goes home.*]

How, Gyll, art thou in? Gett us som lyght.

Uxor Eius
Who makys sich dyn this tyme of the nyght?
I am sett for to spyn; I hope not I myght
Ryse a penny to wyn, I shrew them on hight!
So farys
A huswyff that has bene
To be rasyd thus betwene:
Here may no note be sene
For sich small charys.

Mak
Good wyff, open the hek! Seys thou not what I
bryng?

Uxor
I may thole the[e] dray the snek. A, com in my
swetyng![25]

Mak
Yee, thou thar not rek of my long standyng.

Uxor
By the nakyd nek art thou lyke for to hyng.

Mak
Do way:
I am worthy my mete,
For in a strate can I gett
More then thay that swynke and swette
All the long day.

[*He shows her the sheep.*]

Thus it fell to my lott, Gyll, I had sich grace.

Uxor
It were a fowll blott to be hanged for the case.

Mak
I have skapyd, lelott, oft as hard a glase.[26]

Uxor
Bot so long goys the pott to the water, men says,
At last
Comys it home broken.

Mak
Well knowe I the token,
Bot let it never be spoken;
Bot come and help fast.

I wold he were flayn; I lyst well ete:
This twelmothe was I not so fayn of oone shepe
mete.

Uxor
Com thay or he be slayn, and here the shepe blete . . .

Mak
Then myght I be tane. That were a cold swette!
Go spar
The gaytt-doore.

Uxor
Yis, Mak,
For and thay com at thy bak . . .

Mak
Then myght I by, for all the pak,
The Dewill of the war.[27]

Uxor
A good bowrde have I spied, syn thou can none.
Here shall we hym hyde to thay be gone;
In my credyll abyde. Lett me alone,
And I shall lyg besyde in chylbed, and grone.

Mak
Thou red;
And I shall say thou was lyght
Of a knave childe this nyght.

Uxor
Now well is me day bright,
That ever was I bred!

293 fleece 299 earn, curse 300 Thus fares 302 continually interrupted 303 work 304 chores 305 door 307 don't care about 310 food 311 tight spot 312 labour, sweat 314 chance 315 would be, matter 320 proverb 323 skinned 324 year, one, meal 325 ere, hear, bleat 326 taken 327 bolt 328 main door 329 if 330 get, from, pack (of shepherds) 332 trick, conceived 333 until 334 cradle 335 (as if) in childbed, groan 336 (get) ready 337 delivered 338 boy 339 happy the day 340 born

[25] 'I may suffer [i.e. allow] you to draw the bolt [yourself]. Ah, come in my dear!'

[26] 'I have escaped, Gyll, from many a harder blow [in the past].'

[27] 'The Devil of a bad [lit. worse] time.'

This is a good gyse and a far cast;
Yit a woman avyse helpys at the last.
I wote never who spyse, agane go thou fast.

Mak
Bot I come or thay ryse, els blawes a cold blast![28]
I wyll go slepe.

[*Mak returns to the Shepherds.*]

Yit slepys all this meneye,
And I shall go stalk prevely
As it had never bene I
That caryed thare shepe.

[*He lies down between them.*]

I Pastor
Resurrex a Mortuis![29] Have hald my hand.
Judas carnas dominus,[30] I may not well stand!
My foytt slepys, by Jhesus, and I water fastand.[31]
I thoght that we layd us full nere Yngland.[32]

II Pastor
A ye[a]!
Lord, what I have slept weyll;
As fresh as an eyll,
As lyght I me feyll
As leyfe on a tre.

III Pastor
Benste be here in! So my [hart] qwakes,
My hart is outt of skyn, what so it makys.
Who makys all this dyn? So my browes blakys
To the dowore wyll I wyn. Harke, felows, wakys!
We were fowre:
Se ye awre of Mak now?

I Pastor
We were up or thou.

II Pastor
Man, I gyf God a vowe,
Yit yede he nawre.

III Pastor
Me thoght he was lapt in a wolfe skyn.

I Pastor
So are many hapt now namely within.

II Pastor
When we had long napt, me thoght with a gyn
A fatt shepe he trapt, bot he mayde no dyn.

III Pastor
Be styll:
Thi dreme makes the[e] woode:
It is bot fantom, by the Roode.

I Pastor
Now God turne all to good,
If it be His wyll.

II Pastor
Ryse, Mak, for shame! Thou lyges right lang.

Mak
Now Crystes holy name be us emang!
What is this? For Sant James, I may not well gang!
I trow I be the same. A, my nek has lygen wrang
Enoghe.
Mekill thanks syn yister even,
Now, by Sant Stevyn,
I was flayd with a swevyn,
My hart out of sloghe.

I thoght Gyll began to crok and travell full sad,
Welner at the fyrst cok, of a yong lad
For to mend our flok. Then be I never glad;
I have tow on my rok more then ever I had.
A, my heede!

341 disguise, clever trick 342 woman's advice 343 looks, return 347 creep quietly 349 took away 356 eel 358 leaf 360 (my) skin, whatever caused it 361 noise, As my brows are black 362 door, go, wake up! 364 saw, anything 365 before 367 went, nowhere 368 wrapped 369 dressed, especially 370 trick 374 only an illusion 379 walk 380 will recover, awkwardly 382 since last night 384 tormented, dream 385 (jumped) out of (my) skin 386 cry out, labour 387 well-nigh, cock-crow 388 increase, flock 389 flax, distaff (enough trouble)

28 'Unless I return before they wake up, I'm in for a cold spell [i.e. I'm in for trouble]!'

29 'He rose from the dead!'

30 Unclear: literally 'Judas, flesh, lord'. Bevington (*Medieval Drama*, p. 395) suggests the phrase may be a corruption of '*laudes canas domino*': 'sing praises to the Lord'.

31 'My foot sleeps, by Jesus, I stagger [from] fasting [i.e. lack of food].'

32 'Near England': a nice meta-theatrical allusion, drawing the explicit connection between the biblical shepherds and the medieval actors impersonating them.

A house full of yong tharmes;
The Dewill knok outt thare harnes!
Wo is hym has many barnes,
And therto lytyll brede.

I must go home, by youre lefe, to Gyll, as I thoght.
I pray you looke my slefe that I steyll noght:
I am loth you to grefe, or from you take oght.

III Pastor
Go furth, yll might thou chefe! Now wold I we soght,
This morne,
That we had all oure store.

I Pastor
Bot I will go before;
Let us mete.

II Pastor
Whore?

III Pastor
At the crokyd thorne.

[*Exit Shepherds, Mak returns home.*]

Mak
Undo this doore! Who is here? How long shall I stand?

Uxor Eius
Who makys sich a bere? Now walk in the wenyand![33]

Mak
A, Gyll, what chere? It is I, Mak, youre husbande.

Uxor
Then may we se here the Dewill in a bande,
Syr Gyle:
Lo, he commys with a lote
As he were holden in the throte.
I may not syt at my note,
A hand lang while.

Mak
Wyll ye here what fare she makys to gett hir a glose?
And dos noght bot lakys and clowse hir toose.[34]

Uxor
Why, who wanders, who wakys? Who commys, who gose?
Who brewys, who bakys? What makys me thus hose?
And than,
It is rewthe to beholde,
Now in hote, now in colde,
Full wofull is the householde
That wantys a woman.

Bot what ende has thou mayde with the hyrdys, Mak?

Mak
The last worde that thay sayde when I turnyd my bak,
Thay wold looke that thay hade thare shepe, all the pak.
I hope thay wyll nott be well payde when thay thare shepe lak.[35]
Perde!
Bot how so the gam gose,
To me thay wyll suppose,
And make a fowll noyse,
And cry outt apon me.

Bot thou must do as thou hyght.

Uxor
I accorde me thertyll.
I shall swedyll hym right in my credyll;
If it were a gretter slyght, yit couthe I help tyll.
I wyll lyg downe stright. Com hap me.

Mak
I wyll.

Uxor
Behynde!

391 children 392 brains! 393 (who) has, babies 394 bread (to feed them) 396 (up) my sleeve, to see 398 curse you!, checked 400 stock (of sheep) 401 ahead 402 meet, where? 403 crooked 407 noose 408 Sir Cunning 409 noise 410 As (if) 411 work 412 little 413 hear, a fuss, blow 415 comes, goes? 416 brews, bakes, hoarse? 418 sad 421 lacks 422 shepherds 427 however, game goes 428 They'll suspect me 431 promised, agree 432 swaddle (wrap) 433 (Even) if, deception, could 434 immediately, cover

33 'Who is making such a noise? Now walk [away] in the waning [of the moon]!' A curse, the waning of the moon being an inauspicious time.

34 'And she does nothing [all day long] but lie about and pick [at] her toes.'

35 'I think they will not be well pleased when they find their sheep missing.'

Com Coll and his maroo,
Thay will nyp us full naroo.

MAK
Bot I may cry 'Out! Haroo!'
The shepe if thay fynde.

UXOR
Harken ay when thay call; thay will com onone.
Com and make redy all and syng by thyn oone;
Syng 'lullay' thou shall, for I must grone,
And cry outt by the wall on Mary and John,
For sore.
Syng 'lullay' on fast
When thou heris at the last;
And bot I play a fals cast,
Trust me no more.

[*Enter Shepherds (on the moor).*]

III PASTOR
A, Coll, goode morne. Why slepys thou nott?

I PASTOR
Alas, that ever was I borne! We have a fowll blott.
A fat wedir have we lorne.

III PASTOR
Mary, Godes forbott!

II PASTOR
Who shuld do us that skorne? That were a fowll spott.

I PASTOR
Som shrewe.
I have soght with my doges
All Horbery[36] shroges,
And of xv hoges
Fond I bot oone ewe.

III PASTOR
Now trow me, if ye will, by Sant Thomas of Kent,
Ayther Mak or Gyll was at that assent.

I PASTOR
Peasse, man, be still! I sagh when he went;
Thou sklanders hym yll; thou aght to repent,
Goode spede.

II PASTOR
Now as ever myght I the,
If I shuld evyn here de,
I wold say it were he,
That dyd that same dede.

III PASTOR
Go we theder, I rede, and ryn on oure feete.
Shall I never ete brede the sothe to I wytt.

I PASTOR
Nor drynk in my heede with hym tyll I mete.

II PASTOR
I wyll rest in no stede tyll that I hym grete,
My brothere.
Oone I will hight:
Tyll I se hym in sight:
Shall I never slepe one nyght
Ther I do anothere.

[*They go to Mak and Gyll's house.*]

III PASTOR
Will ye here how thay hak? Oure syre lyst croyne!

I PASTOR
Hard I never none crak so clere out of toyne.[37]
Call on hym.

II PASTOR
Mak, undo youre doore soyne.

MAK
Who is that spak, as it were noyne,
On loft?
Who is that, I say?

436 mate 437 trap, tightly 438 harrow! (help!) 440 soon 441 yourself 442 'lullaby', groan 445 quickly 446 hear 447 unless, shrewd trick 451 wether (castrated ram), lost, forbid! 452 shame 454 dogs 455 bushes 456 fifteen young sheep 457 Found 459 a party to that 460 saw 461 slanders, anything 463 prosper 464 die 467 run 468 bread, until I know the truth 469 until I've seen him 470 greet 471 brothers 472 One (thing), promise 475 (i.e. never in the same place) 476 bark, (Mak) loves to croon! 477 Heard, sing 478 soon 479 noon 480 in the sky (i.e. loudly)

36 Horbury, a town south of Wakefield.

37 As they planned, Mak is singing a lullaby and Gyll is pretending to groan with labour pains.

III PASTOR
Goode felowse, were it day.

MAK
As far as ye may,
Good, spekes soft,

Over a seke womans heede that is at mayll easse;
I had lever be dede or she had any dyseasse.

UXOR
Go to an-othere stede. I may not well qweasse.
Ich fote that ye trede goys thorow my nese,[38]
So hee!

I PASTOR
Tell us, Mak, if ye may,
How fare ye, I say?

MAK
Bot ar ye in this towne to-day?
Now, how fare ye?

Ye have ryn in the myre, and ar weytt yit:
I shall make you a fyre, if ye will sytt.
A nores wold I hyre. Thynk ye on yit,
Well qwytt is my hyre, my dreme this is itt
A seson.
I have barnes, if ye knew,
Well mo then enewe,
Bot we must drynk as we brew,
And that is bot reson.

I wold ye dynyd or ye yode. Me thynk that ye swette.

II PASTOR
Nay, nawther mendys oure mode drynke nor mette.[39]

MAK
Why, syr, alys you oght bot goode?

III PASTOR
Yee, oure shepe that we gett,
Ar stollyn as thay yode. Oure los is grette.

MAK
Syrs, drynkes!
Had I bene thore,
Som shuld have boght it full sore.

I PASTOR
Mary, som men trowes that ye wore,
And that us forthynkes.

II PASTOR
Mak, some men trowys that it shuld be ye.

III PASTOR
Ayther ye or youre spouse, so say we.

MAK
Now if ye have suspowse to Gill or to me,
Com and rype oure howse, and then may ye se
Who had hir;
If I any shepe fott,
Ayther cow or stott;
And Gyll, my wife, rose nott
Here syn she lade hir.
As I am true and lele, to God here I pray,
That this be the fyrst mele that I shall ete this day.

I PASTOR
Mak, as have I ceyll, avyse the[e], I say;
He lernyd tymely to steyll that couth not say nay.[40]

UXOR
I swelt!
Outt, thefys, fro my wonys!
Ye com to rob us for the nonys.

MAK
Here ye not how she gronys?
Youre hartys shuld melt.

UXOR
Outt, thefys, fro my barne! Negh hym not thor!

MAK
Wyst ye how she had farne, youre hartys wold be sore.

482 if only it was . . . 484 Good sir, quietly 485 is sick 486 rather, dead, than 487 breathe 489 high/loudly 494 still wet 496 nurse 497 paid, wages 498 (For) a while 500 enough 503 before you go 505 does something afflict you?, guard 506 walked, loss 508 there 509 someone 510 believe (that) you were there 511 troubles us 512 was you 514 suspicions against 515 search 516 her (the sheep) 517 stolen any sheep 518 heifer 520 since she laid down 523 (hope to), bliss, think carefully 525 faint 526 thieves, home! 527 now 528 Hear 530 baby, don't go near him! 531 suffered

38 'Each step that you take goes through my nose [i.e. sends a pain through my head]'.

39 'Neither drink nor food improves our tempers.'

40 'He who couldn't say no (to other folk's possessions) learned early to steal': proverbial.

Ye do wrang, I you warne, that thus commys before
To a woman that has farne, bot I say no more.

Uxor
A, my medyll!
I pray to God so mylde,
If ever I you begyld,
That I ete this chylde
That lyges in this credyll.

Mak
Peasse, woman, for Godes payn, and cry no so:
Thou spyllys thy brane, and makys me full wo.

II Pastor
I trow oure shepe be slayn. What fynde ye two?

III Pastor
All wyrk we in vayn; as well may we go.
Bot hatters!
I can fynde no flesh,
Hard nor nesh,
Salt nor fresh,
Bot two tome platers.

Whik catell bot this, tame nor wylde,
None, as have I blys, as lowde as he smylde.

Uxor
No, so God me blys, and gyf me joy of my chylde!

I Pastor
We have merkyd amys; I hold us begyld.

II Pastor
Syr, don!
Syr, Oure Lady hym save,
Is youre chyld a knave?

Mak
Any lord myght hym have
This chyld to his son.

When he wakyns he kyppys, that joy is to se.

III Pastor
In good tyme to hys hyppys, and in cele.
Bot who was his gossyppys, so sone rede?

Mak
So fare fall thare lyppys!

I Pastor
[*Aside*] Hark now, a le!

Mak
So God thaym thank,
Parkyn, and Gybon Waller, I say,
And gentill John Horne,[41] in good fay,
He made all the garray,
With the greatt shank

II Pastor
Mak, freyndes will we be, for we ar all oone.

Mak
We? Now I hald for me, for mendes gett I none.
Fare well all thre. [*Aside*] All glad were ye gone!

[*The Shepherds leave the house.*]

III Pastor
Fare wordys may ther be, bot luf is ther none
This yere.

I Pastor
Gaf ye the chyld any thyng?

II Pastor
I trow not oone farthyng.[42]

III Pastor
Fast agane will I flyng,
Abyde ye me there.

[*He goes back in.*]

Mak, take it to no grefe if I come to thi barne.

534 middle/stomach 537 (should) eat 538 lies 539 pain 540 wrecks, brain 543 curse it! 545 soft 547 empty plates 548 No living thing but this (baby) 549 smelled as much as him 551 aimed wrongly 552 completely 554 boy? 555 (be proud to) have 557 grabs 558 hips (i.e. bless him!) 559 godparents, soon ready? 560 lips (i.e. bless them!), lie! 563 faith 564 noise 565 (He) with the long legs 566 united/reconciled (again) 567 look after myself, apologies 569 fair, love 570 year 571 Gave 573 I'll quickly return 575 as no offence, baby

41 These names perhaps refer to local personalities, or stock names for social types.

42 A farthing was the smallest coin of the realm, worth one quarter of an old penny.

MAK
Nay, thou dos me greatt reprefe, and fowll has thou
farne.

III PASTOR
The child will it not grefe, that lytyll day-starne.
Mak, with youre leyfe, let me gyf youre barne
Bot vj pence.

MAK
Nay, do way: he slepys.

III PASTOR
Me thynk he pepys.

MAK
When he wakyns he wepys.
I pray you go hence.

[*I and II Shepherds return.*]

III PASTOR
Gyf me lefe hym to kys, and lyft up the clowtt.
What the Dewill is this? He has a long snowte.

I PASTOR
He is merkyd amys. We wate ill abowte.

II PASTOR
Ill-spon weft, iwys, ay commys foull owte.[43]
Ay, so!
He is lyke to oure shepe!

III PASTOR
How, Gyb, may I pepe?

I PASTOR
I trow kynde will crepe
Where it may not go.[44]

II PASTOR
This was a qwantt gawde, and a far cast.
It was a hee frawde.

III PASTOR
Yee, syrs, wast.
Lett bren this bawde, and bynd hir fast.
A fals skawde hang at the last;
So shall thou.
Wyll ye see how thay swedyll
His foure feytt in the medyll?
Sagh I never in a credyll
A hornyd lad or now.

MAK
Peasse byd I! What! Let be youre fare.
I am he that hym gatt, and yond woman hym bare.

I PASTOR
What dewill shall he hatt, Mak? Lo, God, Makes
ayre!

II PASTOR
Lett be all that! Now God gyf hym care,
I sagh . . .

UXOR
A pratty child is he
As syttys on a wamans kne;
A dyllydowne, perde,
To gar a man laghe.

III PASTOR
I know hym by the eere marke: that is a good tokyn!

MAK
I tell you, syrs . . . Hark!, his noyse was brokyn.
Sythen told me a clerk that he was forspokyn.

I PASTOR
This is a fals wark; I wold fayn be wrokyn.
Gett wepyn!

UXOR
He was takyn with an elfe;
I saw it myself.
When the clok stroke twelf
Was he forshapyn.

II PASTOR
Ye two ar well feft sam in a stede.

576 insult, acted 577 little day-star 578 permission 579 Six pence 581 wakes (i.e. his eyes are open) 582 He'll cry if you wake him 584 kiss, cloth 586 deformed, do wrong to pry 593 cunning trick 594 high fraud, it was 595 Let's burn, slut, tightly 596 false scold (will) 598 bound 599 four feet 600 Saw 601 before this 602 stop it! 603 begat, bore him 604 be called, Mak's heir! 605 sorrow 606 saw . . . 607 As pretty (a) . . . 608 woman's 609 darling 610 make, laugh 612 nose 613 bewitched 614 revenged 615 Get weapons! 616 by 619 exchanged 620 well suited together

43 'Badly spun weft always produces bad cloth': i.e. evil will always be revealed in due course.

44 'I believe that nature will crawl where it cannot run': i.e. it may be slow, but nature will reveal itself in time.

III Pastor
Syn thay manteyn thare theft, let do thaym to dede.

Mak
If I trespas eft, gyrd of my heede.
With you will I be left.

I Pastor
Syrs, do my reede.
For his trespas,
We will nawther ban ne flyte,
Fyght nor chyte,
Bot have done as tyte,
And cast hym in canvas.

[*They go outside and toss Mak in a blanket.*]

Lord, what I am sore, in poynt for to bryst.
In fayth I may no more; therfor wyll I ryst.

II Pastor
As a shepe of vii skore he weyd in my fyst.[45]
For to slepe ay-whore me thynk that I lyst.

III Pastor
Now I pray you,
Lyg downe on this grene.

I Pastor
On these thefys yit I mene.

III Pastor
Wherto shuld ye tene?
Do as I say you.

[*The Angel enters.*]

Angelus cantat 'Gloria in excelsis'; postea dicat:[46]

Angelus
Ryse, hyrd-men heynd! For now is He born
That shall take fro the Feynd that Adam had lorne;
That warloo to sheynd, this nyght is He born.
God is made youre freynd now at this morne.
He behestys
At Bedlem go se:
Ther lygys that fre
In a cryb full poorely,
Betwyx two bestys.

I Pastor
This was a qwant stevyn that ever yit I hard!
It is a mervell to nevyn, thus to be skard.

II Pastor
Of Godes Son of Hevyn he spak upward.
All the wod on a levyn me thoght that he gard
Appere.

III Pastor
He spake of a barne
In Bedlam, I you warne.

I Pastor
That betokyns yond starne.
Let us seke hym there.

II Pastor
Say, what was his song? Hard ye not how he crakyd
it?
Thre brefes to a long.

III Pastor
Yee, mary, he hakt it.
Was no crochett wrong, nor no thyng that lakt it.

I Pastor
For to syng us emong, right as he knakt it,
I can.

II Pastor
Let se how ye croyne.
Can ye bark at the mone?

III Pastor
Hold youre tonges! Have done!

I Pastor
Hark after than.

[*He sings.*]

621 death 622 again, cut off 623 follow my advice 625 curse not quarrel 626 chide 628 toss 629 ready to burst 630 rest 632 anywhere 635 About, think 638 gentle shepherds 639 what Adam had lost 640 warlock, defeat 642 requests (you) 643 Bethlehem 644 lies, noble (one) 647 the strangest voice 648 talk about, scared 649 spoke, above us 650 woods, in a light, made 653 I tell you 654 star 655 seek 656 sang 657 Three short notes to one long, sang 658 note, it lacked nothing 659 sang 660 know (how) 661 croon 662 moon? 664 listen (to me) then

45 'He weighed as much as a sheep of seven-score [i.e. 140] pounds in my hands.'

46 'The Angel shall sing "Glory to God in the highest", then let him say:'

II Pastor
To Bedlem he bad that we shuld gang:
I am full fard that we tary to lang.

III Pastor
Be mery and not sad; of myrth is oure sang;
Ever-lastyng glad to mede may we fang,
Withoutt noyse.

I Pastor
Hy we thedyr for-thy;
If we be wete and wery,
To that chyld and that lady,
We have it not to lose.

II Pastor
We fynde by the prophecy . . . let be your din!,
Of David and Isay, and mo then I myn,
Thay prophecyed by clergy that in a vyrgyn
Shuld He lyght and ly, to sloken oure syn
And slake it
Oure kynde from wo;
For Isay sayd so,
Ecce virgo
Concipiet a chylde that is nakyd.

III Pastor
Full glad may we be, and abyde that day
That lufly to se, that all myghtys may.
Lord, well were me, for ones and for ay,
Myght I knele on my kne, som word for to say
To that chylde.
Bot the angell sayd
In a cryb was He layde;
He was poorly arayd,
Both mener and mylde.

I Pastor
Patryarkes that has bene, and prophetys beforne,
Thay desyryd to have sene this chylde that is borne.
Thay ar gone full clene, that have thay lorne.
We shall se Hym, I weyn, or it be morne,
To tokyn.
When I se Hym and fele,
Then wote I full weyll
It is true as steyll
That prophetys have spokyn:

To so poore as we ar that He wold appere,
Fyrst fynd, and declare by His messyngere.

II Pastor
Go we now, let us fare; the place is us nere.

III Pastor
I am redy and yare; go we in fere
To that bright.
Lord, if thi wylles be,
We are lewde all thre,
Thou grauntt us somkyns gle
To comforth Thi wight.

[*They enter the stable.*]

I Pastor
Hayll, comly and clene; Hayll, yong child!
Hayll, Maker, as I mene, of a madyn so mylde.
Thou has waryed, I weyne, the warlo so wylde;
The fals gyler of teyn now goys he begylde.
Lo, He merys!
Lo, He laghys, my swetyng!
A wel fare metyng.
I have holden my hetyng;
Have a bob of cherys.

II Pastor
Hayll, Sufferan Savyoure, for Thou has us soght.
Hayll, frely foyde and floure, that all thyng has wroght.
Hayll, full of favoure, that made all of noght.
Hayll! I kneyll and I cowre. A byrd have I broght
To my barne.
Hayll, lytyll tyne mop.
Of oure crede Thou art crop:
I wold drynk on Thy cop,
Lytyll day starne.

III Pastor
Hayll, derlyng dere, full of Godhede!
I pray The[e] be nere when that I have nede.

666 afraid, delay too long 667 song 668 bliss as a reward, receive 669 debate 670 Go 671 (Even) if, wet, weary 673 nothing 674 stop 675 Isaiah, than I recall 676 wisdom 677 alight, relieve 681 Behold: a virgin 682 Shall conceive [Isaiah 7:14] 684 lovely (one), is omnipotent 685 I'd be fortunate for ever 690 clothed 691 poor 692 Patriarchs 694 they have lost the chance 695 believe 696 As a sign 697 touch him 699 steel 700 what 704 eager, together 705 bright (one) 707 uneducated 708 something joyful 709 comfort, creature 711 believe, virgin 712 cursed, believe 713 cruel beguiler, is now beguiled 714 (Christ) is merry! 715 laughs 716 very good encounter 717 kept, promise 718 cluster, cherries 719 sovereign saviour 720 noble child, flower 722 kneel, cower 724 tiny moppet 725 Creed, (the) head 726 from your cup 728 divinity

Hayll, swete is Thy chere. My hart wold blede
To se The[e] sytt here in so poore wede,
With no pennys.
Hayll, put forth Thy dall.
I bryng The[e] bot a ball:
Have and play The[e] with all,
And go to the tenys.

MARIA
The Fader of Heven, God omnypotent,
That sett all on seven, His Son has He sent.
My name couth He neven, and lyght or He went.
I conceyvyd Hym full even thrugh myght, as He ment,[47]
And now is He borne.
He kepe you fro wo.
I shall pray Him so.
Tell furth as ye go,
And myn on this morne.

I PASTOR
Fare well, lady, so fare to behold,
With thy childe on thi kne.

II PASTOR
Bot He lyges full cold.
Lord, well is me. Now we go, thou behold.

III PASTOR
For sothe all redy it semys to be told
Full oft.[48]

I PASTOR
What grace we have fun.

II PASTOR
Com furth, now ar we won.

III PASTOR
To syng ar we bun,
Let take on loft!

[*They exit, singing.*]

730 face 731 clothes 732 money 733 hold out your hand 734 only 736 tennis 738 created, in seven (days) 739 did he speak, alighted (in me) 745 remember 751 found 752 saved 753 bound/obliged 754 begin, loudly

47 'I conceived him, indeed, through God's power, as He intended'.

48 'Truly, it seems right to tell our story often.'

Chester (The Paynters and Glaziers), *The Shepherds*

Like the Towneley *Second Shepherds' Play*, this pageant takes the basic detail of the Shepherds' visit to the stable from Luke 2:8–20, but embellishes it lavishly. As in the Towneley pageant, the play explores the universal significance of the Nativity through the experiences of a group of simple working men who are privileged to share in a life-changing event. Only with difficulty do they initially comprehend the mystery to which they are witnesses: as we see from their comic attempts to recall the words of the angelic hymn. But, once comprehended, the message has miraculous effects upon their characters and behaviour. From the quarrelsome figures of the opening exchanges who, like the Towneley Shepherds, are struggling to eke out a living in a rebarbative fallen landscape (although, as their feast suggests, they seem to be rather more prosperous than their Yorkshire counterparts), the Shepherds are transformed by what they experience into witnesses of (and evangelists for) the Incarnation. Their metamorphosis is symbolized not in the nature of the simple gifts which they present to the infant Christ, but in the life choices they make at the close of the play. Each adopts a different form of religious vocation: hermit, anchorite, preacher, changing his literal role as a shepherd for a symbolic one as a 'pastor' of men: a prefiguration of the Christian clergy.

[*Dramatis Personae*: *III Pastors* (three Shepherds; Hankin, Harvey, and Tudd), *Garcius* ('Boy'; Trowle, an apprentice shepherd), *Angelus* (Angel), *Maria*, *Joseph*, *IV Boyes* (servants to the Shepherds)]

Primus Pastor [Hankin]
On wouldes have I walked wylde
Under buskes my bowre to bylde,
From styffe stormes my sheepe to shilde,
My seemely wedders to save.
From comlye Conwaye unto Clyde[1]
Under tyldes them to hyde,
A better shepperd on no syde
Noe yearthlye man maye have.

For with walkynge werye I have mee rought;
Besydes the suche my sheepe I sought.
My taytfull tuppes are in my thought,
Them to save and heale
From the shrewde scabbe yt sought,
Or the rotte, yf yt were wrought.
If the cough had them caught
Of hyt I could them heale.[2]

Loe, here bee my herbes saffe and sownde,
Wysely wrought for everye wounde,
The[y] woulde a whole man bringe to grownde
Within a little whyle;
Of henbane and horehounde,
Tybbe, radishe, and egermonde,
Which bee my herbes save and sounde,
Medled on a rowe.[3]

Here be more herbes, I tell yt you;
I shall recken them on a rowe:
Fynter, fanter, and fetterfowe,
And alsoe penye-wrytte.[4]
This is all that I knowe.
For be yt wether or be yt yowe,
I shall heale them on a rowe
Cleane from theyre hurte.

Here is tarre in a pott
To heale them from the rott;
Well I can and well I wott
The talgh from them take.[5]
And yf sworne yt had the Thursse,[6]
Yett shall the talgh be in my purse,
And the sheepe never the worse
To renne on the rake.

But noe fellowshippe here have I
Save my selfe alone, in good faye;
Therfore after one faste wyll I crye.
But first will I drinke, if I maye.

1 moors 2 bushes, house, build 3 shield 4 wethers (castrated rams) 6 shelters 7 in no place 8 earthly 9 made myself 10 marshes 11 nimble breeding rams 17 safe 19 healthy (i.e. incapacitate) 22 agrimony 24 gathered together 30 ewe 32 Completely 35 know (how to) 40 pasture 41 company 43 someone

[1] Conway and Clwyd: rivers in Wales.
[2] The scab, the rot, and the cough are, respectively, diseases of the skin, the liver, and the lungs common in sheep.
[3] Of the medicinal herbs mentioned (and possibly displayed) here, all are identifiable except 'tybbe'.
[4] Fumitory, (?)fan-weed, feverfew, and pennywort.
[5] Tallow: probably lanolin extracted from wool.
[6] 'Even if the Devil had forbidden it'.

Hic potat Primus Pastor.[7]

Howe, Harvye, howe!
Drive thy sheepe to the lowe.
Thow maye not here excepte I blowe,
As ever have I heale.

Hic Flabit Primus Pastor.[8]

SECUNDUS PASTOR [HARVEY]
Yt is no shame for mee to shewe
How I was set for to sowe
With the fether of a crowe
A clowte upon my heele.

[*They*] *Sitt downe.*

Fellowe, nowe be we well mett.
And though mee thinke us needes,
Had wee Tudd heere by us sett,
Thenn might wee sitte and feede us.

I PASTOR
Yea, to feede us frendly in faye,
How might wee have our service?
Crye thow must lowd, by this daye;
Tudd is deafe and may not well here us.

Secundus Pastor vocat submissa voce:[9]

[II PASTOR]
How, Tudd; come, for thy fathers kyn.

I PASTOR
Naye, faye; thy voyce is wonders dym.
Why, knowys thow not him?
Fye, man, for shame!
Call him Tudd, Tybbys sonne,
And then wyll the shrewe come;
For in good fayth yt is his wonne
To love well his damys name.

II PASTOR
How, Tudd, Tybbys sonne!

TERTIUS PASTOR [TUDD]
Syr, in fayth nowe I come,
For yett have I not all donne
That I have to done;
To seeth salve for our sheepe
And (lest my wiffe should yt weete)
With great gravell and greete
I scowre an ould panne.[10]

Hemlocke and hayriffe, take keepe,
With tarre boyste must bene all tamed,
Penyegrasse and butter for fatt sheepe;
For thys salve am I not ashamed.

Ashamed am I not to shewe
No poynt that longeth to my crafte;
Noe better, that I well knowe,
In land is nowhere lafte.

For, good men, this is not unknowen
To husbandes that benne here abowt:
That eych man muste bowe to his wife,
And commonly for feare of a clowte.

Thus for clowtes now care I;
All ys for feare of our dame keynn.
Now wyll [I] caste my ware hereby,
And hye faste that I were at Hankeynn.

Hankeyn, hold up thy hand and have mee,
That I were on height there by thee.

I PASTOR
Gladly, syr, and thow would bee by me,
For loth me is to denye thee.

II PASTOR
Nowe sythen God hath gathered us together,
With good harte I thanke Him of His grace.
Welcome be thow, well fayre wedder!
Tudd, will we shape us to some solace?

III PASTOR
Solace would best be seene

45 Hey, Harvey! 46 hill 47 hear, unless 48 health 50 just about to sew 52 patch 54 we have need (of something) 57 faith 61 for (the sake of) 62 wonderfully quiet 65 Tib (Elizabeth) 67 habit 68 mother's 72 do 73 boil ointment 74 in case, know 75 stones, grit 76 old pan 77 goosegrass, heed 78 tar-mixture, diluted 79 pennywort 82 aspect belonging to 83 No one 84 left 87 submit 88 blow 89 worry 90 women-folk 91 things 92 go, with Hankin 93 heave me (up) 95 if 96 I would hate to deny you 99 (you) pretty wether! 100 prepare (for) ourselves

7 'Here the First Shepherd drinks.'

8 'Here the First Shepherd blows [on his horn].'

9 'The Second Shepherd calls in a low voice'.

10 Tudd has been mixing sheep-ointment in his wife's saucepan, and has been trying to clean it so that she does not find out.

That we shape us to our supper;
For meate and drinke, well I deeme,
To eych deede is most dere.

I PASTOR
Laye forth, eych man ilych,
What hee hath lafte of his liverye.
And I wyll put forth my pyche
With my parte, firste of us all three.

II PASTOR
And such store as my wife had
In your sight soone shall you see,
At our begininge us to glade;
For in good meate ther is mych glee.

Here is bredd this daye was bacon,
Onyons, garlycke, and leekes,
Butter that bought was in Blacon,[11]
And greene cheese that will greese well your cheekes.

III PASTOR
Ane here ale of Halton I have,[12]
And whot meate I had to my hyer;
A puddinge may noe man deprave,
And a jannock of Lancaster shyre.

Loe, here a sheepes head sowsed in ale,
And a grayne to laye on the greene,[13]
And sowre milke. My wyffe had ordayned
A noble supper, as well is seene.

I PASTOR
Nowe will I caste of my cloacke
And put ont parte of my liverye,
Put owt that I have in my poacke,
And a pigges foote from puddinges purye.[14]

III PASTOR
Abyde, fellowes, and yee shall see here
This hott meate, wee serven yt here;
Gambonns and other good meate in fere,
A puddinge with a pricke in the ende.

I PASTOR
My sotchell to shake out
To sheppardes am I not ashamed.
And this tonge pared rownd aboute
With my teeth yt shalbe atamed.

Tunc commedent, et dicat Primus Pastor:[15]

Byd me doe gladly, and I thee,
For, by God, here is good growsinge;
Come eate with us, God of Heavon hye,
But take noe heede though here be noe howsinge.

II PASTOR
Howsinge ennough have wee here
While that wee have Heavon over our heddes.
Now to weete our mouthes tyme were;[16]
This flackett will I tame, if thow reade us.

III PASTOR
And of this bottell nowe will I bibbe,
For here is bowles of the best.
Such lickour makes men to live;
This game may noe where be leste.

I PASTOR
Fellowes, nowe our bellyes be full,
Thinke wee on him that keepes our flockes.
Blowe thy horne and call after Trowle,
And bydd him, sonne, of our bytlockes.

II PASTOR
Well sayd, Hankyn, by my soothe,
For that shrewe I suppose us seekes.
My horne to lille I wyll not lesse
Tyll that lad have some of our leekes.

III PASTOR
Leekes to his liverye is likinge;
Such a lad no where in land is.

104 For, dear 105 spread out, alike 106 has left, provisions 107 set out my stall 111 please 113 baked today 116 newly made, grease 117 And 118 what 119 criticize 120 Lancashire oatcake 121 pickled 123 sour (i.e. curds) 126 on it 127 wallet/bag 130 food, serve 131 hams, together 132 skewer 133 satchel 135 tongue trimmed 136 tamed 137 if I prosper 138 eating 139 high Heaven 140 housing 144 flask, advise us 145 drink 146 are bowls 148 fun, lost 150 looks after 152 call, for, scraps 155 blow, slack 156 Until 157 desirable

11 Blacon, a village north of Chester.

12 Halton, another nearby village.

13 For 'grayne' Lumiansky and Mills (*Chester Mystery Cycle*, II, p. 108) suggest 'groyne' a pig's snout, or perhaps a whole head.

14 Unclear; either 'pig's foot and puréed sausages' or possibly 'a pig's foot brought out from among sausages (in the bag)'.

15 'Then they shall eat together, and the First Shepherd shall say'.

16 'It's time to wet our mouths'.

Blowe a note for that meetinge
Whyle that horne nowe in thy hand ys.

I Pastor
With this horne I shall make a 'Hooe'
That hee and all Heaven shall here.
Yonder lad that sittes on a lowe
The lowd of this horne shall here.

Tunc cantabit et dicat Garcius:[17]

[Garcius (Trowle)]
Good Lord, looke on mee
And my flocke here as the fed have.
On this wold walke wee;
Are no men here, that noe waye.
All is playne, perdee;
Therfore, sheepe, we mon goe.
Noe better may bee
Of beast that blood and bonne have.

Wotte I not, day or night,
Necessaryes that to mee beelongen.
Tarboyste and tarboll
Yee shall here;
Nettle, hemlock, and butter abydinge,
And my good dogge Dottynolle[18]
That is nothinge cheeffe of his chydinge.

Yf any man come mee bye
And would wytt which waye beste were,
My legge I lifte up whereas I lye
And wishe him the waye easte and west where.
And I rose where I laye,
Me would thinke that travell lost.
For kinge ne duke, by this daye,
Ryse I will not but take my rest here.

Nowe wyll I sitt here adowne
And pippe at this pott like a pope.
Would God that I were downe
Harmeles, as I hastelye hope.
Noe man drinke here shall
Save my selfe, the Devyll of the sope.
All this lottes I seet at little;[19]
Nay yee lades, sett I not by yee.
For you have I manye a fowle fitt.
Thow fowle filth, though thow flytt,
I defye thee!

I Pastor
Trowle, take tent to my talkinge,
For thy tooth here is good tugginge![20]
While thy wedders benne walkinge,
On this loyne thow may have good lugginge.

Garcius
Fye on your loynes and your liverye,
Your liverastes, livers, and longes,
Your sose, your sowse, your saverraye,
Your sittinge withowt any songes!

One this hill I hold mee here.
Noe hape to your meate have I.
But flyte with my fellowes in feare,
And your sheepe full sycerly save I.

II Pastor
For thow saves our sheepe,
Good knave, take keepe.
Sythen thow may not sleepe,
Come eate of this sowse.

Garcius
Nay, the dyrte is soe deepe,
Stopped therin for to steepe;
And the grubbes theron do creepe
At whom at thy howse.

Therfore meate, if I maye,
Of your dightinge to daye
Will I nought by noe waye
Tyll I have my wages.

I wend to have binne gaye
But, see, soe ragged is myne araye;
Aye pinches is your paye
To any poore page.

159 miting (little lad) 163 hill 164 sound 166 they have fed 167 moor 168 in no way 169 empty, by God 172 (i.e. for mortal beasts) 174 belong 175 tar-mixture, tar-ball 177 left-over butter 179 not sparing, barking 181 wants to know 182 wherever 183 eastwards 184 If, (from) where 185 wasted effort 189 pipe 190 down (fromthe hills) 191 unharmed, believe 193 sop/drink 195 lads, I don't care about you 196 Because of you, nasty time 197 argue 202 chewing 203 provisions 204 portions, lungs 205 sauce, pickle, savoury 208 chance of 209 argue, together 210 properly, keep 216 soaked in it 217 maggots 218 home 220 Prepared by you 225 always mean

17 'Then Garcius ['the Boy'] shall sing and say' or 'Then he [I Pastor] sings, and Garcius says'.

18 'Dotty-noll' ('silly-head') is the name of Trowle's dog.

19 'All this noise [i.e. Hankin's horn], I ignore'.

20 'Here's some good work for your teeth!'

III PASTOR
Trowle, boy, for Godes tree,
Come eate a morsell with me;
And then wrastle will wee
Here on this wold.

GARCIUS
That shall I never flee!
Though yt bee with all three
To laye my liverye,[21]
That will I hold.

Tunc ibit ad magistros suos, et dicat:[22]

GARCIUS
Nowe comes Trowle the Trewe;
A torne to take have I tight
With my masters. Or I rewe,
Put him forth that moste is of might.[23]

I PASTOR
Trowle, better thow never knewe.
Eate of this, meate for a knight.

GARCIUS
Naye, spare! Though I spewe,
All upon your heades shall yt light.

II PASTOR
Howe should wee suffer this shame,
Of a shrewe thus to be shente?

III PASTOR
This ladd lusts to be lame
And lose a lymme or hee went.

GARCIUS
Have donne! Beginne wee this game
But warre lest your golyons glent.
That were little dole to our dame,[24]
Though in the myddest of the daye yee were drent.

I PASTOR
False lad, fye on thy face!
One this grownd thow shall have a fall.
Hent one, and hould that thow hasse.
Yf thow happe have, all goe to all![25]

GARCIUS
And this, syrs, here to solace.
Hankyn, sheoparde, shame thee I shall.
Wroth thow art, worse then thow was.
Warre lest thow walter here by the wall.

Tunc projiciat Primum Pastorem, et dicat Secundus Pastor.[26]

II PASTOR
Boye, lest I breake thy bones,
Kneele downe and axe me a boone.
Lest I destroy thee here on these stones,
Sease, lest I shend thee to soone.

GARCIUS
Gole thee to groyns and grownes!
Good were thee thy ould ragges to save soone.
Little dowbt of such drownes,[27]
Lyther tyke, for thy deedes donne.

[*He throws the Second Shepherd.*]

III PASTOR
Owt, alas, hee lyes on his loynes!
But lett mee goe now to that lad.
Sheppardes he shames and shendes,
For last now am I owt shad.

GARCIUS
Both your backes here to mee bendes;
For all your boastes I hould you to bad.
Hould your arses and your hinder loynes;
Then hope I to have as I have hadd.[28]

227 Cross 229 wrestle 231 avoid 236 bout, decided 240 food (fit) for 241 Stop!, If I vomit 242 fall 244 beaten/insulted 245 wants, crippled 246 limb, before, goes 250 (River) Dee, drowned 255 comfort you 258 Beware, sprawl 260 ask, favour 262 destroy, too 266 wretched dog, past deeds 267 side/arse 270 left behind 272 believe you (are) too 273 Hold, backsides

21 'Wager my clothes': Trowle bets his ragged garments against the Shepherds' finer ones that he will win the wrestling match.
22 'Then he shall go to his masters, and say'.
23 'Before I regret it [i.e. before I change my mind and withdraw the wager], bring forward the strongest of you [to fight].'
24 'Beware in case your balls fall off. That would be little comfort for [i.e. would not please] your wife, even if . . . '.
25 'Grab on, and hold what you have. If you have the luck, winner takes all!'
26 'Then he [Trowle] shall throw the First Shepherd, and the Second Shepherd shall say'.
27 'Howl to yourself with grimaces and groans! It would be wise for you to look after your old rags. [There's] little to fear from such loafers [as you]'.
28 'Then I hope/expect to have as much success again [as I had last time]'.

The better in the[e], bore,[29]
As I had before
Of this bovearte,
Yea, hope I more.
Keepe well thy score
For feare of a farte.

Tunc projiciat Tertium Pastorem, et dicat Garci[u]s:[30]

[GARCIUS]
Lye ther, lither, in the lake.
My liverye nowe will I lach:
This curye, this clowt, and this cake.
For yee be cast, now will I catch.

To the Devyll I you all betake,
As traytors attaynt of your tache!
On this would with this will I walke;
All the world wonder on the wache![31]

Et sic recedat Garcius, et dicat Primus Pastor:[32]

[I PASTOR]
Fellowes, this a fowle case ys,
That wee bine thus cast of a knave.
All agaynst our willes hee hase his;
But I must needes hould the harmes that I have.

II PASTOR
That I have needes must I hold;
Of these unhappie harmes ofte here I.
Therfore will I wayte on this would
Upon the wedder, for I am werye.

III PASTOR
Though wee bine werye noe wonder,
What betweene wrastlinge and wakinge.
Ofte wee may bee over though wee be now under.[33]
God amend hit with His makinge.

Tunc sedebunt, et stella apparebit, et dicat Primus Pastor:[34]

What is all this light here
That blasses soe bright here
On my black beard?
For to see this light here
A man may bee afright here,
For I am afeard.

II PASTOR
Feard for a fraye nowe
May wee bee all nowe;
And yett it is night,
Yett seemes yt day nowe.
Never, soothly to saye nowe,
See I such a sight.

III PASTOR
Such a sight seeminge
And a light leeminge
Lettes mee to looke.
All to my deeminge.
From a starre streaminge
Yt to mee stroacke.

GARCIUS
That starre if it stand
To seek will I fond,
Though my sight fayle mee.
While I may live in lond
Why should I not fond,
Yf it will avayle mee?

Tunc respiciens firmamentum dicat Garcius:[35]

A, Godes mightis!
In yonder starre light is;
Of the sonne this sight is,
As yt nowe seemes.

I PASTOR
Hit seemes, as I nowe see,
A bright stare to bee,

277 boaster 279 mark/stance 281 wretch 282 portion, take 283 curry (offal), tripe 284 thrown, take 285 commend you 286 convicted, offence 287 moor 289 business 290 thrown by 291 his (will) 292 put up with the bruises 295 keep watch 296 weary 297 It's no wonder that . . . 298 keeping watch 300 providence 302 blazes 307 fight 312 Saw 313 vision 314 shining 315 Prevents me from looking 316 judgement 318 struck 319 stands (still) 320 strive 324 benefit 327 from, sun (with an unintentional pun on Son) 330 star

29 'The better luck with you, fool'.

30 'Then he [Trowle] shall throw the Third Shepherd, and Garcius shall say'.

31 'All the world, wonder at the watch(men/man)!': Trowle either mocks the shepherds or vaunts himself.

32 'And thus Garcius shall go away and the First Shepherd shall say'.

33 'Another time we may be up, although at the moment we're down.'

34 'Then they shall sit down, and the star shall appear, and the First Shepherd shall say'.

35 'Then, looking towards the sky, Garcius shall say'.

There to abyde.
From yt wee may not flee
But aye gloe on the glee,
Tyll yt downe glyde.

II Pastor
Fellowes, will wee
Kneele downe on your knee
After comford
To the trewe Trinitee,
For to lead us for to see
Our elders Lord?

III Pastor
Our Lord will us lere
In our prayer
Wherto yt will apent;
And why on high here
The eare is soe cleare,
Nowe shall wee be kent.

Garcius
Lord, of this light
Send us some sight
Why that it is sent.
Before this night
Was I never soe afright
Of the firmament.

I Pastor
Ne, fyer! By my faye,
Nowc is it nigh daye;
So was it never.
Therfore I praye
The sooth us to saye,
Or that we desever.

Tunc cantet Angelus: 'Gloria in excelsis Deo et in terra pax hominibus bonae voluntatis.'[36]

Fellowes in feare,
May yee not here
This mutinge on highe?

II Pastor
In 'glore' and in 'glere'?[37]
Yett noe man was nere
Within our sight.

III Pastor
Naye, yt was a 'glorye'.
Nowe am I sorye
Bowt more songe.

Garcius
Of this strange storye
Such mirth is merye;
I would have amonge.

I Pastor
As I then deemed,
'Selsis' it seemed
That hee songe soe.

II Pastor
Whyle the light leemed,
A wreakinge mee weened;
I wyst never whoo.

III Pastor
What songe was this, saye yee,
That he sange to us all three?
Expounded shall yt bee
Erre wee hethen passe;
For I am eldest of degree
And alsoe best, as seemes mee,
Hit was 'grorus glorus' with a 'glee'.
Hit was neyther more nor lasse.

Garcius
Nay, yt was 'glorus glarus glorius';
Methinke that note went over the howse,
A seemely man hee was, and curiouse;
But soone awaye hee was.

I Pastor
Nay, yt was 'glorus glarus' with a 'glo',
And mych of 'celsis' was therto.
As ever have I rest or woo,
Much hee spake of 'glas'.

333 gaze at, happy (thing) 334 goes down 337 seeking comfort 340 the Lord of our fathers 341 instruct 343 What it means 345 air 346 taught 354 nearly (as bright as) 358 Before, split up 359 (all) together 360 hear 361 singing 363 near 367 (That there is not) 370 share in it 375 (divine) vengeance, expected 376 I didn't know who (for). 380 go from here 381 of us all 384 less 386 song 387 very odd 390 much, involved 391 woe

36 'Then the Angel shall sing: "Glory to God in the highest, and on earth, peace, good will towards men"' (Luke 2:13–14).

37 'Glore' and 'glere' are nonsense words: the Shepherds begin to try to make sense of the Angel's Latin.

II Pastor
Naye, yt was neyther 'glas' nor 'glye'.
Therfore, fellowe, nowe stand bye.

III Pastor
By my fayth, hee was some spye,
Our sheepe for to steale.

Or elles hee was a man of our crafte,
For seemely hee was and wounder defte.

Garcius
Nay, hee came by night, all things lefte,
Our tuppes with tarre to teale.

I Pastor
Naye, on a 'glor' and on 'glay' and a 'gly'
Gurd Gabryell when hee so gloryd.
When hee sange I might not be sorye;
Through my brest-bonne bletinge hee bored.

II Pastor
Nay, by God, yt was a 'gloria',
Sayde Gabryell when hee sayde soe.
He had a mych better voyce then I have,
As in Heaven all other have soe.

III Pastor
Wyll [ye] here howe hee sange 'celsis'?
For on that sadly hee sett him;
Nayther singes 'sar' nor soe well 'cis',
Ney '*pax* merye Mawd' when shee had mett him.[38]

Garcius
On tyme hee touched on 'tarre',
And therto I tooke good intent;
All Heaven might not have gonne harre,
That note on high when hee up hent.

I Pastor
And after a '*pax*' or of 'peace',
Up as a pye hee pyped;
Such a loden, this is no lesse,
Never in my life me so lyked.

II Pastor
Upon '*hominibus*' hee muted;
That much mervayle to mee was.
And aye I quoked when hee so whewted;
I durst not hede wher that yt was.

III Pastor
Yett, yett, hee sange more then all this,
For some word is worthye a forder.
For hee sange '*bonae voluntatis*';
That is a cropp that passeth all other.

Garcius
Yett and yett he sange more to;
From my mynde yt shall not starte.
Hee sange alsoe of a '*Deo*';
Me thought that heled my harte.

And that word '*terra*' hee tamed:
Therto I toke good intent.
And '*pax*' alsoe may not be blamed;
For that to this songe I assent.

I Pastor
Nowe pray wee to him with good intent,
And singe I wyll and me umbrace:
That hee will lett us to bee kent,
And to send us of his grace.

II Pastor
Nowe syth I have all my will,
Never in this world soe well I was.
Singe wee nowe, I rede us, shryll
A mery songe us to solace.

Garcius
Singe we nowe; lett see,
Some songe will I assaye.
All men nowe singes after mee,
For musicke of mee learne yee maye.

Tunc cantabunt et postea dicat Tertius Pastor:[39]
(Here singe 'troly, loly, loly, loo'.)

397 trade/profession 398 wonderfully skilled 399 set aside 400 rams, tar, mark (as his) 402 Said 404 breast-bone, singing, bored 410 concentrated 413 (At) one 415 higher 416 lifted up 418 magpie 419 voice, lie 421 'to men', sang 423 shook, called out 425 than 426 worth a lot more 427 (of) 'good will' 428 thing, surpasses 429 too 430 slip 432 healed 434 paid good attention 435 criticized 436 Because, agree 438 proclaim 439 allow, informed 443 vigorously 446 try 448 from 448+ (a popular song refrain)

38 'Sarah', 'Cissy', 'Peace Merry Maud'; Tudd seems to be thinking of characters and names from popular songs.

39 'Then they shall sing and afterwards the Third Shepherd shall say'.

Nowe wend we forth to Bethlem,
That is best our songe to bee,
For to see the starre gleme,
The fruyt alsoe of that mayden free.

I PASTOR
Nowe followe we the starre that shines,
Tyll we come to that holy stable.
To Bethlem boyne the lymes;
Followe we yt withowt any fable.

II PASTOR
Followe we hit and hyes full fast;
Such a frende loth us were to fayle.
Launch on! I will not be the last
Upon Marye for to mervayle.

Hic vadunt versus Bethlem.[40]

III PASTOR
Stynt nowe; goe no moe steppes,
For now the starre beginneth to stand.
Harvye, that good bene our happes
We seene, by our Savyour fonde.

Hic apparet Angelus et dicat:[41]

[ANGELUS]
Sheppardes, of this sight
Be ye not afright,
For this is Godes might;
Takes this in mynde.
To Bethlem nowe right;
There yee shall see in sight
That Christ is borne tonight
To cover all mankynde.

GARCIUS
To Bethlem take wee the waye,
For with you I thinke to wend,
That Prince of Peace for to praye
Heaven to have at our ende.
And singe we all, I read,
Some myrth to His Majestee,
For certayne now see wee it indeede:
The Kinge Sone of Heavon is Hee.

I PASTOR
Sym, sym, securlye
Here I see Marye,
And Jesus Christ fast bye
Lapped in haye.

II PASTOR
Kneele we downe in hye
And praye wee Him of mercye,
And welcome Him worthelye
That woe does awaye.

III PASTOR
Awaye all our woe ys
And many mans moe ys.
Christ, Lord, lett us kys
The cratch or the clothes.

GARCIUS
Solace nowe to see this
Byldes in my brest blys:
Never after to do amys,
Thinge that Him loth ys.[42]

I PASTOR [*seeing Joseph*]
Whatever this ould man that here ys?
Take heede how his head ys whore!
His beard is like a buske of bryers
With a pound of heare about his mouth and more.

II PASTOR
More ys this marveyle to mee nowe,
For to nappe greatly him needes.
Hartles is hee nowe
For aye to his heeles hee heedes.

III PASTOR
Why, with his berde though hit be rough,
Right well to her hee hydes.
Worthye wight, witt would wee nowe;
Wyll ye worne us, worthye in weedes?

449 Bethlehem 451 shine 452 offspring 455 bend our limbs 456 chatter 457 hurry 458 disappoint 460 marvel 461 Stop 463 Harvey, fortunes 464 found 472 recover 476 achieve, death 477 advise 478 joyous song 481 hum, hum, definitely 484 wrapped 485 quickly 488 bring to an end 490 many another man's (too) 491 kiss 492 cradle 494 grows 497 Whoever (is) 498 hoar/grey 499 briar bush 500 hair 501 Greater 502 sleep 503 Without vigour 504 heels (i.e. feet), looks down 506 attends 507 Sir, we'd like to know 508 reject, worthy (one), clothes

40 'Here they shall go toward Bethlehem.'

41 'Here the Angel shall appear and say'.

42 'Anything that is loathsome to Him.'

Maria
Sheppardes, sothlye I see
That my sonne you hyther sent,
Through Godes might in majestye
That in mee light and here is lent.
This man maryed was to mee
For noe sinne in such assent;
But to keep my virginitee,
And truly in non other intent.

Joseph
Good men, Moyses take in mynde;
As he was made through God Allmight,
Ordayned lawes us to bynde
Which that wee should keepe of right;
Man and woman for to bynde
Lawefully them both to light;
To fructifye, as men may fynde,
That tyme was wedded every wight.

Therfore wedded to her I was
As lawe would: her for to lere
For noyse nor slander nor trespasse,
And through that deede the Devill to dere,
As tould mee Gabriell, full of grace.
When I had trussed all my gere
To have fled and to have never seene her face,
By him was I arested there.

For hee sayde to mee sleepinge
That shee lackles was of sinne.
And when I hard that tokeninge,
From her durst I noe waye twynne.
Therfore goes forth and preach this thinge,
All together and not in twynne:
That you have seene your heavonly kinge
Common all mankynde to mynne.

I Pastor
Great God, syttynge in Thy troone,
That made all thinge of nought,
Nowe wee may thanke Thee eychone:
This is Hee that wee have sought.

II Pastor
Goe wee neere anone
With such as we have brought.
Ringe, brooche, or pretiouse stone:
Lett see whether we have ought to proffer.

III Pastor
Lett us doe Him homage.

I Pastor
Whoe shall goe first? The page?

II Pastor
Naye, yee be father in age.
Therfore ye must first offer.

I Pastor
Hayle, Kinge of Heavon soe hye,
Borne in a crybbe;
Mankynd unto Thee
Thow hast made full sybbe.

Hayle, Kynge, borne in a maydens bowre,
Profettes did tell Thow should be our succour;
This clarkes do saye.
Loe, I bringe Thee a bell;
I praye Thee save me from Hell,
Soe that I maye with Thee dwell
And serve Thee for aye.

II Pastor
Hayle, the Emperour of Hell
And of Heaven alsoe;
The Feynd shalt Thow fell,
That ever hath binne fals.

Hayle, the maker of the stare
That stoode us beforne;
Hayle, the blessedes-full baronne
That ever was borne.
Loe, sonne, I bringe Thee a flackett.
Therby hanges a spoone
For to eat Thy pottage with at noone,
As I myselfe full ofte tymes have donne.
With hart I praye Thee to take yt.

III Pastor
Hayle, prince withowten any pere,
That mankynde shall releeve.

512 alighted, laid 513 married 514 that contract 516 for no other reason 519 be bound by 520 justly 522 please 523 multiply 524 everyone was married 526 the law dictated, teach 527 (Rather than), gossip, sin 528 defeat 530 packed, belongings 532 stopped 534 was blameless 535 heard, sign/message 536 dared, depart 537 go 538 separately 540 come, to take care of 541 throne 542 from nothing 543 each one (of us) 547 precious 548 anything to give (Him) 550 boy 551 most senior 556 all part of Your family 557 chamber (i.e. womb) 558 Prophets, salvation 559 scholars 566 destroy 567 been false 568 star 569 in front of us 570 most blessed baby 572 flask 574 soup

Hayle, the fooe unto Lucyfere,
The which beguyled Eve.

Hayle, the graunter of hope,
For one yearth now Thow dwelles.
Loe, sonne, I bringe Thee a cappe,
For I have nothinge elles.

This gifte, sonne, that I give Thee ys but smalle;
And though I come the hyndmost of all,
When Thow shalt men to Thy blys call,
Good Lord, yett thinke one mee.

GARCIUS
My deare, with dryrie unto Thee I mee dresse,
My state on felloweshippe that I doe not lose;
And for to save mee from all yll sicknesse,
I offer unto Thee a payre of my wyves ould hose.

For other jewells, my sonne,
Have I note Thee for to give
That is worthe anythinge at all,
But my good harte whyle I lyve
And my prayers tyll death doth mee call.

THE FIRST BOYE
Nowe to you, my fellowes, this doe I saye,
For in this place, or that I wynde awaye:
Unto yonder chyld lett us goe praye,
As our masterse have donne us beforne.

THE SECOND BOYE
And of such goodes as wee have here,
Lett us offer to this prince so dere,
And to His mother, that mayden clere,
That of her body hasse her borne.

I BOYE
Abyde, syrres, I will goe firste to yonder kinge.

II BOYE
And I will goe nexte to that lordinge.

THE THYRD BOYE
Then will I be last of this offeringe;
This can I saye, noe more.

I BOYE
Nowe, lord, for to give Thee have I nothinge,
Neyther gold, silver, brooch, ne ringe,
Nor noe rich robes meete for a kinge
That I have here in store.

But thoe hit lacke a stopple,
Take Thee here my well fayre bottle,
For yt will hold a good pottle;
In fayth, I can give Thee noe more.

II BOYE
Lord, I know that Thow art of this virgine borne,
In full poore araye sittinge one her arme.
For to offer to Thee have I noe skorne,
Althoo Thou be but a child.

For jewell have I none to give Thee
To mayntayne Thy royall dignitye;
But my hood, take yt Thee,
As Thow art God and man.

THE THYRD BOYE
O noble chyld of thy Father on hye,·
Alas, what have I for to give Thee?
Save only my pype that soundeth so royallye,
Elles truely have I nothinge at all.
Were I in the rocke or in the valey alowe,
I could make this pipe sound, I trowe,
That all the world should ringe
And quaver as yt would fall.

IV BOYE
Nowe, chyld, although Thou be commen from God
And bee Thyselfe God in Thy manhoode,
Yet I knowe that in Thy chyldhood
Thow will for sweetemeat looke.
To pull downe apples, payres, and ploomes,
Ould Joseph shall not neede to hurte his handes;
Because Thow haste not plentye of cromes,
I give Thee here my nuthooke.

I PASTOR
Nowe farewell, mother and maye,
For of synne nought thow wottest.
Thow hast brought forth this daye
Godes Sonne of mightis most.

Wherfore men shall saye:
'Blesed in every coast and place
Be Hee, memoriall for us all.'

581 granter 582 on 586 last in line 587 call men to Heaven 588 remember 589 love, bring myself 590 place in (Your) company 592 old stockings 593 gifts 594 not 612 fitting 614 lacks a stopper 616 measure (of drink) 619 on 620 shame 621 only 630 mountains, below 631 believe 634 come 637 sweet things 638 pears, plums 640 crumbs (i.e. little things) 642 maid/virgin 643 you know nothing 645 powers (the) greatest 648 an example

And that wee may from synne fall
And stand ever in His grace,
Our Lord God bee with thee.

II Pastor
Brethren, lett us all three
Singinge walke homwardlye.
Unkynd will I never in noe case bee,
But preach all that I can and knowe,
As Gabryell taught by his grace mee.
Singinge awaye hethen will I.

III Pastor
Over the sea, and I may have grace,
I will gange and goe abowt nowe
To preach this thinge in every place;
And sheepe will I keepe no more nowe.

Garcius
I read wee us agree
For our mysdeedes amendes to make,
For soe nowe will I;
And to the chyld I wholey mee betake
For aye securlye.
Sheppardes craft I forsake;
And to an anker herby
I will in my prayers wach and wake.[43]

I Pastor
And I an hermitte
To prayse God, to praye,
To walke by stye and by streytt,
In wildernes to walke for aye.
And I shall noe man meete
But for my livinge I shall him praye,
Barefoote one my feete.
And thus will I live ever and aye.[44]

For aye, ever, and alwayse,
This world I fully refuse,
My mysse to amend with monys.
Turne to thy fellowes and kys.

I yelde, for in youth
We have bine fellowes, iwys.
Therfore lend me your mouth,
And frendly let us kysse.

II Pastor
From London to Lowth[45]
Such another shepperd I wott not where is.
Both frend and cowth,
God grant you all His blys.

III Pastor
To that blys bringe you
Great God, if that Thy will bee.
Amen, all singe you;
Good men, farewell yee.

Garcius
Well for to fare, eych frend,
God of His might graunt you;
For here now we make an ende.
Farewell, for wee from you goe nowe.

649 flee/escape 653 homewards 655 understand 656 taught (me) 657 from here (go) 663 sins, atonement 665 wholly dedicate myself 666 Forever, truly 668 an anchorite's cell 672 path, street 673 ever 676 on 679 reject 680 sins, atone for, lamentation 682 agree 683 friends/companions 687 where (there) is 688 companion

[43] Trowle promises to become an anchorite, a religious recluse dedicated to prayer.

[44] Hankin chooses the life of the hermit, who, unlike the anchorite, wanders from place to place begging alms to support his life of prayer. As well as the literal roles, there may well be an allusion here to the lifestyles of the two major religious orders, the sedentary monks and the wandering friars.

[45] Louth, a Lincolnshire town, named here for alliteration, and to indicate a long distance.

York (The Skinners), *The Entry into Jerusalem*

This highly formal pageant demonstrates the close affinities between drama and ceremony which characterize key moments in the Cycle plays. The entry into Jerusalem marks the beginning of the Passion sequence,[1] and, as Christ reminds His disciples (ll. 24–8), also fulfils a number of key prophecies concerning the coming of the Messiah. Acts of healing from Christ's ministry are incorporated into the events, both to increase its dramatic content and to demonstrate His role as redeemer of a 'sick' and fallen world prior to His betrayal and trial.

As Martin Stevens has shown, the pageant draws the city of York itself into its dramatic ambit (see Stevens, *Four Middle English Mystery Cycles*). Christ entering Jerusalem is also simultaneously entering York, and is afforded the sort of ceremonial welcome offered to a visiting English monarch. The city is thus symbolically affirming its own loyalty to Christ even as it represents that of its biblical forebear. The kinds of sacralization of contemporary life and labour which characterize the role of the guilds in their individual pageants is thus expanded to incorporate the whole city collectively. In dramatic terms, the *Entry*, like the later *Crucifixion*, makes great use of the audience as actors in the play that they are witnessing. As Christ and His disciples moved through the street towards the pageant wagon, the audience played the role of the crowds gathered to greet Him, and it would have been from among them that the blind man, Cecus, and the other recipients of His healing called out to Christ for help.

The Skinners processed animal skins into clothes and other goods.

[*Dramatis Personae*: *Jesus*, *Petrus* (the Apostle Peter), *Philippus* (the Apostle Philip), *Janitor* (a civic official of Jerusalem), *VIII Burgensis* (eight Burgesses; chief citizens), *Cecus* (a blind man), *A Pauper*, *Claudus* (a crippled man), *Zache* (Zacheus, the chief publican, or tax-collector).]

JESUS
To Me takis tent and giffis gud hede,
My dere discipulis þat ben here,
I schall ȝou telle þat shal be indede:
My tyme to passe hense it drawith nere,
And by þis skill,
Mannys sowle to save fro sorowes sere
Þat loste was ill.[2]

From Heven to Erth whan I dyssende
Rawnsom to make I made promys,
The prophicie nowe drawes to ende,
My Fadirs wille forsoth it is
Þat sente Me hedyr.
Petir, Phelippe, I schall ȝou blisse,
And go togedir
Unto ȝone castell þat is ȝou agayne.
Gois with gud harte and tarie noȝt,
My comaundement to do be ȝe bayne.
Also I ȝou charge, loke it be wrought:
Þat schal ȝe fynde
An asse þis feste als ȝe had soght,
Ȝe hir unbynde

With hir foole, and to Me hem bring,
Þat I on hir may sitte a space.
So þe prophicy clere menyng
May be fulfillid here in his place:
'Doghtyr Syon,
Loo, þi Lorde comys rydand on an asse
Þe[e] to opon.'

Yf any man will ȝou gaynesaye,
Say þat youre lorde has nede of þam
And schall restore þame þis same day
Unto what man will þam clayme.
Do þus þis thyng.
Go furthe ȝe both and be ay bayne
In My blissyng.

1 give good heed 2 Disciples, are 3 what will indeed happen 4 go from here 5 for this reason 8 descended 9 I promised to redeem (humanity) 10 is about to be fulfilled 13 Peter, Philip, bless 14 Now go 15 ahead of you 16 do not delay 18 As, instruct, done (i.e. do as I say) 19 There 20 tied up thus 21 untie her 22 foal, them 23 for a time 24 So the prophecy's pure meaning 26 Daughter Zion (Israel) 27 comes riding 28 To you [Matthew 21:5] 29 oppose/argue 31 return 35 With

[1] For an account of the Old Testament and Ministry plays in the York Cycle omitted in this anthology, see *The Ordo Paginarum*, above.

[2] 'To save Man's soul, that was lost through evil, from many sorrows.'

PETRUS
Jesu, maistir, evyn at Þy wille
And at Þi liste us likis to doo.
Yone beste whilke Þou desires Þe[e] tille
Even at Þi will schall come Þe[e] too,
Unto Þin esse.   40
Sertis, Lord, we will þedyre all [go]
Þe[e] for to plese.

PHILIPPUS
Lord, Þe[e] to plese we are full bayne
Boþe nyght and day to do þi will.
Go we, broþere, with all oure mayne   45
My Lordis desire for to fulfill,
For prophycye
Us bus it do to Hym by skyll
To do dewly.³

PETRUS
Ʒa, brodir Phelipp, behalde grathely,   50
For als He saide we schulde sone fynde.
Methinke ʒone bestis before myn eye
Þai are þe same we schulde unbynde.
Þerfore frely
Go we to hym þat þame gan bynde,   55
And aske mekely.

PHILIPPUS
The beestis are comen, wele I knawe,
Therfore us nedis to aske lesse leve;
And oure Maistir kepis þe lawe
We may þame take tyter, I preve.   60
For noght we lett,
For wele I watte oure tyme is breve,
Go we þam fett.

JANITOR
Saie, what are ʒe þat makis here maistrie,
To loose þes bestis withoute leverie?   65
Yow semes to bolde, sen noght þat ʒe
Hase here to do;⁴ þerfore rede I
Such þingis to sesse,
Or ellis ʒe may falle in folye
And grette diseasse.   70

PETRUS
Sir, with þi leve, hartely we praye
Þis beste þat we myght have.

JANITOR
To what intente firste shall ʒe saye,
And þan I graunte what ʒe will crave
Be gode resoune.   75

PHILIPPUS
Oure Maistir, sir, þat all may save,
Aske by chesoune.

JANITOR
What man is þat ʒe maistir call,
Swilke privelege dare to hym clayme?

PETRUS
Jesus, of Jewes Kyng and ay be schall,   80
Of Nazareth prophete þe same.
Þis same is He,
Both God and man withouten blame,.
Þis trist wele we.

JANITOR
Sirs, of þat prophette herde I have,   85
But telle me firste playnly, wher is Hee?

PHILIPPUS
He comes at hande, so God me save,
Þat lorde we lefte at Bephage;
He bidis us þere.

JANITOR
Sir, take þis beste with herte full free, 90
And forthe ʒe fare.

And if ʒou thynke it be to don,
I schall declare playnly His comyng
To the chiffe of þe Jewes, þat þei may sone
Assemble same to His metyng.   95
What is your rede?

PETRUS
Þou sais full wele in thy menyng.

36 at your command   37 desire, we are glad to act   38 that You want   39 To You   40 For Your comfort   50 clearly
52 in my sight   55 he who bound them   56 politely   57 common property   58 we have less need to ask permission
59 If, keeps (within)   60 without hindrance, conclude   61 Let nothing stop us   62 short   63 fetch them   64 who,
act authoritatively here   65 permission   66 too   70 offence/trouble   71 earnestly   75 If it is reasonable   77 for a
good reason   82 He is the one we speak of   83 sinless   84 we certainly believe   85 heard   87 nearby   88 Bethpagé
89 waits for us   90 with pleasure   91 go your way   92 done   93 publicly   94 chiefs/leaders   95 together to
meet Him   97 suggestion

³ 'As prophecy impels us to do for Him, by reason.'   ⁴ 'Since you have no business here'.

Do forthe þi dede,

And sone þis beste we schall þe[e] bring
And it restore as resoune will.

Janitor
This tydyngis schall have no laynyng,
But to þe citezens declare it till
Of þis cyte.
I suppose fully þat þei wolle
Come mete þat free.

And, sen I will þei warned be,
Both ȝonge and olde in ilke astate,
For His comyng I will þam mete
To late þam witte, withoute debate.
Lo, wher þei stande,
Þat citezens cheff withoute debate
Of all þis lande.

He þat is rewler of all right
And freely schoppe both see and sande,
He save ȝou, lordyngis gayly dight,
And kepe ȝou in ȝoure semelyte
And all honoure.

I Burgensis
Welcome porter, what novelte?
Telle us þis owre.

Janitor
Sirs, novelte I can ȝou telle
And triste þame fully as for trewe:
Her comes of kynde of Israell
Att hande þe prophette called Jesu,
Lo, þis same day,
Rydand on an asse. Þis tydandis newe
Consayve ȝe may.

II Burgensis
And is þat prophette Jesu nere?
Off Hym I have herde grete ferlis tolde.
He dois grete wounderes in contrees seere,
He helys þe seke, both ȝonge and olde,
And þe blynde giffis þam þer sight
Both dome and deffe, as Hymselffe wolde,
He cures þame right.

III Burgensis
ȝa, v thowsand men with loves fyve
He fedde, and ilkone hadde inowe.
Watir to wyne He turned ryve.
He garte corne growe withouten plogh
Wher are was none.
To dede men als He gaffe liffe,
Lazar was one.

IV Burgensis
In oure Tempill if He prechid
Agaynste þe pepull þat leved wrong,
And also new lawes if He teched
Agaynste oure lawis we used so lang,
And saide pleynlye
The olde schall waste, þe new schall gang,
Þat we schall see.

V Burgensis
ȝa, Moyses lawe He cowde ilke dele
And all þe prophettis on a rowe,
He telles þam so þat ilke a man may fele,
And what þei may interly knowe
Yf þei were dyme.[5]
What þe prophettis saide in þer sawe,
All longis to Hym.

VI Burgensis
Emanuell also by right
Þai calle þat prophette by þis skill,
He is þe same þat are was hyght
Be Ysaye before us till,
Þus saide full clere . . .

VII Burgensis
'Loo, a maydyn þat knew nevere ille
A childe schuld bere.'[6]

100 reason demands 101 hiding 105 noble (man) 106 I intend them to be warned 107 rank/class (of society) 108 Before/of, know 109 doubt 113 in all justice 114 nobly/generously created 115 lords, brightly dressed 116 appropriate (noble) status 118 news 119 this hour (i.e. now) 121 to be true 122 Here, of (the) race of 126 Understand 128 Of, marvels/miracles 129 wonders in many lands 130 heals the sick 131 gives 132 dumb, deaf, as He wishes 133 completely 134 5,000, five loaves 135 enough 136 Water, in great quantities 137 without (use of a) plough 138 before 139 gave 140 Lazarus 142 people who lived/believed sinfully 144 (for) so long 146 old (laws) shall decline, thrive 148 knew in every detail 153 wise sayings 154 relates 155 Emmanuel, justly 156 for this reason 157 was once named 158 To us by (the prophet) Isaiah 159 (Who) thus said clearly (to us) . . . 160 virgin, who never sinned

5 'And He interprets the teachings of all the prophets together so that every man can understand them completely, [even] if they [the teachings] are obscure and difficult [lit. dim].'

6 Isaiah 7:14.

David spake of Hym, I wene,
And lefte witnesse, ȝe knowe ilkone.
He saide þe frute of his corse clene
Shulde royally regne upon his trone,
And þerfore he
Of David kyn and oþir none
Oure kyng schal be.[7]

VIII Burgensis
Sirs, methynketh ȝe saie right wele,
And gud ensampelys furth ȝe bryng,
And sen we þus þis mater fele,
Go we Hym meete as oure owne kyng,
And kyng Hym call.
What is youre counsaill in þis thyng?
Now say ȝe all.

I Burgensis
Agaynste resoune I will noȝt plete,
For wele I wote oure kyng He is.
Whoso agaynst his kyng liste threte,
He is noȝt wise, he dose amys.
Porter, come nere.
What knowlage hast þou of His comyng?
Tels us all here,

And þan we will go mete þat free,
And Hym honnoure as we wele awe
Worthely tyll oure citee,
And for oure soverayne lord Hym knawe,
In whome we triste.

Janitor
Sirs, I schall telle ȝou all on rowe,
And ȝe will lyste.

Of His discipillis, ij þis day
Where that I stode þei faire me grette,
And on ther Maistir halfe gan praye
Oure comon asse þat þei myght gete
Bot for a while,
Wheron þer Maistir softe myght sitte
Space of a mile.

And all þis mater þai me tolde
Right haly as I saie to ȝou,
And þe asse þei have right as þei wolde
And sone will bringe agayne, I trowe,
So þai beheste.
What ȝe will doo avise ȝou nowe,
Þus thinke me beste.

II Burgensis
Trewlye, as for me I say,
I rede we make us redy bowne,
Hym to mete gudly þis day,
And Hym ressayve with grete rennowne
As worthy is.
And þerfore, sirs, in felde and towne
Ȝe fulfille þis.

Janitor
Ȝa, and ȝoure [childer] with ȝou take,
Þoff all in age þat þei be ȝonge,
Ȝe may fare þe bettir for þer sake
Thurgh þe blissing of so goode a kyng,
Þis is no dowte.

III Burgensis
I kan þe[e] thanke for thy saying,
We will Hym lowte.

And Hym to mete I am right bayne
On þe beste maner þat I cane,
For I desire to se Hym fayne
And Hym honnoure as His awne man,
Sen þe soth I see.
Kyng of Juuys we call Hym þan,
Oure kyng is He.

IV Burgensis
Oure kyng is He, þat is no lesse,
Oure awne lawe to it cordis will.
Þe prophettis all bare full witnesse
Qwilke full of Hym secrete gone telle,[8]
And þus wolde say:
'Emang youreselff schall come grete seele
Thurgh God verray.'

162 King David 164 fruit of his holy body (i.e. his offspring) 165 reign, throne 170 you bring forward good examples 171 we feel this way about the matter 176 plead 178 wants to threaten 179 does wrong 182 Tell 184 rightly owe (him) 185 to 186 acknowledge 188 together 189 If you will listen 190 two 191 greeted me politely 192 their Master's behalf requested 195 might sit comfortably 196 (For a) journey of 198 Completely 199 just as they wanted 201 promised 202 consider (among) yourselves 205 to go 207 welcome, honour 209 field 210 do this 211 children 212 (Even) though 213 prosper, their 216 do 218 willing/eager 219 In, can 220 greatly 221 (one of) his servants 223 Jews 225 lie 226 accords 230 joy 231 (the) true God

7 'And therefore only one of David's kin, and no one else, should be our king.'

8 'Who clearly foretold mysteries concerning him'.

V Burgensis
Þis same is He, þer is non othir,
Was us beheest full lange before,
For Moyses saide als oure owne brothir
A newe prophette Good schulde restore.[9]
Þerfore loke ȝe
What ȝe will do, withouten more;
Oure kyng is He.

VI Burgensis
Of Juda come owre kyng so gent,
Of Jesse, David, Salamon;
Also by His modir kynne take tente,
Þe genolagye beres witnesse on,[10]
This is right playne.
Hym to honnoure right as I can
I am full bayne.

VII Burgensis
Of youre clene witte and youre consayte
I am full gladde in harte and þought,
And Hym to mete withouten latt
I am redy, and feyne will noght,
Bot with ȝou same
To Hym agayne us blisse hath brought,
With myrthe and game.

VIII Burgensis
Ȝoure argumentis þai are so clere
I can noȝt saie but graunte þou till,
For whanne I of þat counsaille here
I coveyte Hym with fervent wille
Onys for to see.
I trowe fro þens I schall
Bettir man be.

I Burgensis
Go we þan with processioun
To mete þat comely as us awe,
With braunches, floures, and unysoune
With myghtfull songes her on a rawe.

II Burgensis
Our childir schall
Go synge before, þat men may knawe
To þis graunte we all.

Petrus
Jesu, Lord and Maistir free,
Als Þou comaunde so have we done:
Þis asse here we have brought to Þe[e].
What is Þi wille Þou schewe us sone
And tarie noȝt,
And þan schall we withouten hune
Fulfill Þi þouȝt.

Jesus
I þanke ȝou, breþere, mylde of mode.
Do on þis asse youre cloþis ȝe laye,
And lifte Me uppe with hertis gud
Þat I on hir may sitte þis daye
In My blissing.

Philippus
Lord, Þi will to do allway,
We graunte [þis] þing.

Jesus
Now My breþere, with gud chere
Gyves gode entente, for ryde I will
Unto ȝone cyte ȝe se so nere.
Ȝe shall Me folowe sam and still
Als I are sayde.

Philippus
Lord, as Þe[e] lys[t]e we graunte Þe[e] till
And halde us payde.

Tunc cantant. [*And the processional entry begins*]

Cecus
A, Lorde, þat all þis world has made,
Boþe sonne and mone, nyght and day,

233 (It) was promised us long ago 237 without further (ado) 239 From Judah comes, honourable 240 King Solomon 241 note His mother's kin 242 genealogy bears witness to 244 as well 246 intention 248 delay 249 will not pretend 250 together with you 251 (Go) towards, (Who has) brought us bliss 252 celebration 254 I can do nothing but agree with you 255 advice, hear 256 desire, earnest 257 To see Him once 258 from that moment (on) 261 noble (man), we owe (Him) 262 palms, flowers, harmony 263 vigorous, gathered together 264 children 265 ahead of (us) 271 delay 272 hesitation 274 gentle brothers 275 lay your clothes 277 her 279 perform always 280 agree (to do) 285 said before 287 consider ourselves (already) rewarded 287+ Then they sing 288 Ah, who 289 sun and moon

9 Either 'God shall send us a new prophet' or 'A new prophet shall restore good to us.'

10 As well as coming from the line of David, Solomon, and Jesse on Joseph's side, Christ's descent was said to be pure on his mother's also, as Mary was also of the line of Jesse.

What noyse is þis þat makis me gladde?
Fro whens it schulde come I can noȝt saye,
Or what it mene.
Yf any man walke in þis way
Telle hym me bedene.

PAUPER
Man, what ayles þe[e] to crye?
Where wolde þou be? Þou say me here.

CECUS
A, sir, a blynde man am I
And ay has of tendyr ȝere bene
Sen I was borne.
I harde a voyce with nobill chere
Here me beforne.

PAUPER
Man, will þou oght þat I can do?

CECUS
Ȝa sir, gladly wolde [I] witte
Yf þou couþe oght declare me to
This myrþe I herde, what mene may it
Or undirstande?

PAUPER
Jesu þe prophite full of grace
Comys here at hande,

And all þe cetezens þay are bowne
Gose Hym to mete with melodye,
With þe fayrest processioun
That evere was sene in His Jury.
He is right nere.

CECUS
Sir, helpe me to þe strete hastely,
Þat I may here

Þat noyse, and also þat I myght thurgh grace
My syght of Hym to crave I wolde.

PAUPER
Loo, He is here at þis same place.
Loke þou be bolde,
Crye faste on Hym,with voyce righ[t] high.

CECUS
Jesu, þe sone of David calde,
Þou have mercy.

Allas, I crye; He heris me noȝt.
He has no ruthe of my mysfare.
He turnes His herre, where is His þought?

PAUPER
Cry somwhat lowdar, loke þou noȝt spare,
So may þou spye.

CECUS
Jesu, þe salver of all sare,
To me giffis gode hye.

PHELIPPUS
Cesse, man, and crye noȝt soo,
The voyce of þe pepill gose þe[e] by.
Þe ohte sette still and tente giffe to,
Here passez þe Prophite of Mercye
Þou doys amys.

CECUS
A, David sone, to þe[e] I crye,
Þe Kyng of Blisse.

PETRUS
Lorde, have mercy and late hym goo,
He can noȝt cesse of his crying.
He folows us both to and froo,
Graunte hym his boone and his askyng
And late hym wende.
We gette no reste or þat þis thyng
Be broȝt to ende.

JESUS
What wolde þou, man, I to þe[e] dede
In þis present? Telle oppynly.

CECUS
Lorde, my syight is fro me hydde,
Þou graunte me it, I crye mercy,
Þis wolde I have.

291 where it comes 292 might mean 294 (Let) him quickly tell me 295 ails/afflicts 296 Where do you want to be? 298 always have been, since I was young 300 sound 301 in front of me 302 do you want anything 304 tell me anything 305 what does it mean 306 or imply 309 ready 312 Jewry 315 hear 317 I want to beg Him for my sight 319 Make sure 320 Cry (out) to Him strongly, very loud 321 called 323 hears 324 pity on, misfortune 325 ear/head (away), what is He thinking 326 do not hold back 327 That way you may (yet) see again 328 healer, illness 329 look at me (lit. give good eye) 329+ Philip 331 drowns you out 332 You ought to sit still and pay attention 334 does wrong 337 let, go 340 wish, request 341 go 342 unless 344 What do you want me to do to you 345 In the presence of these people 346 hidden from me

Jesus
Loke uppe nowe with chere blythely,
Þi faith shall þe[e] save.

Cecus
Wirschippe and honnoure ay to Þe[e],
With all þe service þat can be done;
The Kyng of Blisse loved mote He be
Þat þus my sight hath sente so sone,
And by grete skill.
I was are blynde as any stone:
I se at wille.

Claudus
A, wele wer þam þat evere had liffe,
Olde or yonge whedir it were,
Might welde þer lymmes withouten striffe,
Go with þis mirthe þat I see here
And contynewe;
For I am sette in sorowes sere
Þat ay ar newe.

Þou Lord þat schope both nyght and day,
For Thy mercy have mynde on me
And helpe me Lorde, as Þou wele may.
I may noȝt gang
For I am lame, as men may se,
And has ben lang.

For wele I wote, as knowyn is ryffe,
Boþe dome and deffe Þou grauntist þam grace,
And also þe dede þat Þou havyst geven liff;
Therfore graunte me, Lord, in þis place
My lymbis to welde.

Jesus
My man, ryse and caste þe crucchys gode space
Her in þe felde.[11]

And loke in trouthe þou stedfast be,
And folow Me furth with gode menyng.

Claudus
Lorde, lo my crouchis whare þei flee
Als ferre as I may late þam flenge
With bothe my hende!
Þat evere we have metyng
Now I defende,[12]

For I was halte, both lyme and lame
And I suffered tene and sorowes inowe.
Ay-lastand Lord, loved be Þi name,
I am als light as birde on bowe.
Ay be Þou blist,
Such grace hast Þou schewed to me [now]
Lorde, as Þe[e] list.

Zache
Sen firste þis worlde was made of noȝt
And all thyng sette in equite,
Such ferly thyng was nevere non wroght
As men þis tyme may see with eye.
What it may mene?
I can noȝt saye what it may be,
Comforte or tene.

And cheffely of a Prophete new
Þat mekill is profite, and þat of latte
Both day and nyght þai Hym assewe.
Oure pepill same thurgh strete and gatte
Oure olde lawes as nowe þei hatte
And His kepis ȝare.

Men fro deth to liffe He rayse,
The blynde and dome geve speche and sight,
Gretely þerfor oure folke Hym prayse,
And folowis Hym both day and nyght
Fro towne to towne.
Thay calle Hym prophite, be right,
As of renowne.

And ȝit I mervayle of þat thyng,
Of puplicans sen prince am I,

349 a happy face 353 he must be loved 356 before (this) 357 whatever I want 358 happy were those who ever lived 359 whichever 360 (Who) might use their limbs, pain 361 (And) go with this happy procession 362 continue (to do so) 363 But, trapped in many sorrows 364 are always fresh 365 made 366 think of 367 might well do 370 long have been 371 everywhere 372 grant 373 have given life 375 Use of my limbs 378 truly, loyal 379 good intent 380 where they fly 381 As far, throw them 385 crippled, limb 386 enough sorrows 387 worshipped 388 bough 389 (May) You always be blessed 390 showed 392 out of nothing 393 established in equity 398 Happiness or tribulation 399 principally 400 who is a great force (for good), recently 401 (our people) follow Him 402 together, road 403 as they are now called 404 His (law) keep eagerly 405 raised 406 gave 410 justly 411 As is well known 413 publicans (tax-collectors), leader

[11] 'My man, rise and throw your crutches far into the field.'
[12] 'I forbid that we [i.e. the crutches and himself] should ever be reunited.'

Of Hym I cowthe have no knowyng,
Yf all I wolde have comen Hym nere,
Arly and late.
For I am lawe, and of myne hight
Full is þe gate.[13]

Bot, sen no bettir may befalle,
I thynke what beste is for to doo.
I am schorte, ȝe knawe wele all,
Þerfore ȝone tre I will go too
And in it clyme.
Whedir He come or passe me fro,
I schall se Hym.

A, nobill tree þou secomoüre,
I blisse hym þat þe[e] on þe erþe broght.
Now may I see both here and þore
That undir me hid may be noȝt.
Þerfore in þe[e]
Wille I bidde in herte and þought
Till I Hym se.

Unto þe Prophete come to towne
Her will I bide what so befalle.

JESUS
Do, Zache, do faste come downe.

ZACHE
Lorde, even at Þi wille hastely I schall,
And tarie noght.
To Þe[e] on knes, Lord, here I fall,
For synne I wroght;

And welcome, prophete trast and trewe,
With all þe pepull þat to Þe[e] langis.

JESUS
Zache, þi service new schall make þe[e] clene
Of all þe wrong þat þou haste done.

ZACHE
Lorde, I lette noȝt for þis thrang
Her to say sone

Me schamys with synne, but noȝt to mende.[14]
Mi synne forsake þerfore I will.
Halve my gud I have unspendid
Poure folke to geve it till,
Þis will I fayne.
Whom I begylyd, to hym will
I make asith agayne.

JESUS
Thy clere confessioun schall þe[e] clense,
Þou may be sure of lastand lyffe.
Unto þi house, withouten offense
Is graunted pees withouten striffe.
Farewele, Zache.

ZACHE
Lord, Þe[e] lowte ay man and wiffe,[15]
Blist myght þou be.

JESUS
My dere discipulis, beholde and see,
Unto Jerusalem we schall assende.
Man Sone schall þer betrayed be
And gevyn into His enmys hande,
With grete dispitte.
Ther spitting on Hym þer schall þei spende,
And smertly smyte.

Petir, take þis asse Me fro
And lede it where þou are it toke.
I murne, I sigh, I wepe also,
Jerusalem on þe[e] to loke.
And so may þou [rewe]
Þat evere þou þi Kyng forsuke,
And was untrewe.

419 it cannot be helped 422 tree 426 sycamore 427 that planted you in the earth 428 there 429 nothing may be hidden 430 thee 431 wait 433 Until 434 whatever happens 435 Hey!, quickly 438 on (my) knees 439 Because of the sins I have committed 440 trusted and true 441 belong 442 your new service (to me) 444 Do not delay, despite, crowd 448 Half of my unspent wealth 449 to give to the poor 450 happily (do) 451 (he) whom I tricked, 452 restitution 453 full, purify you 454 everlasting 455 your house/family 461 ascend 462 the Son of Man, there 464 despite/hatred 465 they shall spit upon Him 466 fiercely strike (Him) 468 took it from earlier 469 mourn 471 regret

[13] Zacheus seems to move between discussing his general experience and the particular situation in the street in the course of this elliptical speech: 'And yet I wonder at this, that although I am prince of tax-collectors, I could have no knowledge/acquaintance of/with Him [because, as a collector of Roman taxes, I am considered beyond the pale by Jewish society], even if I had come close to Him both early and late [i.e. many times]. For I am lowly [and also, literally, short of stature], and the street is full of those of my height [and above – so that I cannot see Him – and He cannot see me].'

[14] 'I am ashamed of my sin, but not ashamed to repent.'

[15] 'Lord, may everyone [lit. man and woman] always worship you'.

For stone on stone schall none be lefte,
But doune to þe grounde all schal be caste,
Thy game, þi gle, al fro þe[e] refte
And all for synne þat þou done hast.
Þou arte unkynde;
Agayne þi Kyng þou hast trespast,
Have þis in mynde.

PETRUS
Porter, take here þyn asse agayne,
At hande My Lorde comys on His fette.

JANITOR
Behalde where all þi burgeis bayne
Comes with wirschippe Hym to mete.
Þerfore I will
Late Hym abide here in þis strete
And lowte Hym till.

I BURGENSIS
Hayll, Prophette preved withouten pere,
Hayll, Prince of Pees schall evere endure,
Hayll, Kyng comely, curteyse and clere,
Hayll, Soverayne semely, to synfull sure;
To Þe[e] all bowes.
Hayll, Lord lovely oure cares may cure,
All Kyng of Jewes.

II BURGENSIS
Hayll, florisshand floure þat nevere shall fade,
Hayll, vyolett vernand with swete odoure,
Hayll, marke of myrthe oure medecyne made,
Hayll, blossome brigh[t], hayll, oure socoure,
Hayll, Kyng comely.
Hayll, menskfull man, we Þe[e] honnoure
With herte frely.

III BURGENSIS
Hayll, David sone, doughty in dede,
Hayll, rose ruddy, hayll, birrall clere,
Hayll, welle of welthe may make us mede,[16]
Hayll, salver of oure sores sere,
We wirschippe Þe[e].
Hayll hendfull, with solas sere
Welcome Þou be.

IV BURGENSIS
Hayll, blisfull babe, in Bedleme borne,
Hayll, boote of all oure bittir balis,
Hayll, sege þat schoppe boþe even and morne,
Hayll, talker trystefull of trew tales,
Hayll, comely knyght,
Hayll, of mode þat moste prevayles
To save þe tyght.

V BURGENSIS
Hayll, dyamaunde with drewry dight,
Hayll, jasper gentill of Jury,
Hayll, lylly lufsome, lemyd with lyght,
Hayll, balme of boote, moyste and drye,[17]
To all has nede.
Hayll, barne most blist of mylde Marie,
Hayll, all oure mede.

VI BURGENSIS
Hayll, conquerour, hayll, most of myght,
Hayll, rawnsoner of synfull all,
Hayll, pytefull, hayll, lovely light,
Hayll, to us welcome be schall,
Hayll, Kyng of Jues.
Hayll, comely corse þat we Þe[e] call
With mirþe þat newes.

VII BURGENSIS
Hayll, sonne ay schynand with bright bemes,
Hayll, lampe of liff schall nevere waste,
Hayll, lykand lanterne, luffely lemys,
Hayll, texte of trewþe þe trew to taste.[18]
Hayll, Kyng and Sire,
Hayll, maydens chylde þat menskid hir most,
We Þe[e] desire.

VIII BURGENSIS

476 pleasure, joy, snatched from you 477 because of 478 unnatural 479 Against 480 Remember this 482 Nearby, feet 483 burgesses (town elders) 487 to Him 488 proven (to be) peerless 489 eternal peace 490 courteous, pure 491 worthy, sure help to sinners 492 everyone bows 493 who will cure our sorrows 494 Universal King 495 flourishing flower 496 blooming violet 497 centre of happiness, salvation 498 succour 500 noble 502 son of David, heroic in deeds 503 red rose, clear beryl 505 healer, many ills 507 most noble one, many comforts 509 born in Bethlehem 510 cure, bitter woes 511 made 512 trustworthy speaker of true words 514 will that surpasses all else 515 those imprisoned 516 diamond, set with ornaments 517 gentle 518 dear lily, shining 519 medicine of salvation, moist and dry 520 who need it 521 baby, gentle Mary 524 ransomer of all sinners 525 (He who is) full of pity 528 creature (lit. body) 529 ever-renewing happiness 530 sun always shining, beams 531 that never fails 532 fair, shines beautifully 535 virgin's child, honoured

16 'Source of prosperity, (Who) may reward us'.

17 i.e. a universal cure.

18 'Hail, the true Word, (Who will) test the true.'

Hayll, Domysman dredful, þat all schall deme,
Hayll, quyk and dede þat all schall lowte,[19]
Hayll, whom worschippe moste will seme,
Hayll, whom all thyng schall drede and dowte.
We welcome Þe[e],
Hayll, and welcome of all abowte
To owre cete.

Tunc cantant.

537 terrible judge, try 539 most befits 542 all present here 543 city 543+ Then they sing

[19] 'Hail, He to whom all/both the living and the dead shall bow'.

York (The Cutlers), *The Conspiracy*

This and the next four York pageants in this anthology are attributed by J.W. Robinson to a single, anonymous author, referred to only as the 'York Realist', a master of the alliterative line and a dramatist of considerable talent (Robinson, 'The Art of the York Realist'). These pageants depict a series of urgent, anxious encounters, all conducted at night amid scenes of confusion, apprehension, and violent disorder, in which the conspiracy against Jesus is hatched and realized. They effectively dramatize the shuffling of responsibility for Christ's fate between the various courts and jurisdictions of Pilate, the Roman governor of Palestine, King Herod Antipas, and the leaders of the Jewish *Sanhedrin* (Council), the high priests Annas and Caiaphas. This narrative is derived ultimately from biblical sources, and reflects the interplay of political and religious interests in Roman Palestine recorded there, but it is also a feature of the plays with strong local and contemporary resonances. Late medieval towns were themselves patchworks of interlocking and competing jurisdictions and 'liberties' (privileged areas), and York more so than most. Within the city the not always harmonious agenda of a strong city council, the guilds, the civil and ecclesiastical courts, the Minster (cathedral), numerous religious houses, and (at various times in the later fifteenth and sixteenth centuries) the King's Council in the North all vied for ascendancy over the daily affairs of a bustling urban community. In such an environment the various intrigues and rivalries that drive the events of the Passion would probably have struck a painfully familiar chord.

In addition to the biblical sources for this and the following pageants, the dramatist drew on material from two fourteenth-century narrative poems, *The Northern Passion* and *The Gospel of Nicodemus*, as well as introducing characters and events seemingly of his own devising. (See F.A. Foster, ed., *The Northern Passion*, EETS, OS 145, 146, 183 (3 vols. Oxford, 1913–30); W.H. Hulme, ed., *The Middle English Harrowing of Hell and The Gospel of Nicodemus*, EETS, ES 100 (Oxford, 1907).) Among the innovations is the role of the Janitor, not literally the same individual as the Janitor in *The Entry into Jerusalem*, but another representative of the same figure of natural humanity. His instinctive distrust and hostility towards Judas suggest an innate moral discrimination on his part, but he, like the soldiers and Pilate himself, has his own worldly responsibilities and agenda, and eventually allows Judas admittance to Pilate and the high priests, once it is suggested that their safety might be at risk. For several moments, however, the fate of the Conspiracy, and so of humanity, lies in the balance, as the Janitor and Judas exchange insults on the threshold of the palace. In this way the dramatist adds tension to the well-known Passion story, playing the audience's knowledge of future events against the innate tensions realized in performance.

The pageant begins with a lengthy, boastful speech from Pilate of a sort characteristic of the tyrant figures in the Cycle plays. Such speeches fulfil a variety of functions: they gain the attention of a potentially boisterous audience, they mark out the self-regarding nature of tyranny, and – as blasphemous parodies of God's opening speech in the Creation plays – they also identify the speaker as, like Lucifer, an over-reaching impersonator, seeking to claim divine authority for himself. The stress upon the need to suppress disorder in these speeches also tends to undercut the speaker's claims to wield power effectively.

The Cutlers made knives, perhaps a symbolically significant trade for a pageant concerned with treachery and conspiracy.

[*Dramatis Personae*: *Pilatus* (Pontius Pilate, the Roman governor),[1] *Anna* (Annas) and *Caiaphas* (Jewish high priests),[2] *I & II Doctor* (two masters of Jewish law), *I & II Miles* (two Soldiers), *Judas*, *Janitor* (a servant of Pilate's household).]

1 Pilate was Procurator of Judea AD 26–36. In this pageant he, like his biblical equivalent, is anxious not to condemn Jesus without due process of law, and thus resists the obviously partial demands of the high priests. Only the suggestion that Jesus claims to be king – and thus may pose a political threat (ll. 115–16) – provokes his hostility.

2 Annas was high priest and head of the *Sanhedrin* AD 6–15, but retained his title and influence after he relinquished office. John's Gospel reports that Christ, once arrested, was taken first to Annas to be interrogated: see John 18:13. Joseph Caiaphas, the son-in-law of Annas, was high priest and head of the *Sanhedrin* AD 18–36. The New Testament portrays him as an implacable opponent of Jesus, who sought to bring about his death despite the niceties of the law: see John 18:13 and 24; Matthew 57–68; Mark 14:53–65.

Pilatus
Undir þe ryallest roye of rente and renowne,
Now am I regent of rewle þis region in reste;
Obeye unto bidding bud busshoppis me bowne,
And bolde men þat in batayll makis brestis to breste.
To me betaught is þe tent þis towre-begon towne,
For traytoures tyte will I taynte, þe trewþe for to triste.
The dubbyng of my dingnite may noȝt be done downe,
Nowdir with duke nor dugeperes, my dedis are so dreste.[3]
My desire muste dayly be done
With þame þat are grettest of game,
And þeragayne fynde I but fone,
Wherfore I schall bettir þer bone
But he þat me greves for a grume,
Be ware, for wyscus I am.

Pounce Pilatt of thre partis þan is my propir name;[4]
I am a perelous prince to prove wher I peere.
Emange þe philosofers firste ther fanged I my fame,
Wherfore I fell to affecte I fynde noȝt my feere.[5]
He schall full bittirly banne þat bide schall my blame,
If all my blee be as bright as blossome on brere,[6]
For sone his liffe shall he lose, or left be for lame,
Þat lowtes noȝt to me lowly, nor liste noȝt to leere.
And þus sen we stande in oure state
Als lordis with all lykyng in lande,
Do and late us wete if ȝe wate
Owthir, sirs, of bayle or debate
Þat nedis for to be handeled full hate,
Sen all youre helpe hanges in my hande.

Caiphas
Sir, and for to certefie þe soth in youre sight,
As to ȝou for oure soverayne semely we seke.[7]

Pilatus
Why, is þer any myscheve þat musteres his myȝt,
Or malice thurgh meene menn us musters to meke?[8]

Anna
Ȝa, sir, þer is a ranke swayne whos rule is noȝt right,
For thurgh his romour in þis reme hath raysede mekill reke.[9]

Pilatus
I here wele ȝe hate hym; youre hartis are on heght,
And ellis if I helpe wolde his harmes for to eke.[10]
But why are ȝe barely þus brathe?
Bees rewly, and ray fourth youre reasoune.

Caiphas
Tille us, sir, his lore is full lothe.

Pilatus
Be ware þat we wax noȝt to wrothe.

Anna
Why sir, to skyfte fro his skath
We seke for youre socoure þis sesoune.

Pilatus
And if þat wrecche in oure warde have wrought any wrong,
Sen we are warned, we walde witte and wille or we wende.
But and his sawe be lawfull, legge noȝt to lange,
For we schall leve hym, if us list, with luffe here to lende.[11]

I Doctor
And yf þat false faytor youre fortheraunce may fang,
Þan fele I wele þat oure folke mon fayle of a frende.
Sir, þe strenghe of his steven ay still is so strange

1 most royal king, revenue 2 peacetime deputy 3 must those bishops bound to me 4 battle, breasts to burst 10 by, are greatest of all 11 against (my desire), only a few 12 increase their rewards 13 angers me by complaining 14 vicious/savage 15 Pontius, three parts 16 perilous, appear 17 I gained 19 curse, suffer my anger 21 be crippled 22 humbly, willing to learn 23 pomp/authority 24 As lords, the pleasure possible 25 let us know 26 Of either trouble or argument 27 settled quickly (lit. hot) 31 malcontent, gathers 33 evil man, conduct 35 can tell, tempers, raised 37 so utterly angry 38 Be calm, set out 39 To, teaching is abhorrent 41 escape, from his plots 42 help, at this time (lit. season) 43 wretch, jurisdiction 47 may gain your help 48 see, folk (the Jews), lose 49 continues, strong

[3] 'To me is entrusted the keeping of this many-towered town; for traitors I will quickly prosecute, you may trust that to be true! The authority of my office may not be impugned, neither by dukes nor heroic knights, matters are so [well] arranged.'

[4] Pilate explains the (bogus) etymology of his 'three-part' name at the start of *Christ Before Pilate I*.

[5] 'Wherefore I have come to believe that I have no equal.'

[6] '(Even) if my face was as bright as blossom on a briar', i.e. '(I am that dangerous to oppose) even when I am happy'.

[7] 'Sir, to confirm the truth here before you, we approach you as our sovereign, with appropriate formality.'

[8] 'Or any malice committed by evil [possibly 'poor'] men who gather to subdue us?'

[9] 'For, by his reputation, [he] has raised great unrest in this realm.'

[10] 'If I were not to help, his misfortunes would increase.'

[11] 'Since we have been warned, we wish to know about it, and

That but he schortely be schent, he schappe us to schende,[12]
For he kennes folke hym for to call
Grete God son, þus greves us þat gome,[13]
And sais þat he sittande be schall
In high Heven, for þere is his hall.

Pilatus
And, frendis, if þat force to hym fall,
It semes noȝt ȝe schall hym consume.

But þat hymselfe is þe same ȝe saide schulde descende,[14]
Ȝoure seede and ȝou þen all for to socoure.

Cayphas
A, softe, sir, and sese,
For of Criste whan He comes no kynne schall be kenned,
But of þis caytiffe kynreden we knawe þe encrese.[15]
He lykens hym to be lyke God, ay-lastand to lende,
To lifte uppe þe laby, to lose or relesse.

Pilatus
His maistreys schulde move ȝou youre mode for to amende.[16]

Anna
Nay, for swilke mys fro malice we may noȝt us meese,
For he sais he schall deme us, þat dote,
And þat tille us, is dayne or dispite.[17]

Pilatus
To noye hym nowe is youre noote,
But ȝitt þe lawe lyes in my lotte.

I Doctor
And yf ȝe will witt, sir, ȝe wotte
Þat he is wele worthy to wyte.

For in oure Temple has he taught by tymes moo þan tenne,
Where tabillis full of tresoure lay to telle and to trye,
Of oure cheffe mony-changers, butte, curstely to kenne,
He caste þam overe, þat caystiffe, and counted noȝt þerby.[18]

Cayphas
Loo, sir, þis is a perjurye to prente undir penne,
Wherfore make ȝe þat *appostita*, we praye ȝou, to plye.

Pilatus
Howe mene ȝe?

Cayphas
Sir, to mort hym for movyng of men.

Pilatus
Þan schulde we make hym to morne but thurgh ȝoure maistrie.

Latt be, sirs, and move þat no more;
But what in youre Temple betyde?

I Miles
We! Þare, sir, he skelpte oute of score
Þat stately stode selland þer store.[19]

Pilatus
Þan felte he þam fawte before,
And made þe cause wele to be kydde.

But what taught he þat tyme, swilk tales as ȝou telles?

I Miles
Sir, þat oure Tempill is þe toure of his troned sire,

51 teaches, to call him 52 Great God's son, 53 will sit 54 home 55 if he has that power 56 that you will destroy him 58 quiet 61 to live for ever 62 burden, doom or release 67 intention 68 lies, control 70 well, condemn 71 more than ten times 72 tables, be counted, assayed 73 but, cursedly 74 thought nothing of it 75 crime, write down 76 apostate/heretic, surrender 77 What do you mean? 77 execute, sedition 78 mourn 79 Leave it 80 happened 81 Wee!, beat, beyond belief 83 believed them guilty 84 well known/clear 86 tower, enthroned father

will [do] before we go [from here]. But, if his teaching is lawful, do not continue to make allegations about him, because we will allow him, if we want, to live here in peace.'

12 'Unless he is quickly destroyed, he will be likely to destroy us'.

13 'That is what angers us about the man'.

14 'But [rather] that he himself is the one that you said would descend to redeem you and your children [i.e. the Messiah]'.

15 'When Christ does come, no one will know His kin, whereas, we know all about the lineage of this villain's family.'

16 'His powers should persuade you to change your attitude.'

17 'No, because of such crimes [of his], we cannot move from our malice, because he says that he shall judge us, the madman!, and that [claim] is an insult or act of hatred to us.'

18 See, for example, Mark 11:15.

19 'Those [who] were [merely] standing respectably, selling their wares.'

And þus to prayse in þat place oure prophettis
compellis,
Tille Hym þat has poste of prince and of empire;
And þei make *domus domini* þat derand þare dwellis
Þe denn of þe derfenes and ofte þat þei desire.[20]

Pilatus
Loo, is he noght a mad man þat for youre mede
melles,
Sen ȝe ymagyn amys þat makeles to myre?[21]
Ȝoure rankoure is raykand full rawe.

Cayphas
Nay, nay, sir, we rewle us but right.

Pilatus
Forsothe, ȝe ar over-cruell to knawe.

Cayphas
Why, sir? For he wolde lose oure lawe
Hartely we hym hate as we awe,
And þerto schulde ȝe mayntayne oure myght.

For why, uppon oure Sabbott day þe seke makes he
saffe,
And will noȝt sesse for oure sawes to synke so in
synne.

II Miles
Sir, he coueres all þat comes recoveraunce to crave
But in a schorte contynuaunce, þat kennes all oure
kynne.
But he haldis noght oure haly dayes, harde happe
myght hym have,[22]
And therfore hanged be he, and þat by
þe halse.

Pilatus
A, hoo, sir, nowe, and holde in.
For, þoff ȝe gange þus gedy hym gilteles to grave,
Withouten grounde ȝow gaynes noght swilke greffe
to begynne;[23]
And loke youre leggyng be lele,
Withowtyn any tryfils to telle.

Anna
For certayne owre sawes dare we seele.

Pilatus
And þan may we prophite oure pele.

Cayphas
Sir, bot his fawtes were fele,
We mente noȝt of hym for to melle.

For he pervertis oure pepull þat proves his prechyng,
And for þat poynte ȝe schulde prese his pooste to
paire.[24]

II Doctor
Ȝa, sir, and also þat caytiff he callis hym oure kyng,
And for þat cause our comons are casten in care.

Pilatus
And if so be, þat borde to bayll will hym bryng,
And make hym boldely to banne þe bones þat hym
bare.
For-why þat wrecche fro oure wretthe schal not
wryng,
Or þer be wrought on hym wrake.

I Doctor
So wolde we it ware,
For so schulde ȝe susteyne youre seele,
And myldely have mynde for to meke ȝou.

Pilatus
Wele witte ȝe, þis werke schall be wele,
For kende schall þat knave be to knele.

II Doctor
And, so þat oure force he may feele,
All samme for þe same we beseke ȝou.

87 prophets comand us 88 has power over (i.e. God) 91 works for your reward 93 rancour, viciously advancing 94 are only behaving correctly 95 Truly 96 Because, destroy 97 Vigorously, as we are obliged to 98 support 99 Sabbath, cures the sick 100 despite our laws 101 cures, come to beg for health 102 time, kin 104 neck 104 control yourselves 107 ensure, allegations, true 108 lies added 109 claims, certify 110 advance our case 111 if his crimes were (not) many 112 would not have acted against him 113 perverts, who hear 115 himself 116 common people, disturbed 117 that is true, trick, ruin 118 loudly to curse 119 Wherefore, wrath, escape 120 Before, vengeance 120 So do we wish it was 121 maintain your ascendancy 122 If you nobly decide to agree 124 taught, kneel 126 that conclusion, beg

[20] 'And those harmful [ones] who dwell there, they make the House of the Lord [into] a den of iniquity, whenever they want.'
[21] 'Since you think wrongly to destroy that sinless [one]?'
[22] 'And he does not observe our holy days, bad luck may he have'.
[23] 'For, although you rush giddily to condemn him, guiltless, without evidence it is pointless to start such trouble'.
[24] 'For that reason you should move quickly to cut back his power.'

Judas
Ingenti pro inuria: hym, Jesus, þat Jewe,
Unjust unto me, Judas, I juge to be lathe.
For at oure soper as we satte, þe soþe to pursewe,
With Symond Luprus, full sone my skiffte come to scathe.[25]
Tille Hym þer brought one a boyste, my bale for to brewe
That baynly to His bare feete to bowe was full braythe,
Sho anoynte þam with an oynement þat nobill was and newe,
But for þat werke þat sche wrought I wexe woundir wrothe.[26]
And þis, to discover, was my skill:
For of His penys, purser was I,
And what þat me taught was untill,
The tente parte þat stale I ay still.
But nowe for me wantis of my will,
Þat bargayne with bale schall He by.

Þat same oynement, I saide, might same have bene solde
For silver penys in a sowme thre hundereth, and fyne
Have ben departid to poure men as playne pite wolde;[27]
But, for þe poore, ne þare parte priked me no peyne,
But me tened for þe tente parte, þe trewthe to beholde,
That thirty pens of iij hundereth so tyte I schulde tyne.
And, for I mysse þis mcny, I morne on þis molde,
Wherfore for to mischeve þis Maistir of myne
And þerfore faste forþe will I flitte
The princes of prestis untill,
And selle Hym full sone or þat I sitte,
For therty pens in a knotte knytte.
Þus-gatis full wele schall He witte
Þat of my wretthe wreke me I will.
Do open, porter, þe porte of þis prowde place,
That I may passe to youre princes to prove for youre prowe.

Janitor
Go hense, þou glorand gedlyng, God geve þe[e] ille grace,
Thy glyfftyng is so grymly þou gars my harte growe.[28]

Judas
Goode sir, be toward þis tyme, and tarice noght my trace,
For I have tythandis to telle.

Janitor
3a, som tresoune, I trowe,
For I fele by a figure in youre fals face
It is but foly to feste affeccioun in 3ou.
For Mars he hath morteysed his mark,
Eftir all lynes of my lore,
And sais 3e are wikkid of werk
And bothe a strange theffe and a stark.

Judas
Sir, þus at my berde and 3e berk,
It semes it schall sitte yow full sore.

Janitor
Say, bittilbrowed bribour, why blowes þou such boste?
Full false in thy face in faith can I fynde.
Þou arte combered in curstnesse and caris to þis coste,
To marre men of myght haste þou marked in thy mynde.[29]

Judas
Sir, I mene of no malice but mirthe meve I muste.

127 'For a great injury' 128 vile 129 supper, to tell the truth 135 tell you, reason 136 money, purser (treasurer) 137 whatever was brought to me 138 I always stole one tenth 139 as I do not have what I want 140 He will pay for with His ruin 141 all 142 300 silver pennies, then 144 I felt no pain for them 145 I was angry about 146 lose 147 I begrudge it, earth 148 ruin 149 straight out 150 To the princes 151 betray (Jesus), before I rest 152 an agreement sealed 153 Thus 154 I will avenge my anger 155 door 156 good 157 glowering rogue, bad luck 159 helpful, delay, errand 161 guess, look 162 place trust 163 fixed/printed 164 By all my wisdom 165 That, evil of deeds 166 a bold and brazen thief 167 if you bark at my beard thus 168 it will be the worse for you 173 bring happy news

25 '[At the house of] Simon Leprous, my [money-making] scam was brought to nothing.'

26 'Someone brought to Him a box, to provoke my anger [or, bring about my ruin], and [she] was eager to bow to His feet, and she anointed them with an ointment that was noble and fresh. And for that act that she performed I grew wonderfully angry.' See Matthew 26:7. Judas's motives for betraying Christ are not, however, stated there.

27 'Might have been distributed to the poor, as simple pity demands'.

28 'Your glaring is so unpleasant it gives me indigestion.'

29 'Say, beetle-browed villain, why do you blow such boasts? Truly, I see utter treachery [marked] in your face. You are burdened with villainy, and [have] come here intending to ruin great men.'

JANITOR
Say, on-hanged harlott, I holde þe[e] unhende,
Thou lokist like a lurdayne his liffelod hadde loste.
Woo schall I wirke þe[e] away but þou wende.

JUDAS
A, goode sir, take tente to my talkyng þis tyde,
For tythandis full trew can I telle.

JANITOR
Say, brethell, I bidde þe[e] abide,
Þou chaterist like a churle þat can chyde.

JUDAS
3a, sir, but and þe truthe schulde be tryed,
Of myrthe are þer materes I mell,

For thurgh my dedis youre dugeperes fro dere may be drawe.[30]

JANITOR
What, demes þou till oure dukes that doole schulde be dight?[31]

JUDAS
Nay, sir, so saide I noght.
If I be callid to counsaille, þat cause schall be knawen
Emang þat comely companye, to clerke and to knyght.

JANITOR
Byde me here, bewchere, or more blore be blowen,
And I schall buske to þe benke wher baneres are bright
And saie unto oure sovereynes, or seede more be sawen,
Þat swilke a seege as þiselff sewes to þer sight.
[*To Pilate*] My lorde nowe, of witte þat is well,
I come for a cas to be kydde.

PILATUS
We! Speke on, and spare not þi spell.

CAYPHAS
3a, and if us mystir te mell,
Sen 3e bere of bewte þe bell,
Blythely schall we bowe as 3e bidde.

JANITOR
Sir, withoute þis abatyng, þer hoves as I hope
A hyne helte-full of ire, for hasty he is.

PILATUS
What comes he fore?

JANITOR
I kenne hym noght, but he is cladde in a cope,
He cares with a kene face, uncomely to kys.

PILATUS
Go gete hym, þat his greffe we grathely may grope,
So no oppen langage be goyng amys.[32]

JANITOR
Comes on bylyve to my lorde, and if þe[e] liste to lepe,
But uttir so thy langage that þou lette noght þare blys.

JUDAS
That Lorde, sirs, myght susteyne 3oure seele
Þat floure is of fortune and fame.[33]

PILATUS
Welcome, thy wordis are but wele.

CAYPHAS
Say, harste þou, knave, can þou not knele?

PILATUS
[*To Caiaphas*] Loo, here may men faute in you fele,
Late be, sir, youre scornyng, for schame.

[*To Judas*] Bot, bewshere, be no3t abayst to byde at þe bar.

174 unhanged villain, think, ignoble 175 wretch who has lost his livelihood 176 cause you, unless you go 179 order you (to) stop 180 chatter, nagging peasant 181 if, tested 182 my business is beneficial 188 good sir, before, boast 189 bench, banners 190 i.e. before any more time passes 191 man, begs audience 192 who is wise (lit. is the well of wit) 193 heard 194 do not hold back, story 195 if it needs us to get involved 196 would win the prize for beauty 198 any delay, I think there comes 199 man, brim-full, in haste 200 cloak 201 comes, sharp, too ugly to kiss 202 grievance, inquire (about) · 204 Come, hurry 205 utter, spoil 208 only proper 209 do you hear? 210 find fault in you 211 stop 212 abashed, attend

[30] 'For through my deeds your heroic leaders may be saved from harm.'

[31] 'What, do you think that harm will be done to our dukes?'

[32] 'In case public gossip is going against us.' Or, possibly 'So long as none of his words are offensive.'

[33] '[May] that Lord who is the flower of fortune and fame [i.e. God] maintain your authority.'

Judas
Before you, sirs, to be brought, abowte have I bene,
And allway for youre worschippe.

Anna
Say, wotte þou any were?

Judas
Of werke, sir, þat hath wretthid 3ou, I wotte what I meene,
But I wolde make a marchaundyse, youre myscheffe to marre.[34]

Pilatus
And may þou soo?

Judas
Els madde I such maistries to meve.[35]

Anna
Þan kennes þou of som comberaunce oure charge for to chere?
For cosyne, þou art cruell.

Judas
My cause, sir, is kene.
For if 3e will bargayne or by,
Jesus þis tyme will I selle 3ou.

I Doctor
My blissing sone have þou forthy,
Loo, here is a sporte for to spye.

Judas
And Hym dar I hete 3ou in hye,
If 3e will be toward, I telle 3ou.

Pilatus
What hytist þou?

Judas
Judas Scariott.

Pilatus
Þou art a juste man
Þat will Jesus be justified by oure jugement.
But howe-gates bought schall he be? Bidde furthe thy bargayne.

Judas
But for a litill betyng to bere fro þis bente.

Pilatus
Now, what schall we pay?

Judas
Sir, thirti pens and plete, no more þan.

Pilatus
Say, ar 3e plesid of this price he preces to present?

II Doctor
Ellis contrarie we oure consciens, consayve sen we can
Þat Judas knawes hym culpabill.

Pilatus
I call 3ou consent.
But Judas, a knott for to knytt,
Wilte þou to his comenaunt accorde?

Judas
3a, at a worde.

Pilatus
Welcome is it.

II Miles
Take þer of, a traytour tyte![36]

I Miles
Now, leve ser, late no man wete
How þis losell laykis with his lord.

Pilatus
Why, dwellis he with þat dochard whos dedis hase us drovyd?

213 I have been trying to (be) 214 only, honour 214 (of) . . . any danger 217 can you do that? 218 problem, concern us 219 cousin 219 urgent 220 buy (do business) 222 for that 223 see 224 promise, very soon 225 agreeable 226 What is your name? 226 Iscariot 227 Who wants, to be examined 228 How, name 229 Only, reward, carry, place 231 offers 232 go against, perceive 233 knows (Jesus) guilty 233 see (that) 234 to seal a bargain 235 covenant agree 237 Look at that, an eager traitor! 238 dear sir, let, see 239 villain, plays 240 idiot, angered us

34 'Of those events that have angered you, I know what I know, but I want to make a bargain that will end your danger.'

35 'Otherwise I would be mad to begin such a high and dangerous business.'

36 Significantly it is Judas's betrayal of his master that arouses the anger of the soldiers (who are themselves bound by oaths of loyalty to their commander).

I MILES
Þat hase he done, ser, and dose, no dowte is þis day.

PILATUS
Than wolde we knawe why þis knave þus cursidly contryved.

II MILES
Enquere hym, sell ȝe can best kenne if he contrarie.

PILATUS
Say, man, to selle þi maistir what mysse hath he moved?[37]

JUDAS
For of als mekill mony He made me delay,
Of ȝou as I resayve schall but right be reproved.[38]

ANNA
I rede noght þat ȝe reken us, oure rewle so to ray,
For þat þe fales Fiende schall þe[e] fang.[39]

I MILES
When he schall wante of a wraste.

I DOCTOR
To whome wirke we wittandly wrang?

II DOCTOR
Tille hym, bot ȝe hastely hym hang.

III DOCTOR
Ȝoure langage ȝe lay oute to lang!

PILATUS
But, Judas, we trewly þe[e] trast,

For truly þou moste lerne us that losell to lache,
Or of lande thurgh a lirte that lurdayne may lepe.[40]

JUDAS
I schall ȝou teche a token Hym tyte for to take
Wher He is thryngand in þe thrang, withouten any threpe.

I MILES
We knawe hym noght.

JUDAS
Take kepe þan þat caytiffe to catche
The whilke þat I kisse.

II MILES
Þat comes wele þe[e], curious, I cleepe!
But ȝitt to warne us wisely allwayes muste ȝe wacche.
Whan þou schall wende forthwith we schall walke a wilde hepe,[41]
And therfore besye loke now þou be.

JUDAS
Ȝis, ȝis, a space schall I spie us
Al sone as þe sonne is sette, as ȝe see.

I MILES
Go forthe, for a traytoure ar ȝe.

II MILES
Ȝa, and a wikkid man.

I DOCTOR
Why, what is he?

II DOCTOR
A losell, ser, but lewte shuld lye us.

He is trappid full of trayne, þe truthe for to trist,
I holde it but folye his [faythe] for to trowe.

PILATUS
Abide in my blyssing, and late youre breste,
For it is beste for oure bote in bayle for to bowe.

241 (still) does 243 Ask, discover, argues/lies 245 money, denied me 249 Then, lack a means of escape 250 do we knowingly do wrong? 251 To him (Judas), unless 252 You talk too much! 254 teach, (how) to catch the villain 256 sign, to let you catch Him quickly 257 pressed, crowd, trouble 258 do not know what he looks like 258 care 259 (to catch) the one I kiss 259 becomes, strange man, say 260 watch 262 get busy! 263 an opportunity 264 As 267 unless truth should lie 268 full of tricks 269 to trust him 270 stop your clamour 271 welfare, in trouble to agree

37 'What evil has he done, that you are prepared to sell your master?'

38 'As I will receive from you, unless justice is denied.'

39 'I advise you not to try to judge us, or to disparage our authority in this way. For that, may the deceitful Devil take you.' Annas reacts angrily to Judas's suggestion that they might not honour their agreement.

40 'Otherwise the villain may escape, through a trick.'

41 'When you go ahead, we shall follow in a great crowd'.

And, Judas, for oure prophite we praye þe[e] be prest.

Judas
Ȝitt hadde I noght a peny to purvey for my prowe.[42]

Pilatus
Þou schalte have delyveraunce belyve at þi list,
So þat þou schall have liking oure lordschipp to love.
And therfore, Judas, mende þou thy mone,
And take þer þi silvere all same.

Judas
Ȝa, nowe is my grete greffe overe-gone.

I Miles
Be lyght, þan.

Judas
Ȝis, latte me allone,
For tytte schall þat taynte be tone,
And þerto jocounde and joly I am.

Pilatus
Judas, to holde þi behest, be hende for oure happe,
And of us, helpe and upholde we hete þe[e] to have.[43]

Judas
I schall bekenne ȝou his corse in care for to clappe.[44]

Anna
And more comforte in þis case we coveyte not to crave.

I Miles
Fro we may reche þat rekeles, his ribbis schall we rappe,
And make þat roy, or we rest, for rennyng to raffe.[45]

Pilatus
Nay, sirs, all if ȝe scourge hym, ȝe schende noȝt his schappe,
For if þe sotte be sakles, us sittis hym to save.[46]
Wherfore, when ȝe go schall to gete hym,
Unto his body brew ȝe no bale.

II Miles
Our liste is fro leping to lette hym,
But in youre sight, sownde schall we sette hym.

Pilatus
Do flitte nowe forthe till ȝe fette hym,
With solace all same to youre sale.

272 well-being, quick 274 payment soon, pleasure 275 reason 276 stop complaining 278 overcome 279 happy, then 279 let (i.e. leave) 280 traitor, taken 281 therefore, jocund/happy 285 we could not ask for more 290 get 291 do no injury 292 to stop him escaping 293 we shall bring him, intact 294 fetch 295 together to your place

42 'I have not [been paid] a penny yet to provide for my comfort.'
43 'Judas, keep your promise, act skilfully for our benefit, and we promise that you shall have aid and support from us.'
44 'I shall identify his body for you, so that you can drag him off to punishment.'
45 'For, when we catch that madman, we shall rattle his ribs, and make that king writhe [with pain] from his exertions, before we rest.'
46 'No, sirs, even if you scourge him [with whips], do not damage his body [i.e. leave no marks], because, if he is innocent, we will have to release him.'

York (The Bowers and Fletchers), *Christ Before Annas and Caiaphas*

In this and the following Passion pageants, the chief interrogator is aroused from his bed by Christ's captors, symbolizing both the sinful sleep of worldly vanity and, more practically, the disordered nature of the events prompted by the Conspiracy. The pageant also includes the episode of Peter's denial of Jesus and a narrative of the events of Christ's capture in the garden from Malchus, whose ear was severed in the scuffle by Peter, but miraculously restored by Jesus. Christ's silence before his interrogators is an affective element in the dramaturgy of the pageant, but still more powerfully resonant is the violent finale to the interview, when Christ is taken away by the soldiers. This abuse, known conventionally as the 'buffeting' of Jesus, is played out as a macabre version of the children's game 'pops', a violent variation of blind man's buff, in which the seated Christ is blindfolded, and then assaulted by the soldiers, who jeeringly invite him to identify which one of them has hit him. The carnivalesque black humour of the scene is reinforced when the soldiers taunt Christ, who by this time has been beaten unconscious, with cries of 'Wassail!' and jibes that he is asleep, attempting to 'wake' him with further blows.

The pageant is metrically complex, and the manuscript itself may well be corrupt in places, with a number of lines seemingly missing (see 'Textual Variations' towards the end of this volume). To l. 170 the play is predominantly divided into four-line stanzas: once Christ is brought into Caiaphas's presence, twelve-line alliterative stanzas become the norm.

The Bowers and Fletchers made bows and arrows, respectively.

[*Dramatis Personae*: *Cayphas* and *Anna* (Caiaphas and Annas, Jewish high priests), *IV Miles* (four Soldiers), *Petrus* (the Apostle Peter), *I and II Mulier* (two Jewish women, only the first of whom speaks), *Malchus* (servant to Caiaphas), *Jesus*.]

CAYPHAS

Pees, bewshers, I bid no jangelyng ȝe make,
And sese sone of youre sawes, and se what I saye,
And trewe tente unto me þis tyme þat ȝe take,
For I am a lorde, lerned lelly in youre lay.

By connyng of clergy and casting of witte,
Full wisely my wordis I welde at my will,
So semely in seete me semys for to sitte
And þe lawe for to lerne you and lede it by skill,
Right sone.

What wyte so will oght with me
Full frendly, in feyth, am I foune;
Come of, do tyte late me see,
Howe graciously I shall graunte hym his bone.

Ther is nowder lorde ne lady lerned in þe lawe,
Ne bisshoppe ne prelate þat preved is for pris,
Nor clerke in þe courte þat connyng will knawe,
With wisdam may were hym in world is so wise.[1]

I have þe renke and þe rewle of all þe ryall,
To rewle it by right, als reasoune it is.
All domesmen on dese awe for to dowte me
That hase thaym in bandome in bale or in blis;[2]
Wherfore takes tente to my tales, and lowtis unto me.

And therfore, sir knyghtes . . .

Tunc dicunt 'Lorde'.

I charge you chalange youre rightis,
To wayte both be day and by nightis
Of þe bringyng of a boy in to bayle.

1 good sirs, prattling 3 pay good attention 4 greatly learned 5 clerkly wisdom, use 6 use 7 seat (of power), it suits (me) 8 teach, interpret, reason 9 Immediately 10 has any (business) 11 found 12 Come along 13 request 14 nor 15 of proven worth 16 scholar 18 power, realm 19 as is reasonable 20 judges on (the) dais, ought 21 has, (my) jurisdiction 23+ Then they shall say, 'Lord'. 24 look to your responsibilities 25 watch 26 For, villain, prison

[1] 'Who could defend himself so well, or is so worldly wise [as me].'

[2] i.e. in all circumstances.

I Miles
Yis, lorde, we schall wayte if any wonderes walke,
And freyne howe youre folkis fare þat are furth ronne.

II Miles
We schall be bayne at youre bidding, and it not to balk
Yf þei presente you þat boy in a bande boune.

Anna
Why, syr, and is þer a boy þat will noght lowte to youre bidding?

Cayphas
Ya, sir, and of þe coriousenesse of þat karle þer is carping,
But I have sente for þat segge halfe for hethyng.

Anna
What wondirfull werkis workis þat wighte?

Cayphas
Seke men and sori he sendis siker helyng,
And to lame men, and blynde he sendis þer sight.

Of croked crepillis þat we knawe
Itt is to here grete wondering,
How þat he helis þame all on rawe,
And all thurgh his false happenyng.

I am sorie of a sight
Þat egges me to ire,
Oure lawe he brekis with all his myght,
Þat is moste his desire.

Oure Sabott day he will not safe,
But is aboute to bringe it downe,
And therfore sorowe muste hym have,
May he be kacched in felde or towne,
For his false stevyn,
He defamys fowly þe Godhed,
And callis hymselffe God Sone of Hevene.

Anna
I have goode knowlache of þat knafe:
Marie me menys his modir highte,[3]
And Joseph his fadir, as God me safe,
Was kidde and knowen wele for a wrighte.

But o thyng me mervayles mekill overe all,
Of diverse dedis þat he has done . . .

Cayphas
With wicche-crafte he fares withall,
Sir, þat schall ȝe se full sone.

Oure knyghtis þai are furth wente
To take hym with a traye;
By þis I holde hym shente,
He can not wende away.

Anna
Wolde ȝe, sir, take youre reste,
This day is comen on hande,
And with wyne slake youre thirste?
Þan durste I wele warande

Ȝe schulde have tithandis sone
Of þe knyghtis þat are gone,
And howe þat þei have done
To take hym by a trayne.

And putte all þought away,
And late youre materes reste.

Cayphas
I will do as ȝe saie,
Do gette us wyne of þe best.
For, be we ones well wett,
The better we will reste.

I Miles
My lorde, here is wyne þat will make you to wynke,
Itt is licoure full delicious, my lorde, and you like.
Wherfore I rede drely it draughte þat ȝe drynke,
For in þis contre, þat we knawe, iwisse ther is none slyke,

27 any(thing) odd occurs 28 find (out), people, gone 29 command, shirk 30 bound in/with a rope 32 curiousness (cunning) 33 man, half in fun 34 does (he) perform? 35 sick, sorrowful, sure healing 37 crooked cripples 38 hear, incredible 39 together 40 fortune (i.e. through luck alone) 41 regret 42 prompts, anger 43 breaks 44 main intention 45 Sabbath, respect 46 works 48 caught, field 49 voice (teachings) 50 foully 51 God's son 52 knave 54 God save me 55 recognized, well known, carpenter 56 one, I greatly wonder at 57 (the many) different deeds 58 witchcraft, meddles 60 gone out 61 trick 62 Therefore I think he is doomed 63 escape 64 Would you (like to) 65 nearly over 67 I dare say 68 shall 72 do not worry 73 business 76 once I am well watered 78 sleepy 79 if you please 80 advise strongly (that), a glass 81 there is nothing else like it

[3] 'I know that his mother was called Mary'.

Wherfore we counsaile you this cuppe saverly for to kisse.

Cayphas
Do on dayntely, and dresse me on dees,[4]
And hendely hille on me happing,
And warne all wightis to be in pees,
For I am late layde unte napping.

Anna
My lorde, with youre leve, and it like you, I passe.

Cayphas
'Adiew be unte', as þe manere is.

[*Enter I and II Mulier, III and IV Miles, Malchus, Petrus, and Christ (bound).*][5]

I Mulier
Sir knyghtys, do kepe þis boy in bande,
For I will go witte what it may mene,
Why þat yone wighte was hym folowand,
Erly and late, morne and ene.

He will come nere, he will not lette,
He is a spie, I warand, full bolde.

III Miles
It semes by his sembland he had levere be sette
By þe fervent fire to fleme hym fro colde

I Mulier
Ya, but and ȝe wiste as wele as I
What wonders þat þis wight has wrought,
And thurgh his maistir sorssery,
Full derfely schulde his deth be bought.

IV Miles
Dame, we have hym nowe at will
Þat we have longe tyme soughte,
Yf othir go by us still
Þerfore we have no thought.

I Mulier
Itt were grete skorne þat he schulde skape
Withoute he hadde resoune and skill;
He lokis lurkand like an nape,
I hope I schall haste me hym tille.

Thou caytiffe, what meves þe[e] stande
So stabill and stille in þi thoght?
Þou hast wroght mekill wronge in londe,
And wondirfull werkis haste þou wroght.

A lorell, a leder of lawe,
To sette hym and suye has þou soght.
Stande furth and threste in yone thrawe,
Thy maistry þou bryng unto noght.

Wayte nowe! He lokis like a brokke,
Were he in a bande for to bayte,
Or ellis like an nowele in a stok
Full prevaly his pray for to wayte.

Petrus
Woman, thy wordis and thy wynde þou not waste,
Of His company never are I was kende.
Þou haste þe[e] mismarkid, trewly be traste,
Wherfore of þi misse þou þe[e] amende.

I Mulier
Þan gaynesaies þou here þe sawes þat þou saide,
How he schulde clayme to be callid God Sonne,
And with þe werkis þat he wrought whils he walkeþ in þis flodde,
Baynly at oure bydding alway to be bonne?[6]

Petrus
I will consente to youre sawes, what schulde I saye more?
For women are crabbed: þat comes þem of kynde.
But I saye as I firste saide, I sawe Hym nevere are,
But as a frende of oure felawschippe shall ye me aye fynde.

82 kiss with delight **84** skilfully, lay, (the) blankets **85** quiet **86** late going to bed **87** permission, (will) depart **88** 'unto yee', as the fashion is **89** bound **90** (to) find out **91** man over there, following **92** (i.e. all the time) **93** give up **94** declare **95** appearance, rather, sat **96** hot, escape, from **97** If you knew as well as I (do) **99** through (use of), master's sorcery **100** He would pay with a cruel death **102** (He) whom (i.e. Jesus) **103** If other (lesser) men escape us **104** do not care **105** shame **106** Unless **107** lurks, looking, ape **108** think, go quickly to him **109** prompts you (to) **110** thought **111** evil **113** false teacher **114** have you sought to follow **115** push into that crowd **116** powers, will not help you **117** look now!, badger **118** as if he was tied up for baiting **119** an owl on a stump **120** secretly watching for his prey **121** don't waste your breath **122** His (i.e. Jesus's), never known **123** are mistaken, (if) truth be known **124** correct your mistake **125** do you deny **126** claim **130** bad-tempered, that is their nature **131** never saw Him before **132** you shall always find me

4 'Go ahead, carefully, and prepare me [for bed, here] on the dais'.

5 This scene probably took place at ground level, with Annas and Caiaphas remaining on the pageant wagon.

6 'And [do you deny] the deeds that he performed, while he was here, and eagerly agree to be loyal to us?'

MALCHUS
Herke, knyghtis þat are knawen in this contre, as we kenne,
Howe yone boy with his boste has brewed mekill bale.
He has forsaken his maistir before ȝone womenne,
But I schall preve to ȝou pertly and telle you my tale.

I was presente with pepull whenne prese was full prest,
To mete with his maistir with mayne and with myght,
And hurled hym hardely and hastely hym arreste,
And in bandis full bittirly bande hym sore all þat nyght.

And of tokenyng of trouth schall I telle yowe
Howe yone boy with a brande brayede me full nere,
Do move of thez materes emelle yowe,
For swiftely he swapped of my nere.

His maistir, with his myght, helyd me all hole,
That by no syne I cowthe see no man cowþe it witten,
And þan badde hym bere pees in every-ilke bale,
For he þat strikis with a swerd with a swerde schall be streken.[7]

Late se whedir grauntest þou gilte:
Do speke oon, and spare not to telle us,
Or full faste I schall fonde þe[e] flitte,
The soth but þou saie here emelle us.

Come of, do tyte late me see nowe,
In savyng of thyselffe fro schame
3a, and also for beryng of blame.

PETRUS
I was nevere with Hym in werke þat He wroght,
In worde nor in werke, in will nor in dede.
I knawe no corse þat ȝe have hidir brought,
In no courte of this kith, yf I schulde right rede.

MALCHUS
Here sirs, howe he sais, and has forsaken
His maistir to þis woman here twyes,
And newly oure lawe has he taken;
Thus hath he denyed hym thryes.

JESUS
Petir, Petir, þus saide I are,
When þou saide þou wolde abide with Me
In wele and woo, in sorowe and care,
Whillis I schulde thries forsaken be.[8]

PETRUS
Alas þe while þat I come here,
That evere I denyed My Lorde in quarte,
The loke of His faire face so clere
With full sadde sorrowe sheris my harte.

III MILES
Sir knyghtis, take kepe of his karll and be konnand,
Because of sir Cayphas, we knowe wele his þoght.
He will rewarde us full wele, þat dare I wele warand,
Whan he wete of oure werkis, how wele we have wroght.

IV MILES
Sir, þis is Cayphas halle here at hande,
Go we boldly with his boy þat we have here broght.

III MILES
Nay, sirs, us muste stalke to þat stede and full still stande,
For itt is nowe of þe nyght, yf þei nappe oght.
Say, who is here?

I MILES
Say, who is here?

III MILES
I, a frende,
Well knawyn in þis contre for a knyght.

133 Listen 134 boasts, stirred great trouble 135 that woman 136 openly 137 the crowd, thickest 139 grabbed, quickly caught him 140 fiercely bound him in ropes 141 as a sign of truth 142 struck 143 talk about this among you 144 chopped off my ear 145 healed me completely 146 sign (that), understand it 147 told (Peter), bring peace, conflict 148 struck 149 Let's, admit (your) guilt 150 on, don't hesitate 151 quickly, drive you away 152 Unless you tell the truth 153 bearing 157 thought 158 nobody 159 country, interpret correctly 160 Hear 161 twice 162 adopted 163 thrice (three times) 164 Peter, previously 166 prosperity, woe 167 While, thrice 169 living Lord 170 innocent 171 shears (cuts in two) 172 care, rogue, alert 175 learns of 178 go quietly, place 179 night-time, in case 181 as

[7] John 18:26.

[8] An elaboration upon the description in Luke 22:61.

II Miles
Gose furthe, on youre wayes may yee wende,
For we have herbered enowe for tonyght.

I Miles
Gose abakke, bewscheres, ȝe bothe are to blame
To bourde whenne oure busshopp is boune to his bedde.

IV Miles
Why, sir, it were worthy to welcome us home,
We have gone for þis warlowe and we have wele spedde.

II Miles
Why, who is þat?

III Miles
The Jewes Kyng, Jesus by name.

I Miles
A, yee be welcome, þat dare I wele wedde,
My lorde has sente for to seke hym.

IV Miles
Loo, se here þe same.

II Miles
Abidde as I bidde, and be noght adreed.
My lorde, my lorde, my lorde, here is layke, and ȝou list!

Cayphas
Pees, loselles! Leste ȝe be nyse?

I Miles
My lorde, it is wele and ye wiste.

Cayphas
What, nemen us no more, for it is twyes.

Þou takist non hede to þe haste that we hatte here on honde,[9]
Go frayne howe oure folke faris that are furth ronne.

II Miles
My lorde, youre knyghtis has kared as ye þame commaunde,
And thei have fallen full faire.

Cayphas
Why, and is þe foole fonne?

I Miles
Ya, lorde, þei have brought a boy in a bande boune.

Cayphas
Where nowe sir Anna, þat is one and able to be nere?

Anna
My lorde, with youre leve, me behoves to be here.

Cayphas
A, sir, come nere and sitte we bothe in fere.

Anna
Do, sir, bidde þam bring in þat boy þat is bune.

Cayphas
Pese now, sir Anna, be stille and late hym stande,
And late us grope yf þis gome be grathly begune.

Anna
Sir, þis game is begune of þe best,
Nowe hadde he no force for to flee þame.

Cayphas
Nowe, in faithe, I am fayne he is fast,
Do lede in þat ladde, late me se þan.

II Miles
[*To III Miles*] Lo, sir, we have saide to oure sovereyne.
Gose nowe and suye to hymselfe for þe same thyng.

III Miles
Mi lorde, to youre bidding we have ben buxom and bayne,
Lo, here is þe belschere broght þat ye bad bring.

182 Go away! 183 sheltered enough (people) 184 back 185 play, gone 186 it would be best 187 done well 189 I bet 191 Wait, frightened 192 good sport 193 Are you fools? 194 good (news), if you (only) knew 195 the second time 197 find out, are getting on 198 done as you told them 199 had great success, found 201 where (is), is he nearby? 202 I am obliged 203 together 204 bound 206 inquire, game, properly 207 in the best way (possible) 208 them (i.e. the soldiers) 209 glad, captured 210 lead, lad 211 spoken 212 sue 214 good sir [mocking]

9 'You do not respect the urgent business that I have here in hand'.

IV MILES
My lorde, fandis now to fere hym.

CAYPHAS
Nowe I am fayne,
And felawes, faire mott ye fall for youre fynding.

ANNA
Sir, and ye trowe þei be trewe withowten any trayne,
Bidde þayme telle you þe tyme of þe takyng.

CAYPHAS
Say felawes, howe wente ye so nemely by nyȝt?[10]

III MILES
My lorde, was þere no man to marre us ne mende us.

IV MILES
My lorde, we had lanternes and light,
And some of his company kende us.

ANNA
But saie, howe did he, Judas?

III MILES
A, sir, full wisely and wele,
He markid us his maistir emang all his men
And kyssid hym full kyndely his comforte to kele,
By cause of a countenaunce þat karll for to kenne.[11]

CAYPHAS
And þus did he his devere?

IV MILES
Ya, lorde, evere-ilke a dele,
He taughte us to take hym the tyme aftir tenne.

ANNA
Nowe, be my feith a faynte frende myght he þer fynde.

III MILES
Sire, ye myght so have saide hadde ye hym sene þenne.

IV MILES
He sette us to þe same þat he solde us,
And feyned to be his frende, as a faytour,
This was þe tokenyng before þat he tolde us.

CAYPHAS
Nowe trewly, þis was a trante of a traytour.

ANNA
Ȝa, be he traytour or trewe geve we never tale,
But takes tente at þis tyme, and here what he telles.

CAYPHAS
Now sees þat oure howsolde be holden here hole,
So þat none carpe in case but þat in court dwellis.

III MILES
A, lorde, þis brethell hath brewed moche bale.

CAYPHAS
Therfore schall we spede us to spere of his spellis.
Sir Anna, takis hede nowe, and here hym.

ANNA
Say, ladde, liste þe[e] noght lowte to a lorde?

IV MILES
No, sir, with youre leve we schall lere hym.

CAYPHAS
Nay, sir, noght so, no haste,
Itt is no burde to bete bestis þat are bune.
And therfore with fayrenes firste we vill hym fraste,
And sithen forþer hym furth as we have fune.
And telle us som tales, truly to traste.

ANNA
Sir, we myght als wele talke tille it tome tonne.
I warande hym witteles, or ellis he is wrang wrayste,
Or ellis he waitis to wirke als he was are wonne.[12]

III MILES
His wonne was to wirke mekill woo,
And make many maystries emelle us.

215 go about, intimidate 216 good luck to you! 217 if you believe, honest, lies 218 time/details, capture 220 hinder 222 (had) informed us 224 picked out 225 to end his happiness 227 duty, in every respect 228 planned (for) 229 poor friend 231 took us (straight) to 232 pretended, 233 sign 234 deception 235 we do not care whether he is 236 pay attention 237 ensure, kept together 238 talk about this, except those 240 hurry, inquire into his words 242 don't you know how to bow 245 no fun to beat a bound beast 246 fairness, question 247 thereafter, act as we think fit 249 might as well, to an empty barrel 252 habit 253 do great deeds

10 'How was it that you were able to do so well in the dark?'

11 'As a means of letting us know what the man looked like.'

12 'I think he's witless, or else he's twisted wrongly [in the head], or else he is waiting [for a chance] to do as he usually does [i.e. use magic?].'

Cayphas
And some schall he graunte or he goo,
Or muste yowe tente hym and telle us.

IV Miles
Mi lorde, to witte þe wonderes þat he has wroght,
For to telle you the tente it wolde oure tonges tere.

Cayphas
Sen þe boy for his boste is into bale broght,
We will witte, or he wende, how his werkis were.

III Miles
Oure Sabott day, we saye, saves he right-noght,
That he shulde halowe and holde full dingne and full dere.[13]

IV Miles
No, sir, in þe same feste als we the sotte soughte,
He salved þame of sikenesse on many sere sidis seere.

Cayphas
What þan, makes he þame grathely to gange?

III Miles
ȝa, lorde, even forthe in every-ilke a toune
He þame lechis to liffe aftir lange.

Cayphas
A, this makes he by the myghtis of Mahounde.[14]

IV Miles
Sir, oure stiffe Tempill þat made is of stone,
That passes any paleys of price for to preyse,
And it were doune to þe erth and to þe gronde gone,
This rebalde he rowses hym it rathely to rayse.[15]

III Miles
ȝa, lorde, and othir wonderis he workis grete wone,
And with his lowde lesyngis he losis oure layes.

Cayphas
Go lowse hym, and levis þan, and late me allone,
For myselfe schall serche hym and here what he saies.

Anna
Herke, Jesus of Jewes, [we] will have joie
To spille all thy sporte for thy spellis.

Cayphas
Do meve, felawe, of thy frendis þat fedde þe[e] beforne,
And sithen, felowe, of thi fare forþer will I freyne;
Do neven us lightly. His langage is lorne!

III Miles
My lorde, with youre leve, hym likis for to layne,
But and he schulde scape skatheles it wer a full skorne,
For he has mustered emonge us full mekil of his mayne.[16]

IV Miles
Malkus, youre man, lord, þat had his ere schorne.
This harlotte full hastely helid it agayne.

Cayphas
What, and liste hym be nyse for þe nonys,
And heres howe we haste to rehete hym.

Anna
Nowe by Beliall bloode and his bonys,
I holde it beste to go bete hym.

Cayphas
Nay, sir, none haste, we schall have game or we goo.
Boy, be not agaste if we seme gaye.
I conjure þe[e] kyndely and comaunde þe[e] also,
By grete God þat is liffand and laste schall ay,
Yf ȝou be Criste, Goddis Sonne, telle till us two.

254 admit to, before he leaves 255 attend to him 256 describe 257 the tenth part, tear our tongues 260 he completely ignores 262 feast 263 cured, all around him 264 restores them fully to health 265 in every town 266 brings to life those long dead 272 in great number 273 bold lies, breaks 274 loose, then leave, let . . . (with him) 275 interrogate 276 take pleasure 277 spoil, due to your words 278 tell us, supported you 279 other business 280 quickly. He's lost his tongue! 281 he prefers not to talk 282 if, unpunished, great shame 284 Malchus, cut off 285 quickly, healed 286 if he wants to be silly now 287 hear, will quickly correct him 288 Belial (a devil)'s, bones 291 grand (in appearance) 292 encourage gently 293 and will endure for ever 294 If you are, tell us

13 'That [which] he should observe with honour and hold precious and dear to him.'

14 'He does this by the power of Mahound.' Mahound, a corruption of 'Mohammed', was used in the Christian west as the name of a false god or demon.

15 'Our strong Temple that surpasses in praiseworthiness any noble palace, this villain claims to be able to raise up once more, even if it had been razed to the ground.' See Matthew 24:1–2; Mark 3:1–2.

16 'For he has gathered a great number of his supporters [or, shown a great deal of his power] among us.'

Jesus
Sir, þou says it þiselffe, and sothly I saye
Þat I schall go to My Fadir þat I come froo
And dwelle with Hym wynly in welthe allway.

Cayphas
Why, fie on þe[e], faitoure untrewe,
Thy fadir haste þou fowly defamed.
Now nedis us no notes of newe,
Hymselfe with his sawes has he schamed.

Anna
Nowe nedis nowdir wittenesse ne counsaille to call,
But take his sawes as he saieth in þe same stede.
He sclaunderes þe Godhed and greves us all,
Wherfore he is wele worthy to be dede,
And therfore, sir, saies hym þe sothe.

Cayphas
Sertis, so I schall.
Heres þou not, harlott? Ille happe on thy hede!
Aunswere here grathely to grete and to small,
And reche us oute rathely som resoune, I rede.

Jesus
My reasouns are not to reherse,
Nor they þat myght helpe Me are noȝt here nowe.

Anna
Say, ladde, liste þe[e] make verse?
Do telle on belyffe, late us here nowe.

Jesus
Sir, if I saie þe sothe þou schall not assente,
But hyndir, or haste Me to hynge.
I prechid wher pepull was moste in present,
And no poynte in privite, to olde ne ȝonge.
And also in youre Tempill I tolde Myne entente;
Ye myght have tane Me þat tyme for My tellyng,
Wele bettir þan bringe Me with brondis unbrente,
And þus to noye Me be nyght, and also for nothyng.[17]

Cayphas
For nothyng, losell? Þou lies!
Thy wordis and werkis will have a wrekyng.

Jesus
Sire, sen þou with wrong so Me wreyes,
Go spere thame þat herde of My spekyng.

Cayphas
A, þis traitoure has tened me with tales þat he has tolde,
Ȝitt hadde I nevere such hething as of a harlott as hee.[18]

I Miles
What, fye on the[e], beggar, who made þe[e] so bolde
To bourde with oure busshoppe? Thy bane schalle I bee.

Jesus
Sir, if My wordis be wrange or werse þan þou wolde,
A wronge wittenesse I wotte nowe ar ȝe;
And if My sawes be soth þei mon be sore solde,
Wherfore þou bourdes to brode for to bete Me.

II Miles
My lorde, will ȝe here? For Mahounde,
No more now for to neven þat it nedis.

Cayphas
Gose dresse you and dyng ȝe hym doune,
And deffe us no more with his dedis.

Anna
Nay, sir, þan blemysshe yee prelatis estatis,
Ȝe awe to deme no man to dede for to dynge.[19]

297 happily in eternal bliss 298 curse you! 299 you have foully 300 we need no further evidence 301 he has convicted himself 302 (we) need 303 this very place 304 slanders, offends 305 deserves death 306 tell 307 bad luck, head! 308 properly to (everyone) 309 tell us something reasonable 310 to be repeated 312 are you trying to put it into verse? 313 speak up, quickly 314 agree 315 oppose (Me), hang 316 where there were most people 317 never in secret 318 spoke My mind 323 reckoning 324 since you accuse me falsely 325 ask 328 curse you! 329 mock, tormentor 330 untrue, worse, desire 331 false, I see that you are 332 must cost Me dear 333 mock (Me) too much 334 can you hear? 335 enough has been said 336 prepare yourselves, beat him 337 deafen

[17] 'You might have arrested Me there and then for My teachings, [it would have been] much better than to persecute Me at night, secretly [lit. with unburned torches], and all for nothing.'
[18] 'I have never heard such insolence from a villain as [I hear] from him.'

[19] '[If you do that] you defile the office of bishop, for you may not condemn any man to death.' Like the medieval church courts, the Jewish *Sanhedrin* could not pass the death sentence, hence heretics had to be handed over to lay officials for execution.

Cayphas
Why, sir? So were bettir þan be in debate,
Ye see þe boy will noȝt bowe for oure bidding.

Anna
Nowe, sir, ye muste presente þis boy unto sir Pilate,
For he is domysman nere and nexte to þe king,
And late hym here all þe hole, how ye hym hate,
And whedir he will helpe hym or haste hym to hyng.

I Miles
My lorde, late men lede hym by nyght,
So schall ye beste skape oute o skornyng.

II Miles
My lorde, it is nowe in þe nyght,
I rede ȝe abide tille þe mornyng.

Cayphas
Bewschere, þou sais þe beste and so schall it be,
But lerne yone boy bettir to bende and bowe.

I Miles
We schall lerne yone ladde, be my lewte,
For to loute unto ilke lorde like unto yowe.

Cayphas
Ȝa, and felawes, wayte þat ye be ay wakand.

II Miles
Ȝis, lorde, þat warant will wee,
Itt were a full nedles note to bidde us nappe nowe.

III Miles
Sertis, will ye sitte and sone schall ye see
Howe we schall play popse for þe pages prowe.[20]

IV Miles
Late see, who stertis for a stole?
For I have here a hatir to hyde hym.

I Miles
Lo, here is one full fitte for a foole,
Go gete it and sette þe[e] beside hym.

II Miles
Nay, I schall sette it myselffe and frusshe hym also.
Lo here, a shrowde for a shrewe, and of shene shappe.

III Miles
Playes faire, in feere, I schall fande to feste it
With a faire flappe, and þer is one! [*strikes Jesus*], and þer is ij;
And ther is iij; and there is iiij.
Say nowe, with an nevill happe,
Who negheth þe[e] nowe? Not o worde? No!

IV Miles
Dose noddill on hym with neffes, that he noght nappe.[21]

I Miles
Nay, nowe to nappe is no nede,
Wassaille! Wassaylle![22] I warande hym wakande.

II Miles
Ȝa, and bot he bettir bourdis can byde,
Such buffettis schall he be takande.

III Miles
Prophete, Y saie, to be oute of debate,
Quis te percussit, man? Rede, giffe þou may.

IV Miles
Those wordes are in waste, what wenes þou he wate?
It semys by his wirkyng his wittes were awaye.[23]

I Miles
Now late hym stande as he stode in a foles state,
For he likis noȝt þis layke, my liffe dare I laye.[24]

340 Why (not)? It's better than 343 judge, the king's deputy 344 hear everything 345 either help him 346 take 347 avoid scandal 351 teach . . . (how) 352 by my loyalty 353 to each 354 make sure you stay alert 355 Yes, we guarantee 356 would be useless 357 if you will sit down 358 play 'pops', knave's benefit 359 (will) go, stool 360 halter/hood, blindfold 361 fitting for a fool 363 beat 364 villain, good shape 365 Play fair!, go and fasten 366 good blow, a second 368 an evil chance 369 approaches, Not one word? 371 He should not be napping now 372 I think he's awake. 373 unless he can offer better sport 374 He'll take (more) such blows 375 to settle the discussion 376 'Who struck you?' Prophesy, if 377 do you think he understands? 379 as if he were a (court) fool

[20] See headnote.

[21] 'Punch him [on the head?] with [our] fists, to make sure he doesn't fall asleep.'

[22] 'Wassaill': a cry announcing festivities, especially drinking.

[23] 'It seems from his behaviour that his wits are lost.'

[24] 'Because he does not like this game, I would bet my life (on it).'

II MILES
Sirs, us muste presente þis page to ser Pilate,
But go we firste to oure soverayne and see what he saies.

III MILES
My lorde, we have bourded with þis boy,
And holden hym full hote emelle us.[25]

CAYPHAS
Thanne herde ye some japes of joye?

IV MILES
The Devell have þe worde, lorde, he wolde telle us.[26]

ANNA
Sir, bidde belyve þei goo and bynde hym agayne,
So þat he skape noght, for þat were a skorne.

CAYPHAS
Do telle to sir Pilate oure pleyntes all pleyne,
And saie þis ladde with his lesyngis has oure lawes lorne.
And saie þis same day muste he be slayne,
Because of Sabott day þat schal be tomorne,[27]
And saie þat we come oureselffe, for certayne,
And for to fortheren þis fare, fare yee beforne.

I MILES
Mi lorde, with youre leve, us muste wende,
Oure message to make as we maye.

CAYPHAS
[*To Jesus*] Sir, youre faire felawschippe we betake to þe fende,
Goose onne nowe, and daunce forth in þe Devyll way.

383 played 385 did you hear, good jokes? 387 tell them quickly to 389 clearly all our grievances 390 lies, broken 392 tomorrow is the Sabbath 393 (will) come 394 speed matters, you go ahead 397 send, the Devil 398 Go, in the Devil's name

25 'And [have] given him a hard time [lit. made it hot for him] among ourselves.'
26 'The Devil can have any words that he would tell us, my lord'; i.e. he said nothing.
27 In Jewish law, Jesus could not be executed on the Sabbath, when no work must be performed.

York (The Tapiters and Couchers), *Christ Before Pilate I: The Dream of Pilate's Wife*

The pageant reintroduces Satan into the action, paradoxically, in the role of would-be saviour of Jesus's life. Following the events of the Temptation, he appears to have realized that Jesus might indeed be the Son of God, and that His execution might thus bring about the Harrowing of Hell and loss of his own dominion over the souls imprisoned there. Hence he seeks to prevent His death, again using a woman, Pilate's vain wife, Procula, as his vehicle. The action takes place in a number of separate locations, Pilate's hall, Procula's chamber, and the palace courtyard, each of which was probably represented on or around the pageant wagon. Of the characters, Pilate and Procula are both self-regarding sensualists, the former exhibiting lust, drunkenness, and violent anger by turns in the course of the pageant. Procula represents an interesting variant on a misogynistic type, combining elements of the sexual temptress (in her dealings with her husband) with the abusive instincts of the scold (evident in her resentful responses to the Beadle). The Beadle is another representative of natural humanity who, when confronted with Christ's evident spiritual authority, spontaneously worships Him, despite the dangers involved. Christ Himself, as in the previous pageant, maintains a powerfully affective silent presence throughout the action, speaking only once in response to Pilate's questioning.

The pageant is metrically varied, and the manuscript may well be missing several lines (see 'Textual Variants', p. 624). A nine-line stanza is used throughout, but from l. 159 the rhyme-scheme changes from abab bcbbc to abab cdddc.

The Tapiters produced tapestries and ornamental cloths; the Couchers made bedding and bedroom decorations. Procula's bed presumably provided an impressive example of their work.

[*Dramatis Personae*: *Pilatus* (Pontius Pilate, Roman governor), *Uxor Pilati* ('Pilate's Wife': Procula), *Bedellus* ('Beadle': a household official), *Ancilla* ('Hand-maiden' to Procula), *Filius* ('Son' to Pilate and Procula), *Diabolus* (Devil: Satan), *Anna and Cayphas* (Annas and Caiaphas, Jewish high priests), *II Miles* (two Soldiers), *Jesus*.]

PILATUS

Yhe cursed creatures þat cruelly are cryand,
Restreyne you for stryvyng for strengh of my strakis;
Youre pleyntes in my presence use plately applyand,
Or ellis þis brande in youre braynes schalle brestis
and brekis.[1]
Þis brande in his bones brekis,
What brawle þat with brawlyng me brewis;
That wrecche may not wrye fro my werkes,
Nor his sleyghtis noȝt slely hym slakis;
Latte þat traytour noȝt triste in my trewys.[2]
For sir Sesar was my sier and I sothely his sonne,
That exelent emperoure exaltid in hight,
Whylk all þis wilde worlde with wytes had wone,
And my modir hight Pila þat proude was o pight;
O Pila þat prowde, and Atus hir fadir he hight.
This 'Pila' was hadde into 'Atus',
Nowe renkis, rede yhe it right?
For þus schortely I have schewid you in sight
Howe I am prowdely preved 'Pilatus'.

Loo, Pilate I am, proved a prince of grete pride.
I was putte into Pounce þe pepill to presse,
And sithen Sesar hymselffe with exynatores be his
side,
Remytte me to þe remys þe renkes to redresse.
To justifie and juge all þe Jewes,
And yitte am Y graunted on grounde, as I gesse.

[*Enter Uxor Pilati.*]

1 crying 10 Caesar, father, (am) truly 11 exalted on high 12 whom, (his) men, won 13 mother (was) called, of place 14 Of, was her father's name 15 added to 16 people 17 shortly 18 known to be 20 Pontius, repress 21 senators, by 22 Granted, these realms, reform 23 bring justice to 24 granted here, believe

[1] 'Restrain yourselves from your efforts for [fear of] the strength of my strokes [blows]; make your complaints in my presence in the proper manner, or else this sword shall burst and break in your brains.'

[2] 'This sword will break the bones of whatever villain stirs up trouble [for] me with his brawling; that wretch will not escape my vengeance, nor will his tricks slyly set him free. That traitor had better not trust me to be peaceful.'

A, luffe, here lady? No lesse?
Lo sirs, my worthely wiffe, þat sche is,
So semely, loo, certayne scho schewys.

UXOR PILATI
Was nevir juge in þis Jurie of so jocounde generacion,
Nor of so joifull genologie to gentrys enioyned
As yhe, my duke doughty, demar of dampnacion
To princes and prelatis þat youre preceptis perloyned.
Who þat youre preceptis pertely perloyned,
With drede into dede schall ye dryffe hym;
By my trouthe, he untrewly is stonyed
Þat agaynste youre behestis hase honed;
All to ragges schall ye rente hym and ryve hym.

I am dame precious Percula, of prynces þe prise,
Wiffe to ser Pilate here, prince withouten pere.
All welle of all womanhede I am, wittie and wise,
Consayve nowe my countenaunce so comly and clere.
The coloure of my corse is full clere
And in richesse of robis I am rayed,
Ther is no lorde in þis londe, as I lere,
In faith, þat hath a frendlyar feere
Than yhe, my lorde, myselffe þof I saye itt.

PILATUS
Nowe saye itt save may ye saffely, for I will certefie þe same.

UXOR PILATI
Gracious lorde, gramercye, youre gode worde is gayne.

PILATUS
Yhitt for to comforte my corse me muste kisse you madame.

UXOR PILATI
To fulfille youre forward, my fayre lorde, I am fayne.

PILATUS
Howe, howe, felawys! Nowe in faith I am fayne
Of theis lippis so loffely are lappid,
[*To audience*] In bedde is full buxhome and bayne.

UXOR PILATI
Yha, sir, it nedith not to layne,
All ladise we coveyte þan bothe to be kyssid and clappid.

BEDELLUS
My liberall lorde, o leder of lawis,
O schynyng schawe þat all schames escheues,
I beseke you, my soverayne, assente to my sawes,
As ye are gentill juger and justice of Jewes.

UXOR PILATI
Do herke howe þou, javell, jangill of Jewes.
Why, go bette, horosonne boy, when I bidde þe[e].

BEDELLUS
Madame, I do but þat diewe is.

UXOR PILATI
But yf þou reste of thy resoune þou rewis,
For all is a cursed, carle; hase in; kydde þe[e]?[3]

PILATUS
Do mende you madame, and youre mode be amendand,
For me semys it wer sittand to se what he sais.[4]

UXOR PILATI
Mi lorde, he tolde nevir tale þat to me was tendand,[5]
But with wrynkis and with wiles to wend me my weys.

BEDELLUS
Gwisse, of youre wayes to be wendand itt langis to oure lawes.[6]

25 Ah, love, are you here? 26 worthy 27 beautiful, she appears 28 fortunate family 29 lineage, allied to the aristocracy 30 stalwart, judge 31 bishops, ignored your orders 32 presumptuously 33 unto death, drive 34 astonished 35 delayed (in obeying), orders 36 rend, tear 37 prize 39 source of all womanly qualities 40 Perceive, face, fair, pure 41 body 42 the richest robes, dressed 43 have learnt 44 more loving partner 45 though I say it myself 46 you may safely say it 47 thankyou, pleasing 48 to give me pleasure 49 do as you ask 50 Ho, ho, fellows! 51 by these lips, lovely (to be kissed) 52 (she) is 53 should not be hidden 54 ladies, desire, embraced 55 interpreter/maker 56 display, eschews all shame 57 agree, words/request 58 judge 59 villain, prattles about Jews 60 get away, whoreson 61 I'm only doing my duty 67 tricks, to get rid of me

[3] The sense of the second part of Uxor's threat is obscure, perhaps: 'Unless you stop talking, you will regret it, for everything [you say] is vile, you wretch, push off; do you understand?'

[4] 'Compose yourself, madam, and improve your mood, because it seems to me that it would be proper to hear what he has to say.'

[5] 'He never says anything [nice] about me'.

[6] 'Indeed, it is in keeping with our laws that you should go away.'

UXOR PILATI
Loo, lorde, þis ladde with his lawes!
Howe, thynke ye it prophitis wele his prechyng to prayse?[7]

PILATUS
Yha, luffe, he knawis all oure custome,
I knawe wele.

BEDELLUS
My seniour, will ye see nowe þe sonne in youre sight,
For his stately strengh he stemmys in his stremys?
Behalde ovir youre hede how he holdis fro hight
And glydis to þe grounde with his glitterand glemys.
To þe grounde he gois with his bemys
And þe nyght is neghand anone.
Yhe may dome aftir no dremys,[8]
But late my lady here, with all hir light lemys
Wightely go wende till hir wone;

For ye muste sitte, sir, þis same nyght, of lyfe and of lyme.
Itt is noȝt leeffull for my lady by the lawe of this lande
In dome for to dwelle fro þe day waxe ought dymme,
For scho may stakir in þe strete but scho stalworthely stande.[9]
Late hir take hir leve whill þat light is.

PILATUS
Nowe, wiffe, þan ye blythely be buskand.

UXOR PILATI
I am here, sir, hendely at hande.

PILATUS
Loo, þis renke has us redde als right is.

UXOR PILATI
Youre comaundement to kepe to kare for þe[e] Y caste me.
My lorde, with youre leve, no lenger Y lette yowe.[10]

PILATUS
Itt were a rappreve to my persone þat prevely ȝe paste me,
Or ye wente fro this wones or with wynne ȝe had wette yowe.
Ye schall wende forthe with wynne whenne þat ȝe hatte wette yowe.[11]
Gete drinke! What dose þou? Have done!
Come semely, beside me, and sette yowe.
Loke, nowe it is even here þat I are behete you,
Ya, saie it nowe sadly and sone.

UXOR PILATI
Itt wolde glad me, my lorde, if ȝe gudly begynne.

PILATUS
Nowe I assente to youre counsaille so comely and clene.
Nowe drynke, madame, to deth all þis dynne.

UXOR PILATI
Iff it like yowe, myne awne lorde, I am not to lere,
This lare I am not to lere.[12]

PILATUS
Yitt efte to youre damysell, madame.

UXOR PILATI
In thy hande, holde nowe and have here.

ANCILLA
Gramarcy, my lady so dere.

PILATUS
Nowe fares-wele, and walke on youre way.

71 protocol 73 seigneur/lord, sun 74 strength (of) his beams is reduced 75 descends from 76 glittering 77 goes, beams 78 approaching now 80 brightness 81 Quickly, go to her rooms 82 sit (in judgement), limb 83 not lawful 84 once, grows dim 86 leave, while it is light 87 going 89 advised us correctly 95 What are you doing? 96 my beauty 97 what I promised you is here 98 assay (try it!), seriously, quickly 99 please, go first 101 kill all this argument 104 also, hand-maiden 106 Thankyou

[7] 'How does it help to praise his words?'
[8] 'You may not judge once you have been dreaming'. This may be an elaborate way of saying that the judgement will not wait until tomorrow, but must be made before he goes to sleep.
[9] 'As she may stumble in the street unless she stalwartly stands. The Beadle may be diplomatically suggesting that Procula's immediate departure would be in her own best interests, as she will find it more difficult to get to her chamber if it gets any darker.
[10] 'I prepare to leave [now], to obey your command. My lord, with your permission, I will not delay you any further.'
[11] 'It would be a slight upon me if you left me unceremoniously, or crept away from here without first having a drink of wine. You will go happily once you have drunk a little.'
[12] 'If it pleases you, my own lord, I do not need lessons in this subject.'

UXOR PILATI
Now farewele, þe frendlyest, youre fomen to fende.

PILATUS
Nowe farewele, þe fayrest figure þat evere did fode fede,
And farewele, ye damysell, indede.

ANCILLA
My lorde, I comande me to youre ryalte.

PILATUS
Fayre lady, here is schall you lede.
Sir, go with þis worthy in dede,
And what scho biddis you doo loke þat buxsome you be.[13]

FILIUS
I am prowde and preste to passe on apasse,
To go with þis gracious hir gudly to gyde.

PILATUS
Take tente to my tale þou turne on no trayse,
Come tyte and telle me yf any tythyngis betyde.

FILIUS
Yf any tythyngis my lady betyde,
I schall full sone, sir, witte you to say.
This semely schall I schewe by hir side
Belyffe, sir, no lenger we byde.

PILATUS
Nowe fares-wele, and walkes on youre way.

Nowe wente is my wiffe, yf it wer not hir will,
And scho rakis tille hir reste as of nothyng scho rought.
Tyme is, I telle þe[e], þou tente me untill;
And buske þe[e] belyve, belamy, to bedde þat Y wer broght
And loke I be rychely arrayed.

BEDELLUS
Als youre servaunte I have sadly it sought,
And þis nyght, sir, newe schall ye noght,
I dare laye, fro ye luffely be layde.

PILATUS
I comaunde þe[e] to come nere, for I will kare to my couche.
Have in thy handes hendely and heve me fro hyne,
But loke þat þou tene me not with þi tastyng, but tendirly me touche.

BEDELLUS
A, sir, yhe whe wele.

PILATUS
Yha, I have wette me with wyne.
Yhit helde doune and lappe me even [here],
For I will slelye slepe unto synne.
Loke þat no man nor no myron of myne
With no noyse be neghand me nere.

BEDELLUS
Sir, what warlowe yow wakens with wordis full wilde,
Þat boy for his brawlyng were bettir be unborne.

PILATUS
Yha, who chatteres, hym chastise, be he churle or childe,
For and he skape skatheles itt were to us a grete skorne;
Yf skatheles he skape it wer a skorne.
What rebalde þat redely will rore,
I schall mete with þat myron tomorne
And for his ledir lewdenes hym lerne to be lorne.

BEDELLUS
Whe! So, sir, slepe ye, and saies no more.

UXOR PILATI
Nowe are we at home. Do helpe yf ye may,
For I will make me redye and rayke to my reste.

108 to destroy your enemies 109 individual, ever ate food 111 commend, royalty 112 (one) who shall lead you 115 prepared, proceed apace 116 and guide her well 117 pay attention to, don't waver 118 anything (untoward) happens 119 happens to my lady 120 come and tell you 121 I will stay, properly 122 Quickly 124 gone, (even) if she didn't want to 125 goes to, if she had no cares 126 It is time, pay attention to me 127 good friend 128 make sure 129 diligently prepared 130 nothing shall disturb you 131 I wager, once, are lovingly laid 132 go 133 use, skilfully, lift, here 134 handling 135 you weigh well! 136 tuck me up just here 137 sleep deeply, until later 138 servant 139 makes any noise near me 141 he'd wish he was never born 142 punish anyone who talks 143 shame 145 villain, readily, roar 146 meet him, tomorrow 147 evil, teach him how to die 148 say 150 go

[13] 'And make sure you are obedient, whatever she asks [of you].'

Ancilla
Yhe are werie, madame, for-wente of youre way,
Do boune you to bedde, for þat holde I beste.

Filius
Here is a bedde arayed of þe beste.

Uxor Pilati
Do happe me, and faste hense ye hye.

Ancilla
Madame, anone all dewly is dressid.

Filius
With no stalkyng nor no striffe be ye stressed.

Uxor Pilati
Nowe be yhe in pese, both youre carpyng and crye.

Diabolus
Owte! Owte! Harrowe! Into bale am I brought.

This bargayne may I banne,
But yf Y wirke some wile, in wo mon I wonne.[14]
This gentilman, Jesu, of cursednesse He can;
Be any syngne þat I see þis same is Goddis Sonne.
And He be slone oure solace will sese,
He will save man saule fro oure sonde
And refe us þe remys þat are rounde.
I will on stiffely in þis stounde
Unto ser Pilate wiffe, pertely, and putte me in prese.

O woman, be wise and ware, and wonne in þi witte
Ther schall a gentilman, Jesu, unjustely be juged
Byfore thy husband in haste, and with harlottis be hytte.
And þat doughty today to deth þus be dyghted,
Sir Pilate, for His prechyng, and þou,
With nede schalle ye namely be noyed;
Youre stuffe and youre strenghe schal be stroyed,
Youre richesse schal be refte you þat is rude,
With vengeaunce, and þat dare I avowe.[15]

Uxor Pilati
A, I am drecchid with a dreme full dredfully to dowte.
Say childe, rise uppe radly and reste for no roo,
Thow muste launce to my lorde and lowly hym lowte,
Comaunde me to his reverence, as right will Y doo.

Filius
O, what schall I travayle þus tymely þis tyde?
Madame, for the drecchyng of Heven,
Slyke note is newsome to neven
And it neghes unto mydnyght full even.

Uxor Pilati
Go bette, boy, I bidde no lenger þou byde,

And saie to my sovereyne þis same is soth þat I send hym:
All naked þis nyght as I napped
With tene and with trayne was I trapped,
With a swevene þat swiftely me swapped
Of one Jesu, þe juste man þe Jewes will undoo.
She prayes tente to þat trewe man with tyne be noȝt trapped,[16]

But als a domesman dewly to be dressand,
And lelye delyvere þat lede.

Filius
Madame, I am dressid to þat dede,
But firste will I nappe in þis nede,
For he hase mystir of a morne-slepe þat mydnyght is myssand.[17]

Anna
Sir Cayphas, ye kenne wele this caytiffe we have cached

151 weary, tired by walking 152 prepare, for, I believe to be 154 tuck me up, go away quickly 155 anon, duly 156 creeping about, clamour 157 Be quiet, shouting 158 calamity 159 situation, curse 161 He knows (all) about cursedness 162 sign, He is God's son 163 If He is killed, happiness ends 164 man's soul, control 165 and take us from, realms 166 work resolutely, what time is left 167 cunningly, make an attempt 168 watchful, hold 170 beaten by villains 171 resolute (man), condemned 177 tormented 178 ease 179 hurry, bow deeply to him 180 commend, just as I would 181 what do I have to do at this time 183 such talk is annoying to hear 184 it's nearly midnight 185 get on with it! 186 what I tell him is true 188 trouble 189 struck me 190 the Jews want to destroy 192 act like a just judge 193 loyally/correctly, set free, man 194 prepared for 195 as I need to 197 caught

[14] 'Unless I can work some trick, I must live in sorrow.'
[15] '[If this happens] because of His preaching, Sir Pilate and you will be afflicted with poverty; your goods and authority will be destroyed, your riches will be roughly taken from you in vengeance, you have my word for it.'
[16] 'Say that she prays that you take heed that that true man is not trapped by [others'] anger.'
[17] 'He who loses sleep at midnight has to make it up in the morning.'

That ofte-tymes in oure Tempill hase teched untrewly.
Oure meyne with myght at mydnyght hym mached
And hase drevyn hym till his demyng for his dedis undewly;[18]
Wherfore I counsaile þat kyndely we carie
Unto ser Pilate oure prince, and pray hym
That he for oure right will arraye hym
This faitour, for his falsed to flay hym;
For fro we saie hym þe soth I schall sitte hym full sore.[19]

Cayphas
Sir Anna, þis sporte have ye spedely aspied,
As I am pontificall prince of all prestis.
We will prese to ser Pilate, and presente hym with pride
With þis harlott þat has hewed oure hartis fro oure brestis
Thurgh talkyng of tales untrewe. And þerfor, ser knyghtis . . .

Milites
Lorde?

Cayphas
Sir knyghtis þat are curtayse and kynde,
We charge you þat chorle be wele chyned.
Do buske you and grathely hym bynde,
And rugge hym in ropes his rase till he rewe.

I Miles
Sir, youre sawes schall be serued schortely and sone.
Yha, do felawe, be thy feith; late us feste þis faitour full fast.

II Miles
I am douty to þis dede, delyver, have done;
Latte us pulle on with pride till his poure be paste.

I Miles
Do have faste and halde at his handes.

II Miles
For this same is he þat lightly avaunted,
And God Sone he grathely hym graunted.

I Miles
He bese hurled for þe highnes he haunted;[20]
Loo, he stonyes for us, he stares where he standis.

II Miles
Nowe is the brothell boune for all þe boste þat he blowne,
And þe laste day he lete no lordynges myȝt lawne hyme.[21]

Anna
Ya, he wende þis worlde had bene haly his awne.
Als ye are dowtiest today tille his demyng ye drawe hym,
And þan schall we kenne how þat he canne excuse hym.

I Miles
Here, ye gomes, gose a-rome, giffe us gate,
We muste steppe to yone sterne of astate.

II Miles
We muste yappely wende in at þis yate,
For he þat comes to courte, to curtesye muste use hym.

I Miles
Do rappe on, the renkis þat we may rayse with oure rolyng.[22]
Come forthe, sir coward, why cowre ye behynde?

Bedellus
O, what javellis are ye þat jappis with gollyng?

I Miles
A, goode sir, be noȝt wroth, for wordis are as þe wynde.

198 taught 199 retinue, attacked 201 as custom demands, we go 203 will provide for our rights 204 falsehood 206 idea, quickly, noticed 207 (highest) of priests 208 go, proudly 209 cut 210+ Knights 211 courteous 212 chained 214 pull, until he regrets his deeds 215 quickly performed 216 tie up, tightly 217 hurry, get on with it! 218 his strength is gone 219 have (him) tied fast 220 freely boasted 221 claimed seriously to be 223 is astonished at us 226 believed, would be his alone 227 strongest, to, drag 228 if he can, himself 229 people, make way! give us room! 230 go to that star of estate 231 swiftly, go in, gate 232 must behave courteously 234 cower 235 fools, jest with (such) noise 236 like, wind (i.e. merely air)

[18] 'And has driven him to judgement for his improper deeds'.

[19] 'If we tell him [Pilate] the truth, it will be very bad for [Jesus].'

[20] 'He is punished [now] for the authority he aspired to.'

[21] 'Now is the wretch bound, despite all his boasts. He believed that on the Last Day, not even lords would [be able to] overthrow him.'

[22] 'Bang again, that we might wake the men [inside] with our commotion.'

BEDELLUS
I saye, gedlynges, gose bakke with youre gawdes.

II MILES
Be sufferand, I beseke you,
And more of þis matere yhe meke yowe.

BEDELLUS
Why, unconand knaves, an I cleke yowe,
I schall felle yowe, be my faith, for all youre false frawdes.

PILATUS
Say, childe, ill cheffe you! What churlles are so claterand?[23]

BEDELLUS
My lorde, unconand knaves þei crye and þei call.

PILATUS
Gose baldely beliffe and þos brethellis be batt[er]and,
And putte þam in prisoune uppon peyne þat may fall.
Yha, spedely spir þam yf any sporte can þei spell,
Yha, and loke what lordingis þei be.

BEDELLUS
My lorde þat is luffull in lee,
I am boxsom and blithe to your blee.

PILATUS
And if they talke any tythyngis come tyte and me tell.

BEDELLUS
My felawes, by youre faith, can ye talke any tythandis?

I MILES
Yha, sir, sir Cayphas and Anna ar come both togedir
To sir Pilate o Pounce and prince of oure lawe;
And þei have laughte a lorell þat is lawles and liddir.

BEDELUS
My lorde, my lorde!

PILATUS
Howe?

BEDELLUS
My lorde, unlappe yow belyve where ye lye.
Sir Cayphas to youre courte is caried,
And Sir Anna, but a traytour hem taried.
Many wight of þat warlowe has waried,
They have brought hym in a bande his balis to bye.

PILATUS
But are thes sawes certayne in soth þat þou saies?

BEDELLUS
Yha, lorde, þe states yondir standis, for striffe are they stonden.

PILATUS
Now þan am I light as a roo, and ethe for to rayse.
Go bidde þam come in both, and the boye þey have boune.

BEDELLUS
Siris, my lorde geves leve inne for to come.

CAYPHAS
Hayle, prince þat is pereles in price,
Ye are leder of lawes in þis lande,
Youre helpe is full hendely at hande.

ANNA
Hayle, stronge in youre state for to stande,
Alle þis dome muste be dressed at youre dulye devyse.[24]

PILATUS
Who is there, my prelates?

CAYPHAS
Yha, lorde.

237 go, games 238 patient 239 you will learn 240 foolish, if I catch you 241 knock you down, frauds 244 boldly, batter those villains 245 pain of death 246 speedily ask, tell us 247 who they are 248 lovely in brightness 249 to your mood 250 tell of 254 caught, lawless, wicked 255 what? 256 get up 257 come 258 delayed them 259 people, cursed 260 bound, to pay for his evil deeds 261 claims true 262 lords 263 roe (deer), eager to get up 265 gives 266 peerless in renown 268 available 269 authority

[23] 'Say, boy, curse you! What wretches are so clamorous?'

[24] 'All this judgement [i.e. these proceedings] must be arranged under your proper authority.'

Pilatus
Nowe be ȝe welcome, iwiss.

Cayphas
Gramercy, my soverayne. But we beseke you all same
Bycause of wakand you unwarly be noght wroth with þis,
For we have brought here a lorell; he lokis like a lambe.

Pilatus
Come byn, you bothe, and to þe benke brayde yowe.

Cayphas
Nay, gud sir, laugher is leffull for us.[25]

Pilatus
A, sir Cayphas, be curtayse yhe bus.

Anna
Nay, goode lorde, it may not be þus.

Pilatus
Sais no more, but come sitte you beside me in sorowe as I saide youe.

Filius
Hayle, þe semelieste seeg undir sonne sought,
Hayle, þe derrest duke and doughtiest in dede.

Pilatus
Now bene-veneuew, beuscher, what boodworde haste þou brought?
Hase any langour my lady newe laught in þis leede?[26]

Filius
Sir, þat comely comaundes hir youe too,
And sais, al nakid þis nyght as sche napped
With tene and with traye was sche trapped,
With a swevene þat swiftely hir swapped
Of one Jesu, þe juste man þe Jewes will undo.
She beseches you as hir soverayne þat symple to save,
Deme hym noght to deth for drede of vengeaunce.

Pilatus
What, I hope þis be he þat hyder harlid ȝe have.

Cayphas
Ya, sir, þe same and þe selffe, but þis is but a skaunce,
He with wicchecrafte þis wile has he wrought.
Some feende of his sand has he sente
And warned youre wiffe or he wente.

[Pilatus]
Yowe! Þat schalke shuld not shamely be shente,
Þis is sikir in certayne, and soth schulde be sought.

Anna
Yha, thurgh his fantome and falshed and fendes-craft
He has wroght many wondir where he walked full wyde,
Wherfore, my lorde, it wer leeffull his liffe were hym rafte.

Pilatus
Be ye nevere so bryme, ye boþe bus abide
But if þe traytoure be taught for untrewe,
And þerfore sermones you no more.
I will sekirly sende hymselffe fore,
And se what he sais to þe sore.
Bedell, go brynge hyme, for of þat renke have I rewþe.

Bedellus
This forward to fulfille am I fayne in myn herte moved.
Say, Jesu, þe juges and þe Jewes hase me enioyned
To bringe Þe[e] before þam even bounden as Þou arte.
Yone lordyngis to lose Þe[e] full longe have þei heyned,
But firste schall I wirschippe Þe[e] with witte and with will.

273 if we rudely awoke you 275 in, approach the bench 277 you must be courteous 279 soberly 280 most noble man, under the sun 281 dearest, mightiest, deeds 284 that beautiful (one), to you 289 simple (man) 291 think, you have brought here 292 the very same, deception 293 trick 294 demon, as his agent 295 before 296 man, falsely, ruined 297 true, if truth be known 298 magic, deception, fiends' 299 wherever he went 300 lawful, taken from him 301 angry 302 Unless, revealed as a liar 303 speak 304 send for him 305 in answer to the charges 306 Beadle, I have pity 307 This errand greatly moves me 308 have ordered me 310 have long waited to ruin you

[25] 'Lower [i.e. further away from the dais] is [more] appropriate for us.' The priests are anxious to avoid entering the hall, as to do so would pollute their ritual purity and so mean that they cannot take part in the Passover celebrations the next day.

[26] Now 'bienvenue [welcome], good sir, what message have you brought? Has my lady newly caught any sickness here?'

This reverence I do Þe[e] forthy,
For wytes þat wer wiser þan I
They worshipped Þe[e] full holy on hy
And with solempnite sange 'Osanna' till.

I MILES
My lorde þat is leder of lawes in þis lande,
All bedilis to your biding schulde be boxsome and bayne,
And ȝitt þis boy here before yowe full boldely was bowand
To worschippe þis warlowe; methynke we wirke all in vayne.

II MILES
Yha, and in youre presence he prayed hym of pees,
In knelyng on knes to þis knave,
He besoughte hym his servaunte to save.

CAIPHAS
Loo, lord, such arrore amange þem þei have
It is grete sorowe to see, no seeg may it sese.

It is no menske to youre manhed, þat mekill is of myght
To forbere such forfettis þat falsely are feyned,
Such spites in especiall wolde be eschewed in your sight.

PILATUS
Sirs, moves you noȝt in þis matere but bese myldely demeaned,
For yone curtasie I kenne had som cause.[27]

ANNA
In youre sight, sir, þe soth schall I saye,
As ye are prince, take hede I you praye,
Such a lourdayne unlele, dare I laye,
Many lordis of oure landis might lede fro oure lawes.

PILATUS
Saye, losell, who gave þe[e] leve so for to lowte to yone ladde,
And solace hym in my sight so semely þat I saw?

BEDELLUS
A, gracious lorde, greve you noght, for gude case I hadde.
Yhe comaunded me to care, als ye kende wele and knawe,
To Jerusalem on a journay, with seele;
And þan þis semely on an asse was sette
And many men myldely Hym mette,
Als a god in þat grounde þai Hym grette,
Wele semand Hym in waye with worschippe lele.

'Osanna' þei sange, 'þe Sone of David',
Riche men with þare robes þei ranne to His fete,
And poure folke fecched floures of þe frith
And made myrthe and melody þis man for to mete.

PILATUS
Nowe, gode sir, be þi feith, what is 'Osanna' to saie?[28]

BEDELLUS
Sir, constrew it we may be langage of þis lande as I leve,
It is als moche to me for to meve,
Youre prelatis in þis place can it preve,
Als, 'oure saviour and soverayne Þou save us we praye'.

PILATUS
Loo, seniioures, how semes yow? Þe soþe I you saide.

CAYPHAS
Yha, lorde, þis ladde is full liddir, be þis light.
Yf his sawes wer serchid and sadly assaied,
Save youre reverence, his resoune þei rekenne noȝt with right.
This caytiffe þus cursedly can construe us.[29]

BEDELLUS
Sirs, trulye þe trouþe I have tolde
Of þis wighte ȝe have wrapped in wolde.

312 for this reason 313 wiser minds than I 314 devoutly 315 solemnity, sang 'Hosanna' to you 317 beadles 318 bowing 322 begged him 323 error/heresy 324 no one can stop it 326 tolerate, crimes, practised 327 insults, forbidden 332 disloyal rogue, wager 333 might lead into disobedience 335 succour 336 do not grieve, cause 337 go, understand 338 appropriately 339 at that time, noble (man) 340 greeted him 341 as a god, there, greeted 342 fittingly on the road, loyal 345 fetched flowers from the fields 348 translate, as I believe 349 I think that it means . . . 350 confirm 352 What do you think (now)? 353 wicked, by 358 locked up

[27] 'Sirs, do not get excited about this business, but be mild-mannered, for I am sure that he [the Beadle] had some reason for [performing] that courtesy.'

[28] 'Now, good sir, by your faith, what does "Hosanna" mean?'

[29] 'If his words were investigated and seriously examined, save your reverence, his arguments would not accord with the truth. This villain translates [for] us maliciously.'

ANNA
I saie, harlott, thy tonge schulde ȝou holde,
And noght agaynste þi maistirs to meve þus.

PILATUS
Do sese of youre seggyng, and I schall examyne full sore.

ANNA
Sir, demes hym to deth or dose hym away.

PILATUS
Sir, have ye saide?

ANNA
Yha, lorde.

PILATUS
Nowe go sette you with sorowe and care,
For I will lose no lede þat is lele to oure lay.[30]
But steppe furth and stonde uppe on hight
And buske to my bidding, þou boy,
And for þe nones þat þou neven us a noy.

BEDELLUS
I am here at youre hande to halow a hoy,
Do move of youre maistir for I shall melle it with myȝt.[31]

PILATUS
Cry 'Oyas'.

BEDELLUS
Oyas!

PILATUS
Yit efte, be þi feithe.

BEDELLUS
Oyas! (*Alowde*).

PILATUS
Yit lowdar, that ilke lede may light.
Crye pece in this prese, uppon payne þeruppon,
Bidde them swage of þer sweying bothe swiftely and swithe,
And stynte of þer stryvyng and stande still as a stone.
Calle Jesu þe gentill of Jacob, þe Jewe.
Come preste and appere,
To þe barre drawe þe[e] nere,
To þi jugement here,
To be demed for his dedis undewe.

I MILES
Whe, harke how þis harlott he heldis oute of harre,
This lotterelle liste noght my lorde to lowte.

II MILES
Say, beggar, why brawlest þou? Go boune þe[e] to þe barre.

I MILES
Steppe on thy standyng so sterne and so stoute.

II MILES
Steppe on thy standyng so still.

I MILES
Sir cowarde, to courte muste yhe care . . .

II MILES
A lessoune to lerne of oure lawe.

I MILES
Flitte fourthe, foule myght ȝou fare!

II MILES
Say, warlowe, þou wantist of þi will.

FILIUS
O Jesu ungentill, þi joie is in japes,
Þu can not be curtayse, þou caytiffe I calle þe[e],
No ruthe were it to rug þe[e] and ryve þe[e] in ropes.
Why falles þou noȝt flatte here, foule falle þe[e]
For ferde of my fadir so free?
Þou wotte noght his wisdome, iwys,
All thyne helpe in his hande þat it is,
Howe sone he myght save þe[e] fro þis.
Obeye hym, brothell, I bidde þe[e].

360 don't argue against your masters 361 arguing, severely 362 condemn, do away with him 363 have you finished? 367 for now, cry out a cry for me 368 call out a cry 370 'Hear ye!' (the town crier's cry), And again, louder 371 every person, hear 372 crowd 373 stop, noise, quickly 374 efforts 375 (of the race) of Jacob 376 quickly 379 unlawful 380 acts unhinged 381 wretch, doesn't want to bow 382 do you wrangle, move 384 step to your place 387 get going, curse you! 388 you've lost your mind 389 ignoble, you're always joking 391 It would not be a pity to 392 curse you 393 fear, generous/noble 394 you do not understand 395 your only chance of help is 396 easily

[30] 'Now sit down and behave yourself soberly and meekly, for I will not lose anyone who is loyal to my laws.'

[31] 'Tell me your desire, and I shall shout it out with vigour.'

Pilatus
Now Jesu, þou art welcome ewys, as I wene,
Be noȝt abasshed but boldely boune to þe barre;
What seyniour will sewe for þe[e] sore I have sene.[32]
To wirke on þis warlowe, his witte is in warre.
Come preste, of a payne, and appere,
And sir prelatis, youre pontes bes prevyng.
What cause can ye caste of accusyng?
Þis mater ye marke to be meving,
And hendly in haste late us here.

Cayphas
Sir Pilate o Pounce and prince of greate price,
We triste ye will trowe oure tales þei be trewe,
To deth for to deme hym with dewly device.
For cursidnesse yone knave hase in case, if ye knew,
In harte wolde ye hate hym in hye.
For if it wer so,
We mente not to misdo;
Triste, ser, schall ye þerto,
We hadde not hym taken to þe[e].[33]

Pilatus
Sir, youre tales wolde I trowe but þei touche none
entente.[34]
What cause can ye fynde nowe þis freke for to felle?

Anna
Oure Sabbotte he saves not, but sadly assente
To wirke full unwisely, þis wote I riȝt wele,
He werkis whane he will, wele I wote,
And þerfore in herte we hym hate.
Itt sittis you, to strenghe youre estate
Yone losell to louse for his lay.

Pilatus
Ilke a lede for to louse for his lay is not lele.
Youre lawes is leffull, but to youre lawis longis it
Þis faitoure to feese wele with flappes full fele,
And woo may ye wirke hym be lawe, for he wranges
it.[35]
Therfore takes unto you full tyte,
And like as youre lawes will you lede
Ye deme hym to deth for his dede.

Cayphas
Nay, nay, sir, þat dome muste us drede,

It longes noȝt till us no lede for to lose.

Pilatus
What wolde ye I did þanne? Þe Devyll motte you
drawe!
Full fewe are his frendis but fele are his fooes.
His liff for to lose þare longes no lawe,[36]
Nor no cause can I kyndely contryve
Þat why he schulde lose þus his liffe.

Anna
A, gude sir, it raykes full ryffe
In steedis wher he has stirrid mekill striffe
Of ledis þat is lele to youre liffe.[37]

Cayphas
Sir, halte men and hurte he helid in haste,
The deffe and þe dome he delyvered fro doole,
By wicchecrafte, I warande, his wittis schall waste,
For þe farles þat he farith with, loo how þei folowe
yone fole,
Oure folke so þus he frayes in fere.

Anna
The dede he rayses anone;
Þis Lazare þat lowe lay allone,
He graunte hym his gates for to gone,
And pertely þus proved he his poure.

Pilatus
Now, goode siris, I saie, what wolde yhe seme?

401 his mind is confused 402 quickly, or be punished 403 prove your allegations 404 what charges can you bring? 405 this case, begin 406 courteously, hear 409 due process (of law) 410 is planning wickedness 413 intended not to offend 417 to bring down this man 418 does not observe 419 I know very well 420 works when he wants to 422 is best for, authority 423 punish, behaviour 429 determine 431 we must avoid 432 it is not in our power, kill 433 then, (May) . . . take you! 434 but many are his foes 436 legitimately contrive 441 lame, healed 442 dumb, from misery 444 performs 445 thus he terrifies our people 447 Lazarus, was laid low 448 allowed, walk on his way 449 rudely demonstrated, power 450 what do you want?

[32] 'I have seen how the nobles are intent upon destroying you.'
[33] 'Believe us, sir, [if this had not been the case] we would not have brought him to you.'
[34] 'They do not prove [criminal] intent.'
[35] 'It is not legal to kill each person [just] because of his behaviour. It is a matter for your court to deal with this deceiver with fierce blows, and you can cause him great woe, as he broke your laws.' Pilate sees no cause to convict Jesus under Roman civil law, and so suggests that the priests try him for Sabbath-breaking in the Jewish ecclesiastical courts.
[36] 'There is no law that will condemn him to death'.
[37] 'Ah, good sir, it [disorder] spreads everywhere in places in which he has stirred great trouble among folk [previously] loyal to you.'

Caiphas
Sir, to dede for to do hym, or dose hym adawe.

Pilatus
Yha, for he dose wele his deth for to deme?
Go layke you, sir, lightly; wher lerned ye such lawe?
This touches no tresoune, I telle you.
Yhe prelatis þat proved are for price,
Yhe schulde be boþe witty and wise
And legge oure lawe wher it lyse,
Oure materes ye meve þus emel you.

Anna
Misplese noȝt youre persone, yhe prince withouten
pere,
It touches to tresoune, þis tale I schall tell:
Yone briboure full baynly he bed to forbere
The tribute to þe emperoure, þus wolde he compell
Oure pepill þus his poyntis to applye.

Cayphas
The pepull he saies he schall save,
And Criste garres he calle hym, yone knave,
And sais he will þe high kyngdome have.
Loke whethir he deserve to dye.

Pilatus
To dye he deserves yf he do þus indede,
But Y will se myselffe what he sais.
Speke Jesu, and spende nowe þi space for to spede.
Þez lordyngis þei legge þe þou liste noȝt leve on
oure lawes,
They accuse þe[e] cruelly and kene;
And þerfore as a chiftene Y charge þe[e]
Iff þou be Criste, þat þou telle me,
And God Sone þou grughe not to graunte þe[e],[38]
For þis is þe matere þat Y mene.

Jesus
Þou saiste so þiselve. I am sothly þe same
Here wonnyng in worlde to wirke al þi will.
My Fadir is faithfull to felle all þi fame;
Withouten trespas or tene am I taken þe[e] till.

Pilatus
Loo, busshoppis, why blame ye þis boye?
Me semys þat it is soth þat he saies.
Ye meve all þe malice ye may
With youre wrenchis and wiles to wrythe hym away,
Unjustely to juge hym fro joie.

Cayphas
Nought so, sir, his seggyng is full sothly soth,
It bryngis oure bernes in bale for to bynde.

Anna
Sir, douteles we deme als dewe of þe deth,
Þis foole þat ye favour, grete fautes can we fynde
This daye for to deme hym to dye.

Pilatus
Saie, losell, þou lies, be þis light!
Saie, þou rebalde, þou rekens unright.

Cayphas
Avise you, sir, with mayne and with myght,
And wreke not youre wrethe nowe forthy.

Pilatus
Me likes noȝt his langage so largely for to lye.

Cayphas
A, mercy lorde, mekely, no malice we mente.

Pilatus
Noo done is it douteles, balde and be blithe,
Talke on þat traytoure and telle youre entente.
Yone segge is sotell, ye saie;
Gud sirs, wer lerned he such lare?

Cayphas
In faith, we can not fynde whare.

Pilatus
Yhis, his fadir with some farlis gan fare
And has lered þis ladde of his lare.

451 put him to death 453 carry on joking 457 allege/interpret, as it is 459 Do not be angry 461 told (folk), withold 462 taxes, teach/order 463 to practise his preaching 465 he calls himself 467 Decide (now) 470 use your time profitably 471 do not believe in 472 sharply 473 as your lord 477 yourself 478 living in the world 479 end 480 crime or anger (on my part) 482 It seems to me 483 use 484 tricks, deceptions, ruin him 485 to end his joy 486 Not so, (if) his claims are true 487 will bind our children in misery 488 to be worthy of 489 faults 491 by 492 wretch, conclude falsely 493 Consider, strength 494 avenge, wrath, therefore 495 him to speak so freely 497 Now, it (my anger) is done, bold 499 subtle 500 where, such wisdom? 502 dabbled in marvels/magic 503 taught his son, lore

[38] 'And [you] do not grudge to call yourself the Son of God'.

ANNA
Nay, nay, sir, he was but a write, þat we wiste.
No sotelte he schewed þat any segge saw.

PILATUS
Thanne mene yhe of malice to marre hym of myght,
Of cursidnesse convik no cause call yhe knawe?
Me mervellis ye malyngne o mys.[39]

CAYPHAS
Sir, fro Galely hidir and hoo
The gretteste agayne hym ganne goo,
Yone warlowe to waken of woo,
And of þis werke beres witnesse, ywis.

PILATUS
Why, and hase he gone in Galely, yone gedlyng ongayne?

ANNA
Yha, lorde, þer was he borne, yone brethelle, and bredde.

PILATUS
Nowe, withouten fagyng, my frendis, in faith I am fayne,
For now schall oure striffe full sternely be stede.
Sir Herowde is kyng þer, ye kenne,
His poure is preved full preste
To ridde hym or reve hym of rest.
And þerfore, to go with yone gest
Yhe marke us oute of þe manliest men.

CAYPHAS
Als witte and wisdome youre will schal be wroght,
Here is kempis full kene to þe kyng for to care.

PILATUS
Nowe, seniours, I saie yow, sen soth schall be soght,
But if he schortely be sente it may sitte us full sore.
And þerfore, sir knyghtis . . .

[MILITES]
Lorde?

PILATUS
Sir knyghtis þat are cruell and kene,
That warlowe ye warrok and wraste,
And loke þat he brymly be braste.
Do take on þat traytoure you betwene.

Tille Herowde in haste with þat harlott ye hye,
Comaunde me full mekely unto his moste myght.
Saie þe dome of his boy, to deme hym to dye,
Is done upponne hym dewly, to dresse or to dight,
Or liffe for to leve at his liste.
Say ought I may do hym indede,
His awne am I worthely in wede.

I MILES
My lorde, we schall springe on a-spede.
Come þens! To me þis traitoure full tyte.

PILATUS
Bewe sirs, I bidde you ye be not to bolde,
But takes tente for oure tribute full trulye to trete.

II MILES
Mi lorde, we schall hye þis beheste for to halde,
And wirke it full wisely in wille and in witte.

PILATUS
So, sirs, me semys itt is sittand.

I MILES
Mahounde, sirs, he menske you with myght.

II MILES
And save you, sir, semely in sight.

PILATUS
Now in þe wilde vengeaunce ye walke with þat wight,
And fresshely ye founde to be flittand.

504 only a carpenter 505 anyone noticed 509 Galilee, here and there 510 Most (people) flock to him 511 to (be) inspired to evil by 512 bear 513 awkward wretch 514 there, villain, raised 515 deceiving (you) 516 argument be decisively ended 517 Herod 518 known to be enough 519 release (Jesus), deprive 520 prisoner 521 choose for us the 523 are warriors, to go to 525 Unless, quickly, be bad for us 528 bind, twist 529 fiercely, beaten 530 between you 531 To, go 532 Commend, great power 534 Devolves upon him by right 535 his life, to spare, at his pleasure 536 anything, do for him 537 I am at his disposal, all things 538 hurry on apace 539 Let's go! (Bring) to me 540 Good sirs, too bold 541 remember to mention 542 fulfil 544 I think it is fitting 547 for a violent 548 swiftly hurry to go

[39] 'Then do you intend to destroy him by force, since you know of no [legitimate] cause to convict him [in law]? I marvel that you continue to malign him falsely.'

York (The Litsters), *Christ Before Herod*

This pageant represents Christ's interrogation at the court of King Herod Antipas, Tetrarch of Galilee and Peraea, the main account of which is in Luke 23:8–11. Of all the York tyrants, Herod is perhaps the most ridiculous as well as the most vicious-tempered. A pampered and rather dim-witted bully, his interest in Jesus lies in the possibility of entertainment which He seems to offer. Intrigued by what he interprets as Jesus's reputation for conjuring and trickery, Herod seeks by various means to goad Him into performing for his benefit. The contrast between the tyrant's blustering 'byg blure' (loud voice: l. 252) and Christ's silence is perhaps the most effective use of counterpoint in the Cycle. The interrogation culminates in the visually powerful moment (l. 353 onwards) when Jesus is dressed by His tormentors in a white gown (mentioned in the biblical sources but here reinterpreted as an equivalent of the motley coat of the court fool). Rather than symbolizing His folly, the garment effectively symbolizes Christ's purity amid the gaudiness of the Herodian court.

A notable feature of the pageant is the absurd attempt of Herod and his Dukes to reproduce the French language and manners characteristic of the refined chivalric courts of medieval western Europe. The result is a stilted mixture of deference and bluster conducted in a bizarre (and at times almost incomprehensible) Franglais considerably more barbarous than the 'Stratford at Bow' French for which Chaucer gently mocked his Prioress (see *The General Prologue* to *The Canterbury Tales*, l. 125). This motif both creates much of the pageant's cruel humour, and revisits the theme of linguistic self-fashioning begun with the Fall of Lucifer, and given a contemporary social and political resonance in Mak's adoption of a southern accent and manners in the Towneley *Second Shepherds' Play*.

The pageant is metrically very diverse, and the manuscript shows distinct signs of corruption (see 'Textual Variants', p. 624). The main stanza form has fourteen lines, but quatrains and other irregular stanzas also appear frequently. Two locations are employed, Herod's hall (on the pageant wagon) and the approach to his palace (at ground level).

The Litsters were cloth dyers, and so well placed to provide the white garment in which Christ is dressed.

[*Dramatis Personae*: *Rex* (King Herod), *II Dux* (two 'Dukes', members of Herod's court), *Jesus*, *II Miles* (two Soldiers guarding Jesus), *I–III Filius* (Herod's three Sons).]

[REX]
Pes, ye brothellis and browlys in þis broydenesse inbrased,
And freykis þat are frendely your freykenesse to frayne,
Youre tounges fro tretyng of triffillis be trased,[1]
Or þis brande þat is bright schall breste in youre brayne.
Plextis for no plasis but platte you to þis playne,
And drawe to no drolyng but dresse you to drede,
With dasshis.
Traveylis noȝt as traytours þat tristis in trayne,
Or by þe bloode þat Mahounde bledde, with þis blad schal ye blede.
Þus schall I brittyn all youre bones on brede,
Ȝae, and lusshe all youre lymmys with lasschis.

Dragons þat are dredfull schall derke in þer dennes
In wrathe when we writhe, or in wrathenesse ar wapped.
Agaynste jeauntis ongentill have we joined with ingendis,
And swannys þat are swymmyng to oure swetnes schall be suapped,
And joged doune þer jolynes, oure gentries engenderand.[2]
Whoso repreve oure estate we schall choppe þam in cheynes,
All renkkis þat are renand to us schall be reverande.

5 Contest, places, sit down, ground 6 begin, commotion, act soberly 7 (for fear of) blows 8 Work, who trust, deceit 9 blade 10 chop, completely 11 beat, limbs, lashes 12 cower, dens 13 wroth, enveloped in rage 17 reprove, clap, chains 18 running, reverential

[1] 'Peace, you rogues and wretches gathered in this broad place, and [you] friendly folk, [that you may] learn [proper] manliness, restrain your tongues from talking of [mere] trifles'.

[2] 'We have battled against brutish giants with [siege] engines, and swans that are swimming shall be struck [down] at our pleasure, and their joy condemned to enhance our honour.'

Therfore I bidde you sese or any bale be,
Þat no brothell be so bolde boste for to blowes.
And ȝe þat luffis youre liffis, listen to me
As a lorde þat is lerned to lede you be lawes.
And ye þat are of my men and of my menȝe,
Sen we are comen fro oure kyth as ȝe wele knawes,
And semlys all here same in þis cyte,
It sittis us in sadnesse to sette all oure sawes.

PRIMUS DUX
My lorde, we schall take kepe to youre call,
And stirre to no stede but ȝe steven us,
No grevaunce to grete ne to small.[3]

REX
Ya, but loke þat no fawtes befall.

SECUNDUS DUX
Lely, my lord, so we shall,
Ye nede not no more for to nevyn us.

I DUX
Mounseniour, demene you in menske in mynde what I mene
And boune to youre bodword, for so holde I best,[4]
For all þe comons of þis courte bene avoyde clene,
And ilke a renke, as resoune is, are gone to þer reste.
Wherfore I counsaile, my lorde, ȝe comaunde you a drynke.

REX
Nowe certis, I assente as þou sais.
Se ych a qwy is wente on his ways
Lightly, withouten any delayes.
Giffe us wyne wynly and late us go wynke,
And se þat no durdan be done,

Tunc bibit Rex.

I DUX
My lorde, unlase you to lye,
Here schall none come for to crye.

REX
Nowe spedely loke þat þou spie
Þat no noyse be neghand þis none.

I DUX
My lorde, youre bedde is new made, you nedis noȝt for to bide it.

REX
Ya, but as þou luffes me hartely,
Laye me doune softely,
For þou wotte full wele þat I am full tendirly hydid.

I DUX
Howe lye ȝe, my goode lorde?

REX
Right wele, be þis light,
All hole at my desire.
Wherfore I praye ser Satan, oure sire,
And Lucifer, moste luffely of lyre,
He sauffe you all, sirs, and giffe you goode nyght.

[*Enter Soldiers with Christ (bound) at the approach to the palace.*]

I MILES
Sir knyght, ye wote we ar warned to wende
To witte of þis warlowe what is þe kyngis will.[5]

II MILES
Sir, here is Herowde all even here at oure hende,
And all oure entente tyte schall we tell hym untill.

I MILES
Who is here?

I DUX
Who is there?

19 before there is any unpleasantness 20 to boast abroad 23 retinue 24 come, homeland, well know 25 assemble(d), city 26 befits, soberly, declare 27 pay heed to, orders 28 go, place, unless, tell 30 problems arise 31 Loyally 32 need not tell us again 35 common (people), departed 36 is reasonable 37 order yourself 39 every man, gone 40 Quickly 41 Give, pleasingly, nap 42 disturbance is made 42+ Then the King drinks. 43 undress yourself 44 no one 45 see/ensure 46 nearby, midnight 47 wait (for) it 50 soft-skinned 52 wholly as I desire 53 lord 54 countenance 55 save 56 told to go 58 at hand (i.e. nearby) 59 intent, to him 60 famous knights

[3] i.e. 'Nothing is too much trouble (for us).'

[4] 'My lord, if you will condescend to honour in mind [i.e. give some attention to] my advice, prepare [yourself] for going to bed, because I think that is best'.

[5] 'To discover what is the King's will concerning this warlock.'

I MILES
Sir, we are knyghtis kende,
Is comen to youre counsaill þis carle for to kill.

I DUX
Sirs, but youre message may myrthis amende,
Stalkis furthe be yone stretis or stande stone still.

II MILES
Yis certis, ser, of myrthis we mene,
The kyng schall have matteres to melle hym.
We brynge here a boy us betwene,
Wherfore [to] have worschippe we wene.

I DUX
Wele, sirs, so þat it turne to no tene,
Tentis hym and we schall go telle hym.[6]

[*He returns to Herod.*]

My lorde, yondir is a boy boune þat brought is in blame,
Haste you in hye, þei hove at youre ȝates.

REX
What, and schall I rise nowe, in þe Devyilis name,
To stighill amang straungeres in stales of astate?
But have here my hande, halde nowe,
And se þat my sloppe be wele sittande.

I DUX
My lorde, with a goode will Y wolde youe,
No wrange will I witte at my wittande.

But, my lorde, we can tell ȝu of uncouthe tythandes.

REX
Ȝa, but loke ye telle us no tales but trewe.

II DUX
My lorde, þei bryng you yondir a boy boune in a bande
Þat bodus outhir bourdyng or bales to brewe.[7]

REX
Þanne gete we some harrowe full hastely at hande!

I DUX
My lorde, þer is some note þat is nedfull to neven you of new.[8]

REX
Why, hoppis þou þei haste hym to hyng?

II DUX
We wotte noght þer will nor þer wenyng,
But boodword full blithely þei bryng.

REX
Nowe, do þan, and late us se of þere sayng.

II DUX
[*To the Soldiers*] Lo, sirs, ye schall carpe with þe kyng,
And telles to hym manly youre menyng.

I MILES
[*To Herod*] Lorde, welthis and worschippis be with you alway.

REX
What wolde þou?

II MILES
A worde, lorde, and youre willes were.

REX
Well, saye on, þan.

I MILES
My lorde, we fare foolys to flay
Þ[a]t to you wolde forfette.

REX
We, faire falle you þerfore.

I MILES
My lorde, fro ȝe here what we saie
Itt will heffe uppe youre hertis.

REX
Ȝa, but saie what heynde hatte ȝe þore?

61 (Who are) come, fellow 62 unless, may prompt some fun 63 Go away, streets 64 we intend (to bring) fun 65 interest 67 trust to win honour/welcome 70 bound, shame 71 quickly, are coming, gates 72 must I 73 vex (myself), matters of state 74 hold 75 robe, well set 77 I will allow no flaws that I know of 78 strange 80 rope 82 help (i.e. soldiers) 84 Do you think, to hang him? 85 don't know, intention 86 a message, pleasantly 87 see (i.e. hear) 89 boldly, intentions 90 wealth, 91 What do you want?, if you please 92 proceed, fools, punish 93 who offend (against) you, May you have good fortune 94 once you have heard 95 lift, fellow, there 96 law

6 '[Very] well, sirs, just so long as it turns [out to be] no trouble, attend to him [Jesus], and we will go and tell [Herod].'

7 'Who promises either good sport or to cause trouble.'

8 '[T]here is some information that it is necessary to tell you now.'

II MILES
A presente fro Pilate, lorde, þe prince of oure lay.

REX
Pese in my presence, and nemys hym no more!

I MILES
My lorde, he woll worschippe you faine.

REX
I consayve ȝe are ful foes of hym.

II MILES
My lorde, he wolde menske you with mayne,
And therfore he sendis you þis swayne.

REX
Gose tyte with þat gedlyng agayne,
And saie hym a borowed bene sette I noght be hym.[9]

I DUX
A, my lorde, with youre leve, þei have faren ferre,
And for to fraiste of youre fare was no folye.

II DUX
My lorde, and þis gedlyng go þus it will greve werre,
For he gares growe on þis grounde grete velanye.

REX
Why, menys þou þat þat myghtyng schulde my myghtes marre?[10]

I DUX
Nay lorde, but he makis on þis molde mekill maystrie.

REX
Go ynne, and late us see of þe sawes ere,
And but yf þei be to oure bordyng, þai both schalle abye.[11]

II MILES
My lorde, we [were] worthy to blame,
To brynge you any message of mysse.

REX
Why þan, can ye nemyn us his name?

I MILES
Sir, Criste have we called hym at hame.

REX
O, þis is þe ilke selve and þe same:
Nowe, sirs, ye be welcome ywisse.

And in faith I am fayne he is fonne,
His farles to frayne and to fele;
Nowe þes games was grathely begonne.

II MILES
Lorde, lely þat likis us wele.

REX
Ya, but dar ȝe hete hartely þat harlott is he?

I MILES
My lorde, takis hede and in haste ye schall here howe.

REX
Ya, but what menys þat þis message was made unto me?

II MILES
My lorde, for it touches to tresoune, I trowe.

I MILES
My lorde, he is culpabill kende in oure contre
Of many perillus poyntis, as Pilate preves nowe.

II MILES
My lorde, when Pilate herde he had gone thurgh Galyle
He lerned us þat þat lordschippe longed to ȝou,

97 don't mention him again! 98 will, gladly 99 perceive, clearly his enemies 100 do you great honour 101 fellow 102 Return quickly 104 come a long way 105 seek your opinion 106 if, cause worse grief 107 spreads, in this land 109 land, many bold deeds 110 in, hear more of the story 113 (If we brought), evil news 115 home (i.e. in our country) 118 caught 119 investigate, examine 120 begun 121 honestly, greatly pleases us 122 dare, swear 123 hear 124 why was, brought? 126 known to be guilty 127 perilous deeds, proves 128 He (Jesus), through 129 told, belonged

9 'And tell him [Pilate] that I would not give a borrowed bean for him [Jesus].'

10 'What, do you suggest that this little man could threaten my power?'

11 'And, unless we like [what we hear], they shall both pay [for it].'

And or he wiste what youre willis were,
No ferther wolde he speke for to spille hym.

Rex
Þanne knawes he þat oure myghtis are þe more?[12]

I Miles
3a certis, sir, so saie we þore.

Rex
Nowe sertis, and oure frenschippe þerfore
We graunte hym, and no grevaunce we will hym.

And, sirs, ye are welcome, ywisse, as ye wele awe,
And for to wende at youre wille I you warande,
For I have coveite kyndely þat comely to knawe,
For men carpis þat þe carle schulde be konnand.

II Miles
My lorde, wolde he saie you soth of his sawe,
3e saugh nevir slik selcouth, be see nor be sande.[13]

Rex
Nowe gois abakke both and late þe boy blowe,
For I hope we gete some harre hastely at hande.

I Miles
Jerusalem and þe Jewes may have joie
And hele in ther herte for to here hym.

Rex
Saie, beene-venew in bone fay,
Ne plesew & a parle remoy?[14]

II Miles
Nay, my lorde, he can of no bourdyng, þis boy.

Rex
No sir? With þi leve we schall lere hym.

I Filius
Mi lorde, se ther knyghtis þat knawe and are kene,
How þai come to youre courte withoutyn any call.

Rex
3a, sone, and musteris grete maistries, what may þis
bymene?

I Dux
My lorde, for youre myghtis are more þan þe all
They seke you as soverayne, and sertis þat is sene.

Rex
Nowe certis, sen 3e saie so, assaie hym I schall,
For I am fayner of þat freyke þen othir fiftene,[15]
3ae, and hym þat firste fande, faire myght hym fall.

I Miles
Lorde, lely we lereth you no legh,
Þis liffe þat he ledis will lose hym.

Rex
Wele, sirs, drawes you adrygh,
And bewscheris, bryngis 3e hym nygh,
For yif all þat his sleghtis be slye,
3itte or he passe we schalle appose hym.

O, my harte hoppis for joie
To se nowe þis prophette appere.
We schall have goode game with þis boy;
Takis hede, for in haste 3e schall here.

I leve we schall laugh and have likyng
To se nowe þis lidderon her he leggis oure lawis.

II Dux
Harke, cosyne, þou comys to karpe with a kyng,
Take tente and be conande, and carpe as þou knowis.

I Dux
Ya, and loke þat þou be not a sotte of thy saying,
But sadly and sone þou sette all þi sawes.

130 before he knew, opinion was 131 convict 133 there 134 friendship 135 we have no grievance against him 136 well deserve 137 go 138 naturally desire, noble (man) 139 that (he) is cunning/wise 142 get back, breath 143 serious (news), soon 145 health/happiness 146 bienvenue (welcome), 'in good faith' 148 knows nothing of courtly talk 150 these, eager (for action) 151 summons 152 display, mean 153 as, greatest of all 154 seen 155 assay (try) 157 bless him who first caught him 158 tell, lie 159 leads, ruin 160 stand back 161 good sirs, near 162 even if, tricks, sly 163 before he goes, question 164 leaps 166 sport 168 think, (some) fun 169 rogue, interprets 170 cousin, comes 171 wise, truly 172 do not talk like a fool 173 quickly, voice, opinions

[12] 'Then does he acknowledge that our powers are greater [than his]?'

[13] 'My lord, should he tell you the true {extent} of his wisdom, you'd never have seen {i.e. heard of} such marvels, by sea or on sand.'

[14] 'Does it [not] please you to parlé with moi [i.e. talk to me]?'

[15] 'I am more interested in that wretch than in (any) fifteen other men'.

REX
Hym semys full boudisch, þat boy þat þei bryng.

II DUX
Mi lorde, and of his bordyng grete bostyng men blawes.

REX
Whi, þerfore have I soughte hym to see.
Loke, bewsheris, ye be to oure bodis boune.

I DUX
Knele doune here to þe kyng on thy knee.

II DUX
Naye, nedelyngis yt will not be.

REX
Loo, sirs, he mekis hym no more unto me
Þanne it were to a man of þer awne toune.[16]

I DUX
Whe! Go, lawmere, and lerne þe[e] to lowte
Or þai more blame þe[e] to bring.

REX
Nay, dredeles withouten any doute
He knawes noȝt þe course of a kyng.

And her beeis in oure bale, bourde or we blynne;[17]
Saie firste at þe begynnyng withall, where was þou borne?
Do felawe, for thy faith, latte us falle ynne.
Firste of þi ferleis, who fedde þe[e] beforne?
What, deynes þou not? Lo sirs, he deffis us with dynne.
Say, whare ledde ȝe þis lidrone? His langage is lorne.[18]

I MILES
My lorde, his mervaylis to more and to myne
Or musteres emange us both mydday and morne.

II MILES
Mi lorde, it were to fele
Of wonderes, he workith þam so wightely.[19]

I MILES
Whe, man! Momelyng may nothyng avayle,
Go to þe kyng and tell hyme fro toppe unto tayle.

REX
Do bringe us þat boy unto bale,
For lely we leffe hym noȝt lightly.[20]

I DUX
This mop mennes þat he may marke men to þer mede;
He makes many maistries and mervayles emange.

II DUX
V ml. folke faire gon he feede
With fyve looffis and two fisshis to fange.

REX
Howe fele folke sais þou he fedde?

II DUX
V ml., lorde, þat come to his call.

REX
Ȝa, boye? Howe mekill brede he þem bedde?

I DUX
But V looffis, dare I wele wedde.

REX
Nowe be þe bloode þat Mahounde bledde,
What, þis was a wondir at all.

II DUX
Nowe, lorde, ij fisshis blissid he efte
And gaffe þame, and þer none was forgetyn.

174 brutish 175 small talk, make boast 176 (That is) why 177 obedient to our commands 180 bows down 182 idiot 183 Before they bring you to 185 doesn't recognize the figure 186 let us begin 189 Who fed (i.e. raised) you first? 192 great and small 193 Are displayed among 196 mumbling won't help you 197 top to tail (i.e. everything) 200 allot each man's reward 202 5,000, truly, he fed 203 loaves, fishes, only 204 How many . . . ? 205 who came to hear him 206 How much bread, give them? 207 say 209 Here really was a wonder. 210 he also blessed (two fishes) 211 no one

16 'Than to a man of their own town [i.e. than he would to a local nobody].'

17 'Since you are here in our hands, [give us some] sport before we finish'.

18 'What, do you not deign [to speak]? Look, sirs, he deafens us with his din! Say, where have you taken this villain? He's lost his tongue!'

19 'My lord, [his miracles] are so many, he performs them so freely.'

20 'Bring that wretch to suffering, for us, because we do not want to let him off lightly.'

I Dux
3a, lorde, and xij lepfull þer lefte
Of releve whan all men had eten.

Rex
Of such anodir mangery no man mene may.

II Dux
Mi lorde, but his maistries þat musteris his myght.

Rex
But saie, sirs, ar þer sawis soth, þat þei saie?

II Miles
3a, lorde, and more selcouth were schewed to oure sight.
One Lazar, a ladde þat in oure lande lay,
Lay loken undir layre fro lymme and fro light,
And his sistir come rakand in rewfull arraye.
And lorde, for þer raryng he raysed hym full right,
And fro his grath garte hym gang
Evere forthe, withouten any evill.

Rex
We! Such lesyngis lastis to lange.

I Miles
Why, lorde, wene 3e þat wordis be wronge?
Þis same ladde levys us emange.

Rex
Why, there hope Y be dedis of þe Devyll.

Why schulde 3e haste hym to hyng
That sought not newly youre newys?[21]

II Miles
My lorde, for he callis hym a kyng
And claymes to be a kyng of Jewis.

Rex
But saie, is he kyng in his kyth wher he come froo?

I Miles
Nay, lorde, but he callis hym a kyng his caris to kele.

Rex
Thanne is it litill wondir yf þat he be woo,
For to be weried with wrang sen he wirkis wele;[22]
But he schalle sitte be myselfe sen 3e saie soo.
Comes nerre, kyng, into courte. Saie, can 3e not knele?
We schalle have gaudis full goode and games or we goo.
Howe likis þa? Wele lorde, saie! What, devyll, nevere a dele?[23]
I faute in my reverant; *in otill moy*;
I am of favour, loo, fairer be ferre.
Kyte oute yugilment. Uta! Oy! Oy![24]
Be any witte þat Y watte it will waxe werre.

Servicia p(eri)met:[25] Such losellis and lurdaynes as þou, loo,
Respicias timet:[26] What þe Devyll and his dame schall Y now doo?

Do carpe on, carle, for Y can þe[e] cure.
Say, may þou not here me? Oy, man, arte þou woode?
Nowe telle me faithfully before howe þou fore.
Forthe, frende. Be my faith, þou arte a fonde foode.

I Dux
My lorde, it astonys hym, youre steven is so store
Hym had levere have stande stone still þer he stode.

212 twelve basketfuls were left over 213 (To give) as alms 214 No one could imagine (such a banquet) 215 his deeds (are what) display 216 are these things true . . . ? 218 Lazarus, fellow 219 locked, (the) earth, brightness 220 hurrying, sorrowful dress 221 (in response to) her crying 222 grave, made him rise 223 Permanently 224 such lies go on too long 225 do you think these words . . . ? 226 lives among us 227 then I think they are deeds 228 do you hurry . . . ? 230 himself 233 to improve his fortunes 234 if he is sorrowful 236 by me 237 Come near 238 good sport, before 243 From what I know, grow worse 244 wretches 245 wife 246 speak up, help you 247 hear 248 (have) fared/lived 249 foolish thing 250 astonishes, loud 251 He'd rather

21 An obscure statement. Beadle and King, suggesting 'noys' for 'newys', interpret it to mean 'who provoked your anger only recently' (Beadle and King, *York Mystery Plays*, p. 184). But the opposite sense might equally be intended, 'Why [are you] so hasty to punish someone whose crimes are not [simply] recent', i.e. 'Why the sudden hurry to punish him?'

22 'To be unjustly tormented, since he does good deeds'.

23 'How do you like this? Well, lord, say! What, [you] devil, not a word?'

24 Another perplexing mixture of English and cod French, perhaps meaning something like 'I [am] lacking in reverence . . . [pointing to Jesus sitting beside him] '*un autre moi*' [another me!]. I am, look!, far fairer in appearance, *Qui tout jugilment* [Who(ever) of you all judges?], *Ouida, oui, oui* [yes, yes, yes!].'

25 Beadle and King suggest '*saevitia perimet*': glossed as 'savage violence may kill'.

26 'Let him fear and be wary.'

REX
And whedir þe boy be abasshid of Herrowde byg blure
That were a bourde of þe beste, be Mahoundes bloode.[27]

II DUX
My lorde, Y trowe youre fauchone hym flaies
And lettis hym.

REX
Nowe, lely I leve þe[e],
And therfore schall Y waffe it away
And softely with a septoure assaie.
Nowe, sir, be perte, Y þe[e] pray,
For none of my gromys schall greve þe[e].

Si loqueris tibi laus,
Pariter quoque prospera dantur;
Si loqueris tibi fraus,
Fell fex et bella parantur.[28]
Mi menne, ȝe go menske hym with mayne,
And loke yhow þat it wolde seme.

I DUX
Dewcus fayff ser and sofferayne.

II DUX
Sir udins amangidre demayne.[29]

REX
Go aunswer thaym grathely agayne.
What, devyll, whedir dote we or dremys?

I MILES
Naye, we gete noȝt o worde, dare Y wele wedde,
For he is wraiste of his witte or will of his wone.

REX
ȝe saie he lakkid youre lawis as ȝe þat ladde ledde?

II MILES
ȝa, lorde, and made many gaudis as we have gone.

REX
Nowe, sen he comes as a knave and as a knave cledde,
Wherto calle ye hym a kyng?

I DUX
Nay, lorde, he is none,
But an harlotte is hee.

REX
What, devyll, Y ame harde stedde,
A man myght as wele stere a stokke as a stone.

I FILIUS
My lorde, þis faitour so fouly is affrayde,
He loked nevere of lorde so langly allone.[30]

REX
No, sone, þe rebalde seis us so richely arayed
He wenys we be aungelis evere-ilkone.

II DUX
My lorde, Y holde hym agaste of youre gaye gere.[31]

REX
Grete lordis augh to be gay.
[*To Jesus*] Here schall no man do to þe[e] dere,
And therfore yit nemyne in my nere:
For, by the grete god, and þou garre me swere,
Þou had nevere dole or this day.

Do carpe on tyte, karle, of thy kynne.

I DUX
Nay, nedelyngis he nevyns you with none.

REX
Þat schalle he bye or he blynne.

254 broadsword frightens him 255 forestalls, truly, I believe you 256 put 257 try (again) with a sceptre 258 be bold 259 servants, grieve 264 with vigour 265 you, seem 269 are we going mad, or dreaming? 270 (will) get not one word, I bet 271 twisted, or has lost his mind 272 broke, when he was with you? 273 tricks 274 dressed as 275 Why do you call him . . . ? 276 hard-pressed (here) 277 stare (at), stock, or 280 villain 281 thinks, each one 283 ought 284 do harm to you 285 whisper in my ear 286 if you make me swear 287 have never suffered until now 289 will say nothing to you 290 He shall pay for that, goes

[27] 'And if the boy was abashed by Herod's great voice, that would be a great joke, by Mahound's blood!'

[28] 'If you speak well on your own behalf, you will be well treated accordingly, but if you speak badly on your own behalf, poison, filth, and violence will follow.'

[29] Again, these two lines seem to mix cod French with English, and resist convincing interpretation. They might, perhaps, be interpreted as 'Duke's faith, sire and sovereign' and 'Sir Udins [the Duke's own name?], *amant je dire, de-main* [he who loves you, I say, (is) at hand?]'.

[30] '[I think] he's never looked at a lord for so long [before].'

[31] 'I think he is aghast at your fine clothes.'

II Dux
A, leves, lorde . . .

Rex
Lattis me allone!

I Dux
Nowe goode lorde, and ye may, meve you no more,
Itt is not faire to feght with a fonned foode,
But gose to youre counsaille and comforte you þere.

Rex
Thou sais soth. We shall see yf so will be goode,
For certis oure sorowes are sadde.

II Filius
What a devyll ayles hym?
Mi lorde, I can garre you be gladde,
For in tyme oure maistir is madde.
He lurkis, loo, and lokis like a ladde,
He is wode, lorde, or ellis his witte faylis hym.

III Filius
Mi lorde, ȝe have mefte you as mekill as ȝe may,
For yhe myght menske hym no more were he
Mahounde;
And sen it semys to be soo, latte us nowe assaie.

Rex
Loke, bewscheris, ȝe be to oure bodis boune.

I Dux
Mi lorde, howe schulde he dowte us? He dredis not
youre drays.[32]

Rex
Nowe do fourthe, þe Devyll myght hym drawe!
And sen he freyms falsed and makis foule frayes,
Raris on hym rudely, and loke ȝe not roune.

I Filius
Mi lorde, I schall enforce myselffe sen ȝe saie soo.
[*To Jesus*] Felawe, be noȝt afferde nor feyne not
þerfore,
But telle us nowe some truffillis betwene us twoo,
And none of oure men schall medill þam more.
And þerfore by resoune array þe[e],
Do telle us some poynte for thy prowe.
Heris þou not what Y saie þe[e]?
Þou mummeland myghtyng, I may þe[e]
Helpe, and turne þe[e] fro tene, as Y trowe.

II Filius
Loke uppe ladde, lightly, and loute to my lorde here
For fro bale unto blisse he may nowe þe[e] borowe.
Carpe on, knave, kantely, and caste þe to corde here,
And saie me nowe somwhat, þou sauterell, with
sorowe.
Why standis þou as stille as a stone here?
Spare not, but speke in þis place here,
Þou gedlyng, it may gayne þe[e] some grace here.

III Filius
My lorde, þis faitour is so ferde in youre face here
None aunswere in þis nede he nevyns you with none
here.[33]
Do bewshers, for Beliall bloode and his bonys,
Say somwhat, or it will waxe werre.

I Filius
Nay, we gete nouȝt one worde in þis wonys.

II Filius
Do crie we all on hym at onys.

[Al Chylder]
Oȝes! Oȝes! Oȝes!

Rex
O, ȝe make a foule noyse for þe
nonys.

III Filius
Nedlyng, my lorde, it is nevere þe nerre.

I Filius
My lorde, all youre mutyng amendis not a myte,
To medill with a madman is mervaille to me.

291 permission (to speak) 292 do not become angry 293 fight with an idiot 294 counsellors, take comfort 295 speak truly 297 troubles 299 it is timely that [Jesus] 300 lurks, looks, rogue 301 wit fails him 302 tried as best you can 303 (even) if he was 305 obedient to our orders 307 the Devil take him 308 creates falsehoods, strife 309 Roar at him, don't whisper 310 try 311 feign 312 trifles, just between us 313 deal (with you) any further 314 act reasonably 315 something, profit 316 Do you not hear . . . ? 317 mumbling midget 318 save you from pain 319 freely 320 he can bring you 321 bravely, come to an accord 322 little rogue 326 deceiver, in your presence 329 worse 331 once 331+ All the children (Herod's sons) 332 Oyez! (Hear ye!), at this time 333 Necessarily, we are no nearer (success) 334 discussion, improves (things) 335 I wonder at it!

[32] '[W]hy should he fear us [if] he is not frightened by your noise?'

[33] 'He can give you no answer, here, even in his [hour of] need.'

Comaunde youre knyghtis to clothe hym in white
And late hym carre as he come to youre contre.

Rex
Lo, sirs, we lede you no lenger a lite,
Mi sone has saide sadly how þat it schuld be,
But such a poynte for a page is to parfite.

I Dux
Mi lorde, fooles þat are fonde þei falle such a fee.

Rex
What, in a white garmente to goo,
Þus gayly girde in a gowne?

II Dux
Nay, lorde, but as a foole forcid hym froo.

Rex
How saie ȝe, sirs, schulde it be soo?

Al Chylder
Ya, lord.

Rex
We!, þan is þer no more, but boldely bidde þam be boune.[34]

Sir knyghtis, we caste to garre you be gladde,
Oure counsaile has warned us wisely and wele.
White clothis we saie fallis for a fonned ladde,
And all his foly, in faith, fully we feele.

I Dux
We will with a goode will for his wedis wende,
For we wotte wele anowe what wedis he schall were.

II Dux
Loo, here is an haterell here at youre hent,
Alle faciound þerfore foolis to feere.

I Miles
Loo, here a joppon of joie,
All such schulde be gode for a boy.

I Dux
He schalle be rayed like a roye,
And schall be fonne in his folie.

II Dux
We! Thanke þam, evyll motte þou the!

I Miles
Nay, we gete noȝt a worde, wele Y warand.

II Miles
Man, mustir some mervaile to me.

I Dux
What, wene ȝe he be wiser þan we?
Leffe we, and late þe kyng see
Howe it is forcyd and farand.

Mi lorde, loke yf ȝe be paied,
For we have getyn hym his gere.

Rex
Why, and is þis rebalde arayed?
Mi blissing, bewscheris, ȝe bere.

Gose, garre crye in my courte and grathely garre write
All þe dedis þat we have done in þis same degre.
And who fyndis hym greved late hym telle tyte,
And yf we fynde no defaute hym fallis to go free.[35]

I Dux
Oȝes! Yf any wight with þis wriche any werse wate
(Werkis beris wittenesse who so wirkis wrang),[36]
Buske boldely to þe barre his balis to abate,
For, my lorde, be my lewte, will not be deland [lang].

337 let him go, came 338 will delay you no longer 340 can arrangement, boy, is too good 341 mad fools deserve such treatment 343 elegantly dressed, robe 344 as a fool should do 347 try to please you 348 advised 349 befit a simpleton 350 we fully recognize 351 go for his clothes 352 know well enough, wear 353 garment, at hand 354 fashioned to suit fools 355 gippon (tunic) 357 dressed, king 358 revealed in (all) his folly 359 curse you! 361 perform, for me 362 do you believe (that) he is . . . ? 363 (Let's) leave (him) 364 How things are going 365 content 366 brought him, clothes 367 dressed 368 (you have) my blessing 373 wretch, knows worse (crimes) 375 to satisfy his grievance 376 loyalty, judging (for) long

34 'Then there is no more [to be said], but tc boldly tell them to get on with it.'

35 'Go, make a cry in my court, and formally record in writing all the actions that we have taken in this business. And anyone who has been grieved [by Jesus], let him speak up quickly, and if we find no offence in him, then he needs must go free.'

36 'One's deeds always bear witness when one does wrong'.

My lorde, here apperes none to appeyre his estate.

Rex
Wele þanne, fallis hym goo free.
Sir knyghtis, þanne grathis you goodly to gange,
And repaire with youre present and saie to Pilate
We graunte hym oure frenschippe all fully to fang.

I Miles
My lorde, with youre leve þis way schall we lere,
Us likis no lenger to abide here.

II Miles
Mi lorde, and he worþe ought in were,
We come agayne with goode chere.

Rex
Nay, bewscheris, ȝe fynde us not here,
Oure leve will we take at þis tyde

And ȝathely araye us to reste,
For such notis has noyed us or nowe.[37]

I Dux
Ʒa, certis lorde, so holde Y beste,
For þis gedlyng ungoodly has greved you.

II Dux
Loke ȝe bere worde as Ye wotte,
Howe wele we have quitte us þis while.

I Miles
We! Wise men will deme it we dote
But if we make ende of oure note.

Rex
Wendis fourth, þe Devyll in þi throte,
We fynde no defaute hym to flee.[38]

Wherfore schulde we flaye hym or fleme hym
We fynde noȝt in rollis of recorde;
And sen þat he is dome, for to deme hym,[39]
Ware þis a goode lawe for a lorde?

Nay, losellis, unlely ȝe lerned all to late,
Go lere þus lordingis of youre londe such lessons to lere.
Repaire with youre present and saie to Pilate
We graunte hym oure poure all playne to appere,
And also oure grevaunce forgeve we algate
And we graunte hym oure grace with a goode chere.
As touchyng þis brothell, þat brawlis or debate,
Bidde hym wirke as he will, and wirke noght in were.
Go telle hym þis message fro me.
And lede fourth þat mytyng, evyll motte he the.

I Miles
Mi lorde, with youre leve, late hym be,
For all to longe ledde hym have we.

II Miles
What, ȝe sirs, my lorde, will ȝe see?

Rex
What, felawes? Take ȝe no tente what I telle you
And bid you? Þat yoman ye ȝeme.

II Miles
Mi lorde, we schall wage hym an ill way.

Rex
Nay, bewscheris, be not so bryme.
Fare softely, for so will it seme.

I Miles
Nowe, sen we schall do as ye deme,
Adewe, sir.

Rex
Daunce on, in þe Devyll way.

377 no one, speak against his position 378 Well then, he must 379 prepare yourselves 380 return 381 to have (completely) 382 go 383 We (do not) want 384 if he behaves any worse 385 We (will) return, gladly 386 you will 388 promptly prepare 391 Because, evil wretch 392 Be sure to 393 acquitted ourselves 394 think us mad 395 Unless we complete our errand 396 Go away, curse you! 401 Is this . . . ? 402 disloyally 403 land 405 to act freely (in this case) 406 we forgive (him) completely 408 (if there is any) dispute 409 act, but, not in anger 411 midget, curse him! 412 let him stay (here) 413 we've led him for too long 414 will you deal with him? 415 Do you not listen to what 416 servant is your responsibility 417 reward him cruelly 418 angry 419 Act gently, that will look best. 420 command 421 Farewell 422 Get out, curse you!

[37] 'For this business has already begun to annoy us.'
[38] 'We find no crime sufficient to condemn him.'
[39] 'We cannot find in the [legal] record rolls any justification to whip or condemn him [to death], since he remains silent'.

York (The Tilemakers),
Christ Before Pilate II: The Judgement

In the last of the York trial pageants, a new element is introduced into the portrayal of Pilate, fear of Christ's powers, prompted by the (apocryphal) incident of the spontaneously bowing banners (l. 159ff.). Hence he is all the more eager to dismiss the case and see Jesus released. Again, it is only the implicit threat to his own authority contained in Christ's claim to be 'King of the Jews' that provokes him to act against Him. The vicious 'scourging' scene which follows is the most openly ferocious of the acts of violence against Jesus which culminate in His Crucifixion. The mock reverence with which the soldiers treat Him during the scourging parodically echoes the sincere 'hail' lyrics of *The Nativity* and *The Entry*. The missing leaf after l. 438 deprives the manuscript of Pilate's last attempt to avoid condemning Jesus, the offer to release Him in honour of the Passover, and the Jews' insistence that the criminal, Barabas, be released instead.

There is no immediately obvious connection between the Tilemakers' trade and the subject of the pageant.

[*Dramatis Personae*: *Pilatus* (Pontius Pilate), *Anna* and *Caiphas* (Annas and Caiaphas, Jewish high priests) *I–VI Miles* (six Soldiers), *Preco* ('Herald'), *Jesus*, *Barabas*.]

PILATUS
Lordyngis þat are lymett to þe lare of my liaunce,
3e schappely schalkes and schene for to schawe,
I charge 3ou as 3our chiftan þat 3e chatt for no chaunce,
But loke to youre lord here, and lere at my lawe:
As a duke I may dampne 3ou and drawe.
Many bernys bolde are aboute me.
And what knyght or knave I may knawe
Þat list no3t as a lord for to lowte me,
I sall lere hym
In the Develes name, þat dastard, to dowte me.
3a, who werkis any werkes withoute me,
I sall charge hym in chynes to chere hym.

Tharfore, 3e lusty ledes within þis lenght lapped,
Do stynte of 3oure stalkyng, and of stoutnes be stalland
What traytoure his tong with tales has trapped,
That fende for his flateryng full foull sall be falland.
What broll overe-brathely is bralland,
Or unsoftely will sege in þer sales,
Þat caysteffe þus carpand and calland
As a boy sall be broght unto bales.
Þerfore,
Talkes not nor trete not of tales,
For þat gome þat gyrnes or gales,
I myself sall hym hurte full sore.

ANNA
3e sall sytt hym full sore, what sege will assay 3ou;[1]
If he like not youre lordshippe, þat ladde, sall 3e lere hym
As a pereles prince, full prestly to pay 3ou,
Or as a derworth duke with dyntes sall 3e dere hym.

CAIPHAS
3aa, in faythe 3e have force for to fere hym,
Thurgh youre manhede and myght bes he marred.
No chyvalrus chiftan may chere hym
Fro that churll with charge 3e have charred,
In pynyng payne bees he parred.[2]

ANNA
3aa, and with schath of skelpys yll scarred,
Fro tyme þat youre tene he have tasted.[3]

PILATUS
Now certes, as me semes, whoso sadly has soght 3ou,
3oure praysyng is prophetable, 3e prelates of pees.

1 bound, lore, allegiance 2 handsome men, fine, appear 3 chieftain, in no way 5 damn, punish 6 men 8 who doesn't worship me 11 without (my knowledge) 12 chains, punish 13 folk, gathered in this space 14 walking, stand still 15 encumbered 16 fiend, falling 17 arguing too loudly 18 say/speak, halls 20 Like a knave 22 discuss 23 grimaces, moans 28 honourable, blows, pain 29 frighten 30 will he be destroyed 31 succour

[1] 'Whichever man will oppose your wishes, you will treat him (appropriately) badly.'

[2] 'When you have punished (that churl) with rigour, in terrible pain will he be flayed.'

[3] 'Yeah, and badly scarred with wounds from blows, from the time that he tasted your anger.'

Gramercy 3oure goode worde, and ungayne sall it no3t you
That 3e will say the sothe, and for no sege cese.[4]

[*Enter soldiers with Jesus (bound).*]

CAIPHAS
Elles were it pite we appered in þis prees;
But consayve how 3oure knyghtes ere command.

ANNA
3a, my lord, þat leve 3e no lese,
I can telle you, 3ou tydes sum tythandis
Ful sadde.

PILATUS
Se, they bring 3oone brolle in a bande.
We sall here nowe hastely at hand
What unhappe before Herowde he had.

I MILES
Hayll, lovelyest lorde þat evere lawe led 3itt,
Hayll, semelyest undre [sylke] on evere ilka syde,[5]
Hayll, stateliest on stede in strenghe þat is sted 3itt,
Hayll, liberall, hayll, lusty, to lordes allied.

PILATUS
Welcome, what tydandis þis tyde?
Late no langgage lightly nowe lette 3ou.

II MILES
Sir Herowde, ser, it is noght to hyde,
As his gud frende grathely he grete yowe
Forevere.
In what manere þat evere he mete 3ou,
By hymselfe full sone wille he sette 3ou,
And sais þat 3e sall not dissever.

PILATUS
I thanke hym full thraly; and, ser, I saie hym þe same;
But what mervelous materes dyd þis myron þer mell?

I MILES
For all þe lordis langage, his lipps, ser, wer lame;
For any spirringes in þat space no speche walde he spell,
Bot domme as a dore gon he dwell.
Þus no faute in hym gon he fynde,
For his dedis to deme hym to qwell,
Nor in bandis hym brathely to bynde;
And þus
He sente hym to youreself, and assynde
Þat we, youre knyghtis, suld be clenly enclyned,
And tyte with hym to you to trus.

PILATUS
Syrs, herkens, here 3e not what we have oppon hand?
Loo howe þere knyghtes carpe þat to þe kyng cared.
Syr Herowde, þai say, no faute in me fand,
He fest me to his frenschippe, so frendly he fared.
Moreover, sirs, he spake, and noght spared,
Full gentilly to Jesu, þis Jewe,
And sithen to ther knyghtis declared
How fawtes in hym fande he but fewe
To dye.
He taste hym, I telle 3ou, for trewe,
For to dere hym he demed undewe,
And sirs, ye sothly saie I.

CAIPHAS
Sir Pilate, oure prince, we prelatis nowe pray 3ou,
Sen Herowde fraysted no ferþer þis faitour to flaye,
Resayve in 3our sall þer sawes þat I saie 3ou:
Late bryng hym to barre and at his berde sall we baye.[6]

ANNA
3a, for and he wende þus by wiles away,
I wate wele he wirke will us wondre.
Oure men3e he marres þat he may,

40 crowd 41 see, are coming 42 'lies 43 you are due 45 yon/that 47 misfortune, Herod 48 expounded 50 who was ever in power 51 doughty (one) 53 Don't dally with fancy talk 54 it may not be hidden 55 he (Herod) greeted you 57 whatever 59 be parted 60 earnestly 61 servant, meddle in 62 dumb 63 questions, speak 64 dumb, door, did, remain 65 could 66 death 69 assigned 70 properly behaved 71 go 72 listen, in hand 73 these, went 75 bound, he acted 76 spared nothing 78 these 79 found 80 (worthy of) death 81 tested 82 harm, uncalled for 85 intended 86 these 88 (if) he escape, cunning 89 will do wonders (against us) 90 followers, hinders, wherever

4 '[I]t seems to me that whoever has paid sober attention to you (will know) that your praise is appropriate, you peace-loving bishops. Thank you for your good words, and it will profit you [lit. 'not do you no good'], (provided) that you speak the truth and do not leave off for anyone.'

5 'The most handsome of all those nobles present [lit. 'the handsomest in silk'].'

6 'Let him be brought to (the) bar, and we shall accuse him [lit. 'bay at his beard'].'

With his seggynges he settes þam in sondre,
With synne;
With his blure he bredis mekill blondre.
Whills 3e have hym nowe haldes hym undir:
We sall wery hym away yf he wynne.

CAIPHAS
Sir, no tyme is to tarie þis traytour to taste.
Agayne ser Cesar hymselfe he segges, and saies
All þe wightis in this world wirkis in waste
Þat takis hym any tribute: þus his teaching outrayes.
3itt forther he feynes slik affraies,
And sais þat hymself is God Son.
And ser, oure lawe leggis and laye,
In what faytour falsed is fon,
Suld be slayne.

PILATUS
For no schame hym to shende will we shon.[7]

ANNA
Sir, witnesse of þis wanes may be wonne,
Þat will telle þis withowten any trayne.

CAIPHAS
I can reken a rable of renkes full right,
Of perte men in prese, fro this place ar I pas,
Þat will witnesse, I warande, þe wordis of þis wight,
How wikkidly wrought þat þis wrecche has:
Simon, 3arus, and Judas,
Datan and Gamaliell,
Neptalim, Levi, and Lucas,
And Amys þis maters can mell
Togithere.[8]
Þer tales for trewe can they telle
Of this faytour þat false is and felle,
And in legyng of lawes ful lithre.

PILATUS
3a, tussch for youre tales, þai touche not entente.
Þer witnesse I warande þat to witnesse 3e wage,
Some hatred in ther hartis agaynes hym have hent,
And purpose be this processe to putt doun þis page.

CAIPHAS
Sir, in faith, us failith not to fage,
Þai are trist men and true þat we telle 3ou.

PILATUS
Youre swering, seris, swiftely 3e swage,
And no more in this maters ye mell 3ou
I charge.

ANNA
Sir, dispise not þis speche þat we spell you.

PILATUS
If 3e feyne slike frawdis I sall felle 3ou,
For me likis noght youre langage so large.

CAIPHAS
Oure langage is to large, but 3oure lordshipp releve us.
3itt we both beseke you, late brynge hym to barre.
What poyntes þat we putte forth, latt your presence appreve us,
3e sall here how þis harlott heldes out of herre.

PILATUS
3a, butt be wise, witty, and warre.

ANNA
3is, sir, drede 3ou no3t for nothyng we doute hym.

[PILATUS]
Fecche hym, he is noght right ferre.
Do, bedell, buske þe[e] abowte hym.

PRECO
I am fayne,
My lorde, for to lede hym or lowte hym.
Uncleth hym, clappe hym and clowte hym,
If 3e bid me, I am buxhome and bayne.

Knyghtis, 3e er commaundid with þis caityf to care,
And bryng hym to barre, and so my lord badd.

91 teachings, confusion 93 boasting, breeds, chaos 94 While 95 curse, escapes 96 delay, interrogate 97 speaks 98 wastes (their efforts) 99 give, transgresses 100 enormities 102 states and lays (down) 103 falsehood, found 104 (He) should 106 these things, found 107 trickery 108 gather, crowd, worthy men 109 many bold men, before 111 has acted wickedly 112 Jairus 117 These 118 evil 119 expounding, deceitfully 120 are irrelevant 121 you've paid to testify 122 created 124 we cannot deceive 125 trustworthy 126 sirs, stop 130 frauds, punish 131 wild allegations 132 (must) aid us 134 majesty approve 135 here, acts (as if) unhinged 136 shrewd, wary 137 we (don't) suspect him for nothing 138 not very far (away) 139 beadle 142 undress, beat 144 come 145 instructed

7 'If he is without guilt, we will shun condemning him.'

8 The names chosen do not seem to have any specific significance beyond their generally 'Jewish' nature.

I Miles
Is þis thy messege?

[Preco]
ȝa, sir.

[I Miles]
Þan move þe[e] no mare,
For we ar light for to leppe and lede forthe þ[i]s ladd.

II Miles
Do steppe forth; in striffe ert þou stadde,
I uphalde full evyll has þe[e] happed.

I Miles
O man, thy mynde is full madde,
In oure clukis to be clowted and clapped
And closed.

II Miles
Þou bes lassched, lusschyd, and lapped.

I Miles
ȝa, rowted, russhed, and rapped,
Þus thy name with noye sall be noysed.

II Miles
Loo this sege her, my soverayne, þat ȝe for sente.

Pilatus
Wele, stirre noȝt fro þat stede, but stande stille þare.
Bot he schappe som shrewdnesse, with shame bese he shente,
And I will frayst, in faith, to frayne of his fare.[9]

[*The banners bow and the Priests fall to the ground.*]

Caiphas
We! Outte! Stande may I noȝt, so I stare.

Anna
ȝa, harrowe of this traytour, with tene.

Pilatus
Say, renkes, what rewth gars you rare?
Er ye woode or wittles, I wene?
What eyles ȝou?

Caiphas
Out! Slike a sight suld be sene!

Anna
ȝa, allas, conquered ar we clene.

Pilatus
We! Ere ȝe fonde, or youre force fayles ȝou?

Caiphas
A, ser, saugh ȝe noȝt þis sight, how þat þer schaftes schuke,
And thez baneres to this brothell þai bowde all on brede?

Anna
ȝa, ther cursed knyghtes by crafte lete them croke,
To worshippe þis warlowe unworthy in wede.

Pilatus
Was it dewly done þus indede?

Caiphas
ȝa, ȝa, sir, oureselfe we it sawe.

Pilatus
We! Spitte on them, ill mott þai spede!
Say, dastard, þe Devyll mote ȝou drawe,
How dar ȝe
Þer baners on brede þat her blawe
Lat lowte to þis lurdan so lawe?
O, faytouris, with falshed how fare ȝe?

III Miles
We beseke you, and tho senioures beside ȝou, sir, sitte,
With none of oure governaunce to be grevous and gryll,
For it lay not in oure lott þer launces to lett,

146 say 147 pleased, hurry 148 you are in trouble 149 assert, done 151 clutches, hit, struck 152 caught 153 beaten, and surrounded 154 dragged, and struck 155 spoken with anger 156 (is) here 160 I am so stunned 161 carry off 162 what calamity makes you roar? 163 Are you mad 164 ails/afflicts 165 That such a sight should be seen! 166 utterly 167 stupid, strength 168 saw, spears, shook 169 all bowed down 170 deliberately, droop 171 unworthy of clothes (i.e. wicked) 172 duly 174 curse them! 175 rogue, Devil, take you 176 dare 177 blow (in the breeze) 180 who sit beside you 181 conduct, grieved, angry 182 power, prevent

9 'Unless he tries some trick, he is shamefully ruined, and I will strive, in faith, to find out about his conduct.'

And þis werke þat we have wrought, it was not oure will.

PILATUS
Þou lise – harstow, lurdan? – full ille!
Wele þou watte, if þou witnes it walde.

IV MILES
Sir, oure strengh myght noʒt stabill þam stille,
They hilded, for ought we couthe halde,
Oure unwittyng.

V MILES
For all oure fors, in faith, did þai folde,
As þis warlowe worschippe þat wolde,
And us semid, forsoth, it unsittyng.

CAIPHAS
A, unfrendly faytours, full fals is youre fable,
Þis segge with his suitelte to his seett haþ you sesid.

VI MILES
ʒe may say what you semes, ser, bot þer standerdes to stabill,
What freyke hym enforces full foull sall he be fesid.[10]

ANNA
Be þe Devyllis nese, ʒe ar doggydly diseasid;
A, henne-harte, ill happe mot ʒou hente!

PILATUS
For a whapp so he whyned and whesid,
And ʒitt no lasshe to þe lurdan was lente.
Foul fall ʒou.

III MILES
Sir, iwisse, no wiles we have wente.

PILATUS
Shamefully ʒou satt to be shente,
Here combred caystiffes I call ʒou.

IV MILES
Sen ʒou lykis not, my lord, oure langage to leve,
Latte bryng the biggest men þat abides in þis land,
Propirly in youre presence þer pouste to preve;
Beholde þat they helde nott fro þei have þaim in hand.[11]

PILATUS
Now ʒe er ferdest þat evere I fand,
Fy on youre faynte hertis, in feere.
Stir þe[e], no langer þou stande,
Þou bedell, þis bodworde þou bere
Thurgh his towne,
Þe wyghtest men unto were,
And þe strangest þer standerdis to stere,
Hider blithely bid þam be bowne.

PRECO
My soverayne, full sone sall be served youre sawe,
I sall bryng to þer baneres right bigg men and strange.
A company of kevellis in this contre I knawe,
That grete ere and grill, to þe gomes will I gange.

[*He goes to I and II Miles.*]

Say, ye ledis botht lusty and lange,
ʒe most passe to ser Pilate, apace.

I MILES
If we wirke not his wille it wer wrang;
We ar redy to renne on a race
And rayke.

PRECO
Then tarie not, but tryne on a trace,
And folow me fast to his face.

II MILES
Do lede us, us lykes wele þis lake.

184 lies 185 would speak truly 186 hold 187 drooped, could do 188 without our knowledge 189 force, bend 190 as if they would 191 seemed to us, unfitting 192 story 193 cunning, won you to his side 194 think 196 nose, wretchedly diseased 197 hen-heart/coward, curse you! 198 As if struck, whined, groaned 199 was used against 200 Curse you! 201 we've tried no tricks 202 let yourselves be 203 miserable 204 to believe our story 206 strength, prove 208 (the) most cowardly 209 A curse on, all of you 211 message 213 (to warn) the boldest 214 wield 215 (to) hurry 216 performed 217 strong 218 warriors 219 are, fierce, go 220 tall 221 go 222 would be 223 hurry 224 go 225 walk, quickly 227 business

[10] 'But, whoever tries to hold these standards still will have a hard job.'

[11] 'Watch if they don't (also) fail to hold them, once they have them in their hand(s).'

Preco
Lorde, here are þe biggest bernes þat bildis in þis burgh,
Most stately and strange, if with strenght þai be streyned.
Leve me, ser, I lie not; to loke þis lande thurgh,
Þai er myghtiest men with manhode demened.

Pilatus
Wate þou wele, or ellis has þou wenyd?

Preco
Sir, I wate wele withoute wordis moo.

Caiphas
In thy tale be not taynted nor tenyd.

Preco
We! Nay, ser, why shuld I be soo?

Pilatus
Wele þan,
We sall frayst, or they founde us fer fro,
To what game þai begynne for to go.
Sir Cayphas, declare þam ȝe can.

Caiphas
Ȝe lusty ledis, nowe lith to my lare,
Schappe ȝou to þer schaftis þat so schenely her schyne.
If ȝon banners bowe þe brede of an hare,
Platly ȝe be putte to perpetuell pyne.

I Miles
I sall holde þis as even as a lyne.

Anna
Whoso schakis, with schames he shendes.

II Miles
I, certayne I saie as for myne,
Whan it sattles, or sadly discendis
Whare I stande,
When it wryngis or wronge it wendis,
Outher bristis, barkis, or bendes;
Hardly lat hakke of myn hande.

Pilatus
Sirs, waites to þer wightis, þat no wiles be wrought,
Þai are burely and brode, þare bost have þai blowen.

Anna
To neven of þat nowe, ser, it nedis right noght,
For who curstely hym quytes, he sone sall be knawen.

Caiphas
Ȝa, þat dastard to dede sall be drawen,
Whoso fautis, he fouly sall falle.

Pilatus
Nowe, knyghtis, sen þe cokkis has crowen,
Have hym hense with hast fra this halle
His wayes.
Do stiffely steppe on þis stalle,
Make a crye, and cantely þou call,
Evene like as ser Annay þe[e] sais.

Anna
Oyes! Jesu, þou Jewe of gentill Jacob kynne,
Þou nerthrist of Nazareth, now nevend is þi name.
Alle creatures þe[e] accuses. We commaunde þe[e] comme in
And aunswer to þin enemys; deffende now thy fame.

Et Preco, semper post Annam, recitabit judicatur Jesus.[12]

[*The banners bow down, and Pilate stands up, involuntarily.*]

Caiphas
We! Out! We are shente alle for shame!
Þis is wrasted all wrange, as I wene.

Anna
For all þer boste, ȝone boyes are to blame.

Pilatus
Slike a sight was nevere ȝit sene.
Come sytt.

228 men, live, town 229 tested 230 search the whole land 231 are, endowed 232 are you (just) guessing? 233 more 234 false, wrong 237 discover, before they go 238 (i.e. how good they are) 239 instruct 240 fellows, listen 241 Go, brightly here shine 242 by a hair's breadth 243 Immediately, torment 244 straight 245 dishonours himself 246 regarding 247 sinks 249 twists, goes wrong 250 snaps, splinters 251 At once, hack off 252 attend, tricks be done 253 burly, broad 254 no need to speak 255 cursedly fails 256 death, taken 257 whoever fails 259 away 260 on his way 261 bravely, dais 262 loudly 263 Exactly as, tells you 264 Oyez! Jacob's kin 265 lowest 267 name/honour 269 It's all going wrong

12 'And the Beadle declares after Annas, "Let Jesus be judged".'

My comforth was caught fro me clene:
I upstritt, I me myght noȝt abstene
To wirschip hym in wark and in witte.

CAIPHAS
Þerof mervayled we mekill what moved ȝou in mynde,
In reverence of his ribald so rudely to ryse.

PILATUS
I was past all my powre, þogh I payned me and pynd,
I wrought not as I wolde in no maner of wise.
Bot, syrs, my spech wele aspise:
Wightly his wayes late hym wende,
Þus my dome will dewly devyse,
For I am ferde hym, in faith, to offende
In sightes.

ANNA
Þan oure lawe were laght till an ende,
To his tales if ȝe treuly attend,
He enchaunted and charmed oure knyghtis.

CAIPHAS
Be his sorcery, ser (youreselffe þe soth sawe),
He charmed oure chyvalers and with myscheffe enchaunted.
To reverence hym ryally we rase all on rowe;
Doutles we endure not of þis dastard be daunted.[13]

PILATUS
Why, what harmes has þis hatell here haunted?
I kenne to co[n]vyk hym no cause.

ANNA
To all gomes he God Son hym graunted,
And liste not to leve on oure lawes.

PILATUS
Say, man,
Consayves þou noȝt what comberous clause
Þat þis clargye accusyng þe[e] knawse?
Speke, and excuse þe[e] if þou can.

JESUS
Every man has a mouthe þat made is on molde,
In wele and in woo to welde at his will;
If he governe it gudly like as God wolde,
For his spirituale speche hym thar not to spill.
And what gome so governe it ill,
Full unhendly and ill sall he happe;
Of ilk tale þou talkis us untill
Þou accounte sall, þou can not escappe.

PILATUS
Sirs myne,
Ȝe fonne, in faithe, all þe frappe,
For in þis lede no lese can I lappe,
Nor no poynte to putt hym to pyne.

CAIPHAS
Withoute cause, ser, we come not þis carle to accuse hym,
And þat will we ȝe witt as wele is worthy.[14]

PILATUS
Now I recorde wele þe right ȝe will no raþere refuse hym
To he be dreven to his dede and demed to dye;
But takes hym unto you forthe,
And like as youre lawe will you lere,
Deme ȝe his body to abye.

ANNA
O, sir Pilate, withouten any pere,
Do way!
Ȝe wate wele, withouten any were,
Us falles not, nor oure felowes in feere,
To slo no man: youreself þe soth say.

PILATUS
Why suld I deme to dede, þan, withoute deservyng in dede?
But I have herde al haly why in hertes ȝe hym hate.
He is fautles, in faith, and so God mote me spede,
I graunte hym my gud will to gang on his gate.

273 I was overpowered 274 stood up, prevent myself 275 deed, thought 277 villain, abruptly 278 powerless (to resist), struggled 279 wanted to, in no way 280 heed well 281 Quickly, go 282 This (is) my formal judgement 283 afraid 284 Openly 285 would (be) brought 289 knights 290 rose all together 292 crimes, fellow, committed? 293 no reason to 294 claimed (to be) 295 believe in 297 Don't you see what serious charges 298 These priests bring against you? 300 (who) is made on Earth 301 use 302 wishes 303 pious words, he will not fall 304 whoever uses it sinfully 305 ignobly, fare 306 for every word you say to us 309 rave, all of you 310 fellow, falsehood, find 314 not cease against him 315 Until 316 among ourselves 317 allows you 318 pay (the penalty) 320 Don't be foolish! 321 doubt 322 We have no power 323 slay 324 without good cause 325 wholly 326 God help me 327 way

[13] 'We certainly will not endure being frightened by this wretch.'

[14] 'We want you to understand as you should.'

Caiphas
Nought so, ser, for wele ȝe it wate,
To be kyng he claymeth, with croune,
And whoso stoutely will steppe to þat state
ȝe suld deme ser, to be dong doune
And dede.

Pilatus
Sir, trulye þat touched to treasoune,
And, or I remewe, he rewe sall þat reasoune,
And or I stalke or stirre fro þis stede.

Sir knyghtis þat ar comly, take þis caystiff in keping,
Skelpe hym with scourges and with skathes hym scorne.
Wrayste and wrynge hym to, for wo to he be wepyng,
And þan bryng hym before us as he was beforne.

I Miles
He may banne þe tyme he was borne;
Sone sall he be served as ȝe saide us.

Anna
Do wappe of his wedis þat are worne.

II Miles
All redy, ser, we have arayde us.
Have done,
To þis broll late us buske us and brayde us,
As ser Pilate has propirly prayde us.

III Miles
We sall sette to hym sadly sone.

IV Miles
Late us gete of his gere, God giffe hym ille grace.

[They strip and bind Jesus.]

I Miles
Þai ere tytt of tite, lo, take þer his trasshes.

III Miles
Nowe knytte hym in þis corde.

II Miles
I am cant in þis case.

IV Miles
He is bun faste, nowe bete on with bittir brasshis.

[They begin to scourge Jesus with whips.]

I Miles
Go on, lepis, harȝe, lordingis, with lasshes,
And enforce we, þis faitour, to flay hym.

II Miles
Late us driffe to hym derfly, with dasshes,
Alle rede with oure rowtes we aray hym
And rente hym.

III Miles
For my parte, I am prest for to pay hym,

IV Miles
ȝa, sende hym sorow, assaye hym.

I Miles
Take hym, þat I have tome for to tente hym.

II Miles
Swyng to this swyre, to swiftely he swete.

III Miles
Swete may þis swayne for sweght of our swappes.

IV Miles
Russhe on this rebald and hym rathely rehete.

I Miles
Rehete hym, I rede you, with rowtes and rappes.

II Miles
For all oure noy, þis nygard he nappes.

III Miles
We sall wakken hym with wynde of oure whippes.

IV Miles
Nowe flynge to þis flaterer with flappes.

I Miles
I sall hertely hitte on his hippes
And haunch.

330 claim that authority 331 struck 334 remove/go, claim 335 step 337 whips, blows 338 until he weeps for woe 340 curse 341 instructed 342 rip off 343 prepared ourselves 345 ready ourselves 348 clothes, curse him! 349 quickly, snatched off, rags 350 tie, eager, matter 351 bound, blows 352 quickly, chase (him) 353 let's ensure we flay 354 drive, viciously, blows 355 red, blows, decorate 356 tear 358 try 359 time, attend (to) 360 (his) neck, until, sweats copiously 361 fellow, weight, lashes 362 fiercely pursue 364 wretch, sleeps 365 awaken 366 lashes

II Miles
Fra oure skelpes not scatheles he skyppes.

III Miles
3it hym list not lyft up his lippis
And pray us to have pety on his paunch.

IV Miles
To have petie of his paunche he propheres no prayere.

I Miles
Lorde, how likes you þis lake and þis lare þat we lere 3ou?

II Miles
Lo, I pull at his pilche, I am prowd playere.

III Miles
Thus youre cloke sall we cloute to clence you and clere 3ou.

IV Miles
I am straunge in striffe for to stere 3ou.

I Miles
Þus with choppes þis churll sall we chastye.

II Miles
I trowe with þis trace we sall tere you.

III Miles
All þin untrew techyngis þus taste I,
Þou tarand.[15]

IV Miles
I hope I be hardy and hasty.

I Miles
I wate wele my wepon not wast I.

II Miles
He swounes or sweltes, I swarand.

III Miles
Late us louse hym lightyly, do lay on your handes.

IV Miles
3a, for and he dye for this dede, undone ere we all.

I Miles
Nowe unboune is þis broll and unbraced his bandes.

II Miles
O fule, how faris þou now? Foull mott þe[e] fall!

III Miles
Nowe, because he oure kyng gon hym call,
We will kyndely hym croune with a brere.

IV Miles
3a, but first þis purpure and palle
And þis worthy wede salle he were,
For scorne.

I Miles
I am prowd at þis poynte to apper.

II Miles
Latte us clethe hym in þer clothes full clere,
As a lorde þat his lordshippe has lorne.

III Miles
Lange or þou mete slike a men3e as þou mett with þis morne.[16]

IV Miles
Do sette hym in þis sete as a semely in sales.

I Miles
Now thryng to hym thrally with þis þikk þorne.

II Miles
Lo, it heldes to his hede þat þe harnes out hales.

III Miles
Thus we teche hym to tempre his tales.
His brayne begynnes for to blede.

369 he doesn't escape unscathed 370 he doesn't want to 371 pity, stomach/body 373 game, lore 374 tunic 375 cleanse, purify 376 strong, combat, stir 377 chastise 378 action, tire 379 I test 381 think, tough, brisk 382 I don't waste 383 faints, passes out, swear 384 loose, quickly 385 if he dies, are 386 unbound, untied (are) 387 Curse you! 388 called himself 389 appropriately, briar 390 royal garment, cloak 391 garment 393 appear 394 clothe 395 who has lost his lordship 397 seat, a noble(man) in hall 398 thrust, viciously, thick thorn 399 sticks, head, brains leak out 400 moderate his claims

15 Either 'You delay!', or, as Beadle and King suggest (*York Mystery Plays*, p. 206), 'You *Tarandre*!', a reference to a chameleon-like creature capable of changing the colour of its body (a further mocking reference to Christ's wounds).

16 'It will be a long time before you meet another retinue like the one you met this morning.'

IV Miles
3a, his blondre has hym broght to þer bales.
Now reche hym and raught hym in a rede
So rounde,
For his septure it serves indede.

I Miles
3a, it is gode inowe in þis nede,
Late us gudly hym grete on þis grounde.

Ave, riall roy and *rex Judeorum*,
Hayle, comely kyng þat no kyngdom has kende.
Hayll, undughty duke, þi dedis ere dom,
Hayll, man unmyghty þi men3e to mende.

III Miles
Hayll, lord without lande for to lende,
Hayll, kyng, hayll, knave unconand.

IV Miles
Hayll, freyke without forse þe[e] to fende,
Hayll, strang, þat may not wele stand
To stryve.

I Miles
We! Harlott, heve up thy hande,
And us all þat þe[e] wirschip are wirkand
Thanke us, þer ill mot þou þryve.[17]

II Miles
So late lede hym belyve and lenge her no lenger,
To ser Pilate, oure prince oure pride will we prayse.

III Miles
3a, he may synge, or he slepe, of sorowe and angir,
For many derfe dedes he has done in his dayes.

IV Miles
Now wightly late wende on oure wayes,
Late us trusse us, no tyme is to tarie.

[*They go to Pilate.*]

I Miles
My lorde, will 3e listen oure layes?
Here þis boy is 3e bade us go bary
With battis.

II Miles
We ar combered his *corpus* for to cary,
Many wightis on hym wondres and wary,
Lo, his flessh al beflapped þat fat is.

Pilatus
Wele, bringe hym before us as he blisshes all bloo;[18]
I suppose of his seggyng he will cese evermore.
Sirs, beholde upon hight and *ecce homoo*
Þus bounden and bette and broght you before.
Me semes þat it sewes hym full sore;
For his gilte on this grounde is he grevyd;
If 3ou like for to listen my lore

[. . . *One leaf missing from MS here* . . .][19]

[Pilatus]
For propirly by his processe will I preve,
I had no force fro þis felawshippe þis freke for to
fende.[20]

Preco
Here is all, ser, þat 3e for sende.
Wille 3e wasshe whill þe watir is hote?

Tunc lavat manus suas.

Pilatus
Nowe this Barabas bandes 3e unbende,
With grace late hym gange on his gate
Where 3e will.

Barabas
3e worthy men þat I here wate,
God encrece all youre comely estate,
For þe grace 3e have graunt me untill.

402 disorder, these troubles 403 stretch, give him, staff 407 nobly greet, place 408 Hail!, King of the Jews 410 weakling, are dumb 411 unable to support your retinue 413 ignorant 414 fellow, strength, defend yourself 416 fight 417 hold 420 linger 422 complain 423 evil 424 quickly 425 hurry 426 (to) our story? 427 Here (is), batter 428 blows 429 body 430 wonder 431 bruised, wounded 433 speech 434 'Behold, the man' (John 19:5) 435 beaten 436 he has fared very harshly 437 punished 439 prove 441 sent for 442 while, hot 442+ Then he washes his hands 443 bonds, untie 447 noble authority 448 granted to me

17 'And (thank) all of us who are striving to worship you, or may you be cursed!'

18 'Blushes all discoloured (with wounds).'

19 The missing leaf probably contained the call for Jesus to be executed, Pilate's offer that Jesus be the prisoner released to mark the Feast of Passover, and the High Priests' call that another prisoner, Barabas be released instead. The action resumes with Pilate symbolically washing his hands of the responsibility for the death of Jesus (as narrated in Matthew 27:24).

20 'I had no power to protect this fellow from this crowd.'

Pilatus
Here þe jugement of Jesu, all Jewes on þis stede:
Crucifie hym on a crosse and on Calverye hym kill.
I dampne hym today to dy þis same dede,
Þerfore, hyngis hym on hight uppon þat high hill.
And on aythir side hym I will
Þat a harlott ȝe hyng in þis hast,
Methynkith it both reasoune and skill
Emyddis, sen his malice is mast,
Ȝe hyng hym;
Þen hym turmente, som tene for to tast.
Mo wordis I will not nowe wast,
But blynne not to dede to ȝe bryng hym.

Caiphas
Sir, us semys in oure sight þat ȝe sadly has saide.
Now knyghtis þat are conant, with þis catyf ȝe care,
The liffe of þis losell in youre list is it laide.

I Miles
Late us one, my lorde, and lere us na lare.
Siris, sette to hym sadly and sare,
All in cordis his coorse umbycast.

II Miles
Late us bynde hym in bandis all bare.

III Miles
Here is one, full lange will it laste.

IV Miles
Lay on hande here.

V Miles
I powll to my poure is past.
Nowe feste is he, felawes, ful fast;
Late us stere us, we may not long stand here.

Anna
Drawe hym faste hense, delyvere ȝou, have done.
Go, do se hym to dede withoute lenger delay,
For dede bus hym be, nedlyng, be none.
All myrthe bus us move tomorne þat we may,
Itt is sothly oure grette Sabott day;
No dede bodis unberid sall be.

III Miles
We see wele þe soth ȝe us say.
We sall traylle hym tyte to his tree,
Þus talkand.

IV Miles
Farewele, now wightely wende we.

Pilatus
Nowe certis, ȝe are a manly menȝe,
Furth in þe wylde wanyand be walkand.[21]

449 Hear, in 450 Calvary 451 die, death 454 thief, haste 455 reasonable, wise 456 In the middle, greatest 458 taste 460 rest, until 462 cunning/wise 463 placed in your hands 464 alone, say no more 465 keenly 466 bind his body 470 pull, until 472 stir 473 hurry up 475 by noon 476 prepare, (for) tomorrow 477 Sabbath 478 unburied, must be 480 drag, tree (the Cross) 481 talking 482 quickly 484 waning (of the moon)

[21] i.e. 'Go in an inauspicious hour!': a curse.

York (The Pinners), *The Crucifixion*

The Crucifixion is one of the simplest as well as one of the most powerful of the York pageants. A basic, open-topped wagon with a mortise into which the Cross can be fitted is all that is required in terms of set. The only major props are the Cross itself, and the hammers, nails, and ropes used by the Soldiers. The casting requires only five actors; yet the pageant none the less achieves an astonishing dramatization of the central tenets of redemptive theology, and a focus on the agonies of the suffering Christ that were at the heart of late medieval affective piety.

As Jesus spends most of the pageant lying on the Cross on the floor of the wagon, and thus out of sight of the audience at ground level, the focus of attention remains predominantly on the Soldiers. The latter are presented, not as monsters, but as ordinary men, anxious to complete their work without too great exertion, and largely desensitized to the suffering they are causing. In a master-stroke of didactic dramaturgy the playwright allows the audience to identify with the Soldiers, share their practical difficulties as each agonizing stage of the Crucifixion is presented in graphic detail, even to enjoy their jokes (such as the pun on 'saws' and 'sore' at l. 69), until the moment when the Cross is lifted and the powerful icon of the crucified Christ suddenly becomes visible. The audience is thus made to feel their own complicity in the event on an emotional as well as an intellectual level, and to realize the extent of their own sinfulness. Christ's speech of forgiveness at precisely this point consequently comes as an extraordinarily potent reminder of the contemporary relevance of His sacrifice. This speech, in the form of a Passion lyric, and His willingness to submit Himself to the torments of crucifixion (even to the extent of voluntarily lying upon the Cross before being asked) are potent reminders of His willingness to lay down His life for the sake of humanity.

Some of the details of the pageant, notably the inaccurate boring of the holes in the Cross, necessitating the stretching of Jesus's limbs, are taken from the near-contemporary narrative poem *The Northern Passion*. Despite the Soldiers' quick-fire dialogue, the play is actually remarkably regular metrically, being characterized by a dominant twelve-line stanza rhyming ababababcdcd.

The Pinners made pegs, pins, and nails, thereby creating perhaps the most poignant of the associations between sponsoring guild and pageant which characterize the York Cycle.

[*Dramatis Personae*: *I–IV Miles* (four Soldiers), *Jesus.*]

I Miles
Sir knyghtis, take heede hydir in hye,
This dede on-dergh we may noght drawe.
3ee wootte youreselffe als wele as I
Howe lordis and leders of owre lawe
Has geven dome þat þis doote schall dye.

II Miles
Sir, alle þare counsaile wele we knawe.
Sen we are comen to Calvarie
Latte ilke man helpe nowe as hym awe.

III Miles
We are alle redy, loo,
Þat forward to fullfille.

IV Miles
Late here howe we schall doo,
And go we tyte þertille.

I Miles
It may noȝt helpe her for to hone
If we schall any worshippe wynne.

II Miles
He muste be dede, nedelyngis, by none.

III Miles
Þanne is goode tyme þat we begynne.

IV Miles
Late dynge hym doune, þan is he done;
He schall nought dere us with his dynne.

I Miles
He schall be sette and lerned sone,
With care to hym and all his kynne.

1 listen here, quickly 2 idly, draw (out) 4 masters 5 fool 8 ought (to) 10 agreement 11 hear 12 to it 13 here, delay 15 noon 16 (it) is about time 18 trouble, din/noise 19 set (in place), taught (a lesson)

II Miles
Þe foulest dede of all
Shalle he dye for his dedis.

III Miles
That menes crosse hym we schall.

IV Miles
Behalde, so right he redis.

I Miles
Thanne to þis werke us muste take heede,
So þat oure wirkyng be noght wronge.

II Miles
None othir noote to neven is nede,
But latte us haste hym for to hange.

III Miles
And I have gone for gere goode speede,
Bothe hammeres and nayles, large and lange.

IV Miles
Þanne may we boldely do þis dede.
Commes on, late kille þis traitoure strange.

I Miles
Faire myght ȝe falle in feere
Þat has wrought on þis wise.

II Miles
Us nedis nought for to lere
Suche faitoures to chastise.

III Miles
Sen ilke a thyng es right arrayed,
The wiselier nowe wirke may we.

IV Miles
Þe crosse on grounde is goodely graied
And boorede even as it awith to be.

I Miles
Lokis þat þe ladde on lenghe be layde
And made me þane unto þis tree.

II Miles
For alle his fare he schalle be flaied,
That one assaie sone schalle ye see.

III Miles
Come forthe, þou cursed knave,
Thy comforte sone schall kele.

IV Miles
Thyne hyre here schall þou have.

I Miles
Walkes oon! Now wirke we wele.

Jesus
Almyghty God, My Fadir free,
Late þis materes be made in mynde:
Þou badde þat I schulde buxsome be,
For Adam plyght for to be pyned.
Here to dede I obblisshe Me,
Fro þat synne for to save mankynde,
And soveraynely beseke I þe[e]
That þai for Me may favoure fynde.
And fro þe Fende þame fende,
So þat þer saules be saffe
In welthe withouten ende.
I kepe nought ellis to crave.

I Miles
We! Herke, sir knyghtis, for Mahoundis bloode!
Of Adam kynde is all his þoght.

II Miles
Þe warlowe waxis werre þan woode;
Þis doulfull dede ne dredith he noght.

III Miles
Þou schulde have mynde, with mayne and moode,
Of wikkid werkis þat þou haste wrought.

IV Miles
I hope þat he hadde bene as goode
Have sesed of sawes þat he uppe-sought.

I Miles
Thoo sawes schall rewe hym sore,
For all his saunteryng, sone.

21 death 23 means, crucify 27 (We) need say no more 29 quickly 32 bold traitor 33 Good fortune to you all 34 Who, in this way 35 we need no lessons 37 is correctly arranged 38 better 39 well prepared 40 bored (with holes), ought 41 lengthways 42 fastened, cross 43 deeds 44 put to the test 46 grow cold 47 payment/wages 48 Walk on! 49 gracious 50 matters, called (to) mind 52 Adam's, tortured 53 death, sacrifice myself 55 chiefly 56 because of (My death) 57 fiend, defend 58 souls 59 bliss 60 have no other request 62 Adam's kin 63 worse than mad 64 painful death, he does not fear 65 remember, might 67 better 68 (To) have, thought up 69 he will deeply regret 70 babbling

II MILES
Ille spede þame þat hym spare
Tille he to dede be done.

III MILES
Have done belyve, boy, and make þe[e] boune,
And bende þi bakke unto þis tree.

IV MILES
Byhalde, hymselffe has laide hym doune
In lenghe and breede as he schulde bee.

I MILES
This traitoure here teynted of treasoune,
Gose faste and fette hym þan ȝe thre;
And, sen he claymeth kyngdome with croune,
Even as a kyng here have schall hee.

II MILES
Nowe, certis, I schall noȝt feyne
Or his right hande be feste.

III MILES
Þe lefte hande þanne is myne,
Late see who beres hym beste.

IV MILES
Hys lymmys on lenghe þan schalle I lede,
And even unto þe bore þame bringe.

I MILES
Unto his heede I schall take hede,
And with myne hande helpe hym to hyng.

II MILES
Nowe sen we foure schall do þis dede
And medill with þis unthrifty thyng,
Late no man spare for speciall speede
Tille that we have made endyng.

III MILES
Þis forward may not faile;
Nowe are we right arraiede.

IV MILES
This boy here in oure baile
Shall bide full bittir brayde.

I MILES
Sir knyghtis, saie, howe wirke we nowe?

II MILES
Ȝis, certis, I hope I holde his hande.

III MILES
And to þe boore I have it brought
Full boxumly, withouten bande.

I MILES
Strike on þan harde, for Hym þe[e] boght.[1]

II MILES
Ȝis, here is a stubbe will stiffely stande,
Thurgh bones and senous it schall be soght.
This werke is wele, I will warande.

I MILES
Saie, sir, howe do we þore?
Þis bargayne may not blynne.

III MILES
It failis a foote and more,
Þe senous are so gone ynne.

IV MILES
I hope þat marke amisse be bored.

II MILES
Þan muste he bide in bittir bale.

III MILES
In faith, it was overe-skantely scored,
Þat makis it fouly for to faile.

I MILES
Why carpe ȝe so? Faste on a corde
And tugge hym to, by toppe and taile.

III MILES
Ȝa, þou comaundis lightly as a lorde;
Come helpe to haale, with ille haile.

I MILES
Nowe certis þat schall I doo.
[*Aside*] Full snelly as a snayle

71 Curse them 73 bound 75 Behold 76 (in just the right position) 77 convicted 78 fetter/bind 80 have (his crown) 84 performs 85 limbs, stretch 86 bore-hole 90 unprofitable 91 fail to use, the greatest 95 custody 96 endure, torment 98 think 100 (use of a) rope 101 who redeemed you 102 thick nail, strongly 103 sinews, sent 106 business, stop 107 falls short (by) 108 shrunken 109 drilled in the wrong place 110 suffer 111 too carelessly cut 112 unable to work 113 Fasten 114 stretch, head and feet 115 freely, (just) like 116 haul, curse you! 118 swiftly, as a snail

[1] An ironically anachronistic oath, referring as it does to Christ Himself.

III Miles
And I schall tacche hym too,
Full nemely with a nayle.

Þis werke will holde, þat dar I heete,
For nowe are feste faste both his handis.

IV Miles
Go we all foure þanne to his feete,
So schall oure space be spedely spende.

II Miles
Latte see what bourde his bale myght beete,
Tharto my bakke nowe wolde I bende.

IV Miles
Owe! þis werke is al unmeete.
This boring muste all be amende.

I Miles
A, pees man, for Mahounde!
Latte no man wotte þat wondir,
A roope schall rugge hym doune
Yf all his synnous go asoundre.

II Miles
Þat corde full kyndely can I knytte,
Þe comforte of his karle to kele.

I Miles
Feste on þanne faste, þat all be fytte,
It is no force howe felle he feele.

II Miles
Lugge on ʒe both a litill ʒitt.

III Miles
I schalle nought sese, as I have seele.

IV Miles
And I schall fonde hym for to hitte.

II Miles
Owe, haylle!

IV Miles
            Hoo nowe! I halde it wele.

I Miles
Have done, dryve in þat nayle,
So þat no faute be foune.

IV Miles
Þis wirkyng wolde noʒt faile
Yf foure bullis here were boune.

I Miles
Ther cordis have evill encressed his paynes,
Or he wer tille þe booryngis brought.

II Miles
Ʒaa, assoundir are bothe synnous and veynis
On ilke a side, so have we soughte.

III Miles
Nowe all his gaudis nothyng hym gaynes,
His sauntering schall with bale be bought.

IV Miles
I wille goo saie to oure soveraynes
Of all þis werkis howe we have wrought.

I Miles
Nay, sirs, anothir thyng
Fallis firste to youe and me,
Þei badde we schulde hym hyng
On heghte, þat men myght see.

II Miles
We woote wele so ther wordes wore,
But sir, þat dede will do us dere.

I Miles
It may not mende for to moote more,
Þis harlotte muste be hanged here.

II Miles
The mortaise is made fitte þerfore.

III Miles
Feste on youre fyngeres þan, in feere.

IV Miles
I wene it wolle nevere come þore;
We foure rayse it noʒt right to-yere.

119 fasten, to (the Cross) 120 nimbly 121 promise 122 securely fixed 124 time, best spent 125 jest, torment, ease 127 useless 128 altered 130 think about, mystery 131 stretch 137 asunder 133 properly, tie 134 cool 135 ready 136 doesn't matter, terribly, suffers 137 Pull, (more) yet 138 bliss 139 try 140 haul!, Stop there!, think 142 found 144 (even) if four bulls, tied (to it) 145 These, greatly increased 146 bore-holes 147 veins 148 struggled 149 tricks gain him nothing 150 He'll pay for, with suffering 157 know, those were his words 158 harm 159 More debate won't help 161 mortise 162 Grab on, all together 163 believe, there 164 won't, this year (i.e. ever)

I Miles
Say, man, whi carpis þou soo?
Thy liftyng was but light.

II Miles
He menes þer muste be moo
To heve hym uppe on hight.

III Miles
Now certis, I hope it schall noght nede
To calle to us more companye.
Methynke we foure schulde do þis dede
And bere hym to ȝone hille on high.

I Miles
It muste be done, withouten drede.
No more, but loke ȝe be redy,
And þis parte schalle I lifte and leede;
On lenghe he schalle no lenger lie.
Therfore nowe makis you boune,
Late bere hym to ȝone hill.

IV Miles
Thanne will I bere here doune,
And tente his tase untill.

II Miles
We twoo schall see tille aythir side,
For ellis þis werke wille wrie all wrang.

III Miles
We are redy.

IV Miles
Gode sirs, abide,
And late me first his fete up fang.

II Miles
Why tente ȝe so to tales þis tyde?[2]

I Miles
Lifte uppe!

IV Miles
Latte see!

II Miles
Owe! Lifte alang.

III Miles
Fro all þis harme he schulde hym hyde,
And he war God.

IV Miles
Þe Devill hym hang!

I Miles
For grete harme have I hente,
My schuldir is in soundre.

II Miles
And sertis I am nere schente,
So lange have I borne undir.

III Miles
This crosse and I in two muste twynne,
Ellis brekis my bakke in sondre sone.

IV Miles
Laye downe agayne and leve youre dynne,
Þis dede for us will nevere be done.

I Miles
Assaie, sirs, latte se yf any gynne
May helpe hym uppe withouten hone,
For here schulde wight men worschippe wynne,
And noght with gaudis al day to gone.

II Miles
More wighter men þan we
Full fewe I hope ȝe fynde.[3]

III Miles
Þis bargayne will noght bee,
For certis, me wantis wynde.

IV Miles
So wille of werke nevere we wore.
I hope þis carle some cautellis caste.

166 feeble 167 more (of us) 168 heave 173 doubt 174 (Say) no more 175 lead 176 on the ground 177 yourselves ready 179 carry this end 180 attend to his toes 181 attend to (the) 182 go 184 lift up 186 lengthways 187 protect himself 188 If he was/is God 189 done (to) myself 190 dislocated 191 ruined 192 lifted (from) underneath 193 part 194 half 195 stop, din/moaning 196 by us 197 Try (again), device 198 delay 199 strong men win honour 200 jests, play 203 task, never be (finished) 204 I'm out of breath 205 poor (at our) work, were 206 cast some spell (on us)

[2] 'Why are you listening to stories at this time?' i.e. 'Why are you standing idly about (when you should be working)?'

[3] 'I think you will find few stronger men than us.'

II Miles
My bourdeyne satte me wondir soore,
Unto þe hill I myght noght laste.

I Miles
Lifte uppe, and sone he schall be þore,
Therfore feste on youre fyngeres faste.

III Miles
Owe, lifte!

I Miles
We, loo!

III Miles
A litill more.

II Miles
Holde þanne!

I Miles
Howe nowe?

II Miles
Þe werste is paste.

III Miles
He weyes a wikkid weght.

II Miles
So may we all foure saie,
Or he was heved on heght
And raysed in þis array.

IV Miles
He made us stande as any stones,
So boustous was he for to bere.

I Miles
Nowe raise hym nemely for þe nonys
And sette hym be þis mortas heere,
And latte hym falle in alle at ones,
For certis, þat payne schall have no pere.

III Miles
Heve uppe!

IV Miles
Latte doune, so all his bones
Are asoundre nowe on sides seere.

I Miles
Þis fallyng was more felle
Þan all the harmes he hadde.
Nowe may a man wele telle
Þe leste lith of þis ladde.

III Miles
Methynkith þis crosse will noght abide
Ne stande stille in þis mo[r]teyse 3itt.

IV Miles
Att þe firste tyme was it made overe-wyde;
Þat makis it wave, þou may wele witte.

I Miles
Itt schall be sette on ilke a side
So þat it schall no forther flitte.
Goode wegges schall we take his tyde
And feste þe foote, þanne is all fitte.

II Miles
Here are wegges arraied
For þat, both grete and smale.

III Miles
Where are oure hameres laide
Þat we schulde wirke withall?

IV Miles
We have þem here even atte oure hande.

II Miles
Gyffe me þis wegge, I schall it in dryve.

IV Miles
Here is anodir 3itt ordande.

III Miles
Do take it me hidir belyve.

I Miles
Laye on þanne, faste.

III Miles
3is, I warrande.
I thryng þame same, so motte I thryve.
Nowe will þis crosse full stabely stande,
All yf he rave þei will noght ryve.

207 burden, afflicts 208 hold out 209 there 210 firmly 212 past 216 manner 217 brought us to a standstill 218 difficult, carry 219 nimbly, nonce (at this time) 221 once 224 all sides 225 terrible 226 pain, had (until now) 227 count 228 smallest bone 229 hold firm 231 too wide 232 shake 233 wedged 234 move no further 235 wedges 236 fasten the base, well 237 ready 243 already prepared 244 bring 246 knock, together, may I prosper 248 Even if, raves, split

I Miles
Say, sir, howe likis you nowe,
Þis werke þat we have wrought?

IV Miles
We praye youe sais us howe
Ʒe fele, or faynte ʒe ought?

Jesus
Al men þat walkis by waye or strete,
Takes tente ʒe schalle no travayle tyne.
Byholdes Myn heede, Myn handis, and My feete,
And fully feele nowe, or ʒe fyne,
Yf any mournyng may be meete,
Or myscheve mesured unto Myne.
My Fadir, þat alle bales may bete,
Forgiffis þes men þat dois Me pyne.
What þei wirke, wotte þai noght;
Therfore, My Fadir, I crave,
Latte nevere þer synnys be sought,
But see þer saules to save.

I Miles
We! Harke, he jangelis like a jay!

II Miles
Methynke he patris like a py!

III Miles
He has ben doand all þis day,
And made grete mevyng of mercy.

IV Miles
Es þis þe same þat gune us say
That he was Goddis Sone almyghty?

I Miles
Therfore he felis full felle affraye,
And demyd þis day for to dye.

II Miles
Vath, qui destruis templum![4]

III Miles
His sawes wer so, certayne.

IV Miles
And, sirs, he saide to some
He myght rayse it agayne.

I Miles
To mustir þat he hadde no myght,
For all the kautelles þat he couthe kaste.
All yf he wer in worde so wight,
For all his force nowe he is feste.
Als Pilate demed is done and dight,
Therfore I rede þat we go reste.

II Miles
Þis race mon be rehersed right,
Thurgh þe worlde both este and weste.

III Miles
Ʒaa, late hym hynge here stille
And make mowes on þe mone.

IV Miles
Þanne may we wende at wille.

I Miles
Nay, goode sirs, noght so sone,

For certis, us nedis anodir note:
Þis kirtill wolde I of you crave.

II Miles
Nay, nay, sir, we will loke be lotte
Whilke of us foure fallis it to have.

III Miles
I rede we drawe cutte for þis coote,
Loo, se howe sone, alle sidis to save.

IV Miles
The schorte cutte schall wynne, þat wele ʒe woote,
Whedir itt falle to knyght or knave.

251 tell 252 do you (feel) faint? 254 miss none of My suffering 255 Behold, head 256 contemplate, go 257 sorrow, equal 258 misfortune, compared 259 suffering, relieve 260 Forgive, torment Me 261 They know not what they do 263 considered 264 see (that You save) their souls 265 chatters 266 prattles, magpie 267 doing 268 spoke a lot about 269 who told us 271 That's why, suffers, awful torment 272 (is) condemned 274 Those were his words 277 achieve, power 278 spells, could 279 Even if, he spoke, boldly 280 captured 281 (That which), dealt with 283 These events, reported 286 faces at the moon 287 go when we please 289 we need (to do) one more thing 290 cloak 291 decide by lot 292 shall have it 293 draw lots, coat 294 easy (it is), to be fair to all 295 straw

4 'Hah! Thou who would destroy the Temple!': see Mark 14: 58 and 15:29; Matthew 27:40; John 2:19.

[*They draw lots.*]

I Miles
Felowes, ȝe thar noght flyte,
For þis mantell is myne.

II Miles
Goo we þanne hense tyte,
Þis travayle here we tyne.

297 need not quarrel 298 mantle/coat 300 We're wasting our effort here

Albrecht Dürer, *The Harrowing of Hell*, 1510, woodcut. Reproduced courtesy of Dover Publications.

York (The Saddlers), *The Harrowing of Hell*

Despite the title of the pageant, the action takes place, not in Hell itself, but in Limbo, that borderland of Hell in which those who died before Christ's death were imprisoned to await their redemption, denied the presence of God. The Harrowing brings to an end a number of the themes in Christian history preliminary to the Last Judgement. The final battle between God and Satan is settled in favour of the former, not as the heroic joust that some medieval traditions depicted (see, for example, *Piers Plowman*, passus 18), but as a simple show of power. Christ breaks open the gates of Limbo with a command and burst of light, and He finally banishes Satan to Hell with a word, despite the latter's comic bravado and attempts to engage in combat. The central encounter between the two is, however, fought out in the manner of a courtroom disputation, with Satan in the role of cunning lawyer, seeking to retain his dominion through close attention to the small print of his covenant with God. The simple grandeur with which Jesus refutes his claims is in keeping with His portrayal in the earlier earthly trial scenes. The pageant also brings to an end the long sojourn of Adam and Eve and all the Old Testament prophets in Limbo, as Jesus realizes the Redemption of humanity and their liberation from the consequences of the Fall.

The action (the details of which are drawn primarily from The Gospel of Nicodemus) requires a barred cell, at either the foot or the rear of the wagon, representative of Limbo, and an area for the devils and Jesus to use for their debate. Battlements might also have been placed on the upper part of the wagon to represent the walled fortifications of Hell referred to at various points in the pageant (see, for example, l. 140). Given that the pageant was performed for the most part in daylight, the resonant allusions to light and darkness which permeate the text must have been largely symbolic in performance.

[*Dramatis Personae*: *Jesus*, *Adame* (Adam), *Eva* (Eve), *Isaiah* (the prophet), *Symeon* (Simeon), *Johannes Baptista* (John the Baptist), *Moyses* (Moses), *I Diabolus* (First Devil: Rybald), *II Diabolus* (Second Devil: Beelzebub), *Sattan* (Satan), *Belial* (another devil), *David* (King David) *Michael* (The Archangel).]

JESUS
Manne on molde, be meke to Me,
And have thy Maker in þi mynde,
And thynke howe I have tholid for þe[e],
With pereles paynes for to be pyned.
The forward of My Fadir free
Have I fulfillid, as folke may fynde,
Þerfore aboute nowe woll I bee
Þat I have bought for to unbynde.
Þe Feende þame wanne with trayne
Thurgh frewte of erthely foode;
I have þame getyn agayne
Thurgh bying with My bloode.

And so I schall þat steede restore
For whilke þe Feende fell for synne,
Þare schalle mankynde wonne evermore
In blisse þat schall nevere blynne.
All þat in werke My werkemen were,
Owte of thare woo I wol þame wynne,
And some signe schall I sende before
Of grace, to garre þer gamys begynne.
A light I woll þei have
To schewe þame I schall come sone.
My bodie bidis in grave
Till alle thes dedis be done.

My Fadir ordand on þis wise
Aftir His will þat I schulde wende,
For to fulfille þe prophicye[s],
And als I spake My solace to spende.
My frendis þat in Me faith affies,
Now fro ther fois I schall þame fende,
And on the thirde day ryght uprise,
And so tille Heven I schall assende.
Sithen schall I come agayne
To deme bothe goode and ill
Tille endles joie or peyne;
Þus is My Fadirs will.

Tunc cantent.

ADAME
Mi bretheren, harkens to me here,
Swilke hope of heele nevere are we hadde;

1 earth, obedient 3 suffered 4 tormented 5 covenant, gracious 7 busy 8 those I have redeemed, release 9 won them cunning 10 fruit 11 regained 12 buying 14 From which 16 end 17 in (their) deeds laboured for Me 18 woe 20 joys 23 waits 25 ordained in this way 26 follow 28 comfort, dispense 29 put their faith in Me 30 foes, defend 34 bad 35 pain 36+ Then they shall sing. 38 comfort, never before

Foure thowsande and sex hundreth ȝere
Have we bene heere in þis stedde.
Nowe see I signe of solace, seere,
A glorious gleme to make us gladde,
Wherfore I hope oure helpe is nere
And sone schall sesse oure sorowes sadde.

EVA
Adame, my husband hende,
Þis menys solace certayne.
Such light gune on us lende
In Paradise full playne.

ISAIAH
Adame, we schall wele undirstande;
I, Ysaias, as God me kende,
I prechid in Neptalym, þat lande,
And Zabulon, even untill ende.
I spake of folke in mirke walkand
And saide a light schulde on þame lende.
This lered I whils I was levand,
Nowe se I God þis same hath sende.
Þis light comes all of Criste,
Þat seede, to save us nowe.
Þus is my poynte puplisshid.
But Symeon, what sais þou?

SYMEON[1]
Þhis, my tale of farleis feele,
For in þis Temple His frendis me fande.
I hadde delite with Hym to dele
And halsed homely with my hande.
I saide, 'Lorde, late Thy servaunt lele
Pass nowe in pesse to liffe lastand,
For nowe myselfe has sene Thy hele
Me liste no lengar to liffe in lande.'
Þis light þou hast purveyed
To folkes þat liffis in leede,
Þe same þat I þame saide
I see fulfillid in dede.

JOHANNES BAPTISTA
Als voyce criand to folke I kende
Þe weyes of Criste als I wele kanne.
I baptiste Hym with bothe my hande
Even in þe floode of flume Jordanne.
Þe Holy Goste fro Hevene discende
Als a white dowve doune on Hym þanne;
The Fadir voice, my mirthe to mende,
Was made to me even als manne:
'This is My Sone,' He saide,
'In Whome Me paies full wele.'
His light is on us laide,
He comes oure cares to kele.

MOYSES
Of þat same light lernyng have I:
To me, Moyses, he mustered his myght,
And als unto anodir, Hely,[2]
Wher we were on an hille on hight.
Whyte as snowe was His body,
And His face like to þe sonne to sight;
No man on molde was so myghty
Grathely to loke agaynste þat light.
Þat same light se I nowe
Shynyng on us sarteyne,
Wherfore trewly I trowe
We schalle sone passe fro payne.

I DIABOLUS [RYBALD]
Helpe, Belsabub, to bynde þer boyes;
Such harrowe was never are herde in Helle.

II DIABOLUS [BEELZEBUB]
Why rooris þou soo, Rebalde? þou royis,
What is betidde, canne þou ought telle?

I DIABOLUS
What, heris þou noȝt þis uggely noyse?
Þes lurdans þat in Lymbo dwelle,
Þei make menyng of many joies
And musteres grete mirthe þame emell.

42 grat joy 43 light 46 signifies 47 did, shine 48 clearly 50 taught me 51 Naphtali 52 Zebulun (Isaiah 9:1) 53 walking in darkness 55 taught, living 56 sent 57 from Christ 58 seed (offspring of God?) 59 revealed 61 many wonders 62 (Christ's) friends, found 63 delight 64 embraced (Him) lovingly 65 loyal 66 everlasting life 68 I no longer wish 69 provided 70 (this) place (i.e. on earth) 71 told them 73 As (a) voice crying, reveled 75 baptised 76 (the) River Jordan 77 descended 78 dove 79 Father's, to make me glad 80 just like a man's (voice) 82 I am well pleased 84 sufferings, relieve 85 knowledge 86 revealed 87 also, another, Elijah 88 When 90 sun 92 directly at 94 certainly 97 Beelzebub, these boys 98 commotion, heard before 99 roars, raves 100 (has) happened, say anything? 101 hear 103 talk about 104 make, among themselves

[1] For Simeon's story, see Luke 2:25–35.

[2] An allusion to the Transfiguration of Christ, at which Moses and Elijah appeared at Jesus's side, see Matthew 17:1–8 and Mark 9:2–8.

II Diabolus
Mirthe? Nay, nay, þat poynte is paste,
More hele schall þei never have.

I Diabolus
Þei crie on Criste full faste,
And sais He schal þame save.

Belsabub
3a, if He save þame noght, we schall,
For they are sperde in speciall space.
Whils I am prince and principall
Schall þei never passe oute of þis place.
Calle uppe Astrotte and Anaball
To giffe þer counsaille in þis case,
Bele-Berit and Belial;[3]
To marre þame þat swilke maistries mase.
Say to Satan, oure sire,
And bidde þame bringe also
Lucifer, lovely of lyre.

I Diabolus
Al redy, lorde, I goo.

Jesus
Attollite portas, principes,
Oppen uppe, 3e princes of paynes sere,
Et elevamini eternales,[4]
Youre yendles 3atis þat 3e have here.

Sattan
What page is þere þat makes prees
And callis hym kyng of us in fere?

David
I lered levand, withouten lees,
He is a kyng of vertues clere,
A lorde mekill of myght
And stronge in ilke a stoure,
In batailes ferse to fight
And worthy to wynne honnoure.

Sattan
Honnoure? In þe Devel way! For what dede?
All erthely men to me are thrall.
Þe lady þat calles hym lorde in leede
Hadde never 3itt herberowe, house, ne halle.

I Diabolus
Harke, Belsabub, I have grete drede,
For hydously I herde hym calle.

Belliall
We, spere oure 3ates, all ill mot þou spede,
And sette furthe watches on þe wall.
And if he calle or crie
To make us more debate,
Lay on hym þan hardely
And garre hym gange his gate.

Sattan
Telle me what boyes dare be so bolde
For drede to make so mekill draye.

I Diabolus
Itt is þe Jewe þat Judas solde
For to be dede þis othir daye.

Sattan
Owe, þis tale in tyme is tolde,
Þis traytoure trav[es]es us alway.
He schall be here full harde in holde,
Look þat he passe no3t, I þe[e] praye.

II Diabolus
Nay, nay, he will no3t wende
Away or I be ware,
He shappis hym for to schende
Alle Helle or he go ferre.

Sattan
Nay, faitour, þerof schall he faile,
For alle his fare I hym deffie.
I knowe his trantis fro toppe to taile,
He levys with gaudis and with gilery.
Þerby he brought oute of oure bale
Nowe late Lazar of Betannye;
Þerfore I gaffe to þe Jewes counsaille

105 possibility, past 106 comfort 107 eagerly 109 save (i.e. keep) them 110 imprisoned 116 ruin, perform such bold deeds 117 lord 119 face 124 endless (i.e. everlasting) 125 knave, uproar 126 himself, all? 127 taught (when) living, lies 130 struggle 131 fierce battles 134 captive(s) 135 lad (or, ironically 'lady'). land 136 haven 139 lock, curse you! 140 set out watchmen 142 oppose us further 143 fiercely 146 commotion 148 (sold) to his death 149 Oh, this news is timely 150 crosses us 151 captured 152 escapes 154 wary/alert 155 intends, destroy 156 far 158 deeds, defy 159 tricks 160 lives by, games, tricks 161 control 162 recently, Lazarus, Bethany

3 Ashtoreth was a goddess of the Sidonians, see II Kings 23:13; Baal-Berith was a god of the Baalim, Judges 8:33; Belial is a devil; 'Annaball' remains unidentified. All are represented as devils here.

4 'Lift up your heads, O ye gates; and be ye lift up, ye everlasting doors.' Psalms 24:7.

Þat þei schulde alway garre hym dye.
I entered in Judas
Þat forwarde to fulfille,
Þerfore his hire he has:
Allway to wonne here stille.

Belsabub
Sir Sattanne, sen we here þe[e] saie
Þat þou and [þ]e Jewes wer same assente,
And wotte he wanne Lazar awaye
Þat tille us was tane for to tente,
Trowe þou þat þou marre hym maye,
To mustir mightis what he has mente?
If he nowe deprive us of oure praye,
We will ȝe witte whanne þei are wente.

Sattan
I bidde ȝou be noȝt abasshed,
But boldely make youe boune
With toles þat ȝe on traste,
And dynge þat dastard doune!

Jesus
Principes, portas tollite,
Undo youre ȝatis, ȝe princis of pryde,
Et introibit rex glorie,[5]
Þe Kyng of Blisse comes in þis tyde.

Sattan
Owte, harrowe! [What harlot] is hee
Þat sais his kyngdome schall be cryed?

David
Þat may þou in my Sawter see,[6]
For þat poynte of prophicie.
I saide þat He schuld breke
Youre barres and bandis by name,
And on youre werkis take wreke;
Nowe schalle ȝe see þe same.

Jesus
Þis steede schall stonde no lenger stoken:
Opynne uppe, and latte My pepul passe.

[I] Diabolus
Owte! Beholdes, oure baill is brokynne,
And brosten are alle oure bandis of bras.[7]
Telle Lucifer alle is unlokynne.

Belsabub
What þanne, is Lymbus lorne? Allas,
Garre Satan helpe þat we wer wroken;
Þis werke is werse þanne evere it was.

Sattan
I badde ȝe schulde be boune
If he made maistries more.
Do dynge þat dastard doune
And sette hym sadde and sore.

Belsabub
Ȝa, sette hym sore: þat is sone saide,
But come þiselffe and serve hym soo.
We may not bide his bittir braide,
He wille us marre and we wer moo.

Sattan
What, faitours, wherfore are ȝe ferde?
Have ȝe no force to flitte hym froo?
Belyve loke þat my gere be grathed,
Miselffe schall to þat gedlyng goo.
[*To Jesus*] Howe, belamy, abide,
With al thy booste and bere,
And telle to me þis tyde
What maistries makes þou here?

Jesus
I make no maistries but for Myne,
Þame wolle I save, I telle þe[e] nowe.
Þou hadde no poure þame to pyne,
But as My prisounes for þer prowe
Here have þei sojorned, noght as thyne,
But in thy warde: þou wote wele howe.

164 by any means 165 into (the heart of) 166 plan 167 payment 169 hear 170 agreed together 171 won 172 who was given to us to keep 173 can destroy him 174 use powers (such as) he uses? 175 prey 176 tell you, gone 178 ready 179 tools/weapons, trust 182 gates 186 proclaimed 187 Psalter 190 bars, bonds, specifically 191 vengeance 193 fortified 194 Open, people go 195 fortification 196 burst, bands of brass 197 unlocked 198 Limbo lost? 199 Get Satan's, to revenge us 204 make 205 easily said 206 do it to him 207 withstand, attack 208 (even if) there were more of us 209 afraid 210 drive him away 211 armour, prepared 213 Ho!, 'fair friend' (mocking) 214 boast, noise 217 My (people) 219 punish 220 prisoners, benefit 221 your own 222 (temporary) keeping

[5] 'Lift up your heads, O ye gates; . . . and the King of Glory shall come in.' Psalms 24:7.

[6] King David is conventionally credited with authorship of the Psalms.

[7] A paraphrase of Psalms 107:16, 'For he [God] has broken the gates of brass, and cut the bars of iron in sunder.'

SATTAN
And what devel haste þou done ay syne,
Þat never wolde negh þame nere or nowe?

JESUS
Nowe is þe tyme certayne
Mi Fadir ordand before,
Þat they schulde passe fro payne
And wonne in mirthe ever more.

SATTAN
Thy fadir knewe I wele be sight,
He was a write his mette to wynne,
And Marie me menys þi modir hight:
Þe uttiremeste ende of all þi kynne.
Who made þe[e] be so mekill of myght?

JESUS
Þou wikid Feende, latte be thy dynne.
Mi Fadir wonnys in Heven on hight,
With blisse þat schall nevere blynne.
I am His awne Sone,
His forward to fulfille,
And same ay schall We wonne
And sundir whan We wolle.

SATTAN
God Sonne? þanne schulde þou be ful gladde,
Aftir no catel neyd thowe crave!
But þou has leved ay like a ladde,
And in sorowe as a symple knave.

JESUS
Þat was for hartely love I hadde
Unto mannis soule, it for to save.
And for to make þe[e] mased and madde,
And by þat resoune þus dewly to have
Mi Godhede here, I hidde
In Marie modir Myne,
For it schulde noȝt be kidde
To þe[e] nor to none of thyne.

SATTAN
A, þis wolde I were tolde in ilke a toune.
So, sen þou sais God is thy sire,
I schall þe[e] prove be right resoune
Þou motes his men into þe myre.
To breke his bidding were þei boune,
And, for they did at my desire,
Fro Paradise he putte þame doune
In Helle here to have þer hyre.
And thyselfe, day and nyght,
Has taught al men emang
To do resoune and right,
And here werkis þou all wrang.

JESUS
I wirk noght wrang, þat schal þow witte,
If I My men fro woo will wynne.
Mi prophetis playnly prechid it,
All þis note þat [I] nowe begynne.
Þai saide þat I schulde be obitte,
To Helle þat I schulde entre in,
And save My servauntis fro þat pitte
Wher dampned saulis schall sitte for synne.
And ilke trewe prophettis tale
Muste be fulfillid in Mee;
I have þame boughte with bale,
And in blisse schal þei be.

SATTAN
Nowe sen þe[e] liste allegge þe lawes,
Þou schalte be atteynted or we twynne,
For þo þat þou to wittenesse drawes
Full even agaynste þe[e] will begynne.
Salamon saide in his sawes
Þat whoso enteres Helle withynne
Shall never come oute, þus clerkis knawes,
And þerfore, felowe, leve þi dynne.
Job, þi servaunte, also
Þuss in his tyme gune telle
Þat nowthir frende nor foo
Shulde fynde reles in Helle.

JESUS
He saide, full soth, þat schall þou see,
Þat in Helle may be no reles,
But of þat place þan preched he
Where synffull care schall evere encrees.
And in þat bale ay schall þou be
Whare sorowes sere schall never sesse,

223 ever since 224 come near them until 226 ordained 227 escape from 230 carpenter, to earn his food 231 know, (is) called 232 that's the extent of your family 233 taught you to be 234 Fiend, end you noise 236 end 237 own 238 covenant 239 together eternally 240 part, will 242 you needn't want for anything! 243 lived 244 hardship 245 heartfelt 247 baffled 248 those means, duly 251 known 253 I wish this 254 father 256 argue, into the mud (i.e. trouble) 257 command, eager 258 because 260 in(to), recompense 262 together 264 you contradict yourself 266 woe 268 matter 269 die 271 pit 272 damned souls, sin 273 prophet's 274 Me 275 redeemed, suffering 277 like to cite 278 convicted, part 279 those, cite as witnesses 280 will be first to speak against you 281 Solomon, Proverbs 282 (see Proverbs 2:19) 283 (all) scholars know 288 release from (Job 10:21) 292 sorrow, increase 293 torment 294 Where

And for My folke þerfro wer free,
Nowe schall þei passe to þe place of pees.
Þai were here with My wille,
And so schall þei fourthe wende,
And þiselve schall fulfille
Þer wooe withouten ende.

Sattan
Owe, þanne se I howe þou movys emang
Some mesure with malice to melle,[8]
Sen þou sais all schall noȝt gang,
But some schalle alway with us dwelle.

Jesus
Ȝaa, witte þou wele, ellis were it wrang,
Als cursed Cayme þat slewe Abell,
And all þat hastis hemselve to hange,
Als Judas and Archedefell,
Datan and Abiron,[9]
And alle of þare assente,
Als tyrantis everilkone
Þat Me and Myne turmente.

And all þat liste noght to lere My lawe
Þat I have lefte in lande nowe newe:[10]
Þat is my comyng for to knawe,
And to My sacramente pursewe,
Mi dede, My rysing, rede be rawe,
Who will noght trowe, þei are noght trewe.
Unto My dome I schall þame drawe,
And juge þame worse þanne any Jewe.
And all þat likis to leere
My lawe and leve þerbye,
Shall nevere have harmes heere,
But welthe, as is worthy.

Sattan
Nowe here my hande, I halde me paied,
Þis poynte is playnly for oure prowe.
If þis be soth þat þou hast saide
We schall have moo þanne we have nowe.
Þis lawe þat þou nowe late has laide
I schall lere men noȝt to allowe;
Iff þei it take þei be betraied,
For I schall turne þame tyte, I trowe.
I schall walke este and weste,
And garre þame werke wele werre.

Jesus
Naye, Feende, þou schall be feste,
Þat þou schalte flitte not ferre.

Sattan
Feste? þat were a foule reasoune.
Nay, bellamy, þou bus be smytte.

Jesus
Mighill, Myne aungell, make þe[e] boune
And feste yone fende þat he noght flitte.
And, Devyll, I comaunde þe[e] go doune
Into thy selle where þou schalte sitte.

Sattan
Owt! Ay herrowe! Helpe, Mahounde!
Nowe wex I woode oute of my witte.

Belsabub
Sattan, þis saide we are,
Nowe schall þou fele þi fitte.

Sattan
Allas for dole and care,
I synke into Helle pitte!

Adame
A, Jesu, Lorde, mekill is þi myght,
That mekis Þiselffe in þis manere,
Us for to helpe as þou has hight,
Whanne both forfette, I and my feere.
Here have we levyd withouten light
Four thousand and vi c ȝere;
Now se I be þis solempne sight
Howe Thy mercy hath made us clene

295 because, (free) from there 297 consent 298 go forth 306 (Those such) as, Cain 307 who, hang themselves 308 Ahitophel 309 Dathan, Abiram 310 their mind 311 every tyrant 312 torment 313 believe 314 just now 315 acknowledge 316 adhere 317 death, resurrection, rightly 318 believe, true (Christians) 319 judgement 321 learn 322 live thereby 323 harm here 324 happiness 325 am satisfied 326 to our advantage 328 more (prisoners) 329 laid (down) 330 teach, accept 331 accept, betrayed 332 corrupt 334 much worse 335 chained (in Hell) 336 not move far 337 a rotten deal 338 fair friend, struck (down) 339 Michael 340 bind 342 cell, shall stay 344 raving mad 346 suffer your punishment 347 misery, sorrow 350 humbles 351 have said 352 transgressed, spouse 353 lived 354 4,600 years 355 somber 356 free/pure

[8] 'Oh, I see now that you intend to mix some good sense with the malice.'

[9] Cain, the first-born son of Adam and Eve, slew his brother, Abel, and was cursed by God as a consequence (see Genesis 4:1–17). For the suicide of Judas, see Matthew 27:5; for that of Ahitophel, 2 Samuel 17:23. Dathan and Abiram were enemies of Moses (see Numbers 16:27–34).

[10] Jesus here outlines the central tenets of the Apostles' Creed.

EVE
A, Lorde, we were worthy
Mo turmentis for to taste,
But mende us with mercye
Als Þou of myght is moste.

BAPTISTA
A, Lorde, I love Þe[e] inwardly,
That me wolde make Þi messengere
Thy comyng in erth for to crye,
And teche Þi faith to folke in feere;
And sithen before Þe[e] for to dye
And bringe boodworde to þame here,
How þai schulde have Thyne helpe in hye.
Nowe se I all Þi poyntis appere
Als David, prophete trewe,
Ofte tymes tolde untill us;
Of þis comyng he knewe,
And saide it schulde be þus.

DAVID
Als I have saide, ȝitt saie I soo,
Ne derelinquas, Domine,
Animam meam in {In}ferno,[11]
Leffe noght my saule, Lorde, aftir Þe[e]
In depe Helle where dampned schall goo;
Ne suffre nevere saules fro Þe[e] be,
The sorowe of þame þat wonnes in woo
Ay full of filthe, þat may repleye.[12]

ADAME
We thanke His grete goodnesse
He fette us fro þis place.
Makes joie nowe, more and lesse.

OMNIS
We laude God of His grace.

Tunc cantent.

JESUS
Adame, and My frendis in feere,
Fro all youre fooes come fourth with Me
Ȝe schalle be sette in solas seere
Wher ȝe schall nevere of sorowes see.
And Mighill, Myn aungell clere,
Ressayve þes saules all unto þe[e]
And lede þame als I schall þe[e] lere,
To Paradise with playe and plente.
Mi grave I woll go till,
Redy to rise upperight,
And so I schall fulfille
That I before have highte.

MICHILL
Lorde, wende we schall aftir Þi sawe,
To solace sere þai schall be sende.
But þat þer develis no draught us drawe
Lorde, blisse us with Þi holy hende.

JESUS
Mi blissing have ȝe all on rawe,
I schall be with youe wher ȝe wende,
And all þat lelly luffes My lawe,
Þai schall be blissid withowten ende.

ADAME
To Þe[e], Lorde, be lovyng,
Þat us has wonne fro waa.
For solas will we syng
Laus tibi cum gloria etc.

358 to suffer more torment 359 redeem 361 in my heart 362 (You) would make me 363 proclaim 364 all together 366 (the) message 367 soon 368 promises realized 373 yet (again) 376 Leave 377 (the) damned) 382 fetched 383 Make, everyone 383+ Everyone 384 praise, for his 384+ Then they shall sing. 385 (all) my friends 386 foes 387 great comfort 389 Michael 390 Receive 392 happiness 396 previously prophesied 397 following your instructions 398 sent 399 these, make no move against us 400 hand 405 (we will) be praising 406 won us from woe 408 Praise to you with glory

[11] 'For you [O Lord] wilt not leave my soul in Hell.' Psalms 16:10.

[12] A dense passage, perhaps best read as, 'Never suffer [good] souls [who may repent] to be apart from You; which is the sorrow of them who live in the despair [of Hell], always full of filth.'

York (The Carpenters), *The Resurrection*

The Resurrection pageant takes its material from the somewhat contradictory accounts of the visit to the tomb contained in the Gospels: Matthew 28:1–8 and Mark 16:1–8, where only two Marys are involved; Luke 24:1–11, where it is Mary Magdalene, Joanna, and a number of other women who visit the tomb and are confronted by two angels (described only as men in shining garments); and John 20:1–13, where only Mary Magdalene, along with two Apostles, makes the journey, and there are, again, two angels. The pageant picks its way carefully among these varying accounts, and the material in works such as the near-contemporary narrative poem *The Northern Passion*. Although the text does not make explicit precisely what happens when the Angel appears and sings the Easter antiphon '*Christus resurgens*' as Christ rises from the tomb, it seems clear that the events follow the account of Matthew 28:3–4, in which, rather than the Soldiers simply falling asleep, they are stupefied with fear by the Angel (as '(h)is countenance was like lightning and his raiment white as snow./And for fear of him the keepers did shake and became as dead ones'). This is in keeping with their later retelling of events to Pilate and the high priests at ll. 358 and following. Christ's emergence from the tomb, usually involving His symbolic stepping on one of the paralysed soldiers as He climbs out, was a well-established tradition in Christian iconography by this time.

The pageant once more neatly explores spiritual and more worldly concerns in the motives of the Marys and the Jewish authorities. The corrupt administration's attempt to cover up the events by bribing the witnesses has many modern resonances and suggests a powerful cynicism regarding governmental realpolitik and its relationship with the truth (a running theme in the pageant). Yet the Soldiers' inability to lie about events is an endearing feature of their portrayal. The fact that they are rewarded rather than punished for their failure makes the play, for them at least, a human as well as a divine comedy.

Three locations are required, Pilate's hall (on the pageant wagon), the sepulchre of Christ (perhaps a large property at ground level), and the space in between. As Beadle and King suggest (*York Mystery Plays*, pp. 251–2), the Carpenters' association with this pageant is probably explained by the origins of their guild in the Holy Fraternity of the Resurrection.

[*Dramatis Personae*: *Pilatus* (Pontius Pilate), *Anna* and *Caiphas* (Annas and Caiaphas, Jewish high priests), *Centurio* (a Roman Centurion), *I-IV Miles* (four Soldiers), *III Marys* (Mary Magdalene, Mary Cleophas[1], and Mary Salome[2]), *Angelus* (an Angel), *Jesus*.]

PILATUS
Lordingis, listenys nowe unto me:
I comaunde ȝou in ilke degre,
Als domesman chiffe in þis contre,
For counsaill kende,
Atte my bidding ȝou awe to be,
And baynly bende.

And [s]ir Cayphas, chiffe of clergye,
Of youre counsaill late here in hye.
By oure assente sen we dyd dye
Jhesus þis day,
Þat we mayntayne, and stande þerby
Þat werke allway.

CAIPHAS
ȝis, sir, þat dede schall we mayntayne,
By lawe it was done all bedene,
ȝe wotte youreselve, withouten wene
Als wele as we.
His sawes are nowe uppon hym sene
And ay schall be.

ANNA
Þe pepull, sirs, in þis same steede,
Before ȝou saide with a hole-hede
Þat he was worthy to be dede,
And þerto sware.
Sen all was rewlid by rightis rede,
Nevyn it no more.

1 listen 2 each rank 3 chief judges, country 4 renowned as counsellors 5 ought 6 obey 7 chief 8 hear quickly 9 advice, kill 12 action 14 indeed 15 doubt 17 (visited) upon him 20 as one 23 governed, sound advice 24 Discuss

[1] The mother of James and Joses, see Mark 16:1.

[2] The sister of the Virgin Mary, see John 19:25.

PILATUS
To nevyn methinketh it nedfull thyng.
Sen he was hadde to beriyng,
Herde we nowthir of olde ne ȝing
Thithynges betwene.

CAIPHAS
Centurio, sir, will bringe thidings
Of all bedene.

We lefte hym þere for man moste wise,
If any rebelles wolde ought rise
Oure rightwise dome for to dispise
Or it offende,
To sese þame till þe nexte assise,
And þan make ende.

[*Enter Centurio, at ground level.*]

CENTURIO
A, blissid Lorde, Adonay,[3]
What may þes mervayles signifie,
Þat her was schewed so oppinly
Unto oure sight,
Þis day, whanne þat þe man gune dye
Þat Jesus highte?

Itt is a misty thyng to mene.
So selcouth a sight was nevere sene.
Þat oure princes and prestis bedene
Of þis affray
I woll go weten, withouten wene,
What þei can saye.

God save ȝou, sirs, on ilke a side,
Worschippe and welthe in worldis wide;
With mekill mirthe myght ȝe abide
Boght day and nyght.

PILATUS
Centurio, welcome þis tide,
Oure comely knyght.

Ȝe have bene miste us here among.

CENTURIO
God giffe you grace grathely to gang.

PILATUS
Centurio, oure frende full lang,
What is your will?

CENTURIO
I drede me þat ȝe have done wrang
And wondir ill.

CAIPHAS
Wondir ill? I pray þe[e], why?
Declare it to þis company.

CENTURIO
So schall I, sirs, telle ȝou trewly,
Withowten trayne.
Þe rightwise mane þanne mene I by
Þat ȝe have slayne.

PILATUS
Centurio, sesse of such sawe,
Þou arte a lered man in þe lawe,
And if we schulde any witnes drawe
Us to excuse,
To maytayne us evermore þe[e] awe,
And noȝt reffuse.

CENTURIO
To mayntayne trouthe is wele worþi.
I saide ȝou, whanne I sawe Hym dy,
Þat He was Goddis Sone Almyghty
Þat hangeth þore;
Ȝitt saie I soo, and stande þerby
For evermore.

CAIPHAS
Ȝa, sir, such reasouns may ȝe rewe.
Ȝe schulde noght neveyn such note enewe,
But ȝe couthe any tokenyngis trewe
Unto us tell.

CENTURIO
Such woundirfull cas nevere ȝitt ȝe knewe
As now befell.

25 (a) necessary 26 burying 28 News meanwhile 31 as a man 33 contest our righteous judgement 34 transgress 35 seize, assizes (court session) 36 deal decisively (with them) 39 here, openly 41 did die 42 (was) named 43 mysterious, understand 45 What 46 matter 47 discover, doubt 50 (be yours) throughout the world 51 happiness may 52 Both 55 missed 56 to prosper 57 old friend 64 trickery 65 righteous man I mean (he), 68 learned 69 call 70 defend 71 you ought 73 (the) most worthy thing 74 told 73 (the) most worthy thing 74 told 76 there 77 I still say so 79 opinions, regret 80 mention, things, again 81 Unless, can, signs 83 a marvelous thing

3 Adonai: a Hebrew title for God, literally, 'the Lord'.

Anna
We praye þe[e], telle us of what thyng.

Centurio
All elementis, both olde and ȝing,
In ther maneres þai made mornyng
In ilke a stede,
And knewe be countenaunce þat þer kyng
Was done to dede.

Þe sonne for woo he waxed all wanne,
Þe mone and sterres of schynyng blanne,
Þe erthe tremeled and also manne
Began to speke.
Þe stones þat never was stered or þanne
Gune asondir breke,
And dede men rose, both grete and small.

Pilatus
Centurio, beware withall,
ȝe wote oure clerkis þe clipsis þei call
Such sodayne sight.[4]
Both sonne and mone þat sesoune schall
Lak of þer light.

Caiphas
ȝa, and if dede men rose bodily,
Þat myght be done thurgh socery,
Þerfore we sette nothyng þerby
To be abaiste.[5]

Centurio
All þat I tell, for trewthe schall I
Evermore traste.

In þis ilke werke þat ȝe did wirke
Nought allone þe sonne was mirke,
But howe youre vaile raffe in youre kirke,
That witte I wolde.

Pilatus
Swilke tales full sone will make us irke,
And þei be talde.

Anna
Centurio, such speche withdrawe,
Of all þes wordes we have none awe.

Centurio
Nowe, sen ȝe sette noght be my sawe,
Sirs, have gode day.
God graunte you grace þat ȝe may knawe
Þe soth alway.

Anna
Withdrawe þe[e] faste, sen þou þe[e] dredis,
For we schall wele mayntayne oure dedis.

[*Exit Centurio.*]

Pilatus
Such wondir reasouns as he redis
Was nevere beforne.

Caiphas
To neven his noote no more us nedis,
Nowhere even ne morne.

Þerfore loke no manne make ille chere,
All þis doyng may do no dere.
But to beware ȝitt of more were
Þat folke may fele,
We praye you, sirs, of þes sawes sere
Avise ȝou wele.

And to þis tale takes hede in hye,
For Jesu saide even opynly
A thyng þat greves all þis Jury,
And riȝte so may:
Þat he schulde rise uppe bodily
Within þe thirde day.

And be it so, als motte I spede,
His lattar deede is more to drede
Þan is the firste, if we take hede
Or tente þerto.

86 (natural) things, young 87 own ways, mourning 88 on every side 89 showed (by their) behaviour 90 death 91 dark 92 moon, ended 93 like (a) 95 stirred before 96 Broke in two 97 dead 101 at such a time 104 sorcery 108 believe 109 same deed 110 It wasn't only (that), dark 111 How, veil, (was) torn, Temple 112 I'd like to know 113 angry 114 If 116 no fear 117 ignore 118 farewell 121 you are frightened 123 wonderful things, describes 124 never (happened) 125 We need not discuss his news 126 (neither) evening nor morning 127 let, worry 128 behaviour, harm 129 trouble 131 many reports 132 Think carefully 133 quickly 134 publicly 135 grieves, the Jewish people 136 rightly 138 within three days 139 if (he does), may, prosper 140 fear

[4] 'You know that our scholars call such sudden sights "eclipses".'

[5] 'Therefore we don't think there's anything in this to worry about.'

To nevyn þis noote methynke moste nede
And beste to do.

Anna
3a, sir, if all þat he saide soo,
He has no myght to rise and goo,
But if his menne stele hym us froo
And bere away;
Þat were tille us and oþer moo
A foule fraye,

For þanne wolde þei saie evere-ilkone,
Þat he roose by hymselffe allone.
Therfore latte hym be kepte anone
With knyghtes hende,
Unto thre daies be comen and gone
And broght till ende.

Pilatus
In certayne, sirs, right wele 3e saie,
For þis ilke poynte nowe [to] purvaye
I schall ordayne if I may.
He schall not ryse,
Nor none schalle wynne hym þens away
On nokyns wise.

Sir knyghtis, þat are in dedis dowty,
Chosen for chiffe of chevalrye,
As we ay in youre force affie
Boþe day and nyght,
Wendis and kepis Jesu body
With all youre myghte.

And for thyng þat evere be maye,
Kepis hym wele to þe thirde day,
And latis no man takis hym away
Oute of þat stede.
For, and þei do, suthly I saie
3e schall be dede.

I Miles
Lordingis, we saie 3ou for certayne,
We schall kepe hym with myghtis and mayne.
Þer schall no traitoures with no trayne
Stele hym us froo.
Sir knyghtis, takis gere þat moste may gayne,
And lates us goo.

[They go to the Tomb.]

II Miles
3is, certis, we are all redy bowne,
We schall hym kepe till oure rennowne.
On ilke a side latte us sitte doune
Nowe all in fere,
And sone we schall crake his croune
Whoso comes here.

[The Angel enters and stupefies the soldiers, and Jesus rises from the tomb.] Tunc Angelus cantat '[Christus] Resurgens'.[6]

[The III Marys enter.]

Primus Maria [Mary Magdalene]
Allas, to dede I wolde be dight,
So woo in werke was nevere wight,
Mi sorowe is all for þat sight
Þat I gune see,
Howe Criste my Maistir, moste of myght,
Is dede fro me.

Allas þat I schulde se His pyne,
Or yit þat I His liffe schulde tyne,
Of ilke a myscheve He is medicyne
And bote of all,
Helpe and halde to ilke a hyne
Þat Hym on wolde call.

II Maria [Mary Cleophas]
Allas, who schall my balis bete,
Whanne I thynke on His woundes wete?
Jesu, þat was of love so swete
And nevere did ill,
Es dede and graven under þe grete,
Withouten skill.

III Maria [Mary Salome]
Withowten skill þe Jewes, ilkone,
Þat lovely Lorde has newly slayne,
And trespasse did He nevere none

143 discuss this matter, it necessary 145 even if 146 walk 147 Unless, steal 148 carry (him) 149 to us and (many) others 150 terrible situation 151 each one 152 rose 153 guarded immediately 155 Until 158 same, matter, attend (to) 161 steal 162 In no way 163 courageous 164 chief 165 trust in your strength 167 Go, guard 169 whatever happens 173 if 174 dead 178 steal 179 the best weapons 181 prepared 183 for our honour's sake 184 together 185 crack 186 Whoever 187 death, put 188 no one was ever so sorrowful 190 I saw 192 dead (and thus taken) 193 suffering 194 miss 195 misfortune, cure 196 remedy for 197 support for each person 198 who calls on Him 199 relieve my sorrows 200 wet 201 sweet 203 is, buried, earth 204 unreasonably 207 offence

6 'Then the Angel sings "Christ Arising" ' (the Easter antiphon).

In nokyn steede.
To whome nowe schall I make my mone,
Sen He is dede?

I Maria
Sen He is dede, my sisteres dere,
Wende we will on mylde manere
With oure anoynementis faire and clere
Þat we have broght,
To noynte His wondis on sides sere
Þat Jewes Hym wroght.

[II Maria]
Goo we same, my sisteres free,
Full faire us longis His corse to see.
But I wotte noght howe beste may be,
Helpe have we none.
And who schall nowe here of us thre
Remove þe stone?

III Maria
Þat do we noght but we wer moo,
For it is huge and hevy also.

I Maria
[*She sees the Angel*] Sisteris, a ȝonge childe, as we goo
Makand mornyng,
I see it sitte wher we wende to,
In white clothyng.

II Maria
Sistirs, sertis it is noght to hide,
Þe hevy stone is putte beside.

III Maria
Sertis, for thyng þat may betyde,
Nere will we wende,
To layte þat luffely and with Hym bide
Þat was oure frende.

Angelus
Ȝe mournand women in youre þought,
Here in þis place whome have ȝe sought?

I Maria
Jesu, þat to dede is brought,
Oure Lorde so free.

Angelus
Women, certayne here is He noght,
Come nere and see.

He is noght here, þe soth to saie,
Þe place is voide þat He in laye.
Þe sudary here se ȝe may
Was on Hym laide.
He is resen and wente His way,
As He ȝou saide.

Even as He saide, so done has Hee.
He is resen thurgh grete poostee.
He schall be foune in Galile
In flesshe and fell.
To His discipilis nowe wende ȝe,
And þus þame tell.

I Maria
Mi sisteres dere, sen it is soo,
Þat He is resen dede þus froo,
As þe aungell tolde me and yow too:
Oure Lorde so fre,
Hens will I never goo
Or I Hym see.

II Maria
Marie, us thare no lenger layne,
To Galile nowe late us wende.

I Maria
Nought tille I see þat faithfull frende,
Mi Lorde and leche.
Þerfore all þis, my sisteres hende,
Þat ȝe forth preche.

III Maria
As we have herde, so schall we saie.
Marie oure sistir, have goode daye.

I Maria
Nowe verray God, as He wele maye,
He wisse you, sisteres, wele in youre waye,
And rewle ȝou right.

[*Exit II and III Maria.*]

208 no place 209 complaint 211 dear sisters 212 in a humble manner 213 ointments 214 brought 215 anoint, wounds, all over 217 gracious 218 We greatly long, body 219 I don't know what's best 221 which of us . . .? 223 unless there were more (of us) 224 heavy 226 Making 227 where we are heading 229 it cannot be hidden 230 moved aside 231 whatever happens 232 Near 233 look for that lovely (one) 235 mourning 237 death 242 empty 243 shroud, see 244 (That) was 245 risen, gone (on) 248 power 249 found, Galilee 250 skin (i.e. in corporeal form) 254 from the dead 257 (Away from) here 258 Until I see Him 259 we need, stay 261 Not until 262 healer 264 you (must) proclaim 266 farewell 267 true 268 guide 269 govern

Allas, what schall nowe worþe on me.
A weryed wight,
Mi kaytiffe herte will breke in three
Whenne I thynke on þat body free,
How it was spilte.
Both fete and handes nayled tille a tre,
Withouten gilte.

Withouten gilte þe trewe was tane,
For trespas did He nevere none.
Þe woundes He suffered many one
Was for my misse.
It was my dede He was for slayne,
And nothyng His.

How might I, but I loved þat swete,
Þat for my love tholed woundes wete,
And sithen be graven undir þe grete,
Such kyndnes kithe?
Þer is nothing to þat we mete
May make me blithe.

[*Exit I Maria.*]

I MILES
What, oute! Allas, what schall I saie?
Where is þe corse þat herein laye?

II MILES
What ayles þe man? Is he awaye
Þat we schulde tent?

I MILES
Rise uppe and see.

II MILES
Harrowe! For ay
I telle us schente.

III MILES
What devill is þis, what aylis ȝou twoo,
Such noyse and crye þus for to make too?

I MILES
Why, is he gone?

III MILES
Allas, whare is he þat here laye?

IV MILES
Whe! Harrowe! Devill, whare is he away?

III MILES
What, is he þus-gatis fro us wente,
Þat fals traitour þat here was lente,
And we trewly here for to tente
Had undirtane?
Sekirlie, I telle us schente,
Holy, ilkane.

[I MILES]
Allas, what schall we do his day,
Þat þus þis warlowe is wente his waye?
And savely, sirs, I dare wele saie
He rose allone.

II MILES
Witte sir Pilate of þis affraye,
We mon be slone.

III MILES
Why, canne none of us no bettir rede?

IV MILES
Þer is not ellis but we be dede.

II MILES
Whanne þat he stered oute of þis steede,
None couthe it kenne.

I MILES
Allas, harde happe was on my hede
Amonge all menne.

Fro sir Pilate witte of þis dede,
Þat we were slepande whanne he ȝede,
He will forfette withouten drede,
All þat we have.

II MILES
Us muste make lies, for þat is nede,
Oureselve to save.

III MILES
Ȝa, that rede I wele, also motte I goo.

270 happen to me 271 wearied person 272 heart 273 gracious 274 ruined 276 guilt 277 true (one), taken 278 He never committed a crime 280 were for my sins 281 deeds 282 in no way 283 sweet (one) 284 suffered, wet 285 then (to be) buried 286 make known 287 until, meet 288 happy 291 ails, gone 292 attend (to) 294 I believe we're ruined (for ever) 300 thus, gone 301 laid 303 undertaken (to guard him) 304 truly, 305 Completely, each one 308 safely 310 If, Pilate finds out about 311 will be slain 312 give no better advice? 313 no alternative 314 went 315 No one could know it 316 bad luck 318 When 319 sleeping while he went 320 seize, doubt 322 necessary 324 I well advise, may I thrive

IV Miles
And I as: ente þerto alsoo.

II Miles
An hundereth schall I saie, and moo,
Armed ilkone,
Come and toke his corse us froo
And us nere slayne.

I Miles
Nay, certis, I halde þere none so goode
As saie þe soth even as it stoode,
Howe þat he rose with mayne and mode
And wente his way.
To sir Pilate if he be wode
Þis dar I saie.

II Miles
Why, dare þou to sir Pilate goo
With thes tydingis and saie hym soo?

I Miles
So rede I. If he us sloo,
We dye but onys.

III Miles
Nowe he þat wrought us all þis woo,
Woo worthe his bonys!

IV Miles
Go we þanne, sir knyghtis hende,
Sen þat we schall to sir Pilate wende.
I trowe þat we schall parte no frendes
Or þat we passe.

I Miles
And I schall hym saie ilke worde tille ende,
Even as it was.

[*They go to Pilate's hall.*]

Sir Pilate, prince withouten pere,
Sir Cayphas and Anna in fere,
And all ȝe lordyngis þat are here
To neven by name,
God save ȝou all on sidis sere
Fro synne and schame.

Pilatus
ȝe are welcome, oure knyghtis kene,
Of mekill mirthe nowe may ȝe mene,
Therfore some tales telle us betwene
Howe ȝe have wroght.

I Miles
Oure wakyng, lorde, withouten wene,
Is worthed to noȝt.

Caiphas
To noght? Allas, sesse of such sawe.

II Miles
Þe Prophete Jesu, þat ȝe wele knawe,
Is resen and gone for all oure awe,
With mayne and myght.

Pilatus
Þerfore þe Devill hymselffe þe[e] drawe,
Fals recrayed knyght!

Combered cowardis I you call,
Have ȝe latten hym goo fro you all?

III Miles
Sir, þer was none þat did but small
When þat he ȝede.

IV Miles
We wer so ferde, downe ganne we falle
And dared for drede.

Anna
Hadde ȝe no strenghe hym to gaynestande?
Traitoures, ȝe myght have boune in bande
Bothe hym and þame þat ȝe þer fande,
And sessid þame sone.

I Miles
Þat dede all erthely men levand
Myght noȝt have done.

II Miles
We wer so radde everilkone,
Whanne þat he putte beside þe stone,
We wer so stonyed we durste stirre none,
And so abasshed.

325 agree 326 a hundred (men) 327 each one 328 Came 329 nearly 330 nothing's as good 331 tell(ing) the truth, was 332 strength, courage 334 (even) if, mad 338 kill 339 only die once 340 woe 341 Curse his bones! 344 (he and we) won't part as friends 347 Just (exactly) 349 together 352 each side 354 eager knights 355 speak 356 between us 358 watching, doubt 359 Has come to nothing 362 for anything (we could do) 364 take you 365 cowardly 366 wretched 367 let 368 little 370 afraid, we fell 371 cowered in fear 372 to oppose him? 373 bound in rope(s) 374 those you found there 375 seized, soon 376 deed, living 378 scared 380 astonished, not move

Pilatus
What, rose he by hymselfe allone?

I Miles
3a, sir, þat be 3e traste.

IV Miles
We herde never sen we were borne,
Nor all oure faderes us beforne,
Suche melodie mydday ne morne,
As was made þere.

Caiphas
Allas, þanne is oure lawes lorne
For everemare.

II Miles
What tyme he rose goode tente I toke,
Þe erthe þat tyme tremylled and quoke,
All kyndely force þan me forsoke
Tille he was gone.

III Miles
I was aferde, I durste not loke,
Ne myght had none,

I myght not stande, so was I starke.

Pilatus
Sir Cayphas, 3e are a connyng clerke:
If we amysse have tane oure merke,
I trowe same faile.
Þerfore, what schalle worþe nowe of þis werke?
Sais your counsaille.

Caiphas
To saie þe beste forsothe I schal,
That schall be prophete to us all.
3one knyghtis behoves þere wordis agayne-call;
Howe he is miste.
We nolde, for thyng þat myght befall,
Þat no man wiste.

Anna
Now, sir Pilate, sen þat it is soo
Þat he is resynne dede us froo,
Comaundis youre knyghtis to saie, wher þei goo,
Þat he was tane
With xx^{ti} ml. men and mo,
And þame nere slayne.

And therto of our tresorie
Giffe to þame a rewarde forthy.

Pilatus
Nowe of þis purpose wele plesed am I,
And forther, þus:
Sir knyghtis, þat are in dedis dowty,
Takes tente to us,

And herkenes what þat 3e schall saie
To ilke a man both ny3t and daye:
That ten ml men in goode araye
Come 3ou untill,
With forse of armys bare hym awaye
Agaynst your will.

Thus schall 3e saie in ilke a lande,
And þerto on þat same comenaunde
A thousande pounde have in youre hande
To your rewarde:
And frenschippe sirs, 3e undirstande,
Schall not be spared.

Caiphas
Ilkone, youre state we schall amende,
And loke 3e saie as we 3ou kende.

I Miles
In what contre so 3e us sende,
Be nyght or daye,
Wherso we come, wherso we wende,
So schall we saie.

Pilatus
3a, and whereso 3e tarie in ilke contre,
Of oure doyng in no degre
Dois þat no manne þe wiser be
Ne freyne beforne,
Ne of þe sight þat 3e gonne see
Nevynnes it nowþere even ne morne.

383 you can be sure of that 386 music (at any time) 388 our law is lost 390 At the time (that), I saw clearly 391 quaked 392 natural strength 396 paralysed 397 clever scholar 398 have erred in our aim 399 (we all) fail together 400 follow (what shall we do?) 403 profitable 404 must take back their testimony 405 (About) how, missing 406 do not want, anything 407 any man knew (about it) 409 risen 410 wherever 411 taken 412 by 20,000 men and more 413 nearly 414 from, treasury 415 given, for (saying so) 417 furthermore 418 courageous in action 420 listen 422 10,000, well equipped 423 to you 424 carried 427 (to seal) that covenant 429 As 431 lacking (between us) 432 condition/status, improve 433 told you 434 whatever 436 Wherever, go 440 Ensure 441 discover 442 Nor (about) 443 Mention

For we schall mayntayne ȝou alwaye,
And to þe pepull schall we saie
It is gretely agaynste oure lay
To trowe such thing.
So schall þei deme, both nyght and day,
All is lesyng.
Thus schall þe sothe be bought and solde,
And treasoune schall for trewthe be tolde.
Þerfore ay in youre hartis ȝe holde
Þis counsaile clene.
And fares nowe wele both yonge and olde,
Haly bedene.

444 support 446 law 449 lies 450 truth 453 good advice 454 farewell 455 completely, at once

York (The Mercers), *The Last Judgement*

The Mercer's Indenture (1433)

This pageant, based in large part on Christ's account of the Last Judgement in Matthew 25:31–46, formed the spectacular climax to the York Cycle, in which humanity is judged and the world and time itself are brought to an end. An idea of the scale and nature of the production can be gained from the indenture drawn up between the Mercers' Guild and their pageant masters (the four men responsible for 'bringing forth' the pageant) in 1433. This document (printed in Johnston and Rogerson, *REED: York*, I, pp. 55–6), although rather elliptical in some of its detail, lists the props and other hardware used in the pageant, which the company kept and delivered to the pageant masters each year. Most notable are the elaborate costumes for all the leading characters, including the symbolic haloes ('diadems') for the Apostles, the gilded face-mask and bloody shirt ('sirke woundid') for Christ, and the mechanical effects, such as the iron brandreth or grill on which God ascended into Heaven, and the small angels designed to 'run about' on the roof of the pageant wagon through the action of a long cord.

The indenture reveals that, in keeping with iconographic convention, the entrance to Hell was depicted as the mouth of a great beast, probably situated on the front or side of the wagon at ground level. On the wagon itself was the Earth, with thrones of judgement for Jesus and the Apostles. There may well also have been trapdoors through which the Souls could have risen, as if from their graves. Heaven was represented on the upper level of the wagon, where the mechanical angels ran about, and to which Christ returns with the saved souls at the end of the pageant.

First a Pagent with iiij Wheles, Helle mouthe, iij garmentes for iij devels, vi develles faces in iij Vesernes,[1] Array[2] for ij evell saules,[3] þat is to say: ij Sirkes,[4] ij paire hoses, ij vesenes, & ij Chavelers,[5] Array for ij go[o]d saules, þat is to say, ij Sirkes, ij paire hoses, ij vesernes, & ij chavelers, ij paire Aungell Wynges with iren in the endes, ij trumpes[6] of White plate, & ij redes, iiij Aubes[7] for iiij Appostels, iij diademes[8] with iij vesernes for iij Appostels, iiij diademes with iiij Chevelers of yalow[9] for iiij Appostels, A cloude & ij peces of rainbow of tymber, Array for God, that ys to say, a Sirke wounded,[10] a diademe, With a veserne gilted,[11] A grete coster of rede damaske[12] payntid for the bakke syde of the pagent, ij other lesse[13] costers for ij sydes of the Pagent, iij other costers of lewent brede[14] for þe sides of þe Pagent. A litel coster iiij squared to hang at the bakke of God. iiij Irens to bere uppe[15] Heven, iiij smale coterelles[16] & a Iren pynne, A brandreth of Iren[17] that God salle sitte uppon when he salle sty[18] uppe to Heven, With iiij rapes[19] at iiij corners. A Heven of Iren, with a naffe of tre,[20] ij peces of rede cloudes & sternes[21] of gold langing[22] to Heven, ij peces of blu cloudes payntid on bothe sydes, iij peces of rede cloudes, with sunne bemes of golde & sternes for the hiest of Heven, with a lang small border of the same Wurk.[23] vij grete Aungels halding the Passion of God[24], Ane of thame has a fane of latoun[25] & a crosse of Iren in his hede giltid. iiij smaller Aungels gilted holding the Passion. ix smaller Aungels payntid rede to renne[26] about in the Heven. A lang small[27] corde to gerre[28] the Aungels renne aboute, ii shorte rolls of tre[29] to putte forthe the pageant.

1 Masks.
2 Costumes.
3 Evil souls.
4 Shirts.
5 Wigs.
6 Trumpets.
7 Albs.
8 Haloes.
9 Yellow wigs.
10 A shirt marked with Christ's wound in the side.
11 A gilded mask.
12 A hanging made of a richly woven red fabric.
13 Smaller.
14 Broad linen cloth.
15 Support.
16 Cotter-pins.
17 An iron grate.
18 Rise.
19 Ropes.
20 A wooden hub.
21 Stars.
22 Belonging.
23 Workmanship.
24 The Instruments of the Passion, i.e. the hammer, nails, crown of thorns, etc., symbols of the Passion, displayed by the angels during Jesus's account of His suffering at ll. 245–76.
25 A brass vein.
26 Run.
27 Thin.
28 Make
29 Wooden rollers.

The Last Judgement

[*Dramatis Personae*: *Deus* (God the Father and the Son)[1] *III Angelus* (three Angels), *II Anima Bona* (two Good Souls), *II Anima Mala* (two Bad Souls), *II Apostolus* (two Apostles), *III Diabolus* (three Devils).]

DEUS *INCIPIT:*

Firste when I þis worlde hadde wroght:
Woode and wynde and wateris wan,
And all-kynne thyng þat nowe is oght,
Fulle wele Meþoght þat I did þanne.
Whenne þei were made, goode Me þame þoght;
Sethen to My liknes made I man,
And man to greve Me gaffe he noght,
Þerfore Me rewis þat I þe worlde began.

Whanne I had made man at My will,
I gaffe hym wittis hymselve to wisse,
And Paradise I putte hym till,
And bad hym halde it all as his.
But of þe tree of goode and ill
I saide, 'What tyme þou etis of þis,
Manne, þou spedes þiselve to spill;
Þou arte broght oute of all blisse'.

Belyve brak manne My bidding.
He wende have bene a god þerby;
He wende have wittyne of all-kynne thyng,
In worlde to have bene als wise as I.
He ete þe appill I badde schulde hyng,
Þus was he begilid thurgh glotony;
Sithen both hym and his ospring
To pyne I putte þame all forthy.

To lange and late Meþoghte it goode
To catche þois caitiffis oute of care,
I sente My Sone with full blithe moode
Till Erþe, to salve þame of þare sare.
For rewþe of þame He reste on Roode
And boughte þame with His body bare;
For þame He shedde His harte and bloode.
What kyndinesse myght I do þame mare?

Sethen aftirwarde He heryed Hell,
And toke oute þois wrecchis þat ware þareinne;
Þer faughte þat free with feendis feele,
For þame þat ware sounkyn for synne.
Sethen in Erthe þan gonne He dwelle,
Ensaumpill He gave þame Hevene to wynne,
In Tempill Hymselffe to teche and tell,
To by þame blisse þat nevere may blynne.

Sethen have þei founde Me full of mercye,
Full of grace and forgiffenesse,
And þei als wrecchis, wittirly,
Has ledde þer liffe in lithirnesse.
Ofte have þei greved Me grevously,
Þus have þei quitte Me My kyndinesse;
Þerfore no lenger, sekirlye,
Thole will I þare wikkidnesse.

Men seis þe worlde but vanite,
3itt will no manne beware þerby;
Ilke a day þer mirroure may þei se,
3itt thynke þei no3t þat þei schall dye.
All þat evere I saide schulde be
Is nowe fulfillid thurgh prophicie,
Therfore nowe is it tyme to Me
To make endyng of mannes folie.

I have tholed mankynde many a 3ere
In luste and likyng for to lende,
And unethis fynde I ferre or nere
A man þat will his misse amende.
In Erthe I see butte synnes seere,
Therfore Myne aungellis will I sende
To blawe þer bemys, þat all may here
The tyme is comen I will make ende.

Aungellis, blawes youre bemys belyve,
Ilke a creatoure for to call.
Leerid and lewde, both man and wiffe,
Ressayve þer dome þis day þei schall,
Ilke a leede þat evere hadde liffe;

0+ God begins 2 dark 3 every kind (of), anything 4 then 5 I thought they were good 6 in 7 thought nothing of grieving Me 8 it pains Me 14 If you eat 15 bring about your (own) ruin 16 will be 17 broke 18 intended (to) become 19 gained knowledge 23 offspring 24 for that 25 After a (long) time 26 release 28 To Earth, heal, pain 29 compassion, lay on (the) Cross 30 redeemed 32 What more kindness . . .? 33 harrowed 34 therein 35 gracious (one), many devils 36 trapped (there) 37 did He 38 Example, how to achieve 40 buy 43 as wretches, indeed 44 wickedness 46 repaid Me (for) 47 truly 48 will I suffer their 49 (is) but vanity 51 their mirror 55 for Me 58 pleasure, live 59 rarely, (anywhere) 60 repent (for) his sins 61 (nothing) but many sins 63 trumpets, hear 67 learned, simple 68 Receive, their judgement 69 person

1 True to the doctrine of the Trinity, the manuscript lists the character simply as 'Deus'. It is clear, however, that the speaker of the opening lines is God the Father, while the God who judges the Good and Bad Souls from l. 177 onwards is the Son, Jesus.

Bese none forgetyn, grete ne small.
Ther schall þei see þe woundes fyve
Þat My Sone suffered for þem all.

And sounderes þame before My sight,
All same in blisse schall þei not be.
Mi blissid childre, as I have hight,
On My right hande I schall þame see;
Sethen schall ilke a weried wight
On My lifte side for ferdnesse flee.
Þis day þer domys þus have I dight
To ilke a man as he hath served Me.

I ANGELUS
Loved be Þou, Lorde of myghtis moste,
Þat aungell made to messengere.
Thy will schall be fulfillid in haste,
Þat Hevene and Erthe and Helle schalle here.
Goode and ill, every-ilke a gaste,
Rise and fecche youre flessh þat was youre feere,
For all þis worlde is broght to waste.
Drawes to youre Dome, it neghes nere.

II ANGELUS
Ilke a creature, bothe olde and yhing,
Belyve I bidde ȝou þat ȝe ryse;
Body and sawle with you ȝe bring,
And comes before þe high justise.
For I am sente fro Hevene Kyng
To calle ȝou to þis grette assise,
Þerfore rise uppe and geve rekenyng
How ȝe Hym served uppon sere wise.

I ANIMA BONA
Loved be Þou, Lorde, þat is so schene,
Þat on þis manere made us to rise,
Body and sawle togedir, clene,
To come before þe high justise.
Of oure ill dedis, Lorde, Þou not mene,
That we have wroght uppon sere wise,
But graunte us for Thy grace bedene
Þat we may wonne in Paradise.

II ANIMA BONA
A, loved be Þou, lorde of all,
Þat Hevene and Erthe and all has wroght,
Þat with Þyne aungellis wolde us call
Oute of oure graves hidir to be broght.
Ofte have we greved Þe[e], grette and small,
Þeraftir Lorde þou deme us noght,
Ne suffir us nevere to fendis to be thrall,
Þat ofte in Erþe with synne us soght.

I ANIMA MALA
Allas, allas, þat we were borne,
So may we synfull kaytiffis say.
I here wele be þis hydous horne
Itt drawes full nere to Domesday.
Allas, we wrecchis þat are forlorne,
Þat never ȝitt served God to paye,
But ofte we have His flessh forsworne.
Allas, allas, and welaway!

So what schall we wrecchis do for drede,
Or whedir for ferdnes may we flee,
When we may bringe forthe no goode dede
Before Hym þat oure juge schall be?
To aske mercy us is no nede,
For wele I wotte dampned be we,
Allas, þat we swilke liffe schulde lede
Þat dighte us has þis destonye.

Oure wikkid werkis þei will us wreye,
Þat we wende never schuld have bene weten;[2]
Þat we did ofte full pryvely,
Appertly may we se þem wreten.
Allas, wrecchis, dere mon we by:
Full smerte with Helle fyre be we smetyn.
Nowe mon nevere saule ne body dye,
But with wikkid peynes evermore be betyne.

Allas, for drede sore may we quake,
Oure dedis beis oure dampnacioune.
For oure mys menyng mon we make,
Helpe may none excusacioune.
We mon be sette for oure synnes sake
Forevere fro oure salvacioune,
In Helle to dwelle with feendes blake,
Wher never schall be redempcioune.

70 Be 71 five wounds (of Christ) 73 (I shall) divide 74 together 75 promised 72 each wicked person 78 fear 79 their judgement, declared 83 quickly 84 hear 85 each ghost (i.e. soul) 86 fetch, body, companion 88 come, approaches 89 young 92 judge 93 the heavenly 94 assize (i.e. court) 95 an account 96 in every way 97 radiant 98 in 101 evil, don't speak 103 at once 110 do not judge us for that 111 permit, fiends, enslaved 112 pursued 115 hideous horn 117 lost 118 as it pleased Him 121 fear 122 where, terror 124 (to set) before Him 125 will not help us 128 has brought us, destiny 129 betray 131 secretly 132 Openly, written down 133 dearly, pay 134 sharply, stung 135 may, never die 136 tormented 138 are 139 sin(s), moaning 140 excuses won't help 141 must be set 143 black fiends

2 '(Those deeds) that we thought would never be known about'.

II Anima Mala
Als carefull caitiffis may we ryse,
Sore may we wringe oure handis and wepe.
For cursidnesse and for covetise
Dampned be we to Helle full depe.
Rought we nevere of Goddis servise,
His comaundementis wolde we noȝt kepe,
But ofte þan made we sacrafise
To Satanas when othir slepe.

Allas, now wakens all oure were,
Oure wikkid werkis may we not hide,
But on oure bakkis us muste þem bere.
Thei wille us wreye on ilke a side.
I see foule feendis þat wille us feere,
And all for pompe of wikkid pride.
Wepe we may with many a teere,
Allas, þat we þis day schulde bide.

Before us playnly bese fourth brought
Þe dedis þat us schall dame bedene;
Þat eres has herde, or harte has þoght,
Sen any tyme þat we may mene,
Þat fote has gone or hande has wroght,
That mouthe hath spoken or ey has sene,
Þis day full dere þanne bese it boght.
Allas, unborne and we hadde bene!

III Angelus
Standis noght togedir, parte you in two!
All sam schall ȝe noght be in blisse;
Mi Fadir of Hevene woll it be soo,
For many of yowe has wroght amys.
Þe goode on His right hande ȝe goe,
Þe way till Hevene He will you wisse,
3e weryed wightis, ȝe flee Hym froo
On His lefte hande, as none of His.

Deus [Jesus]
Þis wofful worlde is brought till ende,
Mi Fadir of Hevene He woll it be;
Þerfore till Erþe nowe will I wende
Miselve to sitte in mageste.
To deme My domes I woll descende;
Þis body will I bere with Me,
Howe it was dight, mannes mys to mende,
All mankynde þere schall it see.

Mi postelis and My darlyngis dere,
Þe dredefull Dome þis day is dight.
Both Heven and Erthe and Hell schall here
Howe I schall holde þat I have hight:
That ȝe schall sitte on seetis sere
Beside Myselffe to se þat sight,
And for to deme folke ferre and nere
Aftir her werkyng, wronge or right.

I saide also whan I you sente
To suffre sorowe for My sake,
All þo þat wolde þame right repente
Shulde with you wende and wynly wake;
And to youre tales who toke no tente
Shulde fare to fyre with fendis blake.
Of mercy nowe may noȝt be mente,
Butt, aftir wirkyng, welth or wrake.

My hetyng haly schall I fullfille,
Therfore comes furth and sittis Me by
To here þe dome of goode and ill.

I Apostolus
I love Þe[e], Lord God Allmyghty;
Late and herely, lowde and still,
To do Thy bidding bayne am I.
I obblissh me to do Þi will
With all my myght, als is worthy.

II Apostolus
A, myghtfull God, here is it sene
Þou will fulfille Þi forward right,
And all Þi sawes Þou will maynteyne.
I love Þe[e], Lorde, with all my myght,
Þer for us þat has erthely bene
Swilke dingnitees has dressed and dight.

Deus [Jesus]
Comes fourthe, I schall sitte ȝou betwene,
And all fullfille þat I have hight.

Hic ad sedem judicii cum cantu angelorum.[3]

145 sorrowful 147 wickedness, covetousness 149 worked, in God's 152 Satan, while others slept 153 begins 155 backs, carry 157 terrify us 159 tear 160 suffer 161 will be brought out 162 will damn us 163 ears have heard, heart, thought 164 think of 165 foot 166 eye, seen 167 be, bought 168 if (only) we'd not been born! 171 desires it (to be) so 172 done wrong 176 no (servants) of His 179 to Earth 181 deliver My judgements 183 treated, sins to redeem 185 Apostles, dear darlings 187 hear 188 fulfil, that (which) I promised 189 many thrones 190 see 191 far, near 192 according to their deeds 195 who would truly 196 wake with joy 197 (those) who, teaching 198 go to the fire 199 we may not speak 200 bliss or torment 201 promises, wholly 205 early, loud, quiet (i.e. always) 207 dedicate myself 210 covenant, justly 211 words 213 have been on Earth 214 honours, prepared

3 'Here he goes to the seat of judgement, with the song of angels.'

I Diabolus
Felas, arraye us for to fight,
And go we faste oure fee to fange.
Þe dredfull Dome þis day is dight;
I drede me þat we dwelle full longe.

II Diabolus
We schall be sene evere in þer sight
And warly waite, ellis wirke we wrange,
For if þe domisman do us right,
Full grete partie with us schall gang.

III Diabolus
He schall do right to foo and frende,
For nowe schall all þe soth be sought.
All weried wightis with us schall wende,
To payne endles þei schall be broght.

Deus [Jesus]
Ilke a creature, takes entent
What bodworde I to you bringe:
Þis wofull worlde away is wente,
And I am come as crouned Kynge.
Mi Fadir of Hevene, He has Me sente
To deme youre dedis and make ending.
Comen is þe Day of Jugement;
Of sorowe may ilke a synfull synge.

The day is comen of kaydyfnes,
All þam to care þat are unclene,[4]
Þe day of bale and bittirnes;
Full longe abedyn has it bene;
Þe day of drede to more and lesse,
Of ire, of trymbelyng, and of tene,
Þat ilke a wight þat weried is
May say, 'Allas, þis daye is sene'.

Here may ȝe see My woundes wide,
Þe whilke I tholed for youre mysdede.
Thurgh harte and heed, foote, hande, and hide,
Nought for My gilte, butt for youre nede.
Beholdis both body, bak, and side,
How dere I bought youre brotherhede.
Þes bittir peynes I wolde abide;
To bye you blisse þus wolde I bleede.

Mi body was scourged withouten skill,
As theffe full thraly was thrette;
On Crosse þei hanged Me, on a hill,
Blody and bloo, as I was bette,
With croune of thorne throsten full ill.
Þis spere unto My side was sette.
Myne harte-bloode spared noght þei for to spill;
Manne, for thy love wolde I not lette.

Þe Jewes spitte on Me spitously,
Þei spared Me no more þan a theffe.
Whan þei Me strake I stode full stilly,
Agaynste þam did I nothyng greve.
Behalde, mankynde, þis ilke is I,
Þat for ye suffered swilke mischeve.
Þus was I dight for thy folye.
Man, loke, thy liffe was to Me full leffe.

Þus was I dight þi sorowe to slake;
Manne, þus behoved þe[e] to borowed be.[5]
In all My woo toke I no wrake,
Mi will itt was for þe love of þe[e].
Man, sore aught þe[e] for to quake,
Þis dredfull day þis sight to see.
All þis I suffered for þi sake;
Say, man, what suffered þou for Me?

My blissid childre on My right hande,
Youre dome þis day ȝe thar not drede,
For all youre comforte is command;
Youre liffe in likyng schall ȝe lede.
Commes to þe Kyngdome ay-lastand
Þat ȝou is dight for youre goode dede;
Full blithe may ȝe be where ȝe stande,
For meckill in Hevene schall be youre mede.

Whenne I was hungery, ȝe Me fedde;[6]
To slake My thirste youre harte was free.

217 Fellows, prepare 218 to seize our rights 220 delay too long 221 their 222 carefully watch, or 223 the judge does us justice 224 a large proportion (of souls) 229 pay attention 230 message 231 is done away with 232 crowned 236 every sinful (soul) complain 239 sorrow, bitterness 240 awaited 241 great, small 242 anger, trembling, strife 243 wicked 244 to see this day 245 deep wounds 246 suffered 247 heart, flesh 248 not, sin, need 250 dearly, your right to be My brothers 253 unreasonably 254 Like a thief was (it) treated 256 bruised, beaten 257 pierced, wickedly 258 spear, stuck 259 they didn't hesitate 260 for love of you, would not falter 261 spitefully 262 than (they would) a thief 264 I did not get angry 265 I am the same (one) 266 torment 267 treated 268 so dear 269 end 271 suffering, felt no anger 273 you ought to tremble terribly 278 need 279 coming 280 happiness, lead 282 That is prepared for you 284 reward 286 you were generous

4 'The day has come [on which] all those who have been sinful will be overcome with wretchedness.'

5 'Man, it was necessary to do this in order to save you.'

6 See Matthew 25:35–6 for the corporal acts of mercy, enjoined upon all Christians, that Christ outlines here.

Whanne I was clothles, ȝe Me cledde;
Ȝe wolde no sorowe uppon Me see.
In harde presse whan I was stedde,
Of My payns ȝe hadde pitee;
Full seke whan I was brought in bedde,
Kyndely ȝe come to coumforte Me.

Whanne I was wille and werieste
Ȝe herbered Me full hartefully;
Full gladde þanne were ȝe of youre geste,
And pleyned My poverte piteuously.
Belyve ȝe brought Me of þe beste
And made My bedde full esyly;
Þerfore in Hevene schall be youre reste,
In joie and blisse to be Me by.

I ANIMA BONA
Whanne hadde we, Lorde þat all has wroght,
Meete and drinke Þe[e] with to feede,
Sen we in Erþe hadde nevere noght
But thurgh þe grace of Thy Godhede?

II ANIMA BONA
Whanne waste þat we Þe[e] clothes brought,
Or visite Þe[e] in any nede,
Or in Þi sikenes we Þe[e] sought?
Lorde, when did we Þe[e] þis dede?

DEUS [JESUS]
Mi blissid childir, I schall ȝou saye
What tyme þis dede was to Me done:
When any þat nede hadde, nyght or day,
Askid ȝou helpe and hadde it sone.
Youre fre hartis saide þem nevere nay,
Erely ne late, mydday ne none,
But als ofte-sithis as þei wolde praye,
Þame thurte but bide and have þer bone.[7]

[*To Bad Souls*] Ȝe cursid caytiffis of Kaymes kynne,
Þat nevere Me comforte in My care,
I and ȝe forever will twynne,
In dole to dwelle for evermare.
Youre bittir bales schall nevere blynne,
Þat ȝe schall have whan ȝe come þare;
Þus have ȝe served for youre synne,
For derffe dedis ȝe have done are.

Whanne I had mistir of mete and drynke,
Caytiffis, ȝe cacched Me fro youre ȝate.
Whanne ȝe wer sette as sirs on benke,
I stode þeroute, werie and wette;
Was none of yowe wolde on Me thynke,
Pyte to have of My poure state;
Þerfore till Hell I schall you synke;
Weele are ȝe worthy to go þat gate.

Whanne I was seke and soriest
Ȝe visitte Me noght, for I was poure.
In prisoune faste whan I was feste
Was none of you loked howe I lore.
Whenne I wiste nevere where for to reste,
With dyntes ȝe draffe Me fro your dore;
Butte ever to pride þanne were ȝe preste,
Mi flessh, My bloode, ofte ȝe forswore.

Clothles whanne I was ofte, and colde,
At nede of you, ȝede I full naked;
House ne herborrow, helpe ne holde
Hadde I none of you, þof I quaked.
Mi mischeffe sawe ye manyfolde,
Was none of you My sorowe slaked,
Butt evere forsoke Me, yonge and alde,
Þerfore schall ȝe nowe be forsaked.

I ANIMA MALA
Whan had Þou, Lorde þat all thing has,
Hungir or thirste, sen Þou God is?
Whan was it Þou in prisoune was?
Whan was Þou naked or herberles?

II ANIMA MALA
Whan was it we sawe Þe[e] seke, allas?
Whan kid we Þe[e] þis unkyndinesse?
Werie or wette to late Þe[e] passe,
When did we Þe[e] þis wikkidnesse?

DEUS [JESUS]
Caistiffis, als ofte als it betidde

287 you clothed Me 289 hardship, placed 291 bedridden through sickness 293 aghast, wearied 294 sheltered 295 guest 296 sorrowed for, poverty 298 comfortably 300 by my side 302 food, to feed You 305 was it 307 helped 311 anyone in need 312 (for) help 313 generous 314 Early, noon (midnight) 315 as many times, beg 317 Cain's kin 318 sorrow 319 part 321 end 322 there 323 deserved 324 evil, always 325 need, food 326 cast, gate 327 nobles, (the) bench (at dinner) 328 outside, weary, wet 329 would think of Me 330 poor condition 333 sick, most sorrowful 335 (locked up) fast 336 looked how I was doing 337 did not know 338 blows, drove, door 339 intent 341 Without clothes 342 I went about naked 343 shelter, succour 344 (even) though I shivered 345 in many ways 346 eased 348 forsaken 349 has everything 352 shelterless? 354 did we (do You), unkindness? 357 happened

7 'They needed only to ask [you] and they had their wish granted.'

Þat nedfull aught askid in My name,
3e herde þem noght, youre eris 3e hidde,
Youre helpe to þame was no3t at hame.
To Me was þat unkyndines kyd,
Þerfore bere þis bittir blame;
To leste or moste whan 3e it did,
To Me 3e did þe selve and þe same.

Mi chosen childir, comes unto Me,
With Me to wonne nowe schall 3e wende

Þere joie and blisse schall ever be,
3oure liffe in lyking schall 3e lende.
3e cursed kaitiffis, fro Me 3e flee,
In Helle to dwelle withouten ende;
Þer 3e schall nevere butt sorowe see
And sitte be Satanas þe Fende.

Nowe is fulfillid all My forþoght,
For endid is all erthely thyng.
All worldly wightis þat I have wroght,
Aftir þer werkis have nowe wonnyng.
Thei þat wolde synne and sessid noght,
Of sorowes sere now schall þei syng;
And þei þat mendid þame whils þei moght
Shall belde and bide in my blissing.

Et sic facit finem, cum melodia angelorum transiens a loco ad locum.[8]

358 that anyone needy asked (you) 359 heard, ears, covered 360 home 361 done 362 bear 364 the self-same thing 368 live 371 see nothing but 372 beside Satan 373 design 375 folk 376 According to their, dwelling 379 repented, while, could 380 live and endure

8 'And thus He makes an end, with [the] melody of angels crossing from place to place.'

Albrecht Dürer, *The Annunciation*, 1526, drawing. Musée Condé, Chantilly/photo Giraudon.

N-Town, *The Mary Play*

The Mary Play provides an account of the early life of the Virgin Mary, and reflects the fascination with (and devotion to) the Virgin so characteristic of the later medieval period. As well as retelling the story of Mary's miraculous birth (of previously childless parents), her Presentation into the Temple (at which she displays a remarkably precocious knowledge of the Bible), her betrothal to Joseph, the Annunciation, and her visit to her Cousin Elizabeth, the play provides instruction in how to live a good Christian life, and guidance in understanding the Psalms and the origins and significance of acts of devotion such as the *Ave Maria* and the *Magnificat*. The didactic content of the play is highlighted by the figure of Contemplacio (Contemplation), who acts as narrator and expositor of the material, drawing out its significance for the audience, and pointing out those parts of Mary's life that will not be covered. But the play none the less avoids heavy-handed instruction, rooting itself in a plausible – if highly idealized – world in which the recognizably human characters live their lives. It is this mixture of the homely and the sublime (perhaps most obvious in Gabriel's delicate handling of Mary at the Annunciation) which gives the play its distinctive quality, and makes it so typical of the affective lay piety of the period.

Of the events represented, only the Annunciation and the visit to Elizabeth have any biblical basis (in Luke 1:26–58). The remainder of the narrative is drawn from a range of apocryphal and later material such as the Greek Protevangelium, the Pseudo-Matthew, and *The Nativity of Mary* (A. Walker, ed. and trans., *Apocryphal Gospels*, Acts and Revelations, Ante-Nicene Library 16 (Edinburgh, 1890)), The *Legenda Aurea* (*Golden Legend*) of Jacobus de Voragine (ed., Theodor Graesse, 3rd edn, Bresslau, 1890), John Lydgate's *Life of Our Lady* (best consulted in J.A. Lauritis, et al, eds., *A Critical Edition of John Lydgate's Life of Our Lady* (Pittsburgh, Pa., 1961)), and Nicholas Love's *Mirror of the Blessed Life of Jesus Christ* (a translation and adaptation of St Bonaventure's *Meditationes Vitae Christi*, see L.F. Powell, ed., *The Mirrour of the Blessed Lyf of Jesu Christ* (Oxford, 1908)).

How the plays in the N-Town manuscript were staged is not clear, and – given the composite nature of the text – it may well be that the various elements were staged differently. Peter Meredith (*Mary Play*, p. 20) suggests the possibility of place-and-scaffold staging for the *Mary Play*, with separate 'houses' representing the various locations (the Temple, Heaven, the homes of Joachim and Anne, Joseph and Mary, Zacharias and Elizabeth), arranged around a central open space: the *platea* or 'place'. This is a distinct possibility, but the play could be performed more simply, with a single scaffold standing for all the earthly locations, and a higher place (from which, as the stage directions suggest, the Angels must 'descend') representing Heaven. What is clear is that the play utilized a number of impressive 'special effects'. The miraculous blossoming of Joseph's 'wand' may have been achieved with a hollow stick concealing flowers of the sort used by modern conjurors. The appearance of the dove representing the Holy Spirit may have employed the same device, or alternatively the dove may have descended on a wire. The tableau of the Conception (ll. 1374ff), in which the three Persons of the Trinity appear linked to each other and to the Virgin by a network of 'beams', may well have involved rods or streamers representing the rays of celestial light often depicted in medieval iconography, although David Mills has suggested the possibility that the 'beams' were the blasts of trumpets (Mills, 'Concerning a Stage Direction in the *Ludus Coventriae*', *English Language Notes* II (1974), 162–4). Mention of a '*chorus*' in the Temple and the numerous references to the singing of Latin hymns suggest that the playwright could call upon the services of a professional choir (see Rastall, *The Heaven Singing*). A further question concerning staging involves the age of the actor playing the demanding role of Mary herself. It is possible that she would have been played by a young child, although, as recent productions have shown, it is possible for the part to be played most effectively by an adult actor.

The base text used here is British Library MS Cotton Vespasian D.VIII. I have also consulted the photographic facsimile in Meredith and Kahrl, *The N-Town Plays*, and the scholarly editions in Spector, *The N-Town Play*, and Meredith, *The Mary Play from the N-Town Manuscript*, whose suggested separation of the *Mary Play* from the surrounding material I have gratefully followed.

[*Dramatis Personae*: *Contemplacio* (Contemplation, the play's expositor),[1] *Ysakar* (later (ll. 346+ff) *Episcopus*: 'Bishop': the high priest of the Temple), *Joachym* and *Anna* (Joachim and Anne, parents to Mary), *Senior Tribus* (an elder of the Jewish Tribe or House of David), *III Pastores* (three Shepherds, servants of Joachym), *Angelus/Aungel/Gabryel* (the Angel Gabriel), *Maria* (Mary), *Minister* (a priest of the Temple), *Episcopus* (from ll. 595ff this seems to be a second 'Bishop', called Abysakar), *Nuncius* ('Messenger' or Herald of the Temple), *III Generacionis David* (three Men of the House/Line of David), *Joseph*, *Vox* ('Voice'), *Susanne, Rebecca,* and *Sephor* (hand-maidens to Mary), *Virtutes* (one or more of the Angelic Order of 'Virtues'), *Pater*, *Filius*, *Spiritus Sancti* (Father, Son, and Holy Spirit, the three Persons of the Trinity, who appear separately in the Parliament of Heaven section), *Veritas*, *Misericordia*, *Justicia*, *Pax* (Truth, Mercy, Justice, Peace, the 'four daughters of God' representative of the chief qualities of the godhead), *Elizabeth* (cousin to Mary, mother to John the Baptist), *Zachary* (Zacharias, husband to Elizabeth), *Chorus* (Choir), Various *Angels*, *Handmaidens*, and *Priests*.]

CONTEMPLACIO

Cryst conserve þis congregacyon
Fro perellys past, present, and future,
And þe personys here pleand, þat þe pronunciacyon
Of here sentens to be seyd mote be sad and sure:[2]
And þat non oblocucyon make þis matere obscure,
But it may profite and plese eche persone present,
From þe gynnynge to þe endynge so to endure,
Þat Cryst and every creature with þe conceyte be content.

This matere here mad is of þe Modyr of Mercy;
How be Joachym and Anne was here concepcyon,
Sythe offred into þe Temple, compiled breffly,
Than maryed to Joseph, and so, folwyng, þe salutacyon,
Metyng with Elyzabeth, and þerwith a conclusyon,
In fewe wurdys talkyd þat it xulde nat be tedyous
To lernyd nyn to lewd, nyn to no man of reson.
Þis is þe processe; now preserve ȝow Jhesus!

Þerffore of þes I ȝow pray all þat ben here present,
And tak hed to oure talkyn, what we xal say.
I beteche ȝow þat Lorde þat is evyr omnypotent
To governe ȝow in goodnes as He best may.
In Hevyn we may Hym se.
Now God þat is Hevyn Kynge
Sende us all Hese dere blyssynge,
And to His towre He mote us brynge,
Amen, for charyte!

YSAKAR

The prestys of God offre sote ensens
Unto here God and þerfore they be holy.[3]
We þat mynistere here in Goddys presens,
In us xuld be fownd no maner of foly.
Ysakar, prynce of prestys, am I,
Þat þis holyest day here have mynystracyon,
Certyfyenge all tribus in my cure specyaly,[4]
Þat this is þe hyest fest of oure solennyzacyon.

This we clepe *Festum Encenniorum*,[5]
Þe newe fest, of which iii in þe ȝere we exercyse.
Now all þe kynredys to Jerusalem must cum
Into þe Temple of God, here to do sacryfyse.
Tho þat be cursyd my dygnyte is to dysspyse,
And þo þat be blyssyd, here holy sacrefyse to take.[6]
We be *regal sacerdocium*; it perteyneth us to be wysse,
Be fastyng, be prayng, be almes, and at du tyme to wake.[7]

JOACHYM

Now all þis countre of Galyle,
With þis cetye of Nazareth specyal,

1 gathering 2 perils 3 playing 5 poor speaking 7 beginning 8 matter (of the play) 9 made, (i.e. Mary) 10 by, her 11 After that, briefly told 12 married 14 words, should 15 too, nor 16 order (of events) 17 be 18 pay attention 19 commend you (to) 24 tower (i.e. Heaven) 26 priests, sweet incense 27 their 29 kind of sin 31 ministry/service 33 feast, dedication 35 three 36 tribes 40 (a) royal priesthood 42 Galilee 43 city, especially

[1] Given the play's East Anglian origins, its employment of abstractions such as Contemplacio and the Four Daughters of God may suggest a degree of influence from the Morality plays, many of which also originated in the region.

[2] '[So] that the speaking of the words [or doctrine] to be spoken may be sober and sure.'

[3] See Leviticus 21:6: 'They shall be holy unto their God, and not profane the name of their God: for the offerings of the Lord made by fire, and the bread of their God, they do offer: therefore they shall be holy.'

[4] 'Certifying especially (to) all (the) Tribes (of Israel) in my charge'.

[5] *Festum Encaeniorum*: the Feast of the Dedication of the Temple.

[6] 'My responsibility is to refuse [the sacrificial offerings] of those who are cursed [by God], and to accept those of the blessed.'

[7] 'By fasting, by prayer, by [giving] alms, and by waking at the appropriate times [to observe the canonical hours for prayer].'

Þis fest to Jerusalem must go we
To make sacrefyce to God eternal.
My name is Joachym, a man in godys substancyall.
'Joachym' is to say, 'he þat to God is redy';
So have I be and, evyrmore xal,
For þe dredful domys of God sore drede I.

I am clepyd ryghtful; why, wole ȝe se?
For my godys into thre partys I devyde:
On to þe Temple and to hem þat þer servyng be;
Anodyr to þe pylgrimys and pore men, þe iii^{de} for hem with me abyde.[8]
So xulde every curat in þis werde wyde
Ȝeve a part to his chauncel, iwys,
A part to his parochonerys þat to povert slyde,[9]
The thryd part to kepe for hym and his.

But, blyssyd wyff, Anne, sore I drede
In þe Temple þis tyme to make sacryfice.
Becawse þat no frute of us doth procede,[10]
I fere me grettly þe prest wole me dysspice;
Than grett slawndyr in þe tribus of us xulde aryse.
But þis I avow to God with all þe mekenes I can:
Ȝyff of His mercy He wole a childe us devyse,
We xal offre it up into þe Temple to be Goddys man.

Anna
ȝoure swemful wurdys make terys trekyl down be my face;
Iwys, swete husbond, þe fawte is in me.
My name is Anne, þat is to sey 'grace':
We wete not how gracyous God wyl to us be.
A woman xulde bere Cryst, þese profecyes have we;
If God send frute and it be a mayd childe,
With all reverens I vow to His mageste,
Sche xal be here foot-mayd to mynyster here most mylde.

Joachym
Now lete be it as God wole, þer is no more.
Tweyn turtelys for my sacryfice with me I take.
And I beseche, wyff, and evyr we mete more,
Þat Hese grett mercy us meryer mut make.

Anna
For dred and for swem of ȝoure wourdys I qwake.
Thryes I kysse ȝow with syghys ful sad,
And to þe mercy of God mekely I ȝow betake;
And þo þat departe in sorwe, God make þer metyng glad.

Senior Tribus
Worchepful sere Joachym, be ȝe redy now?
All ȝoure kynrede is come ȝow to exorte,
Þat þei may do sacrifice at þe Temple with ȝow,
For ȝe be of grett wurchep as men ȝow report.[11]

Joachym
All synfull, seke, and sory, God mote comforte;
I wolde I were as men me name.[12]
Thedyr in Goddys name, now late us all resorte.
A, Anne, Anne, Anne, God scheeld us fro shame!

Anne
Now am I left alone, sore may I wepe.
A, husbond, ageyn God wel mote ȝow brynge,[13]
And fro shame and sorwe He mote ȝow kepe.
Tyl I se ȝow ageyn, I kannot sees of wepynge.

Senior
Prynce of oure prestys, if it be ȝoure plesynge,
We be com mekely to make our sacrefice.

Ysakar
God do ȝow mede, bothe elde and ȝynge,
Than devowtly we wyl begynne servyse.

There they xal synge þis seqens: 'Benedicta sit beata Trinitas'.[14] *And in þat tyme Ysakar with his ministerys ensensyth þe autere,*[15] *and þan þei make her offryng and Isaker seyth:*

46 wealthy in goods 48 been, shall (be) 49 judgements 50 will 51 parts 54 parish priest, wide world 55 the chancel (of his church) 61 reject 62 slander among, will grow 63 meekness 64 send/create (for) us 65 servant 66 distressing, trickle 67 fault 69 know 70 will, give birth to 71 girl 73 (Temple) servant 74 desires, no more (to say) 75 Two turtle doves 76 if 77 His, will make us merrier 78 distress at, tremble 79 Three times, sighs 80 commend 81 those who 82 Worshipful sir 83 family 86 sick, sorrowful, must 93 cease 94 pleasure 96 God reward you 97 Then

8 'One [third of my income I give] to the Temple and those [priests] who serve there, another [I give] to pilgrims and the poor, the third [I keep] for those who live with me [i.e. my family and household].'

9 'Those parishioners who have fallen into poverty'.

10 'Because we have produced no offspring'.

11 'Because you are of high status, as is commonly reported.'

12 'I wish I was as men describe me.'

13 'Ah, husband, may God bring about your safe return'.

14 'Blessed is the Holy Trinity.'

15 'They purify the altar with incense.'

Comyth up, serys, and offeryth all now,
3e þat to do sacryfice worthy are.

[*To Jaochym*] Abyde a qwyle, sere! Whedyr wytte þu?[16]
Þu and þi wyff arn barrany and bare;
Neyther of 3ow fruteful nevyr 3ett ware.
Whow durste þu amonge fruteful presume and abuse?[17]
It is a tokyn þu art cursyd þare
Whereffore with grett indygnacyon þin offeryng I refuse.

Et refu[n]dit sacrificium Joachim.[18]

Amonge all þis pepyl barreyn be no mo.
Therefore comyth up and offeryth here alle!
Þu, Joachym, I charge þe[e] fast out þe Temple þu go!

Et redit, flendo.[19]

Than with Goddys holy wourde blysse 3ow I shalle.

Ministro cantando:[20]

Adjutorium nostrum in nomine Domini.[21]

CHORUS
Qui fecit Celum et Terram.[22]

MINISTER
Sit nomen Domini benedictum.[23]

CHORUS
Ex hoc nunc et usque in seculum.[24]

EPISCOPUS
Benedicat vos divina majestas et una Deitas:
Pater, et Filius, et Spiritus Sanctus.[25]

CHORUS
Amen.

Signando manu cum Cruce sole[m]niter et recedant tribus extra templum.[26]

[YSAKAR]
Now of God and man blyssyd be 3e alle.
Homward a3en now returne 3e,
And in þis Temple abyde we xalle
To servyn God in Trinyte.

JOACHYM
A, mercyfful Lord, what is þis lyff?
What have I do, Lorde, to have þis blame?
For hevynes I dare not go hom to my wyff,
And amonge my neyborys I dare not abyde for shame.
A, Anne, Anne, Anne, al our joye is turnyd to grame!
From 3oure blyssyd felacheppe I am now exilyd;
And 3e here onys of þis fowle fame,[27]
Sorwe wyl sle 3ow to se me thus revylyd.

But, s[e]n God soferyth thys, us must sofron nede.[28]
Now wyl I go to my sherherdys and with hem abyde,
And þer evyrmore levyn in sorwe and in drede.
Shame makyth many man his hed for to hyde.
Ha, how do 3e, felas? In 3ow is lytel pryde.
How fare 3e and my bestys? Þis wete wolde I veryly.

PRIMUS PASTOR
A, welcom hedyr, blyssyd mayster. We pasture hem ful wyde.
They be lusty and fayr and grettly multyply.

How do 3e, mayster? 3e loke al hevyly.
How doth oure dame at hom? Sytt she and sowyht?[29]

JOACHYM
To here þe[e] speke of here it sleyth myn hert, veryly.

98 sirs 101 are barren 104 sign 122 done 123 sorrow 125 sorrow 126 fellowship 128 sorrow, slay 130 shepherds/shearsmen 131 live 133 how are you, fellows? 135 widely 137 sorrowful 139 hear, her

16 'Wait a moment, sir! Where do you think you are going?'
17 'How dare you presume [to come] and [commit an] abuse among [these] fruitful [people]?'
18 'And he rejects Joachym's sacrifice.'
19 'And he [Joachim] withdraws, weeping.'
20 'The Minister singing'.
21 'Our help is in the name of the Lord.' The words spoken in this ceremony are from the Ordinary of the Mass.
22 'Who made Heaven and Earth.'
23 'Blessed be the name of the Lord.'
24 'From this time, now and for ever.'
25 'May the Divine Majesty and One God bless you: Father, and Son, and Holy Spirit.'
26 'After he has made the sign of the Cross solemnly with his hand, the Tribes shall withdraw from the Temple.'
27 'If you once hear about this terrible shame'.
28 'But, since God permits/ordains this, we must put up with it.'
29 'How is our mistress at home? Does she sit and sew?'

How I and sche doth God Hymself knowyth.
The meke God lyftyth up, þe proude overthrowyht.
Go, do what ȝe lyst. Se ȝoure bestys not stray!

SECUNDUS PASTOR
Aftere grett sorwe, mayster, evyr gret grace growyht.
Sympyl as we kan, we xal for ȝow pray.[30]

TERTIUS PASTOR
Ʒa, to pray for careful; it is grett nede.
We all wul prey for ȝow knelende.
God of His goodnes send ȝow good spede,
And of ȝoure sorwe ȝow sone amende!

JOACHYM
I am nott wurthy, Lord, to loke up to Hefne;
My synful steppys anvenymyd þe grounde.
I, lothfolest þat levyth: Þu, Lord, hyest in Þi setys sefne.[31]
What art Þu? Lord. What am I? Wrecche, werse þan an hownde.
Þu hast sent me shame, which myn hert doth wounde;
I thank Þe[e] more herefore þan for all my prosperite.
Þis is a tokyn Þu lovyst me, now to The[e] I am bounde;
Þu seyst Þu art with hem þat in tribulacyon be.[32]

And hoso have Þe[e], he nedyth not care thanne;
My sorwe is feryng I have do sum offens.
Punchyth me, Lorde, and spare my blyssyd wyff Anne
Þat syttyth and sorwyth ful sore of myn absens.
Ther is not may profyte but prayour to Ʒoure presens.[33]
With prayorys prostrat byfore Þi person I wepe.
Have mende on oure avow for Ʒoure mech magnyficens,
And my lovyngest wyff Anne, Lord, for Þi mercy kepe.

ANNA
A, mercy, Lord, mercy, mercy, mercy!
We are synfolest, it shewyth þat Ʒe send us all þis sorwe.[34]
Why do Ʒe thus to myn husbond, Lord? Why, why, why?
For my barynes? [Ʒ]e may amend þis Þiself, and Þu lyst, tomorwe,[35]
And it plese so Þi mercy; Þee, my Lord, I take to borwe.[36]
I xal kepe myn avow qwhyl I leve and leste.
I fere me I have offendyd Þe[e], myn hert is ful of sorwe.
Most mekely I pray Þi pety, þat þis bale Þu wyl breste.

Here þe aungel descendith þe Hefne syngyng: 'Exultet Celum laudibus, resultet Terra gaudiis, archangelorum gloria sacra canun[t] solennia.'[37]

JOACHYM
Qwhat art þu, in Goddys name, þat makyst me adrad?
It is as lyth abowt me as al þe werd were fere![38]

ANGELUS
I am an aungel of God, com to make þe[e] glad.
God is plesyd with þin helmes and hath herd þi prayere;
He seyth þi shame, þi repreff, and þi terys cler.
God is a vengere of synne, and not nature doth lothe;
Whos wombe þat He sparyth and makyth barreyn her,
He doth to shewe His myth and His mercy bothe.[39]

141 (He) overthrows 143 grows 145 (the) sorrowful, very necessary 146 kneeling 150 poisoned 152 a hound 154 for that 157 whoever has You (with him) 158 done some offence 159 Punish 162 prostrate prayers 163 Remember, great 170 while I live and am able 172 pray (for), sorrow, pass 176 alms(-giving) 177 self-reproof

30 'In our own simple fashion, we shall pray for you.'

31 'I [am] the most loathsome [creature] living, and You, Lord [are] the highest in the seven Heavens.'

32 'You say you are [always] with those in tribulation.' Joachym seems to be recalling such scriptural texts as 'whom the Lord loveth, he correcteth' (Proverbs 3:12), and 'we must through much tribulation enter the kingdom of God' (Acts 14:22).

33 'There is nothing that may profit us but prayers to Your Person.'

34 'We are the sinfullest [of creatures], as is revealed by [the fact] that You send us all this sorrow.'

35 'For my barrenness? You could correct that Yourself, tomorrow, if You wished'.

36 'I take You as my witness, my Lord.'

37 'Let the Heaven rejoice with praises, the Earth resound with joys, they sing in solemn festival to the glory of the archangels.'

38 'It is a bright light around me as if all the world were on fire!'

39 'God is an avenger of sin, and does not loathe nature: those whose wombs He leaves barren here, He does so [in order] to show both His power and His mercy.'

Thu seest þat Sara was nynty ȝere bareyn;
Sche had a son, Ysaac, to whom God ȝaff His blyssynge.
Rachel also had þe same peyn;
She had a son, Joseph, þat of Egypt was kynge.
A strongere þan Sampson nevyr was, be wrytynge,[40]
Nor an holyere þan Samuel, it is seyd thus;
3ett here moderys were bareyn bothe in þe gynnynge.
Þe concepcyon of all swych, it is ful mervelyous.

And in þe lyke wyse, Anne, þi blyssyd wyff,
Sche xal bere a childe xal hygth Mary,
Which xal be blyssyd in here body and have joys fyff,[41]
And ful of þe Holy Goost, inspyred syngulyrly.
Sche xal be offryd into þe Temple, solemply,
Þat of here non evyl fame xuld sprynge thus;[42]
And as sche xal be bore of a barrany body,
So of here xal be bore, without nature, Jhesus,

That xal be savyour unto al mankende.
In tokyn, whan þu come to Jherusalem, to þe Gyldyn Gate,[43]
Þu xalt mete Anne, þi wyff, have þis in þi mende.
I xal sey here þe same, here sorwys to rebate.

JOACHYM
Of þis incomparabyl comfort I xal nevyr forgete þe date!
My sorwe was nevyr so grett, but now my joy is more!
I xal hom in hast, be it nevyr so late.
A, Anne, blyssyd be þat body of þe[e] xal be bore!

Now, farewel, myn shepherdys, governe ȝow now wysly.[44]

PRIMUS PASTOR
Have ȝe good tydyngys, mayster, þan be we glad.

JOACHYM
Prayse God for me, for I am not wourthy.

SECUNDUS PASTOR
In feyth, sere, so we xal, with all oure sowlys sad.

TERTIUS PASTOR
I holde it helpfful þat on of us with ȝow be had.[45]

JOACHYM
Nay, abyde with 3oure bestys, sone, in Goddys blyssynge.

PRIMUS PASTOR
We xal make us so mery now þis is bestad,
Þat a myle on ȝoure wey ȝe xal here us synge.

ANNE
Alas, for myn husbond me is ful wo!
I xal go seke hym, whatsoevyr befalle.
I wote not in Erth which wey is he go.
Fadyr of Hefne, for mercy to ȝoure fete I falle!

ANGELUS
Anne, þin husbond ryght now I was withall,
Þe aungel of God þat bar hym good tydynge.
And as I seyd to hym, so to þe[e] sey I xal:
God hath herd þi preyour and þi wepynge.

At þe Goldyn Gate þu xalte mete hym ful mylde,
And in grett gladnes returne to ȝoure hous.
So be proces þu xalt conseyve and bere a childe
Whiche xal hyght Mary; and Mary xal bere Jhesus,
Which xal be Savyour of all þe werd and us.
Aftere grett sorwe, evyr grett gladnes is had.
Now myn inbassett I have seyd to ȝow thus;
Gooth in oure Lordys name, and in God beth glad.

ANNE
Now blyssyd be oure Lorde and all His werkys ay!
All Heffne and Erthe mut blysse ȝow for this.
I am so joyful, I not what I may say.
Þer can no tounge telle what joye in me is.
I to bere a childe þat xal bere all mannys blys,
And have myn hosbonde ageyn: ho myth have joys more?

181 barren for ninety years 182 Isaac 183 sorrow 187 mothers, beginning 188 such (people) 190 (be) named 196 natural (sexual) conception 200 tell, reduce 201 occasion 203 (go) home 204 Who shall be born of you 206 If you have 208 souls, soberly 211 settled 214 seek, happens 215 he has gone 217 I was with him 218 brought 221 meekly 223 in due course 227 embassy/message 228 go, be 231 (know) not 232 tongue 233 bring 234 who might

40 'There was never a stronger man than Sampson, as the Bible shows us'.
41 'Five Joys': the Five Joys of Mary were traditionally the Annunciation, Nativity, Resurrection, Ascension, and Assumption.'
42 'So that no evil rumours should spread about her'.
43 The Golden, Eastern, Gate of the City of Jerusalem.
44 'Behave yourselves sensibly now.'
45 'I think it sensible that one of us goes with you.'

No creature in Erth is grauntyd more mercy, iwys.
I xal hyȝe me to þe ȝate to be þer before.

Here goth þe aungel aȝen to Hefne.

A, blyssyd be our Lord, myn husbond I se.
I xalle on myn knes and to hym-ward crepe.

JOACHYM
A, gracyous wyff Anne, now fruteful xal ȝe be!
For joy of þis metyng in my sowle I wepe.
Have þis kusse of clennesse and with ȝow it kepe.
In Goddys name now go we, wyff, hom to our hous.

ANNE
Þer was nevyr joy sank in me so depe.
Now may we sey, husbond, God is to us gracyous,
Veryly.

JOACHYM
Ȝa, and if we have levyd wel herebefore,
I pray Þe[e], Lord, Þin ore,
So mote we levyn evyrmore
And, be Þi grace more, holyly.

ANNE
Now homward, husbond, I rede we gon,
Ryth hom al to our place,
To thank God þat sytt in tron,
Þat þus hath sent us His grace.

CONTEMPLACIO
Sovereynes, ȝe han sen shewyd ȝow before,
Of Joachym and Anne, here botherys holy metynge.[46]
How Oure Lady was conseyvid and how she was bore,
We passe ovyr þat, breffnes of tyme consyderynge;[47]
And how Our Lady in here tendyr age and ȝyng
Into þe Temple was offryd, and so forth, proced.
Þis sentens sayd xal be hire begynnyng.
Now þe Modyr of Mercy in þis be our sped!

And as a childe of thre ȝere age here she xal appere
To alle pepyl þat ben here present;
And of here grett grace now xal ȝe here,
How she levyd evyr to Goddys entent
With grace;
That holy matere we wole declare,
Tyl fortene ȝere, how sche dyd fare.
Now of ȝoure speche I pray ȝow spare,
All þat ben in þis place.

Here Joachym and Anne, with Oure Lady betwen hem beyng al in whyte as a childe of iii ȝere age, presente here into þe Temple; thus seyng Joachym:

JOACH[Y]M
Blyssyd be Oure Lord, fayr frute have we now.
Anne, wyff, remembyr wole ȝe
Þat we made to God an holy avow
Þat oure fyrst childe þe servaunt of God xulde be.
The age of Mary, oure dowtere, is ȝerys thre,
Þerfore to thre Personys and on God lete us here present;
Þe ȝonger she be drawyn, þe bettyr semyth me,[48]

And for teryeng of our avow, of God we myth be shent.

ANNE
It is as ȝe sey, husbond, indede.
Late us take Mary, our dowtere, us betwen,
And to þe Temple with here procede.
Dowtere, þe aungel tolde us ȝe xulde be a qwen;
Wole ȝe go se þat Lord ȝoure husbond xal ben,
And lerne for to love Hym, and lede with Hym ȝoure lyff?
Telle ȝoure fadyr and me her, ȝoure answere let sen;
Wole ȝe be pure maydyn, and also Goddys wyff?

MARIA
Fadyr and modyr, if it plesynge to ȝow be,
Ȝe han mad ȝoure avow, so ssothly wole I,
To be Goddys chast servaunt whil lyff is in me.
But to be Goddys wyff, I was nevyr wurthy.
I am þe sympelest þat evyr was born of body.
I have herd ȝow seyd, God xulde have a modyr swete;
Þat I may leve to se hire, God graunt me for His mercy,
And abyl me to ley my handys undyr hire fayr fete.

241 chaste kiss 246 lived 247 Your mercy 249 by 252 enthroned 254 My lords 261 aid 263 are 264 hear 265 (according) to, intent 268 lived 269 stop 275 daughter, years 276 one 278 delaying, punished 282 queen 283 (who) shall be your husband 285 here, let's see 286 (a) pure virgin 292 say 293 live, her 294 enable, feet

[46] 'The holy meeting [of] both Joachym and Anne.'
[47] 'Considering the need for brevity'.
[48] 'The earlier she is admitted, the better it seems to me'.

Et genuflectet ad Deum.[49]

JOACHYM
Iwys, dowtere, it is wel seyd.
3e answere and 3e were twenty 3ere olde!

ANNE
Whith 3oure speche, Mary, I am wel payd.
Can 3e gon alone? Lett se. Beth bolde!

MARIA
To go to Goddys hous, wole 3e now beholde;
I am joyful thedyrward as I may be.

JOACHYM
Wyff, I [am] ryght joyful oure dowtere to beholde.

ANNE
So am I, wys husbond, now in Goddys name go we.

JOACHYM
Sere Prince of Prestes, and it plese 3ow,
We þat were barreyn, God hath sent a childe.
To offre here to Goddys service we mad our avow;
Here is þe same mayde, Mary, most mylde.

[Y]SAKAR
Joachym, I have good mende how I 3ow revyled;
I am ryght joyful þat God hath 3ove 3ow þis grace
To be amonge fruteful; now be 3e reconsylid.
Com, swete Mary, com! 3e have a gracyous face.

Joachym flectendo ad Deum sic dicens:[50]

JOACHYM
Now, Fadyr, and Sone, and Holy Gost,
On God and Personys thre,
We offre to þe[e], Lorde of myghtys most,
Oure dowtere, þi servaunt evyrmore to be.

ANNA
Therto most bounde evyrmore be we.
Mary, in þis holy place leve 3ow we xall;
In Goddys name now up go 3e;
Oure fadyr, oure prest, lo, doth 3ow call.

MARIA
Modyr, and it plese 3ow, fyrst wole I take my leve
Of my fadyr and 3ow my modyr, iwys.
I have a Fadyr in Hefne, þis I beleve;
Now, good fadyr, with þat Fadyr 3e me blysse.

JOACHYM
In nomine Patris, et Filii, et Spiritus Sancti.[51]

MARIA
Amen. Now 3e, good modyr.

ANNE
In nomine Patris, et Filii, et Spiritus Sancti.

MARIA
Amen.

Now, Oure Lord thank 3ow for this.
Here is my fadyr and my modyr bothe,
Most mekely I beseche I may 3ow kys.
Now for3eve me yf evyr I made 3ow wrothe.

Et explexendo osculabit patrem et matrem.[52]

JOACHYM
Nay, dowtere, 3e offendyd nevyr God nor man.
Lovyd be þat Lord, 3ow so doth kepe.

ANNE
Swete dowtyr, thynk on 3oure modyr, An;
3oure swemynge smytyht on myn hert depe.

MARIA
Fadyr and modyr, I xal pray for 3ow and wepe
To God with al myn hert specyaly.
Blysse me day and nyght, evyr her 3e slepe,
Good fadyr and modyr, and beth mery.

JOACHYM
A, ho had evyr suche a chylde!
Nevyr creature 3it þat evyr was bore.
Sche is so gracyous, she is so mylde;
So xulde childyr to fadyr and modyr evyrmore.

ANNE
Than xulde thei be blyssyd and plese God sore.
Husbond, and it plese 3ow, not hens go we xal
Tyl Mary be in þe Temple above thore.
I wold not for al Erthe se here fal.

296 as if 297 satisfied 298 be bold! 300 (to go) that way 307 I remember well 308 given 312 One 316 leave 332 who keeps you so 333 Anne 334 grieving, strike 339 Who 342 So should (all) children (behave) 343 Then, greatly 344 we shall not go from here 345 there 346 her fall

49 'And she shall kneel to God.'
50 'Joachim, kneeling to God, saying thus'.
51 'In the name of the Father, and the Son, and the Holy Spirit.'
52 'And, embracing them, she shall kiss her father and mother.'

Episcopus
Come, gode Mary! Come, babe, I þe[e] call!
Þi pas pratyly to þis plas pretende.
Þu xalt be þe dowtere of God eternall
If þe fyftene grees þu may ascende.
It is meracle if þu do! Now God þe[e] dyffende!
From Babylony to hevynly Jherusalem þis is þe way.[53]
Every man þat thynk his lyff to amende,
Þe fyftene Psalmys in memorye of þis mayde say.

Maria (*et sic deinceps usque ad fine[m] xv*^{fim} *Psalmorum*)[54]
The fyrst degre gostly applyed,
It is holy desyre with God to be.
In trobyl to God I have cryed,
And in sped þat Lord hath herde me.

Ad dominum cum tribularer clamavi;
Et exaudivit me.[55]

The secunde is stody with meke inquysissyon, veryly,
How I xal have knowynge of Godys wylle.
To þe mownteynes of Hefne I have lyfte myn ey,
From qwens xal comyn helpe me tylle.

Levavi oculos meos in montes;
Unde veniat auxilium mihi.[56]

The thrydde is gladnes in mende in hope to be,
That we xall be savyd all thus.
I am glad of these tydyngys ben seyd to me,
Now xal we go into Goddys hous.

Letatus sum in hiis que dicta sunt mihi;
In domum Domini ibimus.[57]

The fourte is meke obedyence as is dette
To Hym þat is above þe planetys sefne.
To Þe[e] I have myn eyn sette
Þat dwellys above þe skyes in Hefne.

Ad te levavi oculos meos;
Qui habitas in celis.[58]

The fyfte is propyr confessyon,
Þat we be nought withowth God thus.
But God in us have habytacyon,
Peraventure oure enemyes shulde swelle us.

Nisi quia Dominus erat in nobis, dicat nunc Israel;
Nisi quia Dominus erat in nobis.[59]

The sexte is confidens in Goddys strenght alon;
For of all grace from Hym comyth þe strem.
They þat trust in God as þe Mownt Syon,
He xal not be steryd endles þat dwellyth in Jherusalem.

Qui confidunt in Domino sicut Mons Syon:
Non commovebitur in eternum qui habitat in Hierusalem.[60]

The sefte is undowteful hope of immortalyte
In oure Lordeis grace and mercy.
Whan oure Lord convertyth oure captivite,
Than are we mad as joyful mery.

In convertendo Dominus captivitatem Syon;
Facti sumus sicut consolati.[61]

The eyted is contempt of veynglory in us,
For Hym þat al mankende hath multyplyed.
But yf oure Lord make here oure hous,
They an laboryd in veyn þat it han edyfied:[62]

348 proceed carefully to this place 350 fifteen steps 351 protect 353 hopes 355 interpreted spiritually 357 distress 358 swiftly 361 humble enquiry 363 lifted my eyes 367 happiness of mind 373 owed 374 seven planets 381 unless 382 swallow 386 stream 387 Mt Zion (Jerusalem) 388 stirred endlessly 391 seventh, certain 392 Lord's 393 redeems 394 made as merry as the joyful 397 eighth 398 increased 399 Unless

53 'This is the path from Babylon to the Heavenly Jerusalem', i.e. out of captivity to freedom.
54 'And thus from the beginning to the end of the fifteen psalms.' As Mary ascends each of the fifteen steps of the Temple, she recites and interprets the opening verse of one of the fifteen Gradual Psalms (Psalms 120-34). The Latin verses are translated into English in the preceding lines.
55 'In my distress I cried unto the Lord, and He heard me.' Psalms 120:1.
56 'I will lift up my eyes unto the hills: from whence cometh my help.' Psalms 121:1.
57 'I was glad when they said unto me, let us go into the house of the Lord.' Psalms 122:1.
58 'Unto Thee lift I up my eyes, O Thou that dwellest in the heavens.' Psalms 123:1.
59 'If it had not been the Lord who was on our side, now may Israel say; / If it had not been the Lord who was on our side, [when men rose up against us].' Psalms 124:1–2.
60 See Psalms 125:1:'They that trust in the Lord shall be as Mount Zion, which cannot be removed but abideth forever.'
61 See Psalms 126:1:'When the Lord turned again the captivity of Zion, we were like them that dream.'
62 'They who have edified it have laboured in vain'.

Nisi Dominus edificaverit domum; in vanum
Laboraveru{n}t qui edificant eam.[63]

The nynte is a childely fer indede,
With a longyng love in oure Lorde þat ay is.
Blyssyd arn all they þat God drede,
Which þat gon in His holy weys.

Beati omnes qui timent Dominum: qui
Ambulant in viis eius.[64]

The tende is myghty soferauns of carnal temptacyon;
For þe fleschly syghtys ben fers and fel.
Ofte ȝough is fowth with, with suech vexacyon;
Þu, seynge God, say so, clepyd Israel.[65]

Sepe expugnaverunt me a juventute mea; dicat
Nunc Israel.[66]

The elefnte is accusatyff confessyon of iniquite,
Of which ful noyous is þe noyis.[67]
Fro depnes, Lord, I have cryed to The[e],
Lord, here in sped my sympyl voys.

De profundis clamavi ad te Domine: Domine
Exaudi vocem meam.[68]

The twelfte is mekenes þat is fayr and softe
In mannys sowle withinne and withowte.
Lord, myn herte is not heyved on lofte,
Nyn myn eyn be not lokynge abowte.

Domine non est exaltatum cor meum;
Neque elati sunt oculi mei.[69]

The threttene is feyth þerwith,
With holy dedys don expresse.
Have mende, Lorde, of Davyth
And of all his swettnes.

Memento Domine David; et omnis
Mansuetudinis eius.[70]

The fourtene is brothyrly concorde, iwys,
Þat norchyth love of creaturys echon.
Se how good and how glad it is,
Bretheryn for to dwelle in on.

Ecce quam bonum et quam jocundum;
Habitare fratres in unum.[71]

The fyftene is gracyous, with on acorde,
Whiche is syne of godly love, semyth me.
Se now, blysse oure Lord,
All þat oure Lordys servauntys be.

Ecce nunc benedicite Dominum:
Omnes servi Domini.[72]

EPISCOPUS
A, gracyous Lord, þis is a mervelyous thynge
Þat we se here all in syght;
A babe of thre ȝer age so ȝynge
To come up þese grecys so upryght!
It is an hey meracle and, by Goddys myght,
No dowth of, she xal be gracyous.

MARIA
Holy fadyr, I beseche ȝow forthryght,
Sey how I xal be rewlyd in Goddys hous.

EPISCOPUS
Dowtere, God hath ȝovyn us Comaundementys Ten,
Which, shortely to say, be comprehendyd in tweyn,

403 ninth, childlike **406** walk **409** tenth, resistance **410** sight of bodily things **418** aid **423** raised on high **424** looking **427** thirteenth **428** openly **429** Remember (King) David **433** fourteenth **434** nourishes love of all creatures **436** in unity **439** fifteenth, unity **440** (a) sign **448** steps so confidently **449** high **450** full of grace **451** painly **452** ruled **453** given **454** in two

63 'Except the Lord build the house, they labour in vain that build it.' Psalms 127:1.

64 'Blessed is every one that feareth the Lord; that walketh in His ways.' Psalms 128:1.

65 'Often youth is fought with by such vexations; Thou, seeing God, called "Israel", say so.'

66 'Many a time have they afflicted me from my youth, may Israel now say.' Psalms 129:1.

67 'The eleventh is the [self]accusatory confession of sin, of which very painful is the torment.' At confession the penitent was enjoined to be ruthless in citing his or her own sins.

68 'Out of the depths have I cried unto Thee, O Lord: Lord, hear my voice.' Psalms 130:1.

69 'Lord, my heart is not haughty, nor mine eyes lofty.' Psalms 131:1.

70 'Lord, remember David and all his [obedience].' Psalms 132:1.

71 'Behold, how good and how pleasant it is for brethren to dwell together in unity.' Psalms 133:1.

72 'Behold, bless ye the Lord, all ye servants of the Lord.' Psalms 134:1.

And þo must be kept of all Crysten men
Or ellys here jugement is perpetual peyn.
Ȝe muste love God severeynly and ȝoure evyn Crystyn pleyn;[73]
God fyrst for His hyȝ and sovereyn dygnyte;
He lovyd ȝow fyrst, love Hym ageyn,
For of love to His owyn lyknes He made the[e].[74]

Love Fadyr, Sone, and Holy Gost:
Love God þe Fadyr, for He gevyth myght;
Love God þe Son, for He gevyth wysdam, þu wost;
Love God þe Holy Gost, for He gevyth love and lyght.
Thre Personys and on God þus love of ryght,
With all þin hert, with all þi sowle, with all þi mende,
And with all þe strenghthis in þe[e] bedyght;
Þan love þin evyn Crystyn as þiself withowtyn ende.

Thu xalt hate nothynge but þe Devyl and synne:
God byddyth the[e] lovyn þi bodyly enmy.
And as for ȝoureself here, þus xal ȝe begynne:
Ȝe must serve and wurchep God here dayly,
For with prayȝer [come] grace and mercy;
Sethe have a resonable tyme to fede;
Thanne to have a labour bodyly,
Þat þerin be gostly and bodely mede.

Ȝoure abydynge xal be with ȝoure maydenys fyve,
Swyche tyme as ȝe wole have consolacyon.

Maria
This lyff me lyketh as my lyve,
Of here namys I beseche ȝow to have informacyon.

Episcopus
There is þe fyrst, Meditacyon;
Contryssyon, Compassyon, and Clennes,
And þat holy mayde, Fruyssyon;
With these blyssyd maydenes xal be ȝoure besynes.

Maria
Here is an holy felacheppe; I fele,
I am not wurthy amonge hem to be.
Swete systerys, to ȝow all I knele,
To receyve me I beseche ȝoure charyte.

Episcopus
They xal, dowtere. And on þe tothere syde se
Ther ben sefne prestys indede,
To schryve, to teche, and to mynystryn to the[e],
To lerne þe[e] Goddys lawys and scrypture to rede.

Maria
Fadyr, knew I here namys, wele were I.

Episcopus
Ther is Dyscressyon, Devocyon, Dylexcyon, and Deliberacyon;
They xal tende upon ȝow besyly,
With Declaracyon, Determynacyon, Dyvynacyon.[75]
Now go, ȝe maydenys, to ȝoure occupacyon,
And loke ȝe tende þis childe tendyrly;
And ȝe, serys, knelyth and I xal gyve ȝow Goddys benyson:
In nomine Patris, et Filii, et Spiritus Sancti.

Et recedet cum ministris suis: omnes virgines dicent: 'Amen'.[76]

[Maria]
To ȝow, fadyr and modyr, I me comende,
Blyssyd be þe tyme ȝe me hedyr brought.

Joachym
Dowtere, þe Fadere of oure feyth þe[e] mot defende,
As He of His myght made all thynge of nowth.

Anne
Mary, to þi sowle solas He sende
In Whos wysdam all þis werd was wrought.
Go we now hens, husbonde so hende,
For owth of care now are we brought.

Hic Joachim et Anna recedent domum.[77]

455 these 456 punishment, pain 459 in return 463 know 465 justly 466 mind 467 placed 470 love your mortal enemy 474 After that 476 spiritual and physical reward 477 hand-maidens 478 At such 479 as much as life itself 480 their 482 Contrition, Purity 483 Fruition (communion with God) 484 business 490 seven priests 491 confess (and absolve), minister 492 teach 493 happy 497 work 499 blessing 501 commend myself 503 may protect you 504 from nothing 505 solace 506 world 507 noble 508 out

73 'You must love God principally, and then your fellow Christians.' (See Matthew 22:37–40.)

74 'For through love He made you in His own image.'

75 Discretion, (religious) Devotion, Dilection (spiritual love), Deliberation (thought), Declaration (clear teaching?), Determination (judgement), Divination (wisdom).

76 'And he shall withdraw with his ministers. All the maidens shall say: "Amen".'

77 'Here Joachym and Anna shall return home.'

MARIA
Be þe Holy Gost at hom be ȝe brought!
(*Ad virgines*) Systerys, ȝe may go do what ȝe xall,
To serve God fyrst here is al my thought.
Beforn þis holy awtere on my knes I fall.

Lord, sefne petycyons I beseche ȝow of here:
Fyrst, þat I may kepe Þi love and Þi lawe;
Þe secunde, to lovyn myn evyn Crystyn as myself
dere;
Þe thrydde, from all þat Þu hatyst me to withdrawe;
The fourte, all vertuys to Þi plesauns knawe;
Þe fyfte, to obey þe ordenaryes of þe Temple echon;
Þe sexte, and þat all pepyl may serve Þe[e] with awe,
Þat in þis holy Tempyl fawte be non.

The sefnte, Lord, I haske with grett fere:
Þat I may se, onys in my lyve,
Þat lady þat xal Goddys Sone bere,
Þat I may serve here with my wyttys fyve,
If it plese Ȝow, and ellys it is not þerwith to
stryve.[78]
With prayers prostrat for þese gracys I wepe.
O, my God, devocyon depe in me dryve
Þat myn hert may wake in Þe[e], thow my body
slepe.

Here þe aungel bryngyth manna in a cowpe of gold, lyke to confeccyons;[79] *þe Hefne syngynge. Þe aungel seyth:*

[ANGELUS]
Merveyle not, mekest maydon, of my mynystracyon;
I am a good aungel sent of God Allmyght
With aungelys mete for ȝoure sustentacyon,
Ȝe to receyve it for natural myght.
We aungellys xul serve ȝow day and nyght.
Now fede ȝow þerwith in Goddys name.
We xal leme ȝow þe lyberary of oure Lordys lawe
lyght,
For my sawys in ȝow shewyth sygnes of shame.[80]

MARIA
To thank oure soveryen Lord not sufficyth my
mende,
I xal fede me of þis fode my Lord hath me sent.
All maner of savowrys in þis mete I fynde,
I felt nevyr non so swete ner so redolent.

ANGELUS
Eche day þerwith ȝe xal be content,
Aunge[lys] alle howrys xal to ȝow apere.

MARIA
Mercy, my makere, how may þis be ment?
I am þe sympelest creature þat is levynge here.

ANGELUS
In ȝoure name, Maria, fyve letterys we han:
M – mayde most mercyfull, and mekest in mende;
A – averte of þe anguysch þat Adam began;
R – regina of regyon, reyneng withowtyn ende;
I – innocent be influens of Jesses kende;
A – advocat most autentyk, ȝoure antecer, Anna.
Hefne and Helle here kneys down bende
Whan þis holy name of ȝow is seyd: Maria.

MARIA
I qwake grettly for dred to here þis comendacyon
Good swete aungel, why wole ȝe sey thus?

AUNGELL
For ȝe xal hereaftere have a salutacyon
Þat xal þis excede, it is seyd amonge us;
The Deyte þat dede xal determyn and dyscus.
Ȝe xal nevyr, lady, be lefte here alone.

MARIA
I crye þe[e] mercy, Lorde, and þin erthe cus,
Recomendynge me to þat Godhyd þat is tryne in
trone.

Hic osculet terram.[81] *Here xal comyn alwey an aungel with dyvers presentys, goynge and comyng, and in þe tyme þei xal synge in Hefne þis hympne: 'Jhesu corona virginum'.*[82] *And after, þer comyth a minister fro þe busschop with a present and seyth:*

509 By 510 To the virgins 512 altar 513 seven prayers, hear 515 as dearly as myself 516 to shun all that You hate 517 all virtues that please You 518 high priests 520 fault 521 ask 522 once, life 524 five wits 530 Almighty 531 angels' food, sustenance 532 bodily strength 537 does not suffice 539 flavours 540 fragrant 543 what does this mean? 544 living 547 averter, anguish 548 queen of (the) region of Heaven 549 through descent from Jesse 550 ancestor 551 their 557 Deity, deed 559 kiss 560 threefold

78 'And otherwise not to involve myself with it.'
79 'A cup of gold, like confections'. Confections were sweet or spicy mixtures often accompanying meat at meals.
80 'We shall teach you the library [i.e. sum total] of God's bright laws, for my words reveal in you signs of humility.'
81 'Here let her kiss the ground.'
82 'The hymn: "Jesus, crown of virgins".'

MINISTER
Prynce of oure prestes, Ysakare be name,
He hath sent ȝow hymself his servyce, indede;
And bad ȝe xulde fede ȝow; spare for no shame;
In þis tyme of mete, no lenger ȝe rede.

MARIA
Recomende me to my fadyr, sere, and God do hym mede.
These vesselys aȝen sone I xal hym sende.
I xal bere it my systerys; I trowe þei have more nede.
Goddys foyson is evyr to His servauntys hendyr þan we wende.[83]

Systerys, oure holy fadyr, Isakare,
Hath sent us hese servyce here ryght now.
Fede ȝow þerof hertyly, I pray ȝow nat spare.
And if owght be leve, specyaly I pray ȝow
That þe pore men þe relevys þerof have now.
Fayn, and I myth, I wolde do þe dedys of mercy.[84]
Pore folk faryn God knowyth how,
On hem evyr I have grett pety.

CONTEMPLACIO
Lo, sofreynes, here ȝe have seyn
In þe Temple of oure Ladyes presentacyon;
She was nevyr occapyed in thyngys veyn,
But evyr besy in holy ocupacyon.

And we beseche ȝow of ȝoure pacyens
Þat we pace þese materys so lythly away;
If þei xulde be do with good prevydens,
Eche on wolde suffyce for an hool day.

Now xal we procede to here dissponsacyon,
Which aftere þis was xiiii ȝere.
Tyme sufficyth not to make pawsacyon;
Hath pacyens with us we besech ȝow her.
And in short spas,
The Parlement of Hefne sone xal ȝe se,
And how Goddys Sone com man xal he;
And how þe Salutacyon aftere xal be,
Be Goddys holy gras.

Tunc venit Abysakar Episcopus.[85]

[EPISCOPUS]
Listenyth, lordyngys, bothe hye and lowe,
And tendyrly takyth heyd onto my sawe.
Beth buxom and benyngne ȝoure busshopp to knowe,
For I am þat lord þat made þis lawe.
With hertys so hende, herkyn nowe!
Ȝoure damyselys to weddyng, ȝa, loke þat ȝe drawe,
Þat passyn xiiii ȝere, for what þat ȝe owe.
Þe lawe of God byddyth þis sawe,
Þat at xiiii ȝere of age,
Every damesel, whatso sche be,
To þe encrese of more plente,
Xulde be browght in good degre
Onto here spowsage.

JOACHYM
Herke now, Anne, my jentyl spowse,
How þat þe buschop his lawe hath tolde;
Þat what man hath a dowtyr in his house
Þat passyth xiiii ȝerys olde,
He muste here brynge, I herde hym rowse
Into þe Tempyl a spowse to wedde.
Wherfor oure dowtyr ryth good and dowse
Into þe Tempyl sche must be ledde,
And þat anoon ryght sone.[86]

ANNE
Sere, I grawnt þat it be so,
Aȝen þe lawe may we not do.
With here togedyr lete us now go;
I hold it ryght weyl done.

JOACHYM
Sere busshopp, here aftyr þin owyn hest,
We have here brought oure dowtyr dere,
Mary, my swete childe; she is ful prest,
Of age she is ful xiiii ȝere.

EPISCOPUS
Welcome, Joachym, onto myn areste,

561 by 562 food from his table 564 mealtime, read 565 reward him 572 anything is left 573 the remains 574 if I can, deeds 576 pity 577 seen 579 with vain things 581 patience 582 pass (over), quickly 583 done, provision 584 whole 585 betrothal 586 fourteen years 587 delay 588 here 589 time 591 Son became 593 grace 595 unto 596 Be, gracious 599 girls, bring 600 as is your obligation 601 orders this rule 603 whosoever 606 To her betrothal 607 gentle 611 say 613 right, sweet 619 well 620 command 622 ready 624 residence

83 'God's plenty is always nearer to His servants than they think.'

84 The seven Acts of Corporal Mercy, enjoined upon all Christians, were to feed the hungry, give drink to the thirsty, shelter travellers, clothe the naked, visit and comfort the sick and those in prison, and bury the dead. See Matthew 25:35–6.

85 'Then comes Bishop Abysakar.'

86 The fact that Mary seems to be living with her parents again here, rather than in the Temple, suggests that the *Mary Play* itself may be a conflation of once separate materials.

Bothe Anne, þi wyff, and Mary clere.
Now Mary, chylde, to þe lawe þu leste
And chese þe[e] a spowse to be þi fere;
Þat lawe þu must fulffylle.

MARIA
Azens þe lawe wyl I nevyr be,
But mannys felachep xal nevyr folwe me;
I wyl levyn evyr in chastyte
Be þe grace of Goddys wylle.

EPISCOPUS
A, fayre mayde, why, seyst, þu so?
What menyth the[e] for to levyn chast?
Why wylt þu not to weddyng go?
Þe cawse þu telle me and þat in hast.

MARIA
My fadyr, and my modyr, sertys, also,
Er I was born, ʒe may me trast,
Thei were bothe bareyn, here frute was do;
They come to þe Tempyl at þe last
To do here sacryfice.
Bycause they hadde nothyr frute nere chylde,
Reprevyd þei wore, of wykkyd and wyllde,
With grett shame þei were revylyd,
Al men dede them dyspyce.

My fadyr and my modyr, thei wepte full sore,
Full hevy here hertys wern of þis dede.
With wepynge eyn þei preyd þerfore,
Þat God wolde socowre hem and sende hem sede.
Iff God wold graunt hem a childe be bore,
They behest þe chylde here lyff xulde lede
In Goddys Temple to serve evyrmore,
And wurchep God in love and drede.
Than God, ful of grace,
He herd here longe prayour,
And þan sent hem both seed and flowre.
Whan I was born in here bowre,
To þe Temple offryd I was.

Whan þat I was to þe Temple brought
And offerde up to God above,
Ther hestyd I, as myn hert thought,
To serve my God with hertyly love.
Clennesse and chastyte myn hert owth
Erthely creature nevyr may shove.[87]
Such clene lyff xuld ʒe nouht
In no maner wyse reprove.
To þis clennesse I me take.
This is þe cawse, as I ʒow tell,
Þat I with man wyll nevyr mell.
In þe servyse of God wyl I evyr dwell;
I wyl nevyr have other make.

EPISCOPUS
A, mercy, God! þese wordys wyse
Of þis fayr mayde clene,
Thei trobyl myn hert in many wyse.
Her wytt is grett and þat is sene.
In clennes to levyn in Godys servise,
No man here blame, non here tene.
And ʒit in lawe þus it lyce:
Þat such weddyd xulde bene.
Who xal expownd þis oute?
Þe lawe doth after lyff of clennes;
Þe lawe doth bydde such maydenes expres
Þat to spowsyng they xulde hem dres.
God help us in þis dowhte!

This ansuere grettly trobelyth me.
To mak avow, to creaturys it is lefful:
Vovete et reddite in Scripture have we;[88]
And to observe oure lawe also it is nedful;
In þis to dyscerne to me it is dredful.
Þerfore to cow[n]cell me in þis cas, I calle
Þe holde and þe wyse, and swiche as ben spedful.[89]
In þis sey ʒoure avyse, I besech ʒow alle.

MINISTER
To breke oure lawe and custom it wore hard indede,
And on þat other syde to do aʒen Scrypture;
To ʒeve sentens in þis degre ʒe must take goo[d]
  hede,
For dowteles þis matere is dyffuse and obscure.
Myn avyse here in þis I ʒow ensure,
Þat we prey all God to have relacyon,

626 listen 627 choose, companion 630 come near 638 Before, trust 639 their fruitfulness was passed 643 were, as 648 eyes 649 succour, seed (a child) 650 born 651 bower (chamber) 661 I promised 669 meddle 671 mate/spouse 675 evident 677 (is) angry (at) her 678 lies 679 such (women) 680 interpret 681 promote (a) 682 expressly 683 prepare themselves 684 doubt/dilemma 685 answer, troubles 686 lawful 692 advice 693 would (be) 694 act against 695 matter 696 doubtless, unclear 697 assure 698 instruction

[87] 'That no earthly creature can ever drive [out].'

[88] 'Vow and restore/return'. Perhaps the allusion is to Psalms 50:14 ('Offer unto God thanksgiving: and pay thy vows unto the most high'), or perhaps Nahum 1:15 ('O Judah, keep thy solemn feasts, perform thy vows)'.

[89] 'The old and the wise, and such as are well-favoured'.

For be prayour grett knowlech men recure;
And to þis I counsell ȝow to ȝeve assygnacyon.

EPISCOPUS
Trewly ȝoure counsell is ryght good and eylsum,
And, as ȝe han seyd, so xal it be.
I charge ȝow, bretheryn and systerys, hedyr ȝe com,
And togedyr to God now pray we
That it may plese His [in]fynyte Deyte
Knowleche in þis to sendyn us.
Mekely eche man falle down on kne,
And we xal begynne: *'Veni creator spiritus'*.[90]

Et hic cantent:[91] *'Veni creator'. And whan 'Veni creator' is don, þe buschop xal seyng:*

Now, Lord God, of lordys wysest of alle,
I pray þe[e], Lorde, knelynge on kne,
With carefull herte I crye and calle,
Þis dowteful dowte enforme Þu me.[92]

ANGELUS
Thy prayour is herd to hyȝ Hevyn halle,
God hath me sent here down to the[e],
To telle þe[e] what þat þu do xalle,
And how þu xalt be rewlyd in iche degre.
Take tent and undyrstond,
This is Goddys owyn byddyng:
Þat all kynsmen of Davyd þe kyng
To þe Temple xul brynge here du offryng,
With whyte ȝardys in þer honde.

Loke wele what tyme þei offere there,
All here ȝardys in þin hand þu take;
Take heed whose ȝerde doth blome and bere,
And he xal be þe maydenys make.

EPISCOPUS
I thank þe[e], Lord, with mylde chere,
Thi wurde xal I werkyn withowtyn wrake;
I xal send for hem bothyn fer and nere,
To werke þi wyl I undyrtake.
Anon it xal be do.
Herk, masangere, þu wend þi way,
Davyd kynsmen, as I þe[e] say,
Byd hem come offyr þis same day,
And brynge white ȝardys also.

[*Nuncius goes outside the Temple and cries out:*]

NUNCIUS
Oy! Al maner men takyth to me tent
That be owgth of kynrede to David þe kyng.
My lord þe busshop hath for ȝow sent,
To þe Temple þat ȝe come with ȝoure offryng.
He chargight þat ȝe hast ȝow, for he is redy bent
Ȝow to receyve at ȝoure comyng.
He byddyth ȝow ferthermore in handys þat ȝe hent
A fayre white ȝerde, everych of ȝow ȝe bryng
In hyght.
Tary not, I pray ȝow,
My lord, as I say ȝow,
Now to receyve ȝow
Is full redy dyght.

JOSEPH
In gret labore my lyff I lede,
Myn ocupasyoun lyth in many place.
For febylnesse of age my jorney I may nat spede.
I thank The[e], gret God, of Thi grace.

PRIMUS GENERACIONIS DAVID
What chere, Joseph? What ys the case
That ye lye here on this ground?

JOSEPH
Age and febylnesse doth me enbrase,
That I may nother well goo ne stond.

SECUNDUS GENERACIO[NIS DAVID]
We be commandyd be the beschoppys sond
That every man of David kynrede
In the Tempyll offyr a wond;
Therfor in this jorney let us procede.

JOSEPH
Me to traveyll yt is no nede.
I prey you, frendys, go forth youre wey.

699 by, receive 700 direction 701 beneficial 702 have 705 Deity 706 send 711 sorrowful 716 every respect 719 of (the house of) David 720 appropriate 721 sticks 722 at the time when 723 your 724 blossom and bear (flowers) 727 fulfil, argument 728 (from) both far 730 done 731 messenger 735 Oyez! 736 in any way related 739 commands, already prepared 741 have 743 held high 749 work takes me to 752 How are you . . .? 754 embrace 755 walk well, stand 756 by the bishop's messenger 758 wand/stick 760 There's no need for me to toil

[90] 'Come creator spirit': a popular hymn.

[91] 'And here let them sing'.

[92] '[God] resolve this difficult dilemma for me.'

Tercius Gener[acionis David]
Ther ys a mayd whos name ys clepyd Mary,
Doughter to Joachym as it is told,
Here to mary thei woll asay
To som man dowty and bold.

Joseph
Benedicite! I cannot undyrstande
What oure prince of prestys doth men,
Þat every man xuld come and brynge with hym a whande.
Abyl to be maryed, þat is not I, so mote I then!
I have be maydon evyr, and evyrmore wele ben.
I chaungyd not ȝet of all my long lyff!
And now to be maryed, sum man wold wen
It is a straunge thynge, an old man to take a ȝonge wyff!

But nevyrþelesse, no doute of, we must forth to towne.
Now, neyborys and kynnysmen, lete us forth go;
I xal take a wand in my hand and cast of my gowne.
Yf I falle, þan I xalle gronyn for wo,
Hoso take away my staff, I say, he were my fo.
Ȝe be men þat may wele ren, go ȝe before.
I am old and also colde, walkyng doth me wo.
Þerfore now wole I, so my staff holde I, þis jurny to wore.

Episcopus
Serys, ȝe xal undyrstande
Þat þis is þe cawse of oure comynge,
And why þat ech of ȝow bryngyth a wande;
For of God we have knowynge,
Here is to be maryde a mayde ȝynge.
All ȝoure roddys ȝe xal brynge up to me,
And on hese rodde þat þe Holy Gost is syttynge,
He xal þe husbond of þis may be.

Hic portent virgas.[93]

Joseph
It xal not be [I], I ley a grote!
I xal abyde behynde prevyly.
Now wolde God I wore at hom in my cote;
I am aschamyd to be seyn, veryly.

I Generacionis David
To wurchep my lord God, hedyr am I come,
Here for to offyr my dewe offrynge.
A fayr white ȝarde in hand have I nome,
My lord sere busshop, at ȝoure byddynge.

II Generacionis David
Off Davythis kynred, sertys, am I com,
A fayr white ȝarde in hand now I bryng.
My lord þe busshop, after ȝoure owyn dom,
Þis ȝarde do I offre at ȝoure chargyng
Ryht here.

III Generacionis David
And I a ȝarde have, both fayr and whyght,
Here in myn hond it is redy dyght;
And here I offre it forth within syght,
Ryght in good manere.

Quartus Generacionis David
I am þe fourte of Davidis kyn,
And with myn offrynge my God I honoure.
Þis fayr whyte ȝarde is offryng myn,
I trost in God of sum socoure.
Com on, Joseph, with offrynge þin,
And brynge up þin as we han oure.
Þu taryst ryth longe behynde, certeyn,
Why comyst not forth to Goddys toure?
Com on, man, for shame!

Joseph
Com? Ȝa, ȝa! God help, full fayn I wolde.
But I am so agyd and so olde
Þat both myn leggys gyn to folde,
I am ny almost lame.

Episcopus
A, mercy, Lord, I kan no sygne aspy.
It is best we go ageyn to prayr.

Vox
He brought not up his rodde ȝet, trewly,
To whom þe mayd howyth to be maryed her.

Episcopus
Whath? Joseph, why stande ȝe there byhynde?
Iwys, sere, ȝe be to blame.

762 named 764 marry, try 766 Bless me! 767 mean 769 May I prosper! 770 virgin always, will be 771 in 776 throw off 777 groan 778 whoever, foe 779 well run 780 pain me 781 complete 788 his rod 789 maid 790 bet, groat (a coin worth 4 pence) 792 were, cottage 793 seen 796 brought 798 David's kin 800 own judgement 801 command 807 fourth 810 trust 812 have ours 813 delay 814 God's tower (i.e. the Temple) 817 aged 818 begin 820 can 823 ought, here 824 What?

93 'Here let them bring their rods.'

JOSEPH
Sere, I kannot my rodde fynde,
To come þer, in trowth, methynkyht shame.

EPISCOPUS
Comyth thens!

JOSEPH
Sere, he may evyl go þat is ner lame:
In soth I com as fast as I may.

EPISCOPUS
Offyr up ȝoure rodde, sere, in Goddys name.
Why do ȝe not as men ȝow pray?

JOSEPH
Now in þe wurchep of God of Hevyn
I offyr þis ȝerde as lely whyte,
Prayng þat Lord of gracyous stewyn,
With hert, with wytt, with mayn, with myght,
And as He made þe sterrys seven,[94]
Þis sympyl offrynge þat is so lyght,
To His wurchep He weldygh evyn;
For to His wurchep þis ȝerd is dyght.
Lord God, I þe[e] pray,
To my herte þu take good hede,
And nothynge to my synful dede;
Aftyr my wyl þu qwyte my mede,
As plesyth to þi pay.

I may not lyfte myn handys heye.

[*The rod bursts into flower, and a dove perches upon it.*]

Lo, lo, lo! What se ȝe now?

EPISCOPUS
A, mercy, mercy! Mercy, Lord, we crye!
Þe blyssyd of God we se art thou.

Et clamant omnes: 'Mercy, mercy!'

A, gracyous God in Hevyn trone,
Ryht wundyrful Þi werkys be!
Here may we se a merveyl one;
A ded stok beryth flourys fre!
Joseph, in hert, withoutyn mone,
Þu mayst be blyth with game and gle,
A mayd to wedde þu must gone,
Be þis meracle I do wel se.
Mary is here name.

JOSEPH
What, xuld I wedde? God forbede!
I am an old man, so God me spede,
And with a wyff now, to levyn in drede,
It wore neyther sport nere game.

EPISCOPUS
Aȝens God, Joseph, þu mayst not stryve.
God wyl þat þu a wyff have.
Þis fayr mayde xal be þi wyve,
She is buxum and whyte as lave.

JOSEPH
A, shuld I have here, ȝe lese my lyff!
Alas, dere God, xuld I now rave?
An old man may nevyr thryff
With a ȝonge wyff, so God me save.
Nay, nay, sere, lett bene!
Xuld I now in age begynne to dote?
If I here chyde she wolde clowte my cote,
Blere myn ey, and pyke out a mote,
And þus oftyntymes it is sene.[95]

EPISCOPUS
Joseph, now as I þe[e] saye,
God hath assygnyd here to þe[e].
Þat God wol have do, sey þu not nay,
Oure Lord God wyl þat it so be.

JOSEPH
Aȝens my God not do I may:
Here wardeyn and kepere wyl I evyr be.
But, fayr maydon, I þe[e] pray,
Kepe þe[e] clene as I xal me.
I am a man of age,
Therfore, sere busshop, I wyl þat ȝe wete

828 Come here! 829 walk, who, almost 834 lily 835 judgement 836 strength 838 trifling, insignificant 839 kindly receive 843 deeds 844 grant my reward 845 it pleases you 849+ And everyone cries: 852 unique miracle 854 complaint 857 By 858 her 862 nor 865 (white) bread 867 if, her, end 868 be passionate? 869 thrive 871 leave it out! 873 chide her, beat my coat (i.e. me) 876 tell you 877 her 881 her guardian 883 chaste

94 'The seven stars': either the seven planets, or the Pleiades.

95 '[She will] trick me, and point out a mote (– i.e. speck of dust – in my eye, to detract attention from the beam in hers]'. The allusion is to Matthew 7:3–5, and refers to the pointing out of minor sins in others to prevent the discovery of major ones in oneself. Joseph is recalling the tricks traditionally ascribed to young wives married to older husbands and reflected in such comic stories as Chaucer's *Wife of Bath's Prologue* and *Merchant's Tale*.

Þat in bedde we xul nevyr mete;
For, iwys, mayden suete,
An old man may not rage.

EPISCOPUS
This holyest virgyn xalt þu maryn now,
3oure rodde floreschyth fayrest þat man may se.
Þe Holy Gost we se syttyht on a bow.
Now 3elde we all preysyng to þe Trenyte.

Et hic cantent: 'Benedicta sit beata Trinitas'.[96]

Joseph, wole 3e have þis maydon to 3oure wyff,
And here honour and kepe as 3e howe to do?

JOSEPH
Nay, sere, so mote I thryff!
I have ryght no nede þerto.

EPISCOPUS
Joseph, it is Goddys wyl it xuld be so;
Sey aftyr me as it is skyl.

JOSEPH
Sere, and to performe His wyl I bow þerto,
For all thynge owyght to ben at His wyl.

EPISCOPUS (*et idem Joseph*)[97]
Sey þan after me: Here I take þe[e], Mary, to wyff,
To havyn, to holdyn, as God His wyll with us wyl make.
And as longe as bethwen us lestyght oure lyff,
To love 3ow as myselff, my trewth I 3ow take.

(Nunc ad Mariam, sic dicens Episcopus.)[98]

Mary, wole 3e have þis man
And hym to kepyn as 3oure lyff?

MARIA
In þe tenderest wyse, fadyr, as I kan,
And with all my wyttys fyff.

EPISCOPUS
Joseph, with þis ryng now wedde þi wyff,
And be here hand now þu here take.

JOSEPH
Sere, with þis rynge I wedde here ryff,
And take here now here for my make.

EPISCOPUS
Mary, mayd withoutyn more stryff,
Onto þi spowse þu hast hym take.

MARIA
In chastyte to ledyn my lyff
I xal hym nevyr forsake,
But evyr with hym abyde.
And, jentyll spowse, as 3e an seyd,
Lete me levyn as a clene mayd.
I xal be trewe, be not dysmayd,
Both terme-tyme and tyde.

EPISCOPUS
Here is þe holyest matremony þat evyr was in þis werd!
Þe hy3 names of oure Lord we wole now syng hy.
We all wole þis solempn dede record
Devowtly: *Alma chorus Domini nunc pangat nomina summi.*[99]

Now goth hom all, in Godys name
Where-as 3oure wonyng was before.
Maydenys, to lete here go alone it wore shame,
It wold hevy 3oure hertys sore.
3e xal blysse þe tyme þat sche was bore,
Now loke 3e at hom here brynge.

MARIA
To have 3oure blyssyng, fadyr, I falle 3ow before.

EPISCOPUS
He blysse 3ow þat hath non hendyng:
In nomine Patris, et Filii, et Spiritus Sancti.

Joseph, þiselph art old of age
And þi wyff of age is 3onge,
And as we redyn in old sage,
Many man is sclepyr of tonge.
Þerfore, evyl langage for to swage,

886 cohabit 887 sweet 888 lust/be passionate 889 marry 891 sit, bough (Joseph's stick) 892 praise 893 as 894 her, ought 895 as I hope to thrive! 898 right (to do) 903 between, lasts 904 pledge, make 907 manner 908 five wits 910 by 911 readily 918 have said 921 i.e. always 924 deed 927 Wherever, dwelling 928 would be shameful 929 sadden 931 her 933 no ending 937 read, (books of) wisdom 938 prone to gossip 939 rumours, forestall

96 'And here let them sing: "Blessed be the Holy Trinity".'

97 '[A]nd Joseph the same': i.e. Joseph repeats the Bishop's words after him.

98 'Now to Mary the Bishop says this.'

99 'Now let the gracious choir sing the highest names of the Lord.' *Alma Chorus Domini* is the sequence for the nuptial mass.

Þat ȝoure good fame may leste longe,
III damysellys xul dwelle with ȝow in stage,[100]
With þi wyff to be evyrmore amonge.
I xal these iii here take:
Susanne, þe fyrst xal be,
Rebecca, þe secunde xal go with the[e],
Sephore, þe thrydde. Loke þat ȝe thre
Þis maydon nevyr ȝe forsake.[101]

SUSANNE
Sere, I am redy att ȝoure wyll
With his maydon for to wende.

REBECCA
Ȝoure byddyng, sere, [I] xall fulffyl,
And folwe þis maydon fayr and hende.

SEPHOR
To folwe hyre it is good skyl,
And to ȝoure byddynge wole I bende.

JOSEPH
Now, sere buschop, hens go I wyl,
For now comyth onto my mende
A matere þat nedful is.

EPISCOPUS
Farewel, Joseph and Mary clere,
I pray God kepe ȝow all in fere
And sende ȝow grace in good manere
To serve þe Kynge of Blysse.

MARIA
Fadyr and modyr, ȝe knowe þis cas,
How þat it doth now stonde with me;
With myn spowse I must forth passe,
And wott nevyr whan I xal ȝow se.
Therfore I pray ȝow here in þis plas
Of ȝoure blyssynge, for charyte,
And I xal spede þe betyr and have more gras
In what place þat evyr I be.
On knes to ȝow I falle.
I pray ȝow, fadyr and modyr dere,
To blysse ȝoure owyn dere dowtere
And pray for me in all manere;
And I for ȝow all.

JOACHYM
Almyghty God, He mote þe[e] blysse,
And my blyssynge þu have also.
In all godnesse God þe wysse
On londe or on watyr, wherevyr þu go!

ANNA
Now God þe[e] kepe from every mysse
And save þe[e] sownd in welth from wo.
I pray þe[e], dowtyr, þu onys me kys
Or þat þi modyr parte þe[e] fro.
I pray to God þe[e] save!
I pray þe[e], Mary, my swete chylde,
Be lowe and buxhum, meke and mylde,
Sad and sobyr, and nothyng wylde,
And Goddys blyssyng þu have.

JOACHYM
Forwel, Joseph, and God ȝow spede,
Wherso ȝe be in halle or boure!

JOSEPH
Almyghty God ȝoure weys lede,
And save ȝow sownd from all doloure.

ANNA
Goddys grace on ȝow sprede.
Farewel, Mary, my swete flowre.
Fareweyl, Joseph, and God ȝow rede.
Fareweyl, my chylde and my tresowre
Farewel, my dowtere ȝyng.

MARIA
Farewel, fadyr and modyr dere,
At ȝow I take my leve ryght here.
God þat sytt in Hevyn so clere
Have ȝow in His kepyng.

JOSEPH
Wyff, it is full necessary þis ȝe knowe,
Þat I and my kynrede go hom before,
For in soth we have non hous of oure owe.
Þerfore I xal gon ordeyn and thanne come ȝow fore.

We ar not ryche of werdly thynge,
And ȝet of oure sustenauns we xal not mys.

940 last 952 her, wise 955 into my mind 956 an important matter 958 in fellowship 963 go away 967 grace 977 water 978 misfortune 980 kiss me once 984 humble 985 Serious 987 Farewell 988 bower (chamber) 990 unhappiness 991 spread 993 guide 994 treasure 1001 (must) go 1002 no, own 1003 arrange (one) 1004 worldly goods 1005 we shall not want for food

100 'Three damsels shall live for a time with you'.

101 Susanne, Rebecca, and Sephora are three of the five companions of the Virgin listed in Pseudo-Matthew. The other two are Abigea and Zahel.

Therfore abydyth here stylle to ȝoure plesynge;
To worchep ȝoure God is all ȝoure blysse.

He þat is and evyr xal be
Of Hefne and Helle ryche kynge,
In Erth hath chosyn poverte,
And all ryches and welthis refusynge.

MARIA
Goth, husbond, in oure Lordys blyssynge;
He mote ȝow spede in all ȝoure nede.
And I xal here abyde ȝoure aȝen-comynge,
And on my Sawtere-book I xal rede.

Now blyssyd be oure Lord for this,
Of Hefne and Erthe and all þat beryth lyff.
I am most bound to Ȝow, Lord, iwys,
For now I am bothe mayde and wyff.

Now, Lord God, dysspose me to prayour
Þat I may sey þe holy Psalmes of Davyth,
Wheche book is clepyd þe Sawtere,
Þat I may preyse The[e], my God, þerwith.
Of þe vertuys þerof þis is þe pygth:
It makyht sowles fayr þat doth it say,
Angelys be steryd to help us þerwith,
It lytenyth therkeness and puttyth develys away.

Þe song of Psalmus is Goddys dete,
Synne is put awey þerby;
It lernyth a man vertuysful to be,
It feryth mannys herte gostly.
Who þat it usyth custommably,
It claryfieth þe herte and charyte makyth cowthe.[102]
He may not faylen of Goddys mercy
Þat hath þe preysenge of God evyr in his mowthe.

O holy Psalmys! O holy book!
Swetter to say than any ony;
Þu lernyst hem love, Lord, þat on þe[e] look,
And makyst hem desyre thyngys celestly.
With these halwyd Psalmys, Lord, I pray The[e] specyaly,
For all þe creatures qwyke and dede,
Þat þu wylt shewe to hem þi mercy,
And to me specyaly þat do it rede.

I have seyd sum of my Sawtere and here I am
At his holy Psalme indede:
Benedixisti domine terram tuam.[103]
In this holy labore, Lord me spede.

JOSEPH
Mary, wyff and mayd most gracyous,
Displese ȝow not, I pray ȝow, so long I have be.
I have hyryd for us a lytyl praty hous,
And þerin ryght hesely levyn wole we.

Come forth, Mary, and folwe me,
To Nazareth now wele we go.
And all þe maydonys bothe fayr and fre,
With my wyff comyth forth also.
Now lystenyth well, wyff, what I tell þe[e]:
I must gon owth hens fer þe[e] fro.
I wyll go laboryn in fer countre,
With trewth to maynteyn oure housholde so;
Þis nyn monthis þu seyst me nowth.
Kepe þe[e] clene, my jentyl spowse,
And all þin maydenys in þin howse,
Þat evyl langage I here not rowse,
For Hese love þat all hath wrought.

MARIA
I pray to God he spede ȝoure way,
And in sowle helth he mote ȝow kepe,
And sende ȝow helth bothe nyth and day.
He shylde and save ȝow from al shenschepe.
Now, Lord of Grace, to Þe[e] I pray,
With morny mood on kne I krepe.
Me save from synne, from tene and tray;
With hert I murne, with eye I wepe.
Lord God of pete,
When I sytt in my conclave
All myn hert on Þe[e] I have.
Gracyous God, my maydenhed save,
Evyr clene in chastyte.

1006 remain 1009 mighty 1011 wealth 1014 return 1015 Psalter (Book of Psalms) 1017 possesses life 1021 say 1023 (i.e. with the Psalms) 1024 essence 1025 purifies the souls who say it 1026 inspired 1027 darkness, drives devils 1028 song 1029 Sin 1030 teaches, virtuous 1031 inspires fear in, spiritual 1032 regularly 1034 lack 1037 sweeter, other 1038 teaches, (to) love 1039 heavenly 1040 holy 1041 living and dead 1044 the complete Psalter 1049 been 1050 hired, little pretty house 1051 comfortably 1057 far away from you 1058 work, distant lands 1059 honesty 1060 nine, not 1063 provoked 1066 spiritual health 1067 night 1068 shield, shame 1070 mournful 1071 trouble 1072 mourn 1073 pity 1074 private room 1076 virginity

[102] 'It purifies the heart and introduces [one] to charity.'

[103] 'Thou hast [blessed] Thy land, O Lord.' Psalms 85:1.

Contemplacio
Fowre thowsand sex undryd foure, I telle,
Man for his offens and fowle foly
Hath loyn ȝerys in þe peynes of Helle,
And were wurthy to ly þerin endlesly;
But thanne xulde perysche ȝoure grete mercye.
Good Lord, have on man pyte;
Have mende of þe prayour seyd by Ysaie;
Lete mercy meke þin hyest mageste.

Wolde God þu woldyst breke þin Hefne myghtye
And com down here into Erth,
And levyn ȝerys thre and threttye,
Thyn famyt folke with þi fode to fede.
To staunche Þi thryste lete Þi syde blede,
For erste wole not be mad redempcyon.
Cum vesyte us in þis tyme of nede;
Of þi careful creaturys, Lord, have compassyon!

A, woo to us wrecchis of wrecchis be,
For God hath haddyd sorwe to sorwe!
I prey Þe[e], Lorde, Þi sowlys com se,
How þei ly and sobbe for syknes and sorwe.
With Þi blyssyd blood from balys hem borwe,
Thy careful creaturys cryenge in captyvyte.
A, tary not, gracyous Lord, tyl it be tomorwe!
The Devyl hath dysceyved hem be his iniquite.

A, quod Jeremye, 'who xal gyff wellys to myn eynes
Þat I may wepe bothe day and nyght
To se our bretheryn in so longe peynes?'[104]
Here myschevys amende may Þi mech myght.
As grett as þe se, Lord, was Adamys contryssyon ryght.
From oure hed is falle þe crowne;
Man is comeryd in synne. I crye to Þi syght:
Gracyous Lord, gracyous Lord, gracyous Lord, come downe!

Virtutes
Lord, plesyth it Þin hyȝ domynacyon,
On man þat Þu made to have pyte.
Patryarchys and prophetys han made supplycacyon,
Oure offyse is to presente here prayerys to The[e].
Aungelys, archaungelys, we thre,
Þat ben in þe fyrst ierarchie,
For man to Þin hy Mageste,
Mercy, mercy, mercy we crye!

The aungel, Lord, Þu made so gloryous,
Whos synne hath mad hym a devyl in Helle,
He mevyd man to be so contraryous;
Man repentyd, and he in his obstynacye doth dwelle.
Hese grete males, good Lord, repelle,
And take man onto Þi grace;
Lete Þi mercy make hym with aungelys dwelle,
Of Locyfere to restore þe place.[105]

Pater
Propter miseriam inopum
Et gemitum pauperum
Nunc exurgam.[106]

For þe wretchydnes of þe nedy
And þe porys lamentacyon,
Now xal I ryse þat am Almyghty.
Tyme is come of reconsyliacyon.
My prophetys with prayers have made supplicacyon,
My contryte creaturys crye all for comforte,
All Myn aungellys in Hefne withowte cessacyon,
They crye þat grace to man myght exorte.

Veritas
Lord, I am Þi dowtere, Trewth,
Þu wylt se I be not lore.
Thyn unkynde creaturys to save were rewthe,
The offens of man hath grevyd Þe[e] sore.
Whan Adam had synnyd, Þu seydest þore
Þat he xulde deye and go to Helle.
And now to blysse hym to resstore?
Twey contraryes mow not togedyr dwelle!

Thy trewthe, Lord, xal leste withowtyn ende,
I may in no wyse fro Þe[e] go.

1078 (For) 4,604 (years) 1079 offence, foul sin 1080 lived 1081 (he is) worthy 1082 then 1084 Isaiah 1085 moderate 1086 break (open) 1087 (Isaiah 64:1) 1088 live (for) thirty-three years 1089 famished, food 1090 thirsty (ones), let 1091 otherwise, made 1092 visit 1093 sorrowful 1094 (who are the most) wretched 1095 added 1096 come (and) see 1097 lie, sob, sickness 1098 redeem them from torment 1100 do not delay 1101 deceived, by 1102 wells, eyes 1104 enduring pains 1105 Their sins 1106 the sea 1107 fallen 1108 burdened with 1110 dominion 1113 role 1118 (i.e. Lucifer) 1120 persuaded, disobedient 1121 (yet) he (Satan) 1122 His great malice, undo 1130 poor's 1135 ceasing 1136 issue forth 1139 unnatural, would be regrettable 1141 you said then 1142 die 1144 two contradictory things may 1145 last

[104] Lamentations 3:48–9.

[105] 'To replenish the places left empty by Lucifer [and his fellows].'

[106] 'For the oppression of the poor, for the sighing of the needy, now will I arise [saith the Lord].' Psalms 12:5.

Þat wretche þat was to Þe[e] so unkende,
He may not have to meche wo.[107]
He dyspysyd Þe[e], and plesyd Þi fo;
Þu art his creatour, and he is Þi creature;
Þu hast lovyd trewthe, it is seyd, evyrmo,
Þerfore in peynes lete hym evyrmore endure.

Misericordia
O, Fadyr of Mercy and God of Comforte,
Þat counsell us in eche trybulacyon,
Lete 3oure dowtere, Mercy, to 3ow resorte,
And on man þat is myschevyd have compassyon
Hym grevyth ful gretly his transgressyon,[108]
All Hefne and Erthe crye for mercy;
Mesemyth þer xuld be non excepcyon,
Ther prayers ben offeryd so specyally.

Trewth sseyth she hath evyr be than,
I graunt it wel, she hath be so.
And þu seyst endlesly þat mercy Þu hast kept for man;
Than, mercyabyl Lorde, kepe us both to.
Thu seyst: '*Veritas mea et misericordia mea cum ipso*'.[109]
Suffyr not Þi sowlys, than, in sorwe to slepe.
Þat Helle-hownde þat hatyth Þe[e], byddyth hym ho.
Þi love, man, no lengere lete hym kepe.

Justicia
Mercy, me merveylyth what ȝow movyth!
Ȝe know wel I am ȝoure systere, Ryghtwysnes.
God is ryghtful and ryghtffulnes lovyth.
Man offendyd Hym þat is endles,
Therfore his endles punchement may nevyr sees.
Also he forsoke his Makere þat made hym of clay,
And þe Devyl to his mayster he ches:
Xulde he be savyd? Nay, nay, nay!

As wyse as is God, he wolde a be;[110]
This was þe abhomynabyl presumpcyon!
It is seyd, ȝe know wel þis of me,
Þat þe ryghtwysnes of God hath no diffynicyon.
Therffore, late þis be oure conclusyon:
He þat sore synnyd ly stylle in sorwe.
He may nevyr make aseyth be reson;
Whoo myght thanne thens hym borwe?

Misericordia
Systyr Ryghtwysnes, ȝe are to vengeabyl;
Endles synne God endles may restore.
Above all hese werkys God is mercyabyl.
Þow he forsook God be synne, be feyth he forsook Hym never þe more;[111]
And þow he presumyd nevyr so sore,
Ȝe must consyder þe frelnes of mankende.
Lerne, and ȝe lyst, þis is Goddys lore:
Þe mercy of God is withowtyn ende.

Pax
To spare ȝoure speches, systerys, it syt;
It is not onest in vertuys to ben dyscencyon.
The pes of God ovyrcomyth all wytt.[112]
Þow Trewth and Ryght sey grett reson,
Ȝett Mercy seyth best, to my pleson.
For yf mannys sowle xulde abyde in Helle,
Betwen God and man evyr xulde be dyvysyon,
And than myght not I, Pes, dwelle.

Therefore mesemyth best ȝe thus acorde,
Than Hefne and Erthe ȝe xul qweme;
Putt bothe ȝoure sentens in oure Lorde
And in His hyȝ wysdam lete hym deme
This is most syttynge me xulde seme
And lete se how we fowre may all abyde.
Þat mannys sowle it xulde perysche, it wore sweme,
Or þat ony of us fro othere xulde dyvyde.

Veritas
In trowthe hereto I consente;
I wole prey oure Lorde it may so be.

Justicia
I, Ryghtwysnes, am wele contente,
For in Hym is very equyte.

1147 unnatural (i.e. humanity) 1149 pleased, foe 1151 eternally 1155 come to You 1161 has always existed 1167 (i.e. Lucifer), cease 1169 what you suggest amazes me! 1170 Righteousness/Justice 1171 just, loves justice 1175 for, chose 1180 limit 1183 sufficient restitution 1184 rescue him from there (Hell) 1185 too vengeful 1187 merciful 1189 badly 1190 frailty 1191 wisdom 1193 stop your argument, (is) proper 1194 for virtues to dispute 1201 agree 1202 satisfy 1203 to 1205 appropriate, I think 1206 live (together) 1212 justice

107 'He may not have too much woe', i.e. no amount would be sufficient punishment for what he has done.
108 'His disobedience distresses Him greatly'.
109 'My truth and My mercy [shall be] with him.' Psalms 89:24.
110 'He [man] wished to be as wise as God'.
111 'Though, through sin, he disobeyed God, he retained his faith in Him'.
112 'The peace of God [which] passeth all understanding'. Philippians 4:7.

MISERICORDIA
And I, Mercy, fro þis counsel wole not fle;
Tyl Wysdam hath seyd, I xal ses.

PAX
Here is God now, here is unyte;
Hefne and Erth is plesyd with Pes.

FILIUS
I thynke þe thoughtys of pes and nowth of
wykkydnes.
This I deme to ses ȝoure contraversy:
If Adam had not deyd, peryschyd had
Ryghtwysnes,[113]
And also Trewth had be lost þerby.
Trewth and Ryght wolde chastyse foly.
Ȝiff another deth come not, Mercy xulde perysch,
Þan Pes were exyled fynyaly.
So tweyn dethis must be, ȝow fowre to cherysch.[114]

But he þat xal deye, ȝe must knawe
Þat in hym may ben non iniquyte,
Þat Helle may holde hym be no lawe,
But þat he may pas at hese lyberte.
Qwere swyche on his, prevyde and se,
And hese deth, for mannys deth, xal be redempcyon.
All Hefne and Erth seke now ȝe.
Plesyth it ȝow þis conclusyon?

VERITAS
I, Trowthe, have sowte þe Erthe, withowt and
withinne,
And in sothe þer kan non be fownde
Þat is of o day byrth, withowte synne,
Nor to þat deth wole be bownde.[115]

MISERICORDIA
I, Mercy, have ronne þe Hevynly regyon rownde
And þer is non of þat charyte
Þat for man wole suffre a deddly wounde.
I cannott wete how his xal be.

JUSTICIA
Sure I can fynde non sufficyent,
For servauntys unprofytable we be echon.
Hes love nedyth to be ful ardent
That for man to Helle wolde gon.[116]

PAX
That god may do, is non but on;[117]
Þerfore þis is Pesys avyse:
He þat ȝaff þis counsell, lete Hym ȝeve þe comforte
alon,
For þe conclusyon in Hym of all þese lyse.

FILIUS
It peyneth Me þat man I mad,
Þat is to seyn, peyne I must suffre fore.
A counsel of þe Trinite must be had,
Whiche of Us xal man restore.

PATER
In Ȝoure wysdam, Son, man was mad thore,
And in wysdam was his temptacyon;
Þerfor, Sone, Sapyens,[118] Ȝe must ordeyn herefore
And se how of man may be salvacyon.

FILIUS
Fadyr, he þat xal do þis must be both God and man;
Lete Me se how I may were þat wede.[119]
And syth in My wysdam he began,
I am redy to do þis dede.

SPIRITUS SANCTUS
I, the Holy Gost, of Ȝow tweyn do procede;[120]
This charge I wole take on Me:
I, Love, to Ȝoure lover xal Ȝow lede.
Þis is þe assent of Oure unyte.

1213 depart from my advice 1214 Wisdom (i.e. Christ), spoken 1217 not 1218 cease 1220 been 1222 does not follow 1223 finally exiled 1225 die 1226 no sin 1227 by 1228 pass at his 1229 where such a one is, search 1231 search (through) 1233 searched 1234 no one 1235 (even) one day old 1237 run 1238 no one so loving 1240 understand, be (resolved) 1242 worthless, each one 1247 Him alone bring 1248 solution, lies in Him 1249 made 1250 for (it) 1251 held 1252 (to decide) which 1253 there 1262 task 1264 agreement

113 'If Adam had not died, then Justice would have perished'.

114 'So two deaths [those of humankind – as a result of sin – and of Christ – to redeem humanity] must occur, if you four are to be reconciled.'

115 'Nor [anyone] who will agree to be bound to that death.'

116 'He who will go into Hell for man's sake will need to have a very fervent love [for humanity].'

117 'There is only one [person] who can do that good [deed]'.

118 Sapience, i.e. wisdom: Christ is addressed as the embodiment of wisdom. God the Father is traditionally associated with power and the Holy Spirit with love and/or virtue.

119 'That garment': i.e. the fleshly body of humanity.

120 As the Athanasian Creed declares, the Holy Spirit is said to proceed from the other two Persons of the Trinity.

MISERICORDIA
Now is þe loveday[121] mad of us fowre fynialy,   1265
Now may we leve in pes as we were wonte.
Misericordia et Veritas obviauerunt sibi,
Justicia et Pax osculate sunt.[122]

Et hic osculabunt pariter omnes.

PATER
From Us, god aungel Gabriel, þu xalt be sende
Into þe countre of Galyle;   1270
The name of þe cyte, Nazareth is kende,
To a mayd, weddyd to a man is she,
Of whom þe name is Joseph, se,
Of þe hous of Davyd bore;
The name of þe mayd fre   1275
Is Mary, þat xal al restore.

FILIUS
Say þat she is withowte wo and ful of grace,
And þat I, þe Son of þe Godhed, of here xal be bore.
Hyȝe þe[e], þu were there apace,
Ellys We xal be there the[e] beffore.   1280
I have so grett hast to be man thore
In þat mekest and purest virgyne.
Sey here she xal restore
Of ȝow aungellys þe grett ruyne.

SPIRITUS SANCTUS
And if she aske þe[e] how it myth be,   1285
Telle here I, þe Holy Gost, xal werke al this.
Sche xal be savyd tho we Oure unyte.
In tokyn here bareyn cosyn, Elyzabeth, is
Qwyk with childe in here grett age, iwys.[123]
Sey here to Us is nothynge impossyble;   1290
Here body xal be so fulfylt with blys
Þat she xal sone thynke þis sownde credyble.

GABR[Y]EL
In Thyn hey inbassett, Lord, I xal go,
It xal be do with a thought.

Beholde now, Lord, I go here to,   1295
I take my flyth and byde nowth.

[*To Mary*] *Ave gracia plena Dominus tecum!*[124]

Heyl, ful of grace, God is with the[e]!
Amonge all women blyssyd art thu.
Here þis name, *Eva*, is turnyd *Ave*;   1300
Þat is to say: withowte sorwe ar ȝe now.[125]

Thow sorwe in ȝow hath no place,
Ȝett of joy, lady, ȝe nede more.
Therfore I adde and sey: 'ful of grace',
For so ful of grace was nevyr non bore.   1305
Ȝett who hath grace, he nedyth kepyng sore,
Therfore I sey: God is with the[e],
Whiche xal kepe ȝow endlesly thore;
So amonge all women blyssyd are ȝe.

MARIA
A, mercy, God! þis is a mervelyous herynge!   1310
In þe aungelys wordys I am trobelyd her.
I thynk how may be þis gretynge?
Aungelys dayly to me doth aper,
But not in þe lyknes of man þat is my fer;[126]
And also thus hyȝly to comendyd be,   1315
And am most unwurthy; I cannot answere;
Grett shamfastnes and grett dred is in me.

GABRYEL
Mary, in þis take ȝe no drede,
For at God grace fownde have ȝe.
Ȝe xal conceyve in ȝoure wombe, indede,   1320
A childe, þe Sone of þe Trynyte,
His name of ȝow, Jhesu clepyd xal be.
He xal be grett, þe Son of þe Hyest clepyd of kende.
And of His fadyr, Davyd, þe Lord xal ȝeve Hym þe se,
Reynyng in þe hous of Jacob, of which regne xal be   1325
non ende.

1265 four, finally   1266 live, as we used to do   1268+ And here they shall kiss each other.   1269 good, sent   1271 known   1274 born   1276 who shall restore all   1279 you must go there quickly   1280 before you   1284 ruin   1285 this might happen   1287 through   1291 fulfilled   1292 news credible   1293 high embassy   1294 done as quick as thought   1295 to her   1296 flight, do not wait   1305 no one born   1306 guarding carefully   1308 therefore   1310 message   1311 here   1312 greeting   1314 companion   1317 humility   1323 by (His) nature   1324 inheritance

[121]   A day set aside for the formal reconciliation of disputes.
[122]   'Mercy and Truth are met together: righteousness and truth have kissed each other.' Psalms 85:10.
[123]   'As a sign of this, her barren cousin Elizabeth is indeed pregnant in her great age.'
[124]   'Hail, full of grace, the Lord is with you.'
[125]   The word-play here reflects the idea that Mary redeemed the sin of Eve (*Eva*), and is therefore her antithesis, and also that Mary redeems humanity 'from woe' (Latin '*a ve*').
[126]   Mary's anxiety that the Angel comes in male form is a further reflection of her modesty and chastity.

MARIA
Aungel, I sey to ȝow,
In what manere of wyse xal þis be?
For knowyng of man I have non now;
I have evyrmore kept, and xal, my virginyte.
I dowte not þe wordys ȝe han seyd to me,
But I aske how it xal be do.

GABRYEL
The Holy Gost xal come fro above to the[e],
And þe vertu of Hym hyest xal schadu þe[e] so.

Therfore þat Holy Gost of þe[e] xal be bore,
He xal be clepyd þe Son of God, sage.
And se, Elyzabeth, ȝoure cosyn, thore,
She hath conseyvid a son in hyre age.
This is þe sexte monyth of here passage,
Of here þat clepyd was bareyn.
Nothynge is impossyble to Goddys usage.
They thynkyth longe to here what ȝe wyl seyn.

Here þe aungel makyth a lytyl restynge and Mary beholdyth hym, and þe aungel seyth:

Mary, come of and haste the[e],
And take hede in thyn entent
Whow þe Holy Gost, blyssyd He be,
Abydyth þin answere and þin assent.
Thorwe wyse werke of dyvinyte,
The Secunde Persone, verament,
Is mad man by fraternyte,
Withinne þiself in place present.

Ferthermore, take hede þis space
Whow all þe blyssyd spyrytys of vertu
Þat are in Hefne byffore Goddys face,
And all þe gode levers and trew
That are here in þis Erthely place
(Thyn owyn kynrede, þe sothe ho knew)
And þe chosyn sowlys þis tyme of grace
Þat are in Helle and byde rescu,

As Adam, Abraham, and Davyd, in fere,
And many othere of good reputacyon,
Þat þin answere desyre to here,
And þin assent to þe Incarnacyon,
In which þu standyst as persevere
Of all mankende savacyon.
Gyff me myn answere now, lady dere,
To all these creaturys comfortacyon.

MARIA
With all mekenes I clyne to þis acorde,
Bowynge down my face with all benyngnyte;
Se here þe hand-mayden of oure Lorde,
Aftyr þi worde be it don to me.

GABRYEL
Gramercy, my lady fre,
Gramercy, of ȝoure answere, on hyght.
Gramercy, of ȝoure grett humylyte,
Gramercy, ȝe lanterne off lyght!

Here þe Holy Gost discendit with iii bemys to Our Lady, the Sone of þe Godhed next with iii bemys to þe Holy Gost, the Fadyr godly with iii bemys to þe Sone, and so entre all thre to here bosom, and Mary seyth:

MARIA
A, now I fele in my body be
Parfyte God and parfyte man,
Havyng al schappe of chyldly carnalyte;
Evyn al at onys, þus God began.

Nott takynge fyrst o membyr and sythe another,
But parfyte childhod ȝe have anon.
Of ȝoure hand-mayden, now ȝe have mad ȝoure modyr.
Withowte peyne in flesche and bon,
Thus conceyved nevyr woman non
Þat evyr was beynge in þis lyff.
O myn hyest Fadyr in ȝoure tron,
It is worthy ȝoure son, now my son, have a prerogatyff.

I cannot telle what joy, what blysse,
Now I fele in my body!
Aungel Gabryel, I thank ȝow for thys!
Most mekely recomende me to my Faderys mercy.
To have be þe modyr of God, ful lytyl wend I!
Now myn cosyn, Elyzabeth, fayn wold I se,
How sche hath conseyvid as ȝe dede specyfy.
Now blyssyd be þe hyȝ Trynyte.

1327 How will this come about? 1328 (carnal) knowledge 1333 overshadow 1335 (the) Wise 1338 pregnancy 1339 she who was called 1341 (the Trinity) wait patiently 1342 come on! 1347 (i.e. Christ) 1348 made, brotherhood 1349 in this present place 1353 who have lived good lives 1355 if truth be known 1356 chosen/elect 1357 await (i.e. at the Harrowing) 1358 (Such) as, fellowship 1362 preserver 1363 mankind's salvation 1366 submit 1370 Thank you 1373 of 1375 perfect 1378 one limb/organ and then 1379 immediately 1381 bone 1383 who ever lived 1384 throne 1385 (such) a distinction 1390 I did not expect! 1392 did

Gabryel
Fareweyl, turtyl, Goddys dowtere dere.
Farewel, Goddys modyr, I þe honowre.
Farewel, Goddys sustyr and his pleynge-fere,
Farewel, Goddys chawmere and his bowre.

Maria
Farewel, Gabryel, specyalye.
Farewel, Goddys masangere expresse.
I thank ȝow for ȝoure traveyl hye.
Gramercy of ȝoure grett goodnes,

And namely of ȝoure comfortabyl massage;
For I undyrstande by inspyracyon,
Þat ȝe knowe by syngulere prevylage,
Most of my sonys Incarnacyon.
I pray ȝow take it into usage,
Be a custom ocupacyon,
To vesyte me ofte be mene passage,
Ȝoure presence is my comfortacyon.

Gabriel
At ȝoure wyl, lady, so xal it be,
Ȝe gentyllest of blood, and hyest of kynrede
Þat reynyth in Erth in ony degre,
Be pryncypal incheson of þe Godhede.

I comende me onto ȝow, þu trone of þe Trinyte.
O, mekest mayde, now þe modyr of Jhesu.
Qwen of Hefne, lady of Erth, and empres of Helle be ȝe;
Socour to all synful þat wole to ȝow sew,
Thour ȝoure body beryth þe babe oure blysse xal renew.
To ȝow, Modyr of Mercy, most mekely I recomende,
And as I began, I ende, with an *Ave* new,
Enjonyd[127] Hefne and Erth – with þat I ascende.

Angeli cantando istam sequenciam: 'Ave Maria, gratia plena, Dominus tecum, virgo serena'.[128] *And þan Mary seyth:*

Maria
Husbond, ryght gracyously now come be ȝe.
It solacyth me sore, sothly, to se ȝow in syth.

Joseph
Me merveylyth, wyff, surely, ȝoure face I cannot se,
But as þe sonne with his bemys quan he is most bryth.

Maria
Husbond, it is as it plesyth oure Lord, þat grace of Hym grew.
Who þat evyr beholdyth me, veryly,
They xal be grettly steryed to vertu.
For þis ȝyfte and many moo, good Lord, gramercy.
Butt, husbond, of oo thynge I pray ȝow most mekely:
I have knowyng þat oure cosyn Elyzabeth with childe is,
Þat it plese ȝow to go to here hastyly;
If owught we myth comforte here, it wore to me blys.

Joseph
A Godys sake, is she with childe, sche?
Than wole here husbond, Zakarye, be mery!
In Montana[129] they dwelle, fer hens, so moty the,
In þe cety of Juda, I knowe it veryly.
It is hens, I trowe, myles two and fyfty;
We are lyke to be wery or we come at þat same.
I wole with a good wyl, blyssyd wyff Mary;
Now go we forthe than in Goddys name.

Maria
Goth, husbond, how it be to ȝow peyne.
This jurny I pray ȝow lete us go fast,
For I am schamfast of þe pepyl to be seyne,
And namely of men, þerof I am agast.
Pylgrymagys and helpyngys wolde be go in hast.[130]
Þe more þe body is peynyd, þe more is þe mede.
Say ȝe ȝoure devocyonys and I xal myn i-cast.
Now in þis jurny, God mote us spede.

Joseph
Amen, amen and evyrmore.
Lo, wyff, lo, how starkly I go before.

Et sic transient circa placeam.

1394 turtle(-dove) 1396 sister, play-fellow 1397 chamber, bower 1399 (sent) especially 1400 great labour 1402 good tidings 1406 make it your habit 1407 by custom 1408 visit, in the mean time 1412 reigns 1417 pray 1418 (that) bears 1423 comforts, sight 1425 sun, when 1426 grew from Him 1428 inspired 1429 gift 1430 one 1433 do anything (to), her 1436 so may I thrive 1439 weary before 1440 will (go) 1442 although, painful 1444 ashamed to be seen by . . . 1445 especially by men 1448 prayers, say mine 1451 strongly

127 'United', although possibly 'Enjovyd': 'which delighted Heaven and Earth', is intended.
128 'With the Angel singing this sequence: "Hail Mary, full of grace, the Lord is with thee, fair virgin".'
129 'In the mountains/hills' (Luke 1:39), here assumed to be a place-name.
130 'Pilgrimages and charitable visits should best be done quickly.'

CO[N]TEMPLACIO
Sovereynes, undyrstondyth þat Kynge Davyd here
Ordeyned foure and twenty prestys of grett devocyon
In þe Temple of God, aftere here apere.
Þei wery[n] clepyd *summi sacerdotes* for here mynistracyon,[131]
And on was prynce of prestys, havynge dominacyon.
Amonge whiche was an old prest clepyd Zakarye,
And he had an old woman to his wyff of holy conversacyon,
Whiche hyth Elizabeth, þat nevyr had childe verylye.

In hese mynistracyon, the howre of incense,
The aungel Gabryel apperyd hym to;
Þat hese wyff xulde conseyve, he ʒaff hym intelligence.
He, seinge hese unwurthynes and age, not belevyd, so
The plage of dompnesse hise lippis lappyd, lo.
Thei wenten hom and his wyff was conseyvenge.
This concepcyon Gabryel tolde oure Lady to,
And in soth sone aftere þat sage sche was sekynge.[132]

And of here tweyners metyng,
Here gynnyth þe proces.
Now God be oure begynnynge
And of my tonge I wole ses.

JOSEPH
A, a, wyff, in feyth I am wery!
Therfore I wole sytt downe and rest me ryght here.
Lo, wyff, here is þe hous of Zakary;
Wole ʒe I clepe Elyzabeth to ʒow to apere?

MARIA
Nay, husbond, and it plese ʒow, I xal go ner.
Now þe blyssyd Trynite be in þis hous.
A, cosyn Elizabeth, swete modyr, what cher?
ʒe grow grett; a, my God, how ʒe be gracyous!

ELIZABETH
Anon as I herd of ʒow þis holy gretynge,
Mekest mayden and þe Modyr of God, Mary,
Be ʒoure breth þe Holy Gost us was inspyrynge;
Þat þe childe in my body enjoyd gretly
And turnyd down on his knes to oure God reverently.
Whom ʒe bere in ʒoure body, þis veryly I ken.
Fulfyllyd with þe Holy Gost, þus lowde I cry:
Blyssyd be þu amonge all women!

And blyssyd be þe frute of þi wombe also,
Þu wurthyest virgyne and wyff þat evyr was wrought.
How is it þat þe Modyr of God me xulde come to,
Þat wrecche of all wrecchis, a whyght wers þan nought?
And þu art blyssyd þat belevyd veryly in þi thought
Þat þe wurde of God xulde profyte in the[e].
But how þis blyssydnes abought was brought,
I cannot thynk nyn say how it myght be.

MARIA
To þe preysynge of God, cosyn, this seyd mut be.
Whan I sat in my lytyl hous onto God praynge,
Gabryel come and seyd to me '*Ave*'.
Ther I conceyvyd God at my consentynge,
Parfyte God and parfyte man at onys beynge.
Than þe aungel seyd onto me
Þat it was sex monethys syn ʒoure conscyvynge;
Þis cawsyth my comynge, cosyn, ʒow to comfort and se.

ELIZABETH
Blyssyd be ʒe, cosyn, for ʒoure hedyr comynge.
How I conseyvyd I xal to ʒow say,
Þe aungel apperyd þe howre of incensynge
Seynge I xulde conseyve, and hym thought nay.
Sethe for his mystrost he hath be dowm alway.
And þus of my concepcyon I have tolde ʒow sum.

MARIA
For þis holy Psalme I begynne here þis day:
Magnificat anima mea Dominum
Et exultavit spiritus meus: in Deo salutari meo[133]

1454 to be present by turns 1456 overall authority 1458 behaviour 1459 (was) named 1460 During, at the time of 1462 (To tell him that), news 1463 disbelieved (it) 1464 curse, dumbness, closed 1468 the meeting of the two (of them) 1469 begins, story 1471 talk, cease 1475 call 1476 near 1478 what news? 1479 great (with child) 1480 As soon as 1482 words 1483 was filled with great joy 1484 knelt 1490 should come to me 1491 being worse, nothing 1495 nor 1496 must be said 1502 conception 1507 he (Zacharias) disbelieved 1508 mistrust, dumb ever since 1510 Therefore

131 'They were named "the highest of priests" because of their duties'.

132 'And, truly, soon after she [Mary] sought [out] that man [Zachary].'

133 Mary and Elizabeth recite and translate the *Magnificat*, the prayer based upon Mary's words to Elizabeth in Luke 1:46–55, which was often included as a devotional work in Psalters. The full text in the Authorized Version reads 'My soul doth magnify the

ELIZABETH
Be þe Holy Gost with joye Goddys Son is in þe[e] cum,
Þat þi spyryte so injouyid þe helth of þi God so.[134]

MARIA
Quia respexit humilitatem ancille sue.
Ecce enim ex hoc beatam me dicent omnes generaciones.

ELIZABETH
For He beheld þe lownes of Hese hand-mayde, ȝe,
Lo ferforthe for þat all generacyonys blysse ȝow in pes.

MARIA
Quia fecit mihi magna qui potens est,
Et sanctum nomen eius.

ELIZABETH
For grett thyngys He made and also myghtyest,
And ryght holy is þe name of Hym in us.

MARIA
Et misericordia eius a progenie in progenies
Timentibus eum.

ELIZABETH
Ȝa, þe mercy of Hym fro þat kynde into þe kynde of pes,
For all þat Hym drede, now is He cum.

MARIA
Fecit potenciam in brachio suo
Disspersit superbos mente cordis sui.

ELIZABETH
The pore in His ryght arme He hath mad so;
Þe prowde to dyspeyre and þe thought of here hertys only.

MARIA
Deposuit potentes de sede
Et exaltavit humiles.

ELIZABETH
The prowde men fro hey setys put He,
And þe lowly upon heyth in þe sete of pes.

MARIA
Esurientes implevit bonis,
Et divites dimisit inanes.

ELIZABETH
Alle þe pore and þe nedy He fulfyllyth with His goodys,
And þe ryche He fellyth to voydnes.

MARIA
Suscepit Israel puerum suum
Recordatus est misericordie sue.

ELIZABETH
Israel for His childe up toke He to cum,
On His mercy to thynk, for Hese þat be.

MARIA
Sicut locutus est ad patres nostros,
Abraham et semini eius in secula.

ELIZABETH
As He spak here to oure forfaderys in clos,
Abraham and to all hese sed of hym in þis werd sa.

MARIA
Gloria Patri, et Filio,
Et Spiritui Sancto.

ELIZABETH
Preysyng be to þe Fadyr in Hevyn, lo,
Þe same to þe Son here be so,
Þe Holy Gost also to ken;

MARIA
Sicut erat in principio et nunc et semper,
Et in secula seculorum, Amen.

1517 lowliness 1518 (so) far that 1529 power 1530 despair, in 1533 high seats 1534 upon high 1537 good things 1530 casts into nothingness 1541 adopted to come (with Him) 1542 those who are His 1545 privately/face to face 1546 his seed, sown

Lord, / And my spirit hath rejoiced in God my Saviour. / For He hath regarded the low estate of His handmaiden: for, behold, from henceforth all generations shall call me blessed. / For He that is mighty hath done to me great things; and holy is His name / And His mercy is on them that fear Him from generation to generation. / He hath sh[o]wed strength with His arm; He hath scattered the proud in the imagination of their hearts. / He hath put down the mighty from their seats, and exalted them of low degree. / He hath filled the hungry with good things; and the rich He hath sent empty away. / He hath [helped] His servant, Israel, in remembrance of His mercy. And He sp[o]ke to our fathers, to Abraham, and to his seed for ever.'

134 'Because your spirit so rejoiced in God's salvation.'

ELIZABETH
As it was in þe begynnynge, and now is, and xal be
for evyr,
And in this werd in all good werkys to abydyn then.

MARIA
This Psalme of prophesye seyd betwen us tweyn,
In Hefne it is wretyn with aungellys hond;
Evyr to be songe and also to be seyn,
Every day amonge us at oure evesong.[135]

But, cosyn Elyzabeth, I xal ȝow here kepe,
And þis thre monethis abyde here now,
Tyl ȝe han childe, to wasche, skore, and swepe,
And in all þat I may to comforte ȝow.

ELIZABETH
A, ȝe Modyr of God, ȝe shewe us here how
We xulde be meke þat wrecchis here be.
All Hefne and Herthe wurcheppe ȝow mow,
Þat are trone and tabernakyl of þe hyȝ Trinite.

JOSEPH
A, how do ȝe, how do ȝe, fadyr Zacharye?
We falle fast in age, withowte oth.
Why shake ȝe so ȝoure hed? Have ȝe þe palsye?
Why speke ȝe not, sere? I trowe ȝe are not wroth.

ELIZABETH
Nay, wys fadyr Joseph, þerto he were ful loth.[136]
It is þe vesytacyon of God; he may not speke, veryly.
Lete us thank God þerffor, both;
He xal remedy it whan it plesyth His mercy.
Come, I pray ȝow specialy.
Iwys, ȝe are welcome, Mary.
For þis comfortabelest comynge, good God, gramercy.

CONTEMPLACIO
Lystenyth, sovereynys, here is conclusyon;
How þe *Ave* was mad, here is lernyd us:
Þe aungel seyd: '*Ave gracia plena Dominus tecum,
Benedicta tu in mulieribus*';
Elyzabeth seyd: '*Et benedictus
Fructus ventris tui*'; thus þe Chirch addyd 'Maria' and
'Jhesus' her.[137]
Who seyth oure Ladyes Sawtere[138] dayly for a ȝer
þus,
He hath pardon ten thowsand and eyte hundryd ȝer.

Than ferther to oure matere for to procede:
Mary with Elizabeth abod þer stylle,
Thre monthys fully, as we rede,
Thankynge God with hertly wylle.

A, Lord God, what hous was þis on,
Þat [held] þese childeryn and here moderys to,
As Mary and Elizabeth, Jhesus and John,
And Joseph and Zakarye also.

And evyr oure Lady abod stylle þus,
Tyl John was of his modyr born.
And þan Zakarye spak, iwus,
Þat had be dowm and his spech lorn.

He and Elizabeth prophesyed as þus,
They mad '*Benedictus*' them beforn;[139]
And so '*Magnificat*' and '*Benedictus*'
Fyrst in þat place þer made worn.

Whan all was don, Oure Lady fre
Toke here leve than aftere this
At Elizabeth and at Zakarie,
And kyssyd John and gan hym blys.

Now most mekely we thank ȝou of ȝoure pacyens,
And beseke ȝou of ȝoure good supportacyon.
If here hath be seyd ore don any inconvenyens,
We asygne it to ȝoure good deliberacy[on],
Besekynge to Crystys precyous Passyon
Conserve and rewarde ȝoure hedyr comynge.
With '*Ave*' we begunne, and '*Ave*' is our conclusyon;
'*Ave Regina Celorum*' to Oure Lady we synge.[140]

1555 remain thereafter 1557 hand 1558 said 1560 serve/look after 1562 scour 1566 Earth, must worship you 1567 (You) who are, tabernacle 1569 are getting very old, truly 1570 palsy 1571 hope 1578 happiest of visits 1580 taught 1585 year 1586 10,800 years of remission 1591 one 1598 who had been dumb, lost 1602 were made 1605 Of 1606 gave 1609 been said 1610 refer 1611 Praying

135 'Evensong': the *Magnificat* was recited during Evensong.

136 'He would be very sorry [to be thought angry].'

137 'The Angel said: "Hail full of grace, the Lord is with you, blessed are you among women"; Elizabeth said: "And blessed be the fruit of your womb", thus the Church added "Maria" and "Jesus" here.' In devotional practice 'Maria' was added after '*Ave*' and 'Jesus' at the end to give the conventional formula of the *Ave Maria* or 'Hail Mary': 'Hail Mary, full of grace, the Lord is with you, blessed are you among women, and blessed is the fruit of your womb, Jesus'.

138 Our Lady's Psalter was an alternative name for the Rosary, the repetition of 150 *Ave Marias* interspersed after every ten repetitions with a *Pater Noster* ('Our Father': 'The Lord's Prayer').

139 *Benedictus Dominus Deus Israel*, often, like the *Magnificat*, printed in Psalters.

140 'Hail the Queen of Heaven', the antiphon used in Nativity processions.

The Tretise of Miraclis Pleyinge (extracts)

The Tretise of Miraclis Pleyinge is an invaluable document for students of medieval drama. Not only is it a sustained assault upon the principles and practice of religious drama, written during the period when the Cycle plays were at their peak, but it also incorporates a putative six-point defence of the religious plays, which the author sets out to refute. The arguments put forward in support of the plays (that they are an aid to worship, that they can convert their audiences from worldliness to true faith, that they inspire true compassion in those who view them and promote affective piety, that they offer a means to instruct those who would otherwise be beyond the reach of the church's teachings (either through lack of learning or sheer apathy), that they provide an acceptable form of entertainment for people who would otherwise find less virtuous ways to spend their time, and that they are an even more effective form of religious story-telling than the visual representations that are the only other 'books' accessible to the unlearned) offer a plausible case for their continuation, and useful evidence of how the plays may have been considered at the time. Even in the hostile environment of the *Tretise*, they are not entirely dispensed with by the author's counter-case.

The word 'myraclis' as it is used in the *Treatise* incorporates the works of God in all their forms, not simply those normally referred to as miraculous, and the objection is to their portrayal in any form of dramatic or semi-dramatic performance. Particular hostility is, however, reserved for performing the events of the Passion, the central feature of the Cycle plays of the great northern towns and cities. In addition to the general objection in principle to recreating 'in play' what God performed 'in earnest', the text levels a number of more detailed criticisms at the nature and effect of performing religious drama, focusing upon the plays' appeal to the emotions rather than the minds of their audiences (a crucial feature of affective piety), their mingling of serious matter with more frivolous material, and their tendency to 'make familiar' religious mysteries in ways that undermined proper respect for divinity.

The text, contained in an early fifteenth-century compilation of Lollard[1] tracts, falls into two parts and was probably the work of two different individuals. The first, more impersonal section (from which the following extracts are taken) was written by a scribe from the Huntingdon area, the second; directed towards 'a friend' who shared some of the religious views of the author, is written in a Northamptonshire dialect. Both sections share a deep hostility to religious drama, although the first is orthodox on most other issues, grounding its objections to acting in a long-standing Christian tradition of anti-theatrical prejudice stretching back to Tertullian's *De Spectaculis*.

The text of *The Tretise* is British Library MS Additional 24202, ff. 14r–21r. I have also consulted the following modern editions: Clifford Davidson, ed., *Tretise of Miraclis Pleyinge* (Kalamazoo, 1993), which provides a lightly modernized version of the whole tract, and Anne Hudson, ed., *English Wycliffite Writings* (Cambridge, 1978), which prints most of the first section in the original spelling.

Here bigynnis a Tretise of Miraclis Pleyinge

Knowe ȝee Cristen men þat, as Crist God and man is boþe weye, trewþ, and lif, as seiþ þe Gospel of Jon,[2] – weye to þe erryinge, trewþe to þe unknowyng and doutyng, lif to þe styynge[3] to Hevene and weryinge,[4] – so Crist dude[5] no þinge to us but efectuely in weye of mercy, in treuþe of ritwesnes,[6] and in lif of ȝildyng[7] everlastynge joye for oure contunuely mornyng[8] and sorwynge in þis valey of teeres. Myraclis þerfore þat Crist dude heere in Erþe, ouþer in Hymsilf ouþer in Hise seyntis,[9] weren so efectuel and in ernest done þat to synful men þat erren[10] þei brouȝten forȝyvenesse[11] of synne,

[1] Lollardy is the name given by scholars to the loosely affiliated heretical groups that grew up in England in the last decades of the fourteenth century. Some at least of their views were inspired by the opinions of the Oxford scholar John Wyclif (*c.*1320–84), who was posthumously condemned as a heretic.

[2] John 14:6: 'Jesus saith unto [Thomas]: I am the way, the truth, and the life: no man cometh unto the Father, but by Me.'

[3] Climbing.

[4] (The) weary.

[5] Did.

[6] Justice.

[7] By exchanging.

[8] Continual mourning.

[9] 'Either Himself or through His saints'.

[10] Who err.

[11] Forgiveness.

settynge hem in þe weye of riȝt bileve;[12] to doutouse[13] men not stedfast þei brouȝten in kunnyng to betere plesen God,[14] and verry[15] hope in God to been stedefast in hym . . . Þanne, syþen myraclis of Crist and of Hyse seyntis weren þus ef[f]ectuel (as by oure bileve we ben in certeyn), no man shulde usen in bourde[16] and pleye þe myraclis and werkes þat Crist so ernystfully wrouȝte to oure helþe;[17] for whoevere so doþ, he erriþ in þe byleve, reversiþ[18] Crist, and scornyþ God. He erriþ in þe bileve, for in þat he takiþ þe most precious werkis of God in pley and bourde, and so takiþ His name in idil,[19] and so mysusiþ oure byleve.[20] A Lord!, syþen an Erþely[21] servaunt dar not takun in pley and in bourde þat þat her Erþely lord takiþ in ernest, myche more we shulden not maken oure pleye and bourde of þo[22] myraclis and werkes þat God so ernestfully wrouȝt to us.[23] For soþely, whan we so doun,[24] drede to synne is takun awey, as a servaunt whan he bourdiþ wiþ his mayster, leesiþ his drede to offendyn hym,[25] namely whanne he bourdiþ wiþ his mayster in þat þat his mayster takiþ in ernest. And riȝt as a nayl smyten in[26] holdiþ two þingis togidere, so drede smyten to Godward[27] holdiþ and susteyneþ oure bileve to Hym.

Þerfore, riȝt as pleyinge and bourdynge of þe most ernestful werkis of God takiþ aweye þe drede of God þat men shulden han in þe same, so it takiþ awey oure bileve, and so oure most helpe of oure savacioun.[28] And, siþ takyng awey of oure bileve is more venjaunce takyng þan sodeyn takyng awey of oure bodily lif,[29] and whanne we takun in bourde and pley þe most ernestful werkis of God as ben Hyse myraclis, God takiþ awey fro us His grace of mekenesse, drede, reverence and of oure bileve, þanne, whanne we pleyin His myraclis as men don nowe on dayes,[30] God takiþ more venjaunce on us þan a lord, þat sodaynly sleeþ his servaunt for he pleyide to homely wiþ hym.[31] And, riȝt as þat lord þanne in dede seiþ to his servaunt, 'Pley not wiþ me, but pley wiþ þi pere!',[32] so whanne we takun in pley and in bourde þe myraclis of God, He, fro us takynge His grace, seiþ more ernestfully to us þan þe forseid lord, 'Pley not wiþ Me but pley wiþ þi pere!'.

Þerfore siche myraclis pleyinge reversiþ Crist. Firste in takyng to[33] pley þat þat He toke into most ernest. Þe second in takyng to myraclis of oure fleyss,[34] of oure lustis and of oure fyve wittis, þat þat God tooc[35] to þe bryngyng in of His bitter deþ,[36] and to techyng of penaunse doynge, and to fleyinge of fedyng of oure wittis and to mortifiyng of hem.[37] And þerfore it is þat seyntis myche noten: þat of Cristis lawȝyng we reden never in Holy Writt,[38] but of His myche penaunse, teris,[39] and schedyng of blod, doying us to witen[40] þerby þat alle oure doyng heere shulde ben in penaunce, in disciplynyng of oure fleyssh, and in penaunce of adversite. And þerfore alle þe werkis þat we don [þat] ben out of alle þes þre,[41] utturly reversen Cristis werkis. And þerfore seiþ Seynt Poul [þ]at 'Ȝif ȝee been out of disciplyne of þe whiche alle gode men ben maad perceneris,[42] þanne avouteris[43] ȝee ben and not sones of God'.[44] And siþ myraclis pleynge reversen penaunce doying, as þei in greet likyng ben don and to grete likyng ben cast biforn,[45] þere as penaunce is in gret mournyng of hert and to greet mournyng is ordeynyd biforne . . .

And syþen no man may serven two lordis togydere,[46] as seiþ Crist in His Gospel,[47] no man may heren at onys efectuely þe voyce of oure Mayster Crist and of his owne lustis. And syþen myraclis pleyinge is of þe lustis of þe fleyssh

12 Correct belief.
13 Doubtful/unsure.
14 'Knowledge how better to please God.'
15 True.
16 Use in game/jest.
17 To aid us.
18 Contradicts.
19 In vain.
20 Perverts our beliefs.
21 Earthly/mortal.
22 Those.
23 For us.
24 Do so.
25 'Loses his fear of offending him'.
26 Driven in (to wood).
27 i.e. when directed towards God.
28 'The greatest aid to our salvation'.
29 'Is [to] take greater vengeance [upon us] than suddenly taking away our very lives'.
30 Do nowadays.
31 'Who suddenly slays his servant because he behaved too familiarly towards him'.
32 Your equal.
33 In
34 Flesh.
35 Took.
36 Death.
37 'And to teaching [us] how to perform acts of penance, and [how to] shun the indulgence of our senses, and [rather] to mortify them.' The distinction is between the (sinful) gratification of the bodily senses (the five wits) and the (proper) denial and mortification of them.
38 'As saints frequently note, we do not read anywhere in the Bible that Christ ever laughed'. The point was made by St John Crysostom, and was taken up by Wyclif.
39 Tears.
40 Intending us to understand.
41 'That do not conform to these three [things]'.
42 Partakers.
43 Adulterers/heretics.
44 Hebrews 12:8: 'But if ye be without chastisement, whereof all are partakers, then are ye bastards, and not sons.'
45 Planned beforehand.
46 At one time.
47 See Matthew 6:24 and Luke 16:13.

and myrþe of þe body, no man may efectuely heeren hem and þe voyce of Crist at onys, as þe voyce of Crist and þe voyce of þe fleysh ben of two contrarious lordis. And so myraclis pleying reversiþ discipline, for as seiþ Seynt Poul, 'Eche forsoþe discipline in þe tyme þat is now is not a joye but a mournynge.'[48] Also, siþen it makiþ to se veyne siȝtis of degyse,[49] aray of men and wymmen by yvil continaunse,[50] eyþer stiryng oþere to leccherie and debatis as aftir most bodily myrþe comen moste debatis, as siche myrþe more undisposiþ a man to paciencie and abliþ to glotonye and to oþere vicis,[51] wherfore it suffriþ not a man to beholden enterly þe ȝerde of God over his heved,[52] but makiþ to þenken on alle siche þingis þat Crist by þe dedis of His Passion badde us to forȝeten. Wherfore siche myraclis pleyinge, boþe in penaunce doyng, in verry discipline, and in pacience reversyn Cristis hestis[53] and dedis.

Also, siche myraclis pleying is scornyng of God, for riȝt as ernestful levyng[54] of þat þat God biddiþ is dispisyng of God, as dide Pharao so bourdfully takyng Goddis biddyngis or wordis or werkis in scornyng of Hym,[55] as dyden þe Jewis þat bobbiden Crist,[56] þanne, syþen þes myraclis pleyeris taken in bourde þe ernestful werkis of God, no doute þat þei scornen God as diden þe Jewis þat bobbiden Crist, for þei lowen[57] at His Passioun as þese lowyn and japen of þe myraclis of God. Þerfore, as þei scorneden Crist, so þeese scorne God. And, riȝt as Pharao, wrooþ[58] to do þat þat God bad hym, dispiside God, so þese myraclis pleyeris and mayntenours leevynge plesingly[59] to do þat God biddiþ, hem scornen God. He, forsoþe, haþ beden us alle to halowyn His name,[60] ȝyvyng drede and reverence in alle mynde of His werkis wiþoute ony pleying or japynge, as al holynesse is in ful ernest. Men þanne pleyinge þe name of Goddis miraclis as plesyngly, þei leeve to do þat God biddiþ hem, so þei scornen His name and so scornyn Hym.

But here aȝenus þei seyen [1] þat þei pleyen þese myraclis in þe worschip of God and so dyden not þes Jewis þat bobbiden Crist. [2] Also ofte siþis[61] by siche myraclis pleyinge ben men convertid to gode lyvynge, as men and wymmen seyng in myraclis pleyinge þat þe Devul by þer aray,[62] by þe wiche þei moven eche on oþe[re] to leccherie and to pride, makiþ hem his servauntis to bryngen hemsilf and many oþere to Helle, and to han fer more vylenye herafter by þer proude aray heere þan þei han worschipe here; and seeynge ferþermore þat al þis worldly beyng heere is but vanite for a while (as is myraclis pleying), wherþoru þei leeven þer pride and taken to hem afterward þe meke conversacioun of Crist and Hise seyntis. And so myraclis pleying turneþ men to þe bileve and not pervertiþ.[63]

Also [3] ofte syþis by siche myraclis pleyinge men and wymmen, seynge þe Passioun of Crist and Hise seyntis, ben movyd to compassion and devocion, wepynge bitere teris,[64] þanne þei ben not scornynge of God but worschipyng. [4] Also prophitable to men and to þe worschipe of God is to fulfillun and sechen alle þe menes by þe whiche men mowen leeve synne[65] and drawen hem to vertues and syþen, as þer ben men þat only by ernestful doynge wylen be convertid to God, so þer ben oþere men þat wylen not be convertid to God but by gamen and pley. And now on dayes men ben not convertid by þe ernestful doyng of God ne of men. Þanne now it is tyme and skilful to assayen to convertyn þe puple[66] by pley and gamen as by myraclis pleynge and oþer maner myrþis. [5] Also summe recreacioun men moten han and bettere it is, or lesse yvele, þat þei han þeyre recreacioun by pleyinge of myraclis þan by pleyinge of oþer japis.[67]

[6] Also, siþen it is leveful[68] to han þe myraclis of God peyntid,[69] why is not as wel leveful to han þe myraclis of God pleyed, syþen men mowen bettere reden þe wille of God and His mervelous werkis in þe pleyinge of hem þan in þe peytnynge, and betere þei ben holden in mennus mynde and oftere rehersid by þe pleyinge of hem þan by þe peytynge, for þis is a deed bok, þe toþer a qu[i]ck.[70]

48 Hebrews 12:11: 'Now no chastening for the present seemeth to be joyous, but grievous [,nevertheless afterward it yieldeth the peaceable fruit of righteousness unto them which are exercised thereby].'

49 'It promotes the spectacle of disguising [i.e. the wearing of costumes].'

50 'Evil continence': i.e. lack of self-restraint.

51 'It renders a man incapable of patience, and provokes [him] to gluttony and to other vices.'

52 'Wherefore [such mirth] prevents a man from recalling the rod [of divine punishment] above his head'.

53 Commands.

54 Deliberate ceasing.

55 See Exodus 5–12.

56 'Who played the bobbiden [buffeting] game with Christ'. See the York *Christ Before Annas and Caiphas* pageant for the treatment of Christ's torment as a game of blind man's buff or pops.

57 'They [the Jews] laughed.'

58 Was unwilling (to the point of rage).

59 'The Miracle-Players and [their] supporters ceasing [in order to pursue their own] pleasure.'

60 'Honour His name'. The reference is to the opening of the Lord's Prayer, 'Our Father which art in Heaven, Hallowed be Thy name'. Matthew 6:9, Luke 11:2.

61 Often-times/frequently.

62 Through their costumes (and behaviour).

63 'Whereby [as a consequence] they abandon their pride and adopt the meek behaviour of Christ and His saints. And so Miracle-playing converts folk to true [Christian] belief and [does] not pervert them.'

64 Bitter tears.

65 'All the means by which folk might [be encouraged to] abandon sin'.

66 People.

67 'Other [secular, and, by implication, more frivolous or ribald] entertainments'.

68 Lawful/permissible.

69 Painted.

70 'They may be more memorable and more frequently thought of if they were performed as drama [rather than merely painted in

To þe first resoun we answeryn seying þat siche myraclis pleyinge is not to þe worschipe of God for þei ben don more to ben seen of þe worlde and to plesyn to þe world þanne to ben sen of God or to plesyn to Hym, as Crist never ensaumplide hem,[71] but onely heþene men þat evere more dishonouren God, seyinge þat to þe worschipe of God, þat is to þe most veleynye of Him.[72] Þerfore, as þe wickidnesse of þe mysbileve of heþene men lyiþ to þemsilf, whanne þei seyn þat þe worschipyng of þeire maumetrie is to þe worschipe of God, so mennus[73] lecherye now on dayes to han þer owne lustus lieþ to hemself whanne þei seyn þat suche miracles pleiyng is to þe worschip of God. For Crist seiþ þat folc of avoutrie sechen siche syngnys as a lecchour sechiþ signes of verrey love[74] but no dedis of verrey love.[75] So, siþen þise myraclis pleyinge ben onely syngnis, love wiþoute dedis, þei ben not onely contrarious to þe worschipe of God, þat is boþe in signe and in dede, but also þei ben gynnys of þe Devvel to cacchen men to byleve of Anticrist, as wordis of love wiþoute verrey dede ben gynnys of þe lecchour to cachen felawchipe to fulfillynge of his leccherie. Boþe for þese myraclis pleyinge been verrey leesyng[76] as þei ben sygnis wiþoute dede and for þei been verrey idilnesse, as þei taken þe myraclis of God in idil aftur þeire owne lust. And certis idilnesse and leesyng been þe most gynnys of þe Dyvul to drawen men to þe byleve of Anticrist . . .

And as anentis[77] þe secound reson, we seyen þat riȝt as a vertuous deede is oþere while occasioun of yvel, as was þe Passioun of Crist to þe Jewis, but not occasioun ȝyven but taken of hem, so yvele dedis ben occasioun of gode dedis oþere while, as was þe synne of Adam occasioun of þe comyng of Crist, but not occasion ȝyven of þe synne but occasion takun of þe grete mercy of God. Þe same wise myraclis pleyinge, al be it þat it be synne, is oþere while occasion of convertyng of men, but, as it is synne, it is fer more occasion[78] of pervertyng of men, not onely of oon synguler persone, but of al an hool comynte,[79] as it makiþ al a puple to ben ocupied in veyn aȝenus þis heeste of þe Psauter book[80] þat seiþ to alle men, and namely to pristis[81] þat eche day reden it in þer servyse, 'Turne awey myn eyen þat þei se not vanytees', and efte, 'Lord, þou hatidest alle waytynge vanytees'.[82] How þanne may a prist pleyn in entirlodies[83] or ȝyve hymsilf to þe siȝt of hem, syþen it is forbeden hym so expresse by þe forseyde heste of God, namely syþen he cursiþ eche day in his service all þo þat bowen awey fro þe hestis of God. But, alas, more harme is, pristis now on dayes most shrewyn hemsilf al day, as a jay þat al day crieþ 'Watte shrewe!',[84] shrewynge hymsilf . . .

And so þes myraclis pleyinge not onely reversiþ feiþ and hope but verry charite by þe whiche a man shulde weylen[85] for his owne synne and for his neyeburs, and namely pristis for it wiþdrawiþ not onely oon persone but alle þe puple fro dedis of charite and of penaunce into dedis of lustis and likyngis and of fedyng of houre wittis.[86] So þanne þes men þat seyen 'Pley we a pley of Anticrist and of þe Day of Dome þat sum man may be convertid þerby' fallen into þe herisie of hem þat, reversyng þe Aposteyl,[87] seyden, 'Do we yvel þingis þat þer comyn gode þingis', of whom, as seiþ þe Aposteyl, 'dampnyng is riȝtwise'.

By þis we answeren to þe þridde resoun seyinge þat siche myraclis playinge ȝyveþ noon occasioun of werrey wepynge and medeful,[88] but þe wepyng þat falliþ to men and wymmen by þe siȝte of siche myraclis pleyinge, as þei ben not principaly for þeire oune synnes, ne of þeire gode feiþ wiþinneforþe,[89] but more of þeire siȝt wiþouteforþ is not alowable byfore God but more reprowable.[90] For, syþen Crist Hymsilf reprovyde þe wymmen þat wepten upon Hym in His Passioun,[91] myche more þei ben reprovable þat wepen for þe pley of Cristis Passioun, leevynge to wepen for þe synnes of hemsilf and of þeire chyldren, as Crist bad þe wymmen þat wepten on Hym.

pictorial form], for [a painting] is a dead book, but [a play] is a living one.' The reference is to the conventional defence of images as 'the books of the poor' through which the illiterate common people could gain access to religious truth.

71 'Cited them as [good] examples [of devotion]'.

72 'But only heathens, who always dishonour God, saying that those things are for God's worship which are [actually] most dishonourable towards Him.'

73 Men's.

74 'The outward appearance of true love'.

75 See Matthew 12:39: 'But He [Jesus] answered and said unto them [the Scribes and Pharisees]: An evil and adulterous generation seeketh after a sign: and there shall no sign be given to it, but the sign of the prophet Jonas.'

76 Truly lies.

77 Against.

78 'Far more frequently the occasion'.

79 A whole community.

80 The Psalter.

81 Priests.

82 See Psalm 119:37: 'Turn away mine eyes from beholding vanity [, and quicken Thou me in Thy way]' and Psalm 31:6:'I have hated them that regard lying vanities.'

83 Interludes.

84 'Watt, curse you!'

85 Weep.

86 'Deeds of lust and pleasure, and the gratification of our senses'.

87 St Paul. See Romans 3:8: 'And not rather (as we be slanderously reported, and as some affirm that we say): Let us do evil, that good may come, whose damnation is just.'

88 True and rewarding weeping.

89 Inwardly.

90 The distinction is drawn between the (virtuous) tears provoked by an inward sense of one's own sins, and the (empty) tears prompted by the mere pretence of (external, bodily) suffering represented by the actor playing Christ on the Cross.

91 See Luke 23:28.

And by þis we answeren to þe furþe resoun,[92] seyinge þat no man may be convertid to God but onely by þe ernestful doyinge of God and by noon veyn pleying, for þat þat þe Word of God worchiþ not ne His sacramentis, how shulde pleyinge worchen þat is of no vertue but ful of defaute? Þerfore riȝt as þe wepyng þat men wepen ofte in siche pley comunely is fals wittnessenge, þat þei lovyn more þe lykyng of þeire body and of prosperite of þe world þan lykynge in God and prosperite of vertu in þe soule, and þerfore, havyng more compassion of peyne þan of synne, þei falsly wepyn for lakkynge of bodily prosperite more þan for lakkyng of gostly,[93] as don dampnyd men in Helle. Riȝt so, ofte syþis þe convertynge þat men semen to ben convertid by siche pleyinge is but feynyd holynesse, worse þan is oþere synne biforehande. For, ȝif he were werryly convertid,[94] he shulde haten to seen alle siche vanyte, as biddiþ þe hestis of God, al be it þat of siche pley he take occasion by þe Grace of God to fle synne and to folowe vertu. And ȝif men seyn heere þat ȝif þis playinge of myraclis were synne, whi wile[95] God converten men by þe occasion of siche pleyinge, heereto we seyen þat God doiþ so for to comenden His mersy to us, þat we þenken enterly hou good God is to us, þat whil we ben þenkynge aȝenus Hym, doynge idilnesse and wiþseyinge Hym, He þenkiþ upon us good, and sendynge us His Grace to fleen[96] alle siche vanyte . . .

And herby we answeren to þe fifte resoun seyinge þat verry recreacion is leeveful, ocupiynge in lasse werkis, to more ardently worschen grettere werkis.[97] And þerfore siche myraclis pleyinge ne þe siȝte of hem is no verrey recreasion but fals and worldly, as provyn þe dedis of þe fautours of siche pleyis þat ȝit nevere tastiden verely swetnesse in God,[98] traveylynge[99] so myche þerinne þat þeir body wolde not sofisen[100] to beren siche a traveyle of þe spirite, but as man goiþ fro vertue into vertue, so þei gon fro lust into lust þat þei more stedefastly dwellen in hem. And þerfore as þis feynyd recreacioun of pleyinge of myraclis is fals equite, so it is double shrewidnesse, worse þan þouy þei pleyiden pure vaniteis. For now þe puple ȝyveþ credence to many mengid leesyngis for oþere mengid trewþis and maken wenen to been gode þat is ful yvel.[101] And so ofte siþis lasse yvele it were to pleyin rebaudye þan to pleyin siche myraclis. And yif men axen[102] what recreacioun men shulden have on þe haliday after þeire holy contemplacioun in þe chirche, we seyen to hem two þingis: oon, þat, ȝif he hadde veryly ocupied hym in contemplacioun byforn, neyþer he wolde aske þat question ne han wille to se vanyte; anoþer we seyn, þat his recreacioun shulde ben in þe werkis of mercy to his neyebore,[103] and in dilityng hym in[104] alle good comunicacion wiþ his neybore, as biforn he dilitid hym in God, and in alle oþere nedeful werkis þat reson and kynde axen.[105]

And to þe laste reson we seyn þat peinture, ȝif it be verry wiþoute mengyng of lesyngis, and not to curious, to myche fedynge mennus wittis, and not occasion of maumetrie to þe puple, þei ben but as nakyd lettris to a clerk to riden þe treuþe.[106] But so ben not myraclis pleyinge þat ben made more to deliten men bodily þan to ben bokis to lewid men.[107] And þerfore, ȝif þei ben quike bookis, þei ben quike bookis to shrewidnesse more þan to godenesse. Gode men þerfore seinge þer tyme to schort[108] to ocupyen hen in gode ernest werkis, and seinge þe day of þer rekenynge neyȝen faste,[109] and unknowyng whan þei schal go hennys,[110] fleen alle siche ydilnessis, hyinge[111] þat þei weren wiþ her spouse Crist in þe blisse of Hevene.

92 The fourth claim.

93 i.e. more for the apparent physical suffering of the actor playing Christ than for the poor spiritual health of the sinner him or herself.

94 Truly converted.

95 Why will.

96 Flee/shun.

97 'True recreation lies in the permissible performance of lesser deeds, [in order] more enthusiastically to [return to] work/perform greater deeds [thereafter]'.

98 'The patrons/supporters of such plays who never tasted true sweetness in God'.

99 Labouring.

100 Suffice.

101 'And therefore, because this pretended recreation of miracle-playing is a false equity [i.e. it pretends to be a virtuous occupation], it is a double villainy, and is [actually] worse than if they performed purely secular [and vain] entertainments. For now the [common] people give credence to many lies because they are mixed up with truths, and [they] believe to be true those things that are completely evil.'

102 Ask.

103 For the Corporal Acts of Mercy see the N-Town *Mary Play*, l. 574 and note.

104 Taking delight in.

105 'That reason and nature demand'.

106 'We say that painting, if it is true, without the mingling in of deception(s), and not too artfully crafted: too much indulging people's senses, and not an occasion for idolatry in the people, then it is just like the unadorned words in which a clerk may read the truth.'

107 Uneducated people.

108 'Their time too short'.

109 'And seeing the day of their death (and judgement) fast approaching'.

110 Leave (this world).

111 Hurrying.

Chester, The Post-Reformation Banns

The Chester Banns were read out on St George's Day to advertise the forthcoming performance on Corpus Christi Day (later, as here, Whitsun). They describe the contents of the pageants and whet the appetites of the audience for what followed. This (late) set from Chester is included here to suggest the ways in which defenders of the Cycle plays sought to adapt them to suit the changing demands of a culture in the grip of religious reform. In an attempt to defend the Cycle against the reformers' charges that the material was largely non-biblical and corrupt in its interpretations, a new set of banns was produced at some point after the onset of the Henrician reformation in the 1530s. These invented a proto-Protestant heritage for the play as the work of an allegedly reform-minded monk, Ranulf Higden (pre-1299–1364) of St Werburgh's Abbey, Chester, and sought to identify it with the origins of the city's own civic identity, through an association with Sir John Arneway, once wrongly thought to be the first mayor of Chester. The new banns attempt to excuse some of the pageants' archaic language and more speculative treatment of events on the grounds of the generally 'backward' and superstitious times in which they were written, but none the less defend the essential value of the Cycle as a fundamentally biblically grounded devotional work.

The text printed here is taken from Huntington Library MS 2, with minor additions from the versions recorded in R. and D. Rogers, *The Breviary of Chester History* (London, 1619) and David Mills, *The Chester Mystery Cycle*.

The Ban[n]es which are Reade Bee-Fore the Beginninge of the Playes of Chester

Reverende lordes and ladyes all
That at this tyme here assembled bee,
By this messange understande you shall
That some tymes there was mayor of this citie
Sir John Arnway, knighte,[1] who most worthilye
Contented him-selfe to sett out in playe
The devise of one Randall, monke of Chester Abbey.[2]

This moonk (moonk-like in Scriptures, well seene![3]
In storyes travilled with the best sorte)
In pageantes set fourth apparently to all eyne
The Olde and Newe Testament with livelye comforth,
Interminglinge there-with, only to make sporte,
Some things not warranted by any writt,
Which to gladd the hearers, he would men to take yt.[4]

This matter he abrevited into playes twenty foure,
And every playe of the matter gave but a taste,
Leavinge for better learning the scircumstance to accomplishe,
For all his proceedinges maye appear to be in haste.
Yet all to-gether unprofitable his labour he did not waste:
For at this daye, and ever, he deserveth the fame
That few monkes deserve, professing that name.

These storyes of the Testamente at this tyme, you knowe,
In a common Englishe tongue never read nor harde.[5]
Yet therof in these pageantes to make open showe.
This moonke – and [no] moonke – was nothinge afeared
With fear of hanging, breninge, or cuttinge off heade,
To sett out that all maye discerne and see.
And parte good be lefte, beleeve you mee.

As in this citie divers yeares the[y] have bene set out,

3 message/announcement 7 work 9 laboured 10 openly, eyes 11 comfort 12 entertainment 13 scriptural text 15 abbreviated 16 a brief hint of the matter 17 (full) circumstances 20 in 21 who profess 25 although no typical monk 26 burning 28 something of value remains 29 performed

1 Sir John Arneway d.1278.

2 See headnote. Higden was the author of a Latin history, the *Polychronicon*.

3 This is probably an ironic assertion, given the widespread Protestant criticisms of 'monkish ignorance'.

4 'Which he wanted people to understand was included only for its entertainment value.'

5 'Were neither read nor heard': the only legally produced Bibles were in Latin until the first official English text was published in 1538.

So at this tyme of Penticoste called Whitsontyde,[6]
Although to all the citie followe labour and coste,
Yet, God givinge leave, that tyme shall you in playe
For three dayes to-gether, begyninge one Mondaye,
See these pagentes played to the beste of theire skill,
Wher[ein] to supplye all wantes shalbe no wantes of good will.[7]

As all that shall see them shall most welcome bee,
So all that do here them we most humbly pray
Not to compare this matter or storie
With the age or tyme wherin we presentlye staye
But in the tyme of ignorance wherin we did straye.[8]
Then doe I compare that, this land through-out,
Non had the like, nor the like dorst sett out.

If the same be likeing to the comens all,
Then our desier is to satisfie; for that is all our gaine.
Yf noe matter or shewe therof special,
Doe not please but misslike the most of the trayne,
Goe backe I saye to the firste tyme, againe.
Then shall you fynde the fyne witt, at this day aboundinge,
At that day and that age had verye small beinge.

Condempne not our matter where grosse wordes you here,
Which ymport at this day small sence or understandinge:
As sometimes 'posty', 'lewtie', 'in good manner', or 'in fere',[9]
With such-like will be uttered in there speeches speakinge.
At this tyme those speeches carried good likeing.
Tho if at this tyme you take them spoken at that tyme,
As well matter as wordes, then is all well and fyne.[10]

This worthy knighte Arnway, then Mayor of this Citie,
This order toke, as declare to you I shall:
That by twentye-fower occupations, artes, craftes, or misterie,
These pageantes shoulde be played after breffe rehearsall;
For every pagente, a car[r]iage to be pro[v]yded withall.
In which sorte we purpose this Whitsontyde
Our pageantes into three partes to devide.

Nowe, you worshippfull Tanners, that of custome olde
The Fall of Lucifer did set out:
Some writers a-warrante your matter; theirfore be boulde
Lustelye to playe the same to all the rowthe.
And, yf any therof stande in any doubte,
Your authour his auther hath.[11] Your shewe let bee!
Good speech, fyne players, with apparril comelye!

Of the Drapers you, the wealthy companye,
The Creation of the Worlde, Adam and Eve,
Accordinge to your wealth, set out wealthilye,
And how Cayne his brother Abell his life did bereave.

The good, symple Waterleaders and Drawers of Deey,
See that your Arke in all poyntes be prepared.
Of Noy and his Children the wholl storye:
And of the Universall Floude, by you shalbe played.

The Sacriffice that faythfull Abraham to his sonne should make
You Barbers and Waxe-chaundlers of aunciente tyme
In the fourth pageante with paines ye doe take.
In decente sorte set out, the storie is fine.
The offeringe of Melchesedeke of breade and wine[12]

31 the city incurs 33 on 37 hear 42 No one, performs now 43 common people 44 desire, profit 46 displeases, audience 47 think back, first performance 49 existence 50 awkward 53 their 54 were popular 59 twenty-four craft guilds 60 brief 61 pageant wagon 63 for performance over three days 66 give authority to 67 crowd 70 fair costumes 74 Cain, take away 75 water-drawers of the river Dee 77 Noah

6 The feast of Pentecost, celebrating the descent of the Holy Spirit upon the Disciples, was held on Whit Sunday.

7 'The goodwill needed to make good the play's shortcomings will not be lacking.'

8 'Do not judge the play by modern standards, but by those of the "ignorant" period in which it was written.'

9 The banns list the already archaic words for 'power', 'loyalty', and 'together'.

10 'If you think [how] they were spoken at that time, both content and words will seem appropriate and good.'

11 'Your author has his own authority [to write]' The banns' anxiety on this point stems from the absence of clear biblical reference to the Fall of Satan in the Bible.

12 Melchisedeck was the priest-king of Salem who gave bread and wine to Abraham on his return from defeating Chedor-Laomer, king of Elam (see Genesis 14:18–20). He operates as a foreshadowing of Christ in the Chester Play and elsewhere.

And the preservation therof set in your playe.
Suffer you not in any poynte the storye to awaye.

Cappers and Lynnen-drapers, see that ye fourth bringe
In well-decked order that worthy storie
Of Balaam and his Asse, and of Balacke the King.[13]
Make the asse to speake, and sett yt out livelye!

Of Octavion the Emperour, that coulde not well alowe
The prophesye of auncient Sibell the sage,[14]
You Wrightes and Sklaters with good players in showe
Lustelye bringe fourth your well-decked carriage.
The beirth of Christ shall all see in that stage.
Yf the Scriptures a-warrant not of the miydwyfe's reporte
The authour telleth his authour, then take it in sporte.[15]

The appearinge Angell and Starr upon Christes beirth,
To Sheapheards, poore, of base and lowe degree,
You Painters and Glaziers, decke out with all meirth
And see that '*Gloria in Excelsis*' be songe merelye.[16]
Fewe wordes in the pageante make meirth truely,
For all that the a[u]thor had to stande uppon
Was 'Glorye to God above, and peace on Earth to Man'.[17]

And you worthy Merchantes-vintners, that nowe have plenty of wine,
Amplifye the storie of those Wise Kinges three,
That through Herodes lande and realme, by the starr that did shine,
Sought the sighte of the Saviour that then borne shoulde be.

And you worshippfull Mercers, though costely and fyne
Yee tryme up your carriage as custome ever was,
Yet in a stable was He borne, that mighty Kinge Devyne,
Poorely in a stable betwixte an oxe and an asse.

You Gouldsmythes and Masons, make comely shewe,
Howe Herode at the retorne of those kinges [did rage],
And howe he slewe the small tender male babes
Beinge under two yeares of age.

You Smythes: honest men, yea, and of honest arte,
Howe Christe amonge the Doctors in the Temple did dispute,
To set out your playe comely yt shalbe your parte.
Get mynstrills to that showe, pipe, tabarte, and flute.

And nexte to this, you the Bowchers of this Citie,
The storie of Sathan that would Christe needs tempte,
Set out as accostomablie have yee:
The Devill in his fethers, all ragge[d] and rente.

The death of Lazarus and his riseing againe,
You of [the] Glovers the wholl occupation,
In pagente with players orderly: let it not be paine,
Finely to advaunce after the best fashion.

The storye howe that to Jerusalem our Saviour toke the waye,
You Corvisors that in nomber manye bee
With your Jerusalem Carriage shall set out in playe.
A commendable true storye, and worthy of memorye.

And how Christe our Savyour at His Last Supper
Gave His bodye and His bloude for redemption of us all
You Bakers see that with the same wordes you utter
As Christe Hym-Selfe spake them, to be a memoriall
Of that death and Passion which in playe ensue after shall.[18]

90 agree to **91** Sybyl **92** Slaters **94** birth **100** merrily **101** (i.e. with scriptural authority) **109** trim/decorate **110** divine **112** Goldsmiths **116** trade **119** minstrels, tabor **120** butchers **121** Satan's temptation of Christ **122** you customarily do **125** whole matter **126** painful **129** shoemakers

13 The story of Balaam and his ass, and Balak, king of Moab, is in Numbers 22–4.

14 In the Chester *Annunciation and Nativity* play, the Sybyl prophesies the Incarnation and Redemption to the Emperor Octavian.

15 The role of the Midwife in the Chester *Nativity* is clearly an embellishment upon the biblical account, but the banns suggest that the author was merely following his source, and that the incident should be taken as light relief.

16 'Glory to God in the highest'.

17 The banns acknowledge that most of the *Shepherds' Play* is an embellishment on the terse biblical description of the Angel's song.

18 The banns carefully subscribe to the Protestant view that the Eucharist is only a memorial of Christ's sacrifice, not (as Catholics believe) a miraculous recreation of it.

The worste of these stories doe not fall to your parte;
Therefore, caste God's loaves abroade with a cheerfull h[e]art.[19]

You Fletchers, Boweyers, Cowpers, Stringers, and Iremongers,
See soberly ye make out Christes dolefull death,
His scourginge, His whippinge, His bloudeshedd, and Passion,
And all the paines He suffered till the last of His breath.
Lordinges, in this storye consisteth our cheeffe fayth
[The ignoraunce wherein hath us many years so blinded;
As though now alle see the pathe playne,
Yet the moste part cannot find it.][20]

As our beleeffe is that Christe after His Passion
Descended into Hell, but what He [did] in that place,
Though our authour set fourth after his opinion,
Yet creditt you the best learned; those he doth not not disgrace.
We wishe that of all sortes the beste you ymbrace.
You Cookes with your carriage see that you do well:
In pagente set out The Harrowinge of Hell.[21]

The Skynners before you after shall playe
The storye of the Resurrection,
Howe Christe from death rose the thirde daye;
Not altered in many poyntes from the olde fashion.

The Saddlers and Fristerers shoulde in theire pagent declare
The appearances of Christe, His travayle to Em[m]aus,
His often speach to the woman and to His disciples deere,
To make His Riseing-againe to all the worlde notorious.

Then see that you Telors with cariage decent
The storye of the Assention formally do frame,
Wherby that gloryous body in cloudes most orient
Is taken up to the heavens with perpetuall fame.

Thus of the Olde and Newe Testament to ende all the storye,
Which our author meaneth at this tyme to have in pleaye,
You Fishemongers to the peagent of The Holy Ghoste[22] well see
That in good order it be done, as hath been all-waye.

And after those ended, yet doth not the storie staye,
But by Prophettes sheweth fourth howe Antechrist shoulde rise
Which you She[a]rmen sett out in moste comely wise.

And then, you Diers and Hewsters, Antichrist bringe out
First with his Doctor, that godlye maye expounde
Who be Antichristes the worlde rounde aboute,
And Enocke and Hely, persons walkinge one grounde,
In partes set you well out, the wicked to confounde;
Which, beinge well understanded Christes worde for to bee,
Confoundeth all Antichristes and sextes of that degree.

The cominge of Christe to geve eternall Judgement,
You Weavers last of all your parte is for to playe.
Domesday we call yt, when the Omnipotente
Shall make ende of this worlde by sentence, I say.
One His righte hand to stande, God grant us that daye,
And to have that sweete worde in melodye:
'Come hether, come hether.' '*Venite Benedicti.*'

To which rest of wayes and seelestial habitation
Grante us free passage, that all to-gether wee,
Accompanied with Angells and endlesse delectation,
Maye contynnally laude God and prayse that Kinge of Glorye.

[The summe of this storie, lordes and ladyes alle,
I have brefly repeated, and how they must be played.
Of one thinge warn you now I shall:
That not possible it is those matters to be contryved

139 Bowyers, Ironmongers 141 bloodshed 143 the focus of our faith 158 Frieze-makers 161 well known 162 Tailors 163 Ascension 164 shining 167 to dramatize 168 pay attention 170 end 173 dyers 176 on, Enoch and Elijah 177 (i.e. actors' roles) 179 sects, kind 183 judgement 186 'Come blessed ones'

19 Small loaves seem to have been thrown to the crowd during the performance.

20 A partisan reference to the coming of the Reformation after centuries of Catholic 'ignorance'.

21 The Harrowing of Hell was an article of the Creed, but, as the banns' anxiety here suggests, it has no basis in Scripture.

22 i.e. the Pentecost Play.

In suche sort and cunning and by such players of price
As at this daye goode players and fyne wittes could devise.

For then should all those persons that as Gods do playe,
In clowdes come down with voyce, and not be seen,
For no man can proportion that Godhead, I saye,[23]
To the shape of man: face, nose, and eyne.
But sithens the face-gylte doth disfigure the man, that deem
A cloudy covering of the man: a voice only to here,
And not God in shappe or persone to appere.
By craftesmen and mean men these pagentes are played,
And to comens and country men accustomably before.
If better men and finer heads nowe come, what can be saide,
But, 'Of comen and countrye players take you the storie'?

And, if any disdaine, then open is the door,
That let him in to heare: pack awaye at his pleasure.
Our playinge is not to get fame or treasure.

All that with qui[e]te minde
Can be contented to tarry,
Be here on Whitson-Monday.
Then beginneth the storie!]

201 gilded-face, conceal 203 shape 204 poor/lowly 208 anyone dislikes (it)

23 'The actors playing God should [ideally] descend in clouds so that only their voices are heard and they are not seen, as no man can properly represent the Godhead.'

Matthew Hutton's Letter to the Mayor and Council of York (1567)

Unsure about the wisdom of continuing to play their (now lost) Creed Play under the new Protestant dispensation brought in with the Elizabethan religious settlement in 1559–60, the mayor and Council of York sent the text to the scholarly dean of York, Matthew Hutton, for his advice. His reply reveals both the (ultimately fatal) suspicion with which reformers viewed the Cycle plays, and a measure of the kind of historical interest in them which was to prompt others (notably in Chester) to copy the play texts and so save them for posterity.

To the right honourable my Lord Mayour of York, and the Right worshipfull his Brethren yeve this.[1]

Salute in Christo, My most humble duetie remembred, etc.,[2]
I have perused the bokes that your Lordshipp with your brethren sent me and as I find manie thinges that I muche like because of th'antiquite,[3] so see I manie thinges that I can not allowe, because they be Disagreinge from the senceritie of the Gospell,[4] the which thinges, yf they shuld either be altogether cancelled or altered into other matter, the wholle drift of the play shuld be altered, and therefor I dare not put my pen unto it, because I want both skill and leisure to ammend it,[5] thoghe in goodwill I assure you, yf I were worthie to geve your lordshipp and your right worshipfull brethren consell:[6] suerlie mine advise shuld be that it shuld not be plaid. For thoghe it was plausible XL [40] yeares agoe, & wold now also of the ignorant sort be well liked; yet now in this happie time of the Gospell,[7] I knowe the learned will mislike it: and how the State will beare with it, I knowe not. Thus beinge bold to utter mine opinion unto your lordshippe, I committ you and your brethren to the tuition of God's spirit.
From Thorneton, the xxiv of March 1567,
Your lordshipps in Christ to command,
Matthew Hutton

1 'Deliver this.'

2 'Greetings in Christ', etc.: a formulaic, honorific opening.

3 'Their age'.

4 'Because they do not conform to the teachings of the Scriptures'.

5 'Because I lack both the talent and the time necessary for the task'.

6 'Counsel/advice'.

7 The post-Reformation period.

Part II

Religion and Conscience: The Moral Plays

Religion and Conscience: The Moral Plays

Introduction

Unlike the pageants from the Cycle plays, the English Moralities or Moral Plays are all independent works designed for performance outside the context of an overarching dramatic structure. They vary as greatly in tone, content, and emphasis as they do in scope. *Mankind* and *Everyman* are small-scale productions, suitable for performance by troupes of between five and seven adult actors, whereas *Wisdom* and *The Castle of Perseverance* (not printed here) are grand affairs calling for large casts and spectacular staging and effects, and *The Play of the Sacrament* employs lavish 'special effects' but requires only a relatively modest cast (this last, the only surviving English Miracle Play, is, however, somewhat different in nature from the Moralities, and so it will be considered separately in the headnote that follows this introduction). What unites these plays, however, is both their didactic purpose and their focus on the nature of the human condition.

Central to the medieval Catholic conception of human identity was the notion of free will. Human beings, it was believed, had the capacity to influence (although not fully to determine)[1] their own fate in the afterlife through the choices they made on Earth; choices influenced by various internal and external forces for good or ill, not least the ever-present threat posed by the Devil. As *Wisdom*, the most overtly philosophical of the plays, carefully outlines, a human being is subject to two antipathetic forces, the desire to know God and behave as He desires, represented by the higher form of reason, and the drive towards pleasure and self-gratification, represented by the senses and the flesh, whose weakness in the face of temptation was then (and remains) proverbial. The medieval self was thus fundamentally conflicted, and it was the business of the Morality drama to explore that conflict and influence its resolution. The methods it used to do so are what gave it its distinct character and form.

It was the *Psychomachia*, an extended allegorical poem by the fourth-century Latin writer Prudentius, that laid out the essential framework within which the Moralities were conceived. It presented the human condition as a battle fought out over the field of the soul by competing forces representing the various virtues and vices characteristic of humankind. We have already encountered this externalization of internal qualities in embryonic form in the debate between the Four Daughters of God in the N-Town *Mary Play*, in which each of the aspects of the divine nature – Truth and Justice, Peace and Mercy – was embodied in human form. The Moralities took this technique and turned it into the central principle of their dramatic construction, allowing internal characteristics such as Pride, Humility, Knowledge, and Understanding, and external forces such as (divine) Mercy, Death, and the World, to fight over the fate of the protagonist in dramatized action.

As their names (most obviously Everyman and Mankind) suggest, the protagonists of these plays are universal figures, whose individual characteristics serve primarily to ally them emblematically with humanity in general. Thus Mankind's physical labours with his spade and Everyman's considerable private wealth and wide circle of friends and relatives, while they give specificity to their portrayal (and may provide hints for characterization and costuming), highlight common aspects of human existence rather than the idiosyncratic features of particular personalities. Whether the overriding metaphor is one of work (as in *Mankind*), isolation and pilgrimage (*Everyman*), or separation and marriage (*Wisdom*), the subject is always fundamentally the human condition.

Each play has its own distinct didactic agenda to pursue within this orthodox Christian outlook. In *Mankind* the lesson to be learned is that it is never too late to repent and seek God's mercy. In *Everyman* it is the rather different point that the whole of life should be spent in preparation for death, so that the fatal dart cannot catch one unprepared. In *Wisdom* the emphasis is upon the need to secure grace through penance and the good offices of the church. In each case, however, the fate of the protagonist is the crucial issue. The classic morality pattern takes him (and it is, typically, a him) under the influence of the Virtues and Vices, through five main stages, from Innocence, through Temptation, to Corruption, Repentance, and eventual Redemption; although this

1 Essential to the salvific process, however, was the element of grace. While good works might predispose a soul for Heaven (and bad deeds could effectively rule it out), God's mercy was essential if the defecit between individual merit and the potentially ruinous legacy of original sin was to be made good.

template is frequently qualified and amended in individual plays. In *Everyman*, for example, the eponymous hero is never tempted into sin; it is his heedlessness of virtue throughout his life that leaves him unprepared for the arrival of Death's summons.

The precise state of the protagonist's moral health at any given moment, and the true nature of the other figures with whom he interacts in the plays, are signalled by a variety of dramatic means. At first glance, the reliance upon allegorical abstractions might suggest a rather simplistic form of dramaturgy, but in fact these plays combine visual effects, acting styles, language, and poetic form in highly sophisticated ways to create their meanings. Characters are distinguished partly by the way they look (a vital feature of small-troupe productions, in which one actor might play a number of different roles, and so costumes and properties such as wigs and beards, rather than the actors themselves, served to differentiate characters), with the Virtues often presented as older men in priestly or scholarly garb, and the (frequently younger) Vices decked out in the latest worldly fashions (see below for a fuller discussion of this idea). Thus the protagonist's condition could be demonstrated by a change of costume. Mankind's surrender to New Guise, Nowadays, and Nought is marked by the shortening of his sober, long 'side gown' into a fashionable jerkin which is as revealing morally as it is physically. Moral status is also reflected by how the characters sound. A highly Latinate vocabulary, sober discourse, and complex, long-lined stanzaic forms are characteristically employed by the Virtues, while the Vices and devils rely on demotic language, scatological jokes, and shorter, more racy, stanzaic forms. Again, this allows the protagonist's shifting allegiance to be demonstrated to the audience as he adopts one or other mode during the course of the play.

Far from being passive witnesses to these shifts, the audiences of the Moral Plays, like those of the Cycles, were themselves drawn into (and implicated in) the action. Central to this process was the role of the Vices and their capacity to captivate both hero and spectator with their corrupting antics. This phenomenon is most obviously evident in *Mankind*, where the watching 'yeomanry' are explicitly invited to join in the singing of a 'Christmas song' which quickly degenerates into scatological obscenity. But it is also present in less overt forms in the other plays, where the antics of the Vices, their verbal dexterity and knockabout humour, are initially presented as more engaging than the ostensibly dour demeanour and didacticism of the Virtues. Like the protagonists, the spectators are allowed to feel as well as see the alluring tug of temptation. Only subsequently are they, like the heroes, encouraged to see the harm that such superficially attractive mischief entails and brought to appreciate the power (and not infrequent beauty) of the Virtues' counsel.

Rather than being set in a specific place (whether that is notionally Bethlehem or Yorkshire) the Moralities are played out in a virtual space, for the most part outside of time and geography. Mankind's field, like Everyman's grave, is anywhere and everywhere. Yet they are capable at any moment of plunging vigorously and directly into the here and now of their audience's own immediate experience. Like the Shepherds of the York and Chester cycles, the allegorical figures of the Moral Plays are familiar and concrete as well as abstract. When the Vices in *Mankind* leave the playing space to make money in the world beyond, they name a number of specific individuals in the local East Anglian communities around Cambridge and Lynn (Norfolk) whom they say they will visit, touching directly (perhaps only playfully, but possibly with a more pointed relevance now lost to us) on local issues and sensitivities. When Mind, Will, and Understanding become corrupted in *Wisdom* their behaviour alludes to what seem to have been very specific incidences of corruption among the nobility, the law courts of Old Holborn (London), and the contemporary 'sex industry' in the Stews of Southwark. This specificity allows the plays to touch upon social and political abuses and to engage with controversial issues on behalf of the communities for which they were written, in the same way as the Towneley *Second Shepherds' Play* spoke powerfully for the poor husbandmen of Yorkshire against the government who over-taxed them and the local gentry who exploited their weakness before the law. But this local interest within the universal drama also embodied a more fundamental philosophical and theologically grounded distrust of the modern, and the *present*, in general. When, in *Wisdom*, Lucifer tempts the three 'Mights' into sin, he does so in the persona of a fashionable courtly gallant, and offers them all the opportunities for self-gratification open to a man of power and wealth in late fifteenth-century England. In *Mankind*, New Guise (the latest fashion) and Nowadays are themselves among the characters conspiring to bring about the hero's downfall. This obsession with modishness reflects not only a sense that the latest fashions offer the best examples of worldliness with which to engage an audience, but also the more powerful sense that the fallen world, by its very nature, is inevitably drifting ever further into corruption and towards the final judgement, and so things 'nowadays' really are the worst that they have ever been. In this respect the plays' didacticism was part of an urgent attempt to bring about the repentance of its audiences: to encourage them, like Everyman, to 'make a good end' before it was all too late.

Further reading

S. Beckwith, 'Ritual, Church, and Theatre: Medieval Dramas of the Sacramental Body', in David Aers, ed., *Culture and History, 1350–1600* (Detroit, 1992), pp. 65–89.

D. Bevington, *From Mankind to Marlowe: The Growth of Structure in the Popular Drama of Tudor England* (Cambridge, Mass., 1962).

J. C. Coldewey, 'The Non-Cycle Plays and the East Anglian Tradition', in R. Beadle, ed., *The Cambridge Companion to Medieval English Theatre* (Cambridge, 1994), pp. 189–210.

T.W. Craik, *The Tudor Interlude* (Leicester, 1958).

C. Cutts, 'The Croxton Play: An Anti-Lollard Piece', *Modern Language Quarterly* 5 (1944), pp. 45–60.

W.A. Davenport, *Fifteenth Century English Drama: The Early Moral Plays and Their Literary Relations* (Cambridge, 1982).

G.M. Gibson, *The Theater of Devotion: East Anglian Drama and Society in the Late Middle Ages* (Chicago, 1989).

R.L. Homan, 'Devotional Themes in the Violence and Humour of *The Play of The Sacrament*', *Comparative Drama* 20 (1986), pp. 327–40.

M.R. Kelley, *Flamboyant Drama: A Study of The Castle of Perseverance, Mankind, and Wisdom* (Carbondale, Ill., 1979).

P.M. King, 'Morality Plays', in R. Beadle, ed., *The Cambridge Companion to Medieval English Theatre* (Cambridge, 1994), pp. 240–64.

J. Marshall, '"Fortune in Worldys Worschyppe": The Satirising of the Suffolks in *Wisdom*', *Medieval English Theatre* 14 (1992), pp. 37–66,

P. Neuss, 'Active and Idle Language: Dramatic Images in *Mankind*', in N. Denny, ed., *Medieval Drama* (London, 1973), pp. 41–68.

R. Potter, *The English Morality Play* (London, 1975).

B. Spivack, *Shakespeare and the Allegory of Evil* (New York, 1958).

E. Streitman, 'The Middle Dutch *Elckerlijc* and the English *Everyman*', *Medium Aevum* 52 (1983), pp. 111–14.

M. Riggio, *The Play of Wisdom: Its Text and Contexts* (New York, 1986).

G. Walker, *The Politics of Performance in Early Renaissance Drama* (Cambridge, 1998).

Simon Bening, *The Mass of St Gregory*, miniature, *c.*1540–50. The J. Paul Getty Museum, Los Angeles, MS. 3.

Croxton, *The Play of the Sacrament*

Unlike the other plays in this section, *The Play of the Sacrament* is a Miracle Play rather than a Morality. It dramatizes the miraculous appearance of Christ in human form from a consecrated Eucharistic Host which is being 'tortured' by a group of Jewish merchants bent upon disproving its divine nature. As it portrays the subsequent conversion of the Jews to Christianity, the play is also a Conversion drama of a kind popular in western continental Europe in the later Middle Ages. Such plays were designed to explore and proclaim the universal truth of Christian doctrine in the face of criticism or disbelief, and so reassure true believers and bolster the faith of doubters and sceptics. Hence, the repeated references to the location and date of the miracle (Heraclia in Aragon, Spain, in 1461) are part of its claim to authenticity – and thus to power – as a narrative of Christian truth. As the central mystery celebrated in the play is the miracle of the Mass, the capacity of the priest to turn the Eucharistic bread literally into the body and blood of Christ through the process of transubstantiation (see the headnote to the Cycle plays section), the unbelievers against whom it was directed may well have been the Lollards and others influenced by the opinions of the fourteenth-century heretic John Wycliff, who denied the real presence, rather than the Jews *per se* (of whom, officially at least, there had been none in England since their expulsion in the thirteenth century). The legend of the miraculous Host is, however, a long-standing one, with versions circulating from as early as the 1430s which linked it with a number of different locations and dates.

The play shares a number of common features with the Cycle plays. It starts with lengthy, alliterative 'boasts' from both the Christian merchant Aristorius and Jonathas, the leader of the Jews, which recall in style and tone the opening speeches of tyrants such as Satan, Herod, and Pilate in the York and Chester plays. The portrayal of the Jews (and Jonathas in particular) is also in the tradition that forged the York Judas, and would later be adapted by Marlowe in *The Jew of Malta* and (with significant variation) by Shakespeare in *The Merchant of Venice*. There has been considerable scholarly debate over whether this tradition can properly be called anti-Semitic in the absence of any English Jews to prompt it,[1] but given the play's debt to continental sources, and the longevity of the tradition, the term seems appropriate in this case. At the very least the potent mixture of slapstick comedy and real violence evident in both the Jonathas scenes in this play and the Scourging and Buffeting scenes in the Cycle plays (the Jews here, like the soldiers who torment Christ, are simultaneously both laughable and truly dangerous) provides a useful index of prevailing anxieties about racial and religious difference in medieval English culture.

As the links between the Jews in this play and the soldiers of the Cycles suggests, it is to the Passion sequence in particular that one must look for the most obvious and powerful correspondences between this play and the civic drama. As the text makes clear at a number of points, when the Jews seek to test the Host through a number of increasingly grotesque acts of violence (on the principle that, if it really is Christ, then it should react) they subject it to a symbolic second Passion. Each stage in the process mirrors an event in the Passion sequence. Aristorius's original theft of the Host re-enacts Judas's betrayal of his master to the High Priests. The stabbing of the wafer, first in its four quarters, then in the centre, repeats the five wounds suffered by Christ on the Cross, one in each limb, then the final thrust with the spear into His side. Jonathas, striking last, thus takes the place of Longinus, the unbeliever converted to Christianity when his eyesight was miraculously restored by the blood flowing from the wound he inflicted. The Crucifixion itself is represented by the fixing of the wafer to the post, just as the deposition from the Cross is repeated in the careful removal of the nails and the taking down of the Host. The placing of the wafer in the cauldron (wrapped in a cloth symbolic of grave-clothes) re-enacts Christ's burial, while the sealing in the oven echoes the descent into Hell and the Harrowing. The final shattering of the oven to reveal the 'image' of Christ thus provides the triumphant Resurrection to complete the sequence.

At least one aspect of the play reflects another dramatic tradition, however. The comic double-act

[1] See, for example, B. Glassman, *Anti-Semitic Stereotypes Without Jews: Images of the Jews in England, 1290–1700* (Detroit, 1975); T.L. Steinberg, 'The Jewish Presence in Middle English Literature', *Christian Jewish Relations* 20 (1987), pp. 29–48; and Miri Rubin, *Gentile Tales: The Narrative Assault On Late Medieval Jews* (New Haven, Conn., 1998).

between the physician Master Brandyche ('Brown-ditch') and his unruly servant Colle, which forms an interlude in the miracle narrative, seems to reflect the folk-traditions of the Mummers' Plays (although a partial debt to the comic servants and pompous masters of classical drama should not be entirely discounted either). A quack doctor frequently appeared in these locally produced fertility dramas to resurrect the hero or his adversary after he had been slain in combat. And a similar delight in comic lists of unlikely-sounding cures and medicines seems to have been central to their performances too (for the Mummers' Plays see E.K. Chambers, *The Medieval Stage* (2 vols, Oxford, 1903), pp. 213ff; Richard Axton, *English Drama of the Early Middle Ages* (London, 1974); A. Brody, *The English Mummers and their Plays* (London, 1970); for a similar delight in lists, see the Chester *Shepherds' Play*, above). The inclusion of this scene in the play may well reflect a further attempt to tailor it for a specifically English rural audience. The interlude is not entirely irrelevant to the surrounding drama, however. It offers a comic counterpoint to the more serious matter that it interrupts in a way reminiscent of the Mak and Gyll scenes in the Towneley *Second Shepherds' Play*. Whereas Master Brandyche brings only a parody of healing, Christ, the true 'medicine for the soul', offers the real thing. Jonathas's immediate rejection of the former, then, acts as a foreshadowing of his later conversion by the latter.

The text poses a number of interesting questions concerning staging. It seems to call for what is known as 'Place and Scaffold' performance, in which a number of 'houses' or 'mansions' (often elevated upon scaffolds) representing specific locations surround a central space known as the *platea* or 'place' (and referred to as such in this play in the stage direction following l. 444). The text seems to require sizeable mansions to represent the homes of Aristorius and Jonathas, and another to represent the parish church, with all the traffic between these locations occurring in the place. If the performance took place in the churchyard or close by, however, the local church itself could be used in lieu of the third scaffold, adding considerable resonance to the final scenes in which the Bishop leads the actors (and audience?) in procession behind the Host to the altar, where the ceremony of reconciliation takes place. The text also calls for a number of spectacular special effects, including a bleeding Host, a cauldron running with blood, and an exploding oven, each of which would have required a substantial investment from any company wishing to perform the play. Most spectacular of all, perhaps, and certainly the most difficult to interpret, is the call for an 'image' of the wounded Christ to emerge from the oven and speak to the Jews. Whether this was intended to be a mechanical prop, or whether an actor played the part, is unclear. The fact that the manuscript lists 'Jh[es]us' among the names of the 'players' (i.e. the *dramatis personae*) may suggest the latter. However, the use of mechanical images in religious drama was not unknown, as the references to the nine small painted angels that 'ran about' in Heaven in the York *Last Judgement* pageant reveals (see *The Mercers' Indenture*, p. 159, above). Nor was it entirely unknown in other religious contexts, as such devices as the Rood of Grace at Boxley Abbey suggest (the 'miraculous' Rood was actually worked surreptitiously by the monks using pulleys and wires, as the reformers gleefully revealed at its destruction in 1538).

The play cannot be dated precisely, but the repeated claim that the events depicted took place in 1461 probably provides a reliable earliest date for its composition. It is conventionally associated, on the strength of the reference to a performance 'at Croxston' in the Banns, with the village of Croxton near Thetford in Suffolk (the nearest of several Croxtons in East Anglia to Babwell Mill, near Bury St Edmunds, which is also mentioned in the text). But the play may well have been designed for touring, and for performance by any number of different companies in and beyond East Anglia. The Banns themselves, and the claim that 'IX may play yt at ease' attached to the cast list, both suggest adaptability to the differing demands of touring troupes. It is perhaps significant that the two references that give the text a local habitation and a name occur outside the play proper, in the Banns and the Master Brandyche interlude (which may well be a later interpolation, as it is not mentioned in the Banns). These may be peculiar to the version copied by the East Anglian scribes into whose hands it came in the mid-sixteenth century, and whose work provides us with the only surviving text.

Although once a free-standing 'book' in its own right, the manuscript became part of a larger anthology of diverse material, now in the library of Trinity College Dublin (Trinity College, Dublin MS F.4. 20, ff. 338r–356r), from which it has only recently been separated once more. For this edition I have used the photographic facsimile of the Trinity manuscript in Norman Davis, ed., *Non-Cycle Plays and the Winchester Dialogues* (Leeds, 1979), and have consulted the modern critical editions in Norman Davis, ed., *Non-Cycle Plays and Fragments*, EETS S.S. 1 (Oxford, 1970); John C. Coldewey, ed., *Early English Drama: An Anthology* (New York, 1993); and David Bevington, ed., *Medieval Drama* (Boston, 1975).

The Na{m}ys and N{u}mbere of the Players[2]: *II Vexillators* (two Flag-bearers, who appear only in the Banns), *Jh{es}us, Episcopus* (a Bishop), *Aristorius, Christianus Mercator* (Aristorius, a Christian Merchant), *{Presbiter,}* (a Priest: Isoder, chaplain to Aristorius), *Clericus* (Clerk: Peter Paul, servant to Aristorius), *Jonathas, Judeus Primus, Magister* (the first Jew, Master), *Jason, Judeus Secundus* (the second Jew), *Jasdon, Judeus Tercius* (the third Jew), *Masphat, Judeus Quartus* (the fourth Jew), *Malchus, Judeus Quintus* (the fifth Jew), *Magister Phisicus* (the Master Physician: Master Brandyche of Brabant), *Coll{e}, Servus* (Colle, the servant (to Brandyche))

[*The Banns*]

PRIMUS VEXILLATOR
Now þe Father and þe Sune and þe Holy Goste,
That all þis wyde worlde hat wrowght,
Save [all] thes semely, bothe leste and moste,[3]
And bryn[g]e yow to the blysse þat He hath yow to-
bowght!
We be ful purposed, wyth hart and wyth thowght,
Off our mater to tell þe entent,
Off þe marvellys þat wer wondursely wrowght
Off þe Holi and Blyssed Sacrament.

SECUNDUS VEXILLATOR
S[o]vereyns, and yt lyke yow to here þe purpoos of
þis play[4]
That [is] representyd now yn yower syght,
Whych in Aragon[5] was doon, þe sothe to saye,
In Eraclea, that famous cyte, aryght:
Therin wonneth a merchaunte of mekyll myght:
Syr Arystorye was called hys name,
Kend full fere wyth mani a wyght;[6]
Full fer in þe worlde sprong hys fame.

I [VEXILLATOR]
Anon to hy[m] ther cam a Jewe,
Wyth grete rychesse for the nonys,
And wonneth in þe cyte of Surrey (þis full trewe!)
Þe wyche had gret plente off precyous stonys.

Of þis Cristen merchaunte he freyned sore,
Wane he wolde have had hys entente:[7]
[Twenty pounds], and merchaundyse mor,
He proferyd for the Holy Sacrament.

II [VEXILLATOR]
But þe Christen marchaunte theroff sed nay,
Because hys profer was of so lityll valewe;
An [hundred pounds] but he wolde pay,
No lenger theron he shuld pursewe.[8]

But mor off ther purpos they gunne speke,
The Holi Sacramente for to bye;
And all for þe wold be wreke,[9]
A gret sume off gold begune down ley.

I [VEXILLATOR]
Thys Crysten merchante consentyd, þe sothe to sey,
And in þe nyght affter, made hym delyveraunce,
Thes Jewes all grete joye made they.
But off thys betyde a straunger chaunce:[10]

They grevid our Lord gretly on grownd,
And put Hym to a [new] Passyon;

1 Son 4 bought for you 5 We fully intend 6 matter/story, essence 7 Of, wonderfully 10 your 12 Heraclea, truly 13 lived 16 far, sprang/spread 18 at that time 19 Syria, this (is) 21 earnestly begged 23 merchandise 26 value 29 more about, began (to) 30 buy 32 sum, (they) laid down 34 he delivered (the Sacrament) 37 grieved, in (that) place

2 In the manuscript this list is placed at the end of the text. The characters are not listed in order of appearance.

3 '[May God] save all these elegant [folk: i.e. the audience], both the highest and the lowest of them.'

4 'My masters, if you would like to hear the intention/nature of this play'.

5 The kingdom of Aragon in Spain.

6 'Known widely by many a person'.

7 'When he tried to get what he wanted'.

8 'Unless he [the Jew] would pay £100, he should not pursue the matter [further].'

9 'And all because they wished to be revenged [upon Christ]'.

10 'But a far stranger event resulted from this'.

Wyth daggers goven Hym many a grevyos wound;
Nayled Hym to a pyller; wyth pynsons plukked Hym doune.

II [VEXILLATOR]
And sythe thay toke þat blysed brede so sownde
And in a cawdron they ded Hym boylde!
In a clothe full just they yt wounde,
And so they ded Hym sethe in oyle.

And than thay putt Hym to a new turmentry:
In a hoote ovyn speryd Hym fast.
There He appyred with woundys blody;
The ovyn rofe asondre and all to-brast.

I [VEXILLATOR]
Thus in our lawe they were made stedfast;
The Holy Sacrament sheuyd them grette favour.
In contrycyon thyr hertys wer cast.
And went and shewyd ther lyves to a confesour.[11]

Thus be maracle of þe Kyng of Hevyn,
And by myght and power govyn to þe prestys mowthe,
In an howshold wer counteryd, iwys, xi.
At Rome þis myracle ys knowen welle kowthe.

II [VEXILLATOR]
Thys marycle at Rome was presented, forsothe,
In the yere of our Lord a M I cccc lxy,
That þe Jewes wyth Holy Sa[c]rament dyd woth,
In the forest seyd of Aragon.

Loo, thus God at a tyme showyd Hym there,
Thorwhe Hys mercy and Hys mekyll myght;
Unto the Jewes He gan appere
That þei shuld nat lesse Hys hevenly lyght.

I [VEXILLATOR]
Therfore, frendys, wyth all your myght
Unto youer gostly father shewe your synne.
Beth in no wanhope, daye nor nyght;
No maner of dowghtys þat Lord put in.

For þat þe dowghtys þe Jewys than in stode;
As ye shall se pleyd both more and lesse
Was yff þe Sacrament were flesshe and blode,
Therfor they put yt to such dystresse.[12]

II [VEXILLATOR]
And yt place yow, thys gaderyng þat here ys,
At Croxtston on Monday yt shall be sen.
To see the conclusyon of this lytell processe,
Hertely welcum shall yow bene.

Now Jhesu yow save fro trey and tene,
To send us Hys hyh[e] joyes of Hevyne.
There myght is wythouton mynd to mene.[13]
Now, mynstrell, blow up wyth a mery stevyn!
Explicit.

39 gave 40 pincers 41 bread 42 cauldron, boiled Him 43 very tightly 44 seethe/boil, oil 45 then, torment 46 shut 47 appeared 48 split asunder, burst 50 showed 51 their hearts 53 by a miracle 54 given, mouth 55 converted, eleven (people) 56 (very) well known 58 1461 59 harm 60 aforesaid 61 Himself 62 Through 63 did 64 lose 66 confess 67 Be, despair 73 If you please, gathering 74 seen 75 narrative 76 be 77 pain/suffering 78 high/great 80 merry voice/noise! 80+ Here ends (the banns)

11 'And went and confessed [the sins of] their [former] lives to a confessor [i.e. a priest]'.
12 'Entertain no doubts of any kind about that Lord; for it was because the Jews doubted whether the Sacrament was [really His] flesh and blood that they inflicted such harm upon it, as you [all], both high and lowly, shall see played [here].'
13 'Beyond the capacity of the human mind to describe.'

Here after foloweth þe Play of þe Conversyon of Ser Jonathas þe Jewe by Myracle of þe Blyssed Sacrament.

ARISTORIUS MERCATOR
Now Cryst, þat ys our Creatour, from shame He cure us;
He maynteyn us with myrth þat meve upon þe mold;
Unto Hys en[d]elesse joye myght He restore us,
All tho þat in Hys name in peas well them hold.
For of a merchante most myght[y], therof my tale ys told;
In Eraclea ys non such, woso wyll understond.

1 (may) He 2 we who move, earth 4 will live in peace 6 there's no one like (me), whoever

For of all Aragon I am most myghty of sylver and of gold;
For, and yt wer a countre to by, now wold I nat wond![14]

Syr Arystory ys my name,
A merchaunte myghty, of a royall araye.
Ful wyde in þis worlde spryngyth my fame,
Fere kend and knowen, þe sothe for to saye.
In all maner of londys, without ony naye,
My merchaundyse renneth, þe sothe for to tell:
In Gene, and in Jenyse, and in Genewaye,[15]
In Surrey, and in Saby, and in Salern I sell;[16]

In Antyoche and in Almayn moch ys my myght,[17]
In Braban and in Brytayn I am full bold,
In Calabre and in Coleyn þer rynge I full ryght,[18]
In Dordrede and in Denmark, be þe c[l]yffys cold;
In Alysander I have abundaw[n]se in the wyde world.
In France and in Farre fresshe be my flower[ys],
In Gyldre and in Galys have I bowght and sold,[19]
In Hamborowh and in Holand moch merchantdyse ys owrys;
In Jerusalem and in Jheryco among the Jewes jentle,
Amo[n]g the Caldeys and Cattlyngys kend ys my komyng;
In Raynes and in Rome to Seynt Petyrs temple
I am knowen certenly for bying and sellyng;

In Mayn and in Melan full mery have I ben;
Owt of Navern to Naples moch good ys þat I bryng;
In Pondere and in Portyngale moche ys my gle;
In Spayne and in Spruce moche ys my spedyng;
In Lombardy and in Lachborn, there ledde ys my lykyng;
In Taryse[20] and in Turkey, there told ys my tale;
And in þe Dukedom of Oryon moche have I in weldyng:
And thus thorowght all þis world sett ys my sale.

No man in thys world may weld more rychesse;
All I thank God of Hys grace, for He þat me sent.
And as a lordys pere thus lyve I in worthynesse,
My curat waytheth upon me to knowe myn entent,
And men at my weldyng; and all ys me lent
My wyll for to worke in thys world so wyde,
Me dare they nat dysplese by no condescent.
And who-so doth, he ys nat able to abyde.

Presbiter
No man shall you tary ne t[r]owble thys tyde,
But every man delygently shall do yow plesance;
And I unto my co[n]nyng to þe best shall hem guyde[21]
Unto Godys plesyng to serve yow to attrueaunce.

For ye be worthy and notable in substance of good;
Of merchauntys of Aragon ye have no pere;
And therof thank God þat dyed on þe Roode,
That was your Makere, and hath yow dere.

Aristorius
Forsoth, syr pryst, yower talkyng ys good!
And therfor, affter your talkyng, I wyll atteyn
To wourshyppe my God that dyed on þe Roode.
Never, whyll þat I lyve, ageyn þat wyll I seyn.
But, Petyr Powle, my clark, I praye the[e] goo wele pleyn
Thorowght all Eraclea, that thow ne wonde,
And wytte yff ony merchaunte be come to þis reyn
Of Surrey or of Sabe or of Shelysdown.[22]

10 appearance 12 known far and wide 13 lands, without denial 14 is carried 18 Brabant (Netherlands) 19 travel 20 Dordrecht (Netherlands), by, cliffs 21 Alexandria, abundance 24 Hamburg (Germany) 25 Jericho 26 Chaldees, Catalans, known 27 Rheims (France) 29 Maine (France), Milan (Italy) 30 Kingdom of Navarre (modern France) 31 ?Pontevedra (Spain), Portugal 32 Prussia, great, prospering 33 Luxemburg, pursued 35 Orleans (Modern France)? 36 sail 37 wield/command 39 peer/equal 40 priest, will 41 command 43 means 45 delay, time 46 pleasure 48 at (your) command 51 Cross 52 holds you dear 53 your 54 endeavour 56 against, speak 57 Peter-Paul, go completely 58 don't delay 59 discover, realm 60 From

[14] 'For I would not hesitate to buy anything, even if it was a [whole] country!'
[15] Genoa (Italy), perhaps Genaissac, near Bordeaux (France), and Geneva (Switzerland).
[16] Syria, Saba (Arabia), Salerno (Italy).
[17] The crusader citadel of Antioch (now Antakya in modern Turkey) and Germany.
[18] Calabria (Italy) and Cologne (Germany).
[19] Faro (Portugal)?/Ferrara (Italy)?, Gelderland (Netherlands), and Galicia (Spain).
[20] Perhaps Tharsia, or the biblical Tarsus (Asia Minor) or Tharshish.
[21] 'And I shall instruct them to the best of my wit/ability'.
[22] Davis suggests Chelidonia in Lycia. A variant of 'Calis-town' (Calais) is also possible.

Clericus
At your wyll for to walke I wyl nat say nay,
Smertly to go serche at þe waterys syde.
Iff ony plesaunt bargyn be to your paye,
As swyftly as I can I shall hym to yow guyde.
Now wyll I walke by thes pathes wyde
And seke the haven, both up and down,
To wette yff ony onknowth shyppes therin do ryde[23]
Of Surrye or of Saby [or] of Shelysdown.

Now shall the merchantys man withdrawe him, and the Jewe Jonathas shall make his bo[a]st.

Jonathas
Now, almyghty Machomet,[24] marke yn þi mageste,
Whose lawes tendrely I have to fulfyll,
After my dethe bryng me to thy hyhe see
My sowle for to save, yff yt be thy wyll;
For myn entent ys for to fulfyll,
As my gloryus god the[e] to honer.
To do agen thy entent, yt shuld gr[e]ve me yll,
Or agen thyn lawe for to reporte.

For I thanke þe[e] hayly, þat hast me sent
Gold, sylver, and presyous stonys;
And abu[n]ddaunce of spycys þou hast me lent,
A[s] I shall reherse before yow onys:
I have amatystys ryche for þe nonys,
And barylls that be bryght of ble,
And saphyre semely, I may show yow attonys,
And crystalys clere for to se;

I have dyamantys derewourthy to dresse,
And emerawdys, ryche I trow they be;
Onyx and achatys both more and lesse,
Topazyouns, smaragdys of grete degre,
Perlys precyous grete plente;
Of rubes ryche I have grete renown;
Crepawdys and calcedonyes semely to se,
A[nd] curyous carbunclys here ye fynd mown.

Spycys I have both grete and smale
In my shyppes, the sothe for to saye:
Gyngere, lycoresse, and cannyngalle,
And fygys fatte to plese yow to paye,
Peper and saffyron and spycys smale,
And datys wole dulcett for to dresse,
Almundys and rys, full every male;
And reysones both more and lesse;

Clovys, greynis,[25] and gynger grene,
Mace, mastyck that myght ys,
Synymone, suger, as yow may sene;
Long peper,[26] and Indas lycorys,
Orengys a[nd] apples of grete apryce,
Pungarnetys, and many other spycys,
To tell yow all I have now, iwys,
And moche other merchandyse of sondry spycys.

Jew Jonathas ys my name;
Jazon and Jazdon þei waytyn on my wyll,
Masfat and Malchus they do the same,
As ye may knowe, yt ys bothe rycht and skyll.
I tell you all, bi dal and by hylle
In Eraclea ys noon so moche of myght,
Werfor, ye owe tenderli to tende me tyll,
For I am chefe merchaunte of Jewes, I tell yow be ryght.

But Jazon and Jazdon, a mater wolld I mene;
Mervelously yt ys ment yn mynde:
Þe beleve of thes Crysten men ys false, as I wene,
For þe beleve on a cake: me thynk yt ys onkynd,
And all they seye how þe prest dothe yt bynd,
And be þe myght of hys word make yt flessh and blode,
And thus be a conceyte þe wolde make us blynd;
And how þat yt shuld be he that deyed upon þe Rode.

62 Quickly 63 good deal, pleasant for you 64 bring (whoever offers it) to you 66 search the harbour 69 distinguished in 70 diligently 71 seat/dwelling 74 honour 75 against your will, terribly 76 speak 77 highly/greatly 78 precious 79 given 80 once 81 amethysts 82 beryls, appearance 83 at once 85 precious diamonds, set 86 emeralds 87 agates 88 topazes, emeralds 89 Pearls 91 Toadstones, chalcedonies 92 carbuncles, may find 95 Ginger, licorice, galingale 96 figs 97 Pepper 98 dates, sweet, use 99 Almonds, rice, sack 100 raisins 101 Cloves 102 gum-mastic, strong 103 Cinnamon 104 Indian 105 oranges, value 106 Pomegranates 110 attend to 112 reasonable 113 by dale . . . (i.e. everyone) 114 no one 115 ought to listen attentively 117 mention 118 it sticks in my mind 120 they, in (i.e. the Host), unnatural 121 priest, conjure 123 by a trick, they 124 (convince us) it is, Cross

23 'To discover if any unknown [i.e. foreign] ships ride [at anchor] there'.

24 A corruption of Mohammed, used generically as the name of a false god, and here assumed to be the god of the Jews.

25 Grains of Paradise (*Amomum meleguetta*).

26 Long pepper is made from *Piper officinarum* (Davis, *Non-Cycle Plays*, p. 153).

JASON
Yea, yea, master, a strawe for talis!
That ma[y] not fale in my beleve;
But, myt we yt gete onys within our pales,[27]
I trowe we shuld sone affter putt yt yn a preve.

JASDON
Now, be Machomete so myght[y], þat ye doon of meve:
I wold I wyste how þat we myght yt gete!
I aver by my grete God, and ellys mote I nat cheve,
But wyghtly the[r]on wold I be wreke!

MASPHAT
Yea, I dare sey feythfulli þat ther feyth [is false]:
That was never he that on Calvery was kyld!
Or in bred for to be blode, yt ys ontrewe als.
But yet wyth ther wyles þei wold we were wyld.

MALC[H]US
Yea, I am myghty Malchus, þat boldly am byld.
That brede for to bete byggly am I bent![28]
Onys out of ther handys and yt myght be exyled,[29]
To helpe castyn yt in care wold I consent.

JONAT[H]AS
Well, syrse, than kype cunsel, I cummande yow all,
And no word of all thys be wyst.
But let us walke to see Arystories hall,
And affterward more counsell among us shall caste.
Wyth hym to bey and to sel I am of powere prest;
A bargyn wyth hym to make I wyll assaye.
For gold and sylver I am nothyng agast
But þat we shall get þat cake to ower paye.[30]

Her shall Ser Isodyr, the prest, speke ont[o] Ser Aristori, seyng on this wise[31] to him; and Jonatas goo do[w]n of[f] his stage.

PRESBITER
Syr, by yowr leve, I may [no] lengere dwell.
It ys fer paste none; yt ys tyme to go to cherche,
There to saye myn evynsong; forsothe as I yow tell,
And syth come home ageyne, as I am wont to werche.

ARISTORIUS
Sir Isydor, I praye yow wallke at yowr wyll.
For to serfe God yt ys well done.
And syt come agen, and ye shall suppe your fyll,
And walke than to your chamber, as ye are wont to doon.

Her shall the marchant men mete with þe Jewes.

JONATHAS
A, Petre Powle, good daye and wele i-mett!
Wer ys thy master, as I the[e] pray?

CLERICUS
Lon[g] from hym have I not lett
Syt I cam from hym, þe sothe for to saye.
Wat tidyng wyth yow, ser, I yow praye,
Affter my master þat ye doo frayne?
Have ye ony bargen þat wer to hys paye?
Let me have knowlech; I shall wete hym to seyn.

JONATHAS
I have bargene[s] royall and ry[c]h
For a marchaunt with to bye and sell;
In all thys lond ys ther non lyke
Of abondaunce of good, as I will tell.

Her shall þe clerk goon to Ser Aristori, saluting him thus:

CLERICUS
All hayll, master, and wel mot yow be!
Now tydyngs can I yow tell:
Þe grettest marchante in all Surre
Is come wyth yow to bey and sell;
This tal ryght wele he me told.
Sir Jonatas ys hys nam,
A marchant of ryght gret fame;
He wolld sell yow, without blame,
P[l]ente of clothe of golde.

125 (such) tales! 126 fall, belief (I don't believe it!) 128 to the test 129 what you suggest 130 wish I knew, get 131 swear, may, prosper 132 eagerly, revenged (on it) 133 truly, their 134 killed 135 bread, untrue as well 136 their wiles, intend, fooled 137 built 140 throw, torment 141 keep counsel (keep this secret) 142 known 144 we shall have 145 buy, well capable 146 try 149 with your permission, stay 150 well past noon 151 Evensong (evening service) 152 then, as is my habit 153 as/when you wish 154 serve 155 then 156 then 157 well met! (a greeting) 159 It's not long since I left him 162 ask 163 pleasing to him 164 know (what) to tell him 167 nothing like them 168 For abundance of goods 173 tale 176 doubt

27 'If we could once get it [the Host] into our hands'.
28 'I'm fully determined to beat that bread!'
29 'If it might once be taken out of their hands'.
30 'I have no doubt that for gold and silver we will get that cake into our hands.'
31 'In this way'.

ARISTORIUS
Petre Powle, I can þe[e] thanke!
I prey þe[e], rychely araye myn[e] hall
As owyth for a marchant of þe banke.
Lete non defawte be fownd at all.

CLERICUS
Sekyrly, master, no m[o]re ther shall!
Styffly about I thynke to stere,
Hasterli to hange your parlowr wyth pall
As longeth for a lordis pere.

Here shall the Jewe merchaunt and his men come to þe Cristen merchaunte.

JONATHAS
All haylle, syr Aristorye, semele to se,
The myghtyest merchaunte of Arigon!
Of yower welfare fayn wet wold we,
And to bargeyn wyth you þis day am I boun.

ARISTORIUS
Sir Jonathas, ye be wellcum unto myn hall!
I pray yow come up and sit bi me,
And tell me wat good ye have to sell,
And yf ony bargeyn mad may be.

JONATHAS
I have clothe of gold, precyous stons, and spycys plente.
Wyth yow a bargen wold I make;
I wold [b]artre wyth yow yn pryvyte.
On lytell thyng, ye wyll me yt take
Prevely in þis stownd;
And I woll sure yow, be thys lyght,
Never dystre[n] yow, daye nor nyght,
But be sworn to yow full ryght,
And geve yow [twenty pounds].

ARISTORIUS
Sir Jonathas, sey me for my sake:
What man[er] of marchandis ys that [ye] mene?

JONATHAS
Yowr God, that ys full mytheti, in a cake!
And thys good anoon shall yow seen.

[ARISTORIUS]
Nay, in feyth, that shall not bene!
I woll not for an hundder pownd
To stond in fere my Lord to tene;
And for so lytell a valew in conscyen[c]e to stond bownd!

JONATHAS
Sir, þe entent ys, if I myght knowe or undertake
If þat he were God Allmyght;
Of all my mys I woll amende make[32]
And doon hym wourshepe bothe day and nyght.

ARISTORIUS
Jonathas, trowth I shall þe[e] tell:
I stond yn gret dowght to do þat dede;
To yow þat bere all for to sell,
I fere me þat I shuld stond in drede!
For, and I unto þe chyrche yede,
And preste or clerke myght me aspye,
To þe Bysshope þei wolde go tell þat dede,
And apeche me of eresye.

JONATHAS
Sir, as for þat, good shyffte may ye make,
And, for a vaylle, to walkyn on a nyght
Wan prest and clerk to rest ben take;
Than shall ye be spyde of no wyght.

ARISTORIUS
Now sey me, Jonathas, be this lyght,
Wat payment þerfor wollde yow me make?

JONATHAS
[Forty pounds], and pay yt ful ryght,
Evyn for þat Lorde sake.

ARISTORIUS
Nay, nay, Jonathas, there-ageyn
I w[o]ld not for an [hundred] pownd!

JONATHAS
Sir, hir ys [yo]wr askyng toolde pleyn;[33]
I shall yt tell yn this stownd.

179 prepare my hall 180 As befits 181 no defect 182 Surely 183 Vigorously, intend, stir myself 184 Hastily, parlour, fine hangings 185 befits 186 handsome, see 188 your, we would eagerly know 196 barter/deal 197 One, take (for) me 198 Secretly, place 199 assure, by . . . (a mild oath) 200 (to) constrain/take action against 201 completely 203 tell 205 mighty 206 anon/immediately 207 be! 208 a hundred 209 risk angering my Lord 210 small a reward 211 so that I can, discover 216 fear 217 buy and sell everything 218 dread 219 if, went 222 impeach, heresy 223 make good provision 224 veil/cover, walk at 225 are gone to their rest 226 seen by no one 229 immediately 230 Lord's 231 in answer 234 count it, place

[32] '[If he were] I would make amends for all my sins'.

[33] 'Sir, here's what you ask for, openly counted out.'

Here is an [hundred pounds], neyther mor no lesse,
Of dokettys good, I dar well saye.
Tell yt ere yow from me passe;
Me thynketh yt a royall araye!

But fyrst, I pray yow, tell me thys:
Off thys thyng whan shall I hafe delyverance?

ARISTORIUS
To-morowe betymes, I shall not myse;
This nyght therfor I shall make purveaunce.

Syr Isodyr he ys now at chyrch,
There sey[y]ng hys evynsong,
As yt [is] hys worshepe for to werche.
He shall sone cum home, he wyll nat be long,
Hys sopere for to eate.
And when he ys buskyd to hys bedde,
Ryght sone hereafter he shal be spedd;
No speche among yow there be spredd!
To kepe yowr toungys, ye nott lett.

JONATHAS
Syr, almyghty Machomyght be wyth yow!
And I shall cum agayn ryght sone.

ARISTORIUS
Jonathas, ye wott what I have sayd, and how
I shall walke for that we have to done.

Here goeth þe Jewys away, and þe preste commyth home.

PRESBITER
Syr, Almyghty God mott be yowr g[u]yde,
And glad yow wheresoo ye rest!

ARISTORIUS
Syr, ye be welcom home thys tyde.
Now, Peter, gett us wyne of the best.

CLERICUS
Syr, here ys a drawte of Romney Red;
Ther ys no better in Aragon,
And a lofe of lyght bred;
It ys holesom, as sayeth þe fesycyon.

[*Exit Peter-Paul.*]

ARISTORIUS
Drynke of[f], Ser Isoder, and be of good chere!
Thys Romney ys good to goo wyth to reste.
There ys no precyouser, fer nor nere,
For all wykkyd metys yt wyll degest.

PRESBITER
Syr, thys wyne ys good at a taste,
And therof have I drunke ryght well.
To bed to gone thus have I cast,
Evyn strayt aftere thys mery mele.

Now, ser, I pray to God send yow good [nyght],
For to my chambere now wyll I gone.

ARISTORIUS
Ser, wyth yow be God Almyght,
And sheld yow ever from yowr fone!

Here shall Aristorius call hys clarke to hys presens.

Howe, Peter! In the[e] ys all my trust,
In especyall to kepe my counsell,
For a lytyll waye walkyn I must.
I wyll not be long; trust as I the[e] tell.

Now prevely wyll I preve my pace,
My bargayn thys nyght for to fulfyll.
Ser Isoder shall nott know of thys case,
For he hath oftyn sacred, as yt ys skyll.
The chyrche key ys at my wyll;
There ys nothyng þat me shall tary.
I wyll nott abyde, by dale nor hyll,
Tyll yt be wrowght, by Saynt Mary!

Here shal he entere þe chirche and take þe Hoost.

Ah, now have I all myn entent!
Unto Jonathas now wyll I fare,
To fulfyll my bargayn have I ment,
For þat mony wyll amend my fare,
As thynkyth me.
But now wyll I passe by thes pathes playne;

236 ducats 237 count, go 238 sight fit for a king 240 Of, have 241 early 242 provision 245 duty 247 supper 248 gone 249 done/finished (for the day) 251 tongues, don't fail 252 Mohammed 255 do 257 comfort, wherever 258 (at) this time 260 draught, Rumney (Greek wine) 262 loaf, (fine) white bread 263 wholesome, physician 264 Drink up! 266 none more precious, far 267 harmful/impure foods, digest 268 to the 270 decided 275 shield/protect, foes 276 Ho! 280 make my way 282 matter 283 consecrated, reasonable[34] 284 disposal 285 hinder 286 delay 289 go 291 improve my situation

[34] The priest has consecrated a large number of wafers and so will not miss one. As l. 387 suggests, the playwright envisages wafers of Holy bread stamped with an image of Christ rather than pieces of ordinary loaf.

To mete wyth Jonathas I wold fayne.
Ah, yondere he commyth yn certayn!
Me thynkyth I hym see.

Welcom, Jonathas, gentyll and trew!
For well and tr[e]wly þou kepyst thyn howre.
Here ys þe Host, sacred newe.
Now wyll I home to halle and bowre.

JONATHAS
And I shall kepe thys trusty treasure
As I wold doo my gold and fee!
[*To the Host*:] Now yn thys clothe I shall the[e] covere,
That no wyght shall the[e] see.

Here shall Arystory goo hys waye; and Jonathas and hys servauntys shall goo to þe tabyll, þus sayng:

JONATHAS
Now, Jason and Jasdon, ye be Jewys jentyll,
Masfatt and Malchus, that myght arn yn mynd,
Thys merchant from the Crysten temple
Hathe gett us thys bred that make us thus blynd.
Now, Jason, as jentyll as ever was the lynde,
Into the forsayd parlowr prevely take thy pase;
Sprede a clothe on the tabyll þat ye shall þer fynd,
And we shall folow after to carpe of thys case.

Now þe Jewys goon and lay the [H]ost on þe tabyll, sayng:

JONATHAS
Syrys, I praye yow all, harkyn to my sawe:
Thes Crysten men carpyn of a mervelows case;
They say þat þis ys Jhesu þat was attayntyd in owr lawe,
And þat thys ys he þat crucyfyed was.

On thes wordys ther law growndyd hath he,[35]
That he sayd on Shere Thursday at hys sopere:
He brake the brede and sayd '*Accipite*',
And gave hys dyscyplys them for to chere.
And more he sayd to them there
Whyle they were all togethere and sum,
Syttyng at the table soo clere:
'*Comedite, corpus meum.*'[36]

And thys powre he gave Peter to proclame,
And how the same shuld be suffycyent to all prechors.
The bysshoppys and curatys saye the same,
And soo, as I understond, do all hys progenytors.[37]

JASON
Yea, sum men in þat law reherse another:
They say of a maydyn borne was hee,
And how Joachyms dowghter shuld be hys mother,
And how Gabrell apperyd and sayd '*Ave!*'
And wyth þat worde she shuld conceyvyd be,
And þat in hyr shuld lyght the Holy Gost,
Ageyns owr law thys ys false heresy;
And yett they saye he ys of myghtys most.

JASDON
They saye þat Jhesu to be owr kyng,
But I wene he bowght þat full dere!
But they make a royall aray of hys uprysyng;
And that in every place ys prechyd farre and nere.
And how he to hys dyscyples agayn dyd appere,
To Thomas, and to Mary Mawdelen,
And syth how he styed by hys own powre;
And thys, ye know well, ys heresy full playn.

MASPHAT
Yea, and also they say he sent them wytt and wysdom
For to understond every langwage,
When þe Holy Gost to them came,[38]
They faryd as dronk men of pymente or vernage;
And sythen how þat he lykenyd hymself a lord of parage:
On hys Fatherys ryght hond he hym sett.
They hold hym wysere þan ever was Syble sage,[39]
And strengere than Alexander, þat all þe wor[l]de ded gett.

298 your appointment 299 newly consecrated 300 bower (chamber) 306 strong 308 that deceives/fools us 309 linden tree (proverbially delicate) 310 go your way 312 discuss 313 word(s) 314 speak 315 convicted under 317 He has based their religion 318 Holy, (Last) Supper 319 'Take' 320 Disciples, comfort 322 one and all 325 St Peter 326 preachers 329 another (part of the Creed) 330 virgin 331 (i.e. Mary) 332 the angel Gabriel, 'Hail' 337 alight 338 paid a high price for that! 339 great thing, Resurrection 342 Magdalene 343 ascended (into Heaven) 344 manifest heresy 348 spiced or sweet wine 349 high birth 351 wiser, the Sibyl[39] 352 conquer

[35] The Jews here begin to list the central elements of the Apostles' Creed.

[36] 'Eat, [this is] My body': Matthew 26:26.

[37] As Davis suggests, it seems likely that those coming after rather than before are intended: perhaps the followers of Christ or the successors of St Peter (i.e. the popes).

[38] See Acts 2:1–47 for the account of the descent of the Holy Spirit upon the Disciples at Pentecost.

[39] The Sibyl at Cumae was renowned throughout the Roman world as a source of (somewhat enigmatic) wisdom.

MALCHUS
Yea, yet they saye as fals, I dare laye my hedde:
How they that be ded shall com agayn to Judgement,
And owr dredfull Judge shalbe thys same brede,
And how lyfe everlastyng them shuld be lent.
And thus they hold, all at on consent,
Because that Phylyppe[40] sayd for a lytyll g[l]osse;
To turne us from owr beleve ys ther entent;
For that he sayd, '*Judicare vivos et mortuos.*'[41]

JONATHAS
Now, serys, ye have rehersyd the substaunce of [their] lawe,
But this bred I wold myght be put in a prefe
Whethere þis be he that in Bosra of us had awe.
There staynyd were hys clothys; þis may we belefe,
Thys may we know: there had he grefe,
For owr old bookys veryfy thus:
Theron he was jugett to be hangyd as a thefe:
'*Tinctis Bosra vestibus.*'[42]

JASON
Yff þat thys be he that on Calvery was mad red,
Onto my mynd, I shall kenne yow a conceyt good:
Surely wyth owr daggars we shall ses on thys bredde,
And so wyth clowtys we shall know yf he have eny blood.

JASDON
Now, by Machomyth so myghty, þat mevyth in my mode![43]
Thys ys masterly ment, thys mattere thus to meve!
And wyth our strokys we shall fray hym as he was on þe Rood,
That he was on-don wyth grett repreve.

MASPHAT
Yea, I pray yow, smyte ye in the myddys of þe cake,
And so shall we smyte þeron woundys fyve!
We wyll not spare to wyrke yt wrake
To prove in thys brede yf þer be eny lyfe.

MALCHUS
Yea, goo we to, than, and take yowr space,
And looke owr daggarys be sharpe and kene;
And when eche man a stroke smytte hase,
In þe mydyll part thereof owr master shall bene.

JONATHAS
When ye have all smytyn, my stroke shalbe sene:
Wyth þis same dagger that ys so styf and strong,
In þe myddys of thys prynt I thynke for to prene!
On lashe I shall hym lende or yt be long.

Here shall the iiij[44] *Jewys pryk þer daggerys in iiij quarters, þus sayng:*

JASON
Have at yt! Have at yt, with all my myght!
Thys syde I hope for to sese!

JASDON
And I shall with thys blade so bryght
Thys other syde freshely afeze!

MASPHAT
And I yow plyght I shall hym not please,
For with thys punche I shall hym pryke!

MALCHUS
And wyth this augur I shall hym not ease:
Another buffett shall he lykke!

JONATHAS
Now am I bold with batayle hym to bleyke,
þe mydle part all for to prene,
A stowte stroke also for to stryke:
In þe myddys yt shal be sene!

353 falsely, wager 356 granted 357 unanimously 358 gloss/commentary 359 beliefs 361 summarized 362 to a test 363 Bozrah 364 stained 365 grief 367 judged 369 red (with blood) 370 tell 371 strike (at) 372 blows 374 masterfully planned, suggest 375 set on him as (if) 376 (So) that, ruined, shame 377 middle 379 take our revenge on it 381 let's get on with it, places 382 ensure 383 has struck 384 shall (strike his) 387 embossed image, pierce 388 One, give him before 390 strike 392 strike straight after 394 spike 395 auger (a carpenter's tool) 396 blow, take 397 battle, frighten (lit. make pale) 399 strong

[40] Probably Philip the Evangelist, the forerunner of St Paul in spreading Christianity among the Gentiles; see Acts 6:1–6, 8:4–8, and 8:26–39.

[41] 'To judge the living and the dead', another element of the Apostles' Creed. See I Peter 4:5, II Timothy 4:1.

[42] Compare Isaiah 63:1: '[Who is this that cometh from Edom] with dyed garments from Bozrah[?]': a passage interpreted in the medieval period as a prophetic allusion to Christ.

[43] 'That wins me over [lit. moves (me) in my mind]!'

[44] Four.

Here þe [H]ost must blede.

Ah, owt, owt! Harrow! What devyll ys thys?
Of thys wyrk I am in were!
It bledyth as yt were woode, iwys!
But yf ye helpe, I shall dyspayre!

JASON
A fyre, a fyre, and that in hast!
Anoon a cawdron full of oyle!

JASDON
And I shall helpe yt were in cast,
All þe iii howrys for to boyle.

MASPHAT
Ye[a], here is a furneys stowte and strong,
And a cawdron therin dothe hong.
Malcus, wher art thow so long,
To helpe thys dede were dyght?

MALCHUS
Loo, here ys iii galons of oyle clere,
Have doon fast; blowe up þe fere!
Syr, bryng that ylke cake nere,
Manly, wyth all yowre mythe.

JONATHAS
And I shall bryng þat ylke cak,
And throwe yt in, I undertake.

[*The Host sticks to his hand.*]

Out, out, yt werketh me wrake!
I may not avoyd yt owt of my hond!
I wylle goo drenche me in a lake.
And yn woodnesse I gynne to wake!
I renne, I lepe over þis lond!

Her he renneth wood, with þe {H}ost in hys hond.

JASON
Renne, felawes, renne, for Cokkys peyn,
Fast we had owr mayster agene!
Hold prestly on thys pleyn
And faste bynd hym to a poste.

JASDON
Here is an hamer and naylys iii, I s[e]ye.
Lyffte up hys armys, felawe[s], on hey,
Whyll I dryve þes nayles, I yow praye,
Wyth strong strokys fast.

[*They fasten the Sacrament to the post.*]

MASPHAT
Now set on, felouse, with mayne and myght,
And pluke hys armes awey in fyght!
Wat? I se he twycche, felouse, aryght!
Alas, balys breweth ryght badde!

Here shall thay pluke þe arme, and þe hand shall hang styll with þe Sacrament.

MALCHUS
Alas, alas, what devyll ys thys?
Now hat he but oon hand, iwys!
Forsothe, mayster, ryght woo me is
Þat ye þis harme have hadde.

JONATHAS
Ther ys no more; I must enduer!
Now hastely to owr chamber lete us goo,
Tyll I may get me sum recuer.
And therfor charge yow everychoon
Þat yt be counsell, that we have doon.

Here shall the lechys man come into þe place, sayng:

COLLE
Aha, here ys a fayer felawshyppe!
Thewh I be nat sh[a]pyn, I lyst to sleppe,
I have a master: I wolld he had þe pyppe,[45]
I tell yow in counsel!
He ys a man of all syence
But of thryffte, I may wyth yow dyspenc[e]![46]
He syttyth wyth sum tapstere in þe spence;
Hys hoode there wyll he sell.[47]

402 amazed/fearful 403 as (if) it 404 Unless 406 (get) a cauldron 407 to throw it in 408 three hours 409 furnace 412 to get this deed done 413 three gallons 414 fire 416 Manfully 419 causes me pain! 420 remove, from 422 begin, fall 423 run 423+ runs mad 424 God's pain (euphemism) 425 Quickly to get, again 426 tightly, ground 427 (i.e. the Host) 429 high 432 fellows 433 fiercely 434 twitches, careful! 435 it's getting worse! 437 only one 438 I'm so sorry! 440 endure 442 recovery/remedy 443 order 444 kept secret 444+ doctor's 446 Although, prepared, slip away 449 (the) sciences 451 tapster/barman, wine-cellar

45 A generic term for a disease: 'I wish he were sick'.

46 'Except for thrift. I can dispense [with the niceties] with you!'

47 'He'd [even] sell his hood [for a drink] there.'

Mayster Brendyche of Braban,
I tell yow, he ys that same man,
Called þe most famous phesy[cy]an
Þat ever sawe uryne.[48]
He seeth as wele at noone as at nyght,
And sumtyme by a candelleyt
Can gyff a jud[g]yment aryght;
As he þat hathe noon eyn.

He ys allso a boone-setter;
I knowe no man go þe better!
In every taverne he ys detter,
Þat ys a good tokenyng!
But ever I wonder he ys so long;
I fere ther gooth sumthyng a-wrong,
For he hath dysa[rv]yde to be hong;
God send never wurse tydyng!

He had a lady late in cure:
I wot be þis she ys full sure!
There shall never Crysten creature
Here hyr tell no tale!
And I stode here tyll mydnyght,
I cowde not declare aryght
My masteris cunyng insyght;
Þat he hat in good ale.

By what devyll ayleth hym so long to tare?
A seek-man myght soone myscary.
Now all þe devyllys of Hell hym wari!
God grante me my boon!
I trowe best we mak a crye:
If any man can hym aspye,
Led hym to þe pylleri;
In fayth, yt shall be don.

Here shall he stond up and make proclamacion, seyng thys:

COLLE
Yff ther be eyther man or woman
That sawe Master Brundyche of Braban,
Or owyht of hym tel can,
Shall wele be quit hys med.

He hath a [c]ut berd and a flatte noose,
A therde-bare gowne and a rent hoose;
He spekyt never good matere nor purpoose.
To þe pyllere ye hym led!

MASTER BRUNDYCHE
What, thu boye, what janglest here?

COLLE
A, master, master, but to your reverence!
I wend never to a seen yowr goodly chere,[49]
Ye tared hens so long.

MASTER BRUNDYCHE
What hast thow sayd in my absence?

COLL[E]
Nothyng, master, but to yowr reverence,
I have told all þis audyense;
[*Aside*] And some lyes among.

But master, I pray yow, how dothe yowr pa[c]yent
That ye had last under yowr medycament?

MASTER BRUNDYCHE
I waraunt she never fele anoyntment.

COLL[E]
Why, ys she in hyr grave?

MASTER BRUNDYCHE
I have gyven hyr a drynke made full well
Wyth scamoly and with oxennell,
Letwyce, sawge, and pympernelle.[50]

COLLE
Nay, than she ys full save!

For now ye ar cum, I dare well saye
Betuyn Dovyr and Calyce þe ryght wey
Dwellth non so cunnyng, by my fey,
In my judgyment.[51]

457 sees (things), noon **458** candle-light **459** diagnosis (as) correctly **460** no eyes (ironic) **461** setter of (broken) bones **463** a debtor **464** sign **465** (why) he **466** something's gone wrong **467** deserved, hanged **468** worse news (i.e. it wouldn't be bad) **469** recently, (his) care **470** by now, taken care of **472** Hear (i.e. she is dead) **473** If **476** has **477** tarry **478** sick man, die **479** curse him! **480** request **481** proclamation **483** lead, pillory **487** can report any news of him **488** They'll be well rewarded **489** beard, nose **490** threadbare, torn hose **491** speaks, sense **492** lead **493** (are you) prattling (about) **494** only (things) respectful to you **496** hence **500** lies here and there **501** patient **503** annoyance/pain **508** completely safe! (ironic) **511** no one, faith

[48] Physicians in this period diagnosed diseases by examining the patient's urine.

[49] 'I thought I'd never see your lovely face again'.

[50] Scammony ('a gum used as a purge': Davis), oxymel (a mixture of vinegar and honey), lettuce, sage, and pimpernel, all herbs used in medicine.

[51] As Dover and Calais are separated only by the English Channel this is somewhat faint praise.

MASTER BRUNDYCHE
Cunnyng? Yea, yea, and with prattyffe
I have savid many a mannys lyfe.

COLLE
On wydowes, maydese, and wyfes
Yowr connyng yow have nyh spent.[52]

MASTER BRUNDYCHE
W[h]ere ys [my] bowg[e]tt wyth drynk profytable?

COLLE
Here, master, master, ware how ye tugg!
The Devyll, I trowe, within shruggys,
For yt gooth 'rebyll-rable'.

MASTER BRUNDYCHE
Here ys a grete congregacyon,
And all be not hole, without negacyon.
I wold have certyfycacyon:
Stond up and make a proclamacion.
Have do faste, and make no pausa[c]yon,
But wyghtly mak a declaracion
To all people þat helpe w[o]lde have.

Hic interim proclamationem faciet.[53]

COLL[E]
All manar off men þat have any syknes,
To Master Brentberecly loke þat yow redresse!
What dysease or syknesse þat ever ye have,
He wyll never leve yow tyll ye be in yow[r] grave.
Who hat þe canker, þe collyke, or þe laxe,[54]
The tercyan, þe quartan,[55] or þe brynny[n]g axs;
For wormys, for gnawyng, gryndy[n]g in þe wombe or in þe boldyro;[56]
All maner red eyn, bleryd eyn, and þe myegrym also;
For hedache, bonache, and therto þe tothache;
The colt-evyll, and þe brostyn men he wyll undertak,[57]
All tho þat [have] þe poose, þe sneke, or þe tyseke.
Thowh a man w[e]re ryght heyle, he cowd soon make hym sek!
Inquyre to þe colkote, for ther ys hys loggyng,
A lytyll besyde Babwell Myll,[58] yf yhe wyll have und[er]stondyng.

MASTER BRUNDYCHE
Now, yff ther be ether man or woman
That nedethe helpe of a phesyscian . . .

COLL[E]
Mary, master, þat I tell can,
And ye wyll understond.

MASTER BRUNDYCHE
Kno[w]est any abut þis plase?

COLL[E]
Ye[a], þat I do, master, so have [I] grase!
Here ys a Jewe, hyght Jonathas,
Hath lost hys ryght hond.

MASTER BRUNDYCHE
Fast to hym I wold inquere.

COLL[E]
For God, master, þe gate ys here.

MASTER BRUNDYCHE
Than to hym I wyll go nere.
My master, wele mot yow be!

JONATHAS
What doost here, felawe? What woldest thu hanne?[59]

MASTER BRUNDYCHE
Syr, yf yow nede ony surgeon or physycyan,
Of yow[r] dyse[se] help yow welle I can,
What hurtys or hermes soever they be.

JONATHAS
Syr, thu art ontawght to come in thus homly,
Or to pere in my presence thus malepertly.

513 practice 515 virgins 517 bag 518 beware, drink 519 moves 520 (i.e. the gurgling of the liquid) 521 (i.e. the audience) 522 whole/healthy, contradiction 523 a declaration 525 Get on with it, delay 526 manfully 528 sickness 529 direct yourselves 530 Whatever 533 burning pains 534 stomach 535 red-eye, bleared, migraine 536 bone-ache, toothache 538 catarrh, head-cold, tuberculosis 539 healthy, sick 540 coal-shed, lodging 546 around, place? 547 grace! 551 Before, way (or lit. his gate) 557 harms 558 ignorant, so casually 559 appear, impertinently

[52] 'You have nearly exhausted your knowledge [with an implied additional sense of "carnal knowledge"].'

[53] 'Here, for a time, he will make proclamation.'

[54] Cancer, colic (stomach pains), and diarrhoea, respectively.

[55] Tertian and quartan were terms for fevers which involved paroxysms every third or fourth day, respectively.

[56] 'Boldyro' is perhaps a euphemism for the penis or testicles.

[57] 'He will take on the colt-evil [a disease of horses which swells the penis] and burst men [i.e. those with hernias]'.

[58] Babwell Mill, near Bury St Edmunds (Suffolk).

[59] 'What are you doing here, fellow? What do you want?'

Voydeth from my syght, and þat wyghtly,
For ye be mysse-avysed!

Coll[e]
Syr, þe hurt of yow hand ys knowen full ryfe,
And my maste[r] have savyd many a manes lyfe.

Jonathas
I trowe ye be cum to make sum stryfe.
Hens fast, lest þat ye be chastysed!

Coll[e]
Syre, ye know well yt can nott mysse;
Men that be masters of scyens be profytable.
In a pott yf yt please yow to pysse,
He can tell yf yow be curable.

[Jonathas]
Avoyde, fealows, I love not yowr bable!
Brushe them hens bothe, and that anon!
Gyff them there reward þat they were gone!

Here shall þe iiij Jewys bett away þe leche and hys man.

Jonathas
Now have don, felawys, and that anon,
For dowte of drede what aftere befall!
I am nere masyd; my wytte ys gon!
Therfor, of helpe I pray yow all.

And take yowre pynsonys þat ar so sure,
And pluck owt the naylys, won and won;
Also in a clothe ye yt cure
And throw yt in þe cawdron, and þat anon.

Here shall Jason pluck owt the naylys and shake þe hond ynto þe cawdron.

Jason
And I shall rape me redely anon
To plucke owt the naylys that stond so fast.
And beare thys bred and also thys bone,
And into the cawdron I wyll yt cast.

Jasdon
And I shall wyth thys dagger so stowte
Putt yt down that yt myght plawe,
And steare the clothe rounde abowte
That nothyng therof shal be rawe.

Masphat
And I shall manly, wyth all my myght,
Make the fyre to blase and brenne,
And sett therundere suche a lyght
That yt shall make yt ryght thynne.

Here shall þe cawdron byle, apperyng to be as bloode.

Malch[u]s
Owt and harow! What devyll ys herein?
All thys oyle waxyth redde as blood,
And owt of the cawdron yt begynnyth to run.
I am so aferd I am nere woode!

Here shall Jason and hys compeny goo to Ser Jonathas, sayng:

Jason
Ah, master, master! What chere ys wyth yow?
I can nott see owr werke wyll avayle.
I beseche yow, avance yow now
Sumwhatt with yowr counsayle!

Jonathas
The best counsayle that I now wott,
That I can deme, farre and nere,
Ys to make an ovyn as redd hott
As ever yt can be made with fere;
And when ye see yt soo hott appere,
Then throw yt into the ovyn fast,
Sone shall he stanche hys bledyng chere!
When ye have donne, stoppe yt; be not agast.

Jasdon
By my fayth, yt shalbe wrowgh[t],
And that anon, in gret hast.
Bryng on fyryng, serys. Here ye nowght?
To hete thys ovyn be nott agast.

Masphat
Here ys straw and thornys kene.
Com on, Malchas, and bryng on fyre,
For that shall hete yt well, I wene.

Here þei kindyll þe fyre.

560 Vanish, quickly 561 ill-advised 562 widely 563 man's 564 trouble 565 Go away, punished 567 science, useful 570 babbling 571 sweep them out 572 (i.e. a beating) 574 fear of what may follow 575 nearly amazed 577 pincers, trusty 578 nails, one by one 579 cover it (the Host) 581 hurry, readily 585 strong 586 boil 587 stir 588 raw (i.e. not boiled away) 589 manfully 590 blaze 592 (i.e. all boiled away) 594 grows 597 how are you? 598 (that) our 599 offer 600 Some advice 601 know 602 judge 603 oven 604 fire 606 it (the Host) 607 Soon, stop, appearance of bleeding 608 block it up, afraid 609 done 611 kindling, sirs, hear 613 sharp thorns

Blow on fast, that done yt were!

MALCH[U]S
Ah, how thys fyre gynnyth to brenne clere!
Thys ovyn ryght hotte I thynk to make.
Now, Jason, to the cawdron þat ye stere
And fast fetche hether that ylke cake.

Here shall Jason goo to þe cawdron and take owt the [H]ost with his pynsonys, and cast it into the ovyn.

JASON
I shall with thes pynsonys, without dowt,
Shake thys cake owt of thys clothe,
And to the ovyn I shall yt rowte
And stoppe hym there, thow he be loth.
The cake I have cawght here, in good sothe;
The hand ys soden, the fleshe from þe bonys;
Now into the ovyn I wyll therwith.
Stoppe yt, Jasdon, for the nonys!

JASDON
I stoppe thys ovyn, wythowtyn dowte;
Wyth clay I clome yt uppe ryght fast,
That non heat shall cum owtte.
I trow there shall he hete and drye yn hast!

Here the ovyn must ryve asunder and blede owt at þe cranys,[60] *and an image appere owt with woundys bledyng.*

MASPHAT
Owt, owt, here ys a grete wondere!
Thys ovyn b[l]edyth owt on every syde!

MALCH[U]S
Yea, þe ovyn on peacys gynnyth to ryve asundre!
Thys ys a mervelows case thys tyde!

Here shall þe image speke to the Juys, sayng thus:

JHESUS
O mirabiles Judei, attendite et videte
Si est dolor [sicut] dolor meus![61]

Oh ye merveylows Jewys,
Why ar ye to yowr kyng onkynd,
And [I] so bytterly bowt yow to My blysse?[62]
Why fare ye thus fule wyth yowre frende?
Why peyne yow Me and straytly Me pynde,
And I yowr love so derely have bowght?
Why are ye so unstedfast in your mynde?
Why wrath ye Me? I greve yow nowght.
Why wyll ye nott beleve that I have tawght,
And forsake your fowle neclygence
And kepe My commandementys in yowr thowght,
And unto My Godhed to take credence?

Why blaspheme yow Me? Why do ye thus?
Why put yow Me to a newe tormentry,
And I dyed for yow on the Crosse?
Why consydere not yow what I dyd crye?
Whyle that I was with yow, ye ded Me velanye.
Why remembere ye nott My bytter chaunce,
How yowr kynne dyd Me avance
For claymyng of Myn enherytaunce?
I shew yow the streytnesse of My grevaunce,
And all to meve yow to My mercy.

JONATHAS
Tu es protector vitae mee; a quo trepidabo?[63]
O Thu Lord, whych art my defendowr,
For dred of The[e] I trymble and quake!
Of Thy gret mercy lett us receyve þe showre;
And mekely I aske mercy, amendys to make.

Here shall they knele down all on ther kneys, sayng:

JASON
Ah, Lord, with sorow and care and grete wepyng,
All we felawys, lett us saye thus
Wyth condolent harte and grete sorowyng:
Lacrimis nostris conscienciam nostram baptizemus![64]

JASDON
Oh Thow Blyssyd Lord of mykyll myght,
Of Thy gret mercy thow hast shewyd us þe path,
Lord, owt of grevous slepe and owt of dyrknes to
lyght,
Ne gravis sompnus irruat.[65]

617 begins 619 go 620 here 623 (in)to, throw 624 even if he's reluctant (to be there) 626 boiled 628 seal it (up) 630 seal 635 split apart into pieces 636+ Jews 640 unnatural/cruel 642 act, foully 643 pain/hurt, tightly confined Me 645 fickle 646 Why do you anger Me 647 what 655 villainy 656 bitter fate 657 treat 659 severity 660 move 664 receive, shower 668 contrite 671 In

60 'The oven must split apart and bleed out of the cracks'.

61 ' O you strange Jews, behold and see if any sorrow is like My sorrow.' See Lamentations 1:12; 'Is it nothing to you, all ye that pass by? Behold, and see if there be any sorrow like unto My sorrow.' Compare also with Christ's speeches in the York *Crucifixion*.

62 'And I so painfully redeemed you for [a place in] My Heaven?'

63 'You are the protector of my life, of whom should I be afraid?' A variation on Psalms 27:1.

64 'With our tears may we baptize our conscience.'

65 'May grievous sleep not attack/seize [us].'

MASPHAT
Oh Lord, I was very cursyd, for I wold know Þy Crede.[66]
I can no men[d]ys make, but crye to The[e] thus:
O gracyows Lorde, forgyfe me my mysdede!
With lamentable hart: *miserere mei, Deus!*

MALCH[U]S
Lord, I have offendyd The[e] in many a sundry wyse.
That styckyth at my hart as hard as a core.
Lord, by þe watere of contrycion lett me aryse:
Asparges me, Domine, ysopo, et mundabor.[67]

JHESUS
All ye that desyryn My servauntys for to be
And to fulfyll þe preceptys of My lawys,
The intent of my commandement knowe ye:
Ite et ostendite vos sacerdotibus Meis.[68]
To all yow þat desyre in eny wyse
To aske mercy, to graunt yt redy I am.
Remember and lett yowr wyttys suffyce,
Et tunc non avertam a vobis faciem Meam.[69]

No Jonathas, on thyn hand thow art but lame,
And ys thorow thyn own cruelnesse.
For thyn hurt þou mayest þiselfe blame:
Thow woldyst preve thy powre Me to oppresse.
But now I consydre thy necesse;
Thow wasshest thyn hart wyth grete contrycyon.
Go to the cawdron, þi care shal be the lesse,
And towche thyn hand, to thy salvacyon.

Here shall Ser Jonathas put hys hand into þe cawdron, and yt shalbe hole agayn; and then say as fo[lo]with:

JONATHAS
Oh Thow my Lord God and Savyowr, osanna!
Thow Kyng of Jewys and of Jerusalem!
O Thow myghty, strong Lyon of Juda,
Blyssyd be the tyme þat Þow were yn Bedlem!
Oh Þou myghty, strong, gloryows and gracyows oyle streme,
Thow myghty conquerrowr of infernall tene,
I am quyt of moche combrance thorowgh Thy meane,[70]
That evere blyssyd mott Þou bene!

Alas þat ever I dyd agaynst Thy wyll,
In my wytt to be soo wood
That I so ongoodly wyrk shuld soo gryll![71]
Aȝens my mysgovernaunce Thow gladdyst me with good:
I was soo prowde to prove The[e] on þe Roode,
And Þou hast sent me lyghtyng þat late was lame.
To bete The[e] and boyle The[e] I was myghty in moode,
And now þou hast put me from duresse and dysfame.

But, Lord, I take my leve at Thy hygh presens,
And put me in Thy myghty mercy.
The Bysshoppe wyll I goo fetche to se owr offens,
And onto hym shew owr lyfe, how þat we be gylty.

Here shall þe master Jew goo to þe Byshopp, and hys men knele styll.

JONATHAS
Hayle, fathere of grace! I knele upon my knee,
Hertely besechyng yow, and interely,
A swemfull syght all for to see
In my howse apperyng verely:
The Holy Sacrament, þe whyche we have done tormentry,
And there we have putt Hym to a newe Passyon;
A chyld apperyng with wondys blody:
A swemfull syght yt ys to looke upon!

EPISCOPUS
Oh Jhesu, Lord, full of goodnesse!
Wyth The[e] wyll I walke with all my myght.
Now, all my pepull, wyth me ye dresse
For to goo see that swymfull syght.

Now all ye peple that here are,
I commande yow, every man,
On yowr feet for to goo, bare,
In the devoutest wyse that ye can.

675 amendment 677 Have mercy on me, God! 678 different ways 679 fruit stone(?) 680 through 682 desire to be 694 need 698 hosanna! (trad. shout of worship) 701 Bethlehem 702 glorious, stream of oil 703 infernal anger/harm 709 misrule, comfort 710 test 711 relief, recently 712 strongly determined 713 suffering, shame 714 of 716 offence 719 entirely 725 painful 728 prepare

[66] i.e. 'I sought to understand the mysteries of Your Creed [by experiment] rather than to believe them through faith.'

[67] '[Sprinkle] me with hyssop, [Lord,] and I shall be clean.' A variation on Psalms 51:7.

[68] 'Go show yourselves unto [my] priests.' Luke 17:14.

[69] 'And then I will not turn My face from you.' See Psalms 27:9, 88:14, 143:7.

[70] 'I am relieved of much encumberence through Your mediation'.

[71] 'That I should do such evil deeds so cruelly!'

Here shall the bisshope entere ynto þe Jewys howse, and say:

O Jhesu, fili Dei,
How thys paynfull Passyon rancheth myn hart!
Lord, I crye to The[e], *miserere mei,*
From thys rufull syght þou wylt reverte.
Lord, we all, wyth sorowys smert,
For thys unlefull work we lyve in langowr.
Now, good Lord, in Thy grace let us be gert,
And of Thy soverreyn marcy send us Thy socowr,
And for Thy holy grace forgyfe us owr errowr.
Now lett Thy pete spryng and sprede!
Thowgh we have be unrygh[t]full, forgyf us our rygore,
And of owr lamentable hartys, good Lord, take hed!

Here shall þe im[a]ge change agayn into brede.

[EPISCOPUS]
Oh Thu largyfluent Lord, most of lyghtnesse,
Onto owr prayers Thow hast applyed!
Thu hast receyvyd them with grett swettnesse;
For all owr dredfull dedys, þou hast not us denyed.
Full mykyll owte Thy name for to be magnyfyed
Wyth mansuete myrth and gret swettnes,
And as gracyows God for to be gloryfyed,
For Thu shewyst us gret gladnes.

Now wyll I take thys Holy Sacrament
Wyth humble hart and gret devocion,
And all we wyll gon with on consent
And beare yt to chyrche wyth sole[m]pne processyon.

Now folow me, all and summe!
And all tho that bene here, both more and lesse,
Thys holy song, *O sacrum convivium,*[72]
Lett us syng all with grett swetnesse.

[*They process to the church, singing.*]

Here shall þe pryst, Ser Isodere, aske hys master what þis menyth.

[PRESBITER]
Ser Arystory, I pray yow, what menyth all thys?
Sum myracle, I hope, ys wrowght be Goddys myght.
The Bysshope commythy [in] processyon with a gret meny of Jewys;
I hope sum myracle ys shewyd to hys syght.
To chyrche in hast wyll I runne full ryght,
For thether, me thynk, he begynnyth to take hys pace.
The Sacrement so semly ys borne in syght.
I hope that God hath shewyd of Hys grace.

ARISTORIUS
To tell yow the trowth I wyll nott lett;
Alas þat ever thys dede was dyght!
An on-lefull bargayn [I] began for to beat:
I sold yon same Jewys owr Lord full ryght
For covytyse of good, as a cursyd wyght.
Woo the whyle that bargayn I dyd ever make!
But yow be my defensour in owr dyocesans syght,
For an heretyke I feare he wyll me tak.

PRESBITER
For sothe, nothyng well-avysed was yowr wytt;
Wondrely was yt wrowght of a man of dyscrescion
In suche perayle yowr solle for to putt!
But I wyll labore for yowr absolucyon.

Lett us hye us fast that we were hens,
And beseche hym of hys benygne grace
That he wyll shew us hys benyvolens
To make amendys for yowr trespas.

Here shall þe merchant and hys prest go to þe chirche, and þe Bysshop shall entre þe chyrche and lay the [H]ost [on] the autere,[73] *sayng thus:*

[EPISCOPUS]
Estote fortes in bello et pugnate cum antico serpente,
Et accipite regnum eternum, et cetera.[74]

My chyldern, ye be strong in batayll gostly
For to fyght agayn the fell serpent
That nyght and day ys ever besy;

734 O Jesus, Son of God 735 wounds 736 have mercy on me 737 pitiful, return/change back 738 painful sorrows 739 unlawful, distress 740 girded/clothed 741 mercy, succour 743 pity, spread 744 been wicked, cruelty 745 heed 746 bountiful, most bright 747 complied 748 sweetness 750 ought, glorified 751 gentle joy 756 one 758 one and all 767 make his way 768 carried 770 resist/hesitate 771 done! 772 unlawful, strike 774 covetousness/greed, goods 775 Woeful was the time 776 Unless, protector, bishop's 778 in no way well-advised 779 Unbelievable, by, (your) discretion 780 peril, soul 785 offence 789 evil

[72] 'O sacred feast!', sung as part of the Vespers for the feast of Corpus Christi.

[73] Altar.

[74] 'Be strong in battle and fight with the old serpent, and receive the eternal kingdom, and so on.' See Revelation 20:2: 'And [an angel] laid hold on the dragon, that old serpent, which is the Devil, and Satan, and bound him [for] a thousand years.'

To dystroy owr sollys ys hys intent.
Look ye be not slow nor neclygent
To arme yow in the vertues sevyn.
Of synnys fo[r]gotyn take good avysement,[75]
And knowlege them to yowr confessor full evyn.

For that serpent, the Devyll, ys full strong
Mervelows myschevos for man to mene,[76]
But that the Passyon of Cryst ys meynt us among,
And that ys in dyspyte of hys infernall tene.
Beseche owr Lord and Savyowr so kene
To put doun that serpent, cumberer of man,
To withdraw hys furyous froward doctryn bydene,
Fulfyllyd of þe fend callyd Levyathan.[77]

Gyff lawrell to that Lord of myght
That He may bryng us to the joyows fruycion:
From us to put the Fend to flyght,
That never he dystroy us by hys temptacion.

PRESBITER
[*To Episcopus*] My fathere under God, I knele unto yowr kne,
In yowr myhty mysericord to tak us in remembrance;
As ye be materyall to owr degre,
We put us yn yowr moderat ordynaunce
Yff yt lyke yowr hyghnes to here owr grevaunce:
We have offenddyd sorowfully in a syn mortall,
Wherfore we fere us owr Lord wyll take vengaunce
Fow owr synnes, both grete and small.

EPISCOPUS
And in fatherhod, that longyth to my dygnyte,
Unto yowr grefe I wyll gyf credens.
Say what ye wyll, in þe name of the Trynyte,
Agayn[s]t God yf ye have wroght eny inconvenyens.

ARISTORIUS
Holy Father, I knele to yow undere *benedycite*,
I have offendyd in the syn of covytys
I sold owr Lordys body for lucre of mony
And delyveryd to the wyckyd, wyth cursyd advyce.
And for that pres[u]mpcion, gretly I agryse
That I presumed to go to the autere
There to handyll þe Holy sacryfyce.
I were worthy to be putt in brennyng fyre.

But, gracyous lord, I can no more
But put me to Goddys mercy and to yowr grace.
My cursyd werkys for to restore,
I aske penaunce now in thys place.

EPISCOPUS
Now, for thys offence that þou hast donne
Aȝens the Kyng of Hevyn and Emperowr of Hell,
Ever whyll þou lyvest, good dedys for to done
And nevermore for to bye nore sell;
Chastys thy body as I shall the[e] tell,
Wyth fastyng and prayng and other good wyrk,
To wythstond the temtacyon of fendys of Hell;
And to call to God for grace looke þou never be irke.

[*To Presbiter*] Also, þou preste, for thy neclygens,
That thou were no wyser in thyn office,
Thou art worthy inpresument for thyn offence;
But be ware ever herafter, and be more wyse.

And all yow [preachers] and curatys that here be,
Of thys dede yow may take example
How that your pyxys[78] lockyd ye shuld see,
And be ware of the key of Goddys temple.

JONATHAS
And I aske Crystendom wyth great devocion;
Wyth repentant hart in all degrees
I aske for us all a generall absolucion.

Here þe Jewys must knele al down.

For that we knele all upon owr knees;
For we have grevyd owr Lord on ground
And put Hym to a new paynfull Passyon,
Wyth daggars styckyd Hym wyth grevos wonde,
New naylyd Hym to a post, and with pynsonys pluckyd Hym down.

791 souls 793 with, seven (cardinal) virtues 795 acknowledge, completely 798 Unless, spread 799 to oppose, anger 800 powerful 801 ensnarer 802 perverse, at once 803 Enacted by 804 Give honour 805 fruition (of Heaven) 806 Fiend 809 great mercy 810 vital, kind 811 gentle 812 hear 813 Mortal Sin 816 belongs, high office 817 credence 819 any offence 820 under (a) blessing 821 covetousness 822 gain of money 823 ill-advisedly 824 (am) horrified 826 handle 833 Against 834 Always while, deeds 836 Chastise 837 praying, works 839 reluctant 842 (of) imprisonment 844 curates 847 look after 852 in this place 854 wound(s)

75 'Think upon the sins [you have] forgotten.'
76 'Is strong/intent to devise incredible mischiefs against mankind'.
77 See Isaiah 27:1: 'In that day the Lord with His sore and great and strong sword shall punish Leviathan the piercing serpent, even Leviathan that crooked serpent; and He shall slay the dragon that is in the sea'.
78 Pyxes: the containers in which the Hosts were kept after consecration.

JASON
And syth we toke that blyssyd bred so sownd
And in a cawdron we dyd Hym boyle.
In a clothe full just we Hym wounde
And so dyd we seth Hym in oyle.

JASDON
And for þat we myght overcom Hym wyth tormentry,
In an hott ovyn we speryd Hym fast.
There He apperyd wyth wo[u]ndys all bloody;
The ovyn rave asunder and all to-brast!

MASPHAT
In Hys law to make us stedfast,
There spake He to us woordys of grete favore.
In contrycyon owr hartys He cast,
And bad take us to a confessor.

MALCHUS
And therefor all we wyth on consent
Knele onto yowr hygh sovereynte;
For to be Crystenyd ys owr intent
Now all owr dedys to yow shewyd have we.

Here shall þe Bysshoppe Crysten the Jewys with gret solempnyte.

EPISCOPUS
Now the Holy Gost at thys tyme mot yow blysse
As ye knele all now in Hys name!
And with the water of baptyme I shall yow blysse
To save yow all from the Fendys blame.
Now, that Fendys powre for to make lame,
In the name of þe Father, þe Son, and þe Holy Gost,
To save yow from the Devyllys flame,
I Crysten yow all, both lest and most.

SER JONATHAS
Now, owr father and byshoppe þat we well know,
We thank yow interly, both lest and most.
Now ar we bownd to kepe Crystys lawe
And to serve þe Fathere, þe Son, and þe Holy Gost,
Now wyll we walke by contre and cos
Owr wyckyd lyvyng for to restore,
And trust in God, of myghtys most,
Never to offend as we have don befor.
Now we take owr lea[v]e at lesse and more;
Forward on owr vyage we wyll us dresse.
God send yow all as good welfare
As hart can thynke or towng expresse!

ARISTORIUS
Into my contre now wyll I fare
For to amende myn wyckyd lyfe;
And to kep the people owt of care,
I wyll teache thys lesson to man and wyfe.

Now take I my leave in thys place.
I wyll go walke, my penaunce to fullfyll,
Now God, aȝens whom I have done thys trespas,
Graunt me forgyfnesse yf yt be Thy wyll.

PRESBITER
For joy of thys, me thynke my hart do wepe,
That yow have gyvyn yow all Crystys servauntys to be,
And Hym for to serve wyth hart full meke,
God, full of pacyens and humylyte.

And the conversacion of all thes fayre men,
Wyth hartys stedfastly knett in on,
Goddys lawys to kepe and Hym to serve bydene,
As faythfull Crystyanys evermore for to gone!

EPISCOPUS
God Omnipotent evermore looke ye serve
Wyth devocion and prayre, whyll þat ye may.
Dowt yt not, He wyll yow preserve
For eche good prayere þat ye sey to Hys pay.
And therfor in every dew tyme loke ye nat delay
For to serve the Holy Trynyte,
And also Mary, that swete may;
And kepe yow in perfyte love and charyte.

Crystys Commandementys x there bee.
Kepe well them; doo as I yow tell.
Almyght[y] God shall yow please in every degre,
And so shall ye save yowr sollys from Hell.
For there ys payn and sorow cruell,
And in Hevyn ther ys both joy and blysse,
More then eny towng can tell.
There angellys syng with grett swetnesse.

856 then 858 tight 859 seethe/boil 860 so 861 thrust, securely 863 split, burst 866 Towards contrition, directed 867 told (us to) take ourselves 868 one mind 870 baptized 871 deeds 875 reproach 880 acknowledge 881 sincerely 884 country, coast (i.e. everywhere) 885 atone for 888 of (you all) 889 journey, prepare ourselves 891 tongue 892 go 894 sorrow 901 given yourselves 904 conduct 905 knit together 906 indeed 907 Christians, go 908 ensure (that) 911 that pleases Him 912 due, look 914 maid 916 ten 918 regard 919 souls

To the whyche blysse He bryng us
Whoys name ys callyd Jhesus,
And in wyrshyppe of thys name gloryows
To syng to Hys honore *Te Deum Laudamus.*

Finis.

Thus endyth the Play of the Blyssyd Sacrament, whyche myracle was don in the forest of Aragon, in the famous cite of Eraclea, the yere of owr Lord God Ml CCCC. lxi, to whom be honowr, Amen.

927 We praise you, O God

Bible Historiale, 1357, London BL Royal MS 17 EVII f.1. The British Library.

Wisdom

Because the manuscript sources of this highly sophisticated moral drama give it no title, it has been variously known as *Wisdom*, *Wisdom: Who is Christ*, and *Mind, Will, and Understanding*. This uncertainty reflects a lack of precise focus in the play itself, which, unlike the other Moralities in this volume, does not have a single protagonist. The plot concerns the battle between Wisdom (Christ) and Lucifer over the fate of Anima, the human soul. The latter has the support of a number of faculties, which are the source of both her strength and her vulnerability: these are the Five Wits, or senses, and the three 'Mights' or powers, Mind, Will, and Understanding. The last three, rather than Anima, are the true protagonists of the drama. It is they who are tempted by Lucifer's blandishments and fall into corruption; Anima merely reflects the results of their decisions in her appearance and attitude, most dramatically when she returns to the stage in her fallen state after l. 902, dressed 'in the most horrible [fashion] . . . fouler than a fiend', and unleashes the seven tiny devils (played by small boys) from under her voluminous skirts.

As the above description suggests, the most striking feature of the play is its use of spectacle, in costume, music, and dance. In this, and in its concern with the intellectual nature of sin and redemption, and its reliance upon lengthy didactic speeches rather than comic action or delineation of character, *Wisdom* points towards the philosophical interests of the later court masque rather than to the Tudor interlude. The three choreographed dumbshows are the most obvious examples of this highly visual and emblematic dramaturgy. Here the social and political consequences of individual sin are demonstrated as Mind becomes Maintenance, Understanding Perjury, and Will Lechery, and each leads in a troupe of dancers to symbolize the manifestations of their respective vices in the noble retinues, law courts, and brothels of fifteenth-century England.

As befitting so spectacular a production, the stage directions in the text are remarkably full and detailed, but the precise auspices for which the play was originally written are less clear. *Wisdom* is commonly dated to the 1460s, largely on the strength of its association with *Mankind* (see below), which can be more securely traced to this period. The East Anglian origins of the text (evident both in its dialect and in the fact that its scribe and earliest owner was a fifteenth-century monk, Thomas Hyngham of Bury St Edmunds, Norfolk) seem clear. But whether it was written for performance in a monastic institution (suggested by its concern with the merits of the contemplative life as opposed to the active – see ll. 394ff), a school (because it employs boy actors), the royal court (because it concerns the abuses of high office, the vices of courtiers, and the law courts in London), or a touring troupe is less evident. Each possibility has its advocates. That the text can be played, with a good deal of doubling, by six adult actors might support the idea of a touring production. But the need for at least thirteen additional dancers and three musicians would seem to militate against the possibility (this assumes that the seven small boys who played the devils also doubled as the Five Wits and the masquers in the troupes of Mind and Understanding, and that one of them played as well the 'shrewd Boy' dragged from the audience by Lucifer following l.550). Perhaps, as Pamela King has suggested ('Morality Plays', pp. 253–4), a performance at Bury Abbey during a visit by the king and court might best account for the complex mixture of concerns and styles exhibited by the play.

The most remarkable stage direction is probably that following l. 752, which calls specifically for six women masquers to play the whores and gallants in the Masque of Lechery. That the sex of the previous troupes was not specified suggests strongly that these are to be different individuals to those in the earlier masques (perhaps the explicit content of this dance was felt to be too risqué to allow the boy actors to take the parts). This is valuable as one of the few surviving references to female actors in the medieval period. That they are associated specifically with the one masque concerned with sexual misrule and licentiousness is probably a telling reflection on prevailing attitudes towards women in the period.

The play draws upon a range of sources. It recalls much of the, so-called, Wisdom literature interpreting biblical texts such as the Song of Songs, and the apocryphal Wisdom of Solomon and Ecclesiasticus. It also draws heavily upon the writings of a number of religious mystics, most notably an English translation of Henry Suso's *Orologium Sapientiae* and Walter Hilton's *Epistle on the Mixed Life*, as well as the anonymous *Novem Virtutes* and a number of treatises attributed to Saints Bernard and Bonaventure.

The text survives in two late fifteenth-century manuscripts, Folger Shakespeare Library MS V. a. 354, the so-called Macro manuscript (so named after one of its previous owners, the eighteenth-century collector, the Reverend Cox Macro (1683–1767) of Bury St Edmunds), which also contains *Mankind*, and Bodleian Library MS Digby 133 (which contains a portion of the text which stops at l. 752). Where necessary I have amended the Macro text in the light of the Digby version (adding the Digby material within square brackets). The Macro text is available in photographic facsimile in D. Bevington, ed., *The Macro Plays: The Castle of Perseverance, Wisdom, Mankind* (Washington, D.C., 1972); and the Digby text in D.C. Baker and J.L. Murphy, eds., *The Digby Plays: Facsimiles of the Plays in Bodley MSS Digby 133 and e Museo 160* (Leeds, 1976). In addition I have consulted the modern editions in Mark Eccles, ed., *The Macro Plays*, EETS os 262 (Oxford, 1969); J.C. Coldewey, ed., *Early English Drama: An Anthology* (New York, 1993); and D. Bevington, ed., *Medieval Drama* (Boston, 1975).

[*Dramatis Personae*: *Wisdom* (Christ, manifested as Divine Wisdom), *Anima* (the Soul), *Mynde, Wyll,* and *Understondyng* (Mind, Will, and Understanding, the three 'Mights' or attributes of the soul), *Lucifer.*
Non-speaking roles: *The Five Wits* (portrayed as virgins), *A 'shrewd' Boy,* 6 *Masked Dancers in Noble Livery* (retainers of Mynde), 6 *Masked Dancers dressed as Jurors* (retainers of Understondyng), 6 *Masked Female Dancers, 3 dressed as Gallants and 3 as Maidens* (retainers of Wyll), *Minstrels* (with trumpets, bagpipe and hornpipe), 7 *Devils* (played by small boys).]

Fyrst entery[th]e Wysdome in a ryche purpull clothe of golde with a mantyll of the same ermynnyde wythin, hawynge abowt Hys neke a ryall hood furred wyth ermyn, wpon Hys hede a cheweler wyth browys, a berde of golde of sypres curlyed,[1] *a ryche imperyall crown þerwpon sett wyth precyus stonys and perlys, in Hys leyfte honde a balle of golde wyth a cros þerwppon*[2] *and in Hys ryght honde a regall schepter,*[3] *thus seyenge:*

[WYSDOM]
Yff ȝe wyll wet þe propyrte
Ande þe resun of My nayme imperyall,
I am clepyde of hem þat in Erthe be
Everlastynge Wysdom, to My noble[y] egalle;
Wyche name acordyst best in especyall
And most to Me ys convenyent,
Allthow eche Persone of þe Trinyte be wysdom eternall
And all thre on everlastynge wysdome togedyre present.[4]

Neverþeles, forasmoche as wysdom ys propyrly
Applyede to þe Sune by resune,
And also yt fallyt to Hym specyally
Bycause of Hys hye generacyon,
Therfor þe belowyde Sone hathe þis sygnyficacyon
Custummaly Wysdom, now Gode, now man,
Spows of þe chyrche and wery patrone,
Wyffe of eche chose sowle. Thus Wysdom begane.

Here entrethe Anima as a mayde, in a wyght clothe of golde gytely purfyled wyth menyver,[5] *a mantyll of blake þerwppeon, a chevele[r] lyke to Wysdom, wyth a ryche chappetelet lasyde behynde hangynge do[wn] wyth to knottys of golde and syde tasselys,*[6] *knelynge down to Wysdom, thus s[eyng]:*

ANIMA
Hanc amavi et exquisivi:[7]
Fro my [yougthe] thys have I sowte
To have to my spowse most specyally,
For a lover of Yowr schappe am I wrote.
Above all hele and bewty þat ever was sowght
I have lovyde Wysdom as for my lyght,
For all goodnes wyth Hym ys broughte.
In wysdom I was made all bewty bryghte.

1 discover, nature 2 meaning 3 by them 4 (equal to) My nobility 10 Son, reason 11 falls 13 beloved 14 Customarily 15 Spouse, true patron 16 Spouse, chosen 20 form, made 21 health

1 'Upon His head a wig with (?) matching eyebrows and a beard of curled [cloth of] Cyprus gold'.
2 i.e. an orb.
3 Sceptre. Wisdom is represented iconographically as Christ the King.
4 'And is most appropriate to Me, although each Person of the Trinity is eternal wisdom, and all three together present one [single] everlasting wisdom.'
5 Perhaps 'gysely' ('elegantly') trimmed with miniver fur is intended.
6 'A rich coronet, laced at the back, with two knots of gold hanging down at the back and two tassels on the sides.' The mixture of white and black reflects Anima's dual capacity for both good and evil.
7 'This have I loved and sought'. Wisdom of Solomon 8:2. The following lines translate the remainder of the apocryphal verse into English.

Off Yowr name þe hye felycyte
No creature knowyt full exposycyon.

WYSDOM
Sapiencia specialior est sole.[8]

I am foundon lyghte wythowt comparyson,
Off sterrys above all þe dysposicyon,
Forsothe of lyght þe very bryghtnes,
Merowre of þe Dyvyne domynacyon,
And þe image of Hys goodnes.

Wysdom ys better þan all wordly precyosnes,
And all þat may dysyryde be
Ys not in comparyschon to My lyknes.
The lengthe of þe yerys in My ryght syde be
Ande in My lefte syde ryches, joy, and prosperyte.[9]
Lo, þis ys þe worthynes of My name.

ANIMA
A, soveren Wysdom, yff Yowur benygnyte
Wolde speke of love, þat wer a game.

WYSDOM
Off My love to speke, yt ys myrable.
Beholde now, Sowll, wyth joyfull mynde,
How lovely I am, how amyable,
To be halsyde and kyssyde of mankynde.
To all clene sowlys I am full hende
And ever present wer þat þey be;
I love My lovers wythowtyn ende
That þer love have stedfast in Me.[10]

The prerogatyff of My love ys so grett
Þat wo tastyt þerof þe lest droppe sure
All lustys and lykyngs worldly xall lett;[11]
They xall seme to hym fylthe and ordure.
They þat of þe hewy burthen of synne hathe cure
My love dyschargethe and puryfyethe clene,
It strengtheth þe mynde, þe sowll makyt pure,
And yewyt wysdom to hem þat perfyghte bene.
Wo takyt Me to spowse may veryly wene,
Yff above all thynge ȝe love Me specyall[y],
That rest and tranqwyllyte he xall sene,
And dey in sekyrnes of joy perpetuall.

The hye worthynes of My love
Angell nor mañ can tell playnly.
Yt may be felt in experyens from above
But not spoke ne tolde as yt ys veryly.
The godly love no creature can specyfye.
[What wre[c]h is that lovyth not this love]
Þat lovyt hys lovers ever so tendyrly
That hys syght from them never can remowe?

ANIMA
O worthy spowse and Soveren fayer,
O swet amyke, owr joy, owr blys!
To Yowr love wo dothe repeyer,
All felycyte yn þat creature ys.
Wat may I yeve Yow ageyn for þis,
O Creator, lover of Yowr creature?
Though be owr freelte we do amys,
Yowr grett mercy ever sparyth reddure.

A, soveren Wysdom, *sanctus sanctorum*,
Wat may I yeve to Yowr most plesaunce?

WYSDOM
Fili, prebe michi cor tuum.[12]
I aske not ellys of all þi substance.
Thy clene hert, þi meke obeysance,
Yeve Me þat and I am contente.

ANIMA
A, soveren joy, my hertys affyance,
The fervowre of my love to Yow I present.

That mekyt my herte, Yowr love so ferwent.
Teche me þe scolys of Yowr dyvynyte.

WYSDOM
Dysyer not to savour in cunnynge to excellent,[13]
But drede and conforme yowr wyll to Me.

26 (the) full 28 formed (of) 29 beyond the power of the stars 30 indeed 31 mirror, power 33 value, riches 34 desired 39 graciousness 40 would be joyous 41 wonderful 44 embraced 53 heavy burden, been cured 56 gives, perfect 59 see 60 die in the certainty 62 (Neither) Angel 64 described, valued, truly 65 God's love 66 (there) is 67 (earthly) lovers 68 cannot take his eyes from 69 fair 70 beloved 71 whoever comes to your love 73 in return 75 through our frailty 76 always spares us punishment 77 Holiest of Holies 80 nothing else 81 obedience 83 allegiance 84 fervour 85 makes meek 86 lessons

8 'Wisdom is unique in nature.' See Wisdom of Solomon 7:15–29.
9 An allusion to the sceptre in His right hand and the orb (of the world) in His left.
10 'Who have remained steadfast in their love for Me.'
11 'Whoever tastes the least drop [of it] shall surely abandon all worldly lusts and desires'.
12 'My son, give me thine heart.' Proverbs 23:26.
13 'Do not desire to know too much rarefied knowledge.'

For yt ys þe heelfull dyscyplyne þat in Wysdam may
be,
The drede of God, þat ys begynnynge.[14]
The wedys of synne yt makyt to flee,
And swete wertuus herbys in þe sowll sprynge.

ANIMA
O endles Wysdom, how may I have knowynge
Off Þi Godhede incomprehensyble?

WYSDOM
By knowynge of yowrsylff ȝe may have felynge
Wat Gode ys in yowr sowle sensyble.
The more knowynge of yowr selff passyble,
Þe more veryly ȝe xall God knowe.

ANIMA
O soveren Auctoure most credyble.
Yowr lessun I attende, as I owe,

I þat represent here þe sowll of man.
Wat ys a sowll, wyll Ȝe declare?

WYSDOM
Yt ys þe ymage of Gode þat all began;
And not only ymage, but Hys lyknes ȝe are.
Off all creaturys þe fayrest ȝe ware
Into þe tyme of Adamys offence.

ANIMA
Lorde, sythe we Thy sowlys y[e]t nowt were þer,
Wy of þe fyrst man bye we þe vyolence?[15]

WYSDOM
For every creature þat hath ben or xall
Was in natu of þe fyrst man, Adame,
Off hym takynge þe fylthe of synne orygynall,
For of hym all creaturys cam.
Than by hym of reson ȝe have blame[16]
And be made þe brondys of Helle.
Wen ȝe be bore fyrst of yowr dame,
Ȝe may in no wyse in Hewyn dwell,

For ȝe be dysvyguryde be hys synne,
Ande dammyde to derkness from Godys syghte.

ANIMA
How dothe grace þan ageyn begynne?
Wat reformythe þe sowll to hys fyrste lyght?

WYSDOM
Wysdam, þat was Gode and man ryght,
Made a full sethe to þe Fadyr of Hewyn
By þe dredfull dethe to Hym was dyght,
Off wyche dethe spronge þe sacrementys sevyn,

Wyche sacramentys all synne wasche awey:
Fyrst, bapte[m] clensythe synne orygynall
And reformyt þe sowll in feythe verray
To þe gloryus lyknes of Gode eternall
Ande makyt yt as fayer and as celestyall
As yt never dyffowlyde had be,
Ande ys Crystys own specyall,
Hys restynge place, Hys plesant see.

ANIMA
I[n] a sowle watt thyngys be
By wyche he hathe hys very knowynge?

WYSDOM
Tweyne partyes: þe on, sensualyte,
Wyche ys clepyde þe flechly felynge.
The [five] owtewarde wyttys to hym be serwynge.[17]
Wan þey be not rewlyde ordynatly
The sensualyte þan, wythowte lesynge,
Ys made þe ymage of synne then of hys foly.

The other parte, þat ys clepyde resone,
Ande þat ys þe ymage of Gode propyrly,
For by þat þe sowll of Gode hathe cognycyon
And be þat Hym serwyt and loveuyt duly.
Be þe neyther parte of reson he knowyt dyscretly
All erthely thyngys how þey xall be usyde,[18]
Wat suffysyth to hys myghtys bodely,
Ande wat nedyt not to be refusyde.

91 weeds 92 virtuous 95 (a) sense (of) 97 knowledge, (you) possess 99 Author/Creator 100 ought 103 created everything 104 (His) image, similitude 105 were 106 Until, Adam's 107 were not there 109 been, shall (be) 110 shares the nature 111 From, orginal sin 112 from, came 114 (fire-)brands 115 born, mother 116 Heaven 117 disfigured 120 restores 121 truly 122 atonement 123 that was appointed for Him 124 spring 126 Baptism 127 renews, true faith 130 As (if), (been) defiled 132 seat/dwelling 134 true knowledge 135 Two, one 136 fleshly sense 138 controlled appropriately 140 through his folly 147 bodily needs 148 must

[14] 'For the wholesome discipline that comes with Wisdom is that the fear of God is the beginning [of all wisdom].' 'The fear of the Lord is the beginning of wisdom: and the knowledge of the holy is understanding': Proverbs 9:10. See also Proverbs 1:7 and Psalms 111:10.

[15] 'Why do we pay violently for the [sins] of the first man?'

[16] 'Then [it is] reasonable that you share in his blame.'

[17] 'The five external senses serve him.'

[18] 'And through [reason] serves and loves [God] properly. By the inferior part of reason [the soul] has innate understanding of how all earthly things should be used.' The superior part of the soul is that which has knowledge of God.

Thes tweyn do sygnyfye
Yowr dysgysynge and yowr aray,
Blake and wyght, fowll and fayer verely,
Every sowll here, þis ys no nay,
Blake by sterynge of synne þat cummyth all-day,
Wyche felynge cummythe of sensualyte,
Ande wyght of knowenge of reson veray
Off þe blyssyde infenyt Deyte.

Thus a sowle ys bothe fowlle and fayer:
Fowll as a best be felynge of synne,
Fayer as a angell, of Hewyn þe ayer,
By knowynge of Gode by hys reson wythin.

ANIMA
Than may I sey thus and begynne
Wyth fyve prudent vyrgyns of my reme;[19]
Thow be þe fyve wyttys of my sowll wythinne.
'*Nigra sum sed formosa, filia Jerusalem.*'[20]

Her entery[th] [five] vyrgynes in white kertyllys and mantelys, wyth chev[elers] and chappelettys, and synge 'Nigra sum sed formosa, filia Jerusalem, si[cut] tabernacula cedar et sicut pelles Salamonis.'[21]

ANIMA
The doughters of Jerusalem me not lake
For þis dyrke schadow I bere of humanyte,
That as þe tabernacull of cedar wythowt yt ys blake
Ande wythine as þe skyn of Salamone full of
bewty.
'*Quod fusca sum, nolite considerare me.*
Quia decoloravit me sol Jovis.'[22]

WYSDOM
Thus all þe sowlys þat in þis lyff be
Stondynge in grace b[e] lyke to thys.

A, *quinque prudentes*, yowr wyttys fyve
Kepe yow clene and ȝe xall never deface,
Ye Godys ymage never xall ryve,
For þe clene sowll [ys] Godys restynge place.

Thre myghtys every Cresten sowll has,
Wyche bethe applyede to þe Trinyte.

MYNDE
All thre here, lo, byfor yowr face!
Mynde.

WYLL
Wyll.

UNDERSTONDYNG
Ande Undyrstondynge, we thre.

WYSDOM
Ȝe thre, declare þan thys,
Yowr syngnyfycacyon and yowr propyrte.

MYNDE
I am Mynde, þat in þe sowle ys
The veray fygure of þe Deyte.
Wen in myselff I have mynde and se
The benefyttys of Gode and Hys worthynes,
How holl I was mayde, how fayere, how fre,
How gloryus, how jentyll to Hys lyknes,

Thys insyght bryngyt to my mynde
Wat grates I [ough] to God ageyn
Þat thus hathe ordenyde wythowt ende
Me in Hys blys ever for to regne.
Than myn insuffycyens ys to me peyn
That I have not werof to yelde my dett,
Thynkynge myselff creature most veyn;
Than for sorow my bren I knett.

Wen in my mynde I brynge togedyr
Þe yerys and dayes of my synfullnes,
The unstabullnes of my mynde hedyr and thedyr,
My oreble fallynge and freellnes,
Myselff ryght nought than I confes,
For by meselff I may not ryse
Wythowt specyall grace of Godys goodnes.
Thus mynde makyt me myselff to dyspyse.

150 appearance, clothes 152 no lie 153 (the) stirring, always 156 infinite Deity 158 like a beast, by 159 heir 161 realm 165 do not disdain me 166 dark 168 Solomon 173 (the) five prudent ones 175 tear 177 three powers/strengths 179 before your eyes 181 then 182 nature 184 true image 187 complete, noble 188 in 190 gratitude, owe 193 my inadequacy pains me 194 nothing with which to repay 195 vain 196 I knot my brows in sorrow 199 fickleness, (straying) here 200 horrible, frailty 201 completely worthless 204 despise

[19] See Matthew 25:1–12.

[20] Song of Songs 1:5. See the next footnote.

[21] Compare Song of Songs 1:5: 'I am black, but comely, O ye daughters of Jerusalem, as the tents of [c]edar, as the curtains/skins of Solomon.'

[22] 'Look not upon me, because I am black, because the sun [of Jove] has [discoloured] me.' See Song of Songs 1:6.

I seke and fynde nowere comforte
But only in Gode, my Creator.
Than onto Hym I do resorte
Ande say, 'Have mynde of me, my Savowr!'
Thus mynde to mynde bryngyth þat fawowre;
Thus, by mynde of me, Gode I kan know.
Goode mynde of Gode yt ys þe fygure;
Ande thys mynde to have all Crysten ow.[23]

Wyll

And I of þe soull am þe Wyll,
Off þe Godhede lyknes and fygure.
Wyt[h] goode wyll no man may spyll,
Now wythowt goode wyll, of blys be sure.
Wat soule wyll gret mede recure,
He must grett wyll have, in thought or dede,
Wertuusly sett wyth consyens pure,
For in wyll stondyt only mannys dede.[24]

Wyll for dede oft ys take;
Therfor þe wyll must weell be dysposyde.
Than þer begynnyt all grace to wake,
Yff wyth synne yt be not anosyde.
Therfor þe wyll must be w[ele] apposyde
Or þat yt to þe mevynge yewe cons[en]t.
The lybrary of reson muyst be wnclosyde
Ande aftyr hys domys to take entent.[25]

Owr wyll in Gode must be only sett
And for gode to do wylfully.
Wan gode wyll resythe, Gode ys in ws knett,
Ande He performyt þe dede veryly.
Off Hym cummyth all wyll sett perfyghtly,
For of owrselff we have ryght nought
But syne, wrechydnes, and foly.
He ys begynner and gronde of wyll and thought.

Than þis goode wyll seyde before
Ys behoveable to yche creature
Iff he cast hym to restore
The soule þat he hath take of cure,
Wyche of God ys þe fygure,
As longe as þe fygure ys kept fayer,
Ande ordenyde ever for to endure
In blys, of wyche ys he þe veray hayer.

Understondyng

The [third] parte of þe soule ys wndyrstondynge,
For by wndyrstondyng I beholde wat Gode ys,
In Hymselff begynny[n]g wythowt begynnynge
Ande ende wythowt ende þat xall never mys.
Incomprehensyble in Hymselff He ys;
Hys werkys in me I kan not comprehende.
How xulde I holly Hym þan þat wrought all þis?
Thus by knowynge of me to knowynge of Gode I
    assende.

I know in angelys He ys desyderable,
For Hym to beholde þe[i] dysyer soverenly;[26]
In Hys seyntys most dylectable,
For in Hymm þe[i] joy assyduly;
In creaturys Hys werkys ben most wondyrly,
For all ys made by Hys myght,
By [Hys] wysdom governyde most soverenly,
And Hys benygnyte inspyryt all soullys wyth lyght.

Off all creaturys He ys lowyde Sovereyn,
For He ys Gode of yche creature,
And þey be His peple þat ever xall reynge,
In wom He dwellyt as Hys tempull sure.
Wan I [of] thys knowynge make reporture
Ande se þe love He hathe for me wrought,
Yt bryngyt me to love þat Prynce most pure,
For, for love, þat Lorde made a man of nought.

Thys ys þat love wyche ys clepyde charyte,
For Gode ys charyte, as awtors tell[es],[27]
Ande woo ys in charyte, in Gode dwellyt he,
Ande Gode, þat ys charyte, in hym dwellys.
Thus wndyrstondynge of Gode compellys
To cum to charyte; than have Hys lyknes, lo!
Blyssyde ys þat sowll þat þis speche spellys:
'*Et qui creavit me requievit in tabernaculo meo*'.[28]

209 favour 215 fall 217 gain great reward 219 virtuously inclined 221 is often taken 222 be well disposed 223 waken 224 damaged 225 examined 229 set in God only 230 act in good will 231 resides, us knit 236 (the) foundation 237 (as I) said 238 necessary for 239 wishes 240 as his responsibility 242 So 244 heir 248 fail 251 hallow/worship 253 by, desired 255 To, saints, delightful 256 assiduously 257 wonderful 260 inspires 261 the beloved sovereign 262 each 264 whom, as (in) 265 declaration 268 As, from 270 authors tell (us) 271 whoever 274 then (to) share 275 utters

[23] 'And all Christians ought to be of this mind.'

[24] 'For men's deeds are judged solely according to the will that prompts them.'

[25] 'Before you consent to its promptings. The sum of reason's teachings must be studied, and you must follow its judgements.'

[26] 'Their principal desire is to behold Him'.

[27] See I John 4:16: 'God is love; and he that dwelleth in love dwelleth in God, and God in him.'

[28] 'And He who created me dwelt in my tabernacle.' Ecclesiasticus 24:9–11.

[Wysdom]
Lo, thes iii myghtys in on Soule be:
Mynde, Wyll, and Wndyrstondynge.
By Mynde of Gode, þe Fadyr knowyng have ye;
By Wndyrstondynge of Gode þe Sone ye have knowynge;
By Wyll, wyche turnyt in[to] love brennynge,
Gode þe Holy Gost, þat clepyde ys lowe:
Not iii Godys but on Gode in beynge.
Thus eche clene soule ys symylytude of Gode abowe.

By Mynde feythe in þe Father have we,
Hoppe in owr Lorde Jhesu by Wndyrstondynge,
Ande be Wyll in þe Holy Gost charyte:
Lo, thes iii pryncypall wertus of yow iii sprynge.[29]
Thys þe clene soule stondyth as a kynge;
Ande abowe all þis ȝe have free wyll;
Off þat be ware befor all thynge,
For yff þat perverte, all þis dothe spyll.[30]

Ye have iii enmyes; of hem be ware:
The Worlde, þe Fleshe, and þe Fende.
Yowr fywe wyttys from hem ȝe spare,
That þe sensualyte þey brynge not yow byhynde.[31]
Nothynge xulde offende Gode in no kynde;
Ande yff þer do, se þat þe nether parte of resone
In no wys þerto lende;
Than þe over parte xall have fre domynacyon.

Wan suggestyon to þe Mynde doth apere,
Wndyrstondynge, delyght not ȝe þerin;
Consent not, Wyll, yll lessons to lere,
Ande than suche steryngys b[e] no syn.
The[i] do but purge þe soule wer ys suche contraversye.
Thus in Me, Wysdom, yowr werkys begynne.
Fyght and ȝe xall have þe crown of glory,[32]
That [is everlastynge] joy, to be parteners þerinne.

Anima
Soveren Lorde, I am bownde to The[e]!
Wan I was nought Þou made me thus gloryus;
Wan I perysschede thorow synne Þou savyde [me];
Wen I was in grett perell Þou kept me, Cristus;
Wen I erryde Þou reducyde me, Jhesus;
Wen I was ignorant Þou tawt me truthe;
Wen I synnyde Þou correcte me thus;
Wen I was hewy Þou comfortede [me] by ruthe;

Wan I stonde in grace Þou holdyste me þat tyde;
Wen I fall Þou reysyst me myghtyly;
Wen I go wyll Þou art my gyde;
Wen I cum Þou reseywyste me most lovynly.
Thou hast anoyntyde [me] with þe oyll of mercy;
Thy benefyttys, Lorde, be innumerable;
Werfor lawde endeles to Þe[e] I crye,
Recomendynge me to Þin endles powre durable.

Here in þe goynge owt þe [Five] Wyttys synge 'Tota pulcra es' et cetera,[33] *they g[oyng] befor, Anima next, and her folowynge Wysdom, and aftyr Hym Mynde, W[yll], and Wndyrstondynge, all iii in wyght cloth of golde, [chevelered] and cr[e]styde in on sute.*[34]

And aftyr þe songe entreth Lucyfer in a dewyllys [aray] wythowt and wythin as a prowde galonte,[35] *seynge thus on thys wy[se]:*

Lucyfer
Owt, harow, I rore!
For envy I lore.
My place to restore
God hath mad a man.
All cum þey not thore,
Woode and þey wore.[36]
I xall tempte hem so sorre,
For I am he þat syn begane.

277 three, one 281 burning love 282 love 283 one 284 the image 286 Hope 288 virtues, from 289 Thus 290 above 294 Fiend 295 protect 297 no way 298 anything does 299 In no way consent to it 300 superior part 301 When the mind is tempted 303 learn 304 promptings 308 partners/sharers 311 through 312 peril, protected 313 erred, restored me 314 taught 315 corrected 316 sorrowful, pity 317 (at) that time 318 raised 319 go (astray), guide 320 receive, lovingly 322 blessings 323 endless praise 324 enduring power 325 roar! 326 scowl 331 (But) I, sorely 332 created sin

[29] See I Corinthians 13:13: 'And now abideth faith, hope, charity, these three; but the greatest of these is charity.'

[30] 'Beware of [free will] above all else, because if that is perverted, all the rest falls.'

[31] 'So that they do not bring you to serve sensuality.' The idea of the three enemies of humanity is defined in the *Meditations* of St Bernard.

[32] See I Timothy 6:12, I Peter 5:4, James 1:12.

[33] 'Thou art [completely] fair [my love, there is no spot in thee].' Song of Songs 4:7.

[34] 'Wearing masks and crests of the same sort.'

[35] i.e. Lucifer wears a devil's costume (perhaps covered in feathers as in the Chester Cycle, and under that the dress of a fashionable courtier, ready for his quick change at ll. 380ff.

[36] 'God has created humanity to fill my place [in Heaven]. They would have to be mad if they did not all go there.'

I was a angell of lyghte;
Lucyfeer I hyght,
Presumynge in Godys syght,
Werfor I am lowest in Hell.
In reformynge of my place ys dyght
Man,[37] [whom] I have in most dyspyght,
Ever castynge me wyth hem to fyght,
In þat Hewynly place he xulde not dwell.

I am as wyly now as than;
Þe knowynge þat I hade, yet I can;
I know all compleccyons of a man
Werto he ys most dysposyde;
Ande þerin I tempte ay-whan;
I marre hys myndys to þer wan,
That whoo ys hym þat God hym began;
Many a holy man wyth me ys mosyde.

Of Gode man ys þe fygure,
Hys symylytude, Hys pyctowre,
Gloryosest of ony creature
Þat ever was wrought;
Wyche I wyll dysvygure
Be my fals conjecture;
Yff he tende my reporture
I xall brynge hym to nought.

In þe soule ben iii partyes iwys:
Mynde, Wyll, Wndyrstondynge of blys,
Fygure of þe Godhede, I know well thys;
And þe flesche of man þat ys so changeable
That wyll I tempte, as I gees.
Thow þat I perwert, synne non ys
But yff þe Soule consent [unto mys],
For in þe Wyll of þe Soule the dedys ben damnable.

To þe Mynde of þe Soule I xall mak suggestyun,
Ande brynge hys Wndyrstondynge to dylectacyon,
So þat hys Wyll make confyrmacyon;
Than am I sekyr inowe
That dethe xall sew of damnacyon;
Than of þe Sowll þe Dewll hath dominacyon.
I wyll go make hys examynacyon,
To all þe dewllys of [Helle] I make awow.

[But], for to tempte man in my lyknes,
Yt wolde brynge hym to grett feerfullnes,
I wyll change me into bryghtn[essse],
And so hym to begyl[e],
Sen I xall schew hym perfyghtnes,
And wertu prov[e it] wykkydnes;
Thus wndyr colors all thynge perverse;
I xall never rest tyll þ[e] Soule I defyle.

Her Lucyfer dewoydyth[38] *and cummyth in ageyn as a goodly galont.*

MYNDE
My Mynde ys wver on Jhesu
That enduyde ws wyth wertu.
Hys doctrine to sue
Ever I purpos.

UNDYRSTONDYNGE
My wndyrstondynge ys in trew
That wyth feyth ws dyd renew.
Hys laws to pursew
Ys swetter to me þan sawowre of þe rose.

WYLL
And my wyll ys Hys wyll veraly
That made ws Hys creaturys so specyally,
Yeldynge [u]nto Hym laude and glory
For Hys goodnes.

LUCYFER
Ye fonnyde fathers, founders of foly,
Ut quid hic statis tota die ociosi?[39]
Ȝe wyll [pyse][40] or ȝe yt aspye.
The Dewyll hath acumberyde yow expres.

Mynde, Mynde, ser, have in mynde thys!

MYNDE
He ys not ydyll þat wyth Gode ys.

LUCYFER
No, ser? I prowe well ys.
Thys ys my suggestyun.

335 Presuming (too much) 339 seeking 340 (So that) in 341 wily 342 knowledge, I still possess 343 aspects 344 What, inclined towards 345 always 346 afflict, brains, their distress 347 he despairs, made 348 by, confounded 350 picture 353 disfigure 355 believes my words 361 guess 362 Though, it is not sinful 363 Unless, wrong 364 (only) in, are deeds damnable 366 pleasure 367 So (long as) 368 certain enough 369 result in 370 Devil, dominion 371 test him 373 my (own) shape 378 virtue (shall) prove (to be) 379 by deception 381 ever/always 382 endowed 383 pursue 385 (that) Truth 388 sweeter, perfume 389 truly 393 foolish old men 395 before you see it 396 clearly overcome you 399 I'll prove (that) he is

37 '[Man] is ordained to take my place'.

38 'Departs'.

39 'Why stand ye here all the day idle?' Matthew 20:6.

40 Piss? Eccles (*Macro Plays*, p. 127) suggests 'perysche/perish'.

All th[y]nge hat dew tymes:[41]
Prayer, fastynge, labour, all thes.
Wan tyme ys not kept, þat dede ys amys,
Þe more pleynerly to yowr informacyon.

Here ys a man þat lywyt wordly,
Hathe wyffe, chylderne, and serwantys besy,
And other chargys þat I not specyfye.
[Is it] leeffull to þis man
To lewe hys labour wsyde truly,
Hys chargys perysche þat Gode gaff duly,[42]
Ande yewe hym to preyer and es of body?
Woso do thus wyth God ys not than.

Mertha plesyde Gode grettly thore.

MYNDE
Ye, but Mar[i]a plesyde Hymm moche more.[43]

LUCYFER
Yet þe lest hade blys for evermore.
Ys not þis anow?

MYNDE
Contemplatyff lyff ys sett before.

LUCYFER
I may not belewe þat in my lore,
For God Hymselff, wan He was man borre,
Wat lyff lede He? Answer þou now.

Was he ever in contemplacyon?

MYNDE
I suppos not, by my relacyon.

LUCYFER
And all Hys lyff was informacyon
Ande example to man.

Sumtyme wyth synners He had conversacyon;
Sumtyme wyth holy also comunycacyon;
Sumtyme He laboryde, preyde; sumtyme
tribulacyon;
Thys was *vita mixta* þat Gode here began;[44]

Ande þat lyff xulde ye here sewe.

MYNDE
I kan not belewe thys ys trew.

LUCYFER
Contemplatyff lyff for to sewe
Yt ys grett drede, and se cause why:
They must fast, wake, and prey, ever new,
Wse harde lywynge and goynge wyth dyscyplyne
dew,[45]
Kepe sylence, wepe, and surphettys eschewe,
Ande yff þey fayll of thys þey offende Gode hyghly.

Wan þey have wastyde by feyntnes,
Than febyll þer wyttys and fallyn to fondnes,[46]
Sum into dyspeyer and sum into madnes,
Wet yt well, God ys not plesyde wyth thys.
Lewe, lewe, suche syngler besynes.
Be in þe worlde, use thyngys nesesse.
The comyn ys best expres.[47]
Who clymyt hye, hys fall gret ys.

MYNDE
Truly, me seme ȝe have reson.

LUCYFER
Aplye yow then to þis conclusyun.

MYNDE
I kan make no replicacyon;
[Your resons be grete.]
I kan not forgett þis informacyon.

403 (the correct) time, wrong 404 plainly, understanding 405 lives a worldly life 406 busy 407 responsibilities 408 lawful for 409 leave his proper labours 411 devote himself, ease 412 Whoever, is not with God 415 (even) the least (i.e. Martha) 416 enough? 417 ranked above (the active) 419 born 420 did He lead 422 to my knowledge 423 instruction 426 holy (people) 427 suffered 429 pursue 430 believe 432 see the reason 435 avoid surfeit 439 despair 440 Understand 441 Leave, strange practices 442 necessary 444 is the greater 445 it seems to me 446 (Give) your answer 447 response 448 arguments, too strong

[41] All things have [their] due times.' 'To every thing there is a season, and a time to every purpose under the Heaven.' Ecclesiastes 3:1.

[42] '[Let] those in his keeping, who God duly gave to him, perish'

[43] The allusion is to Luke 10:38–42. When Christ visited the home of two sisters, one, Martha, laboured to provide food for Him; the other, Mary, sat at His feet listening. Christ commended Mary's behaviour more highly. The story became the basis for many discussions of the merits of the active and contemplative lives in the medieval period.

[44] 'The mixed life', a combination of the active and contemplative, was said by many to be the Christian ideal.

[45] 'Live a life of hardship and follow due discipline'.

[46] 'When they have wasted and fainted away, their wits are enfeebled and they fall prey to folly'.

[47] 'The ordinary life is clearly the best.'

LUCYFER
Thynke þerwppon, yt ys yowr salvacyon.
Now and Wyndyrstondyne wolde have delectacyon,
All syngler devocyons he wolde lett.[48]

Yowr [five] wyttys abrode lett sprede.
Se how [comly] to man ys precyus wede;
Wat worschype yt ys to be manfull in dede;[49]
Þat [bryngeth] in dominacyon.
Off þe symple what profyght yt to tak hede?[50]
Beholde how ryches dystroyt nede;
It makyt man fayer, hym [wele] for to fede;
And of lust and lykynge commyth generacyon.

Wndyrstondynge, tender ye þis informacyon?

UNDERSTONDYNG
In thys I fele in manere of dylectacyon.

LUCYFER
A, ha, ser, then þer make a pawsacyon!
Se and beholde þe worlde abowte.
Lytyll thynge suffysyt to salvacyon;
All maner synnys dystroyt contryscyon;
They þat dyspeyer mercy have grett compunccyon;
Gode plesyde best wyth good wyll, no dowte.

Therfor, Wyll, I rede yow inclyne;
Lewe yowr stodyes, þow ben dywyn;[51]
Yowr prayers, yowr penance (of ipocryttys þe syne!),
Ande lede a comun lyff.
What synne ys in met[e], in ale, in wyn?
Wat synne ys in ryches, in clothynge fyne?
All thynge Gode ordenyde to man to inclyne.
Lewe yowr nyse chastyte and take a wyff.

Better ys fayer frut þan fowll pollucyon.
What seyth sensualite to þis conclusyon?

WYLL
[As] þe fyve wyttys gyff informacyon,
Yt semyth yow resons be goode.

[LUCYFER]
The Wyll of þe Soule hathe fre dominacyon;
Dyspute not to moche in þis wyth reson;
Yet þe nethyr parte to þis taketh sum instruccyon,
And so xulde þe over parte, but he were woode.[52]

WYLL
Me seme, as ȝe sey, in body and soule,
Man may be in þe worlde and be ryght goode.

LUCYFER
[Ya], ser, by Sent Powle!
But trust not þes prechors, for þey be not goode,
For þey flatter and lye as þey wore woode;
Ther ys a wolffe in a lombys skyn.[53]

WYLL
Ya, I woll no more row ageyn þe floode.
I woll sett my soule [on] a mery pynne.

LUCYFER
Be my trowthe, than do ye wyslye.
Gode lowyt a clene sowll and a mery.
Acorde yow iii togedyr by
[And ye may not mysfare.]

MYNDE
To þis suggestyon agre we.

UNDERTONDYNG
Delyght þerin I have truly.

WYLL
And I consent þerto frelye.

LUCYFER
A, ser, all mery þan! Awey care!

Go in þe worlde, se þat abowte;
Geet goode frely, cast no dowte;
To þe ryche ye se men lowly lought.
Yeve to yowr body þat ys nede,
Ande ever be mery; let revell rowte!

451 if, take pleasure 453 wander 454 fine clothes 456 dominion 458 destroy need 459 to eat well 460 from, sexual desire 461 do you favour 462 a kind of pleasure 463 pause 464 around (you) 465 suffice for 466 destroy contrition 467 despair (of) 468 God (is) 471 (the hypocrites' sin!) 472 worldly 473 is (there) in food 475 ordained for, desire 476 over-strict chastity 477 fair fruit 479 report 481 freedom of action 482 too much 487 St Paul 488 these preachers 489 as (if) they were mad 491 row against the tide 492 on a merry course 493 you do wisely 494 loves 495 Agree 496 go wrong 500 Away (with) sorrow! 501 look what's around you 502 Acquire property, don't hesitate 503 bow down low 504 what it desires 505 revel run riot

48 'He would abandon all special acts of devotion.'

49 'How honourable it is to do brave deeds'.

50 'What profit is there in paying attention to simple people?'

51 'Leave your studies: those that are religious'.

52 'Yet the inferior part (of reason) takes some advice on this, and so should the superior part, unless it is mad.'

53 See Matthew 7:15: 'Beware of false prophets, which come to you in sheep's clothing, but inwardly they are ravening wolves.'

MYNDE
Ya, ellys I beschrew my snowte!

UNDERSTONDYNG
And yff I care, cache I þe gowte!

WYLL
And yff I spare, þe Dewyll me spede!

LUCYFER
Go yowr wey than and do wysly.
Change þat syde aray.

MYNDE
I yt dyfye!

UNDERSTONDYNG
We woll be fresche, *hanip la plu joly*![54]
Farwell penance!

MYNDE
To worschyppys I wyll my mynde aplye.

UNDERSTONDYNG
My wndyrstondynge in worschyppys and glory.

WYLL
And I in lustys of lechery,
As was sumtyme gyse of Frawnce.
Wyth 'Wy wyppe,
Farwell', quod I, þe Dewyll ys wppe!

Exiant

LUCYFER
Off my dysyere now have I summe
Wer onys brought into custume,
Then farwell consyens, he wer clumme,
I xulde have all my wyll.
Resone I have made both [deff] and dumme;
Grace ys owt and put arome;
Wethyr I wyll have, he xall cum.
So at þe last I xall hym spyll.
I xall now stere hys mynde
To þat syne made me a fende;
Pryde, wyche ys ageyn kynde
And of synnys hede.
So to covetyse he xall wende,
For þat enduryth to þe last ende;[55]
And onto lechery, and I may hymm rende,
Than am I seker þe Soule ys dede.

That Soule Gode made incomparable,
To Hys lyknes most amyable,
I xall make yt most reprovable,
Ewyn lyke to a fende of Hell.
At hys deth I xall apere informable,
Schewynge hym all hys synnys abhomynable,
Prewynge hys Soule damnable,
So wyth dyspeyer I xall hym qwell.

Wyll in clennes ys mankyn[d],
Verely, þe soule God ys wythin;
Ande wen yt ys in dedly synne,
Yt [is] werely þe Develys place.
Thus by colours [and false gynne]
Many a soule to Hell I wyn.
Wyde to go I may not blyne
Wyth þis fals boy, God gyff hym evell grace!

Her he takyt a [schrewde] boy wyth hym and goth hys wey cryenge.[56]

MYNDE
Lo, me here in a new aray!
Wyppe, wyrre, care awey;
Farwell perfeccyon!
Me semyt myselff most lyghtly, ay!
It ys but honest, no pryde, no nay.
I wyll be freshest, by my fay,
For þat acordyt wyth my complexccyon.

UNDERSTONDYNG
Ande have here [one] as fresche as yow!
All mery, mery, and glade now.
I have get goode, Gode wott how.

506 or I curse 507 gout 508 prosper 510 (sober) long clothing, I defy it! 511 fashionable (and young) 513 (gaining) worldly honour 516 the fashion in France 517 Hey, quick! 518 roused 518+ Exit (Mynde, Wyll, and Understondyng) 519 desire, everything 520 (If it) once became 521 dumb 524 (thrown) out, to wander 525 Wherever, have (reason) 526 ruin 527 stir 528 (that) made, fiend 529 against nature 530 the greatest 531 go 533 unto, if, deliver 534 certain, dead 537 guilty 538 Even 539 with evidence 541 Proving 542 despair, kill 546 truly 547 deception, snares 549 Far, roam, cease 551 I'm here, clothes 552 Quick, hurry 554 attractive, yes 556 faith 557 agrees with 558 here (is) 559 glad 560 gained property, knows

54 Perhaps a French toast, 'All the better for the wine cup (?*hanap*)!'

55 While most sins were conventionally products of youth, avarice was said to endure into old age.

56 Lucifer seizes a 'naughty' boy from among the audience and drags him off with him.

For joy I sprynge, I sckyppe.
Goode makyt on mery, to God avowe.
Farewell consyens, I know not yow!
I am [at eas, hade I inow!]
Truthe on syde I lett hym slyppe.

Wyll
Lo, here on as jolye as ȝe!
I am so lykynge, me seme I fle.
I have atastyde lust: farwell chastyte!
My hert ys evermore lyght.
I am full of felycyte.
My delyght ys all in bewte.
Þer ys no joy but þat in me.
A woman me semyth a hewynly syght.

Mynde
Ande thes ben my syngler solace:
Kynde, fortune, and grace.[57]
Kynde nobley of kynrede me yewyn hase,
Ande þat makyt me soleyn.
Fortune in worldys worschyppe me doth lace.
Grace yewyt curryus eloquens, and þat mase
That all oncunnynge I dysdeyn.[58]

Understondyng
And my joy ys especyall
To hurde wppe ryches, for fer to fall,
To se yt, to handyll yt, to tell yt all,
And [streight] to spare.
To be holde ryche and reyall
I bost, I avawnt wer I xall.
Ryches makyt a man equall
To hem sumtyme hys sovereyngys wer.

Wyll
To me ys joy most [laudable]
Fresche dysgysynge to seme amyable,
Spekynge wordys delectable
Perteynynge onto love.
It ys joy of joys inestymable.
To halse, to kys þe affyable.
A lover ys son perceyvable
Be þe smylynge on me, wan yt doth remove.[59]

Mynde
To [avaunte] thus me semyth no schame,
For galontys now be in most fame.
Curtely personys men hem proclame.
[Moche we be sett bye.]

Understondyng
The ryche [covetouse] wo dare blame,
Off govell and symony thow he bere þe name?[60]
To be fals, men report yt game;
Yt ys clepyde wysdom, 'Ware þat!', quod Ser Wyly.

Wyll
Ande of lechory to make avawnte
Men fors yt no more þan drynke atawnt.[61]
Thes thyngys be now so conversant,
We seme yt no schame.

Mynde
Curyous aray I wyll ever hante.

Understondyng
Ande I falsnes, to be passante.

Wyll
Ande I in lust my flesche to daunte.
No man dyspyes thes; þey be but game.

Mynde
I rejoys of thes; now let ws synge!

Understondyng
Ande yff I spar, ewell joy me wrynge![62]

Wyll
'Have at', quod I, lo, [howe] I sprynge!
Lust makyth me wondyr wylde.

561 jump, skip 562 possessions make one 564 if only I had enough 565 I put truth to one side 566 here's one 567 happy, I'm flying 568 tasted 571 beauty 573 seems to me, heavenly 574 these are 576 has given me noble birth 577 aloof/haughty 582 hoard up, fear of a fall 583 count 584 strictly, save 585 thought (to be), royal 586 boast where I want 588 who were once, superiors 589 the greatest joy is in 590 dressing elegantly, desirable 594 embrace, kiss the willing (ones) 595 easily recognized 596 their 598 most renown 599 Courtly, men call them 600 We're highly thought of 603 deceitful, (merely) sport 604 Sir Wily 607 common 609 elegant, habituate 610 the best 611 tame 615 Let's go 616 wonderfully

57 'Nature, luck, and providence': conventionally the three sources of pride.

58 'Fortune wraps me in worldly honour. Grace gives me ingenious eloquence that amazes [everyone], so I disdain the ignorant.'

59 'When they depart.' Coldewey (*Early English Drama*, p. 88) suggests 'when I undress'.

60 'Who dares to accuse the rich [man] of covetousness, even if he is renowned for usury and simony?' Simony was, strictly, the buying and selling of ecclesiastical offices and privileges, but here may mean simply bribery.

61 'Men consider it no worse than having too much to drink.'

62 'And curse me if I fall behind!'

MYNDE
A tenowr to yow bothe I brynge.

UNDERSTONDYNG
And I a mene for ony kynge.

WYLL
And but a trebull I owtwrynge,
The Devell hym spede þat myrthe exyled!

Et cantant.

MYNDE
How be þis, trow ye nowe?

UNDERSTONDYNG
At þe best, to God avowe.

WYLL
As mery as þe byrde on bow,
I take no thought.

MYNDE
The welfare of þis worlde ys in ws, I ma vowe.

UNDERSTONDYNG
Lett eche man tell hys condycyons howe.

WYLL
Begynne ye, ande have at yow,
For I am aschamyde of ryght nought.

MYNDE
Thys ys a cause of my worschyppe:
I serve myghty lordeschyppe
Ande am in grett tenderschyppe;
Therfor moche folke me dredys.
Men sew to my frendeschyppe
For meyntnance of her schendeschyppe.
I support hem by lordeschyppe.
For to get goode þis a grett spede ys![63]

UNDERSTONDYNG
And I use jerowry,
Enbrace questys of perjury,
Choppe and chonge wyth symonye,[64]
And take large yeftys.
B[e] þe cause never so try,
I preve yt fals, I swere, I lye,
Wyth a quest of myn affye.
The redy wey þis now to thryfte ys![65]

WYLL
A[nd] wat trow ȝe be me?
More þan I take spende I threys iii.[66]
Sumtyme I yeff, sumtyme þey me,
Ande am ever fresche and gay.
Few placys now þer be
But onclennes we xall þer see;
It ys holde but a nysyte.
Lust ys now comun as þe way.[67]

MYNDE
Law procedyth not for meyntnance.[68]

UNDERSTONDYNG
Trowthe recurythe not for habundance.

WYLL
And lust ys in so grett usance,
We fors yt nought.

MYNDE
In us þe worlde hathe most affyance.

UNDERSTONDYNG
Non thre be in so grett aqweynttance.

WYLL
Few þer be outhe of owr allyance.[69]
Wyll þe worlde ys thus, take we no thought!

MYNDE
Thought? Nay, þerageyn stryve I.

UNDERSTONDYNG
We have þat nedyt us, so thryve I.

617 tenor (voice) 618 middle part, (fit) for any 619 treble, squeeze out 620 take him who exiled mirth 620+ And they sing. 623 (a) bough 625 make 626 account for 630 lords 631 stewardship 634 support, corruption 640 gifts 641 just 642 prove 643 paid to follow me 645 by 647 give (to others), they (to) 648 elegant 650 corruption 651 trifle 654 Truth is forestalled by wealth 655 usage 656 We don't notice (it) 657 reliance 658 No three (people) 661 against that 662 what we need

[63] 'This is a great way to acquire goods!'
[64] 'And I use legal corruption, bribe juries to commit perjury, chop and change verdicts for payment.'
[65] 'This is now the easy path to prosperity!'
[66] 'I spend nine times more than I earn.'
[67] 'Lust is now as much used as the main street.'
[68] 'Justice is held back by intimidation.'
[69] 'There are very few who are not loyal to us.'

WYLL
And yff þat I care, never wyve I.
Let them care þat hathe for to sewe!

MYNDE
Wo lordschyppe xall sew must yt bye.[70]

UNDERSTONDYNG
Wo wyll have law must have monye.

WYLL
Ther povert ys þe malewrye,
Thow ryght be, he xall never renewe.[71]

MYNDE
Wronge ys born wpe boldly,
Thow all þe worlde know yt opynly,
Mayntnance ys now so myghty,
Ande all for mede.

UNDERSTONDYNG
The law ys so coloryde falsly
By sleyttys and by perjury,
Brybys be so gredy,
Þat [to] þe pore trowth ys take ryght nought a hede.[72]

WYLL
Wo gett or loose, ye be ay wynnande.
Mayntnance and perjury now stande.
Thei wer never so moche reynande
Seth Gode was bore.

MYNDE
Ande lechery was never more usande
Off lernyde and lewyde in þis lande.

UNDERSTONDYNG
So we thre be now in hande.

WYLL
Ya, and most usyde everywere.

MYNDE
Now wyll we thre do make a dance
Off thow þat longe to owr retenance,
Cummynge in by contenance.
Þis were a dysporte.

UNDERSTONDYNG
Therto I geve acordance
Off thow þat ben of myn affyance.

WYLL
Let se bytyme þe[e], meyntnance.
Clepe in fyrst yowr resorte.

Here entur vi dysgysyde in þe sute of Mynde, with rede berdys, and [Lyons] rampaunt on here crestys, and yche a warder in hys honde; her mynstrall[ys], trumpes, eche answere for hys name.[73]

MYNDE
Let se cum in Indignacyon and Sturdynes,
Males also and Hastynes,
Wreche and Dyscorde expres,
And þe sevente am I, Mayntennance.
Seven ys a numbyr of [discorde] and inperfyghtnes.
Lo, here ys a yomandrye wyth loweday to dres![74]
Ande þe Deule hade swore yt, þey wolde ber wp falsnes[75]
Ande maynten yt at þe best. Þis ys þe Deullys dance![76]

Ande here menstrellys be convenyent,
For trumpys xulde blow to þe Jugemente;
Off batell also yt ys on instrumente,
Yevynge comfort to fyght.
Therfor þey be expedyente

663 I'll never marry 664 who have to pursue (marriage) 669 supported 672 financial reward 674 sleights 675 Bribes 676 Whoever gains, you always win 679 never prospered so well 680 Since God was born 681 used 682 By (the) learned and unlearned 686 those, belong, retinues 687 by gesture (i.e. in dumbshow) 689 agreement 690 my supporters 691 quickly/first 692 Call, your faction 693 Stubbornness 694 Malice, Quick-Temper 695 Vengeance, Open Discord 697 imperfection 701 their, appropriate 702 for, Last Judgement 703 It's also an instrument of battle 704 Giving encouragement

70 'Whoever pursues lordship has to pay for it.'

71 'Where poverty is the malady, even though he is right, he'll never win [the case].'

72 'That truth pays no attention to the poor.'

73 'Here enter six actors dressed in Mynde's livery, with red beards [traditionally Judas's colour], and lions rampant on their [heraldic] crests, and each [actor] has a staff in his hand. Their minstrels have trumpets, and each actor will answer when Mynde says his character's name.' The lions rampant have been seen as allusions to either the de la Pole dukes of Suffolk or the Mowbray dukes of Norfolk (see Eccles, *Macro Plays*, p. 211; Marshall, ' "Fortune in Worldys Worschyppe" '), but they are also conventional symbols of pride.

74 'Look, here's an army to arrange a loveday!' (ironic). Lovedays were held for the formal resolution of disputes.

75 'Even if the Devil had sworn against it, they would support a lie'.

76 A raucous dance associated with the festive Lord of Misrule.

To þes meny of meyntnance.
Blow! lett see 'Madam Regent',[77]
Ande daunce, ye laddys! yowr hertys be lyght.

Lo, þat other spare, thes meny wyll spende.[78]

UNDERSTONDYNG
Ya, wo ys hym xall hem offende!

WYLL
Wo wyll not to hem condescende,
He xall have threttys.

MYNDE
They spyll þat law wolde amende.[79]

UNDERSTONDYNG
Yit mayntnance no man dare reprehende.

WYLL
Thes meny thre synnys comprehende:
Pryde, Invy, and Wrathe in hys hettys.

UNDERSTONDYNG
Now wyll I than begyn my traces.
Jorowr[s] in on hoode beer to facys.
Fayer speche and falsehede in on space ys.
Is it not ruthe?
The quest of Holborn cum into þis placys.[80]
Ageyn þe ryght ever þey rechase[s].[81]
Off wom þey holde not, harde hys grace ys.[82]
Many a tyme have dammyde truthe.

Here entrethe vi jorours in a sute, gownyde, wyth hodys abowt her nekys, hattys of meyntenance þerupon, vyseryde dyversly; here mynstrell, a ba[g]-pyp[e].[83]

UNDERSTONDYNG
Let se fyrst Wronge and Sleyght;
Dobullnes and Falnes, schew yowr myght;
Now Reveyn and Dyscheyit;
Now holde yow here togydyr.
Thys menys consyens ys so streytt
That þey report as mede yewyt beyght.
Here ys þe quest of Holborn, an evyll entyrecte.
They daunce all þe londe hydyr and thedyr.
And I, Perjury, yowr fownder.
Now dance on, ws all! The worlde doth on ws wondyr.

Lo, here ys a menye love wellfare.

MYNDE
Ye, þey spende þat tru men spare.

WYLL
Have þey a brybe, have þey no care
Wo hath wronge or ryght.

MYNDE
They fors not to swere and starre.

WYLL
[Though] all be false, les and mare.

UNDERSTONDYNG
Wyche wey to þe woode wyll þe hare
They knewe, and þey at rest sett als tyghte.[84]
Some seme hem wyse
For þe fadyr of us, Covetyse.

WYLL
Now Meyntnance and Perjury,
Hathe schewyde þe trace of þer cumpeny,
Ye xall se a sprynge of Lechery,
Þat to me attende.
Here forme ys of þe stewys, clene rebaldry.
They [wene] sey sothe wen þat þey lye.
Off þe comyn þey synge eche wyke by and by.
They may sey wyth tenker, I trow, 'Lat amende'.

706 For, retinue 708 lads 711 be obedient 712 threats 714 criticize 715 understand 716 Envy, rages 718 jurors, have two faces in one hood 719 falsehood, in the same place 720 a pity 721 place 722 Against justice 724 (they) have 726 Duplicity, Falsehood 727 Spoliation, Deceit 729 strict 730 as bribery leads them 731 salve 735 (that) loves 736 what, save 737 (If) they have 739 think it nothing, swear, stare 740 less, more 743 think 744 us (all) 747 dance 749 Their, brothels, pure ribaldry 751 For the common men 752 with (the) tinker, 'Let it mend'

77 Perhaps a popular dance tune.

78 i.e. 'When others slack, this group will keep going.'

79 'They ruin what the law tries to correct.'

80 Probably a reference to the inquests convened by the sheriff and justices of Middlesex in High Holborn in London. See Eccles, *Macro Plays*, pp. 211–12.

81 'Rechase' ('assemble'), being a hunting term, plays upon the two senses of 'quest' as jury and hunt.

82 'It's bad luck on those whom they don't favour.'

83 Hats or caps of maintenance bearing the badges of noble patrons were worn by their retainers as signs of their allegiance. 'Vyseryde dyversly' refers to the hoods with faces painted on both the front and the rear, to which Understondyng alludes at l. 718.

84 'Whichever way the hare goes to the woods [proverbially it knew many ways], they know where he's heading and need only to sit tight [and wait].'

Here entreth vi women in sut, [iii] dysgysyde as galontys and iii as matrones, wyth wondyrfull vysurs congruent; here mynstrell, a horne- pype.[85]

Wyll
Cum slepers, Rekleshede and Idyllnes,
All in all, Surfet and Gredynes,
For þe flesche, Spousebreche and Mastres,
Wyth jentyll Fornycacyon.
Yowr mynstrell a hornepype, mete,
Þat fowll ys in hymselff but to þe erys swete.
Thre fortherers of love; 'Hem schrew I!', quod
Bete.[86]
Thys dance of þis damesellys ys thorow þis regyn.

Mynde
Ye may not endure wythowt my meyntenance.

Understondyng
That ys bought wyth a brybe of owr substance.

Wyll
Whow, breydest þou us of þin aqueyntance?
I sett þe[e] at nought!

Mynde
On þat worde I woll tak vengeaunce.
Wer vycys be gederyde, ever ys sum myschance.[87]
Hurle hens thes harlottys! Here gyse ys of France!
Þey xall abey bytterly, by Hym þat all wrought!

Understondyng
Ill spede þe[e] ande þou spare!
Þi longe body bare
To bett I not spare.
Have the[e] ageyn!

Wyll
Holde me not! Let me go! Ware!
I dynge, I dasche, þer, go ther!
Dompe devys, can ye not dare?[88]
I tell yow, outwarde, on and tweyn!

Exiant.

Mynde
Now I schrew yow thus dansaunde!

Understondyng
Ye[a], and ewyll be þou thryvande!

Wyll
No more let us be stryvande.
Nowe all at on!

Mynde
Here was a meny onthryvande.

Understondyng
To þe Deull be þey drywande.

Wyll
He þat ys yll wywande,
Wo hys hym, by þe bon!

Mynde
Leve then þis dalyance
Ande set we a[n] ordenance
Off better chevesaunce
How we may thryve.

Understondyng
At Westmyster, wythowt varyance,
Þe nex terme xall me sore avawnce,
For retornys, for enbraces, for recordaunce.
Lyghtlyer to get goode kan no man on lyve.[89]

Mynde
Ande at þe parvyse I wyll be
A Powlys betwyn ii ande iii,
Wyth a menye folowynge me,
Entret, Juge-Partynge, and To-Supporte.[90]

753 Recklessness 754 Surfeit 755 Adultery, Mistress 757 appropriately 758 ears sweet 760 these, all over the region 762 wealth 763 reproach, your friends? 764 value 767 Throw out, Their manners are 768 pay 769 Curse you unless 771 I'll not fail to beat 774 Get off! 776 Get out, one, two 776+ (The dancers) exit 777 curse, dancing 778 curse you! 779 fighting 780 as one 781 an unprofitable troupe 782 heading 783 badly married 784 Woe is him, bone 786 agreement 787 trading 789 debate 790 Next (law) term, greatly advance 794 2 and 3 p.m.

85 Quite what the 'wonderful, appropriate masks' depicted is not clear, although the symbolic value of the horn-pipe, suggesting the cuckold's horns, is self-evident. Wyll, in the role of Fornication, is the seventh masker.

86 'The furtherers of love; "I curse them", says Betty.'

87 'Where vices are gathered, there's always some mishap.'

88 '[It's supposed to be a] dumbshow, can't you keep quiet?'

89 'By return [of writs], by bribery, by false testimony. An easier way to acquire property no living man knows.'

90 The Parvis was the enclosure in the front of St Paul's Cathedral in London, where the lawyers met to conduct their business (see Chaucer's comments on his Sergeant of Law, *General Prologue*, l. 310ff). Mynde's supporters there are Bribery, Judge-Sharing (giving the judge a share of the profits of any false judgement), and Corrupt Backing (of witnesses).

Wyll
Ande ever þe latter, þe lever me.
Wen I com lat to þe cyte
I walke all lanys and weys to myn affynyte;
And I spede not þer, to þe stews I resort.

Mynde
Ther gettys þou nouhte, but spendys.

Wyll
Yis, sumtyme I take amendys
Off hem þat nought offendys,
I engrose upe here purs.

Mynde
And I arest þer no drede ys,
Preve forfett þer no mede ys,
Ande take to me þat nede ys;
I reke not thow þey curs.

Understondyng
Thow þey curs, [never] þe wers I fare.
Thys day I endyght them I herde of never are;
To-morow I wyll aqwyt them, yff nede were;
Thys lede I my lyff.

Wyll
Ye, but of us iii I have lest care.
Met and drynke and ease, I aske no mare,
Ande a praty wenche, to se here bare;
I reke but lytyll be sche mayde or wyffe.

Mynde
Thys on a soper[91]
I wyll be seen rycher,
Set a noble wyth goode chere
Redyly to spende.

Understondynge
And I tweyn, be þis feer,
To moque at a goode dyner.
I hoope of a goode yer,
For ever I trost Gode wyll send.[93]

Wyll
A[nd] best we have wyne,
Ande a cosyn of myn
Wyth ws for to dyne.
Three nobles wyll I spende frely.

Mynde
We xall acorde well and fyne.

Understondyng
Nay, I wyll not passe schylyngys nyne.

Wyll
No, þou was never but a swyn.
I woll be holdyn jentyll, by Sent Audre of Ely.[94]

Ande now in my mynde I have
My cosyn Jenet *N.*,[95] so Gode me save;
Sche mornyth wyth a chorle, a very knave,
And never kan be mery.
I pley me þer wen I lyst rawe;
Than þe chorle wyll here dysprawe.
[Who] myght make hym thys to lawe,
I wolde onys have hym in þe wyrry.

Mynde
For thys I kan a remedye:
I xall rebuk hym thus so dyspytuusly
Þat of hys lyff he xall [w]ery
And qwak for very fere.
Ande yff he wyll not leve þerby,
On hys bodye he xall abye
Tyll he leve þat jelousy;
Nay, suche chorlys I kan lere.

Understondyng
Nay, I kan better hym qwytte:
Arest hym fyrst to pes for fyght.

797 at the end, better (for) **798** late, City (of London) **799** lanes, friendly to me **800** If, prosper, brothels **801** gain, spend (plenty) **802** extract fines **803** From those **804** gather up, purses **805** where **806** gain (a) forfeit **807** from the needy **808** care, if **810** indict, never heard of **811** acquit, if I have to **812** Thus **814** meat, more **815** pretty, her **816** care, virgin **819** Give, noble (a coin)[92] **821** fellowship **822** jest **823** hope for, year **824** trust **826** cousin **830** spend above 9s **831** (anything) but **832** thought a gentleman **835** suffers, wretch **837** want to have fun **838** insult her **839** take him to law **840** by the throat **841** know **842** spitefully **843** worry **844** tremble **846** he'll pay with his body **848** teach **849** repay

91 'I'll contribute this towards a supper'.

92 In 1465 the noble increased in value from 6s 8d to 10 shillings.

93 An allusion to the proverb 'spend and God will spend (with you).'

94 St Audre, or Ethelreda, founded a monastery in Ely.

95 '*Nomen*': 'name' as in 'N-Town', here the equivalent of the modern 'Janet X'. Perhaps the name of a local woman was inserted in performance.

Than in another schere hym endyght,
He ne xall wete by wom ne howe.[96]
Have hym in þe Marschalsi seyn aryght,[97]
Than to þe Amralte,[98] for þey wyll byght,
A *prevenire facias* than have as tyght,[99]
Ande þou xalt hurle hym so þat he xall have inow.

WYLL
Wat and þes wrongys be espyede?

UNDERSTONDYNG
Wyth þe crose and þe pyll I xall wrye yt[100]
That þer xall never man dyscrey yt
Þat may me appeyere.

MYNDE
Ther ys no craft but we may trye yt.

UNDERSTONDYNG
Mede stoppyt, be yt never so allyede.

WYLL
Wyth yow tweyn wo ys replyede,
He may sey he hathe a schrewde seyer.

MYNDE
Thow woldyst have wondyr of sleyghtys þat be.

UNDERSTONDYNG
Thys make sume ryche and summe never the.

WYLL
Þey must nedys grett goodys gett þe[e].
Now go we to þe wyne!

MYNDE
In trewþe I grante; have at wyth þe[e]!

UNDERSTONDYNG
Ande for a peny or ii, I wyll not fle.

WYLL
Mery, mery, all mery þan be we!
Who þat ws tarythe, curs have he and myn!
[*Enter Wisdom*]

WYSDOM
O thou Mynde, remembyr the[e]!
Turne þi weys, þou gost amyse.
Se what þi ende ys, þou myght not fle:
Dethe to every creature certen ys.
They þat lyve well, þey xall have blys;
Thay þat endyn yll, þey goo to Hell.
I am Wysdom, sent to tell yow thys:
Se in what stat þou doyst indwell.

MYNDE
To my mynde yt cummyth from farre
That dowtles man xall dey.
Ande thes weys we go, we erre.
Wndyrstondynge, wat do ye sey?

UNDERSTONDYNG
I sey, man, holde forthe þi wey!
The lyff we lede ys sekyr ynowe.
I wyll no wndyrstondynge xall lett my pley.
Wyll, frende, how seyst thowe?

WYLL
I wyll not thynke þeron, to Gode avowe!
We be yit but tender of age.
Schulde we leve þis lyve? Ya, whowe!
We may amende wen we be sage.

WYSDOM
Thus many on unabylythe hym to grace.[101]
They wyll not loke, but slumber and wynke.
Þey take not drede before þer face,
Howe horryble þer synnys stynke.
Wen they be on þe pyttys brynke,
Than xall þey trymbull and qwake for drede.

854 they are fierce 856 harry him, enough 857 if, noticed 859 discover 860 (So) that I have to appear 862 Bribery stops (the law), allied 863 whoever has you two to act for him 864 cunning advocate 865 You'd wonder what tricks there are 866 thrive 867 (to) get 872 delays us, my curse 874 yourself 875 reverse your steps 878 end 880 state you remain in 881 Into, far away 882 certainly, die 883 err 886 secure 887 intend (that), prevent 890 young 891 life?, hey! 892 old 894 look, sleep 895 no fear (of what is) 896 their 897 brink of the pit

96 'First have him arrested (for fighting) in order to keep the peace. Then indict him in a court in another county. He won't know by whom or how.'

97 The Marshalsea was the court of the knight marshal which had jurisdiction over the 'Verge', the area surrounding the royal court. The prison of the same name in Southwark was associated with it.

98 The court of the lord admiral.

99 Probably an error for *Praemunire facias*, a writ alleging that the defendant has appealed to a foreign jurisdiction in a matter triable in an English court. With all these suits against him in different courts, the victim will be unable to defend himself effectively, and be forced to surrender or buy off his accusers.

100 'I'll arrange it with the head and tail of a coin [i.e. a bribe]'.

101 'Thus many a person disables themselves from grace.'

Yit Mynde, I sey, yow bethynke
In what perell ye be now! Take hede!

Se howe ye have dy[s]vyguryde yowr soule!
Beholde yowrselff; loke veryly in mynde!

Here Anima apperythe in þe most horrybull wyse, fowlere þan a fende.

MYNDE
Out! I tremble for drede, by Sent Powle!
Thys ys fowler þan ony fende.

WYSDOM.
Wy art þou creature so onkynde,
Thus to defoule Godys own place,
Þat was made so gloryus wythowt ende?
Thou hast made þe Devllys rechace.

As many dedly synnys as ye have usyde,
So many devllys in yowr soule be.
Beholde wat ys þerin reclusyde!
Alas, man, of þi Soule have pyte!

Here rennyt owt from wndyr þe horrybyll mantyll of þe Soull vii small boys in þe lyknes of dewyllys, and so retorne ageyn.[102]

WYSDOM
What have I do? Why lowyste þou not Me?
Why cherysyste þi enmye? Why hatyst þou þi frende?
Myght I have don ony more for þe[e]?
But love may brynge drede to mynde.

Þou hast made the[e] a bronde of Hell
Whom I made þe[e] ymage of lyght.
Yff þe Deull myght, he wolde þe qwell,
But þat mercy expellyt hys myght.
Wy doyst þou, Soule, Me all dyspyght?
Why yewyst þou Myn enmy þat I have wrought?
Why werkyst þou hys consell, by Myn settys lyght?[103]
Why hatyst þou vertu? Why lovyst þat ys nought?

MYNDE
A, Lorde, now I brynge to mynde
My horryble synnys and myn offens,
I se how I have defowlyde þe noble kynde
Þat was lyke to Þe[e] by intellygens.
Wndyrstondynge, I schew to your presens
Owr lyff wyche þat ys most synfull.
Sek yow remedye, do yowr dylygens
To clense þe Soull wyche ys þis fowll.

UNDERSTONDYNGE
Be yow, Mynde, I have very knowenge
That grettly Gode we have offendyde.
Endles peyn worthyi be owr dysyr[v]ynge,
Wyche be owrselff never may be amendyde
Wythowt Gode, in Whom all ys comprehendyde.
Therfor to Hym let us resort;
He lefte up them þat be descendyde.
He ys resurreccyon and lywe; to Hem, Wyll, resort.[104]

WYLL
My wyll was full yowe to syne,
By wyche þe Soule ys so abhomynable.
I wyll retorne to Gode and new begynne,
Ande in Hym gronde my wyll stable,
Þat of Hys mercy He wyll me able
To have þe yiffte of Hys specyall grace,
How Hys seke Soule may be recurable
At þe Jugment before Hys face.

ANIMA
Than wyth yow iii þe Soule doth crye,
'Mercy, Gode!' Why change I nowte,
I þat thus horryble in synne lye,
Sythe Mynde, Wyll, and Wndyrstondynge be brought
To have knowynge þey ill wrought?
What ys þat xall make me clene?
Put yt, Lorde, into my thowte!
Thi olde mercy let me remene.

899 consider 900 peril 901 disfigured 905 unnatural 908 summoned back the Devil 911 concealed 913 done, love 914 do you cherish 917 yourself 919 destroy 920 expels 921 despise Me? 924 worthless? 926 offence 927 defiled, nature 928 in intelligence 931 seek, diligence (try your best) 933 Through, true knowledge 935 we justly deserve 936 by 939 lifts, fallen 941 wholly given (over) 944 firmly ground 945 through, enable 946 gift 947 sick, curable 950 not 953 did wrong 954 is (it) 955 thought/mind 956 recover

[102] See Luke 8:2 for the analogous case of seven devils being cast out of Mary Magdalene.

[103] 'Why do you give to My enemy what I have created [i.e. the soul]? Why do you follow his advice and set little store by Mine?'

[104] 'The Resurrection and the life'. John 11:25.

WYSDOM
Thow þe Soule mynde take
Ande wndyrstondynge of hys synnys allwey,
Beynge in wyll, yt forsake,
Yit thes do not only synnys awey,[105]
But very contrycyon, who þat have may,
Þat ys purger and clenser of synne.
A tere of þe ey, wyth sorow veray,
Þat rubbyt and waschyt þe Soule wythin.

All þe penance þat may be wrought,
Ne all þe preyer þat seyde be kan,
Wythowt sorowe of hert relesyt nought;[106]
That in especyall reformyth man
Ande makyt hym as clene as when he begane.
Go seke þis medsyne, Soull, þat beseke
Wyth veray feythe, and be ye sekyr, than
The vengeaunce of Gode ys made full meke.

By wndyrstondynge have very contrycyon,
Wyth mynde of your synne confessyon make,
Wyt[h] wyll yeldynge du satysfaccyon;
Þan yowr soule be clene, I wndyrtake.

ANIMA
I wepe for sorow, Lorde! I begyn awake,
I that þis longe hath slumberyde in syne.

Hic recedunt demones.

WYSDOM
Lo, how contrycyon avoydyth þe duellys
blake!
Dedly synne ys non yow wythin.

For Gode ye have offendyde hyg[h]ly
Ande yowr modyr, Holy Chyrche, so mylde,
Þerfor Gode ye must aske mercy,
By Holy Chyrch to be reconsylyde,
Trustynge verely ye xall newver be revylyde
Yff ye have yowr charter of pardon by confessyon.
Now have ye foryeffnes þat were fylyde.[107]
Go prey yowr modyr Chyrche of her proteccyon.

ANIMA
O Fadyr of [mercy] ande of comfort,
Wyth wepynge ey and hert contryte,
To owr modyr, Holy Chyrche, I wyll resort,
My lyff pleyn schewenge to here syght.
Wyth Mynde, Undyrstondynge, and Wyll ryght,
Wyche of my Sowll þe partyes be.
To þe domys of þe Chyrche we xall us dyght,
Wyth veray contricyon thus co[m]pleynnyng we.

Here þey go owt, and in þe goynge þe Soule syngyth in þe most lame[n]tabull wyse, wyth drawte notys as yt ys songyn in þe Passyon Wyke:[108]

ANIMA
*Magna velud mare contricio, contricio tua: quis consoletur
tue?*
*Plorans ploravit in nocte, et lacrime ejus in maxillis
ejus.*[109]

WYSDOM
Thus seth Gode mankynde tyll
The nyne poyntys ples Hym all other before.[110]
'Gyff a peny in thy lyve wyth goode wyll
To þe pore, and þat plesythe Gode more
Þa[n] mowyntenys into golde tramposyde wore
Ande aftyr they dethe for the[e] dysposyde.'[111]
Ande all þe goodys þou hast in store
Xulde not profyght so moche wan þi body ys
closyde.

The secunde poynt, Gode seth thus:
'Wepe on tere for My love hertyly,
Or for þe Passyon of Me, Jhesus,
Ande þat plesyt Me more specyally
Than yff þou wepte for þi frendys or goodys worldly

958 in every way 959 forsake (sin) 961 Only true contrition 963 tear, eye 964 scours, washes, inwardly 965 (Not) all, done 968 particularly 970 seek, medicine, beg 971 true faith, certain, then 972 mild 975 due 976 Then 977 to wake 978+ Here the demons depart 979 banishes, black devils 980 no (longer) 983 (of) God 985 rejected 988 for 992 openly revealing, her 994 are the parts 995 judgements, apply ourselves 999 says, to mankind 1000 These nine things 1001 while you live 1002 poor 1006 enclosed (in a coffin) 1008 one tear, from the heart

[105] 'Yet this alone will not remove your sins'.

[106] '[All these] can release nothing without sorrow in the heart'.

[107] 'Now you who were defiled have forgiveness.'

[108] Anima is to sing 'in a lamentable manner, with long drawn-out notes, as it [the verse] is sung during Passion Week'. The following lines were part of the service for Holy Thursday.

[109] Compare Lamentations 2:13 and 1:2: '[Greater than] the sea is thy breach, who can heal you? . . . She weepeth sore in the night, and her tears are on her cheeks'.

[110] Wisdom's speech is drawn from the *Novem Virtutes*, attributed to Richard Rolle. See Eccles, *Macro Plays*, p. 215.

[111] 'Than [if] mountains were turned into gold and donated in your name after your death.'

As moche water as þe se conteynys'.
Lo, contrycyon ys a soveren remedy.
That dystroythe synnys, þat relessyt peynys.

The [third], Gode sethe: 'Suffer pacyenly for My love
Off þi neybure a worde of repreve,
Ande þat to mercy mor dothe Me move
Than þou dyscyplynyde þi body wyth peynys grewe
Wyth as many roddys as myght grow or [þ]rywe
In þe space of [one] days jornye.'
Lo, who suffyryth most for Gode ys most lewe,
Slandyr, repreve, ony adversyte.

The [fourth], Gode sethe: 'Wake on owyr for þe love of Me,[112]
And þat to Me ys more plesaunce
Than yff þou sent xii kyngys free
To My sepulkyr wyth grett puysschaunce
For My dethe to take vengeaunce.'
Lo, wakynge ys a holy thynge.
Þer yt ys hade wyth goode usance,
Many gracys of yt doth sprynge.

The [fifth], Gode sethe: 'Have pyte and compassyon
Off þi neybur wyche ys seke and nedy,
And þat to Me ys more dylectacyon
Than þou fastyde [forty] yer by and by,
Thre days in þe weke, as streytly
As þou cowdys in water and brede'.
Lo, pyte Gode plesyth grettly,
Ande yt ys a vertu soveren, as clerkys rede.

The [sixth], Gode seth on þis wyse:
'Refreyn thy speche for My reverens,
Lett not thy tonge thy evyn-Crysten dyspyse,
Ande þan plesyst [þou] more Myn Excellens
Than yff þou laberyde wyth grett dylygens
Wpon thy nakyde feet and bare
Tyll þe blode folwude for peyn and vyolens
Ande aftyr eche stepe yt sene were'.

The [seventh], Cryst seth in þis maner:
'Thy neybur to ewyll ne sterre not thou,
But all thynge torne into wertu chere,[113]
A[n]d than more plesyst [þou] Me now
Then yf a thowsende tymys þou renne thorow
A busche of thornys þat scharpe were
Tyll þi nakyde body were all rough
Ande evyn rent to þe bonys bare.'

The [eighth], Gode sethe þis man tyll:
'Oftyn pray and aske of Me,
Ande þat plesythe Me more onto My wyll
Than yf My modyr and all sentys preyde for þe[e].'

The [ninth], Gode sethe: 'Lowe Me soverenly,
Ande þat to Me more plesant ys
Than yf þou went wpon a pyler of tre
Þat wer sett full of scharpe prykkys
So þat þou cut þi flesche into þe smale partys.'
Lo, Gode ys plesyde more wyth þe dedys of charyte
Than all þe peynys man may suffer iwys.
Remembyr thes poyntys, man, in þi felycite!

Here entrethe Anima, wyth þe [Five] Wyttys goynge before, Mynde, on þe on[e] syde and Wndyrstondynge on þe other syde and Wyll folowyng, all in here fyrst clothynge, her chapplettys and crestys, and all havying on crownys, syngynge in here commynge in: 'Quid retribuam Domino pro omnibus que retribuit mihi? Calicem salutaris accipiam et nomen Domino invocabo'.[114]

ANIMA
O meke Jhesu, to þe[e] I crye!
O swet Jhesu, my delectacyon!
O Jhesu, þe sune of Vyrgyne Marye,
Full of mercy and compassyon!
My soule ys waschede be Thy Passyon
Fro þe synnys cummynge by sensualyte.
A, be The[e] I have a new resurreccyon.
The lyght of grace I fele in me.

In tweyn myghtys of my soule I The[e] offendyde:
The on by my inwarde wyttys, thow ben gostly;
Þe other by my outwarde wyttys comprehendyde,
Tho be þe [five] wyttys bodyly;

1012 sea contains 1014 remits pains (of penance) 1015 patiently 1016 From, neighbour, reproof 1017 moves Me more to mercy 1018 (if) you, grievous pains 1019 (birch) rods, flourish 1021 safe (from) 1022 slander, (or) any 1024 pleasing 1025 noble kings 1026 sepulchre (in Jerusalem), military strength 1029 when it's done properly 1030 from it 1032 sick and needy 1033 delightful 1034 (if) you fasted, years 1035 strictly 1036 could, on, bread 1038 advise 1039 in this way 1040 Moderate, 1041 slander, fellow Christian(s) 1042 you please 1043 laboured 1045 blood flowed, pain, violence 1046 was seen after each step 1051 ran through 1052 a sharp thorn-bush 1053 lacerated 1054 cut, bare bones 1055 to mankind 1058 saints, prayed 1059 Love Me above all else 1061 wooden pillar 1062 was, spikes 1063 small pieces 1069 son 1075 two powers 1076 those that are spiritual 1078 Those are

112 'Keep a vigil for one hour for love of Me'.

113 'Do not provoke your neighbour to evil, but turn all things into precious virtues'.

114 'What shall I render unto the Lord for all His benefits toward me? I will take the cup of salvation and call upon the name of the Lord.' Psalms 116:12–13.

Wyth þe wyche tweyn myghtys mercy I crye.
My modyr, Holy Chyrche, hath yowe me grace,
Whom ye fyrst toke to yowr mercy,
Yet of myselff I may not satysfye my trespas.

Magna est misericordia tua![115]
Wyth full feyth of foryewenes to Þe[e], Lorde, I come.

WYSDOM

Vulnerasti cor meum, soror mea, sponsa,
In uno ictu oculorum tuorum.[116]

Ye have wondyde My hert, syster, spowse dere,
In þe tweyn syghtys of yowr ey:
By þe recognycyon ye have clere,
Ande by þe hye lowe ye have godly.
It perrysschyt Me hert to here yow crye,
Now ye have forsake synne and be contryte.
Ye were never so leve to Me verelye.
Now be ye reformyde to yowr bewtys bryght.

Ande ther yowr [five] wyttys offendyde has,
Ande to mak asythe be impotent,
My fyve wyttys, þat never dyde trespas,
Hath made asythe to þe Father suffycyent.
Wyth My syght I se þe people vyolent,
I herde hem vengeaunce onto Me call,
I s[m]elte þe stenche of caren here present,
I tastyde þe drynke mengylde wyth gall,

By towchynge I felt peyns smerte.
My handys sprede abrode to halse þi swyre;
My fete naylyde to abyde wyth þe[e], swet herte;
My hert clowyn for þi love most dere;
Myn hede bowhede down to kys þe[e] here;
My body full of holys, as a dovehows.
In thys ye be reformyde, Soule, My plesere,
Ande now ye be þe very temple of Jhesus.

Fyrst ye were reformyde by baptyme of ygnorans
And clensyde from þe synnys orygynall,
Ande now ye be reformyde by þe sakyrment of penance
Ande clensyde from þe synnys actuall.[117]
Now ye be fayrest, Crystys own specyall;
Dysfygure yow never to þe lyknes of þe Fende.
Now ye have receyvyde þe crownnys victoryall
To regne in blys wythowtyn ende.

MYNDE

Have mynde, Soule, wat Gode hath do,
Reformyde yow in feyth veryly.
Nolite conformari huic seculo
Sed reformamini in novitate spiritus sensus vestri:[118]
Conforme yow not to þis pompyus glory
But reforme in gostly felynge.
Ye þat were dammyde by synn endelesly,
Mercy hathe reformyde yow ande crownyde as a kynge.

UNDERSTONDYNG

Take undyrstondynge, Soule, now ye
Wyth contynuall hope in Godys behest.
Renovamini spiritu mentis vestre
Et induite novum hominem, qui secundum Deum creatus est:[119]
Ye be reformyde in felynge, not only as a best,
But also in þe over parte of yowr reasun,
By wyche ye have lyknes of Gode mest
Ande of þat mercyfull very congnycyon.

WYLL

Now þe Soule yn charyte reformyde ys,
Wyche charyte ys Gode verely.
Exspoliantem veterem hominem cum actibus suis:[120]
Spoyll yow of yowr olde synnys and foly
Ande be renuyde in God[es] knowynge ageyn,
That enduyde wyth grace so specyally,
Conservynge in peyn, ever in blys for to reyn.

1080 given 1082 by, atone (for) 1084 forgiveness 1087 wounded 1088 eye(s) 1090 love 1091 perishes kills, hear 1093 dear 1094 beauty 1095 where 1096 incapable of atoning 1097 did 1098 sufficient (for you) 1100 heard, unto 1101 carrion 1102 mingled (see Matthew 27:34) 1103 sharp pains 1104 wide, embrace, neck 1105 nailed 1106 cloven 1107 bowed 1108 (as) full, holes, dovehouse 1109 pleasure 1111 from ignorance 1113 sacrament 1116 Never disfigure yourself into 1117 victorious crown 1119 Remember, done 1123 pompous 1126 command 1131 beast 1132 superior 1133 (most) resemblance to God 1134 merciful (one), true knowledge 1138 divest yourself 1139 renewed, knowledge of God 1140 endowed (you) 1141 Protecting (you) from, reign

115 'For Thy mercy is great.' Psalms 108:4.

116 'Thou hast ravished my heart, my sister, my spouse; . . . with one [stroke/glance] of thine eyes.' Song of Songs 4:9.

117 i.e. those sins actually committed during life (as opposed to original sin, which is inherited).

118 'Be not conformed to this world, but be ye transformed by the renewing of your [spiritual senses].' Romans 12:2.

119 'Be renewed in the spirit of your mind, and . . . put on the new man, which after [God's likeness] is created.' Ephesians 4:23–4.

120 'Put off the old man with his deeds.' Colossians 3:9.

ANIMA
Then wyth yow thre I may sey this
Of owr Lorde, Soveren Person, Jhesus:
Suavis est Dominus universis,
Et miseraciones ejus super omnia opera ijus.[121]
O Thou hye Soveren Wysdam, my joy, *Cristus*,
Hewyn, Erthe, and eche creature
Yelde Yow reverens, for grace pleyntuus
Ye yeff to man, ever to induyr.

Now wyth Sent Powle we may sey thus
Þat be reformyde thorow feythe in Jhesum:
We have peas and acorde betwyx Gode and ws,
Justificati ex fide pacem habemus ad Deum.[122]
Now to Salamonys conclusyon I com:
Timor Domini incium sapiencie.[123]
Vobis qui timetis Deum
Orietur sol justicie:[124]

The tru son of ryghtusnes,
Wyche þat ys [owr] Lorde Jhesu,
Xall sprynge in hem þat drede Hys meknes.
Nowe ye mut every soule renewe.
In grace, and vycys to eschew,
Ande so to ende wyth perfeccyon.
That þe doctryne of Wysdom we may sew,
Sapiencia Patris, grawnt þat for Hys Passyon!

1146 Christ 1147 Heaven 1148 Give, plentiful 1149 give, endure 1151 we (who) are, Jesus 1152 peace, concord 1154 Solomon's 1158 sun/Son 1159 Which is 1160 meekness 1161 must 1164 beg 1165 The wisdom of the Father

[121] 'The Lord is good to all; and His tender mercies are over all His works.' Psalm 144:9.
[122] 'Being justified by faith, we have peace with God.' Romans 5:1.
[123] 'The fear of the Lord is the beginning of [wisdom].' Proverbs 1:7. See also Psalms 111:10, Ecclesiasticus 1:16.
[124] 'Unto you that fear [God] shall the sun of righteousness arise.' See Malachi 4:2.

The Luttrell Psalter (British Library MS), f. 170V. The British Library.

Mankind

Mankind is perhaps the liveliest and most inherently theatrical of the early Moralities. On the strength of internal evidence (the references to new coins and to King Edward at ll. 465–6 and 690–4) it can be safely dated to the period 1465–70 during the reign of Edward IV. Its precise origins cannot be definitively determined, but the distinctive linguistic forms employed (notably the use of 'x' for 'sh' in words such as 'xulde' and 'xall', which was also evident in the N-Town *Mary Play*), suggest that the text has East Anglian origins, and allusions within the play to villages in East Anglia suggest it was intended to be performed in the area around Cambridge and the environs of Lynn in Norfolk. The references to tapsters, an ostler, going out into the 'yard', and the goodman of the house (ll. 274, 733, 562, 468) have led scholars to assume performances in inns or inn-yards were the norm, but these allusions may equally point towards noble or gentry houses in the area. Certainly itinerant performances by a professional company seem likely, given the small size of the cast required (seven adults, or only six if the actor playing Mercy doubles as Titivillus), and the novel means of raising money that the play reveals. The latter is achieved by the simple expedient of pausing the performance just prior to its most arresting theatrical moment, the arrival on-stage of Titivillus, in order to pass around a hat. The devil calls from offstage, while the other Vices assure the audience of the entertaining spectacle he will provide (with his 'big head', which was probably an elaborate mask, and comic antics), and insist that he will not appear until sufficient money is raised to make it worthwhile.

True to the traditions of the Morality Play, *Mankind* takes its eponymous Everyman hero from innocence, through temptation and fall, to repentance and redemption. Also characteristic of the moral drama is the way in which the audience is drawn to share that experience of fall and rise through the manipulation of their affiliations with the characters. In the opening movement of the play, the vigorous language and theatrical exuberance of the Vices (evident in their horseplay and scatological jokes and songs) appear more attractive than the rather heavy didacticism of the old scholar, Mercy, inducing the spectators to share in Mankind's seduction. Once the hero's fall has been engineered, however, the serious consequences of dalliance with sin are signalled by a marked shift in the presentation of the Vices. Both Mischief and New Guise are far more menacing and sinister figures when they return after l. 612, a change marked both visually (by the broken halter around New Guise's neck, and the chains hanging from Mischief's arms) and psychologically (by Mischief's boasts of murder, theft, and what sounds very like the rape of the jailer's wife, and New Guise's declaration that theft and murder are now 'the new fashion'). Mischief's attempt to persuade Mankind to hang himself in despair signals most clearly his devilish associations.

The play is as sophisticated linguistically as it is dramaturgically. While the battle for the soul of Mankind is fought over issues of personal morality, language itself provides both the most effective weapon employed in the struggle, and the principal indicator of its progress. At each point the protagonist's affiliations are signalled not only by the company he keeps, but by the kind of language he employs. While Mercy exerts his influence upon Mankind (during the stages of innocence, repentance, and redemption) he uses the highly Latinate, 'learned' vocabulary and the four-line stanzaic form of the Virtue. Once he has fallen into sin, he quickly adopts the more demotic vocabulary and faster-paced eight-line stanzas of the Vices. Thus the distinctive rhythms and cadences of the spoken word alert the audience at all times to the fortunes of the hero and the status of his soul.

The play survives in a single text, the so-called Macro manuscript, now Folger Shakespeare Library MS Va. 354, which also contains the fuller version of *Wisdom*. For this edition I have used the facsimiles in D. Bevington, ed., *The Macro Plays: The Castle of Perseverance, Wisdom, Mankind* (Washington, D. C., 1972), and J.S. Farmer, ed., *Mankind*, Tudor Facsimile Texts (Amersham, 1914). I have also consulted the following modern editions: M. Eccles, ed., *The Macro Plays*, EETS os 262 (Oxford, 1969); D. Bevington, ed., *Medieval Drama* (Boston, 1975); and John C. Coldewey, ed., *Early English Drama: An Anthology* (New York, 1993).

[*Dramatis Personae*: *Mercy*, *Mischeff* (Mischief, the chief Vice), *Nowadays*, *New Guise* ('New Fashion'), *Nought ('Nothing')* (three Vices), *Mankynde*, *Titivillus* (a devil),[1] *various Minstrels*.]

MERCY

The very Fownder and Begynner of owr fyrst creacyon
Amonge ws synfull wrechys He oweth to be magnyfyede,
Þat for owr dysobedyence He hade non indygnacyon
To sende Hys own Son to be torn and crucyfyede.
Owr obsequyouse servyce to hym xulde be aplyede,
Where He was Lorde of all and made all thynge of nought,
For þe synnfull synnere to hade hym revyvyde
And for hys redempcyon sett Hys own Son at nought.

Yt may be seyde and veryfyede, mankynde was dere bought.
By þe pytuose deth of Jhesu he hade hys remedye.
He was purgyde of hys defawte þat wrechydly hade wrought
By Hys gloryus passyon, þat blyssyde lavatorye.
O soverence, I beseche yow yowr condycyons to rectyfye

2 ought, glorified 3 was not too angry 5 devoted 7 have 9 dearly redeemed 11 purged 12 purifier 13 sovereigns/'my masters'

[1] Titivillus's traditional role was to collect all the idle words spoken in churches (when folk should have been attending to the service) and the Latin errors committed by priests, and store them in a large wallet or bag for use as evidence against the speakers on the Day of Judgement. The idea stems from Christ's words in Matthew 12:36: 'But I say unto you, that every idle word that men shall speak they shall give account thereof on the Day of Judgement.'

And wyth humylite and reverence to have a remocyon
To þis Blyssyde Prynce þat owr nature doth gloryfye,
Þat ȝe may be partycypable of Hys retribucyon.

I have be þe very mene for yowr restytucyon.
Mercy ys my name, þat mornyth for yowr offence.
Dyverte not yowrsylffe in tyme of temtacyon,
Þat ȝe may be acceptable to Gode at yowr goyng hence.
Þe grett mercy of Gode, þat ys of most preemmynence,
Be medyacyon of Owr Lady þat ys ever habundante
To þe synfull creature þat wyll repent hys neclygence.
I prey Gode at yowr most nede þat mercy be yowr defendawnte.

In goode werkys I awyse yow, soverence, to be perseverante
To puryfye yowr sowlys, þat þei not corupte;
For yowr gostly enmy wyll make hys avaunte,
Yowr goode condycyons yf he may interrupte.

O ȝe soverens þat sytt and ȝe brothern þat stonde ryght uppe,[2]
Pryke not yowr felycytes in thyngys transytorye.
Beholde not þe Erth, but lyfte yowr ey wppe.
Se how þe hede þe members dayly do magnyfye,
Who ys þe hede forsoth I xall yow certyfye:
I mene owr Savyowr, þat was lykynnyde to a lambe;
Ande Hys sayntys be þe members þat dayly He doth satysfye
Wyth þe precyose rever þat runnyth from Hys wombe.[3]

Ther ys non such foode, be water nor by londe,
So precyouse, so gloryouse, so nedefull to owr entent,
For yt hath dyssolvyde mankynde from þe bytter bonde
Of þe mortall enmye, þat vemynousse serpente,
From þe wyche Gode preserve yow all at þe Last Judgment!
For sekyrly þe[r] xall be a streyt examynacyon,
The corn xall be savyde, þe chaffe xall be brente.[4]
I besech yow hertyly, have þis premedytacyon.

MYSCHEFFE
I beseche yow hertyly, leve yowr calcacyon.
Leve yowr chaffe, leve yowr corn, leve yowr dalyacyon.
Yowr wytt ys lytyll, yowr hede ys mekyll, ȝe are full of predycacyon.[5]
But, ser, I prey þis questyon to claryfye:
Mysse-masche, dryff-draff.
Sume was corn and sume was chaffe,
My dame seyde my name was Raffe;
Onschett yowr lokke and taken an halpenye.

MERCY
Why com ȝe hethyr, broþer? Ȝe were not dysyryde.

MYSCHEFF
For a wynter corn-threscher, ser, I have hyryde,
Ande ȝe sayde þe corn xulde be savyde and þe chaff xulde be feryde,
Ande, he provyth nay, as yt schewth be þis werse:
'Corn *servit bredibus*, chaffe *horsibus*, straw *fyrybusque*.'[6]
Thys ys as moche to say, to yowr leude wndyrstondynge,
As þe corn xall serve to brede at þe nexte bakynge.
'Chaff *horseybus et reliqua*',[7]
The chaff to horse xall be goode provente,
When a man ys forcolde þe straw may be brent,
And so forth, *et cetera*.

MERCY
Avoyde, goode broþer! Ȝe ben culpable
To interrupte thus my talkyng delectable.

14 a leaning 16 a participant, redemption 18 who mourns 22 generous 24 guardian 27 enemy, boast 30 Don't stake your happiness on 31 eyes upwards 32 head, limbs, glorify 33 tell you truly 39 released 42 strict 43 burnt 44 keep this in mind 45 threshing 46 dallying 50 some 52 open, half-penny 53 desired/sent for 54 hired 55 fired 56 by, verse 58 lewd/unlearned 61 provender 64 Go away!

[2] The distinctions between seated (socially elite) and standing (inferior) spectators suggests that a performance in a great hall is envisaged, with benches along the sides for gentle diners and a large standing crowd around the entrances. See Walker, *The Politics of Peformance in Early Renaissance Drama* ch. 2.

[3] 'With the precious river [of blood] that flows from his side.' For the image of Christ as the bleeding sacrificial lamb, see Revelation 7:9–17; for Christ as the head and Christian believers as the members of the body, see Colossians 1:18; 1 Corinthians 12:27.

[4] For Christ's likening of the Last Judgement to a threshing floor, see Matthew 3:12; Luke 3:17.

[5] 'Your intelligence is small, although your head is large, you're full of preaching.'

[6] Mock Latin, suggesting 'Corn serves for bread, chaff for horses, straw for fires.'

[7] 'And the rest.'

MYSCHEFF
Ser, I have noþer horse nor sadyll.
Therfor I may not ryde.

MERCY
Hye yow forth on fote, brother, in Godys name!

MYSCHEFF
I say, ser, I am cumme hedyr to make yow game,
3et bade 3e me not go out in þe Devllys name
Ande I wyll abyde . . .[8]

[NEW GYSE]
Ande how, mynstrellys, pley þe comyn trace!
Ley on wiyth þi ballys tyll hys bely breste!

NOUGHT
I putt case I breke my neke: how than?

NEW GYSE
I gyff no force, by Sent Tanne!

NOWADAYS
Leppe about lyvely! þou art a wyght man.
Lett ws be mery wyll we be here!

NOUGHT
Xall I breke my neke to schew yow sporte?

NOWADAYS
Therfor ever be ware of þi reporte.

NOUGHT
I beschrew ye all! Her ys a schrewde sorte.
Have þeratt þen wyth a mery chere!

Her[e] þei daunc[e], Mercy seyth:

[MERCY]
Do wey, do wey þis reull, sers! Do wey!

NOWADAYS
Do wey, goode Adam? Do wey?
Thys ys no parte of þi pley.

NOUGHT
3ys, mary, I prey yow, for I love not þis rewelynge.
Cum forth, goode fader, I yow prey!
Be a lytyll 3e may assay.
Anon of wyth yowr clothes, yf 3e wyll play.
Go to! for I have hade a praty scottylynge.

MERCY
Nay, brother, I wyll not daunce.

NEW GYSE
Yf 3e wyll, ser, my brother wyll make yow to
prawnce.

NOWADAYS
Wyth all my herte, ser, yf I may yow avaunce.
3e may assay be a lytyll trace.

NOUGHT
3e, ser, wyll 3e do well,
Trace not wyth þem, be my cownsell,
For I have tracyed sumwhat to fell;
I tell yt ys a narow space.

But, ser, I trow of ws thre I herde yow speke.

NEW GYSE
Crystys curse hade þerfor, for I was in slepe.

NOWADAYS
A[nd] I hade þe cuppe in my honde, redy to goo to
met.
Therfor, ser, curtly, grett yow well.

MERCY
Few wordys, few and well sett!

NEW GYSE
Ser, yt ys þe new gyse and þe new jett.
Many wordys and schortely sett,
Thys ys þe new gyse, every-dele.

MERCY
Lady, helpe! how wrechys delyte in þer synfull weys!

72 'The Common Dance' 73 bellows (bagpipe?), belly 74 What if, what then 75 Don't care, St Anne 76 leap, manly 77 while 79 talk 80 curse, villainous bunch 81 Let's go for it, merrily 82 Stop this behaviour 83 (i.e. old man) 84 none of your business 85 revelling 87 try a little (dancing) 88 off 89 scuttling/capering 91 prance 92 assist you 96 too fiercely 97 (very) confined 99 have, asleep 100 to eat 101 (speak) briefly 102 said 103 fashion 105 in all things

8 A leaf is missing from the manuscript at this point. In the lost portion, Mischief clearly exits and Nowadays, New Gyse, and Nought enter, summoned (as they claim) by Mercy having spoken their names. The action resumes with the two other vices encouraging Nought to dance to music played by the minstrels.

Nowadays
Say not ageyn þe new gyse nowadays!
Þou xall fynde ws sch[r]ewys at all assays.
Be ware! ȝe may son lyke a bofett.

Mercy
He was well occupyde þat browte yow brethern.

Nought
I harde yow call 'New Gyse, Nowadays, Nought,' all
þes thre togethere.
Yf ȝe sey þat I lye, I xall make yow to slyther.
Lo, take yow here a trepett!

Mercy
Say me yowr namys, I know yow not.

New Gyse
New Gyse, I.

[Nowadays]
I, Nowadays.

[Nought]
I, Nought.

Mercy
Be Jhesu Cryst þat me dere bowte,
ȝe betray many men.

New Gyse
Betray! nay, nay, ser, nay, nay!
We make them both fresch and gay.
But of yowr name, ser, I yow prey,
That we may yow ken.

Mercy
Mercy ys my name, by denomynacyon.
I conseyve ȝe have but a lytyll favour in my
communycacyon.[9]

New Gyse
Ey, ey! yowr body ys full of Englysch Laten.
I am aferde yt wyll brest.
'*Pravo te*', quod þe bocher onto me,
When I stale a leg a motun.
ȝe are a stronge cunnyng clerke.

Nowadays
I prey yow hertyly, worschyppull clerke,
To have þis Englysch mad in Laten:

'I have etun a dyschfull of curdys,
Ande I have schetun yowr mowth full of turdys,'
Now opyn yowr sachell wyth Laten wordys
Ande sey me þis in clerycall manere!
Also I have a wyf, her name ys Rachell;
Betuyx her and me was a gret batell;
Ande fayn of yow I wolde here tell
Who was þe most master.[10]

Nought
Thy wyf Rachell, I dare ley twenti lyse.

Nowadays
Who spake to þe[e], foll? Þou art not wyse!
Go and do þat longyth to þin offyce:
Osculare fundamentum![12]

Nought
Lo, master, lo, here ys a pardon bely-mett.
Yt ys grawntyde of Pope Pokett,[13]
Yf ȝe wyll putt yowr nose in hys wyffys sokett,
ȝe xall have forty days of pardon.

Mercy
Thys ydyll language ȝe xall repent.
Out of þis place I wolde ȝe went.

New Gyse
Goo we hens all thre wyth on assent.
My fadyr ys yrke of owr eloquence.[14]
Þerfor I wyll no lenger tary.
Gode brynge yow, master, and blyssyde Mary,
To þe number of þe demonycall frayry![15]

107 Don't speak against 108 us villains in all things 109 soon, buffet/blow 110 employed, brothers 111 heard 112 grovel 113 trip 114 Tell 116 By 122 designation 124 Latinized English 126 'Damn you', butcher 127 stole, of mutton 130 translated into 131 eaten, curds 132 shit, turds 134 tell, scholarly fashion 136 Between, battle 139 wager 20 lice[11] 140 fool 143 to satisfy the belly 145 his wife's hole 147 idle/worthless 149 of one opinion

9 'I see that you take little pleasure in what I am saying.'
10 'I'd gladly hear you tell [me], which of us was the greater master.'
11 Or possibly '20 li's', i.e. £20.
12 'Go and do that which is appropriate to your job [as a fool]: kiss my arse!'
13 'Granted by Pope Wallet': i.e. bought with bribes.
14 'My father [i.e. this priest] is irritated by our eloquence.'
15 'Into the brotherhood of the friary of Hell.'

Nowadays
Cum wynde, cum reyn,
Thow I cumme never ageyn!
Þe Deull put out both yowr eyn!
Felouse, go we hens tyght.

Nought
Go we hens, a Devll wey!
Here ys þe dore, her ys þe wey.
Farwell, jentyll Jaffrey,
I prey Gode gyf yow goode nyght.

Exiant simul, cantent.[16]

Mercy
Thankyde be Gode, we have a fayer dylyverance
Of þes thre onthryfty gestys.
They know full lytyll what ys þer ordynance.
I preve by reson þei be wers þen bestys:

A best doth after hys naturall instytucyon;
ȝe may conseve by there dysporte and behavour,
Þer joy ande delyte ys in derysyon
Of her owyn Cryste, to Hys dyshonur.

Thys condycyon of levyng, yt ys prejudycyall;
Be ware þerof, yt ys wers þan ony felony or treson.
How may yt be excusyde befor þe Justyce of all
When for every ydyll worde we must ȝelde a reson?

They have grett ease, þerfor þei wyll take no thought.
But how þen when þe angell of Hewyn xall blow þe trumpe
Ande sey to þe transgressors þat wykkydly hath wrought,
'Cum forth onto yowr Juge and ȝelde yowr acownte'?

Then xall I, Mercy, begyn sore to wepe;
Noþer comfort nor cownsell þer xall non be hade;
But such as þei have sowyn, such xall þei repe.[17]
Þei be wanton now, but þen xall þei be sade.

The goode New Gyse nowadays I wyll not dysalow.
I dyscomende þe vycyouse gyse; I prey have me excusyde,
I nede not to speke of yt, yowr reson wyll tell it yow.
Take þat ys to be takyn and leve þat ys to be refusyde.[18]

[*Enter Mankynde carrying a spade.*]

Mankynde
Of þe erth and of þe cley we have owr propagacyon.
By þe prouydens of Gode þus be we deryvatt,
To Whos mercy I recomende þis holl congrygacyon:
I hope onto Hys blysse ye be all predestynatt.

Every man for hys degre I trust xall be partycypatt,
Yf we wyll mortyfye owr carnall condycyon
Ande owr voluntarye dysyres, þat ever be pervercyonatt,
To renunce þem and yelde ws wnder Godys provycyon.[19]

My name ys Mankynde, I have my composycyon
Of a body and of a soull, of condycyon contrarye.
Betwyx þem tweyn ys a grett dyvisyon;
He þat xulde be subjecte, now he hath þe victory.

Thys ys to me a lamentable story;
To se my flesch of my soull to have governance.[20]
Wher þe goodewyff ys master, þe goodeman may be sory!
I may both syth and sobbe, þis ys a pytuose remembrance.

O thou, my soull, so sotyll in thy substance,
Alasse, what was þi fortune and þi chaunce
To be assocyat wyth my flesch, þat stynkyng dungehyll?
Lady, helpe! Soverens, yt doth my soull myche yll

To se þe flesch prosperouse and þe soull trodyn wnder fot

154 rain **156** eyes! **157** Fellows, at once **158** in the Devil's way **159** door **163** worthless guests **164** duty **165** worse than beasts **166** instinct **167** understand **170** living **175** trumpet **176** behaved **177** account **180** reap **181** sad **186** our origins **187** derived **188** whole company **189** (pre)destined **194** I am composed **195** of contradictory natures **196** struggle **197** (i.e. the body) **201** sigh, sob, pitiful thought **206** foot

16 'Let them leave together, singing.'

17 Galatians 6:7.

18 'I will not condemn today's virtuous fashions, I criticize [only] those evil fashions: I pray that you will excuse me. I have no need to mention it, really, your own reason demonstrates the point to you. Take what is [good] to take, and leave that which should be rejected.'

19 'Every man will, I believe, share in [this salvation] according to his position in society, provided that we mortify our fleshly natures and [discipline] the desires of our will, that always tend towards perversion, and renounce them, giving ourselves up to God's providence.'

20 'To see my body have control over my soul.'

I xall go to yondyr man and asay hym I wyll.
I trust of gostly solace he wyll be my bote.

All heyll, semely father! Ȝe be welcom to þis house.
Of þe very wysdam ȝe have partycypacyon.
My body wyth my soull ys ever querulose.
I prey yow, for sent charyte, of yowr supportacyon.

I beseche yow hertyly of yowr gostly comforte.
I am onstedfast in lywynge; my name ys Mankynde.
My gostly enmy þe Devll wyll have a grett dysporte
In synfull gydynge yf he may se me ende.[21]

MERCY
Cryst sende yow goode comforte! Ȝe be welcum, my frende,
Stonde wppe on yowr fete, I prey yow aryse.
My name ys Mercy; ȝe be to me full hende.
To eschew vyce I wyll yow avyse.

MANKYNDE
O Mercy, of all grace and vertu ȝe are þe well,
I have herde tell of ryght worschyppfull clerkys.
Ȝe be aproxymatt to Gode and nere of Hys consell;
He hat instytut you above all Hys werkys.

O, yowr lovely wordys to my soull are swetere þen hony.

MERCY
The temptacyon of þe flesch ȝe must resyst lyke a man,
For þer ys ever a batell betwyx þe soull and þe body:
'*Vita hominis est milicia super terram.*'[22]

Oppresse yowr gostly enmy and be Crystys own knyght.
Be never a cowarde ageyn yowr adversary.
Yf ȝe wyll be crownyde, ȝe must nedys fyght.
Intende well and Gode wyll be yow adjutory.

Remember, my frende, þe tyme of contynuance.
So helpe me Gode, yt ys but a chery tyme.[23]
Spende yt well; serve Gode wyth hertys affyance.
Dystempure not yowr brayn wyth goode ale nor wyth wyn.

Mesure ys tresure. Y forbyde yow not þe use.[24]
Mesure yowrsylf ever; be ware of excess.
Þe superfluouse gyse I wyll þat ȝe refuse.
When nature ys suffysyde, anon þat ȝe sese.

Yf a man have an hors and kepe hym not to hye,
He may then reull hym at hys own dysyere.
Yf he be fede overwell he wyll dysobey,
Ande in happe cast his master in þe myre.

NEW GYSE [*from off-stage*]
Ȝe sey trew, ser, ȝe are no faytour.
I have fede my wyff so well tyll sche ys my master.
I have a grett wonde on my hede, lo! and þeron leyth a playster,
Ande anoþer þer I pysse my peson.
Ande my wyf were yowr hors, sche wolde yow all to-banne.
Ȝe fede yowr hors in mesure, ȝe are a wyse man.
I trow and ȝe were þe kyngys palfreyman,
A goode horse xulde be gesumme.[25]

MANKYND[E]
Wher spekys þis felow? Wyll he not com nere?

MERCY
All to son, my brother, I fere me, for yow.
He was here ryght now, by Hym þat bowte me dere,
Wyth oþer of hys felouse; þei kan moche sorow.

They wyll be here ryght son, yf I owt departe.
Thynke on my doctryne; yt xall be yowr defence.
Lerne wyll I am here, sett my wordys in herte.
Wythin a schorte space I must nedys hens.

NOWADAYS
Þe sonner þe lever, and yt be ewyn anon![26]
I trow yowr name ys Do Lytyll, ȝe be so long from hom.

208 comfort, aid 209 proper 210 true, a share 211 quarrelsome 212 holy charity 214 in (my) living 215 take great pleasure 220 (How) to, advise 221 the source 223 His intimate adviser 224 established 225 sweeter than honey 229 Defeat 230 against 231 crowned (in Heaven) 232 helper 233 your time (on Earth) 235 loyalty 236 Unsettle, wine 239 I advise you to 240 satisfied, stop at once 241 too lavishly 242 govern, desire 243 too well 244 perhaps, throw 247 wound, lies, plaster 248 where I piss 249 If, curse 250 moderately 254 too soon 256 know all about 258 teaching 259 while 260 have to leave

21 'In guiding me towards sin, if he can bring me to a bad end.'
22 'The life of man on Earth is a battle.' See Job 5:7, 7:1, 14:1.
23 'Cherry time': the brief duration of a cherry harvest.
24 'Moderation is [the greatest] treasure. I do not forbid you the use [of ale and wine, only the excessive abuse].'
25 'If you were the king's stableman, good horses would be scarce.'
26 'The sooner the better, even if it were right now!'

Yf ȝe wolde go hens, we xall cum everychon,
Mo þen a goode sorte.[27]
Ȝe have leve, I dare well say.
When ȝe wyll, go forth yowr wey.
Men have lytyll deynte of yowr pley,
Because ȝe make no sporte.

NOUGHT
Yowr potage xall be forcolde, ser; when wyll ȝe go dyn?
I have sen a man lost twenti noblys in as lytyll tyme;
Ȝet was not I, be Sent Qwyntyn,
For I was never worth a pottfull a wortys sythyn I was born.
My name ys Nought; I love well to make mery.
I have be sethen wyth þe comyn tapster of Bury.
And pleyde so longe þe foll þat I am ewyn wery.
Ȝyt xall I ber þer ageyn to-morn.[28]

MERCY
[*To Mankind*] I have moche care for yow, my own frende.
Yowr enmys wyll be here anon, þei make þer avaunte.
Thynke well in yow hert, yowr name ys Mankynde;
Be not wnkynde to Gode, I prey yow be Hys servante.

Be stedefast in condycyon; se ȝe be not varyant.
Lose not thorow foly þat ys bowte so dere.[29]
Gode wyll prove yow, son; ande yf þat ȝe be constant,
Of Hys blysse perpetuall ȝe xall be partener.

Ȝe may not have yowr intent at yowr fyrst dysyere.
Se þe grett pacyence of Job [in] tribulacyon;
Lyke as þe smyth trieth ern in þe feere,
So was he triede by Godys vysytacyon.[30]

He was of yowr nature and of yowr fragylyte;
Folow þe steppys of hym, my own swete son,
Ande sey as he seyde in yowr trobyll and adversyte;
'*Dominus dedit, Dominus abstulit; sicut sibi placuit,*
ita factum est; nomen Domini benedictum!'[31]

Moreover, in specyall I gyve yow in charge,
Be ware of New Gyse, Nowadays, and Nought,
Nyse in þer aray, in language þei be large;
To perverte yowr condycyons all þe menys xall be sowte.[32]

Gode son, intromytt not yowrsylff in þer cumpeny.
Þei harde not a masse þi[s] twelmonyth, I dare well say.
Gyff them non audyence; þei wyll tell yow many a lye.
Do truly yowr labure and kepe yowr halyday.

Be ware of Tytivillus, fo[r] he lesyth no wey,
Þat goth invysybull and wyll not be sen.
He wyll ronde in yowr ere and cast a nett before yowr ey.
He ys worst of þem all; Gode lett hym never then!

Yf ȝe dysples Gode, aske mercy anon,
Ellys Myscheff wyll be redy to brace yow in hys brydyll.
Kysse me now, my dere darlynge. Gode sche[l]de yow from yowr fon!
Do truly yowr labure and be never ydyll.

The blyssynge of Gode be wyth yow and wyth all þes worschyppull men!

MANKYNDE
Amen, for sent charyte, amen!

Now blyssyde be Jhesu! my soull ys well sacyatt
Wyth þe mellyfluose doctryne of þis worschyppfull man.
The rebellyn of my flesch now yt ys superatt,
Thankynge be Gode of þe commynge þat I kam.[33]

267 joy in your business **269** soup, dine **271** it wasn't me, St Quentin **272** cabbages **278** their boasts **281** fickle **283** test **284** (a) partaker **287** iron in the fire **294** I instruct you especially **296** Foolish, dress, loose **298** mix **300** pay them no attention **301** keep the holy-days **302** loses **304** whisper **305** prosper **306** displease **307** (Or) else, tie, bridle **308** foes **312** satisfied **313** mellifluous **314** rebellion, suppressed

27 'More than a good many [of us].'

28 'I've been with the common tapster of Bury [St Edmunds] since [we last met], and I've played the fool for so long [there] that even I am weary of it. But I'll go there again in the morning.' The common tapster was the (usually female) owner of a cheap drinking house.

29 'Don't lose through folly what has been bought so dearly [i.e. your salvation].'

30 The testing of Job is related in the biblical book of that name. For the image of testing metals in the fire, see Job 23:10.

31 Compare Job 1:21: '[T]he Lord gave, and the Lord hath taken away; [as was pleasing to him, so it was done], blessed be the name of the Lord'.

32 'They shall seek by all the means they can to pervert your endeavours.'

33 'Thank God that I came when I did.'

Her wyll I sytt and tytyll in þis papyr
The incomparable astat of my promycyon.
Worschypfull soverence, I have wretyn here
The gloryuse remembrance of my nobyll condycyon.

To have remos and memory of mysylff þus wretyn
yt ys,
To defende me from all superstycyus charmys:
'Memento, homo, quod cinis es et in cinerem reverteris.'
Lo, I ber on my bryst þe bagge of myn armys.[34]

NEW GYSE
The wether ys colde, Gode sende ws goode ferys!
'Cum sancto sanctus eris et cum perverso perverteris.'
'Ecce quam bonum et quam jocundum', quod þe Devll to
þe frerys,
'Habitare fratres in unum.'[35]

MANKYNDE
I her a felow speke; wyth hym I wyll not mell.
Thys erth wyth my spade I xall assay to delffe.
To eschew ydullnes, I do yt myn own selffe.
I prey Gode sende yt hys fusyon!

NOWADAYS
Make rom, sers, for we have be longe!
We wyll cum gyf yow a Crystemes songe.

NOUGHT
Now I prey all þe yemandry þat ys here
To synge wyth ws wyth a mery chere;

'Yt ys wretyn wyth a coll, yt ys wretyn wyth a cole',

NEW GYSE and NOWADAYS
Yt ys wretyn wyth a colle, yt ys wretyn wyth a colle,

NOUGHT
'He þat schytyth wyth hys hoyll, be þat schytyth
wyth hys hoyll',

NEW GYSE [and] NOWADAYS
He þat schytyth wyth hys hoyll, he þat schytyth
with his hoyll,

NOUGHT
'But he wyppe hys arse clen, but he wyppe hys ars
clen',[36]

NEW GYSE [and] NOWADAYS
But he wype hys ars clen, but he wype his ars clen,

NOUGHT
'On hys breche yt xall be sen, on hys breche yt xall
be sen.'

NEW GYSE [and] NOWADAYS
On hys breche yt xall be sen, on hys breche yt xall be
sen.

Cantant Omnes
Hoylyke, holyke, holyke! holyke, holyke,
holyke![37]

NEW GYSE
Ey, Mankynde, Gode spede yow wyth yowr
spade!
I xall tell yow of a maryage:
I wolde yowr mowth and hys ars þat þis made
Wer maryede junctly together.[38]

MANKYNDE
Hey yow hens, felouse, wyth bredynge.[39]
Leve yowr derysyon and yowr japyng.
I must nedys labure, yt ys my lyvynge.

NOWADAYS
What ser, we cam but lat hethyr.

Xall all þis corn grow here
Þat ȝe xall have þe nexte ȝer?
Yf yt be so, corn hade nede be dere,
Ellys ȝe xall have a pore lyffe.

NOUGHT
Alasse, goode fadere, þis labor fretyth yow to þe
bon.[40]

316 write, paper 317 nature, promise 319 nature 320 remorse 321 superstitious 328 hear, meddle 329 try to dig 331 foison/plenty 332 Make way, been (away) 333 (and) give 334 yeomanry 336 coal 338 shits, hole 342 seen 343+ They all sing 351 labour 352 here only recently 353 Is this all the corn 355 had better

34 '"Remember, man, you are dust, and to dust you shall return.": Look, I carry the badge of my arms on my breast.' Mankind fastens the paper carrying the scriptural text to his garment. For the sentiments expressed, see Genesis 3:19, Job 34:15.

35 'With the pure thou wilt show yourself pure, and with the froward thou wilt show thyself froward.' Psalms 18:26. '"Behold, how good and how pleasant it is", said the Devil to the friars, "for the brethren to dwell together in unity."' Psalms 133:1.

36 'Unless he wipes his arse clean'.

37 'Everyone sings: "Hoylyke, etc."': the chorus is a scatological parody of 'Holy, holy, holy', suggestive of both 'hole-ly' and 'hole-lick'.

38 'I wish your mouth and his arse, that made this [song], were married jointly together.'

39 'Get you gone, fellows, with reproaches.'

40 'This hard work wears you down to the bone.'

But for yowr croppe I take grett mone.
3e xall never spende yt alonne;
I xall assay to geett yow a wyffe.

How many acres suppose 3e here by estymacyon?

NEW GYSE
Ey, how 3e turne þe erth wppe and down!
I have be in my days in many goode town,
3ett saw I never such another tyllynge.

MANKYNDE
Why stonde ye ydyll? Yt ys pety þat 3e were born!

NOWADAYS
We xall bargen wyth yow and noþer moke nor scorne.
Take a goode carte in herwest and lode yt wyth yowr corne,
Ande what xall we gyf yow for þe levynge?

NOUGHT
He ys a goode starke laburrer, he wolde fayn do well.
He hath mett wyth þe goode man Mercy in a schroude sell.
For all þis he may have many a hungry mele.
3yt woll 3e se he ys polytyke.
Here xall be goode corn, he may not mysse yt;
Yf he wyll have reyn he may overpysse yt;
Ande yf he wyll have comppasse he may overblysse yt
A lytyll wyth hys ars lyke.

MANKYNDE
Go and do yowr labur! Gode lett yow never the!
Or wyth my spade I xall yow dynge, by þe Holy Trinity!
Have 3e non other man to moke, but ever me?
3e wolde have me of yowr sett?
Hye yow forth lyvely, for hens I wyll yow dryffe,

[*Mankind strikes them with his spade.*]

NEW GYSE
Alas, my jewellys! I xall be schent of my wyff!

NOWADAYS
Alasse! and I am lyke never for to thryve,
I have such a buffett.

MANKYNDE
Hens I sey, New Gyse, Nowadays, and Nowte!
Yt was seyde beforn, all þe menys xuld be sought
To perverte my condycyons and brynge me to nought.
Hens, thevys! 3e have made many a lesynge.

NOUGHT
Marryde I was for colde, but now am I warme.
3e are ewyll avysyde, ser, for 3e have don harme.
By Cokkys body sakyrde, I have such a peyn in my arme
I may not chonge a man a ferthynge.[41]

MANKYNDE
Now I thanke Gode, knelynge on my kne.
Blyssyde be Hys name! He ys of hye degre.
By þe subsyde of Hys grace þat He hath sente me
Thre of myn enmys I have putt to flyght.
3yt þis instrument, soverens, ys not made to defende.
Davide seyth, '*Nec in hast{a} nec in gladio salvat Dominus*.'[42]

NOUGHT
No, mary, I beschrew yow, yt ys in *spadibus*.
Therfor Crystys curse cum on yowr *hedybus*
To sende yow lesse myght!

Exiant.

MANKYNDE
I promytt yow þes felouse wyll no more cum here,
For summe of þem, certenly, were summewhat to nere.
My fadyr Mercy avysyde me to be of a goode chere
Ande agayn my enmys manly for to fyght.

I xall convycte þem, I hope, everychon.
3et I say amysse, I do yt not alon.
Wyth þe helpe of þe grace of Gode I resyst my fon

358 I complain greatly 364 any digging like it 365 a pity 366 mock 367 harvest 368 surplus 369 strong 370 at an unlucky moment 372 careful 374 rain, piss over it 375 compost, bless 376 arse (in the same way) 377 thrive 378 strike 379 no one else 380 (join) your gang 381 I'll drive you off 382 jewels (testicles), punished by/deprived of 388 deception 389 I was troubled with cold 390 badly advised 391 God's sacred body (euphemism) 392 change 395 aid 397 (i.e. the spade) 399 'by the spade' 400 'head' 401+ (They shall) go out 402 promise 403 too near 406 defeat 407 wrongly, did 408 foes

41 i.e. 'I cannot lift even the smallest coin.'

42 'Not by the spear or sword does the lord save'. 1 Samuel 17:47.

Ande þer malycyuse herte.
Wyth my spade I wyll departe, my worschyppull soverence,
Ande lyve ever wyth labure to corecte my insolence.
I xall go fett corn for my londe; I prey yow of pacyence;
Ryght son I xall reverte.

[*Exit Mankynde, enter Myscheff.*]

MYSCHEFF
Alas, alasse, þat ever I was wrought!
Alasse þe whyll, I [am] wers þen nought!
Sythyn I was here, by Hym þat me bought,
I am wtterly ondon!
I, Myscheff, was here at þe begynnynge of þe game
Ande arguyde wyth Mercy, Gode gyff hym schame!
He hath taught Mankynde, wyll I have be vane,
To fyght manly ageyn hys fon.

For wyth hys spade, þat was hys wepyn,
Neu Gyse, Nowadays, Nought hath all to-beton.
I have grett pyte to se þem wepyn.

[*The Vices cry out off-stage.*]

Wyll ȝe lyst? I here þem crye.
Alasse, alasse! Cum hether, I xall be yowr borow.
Alac, alac! *Ven*, *ven*! cum hethere wyth sorowe!
Pesse, fayer babys, ȝe xall have a nappyll to-morow!
Why grete ȝe so, why?

NE[W] GYSE
Alasse, master, alasse, my privyte!

MYSCHEFF
A, wher? Alake! Fayer babe, ba me!
Abyde! To son I xall yt se!

NOWADAYS
Here, here, se my hede, goode master!

M[Y]SCHEFF
Lady, helpe! sely darlynge, *ven*, *ven*!
I xall helpe þe[e] of þi peyn;
I xall smytt of þi hede and sett yt on agayn.

NOUGHT
By Owr Lady, ser, a fayer playster!

Wyll ȝe of wyth hys hede! Yt ys a schreude charme!
As for me, I have non harme.
I were loth to forbere myn arme.
ȝe pley *in nomine patris*, choppe![43]

NEW GYSE
ȝe xall not choppe my jewellys, and I may.

NOWADAYS
ȝe, Cristys Crose, wyll ȝe smyght my hede awey?
Ther? Wher on? and on? Oute! ȝe xall not assay.
I myght well be callyde a foppe.

MYSCHEFF
I kan choppe yt of and make yt agayn.

NEW GYSE
I hade a schreude *recumbentibus*, but I fele no peyn.

NOWADAYS
Ande my hede ys all save and holl agayn.
Now towchynge þe mater of Mankynde,
Lett ws have an interleccyon, sythen ȝe be cum hether.
Yt were goode to have an ende.

MYSCHEFF
How, how, a mynstrell! Know ȝe ony out?

NOUGHT
I kan pype in a Walsyngham wystyll, I, Nought, Nought.[44]

MYSCHEFF
Blow apase, and þou xall bryng hym in wyth a flewte.

[*Nought plays the flute/whistle.*]

TITIVILLUS [*off-stage*]
I com wyth my leggys wnder me.

409 malicious hearts 411 discipline my pride 413 return 417 utterly ruined 420 while, gone 424 weeping 426 guardian 427 Alas, come (Latin) 428 Hush, fair babies, an apple 429 weep 430 private parts 431 kiss 432 Too soon I shall see it! 434 (you) poor dear! 436 chop off 437 (That's) a fair cure! 438 off, wicked trick 440 lose 442 if I can help it 443 Christ's Cross 445 fool 446 repair 447 recompense 448 safe and whole 450 consultation 452 anything at all? 454 quickly, flute

[43] 'In the name of the Father . . . chop!', a last blessing before the axe comes down.

[44] A Walsingham whistle. Walsingham is a Norfolk town famous for its shrine to the Virgin.

MYSCHEFF
How, Neu Gyse, Nowadays, herke or I goo!
When owr hedys wer togethere I spake of *si dedero*.[45]

NE[W] GYSE
3o, go þi wey! We xall gaþer mony onto,
Ellys þer xall no man hym se.

Now gostly to owr purpos, worschypfull soverence,
We intende to gather mony, yf yt plesse yowr neclygence,
For a man wyth a hede þat [is] of grett ominpotens.

NOWADAYS
Kepe yowr tayll, in goodnes I prey yow, goode broþer!
He ys a worschyppull man, sers, savyng yowr reverens.
He lovyth no grotys, nor pens of to pens.
Gyf ws rede reyallys yf 3e wyll se hys abhomynabull presens.[46]

NEW GYSE
Not so! 3e þat mow not pay þe ton, pay þe toþer.[47]

At þe goodeman of þis house fyrst we wyll assay.
Gode blysse yow, master! 3e say as yll, ȝet ȝe wyll not sey nay.
Lett ws go by and by and do þem pay.
3e pay all alyke; well mut ȝe fare!

NOUGHT
I sey, New Gyse, Nowadays: '*Estis vos pecuniatus?*'[48]
I haude cryede a fayer wyll, I beschrew yowr *patus*!

NOWADAYS
Ita vere, magister. Cumme forth now yowr *gatus*![49]
He ys a goodly man, sers; make space and be ware!

[*Enter Titivillus.*]

TITIVILLUS
Ego sum dominancium dominus and my name ys Titivillus.[50]
3e þat have goode hors, to yow I sey *caveatis*!
Here ys an abyll felyschyppe to tryse hem out at yowr gatys.

Loquitur ad New Gyse:

Ego probo sic: ser New Gys, lende me a peny!

NEW GYSE
I have a grett purse, ser, but I have no monay.
By þe Masse, I fayll to farthyngys of an halpeny;[51]
3yt hade I ten pound þis nyght þat was.

TITIVILLUS (*loquitur ad Nowadays*)
What ys in þi purse? Þou art a stout felow.

NOWADAYS
Þe Deull have the[e] qwy[tt]! I am a clen jentyllman.
I prey Gode I be never wers storyde þen I am.
Yt xall be otherwyse, I hope, or þis nyght passe.

TITIVILLUS (*loquitur ad Nought*)
Herke now! I say þou hast many a peny.

NOUGHT
Non nobis, Domine, non nobis, by Sent Deny![52]
Þe Duell may daunce in my purse for ony peny;
Yt ys as clen as a byrdys ars.

TITIVILLUS
Now I say yet ageyn, *caveatis*!
Her ys an abyll felyschyppe to tryse hem out of yowr gatys.

Now I sey, New Gyse, Nowadays, and Nought,
Go and serche þe contre, anon yt be sowȝte,
Summe here, summe þer; what yf ȝe may cache owȝte?

458 money for you 459 Otherwise 465 tally (of the money collected) 468 head/patron 469 you may curse 471 good luck to you! 473 while, curse your heads 477 beware! 478 snatch them, gates 478+ (He) speaks to New Guise 479 I prove it, thus 482 last night 482+ (He) speaks to Nowadays 484 reward you 485 provided for 489 (i.e. it's so empty none will get in his way) 490 bird's arse 491 quiet 495 anything?

[45] 'If I give something . . . [I expect something in return]' ,i.e. 'I'm not coming on until I get some money.'

[46] Groats were worth 4 pence, 'pence of two-pence' were single coins worth 2 pence each. 'Ready Royals': Royals were a coin worth 10 shillings, first produced in 1465.

[47] 'You that cannot pay the one may pay the other!'

[48] 'Are you wealthy?'

[49] 'Truly, then, master, come away from your doors [make way at the entrance!].'

[50] 'I am Lord of Lords.' See Deuteronomy 10:17.

[51] 'I am two farthings short of a half-penny', i.e. 'I have no money at all.'

[52] 'Not of our own, Lord, not of our own'. See Psalms 113:9. St Denis is patron saint of France.

Yf þe[e] fayll of hors, take what ȝe may ellys.

NEW GYSE
Then speke to Mankynde for þe *recumbentibus* of my jewellys.

NOWADAYS
Remember my brokyn hede in þe worschyppe of þe fyve vowellys.

NOUGHT
Ȝe, goode ser, and þe sytyca in my arme.

TITIVILLUS
I know full well what Mankynde dyde to yow.
Myschyff hat informyde of all þe matere thorow.
I xall venge yowr quarell, I make Gode avow.
Forth, and espye were ȝe may do harme.

Take W[illiam] Fyde, yf ȝe wyll have ony mo.[53]
I sey, New Gyse, wethere art ȝou avysyde to go?

NEW GYSE
Fyrst I xall begyn at M[aster] Huntyngton of Sauston,
Fro thens I xall go to Wylliam Thurlay of Hauston.
Ande so forth to Pycharde of Trumpyngton.[54]
I wyll kepe me to þes thre.

NOWADAYS
I xall goo to Wyllyham Baker of Waltom.
To Rycherde Bollman of Gayton;[55]
I xall spare Master Woode of Fullburn,
He ys a *noli me tangere*.[56]

NOUGHT
I xall goo to Wyllyam Patryke of Massyngham,
I xall spare Master Alyngton of Botysam
Ande Hamonde of Soffeham,[57]
For drede of '*in manus tuas* qweke'.[58]
Felous, cum forth, and go we hens togethyr.

NE[W] GYSE
Syth we xall go, lett ws be well ware wethere.
If we may be take, we com no more hethyr.
Lett ws con well owr neke-verse, þat we have not a cheke.[59]

TITIVILLUS
Goo yowr wey, a Deull wey, go yowr wey all!
I blysse yow wyth my lyfte honde: foull yow befall!
Com agayn, I werne, as son as I yow call,
A[nd] brynge yowr avantage into þis place.
To speke wyth Mankynde I wyll tary here þis tyde
Ande assay hys goode purpose for to sett asyde.
Þe goode man Mercy xall no lenger by hys gyde.
I xall make hym to dawnce anoþer trace.

Ever I go invysybull, yt ys my jett,
Ande befor hys ey þus I wyll hange my nett
To blench hys syght; I hope to have hys fote-mett.
To yrke hym of hys labur I xall make a frame.
Thys borde xall be hyde wnder þe erth prevely;
Hys spade xall enter, I hope, onredyly;
Be þen he hath assayde,[60] he xall be very angry
Ande lose hys pacyens, peyn of schame.

I xall menge hys corne wyth drawke and wyth durnell;

496 fail (to find) any horses 497 restoration of 498 wells (wounds of Christ?) 499 sciatica 501 thoroughly 503 (Go) forth! 504 more (help) 505 where are you thinking of going 519 aware, where (to) 520 taken (caught) 521 checkmate (fatal blow) 523 (i.e. the 'sinister', Devil's side) 524 warn (you) 525 spoils 527 intentions, ruin 529 dance/tune 530 fashion 532 blind, take his measure 533 trap 534 board, hidden 535 with difficulty 537 to his shame 538 mix, types of weeds

53 The people named in these exchanges were probably all prominent local personalities in the area(s) where the play was intended to be performed. See Eccles, *The Macro Plays*, p. 222. There was a Fydde family in Waterbeach (Cambridgeshire) in the 1450s.

54 Sawston, Hawxton, and Trumpington are all villages south of Cambridge. There were Thirlows in Hawxton in 1450 and Huntingdons in Sawston in the 1420s. There was both a John and a William Pychard in Trumpington in the later fifteenth century.

55 East Walton and Gayton are villages east of Lynn in Norfolk. One William Baker (d.1491) was a resident of the former.

56 'Touch me not': John 20:17. Alexander Wood (d.1479) of Fulbourn (a village east of Cambridge) was a Justice of the Peace in 1471, so the Vices are probably well advised to give him a wide berth.

57 Massingham is a village east of Lynn in Norfolk. A William Allington (d.1479) of Bottisham (east of Cambridge) was a Justice of the Peace in 1457, and Speaker of the House of Commons in 1472, and so was probably another 'untouchable' in the Vice's opinion. There is a village called Swaffham east of Cambridge, and another near Lynn; Hammonds are recorded in each of them.

58 'Into Your hands [O Lord]': Psalms 31:5, according to Luke 23:46 Christ's last words from the Cross, and thus traditionally the last words spoken by a hanged man before execution. Nought will not approach these people for fear of hanging. 'Qweke' is the sound made by the victim's neck breaking.

59 'Neck-verse' was the short piece of Latin (often the opening lines of Psalms 51: '*Miserei me Dominus*', 'Have mercy on me, Lord') recited by clerics in order to prove their status in the secular courts and so claim exemption from capital punishment.

60 'By the time that he has finished trying'.

Yt xall not be lyke to sow nor to sell.
Yondyr he commyth; I prey of cownsell.
He xall wene grace were wane.

MANKYND[E]
Now Gode of Hys mercy sende ys of Hys sonde!
I have brought sede here to sow wyth my londe.
Qwyll I overdylew yt, here yt xall stonde.
In nomine Patris et Filii et Spiritus Sancti now I wyll begyn.[61]
Thys londe ys so harde yt makyth wnlusty and yrke.
I xall sow my corn at wynter and lett Gode werke.

[*Titivillus steals the bag of seeds.*]

Alasse, my corn ys lost! here ys a foull werke!
I se well by tyllynge lytyll xall I wyn.

Here I gyff wppe my spade for now and for ever.

Here Titivillus goth out wyth þe spade.

To occupye my body I wyll not put me in dever.
I wyll here my ewynsonge here or I dyssever.
Thys place I assyng as for my kyrke.
Here in my kerke I knell on my kneys.
Pater noster qui es in Celis.[62]

TITIVILLUS
I promise yow I have no lede on my helys.
I am here ageyn to make þis felow yrke.

Qwyst! pesse! I xall go to hys ere and tytyll þerin.
A schorte preyer thyrlyth Hewyn; of þi preyere blyn.[63]
Þou art holyer þen ever was ony of þi kyn.
Aryse and avent þe[e], nature commpellys![64]

MANKYND[E]
I wyll into þi ȝerde, soverens, and cum ageyn son.
For drede of þe colyke and eke of þe ston
I wyll go do þat nedys must be don.
My bedys xall be here for whosummever wyll ellys.[65]

Exiat.

TITIVILLUS
Mankynde was besy in hys prayere, ȝet I dyde hym aryse.
He ys conveyde, be Cryst, from hys dyvyn servyce.
Wethere ys he, trow ȝe? I wysse I am wonder wyse;
I have sent hym forth to schyte lesynges.
Yff ȝe have ony sylver, in happe pure brasse,
Take a lytyll powder of Parysch and cast over hys face,
Ande ewyn in þe howll-flyght let hym passe.[66]
Titivillus kan lerne yow many praty thyngs.

I trow Mankynde wyll cum ageyn son,
Or ellys I fere me ewynsonge wyll be don.
Hys bedys xall be trysyde asyde, and þat anon.
Ȝe xall a goode sport yf ȝe wyll abyde,
Mankynde cummyth ageyn, well fare he!
I xall answere hym *ad omnia quare*.
Ther xall be sett abroche a clerycall mater.
I hope of hys purpose to sett hym asyde.

MANKYND[E]
Ewynsong hath be in þe saynge, I trow, a fayer wyll.
I am yrke of yt; yt ys to longe be on myle.[67]
Do wey! I wyll no more so oft over þe chyrche-style.
Be as be may, I xall do anoþer.
Of labure and preyer, I am nere yrke of both;
I wyll no more of yt, thow Mercy be wroth.
My hede ys very hevy, I tell yow forsoth.
I xall slepe full my bely and he wore my broþer.

TITIVILLUS
[*To the audience*] Ande ever ȝe dyde, for me kepe now yowr sylence.
Not a worde, I charge yow, peyn of forty pens.
A praty game xall be scheude yow or ȝe go hens.
Ȝe may here hym snore; he ys sade aslepe.

539 suitable 540 keep quiet 541 believe, gone 542 message 544 dig it over 546 (me) exhausted and angry 549 gain 551 no (longer) endeavour 552 hear, Evensong, depart 553 assign, church 554 kneel 556 lead in my heels 558 Hush!, ear, tittle/whisper 561 nature calls! 563 cholic, kidney-stone 565+ Let him leave 568 wonderfully 569 shit lies 570 or perhaps 574 soon 576 cast 577 shall (see) 579 at every question 580 raised 584 no longer come so often 589 my belly-full, even if he was 591 on pain of losing 592 showed 593 sound

61 'In the name of the Father, and the Son, and the Holy Spirit'.

62 'Our Father who art in Heaven', the opening of the Paternoster.

63 'A short prayer pierces Heaven most effectively, [so] stop your praying.'

64 Titivillus induces in Mankind a need to defecate in order to cut short his prayer.

65 'My prayer-beads shall remain here for whoever else may want [to use] them.'

66 'Take a little powder of Paris [an arsenic-based compound?] and rub it over [the coin's] face, and even in the light of evening it will pass [for silver].'

67 'Evensong has, I believe, been going on for a fair while. I am tired of it, it's too long by a mile.'

Qwyst! pesse! þe Deull ys dede![68] I xall goo ronde in hys ere.
Alasse, Mankynde, alasse! Mercy stown a mere!
He ys runn away fro hys master, þer wot no man where;
Moreover, he stale both a hors and a nete.

But ȝet I herde sey he brake hys neke as he rode in Fraunce;
But I thynke he rydyth on þe galouse, to lern for to daunce,
Bycause of hys theft, at ys hys governance.
Trust no more on hym, he ys a marryde man.
Mekyll sorow wyth þi spade beforn þou hast wrought.
Aryse and aske mercy of Neu Gyse, Nowadays, and Nought.
Þei cun avyse þe[e] for þe best; lett þer goode wyll be sought.
Ande þi own wyff brethell, and take þe[e] a lemman.

Forwell, everychon! for I have don my game,
For I have brought Mankynde to myscheff and to schame.

MANKYND[E]

Whope who! Mercy hath brokyn hys neke-kycher, avows,
Or he hangyth by þe neke hye wppon þe gallouse.
Adew, fayer masters! I wyll hast me to þe ale-house
Ande speke wyth New Gyse, Nowadays, and Nought.
A[nd] geett me a lemman wyth a smattrynge face.

[*Enter New Guise with a noose around his neck.*]

NEW GYSE

Make space, for Cokkys body sakyrde, make space!
A ha! well overron! Gode gyff hym ewyll grace!
We were nere Sent Patrykes wey, by Hym þat me bought.

I was twychyde by þe neke; þe game was begunne.
A grace was, þe halter brast asonder; *ecce signum*![69]
The halff ys abowte my neke; we hade a nere rune!
'Beware', quod þe goodewyff when sche smot of here husbondys hede, 'beware!'
Myscheff ys a convicte, for he coude hys neke-verse.
My body gaff a swynge when I hynge wppon þe casse.
Alasse, he wyll hange such a lyghly man, and a fers,
For stelynge of an horse, I prey Gode gyf hym care!

Do wey þis halter! What Deull doth Mankynde here, wyth sorow!
Alasse, how my neke ys sore, I make avowe!

MANKYND[E]

Ȝe be welcom, Neu Gyse! Ser, what chere wyth yow?

NEW GYSE

Well, ser, I have no cause to morn.

MANKYND[E]

What was þat abowte yowr neke, so Gode yow amende?

NEW GYSE

In feyth, Sent Audrys holy bende.[70]
I have a lytyll dyshes, as yt plesse Gode to sende,
Wyth a runnynge ryngeworme.

NOWADAYS

Stonde arom, I prey þe[e], broþer myn!
I have laburryde all þis nyght; wen xall we go dyn?
A chyrche her besyde xall pay for ale, brede, and wyn.
Lo, here ys stoff wyll serve.[71]

NEW GYSE

Now by þe holy Mary, þou art better marchande þen I!

NOUGHT

Avante, knawys, lett me go by!
I kan not geet and I xulde sterve.

{*Enter Mischief, with chains on his arms.*}

594 whisper 595 (has) stolen, mare 597 ox/cow 599 gallows 601 marred/broken 602 earlier 605 betray, mistress 608 Hurrah, neckerchief 612 kissable 613 sacred 614 curse him! 615 St Patrick's Way (Ireland) 616 jerked 618 close shave 620 knew 621 gallow 622 he (who), handsome, fierce 624 Get rid of 627 mourn 630 disease 631 suppurating ringworm 632 Stand back 633 dine 634 nearby 636 merchant 638 get (anything), even if I should

68 'The Devil is dead': proverbial falsely optimistic counsel; 'there's nothing to worry about'.

69 'Behold, a sign!': 'Look, here's the evidence!' He shows the noose.

70 St Audrey's shrine in Ely Cathedral (Cambridgeshire) produced silken neck-bands as health-promoting souvenirs for pilgrims.

71 'Look, here is the stuff that will meet the bill.' Nowadays produces the goods that he has stolen from the church.

MYSCHEFF
Here cummyth a man of armys! Why stonde ȝe so styll?
Of murder and manslawter I have my bely-fyll.

NOWADAYS
What, Myscheff, have þe[e] ben in presun? And yt be yowr wyll,
Me semyth ȝe have scoryde a peyr of fetters.

MYSCHEFF
I was chenyde by þe armys; lo, I have þem here.
The chenys I brast asundyr and kyllyde þe jaylere,
3e, añde hys fayer wyff halsyde in a cornere;
A, how swetly I kyssyde þe swete mowth of hers!

When I hade do, I was myn owȝn bottler;
I brought awey wyth me both dysch and dublere.
Here ys anow for me; be of goode chere!
3et well fare þe new chesance![72]

MANKYNDE
I aske mercy of New Gyse, Nowadays, and Nought.
Onys wyth my spade I remember þat I faught.
I will make yow amendys yf I hurt yow ought
Or dyde ony grevaunce.

NEW GYSE
What a Deull lykyth þe[e] to be of þis dysposycyon?

MANKYNDE
I drempt Mercy was hange, þis was my vysyon,
Ande þat to yow thre I xulde have recors and remocyon,
Now I prey yow hertyly of yowr goode wyll.
I crye yow mercy of all þat I dyde amysse.

NOWADAYS
I sey, New Gys, Nought, Tytivillus made all þis:
As sekyr as Gode ys in Hewyn, so yt ys.

NOUGHT
Stonde wppe on yowr feet! Why stonde ȝe so styll?

NEW GYSE
Master Myscheff, we wyll yow exort
Mankynds name in yowr bok for to report.

MYSCHEFF
I wyll not so; I wyll sett a corte.
Nowadays, mak proclamacyon,
And do yt *sub forma jurys*, dasarde!

NOWADAYS
Oyyt! Oyȝyt! Oyet! All manere of men and comun women
To þe cort of Myschyff othere cum or sen!
Mankynde xall retorn; he ys on of owr men.

MYSCHEFF
Nought, cum forth, þou xall be stewerde.

NEW GYSE
Master Myscheff, hys syde gown may be tolde.
He may have a jakett þerof, and mony tolde.[73]

Nought scribit.

MANKYNDE
I wyll do for þe best, so I have no colde.
Holde, I prey yow, and take yt wyth yow.
Ande let me have yt ageyn in ony wyse.

NEW GYSE
I promytt yow a fresch jakett after þe new gyse.

MANKYNDE
Go and do þat longyth to yowr offyce,
A[nd] spare þat ȝe mow!

NOUGHT
Holde, master Myscheff, and rede þis.

MYSCHEFF
Here ys '*blottybus in blottis,*
Blottorum blottibus istis'.
I beschrew yowr erys, a fayer hande![74]

641 prison 642 gained 645 wife, embraced 647 finished, butler 648 platter 652 once 653 at all 654 (you) any 656 hanged 657 recourse, return 661 surely 664 book (of retainers) 665 summon a (manorial) court 667 in proper legal form, idiot 668 Oyez, whores 669 either come, send (representatives) 670 one 672 accounted for 673 made from it, counted out 673+ Nought writes 674 so (long as) 676 any way 678 what pertains to 679 save what you can

72 'Here's to the new trade!'

73 The Vices introduce Mankind's long gown as evidence in the court, and begin to mock its length and weight.

74 '*Blottybus*, etc.': nonsense Latin, by implication a blotted paper. 'I curse your ears, [this is] good handwriting!' (ironic).

NOWADAYS
3e, yt ys a goode rennynge fyst.
Such an hande may not be myst.

NOUGHT
I xulde have don better, hade I wyst.

MYSCHEFF
Take hede, sers, yt stoude you on hande.

'Carici tenta generalis
In a place þer goode ale ys
Anno regni regitalis
Edwardi nullateni
On 3estern day in Feverere' – þe 3ere passyth fully,
As Nought hath wrytyn; here ys owr Tulli,
'*Anno regni regis nulli*!'[75]

NOWADAYS
What how, Neu Gyse! þou makyst moche [taryynge].
Þat jakett xall not be worth a ferthynge.

NEW GYSE
Out of my wey, sers, for drede of fyghtynge!
Lo, here ys a feet tayll, lyght to leppe abowte!

NOUGHT
Yt ys not schapyn worth a morsell of brede;[76]
Ther ys to moche cloth, yt weys as ony lede.
I xall goo and mende yt, ellys I wyll lose my hede.
Make space, sers, lett me go owte.

MYSCHEFF
Mankynde, cum hethere! God sende yow þe[e] gowte!
3e xall goo to all þe goode felouse in þe cuntre aboute;
Onto þe goodewyff when þe goodeman ys owte.
'I wyll', say 3e.

MANKYNDE
I wyll, ser.

NEW GYSE
There arn but sex dedly synnys, lechery ys non,
As yt may be verefyede be ws brethellys everychon.
3e xall goo robbe, stell, and kyll, as fast as ye man gon.
'I wyll', sey 3e.

MANKYNDE
I wyll, ser.

NOWADAYS
On Sundays on þe morow, erly betyme
3e xall wyth ws to þe all-house erly to go dyn,
And forbere masse and matens, owres and prime.
'I wyll', say 3e.

MANKYNDE
I wyll, ser.

MYSCHEFF
3e must have be yowr syde a longe *da pacem*,
As trew men ryde be þe wey for to onbrace þem,
Take þer monay, kytt þer throtys, thus overface þem.
'I wyll', sey 3e.

MANKYNDE
I wyll, ser.

NOUGHT [*returning with the shortened gown*]
Here ys a joly jakett! How sey 3e?

NEW GYSE
Yt ys a goode jake of fence for a mannys body.
Hay, doog, hay! whoppe whoo! Go yowr wey lyghtly![77]
3e are well made for to ren.

[*Enter Mercy.*]

MYSCHEFF
Tydynngys, tydyngys! I have aspyede on!
Hens wyth yowr stuff, fast we were gon!
I beschrew þe last xall com to hys hom!

684 cursive script 685 cannot be done without 686 had I known 687 concerns you now 698 suitable tail (for the gown) 700 weighs like lead 701 improve 703 gout 704 country 707 only six, is not one 708 us wretches 709 steal, you can 711 early in the morning 712 ale-house 713 forego, the canonical hours 715 peace-maker (a dagger) 716 carve them up 717 cut, overpower 720 protective jacket 722 run 723 spied (some) one 724 we should be gone, quickly! 725 Last one home is cursed!

75 Manorial court records should begin with '*Curia tenta*', but Nought's Latin is flawed. '"The General Court being in session in a place where there is good ale, in the regnal year nought of King Edward the Nothing, on Yesterday in February" – the year passes completely as Nought has written it. Here is our Cicero [the famous rhetorician], " In the regnal year of no one"!'

76 'I wouldn't give you a crumb for its tailoring'.

77 'Hey dog!', etc., huntsmen's cries of encouragement.

Dicant Omnes.
Amen!

MERCY
What how, Mankynde! Fle þat felyschyppe, I yow prey!

MANKYNDE
I xall speke wyth [þee] anoþer tyme, to-morn, or þe next day.
We xall goo forth together to kepe my faders ȝer-day.[78]
A tapster, a tapster! Stow, statt, stow!

MYSCHEFF
A myscheff go wyth! Here I have a foull fall.
Hens, awey fro me, or I xall beschyte yow all.

NEW GYSE
What how, ostlere, hostlere! Lende ws a football!
Whoppe whow! Anow, anow, anow, anow!

MERCY
My mynde ys dyspersyde, my body trymmelyth as þe aspen leffe.
The terys xuld trekyll down by my chekys, were not yowr reverrence.
Yt were to me solace, þe cruell vysytacyon of deth.
Wythout rude behaver I kan [not] expresse þis inconvenyens.
Wepynge, sythynge, and sobbynge were my suffycyens;
All naturall nutriment to me as caren ys odybull.
My inwarde afflixcyon ȝeldyth me tedyouse wnto yowr presens.
I kan not bere yt ewynly þat Mankynde ys so flexybull.

Man onkynde,[79] wherever þou be! for all þis world was not aprehensyble.
To dyscharge þin orygynall offence, thraldam, and captyvyte
Tyll Godys own welbelovyde Son was obedient and passyble.
Every droppe of Hys bloode was schede to purge þin iniquite.
I dyscomende and dysalow þ[in] oftyn mutabylyte,
To every creature þou art dyspectuose and odyble.
Why art þou so oncurtess, so inconsyderatt? Alasse, who ys me!
As þe fane þat turnyth wyth þe wynde, so þou art convertyble.

In trust ys treson; þi promes ys not credyble;
Thy perversyose ingratytude I can not rehers.
To Go[d] and to all þe holy corte of Hevyn þou art despectyble,
As a nobyll versyfyer makyth mencyon in þis verse:
'Lex et natura, Cristus {et} omnia jura
Damnant ingratum, lugent eum fore natum.'[80]

O goode Lady and Moþer of Mercy, have pety and compassyon
Of þe wrechydnes of Mankynde, þat ys so wanton and so frayll!
Lett mercy excede justyce, dere Moþer, amytt þis supplycacyon,
Equyte to be leyde onparty and mercy to prevayll.

To sensuall lyvynge ys reprovable, þat ys nowadays,
As be þe comprehence of þis mater yt may be specyfyede.[81]
New Gyse, Nowadays, Nought wyth þer allectuose ways,
They have pervertyde Mankynde, my swet sun, I have well espyede.

A, wyth þes cursyde cay[tyf]s, and I may, he xall not long indure.
I, Mercy, hys father gostly, wyll procede forth and do my propyrte.[82]
Lady, helpe! þis maner of lyvynge ys a detestabull plesure.
Vanitas vanitatum, all ys but a vanyte.

725+ Let them all say 730 come, slut, come! 732 Go hence, shit upon 733 stableman 735 distracted, trembles 736 trickle 737 would (be) 738 being rude 739 sighing, sustenance 740 is as odious as carrion to me 741 makes me 742 calmly, fickle 743 sufficent 744 sin, slavery 745 willing to suffer 746 your 747 condemn, fickleness 748 despicable, odious 749 discourteous, woe 750 weather-vane, fickle 751 promise 752 perverse, repeat 753 despicable 759 accept 760 justice, aside 763 alluring 764 seen 767 detestable 768 Most vain of vanities

78 'To mark the anniversary of my father's death.'
79 'Unnatural man', with a pun on 'Man-kind'.
80 'Law and nature, Christ, and all justice damn the ingrate, they lament that he was born.'
81 'Sensual living is to blame for everything that is [wrong] nowadays, as an understanding of this matter will make clear [to you].'
82 'He will not stay long with these cursed villains if I can help it. I, Mercy, his spiritual counsellor, will go and fulfil my role.'

Mercy xall never be convicte of hys oncurtes condycyon.
Wyth wepynge terys be nyȝte and be day I wyll goo and never sesse.
Xall I not fynde hym? Yes, I hope. Now Gode be my proteccyon!
My predylecte son, where be ye? Mankynde, *ubi es?*

MYSCHEFF
My prepotent fader, when ȝe sowpe, sowpe owt yowr messe.[83]
Ȝe are all to-gloryede in yowr termys; ȝe make many a lesse.
Wyll ȝe here? He cryeth ever 'Mankynde, *ubi es?*'

NEW GYSE
Hic, hyc, hic, hic, hic hic, hic hic!
Þat ys to sey, here, here, here! ny dede in þe cryke.
Yf ȝe wyll have hym, goo and syke, syke, syke!
Syke not overlong, for losynge of yowr mynde!

NOWADAYS
Yf ȝe wyll have Mankynde, how *domine, domine, dominus*!
Ȝe must speke to þe schryve for a *c(a)pe corpus*,
Ellys ȝe must be fayn to retorn wyth *non est inventur*.[84]
How sey ȝe, ser? My bolte ys schett.

NOUGHT
I am doynge of my nedyngys; be ware how ȝe schott!
Fy, fy, fy! I have fowll arayde my fote.
Be wyse for schotynge wyth yowr takyllys, for Gode wott,
My fote ys fowly overschett.

MYSCHEFF
A parlement, a parlement! Cum forth, Nought, behynde.
A cownsell belyve! I am aferde Mercy wyll hym fynde.
How sey ȝe, and what sey ȝe? How xall we do wyth Mankynde?

NE[W] GYSE
Tysche! A flyes weyng! Wyll ȝe do well?
He wenyth Mercy were honge for stelyng of a mere.
Myscheff, go sey to hym þat Mercy sekyth everywere.
He wyll honge hymselff, I wndyrtake, for fere.

MYSCHEFF
I assent þerto; yt ys wyttyly seyde and well.

NOWADAYS
Qwyppe yt in þi cote; anon yt were don.
Now Sent Gabryellys modyr save þe cloþes of þi schon!
All þe bokys in þe worlde, yf þei hade be wndon.
Kowde not a cownselde ws bett.

Hic exit Myscheff.[85]

MYSCHEFF
How, Mankynde! Cumm and speke wyth Mercy, he is here fast by.

MANKYNDE
A roppe, a rope, a rope! I am not worthy.

MYSCHEFF
Anon, anon, anon! I have yt here redy,
Wyth a tre also þat I have gett.

Holde þe tre, Nowadays, Nought! Take hede and be wyse!

NE[W] GYSE
Lo, Mankynde! do as I do; þis ys þi new gyse.
Gyff þe roppe just to [þy] neke; þis yn myn avyse.

MYSCHEFF
Helpe þisylff, Nought! Lo, Mercy ys here!
He skaryth ws wyth a bales; we may no lengere tary.

NE[W] GYSE
Qweke, qweke, qweke! Alass, my thrott! I beschrew yow, mary!
A, Mercy, Crystys coppyde curse go wyth yow, and Sent Davy!
Alasse, my wesant! Ȝe were sumwhat to nere.

769 convinced 770 cease 772 beloved, where are you? 774 puffed up (with pride), lie 776 here! 777 near-dead in the stream 778 seek 780 Lord 783 shot 784 my necessaries (i.e. urinating) 785 foully covered 786 equipment (i.e. penises) 787 overshot 791 Tush, fly's wing (i.e. a trifle) 792 thinks, hanged, mare 794 I bet, fear 796 Whip it (the noose) 797 your shoe-leather 798 books, opened 799 Couldn't counsel us better 800 close 803 got 806 apply 808 scourges, whip 809 throat 810 abundant 811 throat

83 'My all-powerful father, when you eat, eat up the whole portion.'

84 'You must speak to the sheriff for a [legal writ of] "Take his body" [to empower a search], otherwise you will have to reply "not found [in this jurisdiction]".'

85 Myscheff exits briefly to bring back Mankynde.

Exiant [*all the Vices.*].

MERCY
Aryse, my precyose redempt son! Ʒe be to me full dere.
He ys so tymerouse, me semyth hys vytall spryt doth exspyre.

MANKYNDE
Alasse, I have be so bestyally dysposyde, I dare not apere.
To se yowr solaycyose face I am not worthy to dysyere.

MERCY
Yowr crymynose compleynt wondyth my hert as a lance.
Dyspose yowrsylff mekly to aske mercy, and I wyll assent.
Ʒelde me nethyr gold nor tresure, but yowr humbyll obeysyance,
The voluntary subjeccyon of yowr hert, and I am content.

MANKYNDE
What, aske mercy ȝet onys agayn? Alas, yt were a wyle petycyun.
Ewyr to offend and ever to aske mercy, yt ys a puerilite.
Yt ys so abhominabyll to rehers my iterat transgrescion.
I am not worthy to hawe mercy be no possibilite.

MERCY
O, Mankend, my singler solas, þis a lamentabyll excuse.
The dolorus terys of my hert, how þei begyn to amownt!
O pirssid Jhesu, help þou þis synfull synner to redouce!
Nam hec est mutacio dextre Excelsi; vertit impios et non sunt.[86]
Aryse and aske mercy, Mankend, and be associat to me.
Thy deth schall be my hewynesse; alas, tys pety yt schwld be þus.
Thy obstinacy wyll exclude the[e] fro þe glorius perpetuite.
Ʒet for my lofe ope thy lyppys and sey '*Miserere mei, Deus*!'

MANK[YNDE]
The egall justyse of God wyll not permytte sych a synfull wrech
To be rewyvyd and restoryd ageyn; yt were impossibyll.

MERCY
The justyce of God wyll as I wyll, as Hymsylfe doth precyse:
Nolo mortem peccatoris, inquit,[87] yff he wyll [be] redusyble.

MANK[YNDE]
Þan mercy, good Mercy! What ys a man wythowte mercy?
Lytyll ys our parte of Paradyse were mercy ne were.
Good Mercy, excuse þe inevytabyll objecction of my gostly enmy.
The prowerbe seyth 'þe trewth tryith þe sylfe'.[88] Alas, I hawe mech care.

MERCY
God wyll not make ȝow prevy onto Hys Last Jugement.
Justyce and Equite xall be fortyfyid, I wyll not denye.
Trowthe may not so cruelly procede in hys streyt argument,
But þat Mercy schall rewle þe mater wythowte contraversye.[89]

Aryse now and go wyth me in thys deambulatorye.
My doctrine ys convenient; inclyne yowyr capacite.

813 frightened, life-force **814** bestially behaved **815** comforting, desire **816** guilty confession wounds **818** obedience **820** vile petition **821** Always, childish thing **822** frequent sin **825** sorrowful tears, gather **826** blessed, move, repent **829** sorrow, (it) is (a) pity **830** from eternal glory **831** love, have mercy on me, God **833** revived **834** say precisely **835** repentant **837** where mercy is absent **838** opposition **842** strict **843** opposition **844** cloister (covered walkway) **845** apply your mind (to it)

86 'For this is the change of the right hand of the most High. The wicked are overthrown and are [no more].' See Psalms 77:10, Proverbs 12:7.

87 'Saith the Lord, I have no pleasure in the death of the wicked.' Ezekiel 33:11.

88 'The proverb says, "the truth proves itself".'

89 For the playing out of this argument between the 'four daughters of God', see the N-Town *Mary Play*.

Synne not in hope of mercy; þat ys a cryme notary.
To trust overmoche in a prince yt ys not expedient.

In hope when ȝe syn ȝe thynke to hawe mercy, be ware of þat awenture.
The good Lord seyd to þe lecherus woman of Chanane,
The Holy Gospell ys þe awtorite, as we rede in Scrypture,
'*Vade et iam amplius noli peccare.*'[90]

Cryst preserwyd þis synfull woman takeyn in awowtry;
He seyde to here þeis wordys, 'Go and syn no more',
So to ȝow: go and syn no more. Be ware of weyn confidens of mercy;
Offend not a prince on trust of hys favour, as [I] seyd before.

Yf ȝe fele ȝoursylfe trappyde in þe snare of your gostly enmy,
Aske mercy anon; be ware of þe contynuance.
Whyll a wond ys fresch yt ys prowyd curabyll be surgery,
Þat yf yt procede ovyrlong, yt ys cawse of gret grewans.

MANK[YNDE]
To aske mercy and to hawe, þis ys a lyberall possescion.
Schall þis expedycius petycion ever be alowyd, as ȝe hawe insyght?

MERCY
In þis present lyfe mercy ys plenty, tyll deth makyth hys dywysion;
But whan ȝe be go, *usque ad minimum quadrantem*, ȝe scha[ll] rekyn ȝour ryght.[91]

Aske Mercy and hawe, whyll þe body wyth þe sowle hath hys annexion
Yf ye tary tyll your dyscesse, ȝe may hap of your desyre to mysse.[92]
Be repentant here, trust not þe owr of deth; thynke on þis lessun:
'*Ecce nunc tempus acceptabile, ecce nunc dies salutis.*'[93]

All þe wertu in þe word yf ȝe myght comprehend,
Your merytys were not premyabyll to þe blys abowe,
Not to the lest joy of Hewyn, of ȝour propyr efforte to ascend.
Wyth mercy ȝe may; I tell ȝow no fabyll, Scrypture doth prowe.[94]

MANK[YNDE]
O Mercy, my *suavius solas* and synguler recreatory,[95]
My predilecte spesyall, ȝe are worthy to hawe my lowe;
For wythowte deserte and menys supplicatorie
Ȝe be compacient to my inexcusabyll reprowe.[96]

A, yt swemyth my hert to thynk how onwysely I hawe wroght.
Tytivillus, þat goth invisibele, hyng hys nett before my eye,
And by hys fantasticall visionys sediciusly sowght,
To New Gyse, Nowadayis, Nowght causyd me to obey.

MERCY
Mankend, ȝe were oblivyows of my doctrine m[o]nytor[y]e.
I seyd before, Titivillus wold asay ȝow a bronte.
Be ware fro hensforth of hys fablys delusory.
Þe prowerbe seyth, '*Jacula prestita minus ledunt.*'[97]

Ȝe hawe thre adversaryis and he ys mayster of hem all:
That ys to sey, the Dewell, þe World, þe Flesch and þe Fell.
The New Gyse , Nowadayis, Nowgth, þe World we may hem call;

846 notorious **848** gamble **849** Canaan **850** authority **852** adultery **854** to you (I say), vain **858** wound, proves curable **859** grievance/suffering **860** have (it), great gift **861** expeditious prayer **862** plentiful **864** is united **866** hour **868** virtue, world **873** special beloved, have my love **876** grieves, unwisely **878** treacherously **880** oblivious (to), admonitory **881** try to attack you **882** deceitful lies **885** skin (an adjunct to the Flesh)

90 'Go, and sin no more.' John 8:11.

91 'But once you have gone [i.e. died], "Unto the smallest farthing" you shall [have to] account for your deserts.'

92 'If you wait until [the moment of] your death, you may chance to lose your desires.'

93 'Behold, now is the accepted time, now is the day of salvation.' 2 Corinthians 6:2.

94 'Your own merits are insufficient to entitle you to enter the bliss of Heaven. You cannot ascend even to the least joy of Heaven by your own efforts. [Only] with mercy can you do so, I tell you no lies, Scripture proves [it].'

95 'My sole sweet and unique source of comfort'.

96 'For without my deserving [it], or my having the means to pay for it, you are compassionate towards my inexcusable shame/grounds for reproof.'

97 'Familiar darts sting less.'

And propy[r]ly Titivillus syngnyfyth the Fend of Helle;

The Flesch, þat ys þe unclene concupissens of ȝour body.
These be ȝour thre gostly enmyis, in whom ȝe hawe put ȝour confidens.
Þei browt ȝow to Myscheffe to conclude ȝour temporall glory,
As yt hath be schewyd before þis worcheppyll audiens.

Remember how redy I was to help ȝow; fro swheche I was not dangerus;
Wherfore, goode sunne, absteyne from syn evermore after þis.
Ȝe may both save and spyll ȝowr sowle þat ys so precyus.
Liebere welle, libere nolle, God may not deny iwys.

Be ware of Titivillus, wyth his net and of all enmys will,
Of ȝour synfull delectacion þat grewyth ȝour gostly substans,
Ȝour body ys ȝour enmy; let hym not have hys wyll.
Take ȝour lewe whan ȝe wyll. God send ȝow good perseverans!

Mank[ynde]
Syth, I schall departe, blyse me, fader, her þen I go.
God send ws all plente of Hys gret mercy.

Mercy
Dominus custodit te ab omni malo
In nomine Patris et Filii et Spiritus Sancti. Amen.[98]

Hic exit Mank[ynde].

[Mercy]
Wyrschepyll sofereyns, I hawe do my propirte:
Mankynd ys deliveryd by my faverall patrocynye.
God preserve hym fro all wyckyd captivite
And send hym grace hys sensuall condicions to mortifye.

Now for Hys lowe þat for us receywyd Hys humanite,
Serge ȝour cond[i]cyons wyth dew examinacion.
Thynke and remembyr þe world ys but a wanite,
As yt ys prowyd daly by d[i]verse transmutacyon.

Mankend ys wrechyd, he hath sufficyent prowe.
Therefore God [grant] ȝow all *per suam misericordiam*
Þat ye may be pleyferys wyth þe angellys abowe
And hawe to ȝour porcyon *vitam eternam.* Amen!

888 concupiscence/lusts **892** such, reluctant **894** lose **895** freely to will, freely not to **897** lusts, spiritual soul **900** here, before **904** been true to my nature **905** benevolent protection **907** inclinations **909** Search, consciences, due **910** vanity **911** many changes **913** by His mercy **914** play-fellows, above **915** reward, eternal life

[98] 'The Lord shall preserve thee from all evil [Psalms 121:7], In the name of the Father . . .'

Everyman, title page, The British Library.

Everyman

Everyman has in many ways become the popular archetype of the Morality Play. It uses its universal hero to exemplify a religious and moral lesson: that death comes to everyone, and always unexpectedly, and, when it does, only our good deeds will help to justify us before God. All worldly things, even lifelong friendships and family ties, will be of no avail. It exemplifies this didactic message through a series of encounters between the protagonist and various allegorical figures representing worldly and spiritual values, and it ends with a short sermon from an authority figure, in this case a Doctor of Divinity, who points up the moral for the benefit of anyone who might have missed it in performance. Yet the play is also profoundly unlike most of its counterparts, as a comparison with the other Moralities in this volume will suggest. It has no Vice figures, for example, and so contains none of the ribald, knockabout comedy associated with them. Nor is there, strictly speaking, any real dramatic tension. The tone is unrelentingly serious and didactic, as befits a drama that its printer chose to describe as 'a treatise . . . in the manner of a moral play'. The hero's allegorical trajectory is not the conventional roller-coaster of Temptation, Fall, and Redemption, but a more regular progress through fixed points representative of the ageing process itself. Everyman is surprised at the height of his powers by Death, who allows him a brief respite to settle his affairs before he must succumb to his/her mortal dart. Failing to find help from the bastions of his worldly life (friends, family, and material wealth each desert him in turn), he turns eventually to his long-neglected Good Deeds, who points him towards Knowledge and Confession as the means by which he can set his spiritual account in order before his appearance before the Heavenly court. Through Confession, penitential mortification of the flesh, and the crucial intervention of Priesthood (who administers the sacraments to the dying protagonist), Everyman is eventually in a fit state to face his Maker and Judge. Finally, as he (literally) approaches his grave, his physical and mental faculties desert him: first Beauty and Strength, then Discretion, Five Wits, and finally Knowledge, until he returns to the earth with only Good Deeds for company. The play is thus an essentially simple one, but as recent productions have shown, not undramatic in its capacity to evoke profoundly ironic humour and pathos. It requires a relatively small cast and a simple stage: a grave for Everyman and, perhaps, a high seat for God, being the only large properties required.

Everyman is also unlike its contemporaries in being a direct translation of an earlier dramatic source, the Dutch play *Elckerlijc* ('Everyman'), written in the 1490s. Its international popularity probably stemmed, in part at least, from its stress upon a number of key aspects of late medieval religious culture. The text was described on its title page as 'The *Summoning* of Everyman', and this usefully identifies its highly church-centred outlook. Death is presented as a medieval summoner, serving writs of subpoena to God's court upon unsuspecting humanity, and Good Deeds is to be both the advocate and the chief witness on Everyman's behalf at his final hearing. In keeping with Augustinian theology, the hero's justification will be decided on the strength of a judicious mixture of good works (both worldly and spiritual), and divine grace (mediated through the sacraments of the institutional church). This emphasis on the role of the clergy also marks the play out as characteristic of the late medieval period. Five Wits' bold assertion (at l. 732 and following) that no emperor (nor even any angel!) has the power enjoyed by the lowliest of priests reflects a supreme confidence in the status and capacities of the Catholic church, just as Knowledge's rejoinder, criticizing sinful clergy for their failings, reflects the emphases and agenda of medieval anticlericalism, the call for reform from within. Finally the emphasis on the omnipresence of death, and the need to learn to die well (the play is a dramatization of Everyman's final moments as well as a rumination upon his entire life), embodies the late medieval obsession with the *Ars Moriendi*, or the 'Art of Dying', which was the subject of many popular treatises and sermons.

Everyman is the first of the plays contained in this anthology to survive in its earliest form in a printed edition. It was first published at some point in the 1510s by the London printer Richard Pynson, who produced a second edition between 1525 and 1530. Around 1528–9 a third edition appeared in London, this time from the presses of John Skot, and it was Skot who produced a fourth edition in the first half of the 1530s. The first two printings survive now only in fragmentary form; the first (STC 1064) is now in the Bodleian Library, Oxford, the second (STC 10604.5) is in the British Library. Of the complete texts, the earlier (STC 10606) is also in the British Library, while the later (STC 10606.5) is in the Huntington Library, California. I have also consulted the modern editions in A.C. Cawley, ed., *Everyman and Medieval Miracle Plays* (London, 1959); and D. Bevington, ed., *Medieval Drama* (Boston, 1975).

[*Dramatis Personae: Messenger, God, Dethe* (Death), *Everyman, Felawshyp* (Friendship), *Kinrede* (Kindred/ Family), *Cosyn* (Cousin), *Goodes* (Wealth/Property), *Good Dedes* (Good Deeds), *Knowledge, Confession, Beaute* (Beauty), *Strength, Discrecion* (Discretion), *Fyve Wyttes* (the Five Senses), *Aungel* (Angel), *Doctour* (a Doctor of Theology, acting as the Epilogue), *Priesthood.*[1]

Here beginneth a treatise how the hye Fader of Heven sendeth Dethe to somon every creature to come and gyve a counte of their lyves in this world, and is in maner of a morall playe.

MESSENGER

I pray you all gyve your audyence,
And here this mater with reverence.
By fygure a morall playe:
The Somonynge of Everyman called it is,
That of our lyves and endynge shewes
How transytory we be all daye.
This mater is wonders precyous,
But the entent of it is more gracyous,
And swete to bere awaye,
The story sayth: Man, in the begynnynge
Loke well, and take good heed to the endynge,
Be you never so gay!
Ye thynke synne in the begynnynge full swete,
Whiche in the ende causeth the soule to wepe
Whan the body lyeth in claye.
Here shall you se how Falawshyp and Jolyte,
Both Strengthe, Pleasure, and Beaute,
Wyll fade from the[e] as floure in Maye;
For ye shall here how our Heven Kynge
Calleth Everyman to a generall rekenynge.
Gyve audyence, and here what He doth saye.

[*Exit.*]

God speketh.

GOD

I perceyve, here in My Majeste,
How that all creatures be to Me unkynde,
Lyvynge without drede in worldly prosperyte.
Of ghostly syght the people be so blynde,
Drowned in synne, they know Me not for theyr God.
In worldely ryches is all theyr mynde;
They fere not My ryghtwysnes, the sharpe rod.
My love that I shewed, whan I for them dyed
They forgete clene, and shedynge of My blode rede.
I hanged bytwene two [theves], it cannot be denyed;
To gete them lyfe I suffred to be deed;
I heled theyr fete,[2] with thornes hurt was My heed.
I coude do no more than I dyde, truely.
And nowe I se the people do clene for-sake Me.
They use the seven deedly synnes dampnable,
As pryde, coveytyse, wrath, and lechery
Now in the worlde be made commendable;
And thus they leve of aungelles the Hevenly
    company.
Every man lyveth so after his owne pleasure,
And yet of theyr lyfe they be nothynge sure.
I se the more that I them forbere
The worse they be fro yere to yere.
All that lyveth appayreth faste.
Therfore I wyll, in all the haste,
Have a rekenynge of every mannes persone;
For, and I leve the people thus alone
In theyr lyfe and wycked tempestes,
Veryly they will become moche worse than beestes!
For now one wolde by envy another up ete,[3]
Charyte they do all clene forgete.
I hoped well that every man
In My glory sholde make his mansyon,[4]
And thereto I had them all electe.
But now I se, lyke traytours dejecte,
They thanke Me not for the pleasure that I to them
    ment,
Nor yet for theyr beynge that I them have lent.
I profered the people grete multytude of mercy,
And fewe there be that asketh it hertly.
They be so combred with worldly ryches
That nedes on them I must do justyce,

1 pay attention 3 In the form of 4 Summoning 5 end (i.e. death) 6 always 7 wonderfully 8 intention 9 sweet, remember 12 However happy you are (now) 13 sin, (is) very sweet 15 in the earth 18 flowers 19 Heavenly 20 account/audit 23 unnatural 28 righteousness/justice 30 red blood 32 bring, dead 34 could 39 reject 44 grows increasingly corrupt 47 if 53 home (i.e. in Heaven) 54 chosen 55 abject 56 for, intended 57 existence 59 sincerely 61 necessarily

1 The Priest, who is addressed but does not speak, may remain offstage.

2 'Washed their feet.' See John 13:4–10.

3 'One person will eat another out of envy'.

4 See John 14:2: 'In My father's house are many mansions . . . I go to prepare a place for you.'

On every man lyvynge, without fere.
Where arte thou, Deth, thou myghty messengere?

[*Enter*] *Dethe.*

DETHE
Almyghty God, I am here at your wyll,
Your commaundement to fulfyll.

GOD
Go thou to Everyman
And shewe hym, in My name,
A pylgrymage he must on hym take
Whyche he in no wyse may escape,
And that he brynge with hym a sure rekenynge
Without delay or ony taryenge.

[*Exit God.*]

DETHE
Lorde, I wyll in the worlde go renne over all,
And cruelly out-serche bothe grete and small.
Every man wyll I beset that lyveth beestly
Out of Goddes lawes, and dredeth not foly.
He that loveth rychesse I wyll stryke with my darte,
His syght to blynde, and fro Heven to departe,
Excepte that almes be his good frende,
In Hell for to dwell, worlde without ende.

[*Enter Everyman.*]

Loo, yonder I se Everyman walkynge.
Full lytell he thynketh on my comynge;
His mynde is on flesshely lustes and his treasure,
And grete payne it shall cause hym to endure
Before the Lorde, Heven Kynge.
Everyman, stande styll! Whyder arte thou goynge
Thus gayly? Hast thou thy Maker forgete?

EVERYMAN
Why askest thou?
Woldest thou wete?

DETHE
Ye[a], syr, I wyll shewe you:
In grete hast I am sende to the[e]
Fro God out of His Mageste.

EVERYMAN
What, sente to me?

DETHE
Ye[a], certaynly.
Thoughe thou have forgete Hym here,
He thynketh on the[e] in the Hevenly sp[h]ere,
As, or we departe, thou shalte knowe.

EVERYMAN
What desyreth God of me?

DETHE
That shall I shewe the[e]:
A rekenynge He wyll nedes have
Without ony lenger respyte.

EVERYMAN
To gyve a rekenynge longer layser I crave!
This blynde mater troubleth my wytte.

DETHE
On the[e] thou must take a longe journey;
Therfore thy boke of counte with the[e] thou brynge,[5]
For tourne agayne thou cannot by no waye.
And loke thou be sure of thy rekenynge,
For before God thou shalte answere and shewe
Thy many badde dedes, and good but a fewe;
How thou hast spente thy lyfe, and in what wyse,
Before the chefe Lorde of Paradyse,
Have ado that we were in that waye,
For, wete thou well, thou shalte make none attournay.[6]

EVERYMAN
Full unredy I am suche rekenynge to gyve.
I knowe the[e] not. What messenger arte thou?

DETHE
I am Dethe, that no man dredeth,
For every man I reste, and no man spareth;

62 doubt 68 undertake 69 way 70 honest account (of himself) 71 tarrying/delay 72 run 73 seek out 74 like beasts 75 does not fear sin 76 spear 78 charitable giving 79 for ever 81 He does not expect 87 Why do you ask 88 Do you want to know 96 before, discover 101 I beg (for) more time 102 dark/uncertain, mind 104 account book 105 turn back 108 only a few good (deeds) 109 manner 115 fears no man 116 arrest

5 The book recording all Everyman's deeds during his life.
6 'Get going so that we can be on our way, because you should know that you will have no attorney [to speak for you].'

For it is Goddes commaundement
That all to me sholde be obedyent.

EVERYMAN
O Deth, thou comest whan I had the[e] leest in mynde!
In thy power it lyeth me to save;
Yet of my good wyl I gyve the[e], yf thou wyl be kynde:
Ye[a], a thousande pounde shalte thou have,
And dyfferre this mater tyll an-other daye.

DETHE
Everyman, it may not be, by no waye.
I set not by golde, sylver, nor rychesse,
Ne by pope, emperour, kynge, duke, ne prynces;
For, and I wolde receyve gyftes grete,
All the worlde I myght gete;
But my custome is clene contrary.
I gyve the[e] no respyte. Come hens, and not tary.

EVERYMAN
Alas, shall I have no lenger respyte?
I may saye Deth gyveth no warnynge!
To thynke on the[e], it maketh my herte seke,
For all unredy is my boke of rekenynge.
But twelve yere and I myght have a-bydynge,[7]
My countynge-boke I wolde make so clere
That my rekenynge I sholde not nede to fere,
Wherfore, Deth, I praye the[e], for Goddes mercy,
Spare me tyll I be provyded of remedy!

DETHE
The[e] avayleth not to crye, wepe, and praye;
But hast the[e] lyghtly that thou were gone that journaye,
And preve they frendes yf thou can;
For, wete thou well, the tyde abydeth no man,
And in the worlde eche lyvynge creature
For Adams synne must dye of nature.

EVERYMAN
Dethe, yf I sholde this pylgrymage take,
And my rekenynge suerly make,
Shewe me, for saynt charyte,
Sholde I not come agayne shortly?

DETHE
No, Everyman. And thou be ones there,
Thou mayst never more come here,
Trust me veryly.

EVERYMAN
O gracyous God in the hye sete celestyall,
Have mercy on me in this moost nede!
Shall I have no company fro this vale terestryall
Of myne acqueyn[taun]ce, that way me to lede?

DETHE
Ye[a], yf ony be so hardy
That wolde go with the[e] and bere the[e] company.
Hye the[e] that thou were gone to Goddes magnyfycence,
Thy rekenynge to gyve before His presence.
What, wenest thou thy lyve is gyven the[e],
And thy worldely gooddes also?

EVERYMAN
I had wende so, veryle.

DETHE
Nay, nay, it was but lende the[e].
For, as soone as thou arte go,
Another a whyle shall have it, and than go ther-fro,[8]
Even as thou hast done.
Everyman, thou arte mad! Thou hast thy wyttes fyve,
And here on Erthe wyll not amende thy lyve;
For sodeynly I do come.

EVERYMAN
O wretched caytyfe, wheder shall I flee
That I myght scape this endles sorowe?
Now, gentyll Deth, spare me tyll to-morowe,
That I may amende me
With good advysement.

DETHE
Naye, therto I wyll not consent,
Nor no man wyll I respyte,

121 wealth 123 If (you will) defer, until 125 set (no store) 127 if, great gifts 128 gain 129 completely the opposite 130 hence 133 sick 139 prepared with 141 hurry, quickly 142 test thy friends 143 waits for (proverbial) 145 because of their nature 147 truly 148 holy 149 Can, return soon 150 once 153 high Heavenly throne 154 great need 155 Earthly valley 156 to guide me? 157 anyone, brave 158 keep 161 do you think, given . . . (forever) 163 thought, truly 164 lent (to) 165 gone 175 advice

7 'If I could only have a delay of twelve years'.

8 'Someone else shall have it, for a while, and then lose it [in turn]'.

But to the herte sodeynly I shall smyte
Without ony advysement.
And now out of thy syght I wyll me hy.
Se thou make the[e] redy shortely,
For thou mayst saye this is the daye
That no man lyvynge may scape a-waye. [*Exit.*]

Everyman
Alas, I may well wepe with syghes depe!
Now have I no maner of company
To helpe me in my journey, and me to kepe;
And also my wrytynge is full unredy.
How shall I do now for to excuse me?
I wolde to God I have never be gete!
To my soule a full grete profyte it had be,
For now I fere paynes huge and grete.
The tyme passeth. Lorde, helpe, that all wrought!
For, though I mourne, it avayleth nought:
The day passeth, and is almoost ago.
I wote not well what for to do.
To whome were I best my complaynt to make?
What and I to Felawshyp therof spake,
And shewyd hym of this sodeyne chaunce?
For in hym is all myne affyaunce,
We have in the worlde so many a daye
Be good frendes, in sporte and playe.

[*Enter Felawshyp.*]

I se hym yonder, certaynely.
I trust that he wyll bere me company;
Therfore to hym wyll I speke to ese my sorowe,
Well mette, good Felawshyp, and good morowe!

Felawshyp
Everyman, good morowe, by this daye!
Syr, why lokest thou so pyteously?
If ony thynge be a-mysse, I praye the[e] me saye,
That I may helpe to remedy.

Everyman
Ye[a], good Felawshyp, Ye[a],
I am in greate jeoparde.

Felawshyp
My true frende, shewe to me your mynde;
I wyll not forsake the[e] to my lyves ende,
In the waye of good company.

Everyman
That was well spoken, and lovyngly.

Felawshyp
Syr, I must nedes knowe your hevynesse;
I have pyte to se you in ony dystresse.
If ony have you wronged, ye shall revenged be,
Thoughe I on the grounde be slayne for the[e];
Though that I knowe before that I sholde dye!

Everyman
Veryly, Felawshyp, gramercy.

Felawshyp
Tusshe, by thy thankes I set not a strawe!
Shewe me your grefe, and saye no more.

Everyman
If I my herte sholde to you breke,
And than you to tourne your mynde fro me
And wolde not me comforte whan ye here me speke,
Than sholde I ten tymes soryer be.

Felawshyp
Syr, I saye as I wyll do in-dede.

Everyman
Than be you a good frende at nede!
I have founde you true here-before.

Felawshyp
And so ye shall evermore.
For, in fayth, and thou go to Hell,
I wyll not forsake the[e] by the waye.

Everyman
Ye speke lyke a good frende! I byleve you well.
I shall deserve it, and I maye.

Felawshyp
I speke of no deservynge, by this daye!
For he that wyll saye, and nothynge do,
Is not worthy with good company to go.
Therfore shewe me the grefe of your mynde,
As to your frende moost lovynge and kynde.

Everyman
I shall shewe you how it is:

178 strike 179 warning 180 go 186 protect 187 writing (in the account book) 189 been born 190 would have been 191 great 192 Who created everything 194 gone 197 What if 198 unexpected event 199 my trust 201 Been 208 tell me 213 life's 216 sorrow 218 anyone has 220 Even if I knew in advance 221 thank you 222 There's no need to thank me! 224 open 225 then if you were to 227 sorrier 229 in 230 in the past 235 repay

Commaunded I am to go a journaye;
A longe waye, harde and daungerous,
And gyve a strayte counte, without delaye,
Before the hye Juge, Adonay.[9]
Wherfore, I pray you, bere me company,
As ye have promysed, in this journaye.

FELAWSHYP
This is mater in-dede! Promyse is duty;
But, and I sholde take suche a vyage on me,
I knowe it well, it sholde be to my payne.
Also it make[th] me aferde, certayne.
But let us take counsell here, as well as we can,
For your wordes wolde fere a stronge man.

EVERYMAN
Why, ye sayd yf I had nede
Ye wolde me never forsake, quycke ne deed,
Thoughe it were to Hell, truely.

FELAWSHYP
So I sayd, certaynely,
But suche pleasures be set a-syde, the sothe to saye.
And also, yf we toke such a journaye,
Whan sholde we agayne come?

EVERYMAN
Naye, never agayne, tyll the Daye of Dome.

FELAWSHYP
In fayth, than wyll not I come there!
Who hath you these tydynges brought?

EVERYMAN
In-dede, Deth was with me here.

FELAWSHYP
Now, by God that all hathe bought,
If Deth were the messenger,
For no man that is lyvynge to-daye
I wyll not go that lothe journaye,
Not for the fader that bygate me!

EVERYMAN
Ye promysed other-wyse, parde!

FELAWSHYP
I wote well I say[d] so, truely.
And yet, yf thou wylte ete, and drynke, and make good chere,
Or haunt to women the lusty company,
I wolde not forsake you whyle the daye is clere,
Trust me, veryly.

EVERYMAN
Ye[a], therto ye wolde be redy!
To go to myrthe, solas, and playe
Your mynde wyll soner apply,
Than to bere me company in my longe journaye.

FELAWSHYP
Now, in good fayth, I wyll not that waye.
But, and thou wyll murder, or ony man kyll,
In that I wyll helpe the[e] with a good wyll.

EVERYMAN
O, that is a symple advyse, in-dede.
Gentyll Felawe, helpe me in my necessyte!
We have loved longe, and now I nede;
And now, gentyll Felawshyp, remembre me.

FELAWSHYP
Wheder ye have loved me or no,
By Saynt Johan, I wyll not with the[e] go.

EVERYMAN
Yet, I pray the[e], take the labour and so moche for me
To brynge me forwarde, for saynt charyte,
And comforte me tyll I come without the towne.

FELAWSHYP
Nay, and thou wolde gyve me a newe gowne,
I wyll not a fote with the[e] go.
But, and thou had taryed, I wolde not have lefte the[e] so.
And as now God spede the[e] in thy journaye,
For from the[e] I wyll departe as fast as I maye.

EVERYMAN
Wheder a-waye, Felawshyp? Wyll thou forsake me?

244 strict account 245 judge 248 a serious business 249 voyage/journey 250 painful to me 251 frightened, certainly 253 frighten 255 alive (n)or dead 260 return 261 Judgement 265 redeemed 268 loathsome 269 begat 270 by God 272 make merry 273 keep (the company of) 274 (i.e. ever) 276 (Oh) yeah, you'd be ready for that 277 solace 278 concentrate upon 283 that's foolish talk 288 St John 290 escort me (part of the way) 291 to the edge of 292 (even) if 293 foot 294 stayed here 295 prosper

9 Adonai, 'the Lord': a Hebrew name for God.

Felawshyp
Ye[a], by my faye! To God I be-take the[e].

Everyman
Farewell, good Felawshyp! For the[e] my herte is sore.
A-dewe forever! I shall se the[e] no more.

Felawshyp
In fayth, Everyman, farewell now at the end[ynge]!
For you I wyll remembre that partynge is mournynge. [*Exit.*]

Everyman
Alacke, shall we thus departe indede
(A, Lady, helpe!) without ony more comforte?
Lo, Felawshyp forsaketh me in my moost nede.
For helpe in this worlde wheder shall I resorte?
Felawshyp here-before with me wolde mery make,
And now lyttell sorowe for me dooth he take.
It is sayd, in prosperyte men frendes may fynde,
Whiche in adversyte be full unkynde.
Now wheder for socoure shall I flee,
Syth that Felawshyp hath forsaken me?
To my kynnesmen I wyll, truely,
Prayenge them to helpe me in my necessyte.
I byleve that they wyll do so,
For kynde wyll crepe where it may not go.[10]

[*Enter Kinrede and Cosyn.*]

I wyll go saye, for yonder I se them.
Where be ye now, my frendes and kynnesmen?

Kinrede
Here be we now, at your commaundement.
Cosyn, I praye you shewe us your entent
In ony wyse, and not spare.

Cosyn
Ye[a], Everyman, and to us declare
If ye be dysposed to go ony-whyder;
For, wete you well, [we] wyll lyve and dye to-gyder.

Kinrede
In welth and wo we wyll with you holde,
For over his kynne a man may be bolde.

Everyman
Gramercy, my frendes and kynnesmen kynde.
Now shall I shewe you the grefe of my mynde:
I was commaunded by a messenger
That is a hye kynges chefe offycer;
He bad me go a pylgrymage, to my payne,
And I knowe well I shall never come agayne.
Also I must gyve a rekenynge strayte,
For I have a grete enemy that hath me in wayte,
Which entendeth me for to hynder.

Kinrede
What a-counte is that whiche ye must render?
That wolde I know.

Everyman
Of all my workes I must shewe
How I have lyved, and my dayes spent;
Also of yll dedes that I have used
In my tyme, syth lyfe was me lent,
And of all vertues that I have refused.
Therfore, I praye you, go thyder with me
To helpe to make myn accounte, for saynt charyte.

Cosyn
What, to go thyder? Is that the mater?
Nay, Everyman, I had lever fast brede and water
All this fyve yere and more.

Everyman
Alas that ever I was bore!
For now shall I never be mery
If that you forsake me.

Kinrede
A, syr, what? Ye be a mery man!
Take good herte to you, and make no mone.
But one thynge, I warne you, by Saynt Anne:
As for me, ye shall go alone.

Everyman
My Cosyn, wyll you not with me go?

298 faith, commend 300 adieu/farewell 302 sorrowful 304 (i.e. the Virgin Mary) 306 where shall I go? 308 show 311 help 313 kinsmen/family 316 family, crawl, walk 317 (and) test (that maxim) 321 don't hold back 323 anywhere 324 believe 325 stick with you 326 with, frank 331 commanded (to) on (a) 334 lies in wait for me 335 Who intends to hinder me 340 sinful, done 341 since, lent (to) me 346 rather fast (on) 348 born 352 complaint

10 Proverbial, i.e. family will always get there in the end, however difficult the journey ('blood is thicker than water').

Cosyn
No, by Our Lady! I have the crampe in my to.
Trust not to me, for, so God me spede,
I wyll deceyve you in your moost nede.

Kinrede
It avayleth not us to tyse.
Ye shall have my mayde with all my herte;
She loveth to go to feestes, there to be nyse,
And to daunce, and a-brode to sterte;
I wyll gyve her leve to helpe you in that journey,
If that you and she may a-gree.

Everyman
Now, shewe me the very effecte of your mynde:
Wyll you go with me, or abyde be-hynde?

Kinrede
Abyde behynd? Ye[a], that wyll I, and I maye!
Therfore farewell tyll another daye. [*Exit.*]

Everyman
Howe sholde I be mery or gladde?
For, fayre promyses men to me make,
But whan I have moost nede they me forsake.
I am deceyved; that maketh me sadde.

Cosyn
Cosyn Everyman, farewell now,
For veryly I wyll not go with you.
Also of myne owne an unredy rekenynge
I have to accounte;[11] therfore I make taryenge.
Now God kepe the[e], for now I go. [*Exit.*]

Everyman
A, Jesus, is all come here-to?
Lo, fayre wordes maketh fooles fayne;
They promyse, and nothynge wyll do, certayne.
My kynnesmen promysed me faythfully
For to a-byde with me stedfastly,
And now fast a-waye do they flee;
Even so Felawshyp promysed me;
What frende were best me of to provyde?
I lose my tyme here longer to abyde.
Yet in my mynde a thynge there is:
All my lyfe I have loved ryches.
If that my Good now helpe me myght,
He wolde make my herte full lyght.
I wyll speke to hym in this dystress.
Where arte thou, my Gooddes and ryches?

[*Enter Goodes.*]

Goodes
Who calleth me? Everyman? What hast thou haste?
I lye here in corners, trussed and pyled so hye,
And in chestes I am locked so fast,
Also sacked in bagges. Thou mayst se with thyn eye
I cannot styre; in packes lowe I lye.
What wolde ye have? Lyghtly me saye.

Everyman
Come hyder, Good, in al the hast thou may,
For of counseyll I must desyre the[e].

Goodes
Syr, and ye in the worlde have sorowe or adversyte,
That can I helpe you to remedy shortly.

Everyman
It is another dysease that greveth me;
In this worlde it is not, I tell the[e] so.
I am sent for another way to go,
To gyve a strayte counte generall
Before the hyest Jupyter of all.
And all my lyfe I have had joye and pleasure in the[e].
Therfore, I pray the[e], go with me.
For, paraventure, thou mayst before God Almyghty
My rekenynge helpe to clene and puryfye;
For it is sayd ever amonge
That money maketh all ryght that is wronge.

Goodes
Nay, Everyman, I synge another songe!
I folowe no man in suche vyages;
For, and I wente with the[e],
Thou sholdes fare moche the worse for me.
For bycause on me thou dyd set thy mynde,
Thy rekenynge I have made blotted and blynde;
That thyne accounte thou cannot make truly;
And that hast thou for the love of me!

356 toe 357 God bless me 358 greatest 359 Trying to entice us won't help 360 maid-servant 361 feasts, flirtatious 362 to travel about 363 permission 365 true intent 367 if I can! 378 to this 379 glad/eager 385 would best provide for me 386 waste 389 property 394 tied up (in bags) 396 your (own) eyes 398 tell me quickly 399 haste 400 (your) advice 406 strict final account 407 (i.e. chief God) 410 perhaps 412 people always say 419 illegible 420 clearly read 421 you have (done) through

[11] 'And I have my own unprepared-for reckoning to make'.

EVERYMAN
That wolde greve me full sore,
Whan I sholde come to that ferefull answere.
Up, let us go thyder to-gyder.

GOODES
Nay, not so! I am to brytell, I may not endure.
I wyll folowe [no] man one fote, be ye sure.

EVERYMAN
Alas, I have the[e] loved, and had grete pleasure
All my lyfe-dayes on good and treasure!

GOODES
That is to thy dampnacyon, without lesynge,
For my love is contrary to the love everlastynge.
But, yf thou had me loved moderately durynge,
As to the poore gyve parte of me,
Than sholdest thou not in this dolour be,
Nor in this grete sorowe and care.

EVERYMAN
Lo, now was I deceyved or I was ware,
And all I may wyte my[s]spendynge of tyme![12]

GOODES
What, wenest thou that I am thyne?

EVERYMAN
I had went so.

GOODES
Naye, Everyman, I saye no.
As for a whyle I was lente the[e];
A season thou hast had me in prosperyte.
My condycyon is mannes soule to kyll;
If I save one, a thousande I do spyll.
Wenest thou that I wyll folowe the[e]?
Nay, fro this worlde not, veryle.

EVERYMAN
I had wende otherwyse.

GOODES
Therfore to thy soule Good is a thefe;
For whan thou arte deed, this is my gyse:
Another to deceyve in this same wyse
As I have done the[e], and all to his soules reprefe.

EVERYMAN
O false Good, cursed thou be,
Thou traytour to God, that has deceyved me
And caugh[t] me in thy snare!

GOODES
Mary, thou brought thyselfe in care,
Wherof I am gladde;
I must nedes laugh, I can-not be sadde.

EVERYMAN
A, Good, thou hast had longe my hertely love!
I gave the[e] that whiche sholde be the Lordes above.
But wylte thou not go with me in-dede?
I pray the[e] trouth to saye.

GOODES
No, so God me spede!
Therfore fare-well, and have good daye. [*Exit.*]

EVERYMAN
O, to whome shall I make my mone,
For to go with me in that hevy journaye?
Fyrst Felawshyp sayd he wolde with me gone.
His wordes were very pleasaunt and gaye,
But afterwarde he lefte me alone.
Than spake I to my kynnesmen, all in dyspayre,
An[d] also they gave me wordes fayre;
They lacked no fayre spekynge,
But all forsoke me in the endynge.
Than wente I to my Goodes, that I loved best,
In hope to have comforte; but there had I leest,
For my Goodes sharpely dyd me tell
That he bryngeth many in to Hell.
Than of myselfe I was ashamed;
And so I am worthy to be blamed.
Thus may I well myselfe hate.
Of whome shall I now counseyll take?
I thynke that I shall never spede
Tyll that I go to my Good Dede.
But, alas, she is so weke
That she can nother go nor speke.
Yet wyll I venter on her now.
My Good Dedes, where be you?

[*Enter Good Dedes, crawling.*]

423 dreadful judgement 425 too brittle/fragile 428 in goods 429 deception 430 (i.e. the love of God) 431 during (your life) 433 sorrow 435 before I knew it 437 do you believe I belong to you 438 thought 441 (For) a time 442 nature 443 ruin 446 believed 448 habit 449 way 450 reproof/ruin 454 into trouble 457 heartfelt 463 complaint 464 sad 480 prosper 483 neither walk 484 try her

[12] 'And now I know that I have misspent my time!'

GOOD DEDES
Here I lye, colde in the grounde.
Thy synnes hath me sore bounde,
That I cannot stere.

EVERYMAN
O Good Dedes, I stande in fere!
I must you pray of counseyll,
For helpe now sholde come ryght well.

GOOD DEDES
Everyman, I have understandynge
That ye be somoned a-counte to make
Before Myssyas, of Jherusalem kynge;
And you do by me, that journay with you wyll I take.

EVERYMAN
Therfore I come to you my moone to make.
I praye you that ye wyll go with me.

GOOD DEDES
I wolde full fayne, but I cannot stande, veryly.

EVERYMAN
Why, is there ony-thynge on you fall?

GOOD DEDES
Ye[a], syr, I may thanke you of all!
If ye had parfytely chered me,
Your boke of counte full redy had be.
Loke, the bokes of your workes and dedes eke!
[See] how they lye under the fete,
To your soules hevynes.

EVERYMAN [*Trying to read the book*]
Our Lorde Jesus helpe me!
For one letter here I can-not se.

GOOD DEDES
Here is a blynde rekenynge in tyme of dystres!

EVERYMAN
Good Dedes, I praye you helpe me in this nede,
Or elles I am forever dampned in-dede!
Therfore helpe me to make rekenynge
Before the Redemer of all thynge,
That Kynge is, and was, and ever shall.

GOOD DEDES
Everyman, I am sory of your fall,
And fayne wolde I helpe you, and I were able.

EVERYMAN
Good Dedes, your counseyll I pray you gyve me.

GOOD DEDES
That shall I do, veryly.
Thoughe that on my fete I may not go,
I have a syster that shall with you also,
Called Knowlege, whiche shall with you abyde,
To helpe you to make that dredefull rekenynge.

[*Enter Knowledge.*]

KNOWLEDGE
Everyman, I wyll go with the[e], and be thy gyde,
In thy moost nede to go by thy syde.

EVERYMAN
In good condycyon I am now in every-thynge,
And am holy content with this good thynge,
Thanked be God, my Creature!

GOOD DEDES
And whan [s]he hath brought you there
Where thou shalte hele the[e] of thy smarte,
Than go you with your rekenynge and your Good Dedes togyder
For to make you joyfull at herte
Before the Blessyd Trynyte.

EVERYMAN
My Good Dedes, gramercy!
I am well content, certaynly,
With your wordes swete.

KNOWLEDGE
Now go we togyder lovyngly
To Confessyon, that clensynge ryvere.

EVERYMAN
For joy I wepe; I wolde we were there!
But, I pray you, gyve me cognycyon,
Where dwelleth that holy man, Confessyon?

KNOWLEDGE
In the hous of salvacyon;
We shall fynde hym in that place

488 move 494 Messiah, Jerusalem 495 if you'll take my advice 496 complaint 498 very willingly 499 has something befallen you 500 for all (of it) 501 treated me properly 502 (would) have been 503 also 505 sorrow 513 shall (be) 525 wholly 526 Creator 528 heal, pain(s) 536 river 537 wish 538 knowledge

That shall us comforte, by Goddes grace.
Lo, this is Confessyon. Knele downe and aske mercy,
For he is in good conceyte with God Almyghty.

EVERYMAN
O gloryous fountayne, that all unclennes doth claryfy,
Wasshe fro me the spottes of vyce unclene,
That on me no synne may be sene.
I come with Knowlege for my redempcyon,
Redempte with herte and full contrycyon;
For I am commaunded a pylgrymage to take,
And grete accountes before God to make.
Now I praye you, Shryfte, moder of salvacyon,
Helpe my Good Dedes for my pyteous exclamacyon!

CONFESSION
I knowe your sorowe well, Everyman.
Bycause with Knowlege ye come to me,
I wyll you comforte as well as I can.
And a precyous jewell I wyll gyve the[e]
Called penaunce, voyder of adversyte;
Therwith shall your body chastysed be
With abstynence and perseveraunce in Goddes servyture.
Here shall you receyve that scourge of me,
Whiche is penaunce stronge that ye must endure,
To remembre thy Savyour was scourged for the[e]
With sharpe scourges, and suffred it pacyently;
So must thou, or thou scape that paynful pylgrymage.
Knowledge, kepe Hym in this vyage,
And by that tyme Good Dedes wyll be with the[e].
But in ony wyse be seker of mercy,
For your tyme draweth fast. And ye wyll saved be,
Aske God mercy, and He wyll graunte truely.
Whan with the scourge of penaunce man doth hym bynde,
The oyle of forgyvenes than shall he fynde.

EVERYMAN
Thanked be God for His gracyous werke!
For now I wyll my penaunce begyn.
This hath rejoysed and lyghted my herte,
Though the knottes be paynful and harde, within.

KNOWLEDGE
Everyman, loke your penaunce that ye fulfyll,
What payne that ever it to you be;
And Knowlege shall gyve you counseyll at wyll
How your accounte ye shall make clerely.

EVERYMAN
O eternall God, O hevenly Fygure,
O way of ryghtwysnes, O goodly vysyon,
Whiche dyscended downe in a vyrgyn pure
Bycause He wolde every man redeme,
Whiche Adam forfayted by his dysobedyence:
O blessyd God-heed, electe and hye Devyne,
Forgyve my grevous offence!
Here I crye The[e] mercy in this presence.
O ghostly treasure, O raunsomer and redemer,
Of all the worlde hope and conduyter,
Myrrour of joye, foundatour of mercy,
Which enlumyneth Heven and Erth therby:
Here my clamorous complaynt, though it late be;
Receyve my prayers, [of Thy benignitye!]
Though I be a synner moost abhomynable,
Yet let my name be wryten in Moyses table.
O Mary, praye to the Maker of all thynge,
Me for to helpe at my endynge,
And save me fro the power of my enemy;
For Deth assayleth me strongly.
And, Lady, that I may be meane of thy prayer
Of your Sones glory to be partynere,
By the meanes of His Passion, I it crave.
I beseche you helpe my soule to save!
Knowledge, gyve me the scourge of penaunce:
My flesshe therwith shall gyve acqueyntaunce.
I wyll now begyn, yf God gyve me grace.

KNOWLEDGE
Everyman, God gyve you tyme and space!
Thus I bequeth you in the handes of our Savyour.
Now may you make your rekenynge sure.

EVERYMAN
In the name of the Holy Trynyte,
My body sore punyshed shall be.

[*He scourges himself.*]

Take this, body, for the synne of the flesshe!
Also thou delytest to go gay and fresshe,
And in the way of dampnacyon thou dyd me brynge;
Therfore suffre now strokes of punysshynge.
Now of penaunce I wyll wade the water clere,
To save me from Purgatory, that sharpe fyre.

544 on good terms 545 corruption, purify 552 Confession 558 penance, remover 560 service 561 whip from 562 harsh 565 before 568 all things, certain 569 is running out, If 572 oil/balm, then 575 lightened 576 knots (in the whip) 578 However painful 579 whenever you want 581 image/being 585 (That) which, forfeited through 586 Godhead, Divinity 589 ransomer 590 (the) hope, guide 591 founder 592 illuminates 593 Hear 594 generosity 596 book (of chosen souls) 601 by means 602 Son's, sharer 614 delighted, appear elegant 615 path

[*Good Dedes stands up.*]

GOOD DEDES
I thanke God, now I can walke and go,
And am delyvered of my sykenesse and wo!
Therfore with Everyman I wyll go, and not spare:
His good workes I wyll helpe hym to declare.

KNOWLEDGE
Now, Everyman, be mery and glad!
Your Good Dedes cometh now; ye may not be sad.
Now is your Good Dedes hole and sounde,
Goynge upryght upon the grounde.

EVERYMAN
My herte is lyght, and shal be evermore.
Now wyll I smyte faster than I dyde before.

[GOOD] DEDES
Everyman, pylgryme, my specyall frende,
Blessyd be thou without ende!
For the[e] is preparate the eternall glory.
Ye have me made hole and sounde,
Therfore I wyll byde by the[e] in every stounde.

EVERYMAN
Welcome, my Good Dedes! Now I here thy voyce,
I wepe for very swetenes of love.

KNOWLEDGE
Be no more sad, but ever rejoyce.
God seeth thy lyvynge in His trone above.
Put on this garment to thy behove,
Which is wette with your teres,
Or elles before God you may it mysse,
Whan ye to your journeys ende come shall.

EVERYMAN
Gentyll Knowledge, what do ye it call?

KNOWLEDGE
It is the garment of sorowe.
Fro payne it wyll you borowe.
Contrycyon it is,
That getteth forgyvenes;
It pleaseth God passynge well.

GOOD DEDES
Everyman, wyll you were it for your hele?

[*Everyman puts on the robe.*]

EVERYMAN
Now blessyd be Jesu, Maryes sone,
For now have I on true contrycyon.
And lette us go now without taryenge.
Good Dedes, have we clere our rekenynge?

GOOD DEDES
Ye[a], in-dede, I have [it] here.

EVERYMAN
Than I trust we nede not fere.
Now frendes, let us not parte in twayne.

KNOWLEDGE
Nay, Everyman, that wyll we not, certayne.

GOOD DEDES
Yet must thou led[e] with the[e]
Thre persones of grete myght.

EVERYMAN
Who sholde they be?

GOOD DEDES
Dyscrecyon and Strength they hyght,
And thy Beaute may not abyde behynde.

KNOWLEDGE
Also ye must call to mynde
Your Fyve Wyttes as for your counseylours.

GOOD DEDES
You must have them redy at all houres.

EVERYMAN
How shall I gette them hyder?

KNOWLEDGE
You must call them all togyder,
And they wyll here you incontynent.

EVERYMAN
My frendes, come hyder and be present,
Dyscrecyon, Strengthe, my Fyve Wyttes, and
Beaute!

[*Enter Discrecion, Strength, Fyve Wyttes, and Beaute.*]

620 sickness, woe 625 whole, intact 628 strike (myself) 631 eternal glory is prepared for you 633 situation 637 throne 638 appropriate for you 639 tears 640 lack 644 redeem 646 brings 647 above all things 648 wear 649 Mary's son 651 delay 655 become separated 658 great power 659 Who are they 667 hear, immediately

Beaute
Here at your wyll we be all redy.
What wolde ye that we sholde do?

Good Dedes
That ye wolde with Everyman go,
And helpe hym in his pylgrymage.
Advyse you, wyll ye with him or not in that vyage?

Strength
We wyll brynge hym all thyder,
To his helpe and comforte, ye may byleve me.

Discrecion
So wyll we go with hym all togyder.

Everyman
Almyghty God, loved may Thou be!
I gyve The[e] laude that I have hyder brought
Strength, Dyscrecyon, Beaute, and Fyve Wyttes.
Lacke I nought.
And my Good Dedes, with Knowlege clere,
All be in company at my wyll here.
I desyre no more to my besynes.

Strength
And I, Strength, wyll by you stand in dystres,
Though thou wolde in batayle fyght on the grounde.

Fyve Wyttes
And though it were thrugh the worlde rounde,
We wyll not departe, for swete ne soure.

Beaute
No more wyll I, unto dethes houre,
Whatsoever therof befall.[13]

Discrecion
Everyman, advyse you fyrst of all;
Go with a good advysement and delyberacyon.
We all gyve you vertuous monycyon
That all shall be well.

Everyman
My frendes, harken what I wyll tell;
I praye God rewarde you in His Heven[ly] sp[h]ere.
Now herken all that be here,
For I wyll make my testament
Here before you all present:
In almes halfe my good I wyll gyve with my handes twayne
In the way of charyte, with good entent,
And the other halfe styll shall remayne
In queth, to be retourned there it ought to be.
This I do in despyte of the Fende of Hell,
To go quyte out of his perell
Ever after and this daye.

Knowledge
Everyman, herken what I saye:
Go to Presthode, I you advyse,
And receyve of hym, in ony wyse,
The Holy Sacrament and oyntement togyder.[14]
Than shortly se ye tourne agayne hyder;
We wyll all abyde you here.

Fyve Wyttes
Ye[a], Everyman, hye you that ye redy were.
There is no emperour, kynge, duke, ne baron
That of God hath commycyon
As hath the leest preest in the worlde beynge;
For of the blessyd Sacramentes pure and benygne
He bereth the keyes,[15] and therof hath the cure
For mannes redempcyon (it is ever sure!)
Whiche God for our soules medycyne
Gave us out of His herte with grete pyne.
Here in this transytory lyfe, for the[e] and me,
The blessyd sacramentes seven there be:
Baptym, confyrmacyon, with preesthode good,
And the sacrament of Goddes precyous flesshe and blod,
Maryage, the holy extreme unccyon, and penaunce.
These seven be good to have in remembraunce,
Gracyous sacramentes of hye devynyte.

679 praise **683** for my purpose **684** distress **685** battle **686** anywhere throughout **687** (i.e. whatever the task) **688** the moment of death **691** advice **692** forewarning **699** two hands **700** intention **702** bequest, where **703** Fiend **704** To escape his peril **707** Priesthood **708** however you can **710** return **712** hurry **714** (the same) authority **715** the lowliest priest **717** responsibility **719** healing **720** pain **723** Baptism, Holy Orders **724** the Eucharist

[13] 'Whatever happens as a consequence.'

[14] The Eucharist, received from the priest during the Mass, and Extreme Unction, the final Sacrament, received immediately prior to death.

[15] A reference to Christ's words to the Apostle Peter, 'And I will give unto thee the keys of the Kingdom of Heaven: and whatsoever thou shalt bind on Earth shall be bound in Heaven, and whatsoever thou shalt loose on Earth shall be loosed in Heaven.' Matthew 16:19.

EVERYMAN
Fayne wolde I receyve that holy body,
And mekely to my ghostly fader I wyll go.

FYVE WYTTES
Everyman, that is the best that ye can do.
God wyll you to salvacyon brynge,
For preesthode excedeth all other thynge.
To us Holy Scrypture they do teche,
And converteth man fro synne, Heven to reche.
God hath to them more power gyven
Than to ony aungell that is in Heven.
With fyve wordes he may consecrate
Goddes body in flesshe and blode to make,
And handeleth his Maker bytwene his hande[s].[16]
The preest byndeth and unbyndeth all bandes,
Both in Erthe and in Heven.
[*To Priesthood (offstage?)*] Thou mynystres all the sacramentes seven;
Though we kysse thy fete, thou were worthy!
Thou arte surgyon that cureth synne deedly;
No remedy we fynde under God
But all onely preesthode.
Everyman, God gave preest[s] that dygnyte,
And setteth them in His stede amonge us to be.
Thus be they above aungelles in degree.

[*Exit Everyman to receive the sacrament and extreme unction from Priesthood.*]

KNOWLEDGE
If preestes be good, it is so, suerly.
But whan Jesu hanged on the Crosse with grete smarte,
There He gave out of His blessyd herte
The seven Sacramentes in grete tourment.
He solde them not to us, that Lorde omnypotent!
Therefore Saynt Peter the Apostell doth saye
That Jesus curse hath all they
Whiche God theyr Savyour do by or sell,
Or they for ony money do take or tell.[17]
Synfull preestes gyveth the synners example bad:
Theyr chyldren sytteth by other mennes fyres, I have harde;[18]
And some haunteth womens company
With unclene lyfe, as lustes of lechery.
These be with synne made blynde.

FYVE WYTTES
I trust to God no suche may we fynde.
Therfore let us preesthode honour,
And folowe theyr doctryne for our soules socoure.
We be theyr shepe, and they shepeherdes be,
By whome we all be kepte in suerte.
Peas, for yonder I se Everyman come,
Whiche hath made true satysfaccyon.

GOOD DEDES
Me thynke it is he in dede.

EVERYMAN
Now Jesu be your alder spede!
I have receyved the sacrament for my redempcyon,
And than myne extreme unccyon.
Blessyd be all they that counseyled me to take it!
And now, frendes, let us go with-out longer respyte;
I thanke God that ye have taryed so longe.
Now set eche of you on this Rodde your honde,
And shortely folowe me.
I go before there I wolde be. God be our gyde!

STRENGTH
Everyman, we wyll not fro you go
Tyll ye have done this vyage longe.

DISCRECION
I, Dyscrecyon, wyll byde by you also.

KNOWLEDGE
And though this pylgrymage be never so stronge,
I wyll never parte you fro.
Everyman, I wyll be as sure by the[e]
As ever I dyde by Judas Machabee.[19]

728 Eagerly, (i.e. the Body of Christ) 729 spiritual father (Priesthood) 732 surpasses (in holiness) 733 teach 734 reach 740 bonds 744 surgeon, deadly sin 746 through the priesthood 747 authority 748 to represent Him among us 749 status 750 certainly 751 pain 752 heart 753 torment 756 They have Jesus's curse 757 who, buy 760 heard 762 corrupt living, (such) as 764 no such (bad priests) 766 succour 768 safety 769 Peace/Quiet! 772 the helper of you all 774 then 778 place, hand, Rood/Crucifix 779 quickly 780 where, want to 784 hard

[16] Only priests have the power to consecrate the bread and wine at the mass. Not even angels have that power. The five words are '*Hoc est enim corpus meum*', 'For this is my body', Christ's words at the Last Supper (see Matthew 26:26) spoken by the priest at the moment of consecration.

[17] Knowledge qualifies the encomium of priesthood offered by Fyve Wyttes by condemning those priests who fall short of the ideal, especially those who take money for providing those sacraments which Christ gave freely.

[18] i.e. some married women have children by their clerical lovers and pass them off as their husbands' legitimate offspring.

[19] Judas Maccabeus; see I Maccabees 2:4 and following.

EVERYMAN
Alas, I am so faynt I may not stande!
My lymmes under me do folde.
Frendes, let us not tourne agayne to this lande,
Not for all the worldes golde;
For in to this cave must I crepe
And tourne to erth, and there to slepe.[20]

BEAUTE
What, in to this grave? Alas!

EVERYMAN
Ye[a], there shall ye consume, more and lesse.

BEAUTE
And what, sholde I smoder here?

EVERYMAN
Ye[a], by my fayth, and never more appere.
In this worlde lyve no more we shall,
But in Heven before the hyest Lorde of all.

BEAUTE
I crosse out all this! Adewe, by Saynt Johan!
I take my tappe in my lappe and am gone.

EVERYMAN
What, Beaute, whyder wyll ye?

BEAUTE
Peas, I am defe! I loke not behynde me,
Not and thou woldest gyve me all the golde in thy chest! [*Exit.*]

EVERYMAN
Alas, wherto may I trust?
Beaute gothe fast awaye fro me.
She promysed with me to lyve and dye.

STRENGTH
Everyman, I wyll the[e] also forsake and denye.
Thy game lyketh me not at all.

EVERYMAN
Why, than ye wyll forsake me all?
Swete Strength, tary a lytell space.

STRENGTH
Nay, syr, by the Rode of Grace!
I wyll hye me from the[e] fast,
Though thou wepe to thy herte to-brast.

EVERYMAN
Ye wolde ever byde by me, ye sayd.

STRENGTH
Ye[a], I have you ferre ynoughe conveyde!
Ye be olde ynoughe, I understande,
Your pylgrymage to take on hande.
I repent me that I hyder came.

EVERYMAN
Strength, you to dysplease I am to blame,
Yet, promyse is dette, this ye well wot.

STRENGTH
In fayth, I care not.
Thou arte but a foole to complayne.
You spende your speche, and wast your brayne.
Go thryst the[e] into the grounde! [*Exit.*]

EVERYMAN
I had wende surer I sholde you have founde.[21]
He that trusteth in his Strength,
She hym deceyveth at the length.
Bothe Strength and Beaute forsaketh me,
Yet they promysed me fayre and lovyngly.

DISCRECION
Everyman, I wyll after Strength be gone.
As for me, I wyll leve you alone.

EVERYMAN
Why, Dyscrecyon, wyll ye forsake me?

DISCRECION
Ye[a], in fayth, I wyll go fro the[e],
For whan Strength goth before,
I folowe after ever-more.

EVERYMAN
Yet, I pray the[e], for the love of the Trynyte,
Loke in my grave ones pyteously!

789 collapse **793** return **795** be consumed **796** suffocate **800** reject all this, farewell, John **801** distaff **803** deaf **804** Not (even) if **805** who **808** reject **809** business **811** little while **813** hurry **814** until, bursts **816** escorted you far enough **820** reluctant **821** a promise is a promise **824** waste, words **825** jump **828** eventually **838** once

[20] See Genesis 3:19; 'dust thou art and unto dust thou shalt return'.

[21] 'I believed that I would find you [a] surer ally.'

DISCRECION
Nay, so nye wyll I not come.
Fare-well, everychone! [*Exit.*]

EVERYMAN
O, all thynge fayleth, save God alone:
Beaute, Strength, and Dyscrecyon;
For whan Deth bloweth his blast
They all renne fro me full fast.

FYVE WYTTES
Everyman, my leve now of the[e] I take.
I wyll folowe the other, for here I the[e] forsake.

EVERYMAN
Alas, than may I wayle and wepe!
For I toke you for my best frende.

FYVE WYTTES
I wyll no lenger the[e] kepe.
Now farewell, and there an ende. [*Exit.*]

EVERYMAN
O Jesu, helpe! All hath forsaken me.

GOOD DEDES
Nay, Everyman, I wyll byde with the[e].
I wyll not forsake the[e] in-dede;
Thou shalte fynde me a good frende at nede.

EVERYMAN
Gramercy, Good Dedes! Now may I true frendes se.
They have forsaken me, everychone;
I loved them better than my Good Dedes alone.
Knowlege, wyll ye forsake me also?

KNOWLEDGE
Ye[a], Everyman, whan ye to Deth shall go;
But not yet, for no maner of daunger.

EVERYMAN
Gramercy, Knowlege, with all my herte!

KNOWLEDGE
Nay, yet I wyll not from hens departe
Tyll I se where ye shall be-come.

EVERYMAN
Me thynke, alas, that I must be gone
To make my rekenynge and my dettes paye,
For I se my tyme is nye spent awaye.
Take example, all ye that this do here or se,
How they that I love[d] best do forsake me
Excepte my Good Dedes, that bydeth truly.

GOOD DEDES
All Erthly thynges is but vanyte:[22]
Beaute, Strength, and Dyscrecyon do man forsake,
Folysshe frendes, and kynnesmen, that fayre spake;
All fleeth, save Good Dedes, and that am I.

EVERYMAN
Have mercy on me, God moost myghty,
And stande by me, thou moder and mayde, Holy Mary!

GOOD DEDES
Fere not; I wyll speke for the[e].

EVERYMAN
Here I crye God mercy!

GOOD DEDES
Shorte our ende, and mynysshe our payne;
Let us go and never come agayne.

EVERYMAN
Into Thy handes, Lorde, my soule I commende.
Receyve it, Lorde, that it be not lost.
As Thou me boughtest, so me defende,
And save me from the Fendes boost,
That I may appere with the blessyd hoost
That shall be saved at the Day of Dome.
In manus tuas, of myghtes moost
Forever, *commendo spiritum meum!*[23]

[*Everyman and Good Dedes descend into the grave.*]

KNOWLEDGE
Now hath he suffred that we all shall endure.
The Good Dedes shall make all sure.
Now hath he made endynge.
Me thynketh that I here aungelles synge,

839 close 841 things fail 843 trumpet 844 run 845 leave 846 others 849 protect 854 in need 856 everyone 865 debts 866 nearly 867 hear 870 are only vanity 872 Foolish 878 shorten, lessen 882 redeemed 883 Fiend's boast 884 host 885 Judgement 886 greatest power 888 that (which)

[22] See Ecclesiastes 12:8: 'Vanity of vanities, saith the preacher; all is vanity.'

[23] 'Into thy hands . . . I commend my spirit.' Luke 23:46.

And make grete joy and melody
Where Everymannes soule receyved shall be.

AUNGEL
Come excellente electe spouse to Jesu!
Here above thou shalte go,
Bycause of thy synguler vertue.
Now thy soule is taken thy body fro,
Thy rekenynge is crystall clere.
Now shalte thou in-to the Hevenly sp[h]ere,
Unto the whiche all ye shall come
That lyveth well before the Daye of Dome.

[*Enter Doctour.*]

DOCTOUR
This morall men may have in mynde.
Ye herers, take it of worth, olde and yonge,[24]
And forsake Pryde, for he deceyveth you in the ende.
And remembre Beaute, Fyve Wyttes, Strength, and Dy[s]crecyon,
They all at the last do every man forsake,
Save his Good Dedes there dothe he take.
But be-ware; and they be small,
Before God he hath no helpe at all.
None excuse may be there for Every-man.
Alas, how shall he do than?
For, after dethe, amendes may no man make,
For than mercy and pyte doth hym forsake.
If his rekenynge be not clere whan he doth come,
God wyll saye: *'Ite, maledicti, in ignem aeternum!'*[25]
And he that hath his accounte hole and sounde,
Hye in Heven he shall be crounde.
Unto whiche place God brynge us all thyder,
That we may lyve body and soule togyder.
Therto helpe, the Trynyte!
Amen, saye ye, for saynt Charyte.

FINIS
Thus endith this moral play of Every Man
Imprynted at London in Poule's
Chyrch yarde by me
Johan Skot.

894 chosen 897 from your body 901 Who, virtuously 907 Only 908 if they are (only) few 910 No 911 then 917 crowned 921 holy

24 'You hearers, both old and young, believe [this moral] to be valuable.'

25 '[Then He shall say also unto them on the left hand] "Depart from Me, ye cursed, into everlasting fire".' Matthew 25:41.

Part III

Politics and Morality: The Interludes

Politics and Morality: The Interludes

Introduction

The Interludes gathered together in this section really constitute a sub-genre of the Morality Play, although their similarities with the works in the previous section vary from play to play. They share a number of features with the Moralities, not least their venue. Each of the Interludes which follow (with the exception of the outdoor version of Lindsay's *Thrie Estaitis*) was probably written for performance in the great hall of a royal palace or noble manor house, or the hall of one of the larger London livery companies. Although the great halls of late medieval England varied in shape and size, they shared a number of basic features which gave the interludes their distinctive quality as 'household drama'. The great hall was distinguished by the presence of a dais, usually at one end, upon which the king or noble patron dined in state, and from where he and his immediate entourage would probably have watched the play. At the other end of the hall was the entrance to the kitchen, cellars, and other service rooms of the household, often divided from the hall itself by a partition-wall known as the Screens. Although the hall would have been crowded during a performance, and in the imperfect light of the torches which provided the only illumination would have seemed somewhat chaotic, this was then an auditorium with its own very clear cultural dynamic, a single, organic community with the elite, probably seated, diners at one end, and the lower-status household members crowded around the entrances and exits at the other. As the texts reveal, the plays make clear use of that differentiated audience, with the Vices seeking comradeship with the servants, and the serious moral sentiments being addressed to the patron and his guests (see Twycross, 'Theatricality'; Walker, *Politics of Performance*, ch. 2).

The Interludes are also united by their interest in secular and political concerns, which sets them apart from the Moralities, whose interest was chiefly in the welfare of the human soul. Thus Medwall's *Fulgens* discusses the nature of civic virtue and the role of the aristocracy in public life, while Skelton's *Magnyfycence* anatomizes the role of the sovereign and the nature of good government in the manner of the *speculum principis* ('mirror' or handbook for princes) which was so popular a genre in the Middle Ages. Religion is, however, rarely far from view, even here. Skelton's depiction of one of his vices as a father confessor draws upon a rich seam of anticlerical (and specifically antifraternal) satire, while the author of the anonymous *Godly Queene Hester* uses biblical narrative explicitly to defend the English monasteries against the threat of closure in the late 1520s. With the onset of the Henrician Reformation in the 1530s, national politics and religion became inextricably linked; thus John Heywood's dramas of social and political reconciliation are also pleas for religious orthodoxy and an end to confessional factionalism in troubled times. These themes point towards the concerns of the last plays printed here, the reformed dramas of John Bale and Sir David Lindsay, each of which in its own way sought to reclaim religious drama (hitherto dominated by what Bale saw as 'popish spectacle') for the Protestant cause. In Lindsay's case this religious agenda was welded to a passionate political and social concern that gives a sharp satirical edge to his analysis of the ills of contemporary Scotland.

The intimate relationship between actors and audience which household performance generated is mirrored in the plays. The Interludes do not seek to transport their spectators into a separate play-world, but continually remind them that they are in a great hall, watching a play. Players emerge from among the audience, not merely to suggest the latter's complicity with vice or sin as was the case of the devils of the Cycle plays or the Morality Vices, but claiming actually to *be* members of the crowd. The trick is deftly executed for comic effect in Medwall's *Fulgens and Lucres*, when two household servants (referred to merely as 'A' and 'B') appear to step into the place and join the action. While seemingly anxious not to interfere with the progress of the play, they end up providing it with a comic sub-plot, perhaps the first in English drama. Lindsay revisits the device in *The Thrie Estaitis* to more powerfully unsettling effect, having two representatives of the oppressed underclass step out of the crowd in answer to the player-king's offer to hear the grievances of his subjects. Thus the play is made to appear ambivalently poised between fiction and reality, able to respond explicitly to real social problems, but free to exploit its licence to do so under the guise of moralized 'play' which was characteristic of the Interludes of the period.

As the Moralities demonstrated, the playwrights of this period exhibited a profoundly ambivalent attitude towards the dramatic process in which they were employed, exploiting its capacity to engage the audience's senses and emotions, but mindful all the time of the dangers of that engagement from a moral perspective. Hence it was primarily through the Vices, and the audience's negotiable complicity with them, that the limits of moral drama were explored and expanded. In the work of Bale and Lindsay this interest in the Vices' power to corrupt is given a confessional edge. Bale's most theatrical characters are not merely Vices but *Catholic* Vices, their antics representative, in the playwright's view, not merely of their immorality but of a faith which was itself based upon theatrical 'shows' rather than the truth of the evangelical Word. The audience's engagement with the Vices of *The Three Laws* is thus an engagement with their own unreformed sensibilities, and their capacity to lapse back into idolatry and sin. Bale's plays thus explore a fundamental paradox of reformed drama: they are didactic dramas about the incapacity of play-acting to contain truth.

The outdoor auspices of the version of *The Thrie Estaitis* performed in 1552 and 1554 place it in many ways outside the genre of the Interlude. But the fact that it grew from just such a play, performed in the great hall of James V's palace of Linlithgow in 1540, makes it a fitting text with which to complete this anthology. The ambitious sweep of its action, coupled with its lavish place-and-scaffold staging, demonstrate both the true scope and ambition of the political drama and the extent to which the conditions of staging influence the nature of the play. The fact that we can see clear traces of the earlier Interlude version in the fascinating eye-witness account of its performance sent to Thomas Cromwell by William Eure (see below, pp. 538–40) makes the play doubly valuable as a case study in the archaeology of dramatic composition.

The Interludes differ from Moralities also in the manner of their circulation: all the plays included here have been edited from printed texts. Unlike the Moralities, which were preserved by and large in manuscript form, these plays were published as texts for readers as well as performed as entertainments for audiences, a sign that drama had, among other things, ceased to be a space apart from the everyday world in which moralists could reflect upon the failings of worldliness, and was itself becoming a commodity to be bought and sold in the market-place. The players too were more professional, perhaps members of the household chapel or travelling troupes, who could call upon the specific skills relevant to their trade, whether the singing of the part songs which became a feature of the Interludes, or the increasingly sophisticated tumbling and word-play which is a crucial element of the characterization of the Vices. This new professionalism, coupled with the better acoustics and more intimate staging conditions available in the great halls, allowed the Interlude playwrights (many of whom are identifiable individuals – a further sign of the developing status of the playmaker's craft) to experiment with more sophisticated and subtle effects than were often possible in the outdoor drama. Yet the plays still retain the broad-minded approach to theatre that characterized the Moralities. It would be wrong to underestimate the impact on the drama of the Humanist learning that was gaining ground in the schools, universities, and royal courts during the first half of the sixteenth century. Plays such as Skelton's *Magnyfycence* and Medwall's *Fulgens* show evident signs of their authors' acquaintance with the new learning, as do the plays of John Heywood, who was a part of that circle of writers and scholars around Sir Thomas More that did so much to popularize Humanism in English intellectual culture. But these plays pay as great a debt to late medieval traditions as they do to the theatre of Greece or Rome. It is the spirit of Chaucer rather than that of Plautus that informs the comedy of Heywood or Skelton, and even where the play is set in Ancient Rome (as is *Fulgens*), or has Jupiter among its characters (as does Heywood's *Weather*), the themes discussed are provided by the immediate and passionate struggles of the present rather than the timeless matter of the classical past. These plays are representative of a drama that was intimately rooted in the communities which produced them, their concerns and preoccupations. In this respect they are no different to the religious and moral plays that make up the remainder of this volume.

Further reading

J.B. Altman, *The Tudor Play of Mind* (Berkeley, Calif., 1978).

D. Bevington, *Tudor Drama and Politics: A Critical Approach to Topical Meaning* (Cambridge, Mass., 1968).

M. Bitot, ed., *'Divers Toyes Mengled': Essays on Medieval and Renaissance Culture in Honour of André Lascombes* (Tours, 1996).

N. Caputo, *'Playing With Power': Gli Interludi Tudor e i Percosi della Riforma* (Napoli, 1998).

J. D. Cox and D.S. Kastan, eds, *A New History of Early English Drama* (New York, 1997).

T.W. Craik, *The Tudor Interlude* (Leicester, 1958).

P. Happé, *English Drama Before Shakespeare* (Harlow, 1999).

H.B. Norland, *Drama in Early Tudor Britain, 1485–1558* (Lincoln, Nebr., 1995).

N. Sanders, R. Southern, T.W. Craik, and L. Potter, *The Revels History of Drama in English, Volume Two, 1500–1576* (London, 1980).

W.R. Streitberger, *Court Revels, 1485–1559* (Toronto, 1994).

M. Twycross, 'The Theatricality of Medieval English Plays', in R. Beadle, ed., *The Cambridge Companion to Medieval English Theatre* (Cambridge, 1994), pp. 37–84.

G. Walker, *Plays of Persuasion: Drama and Politics at the Court of Henry VIII* (Cambridge, 1991).

G. Walker, *The Politics of Performance in Early Renaissance Drama* (Cambridge, 1998).

P.W. White, *Theatre and Reformation: Protestantism, Patronage, and Playing in Tudor England* (Cambridge, 1993).

Fulgens and Lucres, title page, woodcut. Reproduced by permission of the Huntington Library, San Marino, California.

Henry Medwall, *Fulgens and Lucres*

Henry Medwall (1461–?1501)

Fulgens and Lucres was not only one of the first English plays to be printed, it was also the first for which an author can be identified. Henry Medwall was born *c.*8 September 1461 in Southwark, a borough on the south bank of the Thames across London Bridge from the City. He was educated at Eton and King's College Cambridge, where he studied Arts and Civil Law, before at some point (perhaps as early as the mid-1480s) joining the household of John Morton, bishop of Ely, the future cardinal, archbishop of Canterbury, and lord chancellor to Henry VII. Medwall's principal role in Morton's service was as a notary public, a drafter and authenticator of legal documents, and as guardian of the archbishop's legal archive. His two surviving plays, *Fulgens and Lucres*, printed by John Rastell at some point between 1510 and 1516, and *Nature*, printed by Rastell's son William in 1530, reveal that he also had a role in providing dramatic entertainments for his employer's household, an interest he may have developed at Eton or Cambridge, both of which had a tradition of performing plays for educational and recreational purposes. Both Medwall's humanist education and his interest in the law are evident in *Fulgens*, with its focus upon questions of morality and social status, and its use of the structure of legal debate in putting cases, replication (l. 2140), and judgement, and concern for such things as 'sureties' (ll. 623ff) and 'jointure' (ll. 924ff). Whether the playwright actually served as chaplain to Morton, as the title page of *Fulgens* claims, is less clear. He certainly took minor clerical orders in 1490, enabling him to be rewarded with clerical livings such as that of Balinghem in the pale of Calais, which he held from August 1492 until 1501. But he may never have proceeded to ordination into the priesthood. The description of Medwall as Morton's chaplain might, then, either have been an error on Rastell's part, or a somewhat inflated recognition of Medwall's association with the chapel through his work as a playwright. Medwall disappears from the surviving documentation after 1501, prompting suggestions that he may have died, at the relatively young age of 40, in that year.

Fulgens and Lucres

Unlike the Moralities, *Fulgens* is a product of humanist education, reflecting classical themes in its exploration of good conduct in this world, rather than preparing its audiences for entry into the next. In this it lays claim, despite its clerical auspices, to be the earliest surviving purely secular play in English. Its main plot is drawn from John Tiptoft, earl of Worcester's English translation (printed by Caxton in 1481) of Buonaccorso da Montemagno's *De Vera Nobilite* ('On True Nobility') of 1428. Its central question, 'does true nobility lie in aristocratic birth and lineage or in personal virtue?', was a traditional one. Chaucer made his old faery woman deliver a lecture on the superiority of 'gentle' conduct over inherited wealth and status in his *Wife of Bath's Tale*, written at the end of the fourteenth century. But the issue gained a new potency with the rise of humanist studies in the universities in the last decades of the fifteenth century, and the growth of a new confidence among men of letters that they had an important role to play alongside the king's noble councillors in the direction of the realm and the upkeep of the commonwealth (the latter is an important term in *Fulgens*). The importance and sensitivity of what may seem to modern audiences a self-evident claim is suggested by the lengths to which Medwall goes to play down the radicalism of his assertions. Lucres and Gayus, A and B, all issue apologies and disclaimers for the content of the play, stating that it concerns no one in what must have been a predominantly aristocratic audience personally, that it concerns matters long ago and far away in imperial Rome, and that no descendants of the protagonists are currently present. Even when dismissing the claims of so obviously decadent a suitor as the aristocratic Cornelius, Lucres assures the spectators that the choice was a difficult one, that her judgement was based merely upon her own 'fantasy' or inclination, and that it should not stand as a general precedent for others to follow. Finally she agrees with the pro-noble servant B that the ideal suitor would be a man of virtue who was also an aristocrat, as he would be worthy of more praise than 'many' (but perhaps significantly not 'all' – both Medwall and Morton were themselves not nobly born) who had more humble origins (ll. 2210–23).

Perhaps the most interesting aspect of the play is, however, not its political content but its dramatic structure. For Medwall added to the social and political dissertation which he adapted from his source an element wholly of his own devising in the form of a comic sub-plot (perhaps the first real sub-plot, rather than merely a comic interlude, in English drama) in the courtship of Joan the Maid by the servants A and B, which mirrors the courtship of Lucres by Gayus and Cornelius, albeit in a lower, more scatological and misogynist register. In the play's most innovative feature, these servants seemingly step out of the audience as the play is about to begin, and get involved in the action.

As Meg Twycross suggests ('Theatricality', p. 79), 'A' and 'B', like the 'N' in N-Town, may well be merely flags of convenience, anonymous markers taken from Medwall's legal experience, adaptable to any household member who took the part (within the play they never refer to each other by name, sticking to the self-referentially vague 'what-calt' ('whatever-your-name-is') instead). The actors could thus be effectively playing themselves, with all the possibilities for in-jokes and extra-dramatic allusions that this would entail. One such possibility has attracted considerable scholarly interest.

Also part of Morton's circle in the 1490s was the young Thomas More, who served as a page in the archbishop's household during 1491–2, when he would have been around 14 years old. William Roper's biography of More recounts his precocious interest in drama during this period, describing how:

> thoughe he was younge of yeares, yeat wold he at Christmas tyde sodenly sometimes steppe in among the players and, never studyeng for the matter, make a parte of his owne there presently among them, which made the lookers on more sporte then all the plaiers beside.[1]

The coincidence of Medwall's play, in which two characters do indeed seem to step in among the players and make parts of their own, having been written for the same household has led to speculation that Roper's anecdote is a mangled recollection of More's having appeared as one of the servants, perhaps, as Nelson suggests, B, who seems (at ll. 360–5) most obviously to insert himself boldly into the action and risk upsetting the play. But, as there is no evidence that *Fulgens* was written for performance during the period when More was in Morton's service, the suggestion must remain unproven.

A and B themselves are creatures of considerable significance in their own right. The technique of introducing supposedly 'real' individuals into the play was to have a considerable dramatic future. What Medwall used for comic effect, Lindsay would revisit in the mid-sixteenth century for political purposes, introducing characters representative of the Scottish commonwealth into his *Satire of the Thrie Estaitis* to voice strident criticisms of clerical and political abuses. The characters also significantly develop the role of the Vice established in the Moral Plays and taken up again in the Interludes of Skelton, Heywood, and Bale in their association with scatological comedy and disrespect for decorum. The 'below stairs' misrule in *Fulgens* is, however, less obviously wedded to strictly moral and didactic purposes. A and B are not dangerous forces whom the protagonist(s) must reject in order to find salvation. Their attempts to ruin the courtships of the main plot are perfunctory and pose no real threat to either a just outcome or Lucres's future happiness. They are more allied to comedy and the processes of drama itself than to the world, the flesh, and the Devil. And, as we have seen, the play is far too secular in its outlook and concerns to worry about the moral implications of comedy. It is more interested in establishing the right recipe for worldly happiness in marriage than in exploring the right way to Heaven.

In both the plot and the sub-plot the women come out on top. Joan humiliates her would-be suitors both intellectually and physically, and Lucres gets the husband she desires (even if it is only the rather wooden Gayus), rather than the noble suitor whom precedent and her father's preference indicate she

1 W. Roper, *The Lyfe of Sir Thomas Moore, Knighte*, ed., E.V. Hitchcock, EETS, 197 (London, 1935), p. 5.

ought to take. In this respect she anticipates the 'strong heroines' of Shakespeare's mature comedies. But it is on its own terms rather than as an anticipation of things to come that the play deserves to be considered. It reveals both the remarkable sophistication of the drama of this period, and its intimate association with the conditions (both physical and cultural) which produced it. Throughout the play there is an ongoing tension between a recognition of the boundaries between actors and audience, play-world and reality, and a mischievous renegotiation of them; an acknowledgement that this is merely an entertainment, distanced from the real concerns of its patron, Cardinal Morton and his principal guests, and a realization that, before such spectators, such material could not help but contribute to political debate.

The play was probably designed for performance in the great hall of Lambeth Palace, the archbishop of Canterbury's London seat, spread over the course of a day's feasting and festivity. As the title page suggests, it is divided into two parts for performance at two separate times, probably accompanying dinner at midday and supper in the evening respectively. The actors were probably, like Medwall, members of Morton's own household, with boys from his chapel choir perhaps taking the female parts, although broader comedy might be achieved if an adult male 'in drag' took the part of Joan. The broad scatological comedy of the A and B scenes, and the evident delight in such devices as the joust at 'farte pryke in cule' (ll. 1165ff), as well as the fashionable courtly basse-dance (ll. 1819ff) and the moral matter of the main plot, certainly indicate the remarkable broad-mindedness of elite culture in this period.

The play survives in a single complete copy of the Rastell print, now held in the Huntington Library, San Marino, California (Huntington Library 62599). This edition is based upon the microfilm copy of that text (STC 17778). I have also consulted two modern scholarly editions, those in Alan H. Nelson, ed., *The Plays of Henry Medwall* (Woodbridge, 1980), and F. Boas and A.W. Reed, eds, *Fulgens and Lucres: A Fifteenth-Century Secular Play* (Oxford, 1926).

Further reading

D. Bevington, *From Mankind to Marlowe* (Cambridge, Mass., 1962).

D. Bevington, *Tudor Drama and Politics: A Critical Approach to Topical Meaning* (Cambridge, Mass., 1968).

T.W. Craik, *The Tudor Interlude* (Leicester, 1958).

R. Godfrey, 'Nervous Laughter in Henry Medwall's *Fulgens and Lucres*', in A. Lascombe, ed., *Tudor Theatre* 3 (Amsterdam, 1996), pp. 81–96 (which advances a case for redating the play to the 1510s).

H.B. Norland, *Drama in Early Tudor Britain, 1485–1558* (Lincoln, Nebr., 1995).

O. Horner, '*Fulgens and Lucres*: An Historical Perspective', *Medieval English Theatre* 15 (1993), pp. 49–86.

A.W. Reed, *Early Tudor Drama: Medwall, the Rastells, and the More Circle* (London, 1926).

M. Twycross, 'The Theatricality of Medieval English Plays', in R. Beadle, ed., *The Cambridge Companion to Medieval English Theatre* (Cambridge, 1994), pp. 37–84.

[*Dramatis Personae: A and B* (spectators, later servants to Gayus and Cornelius respectively), *Fulgens* (Senator of Rome), *Publius Cornelius* (A nobleman, suitor to Lucres), *Lucres* (daughter to Fulgens), *Ancilla* (a 'Maid' to Lucres, named Joan), *Gayus Flaminius* (A man of lowly social origins, a rival suitor to Lucres).]

[*Title Page*]
Here is conteyned a godely[2] *interlude of Fulgens, cenatoure*[3] *of Rome, Lucres his doughter, Gayus Flaminius, and Publius Cornelius, of the Disputacyon of Noblenes, and is devyded in two partyes*[4] *to be played at two tymes. Compyled by mayster Henry Medwall, late chapelayne to the ryght reverent fader in God, Johan Morton, Cardynall and Archebysshop of Caunterbury.*

Intrat A dicens:

[A]
A, for Goddis will,
What meane ye, syrs, to stond so still?

0+ Enter A, saying: 2 silently

[2] Goodly/splendid.

[3] Senator.

[4] Parts.

Have not ye etyn and your fill
And payd no thinge therfore?
Iwys, syrs, thus dare I say,
He that shall for the shott pay
Vouch saveth that ye largely assay
Suche mete as he hath in store.

I trowe your disshes be not bare,
Nor yet ye do the wyne spare,
Therfore be mery as ye fare!
Ye ar welcom eche oon
Unto this house withoute faynynge
But I mervayle moche of one thinge,
That after this mery drynkynge
And good recreacyon

There is no wordes amonge this presse;
Non sunt loquele neque sermones,[5]
But as it were men in sadnes.
Here ye stonde musynge,
Whereaboute I can not tell
Or[6] some els praty damesell
For to daunce and sprynge!

Tell me, what-calt, is it not so?
I am sure here shalbe somewhat ado,
And iwis, I will know it or I go
Withoute I be dryvyn hens.

Intrat B.

[B]
Nay, nay, hardely man, I undertake
No man wyll suche mastryes make,
And it were but for the maner sake!
Thou maist tary by licence[7]
Among other men and see the pley
I warand no man wyll say the[e] nay.

A
I thinke it well evyn as ye say
That no man wyll me greve.
But I pray you, tell me that agayn:
Shall here be a play?

B
Ye[a], for certeyn.

A
By my trouth, therof am I glad and fayn.
And ye will me beleve,

Of all the worlde I love suche sport.
It dothe me so myche plesure and comfort,
And that causith me ever to resort
Wher suche thing is to do.
I trowe your owyn selfe be oon
Of them that shall play.

B
Nay, I am none.
I trowe thou spekyst in derision
To lyke me therto.

A
Nay, I mok not, wot ye well,
For I thought verely by your apparell
That ye had bene a player.[8]

B
Nay, never a dell.

A
Than I cry you mercy:
I was to blame. Lo, therfor, I say
Ther is so myche nyce aray
Amonges these galandis now aday
That a man shall not lightly

Know a player from a nother man.
But now to the purpose wher I began:
I see well here shalbe a play, than!

3 eaten (enough to fill you) 6 bill/reckoning 7 grant, sample extensively 12 each one (of you) 13 deception 14 wonder greatly about 17 crowd 20 musing/in thought 21 about what 22 other pretty girl 23 leap (acrobatically) 24 'whatever-you're called' 25 something happening 26 before 27 Unless, thrown out 27+ Enter B. 28 certainly, wager 33 guarantee, refuse you 35 grieve/annoy 43 to be performed 44 you yourself are one 46 speak 47 liken 50 bit (i.e. 'not at all!') 53 much fine clothing 54 gallants (fashionable courtiers) 55 easily

[5] 'There is no speech nor language [where their voice is not heard].' Psalms 19:3.

[6] A line, stating the first alternative, seems to be missing in the printed text.

[7] 'No one will be so forceful, even if it were just for appearances' sake! You can stay here under licence [i.e. with my permission]'.

[8] Because B is finely dressed, A mistakes him for an actor: a playful allusion to the liberty enjoyed by actors to dress above their social status for the purposes of playing. (A whole series of sumptuary laws regulated the levels of finery appropriate to the different social classes.)

B
Ye[a], that ther shall doutles,
And I trow ye shall like it well.

A
It semeth than that ye can tell
Sumwhat of the mater.

B
Ye[a], I am of counsell.
One tolde me all the processe.

A
And I pray you, what shall it be?

B
By my fayth, as it was tolde me
More than ones or twyse,
As fare as I can bere it awaye
All the substaunce of theyr play
Shall procede this wyse:

When thempire of Rome was in such floure
That all the worlde was subgett to the same,
Than was there an nobill senatour,
And as I remember, Fulgens was his name,
Whiche had a doughter of nobill fame.
And yet, as thauctor sayth in veray dede,
Her nobill vertu dide her fame excede,

All be it there was not one allmost
Thoroughoute all the cyte, yong ne olde,
That of her beaute did not boste.
And over that, her verteuse manyfolde
In suche maner wyse were praysid and tolde
That it was thought she lakkede no thing
To a nobill woman that was accordyng.

Grete labour was made her favour to attayne
In the way of mariage, and among all
That made suche labour were specially twayn
Whiche more than other dyd besily on her call,
On the whiche twayn she sett her mynde especiall,
So that she utterly determyned in her hert
The one of them to have, all other sett aparte.

One of them was called Publius Cornelius,
Borne of noble blode, it is no nay.
That other was one Gayus Flamyneus,
Borne of a pore stocke, as men doth say.
But for all that, many a fayre day
Thorough his grete wisedome and vertueous behavyour
He rulyd the comen wele to his grete honoure.

And how so be it that the vulgare opynion
Hade both these men in lyke favour and reverence,
Supposing they had bene of lyke condycion,
Yet this sayd woman of inestimable prudence
Sawe that there was some maner of difference,
For the whiche her answere she differred and spared
Tyll both theyre condycions were openly declared.

And yet to them both this comfort she gave:
He that coude be founde more noble of them twayne,
In all godely maner her harte sholde he have.
Of the which answere they both were glade and fayne,
For ether of them trustede therby to attayne
Theffecte of his desyre. Yet, when they had do,
One of them must nedis his appetit forgoo.

Hereuppon was areysyd a grete doute and question.
Every man all after as he was affeccionate
Unto the parties seyd his opynion,
But, at the laste, in eschewyng of debate,
This matter was brought before the Cenate,
They to gyve therin an utter sentence
Whiche of these two men sholde have the preeminence.

And finally they gave sentence and awarde
That Gayus Flamyneus was to be commende
For the more nobill man, havynge no regarde
To his lowe byrthe, of the whiche he dyde dyscende,
But onely to his vertue thay dyde therin attende,
Whiche was so grete that of convenience
All the cyte of Rome dyd hym honour and reverence.

A
And shall this be the proces of the play?

B
Ye[a], so I understonde be credible informacyon.

62 matter (of the play), familiar with (the actors) 63 the whole story 66 once, twice 67 far, recall it 69 (in) this way 70 the empire, so flourishing 71 subject 75 the author, truly indeed 79 boast 80 many virtues 81 discussed/assessed 83 that befitted a noble woman 86 two (suitors) 87 did eagerly 88 particularly 90 setting aside the rest 92 undeniable 94 poor family 97 commonwealth/state 98 popular 99 equal 102 degree 103 held back 109 each, trusted 110 The satisfaction 111 necessarily, desire 112 raised, doubt 113 according to his inclination 115 ending the 117 a final 120 commended 122 from 124 accordingly 126 plot

A
By my fayth, but yf it be evyn as ye say,
I wyll advyse them to change that conclusion.
What? Wyll they afferme that a chorles son
Sholde be more noble than a gentilman born?
Nay, beware, for men wyll have therof grete scorn:

It may not be spoken in no maner of case.

B
Yes, suche consyderacions may be layde
That every resonable man in this place
Wyll holde hym therin right well apayde,
The matter may be so well convayde.

A
Let them convay and cary clene than,
Or els he wyll repent that this play began.[9]

How be it, the matter touchith me never a dell,
For I am nether of vertue excellent
Nor yet of gentyl blode. This I know well,
But I speke it onely for this entent:
I wolde not that any man sholde be shent!
And yet there can no man blame us two,
For why in this matter we have nought to do.

B
We? No, God wott, no thing at all,
Save that we come to see this play
As farre as we may by the leve of the marshall.[10]
I love to beholde suche myrthes alway,
For Y have sene byfore this day
Of suche maner thingis in many a gode place
Both gode examples and right honest solace.

This play in like wyse I am sure
Is made for the same entent a[n]d purpose:
To do every man both myrth and pleasure.
Wherfor I can not think or suppose
That they wyll ony worde therin disclose
But suche as shall stond with treuth and reason
In godely maner according to the season.

A
Ye[a], but trouth may not be sayde alway,
For somtyme it causith gruge and despite.

B
Ye[a], goth the worlde so now a day
That a man must say the crow is white?[11]

A
Ye[a], that he must, be God Allmyght.
He must both lye and flater now and than
That castith hym to dwell amonge worldly men.[12]

In some courtis such men shall most wyn!

B
Ye[a], but as for the parish where I abide,
Suche flaterye is abhorride as dedly syn.
And specially lyars be sett asyde
As sone as they may with the faute be spied,
For every man that favoreth and loveth vertue
Wyll suche matter of folke utterly esscheue,

Wherfor I can think these folke wyll not spare
After playne trouth this matier to procede
As the story seyth. Why shulde they care?
I trow here is no man of the kyn or sede
Of either partie, for why they were bore
In the cytie of Rome as I sayd before.

Therfor, leve all this doutfull question
And prayse at the parting evyn as ye fynde.

A
Yes, be ye sure, whan thei have all done
I wyll not spare to shew you my mynd.
Praise who wyll or dispraise, I will not be behynd.
I wyll gest theron what so ever shal befall,
If I can fynd any man to gest withall.

130 affirm, churl (poor man)'s 133 under any circumstances 134 arguments, presented 136 content 137 presented 143 intention 144 punished 146 Because 149 permission 150 entertainments 152 good 154 a similar way 158 any 160 occasion 161 spoken always 162 grudging 163 goes 165 by 166 flatter 168 courts, prosper best 170 abhorred 172 soon, fault (i.e. lying) 174 that kind of people, avoid 176 truth, matter 178 kin, seed/offspring 179 born 181 leave (aside) 182 end, according to your judgement 185 slow 186 joke about it

9 'Let them go [punning on B's 'conveyed'] and carry themselves clean [away], then! Otherwise he who began this play [i.e. Medwall] will repent it.'

10 The Marshal was the household officer responsible for the organization, seating order, and protocol within the great hall during feasts and entertainments.

11 Proverbial: i.e. he must deny what is obviously the truth (to please those in authority).

12 'He [who] wishes to live among men of the world [must do so].'

B
Pees! No moo wordes, for now they come!
The plears bene evyn here at [h]and.

A
So thei be, so [h]elp me God and halydome!
I pray you, tell me where I shall stand.

B
Mary, stand evyn here by me, I warand.
Geve rome there, syrs, for God avowe!
Thei wold cum in if thei myght for you!

A
Ye[a], but I pray the[e], what-calt, tell me this:
Who is he that now comyth yn?

B
Mary, it is Fulgence the Senatour.

A
Ye[a], is?
What? The father of the forseide virgyn?

B
Ye[a], forsoth, he shall this matere begyn.

A
And wher is feyr doughter Lucrece?

B
She comyth anon. I say, hold thy pece!

Intrat Fulgens dicens:

FULGENS
Everlastyng joy with honoure and praise
Be unto our most drad Lord and Savyour,
Whiche doth us help and comfort many ways,
Not lefyng us destitute of His ayde and socour,
But lettith His son shyne on the riche and poore,
And of His grace is ever indifferent
All be yt He diversely commytteth His talent.[13]
To some He lendith the sprete of prophecy,
To some the plenty of tonges eloquence,
To some grete wisdome and worldly policy,
To some litterature and speculatyf science,
To some He geveth the grace of preemynence
In honour and degre, and to some abundance
Of tresoure, riches, and grete inheritaunce.

Every man oweth to take gode hede
Of this distribution, for who so doth take
The larger benefite, he hath the more nede
The larger recompense and thank therfor to make.
I speke these wordes onely for myne owne sake
And for non other person, for I know well
That I am therin chargid, as I shall you tell.

When I consider and call to my remembraunce
The prosperous lyfe that I have allwey
Hyderto endured withoute any grevaunce
Of wordly adversitie, well may I sey
And thynke that I am bound to yeld and pay
Grete prayse and thankes to the Hye Kynge
Of Whom procedith and growith every gode thing

And certes, if I wold not praise of boste
The benefytis that He hath done unto me,
Yet is it well know of lest and most
Thrughoute all Rome [t]hemperiall cyte
What place in the Cenate and honorable degre
I occupye, and how I demean me in the same.
All this can they tell that knowith but my name.

To speke of plenty and grete abundaunce
Of wordly riches therunto belongyng,
Houses of pleasure and grete inheritaunce,
With riche apparell and every other thing
That to a worthy man shold be according,
I am and ever have be in metely gode case,
For the whiche I thank Allmighty God of His grace.

Than have I a wyfe of gode condicyon
And right conformable to myn entent
In every thing that is to be done.
And, how be it that God hath me not sent

188 more 189 players, close to hand 190 the holy land/Christendom? 192 warrant/guarantee 193 Give room, I swear (to) God 194 come, if you let them 197 is (it)? 198 foresaid 199 indeed 201+ Enter Fulgens, saying: 203 dread/feared 205 leaving, succour 206 sun 207 impartial 209 gives, spirit 210 eloquence in many languages 211 political skill 212 philosophy 214 status 216 ought, good heed 222 obliged (to) 225 Hitherto 226 worldly, say 228 High 229 From 230 by boasting 232 by (both the) lowest, highest 233 the imperial city 235 conduct myself 241 appropriate 242 been, moderately 245 obedient

13 'Albeit that he gives different gifts to different people.' The following accounts of the gifts of the Holy Spirit is taken from I Corinthians 12.

An hayr male, whiche were convenient
My name to continew and it to repeyre,
Yet am I not utterly destitute of an heyre,

For I have a doughter in whom I delight
As for the chefe comfort of myn olde age,
And surely my seyd doughter Lucres doth hight.
Men seyth she is as lyke me in visage
As though she were evyn myn owne ymage,
For the whiche cause nature doth me force and
bytide
The more to favour and love here in my mynde.

But yet the principall and grettist occasion
That makyth me to love her as I do
Is this, whiche I speke not of affection
But evyn as the treuth movith me therto:
Nature hath wrought in my Lucres so
That to speke of beaute and clere understanding
I can not thinke in here what shold be lakking.

And besides all that, yet a gretter thing
Whiche is not oft sene in so yong a damesell:
She is so discrete and sad in all demeanyng,
And therto full of honest and verteous counsell
Of here owne mynd, that wonder is to tell
The giftes of nature and of especiall grace.

Am not I gretly bound in this case
To God, as I rehersid you bifore?
I were to voyd of all reson and grace
If I wold not serve and prayse Hym therfore
With due love and drede: He askyth no more.
As far as He will me grace therto send,
The rest of my lif therin will I spend,

Albe yt that I must partely intend
To the promocyon of my doughter Lucres
To some metely mariage, ellis God defend!
She is my chief jewell and riches,
My comfort agayn all care and hevynes,
And also she is now of gode and ripe age
To be a mannes fere by wey of mariage.

Wherfor, if I might see or I dye
That she were bestowid sumwhat accordyng,
Then were my mynd dischargid utterly
Of every grete cure to me belongyng.
It was the chief cause of my hider cummyng
To have a communication in this same matere
With on Cornelius. Cam ther non suche here?[14]

Intrat Publius Cornelius dicens:

CORNELIUS
Yes, now am I come here at the last.
I have taried long, I cry you mercy!

FULGENS
Nay, no offence. Ther is no waste
Nor losse of tyme yet, hardely,
For this is the oure that ye and I
Apoyntid here to mete this other day.
Now shew me your mynd, lete me here what ye say.

CORNELIUS
Than wyll I leve superfluite awey,
For why ye know alredy my minde in substance.

FULGENS
I wot not whether I do, ye or nay.

CORNELIUS
Why, is it now oute of your remembraunce
That my desire is to honour and advaunce
Your doughter Lucres, if she will agree
That I, so pore a man, her husbonde shuld be?

FULGENS
Ye nede not, syr, to use these wordis to me,
For non in this cyte knowith better than I
Of what grete birth or substaunce ye be.
My doughter Lucres is full unworthy
Of birth and goodis to loke so hye,
Savyng that happily her gode condicyon
May her enable to suche a promocyon.

But, if this be youre mynde and suche intent,
Why do ye not laboure to her therfore?
For me semyth it were ryght expedient
That we know therin her mynde before
Or ever we shold commune therof any more,

248 male heir 249 renew 253 is named 254 facial appearance 256 urge, prompt 257 her 258 greatest cause 260 (out) of 264 her, might 267 serious, (her) demeanour 269 (it is) wonderful to report 270 (i.e. that she possesses) 271 obliged 272 told 273 too lacking 278 Albeit, partly attend 279 advancement 280 appropriate, God forbid otherwise 282 against, sorrow 289 companion in 285 before, die 286 fittingly bestowed, in some way 288 responsibility that I carry 291 one 291+ Enter Publius Cornelius, saying: 295 certainly 296 hour 297 Arranged, meet 299 avoid prolixity 300 in essence 301 do not know 307 no one 308 wealth 311 Except, nature/conduct 315 it seems to me 316 (should) know her opinion

14 'Has no such [man] come here?'

For, if she wold to your mynde apply,
No man shalbe so glad therof as I.

CORNELIUS
Suppose ye that I dyde not so begyn
To gete fyrste her favoure?[15] Yes, truste me well!

FULGENS
And what comfort wolde she gyve you therin?

CORNELIUS
By my feyth, no grete comfort to tell,
Save that she abideth to have youre counsell.
For, as she seyth, she will no thing
In suche mater to do withoute your counsell[yng],

Nor other wyse than ye shalbe contente.
And theruppon it was my mynde and desire
To speke with you of her for the same intent
Your gode will in this behalfe to requyre,
For I am so brent in loves fyre
That no thing may my payne aslake
Withoute that ye wyll my cure undertake.

FULGENS
Syr, I shall do you the comfort that I can,
As far as she wil be advised by me.
How be it, certeynly, I am not the man
That wyll take from her the liberte
Of her owne choice: that may not be!
But, when I speke with her, I shall her advyse
To love you before other in all godely wyse.

CORNELIUS
I thanke you, syr, with all myn harte,
And I pray you do it withoute delay.

FULGENS
As sone as I shall fro you departe
I wyll her mynde therin assay,
For I shall think that every howre is twayne
Till I may speke with you agayne.

[*Exit Fulgens.*]

CORNELIUS
Now a wise felow that had sumwhat a brayne,
And of suche thingis had experience,
Such one wolde I with me retayne
To gyve me counseile and assistence.
For I will spare no cost or expence
Nor yet refuse ony laboure or payne
The love of fayre Lucres therby to attayne.

[*To the audience*] So many gode felowes as byn in this
hall,
And is ther non, syrs, among you all
That wyll enterprise this gere?
Some of you can do it if ye lust!
But, if ye wyl not, than I must
Go seche a man elliswhere.

Et exeat [*Cornelius*]. *Deinde loquitur B:*[16]

Now have I spied a mete office for me,
For I wyl be of counsell and I may
With yonder man.

A
Pece, let be!
Be God, thou wyll distroy all the play!

B
'Distroy the play', quod a? Nay, nay,
The play began never till now!
I wyll be doyng, I make God avow,

For there is not in this hondred myle
A feter bawde than I am one.

A
And what shall I do in the meane while?

B
Mary, thou shalt com in anone
With a nother pageant.

A
Who, I?

B
Ye[a], by Saynt Johan.

329 about 330 goodwill, matter, ask 331 burnt 332 quench/reduce 333 Unless 334 what assistance 340 (all) other(s) 343 soon 344 test 345 hour is two 346 Until 347 something (of) a brain 349 employ 350 advice 354 be/are 356 attempt/take on, business 357 wanted to 359 seek, elsewhere 360 suitable job 361 if 364 says he? 366 busy myself 367 within a hundred miles 368 better pimp/pandar 371 scene, St John 372 did

15 'Do you think that I would not have sought her opinion first of all?'

16 'And [Cornelius] shall exit. Then B says'.

A
What? I never uside suche thing before.

B
But folow my counsell, and do no more:

Loke that thou abide here still,
And I shall undertake for to fulfyll
All his mynde withouten delay.
And whether I do so, ye or nay,
At the lest, well dare I undertake
The mariage utterly to mare or to make.

If he and I make any bargeyn
So that I must gyve hym attendaunce,
When thou seest me com in ageyn,
Stond evyn still and kepe thy contenaunce,
For when Gayus Flamyneus comyth in
Than must thou thy pageaunt begyn.

A
Shall ony profyt grow therby?

B
Hold thy pece! Speke not so hye,
Leste any man of this company
Know oure purpose openly
And breke all oure daunce!
For I assure the[e] feithfully,
If thou quyte the[e] as well as I,
This gere shall us both avaunce.

Exeat [B].

A
Nay then, let me alone hardely!
Yf ony advauntage honge therby
I can my selfe thereto apply
By helpe of gode counsell.
This felowe and I be maysterles
And lyve moste parte in ydelnes,
Therefore some maner of besenes
Wolde become us both well.

At the leste wyse, it is mery beynge
With men in tyme of woynge,
For all that whyle they do no thynge
But daunce and make revell,
Synge and laugh with greate shoutynge,
Fyll in wyne with revell routynge.
I trowe it be a joyfull thinge
Amonge suche folke to dwell!

Intrat Fulgens, Lucres, et Ancilla, et dicat:[17]

Fulgens
Doughter Lucres, ye knowe well ynough
What study and care I have for youre promocyon
And what fatherly love I bere to you,
So that I thynke in myne opynyon
It were tyme loste and wastfull occupacyon
This matter to reherse or tell you ony more,
Syth ye it best knowe, as I sayde before.

But the specyall cause that I speke fore
Is touchynge youre mariage. As ye knowe well,
Many folke there be that desyreth sore
And laboureth in that behalve with you to mell.
Ye knowe what is for you, ye nede no counsell.
Howe so be it, yf ye lyste my counseyle to requyre.
I shall be glad to satysfye therein youre desyre.

Lucres
Trought it is, fader, that I am bounde
As moche unto you as ony chylde may be
Unto the fader lyvynge on the grounde,
And where it pleaseth you to gyve unto me
Myne owne fre choyse and my lyberte,
It is the thynge that pleaseth me well,
Sith I shall have therein youre counsell.

And nowe accordynge to this same purpose,
What thynke ye best for me to do?
Ye knowe ryghte well, as I suppose,
That many folke doth me greatly woo,
Amonge the whiche there be specyally twoo
In whome, as I trowe and so do ye,
The choyce of this matter must fynally be.

In that poynt your mynde and myne dothe agre.
But yet, ryght now er I came here,
For Publius Cornelius ye advysed me,

378 least 379 ruin, bring about 380 agreement 381 wait upon him 383 keep a straight face 385 performance 386 loudly 387 In case, crowd 390 (i.e. spoil all our plans) 392 perform, I (do) 395 hangs 398 masterless/without employment 399 idleness 400 business 401 suit 402 At least 403 wooing 405 revelling 407 riotous partying 408 believe it is 414 a waste of effort 419 sorely desire 420 to deal with you in that matter 422 want to ask my advice 424 Truth 426 on Earth 428 free choice 440 (In favour of)

17 'Enter Fulgens, Lucres, and the Maid, and he [Fulgens] shall say'.

As touchinge ye wolde have me only reste there.[18]
Yf that be youre mynde I shall gladly forbere
All other, and only to hym assente
To have me in wedlocke at his commaundemente.

FULGENS
Naye, doughter Lucres, not so I mente,
For though I dyde somwhat to hym enclyne,
Yet for all that it is not myne entente
That ye shulde so thereupon utterly diffyne,
But loke whom ye wyll on Godys blessing and myne.[19]
For, truste ye me verely, it is all one to me
Whether Gayus Flamyneus wedde you or els he.

LUCRES
Than, syth I have so greate lyberte
And so gode choyce, I were unfortunable
And also to unwyse yf I wolde not see
That I had hym whiche is moste honorable.
Wherfore, may it lyke you to be agreable
That I may have respyte to make inquisycyon.
Whiche of this two men is better of condicyon?

FULGENS
I holde me content, that shall be well done.
It may be respyted for a day or twayne,
But in the meane tyme use this provysyon:
Se that ye indyfferently them both entertayne .
Tyll that youre mynde be sett at a certayne
Where ye shall rest now. Can ye do so?

LUCRES
At the leste, my gode wyll shall I put thereto.

FULGENS
Than, syth I have bysynes at whome for to do,
I wyll go thetherwarde as fast as I may.

LUCRES
Is it youre pleasure that I shall with you go?

FULGENS
Nay, I had lever that ye went your way
Aboute this matter.

Et exeat [Fulgens].

LUCRES
Well, God be with you than!
I shall do therein the best that I can.

Et facta aliqua pausatione, dicat Lucres:[20]

LUCRES
I wyll not dysclaunder nor blame no man,
But neverthelesse, by that I here saye,
Pore maydens be dissayved now and than.
So greate dyssemblynge now a daye
There is convayed under wordes gaye,[21]
That if . . .

ANCILLA
Peace, lady, ye must forbere!
Se ye not who cometh here?

LUCRES
Who is it, wot ye ere?

ANCILLA
It is Gayus Flamyneus, parde,
He that wolde your husbonde be.

LUCRES
Ey, gode Lorde! How wyste he
For to fynde me here?

Intrat Gayus Flaminius.

GAYUS
Yes, gode lady, where so ever ye go,
He that lysteth to do his dylygence
In suche manere wyse as I have do,
At the laste he may come to youre presence.
For, who so ever oweth obedyence
Unto love, he hath greate nede
To attendaunce if he wyll spede.[22]

LUCRES
Syr, ye be welcome. What is your mynde?

445 I did not mean that 446 did 447 intention 448 finally decide 450 truly, all the same 451 he (Cornelius) 453 I would be unfortunate 454 too 457 enquiry 460 postponed 462 impartially 463 completely certain 464 decide 465 Of course 466 business, home 467 that way 469 rather 472 slander 473 what I hear said 474 Poor virgins, deceived 479 do you know 482 How did he know 482+ Enter Gayus Flaminius 485 desires, diligent service 486 done 487 Finally 488 owes

18 'Suggesting that you would like me to choose him.'
19 'But, whoever you choose, you have God's blessing and mine.'
20 'And after a certain pause, Lucres shall say'.
21 'There is so much dissembling [deceit] hidden under fine words nowadays'.
22 'He needs to come courting if he wants to prosper.'

Gayus
Why, fayre Lucres, is that your gyse,
To be so straunge and so unkynde
To hym that owith you lovyng servyce?
I trow I have tolde you twyse or thrice
That myn desyre is to mary with you.
Have ye not herde this matter or now?

Lucres
Yes, in veray trouth, I have herde you say
Att dyverse tymes that ye bare me affeccyon:
To suche an intent I say not nay.

Gayus
What nede ye than aske the question
What I wolde with you at this season?
Me semyth ye sholde therin doubt no more
Sith ye know well myn erande before.[23]

Iwys, your strangnes greveth me sore,
But not withstonding, now wyll I sece,
And at this tyme I wyll chide no more
Lest I geve you cause of hevynes.
I cam hyder onely for youre sake, doubtles,
To glade you and please you in all that I can,
And not for to chyde with you as I began.

For thynke it in your mynde, I am the man
That wolde you please in all that I may,
And to that purpose I wyll do what I can
Though ye forbyde it and say therin nay,
In that poynt onely I wyll you disobay.
My hart shall ye have in all godely wise
Whether ye me take or utterly dispise.

And to say that I will folow the gise
Of wanton lovers now aday,
Whiche doth many flatering wordis devise
With gyftis of ringis and broches gay
Theyr lemmans hartis for to betray,
Ye must have me therin excusid,[24]
For it is the thing that I never usid.

Therfore I will be short and playne,
And I pray you hartely, feyre Lucres,
That ye wyll be so to me agayne.
Ye know well I have made labour and besynes
And also desyrid you by wordis expresse
That ye wold vouche save in your harte
To be my wife till deth us departe.

Lo, this is the mater that I come fore:
To know therin your mynde and plesoure,
Whether ye sett by me ony store
To theffect of my seyd desire.
And nothing ellis I wyll require
But that I may have a playne ye[a] or nay,
Whereto I may trust withoute delay.

Lucres
Me thinketh that by that that ye say,
Ye force not what myne answere be![25]

Gayus
A, wyll ye take it that way?
My lady, I ment not so, parde.
Thaffirmatyfe were most lefe to me,
For as ye your self knowith best,
That was and is my principall request.

But ye may say I am a homely gest
On a gentil[wo]man so hastely to call.

Lucres
Nay, nay, syr, that guyse is best!
Ye can not displeyse me with all,
And accordyng to your desire I shall
Evyn as sone as I godely may
Answere you therin withoute delay.

How be it, it can not be done strait way
If I myght gett a realme therby.
Fyrst wyll I my faders mynde assay
Whether he wyll therunto applye.
For, if he like you as well as I,
Your mynde in this behalf shalbe sone easid
If my seyd fader can be content and pleysid.

492 fashion/manner 493 distant 494 owes 497 before 498 very 499 bore/felt for 505 strangeness/formality 506 cease 507 complain/nag you 508 sadness 510 gladden 513 who wants to please you 515 forbid 516 only 519 fashion 521 Who, flattering words 522 gifts, rings, brooches 523 beloveds' hearts 525 practised 528 in return 529 business/effort 530 desired, openly 531 grant 532 death divides us 533 for 534 pleasure 535 place any value on me 536 the satisfaction 537 else, ask 538 a plain yes or no 544 The affirmative (reply), desirable 547 rude guest/fellow 548 abruptly 549 manner 550 displease, with that 552 Even, soon, conveniently may 554 immediately 555 (Even) if I could gain 557 agree 559 eased/relieved 560 pleased

23 'Since you already know my errand.'

24 'You must excuse me from all that'.

25 'I think, from those things that you say, that you do not [really] mind what my answer is!'

Gayus
Gramercy, myne owne swete Lucres.
Of you desire can I no more at all,
Save onely that ye do your besynes
Upon youre fader besily to call,
So that what so ever shal befall,
Within few days I may verily know
To what effect this mater shal grow.

Lucres
Ye shall know by tomorow nyght
What my fader wyll sey therto.

Gayus
Than shall ye make myne harte full light
If it pleyse you so to do.

Lucres
Yes, doubt ye not it shal be so,
And for that cause I wyll even now departe.

Gayus
Now fare well than, myne owne swete harte.

Et exeat Lucres [and Ancilla]. Deinde A accedens ad Gayum Flaminium, dicat ei sic:[26]

A
Syr, ye seme a man of grete honoure,
And that moveth me to be so bolde:
I rede you, adventure not over moche laboure
Upon this woman, leste ye take colde.
I tell you, the mater is bought and solde!
Withoute ye take the better hede,
For all these feyre wordes ye shall not spede!

Gayus
Thynkest thou so in very dede?

A
Ye[a], so helpe me God, and I shall tell you why:
Syr, ryght now, this way as I yede,
This gentylwoman cam even by,
And a fresshe galant in her company.
As God wolde, nere them I stalked
And herde every worde that they talked.

Gayus
But spake they ony worde of me?

A
Nay, nay, ye were no thinge in her thoughte.
They were as besy as they myghte be
Aboute suche a matter as ye have wroughte.
And, by God that me dere boughte,
Loke what answer that ye now have,
Even the same wordes to hym she gave.

Iwys, syr, I am but a pore knave,
But yet I wolde take on me a greate payne
Youre honeste in this matter to save,
Though it be unto me no profyte nor gayne.
But therefore I speke and have dysdayne
To se in a woman suche dyssemblaunce
Towarde a gentylman of youre substaunce.

Gayus
Why, hast thou of me ony acquentaunce?

A
Ye[a], syr, and some tyme ye knewe me,
Though it be now oute of youre remembraunce.

Gayus
By my fayth it may well be,
But never the lesse I thanke the[e].
Me semeth thou woldest that all were well
Betwyxte me and yonder fayre damesell.

A
Ye[a], by God, I wolde fyghte in the quarell
Rather than ye sholde lese youre ente[n]te.

Gayus
I praye the[e], felowe, where doste thou dwell?

A
By my fayth, I am now at myn owne
commaundement;
I lacke a mayster, and that I me repente.
To serve you and please I wolde be fayne
Yf it myght lyke you me to retayne.

561 Thank you 562 I can ask no more 565 happen/result 566 truly 567 conclusion, lead 570 completely happy 571 please(s) 576 moves/prompts 577 advise, do not invest too much 578 in case you come off worst 579 settled already 580 Unless 582 indeed (emphatic) 584 went 586 With, young gallant 587 allowed, crept 593 redeemed me at great cost 598 honesty/reputation 601 dissembling/deception 603 do you know me 608 wish 611 lose what you desire 614 I regret that 615 please (you) 616 employ

26 'And Lucres [and the Maid] shall exit. Then let A, approaching Gayus Flaminius, say to him thus:'

And of one thynge I wyll, a certayne:
I doubte not I shall do you better stede
Towarde this maryage than some other twayne,
And yf I do not, let me be dede!

GAYUS
Well, than wyll I do by thy rede,
And in my servyce thou shalt be
Yf thou canst fynde me any surete.[27]

A
Yes, I can have sureties plente
For my trouth within this place.
Here is a gentilman that wolde truste me
For as moche gode as he hase.[28]

GAYUS
Ye[a], and that is but litle percase,

A
By my fayth, go where he shall,
It is as honest a man as ony in the reall.

I have no more acqueyntaunce within this hall
If I wolde ony frendis assay.
[*Indicates B*] By God, here is one best of all!
I trow he wyll not say me nay.
For he hath knowen me many a day.
Syr, wyll not ye for my trouth undertake?

B
Yes, for God, els I wolde I were bake!
Syr, my maister, wyll ye beleve me?
I dare trust hym for all that I can make,
Yf ye fynde me sufficient surete.
As for his trouth, doubt not ye.
I never coude by hym any thing espie
But that he was as true a man as I.

He and I dwelled many a feyre day
In one scole, and yet I wot well
From thens he bare never away[29]
The worth of an halfe peny that I can tell;
Therfore he is able with you to dwell!
As for his trought, that dare I well saye,
Hardely[30] truste hym therein ye maye.

GAYUS
Upon youre worde I shall assaye,[31]
[*To A*] And, syr, after thi gode deservynge,
So shall I thy wagys pay.
But now to remembre one thinge:
Me thought thou saydist at the begynnynge
That Lucres favoreth better than me
A nother lover. What man is he?

A
Cornelius I wene his name sholde be.

GAYUS
A, then, I knowe him well, by the Rode!
There is not within all this cyte
A man borne of a better blode.
But yet Lucres hath a wytt so gode
That as I thynke she wyll before see
Whether his condicyons therto agree,

And if they do not, fare well he!
But therin I have nought ado.
He shall not be dispraysid for me
Withoute that I be compellid therto.
I can not let hym for to woo
A woman beyng at her owne liberte,
For why it is as fre for hym as for me.

I wyll forbere never the more
Tyll I knowe what shall be the ende.
Go thy waye unto Lucres therfore,
And hertly me unto her recommende.
Prayng her that she wyll me sende
A redy answere of that thing
That she promised me at her departing.

618 service 619 two (men) 620 dead 621 follow your advice 624 aplenty 625 honesty 628 perhaps 630 He, realm 632 try 634 deny me 636 stand surety for me? 637 baked 639 earn 642 see anything about him 643 Except 644 fair 645 school 649 truth/honesty 652 according to your deserts 653 wages 655 said 658 think 659 Cross 661 blood 665 it's 'goodbye' to him! 666 But I'll play no part in that 667 criticized by 668 unless, compelled to do it 669 prevent him from wooing 675 commend me to her 676 Praying 677 speedy

27 A testimonial to good character.

28 'With all the goods he has.' For this comic business A must either first pick out a member of the audience, whom Gayus rejects as a good witness, and then turn to B concealed in the crowd, or pick out B initially, have him rejected at first, and then allow him to find another place in the crowd (possibly concealing his identity in some way in the process) and pick him again.

29 B equivocatingly suggests either that, while he was at school, A never stole anything, or that A never learned anything.

30 'Certainly', with an implied contradictory meaning of 'Hardly [at all]'.

31 'I shall try him on your recommendation.'

A
Mary, I shall, without any tarying.
I knowe myne erand well inow:
Ye shall se me apoynte a metynge
Where she agayne shall speke wyth you.

GAYUS
Than shall I thy wyt alowe
Yf thou can brynge that aboute.

A
Yes, that I shall do, have ye no doubte.

Et exeat Gayus Flaminius, et dicat B:[32]

B
Now, by my trought, I wolde not have thoughte
That thou haddest bene halfe so wyse,
For thou hast this matter featly wrought
And convayed it poynt devyse
To brynge thy selfe to suche a servyce;
I se well thou hast some wytt in thy hede!

A
Ye[a], a lytell. But hast thou spede?

B
Even lyke wyse, have thou no drede,
I have goten a maister for my prowe.
I never thryvede as I shall do now!

A
No? Whiche way?

B
I shall tell the[e] how:
It is no maystry to thryve at all
Under a man that is so liberall.

Ther is now late unto hym fall
So grete goodis by inheritaunce
That he wote never what to do with all,
But lassheth it forth daily escaunce
That he had no dayly remembraunce
Of tyme to come, nor makyth no store,
For he carith not whiche ende goth before.

And, by Oure Lady, I commende hym the more!
Why sholde he those goodis spare,
Sith he laborede never therfore?
Nay, and every man sholde care
For goodis, and specially suche as are
Of gentil blode, it were grete syn,
For all liberalite in them sholde begyn.[33]

Many a pore man therby doth wyn
The chef substauns of his lyving.
My maister were worthy to be a kyng
For liberall expensis in all his deling!
I trow thou shalt se hym com yn
Lyke a rutter somwhat according[34]
In all apparell to hym belongyng.
How moche payeth he, as ye suppose,
For the makyng of a peyre of his hose?

A
Mary, twelve pence were a feyre thing.

B
Ye[a], by the Rode, twenty tymes tolde,
That is evyn twenty shelyngis for the makyng!

A
It can not be so withoute a man wolde
Make them all with sylke and golde!

B
Nay, by Jys, non erthly thing
But evyn the bare cloth and the lynynge!

Save onely that ther is in cuttinge
A new maner of fascyon now a day:
Because they sholde be somwhat straunge,
They moste be strypide all this way
With small slypes of coloures gay,
A codpece before allmost thus large,[35]
And therin restith the gretist charge![36]

679 delay 680 enough 681 arrange, meeting 683 praise 687 had been 688 neatly arranged 689 carried it off perfectly 692 prospered 693 Just the same (as you) 694 advantage 695 thrived (before) 697 takes no skill 698 generous 699 lately, fallen 701 knows 702 squanders, as if 704 saves for the future 705 first (i.e. cares for nothing) 708 he never worked for them 709 if, covet 711 it would be (a) 713 gain 714 chief portion, income 716 dealings 720 did he pay 721 pair 722 good price 723 counted over 724 20 shillings: £1 sterling 725 unless 727 Jesus (they're made from) 728 lining 730 fashion 731 new-fangled 732 striped 733 slips

32 'Let Gayus Flaminius exit, and B shall say'.

33 'For liberality should originate with them [the nobility].'

34 'Looking something like a rutter [a gallant, from the German *ritter*, cavalryman, with implications of rutting: sexual predatoriness]'.

35 'And with a codpiece in front, this large'. The line was no doubt accompanied by a suitably impressive gesture.

36 'And in that lies the greatest cost!' With a bawdy double entendre on the 'charge' of shot in a cannon.

To speke of gowns and that gode chaunge,
Of them he hath store and plenty,
And that the fascyons be new and straunge,
For non of them passith the mydde thy.[37]
And yet he puttyth in a gown communely
How many brode yardis,[38] as ye gesse?

A
Mary, two or thre.

B
Nay, seven and no lesse!

A
By my trouth, that is lyke a lye!

B
But it is as true as ye stond there.
And I shall tell you a reson why:
All that doth that fascyon were,
They have whingis behynd redy to flye,
And a sleve that wolde cover all the body!
Than forty playtis, as I think in my mynde,
They have before, and as many behynde.

A
Well, as for gentilmen, it is full kynde
To have theyr plesyrs that may well paye.[39]

B
Ye[a], but than this grugeth my mynde:
A gentylman shall not were it a daye,
But every man wyll hym self araye
Of the same fascyon, even by and by
On the morow after!

A
Nay, that I defy!
But then I marvell gretly why
You are not garnysshyd after that gyse.

B
There is never a knave in the house save I
But his gowne is made in the same wyse,
And, for bycause I am new come to servyce,
I must for a whyle be content
To were stylle myn olde garment.

A
Ye[a], but abyde: to what intent
Doth thy mayster take in honde
To make hym so moche costely rayment?

B
Mary, that is esy to understonde:
All is done for Lucres sake.
To wedde her he doth his rekenynge make.[40]

A
I put case that she do hym forsake
So that she be my maysters wyf.

B
By my fayth, then I say it wyll make
Many a man to lose his lyf,
For therof wyll ryse a gret stryf.

A
Mary, I pray God send us pes!

B
Be my fayth, it wyll be no lesse
Yf my master have not Lucres.

I can no more, God sped the ryght![41]
Lo, thes folke wyll stryve and fyght
For this womans sake,
And whan thay have done ther uttyrmest,
I wene veryly he shall sped best
That must her forsake!

He is well at ease that hath a wyf,
Yet he is better that hath none, be my lyf!

736 abundant change (of clothes) 740 commonly 741 do you guess 743 likely to be 746 who wear that fashion 747 wings 749 (No fewer) than, pleats 751 completely natural 753 grudges/irritates 754 wear, (for more than) a day 755 dress himself 756 In, reject 758 greatly 759 garnished/dressed 760 no servant, except me 761 way 762 newly, into 764 still wear 767 clothing 768 easy 771 What if 775 arise 776 peace 779 know 782 upmost 783 truly believe, prosper 786 by

37 'The middle of the thigh.' A reference to the sort of revealingly short gown fashionable in the late fifteenth and early sixteenth centuries.

38 A broad yard was a two-yard width of cloth.

39 'Those who can pay get what they want.'

40 'He runs up his account with marrying her in mind'; i.e. the dowry will repay all the initial expenditure.

41 'May God favour the righteous!'

But he that hath a good wyf and wyll forsake her,
I pray God the Devyll take her!

B
Now in gode fayth thou art a made knave.
I se well thou hast wedyd a shrew!

A
The Devyll I have!
Nay, I have marryed two or thre
Syth the tyme that I her lost.

B
And kepist thou them all styll with the[e]?

A
Nay, that wolde not quyte the cost.
To say the trouth, thay fond me most.[42]

B
Than thay have some maner gettynge
By some occupacione, have thay?

A
Syr, thay have a prety waye!
The chef meane of ther levynge
Is lechery . . . lech crafte I wolde say!
Wherein thay labore nyght and day
And ease many a man in some case.

B
And where do thay dwell?

A
Att the Commen Place;[43]
There thou mayst them all fynde!
Goddis mercy, where is my mynde?
By God, I shall be shent!
I shold have gone to Lucres
Abowte my maysters besynes;
Thetherwarde I was bent.

B
By my fayth, my mayster is there
All the whyle that thou arte here,
As I veryly suppose.

A
I shrow thy face, by Saynt Mary!
With thy chaterynge thou doyst me tary
Evyn for the same purpose.

B
I say, whan thou hast with Lucres spoken,
I pray the[e], wyll thou delyver me a token
In myne name to her mayde?

A
Nay, ye muste be ware of that gere,
For I have bene afore you there.

B
Why, hast thou hyr assayed?

A
Ye[a], ye[a], that matyr ys sped full.
I may have her and she wull:
That comfort she me gave.

B
And hast thou no noder comfort att all?
I truste to God than yet I shall
All this matyr save.

How be it, I wyll not the matter begyn
Withoute I were sure she were a virgyn.

A
By my trought, this comfort shall I putt the[e] in:
I cam never on her backe in the way of synne.[44]

Avoyde the place A.

B
Than all is well and fyne
Yf the matter be in that case!
I trust that within a lytyll space
That wenche shall be myne.
I tell you it is a trull of trust

789 mad 793 still 794 repay the cost (of keeping them) 796 means of income 798 cunning 799 means 800 medicine 806 punished 809 I was heading that way 812 truly 813 curse 814 chattering, delay 817 love-token/message 820 before ('I got there first!') 821 tried her? 822 matter, successfully completed 823 if she wishes 825 other 829 Unless I am sure 831+ A leaves the place 833 if that's how things stand 834 time 836 dependable tart

42 'They mostly provided for me.' A's 'marital' history is a thinly disguised allusion to his pimping.

43 Either the Stews in Southwark where the 'common women' (prostitutes) work, or perhaps (as Nelson, *Plays of Henry Medwall*, suggests) the court of Common Pleas in Westminster. If it is the latter, the joke may be 'They're always in court.'

44 This, of course, leaves open the possibility that he has encountered her sinfully from the front.

All to quenche a mannes thrust
Bettyr then ony wyne!

It is a lytyll praty moucet,
And her voyce is as doucett
And as swete as resty porke.
Her face is some what browne and yelow,
But for all that she hath no felow
In syngynge hens to Yorke.

But the worst that grevyth me,
She hath no layser nor lybarte
For an howre or twayne
To be owte of her maystres syght.
I wachyde for her this odyr nyght,
But all was in vayne.

How be it, I thinke that at the laste
I shall come within two stonys caste[45]
Of her, I aske no more.
And yf I do so, then my mate
Shall have no lust therin to prate
As he dyde before.

Come in the maydyn [*Ancilla*].

Cockis body, here she is!
Now wellcome, by Hevyn blys,
The last that was in my thought![46]

ANCILLA
Tusshe, I pray you, let me go!
I have somewhat els to do,
For this howre I have soughte

A man that I sholde speke with all
Fro my maystres.

B
What do you hym call?

ANCILLA
Mayster Gayus or his man.

B
Am not I he that ye wolde have?

ANCILLA
No, no, I wolde have an other knave!

B
Why, am I a knave, than?

ANCILLA
Nay, I sayd not so, perde.
But where trow ye these folkis be?

B
I can not veryly say.
His man went evyn now frome me
And I marvell gretly that ye
Met hym not by the way,
For he is gone to speke with Lucres
From his maystyr.

ANCILLA
What, with my maystres?
Nay!

B
Ye[a], so I harde hym say.

ANCILLA
Goddis mercy, and I was sent
Evyn hedyr for the same intent
To brynge an answere
Of the erande that he is gone fore,
Wherefore now ther is no more
But I must go seche hym there.

B
Nay, tary here a whyle gentyll Jone,
For he wyll come hedyr anone.

ANCILLA
Tary? Why shold I so?

B
Mary, to laugh and talke with me.

ANCILLA
Nay, loke where suche gyglottis be,

837 man's thirst 838 any wine 839 She, pretty little mouse 840 dulcet/sweet 841 sweet, rancid 844 (from) here 845 grieves 846 leisure, liberty 847 hour 848 mistress's 849 waited, other 855 desire, talk/chatter 857 Cock's (God's: euphemism) 858 Heaven's bliss 864 mistress 870 do you think, are 877 heard 882 no alternative 884 Joan 888 (go and) look, wanton women

[45] '[If] I could only come within two stone's throws [of her]'. As 'stones' was slang for testicles, an ejaculatory double entendre is probably also intended.

[46] 'The very person I was thinking about!'

For I am none of them, I warne the[e],
That use so to do.

B
I mene no thinge but good and honest
And for your wele, and you lyst
To assent therunto.

Ancilla
'For my wele', quod a? How may that be?
That is a thinge that I can not se.

B
Mary, this, lo, is myne entent:
I mene, yf ye wolde be content
Or ony wyse agree

For to be my sacrament of penaunce . . .
Ey, God gyve it a very very vengeaunce!
'Of wedlocke' I wolde have sayde!

Ancilla
Tush, by Seynt Jame, ye do but mocke,
To speke to me of ony wedlocke,
And I so yonge a mayde!

B
Why, are ye a mayde?

Ancilla
Ye[a], ellis I were to blame.

B
Where by wote ye?

Ancilla
Mary, for I ame!

B
A, that is a thinge!
Here ye not, syrs, what she sayth?
So resonable a cause thereto she layth!

Ancilla
A straw for your mockynge!
Have ye none to mocke but me?

B
Mocke? Nay, so mote I the,
I mene evyne gode ernest!
Geve me your honde and you shall se
What I wyll promes you.

Ancilla
That way were not best for my prow!

Wold ye hondefast me forth with all?
Nay, be the Roode, fyrst ye shall
Chepe or ever you by!
We must fyrst of the price agre,
For who some ever shall have me,
I promes you faytfully,

He shall me fyrst assure
Of twenty pound londe in joyncture.[47]

B
Why, are ye so costely?
Nay, nay, then ye be not for me.
As prety a woman as ye be
I can some tyme by
For moche les wagis and hyre,
As for the season that I desyre
To have hyr in company[48]

Therefore, yf ye canfynde in youre harte
To leve all sucche joynter aparte
And take me as I am,
I shall do you as greate a pleasure,
And therto I wyll love you oute of mesure,
Els I were to blame.

Ancilla
Ye[a], but oure housholde shall be full small
But yf we have somewhat els with all
Oure charges for to bere.

B
Ye[a], God sende us mery wether!
I may not wed and thryve all together;

889 not one 891 mean/intend 892 benefit, if you wish 894 says he? 898 (in) any way 899 penance 900 give . . . (curse it, doubly!) 901 should 902 James 905 virgin 906 How do you know, because I am 908 Hear 909 an argument, puts forward 911 no one 912 may I prosper 913 I'm being serious 915 promise 916 profit 917 marry/betroth, just like that 919 Always bargain before you buy 922 faithfully 925 costly 928 buy 933 set aside all such jointures 936 immeasurably 937 Otherwise 939 Unless 940 to cover our expenses 941 fine weather (God bless us!) 942 at the same time

47 'He must first guarantee me twenty pounds' worth of land made over in jointure [i.e. legally owned in her name as well as her spouse's].'

48 'I can hire a woman as pretty as you are much more cheaply for as long as I want her.'

I loke not for that gere.

I shall tell you a marvelous case:
I knewe twayne marryed in a place

Dwellyng together in one house,
And I am sure they were not worth a louse
At the begynnynge.
And or ever the yere were do,
They were worth an hondred or two![49]

ANCILLA
That was a marvelous thynge!

But yet I can tell the[e] a gretter marvayle,
And I knewe the persons ryght well:
Syr, I knewe two, certayne,

That when they were wedded, they had in store
Scarce halfe a bed and no more
That was worth an hawe,
And within a yere or twayne
They had so greate encrease and gayne
That at the last they were fayne
To shove theyre hedes in the strawe.[50]

B
Tusshe, ye do but mocke and rayle!
And I promesse you withouten fayle,
Yf ye lyste to have me,
I woot where is an hundred pound in store,
And I ow never a grot[51] therfore!

ANCILLA
All that may be;

I beleve hyt evyn as ye say.
But ye tary me here all day,
I pray you let me goo.
And for my mariage, that is a thing
In the whyche I purpose to geve a sparyng
For a yere or two.

B
'A yere or two', quod a? Nay, God forbede!
Iwis, hyt had be tyme fore you to wedde
Seven or eight yere agoo.

And ye wyst how mery a lyfe
Hyt is to be a wedded wyf,
Ye wold chaunge that mynde.

ANCILLA
Ye[a], so hyt is, as I understonde,
If a woman have a gode husbonde,
But that ys herd to fynde!

Many a man blamyth his wyf, parde,
And she is more to blame than he![52]

B
As true as the Gospell now say ye.
But now tell me one thing:
Shall I have none other answere but this
Of my desyre?

ANCILLA
No syr, iwys,
Not at this metyng.

B
Wyll ye now nede be agoo than?

ANCILLA
Take your leve honestly.

Et conabitur eam osculari.[53]

Se the man!
Let me alone, with sorowe!

B
Mary, so be hyt. But one worde:
I wyll kys the[e] or thou goo.

ANCILLA
The Devyllis torde!
The man is madde, I trowe!

B
So madde I am that nedis I must
As in this poynt have my lust
How so ever I doo.

ANCILLA
Parde, ye may do me that request,
For why it is but good and honest.

943 don't look for, deal 945 two (people) 957 hawthorn berry (very little) 960 pleased 961 heads 962 nag 964 want 965 know 966 (will) pay 968 it 972 delay 975 it was time 977 If you knew 982 hard 988 Regarding 990 gone 994 kiss, before, Devil's turd 997 desire 998 Whatever (else) 1000 only

49 Whether pounds or lice is left deliberately uncertain.

50 i.e. the increase of children reduced them to hiding their heads in the bed-straw (or perhaps to eating it through abject poverty).

51 A groat was a coin worth 4 pence.

52 A seemingly unintentional slip?

53 'And he shall try to kiss her.'

Et osculabitur. Intrat A.[54]

A
Now a felychip, I the[e] beseche,
Set even suche a patche one my breche![55]

B
A wyld feyre therone!

Ancilla
Goddis mercy, this is he
That I have sought so!

A
Have ye sought me?

Ancilla
Ye[a], that have I do!
This gentylman can wytnes bere
That all this owre I have stonde here
Sechyng even for you.

A
Have ye two be togeder so longe?

Ancilla
Ye[a], why not?

A
Mary, then all is wrong,
I fere me so now.

B
Nay, nay, here be to many wytnes
For to make ony syche besynes
As thou wenest, hardely!

Ancilla
Why, what is the mannes thought?
Suppose ye that I wolde be nowght
Yf no man were by?

[A]
Nay, for God, Y ment not so,
But I wolde no man sholde have to do
With you but onely I.

Ancilla
'Have to do', quod a? What call ye that?
Hyt sowndyth to a thing I wote ner what!

[A]
Ey, Godes mercy!
I se well a man must be warre
How he spekyth ther as ye ar,
Ye take it so straungely!

Nay, I mene nothyng but well,
For by my wyll no man shall dele
With you in way of maryage,
But onely I; this wyse I ment!

Ancilla
Ye[a], but though it were youre entent,
Yet ye do but rage

To use suche wordes unto me,
For I am yet at my lyberte.

A
Ye[a], that I know well.
But never the lesse, sythen I beganne
To love you longe before this man,
I have veray greate mervell

That ever ye wolde his mynde fulfyll,
To stonde and talke with hym styll
So long as ye have do.

B
'Before me', quod a? Nay, I make avowe,
I mevyde this matter long byfore you:
How sey ye therto?

Ancilla
I wyll no thinge in the matter say
Lest I cause you to make a fray,
For thereof I wolde be lothe.

A
By Cokkis body, butt who so ever it be
That weddythe her bysydes me,
I shall make hym wrothe!

1001 for fellowship's sake 1003 A wild fire on that! 1005 done 1006 bear witness 1007 hour, stood 1008 searching 1009 been 1013 too many witnesses 1014 such 1015 believe 1016 the man thinking 1017 Do you think I'd be wanton 1018 nearby (to witness) 1023 I don't know what that implies 1025 wary 1026 around you 1029 deal/ negotiate 1031 That's what 1032 intention 1033 rave 1037 since 1039 truly, wonder 1040 satisfy 1042 done 1043 I swear 1044 moved/began 1045 What do you say to that 1047 start a fight 1048 loathed

54 'And she shall be kissed. Enter A.'

55 'Put another similar patch on my breeches [i.e. kiss my arse]!'

B
Ye[a], but he that is so hasty at every worde,
For a medsyn must ete his wyves torde!

ANCILLA
Holde your tongis there I say,
For, and ye make this warke for me,
Ye shall bothe dyspoyntyd be
As fare as I may!

A
By my trouthe, but marke me well:
Yf ever thou with this man dwell
As a woman with here make,
Thou shalt fynde hym the most froward man
That ever thou sawiste sythe the worlde bygan!
For I dare undertake

That forty tymes on a day
Withoute ony cause he wyll the[e] afray
And bete the[e] bake and syde!

ANCILLA
He shall not nede so to do,
For he shall have forty causes and forty too
Yf I with hym abyde.

A
Mary, that ys a remedy accordynge!
But I can tell the[e] an other thynge,
And it is no lye:
Thow maist well be hys weddyd wyf,
But he wyll never love the[e] in his lyf.

ANCILLA
Yet I know a remedy.

A
Howso?

ANCILLA
Mary, I wyll love hym as lytyll agayne!
For every shrewed turne he shall have twayne,
And he were my brother.

B
Iwys, Jone, he spekythe but of males.
There ys no man hens to Cales,
Who so ever be the tother,

That can hym selfe better applye
To please a woman better then I.

ANCILLA
Ye[a], so I harde you say!
But yet, be ye never so wrothe,
There ys never one of you bothe,
For all youre wordes gay,

That shalbe assured of me
Tyll I may fyrst here and se
What ye bothe can do.
And he that can do most maystry,
Be it in cokery or in pastry,
In fettis of warre or dedys of chevalry,
With hym wyll I go.

A
By my trowthe, that lykythe me well.
Ther is no maystry that a man can tell
But I am mete thereto,
Wherefor that wagere I dare well undertake!
Lett me se, wylt thou go coyt for thy ladis sake,
Or what thyng shall we do?

B
Nay, yf thou wylt her with maystry wynne,
With boyes game thou mayst not begyn;
That is not her intent.

A
What is best that we do, than?

B
Mary, canst thou syng?

A
Ye, that I can,
As well as ony man in Kent.

B
What maner of song shall it be?

A
What so ever thou wylt chose the[e],
I holde me well content.

1053 medicine, wife's turd 1055 if you're arguing over me 1056 disappointed 1057 As far as I can arrange it 1058 understand 1060 mate 1061 quarrelsome 1062 saw since 1063 bet 1064 in 1065 assault you 1066 beat, back and sides 1068 more 1073 may 1076 in return 1077 mean act, two (in return) 1078 (Even) if 1079 only (out) of malice 1080 (from) here, Calais 1081 whoever he is 1083 than I can 1084 heard 1087 fine words 1088 certain 1089 hear 1091 show most skill 1092 cookery 1093 feats of arms 1097 fitting for it 1098 accept 1099 play at quoits 1102 boys' games 1109 happy

And yf I mete the[e] not at the close,[56]
Hardely let me the wager lose
By her owne jugement.
Go to now, wyll ye set in?

B
Nay, be the Rode, ye shall begyn.

A
By Seynt Jame, I assent.

Abyde, Jone, ye can gode skyll,
And if ye wolde the song fulfyll
With a thyrd parte,[57]
It wolde do ryght well, in my mynde.

Ancilla
Synge on, hardely, and I wyll not be behynde,
I pray the[e] with all my hert.

Et tunc cantabunt.

B
I am so whorse, it wyll not be.

A
'Horse', quod a? Nay, so mot I the,
That was not the thynge
And a man sholde the trowth saye:
Ye lost a crochet[58] or two by the waye,
To myne understondynge.

B
Why, was I a mynyme before? [59]

A
Ye[a], be the Rode, that ye were and more.

B
Then were ye a mynyme behynde.
Let me se, yet syng agayne,
[*To Ancilla*] And marke whyche of us twayne
Plesyth best your mynde.

Ancilla
Nay, nay, ye shall this matter try
By some other maner of mastry
Than by your syngynge.

B
Let hym assay what mastry he wull.

A
Mary, and my bely were not so full
I wolde wrestell with hym a fayre pull.
That were a game accordynge

For suche valyaunt men as we be!

B
I shrew thyn hert and thou spare me.

Et deinde luctabuntur.[60] [*B throws A.*]

Ancilla
Nay, by my fayth, that was no fall!

B
A, than I se well ye be parcyall,
Whan ye juge so.
Well, I shall do more for your love.
Evyn here I cast to hym my glove
Or ever I hens goo,

On the condycion that in the playne fylde
I shall mete hym with spere and shelde
My lyf theron to jeoparde.
Let me se and he dare take hyt.

Tunc projiciet cirothecam.[61]

A
Yes, hardely, I wyll not forsake hyt.
I am not suche a coward

But I dare mete the[e] at all assays;
Whan shall hyt be do?

B
Even strayght ways
Withoute furthere delay,
And I shrewe his hert that feris

1113 start us off 1116 are skilled (at singing) 1117 complete 1121+ And then they shall sing 1122 hoarse 1135 type of skill 1137 wishes 1138 belly 1139 wrestle, bout 1140 suitable contest 1142 curse, if 1144 partial 1147 throw down (in formal challenge) 1149 open field 1150 shield 1151 risk 1152 if 1155 attempts 1158 fears

56 'And if I'm not still in harmony with you at the end'.

57 Presumably Joan will provide the treble to accompany A and B's tenor and mean. See the three-part harmonies in the Towneley *Second Shepherds' Play*, ll. 182–9, and *Wisdom*, ll. 613–21.

58 A musical note, half a minim.

59 'A minim [half a semi-breve] too quick?'

60 'And then they shall wrestle.'

61 'Then he shall throw down a glove.'

Eyther with cronall[62] or sharpe speris,
This bargyn to assay.

A
And I beshrewe hym for me!
But abyde, now let me se,
Where shall I have a hors?

B
Nay, we shall nede no horse ne mule,
But let us just at farte pryke in cule.[63]

A
Be Seynt Jame, no forse,

Evyn so be it! But where is oure gere?

B
By my fayth, all thing is redy [here]
That belongethe therto.
Com forthe, ye flowre of the frying pane,[64]
Helpe ye to aray us as well as ye can.
And how so ever ye do,

Se that ye juge indifferently
Whiche of us twayne hathe the mastry.

ANCILLA
Yes, hardely, that I shall.
I shall juge after my mynde.
But see ye hold fast behynd
Lest ye troble us in all.

B
Tushe, that is the lest care of fiftene.
And yf I do not, on my game be yt sene![65]
Go to, bynd me fyrst, hardely.
So, lo, now, geve me my spere,
And put me a staffe thorow here;
Than am I all redy.

A
Abyde, who shall helpe to harnys me?

ANCILLA
That shall I do, so mott I the,
With a ryght gode wyll!

A
Soft and fayre! Myne arme is sore,
Ye may not bynd me strayt ther fore.

ANCILLA
Nay, no more I wyll.

I wyll not hurte the[e] for twenty pounde.
Come of now, syt downe on the grounde,
Evyn upon thy tayle.

A
Ey, gode Lorde, whan wyll ye have do?

ANCILLA
Now all is redy: hardely, go to!
Bydde hym bayle, bayle!

A
[*To the audience*] Fall to prayer, syrs, it is nede,
As many of you as wolde me Gode spede,
For this gere stondyth me uppon.

B
Ye[a], and that shall thou fynde or we departe,
And yf thou spare me I shrow thy harte!
Let me se, com on!

Et projectus dicat A:

A
Out, out, alas for payne!
Let me have a pryst or I be slayne
My syn to dysclose.

1159 spears 1160 challenge, try 1163 get a horse? 1165 joust 1166 no worries! 1167 equipment 1170 flower, pan 1171 arm us 1177 keep your arse tight-shut 1178 trouble 1179 least (i.e. very low on my list) 1185 arm 1189 tightly 1192 Come on 1194 have done (stop it!) 1196 Tell him 'charge!' 1198 wish me well 1199 business troubles me 1201 curse 1202+ And (having been thrown) A says 1204 priest 1205 confess

[62] A spear with a less-dangerous, divided head, used in jousting.
[63] 'Fart-prick-in-[the]-arse': a bawdy mock joust which probably involved the two combatants being trussed in a squatting position and hopping towards each other with poles or brooms thrust between their legs to act as spears. The precise role played by the 'fart' element in the equation is not clear. See Peter Meredith (and Meg Twycross), '"Farte Pryke in Cule" and Cockfighting', *Medieval English Theatre* 6 (1984), pp. 30–9. Once trussed, they are helpless when Joan beats them, and have to wait until l. 1249 for Gayus to release them.
[64] A mock-romantic epithet for the (scullery?) maid, Joan.
[65] 'The evidence will be seen on my "game" (Nelson suggests a variant of the French 'jamb', leg or leggings).

B
And bycause he sayth so, it is nede,
For he is not in clene lyfe in dede:
I fele it at my nose . . .

Fo! Fo! etc.

Now ye ar myne, lady!

ANCILLA
Nay, never the more.

B
No? Why so?

ANCILLA
For I am taken up before.

B
Mary, I beshrew your hart therefore!
It shold better content me
That ye had be taken up behynde!

ANCILLA
Nay, nay, ye understond not my mynde
In that poynt.

B
It may well be,
But tell me, how ment ye then?

ANCILLA
Mary, I am sure to an other man
Whose wyfe I intende to be.

B
Nay, I trow, by Cockis Passyon,
Ye wyll not mocke us of that fascyon;
Ye may not, for very shame!

ANCILLA
Shame or not, so shall it be,
And bycause that fore the love of me
Ye two have made this game,
It shall not be done all in vayne,
For I wyll rewarde you bothe twayne,
And ellis I were to blame.
Somewhat thereby ye must nedis wyn,
And therfore to everyche of you wyll I spyn
A new peyre of breches![66]
Take the[e] that fore thy dole!
And bycause he is blacke in the hole,
He shall have as moche!

Et utroque flagellato recedit Ancilla.[67]

A
Oute, alas! What woman was this?

B
It is Lucres mayde.

A
The Devyll it is!
I pray God a vengeance take her!
How saist thou, shall she be thy wyfe?

B
Nay, I had lever she had etyn my knyfe!
I utterly forsake her.

Intrat Gaius.

GAYUS
How, syrs, who hath arayde you thys?

A
Fals thevys, maister, iwys,
And all for your quarell!

GAYUS
What? And this other man too?

A
Ye[a], and ye wolde oure hondes undo,
The matter whe shall tell.

GAYUS
Yes, mary, wyll I. Now tell on:
Who hathe you these wrongis done?

A
Mary, that I shall.

1207 his life hasn't been clean 1208 (I can smell it!) 1209 (B complains about the smell) 1211 already promised (to another) 1218 promised 1221 in, fashion 1229 necessarily win 1230 each 1232 for your portion 1234 the same 1240 rather, eaten 1242 Who's done this to you 1243 Wicked thieves 1246 if, hands

66 She beats their buttocks.

67 'And, when both are beaten, the Maid withdraws.'

Cornelyus servantis, whiche is your enmy,
Espyed me goyng toward Lucres place,
That I coude brynge the matter to passe
Of that gentyl[wo]man, as your desyre was.
They leyd awayte for me in the way,
And so they lefte me in this araye.

GAYUS
Ye[a], but haste thou ony dedely wounde?
That is the thinge that feryth my mynde!

A
I faythe, I was lefte for dede on the grounde,
And I have a grete garce here byhynde
Out of the whiche ther commythe suche a wynde
That yf ye holde a candyll therto
Hyt wyll blowe it oute! That wyll hyt do!

GAYUS
Se to hyt be tyme, by myne advyse,
Lest the wounde fewster within.

A
Then have I nede of a gode surgyn,
For hyt is so depe within the skyn
That ye may put youre nose therin
Evyn up to the harde eyes.

Here is a man that quyt hym as well
For my defence as ever I see.
He toke suche parte that in the quarell
His arme was strykyne of by the harde kne
And yet he slew of them two or thre.

GAYUS
Be they slayne? Nay, God forbyde!

A
Yes, so helpe me God, I warande them dede.

How be it I stonde in grete drede
That yf ever he come in theyr way
They wyll kyt of his arme or his hede,
For so I herde them all thre say. .

GAYUS
Whiche? Thay that were slayne?

A
Ye[a], by this day!
What nedyth me therfore to lye?
He herd it hym selfe as well as I.

GAYUS
Well then, ye lye, both two!

[*Exit B.*]

But now tell me, what hast thou do
As touchynge my commaundement
That I badde the[e] do to Lucres?
Spakyst thou with her?

A
Ye[a], syr, dowtles,
And this is her intent:

Sche commaundyth hyr to you by the same tokyn
That with hyr father she hath spokyn
Accordynge to your requeste,
And so she wyllythe you to be of gode chere,
Desyrynge you this nyght to appere,
Or tomorow at the furthest,

And she wyll mete you here in this place
To gyve you a fynall answare in this case
Whereto ye shall trust.

GAYUS
That is the thing that I desyre!
But sayd she so?

A
Ye[a], be thys fyre,
I tell you verey juste,

In so moche that she bad me say
And warne you that ye shulde purvay
For your owne besenes,

For than it shall determy[n]de be
Whether Publyus Cornelyus or ye
Shall have the preemynence.

GAYUS
All that purpose lykythe me well,
But who shall be here more, canst thou tell?

A
Mary, here shall be Fulgens

1255 laid in wait, road 1256 condition 1257 deadly 1258 frightens 1260 gash 1264 quickly 1265 fester 1266 surgeon 1269 Right up to the eyes 1270 performed 1273 struck off near the knee 1279 cut 1284 both of you 1288 Did you speak 1290 commends herself 1293 wishes 1295 latest 1303 provide 1304 business 1308 I like that plan

And Publius Cornelius hym selfe also,
With dyverse other many moo
Besyde this honorable audyence.
Wherfore, yf ye wyll youre honour save
And your intent in this matter have,
It is best that ye go hens

For to study and call to mynde
Suche argumentis as ye can best fynde
And make your selfe all prest.

Gayus
Thy counsell is gode; be it so,
And evyn thereafter wyll I do,
For I holde it best.

Et exea[n]t Gaius et A. Intrat B.

B
Goddes body, syr[s], this was a fytt!
I beshrew the horys hart yett
When I thinke theron,
And yet the strokys be not so sore
But the shame grevyth me more,
Sith that it was done

Before so many as here be present.
But and I myght take her,
By my trowth I shall make her
This dede to repent!

[*Enter A.*]

A
Yet thou were as gode holde thy pease,
For ther is no remedy doutles;
Therfore lett itt go.
It is to us bothe grete foly and shame
This matter ony more to reherse or name.

B
Well than, be it so.

And yet, because she hathe made me smart,
I trust onys to ryde in her carte,[68]
Be it shame or no.
I can not suffre it paciently
To be rebuked openly
And to be mockyd also.
An other thing grevythe me werst of all:
I shall be shent, that I shall,
Of my mayster too

Because I have ben so long away
Oute of his presence.

A
Nay, nay,

I have harde so muche syth I went hens
That he had lityll mynd to thyn offens.

B
I pray you tell me why.

A
For, as I brought my mayster on hys way,
I harde one of Lucres men say
That thy mayster hathe ben
All this houre at her place,
And that he his answere hase,
This wyse as I mene:

She hathe appoynted hym to be here
Sone, in the evynyng aboute suppere,
An[d] than he shall have a fynall answere
What she entendith to do.
And so than we shal know here intent,
For, as I understond, she wyll be content
To have one of them too.

But furst she wyll nedis know the certayn
Whether is the most noble of them twayne;
This she sayeth alway.

B
Why, that is easy to understonde
Yf she be so wyse as men bere in honde.

A
Ye[a], so I hard you say.

Let me se now, what is your oppynion
Whether of them is most noble of condycion?

1312 more 1319 ready 1322+ And let Gayus and A exit. Enter B 1324 curse, whore's heart still 1326 wounds 1333 you'd be better 1337 discuss 1346 punished 1347 By 1351 given little thought 1357 has 1360 Soon, supper-time 1363 her intentions 1365 two 1366 first, for certain 1367 Which 1370 claim 1373 Whichever

68 Either a euphemism for sexual intercourse or, as Nelson suggests, a reference to the public 'riding' of convicted prostitutes and other felons through the streets in carts. The phrase might thus imply: 'I'd like to be there when she gets what she deserves!'

B
That can I tell hardely:
He that hathe moste nobles[69] in store,
Hym call I the most noble ever more,
For he is most sett by.

And I am sure Cornelyus is able
With his owne goodis to bye a rable
Of suche as Gayus is!
And over that, yf noblenes of kynn
May this womans favour wynn,
I am sure he can not mys.

A
Ye[a], but come hether sone to the ynde of this playe
And thou shalt se wherto all that wyll wey;
It shall be for thy lernynge.

B
Ye[a], cum agayne who wyll for me,
For I wyll not be here, so mot I the!
It is a gentylmanly thinge

That I shulde awayt and com agayne
For other mennys causes and take suche payne!

I wyll not do it, I make God avowe.
Why myght not this matter be endyd nowe?

A
Mary, I shall tell the[e] why:

Lucres and her father may not attende
At this seson to make an ende;
So I hard them say.
And also it is a curteyse gyse
For to respyte the matter this wyse
That the partyes may

In the meane tyme advyse them well,
For eyther of them bothe must tell
And shew the best he can
To force the goodnes of his owne condycion
Bothe by example and gode reason.
I wold not for a swan
That thou sholdest be hens at that season,
For thou shalt here a reyal disputacyon
Bitwext them or thay have do.
An other thing must be considred with all:
These folke that sitt here in the halle
May not attende theretoo:

Whe may not with oure long play
Lett them fro theyre dyner all day;
Thay have not fully dyned.
For and this play where ones overe past,
Some of them wolde falle to fedyng as fast
As thay had bene almost pyned.

But no forse, hardely, and they do.
Ussher, gete them goode wyne therto,
Fyll them of the best.
Let it be do or ye wyll be shent,
For it is the wyll and commaundement
Of the master of the fest.

And therfore we shall the matter forbere
And make a poynt evyn here
Lest we excede a mesure,
And we shall do oure labour and trewe entent
For to play the remenant
At my lordis pleasure.

Finis prime partis.
[*Part Two*]
Intrat A dicens:

A
Muche gode do it you everycheone
Ye wyll not beleve how fast I have gone
For fere that I sholde come to late!
No forse, I have lost but a lytyll swete
That I have taken upon this hete
My colde corage to abate.

But now to the matter that I cam fore:
Ye know the cause therof before;
Your wittis be not so short.
Perde, my felowys and I were here
Today, whan ye where at dyner,
And shewed you a lytyll disport

1377 provided for/highly regarded 1379 buy a (whole) rabble/crowd 1380 such (men) 1383 fail 1384 soon, end 1385 weigh/amount 1386 education 1396 time 1398 courteous fashion 1399 postpone 1404 urge 1406 (even) for 1408 hear, royal/splendid 1409 before, done 1411 (i.e. the audience) 1414 Keep 1416 if, once, finished 1417 eating 1418 As (if), starved 1419 matter, if 1422 done 1424 feast 1426 stop 1429 remaining part 1430+ The end of the First Part, A enters, saying 1433 too 1434 matter, sweat 1435 heat 1441 were, dinner

[69] A noble was a coin worth 80 pence.

Of one Fulgens and his doughter Lucres,
And of two men that made grett besynes
Her husbonde for to be.
She answered to them bothe than:
Loke whiche was the more noble man,
To hym she wolde agre.

This was the substance of the play
That was shewed here today,
All be it that there was
Dyvers toyes mengled yn the same
To styre folke to myrthe and game
And to do them solace,

The whiche tryfyllis be impertinent
To the matter principall,
But never the lesse they be expedient
For to satisfye and content
Many a man with all.

For some there be that lokis and gapys
Only for suche tryfles and japys,
And some there be amonge
That forceth lytyll of suche madnes,
But delytyth them in matter of sadnes
Be it never so longe.

And every man must have hys mynde,
Ellis thay will many fautys fynde
And say the play was nought.
But no force, I car not,
Let them say and spare not,
For God knoweth my thought.

It is the mynde and intent
Of me and my company to content
The leste that stondyth here,
And so I trust ye wyll it alowe.
Ey? Godis mercy, where am I now?
It were almys to wrynge me by the eare,[70]

Bycause I make suche degression
From the matter that I began
Whan I entred the halle.
For, had I made a gode contynuaunce,
I sholde have put you in remembraunce
And to your myndis call

How Lucres wyll come hyder agayne,
And her sayde lovers bothe twayne,
To dyffyne thys question:
Whether of them ys the more noble man.
For theron all this matter began:
It is the chefe foundacyon

Of all thys proces both all and some,
And yf thes players were ons come,
Of this matter will they speke.
I mervell gretely in my mynde
That thay tary so long behynde
Theyre howre for to breke.

But what, syrs! I pray you everychone
Have pacyens, for thay come anone.
I am sure they wyll not fayle
But thay wyll mete in this place
As theyre promys and apoyntment wase,
And ellis I have merveyle.

Let me se, what is now a-cloke?
A, there commyth one. I here hym knoke.
He knokythe as he were wood!
[*To the audience*] One of you go loke who it is.

[*Enter B.*]

B
Nay, nay, all the meyny of them, iwish,
Can not so moche gode.
A man may rappe tyll his naylis ake
Or ony of them wyll the labour take
To gyve hym an answere.

A
I have grete marvell on the[e]
That ever thou wylt take upon the[e]
To chyde ony man here!

No man is so moche to blame as thow
For longe taryinge.

1444 great efforts 1452 Various jests mixed 1453 provoke 1455 trifles, unrelated 1456 main story 1460 look, gape 1461 japes 1463 care little for 1464 serious matter 1465 However long it is 1467 faults 1468 worthless 1469 matter, care 1473 satisfy 1474 least (person) 1475 allow 1481 got straight on with it 1486 define 1487 Which 1490 story, completely 1491 once 1495 To miss their appointment 1500 was 1501 otherwise I'd be amazed 1502 o'clock (the time) 1503 hear, knock 1504 as (if), mad 1506 crowd 1507 (do) so 1508 nails ache 1509 Before 1513 criticize

70 'It would be a good deed to tweak me by the ear'.

B

Ye[a], God avow,
Wyll ye play me that?
Mary, that shall be amended anone:
I am late comen and I wyll sone be gone,
Ellis I shrew my catt.

Kockis body, syr, it is a fayre resone.
I am com hedyr att this season
Only at thy byddynge,
And now thou makyst to me a quarell
As though all the matter were in parell
By my longe taryynge.

Now God be with you, so mote I the,
Ye shall play the knave alone for me!

A

What? I am afrayde,
Iwis, ye are but lewyde!
Turne agayne, all beshrewyde,
Now are you fayre prayde.

B

Why than, is your angyr all do?

A

Ye[a], mary, is it, lo.

B

So is myne too.
I have done clene.
But now, how goyth this matter forth
Of this mariage?

A

By Saynt Jame, ryght nought worth.
I wot nere what thay meane,

For I can none other wise thinke
But that some of them begyn to shrinke
Bycause of ther longe tariage.

B

'Shrynke' now, quod a? Mary, that were mervele![71]
But one thinge of surete I can the[e] tell
As touchynge this mariage:

Cornelius my mayster apoyntyth hym therupone,
And dowtles he wyll be here anone,
In payne of forty pens,
In so muche that he hath devysyde
Certayne straungers fresshly disgisyd
Att his owne exspens

For to be here this nyght also.

A

'Straungers', quod a? What to do?

B

Mary, for to glade with all
This gentylwoman at her hedyr comynge.

A

A, then I se well we shall have a mummynge![72]

B

Ye[a], surely, that we shall!

And therfor never thinke it in thy mynde
That my mayster wyll be behynde
Nor slacke at this bargyn.
Mary, here he commyth, I have hym aspyde.
No more wordis, stonde thou asyde,
For it is he playne.

[*Exit A. Enter Cornelius.*]

CORNELIUS

My frynde, where abowt goist thou all day?

B

Mary, syr, I came heder to asay
Whedyr these folke[73] had ben here.

And yet thay be not come,
So helpe me God and holydome,
Of that I have moche marvaile,
That thay tary so.

1519 curse my cat 1520 good answer 1524 (put) in peril 1527 for all I care! 1530 Come back, you cursed thing 1531 you've been asked politely 1532 anger, done/finished? 1534 completely finished 1535 goes 1536 unprofitably 1537 don't know, intend 1539 hesitate/think again 1540 delay 1541 amazing 1542 for certain 1544 arranged 1546 pence 1548 foreigners, newly disguised 1552 gladden/entertain 1553 when she comes here 1557 slow 1561 plainly 1562 friend, where have you been 1563 here 1564 whether, been 1567 At, great amazement

71 Perhaps, as Nelson suggests, B wilfully mistakes 'shrinks' as a phallic allusion.

72 A general term for an entertainment, generally involving costumes and masks, and often dancing, which encompasses both the folk plays of the Mummers, and the courtly Disguising.

73 i.e. the missing 'mummers'.

Cornelius
Mary, go thi way
And wit where thay wyll or no!

B
Ye[a], God avow, shall I so.

Cornelius
Ye[a], mary, so I say.

B
Yet in that poynt, as semyth me,
Ye do not accordynge to your degre.[74]

Cornelius
I pray the[e], tell me why.

B
Mary, it wolde becom them well inow
To be here afore and to wayte upon you,
And not you to tary

For theyr laysyr and abyde them here
As it were one that were ledde by the eare;
For that I defy!
By this mene you sholde be theyr druge,
I tell you trought, I.

And yet the worst that greveth me
Is that your adversary sholde in you se
So notable a foly.
Therfore witdraw you for a seasone.

Cornelius
By Seynt Johan, thou sayst but reasone.

B
Ye[a], do so hardely,

And whan the tyme drawith upon
That thay be com everychone
And all thinge redy,
Than shall I come streyght away
For to seche you withoute delay.

Cornelius
Be it so, hardely.
But one thinge whyle I thinke therone,
Remember this when I am gone:
Yef hit happon so
That Lucres come in fyrst alone,
Go in hand with her anone,
How so ever thou do,
For to fele her mynde toward me,
And by all meanis possyble to be,
Induce her therunto.

B
Than some token you must gyve me,
For ellis she wyll not beleve me
That I cam from you.

Cornelius
Mary, that is evyn wysely spoken.
Commaunde me to her by the same token:
She knowyth it well inow,

That as she and I walkyde onis togedyr
In her garden hedyr and thedyr,
There happonde a straunge case.
For at the last we dyd se
A byrd sittynge on a holow tre,
An ashe I trow it was.
Anone she prayde me for to assay
Yf I coude start the byrde away.

B
And dyde ye so? Alas, alas!

Cornelius
Why the Devyll sayst thou so?

B
By Cokkis bonis, for it was a kocko!
And men say amonge,
He that throwyth stone or stycke
At suche a byrde, he is lycke
To synge that byrdes songe.

Cornelius
What the Devyll recke I therfore?
Here what I say to the[e] ever more,
And marke thine erand well:
Syr, I had no stone to throw with all,

1577 first, wait 1578 to delay you 1579 leisure, wait for them 1582 drudge/slave 1583 I (do) (emphatic) 1587 withdraw yourself 1588 St John, only reasonably 1590 draws near 1594 seek 1598 if it should happen 1602 discover 1603 means 1609 this same 1611 once 1613 occurred, event 1615 tree 1618 startle/frighten 1621 Cock (God)'s bones, cuckoo 1622 commonly 1623 stick 1624 likely 1625 (i.e. become a cuckold) 1626 care 1627 Hear 1628 remember

74 'You do not [act] according to your status.'

And therfore she toke me her musc ball,[75]
And thus it befell:

I kyst it as strayght as ony pole,
So that it lyghtyde evyn in the hole
Of the holow ashe.
Now, canst thou remember all this?

B
By God, I wolde be loth to do amys,
For some tyme I am full rashe.

Ye say that ye kyst it evyn in the hole
Of the holow ashe as strayte as a pole.
Sayde ye not so?

CORNELIUS
Yes.

B
Well then, let me alone.
As for this erande, it shall be done
As sone as ye be go.

[CORNELIUS]
Fare well then, I leve the[e] here,
And remembyr well all this gere
How so ever thou do.

Et exeat Cornelius.

B
Yes, hardely, this erande shall be spoken.
But how say you, syrs, by this tokene?
Is it not a quaynt thinge?
I went he hade bene a sad man,
But I se well he is a made man
In this message doynge.

But what? Chose he for me,
I am but as a messanger, perde;
The blame shall not be myne but his,
For I wyll his token reporte;
Whether she take it in ernest or sporte
I wyll not therof mys.
Be she wroth or well apayde,
I wyll tell her evyn as he sayde.

Intrat Lucres.

God avow, here she is!
It is tyme for me to be wyse.
Now welcome lady, floure of prise:
I have sought you twyse or thryse
Wythin this houre, iwys.

LUCRES
Me syr? Have ye sought me?

B
Ye[a], that I have, by God that bowght me.

LUCRES
To what intent?

B
Mary, for I have thingis a few
The which I must to you shew
By my maysters commaundement.

Publius Cornelius is hys name,
Your veray lover, in payne of shame,
And yf ye love hym not ye be to blame.
For this dare I say,
And on a boke make it gode:
He lovyd you better than his one hart blode.

LUCRES
Hys harde bloode? Nay, nay.

Half that love wolde serve for me![76]

B
Yet sithe he dyde you fyrst se
In the place where he dwellis,
He had lovyd you so in hys hart
That he settyth not by hym self a fart,
Nor by noo man ellis.

And bycause ye shulde gyve credence
Unto my sayng in hys absence

1630 gave 1632 cast/threw 1633 landed 1643 gone 1646+ And exit Cornelius 1649 strange 1650 thought he was, serious 1651 mad 1653 I don't care what he chooses 1658 lose anything by it 1659 contented 1663 precious flower 1673 true 1676 swear it on a book 1677 loves, own heart's blood 1683 doesn't care a fart for himself

[75] 'Musk-ball': a container for musk (perfume).

[76] Lucres jokingly mishears B to say 'hard' (i.e. 'very') blood, and replies that there's no need to give it all, half will do.

And trust to that I say,
He tolde me tokyns two or thre
Whiche I know well as he tolde me.

LUCRES
Tokyns? What be thay?

B
Let me se, now I had nede to be wyse,
For one of his tokyns is very nyse
As ever I harde tell.
He prayd you for to beleve me
By the same tokyn that ye and he
Walkyd togeder by a holow tre.

LUCRES
All that I know well.

B
A, than I am yet in the ryght way.
But I have som other thyng to say
Towchyng my credence,
Whiche as I thynke were best to be spared,
For happely ye wold not have it declared
Byfore all this audience.

LUCRES
Nay, nay, hardely, spare not:
As for my dedis, I care not
Yf all the worlde it harde.

B
Mary, than shall I procede.
He shewde me also in very dede
How ther satt a byrde,

And than ye delyveryd hym your muskball
For to throw at the byrd with all,
And than as he sayd, ye dyd no wors
But evyn fayr kyst hym on the noke of the ars.

LUCRES
Nay, ther thow lyest falsely, by my fay!

B
Trouth, it was on the hole of thars I shulde say,
I wyst well it was one of the too,
The noke or the hole.

LUCRES
Nay, nor yet so.

B
By my fayth, ye kyst hym or he kyst you
On the hole of thars, chose you now;
This he tolde me sure.
How be it, I speke it not in reprove,
For it was done but for gode love
And for no synfull pleasure.

LUCRES
Nay, nay, man, thow art farr amys!
I know what thyn erande is,
Though thow be neclygent.
Of thy foly thou mayst well abasshe,
For thou shuldis have sayde the holow asshe:
That hole thy mayster ment.

B
By God avow, I trow it was!
I crye you mercy, I have done you trespas.

But I pray you take it in pacyence,
For I mystoke it by necligence.
A myscheef com theron!
He myght have sent you this gere in a letter!
But I shall go lerne myn erande better,
And cum ayen anon.

Et exeat [*B*].

LUCRES
Ye[a], so do hardely!

Now forsoth, this was a lewed message
As ever I harde sith I was bore.
And yf his mayster have therof knowlege
He wyll be angry with hym therfore.
How be it, I will speke therof no more,
For hyt hath ben my condiscyon alwey
No man to hender but to helpe where I may.

Intrat A.

A
Feyr maysters, lyketh it you to know
That my mayster commaunde me to you!

1692 strange/rude 1693 heard 1698 right so far 1700 relating to, trustworthiness 1701 left unsaid 1705 deeds 1706 heard 1712 nothing else 1713 kissed, nick/cleft, arse 1714 faith 1715 the arse 1722 reproof/critically 1723 good/proper 1725 are much mistaken 1728 be ashamed 1729 should 1732 offended you 1734 mistook 1735 a curse on it 1736 matter 1738 again 1741 born 1745 it, habit always 1746 hinder 1747 Fair mistress 1748 commends

LUCRES
Commaundeth you to me?

A
Nay, commaundeth you
to hym!

LUCRES
Wele amendyd, by Saynt Sym![77]

A
Commaundeth he to you, I wolde say,
Or ellis you to he: now chose ye may
Whether lyketh you better!
And here he sendyth you a letter.

Godis mercy, I had it ryght now!
Syrs, is there none there among you
That toke up suche a wrytyng?
I pray you, syrs, let me have it agayne!

LUCRES
Ye ar a gode messanger for certeyne!
But I pray you, syr, of one thyng:

Who is your mayster? Tell me that.

A
Maister what-call-ye-hym . . . Parde, ye wott
Whome I mene well and fyne!

LUCRES
Yet I know not, so mot I go!

A
What? Yes, parde, he that wolde have you so.[78]

LUCRES
I suppose there be many of tho,
Yf I wolde enclyne!

But yet, know I not who ye mene.
I holde best that ye go ageyene
To lerne your maysters name.

A
By my fayth, and I holde it best.
Ye may say I am a homely gest
In ernest and in game.

LUCRES
Abyde, I shall go to you nerehonde:[79]
What ys your owne name, I wolde understonde?
Tell me that or I go!
I trow thou canst not well tell.

A
By my fayth, not verely well,
Bycause ye say so.

Et scalpens caput post modicum intervallum dicat:[80]

By this lyght, I have forgoten!
How be it, by that tyme I have spoken
With som of my company,
I shall be acerteyned of this gere.
But shall I fynde you agayne here?

LUCRES
Ye[a], that thow shalt, happely!

Et exeat A. [*Enter Cornelius.*]

CORNELIUS
Now, fayr Lucres, accordyng to thappoyntement
That ye made with me here this day,
Bycause ye shall not fynde me there neclygent,
Here I am come your wyll to obey,
And redy am I for my selfe to sey
That, as towchyng the degre of noble condycion,
Betwyxt me and Gayus there may be no comparison.

And that shall I shew you by apparent reason
Yf it shall lyke you that I now begynne.

LUCRES
Nay, ye shall spare it for a lytyll season,
Tyl suche tyme that Gayus your adversary come in,
For I wyll gyve you therin none audience
Tyll ye be both toge[d]er in presence.

And in ony wyse, kepe well your patience
Lyke as I have bound you both to the peace.

1753 whichever pleases 1757 picked, document 1764 may I walk (a mild oath) 1766 those 1767 show any inclination 1769 again 1772 rude fellow 1773 (i.e. in all things) 1779 Now you have asked me 1782 companions 1783 correctly informed 1791 concerning, noble status 1793 clear arguments 1795 while 1797 I will not listen to you 1798 (here) in (my) presence

77 'Well corrected!' A has still not got it right, of course.

78 Presumably 'so' would be accompanied by a suitably amorous gesture.

79 'I shall address you more closely [on a more personal matter]'.

80 'And, scratching his head, let him a little later say'.

I forbyde you utterly all maner of violence
Durynge this matter, and also that ye seace
Of all suche wordis as may gyve occasion
Of brallynge or other ongodely condycion.

Cornelius
There shal be in me no suche abusyon
In worde nor dede, I you promyse.

[Enter B.]

But now let me se, what occupation
Or what maner of passe tyme wyll ye devyse
Whyle that these folke dothe tary this wyse?
Wyll ye see a bace-daunce[81] after the gyse
Of Spayne, whyle ye have no thynge to do?
All thynge have I purvaide that belongyth therto!

Lucres
Syr, I shall gyve you the lokynge on.

Cornelius
Wyll ye do so? I aske no more.
Go sone and bidde them come thens anone,
And cause the mynystrellis to come in beffore.

B
Mary, as for one of them, his lippe is sore;
I trow he may not pype, he is so syke.
Spele up tamboryne, ik bide owe frelike![82]

[Enter the dancers,] et deinde corisabunt.

Lucres
Forsothe, this was a godely recreacyon.
But I pray you, of what maner nation
Be these godely creatours?
Were they of Englonde or of Wales?

B
Nay, they be wylde Irissh Portyngales[83]
That dyde all these pleasures.
How be it, it was for my maysters sake,
And he wyll deserve it, I undertake,
On the largest wyse.[84]

Cornelius
Go thy selfe; why stondis thou so?
And make them chere! Let it be do
The best thou canst devyse.

B
Yes, they shall have chere Hevyn hye!
But one thing I promyse you faithfully;
They get no drynke therto.[85]

Exea[n]t [B, dancers, and minstrels. Enter Gayus.] Dicat Lucres:

Lucres
Lo, here thys man ys come now.
Now may ye in your matter procede.
Ye remembre both what I sayde to you
Touchynge myne answere; I trow it is no nede
Ony more to reherse it.

Cornelius
No, in veray dede,
For moche rehersall wolde let the spede[86]
Of all this matter; it nedyth no more.
Let us roundely to the matter we come for.

Lucres
Ye[a], that I pray you as hartly as I can.
But fyrst me semyth it were expedient
That ye both name some indifferent man
For to gyve betwyxt you the forseyde jugement.

Cornelius
Nay, as for that, by myne assent,
No man shall have that office but ye.

Gayus
And I holde me well content that it so be.

1802 cease 1804 brawling, bad behaviour 1805 abuse 1808 devise 1809 (in) this way 1812 arranged 1813 I'll look at it. 1815 come here 1816 minstrels, first 1818 pipe, sick 1819+ And then they shall dance 1822 excellent artists 1830 provide them some hospitality 1834 with it 1834+ and let Lucres say 1842 swiftly 1844 it seems to me 1845 impartial 1848 role

81 Basse-dance: a formal dance performed by one or two couples.
82 'Play up the tambourine [a pipe and tabor, not the modern tambourine], I bid you merrily': a line in Flemish, presumably aimed at one of the many Flemings who, along with French and Italian musicians, formed the basis of the musical establishment in the early Tudor court and its environs.
83 'Wild Irish Portuguese': a nonsense. The 'wild Irish' lived beyond the 'civilized' (i.e. Anglicized) Pale around Dublin.
84 'I dare say he deserves most of the credit.'
85 B puns on cheer: food and drink, and a loud cheer of applause.
86 'Too much discussion will hinder the success'.

LUCRES
Ye[a], but not wythstondyng that ye therto agre
That I sholde this question of nobles diffine,
It is a grete matter whiche, as semyth me,
Pertayneth to a philosopher or ellis a devyne.
How be it, sith the choyse of this matter is myne,
I can be content, under certayne protestacyon,
Whan that I have harde you, to say myne opinion.

Lo, this wyse I mene and thus I do intende:
That what so ever sentence I gyve betwyxt you two
After myne owne fantasie, it shall not extende
To ony other person. I wyll that it be so,
For why no man ellis hath theryn ado.
It may not be notyde for a generall precedent,
All be it that for your partis ye do therto assent.

GAYUS
As touchyng that poynt we holde us well content.
Your sentence shall touche no man but us twayne.
And sith ye shall gyve it by our owne agrement,
None other man ought to have thereat disdayne.
Wherfor all thys dout ye may well refrayne,
And in that matter principall this tyme wolde be spent.

CORNELIUS
Than wyll I begynne.

GAYUS
I holde me well content.

CORNELIUS
Syth ye have promysed, fayre Lucres, heretofore
That to the more noble man ye wyll enclyne,
Vary not fro that worde and I aske no more,
For than shall the victory of this cause be myne,
As it shalbe easy to jugge and diffyne.
For every creature that ony reason hase
Me semyth I durst make hym self jugge in this case,
Save that I fere me the beaute of your face
Sholde therin blynde hym so that he ne myght
Egally disserne the wronge fro the right.
And if he were half so wyse a man in dede
As he reputeth hym self for to be,
Upon your saide answere he sholde not nede
To gaynesay in this matter or travers with me.
My noblenes is knowen thorow all the cyte;
He knoweth hym selfe the noblenes of my kyn,
And at that one poynt my proces I wyll begyne.

Amonge all thistoryes of Romaynes that ye rede,
Where fynde ye ony blode of so gret noblenes
As hath ben the Cornelys wherof I am brede?
And if so be that I wolde therin holde my pease,[87]
Yet all your cornecles beryth gode witnes
That my progenytours and auncetours have be
The chefe ayde and diffence of this noble cyte.

How ofte have myne auncetours in tymes of necessite
Delyverd this cyte from dedely parell,
As well by theyr manhode as by theyr police?
What jeopardi and paine they have suffred in the quarell
Thempire to encrece and for the comune wele[88]
It nedith not the specialties to reherse or name,
Sith every trew Romaine knoweth the same.

In every mannys howse that histories be rife[89]
And wrytten in bookis, as in some placis be
The gestis of Arthur, or of Alexandyrs life,
In the whiche stories ye may evidently se
And rede how Cartage, that royall cyte,
By Cipion of Affrick,[90] my grete graunte-sire,
Subduede was and also ascribede to his empire.

And many other cyties that dyde conspire
Ayenst the noble senatoure makynge resistence,
As often as necessite did it require
They were reducyd unto due obedience,
Eyther by the policy or by the violence
Of my sayde aunceters: thistories be playne
And witnesse that I speke not these wordis in vayne.

My blode hath ever takyn suche payne
To salve garde the comune wele fro ruyn and decay,

1851 decide 1853 Belongs (properly), theologian 1859 opinion 1861 shall be involved 1862 noted/remembered 1868 put away 1875 judge, decide 1876 has any reason 1880 Equally discern 1884 contradict, argue 1888 the histories, Romans, read 1890 Corneliuses, bred 1892 chronicles, bear 1893 forebears, been 1894 defence 1896 Rescued, deadly peril 1897 policy (political skill) 1898 danger 1899 The empire, extend 1900 details 1901 true 1904 deeds, Alexander the Great 1906 Carthage 1907 great-grandfather 1908 incorporated (into) 1913 military action 1914 ancestors 1916 family, always 1917 safeguard

87 'Even if I kept silent about it [myself]'.
88 Both the commonwealth/state and 'the common good'.
89 'In the house of every man who keeps plenty of history books.'
90 Scipio Africanus.

That by one advyse the Cenat dyde ordeyne
Them to be namyd the faders of the contray,
And so were myne auctours reputed alway,
For in every nede they dyde upon them call
For helpe as the chylde doth on the fader naturall.

How be it, to praye them it was no nede at all,
For of their owne myndis they were redy alway.
In tokyn of the same, for a memoriall
Of theyr desertis, the cytie dyde edifye
Triumphall arches, wheruppon ye may
To my grete honour se at this day
Thymages of myn auncetours evyn by and by,[91]
Bycause that theyr noblenes sholde never dye.

In token also that they were worthy
Grete honour and prayse of all the contray,
It is commaunded and used generally
That every cytezen that passith that way
By the sayde images, he must obey
And to that fygures make a due reverence,
And ellis to the lawes he dothe grete offence.

Sith it is so than that of convenience
Suche honoure and homage must nedis be do
To these dede ymagis, than muche more reverence
To me sholde be gevyn: I trow ye thinke so,
For I am theyr very ymage and relyque to
Of theyr flesch and blode, and veray inherytoure
As well of theyr godes as of theyr sayde honoure.

To me they have left many a castell and toure
Whiche in theyr triumphes thay rightfully wan.
To me they have also left all theyr tresoure
In suche abundaunce that I trow no man
Within all Rome, sith it fyrst began,
Had half the store as I understonde
That I have evyn now at ons in my honde.

Lo, in these thyngis my noblenes doth stonde,
Whiche in myne oppynyon suffiseth for this intent.
And I trow there is no man throwgh all this londe
Of Italy, but if he were here present,
He wolde to my sayng in this matter assent,
And gyve unto me the honoure and preeminence,
Rather than make agayne me resistence.

[*To Gayus*] I marvayle gretly what shulde thy mynde insence
To thinke that thy tytle therin sholde be gode.
Parde, thow canst not say for thy deffence
That ever there was gentilmin of thy kyn or blode!
And if there were oone, it wolde be understode
Without it be thy self, whiche now of late
Among noble gentylmen playest check mate.

LUCRES
No more therof, I pray you! Suche wordis I hate,
And I dyde forbid you them at the begynnyng
To eschue thoccasyon of stryfe and debate.

GAYUS
Nay, let hym alone. He spekyth after his lernyng![92]
For I shall answer hym to every thyng
Whan he hath all said, if ye woll here me,
As I thinke ye wyll of your equyte.

CORNELIUS
Abide, I must make an ende fyrst, parde.
To you, swete Lucres, I wolde have said beffore
That, yf ye wyll to my desyre in this matter agre,
Doubtles ye shall blesse the tyme that ever ye were bore.
For riches shall ye have at your will ever more,
Without care or study of laboriouse besynes,
And spend all your dayes in ease and plesaunt idelnesse.

About your owne apparell ye can do non excesse
In my company that sholde displese my mynd.[93]
With me shall ye do non other maner of besynes
But hunt for your solace at the hart and hynde,
And some tyme where we convenient game fynde
Oure hawkis shal be redy to shew you a flight
Whiche shal be right plesaunt and chereful to your sight.

And, yf so be that in huntyng ye have no delyght,
Than may ye daunce a whyle for your disport.
Ye shall have at your pleasure both day and night
All maner of mynstralsy to do you comfort.
Do what thyng ye wyll, I have to support

1918 Senate agreed unanimously 1919 country 1920 forebears 1921 they (the Senate) 1924 minds/volition 1926 deserts/merits 1929 the images/portraits 1930 So that 1935 bow 1936 those 1937 Or else 1940 dead 1942 true image and relic too 1944 goods/wealth 1945 tower 1946 won 1951 once 1952 consist 1953 is sufficient 1956 claims, agree 1958 against 1963 I'd like to know 1964 Unless 1965 (i.e. defeated/ruined them) 1967 did 1968 eschew the cause 1971 will hear 1972 equity/justice 1974 should 1978 worry, effort 1986 pleasing 1990 kinds 1991 have (enough money)

91 'One after the other'.

92 'He speaks according to his [limited] knowledge!'

93 'Nothing that you wear in my company [however excessive] will displease me.'

Our chargis, and over that I may susteyne
At myne owne fyndyng an hundred or twayne.

And as for hym, I am certayn
Hys auncetours were of full poore degre,
All be it that now withyn a yere or twayne,
Bycause that he wold a gentilman be,
He hath hym goten both office and fee,
Whiche, after the rate of hys wrechyd sparyng,[94]
Suffiseth scarsely for hys bare lyvynge.

Wherfore, swete Lucres, it were not accordyng
For your grete beaute with hym to dwell,
For there sholde ye have a threde bare lyvynge
With wrechyd scarcenes, and I have herde tell
That maydens of your age love not ryght well
Suche maner of husbondis, without it be thay
That forceth lytyll to cast them self away.[95]

I mene specyally for suche of them as may
Spede better if they wyll, as ye be yn the case.[96]
And therfore, Lucres, what so ever he wyll say
Hys title agaynst you to force and embrace,
Ye shall do your owen selfe to grete a trespas
Yf ye folow hys part and enclyne therto.
Now say what ye wyll, syr, for I have all doo.

GAYUS
With ryght gode will I shall go to,
So that ye will here me with as grete pacience
As I have harde you: reason wolde soo.
And what so ever I shall speke in this audience,
Eyther of myn owne meritis or of hys insolence,
Yet fyrst unto you all, syrs, I make this request:
That it wolde lyke you to construe it to the best.

For lothe wolde I be as ony creature
To boste of myne owne dedis; it was never my gyse.
On that other syde, loth I am to make ony reportur
Of this mans foly or hym to dispice.
But, never the lesse, this matter towchith me in suche wise
That, what so ever ye thinke in me, I must procede
Unto the veray trouth therof as the matter is in dede.

To make a grete rehersall of that ye have saide
The tyme will not suffre, but, never the lesse,
Two thingis for your self in substaunce ye have layd,
Whiche as ye suppose maketh for your nobles,
Upon the whiche thingis dependith all your processe.
Fyrst, of your auncetours ye allege the noble gestis;
Secondly, the substaunce that ye have of theyr bequestis.

In the whiche thingis onely, by your owne confession,
Standeth all your noblenes: this sayd ye beffore.
Whereunto this I say under the correction
Of Lucres oure jugge here, that ye ar never the more
Worthy in myne oppynion to be callyd noble therfore,
And withoute ye have better causes to shew than these,
Of reson ye must the victory of this matter lese.

To the fyrst parte, as touching your auncetours dedis,
Some of them were noble lyke as ye declare;
Thestoris bereth witnes, I must graunt them nedis.[97]
But yet, for all that, some of them ware
Of contrary di[s]posycion like as ye are,
For they dyde no proffite (no more do ye)
To the comon wele of this noble cytie.

Yf ye wyll the title of noblenes wynne,
Shew what have ye done your self therfore.
Some of your owne meritis let se bryng in,
Yf ever ye dyde ony syth ye were bore.
But surely ye have no suche thyng in store
Of your owne meritis wherby of right
Ye shulde appere noble to ony mannys sight.

But, neverthelesse, I wyll you not blame,
Thowgh ye speke not of your owne dedis at all.
And to say the trowght, ye may not for shame;
Your lyfe is so voluptuouse and so bestiall
In folowynge of every lust sensuall
That I marvaille no thynge in my mynde,
Yf ye leve your owne dedis behynde.

1992 (To meet) our costs, employ 1993 cost, or 200 (servants) 1995 status 1998 gained, salary 2000 basic livelihood 2003 threadbare 2004 poverty 2011 urge, persuade (corruptly) 2012 too, an offence 2015 begin 2017 reason demands it 2018 gathering 2021 favourably 2023 habit 2024 declaration 2025 despise 2026 touches 2028 very 2030 permit 2031 claimed 2032 constitute, nobility 2033 argument 2034 (heroic) deeds 2035 wealth 2039 in no way 2041 unless, arguments 2042 lose 2043 deeds 2046 were 2047 just as 2048 nothing profitable 2053 did any since 2056 any man's 2059 truth 2063 out of the account

94 'Thanks to his wretched thrift'.

95 'Unless it is those [young women] who care little about throwing their lives away.'

96 'Those who could choose better, as you could now.'

97 'The histories bear witness, I needs must grant that.'

He wenyth that by hys proude contenaunce
Of worde and dede, with nyse aray,
Hys grete othys, and open mayntenaunce[98]
Of theftis and murdres every day,
Also hys ryotouse disportis and play,
Hys sloth, his cowardy, and other excesse,
Hys mynde disposed to all unclennesse:
By these thyngis oonly he shall have noblenesse.

Nay, the title of noblenes wyll not ensue
A man that is all gevyn to suche insolence,
But it groweth of longe continued vertu,
As I trust, lady, that youre indifference
Can well diffyne by your sentence.
Hys auncetours were not of suche condicion,
But all contrary to hys disposicyon.

And therfore they were noble withouten faile,
And dyde grete honoure to all the contrey.
But what can theyr sayde noblenes advayle
To hym that takyth a contrary way;
Of whome men spekith every day
So grete dishonoure, that it is marvel
The contrey suffereth hym therin to dwelle?

And, where he to-wyteth me of pore kyn,
He doth me therin a wrongfull offence.
For no man shall thankis or praysyng wyn
By the gyftis that he hath of natures influence.
Lyke wyse I thinke by a contrary sense
That if a man be borne blynde or lame,
Not he hym selfe, but nature therin is to blame.

Therfor he doth not me therin repreve.
And, as for that poynt, this I wott welle,
That both he and I cam of Adam and Eve.
There is no difference that I can tell
Whiche makith oon man an other to excell,
So moche as doth vertue and godely maner,
And therin I may well with hym compare.

How be it, I speke it not for myne one prayse,
But certeynly this hath ever be my condicion:
I have borne unto God all my daies
His laude and prayse with due devocion,
And next that I bere allwayes
To all my neyghbours charitable affeccyon.
Incontynency and onclennes I have had in
    abhominacion,
Lovyng to my frende and faythfull with all,
And ever I have withstonde my lustis sensuall.

One tyme with study my tyme I spende
To eschew idelnes, the causer of syn.
An other tyme my contrey manly I deffend,
And for the victoryes that I have done therin,
Ye have sene your selfe, syr, that I have come in
To this noble cytee twyse or thryse
Crownyd with lawryel as it is the gyse.[99]

By these wayes, lo, I do aryse
Unto grete honoure fro low degre,
And yf myn heires will do likewyse
Thay shal be brought to nobles by me.
But, Cornely, it semyth by the[e]
That the nobles of thyn auncetours everycheon
Shall utterly starve and die in the[e] alone.

And where he to-witeth me on that other syde
Of small possession and grete scarcenes,
For all that, lady, if ye will with me abidde,
I shall assure you of moderate richesse,
And that sufficient for us both, doutles.
Ye shall have also a man accordyng
To youre owne condicions in every thing.

Now, Lucres, I have shewyd unto you a parte
Of my title that I clayme you by,
Besechynge you therfore with all my hart
To considre us both twayne indifferently,
Whiche of us twayne ye will rather alow
More worthy for nobles to marry with you.

LUCRES
Syrs, I have hard you both at large.

2064 believes **2065** fine/foolish clothes **2066** oaths **2067** thefts, murders **2068** riotous behaviour **2069** cowardice **2070** corruption **2071** only **2072** follow **2075** impartiality **2076** decide, judgement **2081** avail **2086** accuses, poor family **2088** thanks, praise **2093** reprove **2095** are descended from **2098** good conduct **2100** my own **2102** given **2103** honour **2104** demonstrate **2105** affection **2106** corruption, held **2108** resisted, sensual lusts **2111** country manfully **2117** from lowly status **2118** heirs **2120** Cornelius, seems **2122** wither **2124** poverty **2125** abide/live **2126** wealth **2128** who matches **2129** character **2132** Begging **2133** impartially **2134** believe **2136** heard, freely

98 Maintenance: the corrupt supporting of followers. See the Towneley *Second Shepherds' Play*, ll. 17–45, and *Wisdom*, ll. 691–740.

99 i.e. he has been awarded formal triumphal entries into the city, crowned with laurel wreaths, to honour his military victories.

CORNELIUS
Nay, abide Lucres, I pray you hertly!
Sithe he leyeth many thynges to my charge,
Suffre that I may therunto repply.

LUCRES
Iwis, replication shall not be necessary
Withoute that ye have some other thing in store
To shew for your self than ye dyde beffore.

CORNELIUS
Why, lady, what thing will ye desyre more
Than I have shewyd to make for noblenes?

LUCRES
Yes, som thyng ther ys that makyth therfore
Better than ye have shewid in your processe.
But now let me se what man of witnes
Or what other proves will ye forth bryng
By the whiche eyther of you may justifie his sayng?

GAYUS
As for my parte, I wyll stonde gladly
To the commune voyce of all the contrey.

LUCRES
And ye lyke wyse, syr?

CORNELIUS
Ye[a], certaynly,
I shall in no wyse your worde dissobey.

LUCRES
Than wyll I betwyxt you both take this way:
I shall go enquyre as faste as I may

What the commune fame wyll theryn reporte,
And, whan I have therof a due evidence,
Than shall I agayne to you resorte
To shew you thopynyon of my sentence
Whome I wyll jugge to have the preemynence.

CORNELIUS
Nay, fayre Lucres, I you requyre;
Let me not now depart in vayne
Not knowyng theffect of my desyre.

LUCRES
Syr, allthough it be to you a payne,
Yet must ye do so evyn both twayne.
Eche of you depart hens to hys owne place,
And take no more labour or payne in this case.

For, as towchyng theffect of my sentence,
I shall go write it by gode advysement
Sone after that I am departed fro hens.
And than to eyther of you both shalbe sent
A copy of the same, to this intent:
That of none other person it shall be sayn
Sith it concerneth but onely unto you twayne.

GAYUS
This is a gode waye as in my mynde.
Ar not ye, syr, content in lyke wyse?

CORNELIUS
I wot nere, yet I wyll prayse as I fynde
And as I have cause; that is evyr my gyse.

GAYUS
Well Lucres, will ye commaunde me ony servyce?

LUCRES
No servyce at all, syr. Why say ye so?
Our Lorde spede you both where so ever ye goo.

Et exeant Publius Cornelus et Gaius Flaminius [*and A*].

Now som mayde, happely, and she were in my case,
Wolde not take that way that I do intend,
For I am fully determyned with Godis grace
So that to Gaius I wyll condyscend,
For in this case I do hym commend
As the more noble man, sith he thys wyse
By meane of hys vertue to honoure doth aryse.

And for all that, I wyll not dispise
The blode of Cornelius: I pray you thinke not so!
God forbede that ye sholde note me that wyse,
For truely I shall honoure them where so ever I go,
And all other that be of lyke blode also.
But unto the blode I wyll have lytyl respect
Where tho condicyons be synfull and abject.

I pray you all, syrs, as meny as be here:
Take not my wordis by a sinistre way.

[*Enter B.*]

2138 alleges, against me 2139 Permit me to reply 2140 (a) formal reply 2141 unless 2142 did 2146 argument 2147 proofs 2148 prove his case 2150 happily accept 2151 common 2156 popular opinion 2158 return 2159 the opinion/verdict 2160 Which of you 2163 result 2165 each of you 2166 from here, home 2168 regarding 2169 good advice 2173 seen 2177 I don't know 2178 always, practice 2179 ask of me any 2182 situation 2184 God's 2185 agree 2190 blood/lineage 2191 interpret me in that way 2195 those characteristics are

B
Yes, by my trouth, I shall witnes bere,
Where so ever I be com a nother day,
How suche a gentylwoman did opynly say
That by a chorles son she wolde set more
Than she wolde do by a gentylman bore.

Lucres
Nay, syr, than ye report me amys!

B
I pray you tell me, how sayd ye than?

Lucres
For God, syr, the substaunce of my wordis was this:
I say evyn as I saide whan I began,
That for vertue excellent I will honoure a man
Rather than for hys blode, if it so fall
That gentil condicyons agre not with all.

B
Than I put case that a gentilman bore
Have godely maners to his birth accordyng.

Lucres
I say, of hym is to be set gret store:
Suche one is worthy more lawde and praysyng
Than many of them that hath their begynnyng
Of low kynred, ellis God forbede!
I wyll not afferme the contrary for my hede,

For in that case ther may be no comparyson.
But, never the lesse, I said this before,
That a man of excellent vertuouse condicions,
Allthough he be of a pore stoke bore,
Yet I wyll honour and commende hym more
Than one that is descendide of ryght noble kyn
Whose lyffe is all dissolute and rotyde in syn.

And therfore I have determyned utterly
That Gaius Flaminius shall have his intent.
To hym onely I shall my self apply
To use me in wedloke at his commaundement,
So that to Cornelyus I wyll never assent,
Allthough he had as grete possession
As ony one man in Cristen region.[100]
I shall in no wyse favour or love hys condicyon,
How be it that his blode requyreth due reverence,
And that shall I gyve hym with all submyssion.
But yet shall he never have the preemynence
To speke of very nobles by my sentence.
Ye be hys servaunt syr; go your way
And report to your mayster evyn as I say.

[*Exit Lucres.*]

B
Shall I do that erand? Nay, let be!
By the Rode, ye shall do it your selfe for me.
I promyse you faythfully,

I wolde my mayster had be in Scotland
Whan he dyd put this matter in her hand
To stond to her jugement!
But, forasmoche as it is so,
That this wrong to hym is doo
By a woman, he must let it goo
And holde hym content.

But he is of suche disposycion
That, whan he hereth of this conclusion,
He wylbe starke madd;
Ye, by my trowth, as made as an hare![101]
It shall make hym so full of care
That he wyll with hym self fare
Evyn as it were a lade!

And so wold not I, so mote I thee!
For this matter, and I were as he,
It shulde never anger me,
But this wold I do:
I wolde let her go in the Mare name!

[*Enter A.*]

[A]
What now, syrs, how goth the game?
What, is this woman go?

B
Ye[a], ye[a], man!

2201 churl's 2203 wrongly 2205 Before God 2209 agree/match 2211 befitting 2212 value 2216 affirm, head 2220 born of poor stock 2223 life, rotted with sin 2226 only, dedicate 2231 way, behaviour 2232 demands 2235 true nobility, verdict 2237 exactly what 2241 been (i.e. far away) 2243 abide by 2245 done 2249 hears 2250 will be furious 2252 sorrow 2253 behave 2254 Just like a madman[102] 2259 in the name of Mary (mild oath) 2260 goes 2261 gone

100 'Christendom'.

101 Hares were proverbially mad (particularly during springtime, hence 'mad as a March hare').

102 For this sense of 'lad' see Shakespeare, *Twelfth Night*, IV, ii, 139.

A

And what way hathe she takyn?

B

By my fayth, my mayster is forsakyn,
And nedis she wyll agre
Unto thy mayster: thus she saieth,
And many causes therfore she leyeth
Why it shulde so be.

A

I marvayle gretely wherof that grue.

B

By my fayth, she saide (I tell the[e] true!)
That she wolde nedis have hym for his vertue
And for none other thynge.

A

Vertue? What the Devyll is that?
And I can tell, I shrew my catt,
To myne understondynge.

[B]

By my fayth, no more can I.
But this she said here opynly;
All these folke can tell.

A

[*To the audience*] How say ye, gode women? Is it your gyse
To chose all your husbondis that wyse?
By my trought, than I marvaile!

B

Nay, this is the fere, so mot I goo:[103]
T[h]at men chise not theyr wyffis so
In placis where I have be.
For wiffis may well complayne and grone,
Albe it that cause have they none
That I can here or se.
But of weddyd men there be ryght fewe
That welle not say the best is a shrew;
Therin they all agree!

I warne you weddyd men everichone
That other remede have ye none
So moche for your ease,
And ye wold study tyll tomorow,
But let them evyn alone, with sorow,
Whan they do you displease.

A

Tusshe, here is no man that settyth a blank[104]
By thy consell or konneth the[e] thank:
Speke therof no more!
They know that remedy better than thow.
But what shall we twayne do now?
I care most therfore.

Me thinketh that matter wolde be wist.

B

Mary, we may goo hens whan we lyst;
No man saith us nay.

A

Why than, is the play all do?

B

Ye[a], by my feyth, and we were ons go
It were do streght wey.

A

And I wolde have thought in vere dede
That this matter sholde have procede
To som other conclusion

B

Ye[a], thou art a maister mery man!
Thou shall be wyse, I wot nere whan![105]
Is not the question

Of noblenes now fully defynde:
As it may be so by a womans mynde?
What woldyst thow have more?
Thow toldest me that other day
That all the substaunce of this play
Was done specially therfor;

Not onely to make folke myrth and game,
But that suche as be gentilmen of name

2264 necessarily 2266 reasons, cites 2268 what caused that 2273 If, curse (i.e. I don't know!) 2279 way 2281 fear 2282 choose, wives that way 2283 places, been 2285 Albeit 2288 best (wife) 2291 remedy 2293 (even) if 2294 avoid them completely 2297 will thank you (for it) 2301 about that 2302 should be known 2303 hence, wish 2304 forbids us 2305 done 2306 if we were to go 2307 It will be finished at once 2308 very 2311 chief among jokers 2315 As (far) as it can 2316 would 2317 (i.e. in the first part)

103 'May I continue to walk': a mild oath.

104 Blanc: a small French coin of little value: i.e. 'no one values your advice'.

105 'I don't know when you'll [ever] be wise.'

May be somwhat movyd
By this example for to eschew
The wey of vyce and favour vertue;
For syn is to be reprovyd

More in them, for the degre,
Than in other parsons such as be
Of pour kyn and birth.
This was the cause principall,
And also for to do with all
This company some myrth.

And, though the matter that we have playde
Be not percase so wele conveyde
And with so gret reason
As thistory it self requyreth,
Yet the auctour therof desyrith
That for this season

At the lest ye will take it in pacience.
And, yf ther be ony offence
(Show us wherein or we go hence)
Done in the same,
It is onely for lacke of connynge,
And not he but his wit runnynge
Is thereof to blame.

And glade wolde he be and ryght fayne
That some man of stabyll brayne
Wolde take on hym the labour and payne
This mater to amende;
And so he wyllyd me for to say.
And that done, of all this play
Shortely here we make an end.

EMPRYNTED AT LONDON BY JOHAN RASTELL, DWELLYNGE ON THE SOUTH SYDE OF PAULYS CHYRCHE, BYSYDE PAULYS CHEYNE.[106]

2322 prompted **2324** way/path **2325** reproved/condemned **2326** owing to their status **2328** poor **2333** perhaps, well performed **2335** the story, demands **2336** author, desires **2337** time **2342** skill (on the author's part) **2343** over-eager brain **2345** very eager **2346** stable/sober **2349** wished

106 Chain.

Magnyfycence, title page, 1530. Cambridge University Library.

John Skelton, *Magnyfycence*

John Skelton (*c.*1460–1529)

John Skelton's precise origins are not known, but he was probably born in the north of England around 1460. He was educated at the University of Cambridge, and gained the title of 'poet laureate' (at this time a qualification in rhetoric rather than a royal appointment) from Cambridge, Oxford, and Louvain. At some point around 1488 he entered the household of Henry VII, and he took holy orders a decade later. His most significant royal appointment was as tutor to the future Henry VIII, a post he held until 1502, when, on the death of Henry's elder brother Prince Arthur, his charge became heir apparent and gained a new household staff. At this point Skelton was pensioned off to the rectory of Diss in Norfolk, where he wrote a number of his more memorable poems, including *Phyllyp Sparowe*, *Ware the Hauk*, and two scurrilous epitaphs on parishioners who had aroused his ire. During the next decade Skelton divided his time between Norfolk and Westminster, and on Henry's accession in 1509 he began a concerted but largely unsuccessful attempt to secure patronage from his former pupil. During the last twenty years of his life, Skelton lived in a tenement in the precincts of Westminster Abbey and wrote a series of satirical works (including *Speke Parott* and *Why Come Ye Nat to Courte?*) reflecting the turbulent political world of the Henrician court and the City of London. Among these is his only surviving play, *Magnyfycence*, probably written in 1519–20 (see below). Skelton died on 21 June 1529 and was buried in St Margaret's church, Westminster.

Magnyfycence

The earliest surviving edition of *Magnyfycence* was printed by William Rastell around 1530, but the play was written considerably earlier, almost certainly between 1515 and 1523, and most probably in 1519–20. Its title page proclaims it to be 'a goodly interlude and a me[r]ry', simultaneously declaring both its morally improving and its entertaining functions in a way that was to become characteristic of early drama publishing. The plot concerns the fate of the eponymous hero, a prince, who begins the play by setting his wealth and happiness under the direction of his moderate and sensible counsellor Measure, but who is subsequently persuaded by Fansy to take into his service a number of other Vices who masquerade as Virtues. These Vices, 'the four C's' (Crafty Conveyaunce, Counterfeit Countenaunce, Cloked Colusyon, and Courtly Abusyon), using their new aliases, contrive to expel Measure from the court and to replace him with Foly, under whose auspices the treasury is exhausted and Felycyte and Lyberte depart. Left bankrupt and helpless before the arrival of Adversyte, Magnyfycence falls prey to Poverte, Dyspare, and (finally) Myschefe, who convinces him that, his sins being so great, there is no hope of divine mercy, and offers him a halter and knife as the means of his self-destruction. Only the timely intervention of Good Hope prevents the hero's suicide, and the subsequent arrival of the virtues Redresse, Sad Cyrcumspeccyon, and Perseveraunce prepares him for restoration to his former majesty.

The play is not based upon a single literary precursor. Rather it applies the conventional Morality formula of Temptation, Fall, and Redemption to a hero who is not a rustic everyman but a prince, and it utilizes the author's thorough understanding of the culture of the royal household. Its sources are thus the numerous works of advice literature addressed to monarchs and the detailed 'books' of regulations and ordinances for the royal household which drew upon them (for the importance of household ordinances for an understanding of the play, see Walker, *Plays of Persuasion*, ch. 3, and Scattergood, 'Skelton's *Magnyfycence*'). It combines the main features of the traditional Moral Play with aspects of the tragic 'Fall of Princes' genre popularized in the fifteenth century by John Lydgate's monumental poem of that title. The play's moral dimension reveals how a human being – any human being – may embrace vice in the mistaken belief that it is virtue, and be morally ruined as a result. The political dimension explores how such personal errors become potentially disastrous weaknesses when exhibited in the prince and played out in the context of the royal court. To this end Skelton deploys the conventional features of personification characteristic of the Moralities, but gives them a new depth and vivacity, by multiplying his Vices into a whole retinue of distinct but overlapping rogueish characterisations.

As Neuss, *Magnificence*, observes, the allegorical personifications are both concrete characters whose role and personality are indicated by their names, and markers of the condition of the protagonist and the progress of the action. Thus Courtly Abusyon is a foppish, immoral courtier, and arrives onstage at the point when the protagonist's court has been infiltrated by the Vices, and Cloked Colusyon is an accomplished conspirator and joins the action at the point when Fansy, Conveyaunce, and Countenaunce collude to gain entry into Magnyfycence's household. Each of the carefully choreographed entrances, exits, and changes of identity symbolizes an axiomatic truth in the didactic economy of the play. Thus when Fansy reappears at l. 909 dressed in his fool's costume, the point is emphasized visually that fancy, when mistaken for largess, leads directly to folly (indeed *is* folly), and that, once embraced, it brings in all the other abuses in its wake.

While the arrival of the Vices onstage signals the progressive degradation of the hero and his court, events offstage chart the intrigue by which Measure is progressively ousted from his position of authority over Lyberte and expelled from the court to be replaced by Fansy and Foly, who give Lyberte free rein.

The play is thus steeped in Skelton's rich knowledge (both practical and theoretical) of the workings of the royal household, and has all the hallmarks of a modern heist or 'caper' movie, in which each stage of a carefully planned robbery is lovingly dramatized in order to demonstrate how the court might be prised open by a determined group of conspirators. In this respect the play is a relatively timeless commentary upon the procedures of the late medieval court. It may also, however, have had a more particular point of focus in a contemporary *cause célèbre*; for the Vices who threaten to ruin Magnyfycence bear a striking resemblance to a group of courtiers known as Henry VIII's 'minions' who were temporarily expelled from the royal household in 1519 as a result of their loose behaviour with the king. One commentator, celebrating their fall, noted that the minions 'were so familier and homely with hym [Henry VIII], and plaied suche light touches with him that they forgat themselves', and condemned their obsession with French manners and attitudes: 'they were all French, in eatyng, drynkyng and apparell, yea and in French vices and bragges, so that all the estates of Englonde were by them laughed at'.[1] The fact that Skelton's Vices wear the latest French fashions and speak in affected French phrases may well be both an echo of the conventional association between courtliness, Frenchness, and vice (as seen, for example, in the York *Christ Before Herod* pageant) and a sharp satirical blow at the newly disgraced minions if, as I believe, the play was written at the time of their fall. A similar effect is achieved by having the Vices litter their conversation with jousting and hawking terms, as the minions had been, until their disgrace, the king's closest companions on the tiltyard and at the chase. Other satirical allusions punctuate the play. There is a running joke about hunting for larks, which, as Neuss observed, is a jibe at the expense of Cardinal Wolsey, whose mistress was named Joan Lark. Similarly the London merchant community, and in particular the Merchant Tailors Company, come in for some barbed comments concerning their wealth and lack of charity.

Like a number of the Moralities, *Magnyfycence* is a remarkably sophisticated linguistic construct. It everywhere displays a fascination with the meaning, implications, and resonance of words. All of the characters play with language, underlining their speech with proverbs and *sententiae*, appealing to written authority (in the case of the Virtues) or popular wisdom (in that of the Vices), singing snatches of popular songs, and spicing their conversation with tradesmen's or huntsmen's cries. The variety of verse forms employed reveals a similar dexterity. As Neuss demonstrates, the lack of measure characteristic of the fallen court is mirrored in the collapse of the ordered four-stress rhyme royal stanza after the arrival of Fansy. Thereafter characters speak in a bravura array of forms ('Skeltonics', 'doggerel rhyme', couplets, alliterative stanzas), until order is once more restored with the return to virtue in the final scenes.

1 Edward Hall, *The Union of the Two Noble and Illustrious Houses of Lancaster and York*, ed. H. Ellis (London, 1809), p. 598.

Performance

There is no external evidence to link the play with a production at court, although, given the nature of its contemporary allusions, this would seem the most fitting place for its performance. An alternative, as Neuss suggested, would be a merchants' hall or noble household in the City, or even one of the Inns of Court, each of which would provide an audience knowledgeable enough to appreciate the play's coterie humour. The staging requires little more than the great hall of a large house decked out for a feast. The only large properties called for are the pallet-bed upon which the fallen hero collapses after l. 1964, and the (stuffed?) owl and dog exchanged by Fansy and Foly during their comic repartee. The remainder of the expenditure necessary for a performance would have been on the elaborate costumes of Magnyfycence himself and the Vices. The roles can all be played, with frequent doubling, by five actors, one of whom may have been a boy (to play the tiny Fansy).

The text printed here is based upon the copy of the *c.*1530 Rastell folio in Cambridge University Library (AB.8.46(4)) (STC 22607). In addition I have consulted the following modern critical additions: John Scattergood, ed., *John Skelton: The Complete English Poems* (Harmondsworth, 1983); R.L. Ramsey, ed., *John Skelton: Magnyfycence*, EETS ES 98 (Oxford, 1908 for 1906); Alexander Dyce, ed., *The Poetical Works of Skelton* (2 vols, London, 1843); P. Happé, ed., *Four Morality Plays* (Harmondsworth, 1979); and Paula Neuss, ed., *Magnificence* (Manchester, 1980).

Further reading

In addition to the editions cited above, helpful material can be found in the following:

W.O. Harris, *Skelton's Magnyfycence and the Cardinal Virtue Tradition* (Chapel Hill, 1965).
A.R. Heiserman, *Skelton and Satire* (Chicago, 1961).
J. Scattergood, 'Skelton's *Magnyfycence* and the Tudor Royal Household', *Medieval English Theatre* 15 (1993), pp. 21–48.
G. Walker, *John Skelton and the Politics of the 1520s* (Cambridge, 1988).
G. Walker, *Plays of Persuasion: Drama and Politics at the Court of Henry VIII* (Cambridge, 1991) (esp. ch. 3).
J.C. Warner, *Henry VIII's Divorce: Literature and the Politics of the Printing Press* (Woodbridge, 1998), ch. 6.

Magnyfycence

A goodly interlude and a mery, devysed and made by Mayster Skelton, poet laureate late deceasyd.

These be the names of the Players:[2] *Felycyte* (Wealthful Felicity or prosperous happiness: the ideal state for a prince), *Lyberte* (Liberty: free will, a quality which may be used for good or ill (see ll. 2099–100)), *Measure* (Moderation in all things, the 'golden' mean necessary for good conduct), *Magnyfycence* (a Prince, the quality defined by Aristotle as characteristic of great men, comprising true magnanimity of spirit, fitting generosity with material wealth, and princely dignity), *Fansy* (Caprice, wilfulness, a force for disorder),[3] *Counterfeit Countenaunce* (False Appearance: a deceiver), *Crafty Conveyaunce* (Guile personified, a skilled thief and 'conveyor' of goods), *Clokyd Colusyon* ('Cloaked' or hidden collusion/conspiracy, an intriguer),[4] *Courtly Abusyon* (the courtly abuses personified),[5] *Foly* (Folly, another fool),[6] *Adversyte* (Adversity), *Poverte* (Poverty,

2 This list of *dramatis personae* appears at the end of the printed text. The grouping of the roles may suggest notes towards doubling.

3 Fansy is a fool, wearing his distinctive costume partially concealed. As Scattergood suggests, he may be intended as a 'natural' fool or simpleton. He is small in stature, perhaps a dwarf of the kind that kings of the period kept in their courts for entertainment, and may have been played by a boy.

4 Colusyon is disguised as a priest throughout the play.

5 Abusyon is a foppish 'gallant', dressed in a parody of the latest fashions.

6 Foly is, as Scattergood suggests, possibly an 'allowed' fool or professional jester. He carries a bauble and wears his fool's costume openly.

dressed as a beggar), *Dyspare* (Despair: here the spiritual sin that denies the possibility of divine mercy), *Myschefe* (Evil: here the will to suicide which follows from despair, armed with a knife and halter), *Good Hope*, *Redresse* (Reform and Renewal personified), *(Sad) Cyrcumspeccyon* (Sober Deliberation: sound judgement, an ally of Measure), *Perseveraunce* (Perseverance).

FELYCYTE
Al thyngys contryvyd by mannys reason,
The world envyronnyd of hygh and low estate,[7]
Be it erly or late, welth hath a season.
Welth is of wysdome the very trewe probate:
A fole is he with welth that fallyth at debate.
But men nowe a dayes so unhappely be uryd
That nothynge than welth may worse be enduryd.[8]

To tell you the cause me semeth it no nede,
The amense therof is far to call agayne.
For when men by welth, they have lytyll drede
Of that may come after, experyence trewe and
playne:
Howe after a drought there fallyth a showre of rayne,
And after a hete oft cometh a stormy colde.
A man may have welth, but not as he wolde,

Ay to contynewe and styll to endure.
But yf prudence be proved with sad
cyrcumspeccyon,
Welthe myght be wonne and made to the lure,[9]
Yf noblenesse were aquayntyd with sober dyreccyon.
But wyll hath reason so under subjeccyon,
And so dysordereth this worlde over all,
That welthe and felicite is passynge small.

But where wonnys Welthe, and a man wolde wyt?
For welthfull Felicite truly is my name.

{Enter Liberty.}

LYBERTE
Mary, Welthe and I was apoynted to mete,
And eyther I am dysseyved or ye be the same.

FELYCYTE
Syr, as ye say. I have harde of your fame;
Your name is Lyberte, as I understande.

LYBERTE
Trewe you say, sir, gyve me your hande.

FELYCYTE
And from whens come ye, and it myght be askyd?

LYBERTE
To tell you, syr, I dare not, leest I sholde be maskyd
In a payre of fetters or a payre of stockys.[10]

FELYCYTE
Here you not howe this gentylman mockys?

LYBERTE
Ye[a], to knackynge ernyst what and it preve?[11]

FELYCYTE
Why, to say what he wyll Lyberte hath leve.

LYBERTE
Yet Lyberte hath ben lockyd up and kept in the
mew.

FELYCYTE
In dede, syr, that Lyberte was not worthe a cue.[12]
Howe be it, Lyberte may somtyme be to large,
But yf Reason be regent and ruler of your barge.

LYBERTE
To that ye say I can well condyssende.
Shewe forth, I pray you, here in what you intende.

3 wealth has its place 4 test 5 fool, falls in dispute 8 there's no need 9 remedy, (i.e. far away) 10 buy/obtain 11 what 14 desires 15 Always 16 endorsed 18 serious control 19 wilfulness 21 are exceedingly 22 if one wanted to know 24 had arranged 25 deceived, you are he 26 heard, reputation 30 lest/in case, trapped 32 Hear 35 cooped up 37 too free 38 Unless, your destiny 39 agree 40 herein, mean

7 '[When] all things are organized by human reason, the world is comprised of those of [both] high and low status'. Felycyte goes on to argue that in such a well-ordered universe relative wealth is an accurate measure of personal wisdom.

8 'But people nowadays are so unfavourably disposed, that nothing is harder to retain than wealth.'

9 'won and trained into obedience [as hawks are trained with baited "lures"]'.

10 Liberty is characteristically anxious to avoid restraint. His fear here is, perhaps, the general one that, once his identity is known, the forces of order will try to repress him.

11 'Yes, but what if it proves to be utterly true?'

12 A coin worth one-eighth of a penny.

FELYCYTE
Of that I intende, to make demonstracyon,
It askyth lesure with good advertysment.
Fyrst, I say, we owght to have in consyderacyon
That Lyberte be lynkyd with the chayne of countenaunce,
Lyberte to let from all maner offence:
For Lyberte at large is lothe to be stoppyd,
But with countenaunce your corage must be croppyd.

LYBERTE
Then thus to you . . .

FELYCYTE
Nay, suffer me yet ferther to say,
And, peradventure, I shall content your mynde.
Lyberte, I wote well, forbere no man there may;
It is so swete in all maner of kynde.
How be it Lyberte makyth many a man blynde;
By Lyberte is done many a great excesse;
Lyberte at large wyll oft wax reklesse.

Perceyve ye this parcell?[13]

LYBERTE
Ye[a], syr, passyng wel.
But and you wolde me permyt
To shewe parte of my wyt,
Somwhat I coulde enferre
Your consayte to debarre,[14]
Under supportacyon
Of pacyent tolleracyon.

FELYCYTE
God forbyd ye sholde be let
Your reasons forth to fet;
Wherfore at lyberte,
Say what ye wyll to me.

LYBERTE
Brefly to touche of my purpose the effecte:[15]
Lyberte is laudable and pryvylegyd from lawe;
Judycyall rygoure shall not me correcte . . .

FELYCYTE
Softe, my frende; herein your reason is but rawe.

LYBERTE
Yet suffer me to say the surpluse of my sawe.
What wote ye where upon I wyll conclude?
I say there is no welthe where as Lyberte is subdude.
I trowe ye can not say nay moche to this:
To lyve under lawe it is captyvyte;
Where Drede ledyth the daunce, there is no joy nor blysse.
Or howe can you prove that there is felycyte,
And you have not your owne fre lyberte
To sporte at your pleasure, to ryn, and to ryde?
Where Lyberte is absent, set welthe asyde.

Hic intrat Measure.[16]

MEASURE
Cryst you assyste in your altrycacyon!

FELYCYTE
Why, have you harde of our dysputacyon?

MEASURE
I parceyve well howe eche of you doth reason.

LYBERTE
Mayster Measure, you be come in good season.

MEASURE
And it is wonder that your wylde insolence
Can be content with Measure presence.

FELYCYTE
Wolde it please you then . . .

LYBERTE
Us to informe and ken.

MEASURE
A, ye be wonders men!
Your langage is lyke the penne
Of hym that wryteth to fast.

FELYCYTE
Syr, yf any worde have past
Me, other fyrst or last,
To you I arecte it, and cast

42 requires, attention 44 continence/self-discipline 45 restrain 47 boldness, cut back 50 no one can live without 51 ways 54 grow 61 with the aid of 62 Of (your) 63 hindered 64 fetch (i.e. explain) 70 Quiet, raw/naive 71 remainder, argument 72 How do you know 73 restricted 74 you can't deny 79 play, run 81 altercation 82 heard 84 Master, at a good moment 85 amazing 86 Measure's 88 teach 89 wonderful/strange 91 too 92 (I) have missed/mistaken 93 either 94 offer it for correction

13 'Do you understand me so far [lit. "this portion" of my case]?'
14 'I could suggest something to counter your argument'.
15 'To suggest briefly the essence of my argument'.
16 'Here Measure enters.'

Therof the reformacyon.

Lyberte

And I of the same facyon.
Howe be it, by protestacyon

Dyspleasure that you none take,
Some reason we must make.

Measure

That wyll not I forsake,
So it in measure be.
Come of, therfore, let se,
Shall I begynne or ye?

Felycyte

Nay, ye shall begynne, by my wyll.

Lyberte

It is reason and skyll
We your pleasure fulfyll.

Measure

Then ye must bothe consent
You to holde content
With myne argument,

And muste you requyre
Me pacyently to here.

Felycyte

Yes, syr, with ryght good chere.

Lyberte

With all my herte intere.

Measure

Oracius to recorde in his volumys olde[17]
With every condycyon Measure must be soght.
Welthe without Measure wolde bere hymselfe to
  bolde;
Lyberte without Measure prove a thynge of nought.
I ponder by nomber;[18] by Measure all thynge is
  wrought,
As at the fyrst orygynall, by godly opynyon;
Whych provyth well that Measure shold have
  domynyon.

Where Measure is myster, plenty dothe none
  offence;
Where Measure lackyth, all thynge dysorderyd is;
Where Measure is absent, ryot kepeth resydence;
Where Measure is ruler, there is nothynge amysse.
Measure is treasure; howe say ye, is it not this?

Felycyte

Yes, questyonlesse, in myne opynyon:
Measure is worthy to have domynyon.

Lyberte

Unto that same I am ryght well agrede,
So that Lyberte be not lefte behynde.

Measure

Ye[a], Lyberte with Measure nede never drede.

Lyberte

What, Lyberte to Measure then wolde ye bynde?[19]

Measure

What ellys? For otherwyse it were agaynst kynde.
If Lyberte sholde lepe and renne where he lyst
It were no vertue, it were a thynge unblyst.

It were a myschefe yf Lyberte lacked a reyne
Where with to rule hym with the wrythyng of a
  rest.
All trebyllys and tenours be rulyd by a meyne.[20]
Lyberte without Measure is acountyd for a beste;
There is no surfet where Measure rulyth the feste;
There is no excesse where Measure hath his helthe;
Measure contynwyth prosperyte and welthe.

Felycyte

Unto your rule I wyll annex my mynde.

Lyberte

So wolde I, but I wolde be lothe

96 I (am), fashion (i.e. mind) 97 on the condition (that) 98 you take no offence 99 argument 100 forbid 101 So (long as) 102 Come on 105 reasonable, proper 108 to accept 112 happily 113 entire heart 115 in every situation 116 behave too boldly 117 would prove worthless 125 thus 126 without question 132 else, would be unnatural 133 run, wanted 134 unblessed/cursed 135 harmful, rein 136 twisting, bridle 137 trebles, tenors, mean 138 considered a beast 139 feast 141 continues/sustains 142 join (i.e. agree)

17 'To cite Horace'. The 'old volumes' cited are probably the *Odes*, II, 10, 5, where the golden mean between extremes of conduct is discussed.

18 'I weigh [all things] by number'. Neuss suggests amending 'I' to 'In', thus turning the line into an echo of Wisdom of Solomon 11:20: 'Thou hast ordained all things by measure, and number, and weight [O Lord].'

19 'Would you bind Liberty to Measure, then?'

20 In music the mean regulates the higher and lower voices.

That wonte was to be formyst now to come
behynde[21]
It were a shame, to God I make an othe,
Without I myght cut it out of the brode clothe,[22]
As I was wonte ever, at my fre wyll.

MEASURE
But have ye not herde say that wyll is no skyll?
Take sad dyreccyon, and leve this wantonnesse.

LYBERTE
It i[s] no maystery . . .

FELYCYTE
Tushe, let Measure procede,
And after his mynde herdely your selfe adresse.
For without Measure, poverte and nede
Wyll crepe upon us, and us to Myschefe lede:
For Myschefe wyll mayster us yf Measure us forsake.

LYBERTE
Well, I am content your wayes to take.

MEASURE
Surely I am joyous that ye be myndyd thus.
Magnyfycence to mayntayne, your promosyon shalbe.[23]

FELYCYTE
So in his harte he may be glad of us.

LYBERTE
There is no prynce but he hath nede of us thre:
Welthe, with Measure, and plesaunt Lyberte.

MEASURE
Nowe pleasyth you a lytell whyle to stande;
Me semeth Magnyfycence is comynge here at hande.

Hic intrat Magnfycence.[24]

MAGNYFYCENCE
To assure you of my noble porte and fame,
Who lyst to knowe, Magnyfycence I hyght.
But Measure, my frende, what hyght this mannys
name?

MEASURE
Syr, though ye be a noble prynce of myght,
Yet in this man you must set your delyght.
And, syr, this other mannys name is Lyberte.

MAGNYFYCENCE
Welcome, frendys, ye are bothe unto me.

But nowe let me knowe of your conversacyon.

FELYCYTE
Pleasyth Your Grace, Felycyte they me call.

LYBERTE
And I am Lyberte, made of in every nacyon.

MAGNYCYCENCE
Convenyent persons for any prynce ryall.
Welthe with Lyberte, with me bothe dwell ye shall,
To the gydynge of my Measure you bothe
commyttynge;
That Measure be mayster us semeth it is syttynge.

MEASURE
Where as ye have, syr, to me them assygned,
Suche order I trust with them for to take,
So that Welthe with Measure shalbe conbyned,
And Lyberte his large with Measure shall make.[25]

FELYCYTE
Your ordenaunce, syr, I wyll not forsake.

LYBERTE
And I my selfe hooly to you wyll inclyne.

MAGNYFYCENCE
Then may I say that ye be servauntys myne.

For by Measure I warne you we thynke to be gydyd;
Wherin it is necessary my pleasure you knowe:
Measure and I wyll never be devydyd,
For no dyscorde that any man can sawe.
For Measure is a meane, nother to hy nor to lawe,
In whose attemperaunce I have suche delyght,
That Measure shall never departe from my syght.

149 sober instruction, leave 150 It doesn't have to be 151 opinion, earnestly direct yourself 162 nearby 163 state 164 I am called 170 tell me about yourselves 172 highly valued 173 royal 175 submitting yourselves 176 fitting 179 combined/allied 181 instruction(s) 182 wholly 186 separated 187 sow 188 middle way, too high, low 189 moderation

21 'I would be reluctant if one who was used to going first should now come last'.

22 Broad cloth was a double-width measure of fabric. To cut out of the broad cloth implies a complete disregard for economy: 'it would be a shame if I couldn't overdo things'.

23 'You will be promoted/appointed to serve Magnyfycence.'

24 'Here Magnyfycence enters.'

25 'And Liberty shall be free [only] in moderation.'

FELYCYTE
Laudable your consayte is to be acountyd,
For welthe without measure sodenly wyll slyde.

LYBERTE
As Your Grace ful nobly hath recountyd,
Measure with Noblenesse sholde be alyde.

MAGNYFYCENCE
Then, Lyberte, se that Measure be your gyde,
For I wyll use you by his advertysment.

FELYCYTE
Then shall you have with you prosperyte resydent.

MEASURE
I trowe good fortune hath annexyd us together
To se howe greable we are of one mynde.
There is no flaterer nor losyll so lyther,
This lynkyd chayne of love that can unbynde.
Nowe that ye have me chefe ruler assyngned,
I wyll endevour me to order every thynge
Your noblenesse and honour consernynge.

LYBERTE
In joy and myrthe your mynde shalbe inlarged,
And not embracyd with pusyllanymyte.
But plenarly all thought from you must be
    dyschargyd,
If ye be lyst to lyve after your fre Lyberte.
All delectacyons aquayntyd is with me;
By me all persons worke what they lyste.

MEASURE
Hem, syr, yet beware of 'Had I wyste!'[26]
Lyberte in some cause becomyth a gentyll mynde,
Bycause course of Measure, yf I be in the way.[27]
Who countyd without me is caste to fer behynde
Of his rekenynge, as evydently we may
Se at our eye the worlde day by day.
For defaute of Measure all thynge dothe excede.

FELYCYTE
All that ye say is as trewe as the Crede.

For, how be it Lyberte to welthe is convenyent,
And from Felycyte may not be forborne,
Yet Measure hath ben so longe from us absent,
That all men laugh at Lyberte to scorne.
Welth and wyt I say, be so threde bare worne,
That all is without measure and fer beyonde the
    mone.

MAGNYFYCENCE
Then noblenesse, I se well, is almoste undone

But yf therof the soner amendys be made;
For dowtlesse I parceyve my magnyfycence
Without Measure lyghtly may fade,
Of to moche lyberte under the offence.[28]
Wherfore, Measure, take Lyberte with you hence,
And rule hym after the rule of your scole.

LYBERTE
What, syr, wolde ye make me a poppynge fole?

MEASURE
Why, were not your selfe agreed to the same,
And now wolde ye swarve from your owne
    ordynaunce?

LYBERTE
I wolde be rulyd and I myght for shame.

FELYCYTE
A, ye make me laughe at your inconstaunce.

MAGNYFYCENCE
Syr, without any longer delyaunce,
Take Lyberte to rule, and folowe myne entent.

MEASURE
It shalbe done at your commaundement.

191 praiseworthy, opinion 192 will soon disappear 194 allied 196 following, advice 198 joined 199 agreeable 200 wretch, wicked 202 nominated me 205 enlarged/set free 206 constrained, cowardice 207 completely, worry, rejected 208 desire, following 209 pleasures are known 210 achieve, desire 212 cases, befits 214 too far 215 In his accounts 216 with, (in) the 217 Through lack of, grow outrageous 220 rejected 221 been 222 mock . . . scornfully 223 threadbare 224 moon (i.e. gone too far) 225 ruined 226 unleash, sooner 228 may easily fade away 231 school/ tutelage 232 chattering fool 233 haven't you already 234 depart from/break, rule 235 if I could without shame 236 inconstancy 237 dalliance/delay 238 my instructions

26 'Ahem! [a cough of reproach], beware of "If only I'd known"!': i.e. 'think now rather than later, because later it will be too late'.

27 'Through [following] the path of measure, provided that I am there [to help].'

28 'Through the fault of too much liberty.'

Itaque Measure exeat locum cum Libertate, et maneat Magnyfycence cum Felicitate.[29]

MAGNYFYCENCE
It is a wanton thynge, this Lyberte.
Perceyve you not howe lothe he was to abyde
The rule of Measure, notwithstandynge we
Have deputyd Measure hym to gyde?
By Measure eche thynge duly is tryde.
Thynke you not thus, my frende Felycyte?

FELYCYTE:
God forbede that it other wyse sholde be!

MAGNYFYCENCE
Ye coulde not ellys, I wote, with me endure.

FELYCYTE
Endure? No, God wote, it were great payne.
But yf I were orderyd by just Measure,
It were not possyble me longe to retayne.

Hic intrat Fansy.[30]

FANSY
Tusche, holde your pece, your langage is vayne.
Please it Your Grace to take no dysdayne
To shewe you playnly the trouth as I thynke.

MAGNYFYCENCE
Here is none forsyth whether you flete or synke![31]

FELYCYTE
From whens come you, syr, that no man lokyd after?

MAGNYFYCENCE
Or who made you so bolde to interrupe my tale?

FANSY
Nowe, *benedicite*, ye wene I were some hafter,
Or ellys some jangelynge Jacke of the Vale;[32]
Ye wene that I am dronken bycause I loke pale.

MAGNYFYCENCE
Me semeth that ye have dronken more than ye have
bled.

FANSY
Yet amonge noble men I was brought up and bred.

FELYCYTE
Nowe leve this jangelynge and to us expounde
Why that ye sayd our langage was in vayne.

FANSY
Mary, upon trouth my reason I grounde,
That without Largesse noblenesse can not rayne;
And that I sayd ones yet I say agayne,
I say without Largesse worshyp hath no place,
For Largesse is a purchaser of pardon and of grace,

MAGNYFYCENCE
Nowe, I beseche the[e], tell me what is thy name?

FANSY
Largesse, that all lordes should love, syr, I hyght.

FELYCYTE
But hyght you Largesse encrease of noble fame?[33]

FANSY
Ye[a], syr, undoubted.

FELYCYTE
Then of very ryght
With Magnyfycence, this noble prynce of myght,
Sholde be your dwellynge, in my consyderacyon.

MAGNYFYCENCE
Yet we wyll therin take good delyberacyon.

FANSY
As in that, I wyll not be agaynst your pleasure.

FELYCYTE
Syr, hardely remembre what may your name
avaunce.

241 tolerate 244 judged 247 otherwise 248 would be difficult 250 to keep me for long 251 language/speech 252 If it pleases 253 tell 255 who, looked for/expected 257 bless you, think I'm a trickster 258 chattering fool 259 drunk, look 262 explain 264 I base my argument 265 liberality, reign/survive 266 what, once/before 267 honour 272 undoubtedly 277 boldly propose, fame enhance

29 'And so let Measure leave the place with Lyberte, and Magnyfycence remain with Felycyte.'

30 'Here Fansy enters.' From what follows it seems clear that he wears a fool's costume only partially covered by a courtier's clothes.

31 'There's no none here who cares whether you float or sink!'

32 'Jack of the Vale' is an insulting nickname used elsewhere by Skelton; see Scattergood, *Poems*, p. 35.

33 'But do you call increase of noble fame "largesse"?' Given that Fansy is supposed to be very small, the emphasis should be on 'large'.

MAGNYFYCENCE
Largesse is laudable, so it in measure be.

FANSY
Largesse is he that all prynces doth avaunce:
I reporte me herein to Kynge Lewes of Fraunce,[34]

FELYCYTE
Why have ye hym named, and all other refused?

FANSY
For, syth he dyed, Largesse was lytell used.

Plucke up your mynde, syr! What ayle you to muse?[35]
Have ye not welthe here at your wyl?
It is but a maddynge, these wayes that ye use,
What avayleth lordshyp, yourselfe for to kyll
With care and with thought howe Jacke shall have Gyl?[36]

MAGNYFYCENCE
What! I have aspyed ye are a carles page.[37]

FANSY
By God, syr, ye se but fewe wyse men of myne age.

But covetyse hath blowen you so full of wynde,
That *colyca passyo* hath gropyd you by the guttys.

FELYCYTE
In fayth, broder Largesse, you have a mery mynd.

FANSY
In fayth, I set not by the worlde two Dauncaster cuttys.[38]

MAGNYFYCENCE
Ye wante but a wylde flyeng bolte to shote at the buttes.[39]
Though Largesse ye hyght, your langage is to large;
For whiche ende goth forwarde ye take lytell charge.[40]

FELYCYTE
Let se this checke yf ye voyde canne.

FANSY
In faythe, els had I gone to longe to scole
But yf I coulde knowe a gose from a swanne.[41]

MAGNYFYCENCE
Wel, wyse men may ete the fysshe, when ye shal draw the pole.[42]

FANSY
In fayth, I wyll not say that ye shall prove a fole,
But ofte tymes have I sene wyse men do mad dedys.

MAGNYFYCENCE
Go shake the[e], dogge, hay, syth ye wyll nedys!

You are nothynge mete with us for to dwell,
That with your lorde and mayster so pertly can prate!
Gete you hens, I say, by my counsell.
I wyll not use you to play with me checke mate.[43]

FANSY
Syr, yf I have offended your noble estate,
I trow I have brought you suche wrytynge of recorde[44]
That I shall have you agayne my good lorde.

278 if 280 I cite the example of 281 ignored 285 madness 290 covetousness/greed 291 colic, gripped, guts 292 brother, merry/madcap 294 lack, arrow, targets 295 too free/uncontrolled 297 if you can escape this charge 302 deeds 303 since you must do so! 304 in no way suitable 305 can impertinently prattle 306 Get, hence 308 rank 310 (as) my

34 Probably Louis XII, who died on 1 January 1515. Perhaps a slight is intended in l. 282 against Louis's successor as king of France, Henry's great rival in conspicuous consumption, Francis I.

35 'Cheer up, sir! What troubles you that makes you so thoughtful?'

36 'How does it advance [your] authority to kill yourself with worry about resolving every minor issue?' 'Jack shall have Jill' was a proverbially happy resolution to a story. See *Love's Labour's Lost*, 5, ii, ll. 862–3.

37 Either 'a churl's servant' (i.e. very low and coarse indeed), or 'a careless servant'.

38 'Truly, I wouldn't give two Doncaster cuts for the whole world.' Doncaster cuts were horses with cropped tails.

39 One of a series of elliptical allusions to Fansy's foolishness. 'A fool's bolt' was proverbially 'soon shot': Magnyfycence is thus suggesting that Fansy is a fool.

40 'You don't care which way up things are.'

41 'Truly, I should have wasted my time at school if I could not tell a goose from a swan'; i.e. this is a childishly easy challenge.

42 'When you have done the fishing': another allegation of folly, this time based upon the proverb 'Fools lade the water and wise men catch the fish.'

43 'I won't employ you to bring about my own ruin.'

44 The letter of recommendation mentioned purports to be from Sad Cyrcumspeccyon, Magnyfycence's absent counsellor, but, as we learn at ll. 531ff, it is really a forgery prepared by Counterfet Countenaunce.

To you recommendeth Sad Cyrcumspeccyon,
And sendeth you this wrytynge closed under sele.

MAGNYFYCENCE
This wrytynge is welcome with harty afeccyon?
Why kepte you it thus longe? Howe dothe he, wele?

FANSY
Syr, thanked be God, he hath his hele.

MAGNYFYCENCE
Welthe, gete you home and commaunde me to Mesure;
Byd hym take good hede to you, my synguler tresure.

FELYCYTE
Is there ony thynge elles your grace wyll commaunde me?

MAGNYFYCENCE
Nothynge, but fare you well tyll sone,
And that he take good kepe to Lyberte.

FELYCYTE
Your pleasure, syr, shortely shall be done.

MAGNYFYCENCE
I shall come to you myselfe, I trowe, this after none.
I pray you, Larges, here to remayne,
Whylest I knowe what this letter dothe contayne.

[*Exit Felycyte.*]

Hic faciat tanquam legeret litteras tacite. Interim superveniat cantando Counterfet Countenaunce suspenso gradu qui viso Magnyfycence sens[i]m retrocedat; a[d] tempus post pusillum rursum accedat Counterfet Countenaunce prospectando et vocitando a longe; et Fansy animat silentium cum manu.[45]

COUNTERFET COUNTENAUNCE
What, Fansy! Fansy!

MAGNYFYCENCE:
Who is that that thus dyd cry?
Me thought he called 'Fansy'.

FANSY
It was a Flemynge hyght Hansy.[46]

MAGNYFYCENCE
Me thought he called 'Fansy' me behynde.

FANSY
Nay, syr, it was nothynge but your mynde.
But nowe, syr, as touchynge this letter . . .

MAGNYFYCENCE
I shall loke in it at leasure better;
And surely ye are to hym beholde,
And for his sake ryght gladly I wolde
Do what I coude to do you good.

FANSY
I pray God kepe you in that mood!

MAGNYFYCENCE
This letter was wryten ferre hence.

FANSY
By lakyn, syr, it hathe cost me pence
And grotes many one or I came to your presence.[47],

MAGNYFYCENCE
Where was it delyvered you? Shewe unto me.

FANSY
By God, syr, beyond the se.

MAGNYFYCENCE
At what place, nowe, as you gesse?

FANSY
By my trouthe, syr, at Pountesse.
This wrytynge was taken me there,
But never was I in gretter fere.

311 S.C. commends himself to you 312 sealed letter 314 How is he, well 315 health 317 special/principal 319 soon 320 (make sure) that he, care of 322 afternoon 324 Whilst I discover 329 behind my back 330 imagination 331 concerning 332 better leisure 333 beholden/obliged 337 far from here 338 By Our Lady 339 groats, before 341 sea 343 Pontoise (France) 344 given (to) 345 fear

45 'Here let him act as if he were reading the letter silently. Meanwhile, let Counterfet Countenaunce come in singing. On seeing Magnyfycence let him retreat on tiptoe, but after a while let Counterfet Countenaunce come again looking about and calling from a distance, and Fansy motions him to be silent with his hand.'

46 'Called Hansy'. Hans was a stock name for a Dutchman/Fleming.

47 A groat was worth 4 pence.

MAGNYFYCENCE
Howe so?

FANSY
By God, at the see syde,
Had I not opened my purse wyde,
I trowe, by Our Lady, I had ben slayne,
Or elles I had lost myne eres twayne.

[MAGNYFYCENCE]
By your soth?

[FANSY]
Ye[a], and there is suche a wache
That no man can scape but they hym cache.
They bare me in hande that I was a spye;
And another bade put out myne eye;
Another wolde myne eye were blerde;[48]
Another bade shave halfe my berde;
And boyes to the pylery gan me plucke,
And wolde have made me Freer Tucke,
To preche out of the pylery hole
Without an antetyme or a stole;[49]
And some bade, 'sere hym with a marke!'
To gete me fro them I had moche warke.

MAGNYFYCENCE
Mary, syr, ye were afrayde.

FANSY
By my trouthe, had I not payde and prayde,
And made largesse, as I hyght,
I had not ben here with you this nyght.
But surely largesse saved my lyfe;
For largesse stynteth all maner of stryfe.

MAGNYFYCENCE
It dothe so sure, nowe and than;
But Largesse is not mete for every man.

FANSY
No, but for you grete estates
Largesse stynteth grete debates;
And he that I came fro to this place
Sayd I was mete for Your Grace;
And in dede, syr, I here men talke
By the way, as I ryde and walke,
Say howe you excede in noblenesse,
If you had with you Largesse.

MAGNYFYCENCE
And say they so, in very dede?

FANSY
With ye[a], syr, so God me spede.

MAGNYFYCENCE
Yet Mesure is a mery mene.

FANSY
Ye[a], syr, a blannched almonde is no bene.[50]
Measure is mete for a marchauntes hall,
But Largesse becometh a state ryall.
What, sholde you pynche at a pecke of grotes?
Ye wolde sone pynche at a pecke of otes![51]
Thus is the talkynge of one and of oder,
As men dare speke it hugger mugger:
A lorde a negarde, it is a shame:
But Largesse may amende your name.

MAGNYFYCENCE
In faythe, Largesse, welcome to me.

FANSY
I pray you, syr, I may so be,
And of my servyce you shall not mysse.

MAGNYFYCENCE
Togyder we wyll talke more of this.
Let us departe from hens home to my place.

FANSY
I folow even after Your Noble Grace.

Hic discedat Magnificens cum Fansy, et intrat Counterfet Countenaunce.[52]

349 two ears 350 Truly?, watch/guard 351 escape, catch 352 claimed 353 ordered 354 blurred/blinded 355 beard 356 pillory, drag 357 Friar Tuck 360 'brand him!' 361 away from them, (hard) work 367 ends 370 nobles 376 would surpass (everyone) 378 truly? 380 happy medium 382 merchants' 383 royal estate 386 other 387 secretly 388 niggard/miser 389 improve, reputation 392 lack

48 As 'to blear someone's eye' also meant to fool them, an alternative or secondary meaning may also be intended.

49 'To preach through the hole in the pillory, without an antetheme [a prefatory theme before a sermon] or a stole [priestly garment].'

50 i.e. 'Just as a blanched almond [a delicacy] is not the same as a humble bean, so the rules that govern ordinary folk should not bind royalty.'

51 'What, should you worry about a handful of small change? You might as well worry about a handful of oats!'

52 'Here let Magnyfycence depart with Fansy, and enter Counterfet Countenaunce.' Fansy follows Magnyfycence but is called back by Counterfet Countenaunce. He eventually leaves after l. 400.

Counterfet Countenaunce
What, I say, herke, a worde.

Fansy:
Do away, I say, the Devylles torde!

Counterfet Countenaunce
Ye[a], but how longe shall I here awayte?

Fansy
By Goddys body, I come streyte;
I hate this blunderyng that thou doste make.

[*Exit Fansy*]

Counterfet Countenaunce
Nowe to the Devyll I the[e] betake,
For in fayth ye be well met.
Fansy hath cachyd in a flye net
This noble man Magnyfycence,
Of Largesse under the pretence.
They have made me here to put the stone,[53]
But nowe wyll I, that they be gone,
In bastarde ryme, after the dogrell gyse,
Tell you where of my name dothe ryse.

For Counterfet Countenaunce knowen am I;
This worlde is full of my foly.
I set not by hym a fly
That can not counterfet a lye,
Swere and stare, and byde therby,
And countenaunce it clenly,[54]
And defende it manerly.
A knave wyll counterfet nowe a knyght,
A lurdayne lyke a lorde to fyght,
A mynstrell lyke a man of myght,
A tappster lyke a lady bryght:
Thus make I them wyth thryft to fyght;
Thus at the laste I brynge hym ryght
To Tyburne[55] where they hange on hyght.

To counterfet I can by praty wayes:
Of nyghtys to occupy counterfet kayes,
Clenly to counterfet newe arayes,
Counterfet eyrnest by way of playes.
Thus am I occupyed at all assayes.
What so ever I do, all men me prayse,
And mekyll am I made of nowe adays.

Counterfet maters in the lawe of the lande,
Wyth golde and grotes they grese my hande,
In stede of ryght that wronge may stande;
And counterfet fredome that is bounde
I counterfet suger that is but [sa]nde;
Counterfet capytaynes by me are mande;[56]
Of all lewdnesse I kyndell the brande.

Counterfet kyndnesse, and thynke dyscayte;
Counterfet letters by the way of sleyght;
Subtelly usynge counterfet weyght;
Counterfet langage, *fayty bone geyte*.[57]
Counterfetynge is a proper bayte;
A counte to counterfet in a resayte,
To counterfet well is a good consayte.

Counterfet maydenhode may well be borne,
But counterfet coynes,[58] is laughynge to scorne:
It is evyll patchynge of that is torne.[59]
Whan the noppe is rughe it wolde be shorne.
Counterfet haltynge without a thorne;.
Yet counterfet chafer is but evyll corne.
All thynge is worse whan it is worne.

What, wolde ye wyves counterfet
The courtly gyse of the newe jet?
An olde barne wolde be underset;

396 hark 397 Get lost! 399 I'll return immediately 400 confused noise 401 I commend you 405 By pretending to be Largesse 407 while 408 irregular, doggerel 409 come from 412 value him at less than 416 manfully 420 An ale-wife 421 (i.e. to hate thrift) 422 them straight 424 pretty/cunning 425 use, keys 426 new disguises(?) 427 earnest, jest 428 occasions 430 I am greatly praised 432 grease . . . (i.e. bribe me) 433 prevail 435 sugar 436 captains, given men 437 kindle, firebrand 438 deceit 440 weights (in retailing) 442 bait 443 total, receipt 445 maidenhood/virginity 448 nap, rough, shorn 449 limping, thorn (in the foot) 450 merchandise 451 worn out 453 fashion 454 propped up from underneath

53 'To place the stones around the fly-net to hold the prey down.' i.e. to complete the trap.

54 'Swear and stare down a challenge, and hold to it and keep a straight face.'

55 Tyburn, the place of public execution in London, close to modern Marble Arch.

56 Perhaps an allusion to the sort of abuses practised by recruiting sergeants and dramatized in the Falstaff scenes in *Henry IV* parts I and II.

57 Perhaps mock French for '*fait à bon geste*': elegantly.

58 Probably a continuation of l. 445: 'coyness': i.e. 'Counterfeiting virginity is tolerable, but counterfeiting shy innocence as well, that's taking the joke too far!' It is possible, however, that a new trick is introduced here, counterfeiting 'coins'.

59 'It's hard to patch that which is torn.' Probably a continuation of the reference to lost virginity.

It is moche worthe that is ferre fet.[60]
'What, wanton, wanton, nowe well ymet!'[61]
'What, Margery Mylke Ducke, mermoset!'
'It wolde be masked in my net.'[62]

It wolde be nyce, thoughe I say nay.
By Crede, it wolde have fresshe aray,
'And therfore shall my husbande pay.'
To counterfet she wyll assay
All the newe gyse, fresshe and gaye,
And be as praty as she may,
And jet it joly as a jay.

Counterfet prechynge, and byleve the contrary;
Counterfet conscyence, pevysshe pope holy;
Counterfet sadnesse, with delynge full madly;
Counterfet holynes is called ypocrysy;
Counterfet reason is not worth a flye;
Counterfet wysdome and workes of foly;
Counterfet Countenaunce every man dothe occupy.

Counterfet worshyp outwarde men may se;
Ryches rydeth, at home is poverte.[63]
Counterfet pleasure is borne out by me,
Coll wolde go clenly and it wyll not be
And Annot wolde be nyce, and laughes 'tehe, wehe'.[64]
Your Cou[n]terfet Countenaunce is all of nysyte,
A plummed partrydge all redy to flye.

A knokylbonyarde wyll counterfet a clarke;
He wolde trotte gentylly, but he is to starke;[65]
At his cloked counterfetynge dogges dothe barke.
A carter a courtyer? It is a worthy warke!
That with his whyp his mares was wonte to yarke;
A custrell to dryve the Devyll out of the derke,
A counterfet courtyer with a knaves marke.

To counterfet this freers have lerned me.
This[66] nonnes nowe and then, and it myght be,
Wolde take in the way of co[u]nterfet charyte,
The grace of God under *benedicite*.
To counterfet thyr counsell they gyve me a fee.
Chanons can not counterfet but upon thre;[67]
Monkys may not for drede that men sholde them se.

Hic ingrediatur Fansy properanter cum Crafty Conveyaunce cum famine multo adinvicem garrulantes; tandem viso Counterfet Countenaunce dicat Crafty Conveyaunce:[68]

CRAFTY CONVEYAUNCE
What! Counterfet Countenaunce!

COUNTERFET COUNTENAUNCE
What! Crafty Conveyaunce!

FANSY
What the Devyll! Are ye two of aquayntaunce?
God gyve you a very myschaunce!

CRAFTY CONVEYAUNCE
Ye[a], yes, syr, he and I have met.

COUNTERFET COUNTENAUNCE
We have bene togyder bothe erly and late.
But Fa[n]sy, my frende, where have ye bene so longe?

455 valued more highly, fetched 456 well met! (a greeting) 457 marmoset (comic term of endearment) 459 fashionable/wanton 460 (the) Creed 463 elegant 465 flaunt herself, jolly/pretty 466 believe 467 peevish/quarrelsome, hypocrite 468 seriousness, dealing/behaving 469 hypocrisy 472 use 473 outwardly 475 supported/justified 478 (pretended) nicety/refinement 479 plumed 480 clumsy oaf, scholar 481 trot like a gentleman, too stiff 483 courtier, work (i.e. that's rich!) 484 lash 485 knave, (ugly enough) to, dark 487 friars taught/learned from 488 nuns, if they can 491 keep their secret 493 see them 497 bad luck!

60 Women were proverbially said to desire goods brought from afar.

61 As Neuss suggests, Countenaunce here seems to mimic an exchange between himself and a would-be fashionable lover.

62 'It' [baby talk for "you"] would [like to both] wear a fashionable veil [that he has brought for her and] / fall into my trap.'

63 'Wealth rides out while poverty stays at home.'

64 The comic rustics Colin and Annot may simply be striving unsuccessfully to ape courtly manners, he in elegant clothes, she in 'nyse' behaviour, but their origins betray them, notably in her coarse laughter. But, as Neuss suggests, there may be a secondary sexual meaning: 'go cleanly' may mean 'copulate without shame' and 'nyse' may imply a flirtatious wantonness reinforced by the wanton laugh (reminiscent of that of Alison in Chaucer's *Miller's Tale*, l. 3740).

65 This stanza mocks the upstart carter who cannot ride a horse like his social superiors.

66 If 'This' is accompanied by an obscene gesture, the stanza becomes a satirical mockery of the sexual misdemeanours of nuns and friars.

67 'Unless there are three of them': perhaps the humour relies on an obscene variant of 'how many cathedral canons does it take to change a light-bulb?'

68 'Here let Fansy come in quickly with Crafty Conveyaunce, talking a great deal, chatting together; finally, on noticing Counterfet Countenaunce, let Crafty Conveyaunce say'.

Fansy
By God, I have bene about a praty pronge . . .
Crafty Conveyaunce, I should say, and I.

Crafty Conveyaunce
By God, we have made Magnyfycence to ete a flye.[69]

Counterfet Countenaunce
Howe could ye do that and [I] was away?

Fansy
By God, man, bothe his pagent and thyne he can play.

Counterfet Countenaunce
Say trouth?

Crafty Conveyaunce
Yes, yes, by lakyn, I shall the[e] warent,
As longe as I lyve, thou haste an heyre parent.

Fansy
Yet have we pyckyd out a rome for the[e].

Counterfet Countenaunce
Why, shall we dwell togyder all thre?

Crafty Conveyaunce
Why, man, it were to great a wonder
That we thre galauntes sholde be longe asonder.

Counterfet Countenaunce
For Cockys harte, gyve me thy hande!

Fansy
By the Masse, for ye are able to dystroy an hole lande.

Crafty Conveyaunce
By God, yet it muste begynne moche of the[e].[70]

Fansy
Who that is ruled by us, it shalbe longe or he thee.

Counterfet Countenaunce
But I say, kepest thou the olde name styll that thou had?

Crafty Conveyaunce
Why, wenyst thou, horson, that I were so mad?

Fansy
Nay, nay; he hath chaunged his, and I have chaunged myne.

Counterfet Countenaunce
Nowe what is his name, and what is thyne?

Fansy
In faythe, Largesse I hyght,
And I am made a knyght.

Counterfet Countenaunce
A rebellyon agaynst Nature
So large a man, and so lytell of stature!
But, syr, howe counterfetyd ye?

[Crafty Conveyaunce]
Sure Surveyaunce I named me.

[Counterfet Countenaunce]
Surveyaunce! Where ye survey
Thryfte hathe lost her cofer kay.

Fansy
But is it not well? Howe thynkest thou?

Counterfet Countenaunce
Yes, syr, I gyve God avowe,
Myself coude not counterfet it better.
But what became of the letter
That I counterfeyted you underneth a shrowde?

Fansy
By the Masse, odly well alowde.

Crafty Conveyaunce
By God, had not I it convayed
Yet Fansy had ben dysceyved.[71]

Counterfet Countenaunce
I wote thou arte false ynoughe for one.

Fansy
By my trouthe, we had ben gone.

501 preparing a subtle trick 504 if 505 role, he (Conveyaunce) 506 I assure you 507 heir apparent 508 chosen, place 510 too 511 gallants, any longer separated 512 God's (euphemism) 513 whole 515 long (time) before he prospers 517 do you think I'm mad, whoreson 523 great 527 coffer key (i.e. thrift is ruined) 529 I swear to God 532 (i.e. secretly) 533 amazingly, received

69 'We've tricked him into something unpleasant.' Proverbially blind people were said to 'eat many a fly'.

70 Either 'it must be inherited from you' (a continuation of the idea that Crafty Conveyaunce is Counterfet Countenaunce's heir apparent), or 'it [the dissimulation] must mainly start with you'.

71 'Fansy would still be frustrated in his purpose.'

And yet, in fayth, man, we lacked the[e],
For to speke with Lyberte.

COUNTERFET COUNTENAUNCE
What, is Largesse without Lyberte?

CRAFTY CONVEYAUNCE
By Mesure mastered yet is he.

COUNTERFET COUNTENAUNCE
What, is your conveyaunce no better?

FANSY
In faythe, Mesure is lyke a tetter
That overgroweth a mannes face,
So he ruleth over all our place.

CRAFTY CONVEYAUNCE
Nowe therfore, whylest we are togyder
Counterfet Countenaunce, nay, come hyder,
I say, whylest we are togyder in same . . .

COUNTERFET COUNTENAUNCE
Tushe, a strawe! It is a shame
That we can no better than so!

FANSY
We wyll remedy it, man, or we go.
For lyke as mustarde is sharpe of taste,
Ryght so a sharpe fansy must be founde,
Wherwith Mesure to confounde.

CRAFTY CONVEYAUNCE
Can you a remedy for a tysyke,
That sheweth yourselfe thus spedde in
 physyke?

COUNTERFET COUNTENAUNCE
It is a gentyll reason of a rake!

FANSY
For all these japes yet that we make . . .

CRAFTY CONVEYAUNCE
Your fansy maketh myne elbowe to ake.

FANSY
Let se, fynde you a better way.

COUNTERFET COUNTENAUNCE
Take no dyspleasure of that we say.

CRAFTY CONVEYAUNCE
Nay, and you be angry and overwharte
A man may beshrowe your angry harte.

FANSY
Tushe, a strawe! I thought none yll.

COUNTERFET COUNTENAUNCE
What, shall we jangle thus all the day styll?

CRAFTY CONVEYAUNCE
Nay, let us our heddes togyder cast.

FANSY
Ye[a], and se howe it may be compast
That Mesure were cast out of the dores.

COUNTERFET COUNTENAUNCE
Alasse, where is my botes and my spores?

CRAFTY CONVEYAUNCE
In all this hast whether wyll ye ryde?

COUNTERFET COUNTENAUNCE
I trowe it shall not nede to abyde.
Cockes woundes! Se, syrs, se, se!

Hic ingrediatur Cloked Colusyon cum elato aspectu, deorsum et sursum ambulando.[72]

FANSY
Cockes armes, what is he?

CRAFTY CONVEYAUNCE
By Cockes harte, he loketh hye.
He hawketh, me thynke, for a butterflye.

COUNTERFET COUNTENAUNCE
Nowe, by Cockes harte, well abyden.
For, had you not come, I had ryden.

541 He's still ruled by Measure 542 Have you plotted no better 543 a skin disease 548 all gathered together 549 it's nothing 550 this 555 phthisic (lung disease) 556 knowledgeable about medicine 557 That's a good argument . . . for a rake! 562 cross/quarrelsome 564 no one 566 put our heads together/confer 567 contrived 568 doors 569 boots, spurs 570 where 571 (i.e. 'we shouldn't delay') 572 see 574 high (in the air) 575 hunts 576 waited (on my part) 577 ridden (to find you)

72 'Here let Cloked Colusyon come in with a proud look, walking up and down.'

CLOKED COLUSYON
Thy wordes be but wynde, never they have no
wayght.
Thou hast made me play the jurde hayte.[73]

COUNTERFET COUNTENAUNCE
And yf ye knewe howe I have mused,
I am sure ye wolde have me excused.

CLOKED COLUSYON
I say com hyder. What are these twayne?

COUNTERFET COUNTENAUNCE
By God, syr, this is Fansy Small Brayne;
And Crafty Convayaunce, knowe you not hym?

CLOKED COLUSYON
'Knowe hym, syr' quod he, yes, by Saynt Sym!
Here is a leysshe of ratches to renne an hare!
Woo is that purse that ye shall share.

FANSY
What call ye him, this?

CRAFTY CONVEYAUNCE
I trowe that he is . . .

COUNTERFET COUNTENAUNCE
Tushe! Holde your pece.
Se you not howe they prece[74]
For to knowe your name?

CLOKED COLUSYON
Knowe they not me? They are to blame.
Knowe ye not me, syrs?

FANSY
No, in dede.

CRAFTY CONVEYAUNCE
Abyde! Lette me se, take better hede!
Cockes harte! It is Cloked Colusyon!

CLOKED COLUSYON
A, syr, I pray God gyve you confusyon!

FANSY
Cockes armes, is that your name?

COUNTERFET COUNTENAUNCE
Ye[a], by the Masse, this is even the same,
That all this matter must under grope.

CRAFTY CONVEYAUNCE
What is this that he wereth? A cope?[75]

CLOKED COLUSYON
Cappe, syr. I say you be to bolde.

FANSY
Se howe he is wrapped for the colde.
Is it not a vestment?

CLOKED COLUSYON
A, ye wante a rope!

COUNTERFET COUNTENAUNCE
Tushe, it is Syr John Double-cloke![76]

FANSY
Syr, and yf ye wolde not be wrothe . . .

CLOKED COLUSYON
What sayst?

FANSY
Here was to lytell clothe.

CLOKED COLUSYON
A, Fansy, Fansy, God sende the[e] brayne!

FANSY
Ye[a], for your wyt is cloked for the rayne.

CRAFTY CONVEYAUNCE
Nay, lette us not clatter thus styll.

CLOKED COLUSYON
Tell me, syrs, what is your wyll?

578 merely wind, weight 585 St Simon! 586 leash (i.e. three), hunting dogs, chase 600 investigate 601 wears, a heavy (clerical) cloak 602 too 604 clerical robe, lack (to hang yourself) 607 too 610 chatter

73 'Jurde hayte': obscure. Neuss suggests a corruption of 'John de Height', 'Lofty John' or 'tall fellow', Scattergood a version of the French '*jeu dehait*' ('joyous game').

74 'Don't you see how they [the audience] press/crowd around.'

75 Neuss suggests that Colusyon wears the cope and biretta ('cappe') of a cardinal.

76 i.e. he, like the other Vices, has more than one layer of clothing, a disguise and his true garb beneath. 'Double-cloak' also metaphorically denotes duplicity.

Counterfet Countenaunce
Syr, it is so that these twayne
With Magnyfycence in housholde do remayne;
And there they wolde ha[v]e me to dwell.
But I wyll be ruled after your counsell.

Fansy
Mary, so wyll we also.

Cloked Colusyon
But tell me where aboute ye go.

Counterfet Countenaunce
By God, we wolde gete us all thyder,
Spell the remenaunt, and do togyder.

Cloked Colusyon
Hath Magnyfycence ony tresure?

Crafty Conveyaunce
Ye[a], but he spendeth it all in Mesure.

Cloked Colusyon
Why, dwelleth Mesure where ye two dwell?
In faythe, he were better to dwell in Hell.

Fansy
Yet where we wonne nowe, there wonneth he.

Cloked Colusyon
And have you not amonge you Lyberte?

Counterfet Countenaunce
Ye[a], but he is a captyvyte.

Clokyd Colusyon
What the Devyll! Howe may that be?

Counterfet Countenaunce
I can not tell you; why aske you me?
Aske these two that there dothe dwell.

[Clokyd Colusyon]
Syr, the playnesse you tell me.

[Crafty Conveyaunce]
There dwelleth a mayster men calleth Mesure . . .

Fansy
Ye[a], and he hath rule of all his tresure.

Crafty Conveyaunce
Nay, eyther let me tell, or elles tell ye.

Fansy
I care not I; tell on for me.

Counterfet Countenaunce
I pray God let you never to thee!

Cloked Colusyon
What the Devyll ayleth you? Can you not agree?

Crafty Conveyaunce
I wyll passe over the cyrcumstaunce
And shortly shewe you the hole substaunce.
Fansy and I, we twayne,
With Magnyfycence in housholde do remay[n]e;
And counterfeted our names we have,
Craftely all thynges upryght to save:
His name Largesse, Surveyaunce myne.
Magnyfycence to us begynneth to enclyne,
Counterfet Countenaunce to have also,
And wolde that we sholde for hym go.

Counterfet Countenaunce
But shall I have myne olde name styll?

Crafty Conveyaunce
Pease! I have not yet sayd what I wyll.

Fansy
Here is a pystell of a postyke![77]

Cloked Colusyon
Tusshe, fonnysshe Fansy, thou arte frantyke!
Tell on, syr; howe then?

Crafty Conveyaunce
Mary, syr, he told us, when
We had hym founde, we sholde hym brynge,
And that we fayled not for nothynge.

Cloked Colusyon
All this ye may easely brynge aboute.

613 are placed 617 what are you trying to achieve 619 Expel everyone else, prosper 626 in 630 tell me plainly 637 detail 638 whole story 642 to make everything seem proper 644 incline 646 wishes 650 foolish, frantic/mad 651 what 654 should not fail

77 'An epistle [letter] with a postscript [or with something written on the back]!'; i.e. 'This story goes on and on!'

Fansy
Mary, the better and Mesure were out.

Cloked Colusyon
Why, can ye not put out that foule freke?

Crafty Conveyaunce
No; in every corner he wyll peke,
So that we have no lyberte;
Nor no man in courte, but he,
For Lyberte he hath in gydyng.

Counterfet Countenaunce
In fayth, and without Lyberte there is no bydyng.

Fansy
In fayth, and Lybertyes rome is there but small.

Cloked Colusyon
Hem! That lyke I nothynge at all.

[Crafty Conveyaunce]
But, Counterfet Countenaunce, go we togyder,
All thre, I say.

Counterfet Countenaunce
Shall I go? Whyder?

[Crafty Conveyaunce]
To Magnyfycence with us twayne,
And in his servyce the[e] to retayne.

Counterfet Countenaunce
But then, syr, what shall I hyght?

Crafty Conveyaunce
Ye and I talkyd therof to nyght.

Fansy
Ye[a], my Fansy was out of owle flyght[78]
For it is out of my mynde quyght.

Crafty Conveyaunce
And nowe it cometh to my remembraunce:
Syr, ye shall hyght Good Demeynaunce.

Counterfet Countenaunce
By the armes of Calys, well conceyved!

Crafty Conveyaunce
When we have hym thyder convayed,
What and I frame suche a slyght
That Fansy with his fonde consayte
Put Magnyfycence in suche a madnesse
That he shall have you in the stede of sadnesse,
And Sober Sadnesse shalbe your name?

Cloked Colusyon
By Cockys body, here begynneth the game!
For then shall we so craftely cary
That Mesure shall not there longe tary.

Fansy
For Cockys harte, tary whylyst that I come agayne.

Crafty Conveyaunce
We wyll se you shortly, one of us twayne.

Counterfet Countenaunce
Now let us go, and we shall, then.

Cloked Colusyon
Nowe let se; quyte you lyke praty men.

{Exit Fansy, Crafty Conveyaunce, and Counterfet Countenaunce.} Hic deambulat {Cloked Colusyon}.[79]

To passe the tyme and order whyle a man may talke
Of one thynge and other to occupy the place,
Then for the season that I here shall walke
As good to be occupyed as up and downe to trace
And do nothynge. How be it full lytell grace
There cometh and groweth of my comynge,
For Clokyd Colusyon is a perylous thynge.

Double delynge and I be all one;
Craftynge and haftynge contryved is by me.
I can dyssemble, I can bothe laughe and grone;
Playne delynge and I can never agre.
But dyvysyon, dyssencyon, dyrysyon; these thre
And I, am counterfet of one mynde and thought,
By the menys of Myschyef to brynge all thynges to nought.

656 if, expelled **657** fellow **658** peek/search **661** under (his) guidance **662** abiding/tolerating (it) **663** place, only **664** I don't like that at all **669** call myself **670** about that last night **674** Demeanour/Behaviour **675** Calais (a mild oath) **677** if, devise, sleight/trick **678** madcap ideas **680** place, seriousness **683** succeed **685** whilst/until **688** acquit yourselves, cunning **689** arrange (things) **692** (It's) as good, pace **694** from **696** identical **697** Trickery, cheating **698** groan **700** derision **702** means

78 i.e. 'My mind was far away'. Fansy picks up on the mention of 'last night', as 'the owl flight' is a synonym for 'the evening'.

79 'Here let [Cloked Colusyon] walk about.'

And though I be so odyous a geste,
And every man gladly my company wolde refuse,
In faythe, yet am I occupyed with the best;
Full fewe that can themselfe of me excuse.
Whan other men laughe than study I and muse,
Devysynge the meanes and wayes that I can,
Howe I may hurte and hynder every man.

Two faces in a hode covertly I bere;
Water in the one hande and fyre in the other.
I can fede forth a fole and lede hym by the eyre:
Falshode-in-Felowshyp is my sworne brother.
By Cloked Colusyon, I say, and none other,
Comberaunce and trouble in Englande fyrst I began:
From that lorde to that lorde I rode and I ran,

And flatered them with fables fayre before theyr face,
And tolde all the myschyef I coude behynde theyr backe,
And made as I had knowen nothynge of the case.
I wolde begyn all myschyef, but I wolde bere no lacke.
Thus can I lerne you, syrs, to bere the Devyls sacke;
And yet, I trowe, some of you be better sped than I
Frendshyp to fayne and thynke full lytherly.

Paynte to a purpose good countenaunce I can,
And craftely can I grope howe every man is mynded.
My purpose is to spy and to poynte every man;
My tonge is with favell forked and tyned.
By Cloked Colusyon thus many one is begyled.
Eche man to hynder I gape and gaspe.
My speche is all pleasure, but I stynge lyke a waspe.

I am never glad but whan I may do yll,
And never am I sory but whan that I se
I can not myne appetyte accomplysshe and fulfyll
In hynderaunce of welthe and prosperyte.
I laughe at all shrewdenes, and lye at lyberte.
I muster, I medle amonge these grete estates;
I sowe sedycyous sedes of dyscorde and debates.

To flater and to flery is all my pretence
Amonge all suche persones as I well understonde
Be lyght of byleve and hasty of credence.
I make them to startyll and sparkyll lyke a bronde.
I move them, I mase them, I make them so fonde,
That they wyll here no man but the fyrst tale;
And so by these meanes I brewe moche bale.

Hic ingrediatur Courtly Abusyon cantando.[80]

Courtly Abusyon
Huffa, huffa taunderum, taunderum tayne, huffa, huffa!

Cloked Colusyon
[*Aside*] This was properly prated, syrs. What sayd a?

Courtly Abusyon
Rutty bully joly rutterkyn, heyda!

Cloked Colusyon
De que pays este vous?

Et faciat tanquem ex{u}at beretum ironice.[81]

Courtly Abusyon
Decke your hofte and cover a lowce.

Cloked Colusyon
Say vous Chaunter 'Venter tre dawce'?[82]

Courtly Abusyon:
Wyda, wyda. Howe sayst thou, man? Am not I a joly rutter?

Cloked Colusyon
Gyve this gentylman rome, syrs, stonde utter!
By God, syr, what nede all this waste?
What is this, a betell, or a batowe, or a buskyn lacyd?[83]

703 guest/fellow 705 used by 706 (there are) very few 710 hood, bear 712 encourage, ear 713 Falsehood 715 Calamity 716 From this . . . to that 719 as (if), nothing about it 720 blame 721 (i.e. do the Devil's work) 722 better accomplished 723 feign, wickedly 724 Paint/pretend (when I want something) 725 discover 726 point (out) 727 flattery, pronged 729 strive (for) and desire 730 pleasant 733 satisfy my desire 735 evil/villainy, with impunity 736 display myself, lords 737 seditious seeds 738 smile ingratiatingly 740 gullible, credulous 741 start, sparkle, firebrand 742 confuse, foolish 743 hear, the first lie they're told 744 torment 745 (tags from courtly songs) 746 prattled, What did he say 747 fine little gallant, oui (more tags) 748 From which country are you 749 roof/ cover, head, louse 751 oui, da (yes, yes) 752 room, aside

[80] 'Here let Courtly Abusyon enter, singing.'
[81] 'And let him ironically pretend to doff his cap.' Colusyon mockingly adopts the French language and manners of the courtier.
[82] 'Can you sing . . . ?' The allusion seems to be to the song '*Votre très douce regaunt pleasaunt*', but Colusyon (perhaps deliberately) misrenders it '*Ventre tres douce*': 'Very soft belly'.
[83] 'A beetle, a boat, or a laced knee-boot?' Colusyon is mocking Abusyon's fashionable boots.

Courtly Abusyon
What? Wenyst thou that I knowe the[e] not, Clokyd Colusyon?

Cloked Colusyon
And wenyst thou that I knowe not the[e], cankard Abusyon?

Courtly Abusyon
Cankard? Jacke Hare,[84] loke thou be not rusty;
For thou shalt well knowe I am nother durty nor dusty.

Cloked Colusyon
Dusty? Nay, syr, ye be all of the lusty.
Howe be it, of scape thryfte your clokes smelleth musty.
But whether art thou walkynge, in fayth unfaynyd?

Courtly Abusyon
Mary, with Magnyfycence I wolde be retaynyd.

Cloked Colusyon
By the Masse, for the cowrte thou art a mete man;
Thy slyppers they swap it, yet thou fotys it lyke a swanne.

Courtly Abusyon
Ye[a], so I can devyse my gere after the cowrtly maner.

Cloked Colusyon
So thou art personable to bere a prynces baner.
By Goddes fote, and I dare well fyght, for I wyll not start.

Courtly Abusyon
Nay, thou art a man good inough but for thy false hart.

Cloked Colusyon
Well, and I be a coward, ther is mo than I.

Courtly Abusyon
Ye[a], in faythe, a bolde man and a hardy.

Cloked Colusyon
A bolde man in a bole of newe ale in cornys.

Courtly Abusyon:
[*Aside*] Wyll ye se this gentylman is all in his skornys?

Cloked Colusyon
But are ye not avysed to dwell where ye spake?

Courtly Abusyon
I am of fewe wordys; I love not to barke.
Beryst thou any rome? Or cannyst thou do ought?[85]
Cannyst thou helpe in faver that I myght be brought?

Cloked Colusyon
I may do somwhat, and more I thynke shall.

Here cometh in Crafty Conveyaunce poyntyng with his fynger, and sayth:

[Crafty Conveyaunce]
Hem, Colusyon!

Courtly Abusyon
Cockys hart! Who is yonde[86] that for the[e] dothe call?

[Crafty Conveyaunce]
Nay, come at ones, for the armys of the dyce!

Courtly Abusyon:
Cockys armys! He hath callyd for the[e] twyce.

Cloked Colusyon
By Cockys harte! And call shall agayne;
To come to me I trowe he shalbe fayne.

Courtly Abusyon
What, is thy harte pryckyd with such a prowde pynne?[87]

Cloked Colusyon
Tushe, he that hath nede, man, let hym rynne.

756 cankered/rusty 759 lustiest/most fashionable 760 because you're a spendthrift 761 where, going, unfeigned? 763 court 764 flap about, step out 765 design, clothes 767 suitable, banner 768 flee 771 bowl, malt-ale 772 scorns/mockery 773 advised 776 into (royal) favour 779 arms, dice (a gambler's oath) 782 obliged

84 A stock name for a lazy, foolish character; the subject of a ballad by John Lydgate.

85 'Do you hold a position of authority [at court]? Or can you do anything [to help me]?'

86 '[That fellow] there'.

87 'Inclined to such proud behaviour.' An allusion to the practice of selecting names from lists by marking them with a pin-prick. Colusyon has been 'pricked out' by pride.

Crafty Conveyaunce
Nay, come away, man; thou playst the Cayser.

[Cloked Colusyon]
By the Masse, thou shalt byde my leyser.

Crafty Conveyaunce
'Abyde, syr', quod he? Mary, so I do.

Courtly Abusyon
He wyll come, man, when he may tende to.

Crafty Conveyaunce
What the Devyll! Who sent for the[e]?

Cloked Colusyon
Here he is nowe, man; mayst thou not se?

Crafty Conveyaunce
What the Devyll, man, what thou menyst?
Art thou so angry as thou semyst?

Courtly Abusyon:
What the Devyll! Can ye agre no better?

Crafty Conveyaunce
What the Devyll! Where had we this joly jetter?

Cloked Colusyon:
What sayst thou, man? Why dost thou not supplye?
And desyre me thy good mayster to be?

Courtly Abusyon
Spekest thou to me?

Cloked Colusyon
Ye[a], so I tell the[e].

Courtly Abusyon
Cockes bones! I ne tell can
Whiche of you is the better man,
Or whiche of you can do most.

Crafty Conveyaunce
In fayth, I rule moche of the rost.

Cloked Colusyon
Rule the roste! Ye[a], thou woldest,
As skante thou had no nede of me.

Crafty Conveyaunce
Nede? Yes, mary. I say not nay.

Courtly Abusyon
Cockes ha[r]te! I trowe thou wylte make a fray.

Crafty Conveyaunce
Nay, in good faythe; it is but the gyse.

Cloked Colusyon
No; for or we stryke, we wyll be advysed twyse.

Courtly Abusyon
What the Devyll! Use ye not to drawe no swordes?

Crafty Conveyaunce
No, by my trouthe; but crake grete wordes.

Courtly Abusyon
Why, is this the gyse nowe adayes?

Cloked Colusyon
Ye[a], for surety; ofte peas is taken for frayes.
But, syr, I wyll have this man with me.

Crafty Conveyaunce
Convey yourselfe fyrst, let se.

Cloked Colusyon
Well, tarry here tyll I for you sende.

Crafty Conveyaunce
Why, shall he be of your bende?

Cloked Colusyon
Tary here; wote ye what I say?

Courtly Abusyon
I waraunt you I wyll not go away.

Crafty Conveyaunce
By Saynt Mary, he is a tawle man.

Cloked Colusyon
Ye[a], and do ryght good servyce he can.
I knowe in hym no defaute
But that the horson is prowde and hawte.

And so they go out of the place.

785 kaiser/caesar (i.e. behave imperiously) 786 wait upon my leisure 788 attend to (it) 791 what do you mean? 794 pretty poseur 795 supplicate/bow to me 799 cannot tell 801 most (for me) 802 roost 804 As if you had little need of me 806 an affray 808 before, we'll think twice 809 Don't you draw swords 810 boast 812 certainly, peace, mistaken 814 Let's see (you) 816 band 819 tall/strong 821 flaw 822 haughty

Courtly Abusyon
Nay, purchace ye a pardon for the pose;
For pryde hath plucked the[e] by the nose
As well as me; I wolde, and I durste . . .
But nowe I wyll not say the worste.

Courtly Abusyon alone in the place.

Courtly Abusyon
What nowe? Let se
Who loketh on me
Well rounde aboute,
Howe gay and howe stoute
That I can were
Courtly my gere.

My heyre bussheth
So plesauntly,
My robe russheth
So ruttyngly,
Me seme I flye
I am so lyght
To daunce delyght.

Properly drest
All poynte devyse,
My persone prest
Beyonde all syse
Of the newe gyse,
To russhe it oute
In every route.

Beyonde Measure
My sleve is wyde,
Al of pleasure
My hose strayte tyde,
My buskyn wyde
Ryche to beholde,
Gletterynge in golde.

Abusyon
Forsothe I hyght;
Confusyon
Shall on hym lyght
By day or by nyght
That useth me:
He can not thee.

A very fon,
A very asse
Wyll take upon
To compasse
That never was
Abusyd before;
A very pore

That so wyll do,
He doth abuse
Hym selfe to to;
He dothe mysse use
Eche man take a fe[88]
To crake and prate;
I befoule his pate.[89]

This newe fonne jet
From out of Fraunce
Fyrst I dyd set,
Made purveaunce
And suche ordenaunce,
That all men it founde
Through out Englonde,

All this nacyon
I set on fyre;
In my facyon
This theyr desyre
This newe atyre;
This ladyes have:
I it them gave.

Spare for no coste:
And yet in dede
It is coste loste
Moche more than nede
For to excede
In suche aray.
Howe be it, I say,

823 catarrh 825 if I dared 828 looks at 830 fine 831 wear 832 my courtly clothes 833 hair spreads out like a bush 835 flaunts/hangs 836 gallantly 837 It seems to me 839 dance (with) 840 dressed 841 perfectly arranged 842 neat 843 measure 845 swagger 846 crowd 850 tightly laced 851 boot(s) 857 fall upon him 859 Who 861 fool 863 undertake 864 attempt 865 What 867 poor (fellow) 868 Who tries to do so 870 excessively 871 misuse 872 everyone 875 foolish style 878 provision 879 ordinance 882 nation 886 attire 888 gave it to them 889 cost 891 money wasted

88 Obscure. Neuss suggests a printer's error for 't'accuse'.

89 Either 'I be-fool his head (i.e. prove him foolish)', or 'I shit upon his head.'

A carlys sonne,
Brought up of nought,
Wyth me wyll wonne
Whylyst he hath ought.
He wyll have wrought
His gowne so wyde
That he may hyde

His dame and his syre
Within his slyve;
Spende all his hyre
That men hym gyve;
Wherfore I preve
A Tyborne checke
Shall breke his necke.

Here cometh in Fansy crayinge:

[FANSY]
Stow, Stow!

[COURTLY ABUSYON]
All is out of harre
And out of trace,
Ay warre and warre
In every place.

But what the Devyll art thou
That cryest 'Stow, stow'?

FANSY
What? Whom have we here, Jenkyn Joly?
Nowe welcom, by the God holy!

COURTLY ABUSYON
What, Fansy, my frende! Howe doste thou fare?

FANSY
By Cryst, as mery as a Marche hare.

COURTLY ABUSYON
What the Devyll hast thou on thy fyste? An owle?

FANSY
Nay, it is a farly fowle.[90]

COURTLY ABUSYON
Me thynke she frowneth and lokys sowre.

FANSY
Torde, man; it is an hawke of the towre![91]
She is made for the malarde fat.[92]

COURTLY ABUSYON
Methynke she is well becked to catche a rat
But nowe what tydynges can you tell? Let se.

FANSY
Mary, I am come for the[e].

COURTLY ABUSYON:
For me?

FANSY
Ye[a], for the[e], so I say.

COURTLY ABUSYON
Howe so? Tell me, I the[e] pray.

FANSY
Why, harde thou not of the fray
That fell amonge us this same day?

COURTLY ABUSYON
No, mary; not yet.

FANSY
What the Devyll! Never a whyt?

COURTLY ABUSYON
No, by the Masse; what, sholde I swere?

FANSY
In faythe, Lyberte is nowe a lusty spere.

COURTLY ABUSYON
Why, under whom was he abydynge?

FANSY
Mary, Mesure had hym a whyle in gydynge,
Tyll, as the Devyll wolde, they fell a chydynge
With Crafty Convayaunce.

896 churl's son 897 from nothing 899 anything 903 mother and father 904 sleeve 905 wages 907 prove 908 setback (i.e. a hanging) 908+ crying 910 Stop! (a cry used in falconry) 911 unhinged 912 control 913 Always worse 917 'Madcap John' (a fool) 920 (i.e. mad) 921 fist 923 frowns, looks sour 926 beaked 934 Not (even) a bit? 935 do I have to swear (it) to you 936 one of the King's Spears (royal bodyguard) 937 serving 939 fell to fighting

[90] 'A marvellous bird.' Despite Fansy's denials, the bird probably is an owl, and thus a suitably ignoble 'hawk' for a fool to own.

[91] 'Shit, man; it's a hawk of the tower!' 'Of the tower' is a technical term from falconry indicating the highest flying position, the implication being that this is the finest of hunting birds.

[92] 'She's [just] made for catching fat wild ducks.'

Courtly Abusyon
Ye[a], dyd they so?

Fansy
Ye[a], by Goddes Sacrament; and with other mo.

Courtly Abusyon
What! Neded that, in the Dyvyls date?[93]

Fansy
Yes, yes; he fell with me also at debate.

Courtly Abusyon
With the[e] also? What! He playeth the state?

Fansy
Ye[a]; but I bade hym pyke out of the gate;
By Goddes body, so dyd I!

Courtly Abusyon
[*Ironically*] By the Masse, well done and boldely.

Fansy
Holde thy pease! Measure shall frome us walke.

Courtly Abusyon
Why, is he crossed than with a chalke?

Fansy
Crossed? Ye[a], checked out of consayte.

Courtly Abusyon
Howe so?

Fansy
By God, by a praty slyght,
As here after thou shalte knowe more.
But I must tary here; go thou before.

Courtly Abusyon
With whom shall I there mete?

Fansy
Crafty Conveyaunce standeth in the strete
Even of purpose for the same.

Courtly Abusyon
Ye[a], but what shall I call my name?

Fansy
Cockes harte! Tourne the[e], let me se thyne aray
Cockes bones! This is all of John de Gay!

Courtly Abusyon
So I am poynted after my consayt.

Fansy
Mary, thou jettes it of hyght.

Courtly Abusyon
Ye[a], but of my name let us be wyse.

Fansy
Mary, Lusty Pleasure, by myne advyse
To name thyselfe; come of, it were done.

Courtly Abusyon
Farewell, my frende.

Fansy
Adue tyll sone.

[*Exit Courtly Abusyon.*]

Fansy
Stowe, byrde, stowe, stowe!
It is best I fede my hawke now.
There is many evyll faveryd, and thou be foule![94]
Eche thynge is fayre when it is yonge; all hayle,
owle!

Lo, this is
My Fansy, iwys.
Nowe Cryst it blysse!
It is, by Jesse,
A byrde full swete,
For me full mete.
She is furred for the hete
All to the fete;

Her browys bent,
Her eyen glent.

941 others too 944 the statesman 945 get out of the door 946 so I did (emphatic) 948 from 949 crossed off the list (no longer relevant)? 950 erased from all favour 951 clever trick 956 Especially for that purpose 958 turn around 959 (i.e. 'Look at Mr Smart!') 960 appointed/dressed 961 strut about haughtily 964 Come on, it's settled 965 Adieu 972 bless it! 976 heat 977 Right down to the feet 979 glinting

93 'Was that necessary, in the Devil's date?' The latter phrase is an oath of the 'in God's name' kind.

94 '[*To the owl*] If you're ugly [and with the obvious pun, 'if you're a bird'] there are a lot of people [i.e. in the audience] with [equally] unfortunate faces!'

Frome Tyne to Trent,
From Stroude to Kent,[95]

A man shall fynde
Many of her kynde,
Howe standeth the wynde,
Before or behynde;

Barbyd lyke a nonne
For burnynge of the sonne;
Her fethers donne.
Well faveryd bonne!

Nowe let me se about
In all this rowte
Yf I can fynde owt
So semely a snowte

Amonge this prese
Even a hole mese[96]
[*To a spectator?*] Pease, man, pease!
I rede we sease.

So farly fayre as it lokys!
And her becke so comely crokys!
Her naylys sharpe as tenter hokys![97]
I have not kept her yet thre wokys,

And howe styll she dothe sytt
Te[w]yt, te[w]yt!
Where is my wyt?[98]
The devyll spede whyt!

That was before I set behynde:
Nowe to curteys, forwith unkynde;
Somtyme to sober, somtyme to sadde,
Somtyme to mery, somtyme to madde;
Somtyme I syt as I were a solempe prowde,
Somtyme I laughe over lowde;
Somtyme I wepe for a gew-gaw,
Somtyme I laughe at waggynge of a straw;
With a pere my love you may wynne,
And ye may lese it for a pynne.
I have a thynge for to say,
(And I may tende therto) for play.
But, in faythe, I am so occupyed
On this halfe and on every syde
That I wote not where I may rest.
Fyrst to tell you what were best,
Frantyke Fansy Servyce I hyght:
My wyttys be weke, my braynys are lyght,
For it is I that other whyle
Plucke down lede, and theke with tyle.[99]
Nowe I wyll this, and nowe I wyll that,
Make a wyndmyll of a mat.
Nowe I wolde . . . and I wyst what . . .
Where is my cappe? I have lost my hat!
And within an houre after,
Plucke downe an house and set up a rafter.
Hyder and thyder, I wote not whyder;
Do and undo, bothe togyder.
Of a spyndell I wyll make a sparre;
All that I make forthwith I marre.
I blunder, I bluster, I blowe, and I blother,
I make on the one day, and I marre on the other.
Bysy, bysy, and ever bysy,
I daunce up and downe tyll I am dyssy;
I can fynde fantasyes where none is.
I wyll not have it so, I wyll have it this.

Hic ingrediatur Foly qu[at]iendo crema et faciendo Multum feriendo tabulas et similia.[100]

FOLY
Maysters, Cryst save everychone!
What Fansy, arte thou here alone?

FANSY
What fonnysshe Foly! I befole thy face.

984 However 986 With a white head-dress, nun 987 Against the 988 dun/dark 989 fair pretty thing 991 crowd 992 discover 993 fine a snout 994 throng 997 cease (looking) 998 amazingly fair, looks 999 is bent so attractively 1001 weeks 1005 (i.e. a curse on wit!) 1006 What 1007 too courteous, immediately 1011 too loudly 1012 over a trifle 1013 shaking 1014 pear 1015 pin 1017 (if I can concentrate for long enough) 1019 side 1027 (i.e. a foolish idea) 1028 if I knew what 1034 spindle, spar 1036 babble 1039 dizzy 1041 that way . . . this way

95 'From the river Tyne [in the north] to the Trent [in the Midlands], from Stroud [Gloucestershire] to Kent': i.e. throughout England.

96 'A whole mess', i.e. a group of diners sharing the same 'mess' of dishes.

97 'Tenter hooks' were used to stretch cloth on a frame.

98 'Tuwhit', an owl call. Fansy, speaking to the bird, realizes he is revealing her owlish nature to the audience and so tries to change the subject.

99 'Pull down [expensive] lead roofing and cover [i.e. replace it] with [less expensive, ceramic] tiles.'

100 'Here let Foly enter [leading a dog], shaking his bauble and making a noise, banging on drums [or tables], and things like that.' While Fansy conceals his fool's garb, Foly wears his openly.

Foly
What frantyke Fansy, in a foles case?
What is this, an owle or a glede?
By my trouthe, she hathe a grete hede.

Fansy
Tusshe, thy lyppes hange in thyne eyen;[101]
It is a Frenche butterflye.

Foly
By my trouthe, I trowe well;
But she is lesse a grete dele
Than a butterflye of our lande.

Fansy
What pylde curre ledest thou in thy hande?

Foly
A pylde curre?

Fansy
Ye[a], so I tell the[e], a pylde curre.

Foly
Yet I solde his skynne to Mackemurre
In the stede of a budge furre.

Fansy
What, fleyest thou his skynne every yere?

Foly
Yes, in faythe, I thanke God I may here.[102]

Fansy
What, thou wylte coughe me a dawe for forty pens?

Foly
Mary, syr, Cokermowthe is a good way hens.

Fansy
What, of Cokermowth spake I no worde.

Foly
By my faythe, syr, the frubyssher hath my sworde.

Fansy
A, I trowe ye shall coughe me a fole.

Foly
In faythe, trouthe ye say we wente togyder to scole.

Fansy
Ye[a], but I can somwhat more of the letter.

Foly
I wyll not gyve an halfepeny for to chose the better.

Fansy
But, broder Foly, I wonder moche of one thynge,
That thou so hye fro me doth sprynge,
And I so lytell alway styll.

Foly
By God, I can tell the[e], and I wyll:
Thou art so feble-fantastycall,
And so braynsyke therwithall,
And thy wyt wanderynge here and there,
That thou cannyst not growe out of thy boyes gere.
And as for me, I take but one folysshe way,
And therfore I growe more on one day
Than thou can in yerys seven.

Fansy
In faythe, trouth thou sayst nowe, by God of Heven!
For so with fantasyes my wyt dothe flete
That wysdome and I shall seldome mete.
Nowe of good Felowshyp, let me by thy [d]ogge.

Foly
Cockys harte, thou lyest; I am no [h]ogge.

Fansy
Here is no man that callyd the[e] hogge nor swyne.

Foly
In faythe, man, my brayne is as good as thyne.

Fansy
The Devyls torde for thy brayne!

1045 fool's costume 1046 falcon 1047 large head 1051 a lot smaller 1053 bald cur 1055 An Irishman (proverbially poor and foolish) 1056 lambskin 1057 do you flay 1058 can hear 1059 make a fool of me 1060 Cockermouth (Cumberland) 1062 furbisher (repair man) 1064 school 1065 I learnt rather more 1066 which (of us) is better 1067 about 1068 tall, have grown 1071 feeble-minded 1072 brainsick 1074 clothes 1077 years 1079 drift/overflow 1081 buy

[101] i.e. 'You're talking so much you cannot see'.
[102] At this point Foly begins to pretend that he is deaf, and 'mishears' all Fansy's subsequent remarks.

FOLY
By my syers soule, I fele no rayne.

FANSY
By the Masse, I holde the[e] madde.

FOLY
Mary, I knew the[e] when thou waste a ladde.

FANSY
[*Aside*] Cockys bonys, herde ye ever syke another?

FOLY
[*Aside*] Ye[a], a fole the tone, and a fole the tother.

FANSY
Nay, but wotest thou what I do say?

FOLY
Why, sayst thou that I was here yesterday?

FANSY
Cockys armys, this is warke, I trowe.

FOLY
What, callyst thou me a donnyshe crowe?

FANSY
Nowe, in good faythe, thou art a fonde gest.

FOLY
Ye[a], bere me this strawe to a dawys nest.

FANSY
What, wenyst thou that I were so folysshe and so fonde?

FOLY
In fayth, ellys is there none in all Englonde.

FANSY
Yet for my fansy sake, I say,
Let me have thy dogge, what soever I pay.

FOLY
Thou shalte have my purse, and I wyll have thyne.

FANSY
By my trouth, there is myne.

FOLY
Nowe, by my trouth, man, take, there is myne;
And I beshrowe hym that hath the worse.

FANSY
Torde, I say! What have I do?
Here is nothynge but the bockyll of a sho,
And in my purse was twenty marke.[103]

FOLY
Ha, ha, ha! Herke, syrs, harke!
For all that my name hyght Foly,
By the Masse, yet art thou more fole than I.

FANSY
Yet gyve me thy dogge, and I am content;
And thou shalte have my hauke to a botchment.

FOLY
That ever thou thryve, God it forfende!
For Goddes cope, thou wyll spende.
Nowe take thou my dogge and gyve me thy fowle.

FANSY
[*To the dog*] Hay, Chysshe, come
hyder!

FOLY
Nay torde, take hym be tyme.

FANSY
What callest thou thy dogge?

FOLY
Tusshe, his name is
Gryme.

FANSY
Come, Gryme! Come, Gryme! It is my praty dogges.

FOLY
In faythe, there is not a better dogge for hogges,
Not from Anwyke unto Aungey.

FANSY
Ye[a], but trowest thou that he be not maungey?

1086 father's, rain 1089 such (i.e. anyone like him?) 1090 one, other 1093 (hard) work 1094 dunnish (dark) 1095 foolish fellow 1096 carry, jackdaw's/fool's 1105 done 1106 buckle, shoe 1112 as a makeweight 1113 If you ever, forbid 1114 cloak 1116 quickly 1118 'It is' (baby talk) 1120 Alnwick (Northumberland), Angers (France) 1121 mangy

103 As a mark was worth 13 shillings and 4 pence, this may well be a lie.

FOLY
No, by my trouthe; it is but the scurfe and the scabbe.

FANSY
What? He hathe ben hurte with a stabbe?

FOLY
Nay, in faythe; it was but a strype
That the horson had for etynge of a trype.

FANSY
Where the Devyll gate he all these hurtes?

FOLY
By God, for snatchynge of puddynges and wortes.

FANSY
What, then he is some good poore mannes curre?

FOLY
Ye[a], but he wyll in at every mannes dore.

FANSY
Nowe thou hast done me a pleasure grete.

FOLY
In faythe, I wolde thou had a marmosete.

FANSY
Cockes harte, I love suche japes.

FOLY
Ye[a], for all thy mynde is on owles and apes;
But I have thy pultre, and thou hast my catell.

FANSY
Ye[a], but thryfte and we have made a batell.

FOLY
Remembrest thou not the japes and the toyes . . .

FANSY
What, that we used whan we were boyes?

FOLY
Ye[a], by the Rode, even the same.

FANSY
Yes, yes, I am yet as full of game
As ever I was, and as full of tryfyls
Nil, *nichelum*, *nihil*, *anglice*, nyfyls.[104]

FOLY
What, canest thou all this L[a]tin yet
And hath so mased a wandrynge wyt?

FANSY
Tushe, man! I kepe some Latyn in store.

FOLY
By Cockes harte, I wene thou hast no more!

FANSY
No? Yes in faythe; I can versyfy.

FOLY
Then I pray the[e] hartely
Make a verse of my butterfly;
It forseth not of the reason, so it kepe ryme.[105]

FANSY
But wylte thou make another on Gryme?

FOLY
Nay, in fayth fyrst let me here thyne.

FANSY
Mary, as for that, thou shalte sone here myne.
Versus: Est snavi snago[106] with a shrewde face; *vilis imago*.

FOLY
Grimbald[*us*][107] gredy snatche a puddyng tyl the rost be redy.

FANSY
By the harte of God, well done!

FOLY
Ye[a], so redely and so sone!

Here cometh in Crafty Conveyaunce.

1122 scurf, scab (skin diseases) 1124 cut 1125 eating, tripe (ox's stomach) 1126 did he get, wounds 1127 blood-sausages, vegetables 1129 (get) in 1133 (i.e. ugly, foolish things) 1134 poultry (bird), cattle (dog) 1135 (i.e. are at odds) 1136 games 1138 Cross 1140 trifles 1143 baffled 1148 about 1153 verses, vile face 1154 until, roast 1156 readily

104 'Nothing, nothing, nothing; in English: nothings.'
105 'It doesn't have to make sense, just so long as it rhymes.'
106 Neuss amends to '*Est Suavis Vago*' and suggests a mock-Latin compliment: 'It is a sweet wag'.
107 Mock-Latin title: 'Gryme-the-bald-one'?

Crafty Conveyaunce
What, Fansy! Let me se who is the tother.

Fansy
By God, syr, Foly, myne owne sworne brother.

Crafty Conveyaunce
Cockys bonys, it is a farle freke;
Can he play well at the hoddypeke?

Fansy
Tell by thy trouth what sport can thou make.

Foly
A, holde thy peas! I have the tothe ake.

Crafty Conveyaunce
The tothe ake! Lo, a torde ye have.

Foly
Ye[a], thou haste the four quarters of a knave.[108]

Crafty Conveyaunce
Wotyst thou, I say, to whom thou spekys?

Fansy
Nay, by Cockys harte, he ne reckys.
For he wyll speke to Magnyfycence thus.

Crafty Conveyaunce
Cockys armys! a mete man for us.

Foly
What, wolde ye have mo folys, and are so many?

Fansy
Nay, offer hym a counter in stede of a peny.

Crafty Conveyaunce
Why, thynkys thou he can no better skyll?

Foly
In fayth, I can make you bothe folys, and I wyll.

Crafty Conveyaunce
What haste thou on thy fyst? A [k]esteryll?

Foly
Nay, iwys, fole; it is a doteryll.

Crafty Conveyaunce
In a cote thou can play well the dyser.

Foly
Ye[a], but thou can play the fole without a vyser.

Fansy
[*To Conveyaunce*] Howe rode he by you? Howe put he to you?[109]

Crafty Conveyaunce
Mary, as thou sayst, he gave me a blurre.
But where gatte thou that mangey curre?

Fansy
Mary, it was his, and now it is myne.

Crafty Conveyaunce
And was it his, and nowe it is thyne?
Thou must have thy fansy and thy wyll,
But yet thou shalt holde me a fole styll.

Foly
Why, wenyst thou that I cannot make the[e] play the fon?

Fansy
Yes, by my faythe, good Syr John.

Crafty Conveyaunce
For you bothe it were inough.[110]

Foly
Why, wenyst thou that I were as moche a fole as thou?

Fansy
Nay, nay; thou shalte fynde hym another maner of man.

Foly
In faythe, I can do mastryes, so I can.

Crafty Conveyaunce
What canest thou do but play Cocke Wat?

1159 strange fellow 1160 simpleton 1162 tooth 1165 Do you know, speak 1166 doesn't care 1170 brass counter 1171 can't tell the difference? 1173 kestrel 1174 plover/idiot 1175 In (the right) clothes, jester 1176 mask 1178 glancing blow/flesh wound 1185 slang: a priest 1189 great deeds 1190 play the fool

[108] Suggesting both 'you're a complete rogue' and 'you deserve to be hanged, drawn, and quartered as one.'

[109] Jousting terms: 'He scored a point against you there, didn't he?'

[110] 'It would take two of you [to make a fool of me].'

Fansy
Yes, yet he wyll make the ete a gnat.

Foly
Yet, yes, by my trouth I holde the[e] a grote
That I shall laughe the[e] out of thy cote.

Crafty Conveyaunce
Than wyll I say that thou haste no pere.

Fansy
Nowe, by the Rode, and he wyll go nere.

Foly
Hem, Fansy! *Regardes, voyes!*

Here Foly maketh semblaunt to take a lowse[111] *from Crafty Conveyaunce showlder*

Fansy
What hast thou founde there?

Foly
By God, a lowse.

Crafty Conveyaunce
By Cockes harte, I trowe thou lyste.

Foly
By the Masse, a Spaynysshe moght with a gray lyste!

Fansy
Ha, ha, ha, ha, ha, ha!

Crafty Conveyaunce
Cockes armes! It is not so, I trowe:

Here Crafty Con{ve}yaunce putteth of{f} his gown.

Foly
Put on thy gowne agayne, for nowe thou has lost.

Fansy
Lo, John a Bonam, where is thy brayne?
Nowe put on, fole, thy cote agayne.

Foly
Gyve me my grote, for thou hast lost.

Here Foly maketh semblaunt to take money of Crafty Conveyaunce, saynge to hym:

Shyt thy purse, dawe, and do no cost.

Fansy
Nowe hast thou not a prowde mocke and a starke?[112]

Crafty Conveyaunce
With yes, by the Rode of Wodstocke Parke!

Fansy
Nay, I tell the[e], he maketh no dowtes
To tourne a fole out of his clowtes.

Crafty Conveyaunce
And for a fole a man wolde hym take.

Foly
Nay, it is I that foles can make;
For be he cayser, or be he kynge,
To felowshyp with Foly I can hym brynge.

Fansy
Nay, wylte thou here nowe of his scoles,
And what maner of people he maketh foles?

Crafty Conveyaunce
Ye[a], let us here a worde or twayne.

Foly
Syr, of my maner I shall tell you the playne:
Fyrst I lay before them my bybyll
And teche them howe they sholde syt ydyll
To pyke theyr fyngers all the day longe;
So in theyr eyre I synge them a songe
And make them so longe to muse
That some of them renneth strayght to the stuse
To thefte and bryboury I make some fall,
And pyke a locke and clyme a wall;
And where I spy a nysot gay
That wyll syt ydyll all the day
And can not set herselfe to warke,
I kyndell in her suche a lyther sparke
That rubbed she must be on the gall
Bytwene the tap[pet] and the wall.

1191 he'll fool you **1192** wager, groat (a coin worth four pence) **1195** come close **1196** Look at this **1198** are lying **1199** moth, grey stripe **1201+** takes off **1203** fool **1206** shut, fool, lose no money **1208** Woodstock (Oxfordshire), a royal palace **1209** doesn't scruple **1210** clothes **1213** emperor **1215** doctrine **1218** plain (truth) **1219** Bible **1220** idle **1221** pick **1222** ear **1224** brothels **1225** pilfering **1226** climb **1227** fine wanton (woman) **1230** wicked **1231** sore place (with sexual connotations) **1232** tapestry (where lovers might hide)

111 'Pretends to take a louse'.

112 'Haven't you received a thorough and splendid mock?'

CRAFTY CONVEYAUNCE
What, horson, arte thou suche a one?

FANSY
Nay, beyonde all other set hym alone.

CRAFTY CONVEYAUNCE
Hast thou ony more? Let se, procede.

FOLY
Ye[a], by God, syr, for a nede
I have another maner of sorte,
That I laugh at for my dysporte;
And those be they that come up of nought,
(As some be not fer[r]e and yf it were well
sought!)[113]
Suche dawys, what soever they be,
That be set in auctorite,
Anone he waxyth so hy and prowde,
He frownyth fyersly brymly browde.
The knave wolde make it koy, and he cowde
All that he dothe muste be alowde;
And 'this is not well done, syr; take hede';[114]
And maketh hym besy where is no nede.
He dawnsys so long 'Hey troly loly',
That every man lawghyth at his foly.

CRAFTY CONVEYAUNCE
By the good Lorde, truthe he sayth.

FANSY
Thynkest thou not so, by thy fayth?

CRAFTY CONVEYAUNCE
'Thynke I not so', quod he? Ellys have I shame,
For I knowe dyverse that useth the same.

FOLY
But nowe, forsothe, man, it maketh no mater,
For they that wyll so bysely smater,
So helpe me God, man, ever at the length
I make hym lese moche of theyr strength.
For with Foly so do I them lede
That wyt he wantyth when he hath moste nede.

FANSY
Forsothe, tell on; hast thou any more?

FOLY
Yes, I shall tell you or I go
Of dyvers mo that hauntyth my scolys.

CRAFTY CONVEYAUNCE
All men beware of suche folys!

FOLY
There be two lyther, rude and ranke:
Symkyn Tytyvell and Pers Pykthanke.[115]
Theys lythers I lerne them for to lere,
What he sayth and she sayth to lay good ere,
And tell to his sufferayne every whyt;
And then he is moche made of for his whyt.
And, be the mater yll more or lesse,
He wyll make it mykyll worse than it is;
But all that he dothe, and yf he reken well,
It is but Foly every dell.

FANSY
Are not his wordys cursydly cowchyd?

CRAFTY CONVEYAUNCE
By God, there be some that he shroudly towchyd;
But, I say, let se and yf thou have any more.

FOLY
I have an hole armory of suche haburdashe in store.
For there be other that Foly dothe use,
That folowe fonde fantasyes and vertu refuse.

FANSY
Nay, that is my parte that thou spekest of nowe.

FOLY
So is all the remenaunt, I make God avowe;

1236 if necessary 1238 pleasure 1243 immediately, haughty 1244 frowns fiercely with angry brows 1245 behave disdainfully 1246 allowed 1248 interferes 1249 dances, (a dance refrain) 1250 laughs 1254 many, behave like that 1256 busily prattle superficially 1257 the end 1258 lose 1260 lacks, most needs it 1263 frequent, lessons 1265 wicked (men), loathsome 1267 These, teach, learn 1268 listen well 1269 sovereign, bit 1270 commended, wit 1272 much 1273 adds it up correctly 1274 bit 1275 wickedly contrived 1276 cunningly touched (wounded) 1278 cheap goods 1280 reject virtue 1282 remainder

[113] 'And some of those [i.e. upstarts] are not far away, if one looked carefully for them!'

[114] Here Foly imitates the haughty tones of the upstart rebuking a servant.

[115] 'Simon Tell-Tale [literally, 'Titivillus', after the devil of that name: see *Mankind*] and Piers the Sycophant.'

For thou fourmest suche fantasyes in theyr mynde
That every man almost groweth out of kynde.

Crafty Conveyaunce
By the Masse, I am glad that I came hyder
To here you two rutters dyspute togyder.

Fansy
Nay, but Fansy must be eyther fyrst or last.

Foly
But whan Foly cometh, all is past.

Fansy
I wote not whether it cometh of the[e] or of me:
But all is foly that I can se.

Crafty Conveyaunce
Mary, syr, ye may swere it on a boke.

Foly
Ye[a], tourne over the lefe, rede there, and, loke
Howe frantyke Fansy fyrst of all
Maketh man and woman in foly to fall.

Crafty Conveyaunce
A, syr, a, a! Howe by that?

Fansy
A peryllous thynge, to cast a cat
Upon a naked man and yf she scrat.

Foly
So how, I say, the hare is squat![116]
For, frantyke Fansy, thou makyst men madde;
And I, Foly, bryngeth them to *qui fuit* gadde,
With *qui fuit* brayne seke I have them brought,
From *qui fuit aliquid* to shyre shakynge nought.[117]

Crafty Conveyaunce
Well argued and surely on bothe sydes!
But for the[e], Fansy, Magnyfycence abydes.

Fansy
Why, shall I not have Foly with me also?

Crafty Conveyaunce
Yes, perde, man, whether ye ryde or go.
Yet for his name we must fynde a shyfte.

Fansy
By the Masse, he shall hyght Consayte.

Crafty Conveyaunce
Not a better name under the sonne.
With Magnyfycence thou shalte wonne.

Foly
God have mercy, good godfather.[118]

Crafty Conveyaunce
Yet I wolde that ye had gone rather;
For as sone as you come in Magnyfycence syght,
All mesure and good rule is gone quyte.

Fansy
And shall we have Lyberte to do what we wyll?

Crafty Conveyaunce
Ryot at lyberte russheth it out styll.

Foly
Ye[a], but tell me one thynge.

Crafty Conveyaunce
What is that?

Foly
Who is mayster of the masshe fat?[119]

Fansy
Ye[a], for he hathe a full dry soule.

Crafty Conveyaunce
Cockes armes! Thou shalte kepe the brewhouse
boule.

Foly
But, may I drynke therof whylest that I stare?

1283 form 1284 becomes unnatural 1288 lost 1291 swear, book 1295 What do you say to that? 1297 if she should scratch 1300 'Someone who' (Latin), roams idly 1301 (is) brainsick 1304 waits (for you) 1306 walk 1307 strategy 1308 Understanding (but also Fancy) 1309 sun 1312 more quickly 1314 completely 1316 always flaunts himself 1320 guard, bowl 1321 sit and watch (it)

116 'So there! The hare is cornered': i.e. 'I've got you!' 'Squat' is a hare-coursing term.

117 'From someone who was something to absolutely nothing.' 'Sheer, shaking' or 'shire-shaking' are both plausible readings. In each case the extreme nature of the nothingness is the point.

118 An allusion to the fact that he has just 'christened' him.

119 Mash-vat: the palace brewing tubs. See Walker, *Plays of Persuasion*, p. 84, fn. 6.

CRAFTY CONVEYAUNCE
When Mesure is gone, what nedest thou spare?
Whan Mesure is gone, we may slee care.

FOLY
Nowe then goo we hens. Away the mare!

[*Exit Fansy and Foly.*]
Crafty Conveyaunce alone in the place.

CRAFTY CONVEYAUNCE
It is wonder to se the worlde aboute,
To se what Foly is used in every place;
Foly hath a rome, I say, in every route.
To put where he lyst, Foly hath fre chace.
Foly and Fansy all where every man dothe face and brace;
Foly fotyth it properly, Fansy ledyth the dawnce,
And next come I after, Crafty Conveyaunce.

Who so to me gyveth good advertence
Shall se many thyngys donne craftely.
By me conveyed is wanton insolence
Pryvy poyntmentys conveyed so properly,
For many tymes moche kyndnesse is denyed
For drede, that we dare not ofte, lest we be spyed.

By me is conveyed mykyll praty ware:
Somtyme, I say, behynde the dore for nede.
I have an hoby can make larkys to dare;
I knyt togyther many a broken threde.
It is grete almesse the hunger to fede,
To clothe the nakyd where is lackynge a smocke,
Trymme at her tayle or a man can turne a socke.[120]

'What howe! Be ye mery'; Was it not well conveyed?[121]
'As oft as ye lyst, so honeste be savyd.'
'Alas, dere harte, loke that we be not perseyvyd!'
Without crafte nothynge is well behavyd.
'Though I shewe you curtesy, say not that I crave',
'Yet convey it craftely, and hardely spare not for me';
So that there knowe no man but I and she.

Thefte also and pety brybery
Without me be full ofte aspyed.
My inwyt delynge there can no man dyscry.
Convey it be crafte, lyft and lay asyde.
Full moche flatery and falsehode I hyde,
And by Crafty Conveyaunce I wyll, and I can,
Save a stronge thefe and hange a trew man.

But some man wolde convey, and can not skyll,
As malypert tavernars that checke with theyr betters;
Theyr Conveyaunce weltyth the worke all by wyll.
And some wyll take upon them to conterfet letters,
And therwithall convey hymselfe into a payre of fetters.
And some wyll convey by the pretence of sadnesse,
Tyll all theyr Conveyaunce is turnyd into madnesse.

Crafty Conveyaunce is no chyldys game:
By Crafty Conveyaunce many one is brought up of nought.
Crafty Conveyaunce can cloke hymselfe frome shame,
For by Crafty Conveyaunce wonderful thynges are wrought.
By Convayaunce Crafty I have brought
Unto Magnyfy[cen]ce a full ungracyous sorte,
For all hokes unhappy to me have resorte.

Here cometh in Magnyfycence with Lyberte and Felycyte.

MAGNYFYCENCE
Trust me, Lyberte, it greveth me ryght sore
To se you thus ruled and stande in suche awe.

LYBERTE
Syr, as by my wyll it shall be so no more.

FELYCYTE
Yet Lyberte without rule is not worth a strawe.

MAGNYFYCENCE
Tushe! Holde your peas; ye speke lyke a dawe;
Ye shall be occypyed, Welthe, at my wyll.

1322 why hold back 1323 slay 1324 Away with melancholy 1325 all around 1327 place, crowd 1328 go, likes, free rein 1329 everywhere, bluster, threaten 1330 steps out, leads 1332 pays good attention 1335 Secret arrangements made 1337 Through fear 1338 much, pretty merchandise 1339 secretly, of necessity 1340 small hawk, larks cower 1342 charity, feed the hungry 1346 like, if honour be maintained 1347 dear heart, perceived 1349 beg(ged) you 1350 don't hold back 1352 petty larceny 1353 often discovered 1354 inward/secret, discover 1355 by, lift 1358 hardened thief, an honest 1359 tries to, lacks the skill 1360 impudent inn-keepers, quarrel 1361 spoils, wilfulness 1364 seriousness 1371 group 1372 wicked rogues 1376 (i.e. is worthless) 1378 employed

120 Either 'make her neat at the back' or 'approach her from behind' 'before a man can turn a sock' (i.e. very quickly). Either way the implication is that these acts of charity have a sexual motive.

121 Here Conveyaunce acts out a dialogue between himself and a 'genteel' lover anxious to protect her reputation.

CRAFTY CONVEYAUNCE
All that ye say, syr, is reason and skyll.

MAGNYFYCENCE
Mayster Survayour,[122] where have ye ben so longe?
Remembre ye not how my Lyberte by Mesure ruled was?

CRAFTY CONVEYAUNCE
In good faythe, syr, me semeth he had the more wronge.

LYBERTE
Mary, syr, so dyd he excede and passe,
They drove me to lernynge lyke a dull asse.

FELYCYTE
It is good yet that Lyberte be ruled by Reason.

MAGNYFYCENCE
Tushe! Holde your peas, ye speke out of season.
Yourselfe shall be ruled by Lyberte and Largesse.

FELYCYTE
I am content so it in Measure be.

LYBERTE
Must Mesure, in the mares name, you furnysshe and dresse?[123]

MAGNYFYCENCE
Nay, nay, not so, my frende Felycyte.

CRAFTY CONVEYAUNCE
Not and Your Grace wolde be ruled by me.

LYBERTE
Nay, he shall be ruled even as I lyst.

FELYCYTE
Yet it is good to beware of 'had I wyst'.

MAGNYFYCENCE
Syr, by Lyberte and Largesse I wyll that ye shall
Be governed and gyded; wote ye what I say?
Mayster Survayour, Largesse to me call.

CRAFTY CONVEYAUNCE
It shall be done.

MAGNYFYCENCE
Ye[a], but byd hym come away
At ones, and let hym not tary all day.

Here goth out Crafty Convayaunce.

FELYCYTE
Yet it is good wysdome to worke wysely by welth.

LYBERTE
Holde thy tonge, and thou love thy helth!

MAGNYFYCENCE
What! Wyll ye waste wynde and prate thus in vayne?
Ye have eten sauce, I trowe, at the Taylers Hall.[124]

LYBERTE
Be not to bolde, my frende; I counsell you, bere a brayne.

MAGNYFYCENCE
And what so we say, holde you content withall.

FELYCYTE
Syr, yet without Sapyence your substaunce may be smal,

For where is no Mesure, how may worshyp endure?

Here cometh in Fansy.

FANSY
Syr, I am here at your pleasure.

Your Grace sent for me, I wene; what is your wyll?

MAGNYFYCENCE
Come hyther, Largesse; take here Felycyte.

FANSY
Why, wene you that I can kepe hym longe styll?

MAGNYFYCENCE
To rule as ye lyst, lo, here is Lyberte.

LYBERTE
I am here redy.

1382 greater 1383 he (Measure), excessively 1403 carry (i.e. use) your brain 1404 Whatever 1405 wisdom, wealth 1406 honour 1410 quiet for long

[122] Surveyor. Conveyaunce's pseudonym is Sure Surveyaunce.
[123] 'Must Measure, in Mary's name [or 'in the name of misery'] provide and arrange for you all?'

[124] Metaphorically: 'You have learnt boldness.' The Merchant Tailors' Company, one of the most ostentatious of the London livery companies, had their hall in Threadneedle Street in the City.

FANSY
What! Shall we
Have Welth at our gydnge to rule as we lyst?
Then fare well thryfte, by Hym that Crosse kyst!

FELYCYTE
I truste Your Grace wyll be agreabyll
That I shall suffer none impechment
By theyr demenaunce, nor loss repryvable.

MAGNYFYCENCE
Syr, ye shall folowe myne appetyte and intent.

FELYCYTE
So it be by Mesure, I am ryght well content.

FANSY
What, all by Mesure, good syr, and none excesse?

LYBERTE
Why, Welth hath made many a man braynlesse.

FELYCYTE
That was by the menys of to moche Lyberte.

MAGNYFYCENCE
What, can ye agree thus and appose?

FELYCYTE
Syr, as I say, there was no faute in me.

LYBERTE
Ye[a], of Jacke a Thrommys bybyll can ye make a glose.[125]

FANSY
Sore sayde, I tell you, and well to the purpose.
What sholde a man do with you? Loke you under [k]ay?

FELYCYTE
I say it is foly to gyve all welth away.

LYBERTE
Whether sholde Welth be rulyd by Lyberte
Or Lyberte by Welth? Let se, tell me that.

FELYCYTE
Syr, as me semeth, ye sholde be rulyd by me.

MAGNYFYCENCE
What nede you with hym thus prate and chat?

FANSY
Shewe us your mynde then, howe to do and what.

MAGNYFYCENCE
I say that I wyll ye have hym in gydynge.

LYBERTE
Mayster Felycyte, let be your chydynge;

And so as ye se it wyll be no better,
Take it in worthe suche as ye fynde.[126]

FANSY
What the Devyll, man, your name shalbe the greter:
For Welth without Largesse is all out of kynde.

LYBERTE
And Welth is nought worthe yf Lyberte be behynde.

MAGNYFYCENCE
Nowe holde ye content, for there is none other shyfte.

FELYCYTE
Then waste muste be welcome, and fare well thryfte!

MAGNYFYCENCE
Take of his substaunce a sure inventory,
And get thou home togyther; for Lyberte shall byde
And wayte upon me.

LYBERTE
And yet for a memory,
Make indentures howe ye and I shal gyde.

FANSY
I can do nothynge but he stonde besyde.

LYBERTE
Syr, we can do nothynge the one without the other.

MAGNYFYCENCE
Well, get you hens than, and sende me some other.

1414 kissed the Cross (i.e. Christ?) 1416 no impediment/harm 1417 Through, behaviour, blameworthy 1418 inclination 1422 means, too 1423 argue 1426 harshly 1427 Lock, key 1429 Why 1435 nagging 1438 reputation, greater 1439 completely unnatural 1440 worth nothing, is lacking 1441 no alternative 1443 wealth, reliable 1445 record 1446 legal agreements 1447 unless he (Lyberte)

[125] 'You can interpret the [proverbial] Fool's Bible'; i.e. you're an accomplished fool.

[126] 'Value it as you find it'; i.e. accept the situation and make the most of it.

FANSY
Whom? Lusty Pleasure, or mery Consayte?

MAGNYFYCENCE
Nay, fyrst Lusty Pleasure is my desyre to have,
And let the other another [time] awayte;
Howe be it, that fonde felowe is a mery knave.
But loke that ye occupye the auctoryte that I you gave.

Here goeth out Felycyte, Lyberte, and Fansy. Magnyfycence alone in the place.

[MAGNYFYCENCE]
For nowe, syrs, I am lyke as a prynce sholde be:
I have Welth at wyll, Largesse, and Lyberte.[127]

Fortune to her lawys can not abandune me,
But I shall of Fortune rule the reyne.
I fere nothynge Fortunes perplexyte.
All honour to me must nedys stowpe and lene.
I synge of two partys without a mene.[128]
I have wynde and wether over all to sayle;
No stormy rage agaynst me can prevayle.

Alexander, of Macedony kynge,[129]
That all the Oryent had in subjeccyon,
Though al his conquestys were brought to rekenynge,
Myght seme ryght wel under my proteccyon
To rayne,[130] for all his marcyall affeccyon,
For I am prynce perlesse provyd of porte,[131]
Bathyd with blysse, embracyd with comforte.

Syrus, that soleme syar was of Babylon,
That Israell releysyd of theyr captyvyte,[132]
For al his pompe, for all his ryall trone,
He may not be comparyd unto me.
I am the dyamounde, dowtlesse, of dygnyte.
Surely it is I that all may save and spyll,
No man so hardy to worke agaynst my wyll.

Porcenya, the prowde provoste of Turky lande,
That ratyd the Romaynes and made them yll rest,[133]
Nor Cesar July, that no man myght withstande,[134]
Were never halfe so rychely as I am drest.
No, that I assure you; loke who was the best.
I reyne in my robys, I rule as me lyst,
I dryve down th[e]se dastardys with a dynt of my fyste.

Of Cato the counte, acountyd the cane,[135]
Daryus, the doughty cheftayn of Perse,[136]
I set not by the prowdest of them a prane.
Ne by non other that any man can rehersse.
I folowe in felycyte without reve[r]sse;
I drede no daunger; I dawnce all in delyte:
My name is Magnyfycence, man most of myght.

Hercules the herdy, with his stobburne clobbyd mase,
That made Cerberus to cache, the cur dogge of Hell,[137]
And Thesius, th[at] prowde was Pluto to face,[138]
It wolde not become them with me for to mell.
For of all barones bolde I bere the bell;
Of all doughty I am doughtyest duke as I deme;
To me all prynces to lowte man be sene.

1454 make sure that you use 1457 laws, abandon 1458 rein 1459 distress/anger (with me) 1460 stoop and bow 1465 East 1466 counted up 1468 martial disposition 1469 proved to be peerless, state 1470 surrounded by 1471 grand lord 1473 throne 1475 diamond 1476 ruin 1477 (is) so 1479 punished, Romans, evil 1481 dressed/prepared 1483 robes, as I choose 1484 wretches, blow from 1486 courageous 1487 do not value, prawn 1488 tell me about 1489 continue 1495 meddle 1496 am the leader 1497 bold (men) 1498 must be seen to bow

127 Heiserman (*Skelton and Satire*, pp. 84ff) notes the similarity between this speech and those of the cycle play tyrants, Herod, Pilate, etc. Magnyfycence has clearly fallen into tyranny by this point in the play.

128 i.e. a song consisting of only a treble and a tenor voice, lacking cohesion (see l. 137, above).

129 Alexander the Great (356–323 BC).

130 '[He] might fittingly rule only under my patronage'.

131 Note the further echoes of the speeches of Pilate, Herod, and the other Cycle Play tyrants here and in what follows.

132 Cyrus the Great (559–529 BC), founder of the Persian empire. For his release of the Israelites, see II Chronicles 36:22–3.

133 Lars Porsenna, the sixth-century BC prince of Clusium who marched on Rome.

134 (Gaius) Julius Caesar (100–44 BC).

135 Probably (Marcus Porcius) Cato the Censor (234–149 BC) 'who was considered knowledgeable'. Cato was the author of a number of speeches and treatises on politics, history, and agriculture, and was considered a source of wisdom in the medieval period on the strength of the *Dicts of Cato*.

136 Darius I, king of Persia (521–486 BC).

137 'Hercules the hardy, with his stout clubbed mace'. Hercules was traditionally depicted carrying a club. His twelfth labour was to subdue (make to 'couche' or cower) Cerberus, the three-headed guardian of Hell.

138 Theseus, the mythical ruler of Athens, journeyed into Hades with his friend Pirithous in an attempt to seize Persephone.

Cherlemayne, that mantenyd the nobles of Fraunce,[139]
Arthur of Albyan, for all his brymme berde,
Nor Basyan the bolde,[140] for all his brybaunce,
Nor Alerycus, that rulyd the Gothyaunce by swerd,[141]
Nor no man on molde, can make me aferd.
What man is so maysyd with me that dare mete,
I shall flappe hym as a fole to fall at my fete.

Galba, whom his galantys garde for agaspe,[142]
Nor Nero, that nother set by God nor man,
Nor Vaspasyan, that bare in his nose a waspe,[143]
Nor Hanyball, agayne Rome gates that ranne,[144]
Nor yet [C]ypyo, that noble Cartage wanne;[145]
Nor none so hardy of them with me that durste crake,
But I shall frounce them on the foretop and gar them to quake

Here cometh in Courtly Abusyon doynge reverence and courtesy.

COURTLY ABUSYON
At your commaundement, syr, wyth all dew reverence.

MAGNYFYCENCE
Welcom, Pleasure, to our Magnyfycence.

COURTLY ABUSYON
Plesyth it Your Grace to shewe what I do shall?

MAGNYFYCENCE
Let us here of your pleasure, to passe the tyme withall.

COURTLY ABUSYON
Syr, then, with the favour of your benynge sufferaunce,
To shewe you my mynde myselfe I wyll avaunce,
If it lyke Your Grace to take it in degre.

MAGNYFYCENCE
Yes, syr; so good man in you I se,
And in your delynge so good assuraunce,
That we delyte gretly in your dalyaunce.

COURTLY ABUSYON
A, syr, Your Grace me dothe extole and rayse
And ferre beyond my merytys ye me commende and prayse.
Howe be it, I wolde be ryght gladde, I you assure
Any thynge to do that myght be to your pleasure.

MAGNYFYCENCE
As I be saved, with pleasure I am supprysyd
Of your langage, it is so well devysed;
Pullyshyd and fresshe is your ornacy.

COURTLY ABUSYON
A, I wolde to God that I were halfe so crafty,
Or in electe utteraunce halfe so eloquent,
As that I myght Your Noble Grace content.

MAGNYFYCENCE
Truste me, with you I am hyghly pleasyd,
For in my favour I have you feffyd and seasyd.[146]
He is not lyvynge your maners can amend;
Mary, your speche is as pleasant as though it were pend,
To here your comon it is my hygh comforte,
Poynt devyse all pleasure is your porte.

COURTLY ABUSYON
Syr, I am the better of your noble reporte.
But of your pacyence under the supporte,
If it wolde lyke you to here my pore mynde . . .

MAGNYFYCENCE
Speke, I beseche the[e]; leve nothynge behynde.

1500 Albion, rugged 1501 plundering 1503 earth 1504 mad enough to oppose me 1505 strike 1507 Nero (37–68), cared neither for 1511 dares to boast 1512 make their hair curl 1512+ (i.e. bowing) 1513 due 1515 should do 1517 benign permission 1519 appropriately/mildly 1522 small-talk 1524 merits 1528 speech, constructed 1529 polished, ornateness 1530 skilful 1531 choice speech 1535 improve 1536 written down 1537 small-talk, greatest 1538 perfectly, pleasant, behaviour 1539 for 1541 opinion 1542 aside

139 The emperor Charlemagne (774–814).

140 Probably Marcus Antonius Aurelius (Bassanius) Caracalla (188–217), Roman emperor 212–17.

141 Alaric, king of the Goths (*c.*370–410).

142 'Galba, who was made to gasp by his knights'. The emperor Servius Sulpicius Galba (*c.*3 BC–AD 69) was murdered by his own praetorian guards.

143 The emperor Titus Flavius Vespasian (9–79) was reputed, perhaps on the strength of his name (*vesper*: wasp), in medieval legend to have been born with a wasp in his nose.

144 Hannibal (247–182 BC) led the Carthaginian army (with its elephants) across the Alps to attack Rome in 211 BC.

145 Probably Scipio Aemilianus Africanus Numantinus (185–129 BC), who sacked Carthage in 146 BC.

146 'Feoffed and seised': legal terms of investiture.

COURTLY ABUSYON
So as ye be a prynce of great myght,
It is semynge your pleasure ye delyte,
And to aqueynte you with carnall delectacyon;
And to fall in aquayntaunce with every newe facyon,
And quyckely your appetytes to sharpe and adresse;
To fasten your fansy upon a fayre maystresse[147]
That quyckely is envyved with rudyes of the rose,
Inpurtured with fetures after your purpose,
The streynes of her vaynes as asure, inde blewe,
Enbudded with beautye and colour fresshe of hewe,
As lyly whyte to loke upon her [l]eyre,
Her eyen relucent as carbuncle so clere,
Her mouthe enbawmed, dylectable, and mery,
Her lusty lyppes ruddy as the chery:
Howe lyke you? Ye lacke, syr, suche a lusty lasse.

MAGNYFYCENCE
A, that were a baby to brace and to basse!
I wolde I had, by Hym that Hell dyd harowe,
With me in kepynge suche a Phylyp Sparowe.[148]
I wolde hauke whylest my hede dyd warke,
So I myght hobby for suche a lusty larke.
These wordes, in myne eyre they be so lustely spoken,
That on suche a female my flesshe wolde be wroken.
They towche me so thorowly and tykyll my consayte,
That weryed I wolde be on suche a bayte.
A Cockes armes! Where myght suche one be founde?

COURTLY ABUSYON
Wyll ye spende ony money?

MAGNYFYCENCE
Ye[a], a thousande pounde.

COURTLY ABUSYON
Nay, nay; for lesse I waraunt you to be sped,
And brought home and layde in your bed.

MAGNYFYCENCE
Wolde money, trowest thou, make suche one to the call?[149]

COURTLY ABUSYON
Money maketh marchauntes, I tell you, over all.[150]

MAGNYFYCENCE
Why, wyl a maystres be wonne for money and for golde?

COURTLY ABUSYON
Why, was not for money Troy bothe bought and solde?
Full many a stronge cyte and towne hath be wonne
By the meanes of money without ony gonne.
A maystres, I tell you, is but a small thynge:
A goodly rybon, or a golde rynge
May wynne with a sawte the fortresse of the holde.
But one thynge I warne you, prece forth and be bolde.

MAGNYFYCENCE
Ye[a], but some be full koy and passynge harde harted.

COURTLY ABUSYON
But, blessyd be our Lorde, they wyll be sone converted.

MAGNYFYCENCE
Why, wyll they then be intreted, the most and the lest?

COURTLY ABUSYON
Ye[a], for *omnis mulier meritrix si celari potest.*[151]

MAGNYFYCENCE
A, I have spyed ye can moche broken sorowe.

1544 fitting 1545 acquaint 1547 whet, direct 1548 mistress 1549 enlivened, redness 1550 Adorned, suitable to 1551 lines, veins, azure, indigo blue 1552 Covered with buds, hue 1553 face 1554 eyes shining 1555 perfumed, delectable 1556 red 1558 babe, embrace, kiss 1561 hawk, head 1562 hunt 1563 ear 1564 satisfied 1565 thoroughly, tickle, fancy 1566 I would love to chew, bait 1569 successful 1573 mistress 1575 been won 1576 gun (fire) 1579 assault, stronghold 1580 press forward 1581 disdainful, exceedingly 1583 persuaded 1585 have known

147 Abusyon goes on to describe the red and white complexion of the perfect late medieval beauty.

148 A generic pet name for a bird. *Philip Sparrow* is also the title of one of Skelton's better-known poems. Sparrows were traditionally associated with lechery.

149 'Make such a woman [obedient] to the call [another hawking term]?'

150 'Money makes everyone a merchant'; i.e. 'everyone has his or her price'.

151 'Every woman is a whore if it can be kept secret.'

COURTLY ABUSYON
I coude holde you with suche talke hens tyll to-
morowe;
But yf it lyke your grace more at large
Me to permyt my mynde to dyscharge,
I wolde yet shewe you further of my consayte

MAGNYFYCENCE
Let se what ye say; shewe it strayte.

COURTLY ABUSYON
Wysely let these wordes in your mynde be wayed.
By waywarde wylfulnes let eche thynge be convayed.
What so ever ye do, folowe your owne wyll;
Be it reason or none, it shall not gretely skyll.
Be it ryght or wronge, by the advyse of me,
Take your pleasure and use fre lyberte;
And yf you se ony thynge agaynst your mynde,
Then some [o]ccacyon or quarell ye must fynde,
And frowne it and face it, as thoughe ye wolde
fyght.
Frete yourselfe for anger and for dyspyte,
Here no man what so ever they say,
But do as ye lyst and take your owne way.

MAGNYFYCENCE
Thy wordes and my mynde odly well accorde.

COURTLY ABUSYON
What sholde ye do elles? Are not you a lorde?
Let your lust and lykynge stande for a lawe.
Be wrastynge and wrythynge, and away drawe.
And ye se a man that with hym ye be not pleased,
And that your mynde can not well be eased,
As yf a man fortune to touche you on the quyke,
Then feyne yourselfe dyseased, and make yourselfe
seke.
To styre up your stomake you must you forge,
Call for a caudell, and cast up your gorge,
With 'Cockes armes! Rest shall I none have
Tyll I be revenged on that horson knave.
A, howe my stomake wambleth! I am all in a swete.
Is there no horson that knave that wyll bete?'

MAGNYFYCENCE
By Cockes woundes, a wonder felowe thou arte;
For ofte tymes suche a wamblynge goth over my
harte,
Yet I am not harte seke, but that me lyst.
For myrth I have hym coryed, beten, and blyst,
Hym that I loved not, and made hym to loute;
I am forthwith as hole as a troute.
For suche abusyon I use nowe and than.

COURTLY ABUSYON
It is none abusyon, syr, in a noble man:
It is a pryncely pleasure and a lordly mynde.
Suche lustes at large may not be lefte behynde.

Here cometh in Cloked Colusyon with Measure.

CLOKED COLUSYON
[*To Measure*] Stande styll here, and ye shall se
That for your sake I wyll fall on my kne.

COURTLY ABUSYON
Syr, Sober Sadnesse cometh; wherfore it be.

MAGNYFYCENCE
Stande up, syr, ye are welcom̄ to me.

CLOKED COLUSYON
Please it Your Grace at the contemplacyon
Of my pore instance and supplycacyon,
Tenderly to consyder in your advertence,
Of our blessyd Lorde, syr, at the reverence,
Remembre the good servyce that Mesure hath you
done,
And that ye wyll not cast hym away so sone.

MAGNYFYCENCE
My frende, as touchynge to this your mocyon,
I may say to you I have but small devocyon.
Howe be it, at your instaunce I wyll the rather
Do as moche as for myne owne father.

CLOKED COLUSYON
Nay, syr; that affeccyon ought to be reserved,
For of Your Grace I have it nought deserved.
But yf it lyke you that I myght rowne in your eyre,
To shewe you my mynde I wolde have the lesse fere.

MAGNYFYCENCE
Stande a lytell abacke, syr, and let hym come hyder.

1586 from now until 1589 more 1590 immediately 1591 weighed 1594 greatly matter 1600 Fret/eat yourself up with 1603 strangely 1604 otherwise 1605 pleasure 1606 twisting, writhing, move 1607 if 1609 hit you where it hurts 1611 pretend 1612 warm drink, vomit (it up again) 1613 And say: 1615 trembles, sweat 1616 beat? 1617 amazing 1618 passes 1619 heart-sick, unless I wish (to be) 1620 pleasure, thrashed, bashed 1621 bow down 1622 completely recovered 1626 unchecked desires 1629 I wonder why 1633 humble entreaty 1634 Carefully 1637 petition 1638 little inclination 1639 request 1641 held in reserve 1643 whisper 1644 fear

Courtly Abusyon
With a good wyll, syr; God spede you bothe togyder.

Cloked Colusyon
Syr, so it is: this man is here by,
That for hym to laboure he hath prayde me hartely.
Notwithstandynge to you be it sayde,
To trust in me he is but dyssayved;
For so helpe me God, for you he is not mete.
I speke the softlyer because he sholde not wete.

Magnyfycence
Come hyder, Pleasure; you shall here myne entent.
Mesure, ye knowe wel, with hym I can not be content:
And surely, as I am nowe advysed,
I wyll have hym rehayted and dyspysed.
Howe say ye, syrs? Herein what is best?

Courtly Abusyon
By myne advyse, with you in fayth he shall not rest.

Cloked Colusyon
Yet, syr, reserved your better advysement,
It were better he spake with you or he wente,
That he knowe not but that I have supplyed
All I can his matter for to spede.

Magnyfycence
Nowe by your trouthe, gave he you not a brybe?

Cloked Colusyon
Yes, with his hande I made hym to subscrybe
A byll of recorde for an annuall rent.

Courtly Abusyon
But for all that, he is lyke to have a glent.

Cloked Colusyon
Ye[a], by my trouthe, I shall waraunt you for me.
And he go to the Dev[y]ll, so that I may have my fee,
What care I?

Magnyfycence
By the Masse, well sayd!

Courtly Abusyon
What force ye, so that ye be payde?

Cloked Colusyon
But yet, lo, I wolde, or that he wente,
Lest that he thought that his money were evyll spente,
That ye wolde loke on hym, thoughe it were not longe.

Magnyfycence
Well cannest thou helpe a preest to synge a songe!

Cloked Colusyon
So it is all the maner nowe a dayes
For to use suche haftynge and crafty wayes.

Courtly Abusyon
He telleth you trouth, syr, as I you ensure.

Magnyfycence
Well, for thy sake the better I may endure
That he come hyder, and to gyve hym a loke
That he shall lyke the worse all this woke.

Cloked Colusyon
I care not howe sone he be refused,
So that I may craftely be excused.

Courtly Abusyon
Where is he?

Cloked Colusyon
Mary, I made hym abyde,
Whylest I came to you, a lytell here besyde.

Magnyfycence
Well, call hym, and let us here hym reason,
And we wyll be comonynge in the mene season.

Courtly Abusyon
This is a wyse man, syr, where so ever ye hym had.

Magnyfycence
An honest person, I tell you, and a sad.

Courtly Abusyon
He can full craftely this matter brynge aboute.

Magnyfycence
Whylest I have hym, I nede nothynge doute.

1650 deceived 1652 quieter, know 1656 rebuked, despised 1659 with due respect to, judgement 1655 legal document, income 1651 glancing blow 1652 for my part 1670 what does it matter to you 1672 poorly 1673 (for) long 1674 priest (i.e. you're a good hypocrite!) 1676 trickery 1677 assure 1680 week 1684 close by here 1686 meanwhile we'll talk 1687 found him 1688 serious (one) 1690 need fear for nothing

Hic introducat Colusion, Mesure, Magnyfycence aspectant{e} vultu elatissimo.[152]

CLOKED COLUSYON
[*To Measure*] By the Masse, I have done that I can,
And more than ever I dyd for ony man
I trowe ye herde yourselfe what I said.

MEASURE
Nay, indeede, but I sawe howe ye prayed,
And made instance for me be lykelyhod.

CLOKED COLUSYON
Nay, I tell you, I am not wonte to fode
Them that dare put theyr truste in me,
And thereof ye shall a larger profe se.

MEASURE
Syr, God rewarde you as ye have deserved!
Byt thynke you with Magnyfycence I shal be
reserved?

CLOKED COLUSYON
By my trouth, I can not tell you that.
But and I were as ye, I wolde not set a gnat
By Magnyfycence, nor yet none of his.
For go when ye shall, of you shall he mysse.

MEASURE
Syr, as ye say.

CLOKED COLUSYON
Nay, come on with me.
Yet ones agayne I shall fall on my kne
For your sake, what so ever befall;
I set not a flye and all go to all.

MEASURE
The Holy Goost be with Your Grace.

CLOKED COLUSYON
Syr, I beseche you let pety have some place
In your brest towardes this gentylman.

MAGNYFYCENCE
I was your good lorde tyll that ye beganne
So masterfully upon you for to take
With my servauntys, and suche maystryes gan make,
That holly my mynde with you is myscontente.
Wherfore I wyll that ye be resydent
With me no longer.

CLOKED COLUSYON
Say somwhat nowe, let se,
For your self.

MEASURE
Syr, yf I myght permytted be,
I wolde to you say a worde or twayne.

MAGNYFYCENCE
What! Woldest thou, lurden, with me brawle
agayne?
Have hym hens, I say, out of my syght!
That day I se hym I shall be worse all nyght.

Here Mesure goth out of the place {with Courtly Abusyon}.

COURTLY ABUSYON [*exiting*]
Hens, thou haynyarde! Out of the dores fast!

MAGNYFYCENCE
Alas! My stomake fareth as it wolde cast.

CLOKED COLUSYON
Abyde, syr, abyde: let me holde your hede.

MAGNYFYCENCE
A bolle or a basyn, I say, for Goddes brede!
A, my hede! But is the horson gone?
God gyve hym a myschefe! Nay, nowe let me alone.

CLOKED COLUSYON
A good dryfte, syr; a praty fete!
By the good Lorde, yet your temples bete.

MAGNYFYCENCE
Nay, so God helpe, it was no grete vexacyon;
For I am panged ofte tymes of this same facyon.

CLOKED COLUSYON
Cockes armes! Howe Pleasure plucked hym forth!

1695 as it appeared 1696 deceive 1698 greater proof 1700 retained (in office) 1702 wouldn't care a gnat 1703 For 1704 he'll miss you 1707 whatever happens 1708 (i.e. however it works out) 1710 pity 1713 To behave so imperiously 1714 used such domineering ways 1715 wholly, dissatisfied 1720 dispute 1723 villain 1724 feels as (if), throw up 1725 head 1726 bowl, basin, by the Sacrament 1728 leave 1729 idea, feat 1731 trouble 1732 pained, in 1733 dragged him off!

152 'Here let Colusyon bring Measure forward, while Magnyfycence looks on with a haughty expression.'

Magnyfycence
Ye[a], walke he must; it was no better worth.

Cloked Colusyon
Syr, nowe me thynke your harte is well eased.

Magnyfycence
Nowe Measure is gone, I am the better pleased.

Cloked Colusyon
So to be ruled by Measure, it is a payne.

Magnyfycence
Mary, I wene he wolde not be glad to come agayne.

Cloked Colusyon
So I wote not what he sholde do here.[153]
Where mennes belyes is mesured, there is no chere;[154]
For I here but fewe men that gyve ony prayse
Unto Measure, I say, nowe a days.

Magnyfycence
Measure? Tut! What the Devyll of Hell!
Scantly one with Measure that wyll dwell.

Cloked Colusyon
Not amonge noble men, as the worlde gothe.
It is no wonder, therfore, thoughe ye be wrothe
With Mesure. Where as all noblenes is, there I have past.
They catche that catche may, kepe and holde fast,
Out of all measure themselfe to enryche;
No force what thoughe his neyghbour dye in a dyche.
With pollynge and pluckynge out of all measure,
Thus must ye stuffe and store your treasure.

Magnyfycence
Yet somtyme, parde, I must use Largesse.

Cloked Colusyon
Ye[a], mary, somtyme: in a messe of vergesse,[155]
As in a tryfyll or in a thynge of nought,
As gyvynge a thynge that ye never bought.
It is the gyse nowe, I say, over all,
Largesse in wordes, for rewardes are but small.
To make fayre promyse, what are ye the worse?
Let me have the rule of your purse.

Magnyfycence
I have taken it to Largesse and Lyberte.

Cloked Colusyon
Than is it done as it sholde be.
But use your largesse by the advyse of me
And I shall waraunt you welth and lyberte.

Magnyfycence
Say on; me thynke your reasons be profounde.

Cloked Colusyon
Syr, of my counsayle this shall be the grounde:
To chose out ii, iii, of suche as you love best,
And let all your fansyes upon them rest.
Spare for no cost to gyve them pounde and peny;
Better to make iii ryche than for to make many.
Gyve them more than ynoughe, and let them not lacke;
And as for all other, let them trusse and packe.
Plucke from an hundred, and gyve it to thre;
Let neyther patent scape them nor fee.[156]
And where soever you wyll fall to a rekenynge,
Those thre wyll be redy even at your bekenynge;
For them shall you have at lyberte to lowte.
Let them have all, and the other go without;
Thus joy without mesure you shall have.

Magnyfycence
Thou sayst truthe, by the harte that God me gave!
For as thou sayst, ryght so shall it be.
And here I make the upon Lyberte
To be supervysour, and on Largesse also;
For as thou wylte, so shall the game go.
For in Pleasure and Surveyaunce and also in the[e]
I have set my hole felycyte;
And suche as you wyll shall lacke no promocyon.

Cloked Colusyon
Syr, syth that in me ye have suche devocyon,
Commyttynge to me and to my felowes twayne
Your Welthe and Felycyte, I trust we shall optayne
To do you servyce after your appetyte.

1734 there was no alternative 1740 bellies, happiness 1744 (There's) hardly one (person) 1745 as things are 1748 They get what they can 1750 No matter if, die, ditch 1751 taxing, stripping 1754 dish, verjuice (acidic fruit drink) 1760 control 1761 given 1765 arguments 1767 two or three (people) 1769 pennies 1772 (i.e. get lost) 1773 take 1775 account (i.e. if you're ever in trouble) 1776 summons 1782 over 1787 those you recommend 1790 succeed 1791 desire

153 'I don't know what business he could have here.'
154 i.e. 'There's no fun when you have to restrict your appetite'.
155 i.e. 'Be generous with something that you don't like'.
156 'Let neither licence [to profit from a restricted trade] nor fee (rent or salary) escape them.' i.e. give them all the financial rewards a prince can bestow.

MAGNYFYCENCE
In faythe, and your servyce ryght well shall I acquyte;
And therfore hye you hens, and take this oversyght.

CLOKED COLUSYON
Nowe Jesu preserve you, syr, prynce most of myght.

Here goth Cloked Colusyon awaye, and leveth Magnyfycence alone in the place.

MAGNYFYCENCE
Thus, I say, I am envyronned with Solace;
I drede no dyntes of fatall Desteny.
Well were that lady myght stande in my grace,[157]
Me to enbrace and love moost specyally;
A, Lorde, so I wolde halse her hartely!
So I wolde clepe her! So I wolde kys her swete!

Here Cometh in Foly.

FOLY
Mary, Cryst graunt ye catche no colde on your fete!

MAGNYFYCENCE
Who is this?

FOLY
Consayte, syr, your owne man.

MAGNYFYCENCE
What tydynges with you, syr? I befole thy brayne pan.

FOLY
By Our Lakyn, syr, I have ben a howkyng for the wylde swan.
My hawke is rammysshe, and it happed that she ran . . .
'Flewe' I sholde say, in to an olde barne
To reche at a rat. I coude not her warne;
She pynched her pynyon, by God, and catched harme.
It was a ronner; nay, fole, I warant her blode warme.[158]

MAGNYFYCENCE
A, syr, thy jarfawcon and thou be hanged togyder!

FOLY
And, syr, as I was comynge to you hyder,
I saw a fox sucke on a kowes ydder,
And with a lyme rodde I toke them bothe togyder.
I trowe it be a frost, for the way is slydder.
Se, for God avowe, for colde as I chydder.

MAGNYFYCENCE
Thy wordes hange togyder as fethers in the wynde.

FOLY
A, syr, tolde I not you howe I dyd fynde
A knave and a carle, and all of one kynde?
I sawe a wethercocke wagge with the wynde.
Grete mervayle I had, and mused in my mynde,
The houndes ranne before, and the hare behynde.
I sawe a losell lede a lurden, and they were bothe blynde.
I sawe a sowter go to supper, or ever he had dynde.

MAGNYFYCENCE
By Cockes harte, thou arte a fyne mery knave!

FOLY
I make God avowe ye wyll none other men have.

MAGNYFYCENCE
What sayst thou?

FOLY
Mary, I pray God your mastershyp to save.
I shall gyve you a gaude of a goslynge that I gave,
The gander and the gose bothe grasynge on one grave.
Than Rowlande the reve ran, and I began to rave,
And with a bristell of a bore his berde dyd I shave.

MAGNYFYCENCE
[*Aside*] If ever I herde syke another, God gyve me shame.

1792 reward 1793 off you go, supervisory role 1795 surrounded by 1796 blows from 1799 embrace 1800 hug, sweetly 1803 skull 1804 Our Lady (euphemism), hawking 1805 wild/ill-trained 1807 pursue, prevent her 1808 trapped, wing 1810 gerfalcon (a large hawk) 1812 cow's udder 1813 limed stick (for catching birds) 1814 there'll be, slippery 1815 I'm shivering with cold 1816 (i.e. you're speaking nonsense) 1817 didn't I tell you 1818 churl 1819 wave 1822 rogue, wretch 1823 cobbler, before he'd had dinner 1827 tell, joke 1828 goose, grazing 1829 reeve/bailiff 1830 boar's bristle, beard 1831 anyone like him

[157] 'That lady [i.e. Destiny] might be well advised'.
[158] 'It [the rat] was a runner [a quick one]; no, fool, I guarantee she's alive.' Perhaps, as Neuss suggests, the (stuffed?) owl looks obviously 'dead' and so elicits a laugh or comment from the audience, prompting Foly to turn on a particular spectator and assure him or her that the bird still lives.

Foly
Sym Sadyglose was my syer, and Dawcocke my dame.
I coude, and I lyst, garre you laughe at a game:
Howe a wodcocke wrastled with a larke that was lame;
The bytter sayd boldly that they were to blame;
The feldfare wolde have fydled and it wolde not frame;
The crane and the curlewe therat gan to grame;
The snyte snyveled in the snowte and smyled at the game.

Magnyfycence
[*Aside*] Cockes bones, herde ye ever suche another?

Foly
Se, syr, I beseche you, Largesse my brother.

Here Fansy cometh.

Magnyfycence
What tydynges with you, syr, that you loke so sad?

Fansy
When ye knowe that I knowe, ye wyll not be glad.

Foly
What, Brother Braynsyke; how farest thou?

Magnyfycence
Ye[a], let be thy japes, and tell me howe
The case requyreth.

Fansy
Alasse, alasse, an hevy metynge!
I wolde tell you and yf I myght for wepynge.

Foly
What, is all your myrthe nowe tourned to sorowe?
Fare well tyll sone, adue tyll to morowe.

Here goth Foly away.

Magnyfycence
I pray the[e], Largesse, let be thy sobbynge.

Fansy
Alasse, syr, ye are undone with stelyng and robbynge!
Ye sent us a supervysour for to take hede;[159]
Take hede of your selfe, for nowe ye have nede.

Magnyfycence
What, hath Sadnesse begyled me so?

Fansy
Nay, madnesse hath begyled you and many mo:
For Lyberte is gone, and also Felycyte.

Magnyfycence
Gone? Alasse ye have undone me!

Fansy
Nay, he that ye sent us, Clokyd Colusyon,
And your payntyd Pleasure, Courtly Abusyon,
And your 'Demenour' with Counterfet Countenaunce,
And your supervysour, Crafty Conveyaunce,
Or ever we were ware, brought us in adversyte,
And had robbyd you quyte from all felycyte.

Magnyfycence
Why, is this the largesse that I have usyd?

Fansy
Nay, it was your fondnesse that ye have usyd.

Magnyfycence
And is this the credence that I gave to the letter?

Fansy
Why, coulde not your wyt serve you no better?

Magnyfycence
Why, who wolde have thought in you suche gyle!

Fansy
What? Yes, by the Rode, syr; it was I all this whyle
That you trustyd, and Fansy is my name;
And Foly, my broder, that made you moche game.

Here cometh in Adversite.

1832 saddlegoose/simpleton, idiot 1833 if I wished 1834 wrestled 1835 bittern (a wading bird) 1836 fieldfare, fiddled, work 1837 fret 1838 snipe, snivelled 1842 what 1844 stop your joking 1845 what's needed 1846 (this is) a sorrowful meeting 1850 ruined through 1853 (Colusyon's alias) 1861 Before, aware (of it) 1862 completely 1864 folly 1865 (i.e. Fansy's forged letter)

[159] i.e. Cloked Colusyon; but it might be, as Dyce suggests, that the surveyor (Crafty Conveyaunce) is intended.

MAGNYFYCENCE
Alas, who is yonder that grymly lokys?

FANSY
Adewe, for I wyll not come in his clokys.

[*Exit Foly.*]

MAGNYFYCENCE
Lorde, so my flesshe trymblyth nowe for drede!

Here Magnyfycence is beten downe and spoylyd from all his goodys and rayment.[160]

ADVERSYTE
I am Adversyte, that for thy mysdede
From God am sent to quyte the[e] thy mede.
Vyle velyarde, thou must not nowe my dynt withstande:
Thou mayst not abyde the dynt of my hande
Ly there, losell, for all thy pompe and pryde;
Thy pleasure now with payne and trouble shalbe tryde.
The stroke of God, Adversyte, I hyght;
I plucke downe kynge, prynce, lorde, and knyght;
I rushe at them rughly and make them ly full lawe;
And in theyr moste truste I make them overthrowe.
Thys losyll was a lorde and lyvyd at his lust,
And nowe lyke a lurden he lyeth in the duste.
He knewe not hymselfe, his harte was so hye;
Nowe is there no man that wyll set by hym a flye.
He was wonte to boste, brage, and to brace;
Nowe he dare he not for shame loke one in the face.
All worldy welth for hym to lytell was;
Nowe hath he ryght nought, naked as an asse.
Somtyme without Measure he trusted in golde;
And now without Mesure he shall have hunger and colde.
Lo, syrs, thus I handell them all
That folowe theyr fansyes in foly to fall:
Man or woman, of what estate they be,
I counsayle them beware of Adversyte.
Of sorowfull servauntes I have many scores:
I vysyte them somtyme with blaynes and with sores;
With botches and carbu[n]ckyls in care I them knyt;
With the gowte I make them to grone where they syt;
Some I make lyppers and lazars full horse;
And from that they love best some I devorse.
Some with the marmoll to halte I them make;
And some to cry out of the bone-ake;
And some I vysyte with brennynge of fyre;
Of some I wrynge of the necke lyke a wyre;
And some I make in a rope to totter and walter;
And some for to hange themselfe in an halter;
And some I vysyte [with] batayle, warre, and murther,
And make eche man to sle other;
To drowne or to sle themselfe with a knyfe:
And all is for theyr ungracyous lyfe.
Yet somtyme I stryke where is none offence,
Bycause I wolde prove men of theyr pacyence.
But nowe a dayes to stryke I have grete cause,
Lydderyns so lytell set by Goddes lawes.
Faders and moders that be neclygent,
And suffre theyr chyldren to have theyr entent,
To gyde them vertuously that wyll not remembre,
Them or theyr chyldren ofte tymes I dysmembre.
Theyr chyldren, bycause that they have no mekenesse,
I vysyte theyr faders and moders with sekenesse;
And, yf I se therby they wyll not amende,
Then Myschefe sodaynly I them sende.
For there is nothynge that more dyspleaseth God
Than from theyr chyldren to spare the rod
Of correccyon, but let them have theyr wyll.
Some I make lame, and some I do kyll,
And some I stryke with a franesy;
Of some theyr chyldren I stryke out the eye;
And where the fader by wysdom worshyp hath wonne
I sende ofte tymes a fole to his sonne.
Wherfore of Adversyte loke ye be ware,
For when I come, comyth sorowe and care.
For I stryke lordys of realmes and landys,
That rule not by mesure that they have in theyr handys,
That sadly rule not theyr howsholde men.

1871 looks so grim? 1873 trembles 1875 give you your reward 1876 Vile old man(?), blow 1877 withstand 1879 tested/purified 1882 roughly 1883 greatest (self-) confidence 1888 brag, bluster 1890 too 1896 whatever 1899 inflict upon them, blisters 1900 boils, inflammations, entangle 1902 lepers, hoarse 1903 separate 1904 mormal (leg-ulcer), limp 1906 burning 1907 strangle 1908 swing, tremble 1910 battle 1911 slay 1914 (there) is no 1915 test men's patience 1917 Villains care so little for 1919 permit, what they desire 1921 injure/separate? 1922 humility 1923 sickness 1925 suddenly 1930 frenzy 1932 honour 1933 for a son 1935 worry 1938 household servants

160 'Robbed of all his property and fine clothing'.

I am Goddys Preposytour; I prynt them with a pen;
Because of theyr neglygence and of theyr wanton vagys,
I vysyte them and stryke them with many sore plagys.
To take, syrs, example of that I you tell
And beware of Adversyte by my counsell.
Take hede of this caytyfe that lyeth here on grounde:
Beholde howe Fortune o[n] hym hath frounde.
For, though we shewe you this in game and play,
Yet it proveth eyrnest, ye may se, every day.
For nowe wyll I from this caytyfe go,
And take myscheffe and vengeaunce of other mo
That hath deservyd it as well as he.
Howe, where art thou? Come hether, Poverte:
Take this caytyfe to thy lore.

[Exit Adversyte.] Here cometh in Poverte.

POVERTE
A, my bonys ake! My lymmys be sore.
Alasse, I have the cyatyca full evyll in my hyppe.
Alasse, where is youth that was wont for to skyppe?
I am lowsy and unlykynge and full of scurffe;
My colour is tawny, colouryd as a turffe.
I am Poverte, that all men doth hate.
I am baytyd with doggys at every mannys gate;
I am raggyd and rent, as ye may se;
Full fewe but they have envy at me.
Nowe must I this carcasse lyft up;
He dynyd with delyte, with Poverte he must sup.
Ryse up, syr, and welcom unto me.

Hic accedat ad levandum Magnyfycence, et locabit eum super locum stratum.[161]

MAGNYFYCENCE
Alasse where is now my golde and fe?
Alasse, I say, where to am I brought?
Alasse, alasse, alasse! I dye for thought.

POVERTE
Syr, all this wolde have bene thought on before;
He woteth not what welth is that never was sore.[162]

MAGNYFYCENCE
Fy, fy, that ever I sholde be brought in this snare!
I wenyd ones never to have knowen of care.[163]

POVERTE
Lo, suche is this worlde! I fynde it wryt,
In welth to beware; and that is wyt.

MAGNYFYCENCE
In welth to beware yf I had had grace,
Never had I bene brought in this case.

POVERTE
Nowe, syth it wyll no nother be
All that God sendeth, take it in gre;
For thoughe you were somtyme a noble estate,
Nowe must you lerne to begge at every mannes gate.

MAGNYFYCENCE
Alasse that ever I sholde be so shamed!
Alasse that ever I Magnyfycence was named!
Alasse that ever I was so harde happed
In mysery and wretchydnesse thus to be lapped!
Alasse that I coude not myselfe no better gyde!
Alasse in my cradell that I had not dyde!

POVERTE
Ye[a], syr, ye[a]; leve all this rage,
And pray to God your sorowes to asswage.
It is foly to grudge agaynst His vysytacyon.
With harte contryte make your supplycacyon
Unto your Maker that made bothe you and me:
And when it pleaseth God, better may be.

MAGNYFYCENCE
Allasse, I wote not what I sholde pray.

POVERTE
Rem[e]mbre you better, syr; beware what ye say,
For drede ye dysplease the hygh Deyte.
Put your wyll to His wyll, for surely it is He
That may restore you agayne to felycyte,
And brynge you agayne out of adversyte.
Therefore Poverte loke pacyently ye take,

1939 prefect 1940 tricks 1941 plagues 1945 frowned 1947 it proves to be true all the time 1949 others 1952 under your instruction 1954 sciatica, badly 1956 unpleasant 1957 clod 1959 baited/chased off 1960 torn 1961 no one envies me 1963 dined 1965 wealth 1967 sorrow 1968 should 1972 written 1973 sensible 1975 situation 1976 different 1977 in good spirit 1978 great lord 1982 unfortunate 1983 wrapped 1987 assuage 1989 prayer 1994 Deity

161 'Here let him approach Magnyfycence to lift him, and let him put him on a bed [or possibly 'a level place'].'

162 'He who has never suffered does not appreciate wealth.'

163 'I used to believe that I would never experience misery.'

And remembre He suffered moche more for your sake,
Howe be it, of all synne He was innocent,
And ye have deserved this punysshment.

MAGNYFYCENCE
Alasse, with colde my lymmes shall be marde!

POVERTE
Ye[a], syr, nowe must ye lerne to lye harde,
That was wonte to lye on fetherbeddes of downe.
Nowe must your fete lye hyer than your crowne.
Where you were wonte to have cawdels for your hede,
Nowe must you monche mamockes and lumpes of brede.
And where you had chaunges of ryche aray,
Nowe lap you in a coverlet, full fayne what you may.[164]
And where that ye were pomped with what that ye wolde,[165]
Nowe must ye suffre bothe hunger and colde.
With curteyns of sylke ye were wonte to be drawe,
Nowe must ye lerne to ly on the strawe.
Your skynne that was wrapped in shertes of Raynes,
Nowe must ye be stormy beten with showres and raynes.
Your hede that was wonte to be happed moost drowpy and drowsy,
Now shal ye be scabbed, scurvy, and lowsy.

MAGNYFYCENCE
Fye on this worlde full of trechery!
That ever noblenesse sholde lyve thus wretchedly.

POVERTE
Syr, remembre the tourne of Fortunes whele,
That wantonly can wynke, and wynche with her hele.[166]
Nowe she wyll laughe; forthwith she wyll frowne;
Sodenly set up and sodenly pluckyd downe.
She dawnsyth varyaunce with mutabylyte,
Nowe all in welth, forthwith in poverte.
In her promyse there is no sykernesse;
All her delyte is set in doublenesse.

MAGNYFYCENCE
Alas, of Fortune I may well complayne.

POVERTE
Ye[a], syr, yesterday wyll not be callyd agayne.
But yet, syr, nowe in this case
Take it mekely, and thanke God of His grace;
For nowe go I wyll begge for you some mete.
It is foly agaynst God for to plete.
I wyll walke nowe with my beggers baggys,
And happe you the whyles with these homly raggys.

Difidendo dicat ista verba:[167]

A, howe my lymmys be lyther and lame!
Better it is to begge than to be hangyd with shame.
Yet many had lever hangyd to be,
Then to begge theyr mete for charyte.
They thynke it no shame to robbe and stele,
Yet were they better to begge, a great dele;
For by robbynge they rynne to '*in manus tuas* quecke';[168]
But beggynge is better medecyne for the necke.
Ye[a], mary, is it, ye[a], so mote I goo.
A Lorde God, howe the gowte wryngeth me by the too!

[Exit Poverte.] Here Magnyfycence dolorously maketh his mone.

MAGNYFYCENCE
O feble Fortune, O doulfull Destyny!
O hatefull happe, O carefull cruelte!
O syghynge sorowe, O thoughtfull mysere!
O rydlesse rewthe, O paynfull poverte!
O dolorous herte, O harde adversyte!
O odyous dystresse, O dedly payne and woo!
For worldly shame I wax bothe wanne and bloo.

Where is nowe my welth and my noble estate?
Where is nowe my treasure, my landes, and my rent?
Where is nowe all my servauntys that I had here a late?

2002 afflicted 2005 higher, head 2006 caudels/warm drinks 2007 munch on scraps 2012 (i.e. in a four-poster bed) 2014 shirts of finest Rennes linen 2024 mingles fickleness with changeability 2026 surety 2027 duplicity 2029 will not return 2033 complain 2035 wrap, plain/rough 2036 withered 2038 rather 2045 twists, toe 2045+ moan 2046 doleful 2047 chance 2048 misery 2049 unheeding sorrow 2052 pale, livid 2055 recently

164 'Now you wrap yourself in a blanket, happy for whatever you can get.'

165 'And where you were pampered with whatever you wanted'

166 'One moment she will wink favourably at you, the next she will kick [at you] with her heel.'

167 Either '*diffidendo*' (despairingly) or '*discedendo*' (as he departs) 'Let him say these words'.

168 'They hurry towards a hanging.' '*In manus tuas* quecke': see *Mankind* l. 517.

Where is nowe my golde upon them that I spent?
Where is nowe all my ryche abylement?
Where is nowe my kynne, my frendys, and my noble blood?
Where is nowe all my pleasure and my worldly good?
Alasse my foly, alasse my wanton wyll!
I may no more speke tyll I have wept my fyll.

{Enter Lyberte.}

LYBERTE
With ye[a], mary, syrs, thus shold it be:
I kyst her swete, and she kyssyd me;
I daunsed the darlynge on my kne;
I garde her gaspe, I garde her gle
With daunce on the le, the le!
I bassed that baby with harte so free;
She is the bote of all my bale.
A, so, that syghe was farre fet!
To love that lovesome I wyll not let;
My harte is holly on her set;
I plucked her by the patlet;
At my devyse I with her met;
My fansy fayrly on her I set;
So merely syngeth the nyghtyngale!

In lust and lykynge my name is Lyberte.
I am desyred with hyghest and lowest degre,
I lyve as me lyst, I lepe out at large;
Of Erthely thynge I have no care nor charge.
I am presydent of prynces; I prycke them with pryde.
What is he lyvynge that Lyberte wolde lacke?
A thousande pounde with Lyberte may holde no tacke.
At Lyberte a man may be bolde for to brake;
Welthe without Lyberte gothe all to wrake.
But yet, syrs, hardely one thynge lerne of me;
I warne you beware of to moche Lyberte:
For *totum in toto* is not worth an hawe.[169]
To hardy, or to moche, to free of the dawe,
To sober, to sad, to subtell, to wyse,
To mery, to mad, to gyglynge, to nyse,
To full of fansyes, to lordly, to prowde,
To homly, to holy, to lewde, and to lowde,
To flatterynge, to smatterynge, to to out of harre,
To claterynge, to chaterynge, to shorte, and to farre,
To jettynge, to jaggynge, and to full of japes,
To mockynge, to mowynge, to lyke a jackenapes.
Thus *totum in toto* groweth up, as ye may se,
By meanes of madnesse and to moche lyberte.
For I am a vertue yf I be well used,
And I am a vyce where I am abused.

MAGNYFYCENCE
A, woo worthe the[e], Lyberte! Nowe thou sayst full trewe;
That I used the[e] to moche sore may I rewe.

LYBERTE
What! A very vengeaunce! I say, who is that?
What brothell, I say, is yonder bounde in a mat?

MAGNYFYCENCE
I am Magnyfycence, that somtyme thy mayster was.

LYBERTE
What, is the worlde thus come to pass?
Cockes armes, syrs, wyll ye not se
Howe he is undone by the meanes of me?
For yf Measure had ruled Lyberte as he began,
This lurden that here lyeth had ben a noble man.
But he abused so his free Lyberte,
That nowe he hath loste all his felycyte.
Not thorowe largesse of lyberall expence,
But by the way of fansy-insolence.
For lyberalyte is most convenyent
A prynce to use with all his hole intent,
Largely rewardynge them that have deservyd:
And so shall a noble man nobly be servyd.
But nowe adayes as hucksters they hucke and they stycke,
And pynche at the payment of a poddynge prycke.[170]
A laudable largesse, I tell you, for a lorde
To prate for the patchynge of a pot sharde!
Spare for the spence of a noble that his honour

2057 clothing 2065 made her gasp, laugh 2066 lea 2067 kissed 2068 remedy for, sorrow 2069 far-fetched 2070 lovely (one), hold back 2071 wholly 2072 collar 2073 arrangement 2075 merrily 2077 by (the) 2078 I like, freely 2079 responsibility 2080 spur them (on) 2082 be no match 2083 escape (all restraint) 2084 ruin 2088 Too, in folly 2090 giggling, wanton 2092 plain/rude 2093 idly prattling, unhinged 2094 jabbering 2095 strutting, fashionable 2096 grimacing, monkey 2101 curse you! 2102 Sorely may I regret (it) 2103 curse it! 2104 wretch, wrapped 2113 through, expenditure 2114 capricious fancy 2117 Generously 2119 like tradesemen, haggle

169 'For "all in all" [everything] is not worth a hawthorn berry.'

170 'And hesitate over the payment of a tiny sum.' A pudding prick was a small skewer used to seal puddings, hence a very cheap item.

myght save,[171]
And spende Cs for the pleasure of a knave.
But so longe they rekyn with theyr reasons amysse
That they lose theyr Lyberte and all that there is.

MAGNYFYCENCE
Alasse that ever I occupyed suche abusyon!

LYBERTE
Ye[a], for nowe it hath brought the[e] to confusyon;
For where I am occupyed and usyd wylfully
It can not contynew long prosperyously.
As evydently in retchlesse youth ye may se
Howe many come to Myschefe for to moche Lyberte.
And some in the worlde, theyr brayne is so ydyll
That they set theyr chyldren to rynne on the brydyll,
In youth to be wanton, and let them have theyr wyll:
And they never thryve in theyr age, it shall not gretly skyll.
Some fall to foly them selfe for to spyll,
And some fall prechynge at the Toure Hyll.[172]
Some hath so moche lyberte of one thynge and other,
That nother they set by father and mother;
Some have so moche lyberte that they fere no synne,
Tyll, as ye se many tymes, they shame all theyr kynne.
I am so lusty to loke on, so freshe and so fre,
That nonnes wyll leve theyr holynes and ryn after me.
Freers, with Foly I make them so fayne
They cast up theyr obedyence to cache me agayne.
At lyberte to wander and walke over all,
That lustely they lepe somtyme theyr cloyster wall.

Hic aliquis buccat in cornu a retro post populum.[173]

Yonder is a horson for me doth rechate.
Adewe, syrs, for I thynke leyst that I come to late.

{Exit Lyberte.}

MAGNYFYCENCE
O Good Lorde, how longe shall I indure
This mysery, this carefull wrechydnesse?
Of worldly welthe, alasse, who can be sure?
In Fortunys frendshyppe there is no stedfastnesse;
She hath dyssayvyd me with her doublenesse.
For to be wyse all men may lerne of me,
In welthe to beware of herde Adversyte.

Here cometh in Crafty Conveyaunce {and} Cloked Colusyon with a lusty laughter.

CRAFTY CONVEYAUNCE
Ha, ha, ha! For laughter I am lyke to brast.

CLOKED COLUSYON
Ha, ha, ha! For sporte I am lyke to spewe and cast.

CRAFTY CONVEYAUNCE
What hast thou gotted, in faythe, to thy share?

CLOKED COLUSYON
In faythe, of his cofers the bottoms are bare.

CRAFTY CONVEYAUNCE
As for his plate of sylver, and suche trasshe,
I waraunt you I have gyven it a lasshe.

CLOKED COLUSYON
What, then he may drynke out of a stone cruyse.

CRAFTY CONVEYAUNCE
With ye[a], syr, by Jesu, that slayne was with Jewes!
He may rynse a pycher, for his plate is to wed.

CLOKED COLUSYON
In faythe, and he may dreme on a daggeswane for ony fether bed.

CRAFTY CONVEYAUNCE
By my trouthe, we have ryfled hym metely well.

CLOKED COLUSYON
Ye[a], but thanke me therof every dele.

2124 hundreds (of nobles) 2125 calculate, flawed logic 2127 practised such abuses 2128 ruin 2131 reckless 2132 from too much 2134 (i.e. give them free reign) 2136 If, it shouldn't surprise us 2137 ruin 2144 nuns, holiness 2145 Friars 2146 throw away 2147 everywhere 2149 blow a summons (a hunting call) 2150 I'm worried in case 2155 deceived 2157 hard 2158 liable to burst 2159 vomit 2160 got, for 2163 blow (i.e. wasted it) 2164 jar 2166 pot, gold-plate is pawned 2167 rough blanket 2168 cleaned him out

[171] 'To argue over the mending of a shard of pot! Resist spending a noble [6 shillings and 4 pence] to save his own honour'.

[172] Tower Hill was the site where noble traitors and others were beheaded.

[173] 'Here someone blows a horn from the back, behind the audience.'

CRAFTY CONVEYAUNCE
Thanke the[e] therof? In the Devyls date!

CLOKED COLUSYON
Leve they pratynge, or els I shall lay the[e] on the pate.

CRAFTY CONVEYAUNCE
Nay, to wrangle, I warant the[e], it is but a stone caste.

CLOKED COLUSYON
By the Messe, I shall cleve thy heed to the waste.

CRAFTY CONVEYAUNCE
Ye[a], wylte thou clenly cleve me in the clyfte with thy nose?

CLOKED COLUSYON
I shall thrust in the[e] my dagger.

CRAFTY CONVEYAUNCE
Thorowe the legge in to the hose.

CLOKED COLUSYON
Nay, horson, here is my glove;[174] take it up and thou dare.

CRAFTY CONVEYAUNCE
Torde! Thou arte good to be a man of warre!

CLOKED COLUSYON
I shall skelpe the[e] on the skalpe; lo, seest thou that?

CRAFTY CONVEYAUNCE
What, wylte thou skelpe me? Thou dare not loke on a gnat.

CLOKED COLUSYON
By Cockes bones, I shall wysse the[e], and thou be to bolde.

CRAFTY CONVEYAUNCE
Nay, then thou wylte dynge the Devyll and thou be not holde![175]

CLOKED COLUSYON
But wottest thou, horson? I rede the[e] to be wyse.

CRAFTY CONVEYAUNCE
Nowe I rede the[e] beware; I have warned the[e] twyse.

CLOKED COLUSYON
Why, wenest thou that I forbere the[e] for thyne owne sake?

CRAFTY COVEYAUNCE
Peas, or I shall wrynge thy be[176] in a brake.

CLOKED COLUSYON
Holde thy hande, dawe, of thy dagger, and stynt of thy dyn,
Or I shal fawchyn thy flesshe and scrape the[e] on the skyn.

CRAFTY CONVEYAUNCE
Ye[a], wylte thou, ha[n]gman? I say, thou cavell!

CLOKED COLUSYON
Nay, thou rude ravener! Rayne beten javel!

CRAFTY CONVEYAUNCE
What, thou Colyn Cowarde, knowen and tryde!

CLOKED COLUSYON
Nay, thou false harted dastarde! Thou dare not abyde.

CRAFTY CONVEYAUNCE
And yf there were none to dysplease but thou and I,
Thou sholde not scape, horson, but thou sholde dye.

CLOKED COLUSYON
Nay, Iche shall wrynge the[e], horson, on the wryst.

CRAFTY CONVEYAUNCE
Mary, I defye thy best and thy worst.

{Enter Counterfet Countenaunce.}

[COUNTERFET COUNTENAUNCE]
What a very vengeaunce nede all these wordys?

2171 strike, head **2172** we're close to fighting **2173** head, waist **2174** crack (i.e. kiss my arse) **2178** strike **2179** look at **2180** teach **2183** twice **2185** twist, rack **2186** Take, from, stop **2187** falchion (sword, here a verb) **2188** tall wretch **2189** brigand, rain-beaten rogue **2190** renowned coward **2194** I

174 Colusyon issues a formal challenge to combat.

175 Ironic: 'I'm sure you'd strike the Devil if you weren't held back!'

176 'Be': it may be, as Neuss suggests, that 'behind' (arse) is intended, although why Conveyaunce should be so coy is unclear.

Go together by the heddys, and gyve me your swordys.

Cloked Colusyon
So he is the worste brawler that ever was borne.

Crafty Conveyaunce
In fayth, so to suffer the[e], it is but a skorne.

Counterfet Countenaunce
Now let us be all one, and let us lyve in rest;
For we be, syrs, but a fewe of the best.

Cloked Colusyon
By the Masse, man, thou shall fynde me resonable.

Crafty Conveyaunce
In faythe, and I wyll be to reason agreable.

Counterfet Countenaunce
Then truste I to God and the Holy Rode,
Here shalbe not great sheddynge of blode.

Cloked Colusyon
By Our Lakyn, syr, not by my wyll.

Crafty Conveyaunce
By the fayth that I owe to God, and I wyll syt styll.

Counterfet Countenaunce
Well sayd; but in fayth, what was your quarell?

Cloked Colusyon
Mary, syr, this gentylman called me javell.

Crafty Conveyaunce
Nay, by Saynt Mary, it was ye called me knave.

Cloked Colusyon
Mary, so ungoodly langage you me gave.

Counterfet Countenaunce
A, shall we have more of this maters yet?
Me thynke ye are not gretly acomberyd with wyt.

Crafty Conveyaunce
Goddys fote! I warant you I am a gentylman borne.
And thus to be facyd I thynke it great skorne.

Counterfet Countenaunce
I cannot well tell of your dysposycyons:
And ye be a gentylman, ye have knavys condycyons.

Cloked Colusyon
By God, I tell you, I wyll not be out facyd.

Crafty Conveyaunce
By the Masse, I warant the[e], I wyll not be bracyd.

Counterfet Countenaunce
Tushe, tushe, it is a great defaute;
The one of you is to proude, the other is to haute.
Tell me brefly where upon ye began.

Cloked Colusyon
Mary, syr, he sayd that he was the pratyer man
Then I was, in opynynge of lockys;
And I tell you, I dysdayne moche of his mockys.

Crafty Conveyaunce
Thou sawe never yet but I dyd my parte,[177]
The locke of a caskyt to make to starte.

Counterfet Countenaunce
Nay, I know well inough ye are bothe well handyd
To grope a gardevyaunce, though it be well bandyd.[178]

Cloked Colusyon
I am the better yet in a bowget.

Crafty Conveyaunce
And I the better in a male.

Counterfet Countenaunce
Tushe, these maters that ye move are but soppys in ale.
Your trymynge and tramynge by me must be tangyd,[179]

2197 agree among yourselves 2199 tolerate 2200 reconciled, peace 2206 Our Lady 2209 wretch 2212 business 2213 burdened 2215 challenged/insulted 2217 If, manners 2219 insulted 2221 too, haughty 2222 briefly what started this 2223 more skilful 2224 picking 2225 insults 2227 spring open 2228 skilful 2230 with a purse, wallet 2231 raise, trifles (bread in ale)

177 'You've never seen me fail to play my part'.
178 'To crack open a treasure-chest, even if it is protected with bands [of iron].'
179 'I must bring some direction to your pointless prattle'.

For had I not bene, ye bothe had bene hangyd,
When we with Magnyfycence goodys made chevysaunce.[180]

MAGNYFYCENCE
And therfore our Lorde sende you a very wengeaunce!

COUNTERFET COUNTENAUNCE
What begger art thou, that thus doth banne and wary?

MAGNYFYCENCE
Ye be the thevys, I say, away my goodys dyd cary.

CLOKED COLUSYON
Cockys bones, thou begger, what is thy name?

MAGNYFYCENCE
Magnyfycence I was, whom ye have brought to shame.

COUNTERFET COUNTENAUNCE
Ye[a], but trowe you, syrs, that this is he?

CRAFTY CONVEYAUNCE
Go we nere and let us se.

CLOKED COLUSYON:
By Cockys bonys, it is the same!

MAGNYFYCENCE
Alasse, alasse, syrs, ye are to blame!
I was your mayster, though ye thynke it skorne,
And nowe on me ye gaure and sporne.

COUNTERFET COUNTENAUNCE
Ly styl, ly styll nowe, with yll hayle!

CRAFTY CONVEYAUNCE
Ye[a], for thy langage can not the[e] avayle.

CLOKED COLUSYON
Abyde, syr, abyde, I shall make hym to pysse.

MAGNYFYCENCE
Nowe gyve me somwhat, for God sake, I crave.

CRAFTY CONVEYAUNCE
In faythe, I gyve the four quarters of a knave.

COUNTERFET COUNTENAUNCE
In faythe, and I bequethe hym the tothe ake.

CLOKED COLUSYON
And I bequethe hym the bone ake.

CRAFTY CONVEYAUNCE
And I bequethe hym the gowte and the gyn.

CLOKED COLUSYON
And I bequethe hym sorowe for his syn.

COUNTERFET COUNTENAUNCE
And I gyve hym Crystys curse.
With never a peny in his purse.

CRAFTY CONVEYAUNCE
And I gyve hym the cowghe, the murre, and the pose.

CLOKED COLUSYON
Ye[a], for *requiem eternam*, groweth forth of his nose.[181]
But nowe let us make mery and good chere.

COUNTERFET COUNTENAUNCE
And to the taverne let us drawe nere.

CRAFTY CONVEYAUNCE
And from thens, to the Halfe Strete,[182]
To get us there some freshe mete.

CLOKED COLUSYON
Why, is there any store of rawe motton?

COUNTERFET COUNTENAUNCE
Ye[a], in faythe, or ellys thou arte to great a glotton.[183]

CRAFTY CONVEYAUNCE
But they say it is a queysy mete:
It wyll stryke a man myscheyously in a hete.

2233 been (here) **2235** curse you! **2236** curse, grumble **2237** carry **2245** stare, spurn **2246** lie, curse you **2247** cannot help you **2248** piss **2253** rack **2257** catarrh conditions **2258** eternal rest, from **2263** mutton (sheep meat)/female flesh **2265** (i.e. it makes one feel sick) **2266** with a fever

180 'Used Magnyfycence's property as the security on a loan.'

181 Proverbially 'hunger drops out of the nose'. The implication here is that Magnyfycence is close to death through hunger and poverty.

182 The Half Street, in Southwark, where the brothels stood. The following lines pun upon eating and whoring, indigestion and venereal disease.

183 'Too great a glutton'; i.e. there is enough to satisfy any normal appetite.

CLOKED COLUSYON
In fay, man, some rybbys of the motton be so ranke
That they wyll fyre one ungracyously in the flanke.

COUNTERFET COUNTENAUNCE
Ye[a], and when ye come out of the shoppe,
Ye shall be clappyd with a coloppe[184]
That wyll make you to halt and to hoppe.

CRAFTY CONVEYAUNCE
Som be wrestyd there that they thynke on it forty dayes,
For there be horys there at all assayes.

CLOKED COLUSYON
For the Passyon of God, let us go thyther!
Et cum festinacione discedant a loco.[185]

MAGNYFYCENCE
Alas, myn owne servauntys to shew me such reproche,
Thus to rebuke me and have me in dyspyght!
So shamfully to me, theyr mayster, to aproche,
That som tyme was a noble prynce of myght.
Alasse, to lyve longer I have no delyght,
For to lyve in mysery, it is herder than dethe.
I am wery of the worlde, for unkyndnesse me sleeth.

Hic intrat Dyspare.[186]

DYSPARE
Dyspare is my name, that Adversyte dothe felowe.
In tyme of dystresse I am redy at hande;
I make hevy hertys, with eyen full holowe.
Of farvent charyte I quenche out the bronde;
Faythe and good hope I make asyde to stonde.
In Goddys mercy, I tell them, is but foly to truste;[187]
All grace and pyte I lay in the dust.

What, lyest thou there lyngrynge, lewdly and lothsome.
It is to late nowe thy synnys to repent.
Thou hast bene so waywarde, so wranglyng, and so wrothsome,
And so fer thou arte behynde of thy rent,
And so ungracyously thy dayes thou hast spent,
That thou arte not worthy to loke God in the face.

MAGNYFYCENCE
Nay, nay, man, I loke never to have parte of His grace,
For I have so ungracyously my lyfe mysusyd;
Though I aske mercy, I must nedys be refusyd.

DYSPARE
No, no; for thy synnys be so excedynge farre,
So innumerable, and so full of dyspyte,
And agayne thy Maker thou hast made suche warre,
That thou canst not have never mercy in His syght.

MAGNYFYCENCE
Alasse my wyckydnesse! That may I wyte!
But nowe I se well there is no better rede,
But sygh and sorowe and wysshe my selfe dede.

DYSPARE
Ye[a], ryd thy selfe rather than this lyfe for to lede.
The worlde waxeth wery of the[e]; thou lyvest to longe.

Hic intrat Myschefe.[188]

MYSCHEFE
And I, Myschefe, am comyn at nede,
Out of thy lyfe the[e] for to lede.
And loke that it be not longe
Or that thy selfe thou go honge
With this halter good and stronge;
Or ellys with this knyfe cut out a tonge
Of thy throte bole, and ryd the[e] out of payne.
Thou arte not the fyrst hymselfe hath slayne.
Lo, here is thy knyfe and a halter, and or we go ferther,
Spare not thy selfe, but boldly the[e] murder.

DYSPARE
Ye[a], have done at ones, without delay.

2267 faith, ribs, rotten/diseased 2268 inflame, wickedly, side/groin 2271 limp 2272 twisted/tormented 2273 whores, all tastes 2275 (for) my 2276 disdain 2277 approach/address 2280 harder 2281 slays me 2282 accompany/follow 2284 hearts sorrowful, eyes 2285 fervent, firebrand 2286 push aside 2288 pity 2289 lingering 2291 angry 2292 far, debt (to God) 2295 expect 2297 necessarily 2298 far too great 2300 against 2302 blame! 2304 dead 2305 (i.e. kill yourself) 2306 grows weary 2307 when needed 2310 Before, hang 2313 Adam's Apple, free yourself from 2314 first (that) 2316 murder yourself

[184] Both 'Struck with a cut of meat' and 'Given the clap/pox by a prostitute'.
[185] 'And let them leave the place hurriedly.'
[186] 'Here Despair enters.'
[187] 'I tell them that it is mere folly to trust in God's mercy'.
[188] 'Here Mischief enters.'

MAGNYFYCENCE
Shall I myselfe hange with an halter? Nay!
Nay, rather wyll I chose to ryd me of this lyve
In styckynge my selfe with this fayre knyyfe.

Here Magnyfycence wolde slee hymselfe with a knyfe.

[MYSCHEFE]
[*Seeing Good Hope*] Alarum, alarum! To longe we abyde!

DYSPARE
Out, harowe! Hyll burneth! Where shall I me hyde?

Hic intrat Good Hope, fugientibus Dyspayre and Myschefe; repente Good Hope surripiat illi gladio, et dicat:[189]

GOOD HOPE
Alas, dere sone! Sore combred is thy mynde,
Thyselfe that thou wolde sloo agaynst nature and kynde.

MAGNYFYCENCE
A, blessyd may ye be, syr! What shall I you call?

GOOD HOPE
Good Hope, syr, my name is; remedy pryncypall
Agaynst all fautes of your goostly foo.
Who knoweth me, hymselfe may never sloo.

MAGNYFYCENCE
Alas, syr, so I am lapped in adversyte
That Dyspayre well nyghe had myscheved me.
For had ye not the soner ben my refuge,
Of dampnacyon I had ben drawen in the luge.

GOOD HOPE
Undoubted ye had lost yourselfe eternally:
There is no man may synne more mortally
Than of wanhope thrughe the unhappy wayes,
By myschefe to brevyate and shorten his dayes.
But, my good sonne, lerne from Dyspayre to flee;
Wynde you from wanhope and aquaynte you with me.
A grete mysadventure thy Maker to dysplease,
Thyselfe myschevynge to thyne endlesse dysease!
There was never so harde a storme of mysery,
But thrughe Good Hope there may come remedy.

MAGNYFYCENCE
Your wordes be more sweter than ony precyous narde,
They molefy so easely my harte that was so harde.
There is no bawme ne gumme of Arabe
More delectable than your langage to me.

GOOD HOPE
Syr, your fesycyan is the grace of God,
That you hath punysshed with his sharpe rod.
Good Hope, your potecary, assygned am I,
That Goddes grace hath vexed you sharply
And payned you with a purgacyon of odyous Poverte,
Myxed with bytter alowes of herde Adversyte.
Nowe must I make you a lectuary softe,
I to mynyster it, you to recyve it ofte,
With rubarbe of repentaunce in you for to rest;
With drammes of devocyon your dyet must be drest,
With gommes goostly of glad herte and mynde,
To thanke God of His sonde; and comforte ye shal fynde.
Put fro you presumpcyon and admyt humylyte,
And hartely thanke God of your Adversyte;
And love that Lorde that for your love was dede,
Wounded from the fote to the crowne of the hede.
For who loveth God can ayle nothynge but good;
He may helpe you, He may mende your mode.
Prosperyte by Hym is gyven solacyusly to man,
Adversyte to hym therwith nowe and than,
Helthe of body his besynesse to acheve,
Dysease and sekenesse his conscyence to dyscryve,
Afflyccyon and trouble to prove his pacyence,
Contradyccyon to prove his sapyence
Grace of assystence His measure to declare,[190]
Somtyme to fall, another tyme to beware;
And nowe ye have had, syr, a wonderous fall,
To lerne you hereafter for to beware withall.
Howe say you, syr, can ye these wordys grope?

2321 Beware, Too 2322 Hell burns, hide myself 2323 dear son, burdened 2324 slay 2327 faults, spiritual enemy 2329 wrapped in 2330 nearly, destroyed 2331 so quickly 2332 lodge/prison 2335 through unhappy means 2336 abbreviate 2338 depart, acquaint yourself 2339 it would be a great mistake 2340 Damaging yourself, distress 2343 spikenard (ointment) 2344 soften 2345 balm, gum arabic (ointments) 2346 words 2347 physician 2348 punished (you) 2349 apothecary 2351 laxative (purgative) 2352 aloes (purgative) 2353 an alectuary (medicine) 2354 administer, receive 2355 rhubarb (a purgative) 2356 small doses, prepared 2357 spiritual gums (ointments) 2358 for, message/gift 2363 (he) who, be affected by 2364 amend, mood 2366 along with it 2367 labour 2368 to reveal 2369 Affliction, test 2370 Contradiction, wisdom 2374 teach 2375 understand

[189] 'Here Good Hope enters as Dyspare and Myschefe are fleeing; let Good Hope swiftly take the knife from him and say'.

[190] '[The] grace of His assistance to reveal His [benign] moderation'.

MAGNYFYCENCE
Ye[a], syr, nowe am I armyd with Good Hope,
And sore I repent me of my wylfulnesse.
I aske God mercy of my neglygence,
Under Good Hope enduryinge ever styll,
Me humbly commyttynge unto Goddys wyll.

GOOD HOPE
Then shall you be sone delyvered from dystresse,
For nowe I se comynge to youwarde Redresse.

Hic intrat Redresse.

REDRESSE
Cryst be amonge you, and the Holy Goste!

GOOD HOPE
He be your conducte, the Lorde of myghtys moste.

REDRESSE
Syr, is your pacyent any thynge amendyd?

GOOD HOPE
Ye[a], syr, he is sory for that he hath offendyd.

REDRESSE
How fele you your selfe, my frend? How is yow
mynde?

MAGNYFYCENCE
A wrechyd man, syr, to my Maker unkynde.

REDRESSE
Ye[a], but have ye repentyd you with harte contryte?

MAGNYFYCENCE
Syr, the repentaunce I have no man can wryte.

REDRESSE
And have ye banyshed from you all dyspare?

MAGNYFYCENCE
Ye[a], holly to Good Hope I have made my repare.

GOOD HOPE
Questyonles he doth me assure
In Good Hope alway for to indure.

REDRESSE
Then stande up, syr, in Goddys name!
And I truste to ratyfye and amende your fame.
Good Hope, I pray you with harty affeccyon
To sende over to me Sad Cyrcymspeccyon.

GOOD HOPE
Syr, your requeste shall not be delayed.

Et exiat [*Good Hope*].

REDRESSE
Now surely, Magnyfycence, I am ryght well apayed
Of that I se you nowe in the state of grace.
Nowe shall ye be renewyd with solace:
Take nowe upon you this abylyment,
And to that I say gyve good advysement.

Magnyfycence accipiat indumentum.[191]

MAGNYFYCENCE
To your requeste I shall be confyrmable.

[REDRESSE]
Fyrst, I saye, with mynde fyrme and stable
Determyne to amende all your wanton excesse;
And be ruled by me, whiche am called Redresse.
Redresse my name is, that lytell am I used
As the world requyreth, but rather I am refused.
Redresse sholde be at the rekenynge in every
accompte,
And specyally to redresse that were out of joynte.
Full many thynges there be that lacketh Redresse,
The whiche were to longe nowe to expresse.
But Redresse is redlesse and may do no correccyon.
Nowe welcome, forsoth, Sad Cyrcumspeccyon.

Here cometh in Sad Cyrcumspeccyon, sayenge:

SAD CYRCUMSPECCYON
Syr, after your message I hyed me hyder streyght,
For to understande your pleasure and also your
mynde.

REDRESSE
Syr, to accompte you; the contynewe of my consayte
Is from Adversyte Magnyfycence to unbynde.

2380 committing myself 2382 towards you 2384 guide 2385 patient 2392 wholly, resort 2393 Without question/doubtless 2396 approve, reputation 2400 repaid/satisfied 2401 Because 2403 garment 2404 attention 2405 conformable/obedient 2410 desires/demands 2412 which is disordered 2414 recount 2415 incapable of offering advice 2417 I came straight here 2419 inform, conclusion, idea 2420 release

191 'Let Magnyfycence receive the garment.'

Sad Cyrcumspeccyon
How fortuned you, Magnyfycence, so far to fal behynde?

Magnyfycence
Syr, the longe absence of you, Sad Cyrcumspeccyon,
Caused me of Adversyte to fall in subjeccyon.

Redresse
All that he sayth of trouthe doth procede,
For where Sad Cyrcumspeccyon is longe out of the way,
Of Adversyte it is to stande in drede.

Sad Cyrcumspeccyon
Without fayle, syr, that is no nay:
Cyrcumspeccyon inhateth all rennynge astray.
But, syr, by me to rule ye fyrst began.

Magnyfycence
My wylfulnesse, syr, excuse I ne can.

Sad Cyrcumspeccyon
Then ye repent you of foly in tymes past?

Magnyfycence
Sothely to repent me I have grete cause.
Howe be it, from you I receyved a letter,
Whiche conteyned in it a specyall clause
That I sholde use Largesse.

Sad Cyrcumspeccyon
Nay, syr, there a pause.

Redresse
Yet let us se this matter thorowly ingrosed.

Magnyfycence
Syr, this letter ye sent to me at Pountes was enclosed.

Sad Cyrcumspeccyon
Who brought you that letter? Wote ye what he hyght?

Magnyfycence
Largesse, syr, by his credence was his name.

Sad Cyrcumspeccyon
This letter ye speke of never dyd I wryte.

Redresse
To gyve so hasty credence ye were moche to blame.

Magnyfycence
Truth it is, syr; for after he wrought me moch shame;
And caused me also to use to moche Lyberte,
And made also Mesure to be put fro me.

Redresse
Then welthe with you myght in no wyse abyde.

Sad Cyrcumspeccyon
A ha! Fansy and Foly met with you, I trowe.

Redresse
It wolde be founde so yf it were well tryde.

Magnyfycence
Surely my welthe with them was overthrow.

Sad Cyrcumspeccyon
Remembre you, therfore, howe late ye were low.

Redresse
Ye[a], and beware of unhappy Abusyon.

Sad Cyrcumspeccyon
And kepe you from counterfaytynge of Clokyd Colusyon.

Magnyfycence
Syr, in Good Hope I am to amende.

Redresse
Use not then your countenaunce for to counterfet.[192]

Sad Cyrcumspeccyon
And from crafters and hafters I you forfende.[193]

Hic intrat Perseveraunce.

Magnyfycence
Well, syr, after your counsell my mynde I wyll set.

Redresse
What, Brother Perceveraunce! Surely well met!

2424 (i.e. is true) **2426** is to be feared **2427** is undeniable **2428** hates, running **2432** Truly **2435** stop there a moment **2436** thoroughly clarified **2437** Pontoise, sealed (see l. 343) **2442** afterwards **2444** dismissed **2448** by, overthrown **2449** recently

[192] 'Don't fall into the habit of deceit.'

[193] 'And I forbid you [to associate with] tricksters and deceivers.'

Sad Cyrcumspeccyon
Ye com hether as well as can be thought.

Perseveraunce
I herde say that Adversyte with Magnyfycence had fought.

Magnyfycence
Ye[a], syr; with Adversyte I have bene vexed,
But Good Hope and Redresse hath mendyd my estate,
And Sad Cyrcumspeccyon to me they have a[nn]exyd.

Redresse
What this man hath sayd, perceyve ye his sentence?

Magnyfycence
Ye[a], syr, from hym my corage shall never flyt.

Sad Cyrcumspeccyon
Accordynge to treuth they be well devysed.

Magnyfycence
Syrs, I am agreed to abyde your ordenaunce:
Faythfull assuraunce with good peradvertaunce.

Perseveraunce
Yf you be so myndyd, we be ryght glad.

Redresse
And ye shall have more worshyp then ever ye had.

Magnyfycence
Well I perceyve in you there is moche sadnesse,
Gravyte of counsell, provydence, and wyt.
Your comfortable advyse and wyt excedyth all gladnesse;
But frendly I wyll refrayne you ferther, or we flyt;
Whereto were most metely my corage to knyt?[194]
Your myndys I beseche you here in to expresse.
Commensynge this processe at Mayster Redresse.

Redresse
Syth unto me formest this processe is erectyd,
Herein I wyll aforse me to shewe you my mynde:
Fyrst, from your magnyfycence syn must be abjected,
In all your warkys more grace shall ye fynde,
Be gentyll, then, of corage, and lerne to be kynde;
For of noblenesse the chefe poynt is to be lyberall,
So that your Largesse be not to prodygall.

Sad Cyrcumspeccyon
Lyberte to a lorde belongyth of ryght,
But wylfull waywardnesse muste walke out of the way.
Measure of your lustys must have the oversyght,
And not all the nygarde nor the chyncherde to play.
Let never negarshyp your noblenesse affray;
In your rewardys use suche moderacyon
That nothynge be gyven without consyderacyon.

Perseveraunce
To the increse of your honour then arme you with ryght,
And fumously adresse you with magnanymyte;
And ever let the drede of God be in your syght,
And knowe your selfe mortal for all your dygnyte.
Set not all your affyaunce in Fortune full of gyle;
Remember this lyfe lastyth but a whyle.

Magnyfycence
Redresse, in my remembraunce your lesson shall rest;
And Sad Cyrcumspeccyon I marke in my mynde:
But, Perseveraunce, me semyth your probleme was best.
I shall it never forget nor leve it behynde,
But hooly to Perseveraunce my selfe I wyll bynde,
Of that I have mysdone to make a redresse,
And with Sad Cyrcumspeccyon correcte my wantonnesse.

Redresse
Unto this processe brefly compylyd,
Comprehendyng the worlde casuall and transytory,
Who lyst to consyder shall never be begylyd
Yf it be regystryd well in memory.
A playne example of worldly vaynglory,
Howe in this worlde there is no sekernesse,
But fallyble flatery enmyxyd with bytternesse.

2457 at the best possible moment 2461 joined 2462 man (i.e. Cyrcumspeccyon) 2463 depart 2464 they (my words) 2465 follow 2466 I assure you, attention 2469 seriousness 2471 comforting 2476 initially, question, directed 2477 try 2478 rejected 2479 (Thus) in, works 2480 of heart 2482 Provided, too unrestrained 2484 be rejected 2486 miser 2487 miserliness, assault 2490 righteousness 2491 passionately, direct yourself 2493 despite all 2494 trust, guileful Fortune 2498 lesson 2500 wholly 2503 discussion, devised 2504 concerning, fickle 2506 recorded 2508 trustworthiness 2509 false flattery, mixed

194 'But, before we go, let me detain you a little longer with a friendly enquiry; where is it best to fix my devotion?'

Nowe well, nowe wo, nowe hy, nowe lawe degre;
Nowe ryche, nowe pore, nowe hole, nowe in dysease;
Nowe pleasure at large, nowe in captyvyte;
Nowe leve, nowe lothe, now please, nowe dysplease;
Now ebbe, now flowe, nowe increase, now dyscrease:
So in this worlde there is no sykernesse,
But fallyble flatery enmyxyd with bytternesse.

SAD CYRCUMSPECCYON
A myrrour incleryd is this interlude,
This lyfe inconstant for to beholde and se:
Sodenly avaunsyd, and sodenly subdude,
Sodenly ryches, and sodenly poverte,
Sodenly comfort, and sodenly adversyte,
Sodenly thus Fortune can bothe smyle and frowne,
Sodenly set up, and sodenly cast downe.

Sodenly promotyd, and sodenly put backe;
Sodenly cherysshyd, and sodenly cast asyde;
Sodenly commendyd, and sodenly fynde a lacke;
Sodenly grauntyd, and sodenly denyed;
Sodenly hyd, and sodenly spyed:
Sodenly thus Fortune can bothe smyle and frowne,
Sodenly set up, and sodenly cast downe.

PERSEVERAUNCE
This treatyse, devysed to make you dysporte,
Shewyth nowe adayes howe the worlde comberyd is,
To the pythe of the mater who lyst to resorte:[195]
To day it is well, to morowe it is all amysse;
To day in delyte, tomorowe bare of blysse;
To day a lorde, to morowe ly in the duste:
Thus in this worlde there is no erthly truste.

To day fayre wether, to morowe a stormy rage;
To day hote, to morowe outragyous colde;
To day a yoman, to morowe made of page;[196]
To day in surety, to morowe bought and solde;
To day maysterfest, to morowe he hath no holde:
To day a man, to-morowe he lyeth in the duste:
Thus in this worlde there is no erthly truste.

SAD CYRCUMSPECCYON
This mater we have movyd you myrthys to make,
Precely purposyd under pretence of play,[197]
Shewyth wysdome to them that wysdome can take:
Howe sodenly worldly welth dothe dekay;
How wysdom thorowe wantonesse vanysshyth away;
How none estate lyvynge of hymselfe can be sure,
For the welthe of this worlde can not indure.

Of the tereste [t]rechery we fall in the flode,
Beten with stormys of many a frowarde blast,
Ensordyd[198] with the wawys savage and wode.
Without our shyppe be sure it is lykely to brast.
Yet of magnyfycence oft made is the mast;[199]
Thus none estate lyvynge of hym[selfe] can be sure,
For the welthe of this worlde can not indure.

REDRESSE
[*To Magnyfycence*] Nowe semyth us syttynge that ye then resorte
Home to your paleys with joy and ryalte.

SAD CYRCUMSPECCYON
Where every thyng is ordenyd after your noble porte.

PERSEVERAUNCE
There to indeuer with all felycyte.

MAGNYFYCENCE
I am content, my frendys, that it so be.

REDRESSE
And ye that have harde this dysporte and game,
Jhesus preserve you frome endlesse wo and shame.
Amen.

2510 high, low 2511 whole/healthy 2513 happy, miserable 2514 decrease 2517 clear mirror/reflection/lesson 2519 Suddenly advanced, subjected 2526 found lacking 2528 hidden 2531 to entertain you 2532 burdened 2542 bound surely to a master 2545 created, to entertain you 2552 worldly treachery 2553 capricious/angry 2554 waves, mad/wild 2555 Unless, burst 2559 fitting, return 2560 palace, royalty 2561 ordained/arranged 2562 endure

[195] '[As] whoever wishes to look to the heart of the matter [will see]'.

[196] 'Today a yeomen [independent small farmer], tomorrow treated like a servant'.

[197] 'Specifically devised in the form of a play'.

[198] 'Besmeared', or perhaps 'sucked in'.

[199] 'Yet we often make magnificence the mainstay of our hopes'.

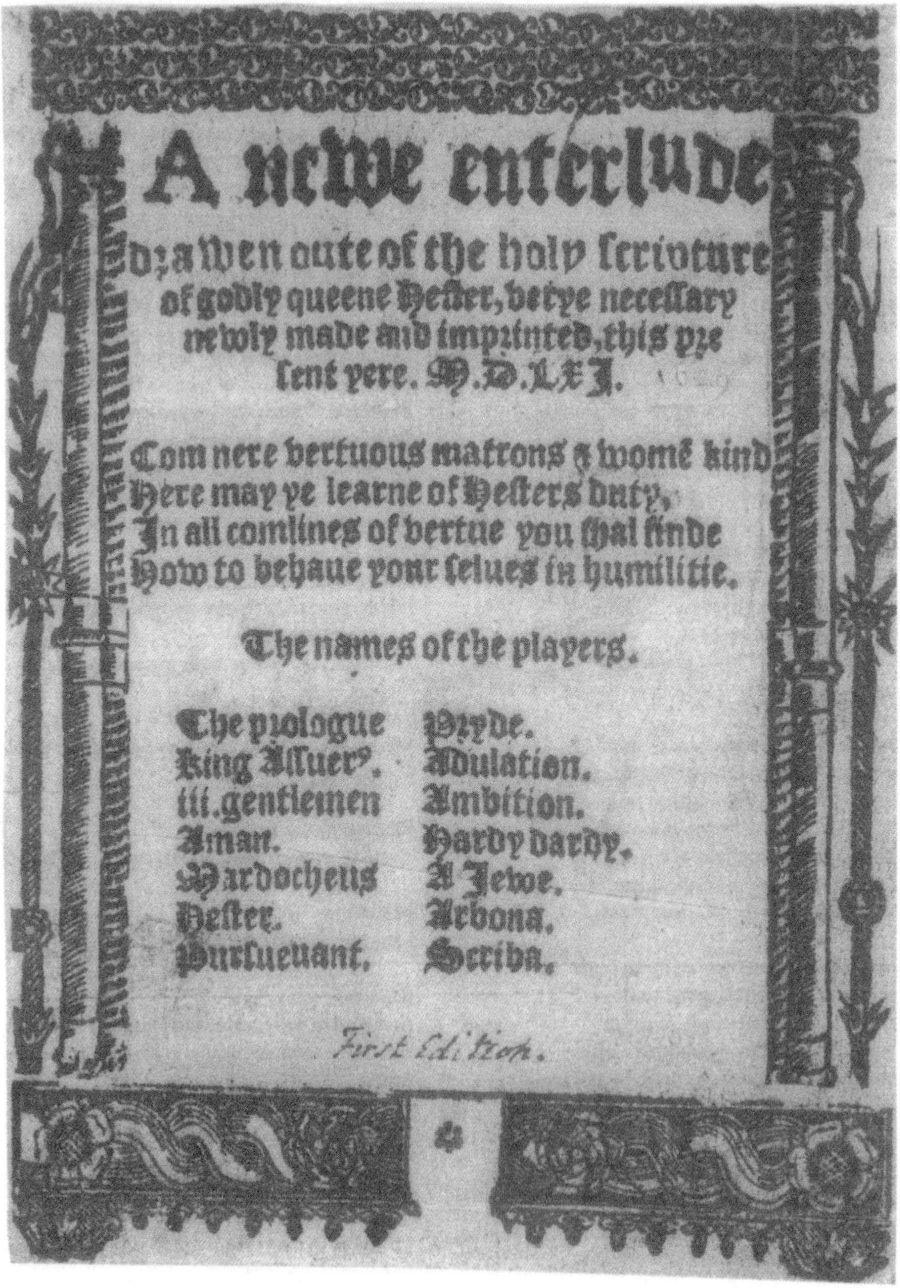

A newe enterlude
drawen oute of the holy scripture
of godly queene Hester, verye necessary
newly made and imprinted, this pre
sent yere. M.D.LXI.

Com nere vertuous matrons & womē kind
Here may ye learne of Hesters duty,
In all comlines of vertue you shal finde
How to behaue your selues in humilitie.

The names of the players.

The prologue
King Assuerus.
iii. gentlemen
Aman.
Mardocheus
Hester.
Pursueuant.

Pryde.
Adulation.
Ambition.
Hardy dardy.
A Jewe.
Arbona.
Scriba.

First Edition.

The Enterlude of Godly Queene Hester, title page, 1561. Reproduced by permission of the Huntington Library, San Marino, California.

The Enterlude of Godly Queene Hester

The only edition of this Interlude seems to have been that entered on the Stationers' Register in 1560/61 and printed in 1561 by the London printers William Pickering and Thomas Hacket. The play itself was, however, probably over thirty years old by that time. It is an adaptation of the events narrated in the biblical book of Esther (and its apocryphal continuation), in which the eponymous Jewish heroine pleads successfully with her husband, King Ahasuerus of Persia, for the lives of her people, who have been condemned to death at the instigation of the evil counsellor Haman. Although the plot is a traditional one, however, its treatment is not. Esther's defence of the Jews is refigured by the anonymous playwright into a defence of the Tudor monastic orders, and the portrayal of Aman/Haman is reworked into a sustained satirical assault upon Henry VIII's chief minister Cardinal Wolsey (see Walker, *Plays of Persuasion*, pp. 102–32). Taken together this suggests that the play formed part of the political and satirical assault upon the cardinal and the policies which he administered which was unleashed at his fall in 1529.

Aman was a popular figure in political satire (his example was also cited in attacks upon Henry's next chief minister, Thomas Cromwell, in the late 1530s) as he fitted ideally the model of the 'evil counsellor'. In a political culture in which kings could not be criticized directly for flawed or unpopular policies, the notion of the 'evil advisor' who had deluded the sovereign into taking the wrong course of action provided a useful means by which critics could voice their opposition and the monarch could alter policy without having to admit that he had erred. This was precisely what occurred in 1529–30, when Henry dismissed Wolsey from office. A number of unpopular taxes and impositions were written off as the results of the cardinal's malign influence, and the king was able to take up the reigns of government once more with a renewed sense of purpose and popularity. Critics of other policies were also able to make a case for their reversal by associating them with the fallen minister, which seems to be what is happening in *Hester*. Wolsey had suppressed a number of small religious houses in the early 1520s to fund new educational establishments in Oxford and Ipswich, and in the late 1520s a far wider suppression was being considered by the crown. Although not complacent about alleged clerical abuses (see, for example, ll. 1082–8), *Hester* offers a strong defence of monasticism on social grounds (stressing the importance of religious houses as centres of poor relief), and seeks to condemn the suppression policy as the result of greed and prejudice on the part of the chief minister Aman/Wolsey.

Aman is, on one level at least, intended as a figure for Wolsey, which allows plenty of scope for in-jokes at the expense of the ostentation of his houses and entourage, his prerogatives as a papal legate, and his origins as the son of an Ipswich butcher (see ll. 372–81, 424–45, and the punning upon 'wool', butchery, and papal bulls). Hester, on the other hand, is probably an idealization of Katherine of Aragon, Henry's resolutely orthodox first wife. Her character is an interesting variation on the popular dramatic subject of female virtue. Hester is presented chiefly as an intercessor with her husband, a venerable role adopted by virtuous royal women throughout the classical and medieval periods; but she is also allowed moments of greater independence. Her refusal to conform to a purely passive role is most evident when she is invited to outline her views on the duties of the ideal queen (ll. 272–95). She boldly replies that the queenly virtues should be precisely the same as the kingly ones, as the queen is very likely to find herself governing the kingdom while her husband is absent on foreign campaigns. In this she looks forward to the more robust secular heroines of the later sixteenth century rather than back to the godly virgins of the religious drama.

The play's other chief addition to its source is the inclusion of the quartet of Vices, Pryde, Ambition, Adulation (flattery), and Hardydardy (loosely and inelegantly translatable as 'foolish business'). Indeed, *Hester* is perhaps unique among the interludes in portraying a trio of ex-Vices, the satirical point being that Pryde, Ambition, and Adulation have all been usurped by Aman, and forced into retirement, bequeathing him all their vicious qualities. Their role in the play is thus, like ageing comedians on the chat-show circuit, to complain that they can no longer perform their proper functions as the younger usurper has taken all the plum perks. Only Hardydardy is a Vice in the traditional sense, enjoying the licence to exchange jokes with high and low characters alike, and drawing others into lively exchanges in his characteristic internally rhymed stanzas. Aman himself, while not a Vice, is vicious in a wholly more malevolent sense. His capacity to lurk in corners, and appear instantly at people's shoulders the moment he is called, foreshadows the mode of Iago and the Machiavellian villains of the playhouse drama.

The play was probably originally performed, like the majority of the Interludes, in the great hall of a palace or manor house, most probably within the court itself, although no record of a production survives. The stage directions call for 'the chapel' to sing a hymn at one point, suggesting that the playwright could call upon the services of a household choir, perhaps even that of the Chapel Royal. The only large prop required is the 'Traverse' into which the king retires, a curtained and canopied throne of the sort occupied by Jupiter in Heywood's *Play of the Weather* (see below).

The text printed here is based upon the 1561 edition (STC 13251), the only surviving copy of which is now in the Devonshire Collection. In addition I have consulted the modern editions in W.W. Greg, ed., *A New Enterlude of Godly Queene Hester* (Louvain, 1904); and J.S. Farmer, ed., *Six Anonymous Plays* (London, 1906).

Further reading

A. Fox, *Politics and Literature in the Reigns of Henry VII and Henry VIII* (Oxford, 1989).
G. Walker, *Plays of Persuasion: Drama and Politics at the Court of Henry VIII* (Cambridge, 1991).

A Newe Enterlude, drawen oute of the Holy Scripture, of Godly Queene Hester, verye necessary, newly made and imprinted, this present yere, MDLXI.

Come nere vertuous matrons and women kind,
Here may ye learne of Hesters duty;
In all comlines of vertue you shal finde
How to behave your selves in humilitie.[1]

The Names of the Players: *The Prologue*, *King Assuerus*,[2] *III Generosus* (Gentlemen: advisors to Assuerus)[3] *Aman*[4] *Mardocheus* (Mordechai, a Jewish dignitary), *Hester* (Esther, niece to Mardocheus), *Pursuevant* (a herald), *Pryde*, *Adulation*, *Ambition*, *Hardy Dardy*,[5] *III Jewes*,[6] *Arbona*,[7] *Scriba* (a royal clerk).

THE PROLOGUE
Divers Philosophers, auncient and sage,
Their clargy and cunnynge to put in practise,
Oft have disputed, by learning and language,
To whome greatest honour men ought to demise,
Or for what cause hie reverence shoulde aryse;
And, amonges manye, some were there doubtlesse,
That concluded honour due unto ryches.

Some also to noble bloude, and high parayge
Affirmed honour dewly to pertayne;
And some to policie and wysedome sage;
And some to power and superiall raigne.
Eche man his reason sayde in certayne.
Over this some said, that vertuous demenoure
To bee excellent, and of moste honour.

The kyng, sitting in a chaire, speaketh to his counsell.

KING ASSUERUS
Of these my lordes we woulde be glad to here,
Which is most worthy honoure to attayne;
By your high reasons we thynke it maye appeare;
To speake, therefore, we praye you, your sentences
plaine;
And, as ye determine, so shall wee, certaine,
Advaunce to honoure, and to promotion applye
Alwayes the best, and that bee most worthye.

2 scholarship 4 grant 5 high 7 (was) due 8 blood, parentage 10 political wisdom 11 superior (i.e. overall authority) 13 virtuous behaviour 15 From 17 wise arguments 18 opinions 20 reward with promotion 21 those who are

1 The play is consciously repackaged for the 1560s as a handbook for virtuous womanhood. Its publication may also, however, reflect contemporary interest in issues of abdicated sovereignty and good and bad counsel evident in plays such as *Gorboduc* (performed at court in 1562).

2 Ahasuerus or Artaxerxes, king of Persia 485–465 BC.

3 It is possible that one of the three *Generosus* is Aman. See the direction following l. 103 and note.

4 The biblical Haman.

5 'Rash daring', or 'foolish business'. See John Skelton, *Speke Parott*, l. 457.

6 The title page lists only 'A Jew', but the text gives lines for 'A Jewe', 'Another Jewe', and 'An Other Jewe' in succession.

7 Harbona or Harbonah, one of Assuerus's court eunuchs.

PRIMUS GENEROSUS
Most drad soveraigne, kinge Assuerus, to your
doughty, weyghty, and sured,[8]
Of riches power, wisdome, vertue, or noble bloude
Which is most soveraigne, and of highest honour?
Me seames as vertue none can be so good,
Not ryches nor power, wisdome nor gentill bludde.
For, wher vertue fayleth, the other be not suer,
But full unstable, and longe cannot indure.

Who so wyll laboure storyes to peruse,[9]
And them with dylligence often will rede,
May see and perceve, how vice dyd confuse
Many noble princes, whiche were, in dede,
Of such magnificence, that we not nede
To doubt of theyre riches, power, and wisdome.
And yet, for lacke of vertue, vice them over came.

SECUNDUS GENEROSUS
Nabuchodonozor, Senacherib, and Salmanasar,[10]
Nero, Dyoclisian, Maxentius also,[11]
All these prynces of hye honoure were,
Of ryches, power, and wysodome; allso
Of noble bloode; yet these and many mo,
For lacke of vertue, to vice dyd fall,
To theyre owne distruction and theyre subjectes all,

TERTIUS GENEROSUS
But then, as me semeth, yt were expedyent,
Amonge all vertues apperteyninge to a prince,
That same to knowe by sume reason urgente;
Which is so necessary to the province,[12]
That wythout yt in no wyse he can convince
Neyther synne nor synners, that unjustly deale,
Nor in good order kepe his common weale.

I GENEROSUS
In myne opynion, that is justice;
A vertu as excellent as may be.
For all thinges it orderith in such wyse,
That where it is, is peace and tranquillitie,
Good order, hygh honour, wealth, and plentye;
And, where it fayleth in the prince or kynge,
The common weale decayeth withoute tariynge.

II GENEROSUS
Besyde justice there muste bee diligence,
In hys owne personne that same to put in ure;
Or els some tyme suche coloured sentence
Under cloke of justice, ye maye be sure
Craftely shall procede from them that have the cure;
Which in processe, may brynge to downfall
The kynge, hys realme, and hys subjectes all.

The judgement of Salamon, in his owne person,
Betwene two women of lyvinge unchaste,[13]
So feared Israell that utterlye noone
Durste once rebell, but they thought it waste
In anye wyse to attempt, eyther fyrst or laste,
Any thynge of displeasure to hys majestye royall,
Fearyng hys wysedome and justice so equall.

III GENEROSUS
If by hys lieutenante had been done the same,
Hys honoure shoulde never have spronge so farre,
Nor so much renowned by noble fame
As it is now, and that both here and there.
Nor yet his subjectes to such awe and feare,
He coulde have dryven, by no meanes at all,
As he dyd by hys justice personall.

And over thys, many a noble man
At the prynces wyll and commaundymente,
To employe justice, dyd the best they can.
And yet the commons unneth coulde be content;
And why? For in their mynde they thyncke,
verament,

27 is lacking, certain 31 ruin 33 we do not need 42 (that of) all their subjects 47 subdue 48 behave unjustly 50 that (virtue) is justice 52 it governs all things 55 it is lacking 56 delay 57 In addition to 58 into practice 59 deceitful/biased 60 under the pretence 61 responsibility 66 frightened, no one at all 67 Dared (to), a waste of time 68 (i.e. at any time) 71 deputy 72 grown so great 74 (i.e. everywhere) 81 scarcely 82 truly

8 As Greg points out, this line is evidently corrupt, and may incorporate words which were cancelled in the original manuscript. The sense should, perhaps, be understood as 'Most dread [doughty, grave, and assured] sovereign, King Assuerus, [you ask] which [of these qualities], power, wisdom, virtue, or noble blood, is the most important, and of the highest honour. It seems to me that none [of these] can be as good as virtue'.

9 'Whoever makes the effort to consult [books of] history'.

10 Nebuchadnezzar, king of Babylon, 604–561 BC; Sennacherib, king of Assyria, 705–681 BC; Shalmaneser, king of Assyria, 727–722 BC. The choice of names (some of which are anachronistic) seems designed to place Assuerus's in a generally ancient and 'exotic' past, rather than anything more historically precise.

11 Born Lucius Domitius Ahenobarbus, the emperor Nero (Nero Claudius Caesar Augustus Germanicus) ruled Rome AD 54–68; Diocletian (Gaius Aurelius Valerius Diocletianus), co-emperor of Rome, AD 284–305; Maxentius (Marcus Aurelius Valerius), briefly succeeded Diocletian, but was defeated by Constantine.

12 'By some urgent means to gain knowledge of that [virtue] which is most important for governing a province'.

13 See I Kings 3 12:16–28.

That either for riches and honour, justis will doe,
And he onely, for the zeale that to justis he hath to.[14]

Wherfore, noble prince, if in youre owne person will ye
Employe justis, the more youre honour shallbe.

King Assuerus
My lordes, we thanke you for youre counsell.
As ye have sayed, so thinke we, verely,
That justis mainteneth ye common weale,
And namely ye prince muste nedes him selfe applye
Unto the same, or els utterly
Shall folowe decay, by warre or els death,
Quoque, si princeps malus populus corvet.[15]

And, over this, if that his lieutenaunt
Shal happen to square from trueth and justice,
Albeit his faire wordes and good semblaunt,
The prince must nedes be circumspect and wise,
That no ambicion nor covetise,
Through great welth and riches inordinat,
Doe erect his corage, for to play checkmate.[16]
For, though it be as well as it may neede,
It shall be thought nay, I assure you, in dede.
Sir, what is your name and progeny?

One of ye gentyllmen must answere, whyche you will.[17]

Aman
I am Aman, sonne of Amadathy,
Of the stocke of Agag, borne lyniallye.

Assuerus
Your learnyng and reason pleaseth us well,
And ye seeme to be of discretion.
We beare ye, therfore, our favour and zeale,
So that, withoute meanes of intercession,
We make you our chaunceloure. Take hede to this lesson:
See ye doe justice, and trueth ever approve,
Or to your destrucion, we shall you soone remove.

Aman
My duty is more nowe then ever it was,
Truly to serve Youre moste noble Grace,
Both nyghte and day, here and in every place. [*Exit.*]

Assuerus
My lordes, as nowe, thus standes the case:
We are comfortles for lacke of a Queene,
Which shoulde be our joye, and chefe solace.
And, to say truth, it hath not been oft seene
But the prince with a princes matched hath beene,
Leaste defaulte of issue shoulde be, which God defende![18]
Therfore, youre counsells firste had, to marry we do intend.

I Generosus
Then let your officers peruse this realme,
And of fayre maidens that be virgins pure,
Of most goodly personages that may be sene,
Gather a great number, that we may make reporte
Unto Your Grace; then may ye be sure
To chose the beste, when ye have them seene,
And that is fittest to be your quene.

Assuerus
Call to us Aman, our trusty chaunceler.

Here entrith Aman with many men awaiting on hym.

Aman
If it please Your Grace, I am here,

Assuerus
Aman, this is the councel of my lordes all:
That our officers in hast we shoulde sende
To peruse this region universall,
From the begynnynge unto the ende,
To seke faire maidens, where so thei may be kende,
And of most goodly personages that maye be sene,
To the intent among them we may chose a quene.
This is our minde, more to speake it shal not nede,
In all that ye may, see it bee done in dede.

89 upholds the commonwealth 94 in addition to 95 deviate 96 Despite, appearance 98 covetousness 102 not to be so 116 the situation is this 118 Who 122 having first heard your 123 search 129 most appropriate 134 universally 136 wherever, found 138 (from) among 139 no more needs to be said

[14] i.e. even if a deputy does his utmost to bring justice, everyone will think that he does so for honour or riches. Only the sovereign is thought to have a genuine zeal for justice in and of itself.

[15] 'Also: "if the prince is evil, the people fall."'

[16] 'Inflates his ambition to defeat [and replace the prince].'

[17] 'Whichever [one] you prefer.' The suggestion seems to be that either there are other *Generosi* present, one of whom proves to be Aman, or that he is one of the three who have spoken so far. If the latter, then *I Generosus* is, perhaps, the best choice, given that he has so far not argued against reliance upon lieutenants.

[18] 'In case there should [otherwise] be a lack of children [and thus heirs to the throne], which God forbid!'

Here the Kyng entryth the travers,[19] *and Aman goeth out.*
Here entreth Mardocheus and a maiden [Hester] *with him.*

[Mardocheus]
I am Mardocheus, borne in Jerusalem,
The sonne of Jaire, and of the stocke of Benjamy,[20]
By Nabuchodonosor brought into this realme
When he did subdue our kyng, Jechony,[21]
And translated the Jewes by conquest and victorye.
Both I and other, in number many one,
Were brought in captivitie, into the realme of
Babilon.

I have here a maiden of the same nacion,
My brothers doughter named Edissa;
But Hester is her common denomination,
And by that well knowen, *nam a deo missa.*[22]
God graunt her grace that persever she maye,
In wisedome and womanhead faythfull to bee,
Her espouse to love in perfecte amitie.

So is it nowe oure kynge Assuerus,
Dyvers Pursevauntes, in great haste hathe sente,
Over all hys realme in these parties nere us.
To seeke faire maidens is his entent,
To chose amonge theym one convenyente
To bee his quene and lady soveraigne,
In love and honour with him for to raigne.

And, for as muche, doughter Hester, that you
Amonge other are appoynted for one,
I thyncke it accordynge, therefore, nowe,
To give you mine advise and instruction.
Attende ye, therfore, without interruption,
And by faithfull mind, and stedfast memorye,
That I shall saye, learne it diligentlye.

Hester
Noble Mardocheus, my father moste kynde,
To that ye shall saye I wyll applye my mynde.

Mardocheus
Than, yf the kinge chose you to his queene,
It is of hys goodnes, bountie, and grace;
And for none youre merites, the truthe to bee seene.
Therefore, to hym repaye muste you needes
obedience,
Trew love, and kyndnes, above personnes all,
Not forged nor fayned, but with affection cordiall.

Breake not the course that queenes have hadde,
In this noble region most part of all,
They have aye bene good, and none of theym badde,
To their prince ever sure, just, and substanciall;
And good to the commons when they dyd call
By mekenes for mercye, to temper the fyre
Of rigors justice in fume or in yre.

Hester
Thys counsell is perfecte, and also so pure,
I graunt it, therfore, and promyse you sure,
It is my whole mynde and hartye desyre
That same to fulfyll, as reason shall requyre.

Pursuevant
I have here of maydens a fayre companye,
Of comlye stature and goodly visage,
Which, to the king, I thynke, by and by,
For to present, and to hys counsell sage,
For their promotion, wealth, and marriage.
Save before, wyth Mardocheus the Jew,
I muste speake for Hester, that is so fayre of hew.

Mardocheus
She is here, redy, and doth attende,
The kynges commaundiment to fullfyll;
And at youre pleasure, forth shall she wende
Wyth out resystance, and by her good wyll.

Pursuevant
Then shall I brynge her the kynge untyll.
Come on, lady Hester, and followe me.
To the kynge shall ye goe with youre cumpany.[23]

Here Aman metythe them in ye place.

145 moved/transported 146 many a one 147 Babylon 148 race 150 name 154 spouse 156 heralds 157 parts/regions 159 appropriate 163 have been chosen 166 Pay attention 168 That (which) 171 as 172 generosity 173 not (owing to), if truth be known 174 you must repay him with 175 True 176 feigned 177 Do not divert from, followed 179 all been 182 With, moderate 183 rigorous, anger, ire 186 heart's desire 190 in due course 193 before that 194 to ask for, hue 197 go 199 unto the king 201+ meets

[19] See headnote.
[20] Mordechai's father, Jair, was one of the tribe of Benjamin. See Esther 2:5.
[21] Jehoiachin, king of Judah at the time of Nebuchadnezzar's conquest of the Jews.
[22] Either 'For she [is] sent from God', or a corruption, perhaps 'a name sent from God'.
[23] The suggestion seems to be that Hester is accompanied by ladies in waiting.

Aman
Syr Pursivaunt, have ye these maydens broughte
For the kynge, lyke as ye had in commaundement?

Pursuevant
Yea, syr, and for them farre have I soughte,
Both in vyllage, towne, and tenemente.
I truste I have done trew service and dylligente.

Aman
So are ye bounde, by very dewty
Of youre allegeaunce and fydelytye.
Se that ye follow us wyth your hole cumpany.

Pursuevant
As ye have sayed, so shall it be.

Then thei go to the Kynge.

Aman
Pleasyth it Youre Grace, accordynge your mynde,
We have made serche all youre regyon,
For goodly maydens of nature fyne and kynde,
And of them have founde, in myne opynyon,
A number ryght fayre, and of complexion
So puer, and of so fayre visage,
That they surmounte all other in personage.

Assuerus
Are they also of suche competent age,
Of suche demeanour and gravitie,
That they be fytte for oure mariage?

Aman
Uppon a profe, Youre Grace shall heare and see,
As well theyr wysedome as theyr beautye.

Assuerus
Sertis they be fayre and goodly eche one;
And, as it maye seme by theyr fyrst countenaunce,
Both by looke and gesture, nature and complexion,
In theym shoulde by kyndnes, myrth, and dalyaunce;
Wysedome, sadnes, and in love perseveraunce;
Constauncie knit wyth comlines, joy to encrease;
Vertue with good demenour, pleasure to put in presse.
But ye, fayre damsell of the highest stature,
And of most ripe age, as shoulde seame,
Of all this companye of most fynest nature:
Tell us your linage, for, as yet we deame,
Your lookes be so lusty, and in love so breme,
If that your demenour hereafter be sene
To that accordynge, ye shalbe our quene.

Hester
Moste noble Prince, as for my linage,
Nor yet my countrey, sertis I can not saye;
My parentes dicessed in myne none age,
So that I never harde yet, unto thys daye,
What coste or countrey, what lande or laye
I was bred in, broughte forth, or borne,

It is to me unknowen, as aye hath bene beforne.
Notwithstandyng, I have had foode and fostring
Of Mardocheus all my lyfe dayes,
Whom I called father in my yonge age,
And so intend to do eftsons and alwaies,
Whome for his frendshippe I have good cause to prayse,
Besechinge Youre Grace, and that moste mekely,
To my sayd foster father, good lorde for to be.

Assuerus
Call in Mardocheus, that we may see his face.

Mardocheus
I am here to attende upon Youre Grace.

Assuerus
Mardocheus, what call you youre daughter?

Mardocheus
If it please Youre Grace, her name is Hester.
Assuringe you, she is a virgin puer,
A pearle undefiled, and of conscience cleare;
Sober, sad, jentill, meke, and demure,
In learninge and litterature, profoundely seene,
In wisdome, eke, semblante to Saba the Quene;[24]
Fytt for any prince to have in marriage,
If his pleasure agree to her personage,

Assuerus
Ye say ryghte well. Then we thynke it expedient

203 As you were told to 207 obliged (to), duty 211 as you wished 217 surpass, appearance 221 (i.e. put them to the test) 223 Certainly 224 appearance 227 sobriety 228 Constancy combined with beauty 229 behaviour, into practice 231 as it seems 234 bright 236 To match that 239 died, nonage (childhood) 241 coast/region, law/faith 243 as it has always been 244 fostering/upbringing 245 From, all the days of my life 247 now 255 (I) assure, pure 257 gentle 258 greatly skilled

[24] The queen of Sheba. See 1 Kings 10:1; 2 Chronicles 9:1.

Some what to prove, by communication,
Her lernynge and her language eloquent:
And by some probleme of hye dubitation,
To knowe her aunswere and consultation.
Howe saye you, Hester, have you ought reade or seene
Of vertues that be best and fittest for a queene?

HESTER
To speake before a king, it is no childes playe,
Therfore, I aske pardon of that I shall saye.

ASSUERUS
We pardone you, what soever ye saye,

HESTER
Then, to bee bolde ryghte well I maye.
No quene there is but by marriage of a prince,
And under covert, according to the lawe.
So that the jurisdiction of the whole province,
To the kynge perteineth, this is the trewe sawe.
Albeit, sometyme more for love than for awe,
The king is content to bee counselled by the queene,
In many sundrye causes, as ofte hath been seene.

Which sentence is sure and grounded with reason.
But yet, not wythstandynge, this is not all;
But eftsons it may chaunce, at sundrye season,
The kynge wyth hys councell, most parte of all,
From this realme to be absente, when warre doth call.
Then the quenes wysdome sadly muste deale
By her grate vertue, to rewle the common weale.

Wherfore, as many vertues be there muste,
Even in the quene as in the prynce,
For feare lest, in warre, sume treason unjust
The realme shoulde subdewe, and falsely convince.
The quene muste savegarde all the hole province.
And so, as muche goodnes aye muste be seene,
As in the kynge, to be in the quene.[25]
And how many vertues longe to a kynge,
Lyke unto Youre Grace, I cannot make recknynge.

ASSUERUS
Then, I doute not, but the wysdome of us two,
Knytte both to gether in parfytte charyte,
All thynges in thys realme shall cumpas so,
By truth and Justice, law and equitye,
That we shall quenche all vice and deformitie.

HESTER
Then, at my beginning I beseche Youre Grace
That I may shew my mynd, whyle I have time and space.

ASSUERUS
Speake at your libertie, I wyll heare it gladlye.

HESTER
Then I wyl be playne, for veritie hath no pere,
And for a pryncipall of thys my tale,
And eke his subjectes, both greate and smale,
In honoure and wealth: yea, all the province,
So riche and so stronge that they maye convince
All their enemyes,[26] where so ever they dwell,
That woulde invade, resiste, or rebell.

And where Goddes servyce and hospitalitie
Doeth decaye, and almes to the poorall,
There may be wealth in places two or three,
But I assure you, the most part, in generall,
Neither have meate nor money, nor strength substancial,
Fytte to doe you service, when ye have nede,
Whiche is no good order, me thynkes in very dede.

Let God alwaye, therfore, have hys parte,
And the poore fedde by hospitalitie;
Eche man his measure, be it pynte or quarte,
And no man to muche, for that is great jeoberdie,

263 test **265** question of great weight and difficulty **266** opinion/advice **267** read anything **269** (i.e. no simple matter) **270** for **273** except through, to **274** by legal authority **276** pertaining, wisdom **279** various **282** sometimes, times **283** the greater part of his council **286** great, govern **290** conquer **291** safeguard **294** belong **295** reckoning (there are so many) **297** United, perfect **298** encompass **300** disorder **302** reveal my opinion **312** poor **314** most of the population **319** (let) the poor (be) fed **321** too, danger

[25] 'And so the queen must display as many virtues as the king.' Perhaps significantly, Katherine of Aragon was left to govern England when Henry VIII and the bulk of his council invaded France in 1513. The victory of her forces over the Scots at Flodden eclipsed the minor battles won by Henry in France.

[26] 'for truth has no equal, both for a prince – the subject of my argument – and for his subjects, great and small, [as it keeps them] in honour and wealth: indeed the whole providence [is made] so rich and strong that they may conquer all their enemies'.

A meane to lose all, as I doe feare me;
For when all is gathered to gether on a heape
It may sone be conveyed, cariage is good cheape.[27]

Thys I speake with trew heart and mynde,
Besechyng Your Grace to take it in good kynde.

Assuerus
Of these matters, another tyme, moore at large
We shall speake, and of dyvers other mo.
Aman, see our servauntes doe accomplishe their
charge,
To awayte upon oure Queene, and that also,
In haste, unto oure waredrobe see ye goe,
For riche apparell of golde and pall,
As well for her selfe as for her ladyes all,

Aman
Than, if it please you to licence the Queene,
As to her pleasure awhyle shall beseeme.

Assuerus
And we, for a season, thys busynesse wyll cease,
And our selfe repose for our pleasure and ease.

Here departith ye Queene and Aman, and all ye maidens.
Here entreth Pride syngynge, poorly arayed.

[Pryde]
To men that be hevy, and wolde faine be mery,
Though they feele smarte:
Oft chance such rekning that with their mouth thei
sing,
Though thei wepe in their hart.

Somtime thei daunce, with mery countenaunce,
When they had lever slepe:
Eke thei laugh and grin, when, by this sunne, I wyn,
In the heart they wepe.

Who so will accord with this double world
Muste use suche artes:
Outwardly kinde, in his heart a fende,
A knave in two partes.

Outward honestie, inward infidelitie,
Bothe rydes on a mule:
In peace he is bolde, but in war he is colde,
That soonest wyll recoyle.

Manye bee that profers, but fewe that offers
Devoutelye in theyr hearte:
They saye they can doe all, but when neede doeth
befall,
They begynne to starte.

He that is double loves alwaye trouble,
And at no tyme wyll cease:
And yet he wyll not fight, by daye or yet by nyghte,
In warre nor in peace.

But such men by battail may get corne and cattell,
Bullyon and plate:
And yf they once get it, let us no moore crave it,
By God, we comme to late,
Eyther to begge or borowe, except shame or sorowe,
Dyspleasure and hate.

Syrs, my name is Pryde, but I have layde asyde
All my goodlye araye:
Ye wynne I lye? There is a cause why
That I goe not gaye.

I tell you at a worde, Aman that newe lorde,
Hath bought up all good clothe,
And hath as many gownes as would serve ten townes
Be ye never so lothe:
And any manne in the towne doe by him a good
gowne,
He is verye wrothe;

And wyll hym strayte tell, the statute of apparell,
Shall teache hym good.[28]
Wherefore by thys daye, I dare not goe gaye;
Threde bare is my hoode.

322 A way of losing everything 324 taken/stolen away 326 with a good nature 327 (at) another, more substantially 328 other (things) too 332 cloth of pall (a rich fabric) 334 (i.e. allow her to depart) 338 sad 343 would rather 344 sun, I believe 346 Whoever wishes to, duplicitous 348 fiend 351 the same mule 353 turn tail 354 There are many who proffer 356 When the need arises 357 start back/hesitate 358 duplicitous 362 battle 363 gold bullion, gold plate 365 too 368 put aside 369 fine clothes 370 You think I'm lying 371 don't dress elegantly 375 (i.e. regardless of who is angered) 376 if 377 He (Aman)

[27] Either 'transporting [things gathered together in one place] is dead easy', or '[such] carrying is a good [i.e. profitable] trade'.

[28] 'And Aman will immediately tell [such a man] that the Statute of Apparel will teach him a lesson.' Statutes of Apparel regulated the kinds of clothing and jewellery that could be worn by the various social classes.

Pryde was wonte to be, a man of jolytye,
Of hye countenaunce and face:
And since Aman rayned, no man hym retayned,
Allmoste in any place.

For Aman, that elfe, woulde no man but hym selfe
Shoulde be proude in dede.
For, as men say, all pryde he taketh away,
Well, God sende him good spede!

[*Enter Adulation.*]

ADULATION
And, as for Adulation, must chaunge his occupation,
It is not worth a pease.

PRYDE
Why so?

ADULATION
For my lorde Aman doeth al that he can,
I assure you, without doubt,
To take up al flatteres, and al crafty clatterers
That dwell fourtye myle aboute.

PRYDE
Yea, but the lawe shal, by order substancial,
Punyshe all those.

ADULATION
Yea, I wil tel you one thing, law now and flatteryng
Aye together gose.

PRYDE
Why so?

ADULATION
For al law, est and west, and adulation in his chest
Aman hathe locked faste;
And, by his crafti pattering, hath turned law into flattering;
So that, fyrst and laste,

The client must pay or the lawyer assaye
The lawe for to clatter.[29]
And when ye wene he saide right, I assure you, by this light,
He doth not els but flatter.

PRYDE
Why so?

ADULATION
For, yf Aman wynkes, the lawyers shrynckes,
And not dare saye yea nor naye.
And, yf he speake the lawe, the other calles hym daw,
No more then dare he say.

So that was law yisterday, is no lawe thys daye.
But flatterynge lasteth always, ye may me beleve.

PRYDE
Dyvines that do preache, me thynkes they should teache,
And flatterynge reprove.

ADULATION
Syr, they have lefte prechyng, and take them to flatteringe,
Moste part of them all.

PRYDE
I marveyle of that.

ADULATION
Do ye marveyle? Mary, I wyll you tell
A cause substantiall.

When they preached, and the truthe teached,
Sume of them caughte a knocke,
And they that should assisted, I wote not how they were brysted,
But they dyd nothynge but mocke.[30]

And that sawe they, and gate them away,
As faste as myghte be.
They solde theyr woll, and purchased a bull,
Wyth a pluralyte.[31]

383 bearing 384 reigned, retains (Pride) 386 little rogue, wants 389 God bless him (ironic) 390 (he) must 391 (i.e. is worthless) 395 employ, sweet-talkers 396 forty miles 400 Always go together 404 cunning speech 409 nothing other than 411 winks (at him), hesitate 413 interprets law correctly, fool 415 That which was, today 417 Theologians 418 condemn 419 have taken up 420 most of them 421 I'm amazed at that 425 received a blow 428 got themselves 429 as they could

29 'Before the lawyer will even begin to discuss the law.'

30 'And those who should have assisted [them], I don't know how they were got at, but [instead of helping] they did nothing but mock.'

31 'They sold their wool [i.e. fleeced their flock], and bought [with a bribe] a papal dispensation permitting them to hold more than one benefice.' Pluralism, the holding by a cleric of more than one parish or other living, was one of the most criticized abuses in the late medieval church.

And lefte predication, and toke adulation,
And what by mendation, and dyspensation,
They gat the nomynation of every good benefyce.
So better by flatterynge then by preachynge,
To wealthe they dyd aryse.
But yet ye muste beware.

Pryde
Where of?

Adulation
That they do not square farre beyonde the marke,
For, yf yt be a good fee, Aman sayeth 'that longeth to me!',
Be yt benefyce or parke.
If he espy to that promotion, he wyll streyt geve him a portion;
A lappe of a thowsande markes.
He shalbe purged cleane, he shall singe neither treble nor meane,
Nor yet speake one worde.

Pryde
Is he well seene in adulation?

Adulation
He is warde of ye occupation,
Without all jestinge boorde;

And no man so hardy, but by hys auctorite,
The same to use.[32]

Here entryth Ambytion.

[Ambytion]
No, for yf he doe, he were better no,
Hys braynes he wyll confewse.

Pryde
Why, who arte thow?

Ambytion
He that can tell how
Aman useth to wurke.

Pryde
Is not Ambytion thy name?

Ambytion
Yes, for God, ye same,
I was wonte to be a great clarke,

Byt, syn Aman bare rewle, neyther horse nor mule
But ys as wyse as I.

Adulation
How so?

Ambytion
For all rewlers and lawes were made by fooles and dawes,
He sayeth, verely.

Ordynances and foundation, without consyderation,
He sayeth, were devysed.
Therfore, hys imagination bringes all out of fashion,
And so all is dysguised.[33]

Sum tyme where was plenty, now ye barnes be empti,
And many men lackes bread.
And wher somtyme was meat, there now is none to get,
But all be gone and dead.

Beggers now do banne, and crye out of Aman,
That evyer he was borne.
They swere by the Roode, he eatyth up all their foode,
So that they gett no good, neyther even nor morne.

And many that be pore, though not from doore to doore
A begginge they dyd goe:
Yet had they releefe, bothe of breade and beefe,
And dryncke also.

And nowe the dore standes shet, and no man can we get,
To worcke neither to fyghte.

432 abandoned preaching, took up 433 mendacity 434 gained, to 436 rise/climb 439 (i.e. go too far) 440 income, belongs 442 looks to (gain) 443 sop/bribe 444 high nor middle ('bass' being the low voice) 446 expert, master of the trade 447 joking apart 450 does, not to 451 confuse/ruin 452 who 453 behaves 454 before 455 was once thought 456 since, gained authority 457 is 459 rule(r)s, idiots 465 barns are empty 466 lack 469 curse, cry out against 472 evening, morning 473 poor 475 charitable relief 477 door, shut 478 Neither to work nor

32 'No man is so brave/foolhardy that he will employ adulation without Aman's permission to do so.'

33 'He says that rules and charters of foundation [i.e. for monasteries and other institutions] were drafted without careful thought, and so he replaces them with new ones of his own devising, and so everything is disfigured.'

Wherefore, yf warre should chaunce, eyther wyth
Scotland or Fraunce,
This geare woulde not goe ryght.[34]

ADULATION
And where is all this become?

AMBYTION
As for that, *dominus vobiscum*, I dare say nothinge but
mum,[35]
Not tyll an other tyme.

PRYDE
All this is out of season, and nothing done by reason,
Nor yet by good ryme.

ADULATION
How say you, Ambition, have ye not provision for to
get promotion
As ye were wonte to do?

AMBYTION
No, by my holydame, for my lorde Aman
Handelles all thynge so

That every office and fee, what so ever it bee,
That maye bee sene and fonde:
By his wit he wyl it featche, and or it fal, he wil it
catche,
That never commeth to the grounde.

So that I repent, that ever I went
Unto the scoles:
For his large commission, maketh me, Ambition,
To dwell amonge fooles.

PRYDE
And is there no remedye?

ADULATION
None that I can spye,
Whyle he doeth raygne.

AMBYTION
Then lette us make merye, even tyll we dye,
And dryve pyne awaye:

PRYDE
I hearde once a Fryer, as trewe a lyer
As anye in the countrey;
Hee preached, veramente, that oure testamente,[36]
Alwaye readye shoulde bee.

ADULATION
For at oure deathe, we shall lacke breathe,
And than, fare well wee!

AMBYTION
Then, mayster Pryde, begynne thys tyde.
Let us here youre fashion.

ADULATION
And ye shall here nexte, even the playne texte,
Of me, Adulation.

PRYDE
Then, by and by, ye shall heare playnely,
Wythout impedimente,
The tenour of my wyll. If ye take heede
thereuntyll:[37]
This is my testament.

Al my presumptuous pryde, whether he goe or ryde,
Nowe or elles than:
My heart and corage, for power and language,
I geve it unto Aman.

Let him kepe of my pryde what he wil, the reste
devide,
Amonge hys whole garde:
And when they have it all, what they wyll dooe
withall,
Advyce them afterwarde.

481 leading 484 untimely/disordered 491 seen, found 492 fetch, before it falls 493 (So) that (it) 495 schools 496 wide jurisdiction 500 die 501 drive away sorrow 502 friar, liar 504 truly 505 Always 506 breath (to make one) 507 it's 'goodbye us!' 516 walk 517 then 521 entourage 523 They can decide later

34 'If there should happen to be a war against either Scotland or France, then this problem could not be corrected'; i.e. there would not be enough able-bodied men about to form an army. The contemporary English nature of the allusion is suggested by the choice of enemies. The reference is to the ending of monastic charitable relief. Previously the poor could gain alms at the monastery gate, and did not have to beg from door to door. Now that Aman has revised their charters and stripped them of their assets, the monasteries no longer offer such charity and the poor are starving.

35 'As for that, "The Lord be with you", I dare say nothing, and keep my mouth shut'.

36 Last will and testament.

37 'The essence of my will'. There is, however, an additional running joke here concerning ecclesiastical singing, from 'tyde' (l. 508) – which can refer specifically to the canonical hours as well as to time generally – through 'playne' and 'playnely' (ll. 510 and 512) – suggesting 'plain-song' – to 'tenor' here.

If pryde have a fall, let them be content withall,
As I am nowe.
For, as for Pryde, lasteth but a tyde,
I assure you.

If to it longe shame, let them, a Goddes name,
Take them bothe:
For, as I feare mee, so muste it needes bee,
Bee they never so lothe.

ADULATION
And I, Adulation, of the same fashion,
At thys tyme present,
To recorde everye man, geve unto Aman,
By thys my testament,

All my subteltie, and forged fydelite,
To hym and hys espyes.
I wot they wyll it use, trew men to confewse,
And that craftely.
And, yf they do in dede, I pray God they may spede,
Even as honestly,

As he that, from steylyng, goth to Sent Thomas
Watryng[38]
In his yong age.
So they from pytter pattour, may cume to tytter
totur,
Even the same pylgrimage.[39]

AMBYTION
And I, Ambytion, had a comission,
By force of a bull,
To gett what I could, but not as I wolde.
Neyther of lambe nor woll,

The bull nor the calfe,[40] coulde please the one halfe
Of my fervente desire.
But ever I thought, by God, there was I woulde have
had
When I was never the nere.[41]

Therfore, all my ambition, to gether in a comission,
Under my seale,
I geve it to Aman, to the intent that Sathan
Maye love hym well:

That, whyle he is here, he maye styll desyre,
And yet never the nere: sometyme to bee,
And when he goeth hence, he maye with him
dispence
By a large facultye.

That for his sines seven, or he come to Heaven,
Wyth out bourde or game,
Sumtyme or tyde, he may for his pryde,
Suffer some shame.

PRYDE
Nowe, by Wades myll,[42] everye mans wyll
Is wonderouslye well!

ADULATION
And, by my holydome, I wene it be wysedome,
For folke often chat, howe men dye in estate,
But so shall not wee.

AMBYTION
No, by Sainct An! But yet my Lorde Aman
Never the better shalbe.

PRYDE
No forse, so God me save! Yf we our wyll myght
have
We woulde he shoulde never thee.

Nowe made is our testament, I praye you be content,
Some myrthe to devyse.

ADULATION
Let us beginne with singynge, and conclude with
drinkynge:
It is the newe gyse.

AMBYTION
Then let us beginne a songe, that wyl last even as
long
As hence to the taverne dore.[43]

526 (it) lasts only for a while 527 if it is shameful, in 531 reluctant 534 may everyone be my witness 536 feigned 537 spies 547 on the strength of 548 but it wasn't what I wanted 556 Satan 558 always 562 sins 569 intestate 571 St Anne 572 Will gain nothing by it 573 No matter 574 thrive

38 'He that goes from stealing to St Thomas-a-Watering [near Southwark, a site for public executions].'

39 'They will go from the first hesitant steps [in crime] to a perilous position [perhaps literally swaying on the gallows] within a single journey.'

40 Punning allusions to papal bulls and the cattle of the same name were common in the period. Skelton referred to Wolsey as 'the bull calf' (*vitulus bubali*) in *Speke Parott*, ll. 348 and 378–80.

41 'But I always thought, by God, that there was something [more] that I wanted, which I was not [even] close to achieving yet.'

42 Wade's Mill: a popular euphemism for the gallows.

43 'As long as the time it takes to get from here to the tavern door.'

Thei depart, singyng, and Aman entreth.

Aman
Moste Noble Prynce, and of highest wysedome,
I do not doubte of youre considar[a]tion,
But that you know what I have bene, eke what I am,
Both in wyll and woorde, and occupation,
Of assured thoughte without adulation,
And as glad to doe service unto Your Grace
As ever I was to live anye tyme or space.

And for the same great malice I do sustayne,
Both of your nobles and communaltie,
To my greate grevaunce and merveylous payne.
And eke further, I feare the jeoperdye
Of my lyfe, goodes, credence, and honestie.
To cease their malyce, unlesse you put in ure
Your power royall, I can not longe endure.[44]

The sclaunderous reportes, the lyes that be made,
The fained dectractions and contumilious,
The rimes, the railinges, so farre sette abrode,
Both payntyd and printyd in moste shamefull wyse
(And, God to recorde, all is but leasinges and lyes),
Was never made on man lyke as is on me,
Only for aplyment of law and equite.[45]

In so much that of late now, in dede,
Before all the commins, upon myne and me,
Moste damnable reportes ware sett a brode,
To my dyshonour and shamefull villany,
And all that were there of that cumpanye,
As I myghte see by theyre countenaunce and voice,
That same alowed and greatly dyd rejoyce.[46]

Wherfore, Noble Prince, I beseche Youre Grace,
Let me be removed, another to have my place.

Assuerus
Aman, we harde wyth deliberation
Uttered, and pronounsed by language cleane,
A very elygante and prudent oracion
Of you as ever to fore was seene,
By whose tenour we knowe what ye meane.
And, have ye no doughte, so shall we for you provide
That youre enemies shall domage you on no syde.

We knowe ryght well the wordes[47] envious to be,
One agaynste an other for fee and office;
But that to regarde in no wyse nede ye,
As longe as ye observe trueth and justyce.
From the which we woulde that in no wyse
Ye shoulde degresse; for, if ye do, in dede,
Youre owne distruction shortly ye shall brede.

But, for youre comforte, harke what I shall tell,
And for more assistance in this that ye do feare,
We make you lieutenaunte to rewle Israell.
Take heare these robes, see ye do them weare,
Eke this golden wande in youre hande to beare,
A token of honour and of estate ryall;
God sende you contynuaunce and well to do with all,

Aman
Noble prynce, accordinge as I am bounde,
I will do you service tyll deathe me confounde,

Assuerus
For a season we wyll, to our solace,
Into our orcharde or some other place,

Here the Kynge entreth the traverse, and Hardy-Dardy entreth the place.

Hardydardy
A proverbe, as men say: a dogge hath a day,
When so ever that it chaunce.
He that wyll drinke wine and hath never a vine,
Muste send or goe to Fraunce.

And, yf he do not, endure he cannot,
He muste nedes shrynke.
Shrinke? yea, say that againe, for it is a greate paine
To be with out drynke.

584 will, word, deeds 588 suffer 589 from, common people 591 danger 592 reputation, honour 596 feigned and insulting detractions 597 abuse, spread around 598 painted/deceitful 599 as God is my witness, deceptions 602 recently 603 commons 604 were published/declared 607 faces, voices 610 removed from office 612 fine language 614 From, before 617 damage, from any quarter 620 you need not worry about that 623 deviate 624 breed/bring on 627 deputy 629 staff 630 royal status 631 perseverance 632 obliged 633 until death destroys me 634 for our entertainment 636 Every dog has his day 637 Whenever that will be

44 'Unless you exert your royal power to stop their malice, I cannot last much longer.'

45 'Was never made against anyone as they are against me, [and] only because I apply the law equitably.'

46 'They all agreed to them and rejoiced.'

47 Farmer suggests a misprint for 'lordes'.

In such case am I, I swere, by Goddes pety!
I lacke both drynke and meate.
But, as I say, a dogge hath a day,
For now I truste to get.
My tyme is come for to get some,
If I be not lett.

It is the common worde Aman is a lorde,
And Aman is of price;
And hath, perdye, all this cuntrie
At his rewle and device.

And I trust to be one of his yemanry,
To weare his bage and marke.
An office I wold beare and it noughte elles wheare,
But the keper of his parke.[48]

AMAN
Me seames ye are not fytte.[49]

HARDYDARDY
Ye wene I lacke wytte?
It may well be so!
Yet a fole, when it doth happe, may somtyme chaunce to stoppe a gappe,
When wyse men wyll not mell.

AMAN
Fooles largely will bourde and tell al theyr thought.

HARDYDARDY
And wyse men well not speke one worde till all become to nought.

AMAN
Fooles will tell all, and that trobleth sore.

HARDYDARDY
And wyse men will say nought at al till al be gone and more.

AMAN
Fooles to idlenes all wayes be preste.

HARDYDARDY
And wyse men use such busines it were better they were at rest.

AMAN
Fooles let the reformation of common wele.

HARDYDARDY
And wyse men be so full of imaginacion they wot not how they deale.[50]

AMAN
Whyse men wolde do ryght, and foles say nay.

HARDYDARDY
And fooles be fayne to fyght when wise men runne away.

AMAN
Fooles spend all tyll they have nought.

HARDYDARDY
And wise men carry all tyll they dare no more crave.

AMAN
Ye are a foole, ye do but clatter.

HARDYDARDY
Many go to scole tyll they can flatter.

AMAN
Leave youre clatter, leste ye cume tardy.

HARDYDARDY
It makes no matter, for my name is Hardydardy.

AMAN
Is youre name Hardydardy?

HARDYDARDY
Yea, yt is it, verily. I wold if it plese ye,
Be one of your yomanrie.

AMAN
As for that, let it passe; we take you for our solace.
And mirthe sumtime to ken.

HARDYDARDY
I wene, be Goddes grace, one foole in a place,
Doth well amonge wise men.

644 such a position, pity 649 prevented 650 rumour (that) 651 great value/authority 652 by God 653 Under, control 654 yeomanry 655 badge (i.e. livery) 660 happen 661 meddle 662 will joke freely 663 comes to 664 (i.e. causes great trouble) 666 ready 668 hinder 670 wise 671 eager 673 dare to desire no more 674 babble 676 come too late 681 will employ you 682 and at times to teach us mirth

48 'I want a job, even if it were only [as] the keeper of his park.' Note the similar concern about maintenance and badges in *Mankind*.

49 'It seems to me that you are not suitable (even for that).'

50 'They don't know what to do.'

Ye must nedes laughe amonge, and if a foole singe a songe.
I holde you than a grote
Some wise man muste be fayn sumtime to take [th]e paine
To do on a fooles cote.

And than, perchaunce, it is not redie.

Aman

Well, ye can speake merely, wherwith I am contente.
Sirs, tarrie you a seasone, se that farre ye not walke,
I will to the kinge, secretly to talke.

[*To Assuerus*] Moste victorius Prince, and of higheste honour,[51]
Primate of the worlde and president chefe,
By whose wisedome and pollityke demeanoure
All the worlde at this day takes relefe,
Both kynge, page, and lorde, yea, in sentence brefe,
No realme nor region able were to stande,
Onles your councell with them be at hande.

Who compelleth lordes to mainteine their nobilite;
Who lerneth knyghtes theyr feates marciall;
Or who religion subdewith to humilite;
Who have craftes and laborers the worlde over all,
In civill cytie or village ryall;
Compelleth eche man to hys order and place;
But only the wisedome and polyce of Your Grace?

Your strength defendith, your wisdome saveth all,
Youre plentye relevithe almoste every man.
Such is your honour and order ryall,
That none other councell at this day canne
Reache nor attaine to know how or whan,
Lyke good order or honorable guise,
As you, by wisdome, dayly do device.

So is it Your Grace, from very base parage
And poore estate, me to hye honour have brought,
For none my vertues, nor wisdome sage,
But onely youre goodes[52] have made me of nought.
God is mi judge, it is ther fore mi thoughte,
And dayly study above all worldly treasure,
That thing to do that is your wealth and plasure.

And, yf it please Your Grace, therfore, to here,
One thynge as I shall make rehersall.
Whan I have saide, I thinke it shall apeare
To your pleasure and profitte substanciall.
And, to be playne, this is it fyrste of all:
A greate number of Jewes with in this realm do dwell;
A people not goode, nor for youre common weale.

They be dispersed over all youre province,
With in them selfe dwellyng, desevered from our nation.[53]
By theyr new lawes they think to convince,
And eke draw unto theyr conversation,
And unto theyr ceremonyes and faction,
Of our people as many as may be,
Intendyng to sub dew all gentilite.[54]

More over, the preceptes of your law
They refuse, and have in great contempte.
They wyll in no wise live under awe
Of any prince, but they wil be exempte.
Wherby good order may sone be interempte,
And occasion is, as I do feare me,
Your subjectes to rebell in hope of lyke liberte.[55]

And Youre Grace knoweth it is [in]expediente
Theyre mallyce to increace thus by sufferance,
For by that may chaunce greate inconvenience,
And to all your realme importune perturbaunce.
For theyre possessions be of substaunce

685 sometimes **686** bet, groat (a coin worth four pence) **688** put on, coat **690** merrily, with which **691** time, don't go too far away **692** (go) to **694** principal ruler **695** wise behaviour **696** comfort **697** (i.e. to put it briefly) **699** Unless they have your guidance **701** teaches, military skills **702** reduces the clergy to humility **704** royal **705** (Who) compels **707** protects **708** relieves/sustains, all **711** when (i.e. anything) **712** similar, fashion **713** devise **714** humble parentage **716** not owing to my virtues **719** continual endeavour **720** that pleases and enriches you **722** relate/describe **727** nor (profitable) for **730** conquer/dominate **731** convert to their lifestyles **736** reject, hold **739** destroyed **743** malice, by tolerating it **744** that may cause **745** invite disorder

51 Aman slips neatly from the couplets in which he spoke to Hardydardy into rhyme royal to address the king, a sign of both his linguistic dexterity and his hypocrisy.

52 Either 'your goodness' or 'the goods/riches that you have given to me'.

53 'Living among themselves, separated from the rest of the nation'. The association between the Jews and the monks and regular clergy of the Tudor period is made all but explicit in this passage.

54 'Subdue [with a possible pun on "sub-Jew"] all the Gentiles [and also gentle/noble behaviour].'

55 'And an occasion/example is offered, I fear, for your [Gentile] subjects to rebel in the hope of gaining similar liberties.'

So greate and so large that I feare at the length
They wyll attempte to subdewe you by strengthe.

My councell, therfore, to avoide jeoperdy,
If that Your Grace, by your power ryall,
Shall geve sentence and plainly decree
To slea these Jewes in your realme over all,
None to escape (let your sentence be generall),
Ye shall by that wynne, to say I dare be bolde,
To your treasure .x. thousande pound of golde.

ASSUERUS
My lorde Aman, we have harde ryght well
All your oration, which is so elegante,
And so well towched that nedes we muste fele
And perceyve your minde, your wordes be so pregnante.
And, as touchinge the Jewes which be so valiaunte,
Both of goodes and greate pocession,[56]
We do agree unto theyre suppression.

We ryghte well perceive that unto them drawe
Much of our people and Jentile nation,
Which, to our honour and also to our lawe,
Muste nedes be a greate derogation;
A meane to bringe all out of facion.
To quenche them, therefore, we be contented well,
In token wherof, holde here a ringe and seale.

AMAN
Of your sentence there shall not lacke one clause,
But all shall be done, and that without pause.
The Pursivauntes call to us shortely.

PURSUEVANT
If it lyke you, we are here.

AMAN
These letters devised we wolde ye shoulde aplye
To bere furth, and that dylligently,
With as much haste as may be,
To the rewlers of every towne and citie,
Streightly commaunding theim all that they maye
The same to execute at their prefixed day.

PURSUEVANT
To his hye pleasure we shall make us preste.
And, tyll it bee done, we wyll take no reste.

AMAN
We be glad we have attained our purpose,
I trust it shall abate the hie corage
Of Mardocheus, and eke all those
That be hys clyantes brynge to repentaunce.

HARDYDARDY
Mary, syr, they be lyke to take penaunce.
It woulde greve any man, yonge or olde of age,
Without his head to goe on pylgrimage.

AMAN
Thei have deserved it, and they shall have it,
It is for theym accordynge.

HARDYDARDY
If I shoulde bewray that some men doe saye,
It were a mad bourdynge.

AMAN
Say what ye lyste.

HARDYDARDY
So woulde I, yf wiste
Ye woulde not angrye.

AMAN
Ye have libertie, as ye pleased be,
To stande or tumble.

HARDYDARDY
Men say, in dede, ye shall lose your head,
And that woulde make you stumble.

AMAN
Why so?

HARDYDARDY
Thei say it is convenient should be fulfilled ye testament
Of Ambition, Adulation, and Pride.
They gave you all their pryde and flatterynge,
And after that, Saint Thomas Watring, there to rest a tide.[57]

747 eventually 752 slay 753 universal 755 £10,000 758 crafted, understand 759 full of meaning 760 strong/bold 764 Gentile 767 to disorder everything 768 subdue/destroy 770 no word shall be ignored 771 (i.e. immediately) 772 quickly 774 apply (yourselves) 775 carry away 778 Strictly 779 pre-arranged 783 haughty spirit 785 clients/ followers 786 likely 790 appropriate 791 reveal 792 joke 793 if (I) thought 794 (be) angry 796 (i.e. to do as you wish) 800 appropriate/likely (that)

56 'Possessions', although perhaps 'possession of lands' is intended here to distinguish it from the ownership of 'goodes'.

57 'To rest a while [once you're hanged].' See n. 38, above.

And men thynke at hoste with them was the Holy
Ghoste.[58]
Wherfore, all that they sayed cannot be take or
sayed,
But as a prophesie.

AMAN
Well, ye are, verely, disposed merely
Now for to talke.
And I am suerly minded secretely,
For my solace to walke.

Et exeat.[59]

Here entreth a Jew and speaketh. [*Enter also II and III Jewe, Mardocheus and Hester*]

[I JEWE]
O lorde, what a thinge is crudelite,
Whan to it is annexed covetous and pride!
It distroyeth both towne and contrey,
Eke all regions on every syde.
All is for him to lyttell, his mouthe is so wide.
His rigour ravenous spares not to spill
Both man and chylde, to have his owne will.

This ravenous wolfe, Aman I do meane,
That hath perswaded the kynge to kill and slea,
And from all this province to avoid cleane
All men and women and children that be
Jewes borne, and of the Jewes consanguinite.
The precept is set up, men to remember,
And it shalbe executed the .xiii. day of December.

Alas that ever shoulde fortune suche rage,
From so cankered a caytyfe to procede!
It is his mynde, my head I ley to gage,
All those to sley, I assure you, in deede,
That wyll not by flattery hys presumptions fede.
He woulde be glorified above creatures all,
And yet, I trust, as Lucifer depe he shal fal.

II JEWE
The Mantuans thought it a greate punishmente
To be proscribed from theyre goodes and lande,
As reciteth Virgill, that poet eloquente,[60]
Much more is our payne, ye may understande,
That shall lose our lyves, unles God take in hande
Us to delyver, or els we not canne
Avoide the murder of this carnifex, Aman.

III JEWE
He shall, by this murder, our goodes wynne,
And him selfe enlarge, his pride to avaunce.
And, when he hath all, he shall be new to begynne,
Ever more to gett by some other chaunce.

MARDOCHEUS
Yet, at the laste, all shall cume to mischaunce,
For, both him and his, God shall make tame,[61]
And, for theyre pride and pyllage, sende them
worldly shame.

HESTER
Mardocheus, wyth youre cumpanye,
We have harde youre lamentation,
To our grefe and displeasure, verely.
Yet we truste by meke supplication,
Fyrste unto God by humble oration,
And than to the king by desyre cordyall,
A meane to fynde for to savegarde ye all.

Call in the chapell to the intent they maye
Syng some holy himpne to spede us this day.

Then the Chappell do singe.

After this prayer and our former abstynens,
To the good Lorde I call for cumforte,
To inspyre the prynce, and his mynd incence,
That I may optayne now, at my resorte,
To redeme the Jewes, all the hole sorte.
Eke to dysclose the falsed, favell, and fraude
Of this cruell Aman, to Thy prayse and laude.

ASSUERUS
O goodly Hester, our most noble Quene,
Of personage pearles, and in wisdome alone,

807 merrily disposed **811** cruelty **812** allied (to) **815** too little **816** doesn't hesitate to ruin **820** banish completely **822** of Jewish blood **823** (for) men **825** occur/chance **826** corrupt **827** intention, I'll bet my head on it **829** feed **831** he shall fall as far as Lucifer did **833** barred from **837** rescue, cannot **838** being murdered by, butcher **839** obtain **840** enrich, advance **841** start afresh **842** opportunity/means **843** come to misfortune **850** prayer **851** heartfelt/pleasing request **852** safeguard **853** the choristers **854** hymn, aid **855** abstinence **857** prompt/inform **858** obtain, going there (to request) **859** whole race **860** falsehood, deceit **863** peerless, unique

58 'And men think that they were familiar with [i.e. inspired by] the Holy Ghost.'

59 'And he shall exit.'

60 Virgil (Publius Vergilius Maro, 70–19 BC), the Roman poet. The allusion is to a story in his *Bucolics*.

61 'For God shall subdue both him and his followers'.

In corage and countenaunce none lyke is seene,
So discrete in dallyance was never none.
Where is your comfort, care can bee none.[62]
Loe, here our wand,[63] approch nere to this place
That we may kisse you, and in our armes embrace.

Here thei kysse.

What aske you, ladye, and what do you demaunde?
Halfe our realme is yours, yf ye commaunde.

HESTER
Noble prince, and our espouse most deare,
Since that to aske ye have geven me libertie,
I besech Your Grace, with heart most entier,
That it may please you this day to dine with me,
Eke my lord Aman I woulde be glad to see
At the same banket for to take repaste.

ASSUERUS
Call us in Aman, that we may go in haste.

[*Enter Aman.*]

AMAN
I am here, ready to atende upon Your Grace.

Here must bee prepared a banket in ye place.

ASSUERUS
Then let us go, while we have tyme and space.
Lady Hester, our moste beloved Quene,
So pewer and so exauisite is thys repaste,
Both of wine and meate, that no better may beene,
Youre mirth eke, and manners so pleasaunte to
attaste,
That for to departe we make no maner haste,[64]
Eke our presence we knowe is to youre pleasure
Farre better than golde or any worldly treasure.

Wherfore, as we sayde, we wolde ye shoulde
demande,
And at your pleasure, your petition make.
The one halfe of our reame, yf ye it cummaund,
We shall with departe, only for your sake,
And of it to you a playne surender make.
And, the more ye aske, wyth lovinge intente,
The more we shall geve, and the better be contente.

HESTER
Noble prynce, your hye magnyficens,
Your bounte, and espieciall grace,
So ofte and so kyndlye doeth incense,
To make request som profite to purchase,
So yet lenger delay were in me greate trespase,[65]
And by that also Your Grace right wel may it
thinke,
That finally your love unto my heart did sinke.

Wherfore, this favoure sence I have obtayned,
Of Your Grace to have any my requeste,
This I do aske with true harte unfayned
And wyth charitie (of all vertues best),
That throw all your reame, both east and west,
As manye as bee of the Jewishe nation
Your Grace wil them pardon at my supplication.

Assurynge you I am of that nacion,
Borne and eke brede in Jerusalem.
Yet I and all they, be one condempnation,
To deathe are determined throughe all this realme,
No remedy, lesse your pardon us redeme.
We woulde rather we myght be solde in bondage
Than thus to peryshe, by fury and outrage.

ASSUERUS
What is he, or what is hys authoritie,
That is so bolde thys acte to attempt?

HESTER
It is Aman, that by cruell envy,
Is oure mortall enymye and wold us enterrupt,
That our lyfe and godes from us were adempte.
Then wold he rule all and if he myght to all get:[66]
And all shoulde not suffice, so hie his heart is set.

Hys pompe and his pryde, so muche is, in dede,
That yf he had all, it coulde him not suffice.
At thys tyme hys treasure youres doeth execede,
And yet content is he in no wyse,

864 heart/spirit 865 behaviour 871 spouse 873 entire/whole 876 banquet 881 pure, exquisite 882 food, be 883 entertainment, experience 889 realm, request 890 give up 891 simple gift 895 bounty/generosity 896 urge/prompt 897 gain 901 since I have obtained this favour 902 From 907 entreaty 908 (that) I am 909 bred 910 all condemned alike 911 sentenced 912 Without remedy, unless 913 into slavery 918 destroy 919 goods, taken away 921 will, high 922 is so great

[62] 'Where your comfort is [offered], no sorrow can exist.'
[63] 'Look, here [is] our staff.' 'And the king held out to Esther the golden sceptre that was in his hand. So Esther drew near and touched the top of the sceptre.' Esther 5:2.
[64] 'That we are in no hurry to leave'.
[65] 'So it would be a great fault on my part to delay further'.
[66] 'If he might get possession of all [property], [then] he would want to *rule* everything [too]'.

But to gette moore daylye he doeth devise.
The commons he extorteth tyll they bee lame.
He takes the profyt and ye beare the name.[67]
But better it were that he shulde suffer payne
Than thus, by crafte, your honour to dystaine.
By his false leasinges, he putteth other in blame,
Deludinge Youre Grace, when he lyst to fayne,
And no man so worthy for to suffer payne
As he him selfe, that by hys poyson and gall
Hath deceyved you, and eke youre commons all.

ASSUERUS
He signified unto me that the Jewes did
Not feede the poore by hospitalitie.
Their possessions, he sayde, were all but hydde,
Amonge them selves lyvyng voluptuouslye,
Thinkyng the same might be, verely,
Much better employed for the common weale
Where now it litle profitteth or never a deale.

HESTER
Noble prince, as for hospitalitye,
Of the Jewes dwellinge in your regyon,
It is with them as alwayes hath bene
Sins the beginning of their possession,
Which God to them gave, of His mere mocion;
Eke great knowledge both of cattell and of grayne
That none to them like houshold coulde maintayne.[68]

Is not of Abraham the hospytallyte
In Scripture noted, and of noble fame,
But one honoringe when he received three,
(The Trenite fygured in the same).[69]
Both Isaake and Jacob had a lyke name,
Of whom the twelve tribes descended be,
Which ever dyd maintaine hospitallyte.

Sinse God, therfore, hath begunne theyre housholde,
And ay hath preserved theyre hospitallite,
I advise no man to be so bolde
The same to dissolve, what so ever he be.
Let God alone, for He shall orderly,
A fine ad finem, both here and there,
Omnia disponere suaviter.

ASSUERUS
O kaytiffe moste crafty, o false dissembler,
With thy flatteringe tonge thou haste deceyved me!
All noble princes by me may be ware
Whom they shall truste and put in auctorite,
Eke whom they shall promote to ryches and dignite.
But we shall teache the[e] good for thine
ingratitude,
And by the[e] all other theyre prince to delude.[70]

AMAN
O lady Hester, moste noble princesse,
Of thine honour and goodnes soveraine,
Extende to me that pitie, or els, doutles,
To deathe I am dressed and mortall payne.
I wotte I have deserved it for certaine,
And againste the[e] my offence is great.
Wherefore, uneth I dare thy goodnesse entreate.

But trueth is, the merite of thys is better,
And God it more accepteth a thousande fold,
Agaynst whome the offence is greater,
And of them that of injurie coulde not tell me.[71]
Wherefore, to speake somewhat it makes me bolde,
To encrease thy merite and rewarde heavenlye,
Save my life, and I thy servaunte shall be.

HESTER
Aman, this matter so heinous is, in dede,
That of our honour we wyll nother speake nor
speede.[72]

AMAN
Alas, then am I utterlye marred!
I must streighte die, it can not be deferred.

927 (i.e. until they are ruined) 930 to bring shame upon 932 wants to deceive 938 hidden 942 Whereas, not at all 945 it always has been 946 Since 947 through his will alone 948 animal (farming) 951 reputation 954 similar reputation 958 always 962 in all places (from here to there) 963 order all things pleasantly 966 by my example, beware 969 well 974 prepared, deadly pain 977 scarcely 987 ruined 988 die immediately

67 'He takes the profit, but [since it is done in your name] you take the blame.'

68 'So that no-one could match them for hospitality.'

69 'By honouring [the] three [guests] he received as if they were only one [this being a representation of the Trinity].' The allusion is to the story in Genesis 18. Abraham is visited by three fair men/angels, but treats them as if they were a single honoured guest, whom he calls 'Lord'. The story was interpreted by Christians as Abraham's instinctive recognition of the Trinitarian nature of God.

70 'And by your example, teach all others not to delude their princes.'

71 A dense passage which seems to mean 'God accepts a thousand times more readily [the petition for mercy] of the person who has been more greatly offended/injured than of them who could not claim to have been injured by me. And this brings greater merit upon the petitioner [too].'

72 Either 'for the sake of my honour' or 'by my honour' (a mild oath), 'I will not speak or do anything to help you.'

ASSUERUS
O thou kaytyffe, canste thou not be contente
With the mischeffe by the[e] done before,
But the quene wylt oppresse, we beinge presente?[73]
What nede we call for evidence moore?
Make him sure and fast, and therto bind him sore.
We will that oure counsell shortlye device,
How we shalbe bestow him, accordynge to justice.

ARBONA
There is in the house of thys traitour, Aman,
A paire of galowes of fiftie cubites hie;[74]
Upon them he had thought, either now or than,
To have caused Mardocheus to die.

ASSUERUS
Leade him hence, and upon them, by and by,
See that ye hange him, and so stoppe his breathe.
Without favoure see he suffer deathe.

[*Exit Arbona with Aman.*]

HARDYDARDY
Other folkes be tardye, as wel as Hardy dardy.
By this reckeninge
A syr, besyde belles, bacon, and somewhat els,
Must nedes have hanginge.

ASSUERUS
Hanginge doe serve, when they that deserve,
Are false feytoures.

HARDYDARDY.
And it commes to lottes of heringes and sprottes,
Which be no tratours,

To hange in the smoke, til they chaunge their cloke
From white to redde.[75]

ASSUERUS
But such do no wronge, wherfore they do not honge
Tyl they be ded.

HARDYDARDY
Ye speake somwhat like, for it toucheth the quicke
To be hanged in good heale.[76]

ASSUERUS
Yet none nede to care that is wyse and ware,
And truly wyll deale.

HARDYDARDY
Have ye not rede, of Naso Ovide,[77]
That eloquent poet?
Nor Valery,[78] which telles merely
The proper feates,

How the smith Perillus, like a *tuta vilus*,[79]
Made a bull of bras?
He had thought, iwis, to have pleased King
 Phalaris,[80]
But yet he did much wurse.

ASSUERUS
Why so?

HARDYDARDY
I wene, by God, he made a rodde
For his owne ars![81]

Phalaris coulde not get with in the bull to shett[82]
(Lo, here beginnes the game!)
Wherefore, in dede, he toke for nede
Perillus, maker of the same.

In he did him turne, and made the fier to burne
And greatly to increace.

993 safe, sorely/tightly 998 later 1005 A nobleman, as well as 1009 is the fate of herrings, sprats 1013 hang 1017 wary 1021 merrily 1022 deeds 1031 the joke 1032 as a necessity 1034 He threw him in

73 'But will try to oppress the queen in our presence?' In the biblical text Haman throws himself onto the couch next to Esther, prompting Assuerus to assume that he is attacking her. 'Then the king returned out of the palace garden . . . and Haman was fallen upon the bed whereon Esther was. Then said the king, will he force the queen also before me in the house?' Perhaps similar business is assumed in the interlude.

74 'A set of gallows fifty cubits (75 feet) high'. A cubit measured 2 spans or 24 finger-breadths.

75 i.e. the skins of the fish will be discoloured by the smoking process.

76 'You say something like the truth, as it is only the living who are hanged while in good health.'

77 Publius Ovidius Naso, 43 BC–*c*. AD 17. The story related is in his *Ars Amatoria*.

78 The Roman Historian Valerius Maximus, fl. 20–30 AD. The story is in his *Factorum*.

79 Tityvyllus, a minor devil (see *Mankind*, above, in which he appears as a character).

80 Phalaris, tyrant of Acragas, c.570–554 BC. He used the brazen bull statue as an engine of torture and execution.

81 i.e. like Aman, he devised the means of his own destruction.

82 'Phalarus couldn't find anyone to shut up inside the bull'.

He cast him in such heate, and eke in such sweate,
He fried him in his greace.

ASSUERUS
What meane you by this?

HARDYDARDY
I wyll tell you, by gis, my hole intencion.
I meane, my master is the fyrste taster
Of his owne invencion.
The gallhouse he made, both hye and brode,
For Mardocheus he them mente;
And now he is faine him selfe, for certaine,
To play the fyrste pagente.

ASSUERUS
He that deserves payne is worthy, certaine,
Even for to have it.

HARDYDARDY
Therfore, God sende all those that will steale mens
clothes,
That once they may goe naked.

[*Enter Arbona.*]

ARBONA
If it please Your Grace, this traitoure, Aman,
We have put to deathe, as was youre
cummaundyment.

ASSUERUS
Then shall we streigthte, as well as we canne,
Bestowe his goodes, for he made no testamente.
Lady Hester, this is our intent:
The house of Aman with all his treasure,
We geve it you; do with all youre pleasure.

HESTER
I thanke Your Grace, with harte entyre.
Nowe, dare I be bolde to shewe you the playnesse
Of my minde, since Mardocheus is heare.
If it please Your Grace, the truth is, doutles,
All be it or now I dyd it not confesse,
This Mardocheus is for certayne,
My fathers brother, no longer I wyll it leyne.
A gentyll man he is, for lynyallye
He is borne of the stocke of Benjaminy.

ASSUERUS
We be ryghte gladde we know his linage;
Hys truth to us before was knowen well.
We wyll him advaunce accordynge hys parage,[83]
Holde, Mardocheus, here is our rynge and seale;
It is our truste ye wyll with justice deale.
We commytte, therfore, unto youre wyse
discrescion,
Of all thys province judgemente and corection.[84]

MARDOCHEUS
I thanke Youre Grace, trustinge ye shall not heare
In all thynges but as justice doth requyre.

HESTER
Noble prince, and our espouse moste deare,
I beseche Youre Grace at my supplycation,
The precepte Youre Grace sente at Amans desyre,
Againste me and all the Jewishe nation,
May be revoked, and, upon convocation,
A new devised by them that can do best,
And that sent forthe, to set the Jewes at reste.

More over, lett the realme be perused
By them that be of your hye councell,
And, if any have the lawe abused
Of all the Jewes with in youre comon weale,
Let them not spare correction to deale,
And strayghtly constrayne them selfe to addresse
To observe that law God gave them by Moses.[85]

The Jewes be the people of God elected,
And weare His badge of cyrcumsicion.
The dayly prayer of that hole secte,
As the Psalmes of David by gostly inspiraction,[86]
Eke holy ceremonies of Gods provision,
To God is vaileable, that nothing greater,
And al the whole realme for them fares the better.

1037 grease 1039 by Jesus, whole 1042 gallows, high, broad 1045 (i.e. be the first to use them) 1051 commandment 1052 immediately 1056 do as you like with it 1057 (my) whole heart 1058 plainness/simplicity 1061 although, before now 1063 conceal 1065 Tribe of Benjamin 1070 hope 1071 discretion 1073 hear (that I have done) 1077 order 1079 consideration/after discussion 1082 (i.e. inquired throughout) 1084 anyone 1091 race 1094 productive, nothing is more so

83 'Promote him to a post befitting his ancestry'. The stress on noble ancestry here is a further blow at the low-born Wolsey.
84 'The judgement and punishment of the whole province.'
85 'And strictly constrain them to keep the laws which God gave them through Moses.'
86 '[Such] as the Psalms written by [King] David under the inspiration of the Holy Spirit'.

ASSUERUS
Stande ye up, Lady, and approche ye neare.
Your petition we graunte it gladlye,

HESTER
Than, if it please Your Grace to heare,
This epistle is made to the sealyng readye.[87]

ASSUERUS
Let it be red, that it maye, by and by,
Be sealed and consigned, and so furthe sent.
And than I truste ye shall be content.

Here the Scrybe doeth reade ye Kinges letter.

SCRIBA
We, Assuerus, Kynge and highe Regent
From India to Ethiopia plaine,[88]
Send gretinge and straighte commaundement
To all the heades and rulers, sertaine,
Wyllyng they should, upon a great payne,
In a hundreth provinces, and seven and twentye,
All men compell to this our decre.

All though it be so our preceptes that be sente
Be of dyverse nature, and playne repugnant,[89]
When ye know our mynd ye shalbe contente
To thinke it no lyghtnes, nor wytte inconstante,
But the necessytie of tymes varyant,[90]
And as cause requereth for the utyllyte
Of our hole reame, heedes and comynalte.

And to the entent ye may know our playne mynde;
The sonne of Amadathy, called Aman,
A Macedone borne, and lyke to theyr owne kynde,
Not of our nacion, as all men tell can,
Whiche, by his sutteltye, both now and than,
Our gentelnes so infecteth for certayne
That neare we were lyke all Jewes to have slayne,

We favored hym, that he was called
Our father, and all men dyd to him honoure.
But his harte wyth pryde so strongly was walled,
That, by his slyght and crafty demeanoure,
Had we not espyed his subtile behavoure,
He wolde have dystroyd Quene Hester, our wyfe,
And from us at the lengthe, have taken our lyfe.

But as for the Jewes, we found them innocente,
And without all blame, though to death they were dyth.
Wherfore Aman, we thought it convenient
To hang hym tyll the death, accordyng to ryght,
Within Susis[91] our noble cetye of myghte.
Not only our dede, nor yet theyr chans nor fate,
But Goddes owne justice, what so ever they prate.

This our precepte and hye cummaundimente
We wolde to all cities ye shoulde declare.
This is our purpose and veri entente:
The Jewes to theyre lawes them selfe shoulde prepare,
Duely to kepe them and not from them square;
And no man to hurt them, see ye remember,
As it was mente the .xiii.day of December,

Dated at Susis, this is certayne,
The .iiii. day of December the .iii. yeare of our raine.

ASSUERUS
This is well, se it be sealed anon,
And that every citie of them may have one.
Now, madam, I truste ye be contente.

HESTER
Yea, and that veramente.
May it now please you your selfe to repose?

ASSUERUS
Very well, save fyrst we wol disclose
Parte of our mynde, which we thinke necessary,
If it be well hard we truste it shall edifye.

1100 read 1101 given (to the heralds), sent out 1105 greeting, strict 1107 upon fear of 1108 127 provinces 1109 decree 1115 utility/benefit 1116 realm, both leaders and commons 1119 Macedonian 1120 Not (one) of 1121 subtlety 1122 corrupted 1123 we nearly 1124 him (so greatly) that 1128 cunning 1130 eventually 1132 condemned 1134 to justice 1135 city 1136 chance/fortune 1140 true intention 1141 dedicate 1142 Duly, (to) deviate 1144 was intended 1146 reign 1150 truly 1151 relax 1152 except 1154 listened to carefully

87 'This letter is drawn up and ready to be sealed.'

88 Either 'to the Plains of Egypt', or 'plainly . . . regent'.

89 'Our last two edicts have been different, indeed mutually contradictory'.

90 'To think it to be no folly [on my part], nor the result of an inconstant mind, but the necessary response to changing circumstances'.

91 Susa/Shushan, one of the capitals of the Persian empire.

My Lordes, by this fygure ye may well se
The multitude hurte by the heades necligence.
If to his pleasure so geven is he,
That he will no paine take nor dilligence.
Who careth not for his cure ofte loseth credence,
A proverbe of olde sume time in usage.
Few men that serve but for theyre owne advauntage.

HESTER
And yet the servantes that bee untrue,
A whyle in the world theyr lyfe may they leade,
Yea, theyr welth and worshippe dayly renewe;
But at the length, I assure you in dede,
Theyr favell and falsehed wyll come abrede,
Whiche shall be to them more bytter than gall.
The hygher they clyme, the deper they fall,

ASSUERUS
Let us, then, cesse thys convocatione,
And this tyme dyssolve this congregation.

HESTER
That lyke as here they have lyved devoutly,
So God Graunt them in Heaven to lyve eternally.[92]

ASSUERUS
To the which we committe all this company.

FINIS

Imprynted at London by Wyllyam Pickerynge and Thomas Hacket, and are to be solde at theyre shoppes.

1155 example 1156 How the populace is 1159 responsibilities, reputation 1160 once commonly used 1161 (There are) few, except 1164 increase/replenish 1166 become public knowledge 1168 climb, deeper 1169 cease this discussion

92 'So that, in the same way as they have lived devoutly here on earth'.

The Four PP, title page, 1533/4. The British Library.

John Heywood, *The Four PP*

John Heywood (*c.*1497–*c.*1578)

John Heywood was born about 1497, possibly in Coventry. By 1519, and perhaps earlier, he had gravitated to court as a musician and singing man, a role he was to play for much of the rest of his life. He was to enjoy considerable royal favour as a chorister, 'player of the virginals' (a keyboard instrument), and court entertainer during the reign of Henry VIII. In 1533, for example, he received a gift of a gilt cup weighing 23 ounces from the king as a reward for his services. At some time about 1522 he married Joan Rastell, daughter of the printer and adventurer John Rastell, and sister of William Rastell, who was to print Heywood's Interludes in the 1530s. Through the Rastells he was to gain access to the wider group of Catholic intellectuals around Sir Thomas More, many of whose cultural and theological views he shared. Unlike More and a number of the other members of his 'circle', however, Heywood did not lose favour during the 1530s, when the religious reforms of the Henrician Reformation began to move the church in a Protestant direction. Despite his own obvious Catholicism, and his musical and dramatic work for the household of Princess Mary (the politically marginalized daughter of Henry's rejected first wife, Katherine of Aragon), Heywood continued to write and play for the court throughout the 1530s, and even produced Interludes (including now lost works such as a 'Masque of King Arthur's Knights' and an Interlude *On the Parts of Man*) for evangelical patrons such as Thomas Cromwell and Archbishop Cranmer of Canterbury. Heywood made no secret of his opposition to the Reformation, however, and his Interludes and poetry of this period voice an eloquent appeal for religious toleration and moderation (see Walker, *Politics of Performance*, ch. 3, and Axton and Happé, *Plays*, introduction) .

William Rastell began to publish Heywood's plays in 1533, beginning with *Johan Johan* ('A mery play betwene John Johan the husbande, Tyb his wyfe, and Syr Johan the preest', a dramatic fabliau translated from a French original) on 12 February, followed on 5 April by *The Pardoner and the Frere* (a satirical attack upon religious controversy). Both of these plays were published anonymously, but *The Play of the We{a}ther* (printed below), published later in 1533, and *The Play of Love* (another exuberant debate play, which appeared in 1534) were both printed with Heywood's name on the title page. It is highly likely that *The Four PP* ('The Four Ps') was also printed by Rastell at this time, but the earliest surviving edition is that of William Middleton of *c.*1544.

Despite being convicted in 1544 of opposing Henry VIII's claim to be head of the Church in England (he seems to have been caught up in a sweep of known Catholic sympathizers in the wake of the so-called Prebendaries' Plot against Cranmer in 1542), Heywood continued to provide music and verses for court entertainments throughout the 1540s and 1550s. Only with the enforcement of the Act of Uniformity in Religion after the accession of Queen Elizabeth did he move into self-imposed exile on the Continent, where he lived in some poverty (his property having been confiscated by the crown in his absence) until his death in Louvain, probably in late 1578.

Further reading

For Heywood's life and career, see:

R. Axton and P. Happé, eds, *The Plays of John Heywood* (Woodbridge, 1991).

R.W. Bolwell, *The Life and Works of John Heywood* (New York, 1966).

A.W. Reed, *Early Tudor Drama: Medwall, the Rastells, Heywood, and the More Circle* (London, 1926).

G. Walker, *Plays of Persuasion: Drama and Politics at the Court of Henry VIII* (Cambridge, 1991).

G. Walker, *The Politics of Performance in Early Renaissance Drama* (Cambridge, 1998).

The Four PP

The Four PP, like all of Heywood's plays except *Johan Johan*, is essentially a dramatized debate, a dispute in the humanist tradition between two or more contending individuals over the merits of their respective vocations or conditions. There is thus no real 'plot' as such, rather events are driven by the arrival of new contributors to the debate or the introduction of new themes for contention. In this play the dispute is over the characters' abilities to direct souls to Heaven. Two religious figures, a Palmer (pilgrim) and a Pardoner, assert the superiority of their vocations as a means of saving souls, first against each other and then against a third party, the Potycary (apothecary), who mischievously suggests that his own lethal quack medicines are a more effective means of sending souls to Heaven than either papal pardons or penitential travel. The resolution of the dispute devolves upon the fourth 'P', the Pedler, who agrees to act as judge. The playful mode of this stage of the debate is demonstrated when the Pedler decides that supremacy should be determined by a lying competition: he who tells the most outrageous lie shall win the day. Two scatological and misogynist stories in the Rabelaisian tradition follow from the Potycary and the Pardoner, but it is the Palmer who triumphs through the apparently innocent observation that he has never seen a woman lose her temper. Both of his rivals spontaneously agree that this is the greatest lie that they have ever heard. Having gained the victory, however, the Palmer proceeds to hand back 'sovereignty' to the others: he will not claim authority over those who do not wish to be ruled. This verdict reveals the more serious purpose behind the Interlude, as the Palmer's refusal to dominate the others prompts the Pedler to issue an eloquent call for religious toleration. Both pardons and pilgrimages (each of which was the subject of hostility from evangelical reformers) are beneficial for the soul, he concludes, provided they are used with good will. But the value of such practices should be left to the church, rather than the ignorant laity, to decide.

The play has no source as such. Some of the comic relics and anticlerical humour are borrowed from a French text, *La farce nouvelle d'un Pardonneur, d'un Triacleur, et d'une Tavernière* (see M. Viollet-Leduc, ed., *Ancien théâtre François* (10 vols, Paris, 1854–7), II, pp. 50–63), and some of the detail as well as the general tone of the treatment of the Pardoner are inspired by Chaucer's *Canterbury Tales* (most notably the *General Prologue*, the *Pardoner's Prologue* and *Tale*, and the *Summoner's Tale*), but the bulk of the material, along with the characters of the Potycary and the Pedler, are the playwright's own invention. Heywood's love of lists, word games, and proverbs (he was to compile a compendium of epigrams in later life), and his delight in acrobatic physical business, are revealed in a number of places. The lists of medicines and herbal remedies at ll. 584–643, and of shrines at ll. 13–50, recall those in the Chester *Shepherds' Play* and the Croxton *Play of the Sacrament*, but again also reflect the author's own reading and experience. Both word-play and acrobatics are frequently associated with the Vices in Interlude drama, but, unlike *The Play of Love* and *We{a}ther*, *The 4PP* does not have a formal Vice among its cast. The duo of the Potycary (with his scatological jokes and delight in athletic demonstrations of misrule) and the Pedlar (with his potent brand of misogynist humour) share Vice-like characteristics, while the Pardoner is a less quick-witted, rather pompous, rogue, and the Palmer is both literally and metaphorically something of an innocent abroad.

The staging requirements of the play are minimal. All that is needed is the space in the centre of a great hall, and the limited number of portable properties that symbolizes each of the characters' vocations. The text printed here is based upon the version published by William Middleton in 1544 (STC 13300), now in the British Library. I have also consulted the facsimiles in J.S. Farmer, ed., *Tudor Facsimile Texts* (London, 1909), and L.M. Clopper and G.R. Proudfoot, eds, *The Four PP*, Malone Society Reprints (Oxford, 1984), and the excellent modern edition in Richard Axton and Peter Happé, eds, *The Plays of John Heywood* (Woodbridge, 1991).

The Play called the Foure PP. A newe and a very mery enterlude of a Palmer, a Pardoner, a Potycary, a Pedlar. Made by Joh[a]n Heewood.

The Names of the Players: *A Palmer* (A Pilgrim),[1] *A Pardoner*,[2] *A Potycary* (an apothecary),[3] *A Pedler.*[4]

PALMER
Nowe God be here! Who kepeth this place?
Now by my fayth I crye you mercy![5]
Of reason I must sew for grace,
My rewdnes sheweth me no[w] so homely.[6]

Wherof your pardon axt and wonne,
I sew you as curtesy doth me bynde
To tell thys, which shal be begonne
In order as may come beste in mynd[e].[7]

I am a palmer as ye se,
Whiche of my lyfe much part hath spent
In many a fayre and farre countre,
As pylgrymes do of good intent.

At Hierusalem have I bene,
Before Chrystes blessed sepulture.
The mount of Calvery have I sene
A holy place ye may be sure.

To Josophat and Olyvete[8]
On fote, God wote, I wente ryght bare.
Many a salt tere dyde I swete
Before thys carkes coulde come there.

Yet have I bene at Rome also
And gone the stacions all arow;[9]
Saynt Peters shryne and many mo
Then yf I tolde all ye do know,

Except that there be any suche
That hath ben there and diligently
Hath taken hede and marked muche,
Then can they speke as much as I.

Then at the Rodes[10] also I was
And rounde about to Amyas,[11]
At Saynt Toncomber and Saynt Tronion,[12]
At Saynt Bothulph and Saynt Anne of Buckston,[13]
On the hylles of Armony where I see Noes arke,
With holy Job and Saynt George in Suthwarke,[14]
At Waltam and at Walsyngam,[15]
And at the good Rood of Dagnam,
At Saynt Cornelys, at Saynt James in Gales,[16]
And at Saynt Wynefrydes Well in Walles,[17]
At our Lady of Boston, at Saynt Edmundes, Byry,[18]

1 is responsible for[5] 3 beg 5 asked (for), won 6 obliges me 12 As well-intentioned pilgrims do 13 Jerusalem 14 sepulchre 19 tear, sweat 20 carcass 23 St Peter's, Rome 25 anyone here (who) 27 remembered 33 Armenia, Noah's Ark 36 Dagenham (Essex)

[1] Pilgrims returning from the Holy Land traditionally carried palm leaves as symbols of their achievement.

[2] A Pardoner or *quaestor* sold papal indulgences, a trade rife with opportunities for corruption, hence pardoners were frequently the subject of anticlerical satire. This one carries a roll of sealed indulgences and a pack full of fraudulent relics.

[3] The Potycary carries a pack filled with his remedies. Like the Pardoner, Heywood's Potycary plays into a number of traditional satirical jibes against apothecaries, notably that their exotic remedies were more frequently fatal than helpful.

[4] A travelling seller of small household items and trinkets. He carries a pack filled with his wares. The frauds associated with this trade were satirized in the figure of Autolycus in Shakespeare's *Winter's Tale.* Heywood's Potycary is, however, a more benign figure.

[5] The Palmer notionally seeks to apologize to the steward or marshal of the hall for his unexpected and dishevelled appearance.

[6] '[As] my rudeness/lack of refinement reveals me to be so lacking in manners.'

[7] 'To tell [my story] which shall be begun in the best possible way.'

[8] The Vale of Jehosaphat near Jerusalem and the Mount of Olives.

[9] 'And gone around the Stations of Rome'. The Stations were a series of pilgrimage sites in and around the Holy City.

[10] Perhaps, as Axton and Happé (hereafter 'A&H') note, the Island of Rhodes, where a relic of the Holy Thorn was kept.

[11] Amiens Cathedral (France), where the head of John the Baptist was enshrined.

[12] St Wilgefortis, commonly called Uncumber because wives wishing to 'un-encumber' themselves of unwanted husbands would pray to her for aid; St Ronion: there was a Scottish saint of this name, but 'Ronion' was popular with satirists owing to the pun *rognon*/kidneys. See the proem to *The Pardoner's Prologue* in Chaucer's *Canterbury Tales.*

[13] St Botulph was a seventh-century saint popular in East Anglia. There was a shrine to St Anne, the mother of the Virgin, in Buxton, Derbyshire.

[14] The location of Job's grave has not been identified; St George's church, Southwark.

[15] Waltham Cross (Essex), site of one of Edward I's 'Eleanor crosses'; Walsingham (Norfolk), site of one of the most popular shrines to the Virgin in Britain.

[16] The tomb of Pope Cornelius in Rome; St James/Santiago de Compostella in Galicia (Spain).

[17] St Winifred's shrine at Holywell (Wales)

[18] Boston (Lincolnshire); the shrine of St Edmund at Bury St Edmunds (Suffolk).

And streyght to Saynt Patrykes purgatory.[19]
At Rydybone and at the blood of Hayles,[20]
Where pylgrymes paynes ryght muche avayles,[21]
At Saynt Davys and at Saynt Denis,[22]
At Saynt Mathew and Saynt Marke in Venis,[23]
At mayster Johan Shorne, at Canterbury,[24]
The great God of Katewade, at Kynge Henry,[25]
At Saynt Savyours, at our lady of Southwell,[26]
At Crome, at Wylsdome and at Muswell,[27]
At Saynt Rycharde and at Saynt Roke,[28]
At at Our Lady that standeth in the oke.[29]
To these with other many one
Devoutly have I prayed and gone,
Prayeng to them to pray for me
Unto the Blessed Trynyte,
By whose prayers and my dayly payne
I trust the soner to obtayne
For my salvacyon grace and mercy.
For be ye sure, I thynke surely,
Who seketh payntes for Crystes sake;
And namely suche as payne do take
On fote to punyshe thy frayle body,
Shall therby meryte more hyely
Then by any thynge done by man.

[*The Pardoner enters.*]

PARDONER
And when ye have gone as farre as ye can,
For all your labour and gostely entente,
Yet welcome home as wyse as ye wente.

PALMER
Why, syr, dyspyse ye pylgrymage?

PARDONER
Nay, for God, syre, then dyd I rage.
I thynke ye ryght well occupyed
To seke these payntes on every syde;
Also your payne I nat disprayse it
But yet I discomende your wit
And, or we go, even so shall ye
If ye in this wyl answere me.
I pray yow shew what the cause is
Ye wente al these pylgrymages.

PALMER
Forsoth this lyfe I dyd begyn
To rydde the bondage of my syn,
For whiche these payntes rehersed or this
I have both sought and sene iwys,
Besechynge them to be recorde
Of all my payne unto the Lorde
That gyveth all remyssyon
Upon eche mans contricyon
And by theyr good mediacyon,
Upon myne humble submyssion
I trust to have in very dede
For my soule helth the better spede.

PARDON[E]R
Nowe is your owne confessyon lyckely
To make your selfe a fole quyckely
For I perceyve ye wolde obtayne
No nother thynge for all your payne
But onely grace your soule to save.
Nowe marke in this what wyt ye have
To seke so farre and helpe so nye!
Even here at home is remedy,
For at your dore my selfe doth dwell,
Who coulde have saved your soule as well
As all your wyde wandrynge shall do
Though ye wente thryes to Jericho.

51 many another one 59 Whoever seeks 61 the frail body 62 merit, highly 65 spiritual ambitions 66 no wiser than when you left 67 do you despise 68 before, I'd be mad to 69 employed 71 don't criticize 72 condemn 76 went (on) 77 vocation 78 rid/escape 79 that I've already named 81 witnesses (before God) 83 remission (of sins) 84 contrition 85 mediation (with God) 88 soul's health, success 89 likely 91 want to 95 when help was so near 97 door 99 long journeying 100 three times

19 St Patrick's church, Lough Derg, Donegal (Ireland), where St Patrick was reputedly granted a vision of Purgatory.

20 Redbourn (Hertfordshire); Hales (Gloucestershire), where a vial of Christ's blood was kept.

21 'Achieves much'. Only deserving cases were allowed to see the precious liquid.

22 The shrine of St David in Pembrokeshire; St Denis, Monmartre, Paris.

23 Perhaps San Matteo, Palermo (Italy); San Marco, Venice.

24 The shrines of John Shorne (a miracle-working priest) in North Marston (Buckinghamshire), and Thomas Beckett (Chaucer's 'hooly blisful martir') at Canterbury (Kent).

25 The Rood at Catway Bridge on the river Stour at Manningtree (Essex); the tomb of Henry VI in St George's Chapel, Windsor (or its former location in Chertsey, Surrey).

26 St Saviour's Abbey, Bermondsey, which had a reputedly miraculous Rood; the church of the Blessed Virgin in Southwell (Nottinghamshire).

27 Crome Hill, near Greenwich, Willesden (Middlesex), and the spring at Muswell Hill (London), all sites dedicated to the Virgin.

28 The shrine of St Richard, Chichester (Sussex); St Rocco, a French saint associated with cures for syphilis.

29 The shrine of the Virgin in Highgate Woods, near London.

Nowe syns ye myght have spedde at home,
What have ye wone by ronnyng at Rome?

PALMER
If this be true that ye have moved,
Then is my wyt in dede reproved.
But let us here fyrste what ye are.

PARDONER
Truly, I am a pardoner.

PALMER
Truely a pardoner, that may be true
But a true pardoner doth nat ensew.
Ryght selde is it sene or never
That treuth and pardoners dwell together.
For be your pardons never so great,
Yet them to enlarge ye wyll nat let
With suche lyes that oftymes, Cryste wot,
Ye seme to have that ye have nat.
Wherfore I went my selfe to the selfe thynge,
In every place and without faynynge
Had as muche pardon there, assuredly,
As ye can promyse me here doutefully.[30]
Howe be it I thynke ye do but scoffe,
But yf ye hadde all the pardon ye kepe of,
And no whyt of pardon graunted
In any place where I have haunted,[31]
Yet of my labour I nothynge repent.
God hathe respect how eche tyme is spent
And, as in His knowledge all is regarded,
So by His goodnes all is rewarded.

PARDONER
By the fyrste parte of this laste tale
It semeth you come late from the ale,
For reason on your syde so farre doth fayle
That ye leve [rea]sonyng and begyn to rayle,
Wherin ye forget your owne parte clerely.
For ye be as untrue as I
And in one poynte ye are beyonde me,
For ye may lye by aucthoryte,
And all that hath wandred so farre
That no man can be theyr controller.[32]
And where ye esteme your labour so muche,
I say yet agayne my pardons be suche
That yf there were a thousande soules on a hepe,
I wolde brynge them all to Haven as good chepe
As ye have brought your selfe on pylgrymage
In the leste quarter of your vyage,
Whiche is farre a thys syde Heven, by God,[33]
There your labour and pardon is od.[34]
With smale cost and without any payne
These pardons bryngeth them to Heven playne.
Geve me but a peny or two pens
And, as sone as the soule departeth hens,
In halfe an houre or thre quarters at moste
The soule is in Heven with the Holy Ghost.

[*The Potycary enters.*]

POTYCARY
Send ye any soules to Heven by water?

PARDONER
If we dyd, syr, what is the mater?

POTYCARY
By God, I have a drye soule shulde thyther.
I praye you let our soules go to Heven togyther!
So bysy you twayne be in soules helth,
May nat a potycary come in by stelth?
Yes, that I wyll, by Saynt Antony,
And, by the leve of thys company,
Prove ye false knaves bothe or we goo,
In parte of your sayenges as thys, lo:
Thou by thy travayle thynkest Heven to gete,
And thou by pardons and relyques countest no lete

101 fared as well 102 running to 103 claimed 104 indeed condemned 108 not necessarily follow 109 seldom 112 exaggerate (their powers), cease 113 knows 114 that (which) 119 Although 120 care for 122 visited 124 knowledge, everyone's 125 observed/considered 128 (i.e. are drunk) 129 fails so badly 130 rail 131 clearly 134 with authority/conviction 137 whereas 139 in, heap (i.e. all together) 140 Heaven, cheaply/easily 142 smallest part, journey 146 clearly 152 (i.e. what of it?) 153 wishes to go there 155 (arguing over) soul's 156 sneak in among you 158 with the permission 161 gain/win 162 relics, think it no difficulty

30 'Whereas I went myself to the very place [i.e. Rome, the source of the Pardoner's pardons], and in every place without deceit, had as much pardon there, certainly, as you can promise [me] here without any certainty.'

31 'And if no hint of a pardon was granted in any place I've visited'.

32 i.e. 'No one can refute your claims, or those of others who have wandered so far.'

33 'And your journey leaves you still a long way from Heaven.' The Pardoner, playing on the financial cost and effort expended on a pilgrimage, claims he can save far more souls far more cheaply.

34 'In this case the pardon you gain is not proportionate to the amount of labour you put in to obtain it.'

To sende thyne owne soule to Heven sure
And all other whome thou lyste to procure.
[*Aside*] If I toke an accyon then were they blanke,[35]
For lyke theves the knaves rob away my thanke.
All soules in Heven havynge relefe
Shall they thanke your craftes? Nay, thanke myn chefe.
No soule, ye knowe, entreth Heven gate
Tyll from the bodye he be separate.
And whom have ye knowen dye honestlye
Without helpe of the potycary?
Nay, all that commeth to our handlynge,
Except ye happe to come to hangynge,
That way perchaunce ye shall nat myster
To go to Heven without a glyster.
But be ye sure I wolde be wo
If ye shulde chaunce to begyle me so.
As good to lye with me a nyght
As hange abrode in the mone lyght.
There is no choyse to fle my hande
But, as I sayd, into the bande!
Syns, of our soules, the multitude
I sende to Heven when all is vewed,
Who shulde but I then all togyther
Have thanke of all theyr commynge thyther?[36]

Pardoner
If ye kylde a thousande in an houre space,
When come they to Heven, dyenge from state of grace?[37]

Potycary
If a thousande pardons about your neckes were teyd,
When come they to Heven yf they never dyed?[38]

Palmer
Longe lyfe after good workes in dede
Doth hynder mannes receyt of mede,
And deth before one dewty done
May make us thynke we dye to sone.
Yet better tary a thynge, then have it,
Then go to sone and vaynly crave it.

Pardoner
The longer ye dwell in communicacion,
The lesse shall you lyke thys ymagynacyon,
For ye may perceyve even at the fyrst chop
Your tale is trapt in such a stop
That at the leste ye seme worste then we.

Potycary
By the Masse, I holde us nought all thre.

[*Enter Pedler.*]

Pedler
By Our Lady, then have I gone wronge!
And yet to be here I thought longe.

Potycary
Brother ye have gone wronge no wyt.
I prayse your fortune and your wyt,
That can dyrecte you so discretely
To plante you in this company,
Thou palmer and thou a pardoner,
I a potycary.

Pedler
And I a pedler.

Potycary
Nowe on my fayth full well watched!
Were the Devyll were we foure hatched?

Pedler
That maketh no mater syns we be matched.
I coulde be mery yf that I catchyd
Some money for parte of the ware in my packe.

Potycary
What the Devyll hast thou there at thy backe?

Pedler
Why, doth thou nat knowe that ever pedler
In every tryfull must be a medler?

163 certainly 164 wish to buy 166 credit 168 principally 173 into our hands 174 happen to be hanged (first) 175 manage 176 suppository 177 sorry 180 moon 181 the only alternative to me 182 noose 184 considered 187 in the space of an hour 189 tied 190 died 193 one's duty (is) done 194 too soon 195 (to) delay, (and) then 196 Than (to) set out too soon 199 (i.e. at first sight) 200 caught, trap 202 consider us worthless 204 I was eager to be here 205 (in) no way 208 bring you to 211 by, observed! 212 Where 213 That's not important 214 received 218 trifle, meddler/trader

35 'If I took a [legal] action [against them], they'd be ruined'.
36 'Who else but me, then, should receive the praise for getting them all there (i.e. to Heaven)?'
37 'How could they get to Heaven, dying out of a state of grace?'
38 The switch of pronoun, from 'you(r)' to 'they' is unsettling, but the same subject seems to be intended.

Specyally in womens tryflynges:
Those use we chefe above all thynges.
Whiche thynges to se, yf ye be disposed,
Beholde what ware here is disclosed.
Thys gere sheweth it selfe in suche bewte
That eche man thynketh it sayth, 'come, bye me'.
Loke were your selfe can lyke to be chooser
Your selfe shall make pryce though I be looser.[39]
Is here nothynge for my father Palmer?
Have ye nat a wanton in a corner
For your walkyng to holy places?
By Cryste, I have herde of as straunge cases!
Who lyveth in love or love wolde wynne
Even at this packe he must begynne,
Where is ryght many a proper token
Of whiche by name parte shall be spoken:
Gloves, pynnes, combes, glasses unspottyd,
Pomanders, hookes, and lasses knotted,[40]
Broches, rynges, and all maner bedes,
Lace rounde and flat for womens hedes,
Nedyls, threde, thymbell, shers, and all such knackes[41]
(Where lovers be, no suche thynges lackes)
Sypers, swathbondes, rybandes, and sleve laces
Gyrdyls, knyves, purses, and pyncases.[42]

POTYCARY
Do women bye theyr pyncases of you?

PEDLER
Ye[a], that they do, I make God a vow.

POTYCARY
So mot I thryve, then for my parte
I beshrewe thy knaves nakyd herte
For makynge my wyfeys pyncase so wyde
The pynnes fall out; they can nat abyde.
Great pynnes must she have one or other,
Yf she lese one she wyll fynde an other;
Wherin I fynde cause to complayne,
New pynnes to her pleasure and my payne.

PARDONER
Syr, ye seme well sene in womens causes
I praye you tell me what causeth this,
That women after theyr arysynge
Be so longe in theyr apparelynge?

PEDLER
Forsoth women have many lettes
And they be masked in many nettes,[43]
As frontlettes, fyllettes, partlettes, and bracelettes,[44]
And then theyr bonettes and theyr poynettes.
By these lettes and nettes the lette is suche
That spede is small whan haste is muche.

POTYCARY
An other cause why they come nat forwarde,
Whiche maketh them dayly to drawe backwarde,
And yet is a thynge they can nat forbere:
The trymmynge and pynnynge up theyr gere,[45]
Specyally theyr fydlyng with the tayle pyn,
And when they wolde have it prycke in,
If it chaunce to double in the clothe,
Then be they wode and swereth an othe,
Tyll it stande ryght they wyll nat forsake it.
Thus though it may nat, yet wolde they make it,
But be sure they do but defarre it,
For when they wolde make it ofte tymes they marre it.
But prycke them and pynne them as myche as ye wyll,
And yet wyll they loke for pynnynge styll.
So that I durste holde you a joynt,
Ye shall never have them at a fall poynt.[46]

PEDLAR
Let womens maters passe and marke myne.
What ever theyr poyntes be, these poyntes be fyne,[47]
Wherfore, yf ye be wyllynge to bye,

220 principally 223 beauty 224 buy 225 where 227 Is there nothing here 228 wanton (woman) 229 (to accompany you) 235 untarnished mirrors 237 brooches, beads 238 heads 243 buy 247 wife's 248 stay (in there) 250 lose 253 experienced, matters 255 rising 256 getting dressed 257 hindrances 264 go 265 resist 267 fiddling, tail (of a gown) 268 stuck in 269 bend 270 mad, oath 271 leave it alone 272 won't straighten/become erect 273 defer, delay 274 ruin 277 bet, jointure/item/member 279 listen to my (business)

39 'You can name your own price, even if I lose money by it.'

40 'Pomanders [balls of perfumed spice], hooks [fasteners for clothes], and knotted lace'.

41 'Needles, thread, thimble(s), scissors, and all such trifles'.

42 'Cypress satin, swaddling bands, ribbons, lace for cuffs, girdles, knives, purses and pin-cases.' 'Pin-case' (a receptacle for pins) was also slang for the vulva, hence the Potycary's extended bawdy riposte.

43 Both 'They wear many veils' and 'They get caught in many snares'.

44 '[Such] as headbands, hairbands, neckbands, and bracelets'.

45 The Potycary returns to his earlier double entendres, playing upon pins/penises and 'gear', clothes/genitalia.

46 'Fasten them completely/fully satisfy them.'

47 The Pedler puns on 'points': the laces for hose which he has for sale in his pack.

Ley downe money, come of quyckely!

PALMER
Nay, by my trouth, we be lyke fryers:
We are but beggers, we be no byers.

PARDONER
Syr, ye maye showe your ware for your mynde
But I thynke ye shall no profyte fynde.

PEDLER
Well, though thys journey acquyte no coste,[48]
Yet thynke I nat my labour loste,
For by the fayth of my body
I lyke full well thys company.
Up shall this packe, for it is playne
I came not hyther al for gayne.
Who may nat play one day in a weke
May thynke hys thryfte is farre to seke.
Devyse what pastyme ye thynke beste
And make ye sure to fynde me prest.[49]

POTYCARY
Why, be ye so unyversall
That you can do what so ever ye shall?

PEDLER
Syr, yf ye lyste to appose me
What I can do then shall ye se.

POTYCARY
Than tell me thys, be ye perfyt in drynkynge?

PEDLER
Perfyt in drynkynge as may be wysht by thynkyng.

POTYCARY
Then after your drynkyng how fall ye to wynkyng?

PEDLER
Syr, after drynkynge, whyle the shot is tynkynge,[50]
Some hedes be swymmyng but myne wyl be synkynge,
And upon drynkynge myne eyse wyll be pynkynge,
For wynkynge to drynkynge is alway lynkynge.

POTYCARY
Then drynke and slepe ye can well do.
But yf ye were desyred therto,
I pray you tell me, can you synge?

PEDLER
Syr, I have some syght in syngynge.

POTYCARY
But is your brest any thynge swete?

PEDLER
What ever my breste be, my voyce is mete.

POTYCARY
That answere sheweth you a ryght syngynge man
Now what is your wyll, good father, than?

PALMER
What helpeth wyll where is no skyll?

PARDONER
And what helpeth skyll where is no wyt?

POTYCARY
For wyll or skyll, what helpeth it
Where frowarde knaves be lackynge wyll?

Leve of thys curyosytie
And who that lyst, synge after me.

Here they singe.

PEDLER
Thys lyketh me well, so mot I the.

PARDONER
So helpe me God, it lyketh nat me!
Where company is met and well agreed
Good pastyme doth ryght well in dede;
But who can syt in dalyaunce?
Men syt in such a variaunce
As we were set or ye came in,
Whiche stryfe thys man dyd fyrst begynne,

282 Lay, come on 283 friars (who renounced all property) 285 if you want 291 I'll close up this pack 292 solely for profit 294 far away (i.e. pointless) 297 skilled in everything 299 challenge 301 perfect (at) 302 wished 303 sleeping 306 eyes, pinking/becoming red 309 asked to (do so) 311 insight/talent 312 breast/lungs (i.e. voice) 313 fitting (for singing) 314 chorister/boaster 316 What use is will 319 quarrelsome 320 leave off/stop, petty argument 321 Whoever wants to 322 may I prosper 327 such argument 328 were doing, before 329 quarrel

48 'Doesn't repay my outlay [i.e. brings me no profit]'.
49 'You'll certainly find me eager [to join in].'
50 'While the coins are still tinkling [in the inn-keeper's hand]'

Allegynge that suche men as use
(For love of God and nat refuse)
On fot to goo from place to place
A pylgrymage callynge for grace,
Shall in that payne with penitence
Obtayne discharge of conscyence;
Comparynge that lyfe for the beste
Enduccyon to our endles reste.[51]
Upon these wordes our mater grewe
For, yf he coulde avow them true,
As good to be a gardener
As for to be a pardoner!
But when I harde hym so farre wyde,
I then aproched and replyed,
Sayenge this: that this indulgence,
Havyng the forsayd penitence,[52]
Dyschargeth man of all offence
With muche more profyt then this pretence.
I aske but two pens at the moste;
I wys this is nat very great coste.
And from all payne without dyspayre,
My soule for his, kepe even his chayre,[53]
And when he dyeth, he may be sure
To come to Heven even at pleasure.
And more then Heven he can nat get,
How farre so ever he lyste to jet.
Then is hys payne more then hys wit,
To wa[l]ke to Heven syns he may syt.
Syr, as we were in this contencion,
In came thys daw with hys invencyon,
Revelynge us, hym selfe avauntynge,[54]
That all the soules to Heven assendynge
Are most bounde to the potycary
Bycause he helpeth most men to dye;
Before whiche deth, he sayeth in dede,
No soule in Heven can have hys mede.

PEDLER
Why, do potycaries kyll men?

POTYCARY
By God, men say so, now and then.

PEDLER
And I thought ye wolde nat have myst
To make men lyve as longe as ye lyste.

POTYCARY
As longe as we lyste, nay, longe as they can!

PEDLER
So myght we lyve without you, than?

POTYCARY
Ye[a], but yet it is necessary
For to have a potycary;
For when ye fele your conscyens redy,[55]
I can sende you to Heven quyckly.
Wherfore concernynge our mater here,
Above these twayne I am best clere,
And yf he lyste to take me so,
I am content you and no mo
Shall be our judge as in thys case:
Whiche of us thre shall take the best place?

PEDLER
I neyther wyll judge the beste nor worste,
For be ye bleste or be ye curste,
Ye know it is no whyt my sleyght
To be a judge in maters of weyght.
It behoveth no pedlers nor proctours
To take on them judgemente as doctours.
But yf your myndes be onely set
To worke for soule helthe, ye be well met,
For eche of you somwhat doth showe
That soules towarde Heven by you do growe.
Then yf ye can so well agree
To contynue togyther all thre,
And all you thre obey on wyll,

338 From, argument developed 339 prove them 340 (It would be) as good 342 wide (of the truth) 344 (i.e. a pardon) 347 (i.e. than the Palmer's claim) 348 pence 349 believe 350 despair 355 likes to swagger (about) 356 greater than 357 since, sit (and still get there) 358 contention/argument 359 fool 362 obliged 365 reward 368 failed 374 conscience 377 clearly the best 380 argument 384 in no way my desire (lit. no trick of mine) 385 weighty matters 386 proctors (minor university officers) 387 doctors (of law) 389 welcome 391 go with your help 394 one

[51] 'Alleging that men who go on pilgrimage for the love of God, not refusing to go on foot from place to place to obtain grace, shall through their efforts, with penitence, obtain the discharge of their consciences [i.e. the remission of sin], claiming that this life is the best preparation for our eternal rest.'

[52] 'Providing that one has the penitential attitude that I have already mentioned'.

[53] 'I'll bet my soul on it, [he'll get to Heaven] and never even have to leave his chair.'

[54] 'Reviling us and praising himself'.

[55] The Potycary's claim rests on his ability to provide the means whereby someone with a clear conscience can commit suicide (while they are in a sinless state) and so ensure that they get straight to Heaven. The flaw in the argument is, of course, that suicide is itself a mortal sin.

Then all your myndes ye may fulfyll
As yf ye came all to one man.
Who shulde goo pylgrymage more then he can?
In that, ye, Palmer, as debite
May clerely dyscharge hym, parde;
[*To the Pardoner*] And for all other syns ones had contryssyon[56]
Your pardons geveth hym full remyssyon.
And then ye, mayster potycary,
May sende hym to Heven by and by.

POTYCARY
Yf he taste this boxe nye aboute the pryme,
By the Masse, he is in Heven or evensonge tyme.[57]
My craft is suche that I can ryght well
Sende my fryndes to Heven and my selfe to Hell.
But, syrs, marke this man, for he is wyse
Who coulde devyse suche a devyce.
For, yf we thre may be as one,
Then be we lordes everychone.
Betwene us all coulde nat be myste
To save the soules of whome we lyste.
But for good order, at a worde,
Twayne of us must wayte on the thyrde.
And unto that I do agree,
For bothe you twayne shall wayt on me.

[PALMER]
What chaunce is this that suche an elfe
Commaunded two knaves be, besyde hym selfe?

PARDONER
Nay, nay, my frende, that wyll nat be
I am to good to wayt on the[e].

PALMER
By Our Lady, and I wolde be loth
To wayt on the better on you both!

PEDLER
Yet be ye sewer for all thys dout,
Thys waytynge must be brought about.
Men can nat prosper wylfully ledde;
All thynge decayed where is no hedde.
Wherfore, doutlesse, marke what I say:
To one of you thre twayne must obey,
And synnes ye can nat agree in voyce
Who shall be hed, there is no choyse
But to devyse some maner thynge
Wherin ye all be lyke connynge
And in the same, who can do beste.
The other twayne to make them preste
In every thynge of hys entente,
Holly to be at commaundement.
And now have I founde one mastry
That ye can do indyfferently;
And is nother sellynge nor byenge,
But even only very lyenge.
And all ye thre can lye as well
As can the falsest devyll in Hell.
And though afore ye harde me grudge
In greater maters to be your judge,
Yet in lyeng I can some skyll,
And yf I shall be judge, I wyll.
And be ye sure without flatery,
Where my consciens fyndeth the mastrye,
Ther shall my judgement strayt be founde,
Though I myght wynne a thousande pounde.[58]

PALMER
Syr, for lyeng though I can do it,
Yet am I loth for to goo to it.

PEDLER
Ye have nat cause to feare to be bolde,
For ye may be here uncontrolled.
And ye[59] in this have good avauntage
For lyeng is your comen usage.
And you in lyenge be well spedde
For all your craft doth stande in falshed.
Ye nede nat care who shall begyn,
For eche of you may hope to wyn.

395 satisfy 396 (i.e. were of one mind) 398 deputy (to go on his behalf) 399 discharge (of that responsibility) 403 in due course 408 listen to 409 plan 412 we cannot fail 414 in order to maintain propriety 415 wait upon/serve 418 a little villain 419 Commanding, in addition to 421 too 423 of you two 424 sure, despite, doubt 427 (are) decayed, where (there is) 430 since, (one) voice 431 alternative 433 equally skilled 435 prepare themselves 437 Wholly 438 skill 439 equally well 440 it's neither 441 lying 444 heard, refuse 446 have some knowledge 447 can 449 greatest skill 450 immediately be given 455 unrestrained 457 regular practice 458 advanced

56 'Once contrition is shown'.

57 'If someone were to taste [the contents of] this box at about Prime [a canonical hour, observed just after sunrise], by the Mass, he'd be in Heaven by the evening service!'

58 '[I'll be an impartial judge] even if someone tries to bribe me with £1,000.'

59 'Ye': it is possible, as A&H suggest, that each of the 'ye's (at ll. 455, 456, and 458 ('you')) is aimed at a different character: Palmer, Pardoner, and Potycary, respectively. But the division, and the order of the recipients, is not a necessary one.

Now speke all thre evyn as ye fynde:
Be ye agreed to folowe my mynde?

PALMER
Ye[a], by my trouth, I am contente.

PARDONER
Now in good fayth, and I assente.

POTYCARY
If I denyed I were a nody,
For all is myne, by Goddes body!

Here the Potycary hoppeth.

PALMER
Here were a hopper to hop for the rynge!
But syr, thys gere goth nat by hoppynge.[60]

POTYCARY
Syr, in this hopynge I will hop so well
That my tonge shal hop as well as my hele.
Upon whiche hoppynge, I hope and nat doute it,
To hop so that ye shall hop[e] without [it].

PALMER
Syr, I wyll neyther boste ne brawll,
But take suche fortune as may fall,
And yf ye wynne this maystry
I wyll obaye you quietly.
And sure I thynke that quietnesse,
In any man is great rychesse
In any maner company
To rule or be ruled indifferently.[61]

PARDONER
By that bost thou semest a begger in dede.
What can thy quyetnesse helpe us at nede?
Yf we shulde starve, thou hast nat, I thynke,
One peny to bye us one potte of drynke.
Nay, yf rychesse myght rule the roste,
Beholde what cause I have to boste:
Lo here be pardons halfe a dosyn,
For gostely ryches they have no cosyn,
And more over to me they brynge
Sufficient succour for my lyvynge.
And here be relykes of suche a kynde
As in this worlde no man can fynde.
Knele down all thre, and when ye leve kyssynge,
Who lyste to offer shall have my blyssynge.
Frendes, here shall ye se evyn anone
Of All Hallows[62] the blessyd jaw bone:
Kys it hardely with good devocion!

POTYCARY
Thys kysse shall brynge us muche promocyon.
Fogh! By Saynt Savyour, I never kyst a wars!
Ye were as good kysse All Hallows ars,
For, by All Halows, me thynketh
That All Halows breth stynketh.[63]

PALMER
Ye judge All Halows breth unknowen;
Yf any breth stynke it is your owne.

POTYCARY
I knowe myne owne breth from All Halows,
Or els it were tyme to kysse the galows.

PARDONER
Nay, syrs, beholde, here may ye se
The great toe of the Trinite.
Who to thys toe any money voweth,
And ones may role it in his moueth,
All hys lyfe after, I undertake,
He shall be ryd of the toth ake.

POTYCARY
I praye you torne that relyke aboute.
Other the Trinite had the goute

466 fool 467 (i.e. the prize is already mine) 468 ring/prize 471 succeed 473 no hop(e) of winning 479 a priceless (asset) 480 kind of 483 when we're in need 485 buy 486 be in charge 488 dozen 489 cousin/equal 490 moreover 492 (holy) relics 494 stopped kissing (the relics) 495 offer (money), blessing 496 immediately 498 eagerly 499 advancement 500 Ugh!, worse (one)! 501 as well advised to, arse 503 breath 504 ignorantly 510 promises 511 roll, mouth 515 Either

60 'This game won't be won by hopping.' The Potycary's hopping is an expression of his excitement, an action traditionally symbolic of folly, and also a visual 'pun' following up the Pedler's suggestion 'each of you may hop(e) to wyn' (l. 461). The hop/hop(e) punning continues in the Potycary's next speech.

61 i.e. 'To accept authority or subservience with equal contentment.'

62 All Hallows, the first of the Pardoner's fraudulent saints, is not, of course, an individual, but the feast day dedicated to all saints, celebrated on 1 November.

63 A&H suggest an allusion here to the church of All Hallows, Honey Lane, in London, which was a centre of evangelical heresy in the 1520s. The 'stinking breath' may thus be a satirical jibe at the preaching conducted there.

Or elles bycause it is thre toes in one,
God made it muche as thre toes alone.[64]

[PARDONER]
Well, lette that passe and loke upon thys.
Here is a relyke that doth nat mys
To helpe the leste as well as the moste:
This is a buttocke bone of Pentecoste.[65]

POTYCARY
By Chryste, and yet for all your boste
Thys relyke hath beshyten the roste.

PARDONER
Marke well thys relyke, here is a whipper.
My frendes, unfayned, here is a slypper
Of one of the Seven Slepers,[66] be sure,
Doutlesse thys kys shall do you great pleasure,
For all these two dayes it shall so ease you
That none other savours shall displease you.

POTYCARY
All these two dayes? Nay, all thys two yere!
For all the savours that may come here
Can be no worse; for, at a worde,
One of the seven slepers trode in a torde.

PEDLER
Syr, me thynketh your devocion is but smal.

PARDONER
Small! Mary, me thynketh he hath none at all.

POTYCARY
What the Devyll care I what ye thynke?
Shall I prayse relykes when they stynke?

PARDONER
Here is an eye toth of the great Turke.
Whose eyes be ones sette on thys pece of worke
May happely lese parte of his eye syght,
But nat all, tyll he be blynde out ryght.

POTYCARY
What so ever any other man seeth,
I have no devocion to Turkes teeth;
For all though I never sawe a greter,
Yet me thynketh I have sene many better.

PARDONER
Here is a box full of humble bees
That stonge Eve as she sat on her knees
Tastynge the frute to her forbydden.
Who kysseth the bees within this hydden
Shall have as muche pardon of ryght
As for any relyke he kyst thys nyght.

PALMER
Syr, I wyll kysse them with all my herte.

POTYCARY
Kysse them agayne and take my parte,
For I am nat worthy. Nay, lette be,
Those bees that stonge Eve shall nat stynge me!

PARDONER
Good frendes, I have ye[s]t here in thys glas
Whiche on the drynke at the weddynge was
Of Adam and Eve undoutedly.
If ye honor this relyke devoutly,
All though ye thurste no whyt the lesse,
Yet shall ye drynke the more, doutlesse.
After whiche drynkynge ye shall be as mete
To stande on your hede as on your fete.

POTYCARY
Ye[a], mary, now I can ye thanke;
In presents of thys the reste be blanke.[67]
Wolde God this relyke had come rather!
Kysse that relyke well, good father.
Suche is the payne that ye palmers take
To kysse the pardon bowle for the drynke sake.
O holy yeste, that loketh full sowr and stale,
For Goddes body helpe me to a cuppe of ale.
The more I be-holde the[e], the more I thurste,

523 shit on the roost/reliquary(?) 524 an excellent one 525 truly 529 no other smells 533 trod, turd 534 piety 538 tooth, a legendary leader 539 Whoever's, once 544 larger 547 stung 549 hidden in this (box) 556 yeast/beer-froth 560 you won't thirst any less 562 able 563 (i.e. you'll be drunk) 566 sooner 570 yeast, sour

64 The joke here seems to be a visual one. Presumably the 'toe bone' is so large that its fraudulence is immediately obvious.

65 Again, not a saint but the annual Jewish harvest feast, at which time the Holy Spirit descended upon the Apostles (see Acts 2:1–47), commemorated on Whit Sunday (seven weeks after Easter) in the Christian calendar.

66 The Seven Sleepers were legendary Christian refugees who reputedly escaped persecution by sleeping in a cave for centuries.

67 'The other relics are nothing compared to this one.'

The oftener I kysse the[e], more lyke to burste,[68]
But, syns I kysse the[e] so devoutely
Hyre me and helpe me with drynke tyll I die!
What, so muche prayenge and so lytell spede!

Pardoner
Ye[a], for God knoweth whan it is nede
To sende folkes drynke, but by Saynt Antony,
I wene he hath sent you to muche all redy.

Potycary
If I have never the more for the[e],
Then be the relykes no ryches to me
Nor to thy selfe, excepte they be
More benefycyall then I can se.
Rycher is one boxe of [t]his tryacle
Then all thy relykes that do no myrakell
If thou haddest prayed but halfe so muche to me
As I have prayed to thy relykes and the[e],
Nothynge concernynge myne occupacion
But streyght shulde have wrought in operacyon;
As as in value I pas you an ace.[69]
Here lyeth muche rychesse in lytell space:
I have a box of rebarb here,
Whiche is as deynty as it is dere.
So helpe me God and hollydam,
Of this I wolde nat geve a dram
To the beste frende I have in Englandes grounde,
Though he wolde geve me xx pounde.
For though the stomake do it abhor,
It pourget[h] you clene from the color
And maketh your stomake sore to walter,
That ye shall never come to the halter.

Pedler
Then is that medycyn a soverayn thynge
To preserve a man from hangynge.

Potycary
If ye wyll taste but thys crome that ye se,
If ever ye be hanged, never truste me.
Here have I *diapompholicus*,
A speciall oyntement as doctours discuse
For a fistela or a canker.
Thys oyntement is even shot anker,
For this medecyn helpeth one and other
Or bryngeth them in case that they nede no other.
Here is a *syrapus de Byzansis*,
A lytell thynge is inough of this,
For even the weyght of one scryppull
Shall make you stronge as a cryppull.
Here be other, as *diosfialios*,
Diagalanga and *sticados*,[70]
Blanka manna, *diospoliticon*,[71]
Mercury sublyme and metridaticon,[72]
Pelitory and *arsefetita*,[73]
Cassy and *colloquintita*;[74]
These be the thynges that breke all stryfe
Betwene mannes sycknes and his lyfe.
From all payne these shall you delever
And set you even at reste for ever.

Here is a medecyn no mo lyke the same,
Whiche comenly is called thus by name:
Alikakabus or *Alkakengy*;[75]
A goodly thynge for dogges that be mangy.
Suche be these medycynes that I can
Helpe a dogge as well as a man.
Nat one thynge here partycularly
But worketh universally,[76]
For it doth me as muche good when I sell it
As all the byers that taste it or smell it.
Now, syns my medycyns be so specyall
And in operacion so generall
And redy to worke when so ever they shall,

575 Hear, before 576 success 580 thanks to you 583 than 584 medicine 585 miracle(s) 592 rhubarb (a purgative) 593 precious, expensive 594 holiness 595 a small measure 597 £20 598 abhors it 599 purges 600 to heave so badly 601 (i.e. be hanged) 602 sovereign/excellent 604 crumb 606 an ointment for ulcers 608 fistula (tubular ulcer), cancer 609 sheet anchor (i.e. reliable) 611 (i.e. it either cures or kills) 612 Byzantine syrup (herbal remedy) 614 scruple (small weight) 615 cripple 616 (an unidentified remedy) 622 end 626 unlike any other

68 'Burst': A&H suggest 'perish through [thirst]'. Alternatively, 'burst through over-drinking'.

69 'If you had prayed half as much to me as I have prayed to you and your relics, there's nothing concerning my vocation that could not have been achieved; therefore I surpass you in value as an ace does the rest of the cards.'

70 A compound of galangale, for stomach pains; *sticardos citrine*, a remedy for chest ailments.

71 White manna-ash (a laxative); *diospoli[tic]on*: a cure-all.

72 Mercuric chloride (used to treat haemorrhoids); *metridaticon*: an ointment used against poisons.

73 Pelleter, a root used in cases of toothache; *asafoetida*: a medicinal gum.

74 Cassia leaves and colocynth/bitter apple (both purgatives).

75 The resin from the winter cherry, used for urinary disorders.

76 'There's not a single thing here that doesn't work universally/on all types of patient'.

So that in ryches I am principall;
If any rewarde may entreat ye,
I besech your mashyp be good to me
And ye shall have a boxe of marmelade,[77]
So fyne that ye may dyg it with a spade.

PEDLER
Syr, I thanke you, but your rewarde
Is nat the thynge that I regarde.
I muste and wyll be indifferent,
Wherfore procede in your intente.

POTYCARY
Nowe yf I wyst thys wysh no synne,
I wolde to God I myght begynne.

PARDONER
I am content that thou lye fyrste.

PALMER
Even so am I, and say thy worste.
Now let us here of all thy lyes
The greatest lye thou mayst devyse,
And in the fewyst wordes thou can.

POTYCARY
Forsoth ye be an honest man.

PALMER
There sayde ye muche but yet no lye.

PARDONER
Now lye ye bothe, by Our Lady
Thy lyest in bost of hys honestie,
And he hath lyed in affyrmynge the[e].

POTYCARY
Yf we both lye and ye say true,
Then of these lyes your parte adew!
And yf ye wyn, make none avaunt
For ye are sure of one yll servaunte.
Ye may perceyve, by the wordes he gave,
He taketh your mashyp but for a knave.
But who tolde true or lyed in dede,
That wyll I knowe or we procede.
Syr, after that I fyrste began
To prayse you for an honest man,
When ye affyrmed it for no lye,
Now by our fayth, speke even truly:
Thought ye your affyrmacio[n] true?

PALMER
Ye[a] mary, I, for I wolde ye knewe
I thynke my selfe an honest man.

POTYCARY
What thought ye in the contrary than?

PARDONER
In that I sayde the contrary,
I thynke from trouth I dyd nat vary.

POTYCARY
And what of my wordes?

PARDONER
I thought ye lyed.

POTYCARY
And so thought I, by God that dyed!
Nowe have you twayne, eche for hym selfe, layde
That none hath lyed out but both truesayd;
And of us twayne none hath denyed,
But both affyrmed that I have lyed.
Now syns both your trouth confes,
And that we both my lye so witnes
That twayne of us thre in one agree;
And that the lyer the wynner must be,
Who coulde provyde suche evydens
As I have done in this pretens?
Me thynketh this mater sufficient
To cause you to gyve judgement
And to gyve me the mastrye,
For ye perceyve these knaves can nat lye.[78]

PALMER
Though nother of us as yet had lyed,
Yet what we can do is untryed,
For yet we have devysed nothynge,
But answered you and geven hyrynge.

PEDLER
Therfore I have devysed one waye
Wherby all thre your myndes may saye.

639 best provided 640 persuade you 641 mastership (honorific title) 643 refined 648 thought, sin 652 hear 654 fewest 658 boast 659 agreeing (with) you 661 adieu/farewell 662 no boast 663 poor 673 I (did), want you to know 680 alleged 688 evidence 689 claim 692 (i.e. the prize) 694 have 697 given hearing (to you) 699 may speak your minds

77 Marmalade was a delicacy thought to have health-promoting properties.

78 The Potycary claims a technical victory, quibbling that in their opening exchange of abuse only he lied, and so he must be the greatest liar.

For eche of you one tale shall tell,
And which of you telleth most mervell
And most unlyke to be true,
Shall most prevayle what ever ensew.

Potycary
If ye be set in mervalynge,
Then shall ye here a mervaylouse thynge;
And though in dede all be nat true,
Yet suer the most parte shall be new.
I dyd a cure no lenger ago
But *Anno domini millesimo*
On a woman yonge and so fayre
That never have I sene a gayre:
God save all women from that lyknes!
This wanton had the fallen syknes,[79]
Whiche by dissent came lynyally,
For her mother had it naturally,
Wherfore this woman to recure
It was more harde ye may be sure.
But though I boste my crafte is suche
That in suche thynges I can do muche,
How ofte she fell were muche to reporte.[80]
But her hed so gydy and her helys so shorte,[81]
That with the twynglynge of an eye
Downe wolde she falle evyn by and by.
But, or she wolde aryse agayne,
I shewed muche practyse, much to my payne.

For the tallest man within this towne
Shulde nat with ease have broken her sowne.
All though for lyfe I dyd nat doute her,
Yet did I take more payne about her
Then I wolde take with my owne syster.
Syr, at the last I gave her a glyster;
I thrust a thampyon in her tewell.
And bad her kepe it for a jewell.
But I knew it so hevy to cary
That I was sure it wolde nat tary,
For where gonpouder is ones fyerd
The tampyon wyll no lenger be hyerd.
Which was well sene in tyme of thys chaunce:
For when I had charged this ordynaunce,
Sodeynly, as it had thonderd,
Even at a clap losed her bumberd.
Now marke, for here begynneth the revell:
This tampion flew x longe myle levell
To a fayre castell of lyme and stone
(For strength I knowe nat suche a one)
Whiche stode upon an hyll full hye,
At fote wherof a ryver ranne bye
So depe, tyll chaunce had it forbyden,
Well myght the *Regent* there have ryden.[82]
But when this tampyon on thys castell lyght,
It put the castels so farre to flyght
That downe they came eche upon other,
No stone lefte standynge, by Goddes mother,
But rolled downe so faste the hyll
In suche a nomber and so dyd fyll
From botom to bryme, from shore to shore,
Thys forsayd ryver so depe before,
That who lyste now to walke thereto,
May wade it over and wet no shoo.
So was thys castell layd wyde open
That every man myght se the token
But in good houre maye these wordes be spoken!
After the tampyon on the walles was wroken,
And pece by pece in peces broken,
And she delyvered, with suche violens
Of all her inconveniens,
I left her in good helth and luste.
And so she doth contynew, I truste.

Pedler
Syr, in your cure I can nothynge tell,
But to our purpose ye have sayd well.

Pardoner
Well syr, then marke what I can say.
I have ben a pardoner many a day,

701 (the) most marvellous (tale) 703 whatever follows from it 704 intent upon marvels 707 certainly 708 performed, longer 709 AD 1000 711 gayer/fairer 712 the same (illness or face?) 714 descent, lineally/by inheritance 716 recover 721 giddy/dizzy, heels 722 twinkling 725 labour/skill 727 revived her from her swoon 731 medicinal suppository 732 tampon/pessary, tail 733 (i.e. look after it carefully) 736 gunpowder, fired 737 plug (in a cannon), heard 738 in this case 739 loaded, cannon 740 if it thundered 741 loosed/shot, bombard (cannon)/bum-beard 743 ten long miles straight 747 by 748 until chance prevented it 749 floated at anchor 750 alighted/fell 751 castellations/walls 756 brim 757 (that was) so deep 759 shoe 763 revenged 766 inconvenience/malady 768 continue/remain 769 I cannot judge your cure

79 'Falling-sickness/epilepsy'. The Potycary's humour here relies upon the fact that sexual intercourse was deemed to be a preventive and treatment for epilepsy. The woman's (and her mother's) frequent bouts of the illness are thus excuses for demanding sex, and the Potycary's reference to his own skill in treating them is thus a sexual boast.

80 'To tell you how frequently she fell sick would be a long story.'

81 To be 'short-heeled' (and thus unbalanced/likely to fall on one's back) was a slang term for wantonness in women.

82 *The Regent*, Henry VIII's great warship, was sunk by the French in 1512, that being the 'chance' that prevented it floating in the river and proving the Potycary's point.

And done greater cures gostely
Then ever he dyd bodely,
Namely thys one which ye shall here,
Of one departed within thys seven yere,
A frende of myne, and lykewyse I
To her agayne was as frendly,
Who fell so syke so sodeynly
That dede she was even by and by,
And never spake with preste nor clerke
Nor had no whyt of thys holy warke,
For I was thens; it coulde nat be.
Yet harde I say she asked for me.
But when I bethought me howe thys chaunced,
And that I have to Heven avaunced
So many soules to me but straungers,
And coude nat kepe my frende from daungers,
But she to dy so daungerously,
For her soule helth especyally;
That was the thynge that greved me soo,
That nothynge coulde release my woo,
Tyll I had tried even out of hande
In what estate her soule dyd stande.
For whiche tryall, shorte tale to make,
I toke thys journey for her sake.
Geve eare, for here begynneth the story.
From hens I went to Purgatory
And toke with me thys gere in my fyste,
Wherby I may do there what I lyste.
I knocked and was let in quyckly,
But, Lord, how lowe the soules made curtesy!
And I to every soule agayne
Dyd gyve a beck, them to retayne,
And axed them thys question than:
Yf that the soule of suche a woman
Dyd late amonge them there appere?
Wherto they sayd she came nat here.
Then ferd I muche it was nat well.
Alas, thought I, she is in Hell!
For with her lyfe I was so acqueynted,
That sure I thought she was nat saynted.[83]
With thys it chaunced me to snese;
'Christe helpe!' quoth a soule, that ley for his fees.[84]
'Those wordes', quoth I, 'thou shalt nat lees.'
Then, with these pardons of all degrees,
I payed hys tole and set hym so quyght
That strayt to Heven he toke his flyght.
And I from thens to Hell that nyght,
To help this woman yf I myght;
Nat as who sayth by outhorite,
But by the waye of entreate.[85]
And fyrst the devyll that kept the gate
I came, and spake after this rate:
'All hayle, syr devyll', and made lowe curtesy.
'Welcome', quoth he, thys smillyngly,
He knew me well and I at laste
Remembered hym syns longe tyme paste.
For as good happe wolde have it chaunce,
Thys devyll and I were of olde acqueyntaunce,
For oft in the play of Corpus Cristi
He hath played the Devyll at Coventry.
By his acqueyntaunce and my behavoure
He shewed to me ryght frendly favoure.
And to make my returne the shorter,
I sayd to this devyll, 'Good mayster porter,
For all olde love, yf it lye in your power,
Helpe me to speke with my lorde and your.'
'Be sure', quoth he, 'no tongue can tell
What tyme thou coudest have come so well,
For this daye Lucyfer fell,[86]
Whiche is our festyvall in Hell.
Nothynge unreasonable craved thys day
That shall in Hell have any nay.
But yet be ware thou come nat in,
Tyll tyme thou may thy pasporte wyn.
Wherfore stande styll, and I wyll wyt
Yf I can get thy save condyt.'
He taryed nat but shortely gat it,
Under seale and the Devyls hande at it
In ample wyse, as ye shall here.

773 spiritual 774 bodily 780 dead, almost immediately 781 priest 782 business 783 elsewhere 785 occurred 786 sent 787 only 789 (i.e. without the last rites) 793 immediately 794 condition 799 gear (i.e. his pardons) 802 curtsey/bowing 804 nod/small bow, repay 805 asked 809 feared 813 sneeze 814 bless you 815 lose (i.e. You'll gain by those words) 816 kinds 817 toll, settled his account so well 819 went from there 821 authority 823 guarded 824 in this manner 825 and (he said) this smilingly 829 as chance would nave it 835 to cut a long story short 838 yours (i.e. Satan) 842 festival/public holiday 844 be denied 846 gain your passport 848 safe conduct/passport 850 with the Devil's signature on it 851 (written) in ample fashion

83 'That I was sure she had not been made a saint [and taken to Heaven].'

84 Either 'who lay here as his reward for taking excessive fees', or 'who lied for his fees (while alive)', probably a jibe at lawyers.

85 A pardoner could only entreat on a soul's behalf, not redeem it on his own authority from Hell. Only in purgatory were his pardons effective.

86 'You could not have come at a better time, because today is the anniversary of Lucifer's fall [from Heaven]'. The contrast with Christ's hostile reception from the devils during the Harrowing of Hell is part of the comedy here.

Thus it began:[87] 'Lucyfere,
By the power of God chyefe Devyll of Hell,
To all the devyls that there do dwell
And every of them, we send gretynge,
Under streyght charge and commaundynge
That they aydynge and assystent be
To suche a pardoner (and named me),
So that he may at lybertie
Passe save without hys jeopardy,
Tyll that he be from us extyncte
And clerely out of Hells precincte;
And hys pardons to kepe savegarde,
We wyll they lye in the porters warde.
Gevyn in the fornes of our palys,[88]
In our hye courte of maters of malys,
Suche a day and yere of our reyne.'

'God save the Devyll!' quoth I for playne.
'I trust thys wrytynge to be sure?'
'Then put thy truste', quoth he, 'in eure,
Syns thou art sure to take no harme.'
Thys devyll and I walket arme in arme
So farre, tyll he had brought me thyther,
Where all the devyls of Hell togyther
Stode in aray, in such apparell
As for that day there metely fell:
Theyr hornes well gylt, theyr clowes full clene,
Theyr taylles well kempt and, as I wene,
With Sothery butter theyr bodyes anoynted;
I never sawe devyls so well appoynted.
The master devyll sat in his jacket,
And all the soules were playnge at racket;
None other rackettes they hadde in hande,
Save every soule a good fyre brande,
Wherwith they played so pretely
That Lucyfer laughted merely,
And all the resedew of the feendes
Dyd laugh full well togytther lyke frendes.
But of my frende I sawe no whyt,
Nor durst nat axe for her as yet.
Anone all this rout was brought in silens,
And I by an usher brought in presens.
Then to Lucyfer, low as I coude,
I knelyd, whiche he so well alowde
That thus he beckte, and, by Saynt Antony,
He smyled on me well favoredly,
Bendynge hys browes as brode as barne durres,
Shakynge hys eares as ruged as burres,
Rolynge hys yes as rounde as two bushels,
Flastynge the fyre out of his nose thryls,
Gnashynge hys teeth so vayngloro[u]sely,
That me thought tyme to fall to flatery.
Wherwith I tolde as I shall tell:

'O plesant pycture,[89] O Prince of Hell,
Feutred in fashyon abominable!
And, syns that is inestimable
For me to prayse the[e] worthyly,
I leve of prays, unworthy
To geve the[e] prays, besechynge the[e]
To heare my sewte, and then to be
So good to graunt the thynge I crave.
And to be shorte, thys wolde I have:
The soule of one which hyther is flytted,
Delivered hens and to me remitted.
And in thys doynge, though al be nat quyt,
Yet some parte I shall deserve it,
As thus: I am a pardoner
And over soules as a controller,
Thorough out the Erth my power doth stande,
Where many a soule lyeth on my hande
That spede in maters as I use them
As I receyve them or refuse them;
Wherby, what tyme thy pleasure is,
I shall requy[t]e any part of thys:
The leste devyll here that can come thyther.'
'Nowe', quoth the Devyll, 'we are well pleased.
Shall chose a soule and brynge hym hyther.
What is hys name thou woldest have eased?'
'Nay', quoth I, 'be it good or evyll,
My comynge is for a she devyll!'
'What calste her', quoth he, 'thou horyson?'
'Forsoth', quoth I, 'Margery Coorson.'
'Now by our honour', sayd Lucyfer,

855 greeting 856 strict order 857 they aid and assist 860 (To) pass safely 861 gone 862 jurisdiction 863 safeguard 864 safekeeping 866 matters of malice 867 reign 868 plainly 869 reliable 870 put it to the test 872 walked 875 stood dressed up 876 was fitting 877 gilded, claws 878 tails, combed 879 Surrey (or sweet) 880 dressed 882 tennis 885 prettily/skilfully 886 merrily 887 residue/remainder 889 evidence/trace 891 silence 892 (the Devil's) presence 894 allowed/liked 895 nodded 896 favourably 897 broad as barn-doors 898 rough as burs 899 eyes, measuring tubs 900 flashing, nostrils 902 resort 905 sheathed, diabolical elegance 906 since it's impossible 908 leave off/stop unworthy (praise) 910 suit 913 flown 914 given into custody 915 matter, I can't repay you fully 916 to some degree, repay 921 direct 923 whenever 924 repay 925 (to) the least (important) 928 released 931 do you call her, whoreson

87 The Pardoner parodies the formal language and protocol of a royal warrant.

88 'Given [i.e. dictated] in the furnace of our palace': a parody signature citing the location where the warrant was drafted.

89 'O image of diabolical perfection': again the Pardoner parodies the form and manner of royal address.

'No devyll in Hell shall witholde her.
And yf thou woldest have twenty mo,
Were nat for justyce they shulde goo;[90]
For all we devyls within thys den
Have more to do with two women
Then with all the charge we have besyde.
Wherfore, yf thou our frende wyll be tried,
Aply thy pardons to women so
That unto us there come no mo.'

To do my beste I promysed by othe,
Whiche I have kepte, for as the fayth goth
At thys dayes to Heven I do procure
Ten women to one man, be sure.
Then of Lucyfer my leve I toke,
And streyght unto the mayster coke
I was hadde into the kechyn,
For Margaryes offyce was ther in.
All thynge handled there discretely,
For every soule bereth offyce metely,[91]
Whiche myght be sene to se her syt
So bysely turnynge of the spyt.
For many a spyt here hath she turned,
And many a good spyt hath she burned,
And many a spyt full hote hath tosted,
Before the meat coulde be halfe rosted.
And, or the meate were half rosted in dede,
I toke her then from the spyt for spede.
But when she sawe thys brought to pas,
To tell the joy wherein she was,
And of all the devyls for joy how then
Dyd rore at her delyvery,
And how the cheynes in Hell dyd rynge,
And how all the soules therin dyd synge,
And how we were brought to the gate,
And how we toke our leve therat,
Be suer lacke of tyme sufferyth nat
To reherse the xx parte of that.
Wherfore, thys tale to conclude brevely,
Thys woman thanked me chyefly
That she was ryd of thys endles deth,
And so we departed on New Market heth.[92]
And yf that any man do mynde her,
Who lyste to seke her, there shall he fynde her.

PEDLER
Syr, ye have sought her wonders well,
And where ye founde her as ye tell,
To here the chaunce ye founde in Hell,
I fynde ye were in great parell.

PALMER
His tale is all muche parellous,
But parte is muche more mervaylous,
As where he sayde the devyls complayne
That women put them to suche payne
By theyr condicions so croked and crabbed,
Frowardly fashonde, so waywarde and wrabbed,
So farre in devision and sturrynge suche stryfe[93]
That all the devyls be wery of theyr lyfe.
This in effect he tolde for trueth,
Wherby muche murvell to me ensueth,
That women in Hell suche shrews can be
And here so gentyll as farre as I se,
Yet have I sene many a myle
And many a woman in the whyle,
Nat one good cytye, towne, nor borough
In Cristendom but I have ben through,
And this I wolde ye shulde understande,
I have sene women fyve hundred thousande
And oft with them have longe tyme maryed,[94]
Yet in all places where I have ben,
Of all the women that I have sene,
I never sawe nor knewe, to my consyens,
Any one woman out of paciens.

POTYCARY
By the Masse, there is a great lye!

PARDONER
I never harde a greater, by Our Lady!

938 more trouble 939 prisoners, otherwise 940 if you want to prove yourself our friend 941 Use 944 as religion fares 945 At the moment 948 master-cook 949 taken, kitchen 950 job, there 954 busily 957 hot, toasted 964 release 965 chains, rattle 966 sing 968 leave at it 970 twentieth 971 briefly 972 principally 973 death 974 separated 975 care about her 977 amazingly 979 adventures you had 980 peril 981 perilous 985 nature, twisted sour 986 naturally quarrelsome, perverse 988 weary 990 (i.e. I'm completely amazed) 991 quarrelsome wretches 992 here (they) are, (can) see 995 city 997 want you to 1000 been 1002 conscience 1003 patience

90 'Were it not for justice [i.e. they are justly imprisoned in Hell]'.

91 'Every soul has an appropriate job [i.e. one relevant to their sins while they were living] there'. Margery's sexual wantonness result in her job being to turn the spit (a slang term for a penis) in the kitchens. 'Burning' was a slang term for passing on a venereal disease.

92 Newmarket Heath, Suffolk, location of the Devil's Dyke, reputedly a gateway to Hell.

93 'So deeply involved in quarrelling and the stirring of trouble'.

94 'had acquaintance'. As A&H observe, a line (perhaps ending in 'tarrying') seems to have been lost prior to this one which would complete the couplet.

PEDLER
A greater! Nay, knowe ye any so great?

PALMER
Syr, whether that I lose or get,
For my parte judgement shall be prayed.

PARDONER
And I desyer as he hath sayd.

POTYCARY
Procede and ye shall be obeyed.

PEDLER
Then shall nat judement be delayd.
Of all these thre, yf eche mannes tale
In Poules Church yarde were set on sale[95]
In some mannes hande, that hath the sleyghte,
He shulde sure sell these tales by weyght,[96]
For as they wey so be they worth.
But which weyth beste; to that now forth.
Syr, all the tale that ye dyd tell
I bere in mynde, and yours as well,
And as ye sawe the mater metely,
So lyed ye bothe well and discretely.
Yet were your lyes with the lest, truste me,
[*To the Potycary*] For yf ye had sayd ye had made fle
Ten tampyons out of ten womens tayles
Ten tymes ten myle to ten castels or jayles,
And fyll ten ryvers ten tymes so depe
As ten of that whiche your castell stones dyde kepe,
[*To the Pardoner*] Or yf ye ten tymes had bodely
Fet ten soules out of Purgatory
And ten tymes so many out of Hell,
Yet, by these ten bonnes, I coulde ryght well
Ten tymes sonner all that have beleved,
Then the tenth parte of that he hath meved.

POTYCARY
Two knaves before one lacketh two knaves of fyve,
Then one and then one, and bothe knaves alyve!
Then two and then two and thre at a cast,
Thou knave and thou knave and thou knave at
laste![97]

Nay, knave, yf ye tryme by nomber,
I wyll as knavyshly you accomber.
Your mynde is all on your pryvy tythe,
For all in ten me thynketh your wit lythe.
Now ten tymes I besech Hym that hye syttes,
Thy wyfes x commaundementes may serch thy v
wittes![98]
Then ten of my tordes in ten of thy teth,
And ten of thy nose, whiche every man seth,
And twenty tymes ten, this wyshe I wolde
That thou haddest ben hanged at ten yere olde:
For thou goest about to make me a slave.
I wyll thou knowe yf I am a gentylman, knave.
And here is an other shall take my parte.

PARDONER
[*To the Potycary*] Nay, fyrste I beshrew your knaves
herte
Or I take parte in your knavery.
I wyll speke fayre, by Our Lady:
[*To the Pedler*] Syr, I beseche your mashyp to be
As good as ye can be to me.

PEDLER
I wolde be glade to do you good
And hym also, be he never so wood.
But dout you nat, I wyll now do
The thynge my consciens ledeth me to.
Both your tales I take farre impossyble,
Yet take I his fa[r]ther incredyble;
Nat only the thynge it selfe alloweth it,
But also the boldenes thereof avoweth it.
I knowe nat where your tale to trye,
Nor yours, but in Hell or Purgatorye.
But hys boldnes has faced a lye
That may be tried evyn in thys companye.

1007 win 1008 I seek judgement 1009 desire (the same) as 1014 skill 1015 in great numbers 1016 weigh 1017 I move on to that 1022 among the losers 1023 fly 1025 jails 1028 bodily 1029 Fetched 1031 bones (i.e. his fingers) 1032 sooner, believed all that 1033 he (the Palmer) claimed 1038 measure/chastise, numbers 1039 overburden/reply 1040 secret (bribe of) 10 per cent from the Palmer 1041 you're obsessed with tens 1042 sits on high 1043 ten, five 1044 turds, teeth 1045 in sees 1048 are trying 1049 I'll show you that 1050 another (i.e. the Pardoner), side 1060 to be utterly impossible 1061 as (the) more incredible 1062 story, confirms it 1063 boldness (of the telling) 1064 test 1066 affirmed

95 St Paul's Churchyard in London was the home of most of the capital's booksellers.

96 i.e. each of these lies would make a best-selling pamphlet.

97 A mathematical fancy of the 'how many beans make five?' variety, offered in riposte to the Pedler's allusion to the tenfold superiority of the Palmer's lie. It was probably accompanied, as A&H suggest, by some lively business as the Potycary arranges the other 'knaves' to illustrate his claims.

98 This line was probably accompanied by gestures which indicate that the 'ten commandments' are his wife's fingers, and his five wits are in either his head or his genitals.

As yf ye lyste to take thys order
Amonge the women in thys border,
Take thre of the yongest and thre of the oldest,
Thre of the hotest and thre of the coldest,
Thre of the wysest and thre of the shrewdest,
[Three of the cheefest and thre of the lewdest,
Thre of the lowest and thre of the hyest,
Thre of the farthest and thre of the nyest,
Thre of the fayrest and thre of the maddest,
Thre of the fowlest and thre of the saddest;
And when all these threes be had a sonder,
Of eche thre two justly by nomber
Shall be founde shrewes, exepte thys fall:
That ye hap to fynde them shrews all.
Hym selfe for trouth all this doth k[n]owe
And oft hath tried some of thys rowe,
And yet he swereth by his consciens,
He never saw woman breke paciens.
Wherfore consydered with true entente,
Hys lye to be so evident
And to appere so evydently,
That both you affyrmed it a ly.
And that my consciens, so depely,
So depe hath sought thys thynge to try,
And tried it with mynde indyfferent,
Thus I awarde by way of judgement:
Of all the lyes ye all have spent,
Hys lye to be most excellent.

PALMER
Syr, though ye were bounde of equyte
To do as ye have done to me,
Yet do I thanke you of your payne,
And wyll requyte some parte agayne.

PARDONER
Mary, syr, ye can no les do
But thanke hym as muche as it cometh to,[99]
And so wyll I do for my parte.
Now a vengeaunce on thy knaves harte!
I never knewe pedler a judge before,
Nor never wyll truste pedlynge knave more.
What doest thou there, thou horson nody?

POTYCARY
By the Masse, lerne to make curtesy,
Curtesy before, and curtesy behynde hym,
And then on eche syde the Devyll blynde hym![100]
Nay, when I have it perfytly
Ye shall have the Devyll and all of curtesy.
But it is nat sone lerned, brother,
One knave to make curtesy to another.
Yet when I am angry that is the worste,
I shall call my mayster 'knave' at the fyrste.

PALMER
Then wolde some mayster perhappes clowt ye.
But, as for me, ye nede nat doute ye;
For I hade lever be without ye
Then have suche besynesse aboute ye.

PARDONER
So helpe me God, so were ye better.
What, shulde a begger be a jetter?
It were no whyt your honestie
To have us twayne jet after ye.

POTYCARY
Syr, be ye sure he telleth you true;
Yf we shulde wayte, thys wolde ensew:
It wolde be sayd, truste me at a worde,
Two knaves made curtesy to the thyrde.

PEDLER
Now by my trouth, to speke my mynde,
Syns they be so loth to be assyned,
To let them lose I thynke it beste.
And so shall ye lyve beste in rest.

PALMER
Syr, I am nat on them so fonde
To compell them to kepe theyr bonde.
And syns ye lyste nat to wayte on me
I clerely of waytynge dyscharge ye.

PARDONER
Mary, syr, I hertely thanke you.

1069 this side (of the hall) 1070 three 1073 most exalted, most common 1075 nearest 1078 are separated out 1080 unless this occurs 1081 happen 1082 Himself (i.e. the Palmer) 1083 row (of spectators) 1089 (of) you 1092 an impartial mind 1094 spoken 1096 in justice 1098 for your trouble 1100 do no less 1101 as it is necessary 1104 (a) pedlar (to be) 1105 again 1106 are you doing, fool? 1107 courtesy/curtsy 1116 strike 1118 rather 1119 trouble with you 1121 swaggerer/man of authority 1122 wouldn't help your reputation a bit 1125 wait on you, follow 1129 assigned/appointed (as servants) 1130 loose/release 1131 in greater peace 1132 so besotted with them 1135 completely, discharge

99 Perhaps there is a further allegation of bribery implied in the Pardoner's words: i.e. 'Pay him whatever the bill amounts to.'

100 These lines must be accompanied by the Potycary bowing low all around his new 'master' the Palmer. The final bow, with its attendant curse, may well be accompanied by a fart. For the association of farts with blinding, see Chaucer's *Miller's Tale*, ll. 619–21.

POTYCARY
And I lyke wyse, I make God avowe.

PEDLER
Now be ye all evyn as ye begoon:
No man hath loste nor no man hath woon.
Yet in the debate wherwith ye began,[101]
By waye of advyse I wyll speke as I can.
I do perceyve that pylgrymage
Is chyefe the thynge ye have in usage,
Wherto in effecte for love of Chryst
Ye have, or shulde have bene, entyst,
And who so doth with suche entent
Doth well declare hys tyme well spent.
And so do ye in your pretence,
If ye procure thus indulgence
Unto your neyghbours charytably,
For love of them in God onely,
All thys may be ryght well applied
To shewe you both well occupyed.
For though ye walke nat bothe one waye,
Yet walkynge thus, thys dare I saye:
That bothe your walkes come to one ende.
And so for all that do pretende,
By ayde of Goddes grace, to ensewe
Any maner kynde of vertue;
As some great almyse for to gyve,
Some in wyllfull pove[r]tie to lyve,
Some to make hye wayes and suche other warkes,
And some to mayntayne prestes and clarkes
To synge and praye for soule departed;[102]
These with all other vertues well marked,
All though they be of sondry kyndes,
Yet be they nat used with sondry myndes,
But as God only doth all those move;
So every man, onely for His love,
With love and dred obediently
Worketh in these vertues unyformely.
Thus every vertue, yf we lyste to scan,
Is pleasaunt to God and thankfull to man.
And who that by grace of the Holy Goste
To any one vertue is moved moste,
That man by that grace that one apply[103]
And therin serve God most plentyfully.
Yet nat that one so farre wyde to wreste,
So lykynge the same to myslyke the reste.
For who so wresteth hys worke is in vayne.
And even in that case I perceyve you twayne,[104]
Lykynge your vertue in suche wyse
That eche others vertue you do dyspyse.
Who walketh thys way for God wolde fynde hym,
The farther they seke Hym, the farther behynde
Hym.[105]
One kynde of vertue to dyspyse another
Is lyke as the syster myght hange the brother.

POTYCARY
For fere lest suche parels to me myght fall,
I thanke God I use no vertue at all!

PEDLER
That is of all the very worste waye!
For more harde it is, as I have harde saye,
To begynne vertue where none is pretendyd,
Then where it is begonne, the abuse to be mended.
How be it ye be nat all to begynne,[106]
One syne of vertue ye are entred in,
As thys: I suppose ye dyd saye true,
In that ye sayd ye use no vertue.
In the whiche wordes, I dare well reporte,
Ye are well beloved of all thys sorte,
By your raylynge here openly
At pardons and relyques so leudly.

POTYCARY
In that I thynke my faute nat great,
For all that he hath I knowe conterfete.

1138 equal/in the same state **1145** enticed/attracted **1146** does so (i.e. goes on pilgrimage) **1148** vocation **1154** on the same road/route **1156** the same destination (i.e. Heaven) **1157** practice **1158** follow **1160** alms/charitable gifts **1161** willing poverty **1165** well known **1166** different **1167** intentions/motives **1168** prompt/motivate **1171** in the same way **1172** understand (it) **1188** perils **1192** practised **1195** sign, have revealed already **1197** (i.e. at least you acknowledge your sins) **1199** (i.e. the audience) **1200** railing/abusing **1201** rudely **1203** he (the Pardoner)

101 i.e. who was most efficacious in helping souls towards Heaven? The Pedler here begins a serious plea for tolerance of religious diversity (albeit within an orthodox Catholic framework).

102 'Some to build and repair main roads and other deeds/projects, and some to pay for the upkeep of priests and scholars who sing [masses] and pray for the souls of the departed [in Purgatory]'. The maintenance of highways and the financial support of chantry priests and Masses were traditional acts of charity practised by the wealthy.

103 'Let him or her apply him or herself through grace to that particular vocation'.

104 'Yet he should not, in liking his own vocation, so distort matters that he dislikes all the rest. For whoever thus distorts things works in vain. And I perceive that you are two [men] in that situation'.

105 'Whoever searches for God in this way, finds that the more they search, the further away from Him they get.'

106 'You do not have to begin entirely from scratch'.

PEDLER
For his and all other that ye knowe fayned,
Ye be nother counceled nor constrayned
To any suche thynge in any suche case
To gyve any reverence in any suche place.
But where ye dout, the truthe nat knowynge,
Belevynge the beste, good may be growynge.
In judgynge the beste no harme at the leste;
In judgynge the worste, no good at the beste.[107]
But beste in these thynges it semeth to me,
To make no judgement upon ye.
But as the churche doth judge or take them,
So do ye receyve or forsake them.
And so be sure ye can nat erre,
But may be a frutfull folower.

POTYCARY
Go ye before and, as I am true man,
I wyll folow as faste as I can.

PARDONER
And so wyll I, for he hath sayd so well,
Reason wolde we shulde folowe hys counsell.

PALMER
Then to our reason God gyve us His grace
That we may folowe with fayth so fermely
His commaundementes, that we maye purchace
Hys love, and so consequently
To byleve Hys churche, faste and faythfully,
So that we may accordynge to His promyse
Be kepte out of errour in any wyse.

And all that hath scapet us here by neglygence,
We clerely revoke and forsake it.
To passe the tyme in thys without offence
Was the cause why the maker dyd make it.
And so we humbly beseche you take it,
Besechynge Our Lorde to prosper you all
In the fayth of Hys churche universall.[108]

FINIS
IMPRYNTED AT LONDON IN FLETESTRETE AT THE
SYGNE OF THE GEORGE BY WYLYYAM MYDDYLTON.

1204 feigned/false 1205 neither advised 1208 (i.e. if a relic is authentic) 1215 accept, reject 1223 firmly 1224 win/gain 1226 believe (in) 1229 escaped, through 1232 (i.e. the playwright)

[107] 'If you assume the best in every situation, you won't miss out if things prove to be false; but if you assume everything is false, then you will never benefit when things turn out to be authentic.'

[108] A resolutely Catholic sentiment with which to end a play during the turbulent early years of the Reformation in England.

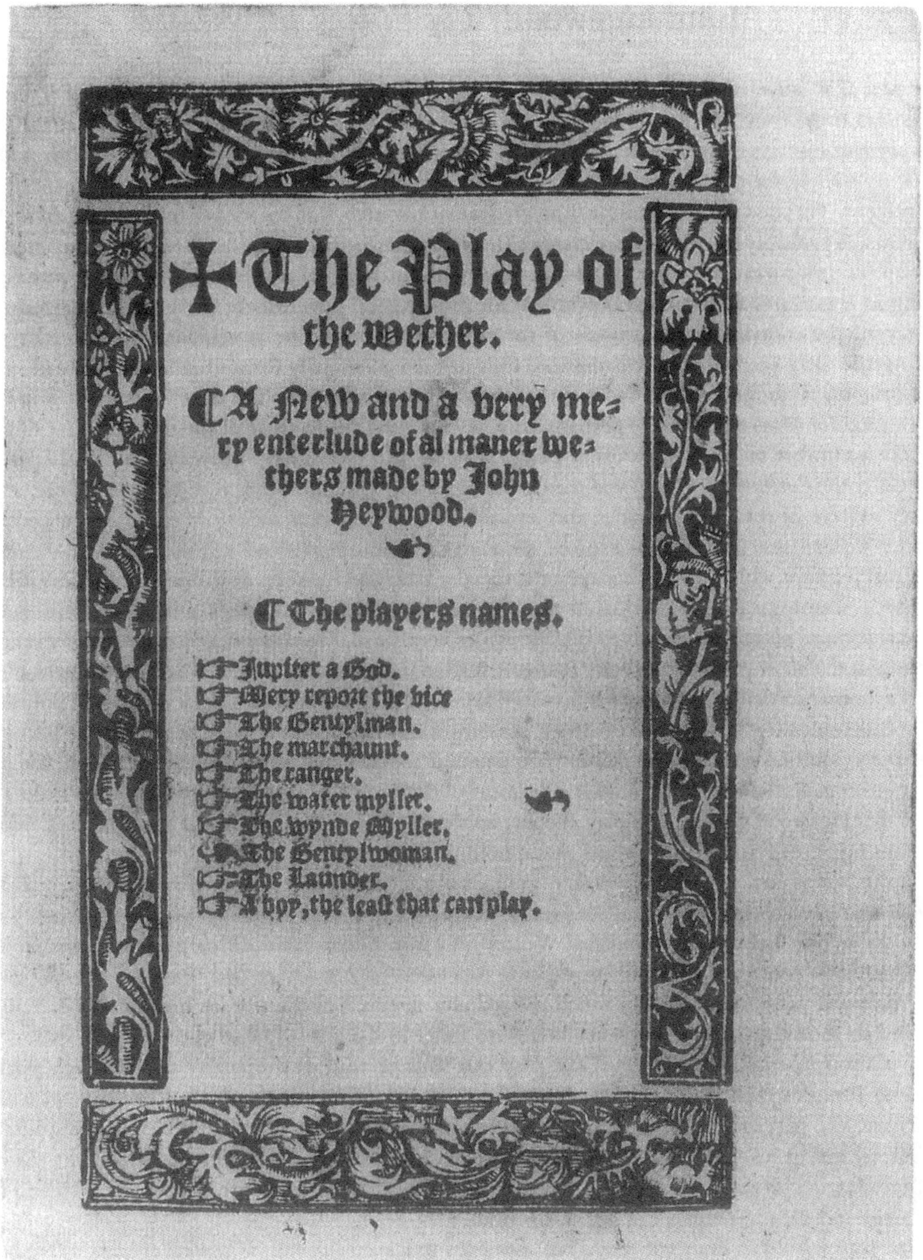
The Play of the wether.

A New and a very mery enterlude of al maner wethers made by John Heywood.

The players names.

Jupiter a God.
Mery report the vice
The Gentylman.
The marchaunt.
The ranger.
The water myller.
The wynde Myller.
The Gentylwoman.
The Launder.
A boy, the least that can play.

The Play of the Weather, title page. Courtesy of the Bodleian Library, Oxford.

John Heywood, *The Play of the Weather*

The plot of *Weather*, like that of *The Four PP*, is not complex, based as it is upon the arrival of a succession of suitors at the court of the god-king Jupiter, each of whom makes self-interested and mutually contradictory requests. As each new character arrives to make a claim for his or her preferred form of weather (and, implicitly for the superiority of his or her profession), the play moves on to another 'scene' or movement. This device has no single, known dramatic source, but the idea of introducing rival suitors to Jupiter was probably borrowed from classical literature, principally the *Ikaromenippus* of the Greek satirist Lucian. The play treats the most inconsequential (and intractable) of subjects, the British weather, but in doing so it explores a fundamental problem for monarchical government: how can a king reconcile and satisfy all the contradictory demands of the subjects for whom he is responsible, especially when, as during the early years of the Reformation, they argue vociferously for mutually antipathetic ends? The god-king's final judgement (he declares that the weather shall remain the same, thus rewarding everyone, albeit only for some of the time) perhaps reflects Heywood's own sense of the impossibility of the task.

Like a number of Heywood's other plays, *Weather* also has much in common with Chaucer's work, especially the *Parliament of Fowls* and the *Canterbury Tales*. Like the latter, it introduces characters who are representative of the various trades and 'estates' of contemporary society (a merchant, a gentleman, a washer-woman) and uses them to explore, through the medium of broad-minded, vernacular comedy, the very real tensions which existed between the social classes and the sexes in the period. Scenes such as Mery Report's scatological humiliation of the Gentylman, or the Launder's withering criticism of the Gentylwoman, permit Heywood to explore issues very similar to those raised by Chaucer in the *Miller's Prologue* and *Tale* or the *Wife of Bath's Prologue*. Indeed, beneath the surface jollity and Heywood's characteristic humanist delight in debate for its own sake, the play does touch upon a number of political issues of intense topicality. On internal evidence, it seems likely that it was written at some point between 1529 and 1533, a period when all the issues upon which it touches (the powers of the sovereign, the problems of a rancorous Parliament, the conflicting claims of the people, the king's marriage) were deeply contentious. For Heywood to produce a play at court on these issues, and in which the king, Jupiter, was such an obvious figure of Henry VIII himself, was a bold political step.

Jupiter's new powers over the weather (granted him by an acrimonious session of the Olympian Parliament) seem clearly designed to reflect Henry VIII's own new-found status as an active monarch after the dismissal of his chief minister, Cardinal Wolsey, in 1529. Thereafter the king made it clear that he would now be in sole control of the decision-making processes, taking advice from Parliament and counsellors, but reserving judgement, in very much the manner declared by Jupiter, to himself alone. This process reached its formal apotheosis in Henry's claim to the title of Supreme Head of the church, granted him by Convocation in 1533. On one level the play can thus be read as supportive of the king's position. In lauding Jupiter's capacity to transcend partisanship and self-interest to reach a solution which satisfies everyone, the playwright offers a message sympathetic to Henry's position. Yet it is significant that Heywood makes his god-king use his powers to leave things as they were rather than introduce radical change. Again Heywood seems to be using his drama to call for tolerance in the face of social and religious divisions and the maintenance of the status quo.

The play is bold in dramatic terms too, not least in the creation of its central character, Mery Report. The latter is listed among the *dramatis personae* as 'the Vice', the first time that the title was used in this formal way, but he is more than just a figure of misrule in the manner of the Morality Vices. The audience is not invited to judge (and condemn) his immoral behaviour from a Christian viewpoint; his engagement with them is more open, more akin to that of the clowns and fools of later sixteenth-century drama. Significantly it is he, rather than Jupiter, who is the play's master of ceremonies, directing the action and setting the tone for the various encounters which he oversees. In a gesture familiar from Medwall's *Fulgens and Lucres*, he enters the action ostensibly from among the audience, but he quickly secures, through his ready wit, the role of Jupiter's squire for the body, and, when he re-enters the place, it is in the fine livery of a royal servant. Thereafter he controls the access of the various suitors to Jupiter, and absorbs them into the bawdy, misogynistic comedy which is his principal contribution to the play. His playful control of the acting space, and his role as the intermediary or 'mean' between the god-king and his subjects, hark back to the role of Measure in Skelton's *Magnyfycence* and forward to that of Diligence in Lindsay's *Satyre of the Thrie Estaitis*. The importance attributed to access and proximity to the monarch in these plays is a reflection of the importance of such matters in Tudor politics itself, a fact highlighted as play politics and 'real' politics are played out in the same physical space: the great hall of the royal palace.

The play itself requires only one major property, the curtained and canopied throne (similar to that used in *Godly Queene Hester*) which Jupiter occupies for most of the play, and which must conceal the musicians who play a song '[with]in' the curtains at l. 178. Otherwise the geography of the great hall itself, with its 'servants' side' at the screens end, and 'elite side' around the dais where the patron dined, could be used to foster the nuanced comedy of manners and etiquette that the interlude at times demands (i.e. ll. 432 and following). The cast required, ten actors with no doubling possible (the entire cast assembles on-stage for the final scene and closing song), strongly suggests that Heywood could call upon the resources of the royal court to furnish his actors. At least one child is required ('the le[a]st [smallest] that can play') for the role of Dick, the Boy; and it may well be that the entire cast (except Mery Report, who may have been played by Heywood himself) was made up of schoolboys and choristers.

The text printed here is based on the version published in 1533 by William Rastell, and now in the Pepys Library (STC 13305). I have consulted two facsimiles, those edited by J.S. Farmer for the *Tudor Facsimile Texts* series (London, 1909) and by T.N.S. Lennam and G.R. Proudfoot for *Malone Society Reprints* (Oxford, 1977), and the modern critical edition in Richard Axton and Peter Happé, eds, *The Plays of John Heywood* (Woodbridge, 1991).

A new and very mery enterlude of all maner wethers made by John Heywood

Jupiter, a god,[1] *The Water Myller*, *Mery Reporte*, the Vice, *The Wynde Myller*, *The Gentylman*, *The Gentylwoman*, *The Marchaunt*, *The Launder* (a washerwoman), *The Ranger* (a forest warden/gamekeeper), *The Boy*, the lest that can play.[2]

Jupiter
Ryght farre to longe as now were to recyte[3]
The auncyent estate wherin our selfe hath reyned,
What honour, what laude gyven us of very ryght,
What glory we have had dewly unfayned
Of eche creature whych dewty hath constrayned,
For above all goddes, syns our fathers fale
We Jupiter were ever pryncypale.

If we so have ben (as treuth yt is in dede)
Beyond the compas of all comparyson,
Who coulde presume to shew, for any mede,
So that yt myght appere to humayne reason,
The hye renowme we stande in at this season?
For, syns that Heven and Erth were fyrste create
Stode we never in suche tryumphaunt estate

As we now do, wherof we woll reporte
Suche parte as we se mete for tyme present,
Chyefely concernynge your perpetuall conforte,[4]
As the thynge selfe shall prove in experyment,
Whyche hyely shall bynde you on knees lowly bent
Soolly to honour oure hyenes day by day.
And now to the mater gyve eare and we shall say.

Before our presens in our hye parlyament,
Both goddes and goddeses of all degrees
Hath late assembled by comen assent
For the redres of certayne enormytees
Bred amonge them thorow extremytees
Abusyd in eche to other of them all,[5]
Namely to purpose in these moste specyall:

2 ancient, reigned 3 worship 4 rightly (and) honestly 5 From, duty 6 father's fall 8 truly 9 limit 10 describe, reward 11 human 12 renown, time 13 since, created 15 will 18 itself, (i.e. as you shall see) 19 highly/greatly 20 solely, highness 24 lately, common 25 redress, enormities/abuses 26 through extreme behaviour 28 In particular, specifically

1 Jupiter became chief of the Roman gods after he deposed his father, Saturn.

2 'The smallest who knows how to act.' The Boy's name is Dick.

3 'It would take much too long now to tell you'.

4 'Chiefly that part of [my power] which concerns your perpetual comfort/well-being'.

5 'Committed by each of them against all of the others'.

Our foresayd father Saturne, and Phebus,
Eolus and Phebe, these four by name,[6]
Whose natures not onely so farre contraryous,
But also of malyce eche other to defame,
Have longe tyme abused ryght farre out of frame
The dew course of all theyr constellacyons,
To the great damage of all Yerthly nacyons,[7]

Whyche was debated in place sayde before.
And fyrste as became our father moste auncyent
Wyth berde whyte as snow, his lockes both cold and hore,
Hath entred such mater as served his entent,
Laudynge his frosty mansyon in the fyrmament
To ayre and yerth as thynge moste precyous,
Pourgynge all humours that are contagyous.[8]

How be yt, he alledgeth that of longe tyme past
Lyttell hath prevayled his great dylygens,[9]
Full oft uppon yerth his fayre frost he hath cast
All thynges hurtfull to banysh out of presens,
But Phebus entendynge to kepe hym in sylens
When he hath labored all nyght in his powres
His glarynge beamys maryth all in two howres.

Phebus to this made no maner answerynge
Wheruppon they both then Phebe defyed.
Eche for his parte leyd in her reprouvynge
That by her showres superfluous, they have tried
In all that she may, theyr powres be denyed.[10]
Wherunto Phebe made answere no more
Then Phebus to Saturne hadde made before.

Anone uppon Eolus all these dyd fle
Complaynynge theyr causes eche one arow,
And sayd, to compare none was so evyll as he,
For when he is dysposed his blastes to blow
He suffereth neyther sone shyne, rayne, nor snow.
They eche agaynste other, and he agaynste all thre,
Thus can these foure in no maner agre

Whyche sene in them selfe, and further consyderynge
The same to redres, was cause of theyr assemble.[11]
And also that we, evermore beynge,
Besyde our puysaunt power of deite,
Of wysedome and nature so noble and so fre,
From all extremytees the meane devydynge,
To pease and plente eche thynge attemperynge,[12]

They have in conclusyon holly surrendryd
Into our handes (as mych as concernynge
All maner wethers by them engendryd)
The full of theyr powrs for terme everlastynge,
To set suche order as standyth wyth our pleasynge,
Whyche thynge, as of our parte, no parte requyred
But of all theyr partys ryght humbly desyred.[13]

To take uppon us wherto we dyd assente.
And so in all thynges wyth one voyce agreable
We have clerely fynyshed our foresayd parleament.
To your great welth whyche shall be fyrme and stable,
And to our honour farre inestymable.
For syns theyr powers, as ours, addyd to our owne
Who can we say know us as we shulde be knowne?[14]

But now, for fyne, the reste of our entent
Wherfore, as now, we hyther are dyscendyd,
Is onely to satysfye and content

31 contradictory 32 through, abuse 33 beyond their normal limits 35 Earthly nations 36 (i.e. the Heavenly Parliament) 37 befitted 38 beard, hoary 39 entered (a bill), interests 40 mansion/orbit, heavens 41 air, earth 42 purging, conditions 43 for (a) 46 presence (i.e. for away) 47 silence 48 he (Saturn), powers 49 mars everything 52 alleged in reproof against her 53 showers, found 56 Than 57 fly (to attack) 58 grievances, by row (in turn) 59 no one could compare to him in evil 60 minded 61 permits, sunshine 66 because we (Jupiter), immortal 67 mighty divine powers 68 generous 71 wholly 73 created 74 total 75 agrees, desire 85 in conclusion 86 at this moment

[6] Saturn and Phoebus (the sun) are the gods associated with cold and heat, respectively; Aeolus (the winds) and Phoebe (the moon) those associated with wind and water. The gods' dispute foreshadows the conflicting demands of the mortal suitors who will appear in person in the Interlude.

[7] As the gods have fallen into disputation, so their planets have been thrown out of their normal orbits, causing damage on Earth through their astrological influence.

[8] Saturn claims that frost is the most beneficial weather for all earthly things as it kills off all contagions.

[9] 'His great efforts have prevailed little'.

[10] 'Their powers [frost and sun] are cancelled out by hers [rain].'

[11] 'It was this state of affairs, once they had seen it for themselves and thought about it, that was the cause of their decision to assemble [in a Parliament] to correct it.'

[12] '[And as we can always] discover the [golden] mean between [harmful] extremes, and moderate everything to bring peace and prosperity to each thing'.

[13] 'Which power was not sought at all on our part, but was [given to us] at the humble entreaty of all of them.'

[14] 'For, since their powers are given to us, and added to our own, who can claim to know us as we deserve [i.e. in our full majesty]?'

All maner people whyche have ben offendyd
By any wether mete to be amendyd.
Uppon whose complayntes, declarynge theyr grefe,[15]
We shall shape remedy for theyr relefe.

And to gyve knowledge for theyr hyther resorte,[16]
We wolde thys afore proclaymed to be
To all our people by some one of thys sorte
Whom we lysste to choyse here amongest all ye.
Wherfore eche man avaunce and we shall se
Whyche of you is moste mete to be our cryer.

Here entreth Mery Reporte.

MERY REPORT
[*To a torch-bearer*] Brother, holde up your torche a lytell hyer!
Now I beseche you my lorde, loke on me furste.
I truste your lordshyp shall not fynde me the wurste.

JUPITER
Why, what arte thou that approchyst so ny?[17]

MERY REPORT
Forsothe, and please your lordshyppe it is I.

JUPITER
All that we knowe very well, but what I?

MERY REPORT
What I? Some saye I am I *perse* I.[18]
But, what maner I so ever be I,
I assure your good lordshyp, I am I.

JUPITER
What maner man arte thou, shewe quyckely.

MERY REPORT
By god, a poore gentylman dwellyth here by.

JUPITER
A gentylman? Thy selfe bryngeth wytnes naye,[19]
Bothe in thy lyght behavour and araye!
But what arte thou called where thou dost resorte?

MERY REPORT
Forsoth, my lorde, mayster Mery Reporte.

JUPITER
Thou arte no mete man in our bysynes
For thyne apparence ys of to mych lyghtnes.

MERY REPORT
Why, can not your lordshyp lyke my maner,
Myne apparell, nor my name nother?

JUPITER
To nother of all we have devocyon.

MERY REPORT
A proper lycklyhod of promocyon!
Well than, as wyse as ye seme to be,
Yet can ye se no wysdome in me.
But, syns ye dysprayse me for so lyghte an elfe,
I praye you gyve me leve to prayse my selfe.
And for the fyrste parte I wyll begyn
In my behavour at my commynge in,
Wherin I thynke I have lytell offendyd,
For sewer my curtesy coulde not be amendyd.
And, as for my sewt your servaunt to be,
Myghte yll have bene myst for your honeste;[20]
For as I be saved, yf I shall not lye,
I saw no man sew for the offyce but I.
Wherfore, yf ye take me not or I go
Ye must anone, whether ye wyll or no.
And syns your entent is but for the wethers
What skyls our apparell to be fryse or fethers?[21]
I thynke it wysdome, syns no man for-bad it
Wyth thys to spare a better, yf I had it.[22]

89 which needs 91 devise (a) 93 beforehand 94 this audience 95 choose 101 approaches so near 103 (i.e. who are you?) 104 *per se*, I am I alone 107 tell (me) 108 who lives near here 105 silly 106 where you come from 113 for our purposes 114 too frivolous 117 (i.e. we like none of them) 118 An excellent chance (ironic) 121 for (being), little rogue 124 entrance 126 surely, courtesy, improved 127 suit/request 130 except me 131 before 132 later, want to, not

15 'When they declare their grievances'.
16 'And [in order] to let them know that they should come here'.
17 Mery Report breaks courtly protocol by walking straight up to Jupiter rather than standing back and waiting to be summoned.
18 Mery Report playfully quips that 'I' is a word 'in itself', and he is only himself.
19 'Your appearance argues that you are not'.
20 'You would have sorely missed it, as far as your reputation is concerned'.
21 'And, since your concern is only the weather [i.e. a trivial matter], what does it matter whether I wear frise [coarse woollen cloth of the sort worn by the poor] or feathers [the height of frivolous extravagance]?'
22 i.e. 'to wear this suit to save a better one [from wearing out], if I had [a better] one, that is.'

And for my name, reportyng alwaye trewly
What hurte to reporte a sad mater merely?
As by occasyon, for the same entent
To a serteyne wedow thys daye was I sent
Whose husbande departyd wythout her wyttynge
(A specyall good lover and she hys owne swettynge)
To whom at my commyng I caste such a fygure,
Mynglynge the mater accordynge to my nature,[23]
That when we departed above all other thynges
She thanked me hartely for my mery tydynges.
And yf I had not handled yt meryly,
Perchaunce she myght have take yt hevely.
But in suche facyon I conjured and bounde her
That I left her meryer then I founde her.[24]
What man may compare to shew the lyke comforte
That dayly is shewed by me, Mery Reporte?
And for your purpose at this tyme ment:
For all wethers I am so indyfferent,
Wythout affeccyon, standynge so up ryght:
Son lyght, mone lyght, ster lyght, twy lyght, torch lyght,
Colde, hete, moyst, drye, hayle, rayne, frost, snow, lightnyng, thunder,
Cloudy, mysty, wyndy, fayre, fowle, above hed or under,
Temperate or dystemperate: what ever yt be,
I promyse your lordshyp all is one to me.

JUPITER
Well, sonne, consydrynge thyne indyfferency,
And partely the rest of thy declaracyon,
We make the[e] our servaunte, and immedyately
We woll thou departe and cause proclamacyon,
Publyshynge our pleasure to every nacyon
Whyche thynge ons done, wyth all dylygens
Make thy returne agayne to this presens.
Here to receyve all sewters of eche degre
And suche as to the[e] may seme moste metely
We wyll thow brynge them before our majeste.
And for the reste, that be not so worthy;
Make thou reporte to us effectually
So that we may heare eche maner sewte at large.
Thus se thow departe, and loke uppon thy charge.

MERY REPORT
Now, good my lorde god, Our Lady be wyth ye!
Frendes, a fellyshyppe, let me go by ye![25]
Thynke ye I may stand thrustyng amonge you there?
Nay by God, I muste thrust about other gere.[26]

Mery Reporte goth out. At thende of this staf the god hath a song played in his trone or Mery Report come in. [27]

JUPITER
Now, syns we have thus farre set forth our purpose,
A whyle we woll wythdraw our godly presens
To enbold all such more playnely to dysclose
As here wyll attende in our foresayde pretens.[28]
And now, accordynge to your obedyens,
Rejoyce ye in us wyth joy most joyfully,
And we our selfe shall joyn in our owne glory.

[Jupiter withdraws.] Mery Report cometh in.

MERY REPORT
Now syrs, take hede, for here cometh goddes servaunt.
Avaunte, carterly keytyfs, avaunt![29]
Why, ye dronken horesons, wyll yt not be?
By your fayth, have ye nother cap nor kne?[30]
Not one of you that wyll make curtsy
To me that am squyre for goddes precyous body![31]

138 merrily 139 it happened, to prove the point 141 died, knowledge 142 (i.e. they really loved each other) 143 created, an impression 146 pleasant news 148 sadly 149 fashion 151 who could match 153 intended 154 impartial 155 bias 156 sun, moon, star 158 under(foot) 160 it's all the same to me 161 son, impartiality 162 partly 164 make (a) 165 (i.e. Making known) 166 Once that's done, diligence 167 to my presence, here 168 suitors, every status 169 fitting 173 kind of petition in full 174 pay attention to your task 179 described, intention(s) 183 obedience 190 curtsey/show respect

23 'Mixing the [sad] news with my [merry] nature'.

24 Double entendres litter this story. 'Cast', 'conjure', and 'handle' all have sexual connotations. The implication is that the widow is only too happy to hear of her husband's death, and uses the opportunity of Mery Report's visit to take a physical form of 'comfort' that her husband could not provide.

25 'In fellowship', addressed to the spectators standing around the exit.

26 'I must exert myself in other matters' (with a sexual innuendo involving both 'thrust' and 'gear').

27 'At the end of this stanza [Jupiter] has a song played in his throne [i.e. by musicians within the curtained area surrounding his throne], before Mery Report comes in.'

28 'To embolden/encourage those who will come here to disclose their grievances in the said matter more fully.'

29 'Get out of the way, unmannerly [lit.: with the manners of a carter] wretches!'

30 'Haven't you got either caps [to take off] or knees [to bow with]?'

31 Squire of the body: a servant who attended to Jupiter's bodily needs in his privy chamber. 'God's precious body' also carries an implied allusion to the embodiment of God in the Eucharistic bread in the Mass.

Regarde ye nothynge myne authoryte?
No 'welcome home', nor 'where have ye be?'?
How be yt, yf ye axyd, I coulde not well tell,
But suer I thynke a thousande myle from Hell.
And on my fayth, I thynke, in my conscyens,
I have ben from Hevyn as farre as Heven is hens,[32]
At Louyn, at London and in Lombardy,[33]
At Baldock, at Barfolde, and in Barbury,[34]
At Canturbery, at Coventre, at Colchester,[35]
At Wansworth and Welbeck, at Westchester,[36]
At Fullam, at Faleborne, and at Fenlow,[37]
At Wallyngford, at Wakefield, and at Waltamstow,[38]
At Tawnton, at Typtre, and at Totnam,[39]
At Glouceter, at Gylford, and at Gotham,[40]
At Hartforde, at Harwyche, at Harrow on the hyll,[41]
At Sudbery, Suthampton, at Shoters hyll,[42]
At Walsyngham, at Wytam, and at Werwycke,[43]
At Boston, at Brystow, and at Berwycke,[44]
At Gravelyn, at Gravesend, and at Glastynbery,[45]
Ynge Gyngiang Jayberd, the paryshe of Butsbery.[46]
The Devyll hym selfe wythout more leasure
Coulde not have gone halfe thus myche I am sure.
But now I have warned them, let them even chose,
For in fayth I care not who wynne or lose.

Here the Gentylman, before he cometh in, bloweth his horne.

MERY REPORT
Now by my trouth, this was a goodly hearyng!
I went yt had ben the gentylwomens blowynge,
But yt is not so as I now suppose,
For womens hornes sounde more in a mannys nose.[47]

GENTYLMAN
Stande ye mery, my frendes, everychone!

MERY REPORTE
Say that to me and let the reste alone.
Syr, ye be welcome, and all your meyny.[48]

GENTYLMAN
Now in good sooth, my frende, God a mercy!
And, syns that I mete the[e] here thus by chaunce,
I shall requyre the[e] of further acqueyntaunce.
And brevely to shew the[e] this is the mater:
I come to sew to the great god Jupyter
For helpe of thynges concernynge my recreacyon,
Accordynge to his late proclamacyon.

MERY REPORT
Mary, and I am he that this must spede.
But fyrste tell me, what be ye in dede?

GENTYLMAN
Fosoth, good frende, I am a gentylman.

MERY REPORTE
A goodly occupacyon, by Seynt Anne!
On my fayth, your mashyp hath a mery lyfe.
But who maketh al these hornes, your self or your wife?[49]
Nay, even in ernest I aske you this questyon.

GENTYLMAN
Now, by my trouth, thou art a mery one!

192 Don't you respect 193 been 194 asked 195 surely, (i.e. far away) 213 this distance 214 told them (of Jupiter's request) 217 thought it was 223 truly (mild oath), bless you! 224 meet 225 I'd like to make your acquaintance 226 briefly 229 recent 230 who must help you 234 mastership 237 merry fellow!

32 As far from Heaven as Heaven is from here'.

33 Louvain (in modern Belgium); Lombardy (Italy).

34 Baldock (Hertfordshire); Barford (perhaps the Cambridgeshire village of that name); Barbary (North Africa).

35 Canterbury (Kent); Coventry (Warwickshire); Colchester (Essex).

36 Wandsworth (Surrey); Welbeck (Nottinghamshire); Chester (Cheshire).

37 Fulham (Middlesex); ?Fulbourn (Cambridgeshire); ?Farnlaw (Northumberland).

38 Wallingford (Berkshire); Wakefield (Yorkshire); Walthamstow (Essex).

39 Taunton (Somerset); Tiptree (Essex); Tottenham (at that time just north of London, in Middlesex).

40 Gloucester; Guildford (Surrey); Gotham (pronounced Gotem: Nottinghamshire).

41 Hertford; Harwich (Essex); Harrow on the Hill (Middlesex).

42 Sudbury (Suffolk); Southampton (Hampshire); Shooters' Hill (near Greenwich).

43 Walsingham (Norfolk); Witham (Essex); Warwick.

44 Boston (Lincolnshire); Bristol; Berwick-upon-Tweed (Northumberland).

45 Gravelines (near Calais, France); Gravesend (Kent); Glastonbury (Somerset).

46 All three names refer to the manors of Ginge Johiberd and Ginges Landri (Great and Little Blunts (Hertfordshire)), where the Heywood family held lands.

47 'For women's horns [i.e. farts] sound more in the nose [than the ear; i.e. smell worse].'

48 Whether or not the Gentylman is indeed accompanied by a retinue would depend on the number of actors available to take the roles. Attendants are not called for by the script.

49 A cuckolded husband was said to grow horns as a result of his wife's adultery.

MERY REPORT
In fayth, of us both I thynke never one sad,
For I am not so mery but ye seme as mad.
But stande ye styll and take a lyttell payne,
I wyll come to you by and by agayne.
[*To Jupiter*] Now, gracyous god, yf your wyll so be.
I pray ye let me speke a worde wyth ye.

JUPITER
My sonne, say on; let us here thy mynde.

MERY REPORTE
My lord, ther standeth a sewter even here behynde,
A gentylman in yonder corner,
And, as I thynke, his name is mayster Horner.
A hunter he is, and comyth to make you sporte,
He wolde hunte a sow or twayne out of this sorte!

Here he poynteth to the women [*in the audience*].[50]

JUPITER
What so ever his mynde be, let hym appere.

MERY REPORTE
Now, good mayster Horner, I pray you come nere.

GENTYLMAN
I am no horner, knave, I wyll thou know yt.

MERY REPORTE
I thought ye had, for when ye dyd blow yt,
Harde I never horeson make horne so goo.
As lefe ye kyste myne ars as blow my hole soo.[51]
Come on your way before the god Jupyter,
And there for your self ye shall be sewter.

GENTYLMAN
Most myghty prynce and god of every nacyon,
Pleasyth your hyghnes to vouchsave the herynge
Of me, whyche, accordynge to [y]our proclamacyon,
Doth make apparaunce in way of besechynge;

Not sole for my selfe, but generally
For all come of noble and auncyent stock;
Whych sorte above all doth most thankfully
Dayly take payne for welth of the comen flocke,[52]

Wyth dylygent study always devysynge
To kepe them in order and unytye,
In peace to labour the encress of theyr lyvynge
Wherby eche man may prosper in plente.

Wherfore, good god, this is our hole desyrynge:
That for ease of our paynes at tymes vacaunt
In our recreacyon: whyche chyefely is huntynge,
It may please you to sende us wether pleasaunt:

Drye and not mysty, the wynde calme and styll,
That after our houndes yournynge so meryly
Chasynge the dere over dale and hyll
In herynge we may folow and to-comfort the cry.[53]

JUPITER
Ryght well we do perceyve your hole request,
Whyche shall not fayle to rest in memory.
Wherfore we wyll ye set your selfe at rest
Tyll we have herde eche man indyfferently,
And we shall take suche order unyversally
As best may stande to our honour infynyte
For welth in commune and ech mannys synguler
profyte.

GENTYLMAN
In Heven and Yerth honoured be the name
Of Jupyter, whome of his godly goodnes
Hath set this mater in so goodly frame
That every wyght shall have his desyre, doutles.

And fyrst for us nobles and gentylmen,
I doute not, in his wysedome to provyde
Suche wether as in our huntynge, now and then,
We may both teyse and receyve on every syde.

Whyche thynge, ones had, for our seyd recreacyon,
Shall greatly prevayle you in preferrynge our helth,
For what thynge more nedefull then our
preservacyon,
Beynge the weale and heddes of all comen welth?[54]

238 neither of us is serious 239 (just) as mad 245 suitor/supplicant 247 horn-blower/cuckolder 249 (I bet) he wants to 253 had (been) 254 blow so (loud) 259 hearing 261 (an) appearance, by 262 only 263 (who) come, lineage 267 unity 268 increase/improvement 269 plenty/abundance 270 whole desire 271 during our leisure time 275 crying, merrily 279 (our) memory 280 wish you (to) 281 impartially 283 as best befits, infinite 284 common, individual 285 Earth 287 good order 288 without doubt 290 (that he will) provide 292 chase, catch (the quarry) 293 once obtained 294 benefit, improving, well-being 295 (is) necessary than

50 This direction suggests that seating may possibly have been segregated by sex.

51 'I'd rather you kiss my arse than blow my [arse] hole like that.'

52 'Daily exert themselves for the good of the common people'.

53 i.e. 'that we may follow close enough to keep them in hearing and to encourage them as they cry.'

54 '[As we are] the well and [river-]heads [i.e. sources] of all common prosperity?'

MERY REPORT
Now I beseche your mashyp, whose hed be you?

GENTYLMAN
Whose hed am I? Thy hed! What seyst thou now?

MERY REPORT
Nay, I thynke yt very trew, so God me helpe,
For I have ever ben, of a lytell whelpe,
So full of fansyes and in so many fyttes,
So many smale reasons and in so many wyttes,
That, even as I stande, I pray God I be dede,
If ever I thought them all mete for one hede.
But, syns I have one hed more then I knew,
Blame not my rejoycynge; I love all thynges new.
And suer yt is a treasour of heddes to have store![55]
One feate can I now that I never coude before.

GENTYLMAN
What is that?

MERY REPORTE
By God, syns ye came hyther
I can set my hedde and my tayle to gyther.[56]
This hed shall save mony, by saynt Mary,
From hens forth I wyll no potycary,
For at all tymys when suche thynges shall myster,
My new hed shall geve myne olde tayle a glyster.
And, after all this, then shall my hedde wayte
Uppon my tayle and there stande at receyte.[57]
Syr, for the reste I wyll not now move you,[58]
But if we lyve ye shall smell how I love yow.
And, syr, touchyng your sewt here: depart when it please you,
For be ye suer, as I can, I wyll ease you.

GENTYLMAN
Then gyve me thy hande, that promyse I take.
And yf for my sake any sewt thou do make,
I promyse thy payne to be requyted
More largely then now shall be recyted. [*Exit.*]

MERY REPORTE
Alas, my necke! Goddes pyty, where is my hed?
By Saynt Eve, I feare me I shall be ded!
And yf I were, me thynke yt were no wonder,
Syns my hed and my body is so farre asonder!

Entreth the Marchaunt.

Mayster Person,[59] now welcome, by my lyfe!
I pray you, how doth my mastres, your wyfe?

MARCHAUNT
Syr, for the presthod and wyfe that ye alledge,
I se ye speke more of dotage then knowledge.
But let pas, syr, I wolde to you be sewter
To brynge me, yf ye can, before Jupiter.

[MERY REPORTE]
Yes, mary can I, and wyll do it in dede.
Tary and I shall make wey for your spede.
[*To Jupiter*] In fayth, good lord, yf it please your gracyous godshyp,
I muste have a worde or twayne wyth your lordshyp.
Syr, yonder is a nother man in place
Who maketh great sewt to speke wyth Your Grace.
Your pleasure ones knowen, he commeth by and by.[60]

JUPITER
Bryng him before our presens sone, hardely.

MERY REPORT
[*To Merchaunt*] Why, where be you? Shall I not fynde ye?
Come a way, I pray God the Devyll blynde ye!

300 since I was a pup **301** fancies **302** (different) minds **303** be (struck) dead **304** able to be crammed into **308** One trick I know now **310** together **311** money **312** will (need), apothecary **313** shall be needed **314** suppository **320** (far as) I can, help **321** accept **323** rewarded **324** generously **326** St Ive **328** apart **330** mistress **332** in dotage/folly **342** certainly

55 'It's surely a great thing to have a store of heads!'
56 The visual comedy accompanying this speech relies upon the Gentylman's face being placed between Mery Report's legs, and thus next to his arse. How this is achieved will require careful thought. Perhaps on bowing low when leaving Jupiter's presence, he might strain his back, leaving him bent double for a time. Mery Report, in helping to straighten him up, could find occasion to prompt his asides to the audience.
57 'Stand ready to receive' (i.e. whatever is discharged as a result of the suppository).
58 'Reveal to you', with a pun on bowel movements which hark back to the suppository.
59 'Parson': Mery Report, perhaps deliberately, mistakes the Merchaunt's long coat for a priest's robes. The subsequent reference to his 'wife' compounds the impudence, as priests should, of course, be celibate, and could not marry.
60 'Once your pleasure is known, he could come to you at once.'

MAR[C]HAUNT
[*To Jupiter*] Most myghty prynce and lorde of lordes all,
Ryght humbly besecheth Your Majeste
Your marchaunt men thorow the worlde all,
That yt may please you of your benygnyte,

In the dayly daunger of our goodes and lyfe,
Fyrste to consyder the desert of our request
(What welth we bryng the rest to our great care and stryfe)
And then to rewarde us as ye shall thynke best.

What were the surplysage of eche commodyte[61]
Whyche groweth and encreaseth in every lande,
Excepte exchaunge by suche men as we be
By wey of entercours that lyeth on our hande?

We fraught from home thynges whereof there is plente,
And home we brynge such thynges as there be scant.
Who sholde afore us marchauntes accompted be?
For were not we, the worlde shuld wyshe and want

In many thynges, whych now shall lack rehersall.[62]
And brevely to conclude, we beseche your hyghnes
That of the benefyte proclaymed in generall
We may be parte takers, for comen encres,

Stablyshynge wether thus, pleasynge Your Grace:
Stormy nor mysty, the wynde mesurable,
That savely we may passe from place to place
Berynge our seylys for spede moste vayleable;[63]

And also the wynde to chaunge and to turne:
Eest, west, north, and south, as beste may be set,
In any one place not to longe to sojourne,
For the length of our vyage may lese our market.

JUPITER
Ryght well have ye sayde, and we accept yt so,
And so shall we rewarde you ere we go hens.
But ye muste take pacyens tyll we have harde mo,
That we may indyfferently gyve sentens.
There may passe by us no spot of neglygence.
But justely to judge eche thynge so upryghte
That ech mans parte maye shyne in the selfe ryghte.

MERY REPORTE
Now syr, by your fayth, yf ye shulde be sworne
Harde ye ever god speke so, syns ye were borne?
So wysely, so gentylly hys wordes be showd.

MERCHAUNT
I thanke Hys Grace, my sewte is well bestowd.

MERY REPORTE
Syr, what vyage entende ye nexte to go?

MERCHAUNT
I truste or myd lente to be to Syo.[64]

MERY REPORTE
Ha, ha, is it your mynde to sayle at Syo?
Nay then, when ye wyll, byr Lady ye maye go,
And let me alone wyth thys. Be of good chere;
Ye may truste me at Syo as well as here;
For, though ye were fro me a thousande myle space,
I wolde do as myche as ye were here in place.
[*Aside*] For, syns that from hens it is so farre thyther,
I care not though ye never come agayne hyther.

MERCHAUNT
Syr, yf ye remember me when tyme shall come,
Though I requyte not all, I shall deserve some.[65]

Exeat Marchaunt.

MERY REPORTE
Now farre ye well, and God thanke you, by Saynt Anne!
[*Aside*] I pray you marke the fasshyon of thys honeste manne:
He putteth me in more truste at thys metynge here,
Then he shall fynde cause why, thys twenty yere.

348 in your benevolence 355 If there was no trade 356 intercourse/trade, in 357 freight/carry 362 briefly 363 to everyone 364 sharers, the common good 365 Establishing 366 (Neither) stormy, moderate 367 safely 371 too, stay 372 a long voyage, lose, sale 375 more (suitors) 376 judgement 378 properly 379 share, be clearly fair 382 revealed 383 in good hands 384 go (on) 386 to 387 by Our Lady 388 this (matter) 390 (away) from me 391 much (for you) (i.e. nothing) 397 nature 399 in twenty years

61 '[Just think] what would be the [excessive] surplus of every commodity'.
62 'Who should be considered more important than us? For, if we did not exist, the world would wish for [and not have] many things, which I will not mention here.'
63 'Keeping our sails [up], to gain the most advantageous speed'.
64 'I hope before mid-Lent [i.e. by the end of March], to be in Chios [an Aegean island].'
65 'Although I will not reward you with all [that you deserve], I shall give you some portion of it': a suitably miserly promise from a merchant.

Here entreth the Ranger.

RANGER
God be here! Now Cryst kepe thys company!

MERY REPORTE
In fayth, ye be welcome evyn very skantely.
Syr, for your comynge, what is the mater?

RANGER
I wolde fayne speke wyth the god Jupyter.

MERY REPORTE
That wyll not be, but ye may do thys:
Tell me your mynde, I am an offycer of hys.

RANGER
Be ye so? Mary, I cry you marcy!
Your maystershyp may say I am homely.
But, syns your mynde is to have reportyd
The cause wherfore I am now resortyd,
Pleasyth it your maystershyp it is so:
I come for my self and suche other mo,
Rangers and kepers of certayne places,
As forestes, parkes, purlews, and chasys,[66]
Where we be chargyd wyth all maner game.
Smale is our profyte, and great is our blame.
Alas for our wages, what be we the nere?
What is forty shyllynges or fyve marke a yere?[67]
Many tymes and oft, where we be flyttynge,
We spende forty pens a pece at a syttynge.
Now for our vauntage whyche chefely is wyndefale,[68]
That is ryght nought; there blowyth no wynde at all,
Whyche is the thynge wherin we fynde most grefe,
And cause of my commynge to sew for relefe,
That the god, of pyty, all thys thynge knowynge,
Maye send us good rage of blustryng and blowynge.
And, yf I can not get god to do some good,
I wolde hyer the Devyll to runne thorow the wood,
The rootes to turne up, the toppys to brynge under.
A myschyefe upon them, and a wylde thunder!

MERY REPORTE
Very well sayd! I set by your charyte
As mych in a maner as by your honeste.
I shall set you somwhat in ease anone.
Ye shall putte on your cappe when I am gone,[69]
For I se ye care not who wyn or lese
So ye maye fynde meanys to wyn your fees.

RANGER
Syr, as in that ye speke as it please ye,
But let me speke wyth the god yf it maye be.
I pray you lette me passe ye.

MERY REPORTE
Why, nay syr, by the Masse, ye[a]!

RANGER
Then wyll I leve you evyn as I founde ye.

MERY REPORTE
Go when ye wyll, no man here hath bounde ye.

Here entreth the Water Myller, and the Ranger goth out.

WATER MYLLER
What the Devyll shold skyl though all the world were dum,
Syns in all our spekynge we never be harde.
We crye out for rayne, the Devyll sped drop wyll cum.
We water myllers be nothynge in regarde.

No water have we to grynde at any stynt.
The wynde is so stronge the rayne can not fall,
Whyche kepeth our myldams as drye as a flynt.
We are undone, we grynde nothynge at all.

The greter is the pyte, as thynketh me,
For what avayleth to eche man hys corne,
Tyll it be grounde by such men as we be?
There is the losse yf we be forborne.

401 scantly 402 the purpose of your visit 407 rude 408 desire 409 have come here 414 are responsible for 416 we're no nearer getting them 418 often, travelling 419 pence each, one meal 420 perks, windfalls 425 a good storm 427 hire, through 428 treetops, bring down 429 (i.e. curse them!) 430 value/esteem 431 much (as I do) (i.e. little) 432 at ease in a moment 434 who wins or loses 435 So long as you 442 would it matter, dumb 443 heard 444 no cursed drop will come 445 held in no regard 446 rate 448 mill-dams/races 451 what use is corn to a man 453 Theirs, neglected

66 'Parks [areas enclosed for private hunting], forest-fringes [used as game reserves], and hunting grounds'.

67 A mark was worth 13 shillings and 4 pence.

68 Rangers were entitled to collect and sell trees and branches blown down by the wind.

69 As A&H note, the Ranger probably tries to put his cap back on here, but Mery Report, enjoying his new-found status, keeps him bareheaded (and thus subservient) for a moment longer.

For, touchynge our selfes, we are but drudgys
And very beggers, save onely our tole,
Whyche is ryght smale, and yet many grudges
For gryste of a busshell to gyve a quarte bole.[70]

Yet, were not reparacyons, we myght do wele:
Our mylstons, our whele with her kogges, and our trindill,[71]
Our floodgate, our mylpooll, our water whele,
Our hopper, our extre, our yren spyndyll.

In thys and mych more so great is our charge,
That we wolde not recke though no water ware,
Save onely it toucheth eche man so large,
And ech for our neyghbour Cryste byddeth us care.[72]

Wherfore my conscyence hath prycked me hyther,
In thys to sewe, accordynge to the cry,
For plente of rayne to the god Jupiter,
To whose presence I wyll go evyn boldely.

MERY REPORTE
Syr, I dowt nothynge your audacyte,
But I feare me ye lacke capacyte,
For, yf ye were wyse, ye myghte well espye
How rudely ye erre from rewls of curtesye.
What, ye come in revelynge and reheytynge,
Evyn as a knave myght go to a beare beytynge!

WATER MYLLER
[*To the audience*] All you bere recorde what favour I have.
Herke how famylyerly he calleth me knave.
Dowtles the gentylman is universall,
But marke thys lesson, syr, you shulde never call
Your felow knave nor your brother horeson,
For nought can ye get by it when ye have done.

MERY REPORTE
Thou arte nother brother nor felowe to me,
For I am goddes servaunt: mayst thou not se?
Wolde ye presume to speke wyth the great god?
Nay, dyscrecyon and you be to farre od.
Byr Lady, these knavys muste be tyed shorter.
Syr, who let you in, spake ye wyth the porter?

WATER MYLLER
Nay, by my trouth, nor wyth no nother man,
Yet I saw you well when I fyrst began.
How be it, so helpe me God and holydam,
I toke you but for a knave as I am.
But mary, now, syns I knowe what ye be,
I muste and wyll obey your authoryte,
And yf I maye not speke wyth Jupiter
I beseche you be my solycyter.

MERY REPORTE
As in that I wylbe your well wyller.
I perceyve you be a water myller,
And your hole desyre, as I take the mater,
Is plente of rayne for encres of water,
The let wherof, ye affyrme determynately
Is onely the wynde, your mortall enemy.

WATER MYLLER.
Trouth it is, for it blowyth so alofte
We never have rayne, or at the moste not ofte.
Wherfore I praye you, put the god in mynde,
Clerely for ever to banysh the wynde.

Entreth the Wynd Myller.

WYND MYLLER
How? Is all the wether gone or I come?
For the Passyon of God, helpe me to some!
I am a wynd myller as many mo be;
No wretch in wretchydnes so wrechyd as we!
The hole sorte of my crafte be all mard at onys,
The wynde is so weyke it sturryth not our stonys,
Nor skantely can shatter the shyttyn sayle
That hangeth shatterynge at a womans tayle.
The rayne never resteth, so longe be the showres
From tyme of begynnyng tyll foure and twenty howres,

454 concerning, slaves 455 except for our toll/fee 458 (it) not (for) repairs 460 mill-pool, water-wheel 461 axle-tree, iron spindle 463 wouldn't care if there was no water 466 prompted me (to come) 467 proclamation 470 don't doubt 471 (mental) capacity/intelligence 472 see 473 break the rules of courtesy 474 quarrelling 475 bear-baiting 476 bear witness 477 familiarly/presumptuously 478 a know-all 480 equal 481 achieve 483 can't you see 485 too far at variance 486 kept on a shorter leash 489 came in 491 thought you were only a servant 495 (i.e. speak for me) 496 well-wisher 499 (the) increase 500 hindrance, resolutely claim 508 other (people) are 509 (is) so 510 class, profession, ruined, once 511 weak, stirs/moves 512 shake, shitten sail 513 flapping 515 (i.e. all day and night)

70 'Which is very small, and yet many [people still] begrudge paying a quart bowl [2 pounds] of grain as a toll on every bushel [64 pounds] we grind for them.'

71 Millstones; cogs; trundle (horizontal wheel).

72 'Except that it concerns every man generally [i.e. not just us], and Christ instructed us all to care for our neighbours' (a specious justification of the Water Myller's self-interest).

And ende whan it shall, at nyght or at none,
An other begynneth as soone as that is done
Such revell of rayne ye knowe well inough
Destroyeth the wynde, be it never so rough;
Wherby, syns our myllys be come to styll standynge,
Now maye we wynd myllers go evyn to hangynge.
A myller? Wyth a moryn and a myschyefe!
Who wolde be a myller? As good be a thefe![73]
Yet in tyme past when gryndynge was plente
Who were so lyke Goddys felows as we?
As faste as God made corne, we myllers made meale.
Whyche myght be best forborne for comyn weale?[74]
But let that gere passe! For I feare our pryde
Is cause of the care whyche God doth us provyde,
Wherfore I submyt me, entendynge to se
What comforte maye come by humylyte.
And now, at thys tyme, they sayd in the crye
The god is come downe to shape remedye.

MERY REPORTE
No doute he is here even in yonder trone.
But in your mater he trusteth me alone,
Wherin I do perceyve by your complaynte
Oppressyon of rayne doth make the wynde so faynte
That ye wynde myllers be clene caste away.

WYND MYLLER
If Jupyter helpe not, yt is as ye say.
But in few wordes to tell you my mynde rounde,
Uppon this condycyon I wolde be bounde
Day by day to say Our Ladyes Sauter:[75]
That in this world were no drope of water
Nor never rayne, but wynde contynuall,
Then shold we wyndemyllers be lordes over all.

MERY REPORT
Come on and assay how you twayne can agre;
A brother of yours, a myller as ye be.

WATER MYLLER
By meane of our craft we may be brothers,
But whyles we lyve shall we never be lovers.
We be of one crafte but not of one kynde:
I lyve by water and he by the wynde.

Here Mery Reporte goth out.

And, syr, as ye desyre wynde contynuall,
So wolde I have rayne ever more to fall,
Whyche two in experyence ryght well ye se
Ryght selde or never to-gether can be.
For as longe as the wynde rewleth, yt is playne,
Twenty to one ye get no drop of rayne;
And when the element is to farre opprest,
Downe commeth the rayne and setteth the wynde at rest.
By this ye se we can not both obtayne,
For ye must lacke wynde or I must lacke rayne.
Wherfore I thynke good, before this audyens,
Eche for our selfe to say or we go hens.
And whom is thought weykest when we have fynysht,
Leve of his sewt and content to be banyssht.

WYND MYLLER
In fayth, agreed. But then, by your lycens,
Our mylles for a tyme shall hange in suspens.
Syns water and wynde is chyefely our sewt
Whyche best may be spared we woll fyrst dyspute.
Wherfore to the see my reason shall resorte
Where shyppes by meane of wynd try from port to port,
From lande to land, in dystaunce many a myle.
Great is the passage and smale is the whyle.
So great is the profyte, as to me doth seme,
That no mans wysdome the welth can exteme.
And syns the wynde is conveyer of all,
Who but the wynde shulde have thanke above all?

WATER MYLLER
Amytte in thys place a tree here to growe[76]
And therat the wynde in great rage to blowe;
When it hath all blowen, thys is a clere case,
The tre removyth no here bred from hys place.

517 another begins 518 excess 521 might as well hang ourselves 522 murain (plague) 524 plentiful 525 God's (chosen) partners 526 flour 529 sorrow 533 provide 538 completely ruined 539 will be as you say 540 opinion clearly 541 would promise 542 Daily, recite, Psalter 546 try (to discover) 548 profession 549 friends 550 nature 555 Very seldom 556 rules 557 (I'll give you odds of) 558 sky, too, troubled 560 obtain (what we want) 563 speak for himself before 564 weakest, finished 565 Leave off/Abandon 566 with your permission 567 stop (while we debate) 568 our chief concern 569 done without 570 sea, travel 571 means, sail 573 distance, time 575 estimate 576 mover 581 moved not a hair's breadth

73 'I might as well be a thief!': an ironic statement, as millers were themselves proverbially associated with theft.

74 'Which could be best done without for the common good?': i.e. God's growing or our milling? The Wynd Myller implies equivalence between the two tasks.

75 For Our Ladies Psalter, see the N-Town *Mary Play*, l. 1590 and note.

76 'Suppose for a moment that a tree was growing here'.

No more wolde the shyppys, blow the best it cowde,
All though it wolde blow downe both mast and shrowde.
Except the shyppe flete uppon the water,
The wynde can ryght nought do: a playne mater.
Yet maye ye on water, wythout any wynde,
Row forth your vessell where men wyll have her synde.
Nothynge more rejoyceth the maryner
Then meane coolys of wynde and plente of water,
For commenly the cause of every wracke
Is excesse of wynde where water doth lacke.
In rage of these stormys the perell is suche,
That better were no wynde then so farre to muche.

WYND MYLLER
Well, yf my reason in thys may not stand,
I wyll forsake the see and lepe to lande.
In every chyrche where goddys servyce is,
The organs beare brunt of halfe the quere, iwys.
Whyche causyth the sounde: or water or wynde?
More-over, for wynde thys thynge I fynde:
For the most parte, all maner mynstrelsy,
By wynde they delyver theyr sound chefly.
Fyll me a bagpype of your water full:
As swetly shall it sounde as it were stuffyd with wull!

WATER MYLLER
On my fayth, I thynke the moone be at the full,
For frantyke fansyes be then most plentefull,
Whych are at the pryde of theyr sprynge in your hed,
So farre from our mater he is now fled.
As for the wynde in any instrument,
It is no percell of our argument.
We spake of wynde that comyth naturally,
And that is wynde forcyd artyfycyally,
Whyche is not to purpose. But, yf it were,
And water in dede ryght nought coulde do there,
Yet I thynke organs no suche commodyte
Wherby the water shulde banyshed be.[77]
And for your bagpypes, I take them as nyfuls.
Your mater is all in fansyes and tryfuls.

WYND MYLLER
By God, but ye shall not tryfull me of so!
Yf these thynges serve not, I wyll reherse mo.
And now to mynde there is one olde proverbe come;
'One bushell of March dust is worth a kynges raunsome.'[78]
What is a hundreth thousande bushels worth than?

WATER MYLLER
Not one myte, for the thynge selfe, to no man.

WYND MYLLER
Why, shall wynde every where thus be objecte?
Nay, in the hye wayes he shall take effecte,
Where as the rayne doth never good but hurt.
For wynde maketh but dust, and water maketh durt.
Powder or syrop, syrs, whyche lycke ye beste?
Who lycketh not the tone maye lycke up the reste.
But, sure, who so ever hath assayed such syppes,
Had lever have dusty eyes then durty lyppes.
And it is sayd syns afore we were borne,
That drought doth never make derth of corne.
And well it is knowen to the most foole here,
How rayne hath pryced corne within this seven yere.[79]

WATER MYLLER
Syr, I pray the[e], spare me a lytyll season
And I shall brevely conclude the[e] wyth reason.
Put case on somers daye wythout wynde to be,
And ragyous wynde in wynter dayes two or thre:
Mych more shall dry that one calme daye in somer
Then shall those thre wyndy dayes in wynter.
Whom shall we thanke for thys when all is done?
The thanke to wynde? Nay, thanke chyefely the sone.
And so for drought: yf corne therby encres,
The sone doth comforte and rype all, dowtles.
And oft the wynde so leyth the corne, God wot,
That never after can it rype, but rot.
Yf drought toke place as ye say, yet maye ye se
Lytell helpeth the wynde in thys commodyte.
But now, syr, I deny your pryncypyll:
Yf drought ever were, it were impossybyll

582 (even if the wind) blew 583 sail 584 Unless, (was) floating 585 clear argument 587 wherever, assigned (sent) 588 sailor 589 moderate cool breezes 590 (ship) wreck 596 is (held) 597 carry half the choir's burden 598 (is it) either 600 musicians 604 wool 605 frantic fancies 606 (i.e. are at their peak) 607 he (your head/mind) 609 part 611 (i.e. wind used by musicians) 612 not relevant (here) 616 consider them, trifles 618 put me off with trifles 623 itself 624 objected to 625 highways, find its use 626 harm 627 mud 628 syrup, like/lick 629 one (dust), other (mud) 630 tried, sips (i.e. tasted mud) 631 rather, muddy 632 has been, before 633 cause 634 (even) the greatest 636 time 637 refute 638 Consider, for example, a summer's 639 raging 643 (Should) the thanks (go), sun 645 ripen 646 blows flat, knows 649 respect 650 main claim (a debating term) 651 prevailed all the time

77 'I think that organs are not of such usefulness [to humanity] that water should be banished for their sake.'

78 Dust (a sign of dry weather) in March is prized as it allows for the early planting of spring crops.

79 'How rain has forced up the price of corn in the past seven years [by spoiling harvests].'

To have ony grayne, for, or it can grow
Ye must plow your lande, harrow, and sow.
Whyche wyll not be, except ye maye have rayne
To temper the grounde, and after agayne
For spryngynge and plumpyng all maner corne.
Yet muste ye have water, or all is forlorne.
Yf ye take water for no commodyte,
Yet must ye take it for thynge of necessyte
For washynge, for skowrynge, all fylth clensynge.
Where water lacketh, what bestely beynge!
In brewyng, in bakynge, in dressynge of meate,
Yf ye lacke water what coulde ye drynke or eate?
Wythout water coulde lyve neyther man nor best,
For water preservyth both moste and lest.
For water coulde I say a thousande thynges mo,
Savynge as now the tyme wyll not serve so.
And, as for that wynde that you do sew fore,
Is good for your wyndemyll and for no more.
Syr, syth all thys in experyence is tryde,
I say thys mater standeth clere on my syde.

WYND MYLLER
Well, syns thys wyll not serve, I wyll alledge the
reste.
Syr, for our myllys, I saye myne is the beste.
My wyndmyll shall grynd more corne in one our
Then thy water myll shall in thre or foure:
Ye[a], more then thyne shulde in a hole yere,
Yf thou myghtest have as thou hast wyshyed here.[80]
For thou desyrest to have excesse of rayne,
Whyche thyng to the[e] were the worst thou
coudyst obtayne,
For, yf thou dydyst, it were a playne induccyon
To make thyne owne desyer thyne owne
destruccyon.
For in excess of rayne, at any flood
Your myllys must stande styll; they can do no good.
And whan the wynde doth blow the uttermost,
Our wyndmylles walke a mayne in every cost.
For, as we se the wynde in hys estate,
We moder our saylys after the same rate.
Syns our myllys grynde so farre faster then yours,
And also they may grynde all tymes and howrs,
I say we nede no water mylles at all,
For wyndmylles be suffycyent to serve all.

WATER MYLLER
Thou spekest of all and consyderest not halfe.
In boste of thy gryste thou arte wyse as a calfe!
For, though above us your mylles grynde farre faster,
What helpe to those from whome ye be myche
farther?
And of two sortes, yf the tone shold be conserved,
I thynke yt mete the moste nomber be served.
In vales and weldes where moste commodyte is,
There is most people:[81] ye must graunte me this.
On hylles and downes, whyche partes are moste
barayne
There muste be few, yt can no mo sustayne.
I darre well say, yf yt were tried even now,
That there is ten of us to one of you.
And where whuld chyefely all necessaryes be,
But there as people are moste in plente?
More reason that you come seven myle to myll,
Then all we of the vale sholde clyme the hyll.
Yf rayne came reasonable, as I requyre yt,
We sholde of your wyndemylles have nede no whyt.

Entreth Mery Reporte.

MERY REPORTE
Stop, folysh knaves! For your reasonynge is suche,
That ye have reasoned even ynough and to much.
I hard all the wordes that ye both have hadde;
[*To the audience*] So helpe me God, the knaves be
more then madde!
Nother of them both that hath wyt nor grace,
To perceyve that both myllys may serve in place.
Betwene water and wynd there is no suche let,
But eche myll may have tyme to use his fet.
Whyche thynge I can tell by experyens.
For I have, of myne owne, not farre from hens,
In a corner to gether, a couple of myllys
Standynge in a marres betwene two hyllys,[82]

652 before 655 soften, later on 656 sprouting, swelling 657 ruined 658 consider, of no value 660 scouring, cleaning of dirt 661 what a beastly life (it is) 662 preparing of food 664 beast 665 (the) greatest, least 666 On water's behalf 667 Except there's no time 668 beg for 669 (It) is, nothing else 670 proved by experience 671 clearly in my favour 672 convince you, put, (of my case) 674 hour 679 worst (thing), could 680 did, induction/beginning 681 desire 685 work most strongly, region 686 the state of the wind 687 moderate/adjust, accordingly 688 much 693 boasting, grinding, as wise 695 very distant 696 sorts (of mills), retained 700 barren 701 (the land) can sustain no more 704 should, necessities 705 where 706 (It is) more reasonable 709 no need at all 711 too 716 hindrance 717 function as it wishes 721 marsh, hills

80 '[Even] if you gained what you wished [for] here.'

81 'And if, of the two kinds [of Miller] only one should be retained, I think it is appropriate that it is the sort that serves the greatest number (of people). In valleys and in rolling fields, where it is most convenient/comfortable to live, that's where the most people are.'

82 The allusion is to his wife's genitals and buttocks.

Not of inherytaunce, but by my wyfe.
She is feofed in the tayle for terms of her lyfe,
The one for wynde, the other for water,[83]
And of them both, I thanke God, there standeth nother,
For, in a good hour be yt spoken,
The water gate is no soner open
But 'Clap!', sayth the wyndmyll, even strayght behynde.
There is good spedde, the Devyll and all they grynde.
But whether that the hopper be dusty,
Or that the mylstonys be sum what rusty,
By the mas, the meale is myschevous musty!
And yf ye thynke my tale be not trusty,
I make ye trew promyse; come when ye lyst,
We shall fynde meane ye shall taste of the gryst![84]

WATER MYLLER
The corne at receyt, happely, is not good.

MERY REPORTE
There can be no sweeter, by the sweet Rood.
Another thynge yet, whyche shall not be cloked,
My water myll many tymes is choked.[85]

WATER MYLLER
So wyll she be, though ye shuld burste your bones,
Except ye be perfyt in settynge your stones.
Fere not the lydger, be ware your ronner.[86]
Yet this for the lydger or ye have wonne her:
Perchaunce your lydger doth lacke good peckyng.[87]

MERY REPORT
So sayth my wyfe, and that maketh all our checkyng.
She wolde have the myll peckt, peckt, peckt every day,
But, by God, myllers muste pecke when they may.
So oft have we peckt that our stones wax ryght thyn,
And all our other gere not worth a pyn.
For wyth peckynge and peckyng I have so wrought,
That I have peckt a good peckynge yron to nought.
How be yt yf I stycke no better tyll her,
My wyfe sayth she wyll have a new myller.
But let this passe, and now to our mater.
I say my myllys lack nother wynde nor water;
No more do yours as farre as nede doth requyre.
But, syns ye can not agree, I wyll desyre
Jupyter to set you both in suche rest
As to your welth and his honour may stande best.

WATER MYLLER
I pray you hertely, remember me.

WYND MILLER
Let not me be forgoten, I beseche ye.

Both myllers goth forth.

MERY REPORT
If I remember you not both a lyke,
I wolde ye were over the eares in the dyke!
Now be we ryd of two knaves at once chaunce.
By Saynt Thomas, yt is a knavyshe ryddaunce.

The Gentylwoman entreth.

GENTYLWOMAN
Now good God, what foly is this!
What sholde I do where so mych people is?
I know not how to passe in to the god now.

MERY REPORT
No, but ye know how he may passe into you!

GENTYLWOMAN
I pray you, let me in at the backe syde.[88]

725 neither stands idle 726 (a mild oath) 727 sooner 728 after/to the rear of 730 grain-chute 731 millstones 732 mass, horribly smelly 733 reliable 735 a means for you to 736 when it's tasted, perhaps 738 concealed 740 no matter how hard you try 741 Unless, preparing, stones/testicles 746 causes, arguments 748 grow, threadbare 749 gear/genitals, pin/penis 751 pecking tool down to nothing 752 don't persist any better 756 demands 758 contentment 762 identically 763 ditch 764 one go 765 bad riddance 767 many, are?

83 '[I own them] not by inheritance [i.e. given to me (at birth) by my parents], but through my wife, who is enfeofed [legally possessed] of them, in an entail [a lease, but also a pun: 'in her tail'] for her lifetime. The one [mill] is for wind, the other for water'.

84 i.e. 'If you don't believe me, you can eat a turd!'

85 With the double entendre: 'My wife's genitals are frequently full.' The Water Myller's subsequent advice is an extended double entendre, implying that Mery Report needs to improve his sexual performance if he is to satisfy his wife and prevent her looking elsewhere for 'corn' to grind.

86 'Don't worry about your ledger [fixed lower millstone], look to your runner [active upper stone/penis].' There may be a further allusion to the kind of fabliau scenario rehearsed in Chaucer's *Miller's Tale*: 'If your own penis is in good order, you won't have to worry about the lodger.'

87 'But consider this about the ledger, before you have won her [over]; it may be that [it] has not been properly tooled with a pecker': i.e. perhaps your grinding equipment isn't meshing properly.

88 'Through the back door': with the obvious sexual connotations.

MERY REPORTE
Ye[a], shall I so, and your foresyde so wyde?
Nay, not yet! But syns ye love to be alone,
We twayne wyll into a corner anone.
But fyrste, I pray you, come your way hyther
And let us twayne chat a whyle to-gyther.

GENTYLWOMAN
Syr, as to you, I have lyttell mater.
My commynge is to speke wyth Jupiter.

MERY REPORT
Stande ye styll a whyle, and I wyll go prove
Whether that the god wyll be brought in love.
[*To Jupiter*] My lorde, how now, loke uppe lustely;
Here is a derlynge come, by saynt Antony!
And yf yt be your pleasure to mary, [89]
Speke quyckly, for she may not tary.
In fayth I thynke ye may wynne her anone,
For she wolde speke wyth your lordshyp alone.

JUPITER
Sonne, that is not the thynge at this tyme ment.
If her sewt concerne no cause of our hyther resorte,[90]
Sende her out of place; but yf she be bent
To that purpose, heare her and make us reporte.

MERY REPORTE
[*Aside*] I count women lost, yf we love them not well,
For ye se god loveth them never a dele.
Maystres, ye can not speke wyth the god.

GENTYLWOMAN
No, why?

MERY REPORTE
By my fayth, for his lordshyp is ryght besy
Wyth a pece of worke that nedes must be doone.
Even now is he makynge of a new moone:[91]
He sayth your old moones be so farre tasted
That all the goodnes of them is wasted;
Whyche of the great wete hath ben moste mater,[92]
For olde moones be leake, they can holde no water.
But for this new mone, I durst lay my gowne,
Except a few droppes at her goyng downe,
Ye get no rayne tyll her arysynge,
Wythout yt nede, and then no mans devysynge
Coulde wyshe the fashyon of rayne to be so good:
Not gushynge out lyke gutters of Noyes flood,
But smale droppes sprynklyng softly on the grounde:
Though they fell on a sponge they wold gyve no sounde.
This new moone shal make a thing spryng more in this while
Then a old moone shal while a man may go a mile.
By that tyme the god hath all made an ende
Ye shall se how the wether wyll amende.
By saynt Anne, he goth to worke even boldely!
I thynke hym wyse ynough, for he loketh oldely.
Wherfore maystres, be ye now of good chere,
For, though in his presens he can not appere,
Tell me your mater and let me alone:
May happe I wyll thynke on you when you be gone.

GENTYLWOMAN
Forsoth the cause of my commynge is this:
I am a woman ryght fayre, as ye se,
In no creature more beauty then in me is,
And, syns I am fayre, fayre wolde I kepe me.

But the sonne in somer so sore doth burne me,
In wynter the wynde on every syde me,
No parte of the yere wote I where to turne me,
But even in my house am I fayne to hyde me.

And so do all other that beuty have,
In whose name at this tyme this sewt I make,
Besechynge Jupyter to graunt that I crave,
Whyche is this: that yt may please hym, for our sake,

To sende us wether close and temperate,

771 when your front-end is so wide 778 (and) find out 781 darling 782 marry 786 what I intend currently 788 the acting space, concerned with 790 consider 792 Mistress 794 done 796 tried out 797 exhausted 799 leaky 800 bet 801 setting/going to bed 803 Unless it is necessary, imagination 805 downpours, Noah's flood 811 improve 813 looks old enough (to be wise) 816 leave it to me 817 Perhaps 821 I want to remain 822 sorely 823 (blows me) on 828 that (which) 830 warm, mild

[89] It may be, as A&H suggest, that there are a series of (perhaps playful, perhaps more pointed) allusions here to Henry VIII's decision to marry Anne Boleyn on 5 January 1533 (hence the possible puns in the oaths to St Anne (l. 812) and St Anthony (l. 781).

[90] 'If her suit does not relate to the cause of our coming here [i.e. the regulation of the weather]'.

[91] A&H suggest that this passage is another extended allusion to Anne (who replaced the old queen/moon, Katherine of Aragon) and her potential to satisfy Henry and produce an heir for him.

[92] 'Which has been the principal cause of the great "wet" [storm]'.

No sonne shyne, no frost, nor no wynde to blow.
Then wolde we get the stretes trym as a parate;
Ye shold se how we wolde set our selfe to show.

MERY REPORT
Jet wher ye wyll, I swere by Saynte Quintyne,
Ye passe them all both in your owne conceyt and myne.

GENTYLWOMAN
If we had wether to walke at our pleasure,
Our lyves wolde be mery out of measure:
One parte of the day for our apparellynge,
Another parte for eatynge and drynkynge,
And all the reste in stretes to be walkynge,
Or in the house to passe tyme wyth talkynge.

MERY REPORT
When serve ye God?

GENTYLWOMAN
Who bosteth in vertue are but daws.[93]

MERY REPORT
Ye do the better, namely syns there is no cause.[94]
How spende ye the nyght?

GENTYLWOMAN
In daunsynge and syngynge
Tyll midnyght, and then fall to slepynge.

MERY REPORT
Why, swete herte, by your false fayth, can ye syng?

GENTYLWOMAN
Nay nay, but I love yt above all thynge.

MERY REPORT
Now, by my trouth, for the love that I owe you,
You shall here what pleasure I can shew you.
One songe have I for you, suche as yt is,
And yf yt were better, ye shold have yt, by gys!

GENTYLWOMAN
Mary syr, I thanke you even hartely.

MERY REPORT
Come on, syrs,[95] but now let us synge lustly.

Here they sing.

GENTYLWOMAN
Syr, this is well done, I hertely thanke you.
Ye have done me pleasure, I make God a vowe.
Ones in a nyght I longe for suche a fyt,[96]
For longe tyme have I ben brought up in yt.

MERY REPORT
Oft tyme yt is sene both in court and towne,
Longe be women a bryngyng up and sone brought down.[97]
So fete yt is, so nete yt is, so nyse yt is,
So trycke yt is, so quycke yt is, so wyse yt is!
I fere my selfe, except I may entreat her,
I am so farre in love I shall forget her.[98]
Now good maystres, I pray you let me kys ye.

GENTYLWOMAN
'Kys me', quoth a! Why nay, syr, I wys ye!

MERY REPORT
What, yes, hardely, kys me ons and no more.
I never desyred to kys you before.

Here the Launder cometh in.

LAUNDER
Why, have ye always kyst her behynde?
In fayth good inough yf yt be your mynde.
And yf your appetyte serve you so to do,
Byr Lady, I wolde ye had kyst myne ars to!

MERY REPORT
To whom dost thou speke, foule hore, canst thou tell?[99]

832 jet/strut, streets, parrot **834** St Quentin **835** surpass, opinion **837** immeasurably merry **838** (would be set aside for) dressing **842** (would) you serve **849** hear **851** (even) if, by Jesus **857** educated, song/promiscuity **860** elegant, it/she (baby talk), wanton **861** pretty **862** fear, unless **865** I tell you **866** once **869** if that's what you like **871** By Our, arse too **872** whore

93 'Those [who] boast of their virtue are merely fools.'

94 'You have no cause to boast of virtue (because you have none).'

95 Probably addressed to the household musicians who would accompany the song(s).

96 'Stanza/bout'. The Gentylwoman sets up the bawdy double entendre between singing and sex which Mery Report develops in the following speech.

97 Both 'brought up (and presented) at court' and 'persuaded to have sex/brought to orgasm'; 'brought down' implies 'dismissed from court', 'morally corrupted', and 'disappointed'.

98 The cruel bathos of 'forget her' is intentional, and part of Mery Report's cynical misogyny.

99 'Have you any idea to whom you are speaking?' Mery Report is now fully enjoying his new status as Jupiter's servant.

Launder

Nay, by my trouth, I syr? Not very well.
But by conjecture this ges I have,
That I do speke to an olde baudy knave.
I saw you dally wyth your symper de cokket;
I rede you beware she pyck not your pokket.
Such ydyll huswyfes do now and than
Thynke all well wonne that they pyck from a man.
Yet such of some men shall have more favour
Then we, that for them dayly toyle and labour.
But I trust the god wyll be so indyfferent.
That she shall fayle some parte of her entent.

Mery Report

No dout he wyll deale so gracyously
That all folke shall be served indyfferently.
How be yt, I tell the[e] trewth, my offyce is suche
That I muste reporte eche sewt, lyttell or muche.
Wherfore, wyth the god syns thou canst not speke,
Trust me wyth thy sewt, I wyll not fayle yt to breke.

Launder

Then leane not to myche to yonder gyglet,
For her desyre contrary to myne is set.
I herde by her tale she wolde banyshe the sonne,
And then were we pore launders all undonne.
Excepte the sonne shyne that our clothes may dry,
We can do no ryght nought in our laundry;
Another maner losse yf we sholde mys
Then of such nycebyceters as she is.[100]

Gentylwoman

I thynke yt better that thou envy me
Then I sholde stande at rewarde of thy pytte.
It is the guyse of such grose queynes as thou art.
Wyth such as I am evermore to thwart,
Bycause that no beauty ye can obtayne,
Therfore ye have us that be fayre in dysdayne.

Launder

When I was yonge as thou art now,
I was wythin lyttel as fayre as thou,
And so myght have kept me, yf I hadde wolde,
And as derely my youth I myght have solde
As the tryckest and fayrest of you all.
But I feared parels that after myght fall,
Wherfore some besynes I dyd me provyde
Lest vyce myght entre on every syde,[101]
Whyche hath fre entre where ydylnesse doth reyne.
It is not thy beauty that I dysdeyne,
But thyne ydyll lyfe that thou hast rehersed,
Whych any good womans hert wolde have perced.
For I perceyve in daunsynge and syngynge,
In eatyng and drynkynge, and thyne apparellynge,
Is all the joye wherin thy herte is set.
But nought of all this doth thyne owne labour get.
For haddest thou nothyng but of thyne owne travayle,[102]
Thou myghtest go as naked as my nayle.
Me thynke thou shuldest abhorre suche ydylnes
And passe thy tyme in some honest besynes.
Better to lese some parte of thy beaute
Then so oft to jeoberd all thyne honeste.
But I thynke, rather then thou woldest so do,
Thou haddest lever have us lyve ydylly to.
And so, no doute, we shulde, yf thou myghtest have
The clere sone banshyt, as thou dost crave.
Then were we launders marde, and unto the[e]
Thyne owne request were smale commodyte.
For of these twayne I thynke yt farre better
Thy face were sone burned and thy clothis the swetter,
Then that the sonne from shynynge sholde be smytten
To kepe thy face fayre and thy smocke beshytten.
Syr, how lycke ye my reason in her case?

Mery Report

Such a raylynge hore, by the holy Mas,
I never herde in all my lyfe tyll now!
In dede I love ryght well the ton of you,
But, or I wolde kepe you both, by Goddes mother,
The Devyll shall have the tone to fet the tother!

874 guess 876 strumpet (simpering coquette) 879 fairly won, steal 887 (whether) small or great 889 mention (but also: ruin) 890 too much, strumpet 894 Unless 899 the object of your pity 900 habit, gross whores 901 argue 905 very nearly 906 wanted (to) 908 prettiest 909 (the) perils 910 I found myself a trade 911 To prevent, enter 912 free entry, reign 913 disdain 914 described 915 pierced 923 business/trade 925 jeopardize, reputation 927 us (honest women), idly too 929 bright sun 930 ruined 931 little advantage 933 sun-burnt, sweeter 934 struck down 936 argument 937 railing whore 939 one (i.e. the Gentylwoman) 941 fetch

100 'It would be a completely different [and much graver] sort of loss if we should be ruined, than if such fashionable minxes as her should lose out.'

101 Proverbially idleness was the foundation and cause of all the other vices.

102 'But you don't obtain any of this through your own labour. If you had nothing except that which you gained by your own efforts'.

LAUNDER
Promise me to speke that the sone may shyne bryght,
And I wyll be gone quyckly for all nyght.

MERY REPORT
Get you both hens, I pray you hartely.
Your sewtes I perceyve and wyll reporte them trewly
Unto Jupyter at the next leysure,
And, in the same, desyre to know his pleasure;
Whyche knowledge hadde, even as he doth show yt,
Feare ye not, tyme inough ye shall know yt.

GENTYLWOMAN
Syr, yf ye medyll, remember me fyrste.[103]

LAUNDER
Then in this medlynge my parte shalbe the wurst.

MERY REPORT
Now I beseche Our Lorde, the Devyll the[e] burst!
Who medlyth wyth many, I hold hym accurst.
Thou hore, can I medyl wyth you both at ones?

Here the gentylwoman goth forth.

LAUNDER
By the Mas, knave, I wold I had both thy stones
In my purs yf thou medyl not indyfferently,
That both our maters in yssew may be lyckly.[104]

MERY REPORT
Many wordes, lyttell mater, and to no purpose,
Suche is the effect that thou dost dysclose.
The more ye byb, the more ye babyll,
The more ye babyll, the more ye fabyll,
The more ye fabyll, the more unstabyll,
The more unstabyll, the more unabyll,
In any maner thynge to do any good.
No hurt though ye were hanged, by the holy Rood!

LAUNDER
The les your sylence, the lesse your credence,
The les your credens, the les your honeste,
The les your honeste, the les your assystens,
The les your assystens, the les abylyte
In you to do ought. Wherfore, so God me save,
No hurte in hangynge suche a raylynge knave!

MERY REPORT
What monster is this? I never harde none suche.
For loke how myche more I have made her to myche,
And so farre at lest she hath made me to lyttell.[105]
Wher be ye launder? I thynke in some spyttell.
Ye shall washe me no gere for feare of fretynge.
I love no launders that shrynke my gere in wettynge.
I pray the[e], go hens and let me be in rest.
I wyll do thyne erand as I thynke best.

LAUNDER
Now wolde I take my leve, yf I wyste how.
The lenger I lyve the more knave you! [*Exit.*]

MERY REPORT
The lenger thou lyvest, the pyte the gretter,
The soner thou be ryd, the tydynges the better!
Is not this a swete offyce that I have,
When every drab shall prove me a knave?
Every man knoweth not what goddes servyce is,
Nor I my selfe knew yt not before this.
I thynke goddes servauntes may lyve holyly
But the Devyls servauntes lyve more meryly.
I know not what god geveth in standynge fees,
But the Devyls servauntes have casweltees
A hundred tymes mo then goddes servauntes have.
For, though ye be never so starke a knave,
If ye lacke money the Devyll wyll do no wurse
But brynge you strayght to a nother mans purse.
Then wyll the Devyll promote you here in this world
As unto suche ryche yt doth moste accord.
Fyrste, *'pater noster qui es in celis'*,
And then ye shall sens the shryfe wyth your helys.[106]
The greatest frende ye have in felde or towne,
Standynge a typ-to shall not reche your crowne.

946 leisure/opportunity I have 948 once obtained 949 soon 952 burst you 953 meddles (sexually), many (women) 954 once 955 testicles 960 talk, babble 961 fable/lie 962 unstable (you become) 965 It wouldn't hurt if 966 less, credibility 967 reputation 968 help you are (with Jupiter) 973 too 975 spittlehouse/hospital 976 no clothes of mine, rubbing (away) 977 clothes/penis, rubbing 981 you are 982 more's the pity 983 gone, the better the news 984 sweet task 985 whore 990 regular wages 991 casual tips and rewards 993 bad/hardened 995 another 997 As befits such rich thieves 1000 tallest 1001 on tip-toe, head

103 Meddle: i.e. take on the matter (but with the sexual connotations that Mery Report takes up in his next speech).
104 'So that both our requests might turn out equally [well].'
105 'For, look how I have magnified her [faults] with my "more"s, and how she has minimized [my virtues] with her "less"s.'
106 'First [you'll be saying] "Our Father who art in Heaven" [the *Paternoster*], and the next moment you'll be swinging your heels above the sheriff's head as if you were censing him [wafting him with incense].' The sheriff was the official responsible for administering capital punishments such as hanging.

The Boy comyth in, the lest that can play.

[Boy]
This same is even he by al lycklyhod[107]
Syr, I pra you, be not you master god?

Mery Report
No, in good fayth, sonne, but I may say to the[e]
I am suche a man that god may not mysse me.
Wherfore, wyth the god yf thou woldest have ought done,
Tell me thy mynde and I shall shew yt sone.

Boy
Forsothe, syr, my mynde is thys, at few wordes:
All my pleasure is in catchynge of byrdes,
And makynge of snow ballys and throwyng the same,
For the whyche purpose to have set in frame,
Wyth my godfather god I wolde fayne have spoken,
Desyrynge hym to have sent me by some token
Where I myghte have had great frost for my pytfallys,
And plente of snow to make my snow ballys.
This onys had, boyes lyvis be such as no man leddys.[108]
O, to se my snow ballys lyght on my felowes heddys,
And to here the byrdes how they flycker theyr wynges
In the pytfale, I say yt passeth all thynges.
Syr, yf ye be goddes servaunt or his kynsman,
I pray you helpe me in this yf ye can.

Mery Report
Alas, pore boy, who sent the[e] hether?

Boy
A hundred boys that stode to-gether,
Where they herde one say in a cry
That my godfather, God Almyghty,
Was come from Heven by his owne accorde,
This nyght to suppe here wyth my lorde.[109]
And farther he sayde, come whoso wull,
They shall sure have theyr bellyes full
Of all wethers, who lyste to crave:
Eche sorte suche wether lyste to have.
And when my felowes thought this wolde be had,
And saw me so prety a pratelynge lad,
Uppon agrement, wyth a great noys
'Sende lyttel Dycke!', cryed all the boys,
By whose assent I am purveyd
To sew for the wether afore seyd.
Wherin I pray you to be good, as thus,
To helpe that god may gyve yt us.

Mery Report
'Gyve boys wether', quoth a! Nonny nonny!

Boy
If god of his wether wyll gyve nonny,
I pray you, wyll he sell ony,
Or lend us a bushell of snow or twayne
And poynt us a day to pay hym agayne?

Mery Report
I can not tell, for, by thys lyght,
I chept nor borowed none of hym this nyght.
But by suche shyfte as I wyll make,
Thou shalte se soone what waye he wyll take.

Boy
Syr, I thanke you. Then I may departe?

The Boye goth forth.

Mery Report
Ye[a], farewell, good sonne, wyth all my harte.
Now such an other sorte as here hath bene
In all the dayes of my lyfe, I have not sene.[110]
No sewters now but women, knavys, and boys,
And all theyr sewtys are in fansyes and toys.
Yf that there come no wyser after thys cry
I wyll to the god and make an ende quyckely.

Oyes, yf that any knave here
Be wyllynge to appere

1002 all likelihood 1005 cannot do without me 1006 want anything done 1007 reveal it to him soon 1011 order 1013 sign 1014 pitfall traps (for birds) 1016 land 1017 flutter 1018 surpasses 1024 (i.e. Mery Report himself) 1028 whoever comes 1029 bellies full (i.e. be satisfied) 1030 whoever cares to ask 1033 knew me to be, talkative 1034 noise 1036 sent (here) 1037 beg 1040 hey ho! 1041 (the boy has understood 'none') 1043 barrel-full 1044 appoint, repay 1046 bought, from 1047 means 1048 action 1054 games 1057 Hear ye

[107] As there is no speech heading here, this line could be allotted to either the Boy or to Mery Report. If the former, it must be addressed either to himself or to the audience concerning Mery Report; if the latter, it is an ironic allusion to the 'greatest friend', given that the Boy is so small.

[108] 'Once we have gained these things, a boy's life would be better than any man's.'

[109] 'My lord': the patron of the feast, perhaps Henry VIII himself.

[110] 'I've never seen such a group of people as I have seen here.'

For wether fowle or clere,
Come in before thys flocke,
And, be he hole or syckly,
Come shew hys mynde quyckly,
And yf hys tale be no lyckly
Ye shall lycke my tayle in the nocke.

All this tyme, I perceyve, is spent in wast
To wayte for mo sewters, I se none make hast.
Wherfore I wyll shew the god all thys procys,
And be delyvered of my symple offys.
[*To Jupiter*] Now lorde, accordynge to your commaundement,
Attendynge sewters I have ben dylygent.
And, at begynnyng as your wyll was I sholde,
I come now at ende to shewe what eche man wolde.
The fyrst sewter before your self dyd appere,
A gentylman desyrynge wether clere,
Clowdy nor mysty nor no wynde to blow,
For hurt in hys huntynge. And then, as ye know,
The marchaunt sewde, for all of that kynde,
For wether clere and mesurable wynde,
As they maye best bere theyr saylys to make spede.
And streyght after thys there came to me, in dede,
An other man, who namyd hym selfe a ranger,
And sayd all of hys crafte be farre brought in daunger
For lacke of lyvynge, whyche chefely ys wynde fall.
But he playnely sayth there bloweth no wynde at al,
Wherfore he desyreth for encrease of theyr fleesys,
Extreme rage of wynde, trees to tere in peces.
Then came a water myller, and he cryed out
For water, and sayde the wynde was so stout
The rayne could not fale, wherfore he made request
For plenty of rayne to set the wynde at rest.
And then, syr, there came a wyndemyller in,
Who sayde for the rayne he could no wynde wyn.
The water he wysht to be banysht all,
Besechynge Your Grace of wynde contynuall.
Then came there an other that wolde banysh all this:
A goodly dame, an ydyll thynge, iwys.
Wynde, rayne, nor froste, nor sonshyne wold she have,
But fayre close wether, her beautye to save.
Then came there an nother that lyveth by laundry,
Who muste have wether hote and clere, here clothys to dry.
Then came there a boy for froste and snow contynuall,
Snow to make snowballys, and frost for his pytfale,
For whyche, God wote, he seweth full gredely!
Your fyrst man wold have wether clere and not wyndy;
The seconde the same, save cooles to blow meanly;
The thyrd desyred stormes and wynde most extremely;
The fourth all in water, and wolde have no wynde;
The fyft no water, but all wynde to grynde;
The syxst wold have none of all these, nor no bright son;
The seventh extremely the hote sone wold have wonne;
The eyght and the last, for frost and snow he prayd.
Byr lady, we shall take shame, I am a frayd!
Who marketh in what maner this sort is led
May thynke yt impossyble all to be sped.
This nomber is smale: there lacketh twayne of ten,
And yet, by the Masse, amonge ten thousand men,
No one thynge could stand more wyde from the tother.
Not one of theyr sewtes agreeth wyth an other.
I promyse you here is a shrewed pece of warke!
This gere wyll trye wether ye be a clarke.
If ye trust to me, yt is a great foly,
For yt passeth my braynes, by Goddes body!

JUPITER
Son, thou haste ben dylygent and done so well,
That thy labour is ryght myche thanke worthy.
But be thou suer we nede no whyt thy counsell,
For in our selfe we have foresene remedy,
Whyche thou shalt se. But fyrst, depart hens quyckly
To the Gentylman and all other sewters here,
And commaunde them all before us to appere.

MERY REPORT
That shall be no lenger in doynge
Then I am in commynge and goynge.

Mery Report goth out.

1061 whole/healthy 1063 likely/plausible 1064 lick, crack 1065 is wasted 1067 reveal to, process/matter 1068 relieved, responsibility 1071 as you told me to at the beginning 1072 wishes 1075 (Neither) cloudy 1077 his kind 1078 moderate 1079 raise 1083 income 1085 plunder/spoils 1086 tear 1088 strong 1089 fall 1092 because of, find 1098 mild, protect 1100 her 1103 greedily/eagerly 1105 cool breezes, moderately 1109 sun 1112 afraid 1113 Whoever considers, crowd behaves 1114 for all, helped 1115 two fewer than ten 1117 further apart 1118 suits 1119 piece of work 1120 test if you're a clerk (i.e. wise) 1122 it's beyond me 1125 sure

JUPITER

Such debate as from above ye have harde,[111]
Suche debate beneth amonge your selfes ye se.
As longe as heddes from temperaunce be deferd,
So longe the bodyes in dystemperaunce be.
This perceyve ye all, but none can helpe save we.
But as we there have made peace concordantly,
So woll we here now gyve you remedy.

Mery Report and all the sewters entreth.

MERY REPORT

If I hadde caught them
Or ever I raught them,
I wolde have taught them
To be nere me.
Full dere have I bought them,
Lorde, so I sought them,
Yet have I brought them
Suche as they be.

GENTYLMAN

Pleaseth yt Your Majeste, Lorde, so yt is:
We, as your subjectes and humble sewters all,
Accordynge as we here your pleasure is,
Are presyd to your presens, beynge pryncypall
Hed and governour of all in every place.
Who joyeth not in your syght no joy can have,
Wherfore we all commyt us to Your Grace
As Lorde of Lordes, us to peryshe or save.

JUPITER

As longe as dyscrecyon so well doth you gyde
Obedyently to use your dewte,
Dout ye not we shall your savete provyde.
Your grevys we have harde, wherfore we sent for ye
To receyve answere, eche man in his degre.
And fyrst to content, most reason yt is,
The fyrst man that sewde, wherfore marke ye this:[112]

Oft shall ye have the wether clere and styll
To hunt in, for recompens of your payne.
Also you merchauntes shall have myche your wyll:
For, oft tymes when no wynde on lande doth remayne,
Yet on the see plesaunt cooles you shall obtayne.
And syns your huntynge maye reste in the nyght,
Oft shall the wynde then ryse, and before day lyght

It shall ratyll downe the wood in suche case
That all ye rangers the better lyve may.
And ye water myllers shall abteyne this grace:
Many tymes the rayne to fall in the valey,
When at the self tymes on hyllys we shall purvey
Fayre wether for your wyndmilles, with such coolys of wynde
As in one instant both kyndes of mylles may grynde.

And for ye fayre women that close wether wold have,
We shall provyde that ye may suffycyently
Have tyme to walke in, and your beauty save.
And yet shall ye have, that lyveth by laundry,
The hote sonne oft ynough your clothes to dry.
Also ye, praty chylde, shall have both frost and snow.
Now marke this conclusyon, we charge you arow:

Myche better have we now devysed for ye all
Then ye all can perceyve or coude desyre.
Eche of you sewd to have contynuall
Suche wether as his crafte onely doth requyre.
All wethers in all places yf men all tymes myght hyer,
Who could lyve by other?[113] What is this neglygens,
Us to atempt in suche inconvenyens?

Now, on the tother syde, yf we had graunted
The full of some one sewt and no mo,
And from all the rest the wether had forbyd,
Yet who so hadde obtayned had wonne his owne wo.
There is no one craft can preserve man so,
But by other craftes, of necessyte,
He muste have myche parte of his commodyte.[114]

1133 beneath (on Earth) 1134 shun temperance/moderation 1135 bodies will be distempered 1137 there (in Heaven) 1140 reached 1150 pressed 1152 Whoever, in seeing you 1154 kill/ruin 1156 do your duty 1157 provide for your safety 1158 grievances 1159 according to his status 1161 much of what you want 1166 sea breezes 1167 stops at night 1169 shake, (a) way 1173 same time, send 1176 mild 1182 by row (i.e. each one) 1184 could 1185 continually 1188 thoughtlessness 1189 To try to persuade us to 1193 gained only his own downfall

[111] 'Such debate above [in Heaven] as you heard about earlier [i.e. at ll. 22–65]'.

[112] 'It is most reasonable to satisfy first the first man who first petitioned us [i.e. the Gentylman], so pay attention to this'.

[113] 'If men could arrange their own weather all of the time in all places, which of them could live together?'

[114] 'There is no single profession that can sustain humankind sufficiently that it does not need to be provided, by other professions, of the greater part of its needs.'

All to serve at ones, and one destroy a nother,
Or ellys to serve one and destroy all the rest:
Nother wyll we do the tone nor the tother,
But serve as many or as few as we thynke best.
And where, or what tyme, to serve moste or lest,
The dyreccyon of that doutles shall stande
Perpetually in the power of our hande.

Wherfore we wyll the hole worlde to attende,
Eche sort, on suche wether as for them doth fall.
Now one, now other, as lyketh us to send.
Who that hath yt, ply yt, and suer we shall[115]
So gyde the wether in course to you all,
That eche wyth other ye shall hole remayne
In pleasure and plentyfull welth, certayne.

GENTYLMAN
Blessyd was the tyme wherin we were borne,
Fyrst for the blysfull chaunce of your godly presens,
Next for our sewt! Was there never man beforne
That ever harde so excellent a sentens

As Your Grace hath gevyn to us all arow.
Wherin your hyghnes hath so bountyfully
Dystrybuted my parte, that Your Grace shall know
Your selfe sooll possessed of hertes of all chyvalry.[116]

MARCHAUNT
Lyke wyse we marchauntes shall yeld us holy
Onely to laude the name of Jupyter
As god of all goddes, you to serve soolly,
For of every thynge, I se, you are norysher.

RANGER
No dout yt is so, for so we now fynde,
Wherin Your Grace us rangers so doth bynde
That we shall gyve you our hertes with one accorde,
For knowledge to know you as our onely lorde.

WATER MYLLER
Well, I can no more but, for our water
We shall geve your lordshyp Our Ladyes Sauter.

WYND MYLLER
Myche have ye bounde us, for, as I be saved,
We have all obteyned better then we craved.

GENTYLWOMAN
That is trew, wherfore Your Grace shall trewly
The hertes of such as I am have, surely.

LAUNDER
[*To the Gentylwoman*] And such as I am (who be as good as you),
His hyghnes shall be suer on, I make a vow.

BOY
Godfather god, I wyll do somwhat for you agayne.
By Cryst, ye may happe to have a byrd or twayne!
And I promyse you, yf any snow come,
When I make my snow ballys, ye shall have some.

MERY REPORT
God thanke Your Lordship. Lo, how this is brought to pas!
Syrs, now shall ye have the wether even as yt was.

JUPITER
We nede no whyte our selfe any farther to bost,
For our dedes declare us apparauntly.
Not onely here on Yerth in every cost,
But also above in the Hevynly company,
Our prudens hath made peace unyversally.
Whyche thynge, we sey, recordeth us as pryncypall
God and governour of Heven, Yerth, and all.

Now unto that Heven we woll make retourne,
Where we be gloryfyed most tryumphantly.
Also we woll all ye that on Yerth sojourne,
Syns cause gyveth cause, to know us your lord onely,[117]
And now here to synge moste joyfully,
Rejoycynge in us; and in meane tyme we shall
Ascende into our trone celestyall.

FINIS

PRINTED BY W. RASTELL
1533
CUM PRIVILEGIO.[118]

1197 once 1198 else 1201 least 1202 direction 1204 whole 1206 as it pleases 1209 united/harmonious 1219 wholly 1221 solely 1222 the nourisher of all things 1228 recite (in your name) 1234 sure of (too) 1236 happen, (as a gift from me) 1239 brought about 1240 as it was before 1241 do not need 1242 clearly reveal our (nature) 1243 Earth, coast/region 1245 prudence 1246 reveals us to be 1250 desire 1254 Heavenly throne

115 'Let each of you use whatever weather comes to hand'.
116 'You shall be the sole possessor of the hearts/loyalty of all noblemen.'
117 i.e. 'Since those on Earth should follow the example of those in Heaven, (you should) acknowledge us as your only lord.'
118 '*Cum Privilegio {Regis}*': '[printed] with royal permission', a legal requirement for all printed books.

John Bale, from *Three Laws*, *c.*1548. Courtesy of the Bodleian Library, Oxford.

John Bale, *Johan Baptystes Preachynge*

John Bale (1495–1563)

John Bale's career as a religious reformer and polemicist was a long and stormy one, and brought him into contact (and frequently into conflict) with many of the most important figures and issues of the period. His early life seems, however, to have been entirely orthodox. He was born in Suffolk in 1495, and from the age of 12 onwards was educated in the Carmelite friary of Norwich. By 1514 he was at Cambridge University, and he also studied at Louvain and Toulouse before obtaining his bachelor's degree in divinity in 1529. During this period he compiled saints' lives and wrote a number of orthodox prayers to the Virgin Mary, as well as developing an interest in the histories of the religious orders. He seemed destined for a successful religious career, and by 1534 was already prior of the Carmelite house at Doncaster. But it was at about this time that he began to show signs of leaning towards Protestantism, perhaps (as he was later to claim) under the influence of Thomas, Lord Wentworth. He renounced his vows and left the order, married, and began a life as a parish priest and preacher, getting into trouble with the church authorities on a number of occasions during the 1530s for the radicalism of his views. He also attracted friends in high places, however, including both John de Vere, fifteenth earl of Oxford, and Thomas Cromwell, Henry VIII's evangelical chief minister.

It was while in de Vere's service that Bale began to write plays and interludes in support of religious reform and the Royal Supremacy. The titles of two now lost works on *The King's Two Marriages* and *The Impostures of Thomas à Beckett* give a flavour of his interests at this time. By 1538, Bale was leading a troupe of actors under Cromwell's patronage, for whom he probably wrote the cycle of Protestant plays on the life of Christ which he intended should replace the Catholic Cycle Plays as a medium of religious instruction for the masses. The two plays printed here form part of that Protestant 'counter-Cycle', much of which, if it was ever completed, is now lost. Bale also wrote a powerful quasi-historical interlude, *King Johan* (1538), designed to support the Royal Supremacy and encourage the king and council towards further radical reform (see Walker, *Plays of Persuasion*, ch. 6). After the fall of Cromwell in 1540, Bale fled to Germany, where he had a number of his plays and other polemical tracts printed. He returned to England following the accession of Edward VI, and became bishop of Ossory in Ireland, where he antagonized the staunchly Catholic population with his sermons and productions of his plays. At the accession of the Catholic Queen Mary in 1553 he was again forced to flee to the Continent, but he returned once more at her death, and lived as a prebendary of Canterbury Cathedral until his own death in November 1563.

Bale was one of the most vigorous advocates of the use of drama for didactic and polemical ends, but he was also a scholar and antiquary of distinction. It is largely due to his efforts that so much information concerning the writers and texts of late medieval England survived the dispersal of the monastic libraries at the Dissolution.

Further reading

L.P. Fairfield, *John Bale: Mythmaker for the English Reformation* (West Lafayette, Ind., 1976).

P. Happé, *John Bale* (New York, 1996).

J.W. Harris, *John Bale: A Study in the Minor Literature of the Reformation* (Urbana, Ill., 1940).

J.N. King, *English Reformation Literature* (Princeton, N.J., 1982).

G. Walker, *Plays of Persuasion: Drama and Politics at the Court of Henry VIII* (Cambridge, 1991).

Johan Baptystes Preachynge

This play, part of Bale's reformed Cycle, is based upon the accounts of John's baptism of Christ which appear in all four of the Gospels; but, as the epigram suggests, it follows chiefly the version in Luke. It is a 'comedy' in the formal sense that it ends happily. Bale changed the emphasis of John's preaching in parts in order to present him as a proto-Protestant figure, setting his focus upon the redeeming power of belief in Christ's divinity against the trust of the Pharisee and Sadducee (types of Bale's Catholic opponents) in the value of good works, ecclesiastical traditions, and the authority of the established church hierarchy.

The play is clearly a flexible piece that could be played either indoors or outside (as it was at the Market Cross in Kilkenny, Ireland, in 1553). The only elaborate property needed would have been the dove which descends after Christ's baptism (a feature borrowed from the Catholic Cycle Plays). The water of baptism might be provided from a convenient bowl or trough, or mimed if necessary. Bale's prosody here is not complex, being based in great part upon rhyme royal stanzas and couplets. As Peter Happé has shown (see Happé, *Plays*) his verse lines are divided by a central caesura, usually after five syllables. To clarify the syntax, I have not reproduced the comma which marks the pause in the printed edition.

The text used here is based upon the earliest surviving version, that printed in *The Harleian Miscellany* I (1744), pp. 97–110, based upon a now lost text of 1538. In addition I have consulted the modern edition in Peter Happé, ed. *The Complete Plays of John Bale* (2 vols, Woodbridge, 1985–6), II, pp. 35–50.

A Brefe Comedy or enterlude of Johan Baptystes Preachynge in the Wyldernesse, openynge the crafty assaultes of the hypocrites, with the gloryouse baptyme[1] *of the Lord Jesus Christ.*
Compyled by Johan Bale, Anno 1538.

The worde of God came unto Johan the sonne of Zachary in the wyldernesse. And he resorted into all the coastes about Jordane, and preached the Batysme of repentaunce for the remyssyon of synnes. Luce iii.[2]

Interlocutores:[3] *Pater Coelestis* (God: 'the Heavenly Father'), *Joannes Baptista* (John the Baptist), *Turba Vulgaris* ((one of the) 'Common Multitude'), *Miles Armatus* (a Soldier), *Publicanus* (a 'Publican': tax-collector), *Pharisaeus* (a Pharisee),[4] *Sadducaeus* (a Sadducee),[5] *Jesus Christus* (Jesus Christ), *Baleus Prolocutor* (Bale the Presenter: the Prologue and Epilogue).

Prefacio.[6]

BALEUS PROLOCUTOR
The kyngdome of Christ wyll now begynne to sprynge,
Which is the preachynge of Hys Newe Testament.
Now shall Messias, which is our Heavenly Kynge,
Apere to the worlde in manhode evydent;
Whose wholsom commynge Johan Baptyst wyll prevent,
Preachynge repentaunce, Hys hygh way to prepare,[7]
Whych we entende before yow to declare.

The Lawe and Prophetes draweth now fast to an ende,[8]
Which were but shaddowes and fygures of Hys commynge.

1 flourish 3 (the) Messiah, who 4 clearly in human form 5 wholesome, foreshadow 9 foreshadowings

1 Baptism.

2 Luke 3:2–3.

3 '[The] Speakers'.

4 The Pharisees were a sect within Judaism dedicated to the strict adherence to and teaching of the Mosaic Law. Jesus singled them out for criticism as hypocrites: see Luke 11:38–48; Matthew 5:20, 15:1–20; Mark 7:1–23. John the Baptist also criticized them: see Matthew 3:7. Bale uses them, with the Sadducees, as types of his Catholic opponents.

5 The Sadducees were an elite group within Jewish society including much of the aristocracy and higher priesthood. They believed in a conservative interpretation of the Torah, the Jewish law. They were distinguished from the Pharisees principally by their rejection of the belief in bodily resurrection. See Matthew 22:23–30.

6 Preface.

7 See Luke 3:3–4: 'And he came into the country about Jordan, preaching the baptism of repentance for the remission of sins / As it is written in the book of the words of Esaias the Prophet, saying, the voice of one crying in the wilderness, Prepare ye the way of the Lord, make His paths straight.'

8 i.e. the time of the Old Law, as described in the Old Testament.

Now shall He approche, that all grace wyll extende
Of cleane remyssyon; our caucyon will He brynge
To pacyfye God, Hys Father everlastynge.
By sheadynge Hys bloude all thynges shall He renewe,
Makynge one people of the Pagane and the Jewe.

For so much as we are geven to noveltees
Of very nature, lete us our selves applye
To accepte these newes and heavenlye verytees,
Which are for our synne most soverayne remedye,
And for our sowles helthe so hyghlye necessarye,
That without knowledge of them, we can not have
A true fayth in Him which dyed our sowles to save.

Whan man had synned, the harde preceptes of the lawe
Moses proclamed, the Prophetes gave monycyons.
But non of them all to the Heavenly Kyngedome drawe,
Tyll Johan Baptyst come with clerar exposycyons.
The publycanes then leave their yll dysposycyons
Unto Christ to come and Hys most holy Gospell.
Where the frowarde sectes contynuallye rebell,

Ye shall se Christ here submyt Hymselfe to baptym
Of Johan Hys servaunt, in most meke humble wyse,
In poornesse of sprete that we shuld folowe hym,[9]
Whose lowlye doctryne the hypocrytes despyse.
Folowe hym therfor, and shurne their devylysh practyse.
Be gentyll in hart, and beare your good intent
Towards Hys Gospell and Godlye Testament.

Incipit Comoedia.[10]

[*Joannes Baptista preaching to Turba Vulgaris, Publicanus, and Miles Armatus.*]

JOANNES BAPTISTA
As a massenger I come to geve yow warnynge
That your Lorde, your Kynge, your Saver and Redemer,
With helth, grace, and pece, to yow ys hydre commynge.
Applye ye therfor, delaye the tyme no longer,
But prepare Hys waye, makynge the rough pathes smother;
Stryke downe the mountaynes, fyll up the valleyes agayne,
For all men shall se their mercyful Saver playne.[11]

The seate of David, whych is the Father Heavenly,
He cometh to possesse as a ruler spirytuall,
And in Jacobs howse to reigne contynually,
Whych is of Hys churche the nombre unyversall
Not only of Jewes but faythfull belevers all.
That congregacyon will He evermore defende,
And of Hys kyngedome shall never be an ende.

TURBA VULGARIS
At these newe tydynges, whom thys good man doth brynge,
My hart within me for joye doth leape and sprynge.

PUBLICANUS
O myghty Maker, what confort to us is thys,
Thyne own Sonne to sende to reforme that is amys!

MILES ARMATUS
Soch confort to me as I can not expresse,
Of tunges though I had thre thousande and no lesse.

JOANNES BAPTISTA
Approche nyghar, fryndes, and tell me what ye saye.

TURBA VULGARIS
Ye tolde us, me thought, we shuld prepare a waye
For the Lordes commynge. Was not your saynge so?

JOANNES BAPTISTA
My preachynge was it, from it can I not go,[12]
For grounded it is on Gods myghty worde, trulye,
Uttered longe afore by the Prophet Esaye.[13]

PUBLICANUS
I praye ye, tell us what ye meane by that waye.

JOANNES BAPTISTA
Your conversacyon, which is in sore decaye.

10 who 11 complete, guarantee 14 shedding, blood 15 Pagans, Jews 16 prone to (favour) 17 (our) very, exert ourselves 18 new, truths 19 most excellent 20 soul's 22 commands 23 instructions 24 lead 25 clearer, interpretations 26 evil 28 Whereas, quarrelsome 33 scorn 34 gentle 36 messenger 37 Saviour 38 hither/here 39 Exert yourselves 40 smoother 43 throne 45 (i.e. Israel) 47 (i.e. Christians) 50 which 52 comfort 53 what is amiss 55 tongues 56 nearer, friends 58 Didn't you say that 63 behaviour/lifestyle

9 'So that we should follow Him in humility of spirit'.

10 'The Comedy begins.'

11 See Luke 3:5–6: 'Every valley shall be filled, and every mountain and hill shall be brought low; and the crooked shall be made straight, and the rough ways shall be made smooth; / And all flesh shall see the salvation of God.'

12 'That was what I preached, I cannot alter it'.

13 See Isaiah 40:3.

Laye apart your wrathe, your covetousnesse and pryde,
Your lustes unlaufull, with your other synnes besyde.
Knowledge your trespace and cease from doynge yll;
Flee mennys tradycyons[14] and Gods hygh lawes fulfyll.
Make ye strayght the pathes, lete every man have hys;
In no wyse revenge whan men use ye amys.
Seke God your father in sprete and veryte,
But not in shaddowes, as doth the Paryse,
Whych by outwarde workes loketh to be justyfyed,
And neyther by faythe not by Gods worde wyll be tryed.
Every depe valleye to moch more hygthe wyll growe;
The mountaynes and hylles shall be brought downe full lowe.[15]

Miles Armatus
What meane ye by that? I pray ye hartely tell.

Joannes Baptista
Mekenesse wyll aryse and pryde abate, by the Gospell.
The symple fysher shall now be notable;
The spirytuall Pharyse a wretche detestable.
The wyse and lerned the Idyote wyll deface;[16]
Synners shall excede the outward payntes in grace.
Abjectes of the worlde in knowledge wyll excell
The consecrate rabyes by vertu of the Gospell.[17]
The poore man by faythe shall very clerely deme
The clause that wyll harde unto the lawer seme.[18]
All that afore tyme untowarde ded remayne,
The rule of Gods worde wyll now make strayght and playne.
The covetouse jourer shall now be lyberall,
The malycyouse man wyll now to charyte fall.
The wratheful hater shall now love ernestlye,
To temperate measure men wyll change glotonye.
Pryde shall so abate that mekenesse wyll prevayle,
Lechery shall lye down and clennesse set up sayle.
Slouthfulnesse shall slyde, and dylygence aryse
To folowe the truthe in godly exercyse.
Prepare ye therfor so fast as ever ye can
To thys Lorde, whych will renue ye every man,
In case ye repent the folye that is past.

Omnes Una
Sory are we for it, and wyll be to our last.

Joannes Baptista
What are ye? Tell me, ych persone severallye.

Turba Vulgaris
I do represent the commen people of Jewry;
In sweate of my browes my lyvynge I procure
By daylye labours, and mynde so to endure.

Publicanus
A publicane I am, and moch do lyve by pollage,
For my offyce is to gather tax and tollage.
Moch am I hated of the Pharyse and Scrybe,
For axyng trybute, it judgynge unlaufull brybe.[19]

Miles Armatus
A soldyour I am, or valeant man of warre,
The lande to defende and hys enemyes to conquarre.
Whan my wages are too lyttle for my expence
To get a botye I spare no vyolence.[20]

Joannes Baptista
For Gods love, repent and turne ye to the Lorde,
That by Him ye maye to Hys kyngedome be restorde.

64 Put aside 65 sins 66 offences/sins 69 abuse you 70 verity/truth 71 Pharisee 72 seeks 73 And (who) 74 much greater height 77 pride be brought low 78 fisherman, honoured 79 (shall become) a 84 understand 86 previously was difficult 88 juror, generous 89 begin to be charitable 91 gluttons will turn to moderation 93 decline, sail (i.e. forge ahead) 94 decline 95 religious devotion 97 For, renew 98 Provided that 99+ All as one (i.e. together) 99 (i.e. forever) 100 in turn 102 By the sweat 103 intend, continue 104 taxation 105 the exacting of tolls 106 by, Pharisees, Scribes 109 its, conquer 110 expenditure/needs 113 restored

14 i.e. those religious practices devised by men and not explicitly demanded in the Bible. Bale's hostility is directed at traditional Catholic practices not grounded in scriptural injunctions, such as pilgrimages, image-worship, and the 'rules' of the regular clergy.

15 Luke 3:5.

16 'The wise and the learned shall be discredited by [the words of] an idiot'.

17 'Sinners shall become more gracious than those who appear outwardly to be saints. The outcasts of the world will become more knowledgeable, by virtue of the Gospel, than the consecrated rabbis [teachers] of the Jewish law.'

18 'The phrase that will seem hard to a lawyer.'

19 'For demanding payment, [as] they judge it to be an illegal bribe [to the Romans].' The Scribes were the doctors and chief interpreters of the Jewish law (the Torah). Their opposition (with that of the Pharisees) to the publicans is noted in Luke 5:30.

20 i.e. 'I use violence to obtain booty without hesitation.'

Ad Deum convertitur Turba Vulgaris et peccata sic confitetur:[21]

Turba Vulgaris
I knowe, Blessed Lorde, by playne experiment
Most nygh unto helth is he that shewyth hys sore.
Wherefor I confesse in place here evydent
The synnefull lyvynge that I have used afore.
A wretched synnar I have bene evermore,
Unthankefull to Thee, to man uncharytable,
And in all my workes both false and deceyvable.

Hunc tunc baptisat Joannes flectentem genua.[22]

Joannes Baptista
Then take my baptyme, whych is a preparacyon
Unto faythe in Christ wherin rest your salvacyon.
To Christes Gospell your conversacyon applye,
And lerne by thys sygne with Hym to lyve and dye.

Turba Vulgaris
Myne usage, ye knowe, is outwarde and externe;
Some godly preceptes for that fayne wolde I lerne.[23]

Joannes Baptista
I will not move ye to offer calfe or gote,
But to charyte, whych is of hyghar note.[24]
With no sacryfyce is God more hyghly pleased
Than with that good hart wherby the poore is eased,
For that He acceptyth as though Hymselfe it had.

Turba Vulgaris
Thys helthsome counsell maketh my hart joyfull and glad.

Joannes Baptista
He that hath two coates, lete hym geve one to the nedye;
And he that hath vytayle, lykewyse releve the hungrye.
Helpe alwayes the poore with herbour, foode, and aparell,
With socour, solace, with doctryne and ghostlye counsell.
These thynges done in faythe maye mollyfye Gods yre.

Turba Vulgaris
Farewell to ye, then, for I have my desyre.

Eo exeunte Publicanus coram Deo peccatum agnoscit.[25]

Publicanus
Thy worde, Blessed Lorde, by this good man declared,
Causeth my conscyence of synne to have remorce,
And to remembre how that I have not spared
The poore to oppresse by crueltie and force.
I consydre yet how I oft have bene horce,
Cryenge for custome, exactynge more than due.
To my neyber, Lorde, I have bene full untrue.

Illum tunc baptisat Joannes incurvantem genua.[26]

Joannes Baptista
Be baptysed, then, in token of repentaunce,
And take to ye faythe with a newe remembraunce,
Thynkynge by thys sygne ye are from hensfourth bounde
Vyces to resyst, acceptynge Christ for your grounde.

Publicanus
Geve me some precept or rule whereon to staye,
That I, in my sort, my Lorde God may obaye.

Joannes Baptista
I wyll not bynde ye your substaunce to dyspence,
But I requyre yow to abstayne from vyolence.
Though your offyce be to gather and to pull,
Yet be no tyrauntes, but rather mercyfull:
A good waye thys were for your estate, I thynke.

Publicanus
Perfourme it I shall; I wolde else I shuld synke.[27]

114 (i.e. experience teaches me) 115 reveals his illness (to the doctor) 116 openly 117 practised 118 sinner 119 Ungrateful, (and) to (my fellow) 120 deceitful 122 rests/lies 123 dedicate your life to 124 sign (i.e. baptism) 125 My practice, external 127 instruct, sacrifice, goat 128 greater importance 130 are aided 131 He received it Himself 132 health-giving 133 needy 134 food 135 shelter, clothes 136 succour 137 soften God's anger 140 to have remorse for my sins 143 hoarse (through) 144 Calling, customs/taxes, (is) due 145 neighbour 148 henceforth committed 149 foundation 150 anchor (my life) 151 according to my class 152 wealth, distribute 154 tax 156 This would be good practice

[21] 'Turba Vulgaris is turned to God and confesses his sins thus'.

[22] 'He then bends his knees [i.e. kneels] and is baptized by John.'

[23] 'I am eager to receive some truly godly instruction for that.'

[24] See Matthew 9:13.

[25] 'When he [Turba Vulgaris] has left, Publicanus acknowledges his sin before God.'

[26] 'He then bends his knees and is baptized by John.'

[27] 'May I be ruined if I don't.'

Joannes Baptista
For your peynes, ye have, appoynted by the emproure,
Your stypende wages; no creature you ought to devoure.
For Gods love, therfor, do no man injury
In taking tollage, advauntage to have therby,
Non otherwyse than it is to yow prescrybed.

Publicanus
By me from hensfourth nought from the poore shall be brybed.

Eo decedente Miles sua confitetur scelera.[28]

Miles Armatus
Experyence doth shewe where as are good monycyons
Maye be avoyded all jeopardy and daunger.[29]
At thys mannys counsell all synneful dysposycyons
I wyll therfor change to a lyfe, I hope, moch better.[30]
No man so wycked, nor so farre out of order,
As I, wretche, have bene, in murther, rape, and thefte.
Swete Lorde, forgeve me and those wayes shall be lefte.

Illum tunc baptisat Joannes in genua procumbentem.[31]

Joannes Baptista
Thys baptyme of myne to yow doth represent
Remyssyon in Christ, in case your synnes ye repent.
In Hys blessed deathe it assureth yow of grace,
Sealynge your pasport unto the hyghar place.

Miles Armatus
My Maker I thanke of Hys most specyall gyfte;
For my usage now shewe me some ghostly dryfte.

Joannes Baptista
Of warre ye have lawes: use them with ryght alwayes.
Do no spoyle, nor rape, take no unlaufull prayes.
The offyce ye have, for the publyque unyte,
Mynde to exercyse to the landes tranquyllyte.[32]
Ye maye thus please God in doynge your feate ryght well.

Miles Armatus
Father, go forewarde, for I moch delyght your counsell.

Joannes Baptista
For the publique peace, Gods lawe doth you permyt
Stronge weapon to weare, but in no case to abuse it.
If ye mynde therfor of God to avoyde the daunger,
For covetouse lucre hurt neyther frynde nor stranger,[33]
But with your wages yche man be satysfyed.

Miles Armatus
Prayse be to the Lorde! I am moch edyfyed.

Eo locum deserente intrant Pharisaeus ac Sadducaeus. Interim Joannes Baptista alloquitur populum.[34]

Joannes Baptista
Of Christ to tell yow, with the dyfference of our Baptym:[35]
I washe in water, but remyssyon is of Him.
My baptyme is a sygne of outwarde mortyfyenge;
A grace is Hys baptyme, of inwarde quyckenynge.
The baptyme of me is the baptyme of repentaunce;
Hys baptyme in faythe bryngeth full recoveraunce.
My doctryne is harde and full of threttenynges;
Hys wordes are demure, replete with wholsom blessynges.
I fear the conscience with terrour of the lawe;
He by the Gospell mannys sowle wyll gentylly drawe.

158 (In return) for, allotted 159 regular wages, overtax 161 for private gain 162 Only as your rules allow 163 stolen 168 (There is) no man 170 left (behind) 172 provided that 176 direction 178 unlawful prey/victims 181 performing your role 182 I delight greatly in 184 Powerful, carry 190 forgiveness, from 191 mortification of the body 192 spiritual (re)birth 193 repentance (of sin) 194 recovery (from sin) 195 threats (of punishment) 196 mild 197 frighten 198 attract/guide

[28] 'He departs and Miles confesses his wickedness.'

[29] 'Experience teaches us that, where there are good forewarnings, all danger and jeopardy are prevented.'

[30] 'In response to this man's advice I will change all [my] sinful tendencies for a [way of] life which is, I hope, much better.'

[31] 'He falls to his knees, and then John baptizes him.'

[32] '[In order to promote] public unity, be sure to exercise the role you have in the interests of peace.'

[33] 'Hurt neither ally nor foe through greed for money'.

[34] 'As he leaves the place, the Pharisee and Sadducee enter. Meanwhile John the Baptist addresses the people.'

[35] '[I shall] describe Christ to you, and the difference between our baptism(s)'.

A knowledge of synne the baptyme of me do teache;[36]
Forgevenesse by faythe wyll He here after preache.
I open the sore, he bryngeth the remedye;
I sturre the conscyence, He doth all pacyfye.
As Esaye sayth, I am the cryars voice;[37]
But He is the worde and message of rejoyce.
The lanterne I am, He is the very lyght;
I prepare the waye, but He maketh all thynges perfyght.

Invicem alloquuntur.[38]

PHARISAEUS
As is said abroade, thys fellawe preacheth newe lernynge.[39]
Lete us dyssemble to understande hys meanynge.

SADDUCAEUS
Wele pleased I am that we examyne hys doynges;
Hys doctrine, paraventure, myght hyndre els our lyvynges.[40]
But in our workynge we must be sumwhat craftye.

PHARISAEUS
Tush! Thu shalt se me undermynde hym very fynelye.

Et vertens se ad Joannem dolose illum aloquitur.[41]

God blesse ye, father, and prospere your busynesse.

JOANNES BAPTISTA
Ye are welcome both, so that ye mynde anye goodnesse.

SADDUCAEUS
No harme we intende; ye maye trust us and ye wyll.

JOANNES BAPTISTA
Ye shewe to the worlde as though ye coulde do no yll,
But the Lorde doth knowe what ye have in your hartes,
And secretlye how ye playe most wycked partes.
Where as sectes remayne the sprete of God cannot be,
Whose kynde is to knytt by a perfyght unyte.

PHARISAEUS
That taunte have I ones bycause I am a Pharyse.

SADDUCAEUS
My parte is no lesse, for I am also a Sadduce.
We wyll thu knowe it, our relygyons are worshypfull.

JOANNES BAPTISTA
Not so worshypfull, but moch more false and deceytfull.
An outwarde pretence ye have of holynesse,
Whych is before God a double wyckednesse.

PHARISAEUS
A very wretche art thu, soch vertuouse men to despyse
As the lawes of God to Hys people doth decyse.[42]
We Pharysees are those whych syt in Moses seate
As interpretours, the holy Scriptures to treate.

JOANNES BAPTISTA
And them ye corrupt with your pestylent tradycyons,
For your bellyes sake have yow false exposycyons.

SADDUCAEUS
What sayst thu to me, whych in one poynt do not swerve
From Moses fyve bokes, but every jote we observe?[43]
Thynkest not us worthy the gloryous name we beare
Of ryghteouse Sadducees? Saye thy mynde wythout feare.

201 wound 202 stir/prompt 204 rejoicing 205 true 206 perfect 207 rumoured 208 intentions 209 doings/behaviour 212 undermine, finely 214 provided, intend any 215 if 216 appear 219 Where there are sects 220 unite/join together 221 only/primarily because 230 discuss/interpret 232 belly's, teachings 235 Do you think we are not

36 'My baptism teaches acknowledgement of sin'.

37 See Isaiah 40:3.

38 'They talk between themselves [privately].'

39 'The new learning' was a phrase used to describe the beliefs of Luther and the evangelicals, usually by its critics.

40 'Otherwise his teachings might, perhaps, hinder our lives [or possibly "our incomes"].'

41 'And, turning to John, he speaks to him deceitfully.'

42 '[Such men] as decide the laws of God for His people.'

43 '[I who] do not swerve one jot/iota from [the teachings of] Moses' five books.' The Pentateuch (the first five books of the Old Testament) were believed to have been written by Moses.

Joannes Baptista
I saye thys unto yow: your observacyons are carnall,
Outwarde workes ye have, but in sprete nothynge at all.
Ye walke in the letter lyke paynted hypocrytes,
Before God ye are no better than Sodomytes.[44]
Synners offendynge of weaknesse, doubt, or ignoraunce,
Of pytie God pardoneth; but where He fyndeth resystence
Agaynst the playne truthe, there wyll He ponnysh most,
For a wyckednesse that is agaynst the Holy Ghost,
And that reigneth in yow, whych never hath forgevenesse.
For enemyes ye are to that ye knowe ryghteousnesse.

Pharisaeus
Avaunt, beggar, avaunt! Becometh it the[e] to prate
So unmannerly agaynst our comely estate,
Whych is knowne to be so notable and holye?
Thu shalt be loked on, I promyse the[e], surelye.

Sadducaeus
Our worthy decrees the knave doth not regarde,
But practyseth newe lawes, soch as were never hearde.
By whose autoryte doest thu teache thys newe lernynge?
Doubt not but shortly thu wylt be brought to a reckenynge.

Joannes Baptista
Ye generacyon of vypers! Ye murtherers of the Prophetes!
Ye Lucifers proude, and usurpers of hygh seates!
Never was serpent more styngynge than ye be,
More full of poyson, nor inwarde cruelte![45]
All your stodye is to persue the veryte;
Soch is your practyse: deceyte and temeryte.
You boast yourselves moch of ryghteousnesse and scyence,
And yet non more vyle, nor fuller of neglygence.
How can ye escape the vengeaunce that is commynge
Upon the unfaythfull whych wyll admytt no warnynge?
Neyther your good workes, nor merytes of your fathers,
Your fastynges, longe prayers, with other holy behavers,[46]
Shall yow afore God be able to justyfye,
Your affeccyons inwarde unless ye do mortyfye.[47]
And therfor shewe fourth the due frutes of repentaunce;
Not in wordes only, but from the hartes habundaunce.
Forsake your malyce, your pryde, and hypocresye,
And now exercyse the frutefull dedes of mercye.[48]

Pharisaeus
It become not the[e] to shew what we shall do,[49]
We knowynge the lawe, and the prophecyes also.
Go teache thy olde shoes, lyke a busye, pratlynge fole,
For we wyll non be of thys newe fangeled scole.[50]
We are men lerned; we knowe the auncyent lawes
Of our forefathers. Thy newes are not worth two strawes.

Sadducaeus
The ofsprynge we are of noble father Abraham,
And have the blessynge so many as of hym cam.
We can not perysh, though thu prate never so myche,
For we are ryghteouse, wele lerned, famouse, and ryche.

237 practices, based on the flesh 241 through 243 punish 246 that (which) you know (is) 247 Does it become you, rail? 248 rudely 250 looked at/investigated 252 heard (before) 253 authority 254 reckoning 255 vipers (poisonous snakes) 256 proud Lucifers, thrones 257 stinging/poisonous 259 study/effort, pursue (violently) 260 temerity 261 wisdom 262 (there is) no one 264 accept 265 merits 266 behaviour 267 justify you before God 269 fruits/products 270 fullness of the heart 278 (i.e. are worthless) 280 (of) all his descendants 281 however much you prattle

44 The Sodomites were the 'abominable' people of Sodom, one of the Cities of the Plain destroyed by God. See Genesis 13:10–13, 18:20–33, 19:1–29. It may be that Bale intends a specific contemporary allusion to the charges of sodomy and sexual abuse frequently levelled against monks by their evangelical critics.

45 See Luke 3:7; Matthew 23:13–39.

46 Bale adds to John's biblical sermon this attack upon the practices of orthodox regular clergy.

47 'Unless you discipline your inward desires (i.e. not those 'outward' desires of the body disciplined by fasting, etc.).'

48 For the acts of Corporal Mercy, see Matthew 25:35–36.

49 'It is not your place to tell us what we should do'.

50 'Oh, go and lecture to your old shoes [it would be just as effective], you interfering, chattering fool, because we will not become members of [your] new-fangled sect.'

JOANNES BAPTISTA
Great folye is it of Abraham so to boost;
Where his fayth is not, the kyndred is sone lost.
Ye are Abrahams chyldren, lyke as was Ismael,[51]
Onlye in the fleshe, to whom no blessynge fell.
It profyteth yow lyttle of Abraham to beare the name
If ye be wycked, but rather it is your shame.
And, as touchynge Abraham, the Lorde is able to rayse
Of stones in the waye, such people as shall Hym prayse.
The Gentyles can He call, whom ye very sore despyse,
To Abraham's true faythe, and graces for them devyse.
No harte is so harde, but He can it mollefye,
No synner so yll, but He maye him justyfye.

PHARISAEUS
Yea, He told the[e] so: thu art next of Hys counsell
And knowest what He myndeth to do in Heaven and in Hell!
Now, forsoth, thu art a jolye Robyne Bell!

SADDUCAEUS
Wyth a lytle helpe, of an heretyke he wyll smell.[52]

JOANNES BAPTISTA
I se it very wele: agaynst Gods truthe ye are bent,
And come not hyther your wicked wayes to repent
For that Prynces sake that will clere us of care;
But your commynge is to trappe me in a snare.

SADDUCAEUS
We know hym not, we nor wyll not knowe hym in dede.
But, whan he shall come, if he do sowe soch sede
As thu hast done here, he maye chaunce to have yll spede.

JOANNES BAPTISTA
Be ware if ye lyst, the axe is put to the rote;
With the Lorde to mocke, it will ye no longar bote.
Every wythered tre that wyll geve no good frute
Shall up (whych are yow of all grace destytute)[53]
And shall be throwne fourth into everlastynge fyre,
Where no helpe can be, for no pryce nor desyre.[54]

PHARISAEUS
A lewde knave art thu: yll doctryne dost thu teache.
We wyll so provyde, thu shalt no longar preache.

SADDUCAEUS
If we do not se for thys gere a dyreccyon,
This fellawe is lyke to make an insurreccyon;
For to hys newe lernynge an infynyte cumpanye
Of worldlye rascalles come hyther suspycyouslye.

PHARISAEUS
In dede they do so, and therfor lete us walke,
Upon thys matter more delyberatlye to talke.

[*Exit Pharisaeus and Sadducaeus.*]

JOANNES BAPTISTA
The nature of these is styll lyke as it hath be:
Blasphemers they are of God and Hys veryte.
Here have I preached the baptyme of repentaunce;
After me He cometh that is of moch more puysaunce.
For all my austeryte of lyfe and godly purpose,
Worthye I am not Hys lachettes to unlose.[55]
He wyll yow baptyse in the Holy Ghost and fyre,
Makynge yow more pure than your heart can desyre.
His fanne is in hande, whych is Gods judgement
Unto Hym commytted by Hys Father omnypotent.
He wyll from Hys floore, which is Hys congregacyon,
Swepe away all fylth and false dyssymulacyon.[56]
Cleane wyll He seclude the disguysed hypocrytes,
And restore agayne the perfyght Israelytes.
He wyll brynge the wheate into Hys barne or grayner,
The chyldren of faythe to the Kyngedome of Hys father;

283 boast 284 claim to kinship 290 by the roadside 291 despise 293 soften 294 (is) so evil, redeem 296 intends 297 (proverbial?) a boaster 301 redeem us from sorrow 303 (i.e. the prince you speak of) 304 seeds (of heresy) 305 bad luck 306 root 307 longer do you good 314 arrange to settle this matter 315 provoke 316 company/crowd 317 rascals/wretches, comes here 319 seriously/purposefully 320 as it always has been 323 power 324 austerity 328 winnowing fan 329 delegated 330 threshing floor 332 He will banish completely 334 granary

51 Ishmael was the illegitimate son of Abraham by the handmaiden Hagar, and thus of lesser status than the patriarch's legitimate sons. See Genesis 16:11–16, 17:1–27.

52 'If we encouraged him a little, he would show signs of heresy.'

53 'Shall [be pulled] up, and you, who are destitute of all grace, are such [trees]'.

54 See Luke 3:16.

55 'I am not worthy to untie the laces of his shoes.' See Luke 3:16.

56 See Luke 3:12.

The c[h]affe unprofytable, whych are the unfaithful sort
Into Hell shall go, to their sorowfull dysconfort.

Jesus Christus
I am Jesus Christ, the sonne of the lyvynge God,
The lyght of Hys glorye, the ymage of Hys substaunce.
Though He to thys daye hath plaged man with the rod,
Yet now for My sake he hath withdrawn all vengeaunce,
All rygour, all fearcenesse, with Hys whole hartes displesaunce,
Sendynge Me hyther, of Hys benyvolence,
To suffer one deathe for all the worldes offence.

The tyme prefixed of My celestyall Father
Is now perfourmed, I reignynge in thys nature,
Borne of a woman, yea of a vyrgyne rather,
Subject to the lawe, for man which is unpure,
From death dampnable hys pardon to procure,
That he maye receyve the hygh inherytaunce
Due to the chyldren of Hys choyce or allowaunce.[57]

If ye will nedes knowe wherfor I am incarnate,
It is to be head of your whole congregacyon,
To make means for ye to pacyfye the hate,
To be the hygh prest that shall worke your salvacyon,
Your gyde, your confort, your helth, your consolacyon.
I come not to judge, nor slee, but all to save;
Come therfor to Me all yow that lyfe wyll have.

I am become flesh, for Myne own promes sake,
Without mannys sede borne, hys kynde to sanctfye;
Of synnars lynage, the synners quarell to take,[58]
Of patryarkes and kynges, as a father and gyde heavenlye,
Poore that ye shuld thynke My kyngedome nothing worldlye,
In flesh to the sprete that the Gospell shuld ye brynge,[59]
Belevynge by Me to have the lyfe everlastynge.

Ye worldlye people, lerne gentylnesse of Me:
Which, though I am God, unto the Father coequal,
I toke thys nature, with all dyscommodyte
My selfe to humble as a creature here mortall,
To rayse ye to God, from your most deadlye fall.
Lete thys example be grafted first in your wytt,
How I for baptyme to Johan My selfe submytt.

Joannes Baptista
By the Holy Ghost assured I am thys houre
That thys man is He whych is of the hyghar poure,
Whom I have preached, the lambe of innocencye,
Whose shoe to unlose, my self is far unworthye.
From whens do ye come? I pray ye, tell to me.

Jesus Christus
From Nazareth thys houre, a cytie of Galyle,
From my mothers howse, the Heavenly Father from hence
To obeye and serve with most due reverence.

Joannes Baptista
Your intent or mynde fayne wolde I understande.

Jesus Christus
To receyve with other the baptyme of thy hande.

Hic protensis manibus baptismo illum prohibet.[60]

Joannes Baptista
Requyre not of me, I desyre The[e], instauntlye,
To presume so farre; for doubtlesse I am unworthye.
I, a carnall synner, ought to have baptyme of The[e],
My Lorde and Saver. And dost thu axe it of me?
Perdon me, swete Lorde, for I wyll not so presume.

Jesus Christus
Without presumpcyon that offyce shalt thu adsume.

340 plagued/punished 342 displeasure 343 through 345 prearranged by 346 arrived 348 who, impure 352 why 355 priest, achieve 357 slay, to save everyone 359 promise's 362 patriarchs 365 through 366 from 368 (human) nature, disadvantages 371 fixed (to grow), mind 374 higher power 375 innocence 376 am completely unworthy 378 Galilee 382 (the) others 383 instantly/now 387 pardon 388 assume/take on

57 i.e. the 'elect', chosen by God for salvation.

58 'Born without [the use of] man's seed in order to sanctify [all those who share] his nature; [born] of a sinful lineage, to take on the sinners' quarrel'.

59 '[I was born] poor, so that you should understand that my kingdom is not a worldly one; [born] in the flesh, so that the Gospel may bring you to the spirit'.

60 'Here [John], with his hands held up, withholds baptism from Him.' For John's initial reluctance to baptize Jesus, see Matthew 3:14.

JOANNES BAPTISTA
The baptyme of me is but a shaddow or type;
Soch is Thy baptyme as awaye all synne doth wype.
I geve but water; the sprete, Lorde, Thu dost brynge.
Lowe is my baptyme; Thyne is an heavenly thynge.
Now Thu art present, it is mete my baptyme ceace;
And Thyne to florysh, all synners bondes to releace.
Me, Thy poore servaunt, replenish here with grace,
And requyre me not to baptyse The[e] here in place.

JESUS CHRISTUS
Johan, suffre Me now in thys to have My wyll,
For us it behoveth all righteousnesse to fulfyll;
That is to say, Me, as wele as these My servauntes,
The great graunde captayne, so wele as hys poore tenauntes.
I come not hither to break the laws of My Father,
As thy baptyme is one, but to confirme them rather.
If I, by the lawe, in yewth was circumcysed,
Why shuld I dysdayne thys tyme to be baptysed?
The Pharysees abhorre to be of the comon sort,
But I maye not so, whych come for all mennys confort.
I must go with them, they are My bretherne all:
He is no good captayne that from hys armye fall.

JOANNES BAPTISTA
They are synners, Lorde, and from good lyvynge wyde.

JESUS CHRISTUS
The more nede is theirs to have Me for their gyde.
I wyll go afore, that they maye folow Me,
Whych shall be baptysed and thynke Me for to be
Their mate or brother, havynge their lyverye token,
Whych is thy baptyme, as thy self here hath spoken.
Take water therefor and baptyse Me thys houre,
That thy baptyme maye take strength of hyghar poure,
The people to marke unto My Kyngedome Heavenlye.

JOANNES BAPTISTA
Then, Blessed Saver, Thy servaunt here sanctyfye.

JESUS CHRISTUS
The man whych have fayth lacketh no sanctyfycacyon
Necessary and mete for hys helth and salvacyon:[61]
Thyne offyce therfor now execute thu on Me.

Hic Joannem sublevat Jesus ac eius baptismo se submittit.[62]

JOANNES BAPTISTA
I baptyse The[e], Lorde, by soch autoryte
As Thy grace hath geven to my poore symplenesse,
Onlye to obeye the hygh request of Thy goodnesse.

In terram procumbens Jesus tunc dicit Deo gratias.[63]

JESUS CHRISTUS
Thys offyce, Father, whych I in thys mortall nature
Do take upon Me at Thy most hygh appoyntment
For mannys salvacyon, here to appeyse Thy hature,
So prospere forewarde that it be to Thy intent
And to Thy people fytte and convenyent,
And that Thu wytsave be Thy most Fatherly poure,
Thy Sonne to commende unto the worlde thys houre.

Descendit tunc super Christum Spiritus Sanctus in columbae specie et vox Patris caelo audietur hoc modo:[64]

PATER CAELESTIS
Thys is Myne Owne Sone and only hartes delyght,
My treasure, My joye, beloved most inteyrlye;
Thys is He whych hath procured grace in My syght
For man that hath done most wylfull trayterye.
Alone is it He that Me doth pacyfye,
For Hys only sake with man am I now content.[65]
To be for ever at a full peace and agrement.

I charge ye, to Hym geve dylygent attendaunce.
Heare Hys monycyons; regarde Hys Heavenly doctryne.

389 prefiguration 390 that it will wipe away 393 fitting (that), cease 394 flourish, release 397 permit 398 For it is appropriate for us all 400 leader, as well, tenants 402 Of which 407 brethren 409 far from good living 410 The greater is their need 413 equal, livery 416 from (the) 417 mark (out for) 420 appropriate 421 perform your role 427 appease Thy hatred 428 advance 430 vouchsafe/grant, power 431 (at) this 433 entirely 435 treachery 439 command, service 440 instructions

61 Bale adds this clear endorsement of the Lutheran doctrine of justification by faith alone to his biblical sources.
62 'Here Jesus lifts up John and submits to his baptism.'
63 'Prostrating Himself, Jesus then voices His thanks to God.'
64 'Then the Holy Spirit descends upon Christ in the form of a dove, and the voice of the Father is heard from heaven in this way'. See Luke 3:22.
65 'Only for His sake am I now content with man.' A further endorsement of the doctrine of salvation by faith in Christ rather than human works.

In mennys tradycyons loke ye have no affyaunce,
Nor in Moses lawe, but as He shall defyne.
Heare Hym, beleve Hym, drawe only after Hys lyne,
For He alone knoweth My purpose towardes yow,
And non els but He; heare Hym therefor only now.

Tunc Caelum inspiciens Joannes incurvat genua.[66]

JOANNES BAPTISTA
O tyme most joyfull, daye most splendiferus!
The clerenesse of Heaven now apereth unto us.
The Father is hearde, and the Holy Ghost is seane,
The Sonne incarnate to puryfye us cleane.
By thys we maye se, the Gospell ones receyved,
Heaven openeth to us, and God is hyghly pleased.
Lete us synge therfor togyther, with one accorde,
Praysynge these same thre as one God and good Lorde.

Et expansis ad Caelum manibus canit Joannes:[67]

Glorye be to the Trynyte,
The Father, the Sonne, and Sprete Lyvynge,
Whych are one God in persones thre,
To whom be prayse without endynge.

BALEUS PROLOCUTOR
Thys vysyble sygne do here to yow declare
What thynge pleaseth God and what offendythe Hys goodnesse.
The worlde hath proude hartes, hygh myndes, wyth soch lyke ware;
God only regardeth the sprete of lowlynesse.
Marke in thys Gospell with the eyes of symplenesse:
Adam by hys pryde ded Paradyse up speare,
Christ hath opened Heaven by Hys great mekenesse heare.

Johan was a preacher; note wele what he ded teache:
Not mennys tradycyons, nor hys owne holye lyfe,
But to the people Christ Jesus ded he preache,
Wyllynge Hys Gospell amonge them to be ryfe,
Hys knowledge heavenly to be had of man and wyfe.
But who receyved it? The sinfull commynalte,
Publicanes, and synners, but no paynted Pharyse.

The waye that Johan taught was not to weare harde clothynge,
To saye longe prayers, nor to wandre in the desart,
Or to eate wylde locusts. No, he never taught soch thynge.[68]
Hys mynde was that faythe shuld puryfye the hart.
My ways, sayth the Lorde, with mennys ways have no part:
Mannys ways are all thynges that are done without fayth,
Gods waye is Hys worde, as the Holy Scripture sayth.

If ye do penaunce, do soch as Johan doth counsell:
Forsake your old lyfe and to the true fayth applye,
Washe away all fylth and folowe Christes Gospell.
The justyce of men is but an hypocresye,
A worke without fayth, an outwarde vayne glorye.
An example here ye had of the Pharysees,
Whom Johan compared to unfruteful, wythered trees.

Geve eare unto Christ, lete mennys vayne fantasyes go,
As the Father bad by Hys most hygh comaundement.
Heare neyther Frances, Benedyct, nor Bruno,[69]
Albert nor Domynyck, for they newe rulers invent.
Beleve neyther Pope, nor prest of hys consent.
Folowe Christes Gospell, and therin fructyfye,
To the prayse of God and Hys Sonne Jesus glorye.

THUS ENDETH THYS BREFE COMEDY OR ENTERLUDE OF JOHAN BAPTYSTES PREACHYNGE IN THE WYLDERNESSE, OPENYNGE THE CRAFTYE ASSAULTES OF THE HYPOCRYTES WITH THE GLORYOUSE BAPTYME OF JESUS CHRIST. COMPYLED BY JOHAN BALE. ANNO M.D.XXXVIII.[70]

441 faith 442 determine 443 follow, lead 445 hear only Him 446 full of splendour 447 purity 448 seen 450 once the Gospel is accepted 452 agreement 455 Living Spirit 458 sign does 460 things 461 favours (only), humility 463 close up (against us) 464 here 468 spread 469 woman 470 common people 471 deceitful 472 harsh 473 wander, desert 475 intention 476 do not accord 483 deed 486 Listen, let 489 rules/rulers 490 who follows him 491 become fruitful 492 the glory of His Son

66 'Then, looking towards Heaven, John kneels down.'

67 'And, holding up his hands to Heaven, John sings'.

68 Bale argues that John's true example was not the harsh material conditions of his life (aspects of which were reflected in the hair shirts, frugal diets, and frequent prayers of the monks, nuns, and friars of Bale's own day) but the message of his teachings. For John's austerity, see Matthew 3:4.

69 Bale goes on to list the founders of the religious orders of his own day. St Francis founded the Franciscan friars, St Benedict the Benedictine monks, and St Bruno the Carthusian friars. St Albert devised the rule followed by the Carmelite friars, and St Dominic founded the Dominican order of friars.

70 1538.

The Three Laws, title page, *c.*1548. Courtesy of the Bodleian Library, Oxford.

John Bale, *The Three Laws*

The Three Laws continues Bale's attempt to create a Protestant drama. Basing his model upon interpretations of the Scripture, Bale dramatizes a universal history consisting of three ages: the Age of Nature, the Age of Moses, and the Age of Christ, each governed by its own distinct law. Each age is, however, subverted by the malignant influence of Infidelitas (Infidelity), the chief Vice of the play, who calls upon the services of three pairs of vicious allies. Like the Pharisee and Sadducee in *John Baptystes Preachynge*, these Vices are symbolic of the Catholic priesthood and what Bale saw as its abuses. Thus Idololatria (a bizarre, transsexual figure) represents the worship of images and false gods in both the Mosaic period and Bale's own day, while Sodomismus represents both the spiritual whoredom of the enemies of Israel and the sexual corruptions (both hetero- and homosexual) alleged against the monks and friars of sixteenth-century England. Bale uses his copious knowledge of church history (gained from his days as an ecclesiastical historian and his studies in numerous monastic libraries) to combine these figures into a coherent assault upon the forces that he saw as obscuring the simple truth of Christ's Gospel throughout history. The end result is galvanized in the fires of his polemical imagination and his deep distrust of cloistered religion into a powerful assault upon the traditions and practices of orthodox spirituality.

The bulk of the play was probably written in *c.* 1538,[1] but was revised for publication in *c.* 1548, when the reference to the death of Henry VIII and the final prayers for Edward VI and his counsellors were added.

The play falls naturally into five acts or movements, and Bale is helpfully forthcoming about the casting and costumes necessary for a production. The printed text contains a doubling plan for five actors, in which the first plays the Prolocutor, Fides Christiana, and Infidelitas; the second Naturae Lex, Avaritia, and Pseudodoctrina; the third Moseh Lex, Idololatria, and Hypocrisis; the fourth Christi Lex, Ambitio, and Sodomismus; and the fifth Deus Pater and Vindicta Dei. The costume notes are as follows: 'Let Idolatry be decked lyke an olde wytche, sodomy lyke a monke of all sectes,[2] Ambycyon lyke a byschop, Covetousnesse [i.e. Avaritia] lyke a Pharyse or spyrituall law[y]er, False Doctryne lyke a popysh doctour, and Hypocresy lyke a graye fryre. The rest of the partes are easye ynough to conjecture.' The Three Laws each carry a symbol of their true natures, given to them by God. Naturae Lex has an emblematic human heart, Moseh Lex the tablets of the Mosaic Law, and Christi Lex a copy of the New Testament. Against the certainty of these fixed symbols the agents of evil appear in a bewildering variety of forms and guises. Infidelitas (true to his name, the most protean of them all) changes from a pedlar to a friar and seems to switch between a clerical and a lay persona depending upon whom he is talking to.

The text printed here is based upon that printed *c.* 1548 by Dirik van der Straten in Wesel (STC 1287). In addition I have consulted the modern edition in Peter Happé, ed., *The Complete Plays of John Bale* (2 vols, Cambridge, 1985–6), II, pp. 65–124.

[*Dramatis personae*: *Baleus Prolocutor* (Bale the Presenter), *Deus Pater* (God the Father), *Naturae Lex* (The Law of Nature), *Moseh Lex* (The Law of Moses), *Christi Lex* (The Law of Christ), *Infidelitas* (Infidelity, the chief Vice), *Sodomismus* (Sodomy), *Idololatria* (Idolatry),[3] *Avaritia* (Avarice), *Ambitio* (both 'Ambition' and 'Vanity'), *Evangelium* (The Gospel/Word of God), *Pseudodoctrina* (False doctrine), *Hypocrisis* (Hypocrisy), *Vindicta Dei* (The Vengeance of God),[4] *Fides Christiana* (Christian Faith).

A Comedy Concerning thre lawes, of Nature,
Moses, and Christ, Corrupted
by the Sodomytes, Pharysees, and Papystes.
Compyled by Johan Bale. Anno M.D. XXXVIII.

[1] The allusion to Cardinal Pole at l. 2047, for example, makes most sense in the context of the cardinal's diplomatic manoeuvres in the late 1530s. See Walker, *Plays of Persuasion*, pp. 194–210.

[2] i.e. in a multi-coloured habit.

[3] Idololatria's name represents a pun, combining both 'idolatry', the abuse alleged by reformers against Catholics as a result of their use of images, and '*latria*', the term used by Catholic theologians to describe the legitimate use of prayers to the Saints. Bale thus uses the name to suggest that even such legitimate devotion is a form of idolatry.

[4] Vindicta Dei is an aspect of Deus Pater, and is played by the same actor. Once he has done his job in vanquishing Infidelitas, he lays aside his rod of punishment and 'becomes' Deus Pater once more.

BALEUS PROLOCUTOR
In ych commen welthe most hygh prehemynence
Is due unto lawes for soch commodyte
As is had by them. For, as Cicero[5] geveth sentence:
Where as is no lawe can no good order be[6]
In nature, in people, in howse, nor yet in citie.
The bodyes above are underneth a lawe;
Who coulde rule the worlde were it not undre awe?

Lyke as Chrysippus,[7] [f]ull clarkely, doth dyffyne,
Lawe is a teacher of matters necessary,
A knowledge of thynges both naturall and devyne,
Perswadynge all truth, dysswadynge all injury;[8]
A gyfte of the Lorde, devoyde of all obprobry,
An wholesom doctryne of men dyscrete and wyse,
A grace from above and a very heavenly practyse.

Our Heavenly Maker, mannys lyvynge to dyrect,
The lawes of Nature, of Bondage, and of Grace,
Sent into thys worlde with vycyousnesse infect,[9]
In all ryghteousnesse to walke before Hys face.
But Infydelyte so worketh in every place
That under the heavens no thynge is pure and
cleane,
So moch the people to hys perverse wayes leane.

The Lawe of Nature hys fylthy dysposycyon
Corrupteth with ydolles and stynkynge Sodometry,
The Lawe of Moses with Avaryce and Ambycyon
He also poluteth; and ever contynually
Christes Lawe he defyleth with cursed hypocresy
And with false doctryne, as wyll apere in presence
To the edyfyenge of thys Christen audyence.

[*Enter Deus Pater, Naturae Lex, Moseh Lex, and Christi Lex.*]

Of Infydelyte God wyll Hymself revenge
With plages of water, of wyldefyre, and of sworde.
And of Hys people due homage He wyll chalenge
Ever to be knowne for their God and good lorde
After that He hath those lawes agayne restorde
To their first bewtye commyttynge them to fayth.
He is now in place: marke therfor what He sayth.
(Exit.)

ACTUS PRIMUS: DE LEGIBUS DIVINUS.[10]

DEUS PATER
I am *Deus Pater*, a substaunce invysyble,
All one with the Sonne and Holy Ghost in essence.
To angell and man I am incomprehensyble,
A strength infynyte, a ryghteousnesse, a prudence,
A mercy, a goodnesse, a truth, a lyfe, a sapyence.
In Heaven and in Earth We made all to Our glory
Man ever havynge in a specyall memory.

Man, I saye agayne, whych is Our owne elect,
Our chosen creature, and servaunt over all,
Above the others peculyarly select
To do Us homage and on Our name to call,
Acknowledgynge Us for hys author princypall,
Indued hym We have with gyftes of specyall grace
And lawes wyll We sende to governe hym in place.

Steppe fou[r]th ye iii Lawes for gydaunce of
mankynde
Whom most inteyrly in hart We love and faver,
And teach hym to walke accordynge to Our mynde,
In clennes of lyfe and in a gentyll behaver.
Depely instruct hym Our mysteryes to saver,
By the workes of fayth all vyces to seclude
And preserve in hym Our Godly symylytude.

NATURAE LEX
Of duty we ought alwayes to be obeysaunt
To Your commaundement, for just it is and
plesaunt.

MOSEH LEX
Your preceptes are true and of perpetuall strength,
On justyce grounded as wyll apere at length.

1 each, pre-eminence 2 usefulness 3 teaches 5 household 6 (i.e. the governors) 7 through fear (of the law) 8 defines in a scholarly way 10 divine 12 shame 21 his (i.e. Infidelity's) 22 his (Infidelity's), nature 23 idols, Sodomy 25 always 27 be shown, (your) presence 29 Upon 30 plagues, wild-fire 31 from, demand 34 beauty 35 (i.e. onstage, pay attention) 40 wisdom 42 Always keeping humanity 45 particularly 47 creator 49 here 50 forward, three 51 entirely, favour 52 (i.e. live) 53 purity, behaviour 54 Thoroughly, savour/relish 55 exclude 56 likeness 57 Through, obedient 59 rules 60 appear

5 Marcus Tullius Cicero (106–43 BC), the poet, rhetorician, and orator. The reference is to *De Legibus* ('On the Laws'), III, 2.3.

6 'Where there is no law, no good order can exist'.

7 The Greek philosopher Chrysippus (*c.*280–207 BC), leader of the Stoics from 232 BC.

8 'Persuading us toward all truth and dissuading us from all injury/wrong-doing'.

9 'In order to regulate human existence in a world corrupted by vice, God sent the Laws of Nature, Bondage, and Grace [i.e. the Laws of Nature, Moses, and Christ]'.

10 'Act One: Concerning the Divine Laws.'

CHRISTI LEX
Proudenesse Ye abhorre with lyke inconvenyentes.
All they are cursed wych go from Your Commaundementes

DEUS PATER
Our Lawes are all one, though yow do thre apere,
Lyke wyse as Our wyll is all one in effect.[11]
But bycause that man in hymself is not clere,
To tyme and persone as now We have respect;
And as thre teachers to hym We yow dyrect.[12]
Though We be but one, in token that We are thre,
Dystyncte in persone and one in the Deyte.

NATURAE LEX
We consydre that for as concernynge man
Foure severall tymes are moch to be respected:
Of innocency first, of hys transgressyon than,
Than the longe season wherin he was afflycted,
Fynally the tyme wherin he was redemed:
Of pleasure is the first, the seconde of exyle,
The third doth ponnysh, the fort doth reconcyle.

MOSEH LEX
Whan angell[13] was made, thys lawe he had by and by,
To serve Yow, hys Lorde, and with laudes to prosecute.
Thys lawe was geven man in tyme of innocency,
In no wyse to eate of the forbydden frute.
These two lawes broken, both they were destytute
Of their first fredome, to their most hygh decaye,[14]
Tyll Your only Sonne ded mannys whole raunsome paye.[15]

CHRISTI LEX
Whan angell in Heaven and man in Paradyse
Those lawes had broken, the lawe of wycked Sathan
Impugned Your lawes by craft and subtyle practyse.
Where Yow sayd 'Eate not', he sayd unto the woman
'Eate. Ye can not dye. As godes ye shall be than.'
By thys first of all Your [lawes] man proved true
And Sathans lawe false, whych he now dayly rue.

DEUS PATER
Lete hym than beware how he Our lawes neglect.
Only to angell and man We gave lyberte
And they onlye fell, becommynge a frowarde sect,
Not by Our mocyon but their owne vanyte.
For that We gave them to their felycyte
Abused they have,[16] to their perpetuall evyll.
Man is now mortall, and angell become a devyll.

Lose man we wyll not, tho[u]gh he from Us doth fal;
Our love towardes hym wyll be moch better than so.
Thu, Lawe of Nature, teache thu hym first of all
Hys Lorde God to knowe, and that is ryght to do.
Charge and enforce hym in the wayes of Us to go.
Thu, Lawe of Moses; and Christes Lawe fynally,
Rayse hym and save hym to Our perpetuall glory.

NATURAE LEX
For tyme of exyle, than, I must be hys teacher.

DEUS PATER
Yea, for thre ages both gyde and governer:
From Adam to Noah, from Noah to Abraham,
And than to Moses, whych is the sonne of Amram.[17]

NATURAE LEX
Where must I remayne, for the tyme I shall be here?

DEUS PATER
In the hart of man hys conscyence for to stere
To ryghteouse lyvynge, and to a just beleve.
In token wherof, thys hart to the[e] I geve.

Hic pro suo signo cor mi[n]istrat.[18]

Thu shalt want no grace to co[n]fort hym with all,
If he to the fayth of My first promyse fall.

61 similar, offences 62 who stray 65 perfect 68 only 69 Distinct, Deity 71 Four distinct periods need to be noted 72 innocence, then/next 76 fourth 78 to perform (acts of) praise 80 way 81 both Adam and Lucifer were 86 guile, subtle 88 then 89 man found Your law to be true 90 he (humanity), regrets 93 disobedient 94 instigation, vanity 99 than that 100 You teach him 101 what (it) 102 Instruct, live 105 During (the) 110 guide 111 Towards, belief/faith 112 As a sign, heart 113 lack 114 keeps/sticks

[11] Like the Trinity itself, God's Laws are both threefold, yet unified.

[12] 'We now take account of the individual circumstances of history and personality, and so send you three [Laws] to him as teachers.'

[13] The allusion is specifically to Lucifer and the fallen angels.

[14] 'Of their original freedom, to their most serious loss/decline'.

[15] 'Did pay humanity's whole ransom.'

[16] 'Those things which We gave them for their happiness they have abused'.

[17] See Exodus 6:20.

[18] 'He shows him a heart for a sign.'

Moseh Lex
Then my course is next, for tyme of hys ponnishment.

Deus Pater
For thre ages more to the[e] must he consent:
From Moses to David, from thens to the Jewes exyle,
And so fourth to Christ, whych wyll man reconcyle.

Moseh Lex
Where shall I, swete Lorde, for that same season dwell?

Deus Pater
With soch harde rulers as wyll the people compell
Our mynde to fulfyll without vayne gaudes or fables.
For a sygne of thys, holde these same stony tables.

Hic pro signo lapideas dat ei tabulas.[19]

All they that observe Our lawes invyolablye
Shall every where prospere, increase, and multyplye.

Christi Lex
Then I perceyve well My course is last of all.

Deus Pater
What though it be so? Yet art Thu pryncypall;
[Over all] the worlde Thy beames shalt Thu extende,
And styll contynue tyll the worlde be at an ende.

Christi Lex
Where shall I, Father, for that same tyme persever?

Deus Pater
With the faythfull sort must Thu contynue ever.
Thu shalt My people returne from farre exyle
And for evermore to My grace reconcyle.
Take thys precyouse boke for a token evydent,
A seale of My covenaunt, and a lyvynge testament.

Hic pro signo dat ei Novum Testamentum.[20]

They that beleve it shall lyve for evermore,
And they that do not wyll rue their folye sore.
Blessed shall he be that yow, My lawes, wyll kepe
In cytie and felde, whether he do worke or slepe.
Hys wyfe shall encreace; hys land shall frutyfye;
And of hys enemyes he shall have vyctorye.
The skye wyll geve rayne whan seasonable tyme shall be;
The workes of hys handes shall have prosperyte.
Cursed shall they be that wyll not Our lawes fulfyll,
Without and within, at market and at myll.
Or corne and cattell they shall have non increase;
Within their owne howse shall sorowes never cease;
Never shall they be without byle, botche, or blayne;
The pestylence and poxe wyll worke them deadly payne.
Shewe thys unto Man and byd hym take good hede
Of Our ryghteousnesse to stande alwayes in drede.
We vysyte the synne and the great abhomynacyon
Of the wycked sort to thirde and fort generacyon.
Thu, Lawe of Nature, instruct hym first of all;
Thu, Lawe of Moses, correct hym for hys fall;
And thu, Lawe of Christ, geve hym a godly mynde,
Rayse hym unto grace, and save hym from the Fynde
Our heavenly blessynge be with yow, everychone.

Omnes Simul.
All prayse and glory to Your Majeste alone.

Christi Lex
Here styll to tarry I thynke it be your mynde.

Naturae Lex
My offyce, ye knowe, is to instruct mankynde.

Moseh Lex
Than God be with yow; we leave ye here behynde.
(*Exeunt*)

FINIT ACTUS PRIMUS.[21]

INCIPIT ACTUS SECUNDUS: NATURAE LEX CORRUPTA.[22]

Naturae Lex
The lawe in effect is a teacher generall;
What is to be done, and what to be layed asyde:
But, as touchynge me, the first Lawe Naturall,
A knowledge I am whom God in man doth hyde,

121 tricks 122 tablets 123 inviolable 124 prosper 125 role 126 if, the most important 129 persevere/remain 130 people, always 131 shall, distant 132 reconcile (them) 133 precious, clear sign 134 living 136 folly sorely 138 field 139 be fertile, bear fruit 141 give 145 no 147 boil, ulcer, blister 148 pox (disease), cause 150 punish 151 (the) third, fourth 156 Fiend (i.e. Satan) 157 each one 159 wait, intention 160 role 163 rejected 164 concerning

19 'Here He gives him tables of stone for a sign.'
20 'Here He gives him the New Testament for a sign.'
21 'Here ends the First Act.'
22 'Here Begins the Second Act: The Law of Nature Corrupted.'

In hys whole workynge to be to hym a gyde,
To honour hys God and seke hys neybers helth,
A great occasyon of peace and publyque welth.

A sore charge I have, mankynde to over se,
And to instruct hym hys Lorde God to obaye.
That Lorde of Heaven graunt I may so do my dewtie
That He be pleased, and man brought to a staye.
Hys bryttle nature, hys slyppernesse to waye,
Moch doth provoke me; but if God set to hande
He shall do full wel, for non maye Hym withstande.

[*Enter Infidelitas, dressed as a pedlar.*][23]

INFIDELITAS
Brom, brom, brom, brom, brom!
Bye brom, bye, bye!
Bromes for shoes and powcherynges,
Botes and buskyns for newe bromes.
Brom, brom, brom!

Marry, God geve ye good even,
And the holyman Saynt Steven
Sende ye a good Newe Yeare.[24]
I wolde have brought ye the paxe,[25]
Or els an ymage of waxe,
If I had knowne ye heare.

I wyll my selfe so handle
That ye shall have a candle
Whan I come hyther agayne.
At thys your soden mocyon,
I was in soch devocyon,
I had nere broke a vayne.[26]

NATURAE LEX
That myght have done ye smart.

INFIDELITAS
No, no, it was but a fart;
For pastyme of my hart
I wolde ye had it forsoth
In serupp or in sowse,
But for noyaunce of the howse,
For easement of your toth.[27]

Now have I my dreame in dede,
God send me wele to spede
And swete Saynt Antony.[28]
I thought I shuld mete a knave,
And now that fortune I have
Amonge thys cumpany.

NATURAE LEX
Why dost thu call me knave?

INFIDELITAS
I sayd I wolde be your slave,
Yf your grace wolde me have,
And do your worke anon.
I wolde so rubbe your botes,
The rofe shuld from the rotes[29]
Whan ye shuld do them on.

NATURAE LEX
Thu art dysposed to mocke;
Sone mayst thu have a knocke,
If thu with me so game.

INFIDELITAS
Your mouth shall kysse my docke,
Your tonge shall it unlocke!
But I saye, what is your name?

NATURAE LEX
I am the Lawe of Nature.

INFIDELITAS
I thought so by your stature,
And by your auncyent gature,
Ye were of soch a rature,
Whan I first heard ye speke.

167 neighbour's, well-being 168 cause, public prosperity 169 serious responsibility, oversee 172 happy state/equilibrium 173 fragile, unreliability, weigh/consider 175 no one 176 Broom 177 Buy (my) broom 178 purse-clasps 179 Boots, half-boots 181 evening 186 you (were) here 193 caused you pain 200 My dream has come true 201 God bless me 203 meet, rogue 204 I've done so 210 boots 212 pull 213 inclined 215 play around 216 arse 221 posture/way of walking 222 nature/status

23 Infidelitas carries a broom, which he pretends to be selling. Given the nature of his spiritual influence, it is appropriate that we see him first as a salesman.

24 St Stephen's feast fell on 26 December.

25 The Pax: the tablet bearing an image of the Crucifixion used during the Mass.

26 'Your sudden move/request startled me so much, while I was at my prayers, that I nearly burst a blood-vessel.'

27 'If it wasn't for the inconvenience that it would cause in the house [through the smell], I would wish that you had it [the fart] preserved in syrup or sauce, to act as a remedy against toothache.'

28 St Anthony, a third-century Egyptian saint, one of the founders of monasticism.

29 'The roof [upper part of the boot] should [come away] from the roots [sole]'.

Ye commoned with God lately,
And now ye are Hys bayly,
Mankynde to rule dyscretely.
Welcome, syr huddypeke!

NATURAE LEX
If thu use soch vyllanye,
I shall dysplease the[e], trulye.

INFIDELITAS
By the Masse, I the[e] defye,
With thy whole cuckoldrye,
And all that with the[e] holde.

NATURAE LEX
Why dost thu me blaspheme,
And so ungodly deme?

INFIDELITAS
For, by thys blessed boke
I went ye had bene a coke,[30]
And that made me so bolde.

For a coke ones havynge age,
With a face demure and sage,
And auncyent to beholde,
As yow have here in place,
With a bearde upon your face,
What is he but a coke-olde?

NATURAE LEX
Ye are dysposed to dallye,
To leape and oversallye
The compasse of your wytte.
I counsell ye yet in season,
Sumwhat to folowe reason,
And gnawe upon the bytte.

INFIDELITAS
Then, after our great madnesse,
Lete us fall to some sadnesse,
And tell me what ye intende.

NATURAE LEX
God sent me unto man
To do the best I can
To cause hym to amende.

Soch creatures as want reason
My rules obye yche season,
And that in every bordre.
The sunne and mone doth move
With the other bodyes above
And never breake their ordre;

The trees and herbes doth growe,
The see doth ebbe and flowe,
And varyeth not a nayle.
The floudes and wholsom sprynges,
With other naturall thynges
Their course do never fayle.

The beastes and byrdes engendre,
So do the fyshes tendre,
Accordynge to their kynde;
Alonlye man doth fall
From good lawes naturall
By a frowarde, wycked mynde.

INFIDELITAS
Now wyll I prove ye a lyar,
Next cosyne to a fryar,
And on the gall ye rubbe.
Ye saye they folowe your lawe,
And varyee not a strawe,
Whych is a tale of a tubbe.

The sunne ones in the clyppes,
Awaye the clerenesse slyppes,
And darkened is the daye.
Of the planetes influence
Aryseth the pestylence
To manye ones decaye.[31]

224 communed/spoke 225 bailiff 227 sir fool 230 I defy you 232 all your allies 234 judge (me) 235 book 238 getting old 241 in this place 243 old cook/cuckold (a laboured pun) 244 waste time 245 overleap/exceed 246 limits 247 while it's possible 249 (i.e. restrain yourself) 251 seriousness 256 lack 257 obey 258 border/region 259 sun, moon 261 order 262 plants 263 sea 264 varies, (i.e. not at all) 265 rivers 267 Never stray from their course 268 birds, multiply 269 tender fishes 270 nature 271 Only humanity alone 273 disobedient/quarrelsome 274 liar 275 cousin (i.e. very like) 276 touch you on a sore point 278 vary/deviate 279 fable (i.e. nonsense) 280 during an eclipse 281 brightness disappears 284 Arises 285 many (a) person's

30 'I thought you were a cook'. If Naturae Lex still carries his symbol of the heart, there may well be a visual joke here, with Infidelitas characteristically mistaking the spiritual symbol for the corporeal main ingredient of a stew.

31 It was popularly believed that eclipses prompted natural catastrophes.

Doth not the see so rage
That non can it aswage,
And swellowe in towne and streate?
The ayre whych geveth breathe
Sumtyme infecteth to deathe
By hys most pestylent heate.

The beastes oft undemure,
Whych were left to mannys cure,
Wyll hym sumtyme devoure:
Thus are your rules forgote
As thynges of slendre note
In creatures, daye and houre.

NATURAE LEX
It is the wyll of God
To use them as a rod
Of Hys just ponnyshment,
Whan Man doth not regarde
The Lorde, nor Hys rewarde,
Nor to Hys lawes consent.

They never are so ronnysh
But whan God doth man ponnysh
For hys unhappynesse.
From God they never fall,
Nor from lawes naturall,
Doynge Hys busynesse.[32]

INFIDELITAS
And yow are the same lawe
That kepe them undre awe
By you[r] most polytyke wytt?

NATURAE LEX
God hath appoynted me
Mankynde to overse
And in hys hart to sytt;

To teache hym for to knowe
In the creatures hygh and lowe
Hys gloryouse Mageste,
And on Hys name to call
Or power celestyall
In hys necessyte;

To thynke Hym everlastynge
And wonderfull in workynge,
And that He createth all,
Both governe and conserve.
From them He never swerve
That to soch fayth wyll fall.[33]

INFIDELITAS
In dede here is good sport:
But why do yow resort
Unto thys present place?

NATURAE LEX
Man alwayes to exhort
To seke all helth and confort
Of the only God of grace;

First in the hartes rejoyce,
And than with open voyce
To worshypp Hym alone,
Knowledgynge Hys Deyte,
Hys power and eternyte,
Whan he shall make hys mone.

INFIDELITAS
I shall kepe ye as well from that
As my grandame kept her cat
From lyckynge of her creame.

NATURAE LEX
What wylt thu kepe me fro?
Tell me ere thu farther go:
Me thynke thu art in a dreame.

INFIDELITAS
From causynge of mankynde
To geve to God hys mynde
Or hys obedyence.

NATURAE LEX
What is thy name? Tell me.

INFIDELITAS
Marry, Infydelyte,
Whych never wyll agre
To your benyvolence.

286 sea 288 swallow up, street 289 air 290 infects (us) 291 its pestilential 292 Often the savage beasts 293 in, care 296 little importance 297 By, (i.e. regularly) 299 (i.e. an instrument) 304 fierce 305 except 306 sin 307 fail/separate 312 wise judgement (ironic) 314 oversee 316 recognize 321 time of need 325 governing, conserving (everything) 333 Only through 335 then 337 Deity 338 eternity 339 he (man), moan/complaint 340 prevent you 341 grandmother 345 dreaming 347 give, thought 352 With

32 i.e. all the instances of apparent misfortune that Infidelitas cites are not breaches of Natural Law but events sent by God to punish human sin.

33 'He will never abandon those who adopt such faith in Him.'

NATURAE LEX
Thu cannyst not kepe me from man.

INFIDELITAS
Yet wyll I do the best I can
To trouble ye now and than,
That ye shall not prevayle.
I wyll cause Ydolatrye,
And most vyle Sodomye
To worke so ongracyouslye
Ye shall of your purpose fayle.

NATURAE LEX
I defye the[e], wycked fynde,
With thy whole venemouse kynde!
God putteth now in my mynde
To fle thy cumpanye.

INFIDELITAS
Ye are so blessed a saynt,
And your self so wele can paynt,
That I must me acquaynt
With yow, no remedye.

NATURAE LEX
Avoyde, thu cruell enemye!
I wyll non of the[e], trulye,
But shurne thy cumpanye,
As I wolde the Devyll of Hell. (*Exit.*)

INFIDELITAS
And are ye gone in dede?
Small Wyttam[34] be your spede;
Except ye take good hede
I wyll be next of your counsell.

Now wyll I worke soch masterye,
By craftes and sutyle polycye,
The Lawe of Nature to poyson
With pestylent Ydolatrye,
And with most stynkynge Sodomye,
That he shall have no foyson.

Where are these vyllen knaves,
The Devyls owne kychyn slaves,
That them I can not se?
I conjure yow both here,
And charge ye to apere,
Lyke two knaves as ye be!

SODOMISMUS ([AS] MONACHUS)[35]
[*Calling from offstage*] *Ambo* is a name full cleane.
Knowe ye not what I meane,
And are so good a clarke?

INFIDELITAS
By Tetragrammaton,[36]
I charge ye, apere anon
And come out of the darke.

Intrant [*Sodomismus and Idololatria*] *simul.*[37]

SODOMISMUS
Have in, than, at a dash,
With swash, myry Annet, swash;[38]
Yet maye I not be to rash
For my holy orders sake.

IDOLOLATRIA ([AS] NECROMANTIC)[39]
Nor I, sonne, by my trouth.
Cha caute a corage of slouth,
And soch a comberouse couth,
Ych wote not what to do.[40]

INFIDELITAS
At Christmas and at Paske
Ye maye daunce the Devyll a maske
Whyls hys great cawdron plawe.
[*To Idololatria*] Yow soch a prati mynyon,
[*To Sodomismus*] And yow now in relygyon,
Soch two I never sawe.

Is not thy name Ydolatrye?

359 wickedly (that) 361 fiend 366 describe (fraudulently) 367 associate with you 368 there's no alternative 370 I want nothing to do with you 371 shun 376 your closest adviser 377 achieve, control 378 subtle tricks 382 prosperity 383 villainous 384 kitchen 387 appear 389 *Both*, good 391 scholar 395 Come 397 too 399 son 403 Easter 404 masque 405 cauldron boils 406 pretty companion 407 as a friar/monk

34 Happé notes a pun here: both 'little wit' and Little Witham, a village in Essex.
35 'Dressed as a monk'.
36 The 'four letters' of the name of God: 'YHVH' (for Yahweh), used in conjuration.
37 'They enter together.'
38 As Happé suggests, 'Swash, Merry Annet' may be a song refrain.
39 'Dressed as a Necromancer [a conjurer of the Dead]'.
40 'I caught a spirit from Sloth and such a burdensome nature that I don't know what to do.' Idololatria adopts a southern dialect (employing the southern forms 'ych' and 'cha' for 'I') here for comic effect.

SODOMISMUS
Yes, an wholsom woman, verelye,
And wele seane in phylosophye;
Mennys fortunes she can tell.
She can by sayenge her *Ave Marye*,
And by other charmes of sorcerye,
Ease men of toth ake, by and bye,
Yea, and fatche the Devyll from Hell.

She can mylke the cowe and hunte the foxe,
And helpe men of the ague and poxe,
So they brynge moneye to the boxe,
Whan they to her make mone.
She can fatch agayne all that is lost,
And drawe drynke out of a rotten post,[41]
Without the helpe of the Holye Ghost:
In workynge she is alone.

INFIDELITAS
What, sumtyme thuy wert an he!

IDOLOLATRIA
Yea, but now ych am a she,
And a good mydwyfe, *per De*,
Yonge chyldren can I charme,
With whysperynges and whysshynges,
With crossynges and with kyssynges,
With blasynges[42] and with blessynges,
That spretes do them no harme.

INFIDELITAS
Then art thu lyke to Clisthenes,
To Clodius and Euclides,
Sardinapalus and Hercules,[43]
Whych themselves oft transfourmed
Into a womannys lyckenes,
With agylyte and quyckenes.
But they had Venus syckenes,
As writers have declared.

SODOMISMUS
Lete her tell fourth her matter.

IDOLOLATRIA
With holye oyle and watter,
I can so cloyne and clatter,
That I can, at the latter,
Manye suttyltees contryve.
I can worke wyles in battle,
If I do ones but spattle,
I can make corne and cattle,
That they shall never thryve.

Whan ale is in the fatt,
If the bruar please me natt,
The cast shall fall downe flat,
And never have any strength.
No man shall tonne nor bake,
Nor meate in season make,
If I agaynst hym take,
But lose hys labour at length.

Their wellys I can up drye,
Cause trees and herbes to dye,
And slee all pullerye
Where as men doth me move.
I can make stoles to daunce,
And earthen pottes to praunce,
That non shall them enhaunce,
And do but cast my glove.[44]

I have charmes for the plowgh,
And also for the cowgh;

410 truly 411 schooled 412 Men's 413 saying, 'Hail Mary' 415 Relieve, toothache 416 fetch/summon 418 fever 419 cash-box 424 unique 425 (i.e. You used to be male) 427 by God! 429 wishings 432 (evil) spirits 437 likeness 438 agility 439 sickness (i.e. lust) 441 story 442 oil, water 443 feign, babble 444 by the time I'm finished 445 subtleties/tricks 446 perform wonders 447 spit 450 vat 451 brewer doesn't please me 452 product (i.e. beer), be ruined 454 brew 457 (he'll) waste his time 458 wells, dry up 459 plants 460 slay, poultry 461 When men anger me 462 stools 463 prance 466 plough 467 cow

41 Perhaps the equivalent of 'Get blood from a stone.'

42 'Blazings'. Happé suggests a reference to the light of candles. Idololatria is listing the trappings and ritual practices of the Catholic faith.

43 The classical cross-dressers listed are Calisthenes, the historian of Alexander the Great's eastern campaigns (perhaps an allusion to Alexander and his companions' adoption of 'effeminate' eastern dress); Clodius Publius (d.52 BC), who dressed in women's clothes at the festival of the Good Goddess in Rome in 62 BC; Euclides, the son of Hippocrates, tyrant of Syracuse; Sardanapalus (Assur-bani-pal), king of Assyria in the seventh century BC (who, according to John Skelton's translation of *The Bibliotheca Historica of Diodorus Siculus* (I, 166), 'addressed himself like unto a nice mistress, passing wanton of corage, feigned to speak in a feminine voice . . . and many times abused his body, sometime with active delectation as man, and sometime with passive pollutions suffered to be lain by as a woman'); and the Greek hero Hercules (who was made to dress and work as a handmaiden by Omphale, queen of Lydia). See n. 73 for the source of this list.

44 'No one will prosper: I only have to throw down my glove [to make it so].'

She shall geve mylke ynowgh,
So longe as I am pleased.
Apace the mylle shall go,
So shall the credle do,
And the musterde querne also,
No man therwith dyseased.

Infidelitas
Than art thu for me fytt!

Sodomismus
The woman hath a wytt,
And by her gere can sytt,
Though she be sumwhat olde.
It is myne owne swete bullye,
My muskyne[45] and my mullye,
My gelover and my cullye,
Yea, myne owne swetehart of golde.

Infidelitas
I saye yet not to bolde.

Idololatria
Peace, fondelinge, tush, a button!

Infidelitas
What, wylt thu fall to mutton,
And playe the hungry glutton,
Afore thys cumpanye?
Ranke love is full of heate;
Where hungry dogges lacke meate
They wyll durty puddynges eate
For want of befe and conye.

Hygh, mynyon, for monye,
As good is draffe as honye,'
Whan the daye is whote and sonnye,
By the blessed Rode of Kent.[46]

Sodomismus
Saye fourth your mynde, good mother,
For thys man is non other
But our owne lovynge brother,
And is very wele content.

Idololatria
I never mysse but paulter
Our Blessed Ladyes Psaulter[47]
Before Saynt Savers aulter,
With my bedes ones a daye.
And thys is my commen cast,
To heare Masse first or last,
And the Holy Frydaye fast,
In good tyme mowt I it saye.[48]

With blessynges of Saynt Germyne,[49]
I wyll me so determyne
That neyther foxe nor vermyne
Shall do my chuckens harme.
For your gese seke Saynt Legearde,[50]
And for your duckes Saynt Lenarde,[51]
For horse take Moyses yearde,
There is no better charme.

Take me a napkyn folte,
With the byas of a bolte,[52]
For the healynge of a colte,
No better thynge can be.
For lampes and for bottes[53]
Take me Saynt Wylfrides knottes,[54]
And holy Saynt Thomas lottes,[55]
On my lyfe I warande ye.

For the cowgh take Judas eare,[56]
With the parynge of a peare,
And drynke them without feare
If ye wyll have remedy.

468 enough 470 Quickly, mill 471 corn-cradle (a tool used in harvesting) 472 mustard-mill 473 will be disadvantaged 474 Then you're just the person I'm looking for 476 and she knows her trade 478 she is (baby talk), lover/dear 480 gilly-flower 481 sweetheart 482 Don't go too far (in trying to seduce Sodomismus) 483 Quiet, fool, (that's just) a trifle 484 start to pursue old flesh 486 In front of 487 Foul 489 blood-puddings/sausages (proverbial) 490 lack, rabbit 491 Ah well, friend 492 (i.e. beggars can't be choosers) 493 hot, sunny 495 Speak 497 Than 499 mumble 501 St Saviour's altar 502 once 503 usual practice 509 vermin 510 chickens 511 geese 513 Moses's staff 523 cough (lung disease) 524 peelings

45 Muskyne, mullye and cullye are baby-talk terms of endearment.

46 Probably, as Happé suggests, the Rood of Grace of Boxley, Kent: a 'miraculous' image (which proved, on inspection, to be worked mechanically) destroyed by Henry VIII's commissioners in 1538.

47 For Our Lady's Psalter, see the N-Town *Mary Play*, l. 1590.

48 Either a general superstitious saying: 'May it bring me good fortune', or Bale may be mocking the ritualistic nature of popular religious practice: 'If I say (the Psalter) quickly enough.'

49 St Germain, a fifth-century French saint.

50 St Leger, a seventh-century bishop of Autun.

51 St Leonard, patron saint of domestic animals.

52 'Take a napkin folded along the bias of the cloth'.

53 Lampass: a mouth infection in horses; bottes: worms.

54 St Wilfrid, a seventh-century Yorkshire saint.

55 The theologian St Thomas Aquinas's 'lots'. Happé suggests the allusion is to the spells performed using Aquinas's works.

56 'Jew's ear', a medicinal fungus.

Thre syppes are for the hyckock,
And vi more for the chyckock;
Thus maye my praty pyckock
Recover, by and by.

If ye cannot slepe, but slumber,
Geve otes unto Saynt Uncumber,[57]
And beanes in a serten number
Unto Saynt Blase[58] and Saynt Blythe;[59]
Geve onyons to Saynt Cutlake,[60]
And garylyke to Saynt Cyryake,[61]
If ye wyll shurne the head ake,
Ye shall have them at Queen-hythe.

A dramme of a shepes tyrdle,
And good Saynt Frances gyrdle,
With the hamlet of an hyrdle,[62]
Are wholesom for the pyppe.
Besydes these charmes afore,
I have feates many more
That I kepe styll in store
Whome now I over hyppe.

INFIDELITAS
It is a spoart, I trowe,
To heare how she out blowe
Her witche craftes on a rowe.
By the Masse, I must nedes smyle!
Now, I praye the[e], lete me knowe
What sedes that thu cannyst sowe
Mankynde to over throwe,
And the Lawe of Nature begyle.

SODOMISMUS
My selfe I so behave,
And am so vyle a knave,
As nature doth deprave
And utterlye abhorre.
I am soche a vyce, trulye,
As God in Hys great furye
Ded ponnysh most terryblye
In Sodome and in Gomorre.[63]

In the flesh I am a fyre,
And soch a vyle desyre,
As brynge men to the myre
Of fowle concupyscence.
We two togyther beganne
To sprynge and to growe in manne,
As Thomas of Aquyne scanne
In the fort boke of hys sentence.

I dwelt amonge the Sodomytes,
The Benjamytes, and Madyanytes,[64]
And now the Popysh hypocrytes
Embrace me every where.
I am now become all spyrytuall,
For the clergye at Rome, and over all,
For want of wyves, to me doth fall,
To God they have no feare.

The chyldren of God I ded so move,
That they the doughters of men ded love,[65]
Workynge soch wayes as ded not behove,
Tyll the floude them over went.
With Noes sonne Cham I was half joyned,[66]
Whan he hys dronken father scorned.
In the Gomorytes I also reigned,
Tyll the hand of God them brent.

I was with Onan not unacquaynted,[67]
Whan he on the grounde hys increase shed.
For me hys bretherne Joseph accused,[68]
As Genesis doth tell.

527 hiccoughs 528 six, whooping-cough 529 peacock (term of endearment) 532 oats, 533 beans, certain 537 avoid 538 by them, the London docks 539 dram, sheep's turd 540 St Francis of Assisi, girdle/rope 542 illness (generic) 543 mentioned before 545 saved up 546 Which, pass over 547 good fun 548 boasts about 549 all together 550 have to smile 552 seeds, sow 561 Did 565 brings, mire/swamp 565 lust 567 (i.e. he and Idololatria) 569 Thomas Aquinas discusses 570 fourth, *Sententiae* 575 (i.e. religious) 577 lack 578 Of 579 did 581 were not natural 582 (Noah's) flood 585 People of Gomorrah 586 burnt 588 spilled his seed

57 St Wilgefortis, popularly known as Uncumber as she would 'un-encumber' unhappy wives of their husbands. Perhaps the implication is that the wife cannot sleep for the husband's snoring and so can only 'slumber' fitfully.

58 St Blaise, a fourth-century Armenian saint.

59 St Blitharius, a seventh-century Scottish saint.

60 St Guthlac, a seventh-to-eighth-century English saint.

61 St Cyriacus of Jerusalem (d.133).

62 Happé suggests an 'amulet' and a sheep-hurdle.

63 Gomorrah. See Genesis 18:20–19:30.

64 For the children of Benjamin, see Judges 20; for the Midianites, see Judges 6:1.

65 See Genesis 6:1–4.

66 Ham, see Genesis 9:22–4.

67 See Genesis 39:8–10.

68 'Because of me Joseph was accused by his brothers'. See Genesis 37:2.

David ones warned all men of us two,
'Do not as mules and horses wyll do.'[69]
Confounded be they that to ymages go,
Those are the wayes to Hell.

Both Esaye and Ezechiel,
Both Hieremy and Daniel,
Of us the abhomynacyons tell,
With the prophetes everychon.[70]
For us two God strake with fyre and watter,
With battayle, with plages and fearfull matter,
With paynefull exyle, than, at the latter,
Into Egipt and Babylon.

As Paule to the Romanes testyfye,[71]
The gentyles after Idolatrye
Fell to soch bestyall Sodomye
That God ded them forsake.
Who foloweth us, as he confesse,
The kyngedom of God shall never possesse;
And as the Apocalyps expresse[72]
Shall synke to the burnynge lake.

We made Thalon and Sophocles,
Thamiras, Nero, Agathocles,
Tiberius, and Aristoteles,[73]
Themselves to use unnaturallye:
I taught Aristo and Fulvius,
Semiramis and Hortensius,
Crathes, Hyliscus, and Pontius
Beastes to abuse most monstruouslye.[74]

INFIDELITAS
Marry, thu art the Devyll hymselfe!

IDOLOLATRIA
If ye knewe how he coulde pelfe,
Ye wolde saye he were soch an elfe,
As non under Heaven were els.

INFIDELITAS
The fellawe is wele decked,
Dysgysed and wele necked,
Both knavebalde and pyepecked,[75]
He lacketh nothynge but bels.

SODOMISMUS
In the first age I beganne,
And so perseverde with manne,
And styll wyll, if I canne,
So longe as he endure.
In monkysh sectes renue,
And popysh prestes contynue,
Whych are of my retynue,
To lyve I shall be sure.

Cleane marryage they forbyd,
Yet can not their wayes be hyd;
Men knowe what hath betyd,
Whan they have bene in parell.
Oft have they buryed quycke
Soch as were never sycke.
Full many a propre trycke,
They have to helpe their quarell.

In Rome to me they fall,
Both byshopp and cardynall,
Monke, fryre, prest, and all,
More ranke they are than antes.

599 Because of, struck 600 battle 601 painful, end 602 Egypt 614 abuse 620 steal/plunder 622 like no one else 623 well dressed 626 bells (to complete a fool's costume) 631 renewed 636 hidden 637 has occurred 638 peril (of being found out) 639 alive 640 sick 641 proper 645 friar, priest 646 lustful, ants

69 Psalms 32:9. 'Be ye not as the horse, or as the mule, which have no understanding: whose mouth must be held in with bit and bridle, lest they come near unto thee.'

70 See Isaiah 3 and following; Ezekiel 16:49–63; Lamentations 1–22; Daniel 11:3–36.

71 'Testifies'. See Romans 1:22–7.

72 'As Revelation reveals': see Revelation 14:9–11.

73 Sophocles (*c.*496–406 BC), the Greek dramatist and poet; Thamyris the Greek bard; the Emperor Nero Claudius Caesar (who reigned AD 54–68); Agathocles, tyrant of Syracuse (361–289 BC). The inclusion of the Greek philosopher Aristotle (384–322 BC) among the self-abusers is perhaps the result of a scurrilous medieval tradition concerning his combative marital life. Tiberius Julius Caesar Augustus was Roman emperor AD 14–37. His last years were spent in sensual indulgence on the isle of Capri. Thalon remains unidentified. These figures are all listed in Ravisius Textor, *Officina* (Paris, 1520). Bale also took his list of cross-dressers at 11. 433–5 from Textor's book.

74 Ariston of Chios, a Greek philosopher of the third century BC. 'Fulvius' is perhaps Marcus Fulvius Nobilior, military commander and censor of the first century BC. Semiramis was the legendary queen of Assyria, daughter of the goddess Derceto, who was raised by doves and eventually turned into one on her death. Hortensius may be Hortensius Quintus, dictator of Rome from *c.*287 BC, or possibly Quintus Hortalus Hortensius (114–50 BC), the Roman jurist. Crates was one of the earliest Greek poets. Hyliscus and Pontius remain mysterious, although the latter may be Pilate. Textor lists these names among his practitioners of bestiality and related vices.

75 'Both bald like a knave, and multi-coloured, like a magpie'.

Example in Pope Julye,[76]
Whych sought [to] have in hys furye
Two laddes, and to use them beastlye,
From the Cardynall of Nantes.[77]

INFIDELITAS
Well yow two are for my mynde,
Steppe fourth and do your kynde.
Leave never a poynt be hynde
That maye corrupt in man
The lawe wryt in hys hart:
[*Ad Sodo.*:][78] In hys flesh do thy part,
[*Ad Idol.*:][79] And hys sowle to pervart
Do thu the best thu can.

Here have I pratye gynnes,
Both brouches, beades, and pynnes,
With soch as the people wynnes
Unto ydolatrye.
[*Ad Idol.*:] Take thu part of them here,
Beades, ryngs, and other gere,
And shortlye the[e] bestere
To deceyve man properlye.

Take thys same staffe and scryppe,
With a God here of a chyppe,[80]
And, good beldame, forewarde hyppe,
To set fourth pylgrymage.
[*Ad Sodo.*:] Set thu fourth sacramentals,
Saye dyrge, and synge for trentals,[81]
Stodye the Popes decretals,
And mixt them with buggerage.

Here is a stoole for the[e],
A ghostlye father to be;
To heare *Benedicite*,
A boxe of creame and oyle.
[*Ad Idol.*:] Here is a purse of rellyckes,
Ragges, rotten bones, and styckes,
A taper with other tryckes,
Shewe them in every soyle.

SODOMISMUS
I wyll corrupt Gods image
With most unlawfull usage,
And bryng hym into dottage,
Of all concupyscence.

IDOLOLATRIA
Within the flesh thu art,
But I dwell in the hart,
And wyll the sowle pervart
From Gods obedyence.

INFIDELITAS
Spare non abhomynacyon,
Nor detestable fashyon,
That mannys ymagynacyon
By wytt maye comprehende.
To quycken our spretes amonge
Synge now some myry songe,
But lete it not be longe,
Least we to moch offende.

Post cantionem Infidelitas alta voce dicet:[82]

Oremus, Omnipotens sempiterne Deus, qui ad imaginem
et similitudinem nostram formasti laicos, da quaesumus
ut sicut eorum sudoribus vivimus ita eorum uxoribus,
filiabus et domicellis perpetuo frui mereamur. Per dominum
nostrum Papam.[83]

[*Exeunt Sodomismus and Idololatria.*]

INFIDELITAS
Now are these whoresons forth;
It wyll be somwhat worth
To se how they wyll wurke,
The one to poyson the hart,
The other the outwarde part
Ingenyously wyll lurke.

648 furious lust 649 boys, bestially 651 my kind of people 652 what comes naturally 653 untouched 655 written 657 soul, pervert 659 clever traps 660 broaches 661 things which entice people 665 quickly stir yourself 667 bag (of a pilgrim) 669 old woman, hobble off 671 promulgate ceremonies 673 Study/ordinances 674 mix, buggery 675 (clerical) stole 678 chrism (for baptisms) 681 candle 682 land 685 dotage/idiocy 686 lust 689 pervert 694 conceive 695 enliven, spirits 696 merry 699 too 704 gone 705 worth something 709 lurk (in)

76 Pope Julius II (1503–13).
77 For this story, see Bale's *Mystery of Iniquity* (Geneva, 1545).
78 'To Sodomismus'.
79 'To Idololatria'.
80 A wooden image of Christ or a saint.
81 Dirge: the Office for the Dead; Trental: a set of thirty requiem Masses.
82 'After the song, Infidelitas shall say in a high voice'.
83 'Let us pray, Almighty and eternal God, Who has formed the layfolk in our image and likeness, grant, we pray, that [just] as we live by their sweat, so may we merit the endless enjoyment of their wives, daughters, and maidservants, through our lord, the pope.'

The Lawe of Nature they wyll
Infect, corrupt, and spyll
With their abhomynacyon,
Idolatry with wyckednesse,
And Sodomy with fylthynesse,
To hys most utter dampnacyon.

These two wyll hym so use,
Ich one in their abuse,
And wrappe hym in soch evyll,
That by their wycked cast
He shall be at the last
A morsell for the Devyll.

Now underneth her wynges
Idolatry hath kynges
With their nobylyte,
Both dukes, lordes, knyghtes, and earles,
Fayre ladyes with their pearles,
And the whole commenalte.

Within the bownes of Sodomye
Doth dwell the spirytuall clergye,
Pope, cardinall, and pryst,
Nonne, chanon, monke, and fryre,
With so many els as do desyre
To reigne undre Antichrist.

Detestynge matrymonye,
They lyve abhomynablye,
And burne in carnall lust.
Shall I tell ye farther newes?
At Rome for prelates are stewes
Of both kyndes: thys is just!

The Lawe of Nature, I thynke,
Wyll not be able to wynke
Agaynst the assaultes of them,
They havynge so hygh prelates,
And so manye great estates
From hens to Hierusalem.

Pause now a lyttle whyle;
Myne eares doth me begyle
If I heare not a sounde.

710

715

720

725

730

735

740

745

Yon folke hath sped, I gesse,
It is so, by the Messe!
Awaye now wyll I rounde. (*Exit.*)

[*Enter Law of Nature, dressed as a leper.*[84]]

NATURAE LEX
I thynke ye marvele to se soch alteracyon
At thys tyme in me, whom God left here so pure.
Of me it cometh not, but of mannys operacyon,
Whome dayly the Devyll to great synne doth allure.
And hys nature is full bryttle and unsure.
By hym have I gote thys fowle dysease of bodye,
And, as ye se here, am now throwne in a leprye.

I wrought in hys hart, as God bad ernestlye,
Hym oft provokynge to love God over all
With the inner powers. But the false Idolatrye
Hath hym perverted by slayghtes dyabolycall,
And so hath Sodomye, through hys abuses carnall,
That he is now lost, offendynge without measure,
And I corrupted, to my most hygh dyspleasure.

I abhorre to tell the abusyons bestyall
That they daylye use whych boast their chastyte;
Some at the aulter to incontynency fall,
In confessyon some full beastly occupyed be.
Amonge the close nonnes reigneth thys enormyte:
Soch chyldren slee they as they chaunce for to have,
And in their prevyes provyde them of their grave.[85]

Ye Christen rulers, se yow for thys a waye:
Be not illuded by false hypocresye;
By the stroke of God the worlde wyll els decaye.
Permyt prestes rather Gods lawfull remedye,
Than they shuld incurre most bestyall Sodomye.
Regarde not the Pope, nor yet hys whorysh
kyngedom,
For he is the master of Gomor and of Sodome.

With man have I bene, whych hath me thus defyled
With Idolatrye and uncleane Sodomye,
And worthye I am from God to be exyled.
Pytie me yet, Lorde, of Thy most bownteouse mercye:
I wyll fourth and mourne tyll Thu sende remedye.

711 kill 717 Each, by 719 effort(s) 727 commonalty/people 728 bounds/jurisdiction 737 more 738 (there) are brothels 739 (i.e. hetero- and homosexual) 741 ignore 743 having (on their side) 745 here, Jerusalem 747 Unless my ears deceive me 749 succeeded 751 go 752 you're amazed 754 It's not my fault, the result of 756 fragile, unreliable 758 leper-house 762 diabolical tricks 767 (those who) boast (of) 768 altar, copulation 770 enclosed/cloistered 773 find a remedy for this 774 deluded 775 otherwise 776 (i.e. marriage) 777 fall into 779 Gomorrah

84 Leprosy here is both literal (associated as it was with syphilis, and hence the influence of Sodomismus and sexual promiscuity) and symbolic of spiritual corruption.

85 'They [the nuns] murder any babies they happen to give birth to, and bury them in their privies/cesspits.'

Promyse hast Thu made to a gloryouse lyberte
To brynge Heaven and Earth: than wylt Thu, I trust, restore me. [*Exit.*]

FINIT ACTUS SECUNDUS.[86]

INCIPIT ACTUS TERTIUS: MOSEH LEX CORRUPTA.[87]

MOSEH LEX
The Lorde, perceyvynge Hys first Lawe thus corrupted
With uncleane vyces, sent me, Hys Lawe of Moses,
To se hym for synne substancyallye corrected,
And brought in agayne to a trade of godlynes.
For I am a lawe of rygour and of hardenes:
I strayghtly commaunde, and, if it be not done,
I thretten, I curse, and slee in my anger sone.

To God I requyre a perfyght obedyence,
Condempnynge all soch as do it not in effect.
I shewe what synne is; I burden sore mannys conscyence;
To hym am I death whan hys lyfe is infect.
Yet, if he take hede, to Christ I hym dyrect,
Forgevenesse to have, with lyght, helth, and salvacyon,
Least he shuld dyspayre and fall into dampnacyon.

[*Enter Infidelitas, dressed as a grey friar.*]

INFIDELITAS
Ha, ha, ha, ha, ha, ha, ha, ha, ha, ha, ha!
'A pastyme', quoth a! I knowe not the tyme nor whan
I ded laugh so moch sens I was an honest man!
Beleve me and ye wyll, I never sawe soch a sport.
I wolde ye had bene there that ye myght have made the fort.[88]

MOSEH LEX
Where woldest have had me? Tell me, good brother myne.

INFIDELITAS
At the Mynorasse, ser, late yester nyght at complyne.[89]

MOSEH LEX
At the Mynorasse? Why, what was there ado?

INFIDELITAS
For soch an other wolde I to Southampton go.
In dede yester daye it was their dedycacyon,[90]
And thydre in Gods name came I to se the fashyon.
An olde fryre stode forth with spectacles on hys nose,
Begynnynge thys Anteme, a my fayth, I do not glose,
[*Singing*:] '*Lapides preciose*'.[91]

MOSEH LEX
And what ded folowe of thys?

INFIDELITAS
I shall tell ye, ser, by Gods blys.
Then came Dame Isbell, an olde nonne and a calme,
Crowynge lyke a capon, and thus began the Psalme:
[*Sings*:] '*Saepe expugnaverunt me a juventute mea.*'[92]

MOSEH LEX
And what includeth thys mysterye?

INFIDELITAS
A symple problem of bytcherye.
Whan the fryre begonne a[f]ore the nonne
To synge of precyouses stones,
'From my youth', sayt she, 'they have confort me',
As it had bene for the nones.

MOSEH LEX
I assure the[e] playne, I set not by soch gaudes;[93]
Thy usage shewe the[e] to be brought up amonge baudes.

INFIDELITAS
It was a good world whan we had soch wholsom storyes

784 (go) forth **785** of **789** him (man) **790** practice **791** rigour, severity **792** strictly **793** slay, soon **797** corrupted **798** I guide him **800** Lest/In case, despair **802** says he **804** if **806** would (you) **808** what happened there **809** Southampton (Hampshire) **811** there **812** friar stood **813** Anthem, deceive you **815** from **817** Isobel, loose (woman) **820** What did this rite involve **821** whoredom **822** before **825** if it was relevant **827** behaviour, whores

86 'Here ends the Second Act.'

87 'Here begins the Third Act: The Law of Moses Corrupted.'

88 'Fourth'. The other three (as what follows makes clear) are the nun, the friar, and Infidelitas himself.

89 'At the Minories-without-Aldgate [the Franciscan priory to the east of London], last night at Compline [the last canonical hour of the day].'

90 'The ceremony of dedication for the church'.

91 'Precious stones', the beginning of the dedicatory Anthem. There is also a Latinate pun on 'stones' (testicles) which gives the story its bawdy humour.

92 'Many a time have they afflicted me from my youth.' Psalms 129:1. Again the bawdy double entendre provides the humour.

93 'I am not interested in such jokes'.

Preached in our churche on sondayes and other feryes.

With us was it merye
Whan we went to Berye,[94]
And to Our Lady of Grace,[95]
To the bloude of Hayles,[96]
Where no good chere fayles,
And other holye place.

Whan the prestes myght walke,
And with yonge wyves talke,
Than had we chyldren plentye;
Than cuckoldes myght leape
A score on a heape;
Now is there not one to twentye.[97]

Whan the monkes were fatte
And ranke as a ratte,
With bellyes lyke a bore,
Then all thynges were dere,
Both befe, breade, and bere;
Now grudge the jourers sore.

Whan byshoppes myght burne,
And from the truth turne
The syllye, symple sowle,
Than durst no man creake,
Open mouthe, nor speake
Of Christ, nor yet of Powle.

Now are the knaves bolde
With Scriptures to holde,
And teache them every where,
The carter, the sowter,
The bodger, the clowter,
That all wyll awaye, I fere.

At us so they pulle,
Our lyvynges are dulle,
We are now lyke to fall;
If we do not fyght
For the churches ryght,
By the Messe, we shall lose all!

But I praye ye, ser, tell me: what is your name?

MOSEH LEX
The Lawe of Moses: to lye I were to blame.

INFIDELITAS
In these same partyes what do ye now intende?

MOSEH LEX
Mankynde to refourme, that he hys lyfe amende.
I shewe what synne is and what thynge pleaseth God;
I confort the just, and the yll I ponnysh with [the] rod.[98]
The commen people have thought it commodyouse
Dyverse goddes to have with rytes superstycyouse;
My commaundement is to seke one God alone,
And in all their nedes to Hym to make their mone.
Amonge the gentyles was it thought non injurye,
If a man wer hurt, to slee hys adversarye:
Thys thynge I forbyd, and saye, 'Thu shalt not kyll:
Lawe is the revenger, the man maye do no yll.'
Some persones there are that inordynatlye love;
Those are perswaded all thynges them to behove
Whych I inhybyte, saynge contynuallye,
'No rape shalt thu do, nor yet commyt advouterye;
Thu shalt do no theft nor covete that is not thyne;
Agaynst thy neyber shalt thu not falsely dyffyne'.

INFIDELITAS
We may do nothynge if we be pynned in thus;
Neyther yow nor God to that hard trade shall brynge us!
We must have one God, and worshypp Hym alone?
Marry, that in dede wolde make a Turke to grone!
If we be stryken, we maye not stryke agayne?
A proper bargayne, and dyscretelye uttered playne![99]
For cumpanyes sake ye saye we maye not love:
I defye your worst, and to yow there is my glove![100]

829 Sundays, holy days 834 is lacking 838 aplenty 840 twenty all together 843 lustful, rat 844 boar 845 precious 846 beer 847 greedy men complain 848 burn (heretics) 850 soul 851 dared, object 853 St Paul 857 shoemaker 858 repair-man, clothes-maker 859 be lost 861 incomes, low 862 likely, fail 867 if I lied 868 parts, intend (to do) 871 evil 872 convenient 873 worship 875 complaint/prayer 876 no crime 877 slay 879 must 881 are acceptable for them 882 prohibit, saying 883 adultery 884 covet, (which) is 885 neighbour, bear false witness 886 pinned in (by rules) 889 groan 890 back

94 The shrine of St Edmund in Bury St Edmunds (Suffolk).

95 The Rood of Grace in Boxley (Kent).

96 Hailes Abbey (Gloucestershire), where a vial of Christ's blood was kept. All of the sites Infidelitas mentions were pilgrimage centres.

97 'Nowadays fewer than one in twenty men are cuckolds.'

98 In what follows Moseh Lex outlines the Ten Commandments.

99 'That's a good deal, and discreetly spoken!' (ironic).

100 He throws down his glove in challenge.

MOSEH LEX
What, thu wylt not fyght? Thy wyttes are better than so.

INFIDELITAS
In the quarell of love, I shall prove ye ere I go;
By the Messe, I thynke to put ye to your fence.

MOSEH LEX
Thu were moch better to kepe thy pacyence.

INFIDELITAS
Naye, by Cockes sowle, frynd, I must lay ye on the coate.
In loves cause to fyght ye maye sone have me a floate.
Naye, have at your pylche! Defende ye, if ye maye.

MOSEH LEX
Soch a fole art thu as seke thyne owne decaye.
If I ones meddle, to the[e] it wyll be death.
Dedyst thu never hear that lawe sleath in hys wreath?

INFIDELITAS
By the Blessed Lorde, than wyll I playe Robsons part.

MOSEH LEX
Whye, what part wylt
thu playe?

INFIDELITAS
By Cockes sowle, geve over so sone as I fele smart.[101]

MOSEH LEX
It wyll be to late If I ones cupple with the[e].

INFIDELITAS
Then lete me alone, and we shall sone agre,
And I shall be glad to be acquaynted with ye.

MOSEH LEX
Acquayntaunce, good fellawe, thu mayst sone have of me!

INFIDELITAS
The worst fault I have, I am hastye now and than;
But it is sone gone, I toke it of a woman.
But what meane those tables that ye have in your hande?

MOSEH LEX
Kepe sylence a whyle and thu shalt understande.
Thre thynges I declare, the first are the preceptes morall,
Next the lawes judycial, and last the rytes ceremonyal.
The morall preceptes are Gods Commaundementes Ten,
Whych ought evermore to be observed of all men.
The lawes of Nature the morall preceptes declare,
And the plesaunt workes to God they teache and prepare.
They sturre man to fayth, and provoke hym also to love,
To obeye, to serve, and to worshypp God above.
In two stonye tables God wrote them first of all,
That they shuld remayne as thynges contynuall.
The first hath but thre, whych tende to Gods hygh honour;[102]
Seven hath the seconde, and they concerne our neybour.
The first doth expounde the first lawe naturall;
The next the other, makynge them very formall.
In sprete is the first, that we shuld God honour and love;[103]
To outward workynge the seconde doth us move,
Forbyddynge all wronges, preservynge just marryage,
Norryshynge true peace and other godly usage.

INFIDELITAS
What is the effect of your lawes judycyall?

MOSEH LEX
Soch thynges to commaunde as are cyvyle or temporall.
From vyce to refrayne and outwarde injurye,
Quyet to conserve and publyque honestie:

894 You know better than that 895 a quarrel about 896 on the defensive 897 You'd do better 898 God's (euphemism), strike 899 get me started 900 jacket 901 ruin 902 once get involved 903 Did, slays, wrath 904 a coward's role 906 too, join/get to grips 910 impetuous 911 got it from 912 (stone) tablets 917 by 919 works pleasing to God 920 stir/inspire 927 clear 929 behaviour, direct 931 Nourishing 933 civic, worldly 935 To keep the peace

101 'Any pain.'

102 i.e. the first tablet, containing the three spiritual commandments concerning worship of God.

103 'The first [tablet] deals with the spirit'.

These are to support the lawes of the seconde table.
Ceremonyall rytes are also commendable,
In holy dayes, garmentes, temples, and consecracyons,
Sacryfyces and vowes, with offerynges and expiacyons,[104]
Whych are unto Christ as fygurs, types, and shadowes.
As Paule doth declare, in hys Pystle to the Hebrues,[105]
These are only fygures and outwarde testymonyes,
No man is perfyght by soch darke ceremonyes:
Only perteyne they unto the thirde Commaundement
Of the Sabboth daye, tyll Christ the Lorde be present,
In Hys death endyng the whole Judaycal presthode.

INFIDELITAS
Good dayes myght ye have, ye speake it full wele by the Rode.
A am a poore lad, and by my trouth bent ernestyle
To wayte upon ye and to be your very lackye.

MOSEH LEX
What art thu called, I praye the[e], hartelye?

INFIDELITAS
Graye fryre am I non, by the Messe; I can not flatter.
I am Infydelyte, to tell the truth of the matter.

MOSEH LEX
And hast thu so longe dyssembled thus with me?

INFIDELITAS
Yea, for advauntage, to smell out your subtylyte.

MOSEH LEX
Avoyde, hens, I saye, thu false Infydelyte!

INFIDELITAS
Naye, that I wyll not, by Yngham Trynyte.[106]

MOSEH LEX
Wylt thu not, in dede? Than wyll I fet hyther the poure
Of judges and kynges to subdue the[e] within thys houre. (*Exit.*)

INFIDELITAS
Soch knyghtes wyll I have as shall confounde them all,
As Sadducees and Scrybes, with the sect pharysaycal.
By helpe of my chyldren Idolatry and Sodomye,
The Lawe of Nature I kest ones in a leprye.
I have yet two more, Ambycyon and Covetousnes,
Whych wyll do as moch to the Lawe of Moses.
Where are my whoresons that they come not awaye?

[*Enter Avaritia and Ambitio.*]

AVARITIA ([AS] JURISCONSULTUS)[107]
Yea, whoreson, on thy face, even in thy best araye!
I wyll thu knowe it, I am a worshypfull doctour,
A scrybe in the lawe, and a profytable proctour.

INFIDELITAS
Goppe, with a vengeaunce! How comest thu so aloft?[108]

AVARITIA
I shall tell the[e], man, if thu wylt commen more soft,
By fayned flatterye and by coloured adulacyon;
Ambycyon here also rose out of a lyke foundacyon.

INFIDELITAS
Come, axe me blessynge, lyke praty boyes, apace.

AMBITIO
I wyll not bowe, sure, to soch a folysh face.

INFIDELITAS
Axe blessynge, I saye, and make me no more ado.

938 vestments 940 images, foreshadowings 942 symbols 943 perfected, unclear/imperfect 944 They only relate to 946 Judaical 948 I, determined 949 slave 950 are 951 I'm no Franciscan 959 subtlety/tricks 955 hence/get away 957 fetch, power 960 the Pharisees 962 threw, leper-house 964 the same 965 here 966 (a turd in) thy, clothes 968 advocate/lawyer 970 converse, quietly 971 feigned, deceitful, flattery 972 from similar origins 973 ask my, nice boys, quickly

104 Expiatory prayers.

105 'Epistle': see Hebrews 8–10, especially 10:1, 'For the law having a shadow of good things to come, and not the very image of the things, can never with those sacrifices which they offered year by year continually make the comers thereunto perfect.'

106 Holy Trinity College, Ingham (Norfolk).

107 'Dressed as a clerical lawyer'.

108 'Geddup, curse you [a carter's cry to his horse]! How come you're so haughty?'

AMBITIO
Unsemelye were it, we prelates shuld do so.

AVARITIA
For no compulsyon wyll I do it, be swete Marye.

INFIDELITAS
I must fatche ye in, there is no remedye.
A, noughty whoresons, have I brought ye up hytherto?
And knowe not your father? Ye shal drynke both ere I go![109]

[*Infidelitas thrashes them.*]

AMBO SIMUL.
Nomore at thys tyme! Forsoth, we crye a mercye!

INFIDELITAS
Downe on your knees, than, and axe me blessyng shortely.

AMBO SIMUL.
Blesse me, gentyll father, for swete Saynt Charyte.

INFIDELITAS
Aryse noughty knaves; God lete ye never to thee!
Though amonge our selves, we murmour, bragge, and face,
Somtyme for lucre, somtyme for the hyghar place,
Yet for advauntage, in thys we all agre,
To blynde the rulers, and deceyve the commynalte.

AVARITIA
Art advysed of that? By the Messe, we are in dede;
Yet of our knaveryes, the foles wyll never take hede.

To labour with a spade
Our colour wolde it fade;
We maye not with that trade,
We love so moch our ease.
We must lyve by their sweate,
And have good drynke and meate,
Whan they have not to eate
The substaunce of a pease.

We leade them in the darke,
And so their conscyence marke,
That sturdy they are and starke,
In every wycked evyll.
We teache ydolatrye,
And laugh full merelye
To [see] ych cumpanye
Ronne headlondes to the Devyll.

If we maye have the tythynges,
And profytable offerynges,
We care not to what doynges
They customablye fall.
We are soch mercenaryes
And subtyle propryetaryes
As from the flock all carryes
The wolle, skynne, flesh and all.

In our perambulacyons
We loke for commendacyons
And lowlye salutacyons
In temple, howse, and strete.
Our lowsye Latyne howres,
In borowes and in bowres,
The poore people devowres,
And treade them undre fete.

AMBITIO
I am Ambycyon,
Whose dysposycyon
Is honour to appete.
I gape for empyre,
And worshypp desyre,
As Minos ded in Crete.[110]

I loke up aloft,
And love to lye soft,
Not carynge for my flocke,
Have I ones the flese,
With pygges, lambes, and gese,
They maye go turne a socke.

976 unseemly **977** by **978** fetch/drag **984** thrive **985** boast **986** money, precedence **988** common people **989** Do you know that? **990** fools **992** (i.e. would make us ill) **993** (meddle) with **994** We love comfort too much **995** (i.e. the common people's) **998** pea **999** into ignorance **1000** stain/influence **1001** determined, hardened **1004** merrily **1006** Run headlong **1007** tithes **1008** gifts (to shrines, etc.) **1010** habitually **1012** hoarders of property **1013** we steal all **1015** wanderings **1019** lousy **1020** towns, bedrooms **1021** devour (the wealth of) **1022** (we) tred, foot **1025** Is to crave honour **1026** lust, dominion **1027** desire to be honoured **1029** (i.e. behave haughtily) **1032** Once I get the fleece/loot **1034** (i.e. I don't care what they do)

[109] 'You'll both suffer [equivalent of the modern "take your medicine"] before you go!'

[110] Minos, king of Crete, who made peace with Athens only when offered an annual tribute of young virgins to feed to the Minotaur.

Lucifer I made
So hyghly to wade,
To God he wolde be equall.
Of Adam and Eve
I slewe the beleve,
And caused them to fall.

What nede I rehearce
The gyauntes most fearce,
With the buylders of Babell?
Nemrod the tyraunt,[111]
With them there applyaunt
Agreed to my counsell.

From me wolde not go
Cruell Pharao,
No more wolde Amalech,
Saul, Achitophel,
Absolon, Jesabel,
Nor Adonisedech.[112]

I made Roboam
And Hieroboam,
With Nabuchodonosor,
Triphon, Alchimus,
And Simon Magus,[113]
To abuse them evermor.

In pryde I excede,
And no people fede,
But with lyes for advauntage.
As Mantuane tell,[114]
To leade men to Hell
Is my most commen usage.

Hygh thynges I attempt,
And wyll me exempt
From prynces jurysdyccyon
As brynge to the Devyll
Without anye contradyccyon.

INFIDELITAS
Here is a prelate even for myne owne touth;
Soch an other is not in the whole south!
Clappe thu somwhat more as thu hast begunne;
I lyke wele your talkynge, by the holy nunne![115]

AVARITIA
I Covetyse am,
The Devyll or hys dam,
For I am insacyate,
I ravysh and plucke,
I drawe and I sucke,
After a wolvysh rate.

Father nor mother,
Syster nor brother,
I spare not in my moode.
I feare neyther God,
Nor Hys ryghtfull rod,
In gatherynge of goode.

Both howse and medowe
From the poor wydowe,
I spare not for to take;
Ryght heyres I rob,
And as bare as Job
The fatherles I make.[116]

With me toke Nadab,
Nabal and Achab,
With all the clergye of Bell;

1036 To become so ambitious **1039** killed their faith (in God) **1041** tell you (about) **1042** giants **1045** favourable/friendly **1046** (They) agreed **1058** practise abuses **1061** Except, for (my own) **1062** tells/reports **1064** practice **1066** I will exempt myself **1068** bring (folk) **1071** after my taste **1072** (i.e. he's unique!) **1073** keep talking **1076** wife/mother **1077** insatiable **1080** Just like a wolf **1086** acquiring property (for myself) **1089** I don't hesitate **1090** Legitimate heirs **1092** fatherless

[111] For the giants who bred with the daughters of humanity, see Genesis 6:4; for the builders of the Tower of Babel, Genesis 11:1–9; for Nimrod, Genesis 10:8–10. All of these are cited as victims of over-ambition.

[112] For Pharaoh, see Exodus 1–14; for Amalech, who, like Pharaoh, opposed the progress of Moses and the Israelites to the Promised Land, see Exodus 17; for Saul, who kept plunder against God's wishes, see 1 Samuel 8–15; for Absalon and Ahithophel, rebels against King David, see 2 Samuel; for Jezabel, 1 Kings 21:5–25; for Adoni-zedek, king of Jerusalem and an enemy of Joshua, Joshua 10:1–27.

[113] A further list of proud and ambitious opponents of God's wishes. For Rehoboam, the son of Solomon, who provoked the Tribes to rebel against him, and Jeroboam, who led the Kingdom of Judah against Rehoboam, see 1 Kings 12–14; for Nebuchadnezzar, king of Babylon (who, for his arrogance, was driven mad by God and forced to live for a time like a beast), see 2 Kings 25 and Daniel 1–4; for the usurper Tryphon and Alcimus, the advisor who was opposed by Judas Maccabeus, see I Maccabees 7–11; for Simon Magus, who falsely claimed divine powers for himself, see Acts 8:9–24.

[114] Johannes Baptista Spagnolo Mantuanus (1448–1516), the author of Latin *Eclogues*.

[115] Probably a reference to Elizabeth Barton, the 'Nun of Kent', who was executed for treason in 1534 for speaking against Henry VIII's divorce and the direction of religious policy.

[116] For Job's poverty, see the biblical Book of Job, *passim*.

Judas and Giezi,
With the sonnes of Heli,
And the sonnes of Samuel.[117]

Jannes and Jambres,
Also Diotrephes
Wrought wylfull wyckednesse;
So ded Menelaus,
With false Andronicus,
And all for covetousnesse.[118]

AMBITIO
With vyces seven
I close up Heaven,
And speare up Paradyce;
I oppen Hell
By my counsell,
Maynteynynge every vyce.

AVARITIA
For sylver and golde
With falsehed I holde,
Supportynge every evyl.
I have it in awe
For to choke the lawe,
And brynge all to the Devyll.

INFIDELITAS
By the Blessed Trynyte,
No men more fyt for me
To do my busynes;
Ambycyon to begyle,
And Avaryce to defyle
The Lawe of Moyses.
Tell me first of all what wylt thu do, Ambycyon?

AMBITIO
I am thyne owne chylde, thu knowest my
dysposycyon;
I wyll sure do as ded the Phylystynes.

INFIDELITAS
Why, what ded those
knaves?

AMBITIO
They stopped up Abrahams pyttes, as
Genesis diffines,
With mudde and with myre, and left them full
uncleane.[119]

INFIDELITAS
By that same practyse tell me what thu dost meane.

AMBITIO
With fylthy gloses and dyrty exposycyons
Of Gods lawe wyll I hyde the pure dysposycyons.
The keye of knowledge I wyll also take awaye,
By wrastynge the text to the Scriptures sore
decaye.[120]

INFIDELITAS
And what wylt thu do, my fellawe Covetousnes?

AVARITIA
A vayle wyll I sprede upon the face of Moses,
That non shal perceyve the clerenes of hys
contenaunce,

1107 lock up (the gates of) 1110 supporting 1112 falsehood, ally myself 1114 through fear 1118 are more suitable 1124 nature 1125 Philistines 1129 interpretations 1130 statement 1132 twisting 1134 veil 1135 no one, clarity, face

117 Most of the individuals named in this stanza aroused the anger of God by seeking personal gain. Nadab the son of Aaron died for offering improper 'strange fire' to God (see Leviticus 10:1–2). Nabal (whose name means 'fool') was a sheep-farmer who insulted David while drunk (1 Samuel 25:2–42). Achab, king of Samaria, was the husband of Jezebel, who aroused God's anger by acquiring the vineyard of Naboth (1 Kings 21). Bel was a god of the Babylonians (see Jeremiah 50:2 and 51:44, and the apocryphal book The Idol Bel and the Dragon, *passim*). For Judas Iscariot's betrayal of Christ, see, for example, Matthew 26:14; Mark 14:10; John 6:70–1 and 18:2–3; Luke 22:3–4; and the York pageant of *The Conspiracy*, above. Geharzi, servant to the Prophet Elisha, covetously extracted money for himself from Naaman the Syrian, whom the prophet had cured of leprosy. As a result Naaman's leprosy was visited upon Geharzi (2 Kings 5:1–27). Hophni and Phinehas, the sons of Eli, aroused divine anger by abusing the sacred offerings for their own profit (I Samuel 2:12–36). Joel and Abia, the sons of Samuel, were judges in Beersheba, who 'walked not in his ways, but turned aside after lucre, and took bribes and perverted judgement' (1 Samuel 8:1–5).

118 According to 2 Timothy 3:8, Jannes and Jambres were the names of the Egyptian magicians who opposed Moses in Exodus 7:11–22. Diotrephes (described as 'loving to have the pre-eminence') was an opponent of St Paul (see 3 John 9). Menelaus was a corrupt priest who plundered sacred vessels from the Temple to fund his activities; Andronicus was the king's deputy who supported him; see 2 Maccabees 4:23–34.

119 For the Philistines' blocking of the wells used by Abraham and subsequent pollution of the water supply, see Genesis 26:15–18.

120 Bale interprets the story of Abraham's wells as foreshadowing the Catholic clergy's 'polluting' the purity of the Gospels with centuries of critical interpretation and argument.

Whych is of the lawe the meanyng and true ordynaunce.[121]

INFIDELITAS
Why, what wyll ye saye unto the Ten Commaundementes?

AMBITIO
We must poyson them with wyll workes and good intentes,
Where as God doth saye, 'No straunge goddes thu shalt have',
With sayntes worshyppynge that clause we wyll deprave.
And, though He commaunde to make no carved ymage,
For a good intent yet wyll we have pylgrymage.
Though He wyll us not to take Hys name in vayne,
With tradycyons yet therunto wyll we constrayne.[122]
No Sabboth wyl we with Gods worde sanctyfye,
But with lyppe labour and ydle ceremonye.
To father and mother we maye owe non obedyence,
Our relygyon is of so great excellence.
Though we do not slee, yet maye we heretykes burne,
If they wyll not sone from Holy Scripture turne.
What though it be sayd, 'Thu shalt do no fornycacyon',
Yet wyll we mayntene moch greatter abhomynacyon.
Tho[u]gh theft be forbyd, yet wyll we contynuallye
Robbe the poore people through prayer and purgatorye.
God hath inhybyted to geve false testymonye,
Yet we wyll condempne the Gospell for heresye.
We shuld not covete our neybers howse nor wyfe,
Hys servaunt nor beast, yet are we therin most ryfe.
Of men make we swyne by the draffe of our tradycyons,[123]
And cause them nothynge to regard but superstycyons.
As dogges unresonable on most vyle carren fede,
So wyll we cause them seke ydolles in their nede;
And alwayes their grounde shall be for a good intent.

INFIDELITAS
More myscheves, I trowe, the Devyll coulde not invent
Than yow two can do! By the Messe, ye are alone!
Lyttle coulde I do, were ye ones from me gone.
To the corruptynge of the Lawe of Moyses,
Go forwarde, therfor, in your decytfulnes.

AVARITIA
With superstycyons the Jewes ceremonyall lawes
I wyll so handle they shall not be worth two strawes.
The lawes judycyall through cawtels and delayes
I wyll also drowne to all ryghteouse mennys decayes.
To set thys forwarde we must have sophystrye,
Phylosophye and logyck, as scyence necessarye.
The byshoppes must holde their prestes in ignoraunce
With longe Latyne houres, least knowledge to them chaunce;[124]
Lete them have longe mattens, longe evensonges, and longe Masses;
And that wyll make them as dull as ever were asses;
That they shall never be able to prophecye,
Or yet preach the truth to our great injurye.
Lete the cloysterers be brought up ever in sylence,
Without the Scriptures in payne of dysobedyence.
Se the laye people praye never but in Latyne;
Lete them have their Crede and servyce all in Latyne,
That a Latyne beleve maye make a Latyne sowle:
Lete them nothynge knowe of Christ nor yet of Powle.
If they have Englysh, lete it be for advauntage,
For pardons, for dyrges, for offerynges, and pygrymage.
I recken to make them a newe Crede in a whyle.
And all in Englysh, their conscyence to begyle.

INFIDELITAS
Rehearce unto me the artycles of that Crede.

1136 instruction 1138 evil, intentions 1140 corrupt 1143 wishes 1146 (i.e. mere words, vain rites) 1149 kill 1150 soon betray the Gospel 1154 fees for prayers for the dead 1155 prohibited us from giving 1158 active 1160 to care for nothing 1161 carrion 1162 (to) run to idols 1163 motive, well-intentioned 1164 mischiefs 1165 unique 1166 if you were once 1171 tricks 1172 the ruin of righteous men 1173 sophistry/scholastic learning 1174 logic, essential disciplines 1175 keep 1177 matins 1181 (i.e. monks and nuns) 1185 faith, soul 1187 (our) advantage 1191 Repeat

121 When Moses returned from speaking with God, he wore a veil so that his followers could not see his transfigured face. St Paul interpreted this allegorically as an allusion to the veil placed over religious truths until the coming of Christ; see Exodus 34:35 and 2 Corinthians 3:15–16.

122 'We will force people to do otherwise through our customary rites.'

123 'We turn men into swine through the pig-swill of our ceremonies and customs'.

124 'To make sure that they don't happen to learn anything'.

AVARITIA
The artycles are these, geve eare and take good hede:

First they shall beleve in our holy father Pope;
Next in hys decrees and holy decretals;
Then in holy church, with sencer, crosse, and cope,
In the ceremonyes and blessed sacramentals;
In Purgatory then, in pardons, and in trentals,
In prayinge to sayntes, and in Saynt Frances whoode,
In our Lady of Grace, and in the Blessed Roode.

They shall beleve also in rellyckes and relygyon,
In Our Ladyes Psalter, in fre wyll and good wurkes,
In the Ember Dayes,[125] and in the Popes remyssyon,[126]
In bedes and in belles, not used of the Turkes,
In the golden masses agaynst soch spretes as lurkes,
With charmes and blessynges. Thys Crede wyll brynge in money;
In Englysh therfor we wyl it clarkely conveye.

INFIDELITAS
Yea, and burne the knaves that wyll not beleve that Crede,
That into the dytche the blynde the blynde maye lede.

AMBITIO
Then I holde it best that we alwayes condempne
The Byble readers least they our actes contempne.

INFIDELITAS
Yea, never spare them, but evermore playe the bytar,
Expressynge alwayes the tropes and types of thy mytar.[127]

AMBITIO
Why, what dost thu thynke my mytar to sygnyfy?

INFIDELITAS
The mouth of a wolfe, and that shall I prove by and by:
If thu stoupe downewarde, loo, se how the wolfe doth gape,
Redye to devoure the lambes, least any escape.
But thy wolvyshnesse by thre crownes wyll I hyde,
Makynge thu a Pope, and a captayne of all pryde.
That whan thu doest slee soch as thy lawes contempne
Thu mayst saye, 'Not I, but the powers ded them condempne'.
These labels betoken the lawes of 'se-non' and 'can-non'.[128]

AMBITIO
I trowe thu woldest saye the two lawes cyvyle and canon?

INFIDELITAS
As I spake, I thought, and styll thynke, by Saynt Johan.
Yea, persecute styll the i[n]structers of the people,
And thu, Covetousnesse, let no bell rynge in steple
Without a profyght. Tush, take moneye every whear,
So nygh clyppe and shave that thu leave never a heare.

AVARITIA
I caused the Pope to take but now of late,
Of the graye fryres to have canonyzate
Franciscus de Pola, thre thousand duckates and more;[129]
And as moch besydes he had not longe afore
For a cardynall hatte of the same holy order.
Thus drawe we to us great goodes from every border.
Pope Clement and Seventh payed ones for hys papacye[130]
Thre hondred thousand good duckates of lawful monye.

INFIDELITAS
I marvele how he coulde come to so moch good.

1194 canon laws 1195 censer 1198 hood 1200 relics 1203 beads, (even by) Turks 1204 lurk about 1206 spread it through scholarship 1208 (proverbial) 1210 condemn 1211 biter (i.e. bite like a wolf) 1215 stoop 1217 (i.e. the pope's triple crown) 1220 higher powers 1222 civil 1223 No, I meant what I said 1226 profit, everwhere 1227 cut, hair 1229 canonized 1231 before 1235 money

125 The Ember Days were the days of fasting in the church calendar.
126 The pope's power to grant remission from sin.
127 'Revealing the symbolic significance of your mitre.' The two segments of the mitre, when tilted forward, resemble the jaws of a wolf.
128 '"See nothing" and "do nothing".'
129 Franciscus de Paola (1416–1507), who founded the Friars Minor, and was canonized in 1519.
130 Clement VII was pope 1523–34.

Avaritia
Yes, yes, by pollage, and by shedynge Christen blood.
Crosers and mytars in Rome are good merchandyce,
And all to lyttle to maynteyne their pompe and vyce.

Ambitio
The Pope for whoredom hath in Rome and Viterbye[131]
Of golde and sylver a wonderfull substaunce yearlye.
Tush, they be in Englande that moch rather wolde to dwell
Whores in their dyoceses tha[n] the readers of Christes Gospell.[132]

Infidelitas
They do the better, for by them they maye have profyght;
As for the other, do trouble them daye and nyght.
Well now, steppe forewarde and go do your busynes
To the corruptynge of the Lawe of Moyses.

Avaritia
Doubt not but we shall make hym a crepple blynde.

Infidelitas
Synge then at our farwel to recreate our mynde.

Finita cantiuncula exeunt ambo.[133]

Infidelitas
Now am I left alone,
And these ii merchauntes gone,
Their myschefes to conclude.
I thynke within a whyle
They wyll trappe and begyle
The worthy lawe of Jude.

Ambycyon first of all,
With hys rytes bestiall,
Wyll make the people swyne.
In draffe wyl he them lede,
And with tradycyons fede
Where they shall suppe or dyne.

Covetousnes wyll warke
That many one shall barke
Lyke dogges agaynst the truth.
Some shall Gods worde defyle
And some wyll it revyle,
Soch beastlynesse ensuth.

Ambycyon hath thys houre
All the whole spirytuall poure,
And maye do what hym lust.
Now Covetousnesse doth rule,
And hath both horse and mule,
All matters by hym dyscust.

Now byshopryckes are solde
And the Holy Ghost for gold
The Pope doth bye and sell.
The truth maye not be tolde
Undre paynes manyfolde
With sendynges downe to Hell.

The people prestes do famysh
And their goodes from them ravysh,
Yea, and all the worlde they blynde.
All prynces do they mock,
And robbe the syllye flocke,
Nothynge they leave behynde.

On the face of Moyses
A vayle they have cast, doughtles,
The lyght of the lawe to hyde,
Least men to Christ shuld comme
From ceremonyes domme
As to their heavenly gyde.

The lawe can never be
At anye lyberte
Where soch two enemyes raigne.
Now is it tyme to walke;
Of thys more wyll I talke
Whan I come hyther agayne. (*Exit.*)

[*Enter Moseh Lex, crippled and blind.*]

Moseh Lex
If pytie maye move your gentyll Christen hartes,

1237 (over-)taxation, shedding 1238 croziers, mitres (i.e. bishoprics) 1239 everything is too little 1244 them (whores) 1248 a blind cripple 1249 entertain 1251 two 1255 Judah 1259 pig-swill 1262 work 1267 will ensue 1269 power 1270 he likes 1273 are within his purview 1280 Priests starve the people 1281 steal 1284 simple 1287 veil 1289 Lest 1290 dumb 1294 reign

131 Viterbo, the pope's alternative residence.

132 'There are bishops in England who would rather have whores live in their diocese than preachers of the Gospel.'

133 'When the little song is finished, they go out.'

Lete it now sturre ye to mourne thys heavye chaunce.
Two enemyes with me have played most wycked partes
And left me starke blynde, God knoweth to my sore grevaunce,
And I thynke also to your more hynderaunce.
To leade yow to Christ somtyme a gyde I was;
Now am I so blynde, I can not do it, alas!

Most rygorously those enemyes now of late
Ded fall upon me and spoyle me of my syght.
One was Ambycyon, whych ever ought me hate,
And Covetousnesse the other enemye hyght.
Now for soth and God, in their most cruell spyght
The one made me blynde, the other made me lame.
And whan they had done, ther at they had great game.

Thus a blynde crypple I wander here alone,
Abydynge the tyme and grace of restauracyon
By the Sonne of God, to whom I make my mone,
My cause to pytie and graunt me supportacyon;
Least I be left here to utter desolacyon
And extreme decaye, without any remedye,
If he ded not helpe, of goodnesse and of mercye.

Ye Christen prynces, God hath geven yow the poure
With scepture and swerde all vyces to correct.
Let not Ambycyon nor Covetousnesse devoure
Your faythfull subjectes, nor your offycers infect.
Have to your clergye a dylygent respect,
And se they do not corrupt the lawes of God,
For that doth requyre a terryble, heavye rod.

God gave me to man, and left me in tables of stone,
That I of hardenesse a lawe shuld specyfye;
But the Pharysees corrupted me anone,
And toke from me cleane the quyvernesse of bodye
With clerenesse of syght and other pleasures manye.
Now wyll I to Christ, that He maye me restore
To more perfeccyon than I ever had afore.

FINIT ACTUS TERTIUS.[134]

INCIPIT ACTUS QUARTUS: CHRISTI LEX CORRUPTA.[135]

EVANGELIUM
Unfaythfulnesse hath corrupted every lawe
To the gret decaye of Adams posteryte.
Were it nott for me, whych now do hyther drawe,
All flesh wolde perysh, no man shuld saved be.
I am Christes Gospell, and infallybyle veryte;
Soch a power of God as saveth all that beleve,
No burdene nor yoke that any man wyll greve.

In the bloude of Christ I am a full forgevenesse,
Where fayth is grounded with a sure confydence.
I am soch a grace, and so hygh tydynges of gladnesse,
As rayse the synner and pacyfye hys conscyence.
I am sprete and lyfe, I am necessarye scyence.
I requyre but love for mannys justyfycatyon,
With a fayth in Christ for hys helth and salvacyon.

[*Enter Infidelitas.*]

INFIDELITAS
Gods beneson have ye! It is joye of your lyfe.
I have hearde of ye, and of my mastres your wyfe.

EVANGELIUM
If thu heardest of me, it was by the voyce of God.

INFIDELITAS
Naye, he that spake of ye was sellynge of a cod
In an oyster bote, a lyttle beyonde Quene-hythe;
A northen man was he, and besought ye to be lythe.

EVANGELIUM
If he spake of me, he was some godly preacher.

INFIDELITAS
Naye ser, by the Roode, nor yet a wholsom teacher.

EVANGELIUM
After what maner ded he speake of me? Tell.

INFIDELITAS
He swore lyke a man, by all contententes of the Gospell;
He swore and better swore, yea, he ded sweare and sweare agayne.

1299 stir/prompt, sorrowful 1302 it is also, greater 1303 guide 1306 did rob 1307 owes 1308 was called 1309 truth, spite 1311 fun 1313 restoration 1314 moan/complaint 1319 power 1325 that calls for, (i.e. punishment) 1329 vitality 1332 greater 1333 (i.e. Infidelity) 1334 successors 1337 infallible truth 1338 from God 1339 (I am) no burden 1344 knowledge 1345 only, salvation 1346 (humanity's) health 1347 blessing 1348 mistress 1351 (see l. 538) 1352 (he) begged 1356 the contents

[134] 'Here ends the Third Act.'

[135] 'Here begins the Fourth Act: The Law of Christ Corrupted.'

EVANGELIUM

That speakynge is soch as procureth eternall payne.[136]
Wyll not the people leave that most wycked folye,
And it so dampnable? To heare it I am sorye.
But, what dedyst thu meane whan thu spakest of my wyfe?

INFIDELITAS

Nothynge; but I thought it was joye of your lyfe
That ye were so good to your neybers as ye are.

EVANGELIUM

Why, how good am I? Thy fantasye declare.

INFIDELITAS

Ye ease them amonge, if it be as I heare:[137]
Whan ye are abroade, there is fyne myry cheare.[138]

EVANGELIUM

As thu art, thu speakest, after thy hartes abundaunce,[139]
For as the man is, soch is hys utteraunce.
My wyfe is the church, or Christen congregacyon,
Regenerate in sprete, doynge no vyle operacyon;
Both cleane and holy, without eyther spott or wryncle
The Lambe with Hys bloude ded her wash and besprynclе.
Thys is not the church of dysgysed hypocrytes,
Of apysh shavelynges, or papystycall sodomytes;[140]
Nor yet, as they call it, a temple of lyme and stone,[141]
But a lyvysh buyldynge, grounded in fayth alone
On the harde rocke Christ, whych is the sure foundacyon:[142]
And of thys church some do reigne in every nacyon,
And in all contrayes, though their nombre be but small.

INFIDELITAS

Their nomber is soch as hath ronne over all;
The same Danes are they men prophecy of playne,
Whych shuld over ronne thys realme yet ones agayne.

EVANGELIUM

What Danes speakest thu of? Thy meanynge shewe more clerlye.

INFIDELITAS

Dane Johan, Dane Robert, Dane Thomas, and Dane Harrye;[143]
These same are those Danes that laye with other mennys wyves,
And occupyed their landes to the detryment of their lyves.
These are accounted a great part of the churche,
For in Gods servyce they honourablye wurche,
Yellynge and cryenge tyll their throtes are full sore.

EVANGELIUM

That church was descrybed of Esaye longe afore:[144]
'Thys people', sayth God, 'with ther lyppes honour Me',
In vayne worshyp they, teachynge mennys fatuyte.
Apparaunt is that church and open to the eyes;
Their worshyppynges are in outwarde ceremonyes,
That counterfet church standeth al by mennys tradycyons,
Without the Scriptures and without the hartes affeccyons.
My church is secrete and evermore wyll be,
Adorynge the Father in sprete and in veryte.
By the worde of God thys church is ruled onlye,
And doth not consyst in outwarde ceremonye.
Thys congregacyon is the true church mylytaunt;
Those counterfet desardes are the very church malygnaunt,

1360 If it (is) 1361 did, spoke 1364 What are you talking about 1366 away from home, merry 1370 vile deeds 1371 blemish 1372 (i.e. Christ), shower 1376 living 1378 some (members) 1379 only 1382 overwhelm 1387 considered (to be) 1388 works 1392 men's folly 1393 visible 1394 physical 1395 only 1401 militant 1402 fools, malignant

136 'Speaking like that [i.e. swearing] is something which gains one eternal pain.'.

137 'You let your wife satisfy your neighbours [sexually]'.

138 Infidelitas deliberately misunderstands the mystical relationship between Christ and the church (described by St Paul in Ephesians 5:25 as analogous to the relationship between a husband and wife) as a literal marriage. Thus he mocks the church's love for all men as whoredom, and Christ as a cuckold. It is typical of Vices to misinterpret spiritual things as if they were physical.

139 'Your words reveal you for what you are'.

140 'Ape-like shaved things [i.e. the tonsured clergy] or popish perverts'.

141 i.e. 'The true church is not a physical building either (but a gathering of true believers).'

142 See 1 Corinthians 10:4.

143 i.e. Don/Dom: 'father', a monk's formal title.

144 'By Isaiah long ago'. See Isaiah 29:13.

To whom Christ wyll saye, 'I knowe non of your sort.'[145]

INFIDELITAS
Moch are they to blame that ther bretherne so report.

EVANGELIUM
Soch are no bretherne, but enemyes to Christes blode,
As put salvacyon in shaven crowne, mytar, or whode.[146]

INFIDELITAS
I praye ye, how longe have your swete spowse contynued?

EVANGELIUM
Sens the begynnynge, and now is in Christ renued:
Adam had promyse of Christes incarnacyon,
So had Abraham, with hys whole generacyon,
Whych was unto them a preachynge of the Gospell
Into salvacyon and delyveraunce from Hell.

INFIDELITAS
By thys tyme I hope ye have a fayre increase?

EVANGELIUM
She is not barren, but beareth, and never cease.
The Corinthes first Epystle hath thys clere testymony:
'In *Christo Jesu per Evangeliu{m} vos genui*:'[147]
'I have begote yow in Jesu Christ', sayth Powle,
'By the Gospel preachynge to the confort of your sowle.'

INFIDELITAS
Than are ye a cuckolde, by the blessed holy Masse!
As I sayd afore, so cometh it now to passe.
For I am a prophete by hygh inspiracyn led.
Now lyke I my self moch better than I ded.
Ye sayt that Saynt Paule begate your wyfe with chylde!

EVANGELIUM
By mysunderstandynge thu art ungracyously begylde.
An only mynyster was Paule in that same doynge;
That he therin ded was by the Gospell preachynge.
Hys mynde is the Gospell to have done that operacyon,[148]
And thys must thu holde for no carnall generacyon.[149]

INFIDELITAS
Marry, so they saye, ye fellawes of the newe ler[n]ynge
Forsake holy church, and now fall fast to wyvynge.[150]

EVANGELIUM
Naye, they forsake whoredome with other dampnable usage,
And lyve with their wyves in lawfull marryage,
Whyls the Popes oyled swarme raigne styll in their olde buggerage.

INFIDELITAS
Yea, poore marryed men have very moch a do;
I counte hym wysest that can take a snatche and to go.[151]

EVANGELIUM
Thu semest one of them that detesteth matrymonye,
Whych is afore God a state both just and holye.
Of soch as thu art, Saynt Paule ded prophecye,[152]
By the Holy Ghost, that a serten cumpanye
In the latter dayes from the truth of God shuld fall,
Attendynge to spretes of errour dyabolycall:
Whych in hypocresy wyll teache lyes for advauntage
With marked conscyences inhybytynge marryage.
Thu aperest by thy frutes to be Infydelyte.

INFIDELITAS
I am non other but even the very he,
And hyther now come I to commen the matter with ye.

1407 has, existed 1408 Since, renewed 1413 have increased greatly in numbers 1414 She (the true church) is fruitful 1425 Paul was merely a minister 1426 What he did 1429 (i.e. evangelicals) 1433 Whilst, anointed 1436 You seem to be 1441 spirits 1443 soiled 1444 (i.e. your deeds) 1446 discuss

145 Christ's words to all sinners on Judgement Day. See Matthew 25:41.

146 '[Folk] who trust that salvation will come from wearing a shaven head, mitre, or hood.'

147 1 Corinthians 4:15.

148 'He wanted the Gospel [to inspire the Church with life]'.

149 'And you must believe that to be no fleshly [sexual] act.'

150 'Marriage': a reference to the Protestant belief in clerical marriage.

151 'Who can take sexual satisfaction where he can and then move on.'

152 Romans 1:21–32.

EVANGELIUM
Avoyde, cursed fynde, and get the[e] out at the gates!

INFIDELITAS
Naye, first wyll I serve ye as I lately served your mates;
And hens wyll I not, for thys place is for me.
Who shuld here remayne but Infydelyte?

EVANGELIUM
Well, than, for a tyme I must depart from hens.
But thys first wyll I saye before thys audyens:
Easyer wyll it be concernynge ponnyshment
To Sodom and Gomor in the Daye of Judgement,
Than to those cyties that resyst the veryte
At the suggestyons of Infydelyte.
That people wyll be for ever and ever lost,
For it is the great synne agaynst the Holy Ghost.
In the Olde Lawe first the Father Hys mynde expres;
Than came Hys Sonne Christ and made it more manyfest;
And now the Holy Ghost is come to close up all.
If He be not heard, extreme dampnacyon wyll fall.
No prayer remayneth, nor expyacyon for synne,
To them that no profyght of the worde of God wyll wynne.
Take good hede therfor, and saye that ye have warnyng. (*Exit.*)

INFIDELITAS
God sende your mother of yow to have a fondelynge![153]
By the Masse, I thynke he is wele out of the waye.
Now wyll I contryve the dryft of another playe.
I must worke soch wayes Christes lawe maye not contynue.
In a whyle am I lyke to have non els of my retynue.
Companyons I want to begynne thys tragedye;
Namely False Doctryne, and hys brother Hypocresye.
They wyll not be longe, I suppose now, verelye.
By Cockes sowle, me thynke I se soch a cumpanye.
Hem, I saye! Chyldren, wyll not my voyce be hearde?
As good is a becke as is a *dewe vow garde*.[154]
By my honestie, welcome, myne owne companyons both!

Intrant [*Pseudodoctrina and Hypocrisis.*]

PSEUDODOCTRINA
Thu shalt sure have a lyvery of the same cloth.
Gramercyes, by God, my olde frynde, Infydelyte!

HYPOCRISIS
What, brother Snyp Snap, how gothe [the] wor[l]de with the[e]?

INFIDELITAS
What, fryre Flyp Flap, how saye ye to *Benedicite*?[155]

HYPOCRISIS
Marry, nothynge but well, for I crye now advauntage.

INFIDELITAS
At her purse or arse? Tell me, good fryre Succage.

HYPOCRISIS
By the Messe, at both, for I am a great penytensar,[156]
And syt at the pardon. Tush, I am the Popes owne vycar;
If thu lackest a pece, I knowe where thu mayst be sped
With c[h]oyse of a score, and brought even to thy bed.

PSEUDODOCTRINA
Art thu not ashamed to talke so lyke a knave?

HYPOCRISIS
No, for it is soch gere as the holyest of us wyll have;
Pope, cardynall, byshop, monke, chanon, prest, and fryre,
Not one of ye all but a woman wyll desyre.

1447 fiend 1448 treat 1449 hence, mine 1452 audience 1454 For, at 1455 for, truth 1462 result 1463 expiation 1464 gain 1468 plot 1470 no one else for 1471 lack 1473 hope, truly 1474 God's (euphemism) 1475 Ahem! 1478 livery 1479 Thankyou, friend 1482 see some 1483 friar Suckage 1486 piece (of flesh)/a whore 1487 twenty 1489 such matter

153 'May your mother have come by you as a foundling!' (a curse).

154 'A nod is as good as a courtly [French] greeting.'

155 Hypocrisis and Infidelitas identify each other as brother friars – both thieves or tricksters (flip-flop: flim-flam?).

156 'Penitenser': a priest licensed to hear confession and give penance.

PSEUDODOCTRINA
Our orders permyt us not to have them in marryage.

HYPOCRISIS
No, but ye fatche them in by an other carryage:
Ye do even as we do; we both are of one rate.

INFIDELITAS
By the Messe, I laugh to heare thys whoreson prate.

PSEUDODOCTRINA
What fashyon use ye? To us here intymate.

HYPOCRISIS
Ego distinguo whether ye wyll have Lyons or Parys.[157]

PSEUDODOCTRINA
Of them both to shewe, it wyll not be farre amys.

HYPOCRISIS
In Parys we have the mantell of Saynt Lewes[158]
Whych women seke moch for helpe of their barennes;
For be it ones layed upon a womannys bellye,
She go thens with chylde,[159] the myracles are seane there daylye.
And besydes all thys, ye wolde marvele in confessyon
What our fathers do to assoyled them of transgressyon.
Johan Thessecclius[160] assoyled a yonge woman ones
Behynde the hygh aulter tyll she cryed out of her bones.
And as for Lyons, there is the length of our Lorde
In a great pyller. She that wyll with a coorde
Be fast bounde to it and take soch chaunce as fall
Shall sure have chylde, for within it is hollowe all.[161]
Tush, I coulde tell ye of moch more wondre than this;
In course to heare them I thynke ye wolde ye blys.[162]

PSEUDODOCTRINA
As thu hast begunne, go forewarde in it and tell.

INFIDELITAS
Soch a knave, I suppose, is not from hens to Hell.

HYPOCRISIS
In our relygyon was an holye, Popysh patryarke
Whych of all bawdrye myght be the great monarke;
The nonnes to confesse he went from place to place,
And two hondred of them he broached in that space.[163]
Many spyces he eate hys currage to pro[v]oke;
Soch a fellawe was he, as of that gere had the stroke.[164]

PSEUDODOCTRINA
Now somewhat wyll I tell to confirme thy tale withall.
In Kynge Ferdynands[165] tyme in Spayne was a cardynall,
Petrus Mendoza was the very man that I meane;[166]
Of lemans he had great nombre besydes the quene.[167]
One of hys bastardes was earle, an other was duke,
Whom also he abused and thought it no rebuke.
Joannes Cremona, an other good cardynall,
For reformacyon of the clergye spyrituall,
Came ones into Englande to dampne prestes matrymonye,
And the next nyght after was taken doynge bytcherye.[168]

1493 other means **1494** kind **1496** make known **1498** too far wrong **1500** in, barrenness **1504** purge, sin **1505** once **1506** altar, until, (i.e. earnestly) **1507** the height (marked out) **1508** pillar, cord **1509** accept whatever happens **1514** There's not such a knave **1516** (i.e. the best/worst of all) **1517** nuns **1519** ate, courage/virility, stimulate **1521** something **1524** lovers **1529** damn clerical marriage **1530** discovered whoring

157 '"I make a distinction": do you want to choose Lyons or Paris practice?'

158 The mantle of St Louis, patron saint of France.

159 'She leaves there pregnant'.

160 'John Thessecclius' (perhaps a corruption of 'The Ecclesius': 'John (of) the Church') may have been an invention of Bale's.

161 'Completely hollow': the idea is, as with the mantle of St Louis, that the priests will rape the woman while she is incapacitated and thus provide the 'miraculous' pregnancy themselves.

162 'You'd need to bless yourself to hear them all' (i.e. 'you would think it was wonderful').

163 'He served there': the *double entendre* is explicit.

164 'He was the best equipped in that department': again an obvious anatomical *double entendre*.

165 Ferdinand of Aragon (1479–1516).

166 Petrus Mendoza (1428–95).

167 Queen Isabella of Castile (1474–1504).

168 John of Crema (Cremona), papal legate to England in 1125, who 'in the council . . . dealt most severely with the matter of priests' wives, saying that it was the greatest sin to rise from the side of a whore and go to make the Body of Christ. Yet . . . on the very same day he had made the Body of Christ, he was discovered with a whore.' Henry of Huntingdon, *Historia Anglorum*, ed. D. Greenway (Oxford, 1996), pp. 473–5.

Doctor Eckius also, whych fearcely came to dyspute[169]
In Lipsia with Luther, mydynge there hym to confute
For marryage of prestys, thre chyldren had that yeare.
By thys maye ye se that sumtyme we make mery cheare!

INFIDELITAS
Marry, that ye do; I shall beare ye recorde now.
But how wyll ye answere for breakynge of your vow?

PSEUDODOCTRINA
We never breake vowe so longe as we do not marrye,
Though we in whoredome be never so bolde and busye.

INFIDELITAS
By your order, than, ye maye walke moch at large.
What hast thu, Hypocresye, to laye for thy dyscharge?

HYPOCRISIS
Saynt Frances habyte, with the holy gyrdle and whode;
Non can go to Helle that therin dy, by the Rode;[170]
In case Saynt Frances be sure upon their syde,
Els maye they fortune to be of their purpose wyde.
For I reade of one that shuld have gone to the Devyll
But the spretes of Helle coulde do to hym non evyll
Tyll St Frances came and toke from hym hys cowle;
Then went he to Helle, the fryres ded heare hym howle!
I wyll therfor serve St Frances with hart and mynde,
With dayly memoryes that he maye be my frynde;
And than I care not for all the devyls in Hell.
That I have tolde yow is more true than the Gospel.

INFIDELITAS
Then are ye more sure than monkes for your heretage,
For their landes are here, but ye clayme Heaven for advauntage.

PSEUDODOCTRINA
Yet is it to them a ve[r]y plesaunt thynge
Their abbot at home to be called lorde and kynge.

INFIDELITAS
Naye, monke and chorle, for here is no kynge but one;
If he be a kynge, hys mace is a marybone
And hys crowne a cow torde! Soch knaves as come from the cart
Must be called kynges for playenge a popysh part.[171]

PSEUDODOCTRINA
It become not the Romysh Pope so to lurche,
Consyderynge he is the hyghest of the churche.

INFIDELITAS
If he be the hyghest, than is he the wether cocke.

PSEUDODOCTRINA
Ah, now I perceyve thu art dysposed to mocke;
Of all holy churche he is the pryncypall heade.

INFIDELITAS
Marry, that is true; he sendeth out bulles undre lead,
And he hath two keyes, the one to open Hell,
The other speareth Heaven; thus do newe heretykes tel.[172]
They report also that dogges have no devocyon
To hys holy lawes, nor to hys olde instruccyon.

PSEUDODOCTRINA
Why shuld dogges hate hym? Make that more evydent.

INFIDELITAS
They love no pese porrege, nor yet reade hearynges in Lent,
Stock fysh nor oysters, but curse hym body and bone,
And wolde hys reade sprottes and rotten fysh were gone.[173]
Tush, I heare them, I, and that maketh me full sad.

1534 we have a great time 1535 I'll swear to it 1540 to offer in your defence 1541 hood 1542 die 1543 If they do 1544 to fail in their plans 1553 inheritance 1554 (your) profit 1558 he (an abbot), marrow-bone 1559 turd, low origins 1561 doesn't become, lie 1566 authenticated by lead seals 1568 (i.e. reformers)

169 Johann Maier von Eck (1486–1543), the Catholic scholar who disputed with Luther in Leipzig in 1519.
170 It was popularly believed that anyone buried in a Franciscan habit would not go to Hell.
171 i.e. low-born clerics cannot claim real authority; they gain status only through the backing of the pope.
172 A reference to St Peter's keys of the Kingdom of Heaven, symbolic of the powers to bind and loose souls granted him by Jesus (see Matthew 17:19). Here the powers are mockingly declared only to be negative, to lock up Heaven and open Hell.
173 Peas porridge, red herrings, dried salt-fish, oysters, and red sprats were among the foods permitted to be eaten on fast days.

HYPOCRISIS
Eyther thu doest mock, or els thu art sure mad.

INFIDELITAS
I heare the people complayne very moch of the[e].

PSEUDODOCTRINA
What is their pratlinge? I praye the[e] hartely, tell me.

INFIDELITAS
They saye thu teachest nothyng but lowsy tradycions,
And lyes for lucre, with damnable superstycyons.
And thus they conclude that the draffe of popysh prystes
Is good ynough for swyne, by whom they meane the papystes.
Yea, and they saye also, the dyet of men is all
To most vyle carren, the dogges wyll sonest fall.[174]

PSEUDODOCTRINA
Than do they compare the papystes unto dogges?

INFIDELITAS
Marry, that they do, and to soch swynysh hogges
As in swyll and sosse are brought up all their lyfe.
Soch are the papystes, they saye, both man and wyfe.
They saye of the[e] also, that thu art a noughty knave;
By prowlynge and lyenge ye fryers wolde all have;
Thyne order, they saye, is spronge even out of Hell,
And all thys knowledge they have now of the Gospell.

HYPOCRISIS
Why, where is he now? I besych the[e], hartely, tell.

INFIDELITAS
By the Messe, abroade, and, I warande ye, maketh revell.
I commoned with hym, and he ded us despyse;
Agaynst hym therefor sumwhat must we devyse.

PSEUDODOCTRINA
Marry that must we, or els it wyll be wronge;
He wyll sure destroye us if we do suffer hym longe.
Nedes must we serve hym as we ones served Christ.

INFIDELITAS
Why, mad brayned whoresons, how ded ye handle Christ?

PSEUDODOCTRINA
As he preached here, we followed from place to place
To trappe Hym in snare, and Hys doctryne to deface.
Than founde we the meanes to put Hym so to death
Least He agaynst us shuld open any more breath;
And we set foure knyghtes to kepe Hym downe in Hys grave
That He never more our lyvynge shuld deprave.[175]
And thus must we serve the Gospell, no remedye,
Els wyll he destroye our lyvynge perpetuallye.
Better one were lost than we shuld perysh all,
As Cayphas ones sayd in counsell pharysaycall.[176]

INFIDELITAS
By God, and wele sayd! Whan ye have hym in hys grave,
Stampe hym downe tyll he shyte, and serve hym lyke a knave.

HYPOCRISIS
We must so ordre hym that he go nomore at large.

PSEUDODOCTRINA
Foure knyghtes wyl we hyre whom we shall streyghtly charge
To kepe hym downe harde. The first are ambycyouse prelates,
Then covetouse lawers that Gods worde spyghtfully hates,
Lordes without lernynge, and justyces unryghtfull:
These wyll kepe hym downe, and rappe hym on the scull.
Ther someners and ther scribes I warande ye shal stere
With balyves and catchpolles to holde hym downe every where.[177]
I trowe Rugge and Corbet at Norwych wyll do their part,

1576 surely 1580 lie, money 1581 pig-swill 1587 dog-food 1590 wandering, lying 1593 he (i.e. Evangelium) 1594 having a good time 1595 spoke 1599 do to him 1604 (i.e. say any more) 1607 (there's) no alternative 1608 Otherwise he'll 1612 shits himself 1613 goes free no longer 1614 strictly instruct 1617 unjust 1619 instruct/guide

174 '[Turned] to the most vile carrion, that only dogs could relish.'

175 For the setting of the guard at Christ's tomb, see the York *Resurrection* pageant.

176 For Caiaphas's counsel to the Pharisees, see John 18:14.

177 The summoners, bailiffs, and catch-poles (sheriff's officers) were all servants of the ecclesiastical courts who would pursue heretics.

With Wharton of Bongaye, and for my sake put hym to smart.[178]

HYPOCRISIS
And I wyll rayse up in the unyversytees
The seven slepers there to advaunce the Popes decrees:
As Dorbel and Duns, Durande and Thomas of Aquyne,
The Mastre of *Sentens*, with Bachon the great devyne,
Henricus de Gandova and these shall read *ad clerum*,
Aristotle and Albert, *de secretis mulierum*,
With the commentaryes of Avicen and Averoyes,
And a *Phebo Phebe* whych is very good for boyes.[179]

INFIDELITAS
Yea, and lete the Pope, as Gods owne vycar here,
In hys hande iii crosses, and iii crownes on hys head bere,
Hys power betokenynge in Heaven, in Earth, and in Hell,
That he maye commaunde all kynges to subdue the Gospell.

PSEUDODOCTRINA
Hysselfe maye do that, he nede commaunde non other.
Is not he the head of the holy church, our mother?
Maye not he make payntes and devyls at hys owne pleasure,
Whych hath in hys handes the keyes and churches treasure,
So wele as he made Saynt Herman first a saynt,
And twenty years after of heresye hym attaynt?[180]
First he sent hym to Heaven by hys canonyzacyon,
And from thens to Helle by an excommunycacyon.
We reade of Formosus that, after he was dead,
One Pope hys fyngars, an other cut of hys head,
And threwe hys carkas into the floude of Tyber,
With the head and fyngars, as Platina doth remember,[181]
In token that he is judge over quyck and dead,
And maye dampne and save by hys pardons undre lead.
Sylvester the Seconde to the Devyll hymself ones gave
For that hygh offyce that he myght dampne and save.
He offered also hys stones to Sathan, they saye,
For prestes chastyte, and so went their marryage awaye.[182]

[*Enter Evangelium.*]

HYPOCRISIS
Here is one commynge, enquyre what he intende.

INFIDELITAS
Ha, it is the Gospell! From hym God us defende!
(*Exit secreto.*)[183]

PSEUDODOCTRINA
Shewe me, brother myne, who ded the[e] hyther sende?

EVANGELIUM
The Father of Heaven of Hys mere benyvolence.
I desyre therfor to have fre audyence.

PSEUDODOCTRINA
Ye mynde, than, to preache afore thys cumpanye?

EVANGELIUM
In the lawes of God wolde I instruct them gladlye;

1632 three 1633 symbolizing 1635 He can do that himself 1640 convicted 1653 someone 1655 Who sent you here 1656 by 1658 intend

178 William Repps or Rugg was bishop of Norwich 1536–50. For John Corbet, see Bale's *Actes of Englysh Votaryes* (Antwerp, 1546), II, 83. Richard Wharton of Bungay (Norfolk), was an agent of Cromwell's. As Happé notes, he comes in for further criticism from Bale in his *Yet a Course at the Romish Foxe* (Zurich, 1543), fol. V.

179 In this stanza Bale mocks some of the leading Catholic scholars and authorities of the medieval period; Nicholas de Orbelis (1400–73); Duns Scotus (*c.*1265–1308); Durandus of St Pourcain (1270–1334); St Thomas Aquinas (1225–74), (Peter Lombard) the author ('master') of the *Sententiae*, a set text in theology schools; Roger Bacon (*c.*1220–90); Henry of Ghent (d.1293); St Albertus Magnus (1193–1280), to whom the *de Secretis Mulierum* ('On the Secrets of Women') was attributed. The Greek philosopher Aristotle (384–322 BC), and the Arab philosophers Avicenna (980–1037) and Averoes (1126–98), are included owing to their influence on medieval Catholic thought. '*Phebo phebe*' is the opening of Alanus de Insulis's textbook *Doctrinale Minus*.

180 Bale makes the same claim, that Boniface VIII (pope 1294–1303) posthumously burned St Herman for heresy, in *The Image of Bothe Churches* (Antwerp, 1546), Cii(v).

181 Bartolomeo Platina's *History of the Lives of the Popes* (Paris, 1505) narrates how Steven VI (pope 896–7) disinterred the body of his predecessor Formosus (who occupied the papal throne 891–6) and tried it for perjury and other crimes. Formosus was found guilty and the body mutilated. It was subsequently thrown into the river Tiber by Steven's successor Sergius III (pope 904–11).

182 The story that Silvester II (pope 999–1003) offered his testicles to Satan in return for the doctrine of clerical celibacy may be Bale's own invention.

183 'He exits secretly.'

For non other waye there is unto salvacyon,
But the worde of God in every generacyon,
That quyckeneth, that saveth, that bryngeth unto Heaven,
As before Hys death Christ taugh[t] the Apostle aleven.

PSEUDODOCTRINA
Preache here thu shalt not, without the auctoryte
Of Pope or byshopp, or of some of their affynyte.

EVANGELIUM
Gods worde never taketh hys autoryte of man.

PSEUDODOCTRINA
Thu shalt not here preache, do thu the best thu can.

HYPOCRISIS
Gods blessynge on your good hart, it is spoken even like a man.
Ye knowe thys daye, ser, we have a full holy feast,
And must go processyon with the blessed Rode of Reast.[184]
We have longe mattens, longe laudes, longe houres, longe pryme;
Masse, evensonge, co[m]plyne and all must be done in tyme;
Sensynge of the aulters, and castynge of holy water,
Holy breade makynge, with other necessary matter.

EVANGELIUM
Have God commaunded any soch thynges to be done?

PSEUDODOCTRINA
What is that to the[e]? Go meddle thu with olde shone!
Cannyst thu saye but they are good sygnyfycacyons?[185]

EVANGELIUM
I saye they are frutes of your ymagynacyons,
To brynge in lucre and darken Gods hygh glorye.
Of yow God doth axe no soch vayne beggerye.
Christ never sent Hys to shewe sygnyfycacyons,
But Hys lyvynge worde to all the Christen nacyons.
Ye forsake the Lorde, as Esaias doth tell,
And hyghly blaspheme the holie of Israel.
In hys first chaptre thys horryble sentence is:
Quis haec frustranea quaesivit de manibus vestris;
'Who hath requyred of yow soch sacryfyce?
In vayne offer yow that uncommaunded servyce.
Your incense to Me is great abhomynacyon;
I sore abhorre it and moch detest your fashyon.
Whan ye praye to Me, I geve ye non attendaunce,
But avert My face, sayth God, and My countenaunce.'[186]
By thys ye maye se that the Lorde doth not regarde
Your mangy mutterynge, ney[t]her graunt it any rewarde.
No man wylleth Paule to speake in the congregacyon
In a straunge language without interpretacyon.
In your Latyne houres the flocke do ye not consydre
But declare your selves to be Romysh all togydre.
'Be not led about', sayth Paule, 'by an straunge lernynge.'[187]
What els is your doctryne but a blynde, Popysh thynge?
He testyfyeth also, *Non enim ut baptizarem*
Misit me Christus, sed ut evangelizarem:
'Christ hath not me sent that I shuld baptyse', sayth Paule,
'But to preach Hys worde to the confort of mannys sowle'.[188]
Loo, though baptyme be a thynge very necessarye,
Yet must it geve place to Gods worde, no remedye.
Why, than, preferre ye your draffysh ceremonyes
To the Gospell preachynge? O dampnable injuryes!

HYPOCRISIS
Why suffer ye hym to pratle here so longe?

PSEUDODOCTRINA
Get the hens shortly, or with the[e] it wyll be wronge.

Intrat [*Infidelitas.*]

1662 gives life 1663 eleven Apostles 1665 faction 1666 needs no permission from men 1667 however hard you try 1671 matins 1673 Censing, sprinkling 1676 shoes (i.e. get lost!) 1678 (i.e. the products) 1679 money 1680 ask 1681 (out) His (Disciples), symbols 1682 But (to preach) 1691 pay, no attention 1694 mangy/rotten 1695 Paul instructs that no man 1696 interpreting it 1706 concede pride of place 1707 worthless 1709 chatter 1710 You'll suffer for it

184 '[In] procession': Happé suggests the allusion is to the Cross of Wrest, a village in Bedfordshire.
185 'Can you deny that these are good symbols?'
186 A paraphrase of Isaiah 1:11–15.
187 Hebrews 13:9.
188 'For Christ sent me not to baptize, but to preach the Gospel': 1 Corinthians 1:17.

INFIDELITAS
Peace be here, and God, mastre doctour, by your leave,
That I maye declare a pardone here in my sleve,
Of Our Lady of Boston, Ingham, and Saynt Johannes frarye,[189]
With the indulgence of blessyd Saynt Antonye.

PSEUDODOCTRINA
Wele take thy pleasure, and do it hardelye.

HYPOCRISIS
Syr, he doth me wro[n]ge, for thys daye it is my stacyon
To preache my brotherhede and gather my lymytacyon.[190]

PSEUDODOCTRINA
Who first speake, first spede;[191] steppe fourth and reade thy pardon,
And whan he hath done, your course is Father Warden.[192]

EVANGELIUM
What course appoynt ye for preachyng of the Gospel?

PSEUDODOCTRINA
I wolde thy Gospell and thu were both now in Hell.

EVANGELIUM
Why, and shall thys baggage put by the word of God?

PSEUDODOCTRINA
Thu wylt not be answered tyll thu fele a sharper rod.

INFIDELITAS
Good Christen people, I am come hyther, verelye,
As a true p[r]octour of the howse of Saynt Antonye.
Of cleane remyssyon I have brought ye indulgence,
A pena et culpa – for all your synne and offence,
By the auctoryte of Pope Leo and Pope Clement,
Pope Bonyface, Pope Pius, Pope Johan, and Pope Innocent.[193]
And here I blesse ye with a wynge of the Holy Ghost,
From thonder to save ye, and from spretes in every coost.
Lo, here is a belle to hange upon your hogge,
And save your cattell from the bytynge of a dogge.
So many as wyll come to thys holy fraternyte,
Come paye your moneye, and ye shall have letters of me.

PSEUDODOCTRINA
Lete me have a letter, for I wyll be a brother.

HYPOCRISIS
Then geve me a belle, for I wyll be an other.

EVANGELIUM
O dampnable leadynge of Babylonicall Sodomytes!
Your selves ye declare to be shamefull hypocrytes.
Lorde, pytie thy people, and take awaye these gydes,
These scorners, these robbers, these cruell homycydes.
Soch prophetes are they as God ded never sende;
As Hieremy sayth, they dampnable wayes pretende.[194]
Wo, hypocrytes, wo! For here ye tryfle and mocke
With Christen people, and the Kyngedom of Heaven uplocke.
Ye count it a game to lose that Christ hath bought
With Hys precyouse bloud, and here most derely sought.
O ye are wretches and pestylent Antichristes,
Mynysters of Dagon,[195] and most deceytfull papystes.
Lyke ravenouse wolves, poore wydowes ye devoure;
By tyttle of prayer eternall, dampnacyon is youre[s].
Youre owne dreames ye folowe, but matter moch more wayghtye
Ye do not esteme, as judgement, faythe, and mercye.

1711 master 1712 sleeve 1715 do as you wish 1716 responsibility 1720 What provision do you make 1722 set aside 1725 spokesman for 1726 complete remission (of sins) 1727 From penalty and guilt 1731 coast/region 1733 biting 1734 As 1735 letters (of remission) from 1739 You reveal yourselves 1740 pity 1741 murderers 1745 lock up 1746 think, what 1751 (false) title/authority 1753 (matters such) as

189 Boston (Lincolnshire); Ingham (Norfolk); perhaps the Priory of St John, north of Smithfield, London.

190 'My revenue from my allotted territory.' A 'limitor' (begging friar) was so named after the 'limitation' or area within which he had a licence to beg.

191 'Who speaks first, prospers first'.

192 'When he has finished, your course of action is [to appeal to] the Warden [for your loss of begging rights].'

193 There were many popes in the Middle Ages with these names. It is not clear that any specific individuals are intended.

194 See Jeremiah 2, *passim*.

195 Dagon: a god of the Philistines; see, for example Judges 16:23; 1 Maccabees 10:83–4.

Wo, Pharysees, wo! Ye make cleane outwardlye,
But inwardes ye are full of covetousnesse and baudrye.
Paynted tumbes are ye, ap[e]rynge ryght bewtyfull,[196]
But within ye stynke, and have thoughtes very shamefull.
Ye slewe the prophetes, your doynges yet beare wytnesse:
How thynke ye to avoyde that poynt of unryghteousnesse?
Oh ragynge serpentes, and vyperouse generacyon,[197]
How can ye escape the daunger of dampnacyon?

PSEUDODOCTRINA
Who made the[e] so bolde to medle within my cure,
And teache newe lernynge? An heretyke art thu, sure!
If due serch were made, we shuld fynde the[e], I thynke, no pryst.[198]

EVANGELIUM
Yes, anoynted of God, but no popysh Antichrist.

PSEUDODOCTRINA
Here I attache the[e] for a busye scysmatyke,
And wyll the[e] accuse for an haynouse heretyke.
Laye handes upon hym, and depryve hym of thys aparell.

Hic veste spoliatum sordidioribus induunt.[199]

Loo, thus wyll I handle all them that shall take thy quarell.
Holde, awaye with thys gere, and laye it fourth asyde!

HYPOCRISIS
Naye, tarry brother myne, for away shalt thu not slyde.

EVANGELIUM
I am not goynge; why doest thu slaunder me?

INFIDELITAS
Burne hym to ashes, and shewe to hym no pytie.

PSEUDODOCTRINA
Brent shall he not be if he wyll nomore do so.
Fellawe, how sayst thu? Wylt thu here abjure or no?

EVANGELIUM
I wyll neyther abjure, nor yet recant Gods glorye.

PSEUDODOCTRINA
I offered the[e] reason, and therto thu wylt not applye.
Wele, get the[e] forewarde, for thu shalt sure dye.
The temporall power shall judge the[e] to the fyre
At our accusement and holy relygyouse desyre.

EVANGELIUM
Though yow for my sake impryson men cruellye,
Famysh them, stocke them, and them with fagotes frye,[200]
Hurt me ye shall not, for I can never dye,
And they fo[r] my sake shall lyve pe[r]petuallye.

PSEUDODOCTRINA
Here is a pratynge! With a vengeaunce, hens!

HYPOCRISIS
Thys horryble heretyke now shall we well recompens.

Exeunt cum eo.[201]

INFIDELITAS
Yea, burne hym wele, fryre, and lete hym no longer raygne.
Laye on grene fagotes to put hym to the more payne.
By the Messe, I laugh to se how thys gere doth wurke.
He is lyke of them to have nomore grace than a Turke,[202]
For soch knaves they are as a man shall not lyghtly fynde,

1754 make (yourselves) clean 1755 bawdry/sins 1762 jurisdiction 1766 arrest, schismatic/heretic 1767 heinous 1768 these clothes 1769 treat, support your claims 1771 slip 1774 (i.e. agree to stop preaching heresy) 1777 agree 1778 surely die 1780 accusation 1782 starve 1785 What a lot of nonsense, hence! 1786 repay 1787 friar, reign 1788 green/unseasoned, greater 1789 work/progress 1791 easily

196 'Painted tombs': i.e. 'whited sepulchres' or hypocrites; see Matthew 23:27.

197 Viperous/snake-like; see, for example, Matthew 3:7.

198 'Not to be a real priest [and so not entitled to preach].'

199 'Here, removing his clothes, they put more sordid/dirty ones on him.'

200 'Burn them with faggots [lumps of wood]'.

201 'They go out with him.'

202 'He's likely to get no more grace from them than he would from a Turk'.

And rake Hell over, companyons they are to my mynde.
My busynesse all is now at a good conc[l]usyon,
That I have here brought these iii lawes to confusyon;
Now shall I be able to lyve here peaceablye,
And make frowlyke chere, with 'Hey how, fryska jolye!'[203]
The Lawe of Nature I kest first in a leprye
By the secrete helpe of Ydolatrye and Sodomye.
The Lawe of Moses I made a crypple blynde,
Avaryce and Ambycyon to helpe me were not behynde.
And now Christes Lawe I have brent for heresye,
By helpe of False Doctryne and my cosyne Hypocresye.
On these same iii Lawes all other lawes depende
And can not prevayle nowe these are at an ende.
If Christen governers do not these lawes upholde
Their cyvyle ordynaunces wyll sone be very colde.
Well, thys valeaunt George hath made them all to stoupe;
Cheare now may I make, and set cocke on the houpe.
Fyll in all the pottes, and byd me welcome, hostesse,
And go call me hyther myne owne swete mynyon Besse!

FINIT ACTUS QUARTUS.[204]

INCIPIT ACTUS QUINTUS: RESTAURATIO LEGUM DIVINARUM.[205]

VINDICTA DEI
Quid gloriaris in malicia qui potens es in iniquitate?[206]

Thu vengeable wretche, replete with poyson and vyce,
Why doest thu thus rejoyce in crueltie and malyce?
Thynkest thu that God slepeth and wyll not Hys defende,
And that thy myschefe shall never have an ende?
The bloude of innocents to Hym for vengeaunce call,
And therfor thys houre must I fearcely upon the[e] fall.

INFIDELITAS
Thu sprete of the ayre, I strayghtly conjure the[e] here,
By Panton and Craton,[207] and charge the[e] to com no nere.

VINDICTA DEI
Thynkest thu to stoppe me with thy folysh conjuracyon,
Whom God sendeth hyther for thy abhomynacyon?

INFIDELITAS
What art thu called? Thy name to me rehearce.

VINDICTA DEI
I am Vindicta Dei, in ponnyshment most fearce;
With water, with swerde, and with fyre I must the[e] pearce.

INFIDELITAS
Be good in thy offyce, and thu shalt have moneye and meate.

VINDICTA DEI
By fylthy rewardes thu cannyst not me intreate,
But that I wyll do as God hath me commaunded;
For if worldly gyftes my furye myght have changed
The unyversall worlde had not bene drowned with water,
Nor Sodome and Gomor with so fyery fearfull matter,
Nor yet the Israelytes with terrour of the sworde,
With hungre and pestylence in the anger of Gods worde.
Pharao in Egipte the plages had never felt
Might I have bene stopped for sylver or for gelte.
In Egipte I brought ten terryble ponnyshmentes[208]
Upon the people, for breakynge Hys Commaundementes.

1792 Even if he were to rake 1796 merry 1797 threw, leper-house 1800 slow 1801 burnt 1802 cousin 1803 three 1804 (So) cannot 1806 regulations, (i.e. dead) 1807 St George (hero), submit 1808 (i.e. live recklessly) 1809 Fill up 1812 vengeful 1814 defend His (followers) 1817 fiercely 1818 air, strictly 1819 come no nearer 1824 pierce 1825 good (to me) 1829 whole, would not have been

203 A song tag.
204 'Here ends the Fourth Act.'
205 'Here begins the Fifth Act: The Restoration of the Divine Laws.'
206 'Why boastest thou thyself in mischief, you who are strong in iniquity?' A paraphrase of Psalms 51:1–3.
207 The elements of the word '*Pantocraton*': 'ruler of all', here perhaps intended as the name of the Devil, used in conjuration, but effectively reminding the audience of God's role as true 'ruler of all'.
208 See Exodus 7:17–11:10.

Their wholsom waters I tourned into bloude;
I multyplyed frogges to poyson therwith their foude;
I made waspes and dranes them grevously to stynge,
And all kyndes of flyes sone after ded I in brynge;
Upon their cattel I threwe the foule pestylence,
Both botche, byle, and blayne they had for their offence;
Lyghtenynges and haylynges destroyed their corne and frute;
A swarme of hungry locustes their pastours destytute.
The space of thre dayes I gave them palpable darkenesse;
I slewe the first goten of man and beast for thy rudenes:
For I never stryke but for the[e], Infydelyte.

INFIDELITAS
'Stryke for me', quoth a? By the Mary Masse, I defye the[e]!

VINDICTA DEI
What, thu wylt not so, thy braynes are not so lyght.

INFIDELITAS
Anger me not to moch; for if thu do, I fyght.

VINDICTA DEI
All that wyll not helpe thy wycked workynges now;
Whan the stronger come, the weaker must nedes bowe.
The Lawe of Nature infected thu hast with a leprye.

INFIDELITAS
Naye, it was not I, but that wytche Idolatrye,
And that polde, shorne knave that men call Sodomye.

VINDICTA DEI
Of whom spronge they first but of Infydelyte?
Therfor thu shalt have the plage of penalte
Whych they first tasted for their inyquyte.
For these two vyces I drowned the worlde with water;
In token wherof I plage the[e] with the same matter.

Hic Infidelitatem lympha percutit.[209]

INFIDELITAS
Tush! I defye thy worst. Thys shall not dryve me hence,
For after the floude with Cham had I resydence,[210]
And so contynued tyll Moyses lawe came in,
With hys jolye tryckes a newe rule to begyn.

VINDICTA DEI
And hym thu corruptedest with Avaryce and Ambycyon,
And so dedst leave hym in myserable condycyon.
Thu shalt have, therfor, that than to them was due.
Most terryble battayle the Israelytes untrue
That tyme ded suffer for their infydelyte;
Wherfor with thys swerde I justlye bannysh the[e]
Bycause thu shalt here geve place to Christes Gospel.

Gladio Infidelitatem denuo cedit.[211]

INFIDELITAS
Yet wyll I not hens, but agaynst ones rebell.
Ded not I remayne with Judas and other more?

[VINDICTA DEI]
Whan Christ preached here and taught them, [thu] vext Hym sore.

[INFIDELITAS]
Yes, and after that was I with Simon Magus,
With Saunder Coppersmyth, with Elimas and Demetrius.[212]
And now I persever amonge the ranke rable of papystes,
Teachyng ther shorlynges to playe the Antichrystes.

VINDICTA DEI
The innocent bloude of payntes contynuallye
Doth call unto God to revenge their injurye,
Agaynst false doctryne and cursed hypocresye,
Whom thu hast raysed the glory of the Gospell
To darken, and hys fryndes most myserably to quell.
Wherfor thu shalt have lyke as thu hast deserved,
For thy wycked doynges thy ponyshment now doubled.

1838 food 1839 drones/bees 1842 ulcer, boil, blister 1843 hail-storms 1844 stripped bare their pastures 1845 (For) the 1846 first begotten son 1850 too 1852 surrender 1855 bald 1856 From, from 1857 punishment 1862 flood 1867 that (which) then 1868 battle(s) 1869 (At) that 1872 once again 1874 vexed 1878 little shaven ones

209 'Here he throws water on Infidelitas.'

210 Ham (son of Noah). See Genesis 9:18–10:32.

211 'With a sword he strikes Infidelitas a second time.'

212 All these individuals set themselves against the work of Paul and the Apostles. For Simon Magus, see l. 1057, above; for Alexander the coppersmith, 2 Timothy 4:14; for Elimas, a sorcerer, Acts 13:8–12; and for Demetrius, a silversmith, Acts 19:24–41.

Ignis ipsum precedet, the prophete David sayth thus:
Atque inflammabit in circuitu inimicos eius:[213]
'A consumynge fyre shall ronne before the judge,
Hys enemyes consumynge', they shal fynde no
refuge.
Ob scelera et culpas hominum ritusque nephandos
In cineres ibit tellus, tenuemque favillam,[214]
As Mantuan writeth, for the wyckednesse of the[e]
The Earth to ashes by fyre shall turned be.

Ignis flamma Infidelitatem locum exire coget.[215]

Infidelitas
Credo, credo, credo, I saye, credo, credo, credo!
To the Devyll of Helle, by the Messe, I wene I go.

Exit [*Infidelitas, Vindicta Dei becomes Deus Pater.*]

Deus Pater
As ye have seane here how I have strycken with fyre
The pestylent vyce of Infydelyte,
So wyll I destroye in the fearcenesse of Myne yre
All sectes of errour with their enormyte,
Whych hath rysen out of that inyquyte.
For as it is sayd that My hande hath not sett
Shall up by the rote, no power maye it lett.[216]

The Apostle Johan in the Apocalyps doth saye
He sawe a newe Heven and a newe Earth
aperynge,[217]
The olde Earth and see were taken cleane awaye;
That Heaven is mannys fayth, that Earth hys
understandynge,
Whom We have renued by Our most secret
workynge;
The olde cancred Earth exylynge with the see,
Whych is superstycyon and infydelyte.

A new Hierusalem the sayd Johan also se,
As a bewtyfull bryde prepared to her husbande.[218]
Our true faythfull churche is that same fayr cytie
Whom We have clensed by the power of Our ryght
hande,
As a spouse to Christ in every Christen lande,
Bannyshynge the sectes of Babylonicall poperye,
That she in the sprete maye walke to our glorye.

Resort ye thre Lawes, for yow wyll I clere also
Of soch infeccyons as by Infydelyte
Ye have receyved, that ye with her maye go
Declarynge the wayes of Christen lyberte,
That Us she maye take without perplexite
For her only God, and be Our people styll
In Our lawes walkynge accordyng to Our wyll.

Omnes Simul.
At Your commaundement we are, most blessed
Lorde,

Deus Pater
Approche nyghar than and ye shall be restorde.

Thu, Lawe of Nature, We first begynne with the[e],
Restorynge the[e] agayne to thy first puryte.
Avoyde Idolatrye, avoyde vyle Sodomye;
We charge ye nomore thys lawe to putryfye.
Kepe styll that same hart for a sygne perpetuall
That thu wert written in mannys hart first of all.

Thu, Law of Moses, geve Me that vayle from the[e],
No longar shalt thu neyther blynde nor croked be.
Hens thu, Ambycyon, and cursed Covetousnes!
I here bannysh yow from thys lawe ever, doughtles.
Lose not those tables whych are a token true,
That thu in the flesh shalt evermore contynue.

Thu, Lawe of the Gospell, though thu be last of all,
In operacyon yet thu art the pryncypall.
From the[e] I exyle Hypocresy and False Doctryne,
With all that depende upon the papystycall lyne.
Reserve the same boke for a sygne of heavenly poure,
For that boke thu art that Johan from Heaven ded
devoure.[219]

Naturae Lex
Everlastynge prayse to Thy gloryouse Majeste!

1888 run 1894 I believe 1898 my anger 1899 enormity/abuses 1901 that (which) 1907 renewed 1908 cankered 1917 Come back 1925 nearer 1928 Go away 1929 putrify/corrupt 1930 for ever, sign 1932 veil 1933 crooked/crippled 1935 (for) ever, doubtless 1936 true sign 1942 keep, book, power

[213] Psalms 97:3: 'A fire goeth before him, and burneth up his enemies round about.'

[214] 'Because of the wickedness and guilt of men and their forbidden rites, the world shall become ashes of the finest [i.e. smallest] sort.' Mantuan, *De Suorum Temporum Calamitatibus*.

[215] 'The flame of the fire causes Infidelitas to flee from the place.'

[216] See Matthew 15:13, and earlier uses of the image in 2 Chronicles 7:20 and Ezekiel 17:5–24.

[217] See Revelation 21:1.

[218] See Revelation 21:2.

[219] 'The book that St John read passionately.' See Revelation 5:1 and following.

MOSEH LEX
Our Heavenly Governour, great is Thy gracyouse pytie!

CHRISTI LEX
Of mankynde Thu art the eternall felycyte!

NATURAE LEX
Now leavest Thy servauntes in Thy perpetuall peace;
To do The[e] servyce from hens wyll we not ceace.

MOSEH LEX
For our eyes have seane what Thu hast now prepared
For Thy peoples helth, whych hath bene here declared.

CHRISTI LEX
A lyght Thu hast sent whych is Thy joyouse Gospell,
To the consolacyon of the Howse of Israel.

NATURAE LEX
In rejoyce of thys, make we some melodye.

MOSEH LEX
The name of our God to prayse and magnyfye.

CHRISTI LEX
I assent therto, and wyll synge very gladlye.

Hic ad Dei gloriam cantabunt 'In exitu Israel de Aegypto', vel aliud simile.[220]

DEUS PATER
Now have We destroyed the kyngedom of Babylon,[221]
And throwne the great whore into the bottomlesse pyt,
Restorynge agayne the true fayth and relygyon
In the Christen churche, as We have thought it fyt,
Depurynge these lawes so to contynue yt.
Man is Our creature, and hath grace in Our syght,
To dwell with hym now is Our whole hartes delyght.

Man is Our people, hys God We are agayne,
With hym wyll We have contynuall resydence.
Awaye wyll We wype from hym all s[o]rowe and payne:
He shall no longar dyspayre for hys offence,
Nor have in hys sowle any carefull doubt of conscyence,
The olde popyshnesse is past whych was dampnacyon;
We have now renued Our Christen congregacyon.

[*Enter Fides Christiana.*]

Stande fourth Christen Fayth, and take Our advertysement:
We here appoynt the[e] to governe Our congregacyon.
Se thu do nothynge without the admonyshment
Of these thre Lawes here. Enprent their declaracyon
Of My swete promyses, and than make thu relacyon
To My folke agayne, that they maye walke to Me
Without popysh dreames in a perfyg[h]t lyberte.

FIDES CHRISTIANA
Most heavenly Maker, in that Thu doest commaunde me
Evermore wyll I full prompt and dylygent be.

DEUS PATER
Thu, Lawe of Nature shalt teache man God to knowe,
And that to refuse wherby any yll maye growe.

NATURAE LEX
From thys Your precept shall I not varye, I trowe.

DEUS PATER
Teache thu hym also to worshyp one God above,
And hys poore neyber to prosecute with love.

MOSEH LEX
I hope, blessed Lorde, to do as me shall behove.

DEUS PATER
And thu shalt teache hym to love God in hys hart,
And those to forgeve by whom he suffereth smart.

CHRISTI LEX
In Your appoyntmentes wyll I do also my part.

1946 felicity/happiness 1947 (you) leave 1953 celebration 1960 Purifying 1966 despair 1967 sorrowful 1969 renewed 1970 instruction 1973 Imprint (in your memories) 1976 perfect 1977 do 1979 shall, to know God 1980 to refuse anything 1981 deviate 1983 treat 1986 from, hurt

[220] 'Here to the glory of God, they shall sing "When Israel came out of Egypt", or something similar.'

[221] Revelation 19:14.

Deus Pater
[*To Naturae Lex*] Worke thu in the hart a knowledge necessarye;
[*To Moseh Lex*] In the flesh worke thu by outwarde ceremonye;
[*To Christi Lex*] Change thu to the spret the workynges of these two,
And cause Our people in a perfyght waye to go.
Take hede, Christen Fayth, to the teachynges of these thre,
And move Our people to walke in the veryte.
The promyses We made in all these thre ar Gospell,
We wolde thu shuldest so to Our congregacyon tell.
Our everlastynge blessynge be with yow evermore.

Omnes Simul.
To Thy swete name, Lorde, prayse and perpetuall honoure!

Fides Christiana
It hath pleased God to put me in thys offyce
To governe Hys churche and Christen congregacyon,
And therin to do as ye shall me entyce.
Geve me, I praye yow, soch wholsom exhortacyon
As maye be to Man a clere edyfycacyon,
And I wyll be glad to take your advertysement
As it shall become any chylde obedyent.

Christi Lex
Ye speake it full wele, than marke what shall be sayed,
And dylygentlye loke that it be obeyed.

Naturae Lex
The effect of me is for to knowe the Lorde
Everlastynge, stronge, most gracyouse, and godlye,
And, as touchynge man, to have fraternall concorde,
Faver to norrysh, and to do non injurye,
To kepe covenauntes made, and love true matrymonye.
These noble effectes so temper yow in man
That them to fulfyll he do the best he can.

Moseh Lex
The effect of me is for to worshyp the Lorde
As one God alone, and to fle from Idolatrye;
Not to slee nor stele, nor yet to beare false recorde;
To shewe what is synne and to seke the remedye;
Publyque peace to holde, and sore to ponnysh the gyltye.
From these good effectes se that man never swerve;
Than shall he be sure that God wyll hym preserve.

Christi Lex
The effect of me is for to love the Lorde
In the innar sprete, and to faver frynde and enmye,
And in all poyntes els with Gods wyll to accorde;
To preache remyssyon, to save and to justyfye;
In Christ all to seke: lyfe, justyce, peace, and mercye.
These heavenly effectes in man so incorporate
That he maye in sprete be newlye regenerate.

Fides Christiana
More swete than honye are your thre exhortacyons,
And regestred they be in my memoryall.
Now wyll I forewarde to all the Christen nacyons,
And se in effect these lawes observed all,
To the abolyshment of the dreames papystycall.
Now the lyght is come, the darkenesse dyeth awaye;
I trust in the Lorde men wyll walke in the daye.

Good Christen people, to these thre lawes applye:
First knowe that ye have a lyvynge God above,
Than do Hym honour and Hys name magnyfye;
Worshyp Hym in spret, as the Gospel yow doth move;
Than obeye your kynge lyke as shall yow behove,
For he in hys lyfe that Lorde doth represent
To savegarde of the just and synners ponnyshment.

So that ye regarde soch lawes as he doth make,
For they are of God as Salomon doth report.
Of these lawes doubtles those lawes their groundynges take
To the publyque welth to geve ayde, strength, and confort,
For preservacyon of all the Christen sort.
In no case folowe the wayes of Reygnolde Pole;[222]
To hys dampnacyon he doubtles playeth the fole.

Have a due respect unto your contreye natyve,
Whych hath brought ye up and geven ye norryshment,
Even from your cradles to these dayes nutrytyve,

1993 truth 2002 edification/benefit 2003 instruction 2009 brotherly 2010 Favour, nourish, no 2016 slay, steal, witness 2019 deviate 2022 friend and enemy (alike) 2023 other matters 2024 remission (of sin) 2029 recorded, memory 2033 dies 2034 daylight 2039 Then, as is right for you 2041 safeguard 2043 from God 2044 foundations 2048 fool 2051 nourishing times

[222] Cardinal Reginald Pole, an English Catholic exile employed by the popes to foment rebellion during the reigns of Henry VIII and his son Edward VI. On the accession of the Catholic Queen Mary he returned to England as papal legate.

So that ye maye do, to her welth and preferment,
Mynyster to her no hatefull detryment.
A dogge to hys frynde wyll never be unlovynge;
Lete reason in ye not lose hys naturall workynge.

NATURAE LEX
Who lyveth without lawe shal perysh without lawe,
And therfor we have thre Lawes to yow descrybed,
That after their lyve ye shuld in your lyvynge drawe.
We have also shewed how they have bene corrupted
By fowle idolaters, and Sodomytes poluted,
By covetouse prestes, and by ambycyouse prelates,
Hypocryticall fryres, false doctours, and false curates.

MOSEH LEX
Who hath restored these same thre Lawes agayne
But your late Josias and valeaunt Kynge Henrye?[223]
No prynce afore hym toke ever yet soch payne
From Englande to bannysh Idolatrye and fowle Sodomye,
Covetousnes, Ambycyon, False Doctryne, and Hypocresye.
It was he that brought Christes veryte to lyght
Whan he put the Pope with hys fylthynes to flyght.[224]

CHRISTI LEX
From dampnable darkenesse, as my brother here doth saye,
He hath delyvered thys realme of Englande godlye,
Bryngynge hys subjectes into the true path waye
Of their sowles savegarde if they now folowe it wyselye;
And left them he hath, the same waye styl to fortyfye,
Hys noble sonne Edwarde, soch a kynge of God elect
As questyonles wyll perfourme it in effect.

FIDES CHRISTIANA
Praye all to the Lorde for the longe contynuaunce
Of Hys Graces lyfe in thys worldes habytacyon;
And that of hys nobles he have true mayntenaunce
In the pryncyples of thys most worthy foundacyon,
That he maye to Christ brynge us from desolacyon.
Praye for Quene Kateryne, and the noble Lorde Protectour,[225]
With the whole counsell that God be their directour.
Amen.

2053 nothing detrimental **2058** follow **2074** still **2076** doubtless, perform **2078** (i.e. Edward VI) **2079** from, support

[223] Henry VIII (1509–47).
[224] i.e. through the break with Rome and Henrician Reformation of the 1530s.
[225] Katherine Parr (Henry VIII's sixth wife, who survived him and became a significant figure during the reign of his son Edward VI) and Sir Edward Seymour, Protector Somerset, Edward VI's first chief minister (and regent in all but name).

ANE
SATYRE OF
THE THRIE ESTAITS,
in commendation of vertew
and vituperation of vyce.
Maid be Sir Dauid Lindesay of the
Mont, alias, Lyon King
of Armes.

IVSTITIA. RELIGIO.

SVVM CVIQ. DEVM COLE
HIS SVFFVLTA DVRANT

H C

AT EDINBVRGH
PRINTED BE ROBERT
CHARTERIS.
1602.

Ane Satyre of the Thrie Estaitis, title page, 1602. Courtesy of the Bodleian Library, Oxford.

Sir David Lindsay, *Ane Satyre of the Thrie Estaitis*

Sir David Lindsay of the Mount (c.1486–1555)

Sir David Lindsay of the Mount, the son of a wealthy family with lands around Cupar in Fife and in Lothian, spent most of his adult life in and around the Scottish royal court. He was probably the 'one called Lindsay' who was recorded in the household accounts for 1508, and was certainly at court in October 1511 when he was rewarded for his involvement in a play performed before James IV and Queen Margaret at Holyrood Abbey with the gift of a 'play coat' of blue and yellow taffeta. His involvement in both the entertainments and the politics of the court is well documented thereafter.

After the death of James IV in 1513, Lindsay served in the household of the infant James V, acting as usher, entertainer, companion, and (if his own account is to be believed) surrogate father to the young king. During the turbulent factional struggles of the 1520s he was exiled from court for a time, as Archibald Douglas, sixth earl of Angus, gained control of the court, but Lindsay was restored to favour by the end of the decade, and took on a number of important diplomatic and political roles. By 1532 he was Snowden Herald, and in 1540 he became Lyon King of Arms, the chief Scottish herald, one of whose duties was to sit at the foot of the throne in Parliament and act as formal intermediary between the king and his subjects during the sessions. The insights into national politics and court life which this post and his intimate relationship with the king gave him are reflected in the strongly political nature of his writing, as is his intense belief in the king's responsibility for the welfare of his subjects.

Perhaps the defining moment in Lindsay's development as a political dramatist came in 1542 with the death of James V, which plunged Scotland into another long period of regency government and political uncertainty. The consequences for Scotland of the lack of strong government are one of the central issues explored in his only surviving dramatic text, *Ane Satyre of the Thrie Estaitis*. In addition to his dramatic writings, Lindsay also wrote a number of long narrative poems, including *The Dreme*, *The Complaynt*, and *The Testament and Complaynt of Our Soverane Lordis Papyngo* (Parrot) in the late 1520s, and *The History of Squyer Meldrum* and *The Monarche*, both roughly contemporary with the text of *Ane Satyre* from the early 1550s.

Ane Satyre of the Thrie Estaitis

Ane Satyre is unique among the Interludes of the period in that three known performances are recorded, each of which presented a substantially different version of the text. The first, as early as 1540, was a great hall performance in James V's royal palace at Linlithgow. No script has survived of this version, but a detailed eye-witness account of the production exists and is printed here, along with a covering letter describing the context of the performance sent by the English commander of Berwick, Sir William Lyall, to Henry VIII's lord privy seal, Thomas Cromwell. The dramatic action described is sufficiently close to that of the play to suggest that this was an embryonic form of what was later to become *Ane Satyre*. The second and third performances, both produced outdoors, came in the early 1550s. The first was on Castle Hill in Lindsay's home town of Cupar in Fife on 7 June 1552, the second on the Greenside, Calton Hill, Edinburgh, probably on 12 August 1554. On the latter occasion, the regent, Mary of Guise, and 'a great part of the Nobility' of Scotland were present to witness the production. It is clear that Lindsay rewrote the 1540 play for the Cupar performance, significantly expanding the scope of the action, and including a much wider cast and greater coverage of social issues, and that he amended the play again for its performance in the capital. Two versions of the text survive, each combining elements of the two later performances. The fuller version is that printed by Henry Charteris in Edinburgh in 1602, but there is an earlier, shorter (and substantially reorganized) version in the Bannatyne Manuscript (an anthology of Scottish verse and drama), which contains the Banns for the Cupar performance and a number of the bawdier passages omitted in the printed text.

The 1540 Interlude seems to offer a brief Morality Play, in which the main comic element is provided by the antics of boastful courtiers, before the King is asked to answer the petition for justice by the Poor Man, who speaks on behalf of the rural poor. The play seems to have ended with a declaration on the part of the King that justice would be done, a conclusion which provided James V with an opportunity to berate his bishops on the need for real reforms in the government and conduct of the clergy. The fuller, outdoor drama of the 1550s is divided into two sections, separated by an interval and preceded by the Banns. The Cupar Banns offer a brief play in miniature, a 'taster' of the drama to come which focuses on traditional comic stereotypes and bawdy action in a way likely to draw in a crowd. The first half of the play itself significantly expands the events of the 1540 Interlude, providing a self-contained Morality Play in which the hero, *Rex Humanitas* (King Humanity), is tempted by his young companions (Wantonnes, Placebo, and Solace) to embrace Sensualitie, and subsequently to adopt the more dangerous Vices Flatterie, Falset (Falsehood), and Dissait (Deceit). Under their influence Gude Counsall, Chastitie, and Veritie are excluded and persecuted, and the church and state fall ever further into corruption. Only the arrival of Divyne Correctioun (an avenging angel sent from God) scatters the Vices and restores good order to the court. The second half of the play places the reformation of king and court in a wider context. A Parliament is summoned (the event which gives the play its name, the Thrie Estaitis being the three social classes traditionally entitled to a place in Parliament: the noblemen (Temporalitie), the higher clergy (Spiritualitie), and wealthy burgesses (represented by Merchand, the Merchant), who are joined in the course of the play by the fourth Estate, the commons, represented by Johne the Common-weill), and Acts are devised to extend the reformation to all aspects of Scottish social and religious life.

Lindsay rewrote *Ane Satyre* at a time of profound social, economic, and religious turmoil in Scotland. Left without a king after James V's death in 1542, the realm was still coping with the poverty, famine, and consequent social dislocation caused by the disastrous war with England in the 1540s, and was struggling through the early stages of a religious reformation. The sense of a realm locked in a lengthy and intractable crisis of self-confidence pervades the play at every level (for a fuller account of the play's politics, see Walker, *The Politics of Performance*, ch. 4, and Lyall, *Ane Satyre*, Introduction). Scotland is portrayed as a nation in the latter stages of potentially terminal decline, its secular rulers wedded to sensuality, its clergy to self-interest and financial and spiritual corruption, and its common people ground down by over-taxation and neglect. The situation is presented visually by the powerful symbol of misrule that begins the second half of the play: the Thrie Estaitis walking backwards to Parliament, each one led by its characteristic Vice. Here indeed is a world turned upside-down. All the forces for change have to arrive from elsewhere, Gude Counsall and Chastitie from across the sea, Veritie and the New Testament from England, and Correctioun from Heaven. It is only the threat of final judgement and punishment that shocks the King into reforming himself and setting about the recuperation of his broken realm.

The play is informed by a passionate concern for the sufferings of the rural poor, and a fierce condemnation of the Catholic clergy whom Lindsay clearly blamed for the greater part of the nation's misery. There is a genuine radicalism to many of the reforms proposed in the parliamentary programme of part 2 (the abolition of death duties on rented lands, the establishment of a northern college of justice funded by the suppression of all the Scottish nunneries, and the advocacy of clerical marriage, with its remarkable stipulations barring intermarriage between the clergy and the nobility, which would have initiated a separate caste of clerical families). But the play is not the work of a zealot. Lindsay was fully aware of the limitations upon reform and the imperfect nature of the world. Thus Flatterie and Public Oppressioun ultimately escape punishment, and Foly returns to the stage to have (almost) the last word. There is also a pragmatism to events, reflective, no doubt, of Lindsay's long experience of royal service: Scrybe and the herald Diligence both complain about their lack of wages, Rex is allowed to maintain his milder vices (a taste for gambling games, music, and outdoor sports), and even the clerical abuse of pluralism (whereby an individual holds more than one benefice at a time) is allowed to continue in the specific case of princes of the royal blood (a pragmatic acceptance that the crown needed to supplement its income somehow, even at the expense of the church).

There is, however, a thoroughgoing radicalism to Lindsay's dramatic techniques in his combination of conventional Morality elements with the language and iconography of other cultural forms. The play explores the limits of dramatic performance, and freely transgresses the porous boundaries between 'drama's' playful representations and the more earnest spectacles of judicial and confessional 'theatre'. Lindsay absorbs within his drama two sermons (one delivered 'straight', the second – spoken by Foly – a parodic *sermon joyeux* in the French tradition), a meeting of Parliament and a formal declaration of a programme of legislative Acts, and three public executions (one made more realistic, as the stage directions insist, by the actor himself being hoisted up, rather than an effigy, and a black bird being released, symbolic of his evil soul, at the moment of his death). There are also a number of minor rituals and acts, ranging from Johne the Common-weill's recitation of the Creed and his impromptu trial for heresy, to the mock-baptisms of the Vices, each of which is faithfully reproduced with its familiar rhetoric and iconography intact. In this way the play remains ambiguously placed between the spheres of the real and the imagined, a point emphasized by the fact that the Cupar Banns begin by announcing that a meeting of Parliament, rather than a play, will take place for the audience's delectation.

The most powerful instance of this blurring of the play-world and the world of the audience occurs during the Interlude between the acts, when, in this curiously liminal moment (performed 'the principal players being out of their seats', and while the audience is encouraged to attend to its needs for refreshment), the Pauper steps into the playing space as if from among the audience (a feat repeated by Johne early in part 2), forcing the fictional reformers to consider the concerns of the contemporary Scottish poor, and equally bringing the plight of their oppressed neighbours to the attention of the elite spectators. Similarly, when the Vices are finally hanged, their last speeches draw the audience into complicity with their crimes by the simple, but deeply unsettling, stratagem of naming real individuals in the Cupar and Edinburgh communities allegedly guilty of the same abuses.

The most shocking element of the play to modern readers is, however, likely to be Lindsay's vocabulary and tone rather than his political engagement. The play is often startlingly frank in its use of sexual and scatological language, mixing the broad and obscene comedy of Foly and the Vices, and the wives' remarkable openness about their sexual needs, with the high moral tone and elevated discourse of Chastitie and Veritie and the sermon of the Doctour of divinity. This mixture of material reveals the broad-mindedness of court culture in this period, which was clearly untroubled by the kinds of anxiety about generic integrity and sustained seriousness of tone which would exercise the theorists of later ages. In metrical terms the play is also diverse, alternating different stanza forms to indicate both moral shifts of character and the allegiances of individuals. The Vices characteristically employ a number of tail-rhyme (*rime coueé*) stanzas (rhyming aaabcccb or aabccb), while the Virtues favour eight-line (abab bcbc) stanzas, and both employ couplets, shifting between three-, four-, and five-stress lines.

The staging requirements for the outdoor productions were clearly spectacular and expensive. The costumes of the large cast would alone make for a sumptuous display, but their effects were clearly enhanced by place-and-scaffold staging on an impressive scale. A number of the leading characters had their own 'chairs' on scaffolds, notably Rex himself, and probably Sensualitie and Spiritualitie too, while the Parliament would have required elevated seating for both Rex and Correctioun, as well as places for the court officials, a 'bar' at which Johne can enter his pleas for reform, and benches for the Thrie Estaitis themselves. In addition the stage directions indicate that there was a 'Pavilion' which acted as a dressing room for the cast, a pulpit, from which the sermons were delivered, two sets of stocks in which Veritie and Chastitie are imprisoned, and a 'stank' or ditch filled with water across which Johne must jump (although, as the stage directions helpfully note, it does not matter if he falls in), and through which the Taylour's and Sowtar's Wives wade in search of drink. Given the fluidity of the action, and the likelihood that many of the actors remained in full view throughout the play, I have not added entrances and exits to the text where they are not stated in the original(s) or obvious from the dialogue.

The text of the Description of the 1540 Interlude is based on that contained in BL MS Reg. 7. C. xvi, ff. 136–9. The text of the play itself is based upon the Charteris edition of 1602 (STC 15681) with material (printed within square brackets) supplied from the version in the Bannatyne Manuscript (National Library of Scotland MS Adv. 19.1.1 ff. 164r–210r) where it supplements the Charteris text or offers more satisfactory readings. In addition I have consulted the full or partial modern editions in the following: D Hamer, ed., *The Works of Sir David Lindsay of the Mount* (4 vols, Edinburgh, 1931–6), volumes II and IV; P. Happé, ed., *Four Morality Plays* (Harmondsworth, 1979); R.D.S. Jack and P.A.T. Rozendaal, eds., *The Mercat Anthology of Early Scottish Literature, 1375–1707* (Edinburgh, 1997); and R. Lyall, ed., *Ane Satyre of the Thrie Estaitis* (Edinburgh, 1989).

Further reading

C. Edington, *Court and Culture in Renaissance Scotland: Sir David Lindsay of the Mount* (Amherst, Mass., 1994).

J.S. Kantrowitz, *Dramatic Allegory: Lindsay's 'Ane Satyre of the Thrie Estaitis'* (Lincoln, Nebr., 1975).

J.D. McClure, 'A Comparison of the Bannatyne MS and the Quarto Texts of Lindsay's *Ane Satyre of the Thrie Estaitis*', in D. Strauss and H.W. Dressler, eds, *Scottish Language and Literature, Medieval and Renaissance* (Frankfurt, 1986), pp. 409–22.

J.J. McGavin, 'The Dramatic Prosody of Sir David Lindsay', in R.D.S. Jack and K. McGinley, eds, *Of Lion and Unicorn* (Edinburgh, 1993), pp. 39–66.

A.J. Mill, 'Representations of Lyndsay's *Satyre of the Thrie Estaitis*', *Publications of the Modern Language Association of America* 47 (1932), pp. 636–51.

A.J. Mill, 'The Original Version of Lyndsay's *Satyre of the Thrie Estaitis*', *Studies in Scottish Literature* 6 (1968–9), pp. 67–75.

G. Walker, *The Politics of Performance in Early Renaissance Drama* (Cambridge, 1998), ch. 4.

J.H. Williams, 'Shady Publishing in Sixteenth-Century Scotland: The Case of David Lyndsay's Poems', *Bibliographical Society of Australia and New Zealand Bulletin* 16 (1992), pp. 97–106.

The Description of the 1540 Interlude

To the Right Honorable and my very goode Lorde, my Lordes Prevy Seale,

[f.137r] Pleas it your goode Lordeshipe to be advertisede[1] that at the meating whiche I had with twoe gentle men of the King of Scotts Counsaile at Caldstreme[2] for suche buysynes[3] as I have advertised your lordshipe of in myn other lettre with of our procedings in the same. I hade diverse commynyngs[4] with Mr Thomas Bellendyn, one of the saide [C]oun[ce]llours for Scotlande, a man by estymacion apperaunte[5] to be of thage of fiftye yeres or above, and of gentle and sage conversacion, specially touching the staye[6] of the spritualtie[7] in Scotlande. And, gathering hym to be a [man] inclyned to the soorte used in our soverains Realme of England,[8] I dide soe largely breke with hym in thoes behalves[9] as to move to knowe of hym of whate mynde the King and counsaile of Scotland was inclyned unto concernyng the Busshope of Rome,[10] and for the reformacion of the mysusing[11] of the spritualtie in Scotlande, wherunto he genttlie and lovinglie aunswered, shewing hym self well contented of that commynyng, [and] did saye that the King of Scotts hym self, with all his temporall Counsaille was gretely geven[12] to the reformacion of the mysdemeanours of Busshops, Religious persones[13], and preists within the Realme. And so muche that by the Kings pleasour, he being prevey therunto,[14] thay have hade ane enterluyde[15] played in the feaste of the Epiphanne of Our Lorde laste paste,[16] before the King and Quene at Lighgive,[17] and the hoole counsaile, spirituall and

1 Informed.

2 Coldstream, a town on the river Tweed, south-west of Berwick.

3 Business.

4 'Communings': discussions.

5 Appearing.

6 Restriction/reform.

7 Clergy.

8 i.e. Eure took Bellendon to be of a reformist disposition.

9 'I frankly broached the subject with him of those matters'.

10 The pope. Because they denied the supremacy of the pope, Henry VIII's government insisted he be referred to only as the bishop of Rome.

11 Abuses.

12 'Greatly given [i.e. strongly inclined].'

13 i.e. the regular religious, monks, nuns, and friars.

14 'Privy to [i.e. part of] [the plan]'.

15 Interlude.

16 The most recent feast of the Epiphany, i.e. 6 January 1540.

17 Linlithgow, a royal palace and town, west of Edinburgh.

temporall.[18] The hoole matier whereof concluded upon the Declaracion of the noughtines[19] in Religion, the presumpcion of busshops, the collucion[20] of the spirituall courts (called the concistory courts in Scotland), and mysusing of preists. I have obteigned a noote frome a Scotts man of our sorte, being present at the playing of the saide enterlutyde, of theffecte thereof, which I doe sende unto your lordshipe by this berer.[21] My lorde, the same Mr Bellendyn shewed me that after the said enterluyd fynished, the King of Scotts dide call upon the Busshope of Glascoe being Chauncelour,[22] and diverse other busshops, exorting thaym[23] to reform thair facions and maners of lyving,[24] saying that oneles thay soe did, he wold sende sex of the proudeste of thaym unto his uncle of England, and, as thoes wer ordoured, soe he wold ordour all the reste that wolde not a mende.[25] And therunto the Chauncelour shuld aunswer, and say unto the King that one worde of His Graces mouthe shuld suffice thayme to be at commaundement,[26] and the King haistely and angrely[27] aunswered that he wold gladely bestowe any words of his mouthe that could a mend thaym. I am alsoe advertised by the same Mr Bellendyn that the King of Scottes is fully mynded to expell all spirituall men from having any auctoritie by office under His Grace, either in household or elles-where within the Realme, and daily studiethe and devisithe for that entente.[28]

At the Kinges Majesties Castell of Berwike,[29] the 26th day of January (1540),
Your Lordships, at commaundement,
Wyllm Eure.

[f. 138r]

The Copie of the nootes of the interluyde

In the first entres come in Solaice, whose parte was but to make mery, sing ballettes[30] with his ffelowes, and drinke at the interluydes[31] of the play, whoe shewede[32] firste to all the audience the playe to be played, whiche was a generall thing, meanyng nothing in speciall to displease noe man, praying therfor noe man to be angre with the same.[33] Nexte come in a King, whoe passed to his throne, having noe speche to thende of the playe, and thene to ratifie and approve as in playne parliament all thinges doon by the reste of the players whiche represented the Thre Estes.[34] Withe hym come his courtiours Placebo, Pikthanke, and Flatterye,[35] and suche a like garde,[36] one swering he was the lustiest, starkeste,[37] best proporcioned and moste valiaunte man that ever was, an other swearing he was the beste with longe bowe, crosebowe, and culverein[38] in the world, an other swearing he was the best juster[39] and man of armes in the world, and soe furthe during thair partes. Ther after came in a man, armed in harnes,[40] with a sword drawn in his hande, a Busshope, a Burges man,[41] and Experience, clede like a doctour,[42] whoe sete thaym all down on the

[18] 'The entire Royal Council, both the spiritual lords [bishops, priors, and abbots] and the temporal [lay] lords.'

[19] Naughtiness/abuses.

[20] Collusion/corruption.

[21] The bearer of the letter.

[22] Gavin Dunbar, archbishop of Glasgow and chancellor of Scotland.

[23] Them.

[24] Either 'their fashions and manners of living', i.e. lifestyles, or 'factions, and manners of living', their divisions and intrigues and their lifestyles.

[25] 'Unless they did so, he would send six of the proudest of them to his uncle [the king] of England [Henry VIII], and, whatever Henry did with them, he [James] would do with all the rest who would not amend [reform] themselves.'

[26] 'Would secure their obedience'.

[27] 'Hastily [quickly] and angrily'.

[28] 'Studies and plans every day to achieve that end.'

[29] Berwick Castle (Northumberland).

[30] Ballads.

[31] 'During the intervals'.

[32] Described.

[33] i.e. the play had no personal or specific satirical targets, so no one should take offence; a traditional defence of political satire in the period.

[34] The Three Estates of Parliament, the temporal and spiritual peers and the burgesses.

[35] Placebo ('I will please'), Reward-Seeker, and Flattery.

[36] Crew.

[37] Strongest.

[38] Culverin (small firearm).

[39] Jouster.

[40] Harness (body-armour).

[41] Burgess.

[42] Dressed like a doctor of law.

deis,[43] under the King. After thayme come a Poor Man, whoe did goe upe and downe the scaffald, making a hevie[44] complaynte, that he was heryed[45] throughe the courtiours taking his fewe[46] in one place, and alsoe his tackes[47] in an other place, wher throughte he hade s[k]ayled[48] his house, his wife and childeren beggyng their brede, and soe of many thousaund in Scotlande, whiche wolde make the Kynges Grace lose of men if His Grace stod neide,[49] saying thair was noe remedye to be gotten; for thoughe he wolde suyte[50] to the Kinges Grace, he was naither acquaynted with Controuller nor Treasurer,[51] and withoute thaym myght noe man gete noe goodenes of the King. And after he spered for the King,[52] and when he was showed to the man that was King in the playe, he aunsuered and said he was noe king, ffor ther is but one King, whiche made all and governethe all, Whoe is eternall, to Whome he and all erthely kinges ar but officers, of the whiche thay muste make recknyng,[53] and so furthe muche moor to that effecte.[54] And thene he loked to the King and saide he was not the King of Scotland, for ther was an other King in Scotlande, that hanged John Armestrang with his fellowes, and Sym the Larde,[55] and many other moe, which had pacified the countrey, and stanched thifte,[56] but he had lefte one thing undon, whiche perteyned aswell to his charge as th[other].[57] [f.138v] And, whene he was asked what that was, he made a long narracion of the oppression of the poor by the taking of the corse presaunte beistes,[58] and of the herying of poor men by concistorye lawe, and of many other abussions of the spritual[itie] and churche, withe many long stories and auctorities. [And] thene the Busshope roise and rebuked hym, saying [it] effered not to hym to speake such matiers,[59] comaundinge hym scilence, or elles to suffer dethe for it, by thair lawe. Therafter roise the man of armes, all[ed]ginge the contrarie, and commaunded the poor man to speake, saying thair abusion hade been over longe suffered, withoute any law. Thene the Poor Man shewed the greate abusion of busshopes, Prelettes, Abbottes, reving[60] menes[61] wifes and doughters, and holding thaym, and of the maynteynyng of thair childer, and of thair over bying of lordes and barrons eldeste sones to thair doughters,[62] where thoroughe the nobilitie of the blode of the Realme was degenerate,[63] and of the greate superfluous rentes that perteyned to the churche, by reason of over muche temporall landes given to thaym, whiche thaye proved that the Kinge might take boothe by the canon lawe, and civile lawe, and of the greate abomynable vices that reiagne in clostures,[64] and of the common bordelles[65] that was keped in closturs of nunnes. All this was provit by Experience. And also was shewed th'office of a busshope,[66] and producit the Newe Testament with the auctorities to that effecte. And thene roise the Man of Armes and the Burges, and did saye that all that was producit by the Poor Man and Experience was reasonable, of veritie and of greate effecte, and verey expedient to be reafourmede[67] with the consent of parliament. And the Busshope said he wold not consent therunto. The Man of Armes and Burges saide thay wer twoe, and he bot[68] one, wherfor thair voice shuld have mooste effecte. Theraftre the King in the playe ratefied, approved, and confermed all that was reheresed.[69]

43 Dais.
44 Sorrowful
45 Harried/oppressed.
46 Feu, a fixed rent on land.
47 Tax.
48 'Skail': to break up or disperse a home.
49 'And so have many thousands of men in Scotland, which would leave the king short of men if His Grace stood in need [of raising an army]'.
50 Take his suit.
51 The chief officers of the royal household, who controlled access to the King.
52 'Asked for the king'.
53 An account (of their performance).
54 'And a lot more to the same effect.'
55 The two border reivers (bandits), John Armstrong of Gilknockie, hanged at Carlinrigg in 1530, and Simon Armstrong, alias 'Sym the La[i]rd', hanged in 1536, both under James V's jurisdiction.
56 'Stopped theft'.
57 'Which was as important a part of his responsibilities as the rest.'
58 Animals taken as 'corpse presents', mortuary fees paid on the death of the owner.
59 'It was not his role to raise such subjects'.
60 Stealing/kidnapping.
61 Men's.
62 The complaint that prelates were able to use large cash dowries to 'buy up' the sons of noblemen as husbands for their illegitimate daughters, thus 'polluting' noble blood-lines, is a theme returned to in the 1552–4 play.
63 Contaminated.
64 Cloisters, i.e. monasteries, friaries, and convents.
65 Brothels.
66 'It was revealed what the responsibilities of a bishop [really] were'.
67 Reformed.
68 Only.
69 'All that had been said to that point.'

Ane Satyre of the Thrie Estaitis (the 1552–4 text)

[*Dramatis Personae*: *In the Cupar Banns*: *Nuntius* (the Messenger: acts as Prologue and Epilogue), *Cotter* (a smallholder), *Cotter's Wife*, *Auld Man* (Old Man), *Bessy* (The Auld Man's young wife), *Courteour*, *Fynlaw of the Fute Band* (Finlay of the Infantry Company),[1] *Marchand* (a wealthy Merchant), *Clerk* (a scholar), *Fule* (the Fool).[2]

In the Play: Diligence,[3] *Rex Humanitas* (King Humanity),[4] [Courtiers to Rex:] *Wantonnes*,[5] *Placebo* ('I will please'),[6] *Solace* (Pleasure), *Sensualitie* (a seductive noblewoman),
[Sensualitie's Ladies:] *Hamelines* (Sluttishness), *Danger* (Haughtiness), *Fund-Jonet* (Foundling Janet),[7]
[The Vices:] *Flatterie*,[8] *Falset* (Falsehood), *Dissait* (Deceit),
[The Female Virtues:] *Veritie* (Truth: the Protestant version of biblical truth), *Chastitie*,
[The Three Estates:] *Spiritualitie* (the higher clergy), *Temporalitie* (a nobleman), *Merchand* (Merchant),
[The Clergy:] *Bishops*, *Abbot*, *Persone* (a Parson/Parish Priest), *Priores* (a Prioress), *Freir* (a Friar),
[The Tradesfolk:] *Sowtar* (a shoemaker), *Sowtar's Wyfe*, *Taylour*, *Taylour's Wyfe*, *Jennie* (Taylour's daughter),
[The Male Virtues:] *Discretioun* (Discretion: sound judgement), *Correctioun's Varlet* (page to Divyne Correctioun), *Divyne Correctioun* (God's avenging angel),[9] *Gude Counsall* (Good Counsel, advisor to princes),
[The Oppressed Poor:] *Pauper* (a beggar, formerly a cotter), *Johne the Common-weill* (John the Commonwealth, representative of the Scottish common people),
[The Minor Crooks:] *Pardoner*,[10] *Wilkin* (Wilkin Widdiefowl ('Gallowsbird'), the Pardoner's servant), *Covetice* (Greed), *Public Oppressioun* (a corrupt landowner), *Common Thift* (Petty Theft),
[The Officers of the Parliament:] *II Sergeants* (Beadles), *Scrybe* (the Clerk of the Parliament), *Doctour* (a Theologian), *II Licents* (university Masters graduates, licensed to preach), *Batcheler* (university BA graduate), *Trumpet* (a Trumpeter), *Dempster* (a court official), *Foly* (Folly: a fool), *Glaiks* and *Stult* (Foly's children).]

The Proclamatioun maid in Cowpar of Fyffe

[Nuntius]
Richt famous pepill, ye sall undirstand
How that ane prince richt wyiss and vigilent
Is schortly for to cum in to this land,
And purpossis to hald ane Parliament.
His Thre Estaitis thairto hes done consent,
In Cowpar town in to thair best array,
With support of the Lord Omnipotent,
And thairto hes affixt ane certaine day.
With help of Him that rewlis all abone,
That day salbe within ane litill space.
Our purposs is, on the sevint day of June,
Gif weddir serve and we haif rest and pece,
We sall be sene in till our playing place,
In gude array abowt the hour of sevin.
Off thriftiness that day I pray yow ceiss,
Bot ordane us gude drink aganis allevin.

2 wise 3 soon 4 intends 5 have consented 6 Cupar (Fife) 8 appointed 9 rules, above 11 seventh 12 If the weather is suitable 13 acting 15 cease 16 provide, for 11 a.m

1 Finlaw is a traditional satiric figure, the braggart soldier or '*Miles Gloriosus*'. He proves ultimately to be a coward.

2 Probably the same character as Foly in the play proper, he is dressed in the traditional fool's costume and sports a spectacularly large codpiece, the source of much of his bawdy humour.

3 Like Nuntius, Diligence acts as prologue and herald in the play, stage-managing events and acting as a link between play and audience.

4 Both the king of Scotland and (in part 1 at least) a youthful everyman.

5 The first of the three (minor) court Vices, Wantonnes represents lust for life and hedonism rather than anything more culpable.

6 Placebo is a courtly yes-man, but falls short of the self-interested dishonesty of Flatterie.

7 There seems to have been a real individual of this name in the Scottish court at the time the play was performed.

8 Flatterie spends most of the play disguised as a friar.

9 Like St Michael the Archangel, Correctioun has wings and carries a sword. He represents the divine punishment visited upon erring nations.

10 Robert Rome-Raker. The name implies both 'Runner-to-and-from-Rome' and also, perhaps, 'rake' in the more modern sense of 'libertine'. He is a corrupt pardoner in the Chaucerian mould.

Fail nocht to be upone the Castell Hill
Besyd the place quhair[11] we purpoiss to play.
With gude stark wyne your flacconis see ye fill,
And hald yourself the myrieast that ye may.
Be not displeisit quhat evir we sing or say,
Amang sad mater howbeid we sumtyme relyie.
We sall begin at sevin houris of the day,
So ye keip tryist, forsuth, we sail nocht felyie.[12]

Cotter
I salbe thair with Goddis grace,
Thocht thair war nevir so grit ane prese
And formest in the fair,
And drink ane quart in Cowpar toun
With my gossep Johnne Williamsoun,
Thocht all the nolt sowld rair.

I haif ane quick divill to my wyfe,
That haldis me evir in sturt and stryfe,
That warlo, and scho wist
That I wald cum to this gud toun,
Scho wald call me fals ladrone loun,
And ding me in the dust.

We men that hes sic wickit wyvis,
In grit langour we leid our lyvis,
Ay dreifland in diseiss.
Ye preistis hes grit prerogatyvis,
That may depairt ay fra your wyvis,
And cheiss thame that ye pleiss.

Wald God I had that liberty,
That I micht pairt, als weill as ye,
Withowt the Constry law.
Nor I be stickit with ane knyfe,
For to wad ony uder wyfe;
That day sowld nevir daw!

Nuntius
War thy wyfe deid, I see thow wald be fane.

Cotter
Ye[a], that I wald, sweit sir, be Sanct Fillane![13]

Nuntius
Wald thow nocht mary fra hand ane uder wyfe?

Cotter
Na, than the dum divill stik me with ane knyfe!
Quha evir did mary agane, the Feind mot fang
thame,
Bot as the preistis dois ay, stryk in amang thame.

Nuntius
Than thow mon keip thy chestety, as effeiris?

Cotter
I sall leif chest as abbottis, monkis, and freiris.
Maister, quhairto sowld I my self miskary[14]
Quhair I, as preistis, may swyve and nevir mary.

[Enter Cotter's Wife.]

Wyfe
Quhair hes thow bene, fals ladrone loun?
Doyttand and drinkand in the toun.
Quha gaif the[e] leif to cum fra hame?

Cotter
Ye gaif me leif, fair lucky dame.

Wyfe
Quhy hes thow taryit heir sa lang?

Cotter
I micht not thrist owtthrow the thrang,
Till that yone man the play proclamit.

Wyfe
Trowis thow that day, fals cairle defamit,[15]
To gang to Cowpar to see the play?

Cotter
Ye[a], that I will deme, gif I may.

Wyfe
Na, I sall cum thairto sickerly,
And thow sall byd at hame and keip the ky.

19 strong, flagons 20 behave, merriest 21 displeased 22 serious matter, joke 26 though, great a crowd 27 foremost 29 companion 30 cattle should roar 31 living, for 32 keeps, trouble 33 witch, if she knew 34 good 35 lazy wretch 36 knock 37 wicked 38 lead 39 miserable, discomfort 40 prerogatives/liberties 41 part 42 choose, please 45 consistory (ecclesiastical court) 46 May I be stabbed 47 If I wed another 48 dawn 49 happy 51 immediately 53 may seize them 54 priests always do, thrust 55 must, chastity, as is correct 56 live (as) chaste 58 fornicate 60 Fooling around 61 permission 63 delayed 64 push through the crowd 65 that, proclaimed 69 certainly 70 stay, look after the cow

11 Where. 'Qu' is the Middle Scots equivalent of 'Wh'.
12 'If you keep our arrangement, truly, we shall not fail.'
13 St Fillan, an eighth-century Perthshire saint.
14 'Sir, why [to what end] should I ruin myself . . . ?'
15 'Do you intend, false defamed fellow'.

Cotter
Fair lucky dame, that war grit schame,
Gif I that day sawld byid at hame.
Byid ye at hame, for, cum ye heir,
Ye will mak all the toun a steir.
Quhen ye ar fow of barmy drink
Besyd yow nane may stand for stink.
Thairfoir, byid ye at hame that day,
That I may cum and see the play.

Wyfe
Fals cairle, be God, that sall thow nocht,
And all thy crackis sall be deir coft.
Swyth, cairle, speid the[e] hame speidaly,
Incontinent, and milk the ky,
And muk the byre or I cum hame.

Cotter
All salbe done, fair lucky dame.
I am sa dry, dame, or I gae,
I mon ga drink ane peny or twae.

Wyfe
The Divill a drew sall cum in thy throte.
Speid hand, or I sall paik thy cote,
And to begin, fals cairle, tak thair ane plate!

Cotter
The Feind ressaif the handis that gaif me that.
I beseik yow, for Goddis saik, lucky dame,
Ding me na mair this day till I cum hame,
Than sall I put me evin in to your will.

Wyfe
Or evir I stynt thow sall haif straikis thy fill.

Heir sal the Wyfe ding the Carle, and he sall cry Goddis mercy.

[Cotter]
Now wander and wa be to thame all thair lyvis,
The quhilk ar maryit with sic unhappy wyvis.

Wyfe
I ken foure wyvis, fals ladrone loun,
Baldar nor I dwelland in Cowpar toun.

Cotter
Gif thay be war, ga thow and thay togidder.
I pray God nor the Feind ressaif the fidder.

[*She chases him off. Enter Fynlaw.*]

Fynlaw of the Fute Band
Wow, mary, heir is ane fellone rowt!
Speik, schiris, quhat gait may I get owt?
I rew that I come heir.
My name, schiris, wald ye undirstand,
Thay call me Findlaw of the Fute Band:
A nobill man of weir.
Thair is na fyifty in this land
Bot I dar ding thame hand for hand.
Se, sic ane brand I beir!

Nocht lang sensyne besyd ane syik,
Upoun the sonny syd of ane dyk,
I slew with my richt hand
Ane thousand, ye[a], and ane thousand to.
My fingaris yit ar bludy, lo,
And nane durst me ganestand.

Wit ye, it dois me mekill ill
That can nocht get fechting my fill,
Nowdir in peax nor weir?
Will na man for thair ladyis saikis
With me stryk twenty markit straikis
With halbart, swerd, or speir?

Quhen Inglismen come in to this land
Had I bene thair with my bricht brand,
Withowttin ony help
Bot myne allane, on Pynky Craiggis[16]
I sowld haif revin thame all in raggis
And laid on skelp for skelp.

71 would be 72 should be 74 stir up all the town 75 full/drunk, frothy 76 no one 80 wisecracks, dearly paid for 81 Get out, speedily 82 At once 83 clean out the cowshed, before 85 go 86 must, pennyworth 87 (i.e. not a drop) 88 Hurry up, thrash 89 a blow 90 take, gave 91 sake 94 your fill of blows 95 wonder, woe 96 ill-favoured 98 Bolder than I (am) 99 worse 100 take the lot 101 terrible crowd 102 sirs, way 103 rue/regret 105 foot (infantry company) 106 war 107 not fifty 108 hand-to-hand 109 sword 110 since, stream 111 sunny, wall 113 too/more 114 are still bloody 115 stand against me 116 Do you know 117 can't get enough fighting 118 Neither, peace 119 sakes 120 formal blows 121 halberd (a pole-axe) 122 Englishmen 125 alone 126 torn 127 blow

16 Pinkie Cleuch (ravine), where the Scottish forces were disastrously defeated by an English army led by the earl of Somerset in 1547.

Sen nane will fecht, I think it best
To ly doun heir and tak me rest,
Than will I think nane ill.
I pray the grit God of His grace
To send us weir and nevir peace,
That I may fecht my fill.

Heir sall he ly doun. [*Enter the Fule.*]

Fule
My Lord, be Him that ware the croun of thorne,
A mair cowart was nevir, sen God was borne.
He lovis him self, and uthir men he lakkis.
I ken him weill, for all his boistis and crakkis.
Howbeid he now be lyk ane captane cled,
At Pyncky Clewch he was the first that fled.
I tak on hand, or I steir of this steid,
This crakkand cairle to fle with ane scheip heid.

Heir sall the Auld Man cum in, leidand his Wyfe in ane dance.

[Auld Man]
Bessy my hairt, I mon ly doun and sleip,
And in myne arme se quyetly thow creip.
Bessy my hairt, first lat me lok thy cunt,
Syne lat me keip the key as I was wount.

Bessy
My gud husband, lock it evin as ye pleiss;
I pray God send yow grit honor and eiss.

Heir sall he lok hir cunt and lay the key under his heid. He sall sleip and scho sall sit besyd him. [*Enter the Courteour, Marchand, and Clerk.*]

Courteour
Lusty lady, I pray yow hairtfully,
Gif me licence to beir yow cumpany.
Ye sie I am ane cumly courteour,
Quhilk nevir yit did woman dishonour.

Marchand
My fair maistres, sweitar than the lammer,
Gif me licence to luge in to your chalmer.
I am the richest marchand in this toun:
Ye sall of silk haif kirtill, hude, and goun.

Clerk
I yow beseik, my lusty lady bricht,
To gif me leif to ly with yow all nicht,
And of your quoman lat me schut the lokkis,
And of fyne gold ye sall ressaif ane box.

Fule
Fair damessell, how pleiss ye me?
I haif na mair geir nor ye sie.[17]
Swa lang as this may steir or stand,
It sall be ay at your command.
Na, it is the best that evir ye saw.

Bessy
Now welcome to me aboif thame aw!
Was nevir wyf sa straitly rokkit?
Se ye not how my cunt is lokkit?

Fule
Thinkis he nocht schame, that brybor blunt,
To put ane lok upoun your cunt?

Bessy
Bot se gif ye can mak remeid,
To steill the key fra undir his heid.

Fule
That sall I do, withowttin dowt.
Lat se gif I can get it owte;
Lo, heir the key, do quhat ye will.

Bessy
Na than, lat us ga play our fill.

Heir shall thay go to sum quyet place. [*Exeunt Courteour and Marchand.*]

Fynlaw of the Fute Band
[*Waking*] Will nane with me in France go to the weiris,
Quhair I am captane of ane hundreth speiris?
I am sa hardy, sturdy, strang, and stowt,
That owt of Hell the Divill I dar ding owt.

Clerk
Gif thow be gude or evill I can not tell;

130 no 135 greater coward 136 criticizes 137 boasts, claims 138 dressed like a captain 140 undertake, leave this place 141 boasting, scare off, sheep's 142 heart 144 lock up (in a chastity belt) 146 please 147 ease/comfort 148 earnestly 149 keep 150 see, fine 152 mistress, sweeter, amber 153 lodge, chamber 155 dress, hood 158 genitals, shoot/pick 160 How do I please you 162 So, stir 164 isn't it 165 above them all! 166 tightly restricted 168 blunt villain 170 remedy 173 Let's see 177 spearmen 178 strong, brave 179 I dare drive out

17 'I have no more property/equipment than you can see here.' He points, no doubt, to his unfeasibly large codpiece.

Thay ar not sonsy that so dois ruse thame sell.
At Pyncky Clewch I knew richt woundir weill
Thow gat na creddence for to beir a creill.
Sen sic as thow began to brawll and boist,
The commoun weill of Scotland hes bene loist.
Thow cryis for weir, bot I think peax war best.
I pray to God till send us peice and rest,
On that conditioun that thow and all thy fallowis
War be the craiggis heich hangit on the gallowis,
Quha of this weir hes bene the foundament.
I pray to the grit God Omnipotent
That all the warld and mae mot on thame wounder,
Or ding thame deid with awfull fyre of thunder.

FYNLAW
Domine doctor, quhair will ye preiche to morne?
We will haif weir and all the warld had sworne.
Want we weir heir, I will ga pass in France,
Quhair I will get ane lordly governance.

CLERK
Sa quhat ye will, I think seuer peax is best.
Quha wald haif weir, God send thame littill rest.
Adew crakkar, I will na langar tary:
I trest to see the[e] in ane firy fary.
I trest to God to see the[e] and thy fallowis
Within few dayis hingand on Cowpar gallowis.
[*Exit.*]

FYNLAW
Now art thow gane; the dum divill be thy gyd!
Yone brybour was sa fleit he durst not byid.
Be woundis and Passionis, had he spokkin mair ane word,
I sowid haif hackit his heid af with my swerd.

Heir sall the Gudman [*i.e. Auld Man*] *walkin*[18] *and cry for Bessy.*

[AULD MAN]
My bony Bessy, quhair art thow now?
My wyfe is fallin on sleip, I trow.
Quhair art thow Bessy, my awin sweit thing,
My bony, my hairt, my dayis darling?
Is thair na man that saw my Bess?
I trow scho be gane to the Mess.
Bessy my hairt, heiris thow not me?
My joy, cry 'keip', quhairevir thow be.
Allace for evir, now am I fey,
For of hir cunt I tynt the key!
Scho may call me ane jufflane jok:
Or I swyve I mon brek the lok.

BESSY
Quhat now, gudman, quhat wald ye haif?

AULD MAN
No thing, my hairt, bot yow I craif.
Ye haif bene doand sum bissy wark?

BESSY
My hairt, evin sewand yow ane sark
Of Holland claith, baith quhyt and tewch.
Lat pruve gif it be wyid annewch.

Heir sall scho put the sark ovir his heid, and the Fule sall steill[19] *in the key agane.*

AULD MAN
It is richt verry weill, my hairt,
Oure Lady, lat us nevir depairt.
Ye ar the farest of all the flok.
Quhair is the key, Bess, of my lok?

BESSY
Ye reve, gudman, be Goddis heid,
I saw yow lay it undir your heid.

AULD MAN
Be my gud faith, Bess, that is trew.
That I suspectit yow, sair I rew.
I trow thair be no man in Fyffe
That evir had sa gude ane wyfe.
My awin sweit hairt, I ha[l]d it best
That we sitt doun and tak us rest.

FYNLAW
Now is nocht this ane grit dispyte,
That nane with me will fecht nor flyte.
War Golias in to this steid[20]

181 lucky, elevate themselves 182 wonderfully 183 basket 184 Since such, boast 185 lost/ruined 186 would be 188 fellows 189 by the necks, high 190 cause 192 more 194 Master, tomorrow 195 even if, sworn (against it) 196 If we lack 197 command 198 surely 200 boaster 201 trust, great confusion 203 hanging 204 gone, guide 205 scared 206 (God's) wounds, another 207 should, hacked, off 208 bonnie 209 asleep 211 day's 213 Mass 214 don't you hear me 215 'tweet' 216 doomed 217 I've lost 218 fumbling fool 219 Before I have sex, must break 220 husband 221 only you 222 doing, busy 223 sewing, shirt 224 fine Dutch, white, tough 225 Let's see, wide enough 227 part 228 fairest 230 rave 233 I sorely regret 238 shame 239 fight, argue

18 Waken.
19 Sneak.
20 'Were Goliath in this place'. See I Samuel 17 for David's giant opponent.

I dowt nocht to stryk of his heid.
This is the swerd that slew Gray Steill[21]
Nocht half ane myle beyond Kynneill.
I was that nobill campioun
That slew Schir Bews of Sowth Hamtoun.[22]
Hector of Troy, Gawyne,[23] or Golias
Had nevir half sa mekle hardiness.

Heir sall the Fuile cum in with ane scheip heid on ane staff and Fynlaw sall be fleit.[24]

[FYNLAW]
Wow, wow, braid *benedicitie*!
Quhat sicht is yone, schiris, that I see?
I{n} nomini Patris et Fillii.
I trow yone be the spreit of Gy.[25]

Na, faith, it is the spreit of Marling,
Or sum scho gaist, or Gyr Carling.[26]
Allace for evir, how sall I gyd me?
God sen I had ane hoill till hyd me.
Bot dowt my deid yone man hes sworne,
I trow yone be grit Gowmakmorne.[27]
He gaippis, he glowris; howt, welloway!
Tak all my geir and lat me gay!
Quhat say ye, schir, wald ye have my swerd?
Ye[a], mary, sall ye at the first word,
My gluvis of plait and knapskaw to.
Your pressonar I yeild me; lo,
Tak thair my purss, my belt, and knyfe.
For Goddis saik, maister, save my lyfe.
Na, now he cumis evin for to sla me.
For Godis saik, schiris, now keip him fre me.
I see not ellis bot tak and slae.
Wow, mak me rowme and lat me gae!

[*Fynlaw runs away.*]

NUNTIUS
As for this day, I haif na mair to say yow.
On Witsone Tysday cum see our play, I prey yow.
That samyne day is the sevint day of June,
Thairfoir, get up richt airly and disjune.
And ye ladyis, that hes na skent of leddir,
Or ye cum thair, faill nocht to teme your bleddir.
I dreid, or we haif half done with our wark,
That sam of yow sall mak ane richt wait sark. [*Exit.*]

243 Kinneil (Linlithgowshire) 244 champion 247 so great courage 248 broad blessing 249 sirs 250 In the name of the Father and Son 252 Merlin 254 Alas, what shall I do 255 send, hole 256 doubtless, death 258 gapes, glowers 259 go 261 you shall 262 gloves, plate-metal, head-guard 263 prisoner 264 purse 266 slay 267 from 268 nothing, capture, death 269 get out of the way 270 tell 271 Whit Tuesday 273 early, have breakfast 274 no lack of genitals 275 empty, bladder 277 some, wet dress

[*The Play: Part One*]

DILIGENCE
The Father and founder of faith and felicite,
That your fassioun formed to His similitude,[28]
And His Sone, our Saviour, scheild in necessitie,
That bocht yow from baillis [ransonit on the Rude],
Repleadgeand His presonaris with His hart-blude,
The Halie Gaist, governour and grounder of grace,
Of wisdome and weilfair baith fontaine and flude,
[Save] yow all that I sie seasit in this place,
And scheild yow from sinne;
And with His spreit yow inspyre,
Till I have shawin my desyre.
Silence, soveraine[s], I requyre;
For now I begin.

Pausa.

Tak tent to me, my freinds, and hald yow coy,

3 (our) shield 4 redeemed, affliction, ransomed 5 Redeeming 6 Ghost/Spirit, foundation 7 source and spring 8 seated 10 spirit 11 shown/revealed 12 request 13+ Pause 14 Pay attention, keep quiet

21 Sir Greysteel, a giant knight from popular Scottish romances.
22 Bevis of Hampton, the hero of medieval romance.
23 Sir Gawain, a knight of the Round Table and hero of many medieval romances.
24 'put to flight.'
25 The ghost of Guy (or Guido) of Alet, another literary character.
26 'Or some she-ghost or Gyr Carling [the Scottish variant of Hecate].'
27 Goll Mac Morna, a legendary Irish hero.
28 'Who formed you in His image'.

For I am sent to yow as messingeir
From ane nobill and rycht redoubtit roy,
The quhilk hes bene absent this monie yeir,
Humanitie, give ye his name wald speir:
Quha bade me shaw to yow, but variance,
That he intendis amang yow to compeir,
With ane triumphant, awfull ordinance,

With crown and sword and scepter in his hand,
Temperit with mercie quhen penitence appeiris.
Howbeit that hee lang tyme hes bene sleipand,
Quhairthrow misreull hes rung thir monie yeiris,
That innocentis hes bene brocht on thair beiris,
Be fals reporteris of this natioun.
Thocht young oppressouris at the elder leiris,[29]
Be now assurit of reformatioun.

Sie no misdoeris be sa bauld
As to remaine into this hauld:
For quhy, be Him that Judas sauld,
Thay will be heich hangit.
Now faithfull folk for joy may sing;
For quhy it is the just bidding
Of my soveraine lord, the King
That na man be wrangit.

Thocht he, ane quhyll into his flouris,
Be governit be vylde trompouris,
And sumtyme lufe his paramouris,
Hauld ye him excusit.
For, quhen he meittis with Correctioun,
With Veritie and Discretioun,
Thay will be banisched aff the toun,
Quhilk hes him abusit.

And heir, be oppin proclamatioun,
I wairne in name of his magnificence,
The Thrie Estaitis of this natioun,
That thay compeir with detfull diligence,
And till His Grace mak thair obedience.
And first I wairne the Spritualitie,
And sie the burgessis spair not for expence:
Bot speid thame heir with Temporalitie.

Als I beseik yow famous auditouris,
Conveinit in this congregatioun,
To be patient the space of certaine houris,
Till ye have hard our short narratioun.
And als we make yow supplicatioun,
That na man tak our wordis intill disdaine,
Althocht ye hear, be declamatioun,
The common weill richt pitiouslie complaine.

Rycht so the verteous Ladie Veritie
Will mak ane pitious lamentatioun:
Als for the treuth sho will impresonit be
And banischit lang tyme out of the toun:
And Chastitie will mak narratioun
How sho can get na ludging in this land,
Till that the heavinlie King Correctioun
Meit with the king and commoun, hand for hand.

Prudent peopill, I pray yow all,
Tak na man greif in speciall,
For wee sall speik in general,
For pastyme and for play.
Thairfoir, till all our rymis be rung
And our mistoinit sangis be sung,
Let everie man keip weill ane toung,
And everie woman tway.

[*Enter Rex Humanitas.*]

REX HUMANITAS
O Lord of Lords, and King of Kingis all,
Omnipotent of power, Prince but peir,
Ever ringand in gloir celestial:
Quha, be great micht, and haifing na mateir,
Maid Heavin and Eird, fyre, air, and watter cleir.
Send me Thy grace, with peace perpetuall,
That I may rewll my realme to Thy pleaseir,
Syne bring my saull to joy angelicall.

Sen Thow hes givin mee dominatioun
And rewll of pepill subject to my cure,
Be I nocht rewlit be counsall and ressoun,
In dignitie I may nocht lang indure.

16 renowned king 17 many (a) year 18 if, would ask 19 instructed, without doubt 20 appear 21 authority/power 23 Tempered/moderated 24 has, sleeping 25 misrule has reigned, these 26 to, biers/coffins 27 By rumour-mongers 29 assured 30 offenders, bold 31 place 32 Because, sold 33 hanged high 37 wronged 38 Though, while, maturity 39 vile deceivers 40 for a time, love 41 excused 42 meets 44 from 45 Who, have abused him 46 by open/public 47 warn/instruct 49 present themselves, dutiful 52 burgesses (townsfolk) 54 Also, beseech, audience 55 Gathered, crowd 56 (for) the space, hours 59 disdainfully 64 imprisoned 65 banished 67 lodging 71 No one take particular offence 72 only generally 74 rhymes 75 tuneless songs 76 guard, a (i.e. his) tongue 77 two 79 without equal 80 reigning, glory 81 having no matter (Himself) 82 Earth 87 authority 88 If I am not

29 'Although young oppressors learn from their elders'.

I grant my stait my self may nocht assure,
Nor yit conserve my lyfe in sickernes.
Have pitie, Lord, on mee, Thy creature,
Supportand me in all my busines.

I Thee requeist, quha rent wes on the Rude,
Me to defend from the deidis of defame:
That my pepill report of me bot gude,
And be my saifgaird baith from sin and shame.
I knaw my dayis induris bot as ane dreame,
Thairfoir, O Lord, I hairtlie The[e] exhort,
To gif me grace to use my diadeame
To Thy pleasure and to my great comfort.

[Heir sall the King pass to royall sait[30] *and sit with ane grave countenance till Wantones* [*and Placebo*] *cum.*]

Wantonnes
My soveraine Lord and Prince but peir,
Quhat garris yow mak sic dreirie cheir?[31]
Be blyth sa lang as ye ar heir,
And pas tyme with pleasure:
For als lang leifis the mirrie man
As the sorie, for ocht he can:[32]
His banis full sair, sir, sall I ban
That dois yow displeasure.

Sa lang as Placebo and I
Remaines into your company,
Your Grace sall leif richt mirrely;
Of this haif ye na dout.
Sa lang as ye have us in cure,
Your Grace, sir, sall want na pleasure:
War Solace heir, I yow assure,
He wald rejoyce this rout.

Placebo
Gude brother myne, quhair is Solace,
The mirrour of all mirrines?
I have great mervell, be the Mes,
He taries sa lang.
Byde he away, wee ar bot shent:
I ferlie how he fra us went.
I trow he hes impediment
That lettis him [to] gang.

Wantonnes
I left Solace, that same greit loun,
Drinkand into the burrows toun:
It will cost him halfe of ane croun,
Althocht he had na mair.
And als he said hee wald gang see
Fair Ladie Sensualitie,
The beriall of all bewtie
And portratour preclair.

[*Enter Solace, at a distance.*]

Placebo
Be God, I see him at the last,
As he war chaist, rynnand richt fast;
He glowris evin as he war agast,
Or fleyit of ane gaist.
Na, he is wod drunkin, I trow.
Se ye not that he is wod fow?
I ken weill be his creischie mow
He hes bene at ane feast.

Solace
Now, quha saw ever sic ane thrang?
Me thocht sum said I had gain wrang.
Had I help, I wald sing ane sang
With ane rycht mirrie noyse.
I have sic pleasour at my hart,
That garris me sing the tr[i]bill pairt:
Wald sum gude fallow fill the quart
It wald my hairt rejoyce.

Howbeit my coat be short and nippit,
Thankis be to God I am weill hippit,[33]
Thocht all my gold may [sone] be grippit
Intill ane pennie pursse.
Thocht I ane servand lang haif bene,
My purchais is nocht worth ane preine:

90 acknowledge, make sure 91 surety 93 Supporting 94 torn 95 deeds, imfamy 96 only good 97 safeguard/protector 98 endure/pass 100 diadem/crown 104 happy 108 I shall sorely curse his bones 112 live 114 in charge 116 Were 117 cheer, company 120 by the Mass 121 delays 122 If he stays away, ruined 123 I'm amazed 124 has 125 prevents him coming 126 idler 127 burgh (town) 132 beryl (jewel), beauty 133 fairest of appearance 135 (being) chased, running 136 glowers 137 frightened, ghost 138 mad drunk 139 mad with drink 140 greasy mouth 142 throng 143 gone wrong (got lost) 147 treble 148 fellow, pot 150 tight 152 soon, gripped 153 In 154 servant 155 wealth, prawn/pin (i.e. little)

[30] Seat/throne.

[31] 'What causes you to have such a miserable face?'

[32] 'For the merry man lives as long as the sombre one, for all his efforts.'

[33] 'I have good hips'. His hips would be shown off by the short, tight-fitting coat.

I may sing *Peblis on the Greine*,[34]
For ocht that I may tursse.

Quhat is my name; can ye not gesse?
Sirs, ken ye nocht Sandie Solace?
Thay callit my mother Bonie Besse,
That dwelt betwene the bowis.
Of twelf yeir auld sho learnit to swyfe,
Thankit be the great God on lyve:
Scho maid me fatheris four or fyve:
But dout, this is na mowis.

Quhen ane was deid, sho gat ane uther;
Was never man had sic ane mother.
Of fatheris sho maid me ane futher
Of lawit men and leirit.
Scho is baith wyse, worthie, and wicht,
For scho spairis nouther kuik nor knycht:
Yea, four and twentie on ane nicht,
And ay thair eine scho bleirit.[35]

And gif I lie, sirs, ye may speir.
Bot, saw ye nocht the King cum heir?
I am ane sportour and playfeir
To that royall young king.
He said he wald, within schort space,
Cum pas his tyme into this place:
I pray The[e], Lord, to send him grace,
That he lang tyme may ring.

PLACEBO
Solace, quhy taryit ye sa lang?

SOLACE
The Feind a faster I micht gang![36]
I micht not thrist out throw the thrang
Of wyfes fyftein f[i]dder.
Then for to rin I tuik ane rink,
Bot I felt never sik ane stink:
For our Lordis luif, gif me ane drink,
Placebo, my deir br[ud]er.

[*Heir sall Placebo gif Sollace ane drink.*]

REX
My servant Solace, quhat gart yow tarie?

SOLACE
I wait not, sir, be sweit Saint Marie!
I have bene in ane feirie farie,
Or ellis intill ane trance.
Sir, I have sene, I yow assure,
The fairest earthlie creature
That ever was formit be nature,
And maist for to advance.

To luik on hir is great delyte,
With lippis reid and cheikis quhyte.
I wald renunce all this warld quyte
For till stand in hir grace.
Scho is wantoun and scho is wyse,
And cled scho is on the new gyse;
It wald gar all your flesche up ryse,
To luik upon hir face.

War I ane king, it sould be kend,
I sould not spair on hir to spend,
And this same nicht for hir to send
For my pleasure.
Quhat rak of your prosperitie
Gif ye want Sensualitie?
I wald nocht gif ane sillie flie
For your treasure.

REX
Forsuith, my friends, I think ye are not wyse
Till counsall me to break commandement
Directit be the Prince of Paradyce:
Considering ye knaw that my intent
Is for till be to God obedient,
Quhilk dois forbid men to be lecherous.
Do I nocht sa, perchance I will repent.
Thairfoir, I think your counsall odious,

157 anything, profit 158 guess 159 Sandy (Alexander) 161 arches (of a bridge?) 162 from the age of 12 163 the living God 164 provided for me 165 Truly, no lie 168 a crowd 169 uneducated, learned 170 strong 171 spares, cook 172 in 174 ask 176 gaming companion, playfellow 178 space (of time) 181 reign 189 push through 185 (all) together 186 run, took a course 187 experienced, such 188 love 189 brother 190 made (i.e. what kept you?) 191 don't know 192 complete confusion 196 formed 197 most praiseworthy 199 lips, white 200 renounce, completely 205 look 206 known 210 What does your prosperity matter 211 lack 212 give, fly (i.e. nothing) 216 Given 218 to 220 If I don't do so, I'll regret it

34 Perhaps a popular song, or, as Jack suggests, a deliberate confusion of two songs, 'Peblis to the Play' and 'Christ's Kirk on the Green'.

35 'And she always made fools of them [lit. bleared their eyes].'

36 'I couldn't go any faster, [by] the Devil!'

The quhilk ye gaif mee till,
Becaus I have bene to this day
Tanquam tabula rasa:[37]
That is als mekill as to say,
Redie for gude and ill.

PLACEBO
Beleive ye that we will begyll yow,
Or from your vertew we will wyle yow,
Or with evill counsall overseyll yow,
Both into gude and evill?
To tak Your Graces part wee grant
In all your deidis participant,
Sa that ye be nocht ane young sanct
And syne ane auld devill.

WANTONNES
Beleive ye, sir, that lecherie be sin?
Na, trow nocht that: this is my ressoun quhy:
First at the Romane Kirk will ye begin,
Quhilk is the lemand lamp of lechery:
Quhair cardinals and bischops generally
To luif ladies thay think ane pleasant sport,
And out of Rome hes baneist Chastity,
Quha with our prelats can get na resort.

SOLACE
Sir, quhill ye get ane prudent queine,
I think Your Majestie serein
Sould have ane lustie concubein,
To play yow withall:
For I knaw be your qualitie,
Ye want the gift of chastitie.
Fall to, *in nomine Domini*;[38]
This is my counsall.

I speik, sir, under protestatioun
That nane at me haif indignatioun:
For all the prelats of this natioun,
For the maist part,
Thay think na schame to have ane huir,
And sum hes thrie under thair cuir:
This to be trew I'le yow assuir,
Ye sall heir efterwart.

Sir, knew [ye] al the mater throch,
To play ye wald begin:
Speir at the monks of Bamirrinoch,[39]
Gif lecherie be sin.

PLACEBO
Sir, send ye for Sandie Solace,
Or ells your monyeoun Wantonnes,
And pray my Ladie Priores,
The suith till declair:
Gif it be sin to tak [ane] Kaity,
Or to leif like ane bummillbaty.
The Buik sayis *'Omnia probate'*[40]
And nocht for to spair.

[*Heir sall entir Dame Sensualitie with her Maydynnis*[41] *Hamlines and Danger.*]

SENSUALITIE
Luifers, awalk! Behald the fyrie spheir,
Behauld the naturall dochter of Venus:
Behauld, luifers, this lustie ladie cleir,
The fresche fonteine of knichtis amorous,
Repleit with joyis dulce and delicious.
Or quha wald mak to Venus observance
In my mirthfull chalmer melodious,
Thair sall thay find all pastyme and pleasance.

Behauld my heid, behauld my gay attyre,[42]
Behauld my halse, lu[f]sum and lilie quhite:
Behauld my visage, flammand as the fyre,
Behauld my papis of portratour perfyte.
To luke on mee luifers hes greit delyte;
Rycht sa hes all the kinges of Christindome:
To thame I haif done pleasouris infinite,
And speciallie unto the Court of Rome.

222 gave to me 225 as much 227 beguile 228 wile/trick 229 beguile 231 side, agree 233 a young saint 234 then (later), old 237 church 238 shining 241 have banished 242 access 243 until 244 serene 245 concubine/mistress 247 nature 248 lack 255 (it is) no shame, whore 256 control 257 I'll assure you 258 afterwards 259 the whole matter 264 minion/companion 266 truth 267 a slut 268 live, idle fool 270 spare/hesitate 271 Lovers awake, sphere 272 daughter 274 fountain, knights 275 sweet 276 whoever wants to worship 278 pleasure 279 head 280 neck, lovely 281 flaming (i.e. red) 282 breasts, perfect appearance

37 'Like a razed [wax] tablet': i.e. a blank page, ready to be written on by others.
38 'Get on with it, in the name of the Lord'.
39 Balmerino, a Cistercian house five miles from Cupar.
40 'The Bible says "test everything" ': a reference to I Thessalonians 5:21, here deliberately misinterpreted as an injunction to try out every pleasure.
41 Maidens.
42 Note the potentially blasphemous echoes of Christ's speech from the Cross in the York *Crucifixion* pageant. Sensualitie here offers herself as an icon for the worship of lovers.

Ane kis of me war worth in ane morning
A milyioun of golde to knicht or king.
And yit I am of nature sa towart
I lat no luiffer pas with ane sair hart,
Of my name wald ye wit the veritie,
Forsuith, thay call me Sensualitie.
I hauld it best now or we farther gang,
To Dame Venus let us go sing ane sang.

Hamelines
Madame, but tarying,
For to serve Venus deir
We sall fall to and sing.
Sister Danger, cum neir.

Danger
Sister, I was nocht sweir
To Venus observance.
Howbeit I mak dangeir,
Yit be continuance
Men may have thair pleasance.
Thairfoir let na man fray.
We will tak it, perchance,
Howbeit that wee say nay.

Hamelines
Sister, cum on your way,
And let us nocht think lang:
In all the haist wee may
To sing Venus ane sang.

Danger
Sister, sing this sang I may not,
Without the help of gude Fund-Jonet:
Fund-Jonet, hoaw! Cum tak a part.

[*Enter Fund-Jonet.*]

Fund-Jonet
That sall I do with all my hart;
Sister, howbeit that I am hais,
I am content to beir a bais.
Ye twa sould luif me as your lyfe,
Ye knaw I lernit yow baith to swyfe:
In my chalmer, ye wait weill quhair,
Sen syne, the Feind ane man ye spair![43]

Hamelines
Fund-Jonet, fy, ye ar to blame!
To speik foull wordis think ye not schame?

Fund-Jonet
Thair is ane hundreth heir sitand by
That luifis geaping als weill as I,
Micht thay get it in privitie:
Bot quha begins the sang, let se.

Rex
Up, Wantonnes, thow sleipis to lang!
Me thocht I hard ane mirrie sang.
I the[e] command in haist to gang
Se quhat yon mirth may meine.

Wantonnes
I trow, sir, be the Trinitie,
Yon same is Sensualitie,
Gif it be scho sune sall I sie
That soverane sereine.

Heir sall Wanton[n]es ga spy thame[44] *and cum agane to the King.*

Rex
Quhat war thay yon, to me declair.

Wantonnes
Dame Sensuall, baith gude and fair.

Placebo
Sir, scho is mekill to avance,
For scho can baith play and dance,
That perfyt patron of plesance,
Ane perle of pulchritude:
Soft as the silk is hir quhite lyre,
Hir hair is like the goldin wyre:
My hart burnis in ane flame of fyre,
I sweir yow, be the Rude.

I think scho is sa wonder fair
That in the Earth scho hes na compair.
War ye weill leirnit at luffis lair,
And syne had hir anis sene,
I wait, be Cokis Passioun,

288 million (pounds) in 289 so generous/wanton 290 let, sore/sorry 291 know 293 before we go any further 295 without delay 299 not reluctant 301 Although I act disdainfully 302 by perseverance 304 fear 315 hoarse 316 bass (voice) 318 taught, fornicate 319 (bed)chamber 323 sitting nearby 324 love sex as much as I do 325 If they could, secretly 327 too long 330 mean 333 If, soon, see 337 much to be praised 340 pearl of beauty 341 complexion 346 no equal 347 taught in lovers' lore 348 seen her once 349 by God's Passion (euphemism)

43 'Since then you spare no man, by the Devil!'

44 'Go to look at them'.

Ye wald mak supplicatioun,
And spend on hir ane millioun,
Hir lufe for till obteine.

SOLACE
Quhat say ye, sir? Ar ye content
That scho cum heir incontinent?
Quhat vails your kingdome and your rent,
And all your great treasure,
Without ye half ane mirrie lyfe,
And cast asyde all sturt and stryfe?
And, sa lang as ye want ane wyfe,
Fall to and tak your pleasure!

REX
Gif that be trew quhilk ye me tell,
I will not langer tarie,
Bot will gang preif that play my sell,
Howbeit the warld me warie.
Als fast as ye may carie
Speid with all diligence:
Bring Sensualitie,
Fra-hand, to my presence.

Forsuth, I wait not how it stands,
Bot, sen I hard of your tythands,
My bodie trimblis, feit and hands,
And quhiles is hait as fyre.
I trow Cupido, with his dart,
Hes woundit me out-throw the hart;
My spreit will fra my bodie part,[45]
Get I nocht my desyre.

Pas on away with diligence,
And bring hir heir to my presence:
Spair nocht for travell nor expence,
I cair not for na cost.
Pas on your way schone, Wantonnes,
And tak with yow Sandie Solace,
And bring that ladie to this place,
Or els I am bot lost.

Commend me to that sweitest thing,
And present hir with this same ring,
And say I ly in languisching,
Except scho mak remeid.
With siching sair I am bot schent,
Without scho cum incontinent,
My heavie langour to relent,
And saif me now fra deid.

WANTONNES
Or ye tuik skaith, be Gods goun,
I lever thair war not, up nor doun,
Ane tume cunt into this toun,
Nor twentie myle about.
Doubt ye nocht, sir, bot wee will get hir,
Wee sall be feirie for till fetch hir,
Bot faith wee wald speid all the better,
Till gar our pursses rout.

SOLACE
Sir, let na sorrow in yow sink,
Bot gif us ducats[46] for till drink
And wee sall never sleip ane wink
Till it be back or eadge.[47]
Ye ken weill, sir, wee have no cunye.

REX
Solace, sure that sall be no sunyie;
Beir ye that bag upon your lunyie:
Now sirs, win weill your wage.
I pray yow speid yow sone againe.

WANTONNES
Ye[a], of this sang, sir, wee ar faine,
Wee sall nether spair [for] wind nor raine,
Till our days wark be done.
Fairweill, for wee ar at the flicht.
Placebo, rewll our Roy at richt:
We sall be heir, man, or midnicht,
Thocht wee marche with the mone.

Heir sall thay depairt singand[48] mirrelly.

WANTONNES
Pastyme with pleasance and greit prosperitie,
Be to yow, soveraine Sensualitie.

SENSUALITIE
Sirs, ye ar welcum. Quhair go ye, eist or west?

350 (i.e. beg her) 354 immediately 355 What use is 357 Unless 358 trouble 359 lack 360 (i.e. Get stuck in!) 363 try that game myself 364 blame me 369 don't know 370 news 371 trembles, feet 372 sometimes, hot 374 through 376 Unless I get 381 soon 384 utterly 388 Unless, remedy 389 sighing sorely, almost ruined 390 Unless 391 relieve 393 Before, took harm, gown 394 I'd rather 395 empty/unused 398 wonderfully eager 400 jingle 405 cash 406 hindrance 407 back 408 earn 413 about to fly/depart 414 correctly 419 east

45 Spirit. There may be an early version of the bawdy Shakespearean pun spirit/semen implicit here.

46 Italian coins.

47 'By whatever means [lit. whether by the back or the edge of the sword]'.

48 Singing.

WANTONNES
In faith, I trow we be at the farrest.

SENSUALITIE
Quhat is your name? I pray you, sir, declair.

WANTONNES
Marie, Wantonnes, the Kings secretair.

SENSUALITIE
Quhat king is that quhilk hes sa gay a boy?

WANTONNES
Humanitie, that richt redoutit roy,
Quhilk dois commend him to yow hartfulie,
And sends yow heir ane ring with ane rubie,
In takin that, abuife all creatour,
He hes chosen yow to be his paramour.
He bade me say that he will be bot deid,
Without that ye mak haistelie remeid.

SENSUALITIE
How can I help him, althocht he suld forfair?
Ye ken richt weill I am na medcinair.

SOLACE
Yes, lustie ladie, thocht he war never sa seik,
I wait ye beare his health into your breik:
Ane kis of your sweit mow in ane morning
Till his seiknes micht be greit comforting;
And als he maks yow supplicatioun,
This nicht to mak with him collatioun.

SENSUALITIE
I thank His Grace of his benevolence.
Gude sirs, I sall be reddie evin fra hand;
In me thair sall be fund na negligence,
Baith nicht and day, quhen His Grace will demand.
Pas ye befoir and say I am cummand,
And thinks richt lang to haif of him ane sicht.
And I to Venus do mak ane faithfull band,
That in his arms I think to ly all nicht.

WANTONNES
That sal be done, bot yit, or I hame pas,
Heir I protest for Hamelynes, your las.

SENSUALITIE
Scho salbe at command, sir, quhen ye will:
I traist scho sall find yow flinging your fill.

WANTONNES
Now hay, for joy and mirth I dance!
Tak thair ane gay gamond of France:
Am I nocht worthie till avance,
That am sa gude a page,
And that sa spedelie can rin
To tyst my maister unto sin?
The Fiend a penny he will win
Of this his mariage.

I rew richt sair, be Sanct Michell,
Nor I had pearst hir my awin sell:
For quhy yon king, be Bryds bell,[49]
Kennis na mair of ane cunt
Nor dois the noveis of ane freir!
It war bot almis to pull my eir,
That wald not preif yon gallant ger.[50]
Fy that I am sa blunt!

I think this day to win greit thank;
Hay, as ane brydlit cat I brank . . .[51]
Alace, I have wreistit my schank![52]
Yit I gang, be Sanct Michaell!
Quhilk of my leggis, sirs, as ye trow,
Was it that I did hurt evin now?
Bot quhairto sould I speir at yow?
I think thay baith ar haill.

[*To Rex*] Gude morrow, maister, be the Mes!

420 at the end (of our journey) 422 secretary 423 so fine a servant 424 renowned 425 commends himself 427 token, above 428 lover 430 hasty 431 die 432 doctor 433 sick 434 in your crack (genitals) 435 mouth 438 to dine with him 439 for 441 found 443 coming 444 I hope to see him soon 445 vow 447 but yet, before 448 I make a bid, lass (maid) 450 trust, enough jigging 452 gambade (French dance) 453 to promote 456 entice 457 he'll not gain a penny 459 regret, St Michael the Archangel 460 That I didn't pierce/penetrate her myself 462 Knows no more about 463 a friar's novice 464 would be an act of charity 473 why ask you? 474 healthy 475 Mass

49 St Bride (or Bridget), who began life as a milkmaid, and was thus conventionally depicted with a cow and bell.

50 '[I] who would not put [Sensualitie's] magnificent equipment to the test.'

51 Either: 'I strut like a cat in a bridle [collar]', or, reading 'bry[n]dlit' for 'brydlit', 'I strut like a mongrel cat' (i.e., inappropriately and above its station); an ironic revelation of Wantonnes's misplaced arrogance.

52 'I've twisted my leg!' Wantonnes seems to injure himself, but then (to his own surprise) continues dancing ('I'm still going, by St Michael!'), forgetting which leg it was that he hurt. Such nonsensical fooling is typical of the more physical Vice roles.

REX
Welcum, my minyeon, Wantonnes:
How hes thow sped in thy travell?

WANTONNES
Rycht weill, be Him that herryit Hell:
Your erand is weill done.

REX
Then, Wantonnes, how weill is mee!
Thow hes deservit baith meit and fie,
Be Him that maid the mone.

Thair is ane thing that I wald speir;
Quhat sall I do quhen scho cums heir?
For I knaw nocht the craft perqueir
Of luifers gyn.
Thaifoir at lenth ye mon me leir,
How to begin.

WANTONNES
To kis hir and clap hir, sir, be not affeard;
Sho will not schrink, thoct ye kis hir ane span within the baird.
Gif ye think that sho thinks shame, then hyd the bairns eine
With hir taill, and tent hir weil, ye wait quhat I meine![53]
Will ye leif me, sir, first for to go,
And I sall leirne yow all kewis how to do?

REX
God forbid, Wantonnes, that I gif the[e] leife.
Thou art over perillous ane page sic practiks to preife.

WANTONNES
Now, sir, preife as ye pleis, I se hir cumand;
Use your self gravelie, wee sall by yow stand.

Heir sall Sensualitie cum to the King and say:

SENSUALITIE
O Queene Venus, unto thy celsitude
I gif gloir, honour, laud, and reverence:
Quha grantit me sic perfite pulchritude,
That princes of my persone have pleasance.
I mak ane vow with humbill observance,
Richt reverentlie thy tempill to visie,
With sacrifice unto thy [deitie].

Till everie stait I am so greabill,
That few or nane refuses me at all:
Paipis, patriarks, or prelats venerabill,
Common pepill, and princes temporall,
Ar subject all to me, Dame Sensuall.
Sa sall it be ay quhill the warld indures,
And speciallie quhair youthage hes the cures.

Quha knawis the contrair?
I traist few in this companie,
Wald thay declair the veritie,
How thay use Sensualitie,
Bot with me makis repair.

And now my way I man avance
Unto ane prince of great puissance,
Quhom young men hes in governance,
Rolland into his rage.
I am richt glaid, I yow assure,
That potent prince to get in cure,
Quhilk is of lustines the luir,
And greitest of curage.

Heir sall scho mak reverence and say:

O potent Prince of pulchritude preclair,
God Cupido preserve your celsitude:
And Dame Venus mot keip your court from cair,
As I wald sho suld keip my awin hartblud.

REX
Welcum to me, peirles in pulchritude,
Welcum to me, thow sweiter nor the lamber,
Quhilk hes maid me of all dolour denude.
Solace, convoy this ladie to my chamber.

Heir sall scho pass to the chalmer and say:

477 How did you get on, labour 478 harrowed 480 how happy I am 481 food and wages 482 moon 485 skills by heart 486 of lovers' art 487 must teach me at length 489 embrace 493 Will you let me go first 494 teach you the right cues 495 permission 496 to try such practices 497 coming 498 Behave 499 majesty 500 glory, praise 504 visit 506 agreeable 511 always, while 512 the young have authority 513 Who knows different? 515 If they would 517 keep company 518 I must make my way 519 power 521 rolling, madness 523 under my control 524 lure 525 desire 526 fairest beauty 528 May Dame Venus 529 heart-blood 530 peerless 531 sweeter than amber 532 freed me from depression 533 convey/escort

53 'She will not resist, even of you kiss her a span within the beard/baird [either "bodice" or "beard"/pubic hair]. If you think that she is embarrassed, then cover the baby's eyes with the tail of her smock and give her a good seeing to, you know what I mean!'

Sensualitie
I gang this gait with richt gude will.
Sir Wantonnes, tarie ye stil:
And Hamelines, the cap yeis fill,
And beir him cumpanie.

[Hamelines]
That sall I do, withoutin dout,
And he and I sall play cap out.

Wantonnes
Now ladie, len me that batye tout:
Fill in, for I am dry.

Your dame be this, trewlie,
Hes gotten upon the gumis.
Quhat rak thocht ye and I
Go junne our justing lumis?[54]

Hamelines
Content I am with [richt] gude will,
Quhen ever ye ar reddie,
[All] your pleasure to fulfill.

Wantonnes
Now weill said, be Our Ladie!

Ile bair my maister cumpanie,
Till that I may indure:
Gif ye be quisland wantounlie,
We sall fling on the flure.

Heir sall thay pass all to the chalmer and Gude Counsale [*who enters here*] *sall say:*

Gude Counsall
Immortall God, maist of magnificence,
Quhais majestie na clark can comprehend,
Must save yow all that givis sic audience,
And grant yow grace Him never till offend,
Quhik on the Croce did willinglie ascend,
And sched His pretious blude on everie side:
Quhais pitious Passioun from danger yow defend,
And be your gratious governour and gyde.

Now, my gude freinds, considder I yow beseik
The caus maist principall of my cumming:
Princis or potestatis ar nocht worth ane leik,
Be thay not gydit be my gude governing.
Thair was never empriour, conqueror, nor king,
Without my wisdome that micht thair wil avance.
My name is Gude Counsall, without feinyeing;
Lords for lack of my lair ar brocht to mischance.

Finallie, for conclusioun,
Quha halds me at delusioun
Sall be brocht to confusioun:
And this I understand.
For I have maid my residence
With hie princes of greit puissance
In Ingland, Italie, and France,
And monie uther land.

Bot out of Scotland, wa, alace,
I haif bene fleimit lang tyme space,
That garris our gyders all want grace,
And die befoir thair day;[55]
Becaus thay lychtlyit Gude Counsall,
Fortune turnit on thame hir saill,
Quhilk brocht this realme to meikill baill,
Quha can the contrair say?

My Lords, I came nocht heir to lie.
Wa is me for King Humanitie,
Overset with Sensualitie,
In th'entrie of his ring,
Throw vicious counsell insolent.
Sa thay may get riches or rent
To his weilfair thay tak na tent,
Nor quhat sal be th'ending.

Yit in this realme I wald mak sum repair,
Gif I beleifit my name suld nocht forfair:
For, wald this King be gydit yit with ressoun,
And on misdoars mak punitioun,
Howbeit I haif lang tyme bene exyllit,

536 you fill the cup 537 keep 539 a drinking game 540 lend, lusty (one) 541 fill it up 551 For as long as 552 whistling wantonly 553 thrash about, floor 555 no scholar 558 Cross 559 precious 560 protect 561 gracious 563 principal cause 564 governors, leek 566 emperor 567 carry out their wishes 568 feigning 569 teaching, misfortune 571 in derision 577 many another 578 woe, alas 579 driven out 580 makes, rulers, lack 582 belittled 584 suffering 589 at the start of, reign 592 pay no attention 593 (consider) the consequences 594 stay a while/reform things 595 perish 597 punish wrong-doers 598 exiled

54 'Your mistress has, by now, got it on her lips, so what does it matter if you and I join [go to it with] our jousting equipment?'

55 'Before their time'. Recent Scottish history was blighted by the early deaths of kings and subsequent minority governments. In Lindsay's lifetime both James IV and James V had died relatively young.

I traist in God my name sall yit be styllit.
Sa, till I se God send mair of His grace,
I purpois till repois me in this place.

Heir entiris Flattery, new landit out of France, and stormested at the May.[56]

Flatterie
Mak roume, sirs, hoaw, that I may rin!
Lo, se quhair I am new cum [in],
Begaryit all with sindrie hewis:
Let be your din till I begin,
And I sall schaw yow of my newis.

Throuchout all Christindome I have past,
And am cum heir now at the last,
Tostit on sea ay sen Yuill Day,
That wee war faine to hew our mast,
Nocht half ane myle beyond the May.

Bot now amang yow I will remaine:
I purpois never to sail againe,
To put my lyfe in chance of watter:
Was never sene sic wind and raine,
Nor of schipmen sic clitter clatter.

Sum bade 'haill!', and sum bade 'standby
On steirburd!', 'hoaw!'; 'aluiff; fy, fy!'
Quhill all the raipis beguith to rattil:
Was never roy sa fleyd as I,
Quhen all the sails playd brittill brattill.

To se the waws it was ane wonder,
And wind that raif the sails in sunder:
Bot I lay braikand like ane brok,
And shot sa fast, above and under,
The Devill durst not cum neir my dok.

Now am I scapit fra that effray,
Quhat say ye, sirs, am I nocht gay?
Se ye not Flatterie, your awin fuill,
That yeid to mak this new array?
Was I not heir with yow at Yuill?
Yes, be my faith, I think on weill.
Quhair ar my fallows that wald nocht fail?[57]
We suld have cum heir for ane cast.
Hoaw, Falset, hoaw!

[Enter Falset.]

Falset
Wa, [serve] the Devill!
Quha is that that cryis for me sa fast?

Flatterie
Quhy, Falset, brother, knawis thou not me?
Am I nocht thy brother, Flattrie?

Falset
Now welcome, be the Trinitie:
This meitting cums for gude.
Now let me bresse the[e] in my armis.
Quhen freinds meits, harts warmis,
Quod Jok, that frelie fud.

How happinit yow into this place?

Flatterie
Now, be my saul, evin on a cace.
I come in sleipand at the port,
Or evir I wist, amang this sort.
Quhair is Dissait, that limmer loun?

Falset
I left him drinkand in the toun.
He will be heir incontinent.

Flatterie
Now, be the Haly Sacrament,
Thay tydingis comforts all my hart:
I wait Dissait will tak my part.
He is richt craftie as ye ken,
And counsallour to the merchand men.
Let us ly doun heir baith and spy
Gif wee persave him cummand by.

[Enter Dissait.]

599 honoured 601 repose (remain) 602 run 604 trimmed, sundry colours 605 Be quiet 606 show/tell 607 passed 609 Tossed, Yule (Christmas) 610 glad, cut down 614 at risk in 616 noise 618 starboard, track to windward 619 ropes began 620 so scared/whipped 621 rattled 622 waves 623 ripped, apart 624 farting, badger 626 arse 627 escaped, affray 629 own fool 630 went/worked, set-up 634 a throw (i.e. game of dice) 635 (i.e. curse you!) 636 shouts, loud 640 This is a lucky meeting 641 embrace 642 warm 643 splendid fellow 644 What brought you 645 soul, by luck 648 roguish 652 That news 653 I think 656 look 657 coming

56 'Driven by a storm to harbour on the Isle of May [in the Firth of Forth].'

57 i.e. 'who said they'd definitely be here.'

Dissait
Stand by the gait, that I may steir!
Aisay, Koks bons, how cam I heir?
I can not mis to tak sum feir,
Into sa greit ane thrang.
Marie, heir ane cumlie congregatioun!
Quhat, ar ye, sirs, all of ane natioun?
Maisters, I speik be protestatioun,
In dreid ye tak me wrang.[58]

Ken ye not, sirs, quhat is my name?
Gude faith, I dar not schaw it for schame.
Sen I was clekit of my dame,
Yit was I never leill.
For Katie Unsell[59] was my mother,
And Common Theif my foster brother:
Of sic freindship I had ane fither,
Howbeit I can not steill.

Bot yit I will borrow and len,
As be my cleathing ye may ken
That I am cum of nobill men;
And als I will debait
That querrell[60] with my feit and hands.
And I dwell amang the merchands:
My name, gif onie man demands,
Thay call me Dissait.

[*Seeing Falset*] *Bon-jour*, brother, with all my hart;
Heir am I cum to tak your part,
Baith into gude and evill.
I met Gude Counsall be the way,
Quha pat me in ane felloun fray:
I gif him to the Devill!

Falset
How chaipit ye, I pray yow tell?

Dissait
I slipit into ane bordell,
And hid me in a bawburds bed.
Bot suddenlie hir schankis I sched,
With hoch hurland amang hir howis:
God wait gif wee maid monie mowis!
How came ye heir, I pray yow tell me?

Falset
Marie, to seik King Humanitie.

Dissait
Now, be the gude ladie that me bair,
That samin hors is my awin mair![61]
Now with our purpois let us mell:
Quhat is your counsall, I pray yow tell?
Sen we thrie seiks yon nobill king,
Let us devyse sum subtill thing:
And als, I pray you as my brother,
That we ilk ane be trew to uther.
I mak ane vow with all my hart,
In gude and evill to tak your part.
I pray to God, nor I be hangit,
Bot I sall die or ye be wrangit.

Falset
Quhat is thy counsall that wee do?

Dissait
Marie, sirs, this is my counsall, lo:
Till tak our tyme, quhill wee may get it,
For now thair is na man to let it:
Fra tyme the King begin to steir him,
Marie, Gude Counsall I dreid cum neir him,
Ane be we knawin with Correctioun,
It will be our confusioun.
Thairfoir, my deir brother, devyse
To find sum toy of the new gyse.

Flatterie
Marie, I sall finde ane thousand wyles:
Wee man turne our claithis, and change our stiles,
And disagyse us, that na man ken us.
Hes no man clarkis cleathing to len us?
And let us keip grave countenance,
As wee war new cum out of France.

658 Out of the way, come through **659** God's bones (euphemism) **660** find some company **661** crowd **662** here's **663** race/country **668** snatched from, mother **669** honest **672** plenty **674** lend **675** by my clothing **677** (i.e. fight) **678** feet **680** any **686** put, terrible state **688** How did you escape **689** bordello (brothel) **690** whore's **691** legs, parted **692** great thrusting, between, thighs **693** knows, pulled many faces **696** who gave birth to me **698** meddle (let's discuss it) **700** seek **707** before you are wronged **710** Seize our chance **711** hinder **712** stir himself **714** if we are recognized by **715** ruin **717** trick **718** tricks **719** reverse, clothes, names **720** disguise **722** serious faces

58 'I speak fearfully and only on the understanding that you won't take me the wrong way.'
59 'Unhallowed Katie', a caricature name for a prostitute.
60 i.e. that he is a nobleman.
61 'That same horse is my own mare': i.e. 'That's exactly my intention too.'

DISSAIT
Now, be my saull, that is weill devysit.
Ye sall se me sone disagysit.

FALSET
And as sall I, man, be the Rude:
Now sum gude fallow len me ane hude.

Heir sall Flattry help his twa marrowis[62] [*to disguise themselves*].

DISSAIT
Now am I buskit and quha can spy,
The Devill stik me, gif this be I?
If this be I, or not, I can not weill say,
Or hes the Feind or farie-folk borne me away?

FALSET
And gif my hair war up in ane how,
The Feind ane man wald ken me, I trow:
Quhat sayis thou of my gay garmoun?

DISSAIT
I say thou luiks evin like ane loun.
Now, brother Flatterie, quhat do ye?
Quhat kynde of man schaip ye to be?

FLATTERIE
Now, be my faith, my brother deir,
I will gang counterfit the freir.

DISSAIT
A freir? Quhairto? Ye can not preiche.

FLATTERIE
Quhat rak, man? I can richt weill fleich.
Perchance I'le cum [to] that honour,
To be the Kings confessour.
Pure freirs are free at any feast,
And marchellit ay amang the best.
Als God hes lent to them sic graces,
That bischops puts them in thair places,
Out-throw thair dioceis to preiche.
Bot ferlie nocht, howbeit thay fleich,
For, schaw thay all the veritie,
Thaill want the bischops charitie.
And, thocht the corne war never sa skant,
The gudewyfis will not let freirs want:
For quhy thay ar thair confessours,
Thair heavinlie, prudent counsalours,
Thairfor, the wyfis plainlie taks thair parts,
And shawis the secreits of thair harts
To freirs with better will, I trow,
Nor thay do to thair bed-fallow.

DISSAIT
And I reft anis ane freirs coull,
Betuix Sanct-Johnestoun and Kinnoull:[63]
I sall gang fetch it, gif ye will tarie.

FLATTERIE
Now play me that of companarie!
Ye saw him nocht this hundreth yeir,
That better can counterfeit the freir.

DISSAIT
Heir is thy gaining, all and sum:
That is ane koull of Tullilum.[64]

FLATTERIE
Quha hes ane [porteus] for to len me?
The Feind ane saull, I traw, will ken me.

FALSET
Now gang thy way quhair ever thow wil,
Thow may be fallow to Freir Gill:
Bot with Correctioun gif wee be kend,
I dreid wee mak ane schamefull end.

FLATTERIE
For that mater I dreid nathing;
Freiris ar exemptit fra the King:
And freiris will reddie entries get,
Quhen lords ar haldin at the get.

FALSET
Wee man do mair yit, be Sanct James!
For wee mon all thrie change our names.
Hayif me and I sall baptize thee.

724 devised 727 hood 728 clothed 729 stab, if this is me 732 cap 733 (i.e. no one would) 734 garment 737 do you intend 741 What does that matter, flatter 744 welcome 745 placed by the marshal 747 as their surrogates 748 Throughout 749 don't be amazed 750 if they reveal the truth 751 lose 752 scarce 753 women, lack 759 Than 760 Once I stole, cowl 763 Do that for me for friendship's sake 766 earnings 767 a breviary 768 no one will know me 775 exempt from royal authority 776 get easy entry 777 held back, gate 778 must 780 christen

62 Companions.

63 'Between Perth and Kinneil Palace [20 miles west of Edinburgh]'.

64 A cowl from the Carmelite house of Tullilum, near Perth. Dissait has clearly exited and returned with the cowl between ll. 764 and 766.

Dissait
Be God and thair about may it be.
How will thou call me, I pray the[e] tell?

Falset
I wait not how to call my sell!

Dissait
Bot yit anis name the bairns name.

Falset
Discretioun, Discretioun, in Gods name!

Dissait
I neid nocht now to cair for thrift,
Bot quhat salbe my Godbairne gift?

Falset
I gif yow all the devilis of Hell!

Dissait
Na, brother, hauld that to thy sel!
Now sit doun, let me baptise the[e]:
I wait not quhat thy name sould be.

Falset
Both yit anis name the bairns name.

Dissait
Sapience, in ane warlds schame!

Flatterie
Brother Dissait, cum baptize me.

Dissait
Then sit doun lawlie on thy kne.

Flatterie
Now, brother, name the bairns name.

Dissait
Devotioun, [in] the Devils name!

Flatterie
The Devill resave the[e], lurdoun loun;
Thow hes wet all my new schavin croun.

Dissait
Devotioun, Sapience, and Discretioun,
Wee thre may rewll this regioun.
Wee sall find monie craftie things
For to begyll ane hundreth kingis.
For thow can richt weil crak and clatter,
And I sall feinye, and thow sall flatter.

Flatterie
Bot I wald have, or wee depairtit,
Ane drink to mak us better hartit.

Now the King sall cum fra his chamber.

Dissait
Weill said, be Him that herryit Hell,
I was evin thinkand that my sell.
Now, till wee get the Kings presence,
Wee will sit doun and keip silence.
I se ane [yonder]; quhat ever he be,
I'le wod my lyfe, yon same is he!
Feir nocht, brother, bot hauld yow still
Till wee have hard quhat is his will.

Rex
Now, quhair is Placebo and Solace?
Quhair is my minyeoun, Wantonnes?
Wantonnes, hoaw, cum to me sone!

[Enter Wantonnes and Hamelines; Danger, Solace, and Placebo follow at a distance.]

Wantonnes
Quhy cryit ye, sir, till I had done?

Rex
Quhat was ye doand, tell me that?

Wantonnes
Mary, leirand how my father me gat.
I wait nocht how it stands, but doubt.
Me think the warld rinnis round about.[65]

Rex
And sa think I, man, be my thrift:
I see fyfteine mones in the lift.

781 (i.e. that's what we'll do) 782 What 784 yet once, baby's 786 care about 787 godchild's 789 keep that for yourself 793 Wisdom 795 lowly 798 receive 799 new-shaven (friar's) tonsure 804 boast, chatter 805 feign 808 harried (i.e. Christ) 810 get (into) 812 (some) one 813 wager 818 soon 819 called 820 were, doing 821 learning, begot me 824 may I thrive 825 sky

65 'I don't know how things are [with the double entendre "I don't know if I still have an erection"]. I think the world is spinning round.' Wantonnes is still reeling from his sexual exertions with Hamelines.

[WANTONNES
Lat Hamelines, my lass, allane
Scho bendit up ay twa for ane.][66]

HAMELINES
Gat ye nocht quhilk ye desyrit?
Sir, I beleif that ye ar tyrit.

DANGER
Bot, as for Placebo and Solace,
I held them baith in mirrines.
[Howbeid I maid it sumthing tewch,
I fand thame chalmer-glew annewch.[67]

SOLACE
Mary, thaw wald gar ane hundreth tyre;
Thow hes ane cunt lyke ane quaw-myre.

DANGER
Now fowll fall yow, it is na bourdis,
Befoir ane king to speik fowll wourdis.
Or evir ye cum that gait agane,
To kiss my cloff ye salbe fane.]

SOLACE
Now schaw me, sir, I yow exhort,
How ar ye of your luif content?
Think ye not this ane mirrie sport?

REX
Yea, that I do in verament!
Quhat bairnis ar yon upon the bent?
I did nocht se them all this day.

WANTONNES
Thay will be heir incontinent.
Stand still and heir quhat thay will say.

Now the vycis cums and maks salutatioun, saying:

DISSAIT
Laud, honor, gloir, triumph, and victory
Be to Your maist excellent Majestie.

REX
Ye ar welcum, gude freinds, be the Rude;
Appeirandlie ye seime sum men of gude.
Quhat ar your names? Tell me without delay.

DISSAIT
Discretioun, sir, is my name, perfay.

REX
Quhat is your name, sir, with the clipit croun?

FLATTERIE
But dout, my name is callit Devotioun.

REX
Welcum, Devotioun, be Sanct Jame.
Now, sirray, tell quhat is your name.

FALSET
Marie, sir, thay call me . . . quhat call thay me?
[I wat not weill, but gif I lie.]

REX
Can ye nocht tell quhat is your name?

FALSET
I kend it quhen I cam fra hame.

REX
Quhat gars ye can nocht schaw it now?

FALSET
Marie, thay call me Thin Drink,[68] I trow.

REX
Thin Drink? Quhat kynde of name is that?

DISSAIT
Sapiens, thaw servis to beir ane plat.
Me think thow schawis the[e] not weill wittit.

FALSET
Sypeins, sir, Sypiens! Marie, now ye hit it!

826 alone **828** what you desired **829** tired **831** favoured them both equally **834** you'd tire a hundred men **835** quagmire **836** it's no joke **839** crack, glad **843** truly **844** young people, field **846** immediately **851** apparently, goods/virtue **853** by (my) faith **854** clipped (short-cut) **859** unless I lie **861** knew, home **862** unable to reveal it now **865** deserve, a slap **866** reveal yourself to be, witted

66 'She drew up/arched her back [like a bow] two for one': i.e. 'good enough for two people', or 'twice for every once that I could manage'.

67 'Even if I played hard to get [lit. made it somewhat tough], I gave them enough sexual satisfaction [lit. "bedroom glee"].'

68 As he reveals at l. 867, Falset mistakes 'sapience' for 'sypeins', the sediment-filled wine at the bottom of a cask or bottle, and consequently transmutes this into 'thin (or poor) drink'.

FLATTERIE
Sir, gif ye pleis to let [me] say,
His name is *Sapientia*.

FALSET
That same is it, be Sanct Michell!

REX
Quhy could thou not tell it thy sell?

FALSET
I pray Your Grace, appardoun me,
And I sall schaw the veritie:
I am sa full of Sapience,
That sumtyme I will tak ane trance:
My spreit wes reft fra my bodie,
Now heich abone the Trinitie.

REX
Sapience suld be ane man of gude.

FALSET
Sir, ye may ken that be my hude.

REX
Now have I Sapience and Discretioun,
How can I faill to rewll this regioun?
And Devotioun to be my confessour.
Thir thrie came in ane happie hour.
[*To Dissait*] Heir I mak the[e] my secretar,
[*To Falset*] And thou salbe my thesaurar,
[*To Flatterie*] And thow salbe my counsallour
In spirituall things and confessour.

FLATTERIE
I sweir to yow, sir, be Sanct An,
Ye met never with ane wyser man,
For monie a craft, sir, do I can,
War thay weill knawin.
Sir, I have na feill of flattrie,
Bot fosterit with phil[o]sophie,
Ane strange man in astronomie,
Quhilk salbe schawin.

FALSET
And I have greit intelligence
In quelling of the quintessence.[69]
Bot, to preif my experience,
Sir, len me fourtie crownes,
To mak multiplicatioun.
And tak my obligatioun,
Gif wee mak fals narratioun,
Hauld us for verie lownes.

DISSAIT
Sir, I ken be your physnomie
Ye sall conqueis, or els I lie,
Danskin, Denmark, and Almane,
Spittelfeild, and the realme of Spane.
Ye sall have at your governance,
Ranfrow and all the realme of France,
Yea, Rugland and the toun of Rome,
Castorphine, and al Christindome.
Quhairto, Sir, be the Trinitie,
Ye ar ane verie *A-per-sie*.

FLATTERIE
Sir, quhen I dwelt in Italie
I leirit the craft of palmistrie.
Schaw me the lufe, sir, of your hand,
And I sall gar yow understand
Gif Your Grace be infortunat,
Or gif ye be predestinat.
I see ye will have fyfteine queenes,
And fyfteine scoir of concubeines.
The Virgin Marie saife Your Grace,
Saw ever man sa quhyte ane face,
Sa greit ane arme, sa fair ane hand;
Thairs nocht sic ane leg in al the land.
War ye in armis, I think na wonder
Howbeit ye dang doune fyfteine hunder.[70]

DISSAIT
Now, be my saull, that's trew thow sayis,
Wes never man set sa weill his clais:
Thair is na man in Christintie
Sa meit to be ane king as ye.

869 Sapience (Latin) 872 pardon 875 fall into 876 ravished from 877 high above 878 should 885 treasurer 888 St Anne 892 no understanding 893 brought up in 894 extraordinarily able 895 shown 898 prove/test 900 (an alchemical process) 901 promise 902 (i.e. if we lie) 903 absolute rogues 904 facial features 905 conquer 906 Danzig, Germany 907 Spittlefield (London), Spain 909 Renfrew (Scotland) 910 Rutherglen (Lanarkshire) 911 Corstorphine, near Edinburgh 912 In addition to which 913 paragon (of princes) 915 learned 916 palm 918 ill-fated 919 predestined (to prosper) 921 (i.e. 300) 922 save 923 white 929 suited his clothes so well 930 Christendom 931 meet (fitting)

69 'In distilling the quintessence': i.e. the mysterious 'fifth element' (after air, water, fire, and earth) sought by alchemists.

70 'If you were in arms I wouldn't be surprised if you struck down fifteen hundred [foes].'

FALSET
Sir, thank the Haly Trinitie,
That send us to your cumpanie:
For God, nor I gaip in ane gallows,[71]
Gif ever ye fand thrie better fallows.

REX
Ye ar richt welcum, be the Rude,
Ye seime to be thrie men of gude.

Heir sall Gud Counsell schaw himself in the feild.

Bot quha is yon that stands sa still?
Ga spy and speir quhat is his will.
And, gif he yearnis my presence,
Bring him to mee with diligence.

DISSAIT
That sall we do, be Gods breid;
We's bring him eather quick or deid.

REX
I will sit still heir and repois.
Speid yow agane to me, my jois.

FALSET
Ye[a], hardlie, Sir, keip yow in clois
And quyet till wee cum againe.
Brother, I trow be Coks toes,
Yon bairdit bogill cums fra ane traine.

DISSAIT
Gif he dois sa, he salbe slaine.
I doubt him nocht, nor yit ane uther:
Trowit I that he come for ane traine,
Of my freindis I sould rais ane futher.

FLATTERIE
I doubt full sair, be God Him-sell,
That yon auld churle be Gude Counsell:
Get he anis to the Kings presence,
We thrie will get na audience.

DISSAIT
That matter I sall tak on hand,
And say it is the Kings command
That he anone devoyd this place,
And cum nocht neir the Kings grace:
And that under the paine of tressoun.

FLATTERIE
Brother, I hauld your counsell ressoun.
Now let is heir quhat he will say:
Auld lyart beard, gude day, gude day.

GUDE COUNSALL
Gude day againe, sirs, be the Rude.
The Lord mot make yow men of gude.[72]

DISSAIT
Pray nocht for us to lord nor ladie,
For we ar men of gude alreadie.
Sir, schaw to us quhat is your name.

GUDE COUNSALL
Gude Counsell thay call me at hame.

FALSET
Quhat says thow, carle, ar thow Gude Counsell?
Swyith, pak the[e] sone, unhappie unsell.[73]

GUDE COUNSALL
I pray yow, sirs, gif me licence
To cum anis to the Kings presence,
To speik bot two words to His Grace.

FLATTERIE
Swyith, hursone carle, devoyd this place!

GUDE COUNSALL
Brother, I ken yow weill aneuch,
Howbeit ye mak it never sa teuch:
Flattrie, Dissait, and Fals Report,
That will not suffer to resort
Gude Counsall to the Kings presence.

DISSAIT
Syith, hursun carle, gang pak the[e] hence!
Gif ever thou cum this gait agane,
I vow to God thou sall be slane.

Heir sall thay hurle away Gude Counsall.

933 sent 935 found 940 desires (to enter) 942 bread 943 We shall, alive 944 repose (wait) 945 hurry back, friends 946 inside 947 quiet 948 God's (euphemism) 949 bearded goblin, for trouble 951 fear 952 If I believed 953 crowd 954 sorely 955 old 956 If he once gets 957 no (further) access (to Rex) 960 at once, depart from 963 reasonable 965 grey/grizzled 969 goods/property 974 permission 976 just 978 well enough 979 However much you brazen it out

71 '[I swear] before God, may I gape in the gallows'.
72 'May the Lord make you good men/men of God.'
73 'Get out, get going quickly, ill-fated villain.'

[Gude Counsall]
Sen at this tyme I can get na presence,
Is na remeid bot tak in patience.[74]
Howbeit, Gude Counsall haistelie be nocht hard
With young princes, yit sould thay noch[t] be skard,
Bot, quhen youthheid hes blawin his wanton blast,
Then sall Gude Counsall rewll him at the last.

Now the Vycis gangs to ane counsall.[75]

Flatterie
Now, quhill Gude Counsall is absent,
Brother, wee mon be diligent;
And mak betwix us sikker bands,
Quhen vacands fallis in onie lands,
That everie man help weill his fallow.

Dissait
I had, deir brother, be Alhallow,
Sa ye fische nocht within our bounds.[76]

Flatterie
That sall I nocht, be Gods wounds,
Bot I sa plainlie tak your partis.

Falset
Sa sall wee thyne with all our hartis.
Bot haist us quhill the King is young.
Let everie man keip weill ane toung,
And in ilk quarter have ane spy
Us till adverteis haistelly
Quhen ony casualities
Sall happin into our countries.
And let us mak provisioun,
Or he cum to discretioun:
Na mair he waits now nor ane sant
Quhat thing it is to haif or want.[77]
Or he cum till his perfyte age,
We sall be sikker of our wage:
And then let everie carle craif uther.

Dissait
That mouth speik mair, my awin deir brother.
For God, nor I rax in ane raip,
Thaw may gif counsall to the Paip!

Now thay returne to the King.

Rex
Quhat gart you bid sa lang fra my presence?
I think it lang since ye depairtit thence.
Quhat man was yon with ane greit boustous beird?
Me thocht he maid yow all thrie very feard.

Dissait
It was ane laidlie, lurdan loun,
Cumde to break buithis into this toun.
Wee have gart bind him with ane poill,
And send him to the theifis hoill.

Rex
Let him sit thair with ane mischance,
And let us go to our pastance.

Wantonnes
Better go revell at the rackat,
Or ellis go to the hurlie hackat,
Or then to schaw our curtlie corsses,
Ga se quha best can rin thair horsses.

Solace
Na, Soveraine, or wee farther gang,
Gar Sensualitie sing ane sang.

Heir sall the Ladies sing ane sang, the King sall ly doun amang the Ladies, and then Veritie sall enter.

Veritie
Diligite Justitiam qui judicatis terram.[78]

Luif Justice, ye quha hes ane judges cure
In Earth, and dreid the awful judgement

986 no access (to Rex) **988** not heard immediately **989** scared **990** youth, blown **993** must **994** between, firm agreements **995** (lucrative) vacancies, appear **996** help his fellow (to gain them) **997** Allhallows **1000** take your side **1002** hurry **1004** each region **1005** quickly inform us **1006** casual income (perks) **1007** territories **1009** Before he (Rex) **1012** maturity **1013** sure **1014** beg from each other **1015** (i.e. I like what you say) **1016** may I stretch, rope **1018** made, stay, (away) from **1022** loathsome, lazy rogue **1023** Come, break into shops **1024** tied him to a pole **1025** thieves hole (i.e. jail) **1026** with bad luck (i.e. curse him!) **1027** pastimes **1028** (i.e. play tennis) **1029** sledging **1030** courtly bodies **1031** can best race **1035** has, authority

74 'There's no alternative but to put up with it patiently.'

75 'Go into a huddle [for discussion].'

76 'So long as you don't fish within our territory': i.e. don't work on our patch.

77 'At the moment he knows no more than a saint does about what it is to have or lack [property].'

78 'Dedicate yourselves to Justice, you who are judges of the Earth.' See Wisdom of Solomon 1:1.

Of Him that sall cum judge baith rich and pure,
Rycht terribilly with bludy wounds rent.
That dreidfull day into your harts imprent;
Belevand weill how and quhat maner ye
Use justice heir til uthers, thair at lenth
That day, but doubt, sa sall ye judgit be.[79]

Wo than, and duill be to yow princes all,
Sufferand the pure anes for till be opprest:
In everlasting burnand fyre ye sall
With Lucifer richt dulfullie be drest.
Thairfoir, in tyme for till eschaip that nest,
Feir God; do law and justice equally
Till everie man; se that na puir opprest
Up to the Hevin on yow ane vengence cry.[80]

Be just judges without favour or fead,
And hauld the ballance evin till everie wicht.[81]
Let not the fault be left into the head,
Then sall the members reulit be at richt,
For quhy subjects do follow day and nicht
Thair governours, in vertew and in vyce.
Ye ar the lamps that sould schaw them the licht
To leid them on this sliddrie rone of yce.

Mobile mutatur semper cum principe vulgus.[82]

And, gif ye wald your subjectis war weill gevin,
Then verteouslie begin the dance your sell,
Going befoir, then they anone, I wein,
Sall follow yow, eyther till Hevin or Hell.
Kings sould of gude exempils be the well.
Bot, gif that your strands be intoxicate,
In steid of wyne thay drink the poyson fell:
Thus pepill follows ay thair principate.

Sic luceat lux vestra coram hominibus ut videant opera vestra bona.[83]

And specially ye princes of the preists,
That of peopill hes spiritual cuir,
Dayly ye sould revolve into your breistis[84]
How that thir haly words ar still maist sure.
In verteous lyfe gif that ye do indure,
The pepill wil tak mair tent to your deids
Then to your words; and als baith rich and puir
Will follow yow baith in your warks and words.

Heir sal Flatterie spy Veritie with ane dum countenance.

Gif men of me wald have intelligence,
Or knaw my name, thay call me Veritie.
Of Christis law I have experience,
And hes oversaillit many stormie sey.
Now am I seikand King Humanitie,
For of His Grace I have gude esperance.
Fra tyme that he acquaintit be with mee,
His honour and heich gloir I sall avance.

Heir sall Veritie pas to hir sait.

Dissait
Gude day, father, quhair have ye bene?
Declair till us of your novels.

Flatterie
Thair is now lichtit on the grene
Dame Veritie, be buiks and bels![85]

Bot cum scho to the Kings presence,
Thair is na buit for us to byde.[86]
Thairfoir, I red us all go hence.

Falset
That will we nocht yit, be Sanct Bryde:
But wee sall ather gang or ryde
To Lords of Spritualitie,

1038 torn, bloody wounds **1039** imprint (i.e. remember) **1040** Believing **1043** dole (grief) **1044** suffering, poor ones **1045** burning **1046** dolefully, provided for **1047** resting place **1051** enmity **1053** (i.e. Make sure the governor isn't sinful) **1054** be ruled properly **1057** light **1058** slippery patch of ice **1060** want, to be inclined to virtue **1061** (i.e. set the right example) **1062** I believe **1064** should, well-spring/origin **1065** streams, toxic/poisoned **1066** Instead, deadly **1067** always follow their princes **1069** church leaders **1070** for, responsibility **1072** certain **1073** if you continue **1074** pay more attention, deeds **1076** works **1077** would learn about me **1080** sailed over, sea **1081** seeking **1082** hope **1083** From (the) time **1084** high glory **1084+** seat/throne **1086** Tell us your news **1087** alighted **1091** advise us (to) **1093** either walk

79 'To others here [on Earth], for you will be judged, certainly, in due course on that Day [of Judgement].'
80 'See that no poor oppressed folk cry to Heaven for vengeance upon you.'
81 Person: i.e. an allusion to the scales of Justice: 'be impartial'.
82 'The fickle crowd always changes with the prince': an often-quoted maxim supposedly coined by the Emperor Theodosius (AD 378–95).
83 'Let your light so shine before men that they may see your good works.' Matthew 5:16.
84 'Turn over in your breasts [i.e. remind yourselves] each day'.
85 Books and bells (the paraphernalia of the Catholic rite of anathema or cursing).
86 'If she gets to the King's presence, there'll be no point in our sticking around.'

And gar them trow yon bag of pryde
Hes spokin manifest heresie.

Heir thay cum to the Spritualitie.

FLATTERIE
O reverent fatheris of the Sprituall Stait,
Wee counsall yow be wyse and vigilant:
Dame Veritie hes lychtit now of lait,
And in hir hand beirand the New Testament.
Be scho ressavit, but doubt wee ar bot schent.[87]
Let hir nocht ludge thairfoir, into this land,
And this wee reid yow do incontinent,
Now, quhill the King is with his luif sleipand.

SPRITUALITE
Wee thank yow, freinds, of your benevolence:
It sall be done evin as ye have devysit.
Wee think ye serve ane gudlie recompence,
Defendand us that wee be nocht supprysit.
In this mater wee man be weill advysit,
Now quhill the King misknawis the Veritie.
Be scho ressavit, then wee will be deprysit.
Quhat is your counsell, brother, now let se?

ABBOT
I hauld it best that wee incontinent
Gar hauld hir fast into captivitie,
Unto the thrid day of the Parlament,
And then accuse hir of hir herisie:
Or than banische hir out of this cuntrie.
For, with the King gif Veritie be knawin,
Of our greit gloir wee will degradit be,
And all our secreits to the commouns schawin.

PERSONE
Ye se the King is yit effeminate,
And gydit be Dame Sensualitie,
Rycht sa with young counsall intoxicate,[88]
Swa at this tyme ye haif your libertie.
To tak your tyme I hauld it best for me,
And go distroy all thir Lutherians,[89]
In speciall yon Ladie Veritie.

SPRITUALITE
Schir Persone, ye sall be my commissair
To put this mater till executioun.
And ye, sir Freir, becaus ye can declair
The haill processe,[90] pas with him in commissioun.
Pas all togidder with my braid bennisoun,
And, gif scho speiks against our libertie,
Then put hir in perpetuall presoun,
That scho cum nocht to King Humanitie.

Heir sall thay pas to Verity.

PERSONE
Lustie Ladie, we wald faine understand
Quhat earand ye haif in this regioun.
To preich or teich quha gaif to yow command,
To counsall kingis how gat ye commissioun?
I dreid, without ye get ane remissioun,
And syne renunce your new opiniones,
The Spirituall Stait sall put yow to perdition,
And in the fyre will burne yow, flesche and bones.

VERITIE
I will recant nathing that I have schawin:
I have said nathing bot the veritie.
Bot with the King fra tyme that I be knawin,
I dreid ye spaiks of Spritualitie
Sall rew that ever I came in this cuntrie.
For, gif the veritie plainlie war proclamit,
And speciallie to the Kings Majestie,
For your traditions ye wilbe all defamit.[91]

Heir the Vycis gais to the Sprituall Estait and lyis upoun Veretie,[92] desiring hir to be put in captivitie, quhilk is done with diligence.

FLATTERIE
Quhat buik is that, harlot, into thy hand?
Out, walloway, this is the New Testment,

1095 make them believe 1100 carrying 1102 lodge (live) 1103 advise 1104 lover 1105 for 1106 devised 1107 deserve, goodly 1108 overcome 1109 must 1110 misunderstands/is ignorant of 1111 no longer valued 1115 Until, third 1119 deprived 1120 revealed 1121 still under the influence of women 1125 seize your opportunity 1127 And especially Lady Veritie there 1128 Sir Parson, commissioner 1129 into 1131 as co-investigator 1132 broad blessing 1134 prison 1136 eagerly wish to 1137 errand/purpose 1138 who told you to 1139 permission 1140 unless you get a pardon 1141 then, renounce 1142 punishment 1144 said 1145 but 1146 Once I am known 1147 rungs (of a ladder) 1149 proclaimed 1152 in

87 'If she is received [at court], it's certain we're done for.'
88 'And also drunk with the advice of his young friends'.
89 Lutherans: followers of the German reformer Martin Luther (1483–1586).
90 'The whole story'.
91 'You will be reviled for your traditional practices.'
92 'Here the Vices go to the Spiritual Estate and tell lies about Veritie'.

In Englisch toung, and printit in England!
Herisie, herisie; fire, fire, incontinent!

Veritie
Forsuith, my freind, ye have ane wrang judgement,
For in this buik thair is na heresie,
Bot our Christs word, baith dulce and redolent,
And springing well of sinceir veritie.

Dissait
Cum on your way: for all your yealow locks,
Your wantoun words, but doubt, ye sall repent.
This nicht ye sall forfair ane pair of stocks,
And syne the morne be brocht to thoill judgement.

Veritie
Four our Christs saik I am richt wall content
To suffer all thing that sall pleis His grace;
Howbeit ye put ane thousand to torment,
Ten hundreth thowsand sall rise into thair place.

Veritie sits down on hir knies and sayis:

Get up, Thow sleipis all too lang, O Lord,[93]
And mak sum ressonabill reformatioun
On them that dois tramp doun Thy gracious word,
And hes ane deidlie indignatioun
At them quha maks maist trew narratioun.
Suffer me not, Lord, mair to be molest.
Gude Lord, I mak The[e] supplicatioun,
With Thy unfreinds let me nocht be supprest.

Now, Lords, do as ye list,
I have na mair to say.

Flatterie
Sit doun and tak yow rest,
All nicht till it be day.

Thay put Veritie in the stocks and returne to Spritualitie.

Dissait
My Lord, wee have with diligence
Bucklit up weill yon bledrand baird.

Sprituality
I think ye serve gude recompence;
Tak thir ten crowns for your rewaird.

Veritie
The prophesie of the Propheit Esay
Is practickit, alace, on mee this day,
Quha said the veritie sould be trampit doun
Amid the streit, and put in strang presoun.
His fyve and fyftie chapter, quha list luik,[94]
Sall find thir words writtin in his buik.
Richt sa Sanct Paull wrytis to Timothie,
That men sall turne thair earis from veritie.[95]
Bot in my Lord God I have esperance;
He will provide for my deliverance.
Bot ye princes of Spritualitie,
Quha sould defend the sinceir veritie,
I dreid the plagues of Johnes Revelatioun
Sall fal upon your generatioun.[96]
I counsall yow this misse t'amend,
Sa that ye may eschaip that fatall end.

Heir sall entir Chastitie and say:

Chastitie
How lang sall this inconstant warld indure?
That I sould baneist be sa lang, alace!
Few creatures or nane takis on me cure,
Quhilk gars me monie nicht ly harbrieles.
Thocht I have past all yeir fra place to place,
Amang the Temporal and Spirituall staits
Nor amang Princes I can get na grace,
Bot boustuouslie am halden at the getis.

Diligence
Ladie, I pray yow, schaw me your name.
It dois me noy, your lamentatioun.

Chastitie
My freind, thairof I neid not to think shame;
Dame Chastitie, baneist from town to town.

1158 sweet, fragrant 1160 yellow hair 1162 endure 1163 (in) the morning, suffer 1172 Against, make 1173 molested 1175 by, enemies, oppressed 1181 Buckled (tied), blathering bard 1182 deserve 1184 Isaiah 1185 put into practice 1186 trampled 1187 street 1192 hope 1198 to amend this error 1199 escape 1201 banished for so long 1202 take care of me 1203 to lie shelterless for many nights 1204 year 1207 roughly, kept out 1209 It annoys/grieves me

93 For the appeal to God to awake, see Psalms 43:22–3.

94 'Who wants to look it up, it's in the fifty-fifth chapter'. Actually Isaiah 59:4: 'And judgement is turned away backward, and justice standeth far off; for truth is fallen in the street, and equity cannot enter.'

95 'And they shall turn away their ears from the truth, and shall be turned unto fables.' II Timothy 4:4.

96 For the plagues described by St John, see Revelation 22:18.

Diligence
Then pas to ladies of religioun,
Quhilk maks thair vow to observe chastitie:
Lo, quhair thair sits ane Priores of renown
Amang the rest of Spritualitie.

Chastitie
I grant yon ladie hes vowit chastitie,
For hir professioun thairto sould accord.
Scho maid that vow for ane abesie,
Bat nocht for Christ Jesus, our Lord.
Fra tyme that they get thair vows, I stand ford,
Thay banische hir out of thair cumpanie:
With Chastitie thay can mak na concord,
Bot leids thair lyfis in sensualitie.

I sall observe your counsall gif I may:
Cum on and heir quhat yon ladie will say.

Chastitie passis to the Ladie Priores, and sayis:

My prudent lustie Ladie Priores,
Remember how ye did vow chastitie.
Madame, I pray yow of your gentilnes
That ye wald pleis to haif of me pitie,
And this ane nicht to gif me harberie:
For this I mak yow supplicatioun.
Do ye nocht sa, Madame, I dreid, perdie,
It will be caus of depravatioun.

Priores
Pas hynd, Madame, be Christ ye cum nocht heir;
Ye ar contrair to my cumplexioun.
Gang seik ludging at sum auld monk or freir,
Perchance thay will be your protectioun.
Or to prelats mak your progressioun,
Quhilks ar obleist to yow als weill as I.
Dame Sensuall hes gevin directioun
Yow till exclude out of my cumpany.

Chastitie
Gif ye wald wit mair of the veritie,
I sall schaw yow be sure experience,
How that the Lords of Sprituality
Hes baneist me, alace, fra thair presence.

Chastitie passes to the Lords of Spritualitie.

My Lords, laud, gloir, triumph, and reverence
Mot be unto your halie Sprituall Stait.
I yow beseik, of your benevolence,
To harbry mee that am sa desolait.

Lords, I have past throw mony uncouth schyre,
Bot in this land I can get na ludgeing.
Of my name, gif ye wald haif knawledging,
Forsuith, my lords, thay call me Chastitie.
I yow beseik, of Your Graces bening,
Gif me ludging this nicht for charitie.

Spritualite
Pas on, madame, we knaw yow nocht;
Or, be Him that the warld [hes] wrocht,
Your cumming sall be richt deir coft,
Gif ye mak langer tarie.

Abbot
But doubt wee will baith leif and die
With our luif, Sensualitie.
Wee will haif na mair deall with the[e]
Then with the Queene of Farie.

Persone
Pas hame amang the nunnis and dwell,
Quhilks ar of chastitie the well.
I traist thay will with buik and bell
Ressave yow in thair closter.

Chastitie
Sir, quhen I was the nunnis amang,
Out of thair dortour thay mee dang,
And wald nocht let me bide sa lang
To say my *Pater Noster*.

I se na grace thairfoir to get.
I hauld it best, or it be lait,
For till go prove the Temporall Stait,
Gif thay will mee resaif.
Gud day, my Lord Temporalitie,
And yow, Merchant of gravitie:
Ful faine wald I have harberie,
To ludge amang the laif.

1214 Prioress 1217 should conform to it 1218 (only) to gain the post of abbess 1219 But not 1220 make, I guarantee it 1221 her (Chastitie) 1222 cannot agree 1223 lead, lives 1229 on 1230 one, shelter 1232 so, by God 1233 the loss of (your) job 1234 Go away 1235 contrary, nature 1236 Go (and) seek lodging 1238 journey 1239 obligated, as well 1240 given 1241 to 1242 know 1247 Must 1249 harbour (shelter), desolate 1250 strange lands 1252 knowledge 1253 Truly 1254 benign 1258 dearly bought 1259 delay 1260 live 1261 love 1262 dealings 1264 Go home 1265 source/origin 1266 trust 1267 cloister 1269 dormitory, drove 1271 'Our Father' 1273 consider, before, late 1274 test 1275 receive 1278 eagerly 1279 rest (of you)

Temporalitie
Forsuith, wee wald be weil content
To harbrie yow with gude intent,
War nocht we haif impediment:
For quhy we twa ar maryit.
Bot wist our wyfis that ye war heir,
Thay wald mak all this town on steir.
Thairfoir, we reid yow rin areir,
In dreid ye be miscaryit.

Chastitie
Ye men of craft of greit ingyne,
Gif me harbrie, for Christis pyne,
And win Gods bennesone and myne,
And help my hungrie hart.

Sowtar
Welcum, be Him that maid the mone,
Till dwell with us till it be June.
We sall mend baith your hois and schone,
And plainlie tak your part.

Taylour
Is this fair Ladie Chastitie?
Now welcum, be the Trinitie.
I think it war ane great pitie
That thou sould ly thairout.
Your great displeasour I forthink.
Sit doun, Madame, and tak ane drink,
And let na sorrow in yow sink,
Bot let us play cap out.

Sowtar
Fill in and play [drink about],
For I am wonder dry.
The Devill snyp aff thair snout
That haits this company.

Heir sall thay gar Chestety sit down and drink [*Enter Jennie, Taylours Wyfe, and Sowtars Wyfe.*]

Jennie
Hoaw Mynnie, Mynnie, Mynnie!

Taylours Wyfe
Quhat wald thow, my deir dochter, Jennie?
Jennie, my joy, quhair is thy dadie?

Jennie
Mary, drinkand with ane lustie ladie,
Ane fair young mayden cled in quhyte,
Of quhom my dadie taks delyte.
Scho hes the fairest forme of face,
Furnischit with all kynd of grace.
I traist gif I can reckon richt,
Scho schaips to ludge with him all nicht.

Sowtars Wyfe
Quhat dois the Sowtar, my gudman?

Jennie
Mary, fillis the cap and tumes the can.
Or he cum hame, be God, I trow,
He will be drunkin lyke ane sow.

Taylours Wyfe
This is ane greit dispyte, I think,
For to resave sic ane kow-clink.
Quhat is your counsell that wee do?

Sowtars Wyfe
Cummer, this is my counsall, lo:
Ding ye the tane, and I the uther.

Taylours Wyfe
I am content, be Gods mother!
I think, for mee, thay huirsone smaiks,
Thay serve richt weill to get thair paiks.
Quhat master Feind neids all this haist?
For it is half ane yeir almaist
Sen ever that loun laborde my ledder.[97]

Sowtars Wyfe
God, nor my trewker mence ane tedder,[98]
For it is mair nor fourtie dayis,
Sen ever he cleikit up my clayis.
And last quhen I gat chalmer glew,
That foull Sowter began till spew.

1282 were it not that 1283 married 1284 if our wives found out 1285 stir up 1286 advice, run away 1287 for fear, harmed 1288 ingenuity 1289 pain 1290 blessing 1294 hose, shoes 1299 outside 1300 discomfort, regret 1306 snip/cut, nose 1308 mummy 1309 What do you want 1310 daddy 1311 drinking 1312 clad 1313 in 1315 furnished/provided 1317 intends 1318 husband 1319 empties 1321 drunken 1322 shame to us 1324 whore 1325 Companion 1326 one 1328 useless sons of bitches 1329 deserve, a thrashing 1330 What the Devil's the rush 1331 almost half a year 1334 more than 1335 since, pulled, clothes 1336 the last time, got any sexual attention 1337 to vomit

97 'Toiled at my leather': i.e. satisfied me sexually.

98 'May my trickster [husband] grace the gallows'.

And now thay will sit doun and drink
In company with ane kow-clink!
Gif thay haif done us this dispyte,
Let us go ding them till thay dryte.

Heir the Wifis sall chase away Chastitie.

Taylours Wyfe
Go hence, harlot, how durst thow be sa bauld
To ludge with our gudemen but our licence?
I mak ane vow to Him that Judas sauld,
This rock of myne sall be thy recompence.
Schaw me thy name, dudron, with diligence.

Chastitie
Marie, Chastitie is my name, be Sanct Blais.[99]

Taylours Wyfe
I pray God nor He work on the[e] vengence,
For I luifit never Chastitie all my dayes.

Sowtars Wyfe
Bot my gudman, the treuth I sall the[e] tell,
Gars mee keip chastitie sair agains my will.
Becaus that monstour hes maid sic ane mint,
With my bedstaf that dastard beirs ane dint.[100]
And als I vow, cum thow this gait againe,
Thy buttoks salbe beltit, be Sanct Blaine.[101]

Heir sall thay speik to thair gudemen and ding them.

Taylours Wyfe
Fals hurson carle, but dout thou sall forthink
That evar thow eat or drink with yon kow-clink.

Sowtars Wyfe
I mak ane vow to Sanct Crispine,[102]
Ise be revengit on that graceles grume:
And, to begin the play, tak thair ane flap!

Sowtar
The Feind ressave the hands that gaif mee that!

Sowtars Wyfe
Quhat now, huirsun, begins thow for til ban?
Tak thair ane uther upon thy peild harne-pan!
Quhat now, cummer, will thow nocht tak my part?

Taylours Wyfe
That sal I do, cummer, with all my hart.

Heir sall thay ding thair gudemen, with silence.

Taylour
Alace, gossop, alace! How stands with yow?
Yon cankart carling, alace, hes brokin my brow.
Now weils yow, preists, now weils yow all your lifes,
That ar nocht weddit with sic wickit wyfes.

Sowtar
Bischops ar blist, howbeit that thay be waryit,
For thay may fuck thair fill and be unmaryit.
Gossop, alace, that blak band we may wary,
That ordanit sic puir men as us to mary.
Quhat may be done bot tak in patience?
And on all wyfis weill cry ane loud vengence.

Heir sall the Wyfis stand be the watter syde and say:

Sowtars Wyfe
Sen of our cairls we have the victorie,
Quhat is your counsell, cummer, that be done?

Taylours Wyfe
Send for gude wine and hald our selfis merie,
I hauld this ay best, cummer, be Sanct Clone.[103]

Sowtars Wyfe
Cummer, will ye draw aff my hois and schone,
To fill the quart I sall rin to the toun.

Taylours Wyfe
That sal I do, be Him that maid the mone,
With all my hart, thairfoir, cummer, sit doun.

1340 injury/shame 1341 crap themselves 1342 bold 1343 without our permission 1344 sold 1345 distaff 1346 slut, quickly 1348 that He 1349 loved 1351 greatly against 1352 attempt (with Chastitie) 1355 thrashed with a belt 1356 doubtless you'll regret 1359 I'll, revenged, fellow 1360 a blow 1361 gave 1362 to curse 1363 bald head 1366 companion, how are things 1367 shrewish hag 1368 prosper 1369 married, wicked 1370 blessed, cursed (too) 1371 all they want, unmarried 1372 black contract, curse 1373 commanded 1374 suffer (it) patiently 1378 merry 1380 pull off, hose, shoes 1381 jug

99 St Blais, a fourth-century saintly healer.

100 'That dastard will take a blow from my bedstaff [the rod used for smoothing sheets].'

101 St Blane, an early Scottish saint, with a pun on 'blain', sore or inflammation.

102 St Crispin, patron saint of shoemakers.

103 Perhaps St Cluanus (St Mochua), a sixth-century Irish saint.

Kilt up your claithis abone your waist,
And speid yow hame againe in haist,
And I sall provyde for ane paist,
Our corsses to comfort.

Sowtars Wyfe
Then help me for to kilt my clais.
Quhat gif the padoks nip my tais?
I dreid to droun heir, be Sanct Blais,
Without I get support.

Sho lifts up hir clais above hir waist and enters in the water.

Cummer, I will nocht droun my sell.
Go east about the nether mill.

Taylours Wyfe
I am content, be Bryds bell,
To gang with yow quhair ever ye will.

Heir sall thay depairt and pas to the Palyeoun.[104]

Diligence
[*To Chastitie*] Madame, quhat gars yow gang sa lait?
Tell me how ye have done debait,
With the Temporall and Spirituall Stait?
Quha did yow maist kyndnes?

Chastitie
In faith, I fand bot ill and war,
Thay gart mee stand fra thame askar.
Evin lyk ane begger at the bar,
And fleimit mair and lesse.

Diligence
I counsall yow, but tarying,
Gang tell Humanitie the King.
Perchance hee, of his grace bening,
Will mak to yow support.

Chastitie
Of your counsell I am content
To pas to him incontinent,
And my service till him present,
In hope of sum comfort.

Heir sall thay pas to the King.

Diligence
Hoaw, Solace! Gentil Solace, declair unto the King
How thair is heir ane ladie fair of face,
That in this cuntrie can get na ludging;
Bot pitifullie flemit from place to place,
Without the King, of his speciall grace,
As ane servand hir in his court resaif.
Brother Solace, tell the King all the cace,
That scho may be resavit amang the laif.

Solace
Soverane, get up and se ane hevinlie sicht,
Ane fair ladie in quhyt abuilyement.
Scho may be peir unto ane king or knicht,
Most lyk ane angell be my judgment.

Rex
I sall gang se that sicht incontinent.
Madame, behauld gif ye have knawledging
Of yon ladie, or quhat is hir intent.
Thairefter wee sall turne but tarying.

Sensualitie
Sir, let me se quhat yon mater may meane,
Perchance that I may knaw hir be hir face.
But doubt this is Dame Chastitie, I weine.
Sir, I and scho cannot byde in ane place.
But, gif it be the pleasour of Your Grace
That I remaine into your company,
This woman richt haistelie gar chase,
That scho na mair be sene in this cuntry.

Rex
As evir ye pleis, sweit hart, sa sall it be.
Dispone hir as ye think expedient:
Evin as ye list to let hir live or die;
I will refer that thing to your judgement.

Sensualitie
I will that scho be flemit incontinent,
And never to cum againe in this cuntrie.
And, gif scho dois, but doubt scho sall repent,
As als perchance a duilfull deid sall die.

1384 tie, above 1386 pastry 1387 bodies 1389 toads, toes 1390 fear 1391 Unless 1392 drown 1393 lower 1396 walk so late (at night) 1397 made trial of 1400 only bad and worse 1401 made, apart 1402 the (courtroom) bar 1403 drove (me) away 1404 without 1406 benign 1415 driven 1416 Unless 1417 servant, employ her 1418 the whole story 1419 received, rest (of the court) 1421 white clothing 1422 the equal of 1424 (and) see 1425 knowledge 1430 I believe 1431 abide 1433 in 1434 quickly chase away 1437 Dispose of her 1442 does, without doubt 1443 doleful death

104 The pavilion which acted as a dressing room for the players.

Pas on, Sir Sapience and Discretioun,
And banische hir out of the Kings presence.

Dissait
That sall we do, Madame, be Gods Passioun!
Wee sall do your command with diligence,
And at your hand serve gudely recompence.
Dame Chastitie, cum on, be not agast;
We sall rycht sone, upon your awin expence,
Into the stocks your bony fute mak fast.

Heir sall they harll[105] *Chastitie to the stoks, and scho sall say:*

[Chastitie]
I pray yow, sirs, be patient,
For I sall be obedient
Till do quhat ye command,
Sen I se thair is na remeid,
Howbeit it war to suffer deid,
Or flemit furth of the land.

I wyte the Empreour Constantine,[106]
That I am put to sic ruine
And baneist from the Kirk:
For, sen he maid the Paip ane king,
In Rome I could get na ludging,
Bot heidlangs in the mirk.

Bot Ladie Sensualitie
Sensyne hes gydit this cuntrie,
And monie of the rest.
And now scho roulis all this land,
And hes decryit at hir command,
That I suld be suppress.

Bot all comes for the best,
Til him that lovis the Lord:
Thocht I be now molest
I traist to be restorde.

Heir sall they put hir in the stocks.

[Chastitie]
Sister, alace, this is ane cairful cace,
That we with princes sould be sa abhorde.

Veritie
Be blyth, sister. I wast within schort space
That we sall be richt honorablie restorde,
And with the King we sall be at concorde,
For I heir tell Divyne Correctioun
Is new landit, thankit be Christ our Lord.
I wait hee will be our protectioun.

H[e]ir sall enter Corrections Varlet.

Varlet
Sirs, stand abak and hauld yow coy,
I am the King Correctiouns boy,
Cum heir to dres this place.
Se that ye mak obedience
Untill his nobill excellence
Fra tyme ye se his face.

For he maks reformatiouns
Out-throw all Christin natiouns,
Quhair he finds great debaits.
And, sa far as I understand,
He sall reforme into this land
Evin all the Thrie Estaits.

God furth of Heavin hes him send
To punische all that dois offend
Against His Majestie,
As lyks him best to tak vengence,
Sumtyme with sword and pestilence,
With derth and povertie.

Bot, quhen the peopill dois repent,
And beis to God obedient,
Then will he gif them grace.
Bot thay that will nocht be correctit,
Rycht sudanlie will be dejectit,
And fleimit from his face.

Sirs, thocht wee speik in generall,
Let na man into speciall
Tak our words at the warst:
Quhat ever wee do, quhat ever wee say,
I pray yow tak it all in play,
And judg ay to the best.

1448 deserve 1451 bonny foot 1454 To 1455 no remedy (alternative) 1456 Even if, death 1457 (to be) exiled from 1463 (thrown) headlong, dark 1465 (has) for some time 1466 many 1467 rules 1468 decreed 1472 Although, molested 1473 trust 1474 sad situation 1476 happy, knew 1481 know 1482 be quiet 1484 prepare 1487 Once you have seen 1489 Throughout 1490 wherever 1492 within 1494 has sent him forth out 1495 does 1499 famine 1501 are 1504 suddenly cast down 1506 in general (terms; i.e. of everyone) 1507 especially 1508 as maliciously inclined

105 Haul.

106 'I blame the Emperor Constantine'. Constantine I (Flavius Valerius Constantinus, *c.* AD 274–337) was thought to have given the Roman church control of the lands in Italy in AD 330, through the 'Donation of Constantine', thus initiating its role as a landowner and beginning its interest in worldly concerns.

For silence I protest,
Baith of lord, laird, and ladie.
Now I will rin but rest
And tell that all is ready.

Dissait
Brother, heir ye yon proclamatioun?
I dreid full sair of reformatioun,
Yon message maks me mangit.
Quhat is your counsell, to me tell.
Remaine wee heir, be God Him-sell,
Wee will be all thre hangit.

Flatterie
Ile gang to Spritualitie,
And preich out-throw his dyosie,
Quhair I will be unknawin.
Or keip me closse into sum closter,
With mony piteous *Pater Noster*,
Till all thir blasts be blawin.

Dissait
Ile be weill treitit, as ye ken,
With my maisters, the merchand men,
Quhilk can mak small debait.
Ye ken richt few of them that thryfes,
Or can begyll the landwart wyfes,
But me, thair man, Dissait.

Now, Falset, quhat sall be thy schift?

Falset
Na, cuir thow nocht, man, for my thrift.
Trows thou that I be daft?
Na, I will leif ane lustie lyfe,
Withoutin ony sturt and stryfe,
Amang the men of craft.

Flatterie
I na mair will remaine besyd yow,
Bot counsell yow rycht weill to gyde yow.
Byd nocht on Correctioun.
Fair-weill, I will na langer tarie.
I pray the alrich Queene of Farie
To be your protectioun.

Dissait
Falset, I wald wee maid ane band:
Now, quhill the King is yit sleipand,
Quhat rak to steill his box?

Falset
Now, weill said, be the Sacrament:
I sall it steill incontinent,
Thocht it had twentie lox.

Heir sal Falset steill the Kings box with silence.

Lo, heir the box! Now let us ga;
This may suffice for our rewairds.

Dissait
Yea, that it may, man, be this day,
It may weill mak [us] landwart lairds.
Now let us cast away our clais,
In dreid sum follow on the chase.

Falset
Rycht weill devysit, man, be Sanct Blais.
Wald God wee war out of this place!

Heir sall thay cast away thair conterfit clais.

Dissait
Now, sen thair is na man to wrang us,
I pray yow, brother, with my hart,
Let us ga part this pelf amang us,
Syne haistely we sall depart.

Falset
Trows thou to get als mekill as I?
That sall thow nocht, I staw the box,
Thou did nathing bot luikit by,
Ay lurkeand lyke ane wylie fox.

Dissait
Thy heid sall beir ane cuppill of knox,
Pellour, without I get my part.
Swith, huirsun smaik, ryfe up the lox,
Or I sall stick the[e] throuch the hart.

Heir sall thay fecht with silence.

1514 without 1517 sorely 1518 confused/mad 1523 diocese/region 1524 unknown 1525 close, cloister 1527 (i.e. until they're finished) 1528 treated 1530 can hardly argue (with me) 1531 thrives 1532 beguile, country 1533 Without (the help of) me 1534 what will you do 1535 Don't worry about me 1536 stupid 1537 live 1539 craftsmen 1540 no longer 1541 look after yourselves 1542 Don't wait for 1544 elvish 1546 agreement 1548 What about stealing 1551 locks 1555 country gentlemen 1556 throw, clothes 1557 fear, someone will pursue us 1558 Good thinking! 1559+ (i.e. their disguises) 1560 wrong 1562 booty 1563 Afterwards 1564 Do you expect 1565 stole 1566 act as look-out 1567 lurking 1568 couple, blows 1569 Villain, unless 1570 rip off 1571+ fight

FALSET
Alace, for ever, my eye is out!
Walloway, will na man red the men?

DISSAIT
Upon thy craig tak thair ane clout,
To be courtesse I sall the[e] ken.

Fair-weill, for I am at the flicht,
I will nocht byde on ma demands.
And wee twa meit againe this nicht,
Thy feit salbe w[i]rth fourtie hands.[107]

Heir sal Dissait rin away with the box throuch the water.
[*Enter Correction.*]

DIVYNE CORRECTIOUN
Beati qui esuriunt et sitiunt justitiam.[108]

Thir ar the words of the redoutit Roy,
The Prince of Peace, above all kings King,
Quhilk hes me sent all cuntries to convoye,
And all misdoars dourlie to doun thring.
I will do nocht without the conveining
Ane Parleament of the Estaits all:
In thair presence I sall, but feinyeing,
Iniquitie under my sword doun thrall.

Thair may no prince do acts honorabill,
Bot gif his counsall thairto will assist.
How may he knaw the thing maist profitabil
To follow vertew and vycis to resist,
Without he be instructit and solist?
And, quhen the king stands at his counsell sound,
Then welth sall wax and plentie as he list,
And policie sall in his realme abound.

Gif ony list my name for till inquyre,
I am callit Divine Correctioun.
I fled throch mony uncouth land and schyre,
To the greit profit of ilk natioun.
Now am I cum into this regioun
To teill the ground that hes bene lang unsawin,
To punische tyrants for thair transgressioun,
And to caus leill men live upon thair awin.[109]

Na realme nor land but my support may stand,
For I gar kings live into royaltie.
To rich and puir I beir ane equall band,
That thay may live into thair awin degrie.
Quhair I am nocht is no tranquillitie.
Be me tratours and tyrants ar put doun,
Quha thinks na schame of thair iniquitie
Till thay be punisched be mee, Correctioun.

Quhat is ane king? Nocht bot ane officiar,
To caus his leiges live in equitie:
And under God to be ane punischer
Of trespassours against His majestie.
Bot, quhen the king dois live in tyrannie,
Breakand justice for feare or affectioun,
Then is his realme in weir and povertie,
With schamefull slauchter but correctioun.

I am ane judge richt potent and seveir,
Cum to do justice monie thowsand myle.
I am sa constant baith in peice and weir,
Na bud nor favour may my sicht oversyle.
Thair is, thaifoir, richt monie in this Ile
Of my repair but doubt that dois repent:
Bot verteous men, I traist, sall on me smyle,
And of my cumming sall be richt weill content.

GUDE COUNSALL
Welcum, my Lord, welcum ten thousand tyms
Till all faithfull men of this regioun:
Welcum for till correct all falts and cryms
Amang this cankred congregatioun.
Louse Chastitie, I mak supplicatioun;
Put till fredome fair Ladie Veritie,
Quha, be unfaithfull folk of this natioun,
Lyis bund full fast into captivitie.

CORRECTIOUN
I mervel, Gude Counsell, how that may be,
Ar ye nocht with the King familiar?

1573 separate 1574 neck, blow 1575 courteous, teach 1576 I'm off! 1577 wait for more 1578 If 1581 renowned 1583 guide 1584 severely, knock down 1585 nothing 1588 subjugate 1593 Unless, encouraged 1594 holds with 1595 grow, wishes 1596 political wisdom 1597 anyone wishes 1599 flew, strange, shires 1602 cultivate, unsown 1605 without 1606 behave regally 1607 covenant 1608 (peacefully) in their own estates 1613 Nothing, officer (deputy) 1614 subjects (to) 1618 Breaking 1619 war/strife 1620 slaughter without 1621 powerful, severe 1624 bribe, blur my sight 1625 Isle (Britain) 1626 who repent of my arrival 1629 times 1630 To 1631 faults, crimes 1632 corrupt 1633 loose, (free), I beg you 1634 release 1636 bound very tightly in 1637 I am amazed 1638 intimate

[107] i.e. 'You'd do better to run away than to fight.'
[108] 'Blessed are they [who] hunger and thirst after righteousness [for they shall be filled].' Matthew 5:6.
[109] 'And to enable true men to sustain themselves.'

Gude Counsall
That I am nocht, my Lord, full wa is me,
Bot lyke ane begger am halden at the bar:
Thay play bo-keik evin as I war ane skar.[110]
Thair came thrie knaves in cleithing counterfeit,
And fra the King thay gart me stand affar,
Quhais names war Flattrie, Falset, and Dissait.

Bot quhen thay knaves hard tell of your cumming,
Thay staw away, ilk ane ane sindrie gait,
And cuist fra them thair counterfit cleithing.
For thair leving full weill thay can debait.[111]
The merchandmen thay haif resavit Dissait;
As for Falset, my Lord, full weill I ken,
He will be richt weill treitit, air and lait,
Amang the maist part of the crafts men.

Flattrie hes taine the habite of ane freir,
Thinkand to begyll Spiritualitie.

Correctioun
But doubt, my freind, and I live half ane yeir,
I sall search out that great iniquitie.
Quhair lyis yon ladyes in captivitie?
How now, sisters? Quha hes yow sa disgysit?

Veritie
Unfaithfull members of iniquitie
Dispytfullie, my lord, hes us supprysit.

Correctioun
Gang put yon ladyis to thair libertie
Incontinent, and break doun all the stocks:
But doubt thay ar full deir welcum to mee.
Mak diligence, me think ye do bot mocks!
Speid hand, and spair nocht for to break the locks,
And tenderlle tak them up be the hand.
Had I them heir, thay knaves suld ken my knocks
That them opprest and baneist aff the land.

Thay tak the ladies furth of the stocks, and Veritie sall say:

Veritie
Wee thank you, sir, of your benignitie.
Bot, I beseik Your Majestie Royall,
That ye wald pas to King Humanitie,
And fleime from him yon Ladie Sensuall,
And enter in his service Gude Counsell,
For ye will find him verie counsalabill.

Correctioun
Cum on, sisters, as ye half said I sall,
And gar him stand with yow thrie, firme and stabill.

Correctioun passis towards the King, with Veritie, Chastitie and Gude Counsell.

Wantonnes
Solace, knawis thou not quhat I se?
Ane knicht or ellis ane king, thinks me,
With wantoun wings as he wald fle.
Brother, quhat may this meine?
I understand nocht, be this day,
Quhidder that he be freind or fay.
Stand still and heare quhat he will say,
Sic ane I haif nocht seine.

Solace
Yon is ane stranger, I stand forde.
He semes to be ane lustie lord.
Be his heir-cumming for concorde,
And be kinde till our King,
He sall be welcome to this place,
And treatit with the Kingis Grace.
Be it nocht sa, we sall him chace
And to the Divell him ding.

Placebo
I reid us put upon the King,
And walkin him of his sleiping.
Sir, rise and se ane uncouth thing!
Get up, ye ly too lang!

1639 woe 1640 held back 1642 disguise 1643 apart 1645 those 1646 stole, each by a different way 1647 cast 1649 received/taken in 1651 early, late 1653 taken 1654 Thinking 1658 disfigured 1659 limbs/minions 1660 Contemptuously, overcome 1664 you are messing about 1665 Hurry 1667 know/feel 1672 drive away 1674 open to advice 1675 have, shall (do) 1679 fly 1682 whether, foe 1684 (i.e. I've never seen anyone like him) 1685 I guarantee it 1687 If, (is) for amity 1690 well-treated (by) 1692 Devil 1693 advise, go to 1694 waken, from 1695 strange

110 'They play bo-peep [with me], even as if I were a scarecrow.' As Jack notes, Gude Counsall portrays himself as suffering the kind of cruel blindfolded 'game' inflicted on Christ during the 'Buffeting'. See the York pageant of *Christ Before Annas and Caiaphas*, above.

111 'When it comes to making a living, they can look after themselves [very successfully].'

SENSUALITIE
Put on your hude, John Fule, ye raif.
How dar ye be so pert, sir knaif,
To tuich the King? Sa Christ me saif,
Fals huirsone, thow sall hang.

CORRECTIOUN
Get up, sir King, ye haif sleipit aneuch
Into the armis of Ladie Sensual.
Be suir that mair belangis to the pleuch,[112]
As efterward, perchance, rehears I sall.
Remember how the King Sardanapall,[113]
Amang fair ladyes tuke his lust sa lang,
Sa that the maist part of his leiges al
Rebeld, and syne him duilfully doun thrang.

Remember how, into the tyme of Noy,
For the foull stinck and sin of lechery,
God, be my wande did al the warld destroy.
Sodome and Gomore richt sa, full rigorously,[114]
For that vyld sin war brunt maist cruelly.
Thairfoir, I the[e] command, incontinent,
Banische from the[e] that huir Sensualitie,
Or els, but doubt, rudlie thow sall repent.

REX
Be quhom have ye sa greit authoritie?
Quha dois presume for til correct ane king?
Knaw ye nocht me, greit King Humanitie,
That in my regioun royally dois ring?

CORRECTIOUN
I have power greit princes to doun thring,
That lives contrair the Majestie Divyne:
Against the treuth quhilk plainlie dois maling,
Repent they nocht, I put them to ruyne.

I will begin at thee, quhilk is the head
And mak on the[e] first reformatioun.
Thy leiges than will follow the[e] but pleid.
[*To Sensualitie*] Swyith, harlot, hence without
dilatioun!

SENSUALITIE
My Lord, I mak yow supplicatioun:
Gif me licence to pas againe to Rome;
Amang the princes of that natioun,
I lat yow wit my fresche beautie will blume.

Adew, Sir King, I may na langer tary;
I cair nocht that, als gude luife cums as gais,
I recommend yow to the Queene of Farie.
I se ye will be gydit with my fais.
As for this king, I cure him nocht twa strais:
War I amang bischops and cardinals,
I wald get gould, silver, and precious clais
Na earthlie joy but my presence avails.

Heir sall scho pas to Spiritualitie.

My Lords of the Sprituall Stait,
Venus preserve yow, air and lait;
For I can mak na mair debait,
I am partit with your King;
And am baneischt this regioun,
Be counsell of Correctioun:
Be ye nocht my protectioun,
I may seik my ludgeing.

SPIRITUALITIE
Welcum, our dayis darling,
Welcum with all our hart.
Wee all, but feinyeing,
Sall plainly tak your part.

Heir sal the Bishops, Abbots, and Persons kis the Ladies.

CORRECTIOUN
Sen ye ar quyte of Sensualitie,
Resave into your service Gude Counsall;
And richt sa this fair ladie, Chastitie,
Till ye mary sum queene of blude-royall.
Observe then chastitie matrimoniall,
Richt sa resave Veritie be the hand,
Use thair counsell, your fame sall never fall,
With thame, thairfoir, mak ane perpetuall band.

1697 rave 1698 dare, cheeky 1699 touch 1701 enough 1706 took 1707 subjects 1708 rebelled, threw down/deposed 1709 Noah 1711 rod 1713 vile, were burnt 1716 ruefully 1718 does, to 1720 reign 1721 throw down 1722 (Those) who live contrary (to) 1723 do malign 1724 (If) they don't repent 1727 subjects, then, without debate 1728 Get out, delay 1732 let, know, bloom 1734 I don't care about, as goes 1736 guided by, foes 1737 (i.e. Correction), care (about), straws 1738 Were 1739 gold, clothes 1740 (There is) no, unless 1742 early 1743 I can influence things no further 1744 separated from 1747 If you are not 1748 must search (for) 1749 day's (i.e. light of our lives) 1753 Since, rid 1754 Receive 1756 Until 1757 thereafter, marital faithfulness 1759 (and) your 1760 them, agreement

112 'There's more to be said on that matter [lit. more belongs to the plough]'.

113 Sardanapulus (Assur-bani-pal), Assyrian king of the seventh century BC, renowned for his sensual indulgence.

114 Sodom and Gomorrah (see Genesis 18:19–19:29).

Heir sall the King resave Gude Counsell, Veritie, and Chastitie.

Now, sir, tak tent quhat I will say:
Observe thir same, baith nicht and day,
And let them never part yow fray.
Or els, withoutin doubt,
Turne ye to Sensualitie,
To vicious lyfe and rebaldrie,
Out of your realme richt schamefullie,
Ye sall be ruttit out,

As was Tarquine, the Romane king,[115]
Quha was, for his vicious living,
And for the schamefull ravisching
Of the fair chaist Lucres,
He was [di]graidit of his croun,
And baneist aff his regioun.
I maid on him correctioun,
As stories dois expres.

Rex
I am content to your counsall t'inclyne,
Ye beand of gude conditioun.
At your command sall be all that is myne,
And heir I gif yow full commissioun
To punische faults and gif remissioun;
To all vertew I salbe consociabill.
With yow I sall confirme ane unioun,
And at your counsall stand ay firme and stabill.

The King imbraces Correctioun with a humbil countenance.

Correctioun
I counsall yow incontinent
To gar proclame ane Parliament
Of all the Thrie Estatits.
That thay be heir with diligence,
To mak to yow obedience,
And syne dres all debaits.

Rex
That salbe done but mair demand,
Hoaw, Diligence, cum heir fra hand,
And tak your informatioun:
Gang warne the Spiritualitie,
Rycht sa the Temporalitie,
Be oppin proclamatioun,

In gudlie haist for to compeir
In thair maist honorabill maneir,
To gif us thair counsals:
Quha that beis absent, to them schaw
That thay sail underly the law,
And punischt be that fails.

Diligence
Sir, I sall baith in bruch and land,
With diligence do your command,
Upon my awin expens.
Sir, I have servit yow all this yeir,
Bot I gat never ane dinneir
Yit for my recompence.

Rex
Pas on, and thou salbe regairdit,
And for thy service weill rewairdit,
For quhy, with my consent,
Thou sall have yeirly for thy hyre,
The teind mussellis of the Fer[n]ie Myre,[116]
Confirmit in Parliament.

Diligence
I will get riches throw that rent
Efter the Day of Dume:
Quhen, in the colpots of Tranent,
Butter will grow on brume!

All nicht I had sa meikill drouth,
I micht nocht sleip ane wink.
Or I proclame ocht with my mouth,
But doubt I man haif drink.

Correctioun
Cum heir, Placebo and Solace,
With your companyeoun, Wantonnes.
I knaw weill your conditioun:

1763 from you 1765 (If) you turn (again) 1766 ribaldry 1768 rooted/driven 1770 lifestyle 1771 rape 1773 deprived 1776 relate 1777 to follow 1778 being 1782 agreeable 1790 prepare, issues for debate 1791 without further 1792 at once 1796 open/public 1797 goodly, be present 1798 manner 1800 tell them 1801 be subject to 1802 all who fail shall be punished 1803 burgh/town, country 1805 own expense 1807 a coin 1809 looked upon favourably 1810 rewarded 1812 fee 1814 Confirmed 1815 through, fee 1816 After Doomsday 1817 coal-pits 1818 broom bushes (i.e. never) 1819 so great a thirst 1821 anything 1822 must

[115] The story of Sextus Tarquinus and his rape of Lucretia is narrated in Livy's *Histories*, and forms the subject of Shakespeare's *Rape of Lucrece*.

[116] 'The tithe of mussels [i.e. one tenth of all mussels gathered] from the Ferny Mire'. As the latter was an inland area just west of Cupar, there are unlikely to be any mussels gathered there, hence Diligence's subsequent complaint.

For tysting King Humanitie
To resave Sensualitie,
Ye man suffer punitioun.

WANTONNES
We grant, my Lord, we have done ill,
Thairfoir wee put us in your will.
Bot wee haife bene abusit:
For, in gude faith, sir, wee beleifit,
That lecherie had na man greifit,
Becaus it is sa usit.

PLACEBO
Ye se how Sensualitie,
With principals of ilk cuntrie,
Bene glaidlie lettin in,
And with our prelatis mair and les.
Speir at my Ladie Priores,
Gif lechery be sin.

SOLACE
Sir, wee sall mend our conditioun,
Sa ye give us remissioun,
Bot give us live to sing:
To dance, to play at chesse and tabils,
To reid stories and mirrie fabils,
For pleasure of our king.

CORRECTIOUN
Sa that ye do na uther crime,
Ye sall be pardonit at this tyme,
For quhy, as I suppois,
Princes may sumtyme seik solace
With mirth and lawfull mirrines,
Thair spirits to rejoyis.
And richt sa halking and hunting
Ar honest pastimes for ane king
Into the tyme of peace:
And leirne to rin ane heavie spear,
That he into the tyme of wear
May follow at the cheace.

REX
Quhair is Sapience and Discretioun?
And quhy cums nocht Devotioun nar?

VERITIE
Sapience, sir, was ane verie loun,
And Discretioun was [nyne tymes] war.
The suith, sir, gif I wald report,
Thay did begyle Your Excellence,
And wald not suffer to resort
Ane of us thrie to your presence.

CHASTITIE
Thay thrie war Flattrie and Dissait,
And Falset, that unhappie loun,
Against us thrie quhilk maid debait
And banischt us from town to town.
Thay gart us twa fill into sowne,
Quhen thay us lockit in the stocks:
That dastart knave, Discretioun,
Full thifteouslie did steill your box.

REX
The Devill tak them, sen thay ar gone!
Me thocht them ay thrie verie smaiks.[117]
I make ane vow to Sanct Mavane,[118]
Quhen I them finde, thays bear thair paiks.
I se they have playit me the glaiks.
Gude Counsall, now schaw me the best,
Quhen I fix on yow thrie my staiks
How I sall keip my relme in rest.

GUDE COUNSALL
Initium sapientiae est timor Domini.[119]

Sir, gif Your Hienes yearnis lang to ring,[120]
First dread your God abuif all uther thing.
For ye ar bot ane mortall instrument
To that great God and King Omnipotent.
Preordinat be His divine Majestie,
To reull His peopill intill unitie.

1826 enticing 1827 receive 1828 must, punishment 1831 abused 1832 believed 1833 grieved 1834 so commonly practised 1836 princes 1837 let into (their company) 1839 Ask 1841 amend, behaviour 1842 If 1843 leave (permission) 1844 backgammon 1845 merry fables 1847 So long as 1849 suppose 1852 rejoice 1853 hawking 1856 run (with) (i.e. joust) 1858 join in the charge 1860 near 1862 worse 1863 truth 1867 Those 1868 ill-favoured 1869 opposed 1871 fall into a swoon 1872 dastardly 1873 thievingly 1878 they'll get their deserts 1879 made a fool of me 1881 (i.e. I rely completely on you) 1882 peace 1885 above 1888 preordained 1889 rule, in unity

117 'They always seemed to me to be complete villains.'

118 St Mevenna, a sixth-century Cornish saint.

119 'The fear of the Lord is the beginning of wisdom.' Psalms 111:10 and Proverbs 9:10.

120 'If Your Highness desires to reign for a long time'.

The principall point, sir, of ane kings office
Is for to do to everilk man justice,
And for to mix his justice with mercie,
But rigour, favour, or parcialitie.
Forsuith, it is na littill observance,
Great regions to have in governance.
Quha ever taks on him that kinglie cuir,
To get ane of thir twa he suld be suir:
Great paine and labour, and that continuall,
Or ellis to have defame perpetuall.
Quha guydis weill, they win immortall fame,
Quha the contrair, they get perpetuall schame:
Efter quhais death, but dout, ane thousand yeir
Thair life at lenth rehearst sall be perqueir.
The Chroniklis to knaw I yow exhort,[121]
Thair sall ye finde baith gude and evill report.
For everie prince efter his qualitie,
Thocht he be deid, his deids sall never die.
Sir, gif ye please for to use my counsall,
Your fame and name sall be perpetual

Heir sall the messenger, Diligence, returne and cry 'a Hoyzes,[122] a hoyzes, a Hoyzes!', and say:

[Diligence]
At the command of King Humanitie,
I wairne and charge all members of Parliament,
Baith Sprituall Sta[i]t and Temporalite,
That till His Grace thay be obedient,
And speid them to the court incontinent,
In gude ordour arrayit royally.
Quha beis absent or inobedient,
The Kings displeasure thay sall underly.

[*To the audience*] And als I mak yow exhortatioun,
Sen ye haif heard the first pairt of our play,
Go tak ane drink and mak collatioun,
Ilk man drink till his marrow, I yow pray.
Tarie nocht lang, it is lait in the day.
Let sum drink ayle and sum drink claret wine:
Be great Doctors of Physick I heare say
That michtie drink comforts the dull ingine.

And ye ladies that list to pisch,
Lift up your taill, plat in ane disch,
And, gif that your [quhislecaw] cryis 'quhisch',
Stop in ane wusp of stray.
Let nocht your bladder burst, I pray yow,
For that war evin aneuch to slay yow;
For yit thair is to cum, I say yow,
The best pairt of our play.

Now sall the pepill mak collatioun, then beginnis the Interlude, the Kings, Bischops, and principall players being out of their seats.

[The Interlude]

Pauper
Of your almis, gude folks, for Gods luife of Heavin,
For I have motherless bairns, either sax or seavin.
Gif ye'ill gif me na gude, for the luife of Jesus,
Wische me the richt way till Sanct Androes.

Diligence
Quhair have wee gottin this gudly companyeoun?
Swyith out of the feild, fals raggit loun!
God wait gif heir be ane weill keipit place,
Quhen sic ane vilde begger carle may get entres.
Fy on yow, officiars, that mends nocht thir failyies!
I gif yow all till the Devill, baith Provost and bailyies.
Without ye cum and chase this carle away,
The Devill a word yeis get mair of our play![123]
Fals huirsun raggit carle, quhat devil is that thou rugs?

1891 every 1893 Without 1894 no small task 1896 responsibility 1897 one of two (things), sure 1899 shame/ignominy 1900 Whoever rules well 1902 After whose 1903 length, retold thoroughly 1906 according to his nature 1907 dead, deeds 1911 warn/instruct 1915 clothed 1916 Whoever is 1917 be subjected to 1920 prepare some food 1921 (a toast) to his friend 1924 medicine 1925 strong, dull mind 1926 need to piss 1927 splash 1928 anus, 'squelch' 1929 stuff, whisp, straw 1931 enough 1932 tell 1934 charity, love 1935 babies, six or seven 1936 give 1937 Show, St Andrews (in Fife) 1938 fellow (ironic) 1939 ragged 1940 knows, kept/ordered 1941 gain entry 1942 correct, faults 1943 mayor, magistrates 1945 you're calling up

121 'I advise you to read the chronicles'.
122 'Oyez!/Hear ye!', the call of the town crier.
123 'You'll get not a word more of our play, by the Devil!'

PAUPER
Quha Devil maid the[e] ane gentill man, that wald not cut thy lugs?[124]

DILIGENCE
Quhat now? Me thinks the carle begins to crack.
Swyith carle, away; or, be this day, Ise break thy back!

Heir sall the Carle clim up and sit in the Kings tchyre.[125]

Cum doun, or, be Gods croun, fals loun, I sall slay the[e].

PAUPER
Now sweir be thy brunt schinis, the Devill ding them fra the[e].
Quhat say ye till thir court dastards? Be thay get hail clais,
Sa sune do thay leir to sweir and trip on thair tais.[126]

DILIGENCE
Me thocht the carle callit me knave, evin in my face.
Be Sanct Fillane,[127] thou salbe slane, bot gif thou ask grace.
Loup doun or, be the gude Lord, thow sall los thy heid.

PAUPER
I sal anis drink or I ga, thocht thou had sworne my deid.

Heir Diligence castis away the ledder.[128]

DILIGENCE
Loup now, gif thou list, for thou hes lost the ledder.

PAUPER
It is full well thy kind to loup and licht in a tedder.
Thou sal be faine to fetch agane the ledder or I loup.
I sall sit heir into this tcheir till I have tumde the stoup.

Heir sall the Carle loup aff the scaffald.

DILIGENCE
Swyith, begger bogill, haist the[e] away!
Thow art over pert to spill our play.

PAUPER
I will not gif for al your play worth an sowis fart,[129]
For thair is richt lytill play at my hungrie hart.

DILIGENCE
Quhat Devill ails this cruckit carle?

PAUPER
Marie, meikill sorrow;
I can not get, thocht I gasp, to beg nor to borrow.

DILIGENCE
Quhair, devill, is this thou dwels, or quhats thy intent?

PAUPER
I dwell into Lawthiane, ane myle fra Tranent.[130]

DILIGENCE
Quhair wald thou be, carle, the suth to me schaw?

PAUPER
Sir, evin to Sanct Androes for to seik law.

DILIGENCE
For to seik law, in Edinburgh was the neirest way.

PAUPER
Sir, I socht law thair this monie deir day,
Bot I culd get nane at Sessioun nor Seinye:[131]
Thairfoir the mekill dum devill droun all the meinye!

DILIGENCE
Shaw me thy mater, man, with al the circumstances,
How that thou hes happinit on thir unhappie chances.

1948 boast 1949 I'll 1951 burnt shins 1956 leap, lose 1957 death 1959 jump, land, hangman's noose 1961 emptied, jug 1962 goblin 1963 eager, ruin 1965 in 1966 crooked/broken 1970 truth 1971 St Andrews (Fife) 1972 best place 1973 sought 1975 crowd (of them)

124 'Who the Devil made you a gentleman and would not cut off your ears?' Cut ears would mark one out as a criminal.
125 Chair/throne.
126 'What do you say to/about these court villains? No sooner do they get [a] whole [suit of] clothes, but they immediately learn to swear and swagger about on their toes.'
127 St Fillan, a local eighth-century Fife saint.
128 Ladder.
129 'I wouldn't give a sow's fart for your play.'
130 Tranent in Lothian lies just to the east of Edinburgh, across the Firth of Forth from Fife. It was an area badly ravaged by English raids in the late 1540s.
131 'Sessioun': the secular court of Session; 'Seinye': the ecclesiastical Consistory court.

PAUPER
Gude-man, will ye gif me your charitie,
And I sall declair yow the black veritie.
My father was ane auld man and ane hoir,
And was of age fourscoir of yeirs and moir,
And Mald, my mother, was fourscoir and fyfteine,
And with my labour I did thame baith susteine.
Wee had ane meir that caryit salt and coill,
And everie ilk yeir scho brocht us hame ane foill.
Wee had thrie ky that was baith fat and fair,
Nane tydier into the toun of Air.
My father was sa waik of blude and bane
That he deit, quhairfoir my mother maid great maine.
Then scho deit within ane day or two,
And thair began my povertie and wo.
Our gude gray meir was baittand on the feild,
And our lands laird tuik hir for his hyreild.[132]
The vickar tuik the best cow be the head,
Incontinent, quhen my father was deid.
And, quhen the vickar hard tel how that my mother
Was dead, fra-hand he tuke to him ane uther.
Then Meg, my wife, did murne both evin and morow,
Till at the last scho deit for verie sorow.
And quhen the vickar hard tell my wyfe was dead,
The thrid cow he cleikit be the head.
Thair umest clayis that was of rapploch gray,[133]
The vickar gart his clark bear them away.
Quhen all was gaine, I micht mak na debeat,
Bot with my bairns past for till beg my meat.
Now have I tald yow the blak veritie,
How I am brocht into this miserie.

DILIGENCE
How did the person, was he not thy gude freind?

PAUPER
The Devil stick him! He curst me for my teind,
And halds me yit under that same proces
That gart me want the Sacrament at Pasche.[134]
In gude faith, sir, thocht [ye] wald cut my throt,
I have na geir except ane Inglis grot,
Quhilk I purpois to gif ane man of law.

DILIGENCE
Thou art the daftest fuill that ever I saw!
Trows thou, man, be the law to get remeid
Of men of kirk?[135] Na, nocht till thou be deid.

PAUPER
Sir, be quhat law, tell me quhaifoir or quhy
That ane vickar sould tak fra me thrie ky?

DILIGENCE
Thay have na law exceptand consuetude,
Quhilk law to them is sufficient and gude.

PAUPER
Ane consuetude against the common weill,
Sould be na law, I think, be sweit Sanct Geill.[136]
Quhair will ye find that law, tell gif ye can,
To tak thrie ky fra ane pure husband man?
Ane for my father, and for my wyfe ane uther,
And the thrid cow he tuke for Mald, my mother.

DILIGENCE
It is thair law, all that they have in use,
Thocht it be cow, sow, ganer, gryse, or guse.

PAUPER
Sir, I wald speir at yow ane question:
Behauld sum prelate of this regioun,
Manifestlie during thair lustie lyfis,
Thay swyfe ladies, madinis, and uther men wyfis,
And sa thair cunts they have in consuetude.
Quidder say ye that law is evill or gude?

DILIGENCE
Hald thy toung man, it seims that thou war mangit,
Speik thou of preists, but doubt thou will be hangit.

1980 grey-haired 1981 more (i.e. over 80) 1982 (i.e. 95) 1984 mare, carried, coal 1985 produced a foal 1986 cows 1987 better, Ayr (west Scotland) 1988 weak, bone 1989 died, moan 1902 grazing 1997 took 1998 mourn, evening, morning 2001 grabbed 2003 made 2004 gone, couldn't argue 2005 went, food 2008 parson 2009 excommunicated, (unpaid) tithe 2010 legal action 2012 throat 2013 property, groat (worth 4 pence) 2014 intend, give to 2020 excepting custom (tradition) 2025 husbandman (small farmer) 2028 they claim everything 2029 gander, suckling pig, goose 2033 fornicate with, virgins 2034 in use (through custom) 2036 mad

132 'And our landlord took her for his heriot [the fee payable in kind on the death of the tenant-in-chief; usually the best animal on the farm].'

133 'The uppermost garments that were made of grey homespun'. 'The umest clayis' was another mortuary duty payable in kind to the parish priest.

134 'Which meant that I could not receive the Sacrament at Easter.' Excommunicates were denied communion until they were formally reconciled with the church.

135 'Do you think you'll get redress against churchmen through the courts?'

136 St Giles, patron saint of the City of Edinburgh.

PAUPER
Be Him that buir the cruell croun of thorne,
I cair nocht to be hangit, evin the morne.

DILIGENCE
Be sure, of preistis thou will get na support.

PAUPER
Gif that be trew, the Feind resave the sort!
Sa, sen I se I get na uther grace,
I will ly doun and rest mee in this place.

Pauper lyis doun in the feild. Pardoner enters.

PARDONER
Bona dies, Bona dies!

Devoit peopill, gude day I say yow!
Now tarie any lytill quhyll, I pray yow,
Till I be with yow knawin:
Wait ye weill how I am namit?
Ane nobill man and undefamit
Gif all the suith war schawin.

I am Sir Robert Rome-Raker,
Ane perfite publicke pardoner,
Admittit be the Paip.
Sirs, I sall schaw yow for my wage
My pardons and my pilgramage,
Quhilk ye sall se and graip.

I give to the Devill with gude intent
This unsell, wickit New Testament,
With them that it translaitit!
Sen layik men knew the veritie,
Pardoners gets no charitie,
Without that thay debait it

Amang the wives, with wrinks and wyles,
As all my marrowis men begyles,
With our fair fals flattrie:
Yea, all the crafts I ken perqueir,
As I was teichit be ane freir
Callit Hypocrisie.

Bot now, allace, our greit abusioun
Is cleirlie knawin till our confusioun,
That we may sair repent.
Of all credence now am I quyte,
For ilk man halds me at dispyte,
That reids the New Testment.

Duill fell the braine that hes it wrocht,
Sa fall them that the Buik hame brocht:
Als I pray to the Rude
That Martin Luther, that fals loun,
Black Bullinger, and Melancthoun,[137]
Had bene smorde in their cude!

Be Him that buir the crowne of thorne,
I wald Sanct Paull had never bene borne,
And als I wald his buiks
War never red into the Kirk,
Bot amangs freirs into the mirk,
Or riven amang ruiks.

Heir sall he lay doun his geir upon ane buird[138] *and say:*

My patent pardouns ye may se,
Cum fra the [Can] of Tartarie,
Weill seald with oster-schellis.[139]
Thocht ye have no contritioun,
Ye sall have full remissioun,
With help of buiks and bellis.

Heir is ane relict, lang and braid,
Of Fine Macoull the richt chaft blaid,[140]
With teith and al togidder.
Of Collings cow heir is ane horne,
For eating of Makconnals corne,
Was slaine into Balquhidder.[141]

Heir is ane coird baith great and lang,
Quhilk hangit Johne the Armistrang,[142]

2038 wore **2039** tomorrow **2041** take them all **2044** Good day **2045** Devout **2046** while **2047** While I introduce myself **2049** of good reputation **2053** appointed **2056** grasp/touch **2058** unhallowed **2059** translated **2060** lay **2062** Unless, fight for it **2063** tricks **2064** (business) partners **2066** know thoroughly **2067** taught **2070** to **2071** sorely **2072** deprived **2075** Dole befall **2076** (And) the same befall those **2080** smothered, cradles **2085** in the dark **2086** torn to pieces by rooks **2088** Khan **2090** repentance

[137] Heinrich Bullinger (1504–75) and Philip Melanchthon (1497–1560); like Luther, leading Protestant reformers.
[138] Board/trestle table.
[139] 'Oyster-shells': the sign worn by those who had been on pilgrimage to St James, Compostella.
[140] 'The right jaw-bone of Fin MacCoull [the legendary Irish hero]'.
[141] The story of Collins's cow and MacConnell's corn in Balquhidder (Perthshire) is unknown. It may, perhaps, have been a suitably obscure invention of Lindsay's.
[142] For Armstrong, see the Description of the 1540 Interlude, n. 55.

Of gude hemp soft and sound.
Gude halie peopill, I stand ford,
Quha ever beis hangit with this cord,
Neids never to be dround.

The *culum* of Sanct Bryds kow,
The gruntill of Sanct Antonis sow,
Quhilk buir his haly bell:
Quha ever he be heiris this bell clinck,
Gif me ane ducat for till drink,
He sail never gang to Hell,

Without he be of Baliell borne.
Maisters, trow ye that this be scorne?
Cum, win this pardoun, cum!
Quha luifis thair wyfis nocht with thair hart,
I have power them for till part.
Me think yow deif and dum!

Hes naine of yow curst wickit wyfis
That halds yow into sturt and stryfis?
Cum tak my dispensatioun.
Of that cummer I sall mak yow quyte,
Howbeit your selfis be in the wyte,
And mak ane fels narratioun.

Cum win the pardoun, now let se,
For meill, for malt, or for monie,
For cok, hen, guse, or gryse:
Of relicts heir I have ane hunder.
Quhy cum ye nocht? This is ane wonder.
I trow ye be nocht wyse.

Sowtar
Welcum hame, Robert Rome-Raker,
Our halie patent pardoner;
Gif ye have dispensatioun
To pairt me and my wickit wyfe,
And me deliver from sturt and stryfe,
I mak yow supplicatioun.

Pardoner
I sall yow pairt but mair demand
Sa I get mony in my hand,
Thairfoir let se sum cunye.

Sowtar
I have na silver be my lyfe,
Bot fyve schillings and my schaipping knyfe,[143]
That sall ye have, but sunye.

Pardoner
Quhat kynd of woman is thy wyfe?

Sowtar
Ane quick devill, sir, ane storme of stryfe,
Ane frog that fyles the winde:
Ane fistand flag, a flagartie fuffe,
At ilk ane pant scho lets ane puffe,
And hes na ho behind.

All the lang day scho me dispyts,
And all the nicht scho flings and flyts,
Thus sleip I never ane wink.
That cockatrice, that commoun huir,
The mekill Devill may nocht induir
Hir stuburnnes and stink.

Sowtars Wyfe
Theif carle, thy words I hard rycht weill!
In faith my freindschip ye sall feill,
And I the[e] fang!

Sowtar
Gif I said ocht, dame, be the Rude,
Except ye war baith fair and gude,
God nor I hang!

Pardoner
Fair dame, gif ye wald be ane wower,
To part yow twa I have ane power.
Tell on, ar ye content?

Sowtars Wyfe
Ye[a], that I am, with all my hart!
Fra that fals huirsone till depart,
Gif this theif will consent.
Causses to part I have anew,
Becaus I gat na chamber-glew,
I tell yow verely.

2102 holy, I guarantee it 2103 is 2104 drowned 2105 anus, St Bridget's cow 2106 snout, St Anthony's 2107 carried 2108 whoever hears 2109 (If he) gives 2111 Unless, Belial (a devil) 2112 Do you think I'm joking? 2115 divorce 2116 deaf 2117 none 2118 brings you trouble 2120 friend (ironic) 2121 wrong 2122 bear false witness 2124 meal 2125 suckling pig 2126 hundred 2130 open/honest 2135 without further ado 2137 cash 2140 without delay 2142 living 2143 defiles/pollutes the air 2144 belching slut, whorish stinker 2145 every, fart 2146 pause 2147 despises 2148 scolds 2150 a legendary monster, whore 2151 endure 2152 stubbornness 2154 feel 2155 If I get my hands on you! 2156 anything 2158 May I hang, by God! 2159 suitor (to me) 2165 enough 2166 sexual satisfaction

[143] Shaping knife (one of the tools of his trade).

I mervell nocht, sa mot I lyfe,
Howbeit that swingeour can not swyfe,
He is baith cauld and dry.[144]

Pardoner
Quhat wil ye gif me for your part?

[Sowtars Wyfe]
Ane cuppill of sarks, with all my hart,
The best claith in the land.

Pardoner
To part sen ye ar baith content,
I sall yow part incontinent,
Bot ye mon do command.

My will and finall sentence is,
Ilk ane of yow uthers arsse kis.
Slip doun your hois. Me thinkis the carle is glaikit!
Set thou not by, howbeit scho kisse and slaik it.

Heir sall scho kis his arsse with silence.

Lift up [her] clais, kis hir hoill with your hart.

Sowtar
I pray yow, sir, forbid hir for to fart.

Heir sall the Carle kis hir arsse with silence.

Pardoner
Dame, pas ye to the east end of the toun,
[*To the Sowtar*] And pas ye west, evin lyke ane cuckald loun.
Go hence, ye baith, with Baliels braid blissing.
Schirs, saw ye ever mair sorrowles pairting?

[*Exit Sowtar and his Wyfe.*] *Heir sal the Boy cry aff*[145] *the hill:*

Wilkin
Hoaw, maister, haow! Quhair ar ye now?

Pardoner
I am heir, Wilkin Widdiefow.

Wilkin
Sir, I have done your bidding,
For I have fund me ane great hors bane,
Ane fairer saw ye never nane,
Upon Dame Fleschers midding.

Sir, ye may gar the wyfis trow,
It is ane bane of Sanct Bryds cow,
Gude for the fever quartane.[146]
Sir, will ye reull this relict weill,
All the wyfis will baith kis and kneill
Betuixt this and Dumbartane.[147]

Pardoner
Quhat say thay of me in the toun?

Wilkin
Sum sayis ye ar ane verie loun:
Sum sayis *Legatus natus*;[148]
Sum sayis y'ar ane fals Saracene,
And sum sayis ye ar for certaine
Diabolus incarnatus.

Bot keip yow fra subjectioun
Of the curst King Correctioun:
For, be ye with him fangit.
Becaus ye ar ane Rome-raker,
And commoun publick cawsay paker,
But doubt ye will be hangit.

Pardoner
Quhair sall I ludge into the toun?

Wilkin
With gude kynde Christiane Anderson,[149]
Quhair ye will be weill treatit.
Gif ony limmer yow demands,
Scho will defend yow with hir hands,
And womanlie debait it.

Bawburdie says, be the Trinitie,
That scho sall beir yow cumpanie,
Howbeit ye byde ane yeir.

2168 may 2169 rogue, perform sexually 2172 shirts 2173 cloth 2176 do as I tell you 2179 hose, stupid 2180 satisfy (the ritual) 2181 her hole 2184 cuckold fool 2188 gallows-bird 2190 horse-bone 2192 Mrs Butcher's midden (dunghill) 2193 believe 2196 employ 2202 Saracen 2204 the Devil incarnate 2207 caught by him 2208 a traveller to (and from) Rome 2209 street-walker 2211 lodge in 2214 villain, comes looking for you 2217 Whore 2219 stay (for)

144 'Cold and dry'. Medieval medical theory suggested that an abundance of these humours made one Melancholic and prone to impotence.
145 From.
146 A serious fever whose symptoms worsened every fourth day.
147 'Between here and Dunbarton [a town west of Glasgow].'
148 A bishop or cardinal holding the title of papal legate, who could act in the pope's name within his own diocese (as opposed to a legate *a latere*, whose remit was wider).
149 Perhaps, as Lyall suggests, the name of a local whore.

Pardoner
Thou hes done weill, be Gods mother!
Tak ye the taine and I the tother,
Sa sall we mak greit cheir.

Wilkin
I reid yow speid yow heir,
And mak na larger tarie.
Byde ye lang thair but weir,
I dreid your weird yow warie.[150]

Heir sall Pauper rise and rax him.[151]

Pauper
Quhat thing was yon that I hard crak and cry?
I have bene dreamand and dreveland of my ky.
With my richt hand my haill bodie I saine,[152]
Sanct Bryd, Sanct Bryd, send me my ky againe!
I se standa[n]d yonder ane halie man,
To mak me help let me se gif he can.
Halie maister, God speid yow and gude morne.

Pardoner
Welcum to me, thocht thou war at the horne.
Cum win the pardoun, and syne I sall the saine.

Pauper
Wil that pardoun get me my ky againe?

Pardoner
Carle, of thy ky I have nathing ado.
Cum win my pardon, and kis my relicts to.

Heir sall he sain him with his relictis.[153]

Pardoner
Now lows thy pursse and lay doun thy offrand,
And thou sall have my pardon evin fra-hand.
With raipis and relicts I sall the[e] saine againe,
Of gut or gravell thou sall never have paine.
Now win the pardon, limmer, or thou art lost.

Pauper
My haly father, quhat wil that pardon cost?

Pardoner
Let se quhat mony thou bearest in thy bag.

Pauper
I have ane grot heir, bund into ane rag.

Pardoner
Hes thou na uther silver bot ane groat?

Pauper
Gif I have mair, sir, cum and rype my coat.

Pardoner
Gif me that grot, man, gif thou hest na mair.

Pauper
With all my heart, maister; lo, tak it thair.
Now let me se your pardon, with your leif.

Pardoner
Ane thousand yeir of pardons I the geif.

Pauper
Ane thousand yeir? I will not live sa lang!
Delyver me it, maister, and let me gang.

Pardoner
Ane thousand yeir I lay upon thy head,
With *totiens quotiens*;[154] now mak me na mair plead,
Thou hast resaifit thy pardon now already.

Pauper
Bot I can se na thing, sir, be Our Lady!
Forsuith, maister, I trow I be not wyse,
To pay ere I have sene my marchandryse.
That ye have gottin my groat full sair I rew.
Sir, quhidder is your pardon, black or blew?
Maister, sen ye have taine fra me my cunyie,
My marchandryse schaw me, withouttin sunyie.
Or to the bischop I sall pas and pleinyie
In Sanct Androis, and summond yow to the Seinyie.

Pardoner
Quhat craifis the[e], carle? Me thinks thou art not wise.

2221 one, other 2223 advise you (to) 2224 delay 2227 chatter 2228 dreaming, raving 2231 standing 2233 bless you 2234 outlawed 2235 then I'll bless you 2239 loosen, offering 2241 ropes 2242 gout, gallstones 2246 groat (a coin worth 4 pence), bound 2248 search 2752 give 2256 ask for nothing more 2257 received 2260 before, merchandise 2261 sorely, rue 2263 cash 2264 delay 2265 complain 2267 craves (demands)

150 'If you stay there long, doubtless you'll rue your fate, I fear.'
151 Stretch himself.
152 'I bless my whole body with the sign of the Cross'.
153 Relics.
154 'As often as . . . so often': a formulaic tag in indulgences.

Pauper
I craif my groat, or ellis my marchandrise.

Pardoner
I gaif the[e] pardon for ane thowsand yeir.

Pauper
How shall I get that pardon? Let me heir.

Pardoner
Stand still and I sall tell the haill storie.
Quhen thow art deid and gais to Purgatorie,
Being condempit to paine a thowsand yeir,
Then sall thy pardoun the[e] releif, but weir.
Now be content. Ye ar ane mervelous man!

Pauper
Sall I get nathing for my grot quhill than?

Pardoner
That sall thou not, I mak it to yow plaine.

Pauper
Na? Than, gossop, gif me my grot againe.
Quhat say ye, maisters? Call ye this gude resoun,
That he sould promeis me ane gay pardoun,
And he resave my money in his stead,
Syne mak me na payment till I be dead?
Quhen I am deid, I wait full sikkerlie,
My sillie saull will pas to Purgatorie.
Declair me this, now God nor Baliell bind the[e],
Quhen I am thair, curst carle, quhair sall I find the[e]?
Not into Heavin, bot rather into Hell.
Quhen thou are thair, thou can not help thy sel.
Quhen will thou cum my dolours till abait?
Or I the[e] find, my hippis will get ane hait.
Trowis thou, butchour, that I will by blind lambis?
Gif me my grot; the Devill dryte in thy gambis!

Pardoner
Suyith, stand abak, I trow this man be mangit!
Thou gets not this, carle, thocht thou suld be hangit.

Pauper
Gif me my grot, weill bund into ane clout,
Or, be Gods breid, Robin sall beir ane rout.

Heir sall they fecht with silence, and Pauper sal cast doun the buird, and cast the relicts in the water.

Diligence
Quhat kind of daffing is this al day?
Suyith, smaiks, out of the feild, away!
Into ane presoun put them sone,
Syne hang them quhen the play is done.

[Part Two]

Heir sall Diligence mak his Proclamatioun.

[Diligence]
Famous peopill, tak tent and ye sall se
The Thrie Estaitis of this natioun
Cum to the court with ane strange gravitie.
Thairfoir, I mak yow supplicatioun:
Till ye have heard our haill narratioun,
To keip silence and be patient, I pray yow.
Howbeit we speik be adulatioun,
Wee sall say nathing bot the suith, I say yow.

Gude verteous men that luifis the veritie,
I wait thay will excuse our negligence:
Bot vicious men, denude of charitie,
As feinyeit fals flattrand Saracens,
Howbeit thay cry on us ane loud vengence,
And of our pastyme make ane fals report,
Quhat may wee do bot tak in patience,
And us refer unto the faithfil sort?

Our Lord Jesus, Peter, nor Paull,
Culd not compleis the peopill all,
Bot sum war miscontent.
Howbeit thay schew the veritie,
Sum said that it war heresie,
Be thair maist fals judgement.

Heir sall the Thrie Estaitis cum fra the palyeoun, gangand backwart, led be thair Vyces.[155]

2271 whole **2274** relieve you, doubtlessly **2276** until then **2281** place **2283** know, certainly **2284** simple/holy **2289** sorrows to end **2290** heat **2291** buy, lambs (i.e. rotten goods) **2292** shit on, tricks **2293** distracted **2295** cloth **2296** bread, a blow **2297** folly **2299** prison **2305** whole **2307** in pretence **2309** love truth **2311** without **2312** deceiving, flattering **2314** performance **2318** could, please **2319** unhappy

155 'Walking backwards'. Covetice and Sensualitie lead Spiritualitie, Falset and Dissait Marchand, and Public Oppressioun Temporalitie.

WANTONNES
Now braid *benedicite*,
Quhat thing is yon that I se?
Luke, Solace, my hart!

SOLACE
Brother Wantonnes, quhat thinks thow?
Yon ar the Thrie Estaitis, I trow,
Gangand backwart!

WANTONNES
Backwart? Backwart? Out, wallaway!
It is greit schame for them, I say,
Backwart to gang.
I trow the King Correctioun
Man mak ane reformatioun,
Or it be lang.

Now let us go and tell the King.

Pausa.[156]

[*To Rex*] Sir, wee have sene ane mervelous thing,
Be our judgement:
The Thrie Estaitis of this regioun
Ar cummand backwart throw this toun
To the Parlament.

REX
Backwart? Backwart? How may that be?
Gar speid them haistelie to me,
In dreid that thay ga wrang.

PLACEBO
Sir, I se them yonder cummand,
Thay will be heir evin fra hand,
Als fast as thay may gang.

GUDE COUNSELL
Sir, hald you stil and skar them nocht,
Till ye persave quhat be thair thocht,
And se quhat men them leids.
And let the King Correctioun.
Mak ane scharp inquisitioun,
And mark them be the heids.

Quhen ye ken the occasioun
That maks them sic persuasioun,
Ye may expell the caus.
Syne them reforme as ye think best,
Sua that the realme may live in rest,
According to Gods lawis.

Heir sall the Thrie Estaitis cum and turne thair faces to the King.

SPIRITUALITIE
Gloir, honour, laud, triumph, and victorie
Be to Your michtie prudent Excellence.
Heir ar we cum, all the Estaits Thrie,
Readie to mak our dew obedience,
At your command with humbill observance,
As m[a]y pertene to Spiritualitie,
With counsell of the Temporalitie.

TEMPORALITIE
Sir, we with michtie curage at command
Of Your superexcellent Majestie,
Sall mak service baith with our hart and hand,
And sall not dreid in thy defence to die.
Wee ar content, but doubt, that wee may se
That nobill heavinlie King Correctioun,
Sa he with mercie mak punitioun.

MERCHAND
Sir, we ar heir, your burgessis and merchands.
Thanks be to God that we may se your face,
Traistand wee may now into divers lands,
Convoy our geir with support of Your Grace.
For now, I traist, wee sall get rest and peace,
Quhen misdoars ar with your sword overthrawin
Then may leil merchands live upon thair awin.

REX
Welcum to me, my prudent Lords all,
Ye ar my members, suppois I be your head.
Sit doun, that we may with your just counsall,
Aganis misdoars find soveraine remeid.
Wee sall nocht spair for favour nor for feid,
With your avice to mak punitioun,
And put my sword to executioun.

CORRECTIOUN
My tender freinds, I pray yow with my hart,
Declair to me the thing that I wald speir.

2325 look 2334 Before long 2339 coming 2347 frighten 2348 thought/intention 2349 lead them 2352 Make note of the problem in proper legal form 2353 reason 2354 behave this way 2360 mighty 2362 due 2364 pertain 2372 So (long as) he 2373 burgesses (civic worthies) 2375 Trusting (that) 2376 Transport, goods 2379 loyal, by their own efforts 2381 believe that I am 2383 Against, effective remedy 2384 hold back, enmity 2385 advice 2388 would

156 'A pause' (while they go to Rex's scaffold).

Quhat is the caus that ye gang all backwart?
The veritie thairof faine wald I heir.

Spiritualitie
Soveraine, we have gaine sa this mony a yeir.
Howbeit ye think we go undecently,
Wee think wee gang richt wonder pleasantly.

Diligence
Sit down, my Lords, into your proper places:
Syne let the King consider all sic caces.
Sit down, sir Scribe, and sit doun Dampster to,[157]
And fence the court as ye war wont to do.

Thay ar set doun, and Gude Cownsell sal pas to his seat.

Rex
My prudent Lords of the Thrie Estaitis,
It is our will abuife all uther thing
For to reforme all them that maks debaits
Contrair the richt, quhilk daylie dois maling,
And thay that dois the Common-weil doun thring.
With help and counsell of King Correctioun,
It is our will for to mak punisching,
And plaine oppressours put to subjectioun.

Spiritualitie
Quhat thing is this, sir, that ye have devysit?
Schirs, ye have neid for till be weill advysit.
Be nocht haistie into your executioun,
And be nocht our extreime in your punitioun.
And, gif ye please to do, sir, as wee say,
Postpone this Parlament till ane uther day.
For quhy the peopill of this regioun
May nocht indure extreme correctioun.

Correctioun
Is this the part, my Lords, that ye will tak,
To mak us supportatioun to correct?[158]
It dois appeir that ye ar culpabill,
That ar nocht to Correctioun applyabill.
Suyith, Diligence, ga schaw it is our will
That everilk man opprest geif in his bill.

Diligence
All maneir of men I wairne that be opprest,
Cum and complaine, and thay salbe redrest.
For quhy it is the nobill Princes will,
That ilk compleiner sall gif in his bill.

[*Enter Johne the Common-Weill.*]

Johne the Common-Weill
Out of my gait, for Gods saik let me ga!
Tell me againe, gude maister, quhat ye say.

Diligence
I warne al that be wrangouslie offendit,
Cum and complaine, and thay sall be amendit.

Johne
Thankit be Christ that buir the croun of thorne,
For I was never sa blyth sen I was borne.

Diligence
Quhat is thy name, fallow? That wald I feil.

Johne
Forsuith, thay call me Johne the Common-Weil.
Gude maister, I wald speir at you ane thing:
Quhair traist ye I sall find yon new cumde King?

Diligence
Cum over, and I sall schaw the[e] to His Grace.

Johne
Gods bennesone licht on that luckie face!
Stand by the gait, let se gif I can loup.
I man rin fast, in cace I get ane coup.

Heir sall Johne loup the stank[159] or els fall in it.

Diligence
Speid the away, thou taryis all to lang.

Johne
Now, be this day, I may na faster gang.

2391 walked this way **2392** improperly **2393** wonderfully **2397** open the proceedings **2399** above **2401** act wickedly **2402** who, throw down **2406** devised **2409** over/too **2416** culpable/guilty **2417** conformable **2418** go **2419** give in, petition **2421** gain redress **2426** wrongfully **2427** amended **2429** happy **2430** know **2433** Where do you think, arrived **2435** blessing, alight **2437** must, fall

[157] 'Dempster too.' The Dempster was the court official who declared the judgements reached during the session.
[158] 'Is this how you intend to help us to reform matters, my Lords?'
[159] Ditch.

JOHNE
Gude day, gud day, grit God saif baith Your Graces,
Wallie, wallie fall thay twa weill fairde faces.[160]

REX
Shaw me thy name, gude man, I the[e] command.

JOHNE
Marie, Johne the Common-weil of fair Scotland.

REX
The Common-weil hes bene amang his fais.

JOHNE
Ye[a], sir, that gars the Common-weil want clais.

REX
Quhat is the caus the Common-weil is crukit?

JOHNE
Becaus the Common-weill hes bene overlukit

REX
Quhat gars the[e] luke sa with ane dreirie hart?

JOHNE
Becaus the Thrie Estaits gangs all backwart.

REX
Sir Common-weill, knaw ye the limmers that them leids?

JOHNE
Thair canker cullours, I ken them be the heads:
As for our reverent fathers of Spiritualitie,
Thay ar led be Covetice and cairles Sensualitie.
And as ye se, Temporalitie hes neid of correctioun,
Quhilk hes lang tyme bene led be Publick Oppressioun:
Loe quhair the loun lyis lurkand at his back.
Get up, I think to se thy craig gar ane raip crack.
Loe, heir is Falsset and Dissait, weill I ken,
Leiders of the merchants and sillie crafts-men.
Quhat mervell thocht the Thrie Estaits backwart gang,
Quhen sic an vyle cumpanie dwels them amang,
Quhilk hes reulit this rout monie deir dayis,
Quhilk gars John the Common-weill want his warme clais.
Sir, call them befoir yow and put them in ordour,
Or els John the Common-weil man beg on the bordour.[161]
Thou feinyeit Flattrie, the Feind fart in thy face:
Quhen ye was guyder of the Court we gat litill grace.
Ryse up Falset and Dissait, without ony sunye,
I pray God nor the Devils dame dryte on thy grunye.
Behauld, as the loun lukis evin lyke a thief!
Monie wicht warkman thou broat to mischief.
My soveraine Lord Correctioun, I mak yow supplication,
Put thir tryit truikers from Christis congregation,

CORRECTIOUN
As ye have devysit, but doubt it salbe done.
Cum heir, my Sergeants, and do your debt sone.
Put thir thrie pellours into pressoun strang,
Howbeit ye sould hang them, ye do them na wrang.

I SERGEANT
Soverane Lords, wee sall obey your commands:
[*To II Sergeant*] Brother, upon thir limmers lay on thy hands.
[*To a Vice*] Ryse up sone loun! Thou luiks evin lyke ane lurden,
Your mouth war meit to drink an wesche jurden.

II SERGEANT
Cum heir, gossop, cum heir, cum heir;
Your rackles lyfe ye sall repent.
Quhen was ye wont to be sa sweir?
Stand still and be obedient.

I SERGEANT
Thair is nocht in all this toun,
(Bot I wald nocht this taill war tald),
Bot I wald hang him for his goun,

2444 foes 2445 lack clothes 2446 crooked (broken) 2447 neglected 2448 look, sorrowful 2450 rogues, lead them 2451 corrupt deceits 2452 reckless 2456 lies lurking 2457 neck crack a rope 2459 simple 2460 It's no wonder that 2462 ruled, long days 2468 any delay 2469 that, shit, snout 2470 looks 2471 strong workman, brought 2473 Expel these proven villains 2475 duty 2476 thieves 2480 rogue 2481 fit, full chamber-pot 2483 reckless 2484 reluctant 2486 no one 2487 story, told 2488 gown

160 'Good luck, good luck befall those two well-favoured faces.'
161 'Must beg along the border [with England; a wild, lawless region].'

Quhidder that it war laird or la[w]d.
I trow this pellour be spur-ga[w]d.
Put in thy hand into this cord.
Howbeit I se thy skap skyre ska[w]d,
Thou art ane stewat, I stand foird.

Heir sall the Vycis be led to the stocks.

II Sergeant
Put in your leggis into the stocks,
For ye had never ane meiter hois.
Thir stewats stinks as thay war broks!
Now ar ye sikker, I suppois.

Pausa.

My Lords, wee have done your commands.
Sall wee put Covetice in captivitie?

Correctioun
Ye[a], hardlie lay on them your hands,
Rycht sa upon Sensualitie.

Spiritualitie
Thir is my grainter and my chalmerlaine,
And hes my gould and geir under hir cuiris.
I mak ane vow to God I sall complaine
Unto the Paip how ye do me injuris.

Covetice
My reverent fathers, tak in patience,
I sall nocht lang remaine from your presence.
Thocht for ane quhyll I man from yow depairt,
I wait my spreit sall remaine in your hart,
And quhen this King Correctioun beis absent
Then sall we twa returne incontinent.
Thaifoir, adew.

Spiritualitie
Adew, be Sanct Mavene.
Pas quhair ye will, we ar twa naturall men.

Sensualitie
Adew, my Lord . . .

Spiritualitie
Adew, my awin sweit hart.
Now duill fell me, that wee twa man depart.

Sensualitie
My Lord, howbeit this parting dois me paine,
I traist in God we sal meit sone agane.

Spiritualitie
To cum againe, I pray yow, do your cure:
Want I yow twa, I may nocht lang indure.

Heir sal the Sergeants chase them away, and thay sal gang to the seat of Sensualitie.

Temporalitie
My Lords, ye knaw the Thrie Estaits
For Common-weill suld mak debaits.
Let now amang us be devysit
Sic Actis that with gude men be praysit,
Conforming to the common law,
For of na man we sould stand aw.
And for till saif us fra murmell,
Schone Diligence, fetch us Gude Counsell,
For quhy he is ane man that knawis
Baith the cannon and civil lawis.

Diligence
Father, ye man incontinent
Passe to the Lords of Parliament,
For quhy thay ar determinat all,
To do na thing [bot] by your counsall.

Gude Counsall
That sal I do within schort space,
Praying the Lord to send us grace
For till conclude or wee depart,
That they may profeit efterwart,
Baith to the Kirk and to the King.
I sall desyre na uther thing.

Pausa.

My Lords, God glaid the cumpanie.
Quhat is the caus ye send for me?

Merchand
Sit doun and gif us your counsell,
How we sall slaik the greit murmell
Of pure peopill that is weill knawin,
And as the Common-weill hes schawin.
And als wee knaw it is the Kings will

2489 commoner 2490 thief, spur-maddened 2492 cancer-scarred scalp 2493 stinker, I guarantee it 2495 more appropriate hose 2496 like badgers 2497 secure, believe 2502 granary-keeper, chamberlain 2503 gold, goods, in their keeping 2505 injuries 2507 (away) from 2508 must 2510 is gone 2512 adieu (farewell) 2513 (i.e. two of a kind) 2515 sorrow befall, must separate 2518 best 2519 If I lack 2521 On behalf glass of 2523 (will) be praised 2525 (in) awe 2526 complaints 2529 clerical and lay laws 2532 all determined 2537 be profitable thereafter 2540 gladden 2543 end 2545 shown

That gude remeid be put thairtill.
Sir Common-weill, keip ye the bar;
Let nane except your self cum nar.

Johne
That sall I do as I best can.
I sall hauld out baith wyfe and man.
Ye man let this puir creature
Support me for till keip the dure.
I knaw his name full sickerly,
He will complaine als weill as I.

Gude Counsall
My worthy Lords, sen ye have taine on hand
Sum reformatioun to mak into this land,
And als ye knaw it is the Kings mynd,
Quha till the Common-weil hes ay bene kynd,
Thocht reif and thift wer stanchit weill aneuch,
Yit sumthing mair belangis to the pleuch.
Now into peace ye sould provyde for weirs,
And be sure of how mony thowsand speirs
The King may be quhen he hes ocht ado.
For quhy, my Lords, this is my ressoun, [lo]:
The husband-men and commons thay war wont
Go in the battell formest in the front.
Bot I have tint all my experience
Without ye mak sum better diligence;
The Common-weill mon uther wayis be styllit,
Or, be my faith, the King wilbe begyllit.
Thir pure commouns, daylie as ye may se,
Declynis doun till extreme povertie:
For sum ar hichtit sa into thair maill,
Thair winnung will nocht find them water kail.
How prelats heichts thair teinds it is well knawin,
That husband-men may not weill hald thair awin,
And now begins ane plague amang them new,
That gentill men thair steadings taks in few.[162]
Thus man may pay great ferme, or lay thair steid,
And sum ar plainlie harlit out be the heid,
And ar distroyit without God on them rew.

Pauper
Sir, be Gods breid, that taill is verie trew!
It is weill kend I had baith nolt and hors,
Now all my geir ye se upon my cors.

Correctioun
Or I depairt I think to mak ane ordour.

Johne
I pray yow, sir, begin first at [the] bordour.
For how can we fend us aganis Ingland,
Quhen we can nocht, within our native land,
Destroy our awin Scots common traitor theifis,
Quha to leill laborers daylie dois mischeifis?
War I ane king, my Lord, be Gods wounds,
Quha ever held common theifis within thair bounds,
Quhairthrow that dayly leilmen micht be wrangit,
Without remeid thair chiftanis suld be hangit,
Quhidder he war ane knicht, ane lord, or laird,
The Devill draw me to Hell and he war spaird.

Temporalitie
Quhat uther enemies hes thou? Let us ken.

Johne
Sir, I compleine upon the idill men,
For quhy, sir, it is Gods awin bidding,
All Christian men to wirk for thair living.
Sanct Paull, that pillar of the Kirk,
Sayis to the wretchis that will not wirk,
And bene to vertews [labour] laith,
'*Qui non laborat non manducet.*'[163]
This is, in Inglische toung or leit,
'Quha labouris nocht, he sall not eit'.
This bene against the strang beggers,[164]
Fidlers, pypers, and pardoners,
Thir jugglars, jestars, and idill cuitchours,
Thir carriers and thir quintacensours,
Thir babil-beirers and thir bairds,
Thir sweir swyngeours with lords and lairds

2547 thereto 2548 guard the bar 2549 near 2551 keep 2552 (i.e. Pauper) 2553 door (entrance) 2554 truly 2556 taken on 2558 intention 2560 robbery, ended, enough 2561 remains to be done 2562 in time of, prepare, wars spearmen (foot soldiers) 2564 may summon, anything to do 2566 used (to) 2567 foremost 2568 lost 2569 Unless 2570 must, organized 2574 have their rents raised so high 2575 profits, buy, water-cress 2576 raise, tithes 2578 a new plague 2580 rents, lose, farm 2581 hurled, head 2582 take pity on them 2584 cattle, horses 2585 body/person 2588 defend ourselves against 2591 honest, mischief 2593 tolerated, territories 2594 wronged 2595 these landowners 2597 if he were spared 2599 idle 2604 loathe to do virtuous labour 2606 language 2610 idle gamblers 2611 sycophants, alchemists 2612 bauble-bearers (fools), bards 2613 bold villains

162 'Gentlemen place their farmsteads in feu:' i.e. let them out at a fixed rent with a large lump-sum payment at the start of the rental period.

163 'If any would not work, neither should he eat.' II Thessalonians 3:10.

164 'This speaks against the strong beggars [i.e. those who could work but choose to beg instead]'.

Ma then thair rents may susteine,
Or to thair profeit neidfull bene,[165]
Quhillk bene ay blythest of discords,
And deidly feid amang thar lords.
For then they sleutchers man be treatit,
Or els thair querrels undebaitit.[166]
This bene against thir great fat freiris,
Augustenes, Carmeleits, and Cordeleirs,[167]
And all uthers that in cowls bene cled,
Quhilk labours nocht and bene weill fed.
I mein nocht laborand Spiritualie,
Nor for thair living corporallie,
Lyand in dennis lyke idill doggis,
I them compair to weil fed hoggis!
I think they do them selfis abuse,
Seing that thay the warld refuse:
Haffing profest sic povertie,
Syne fleis fast fra necessitie.
Quhat gif thay povertie wald professe,
And do as did Diogenes?[168]
That great famous philosophour,
Seing in earth bot vaine labour,
Alutterlie the warld refusit
And in ane tumbe himself inclusit,
And leifit on herbs and water cauld;
Of corporall fude na mair he wald.
He trottit nocht from toun to toun
Beggand to feid his carioun.
Fra tyme that lyfe he did profes,
The wa[r]ld of him was cummerles.
Rycht sa of Marie Magdalene,[169]
And of Mary th'Egyptiane,[170]
And of auld Paull, the first hermeit:[171]
All thir had povertie compleit.
Ane hundreth ma I micht declair,
Bot to my purpois I will fair,
Concluding sleuthfull idilnes,
Against the Common-weill expresse.

Correctioun
Quhom upon ma will ye compleine?

Johne
Marie, on ma and ma againe.
For the pure peopill cryis with
The infetching of Justice airis:
Exercit mair for covetice
Then for the punisching of vyce.
Ane peggrell theif that steillis ane kow
Is hangit; bot he that steillis ane bow,
With als meikill geir as he may turs,
That theif is hangit be the purs.
Sic pykand peggrall theifis ar hangit,
Bot he that all the warld hes wrangit,
Ane cruell tyrane, ane strang transgressour,
Ane common publick plaine oppressour,
By buds may he obteine favours
Of tresurers and compositours.
Thocht he serve greit punitioun,
Gets easie compositioun: settlement
And throch laws consistoriall,
Prolixt, corrupt, and pertiall,
The common peopill ar put sa under,
Thocht thay be puir, it is na wonder.

Correctioun
Gude Johne, I grant all that is trew,
Your infortoun full sair I rew.
Or I pairt aff this natioun,
I sall mak reformatioun.

2614 More 2616 happiest about disputes 2617 feuds, their 2618 these idlers, looked after 2622 clad 2624 labouring 2625 physically 2627 Lying, dens 2629 reject 2630 professed (i.e. taken vows of) poverty 2631 quickly flee from hardship 2635 only 2636 completely rejected the world 2737 barrel, enclosed 2638 lived, cold 2639 bodily food, would (have) 2640 trotted 2641 Begging, flesh 2643 he had no affection for 2647 (lived in) complete poverty 2648 more 2649 return 2650 slothful 2651 (To be) explicitly against 2655 exactions, the courts of Assize 2656 Exercised, more 2658 petty thief 2659 (whole) herd 2660 much property, carry off 2661 purse (i.e. only fined) 2662 small-time thieving 2663 wronged 2664 tyrant 2666 bribes 2667 accountants 2668 deserves 2669 an easy (financial) settlement 2670 consistory court laws 2671 over-complicated, partial 2675 misfortune 2676 Before I leave

165 'Or are necessary for their profit'. Johne continues his attack upon the hordes of superfluous retainers whom he sees as hanging around the households of lords.

166 If there were no feuds, the bards, minstrels, and entertainers would get no opportunities to celebrate their patrons' victories or revile their enemies.

167 The Augustinians, Carmelites, and Franciscans were three of the four major orders of friars (the Dominicans were the fourth).

168 The philosopher Diogenes the Cynic (*c.*400–*c.*325 BC), who, rejecting the world completely, reputedly lived in a barrel.

169 Medieval legend held that Mary Magdalene adopted a contemplative life in the desert after the Crucifixion. The Digby play of Mary Magdalen recounts her story.

170 Mary of Alexandria, who converted to Christianity and became a contemplative.

171 St Paul the Hermit, whose saintly life in the desert was the subject of a tract by St Jerome.

And als, my Lord Temporalitie,
I yow command in tyme that ye
Expell Oppressioun aff your lands.
And als I say to yow merchands,
Gif ever I find be land or sie,
Dissait be in your cumpanie,
Quhilk ar to Common-weill contrair,
I vow to God I sall not spair
To put my sword to executioun,
And mak on yow extreme punitioun.
Mairover, my Lord [Temporalitie],
In gudlie haist I will that ye
Set into few your temporall lands
To men that labours with thair hands,
Bot nocht to ane gearking gentill man,
That nether will he wirk, nor can,
Quhair throch the policy may incresse.

Temporalitie
I am content, sir, be the Messe,
Swa that the Spiritualitie
Sets thairs in few als weill as wee.

Correctioun
My Spirituall Lords, ar ye content?

Spiritualitie
Na, na, wee man tak advysement.
In sic maters for to conclude
Ovir haistelie, we think nocht gude.

Correctioun
Conclude ye nocht with the Common-weil,
Ye salbe punischit be Sanct Geill.

Heir sall the Bischops cum with the Freir.

Spiritualitie
Schir, we can schaw exemptioun
Fra your temporall punitioun,
The quhilk wee purpois till debait.

Correctioun
Wa than, ye think to stryve for stait.
My Lords, quhat say ye to this play?

Temporalitie
My soveraine Lord, we will obay,
And tak your part with hart and hand,
Quhat ever ye pleis us to command.

Heir sal the Temporal Stait sit doun on thair kneis and say:

Bot wee beseik yow, Soveraine,
Of all our cryms that ar bygaine
To gif us ane remissioun,
And heir wee mak to yow conditioun
The Common-weill for till defend,
From hence-forth till our lives end.

Correctioun
On that conditioun I am content
Till pardon yow, sen ye repent.
The Common-weill tak be the hand
And mak with him perpetuall band.

Heir sall the Temporal Staits, to wit, the Lords and Merchands, imbreasse[172] Johne the Common-weill.

Johne, have ye ony ma debaits
Against the Lords of Spirituall Staits?

Johne
Na, sir, I dar nocht speik ane word.
To plaint on preistis, it is na bourd.

Correctioun
Flyt on thy fow fill, I desyre the[e],
Swa that thou schaw bot the veritie,

Johne
Grandmerces, then I sall nocht spair,
First to compleine on the vickair.
The pure cottar being lyke to die,
Haifand young infants, twa or thrie,
And hes twa ky but ony ma,
The vickar most half ane of thay,
With the gray frugge that covers the bed,
Howbeit the wyfe be purelie cled.
And, gif the wyfe die on the morne,
Thocht all the bairns sould be forlorne,
The uther kow he cleiks away
With the pure cot of raploch gray.
Wald God this custome war put doun,
Quhilk never was foundit be ressoun.

2682 sea 2690 feu 2692 work-shy 2694 good government, increase 2699 advice 2705 punishment/jurisdiction 2707 supremacy 2713 crimes, in the past 2715 a pledge 2725 complain against, no joke 2726 complain all you like 2727 speak only truth 2728 Thank you 2729 vicar 2730 peasant farmer 2731 Having 2732 and no more 2733 them (a cow) 2734 quilt 2735 clad 2738 snatches 2739 coat, grey homespun 2740 abolished

172 Embrace.

Temporalitie
Ar all thay tails trew that thou telles?

Pauper
Trew, sir, the Divill stick me elles!
For, be the Halie Trinitie,
That same was practeisit on me.
For our vickar, God give him pyne,
Hes yit thrie tydie kye of myne:
Ane for my father, and for my wyfe ane uther,
And the thrid cow he tuke for Mald, my mother.

Johne
Our Persone heir, he takis na uther pyne,
Bot to ressave his teinds and spend them syne,
Howbeit he be obleist be gude ressoun,
To preich the Evangell to his parochoun.
Howbeit thay suld want preiching sevintin yeir,
Our persoun will not want ane scheif of beir.

Pauper
Our bishops with thair lustie rokats quhyte,
Thay flow in riches royallie and delyte:
Lyke Paradice bene thair palices and places,
And wants na pleasour of the fairest faces.
Als thir prelates hes great prerogatyves,
For quhy thay may depairt ay with thair wyves,
Without ony correctioun or damnage,
Syne tak ane uther wantoner, but mariage.
But doubt I wald think it ane pleasant lyfe,
Ay on quhen I list to part with my wyfe,
Syne tak ane uther of far greiter bewtie.
Bot ever alace, my lords, that may not be,
For I am bund, alace, in mariage;
Bot thay lyke rams rudlie in thair rage,
Unpysalt rinnis amang the sillie yowis,[173]
Sa lang as kynde of nature in them growis.

Person
Thou lies, fals huirsun, raggit loun:
Thair is na priests in all this toun,
That ever usit sic vicious crafts.

Johne
The Feind ressave thay flattrand chafts!
Sir Dominie, I trowit ye had be dum.
Quhair Devil gat we this ill fairde blaitie bum?

Person
To speik of preists, be sure, it is na bourds:
Thay will burne men now for rakles words,
And all thay words ar herisie in deid.

Johne
The mekil Feind resave the saul that leid.
All that I say is trew, thocht thou be greifit,
And that I offer on thy pallet to preif it.

Spiritualitie
My Lords, quhy do ye thoil that lurdun loun
Of Kirk-men to speik sic detractioun?
I let yow wit, my Lords, it is na bourds,
Of prelats for till speik sic wantoun words.

Heir Spiritualitie fames[174] *and rages.*

Yon villaine puttis me out of charitie!

Temporalitie
Quhy, my Lord, sayis he ocht bot verity?
Ye can nocht stop ane pure man for till pleinye,
Gif he hes faltit, summond him to your Seinye.

Spiritualitie
Yea, that I sall. I sall mak greit God a vow,
He sall repent that he spak of the kow.
I will not suffer sic words of yon villaine.

Pauper
Than gar gif me my thrie fat ky againe.

Spiritualitie
Fals carle, to speik to me stands thou not aw?

Pauper
The Feind resave them that first devysit that law!
Within an houre efter my dade was deid
The vickar had my kow hard be the heid.

Person
Fals huirsun carle, I say that law is gude,
Becaus it hes bene lang our consuetude.

2743 stab, otherwise **2745** practised **2746** sorrow **2751** tithes, and then spend them **2752** obliged **2753** Gospel, parishioners **2754** lack, seventeen **2755** sheaf, barley (in tithe) **2756** white rockets (surplices) **2758** palaces, homes **2759** (they) lack **2762** punishment or condemnation **2763** (even) more wanton, without **2766** beauty **2768** bound **2769** frenzy **2771** natural inclination prompts **2774** behaviour **2775** flattering jaws **2776** Sir Lord (ironic), thought, dumb **2777** idler **2779** careless **2781** lied **2782** grieved/angered **2783** head **2784** suffer **2788** puts **2789** anything **2790** from complaining **2791** lied, Consistory Court **2793** what he said about **2796** aren't you afraid **2798** dad

[173] 'Run with their [erect] penises on show among the silly ewes'.

[174] 'Foams [at the mouth]'.

Pauper
Quhen I am Paip, that law I sal put doun:
It is ane sair law for the pure commoun.

Spiritualitie
I mak an vow, thay words thou sal repent.

Gude Counsall
I yow requyre, my Lords, be patient.
Wee came nocht heir for disputatiouns;
Wee came to make gude reformatiouns.
Heirfoir, of this your propositioun,
Conclude and put to executioun.

Merchand
My Lords, conclud that al the temporal lands
Be set in few to laboreris with thair hands,
With sic restrictiouns as sall be devysit,
That thay may live and nocht to be supprysit,
With ane ressonabill augmentatioun:
And quhen thay heir ane proclamatioun
That the Kings Grace dois mak him for the weir,
That thay be reddie with harneis, bow, and speir.
As for myself, my Lord, this I conclude.

Gude Counsall
Sa say we all, your resoun be sa gude.
To mak an Act on this we ar content.

Johne
On that, sir Scribe, I tak an instrument.
Quhat do ye of the corspresent and kow?

Gude Counsall
I wil conclude nathing of that as now,
Without my Lord of Spiritualitie
Thairto consent, with all this haill cleargie.
My Lord Bischop, will ye thairto consent?

Spiritualitie
Na, na, never till the Day of Judgement!
Wee will want nathing that wee have in use,
Kirtil nor kow, teind lamb, teind gryse, nor guse.

Temporalitie
Forsuith, my Lord, I think we suld conclude.
Seing this kow ye have in consuetude,
Wee will decerne heir that the Kings Grace
Sall wryte unto the Paipis holines:
With his consent be proclamatioun,
Baith corspresent and cow we sall cry doun.

Spiritualitie
To that, my Lords, wee plainlie disassent:
Noter,[175] thairof I tak ane instrument.

Temporalitie
My Lord, be Him that al the warld hes wrocht,
Wee set nocht by quhider ye consent or nocht:
Ye ar bot ane Estait and we ar twa,
Et ubi major pars ibi tota.[176]

Johne
My Lords, ye haif richt prudentlie concludit.
Tak tent now how the land is clein denudit
Of gould and silver, quhilk daylie gais to Rome,
For buds, mair then the rest of Christindome.
War I ane king, sir, be Coks Passioun,
I sould gar mak ane proclamatioun,
That never ane penny sould go to Rome at all,
Na mair then did to Peter nor to Paull.
Do ye nocht sa, heir for conclusioun,
I gif yow all my braid black malesoun.

Merchant
It is of treuth, sirs, be my Christindome,
That mekil of our money gais to Rome.
For we merchants, I wait, within our bounds,
Hes furneist preists ten hundreth thowsand punds
For thair finnance; nane knawis sa weill as wee.
Thairfoir, my Lords, devyse sum remedie.
For throw thir playis and thir promotioun,
Mair for denners nor for devotioun,
Sir Symonie hes maid with them ane band,[177]
The gould of weicht thay leid out of the land.
The Common-weil thair throch bein sair oppest;
Thairfoir devyse remeid as ye think best.

2803 sore (harsh) 2811 manual workers 2813 subject to (unexpected) taxes and fees 2814 annual increase in rent 2816 prepare himself, war 2817 armour 2821 I want this documented 2822 will you do about, mortuary fee 2823 at present 2824 unless 2825 whole clergy 2828 we currently enjoy 2829 Girdle, tithe lamb, suckling pig 2832 decide 2835 denounce/abolish 2836 disagree 2839 we do not care whether 2843 completely denuded 2845 bribes, than (to) 2849 St Peter or St Paul 2851 broad curse 2855 furnished (given to), pounds 2856 upkeep, no one knows 2858 pleas 2859 coins 2860 agreement 2861 weight, take 2862 through that

[175] Notary: the Notary Public was the clerk of the court. He seems to be the same character as the Scribe.
[176] 'And where the greater part is, there is the whole.' A legal principle whereby a majority decision is taken to be the view of the whole assembly.
[177] The sin of buying and selling ecclesiastical offices and preferments, named after Simon Magus. See Acts 8:9–24.

GUDE COUNSALL
It is schort tyme sen any benefice
Was sped in Rome except greit bischopries.[178]
Bot now for ane unworthie vickarage
Ane preist will rin to Rome in pilgrimage.
Ane cavell, quhilk was never at the scule,
Will rin to Rome and keip ane bischops mule,
And syne cum hame with mony colorit crack,
With ane buirdin of benefices on his back;
Quhilk bene against the law, ane man alane
For till posses ma benefices nor ane.
Thir greit commends,[179] I say withoutin faill,
Sould nocht be given bot to the blude royall.
Sa I conclude, my Lords, and sayis for me,
Ye sould annull all this pluralitie.[180]

SPIRITUALITIE
The Paip hes given us dispensatiouns.

GUDE COUNSALL
Yea, that is be your fals narratiouns.
Thocht the Paip for your pleasour will dispence,
I trow that can nocht cleir your conscience.
Advyse, my Lords, quhat ye think to conclude.

TEMPORALITIE
Sir, be my faith, I think it verie gude,
That fra hence furth na preistis sall pas to Rome,
Becaus our substance thay do still consume
For pleyis and for thair profeit singulair,
Thay haif of money maid this realme bair.
And als I think it best, be my advyse,
That ilk preist sall haif bot ane benefice.
And gif thay keip nocht that fundatioun,
It sall be caus of deprivatioun.

MERCHANT
As ye haif said, my Lord, we wil consent.
Scribe, mak an Act on this incontinent.

GUDE COUNSALL
My Lords, thair is ane thing yit unproponit,
How prelats and preistis aucht to be disponit.
This beand done, we have the les ado.
Quhat say ye, sirs? This is my counsall, lo,
That, or wee end this present Parliament,
Of this mater to tak rype advysement.
Mark weill, my Lords, thair is na benefice
Given to ane man bot for ane gude office.
Quha taks office and syne thay can nocht us it,
Giver and taker, I say, ar baith abusit.
Ane bischops office is for to be ane preichour,
And of the law of God ane publick teachour.
Rycht sa the persone unto his parochoun,
Of the Evangell sould leir them ane lessoun.
Thair sould na man desyre sic dignities,
Without he be abill for that office.
And for that caus I say, without leising,
Thay have thair teinds, and for na uther thing.

SPIRITUALITIE
Freind, quhair find ye that we suld prechours be?

GUDE COUNSALL
Luik quhat Sanct Paul wryts unto Timothie.
Tak thair the Buik: let se gif ye can spell.

SPIRITUALITIE
I never red that, thairfoir reid it your sel.

Counsall sall read thir wordis on ane Buik:

[GUDE COUNSALL]
'Fidelis sermo, si quis Episcopatum desiderat, bonum
opus desiderat. Oportet {ergo}, eum irreprehensibilem
esse, unius uxoris virum, sobrium, prudentem,
ornatum, pudicum, hospitalem, doctorem:
non vinolentum, non percussorem, sed modestum.'[181]

That is: 'This is a true saying, If any man desire the office
of a Bishop, he desireth a worthie worke:
a Bishop, therefore, must be unreproveable,
the husband of one wife, etc.'

2868 wretch, school **2869** look after (to win favour) **2870** dishonest boasts **2871** burden **2872** alone **2873** more **2875** except, those of royal blood **2879** lies **2885** wealth, use up **2886** pleas, personal profit **2887** bare **2890** establishment **2891** loss of office **2894** still to be discussed **2895** disposed (provided for) **2896** being, less to do **2899** mature advice **2900** Remember **2901** good purpose **2902** fulfil its responsibilities **2903** abused **2904** preacher **2906** parishioners **2907** Gospel, teach **2909** capable **2910** lying

178 'Not so long ago, it was only great bishoprics that had to be negotiated in Rome.'

179 A *Commendam* was a dispensation to hold more than one benefice at a time.

180 Pluralism was the holding of multiple benefices.

181 'This is a true saying: If a man desire the office of a bishop, he desireth a good work. A bishop, then, must be blameless, the husband of one wife, vigilant, sober, of good behaviour [and] appearance, given to hospitality, apt to teach. Not given to wine, no striker, [not greedy of filthy lucre], but patient, [not a brawler, not covetous].' I Timothy 3:1–3.

SPIRITUALITIE
Ye temporall men, be Him that heryit Hell,
Ye are ovir peart with sik maters to mel.

TEMPORALITIE
Sit still, my Lord, ye neid not for till braull,
Thir ar the verie words of th'Apostill Paul.

SPIRITUALITIE
Sum sayis, be Him that woare the croun of thorne,
It had been gude that Paull had neir bene borne.

GUDE COUNSALL
Bot ye may knaw, my Lord, Sanct Pauls intent.
Schir, red ye never the New Testament?

SPIRITUALITIE
Na sir, be him that our Lord Jesus sauld,
I red never the New Testament nor Auld.
Nor ever thinks to do sir, be the Rude!
I heir freiris say that reiding dois na gude.

GUDE COUNSALL
Till yow to reid them, I think it is na lack,[182]
For anis I saw them baith bund on your back;
That samin day that ye was consecrat.[183]
Sir, quhat meinis that?

SPIRITUALITIE
The Feind stick them that wat!

MERCHANT
Then, befoir God, how can ye be excusit;
To haif ane office and waits not haw to us it?
Quhairfoir war gifin yow all the temporal lands,
And all thir teinds ye haif amang your hands?
Thay war givin yow for uther causses, I weine,
Nor mummil Matins and hald your clayis cleine.
Ye say to the Appostils that ye succeid,
Bot ye schaw nocht that into word nor deid.
The law is plaine: our teinds suld furnisch teichours.

GUDE COUNSALL
Yea, that it sould, or susteine prudent preichours.

PAUPER
Sir, God nor I be stickit with ane knyfe,
Gif ever our Persoun preichit in all his lyfe.

PERSOUN
Quhat Devil raks the[e] of our preiching,
undocht?[184]

PAUPER
Think ye that ye suld have the teinds for nocht?

PERSON
Trowis thou to get remeid, carle, of that thing?

PAUPER
Yea, be Gods breid, richt sone, war I ane king.

PERSON
Wald thou of prelats mak deprivatioun?

PAUPER
Na, I suld gar them keip thair fundatioun.
Quhat Devill is this? Quhom of sould Kings stand
aw
To do the thing that they sould be the law?
War I ane king, be Coks deir Passioun,
I sould richt sone mak reformatioun.
Failyeand thairof, Your Grace sould richt sone finde
That preists sall leid yow lyke ane bellie blinde.

JOHNE
Quhat gif King David[185] war leivand in thir dayis
The quhilk did found sa mony gay abayise?
Or out of Heavin quhat gif he luikit doun,
And saw the great abominatioun,
Amang thir abesses and thir nunries,
Thair publick huirdomes and thair harlotries?
He wald repent he narrowit sa his bounds,
Of yeirlie rent thriescoir of thowsand pounds.
His successours maks litill ruisse, I ges,
Of his devotioun or of his holiness.

[ABBOT][186]
How dar thou, carle, presume for to declair,

2925 harrowed 2926 too presumptuous, meddle 2927 to brawl 2930 never 2936 reading does 2938 once, bound 2940 means, know 2942 not know how to use it 2943 were given 2945 purposes 2946 Than to mumble, keep, clothes 2947 are successors 2948 in 2949 pay for 2951 may I 2958 fulfil their responsibilities 2959 of whom, be afraid 2963 Failing that 2964 blindfolded man 2965 was living 2966 fine abbeys 2967 looked 2969 abbeys, nunneries 2971 depleted his resources 2973 make little boast, guess

182 'It would be no bad thing for you to read them'.

183 'The same day that you were consecrated.' Part of the consecration service for bishops involved the Bible being held over the candidate's head.

184 'What the Devil do you know about preaching, wretch?'

185 David I (1124–53).

186 Charteris has 'Abbas(se)'.

Or for to mell the[e] with sa heich a mater?
For in Scotland thair did yit never ring,
I let the[e] wit, ane mair excellent king.
Of holines he was the verie plant,
And now in Heavin he is ane michtfull Sanct,
Becaus that fyftein abbasies he did found,
Quhair-throw great riches hes ay done abound
Into our Kirk and daylie yit abunds.
Bot kings now, I trow, few abbasies founds
I dar weill say thou art condempnit in Hel,
That dois presume with sic maters to mell.
Fals huirsun carle, thou art ovir arrogant
To judge the deids of sic ane halie sanct.

JOHNE
King James the first,[187] roy of this regioun,
Said that he was ane sair sanct to the croun.
I heir men say that he was sumthing blind,
That gave away mair nor he left behind.
His successours that halines did repent,
Quhilk gart them do great inconvenient.

[ABBOT]
My Lord Bishop, I mervel how that ye
Suffer this carle for to speik heresie!
For, be my faith, my Lord, will ye tak tent,
He servis for to be brunt incontinent.
Ye can nocht say bot it is heresie,
To speik against our law and libertie.

SPIRITUALITIE
Sancte Pater, I mak yow supplicatioun:
Exame yon carle syne mak his dilatioun.[188]
I mak ane vow to God omnipotent,
That bystour salbe brunt incontinent.

[FLATTERIE]
Venerabill father, I sall do your command:
Gif he servis deid, I sall sune understand.

Pausa.

Fals huirsun carle, schaw furth thy faith.

JOHNE
Me think ye speik as ye war wraith.
To yow I will nathing declair,
For ye ar nocht my ordinair.[189]

FLATTERIE
Quhom in trowis thou, fals monster mangit?

JOHNE
I trow to God to se the[e] hangit!
War I ane King, be Coks Passioun,
I sould gar mak ane congregatioun,
Of all the freirs of the four ordours,
And mak yow vagers on the bordours.
[*To Correctioun*] Schir, will ye give me audience,
And I sall schaw your excellence,
Sa that Your Grace will give me leife,
How into God that I beleife.

CORRECTIOUN
Schaw furth your faith and feinye nocht.

JOHN
I beliefe in God that all hes wrocht,[190]
And creat everie thing of nocht;
And in His Son our Lord Jesu,
Incarnat of the Virgin trew,
Quha under Pilat tholit Passioun
And deit for our salvatioun;
And on the thrid day rais againe,
As Halie Scriptour schawis plane.
And als, my Lord, it is weill kend,
How he did to the Heavin ascend,
And set him doun at the richt hand
Of God the Father, I understand;
And sall cum judge on Dumisday.
Quhat will ye mair, sir, that I say?[191]

CORRECTIOUN
Schaw furth the rest: this is na game.

JOHNE
I trow *Sanctam Ecclesiam*,[192]

2976 high (serious) **2979** source **2980** powerful **2982** always abounded **2983** abounds **2990** sore (harmful) **2991** somewhat **2992** more than **2998** deserves, burnt **3001** Holy father **3009** loud-mouth **3011** In whom do you believe **3014** assembly **3016** vagrants **3019** permission **3021** don't feign **3023** created, from nothing **3026** suffered **3027** died **3028** rose **3029** plainly shows

[187] James I (1405–37).
[188] 'Examine that fellow, then let him declare his beliefs.' Spiritualitie and Flatterie subject Johne to an impromptu heresy trial.
[189] Ordinary: the bishop with overall jurisdiction over an individual.
[190] Johne's declaration of faith follows the Apostle's Creed.
[191] Johne has stopped short at the point where he should declare belief in the church on Earth.
[192] 'The Holy Church': Johne significantly omits the word 'Catholic' contained in the Creed.

Bot nocht in thir bischops nor thir freirs,
Quhilk will for purging of thir neirs,
Sard up the ta raw and doun the uther:
The mekill Devill resave the fidder!

Correctioun
Say quhat ye will, sirs, be Sanct Tan,
Me think Johne ane gude Christian man.

Temporalitie
My Lords, let be yow disputatioun.
Conclude with firm deliberatioun
How prelats fra thyne sall be deponit.

Merchand
I think for me evin as ye first proponit,
That the Kings Grace sall gif na benefice,
Bot till ane preichour that can use that office.
The sillie sauls that bene Christis scheip
Sould nocht be givin to gormand wolfis to keip.
Quhat bene the caus of all the heresies
Bot the abusioun of the prelacies?
Thay will correct and will nocht be correctit,
Thinkand to na prince thay wil be subjectit.
Quhairfoir I can find na bette remeid,
Bot that thir Kings man take it in thair heid,
That thair be given to na man bischopries,
Except thay preich out-throch thair diosies,
And ilk persone preich in his parochon:
And this I say for finall conclusion.

Temporalitie
Wee think your counsall is verie gude,
As ye have said, wee all conclude.
Of this conclusioun, Noter, wee mak ane Act.

Scrybe
I wryte all day, bot gets never ane plack!

Pauper
Och, my Lords, for the Halie Trinitie,
Remember to reforme the Consistorie.
It hes mair neid of reformatioun
Nor Ploutois court,[193] sir, be Coks Passioun!

Person
Quhat caus hes thou, fals pellour, for to pleinye?
Quhair was ye ever summond to thair Seinye?

Pauper
Marie, I lent my gossop my mear to fetch hame
coills,
And he hir drounit into the querrell hollis.
And I ran to the Consistorie for to pleinye,
And thair I happinit amang ane greidie meinye.
Thay gave me first ane thing thay call *citandum*,[194]
Within aucht dayis I gat bot *lybellandum*,[195]
Within ane moneth I gat *ad opponendum*,[196]
In half ane yeir I gat *interloquendum*,[197]
And syne I gat, how call ye it? *ad replicandum*,[198]
Bot I could never ane word yit understand him.
And than thay gart me cast out many plackis,
And gart me pay for four and twentie actis.
Bot, or thay came half gait to *concludendum*,
The Feind ane plack was left for to defend him.[199]
Thus thay postponit me twa yeir with thair traine,
Syne *hodie ad octo* had me cum againe;
And than thir ruiks thay roupit wonder fast,
For sentence silver thay cryit at the last.
Of *pronunciandum*[200] thay maid me wonder faine,
Bot I gat never my gude gray meir againe.

Temporalitie
My Lords, we mon reforme thir Consistory lawis,
Quhais great defame above the heavins blawis.
I wist ane man in persewing of ane kaw,
Or he had done, he spendit half ane bow.
Sa that the kings honour wee may avance,
Wee will conclude as they have done in France:[201]
Let sprituall maters pas to Spritualitie,
And temporall maters to Temporalitie.
Quha failyeis of this sall cost them of thair gude;
Scribe, mak ane Act for sa wee will conclude.

3039 nethers(?) **3040** copulate, one row **3041** take the lot of them **3042** St Anne **3044** put aside **3046** from now on, provided for **3047** proposed **3049** to **3050** sheep **3051** greedy **3053** bishops **3056** better **3058** bishoprics **3059** throughout **3060** parson, parish **3065** a fourpenny piece **3070** thief, complain **3072** mare, coals **3073** drowned, quarry-pits **3075** fell, greedy crew **3077** eight **3082** coins **3084** halfway to a conclusion **3086** postponed, tricks **3087** 'a week today' **3088** rooks, croaked **3089** judgement fees, cried **3091** mare **3094** pursuing **3095** spent, herd **3098** matters **3100** fails in this, goods

193 'Than the court of Pluto [lord of the classical underworld]'.
194 The opening word of a citation or summons.
195 The opening of a plea.
196 The formal response to a plea.
197 An interim decree.
198 The plaintiff's response to an *ad opponendum*.
199 'I'd not got a fourpenny piece left to pay for my defence, by the Devil.'
200 The opening of a pronouncement or final judgement.
201 The powers of the French ecclesiastical courts over the laity had been limited by the Edict of Villers-Cotterets (1539).

Spiritualitie
That act, my Lords, plainlie I will declair:
It is againis our profeit singulair.
Wee will nocht want our profeit, be Sanct Geill!

Temporalitie
Your profeit is against the common-weil.
It salbe done, my Lords as ye have wrocht:
We cure nocht quhidder ye consent or nocht.
Quhairfoir servis then all thir temporall judges,
Gif temporall maters sould seik at yow refuges?
My Lord, ye say that ye ar sprituall,
Quhairfoir mell ye than with things temporall?
As we have done conclude, sa sall it stand.
Scribe, put our Acts in ordour evin fra hand.

Spiritualitie
Till all your Acts plainlie I disassent,
Notar, thairof I tak ane instrument.

Heir sall Veritie and Chastitie mak thair plaint[202] *at the bar.*

Veritie
My Soverane, I beseik your excellence,
Use justice on Sprituallitie,
The quhilk to us hes done great violence.
Becaus we did rehers the veritie,
Thay put us close into captivitie,
And sa remanit into subjectioun:
Into great langour and calamitie,
Till we war fred be King Correctioun.

Chastitie
My Lord, I haif great caus for to complaine.
I could get na ludging intill this land:
The Spirituall Stait had me sa at disdaine.
With Dame Sensuall thay have maid sic ane band,
Amang them all na freindschip, sirs, I fand.
And, quhen I came the nobill [nunnis] amang,
My lustie Lady Priores fra hand
Out of dortour durlie scho me dang.

Veritie
With the advyse, sir, of the Parliament
Hairtlie we mak yow supplicatioun:
Cause King Correctioun tak incontinent
Of all this sort examinatioun.
Gif thay be digne of deprivatioun,
Ye have power for to correct sic cases;
Chease the maist cunning clerks of this natioun,
And put mair prudent pastours in thair places.
My prudent Lords, I say that pure craftsmen
Abufe sum prelats ar mair for to commend.
Gar exame them, and sa ye sall sune ken,
How thay in vertew bischops dois transcend.

Scribe
Thy life and craft mak to thir Kings kend,
Quhat craft hes thow, declair that to me plaine.

Taylour
Ane tailyour, sir, that can baith mak and mend:
I wait nane better into Dumbartane.[203]

Scribe
Quhairfoir of tailyeours beirs thou the styl?

Taylour
Becaus I wait is nane within ane myll,
Can better use that craft as I suppois:
For I can mak baith doublit, coat, and hois.

Scribe
How cal thay you, sir, with the schaiping knife?

Sowtar
Ane sowtar, sir, nane better into Fyfe.

Scribe
Tel me quhairfoir ane sowtar ye ar namit?

Sowtar
Of that surname I neid nocht be aschamit,
For I can mak schone, brotekins, and buittis.
Gif me the coppie of the Kings cuittis,
And ye sall se richt sune quhat I can do:
Heir is my lasts, and weill wrocht ledder to.[204]

Gude Counsall
O Lord my God, this is an mervelous thing,

3103 individual profits 3107 care 3108 what is the point of 3109 can be dealt with by you 3119 preach 3120 tightly 3121 remained in 3122 distress 3123 freed 3125 in 3126 in 3128 found 3131 dormitory, fiercely, drove 3136 worthy 3138 choose 3141 Are more praiseworthy than some bishops 3142 examine 3143 exceed bishops in virtue 3144 make known to 3145 What is your trade 3148 Why are you called a tailor 3151 hose 3153 shoemaker 3154 named 3156 shoes, half-boots, boots 3156 mould, ankles

202 Complaint.

203 'I think there's none better from here to Dumbarton [on the west coast of Scotland].'

204 'Here are my lasts [a cobbler's anvils] and well-made leather to [go with them].'

How sic misordour in this realme sould ring.
Sowtars and tailyeours thay ar far mair expert
In thair pure craft and in thair handie art,
Nor ar our prelatis in thair vocatioun:
I pray yow, sirs, mak reformatioun.

VERITIE
Alace, alace, quhat gars thir temporal kings
Into the Kirk of Christ admit sic doings?
My Lords, for lufe of Christs Passioun,
Of thir ignorants mak deprivatioun,
Quhilk in the court can do bot flatter and fleich,
And put into thair places that can preich.
Send furth and seik sum devoit, cunning clarks
That can steir up the peopill to gude warks.

CORRECTIOUN
As ye have done, madame, I am content.
Hoaw, Diligence pas hynd incontinent,
And seik out-throw all towns and cities:
And visie all the universities.
Bring us sum Doctours of Divinitie,
With licents[205] in the law and theologie,
With the maist cunning clarks in all this land.
Speid sune your way, and bring them heir fra hand.

DILIGENCE
Quhat gif I find sum halie provinciall,
Or minister of the gray freiris all,
Sall I bring them with me in cumpanie?

CORRECTIOUN
Cair thou nocht quhat estait sa ever he be,
Sa thay can teich and preich the veritie.
Maist cunning clarks with us is best beluifit,
To dignitie thay salbe first promuifit.
Quhidder thay be munk, channon, preist or freir,
Sa thay can preich, faill nocht to bring them heir.

DILIGENCE
Than fair-weill, sir, for I am at the flicht.
I pray the Lord to send yow all gude nicht.

Heir sall Diligence pas to the Palyeoun.

TEMPORALITIE
Sir, we beseik Your Soverane Celsitude
Of our dochtours to have compassioun.
Quhom wee may na way marie, be the Rude,
Without wee mak sum alienatioun
Of our land for thair supportatioun.[206]
For quhy the markit raisit bene sa hie
That prelats dochtours of this natioun,
Ar maryit with sic superfluitie,
Thay will nocht spair to gif twa thowsand pound,
With thair docthtours to ane nobill man,
In riches sa thay do superabound.
Bot we may nocht do sa, be Sanct Allane,[207]
Thir proud prelats our dochters sair may ban,[208]
That thay remaine at hame sa lang unmaryit;
Schir, let your barrouns do the best thay can,
Sum of our dochtours, I dreid, salbe miscaryit.

CORRECTIOUN
My Lord your complaint is richt ressonabill,
And richt sa to our dochtours profitabill;
I think, or I pas aff this natioun,
Of this mater till mak reformatiom

Heir sall enter Common Thift.

THIFT
Ga by the gait, man, let me gang.
How Devill came I into this thrang?
With sorrow I may sing my sang,
And I be taine.
For I have run baith nicht and day,
Throw speid of fut I gat away,
Gif I be kend heir, wallaway,
I will be slaine.

PAUPER
Quhat is thy name, man, be thy thrift?

3161 disorder, reign 3163 poor 3164 Than 3170 cajole 3171 those (who) 3172 devout, learned clerks 3173 stir up/inspire 3175 hence 3177 visit 3181 Hurry soon 3182 bishop 3183 (i.e. the Franciscans) 3186 of what estate 3187 so (long as) 3188 beloved 3189 promoted 3190 monk, canon 3192 I'm about to fly 3194 Majesty 3195 daughters 3196 marry off 3199 market, raised, high 3200 bishop's daughters 3201 excessive expense 3202 They (the bishops) 3204 They are so excessively wealthy 3207 unmarried 3208 barons 3209 ruined 3214 Get out of the way, pass 3215 (the) Devil, throng 3217 If, taken/arrested 3219 Though, foot, got 3220 recognized

205 Those licensed (by virtue of their Masters' degrees) to preach publicly.
206 'Unless we alienate [give away] some part of our lands to support them.'
207 St Allan (or Elia), a sixth-century Cornish/Breton saint.
208 'Our daughters may sorely curse these proud prelates'.

Thift
Huirsun, thay call me Common Thift:
For quhy I had na uther schift,
Sen I was borne.
In Eusdaill[209] was my dwelling place,
Mony ane wyfe gart I cry 'alace';
At my hand thay gat never grace,
Bot ay forlorne.

Sum sayis ane king is cum amang us,
That purpois to head and hang us:
That is na grace gif he may fang us
Bot on an pin.
Ring he, we theifis will get na gude,
I pray God and the Halie Rude,
He had bene smoird into his cude,
And all his kin.

Get this curst King me in his grippis,
My craig will wit quat weyis my hippis:
The Devill I gif his toung and lippis,
That of me tellis.[210]
Adew, I dar na langer tarie,
For, be I kend, thay will me carie,
And put me in ane fierie farie,
I se nocht ellis.

I raif, be Him that herryit Hell,
I had almaist forget my sell:
Will na gude fallow to me tell,
Quhair I may finde
The Earle of Rothus best haiknay?[211]
That was my earand heir away:
He is richt starck, as I heir say
And swift as winde.

Heir is my brydill and my spurris,
To gar him lance ovir land and furris
Micht I him get to Ewis-durris,[212]
I tak na cuir.
Of that hors micht I get ane sicht,
I haife na doubt yit or midnicht,
That he and I sould tak the flicht
Throch Dysert Mure.[213]

Of cumpanarie tell me, brother,
Quhilk is the richt way to the Strother?
I wald be welcum to my mother,
Gif I micht speid.
I wald gif baith my coat and bonet
To get my Lord Lindesayis broun jonet.[214]
War he beyond the watter of Annet,
We sould nocht dreid.

[*He discovers Oppressioun in the stocks.*]

Quhat now, Oppressioun, my maister deir!
Quhat mekill Devill hes brocht yow heir?
Maister, tell me the caus perqueir,
Quhat is that ye have done.

Oppressioun
Forsuith, the Kings Majestie
Hes set me heir as ye may se:
Micht I speik [with] Temporalitie,
He wald me releife sone.

I beseik yow, my brother deir,
Bot halfe ane houre for to sit heir.
Ye knaw that I was never sweir
Yow to defend.
Put in your leg into my place,
And heir I sweir, be Gods grace,
Yow to releife within schort space,
Syne let yow wend.

Thift
Than, maister deir, gif me your hand,
And mak to me ane faithfull band,
That ye sall cum agane fra hand,
Withoutin fail.

3224 alternative **3227** Many, I made cry out **3229** (were) always **3231** intends, behead **3232** seize **3234** If he reigns **3236** smothered, cradle **3238** If this cursed king gets me **3246** I'm raving **3251** errand in these parts **3252** strong **3254** bridle **3255** race, furrows **3257** I'd have no worries **3258** if I could get a sight **3262** Out of fellowship **3263** Struthers, south of Cupar **3268** Annat Burn (South Perthshire) **3272** whole reason **3277** relieve **3280** reluctant **3285** go on your way

209 Ewesdale, the valley of the river Ewes in Dumfriesshire, a lawless border region, home to John Armstrong (see 'Description of the 1540 Interlude', n. 55).
210 'My neck will know how much my hips weigh [i.e. as I am hanged]. I give [to] the Devil the tongue and lips of him/anyone who informs on me.'
211 'The Earl of Rothes's best riding-horse'. George Leslie, earl of Rothes (*c.* 1495–1558), was sheriff of Fife from 1540.
212 A pass linking Teviotdale and Ewesdale.
213 As Lyall observes, Dysart Moor (Fifeshire) lies on the road from Leslie House (Rothes's seat) to the nearest crossing of the river Forth at Kinghorn.
214 'My Lord Lindsay's brown jennet [a small horse].' The Lindsays, earls of Crawford, had their seat at Struthers Castle.

OPPRESSIOUN
Tak thair my hand richt faithfullie
Als I promit the[e] verelie,
To gif to the[e] ane cuppill of kye
[In Liddisdaill.[215]

Heir sall Common Thift put his feit in the stokkis and Oppressioun sall steill away and betra[y] him.

[OPPRESSIOUN]
Bruder, tak patience in thy pane,
For I sweir the[e], be Sanct Fillane,
We twa sall nevir meit agane,
In land nor toun.

THIFT
Maister, will ye[e] not keip conditioun,
And put me forth of this suspitioun?

OPPRESSIOUN
Na, nevir quhill I get remissioun.
A-dew to my companyeoun:

I sall commend the[e] to thy dame.

THIFT
Adew than, in the Divillis name,
For to be fals thinkis thow na schame,
To leif me in this pane?
Thow art ane loun, and that ane liddir.

OPPRESSIOUN
Bo, man, I will go to Baquihiddir.
It sall be Pasche, be Goddis moder,
Or evir we meit agane.]

Haif I nocht maid ane honest schift,
That hes betrasit Common Thift?
For thair is nocht under the lift
Ane curster cors.
I am richt sure that he and I
Within this hal[f] yeir craftely
Hes stolen ane thowsand scheip and ky,
By meiris and hors.

Wald God I war baith sound and haill,
Now liftit into Liddisdaill:
The Mers sould find me beif and kaill,[216]
Quhat rak of bread!
War I thair liftit with my lyfe,
The Devil sould stick me with ane knyfe
And ever I come againe to Fyfe
Quhill I war dead.

Adew, I leife the Devill amang yow,
That in his fingers he may fang yow,
With all leill men that dois belang yow.
For I may rew
That ever I came into this land,
For quhy ye may weill understand,
I gat na geir to turne my hand:
Yit anis, adew! [*Exit.*]

Heir sall Diligence convoy[217] the thrie Clarks.

DILIGENCE
Sir, I have brocht unto Your Excellence
Thir famous clarks of greit intelligence:
For to the common peopill thay can preich,
And in the scuilis in Latine toung can teich.
This is ane Doctour of Divinitie,
And thir twa Licents, men of gravitie.
I heare men say their conversatioun
Is maist in divine contemplatioun.

DOCTOUR
Grace, peace, and rest from the Hie Trinitie
Mot rest amang this godlie cumpanie:
Heir ar we cumde as your obedients,
For to fulfil your just commandements.
Quhat evir it please Your Grace us to command,
Sir, it sall be obeyit evin fra hand.

REX
Gud freinds, ye ar richt welcome to us all:
Sit down all thrie and geif us your counsall.

3291 promise 3292 cows 3294 Brother 3298 our agreement 3299 out, suspicion (of you) 3302 your wife 3306 a lazy one at that 3307 Balquhidder (Perthshire) 3308 Easter 3310 confession/trick 3311 have betrayed 3312 heavens 3313 more cursed (wicked) body 3316 sheep, cows 3317 Not counting mares 3319 lifted (transported) 3321 Who cares about 3325 Until 3328 who belong to you 3332 try my luck 3333 Once again, adieu 3337 schools 3340 speech/lifestyles 3341 Mostly involves 3343 May 3344 come 3347 obeyed

215 Liddisdale, like Ewesdale, was a valley in Dumfriesshire renowned for banditry.

216 'The Merse [a rich farming area in Berwickshire] should provide me with beef and kale [vegetables]'.

217 Bring in, escort.

CORRECTIOUN
Sir, I give yow baith counsal and command:
In your office use exercitioun:
First that ye gar search out throch all your land
Quha can nocht put to executioun
Thair office efter the institutioun
Of godlie lawis, conforme to thair vocatioun.
Put in thair places men of gude conditioun,
And this ye do without dilatioun.

Ye ar the head, sir, of this congregatioun,
Preordinat be God Omnipotent,
Quhilk hes me send to mak yow supportatioun,
Into the quhilk I salbe diligent.
And quha-saever beis inobedient,
And will nocht suffer for to be correctit,
Thay salbe all deposit incontinent,
And from your presence they sall be dejectit.

GUDE COUNSALL
Begin first at the Spritualtie,
And tak of them examinatioun
Gif they can use their divyne dewetie.
And als I mak yow supplicatioun,
All thay that hes thair offices misusit,
Of them make haistie deprivatioun,
Sa that the peopill be na mair abusit.

CORRECTIOUN
Ye ar ane prince of Spritualitie.
How have ye usit your office, now let se?

SPIRITUALITIE
My Lords, quhen was thair ony prelats wont
Of thair office till ony king mak count?[218]
Bot, of my office gif ye wald have the feill,
I let yaw wit I have usit it weil.
For I tak in my count twyse in the yeir,
Wanting nocht of my teind ane boll of beir.
I gat gude payment of my temporall lands,
My buttock-maill, my coattis, and my offrands,[219]
With all that dois perteine my benefice.
Consider now, my Lord, gif I be wyse.
I dar nocht marie contrair the common law.
Ane thing thair is, my Lord, that ye may knaw:
Howbeit I dar nocht plainlie spouse ane wyfe,
Yit concubeins I have had four or fyfe.
And to my sons I have givin rich rewairds
And all my dochters maryit upon lairds.
I let yow wit, my Lord, I am na fuill,
For quhy I ryde upon ane amland muill,
Thair is na temporall lord in all this land,
That maks sic cheir, I let yow understand.
And als, my Lord, I gif with gude intentioun,
To divers temporall lords ane yeirlie pensioun,
To that intent that thay with al thair hart,
In richt and wrang sal plainlie tak my part.
Now have I tauld yow, sir, on my best ways,
How that I have exercit my office.

CORRECTIOUN
I weind your office had bene for til preich,
And Gods law to the peopill teich.
Quhairfoir weir ye that mytour, ye me tell?

SPIRITUALITIE
I wat nocht, man, be Him that herryit Hel.

CORRECTIOUN
That dois betakin that ye with gude intent
Sould teich and preich the Auld and New
    Testament.

SPIRITUALITIE
I have ane freir to preiche into my place:
Of my office ye heare na mair quhill Pasche.

CHASTITIE
My Lords, this Abbot and this Priores,
Thay scorne thair gods: this is my reason quhy
Thay beare an habite of feinyeit halines,
And in thair deid thay do the contrary.
For to live chaist thay vow solemnitly,
Bot fra that thay be sikker of thair bowis[220]
Thay live in huirdome and in harlotry.
Examine them, sir, how thay observe thair vowis.

3351 exert yourselves 3353 into practice 3354 after 3355 relevant to 3357 delay 3359 Preordained 3360 sent me to aid you 3362 whoever is 3364 deposed 3365 thrown out 3368 duty 3370 misused 3377 an understanding 3378 I'll let you know 3379 make my accounts 3380 Lacking, measure of barley 3381 from 3383 (to) my 3386 marry 3388 marry 3390 to lairds (landowners) 3391 no fool 3392 while, ambling mule 3394 has so pleasant a lifestyle 3395 give 3396 yearly 3400 exercised 3401 believed 3403 wear, mitre 3404 don't know 3405 betoken (symbolize) 3407 in 3408 until Easter 3411 feigned 3412 deeds 3413 solemnly

218 'When did prelates ever have to account for their activities to kings?'

219 Buttock-mail: a fine paid by those found guilty of fornication; coats: a tax for ratifying wills, and offerings.

220 'But, from the moment that they are sure of their papal bulls [establishing them in office]'.

Correctioun
Sir Scribe, ye sall at Chastities requeist
Pas and exame yon thrie in gudlie haist.

Scribe
Father Abbot, this counsall bids me speir
How ye have usit your abbay thay wald heir.
And als thir Kings hes givin to me commissioun
Of your office for to mak inquisitioun.

Abbot
Tuiching my office, I say to yow plainlie,
My monks and I, we leif richt easelie:
Thair is na monks from Carrick to Carraill[221]
That fairs better and drinks mair helsum aill.
My prior is ane man of great devotioun:
Thairfoir daylie he gets ane double portioun.

Scribe
My Lords, how have ye keipit your thrie vows?[222]

Abbot
Indeid richt weill, till I gat hame my bows.
In my abbay quhen I was sure professour,
Then did I liefe as did my predecessour.
My paramours is baith als fat and fair,
As ony wench into the toun of Air.
I send my sons to Pareis to the scullis,
I traist in God that thay salbe na fuillis.
And all my douchters I have weill providit,
Now judge ye gif my office be weill gydit.

Scribe
Maister Person, schaw us gif ye can preich.

Person
Thocht I preich not, I can play at the caiche.
I wait thair is nocht ane amang yow all
Mair ferilie can play at the fut-ball;
And for the carts, the tabils, and the dyse,
Above all persouns I may beir the pryse.
Our round bonats we mak them now four-nuickit,
Of richt fyne stuiff, gif yow list cum and luik it.
Of my office I have declarit to the[e]:
Speir quhat ye pleis, ye get na mair of me.

Scribe
Quhat say ye now, my Ladie Priores?
How have ye usit your office, can ye ges?
Quhat was the caus ye refusit herbrie
To this young lustie ladie, Chastitie?

Priores
I wald have harborit hir with gude intent,
Bot my complexioun thairto wald not assent:
I do my office efter auld use and wount,
To your Parliament I will mak na mair count.

Veritie
Now caus sum of your cunning clarks
Quhilk ar expert in heavinlie warks,
And men fulfillit with charitie
That can weill preiche the veritie,
And gif to sum of them command
Ane sermon for to make fra-hand.

Correctioun
As ye have said, I am content
To gar sum preich incontinent.

Pausa.

Magister noster, I ken how ye can teiche,
Into the scuillis and that richt ornatlie:
I pray yow now that ye wald please to preiche,
In Inglisch toung, land folk to edifie.[223]

Doctour
Soverane, I sall obey yow humbillie,
With ane schort sermon presentlie in this place:
And schaw the word of God unfeinyeitlie,
And sinceirlie as God will give me grace.

Heir sall the Doctour pas to the pulpit and say:

Si vis ad vitam ingredi, serva mandata.[224]

3423 Touching (concerning) 3424 easily/comfortably 3428 portion (of food) 3429 kept 3430 (papal) bulls 3431 securely installed 3432 live 3433 mistresses are 3434 Ayr 3435 Paris, schools 3437 provided (for) 3440 catch (hand tennis) 3442 nimbly, football 3443 cards, backgammon, dice 3444 prize (i.e. I am the best) 3445 bonnets, four-cornered 3446 material, look (at) 3450 remember 3451 shelter 3454 nature 3455 old custom, desire 3456 account 3458 spiritual matters 3459 filled 3465 our teacher 3466 ornately/skilfully 3471 unfeignedly

221 'From Carrick [Argyllshire, on the west coast of Scotland] to Crail [Fifeshire, on the east coast]'.

222 The three vows were of poverty, chastity, and obedience.

223 'In lowland Scots to edify the country folk'.

224 'If you will enter into life, keep the Commandments'. Matthew 19:17.

Devoit peopill, Sanct Paull the preichour sayis,[225]
The fervent luifis and fatherlie pitie
Quha God almichtie hes schawin mony wayis
To man in his corrupt fragilitie,
Exceids all luife in Earth, sa far that we
May never to God mak recompence conding:
As quha sa lists to reid the veritie,
In Halie Scripture he may find this thing.

Sic Deus dilexit mundum.[226]

Tuiching nathing the great prerogative
Quhilk God to man in his creatioun lent;
How man of nocht creat superlative
Was to the image of God Omnipotent.[227]
Let us consider that speciall luife ingent
God had to man quhen our foir-father fell,
Drawing us all in his loynis immanent,[228]
Captive from gloir in thirlage to the Hel.

Quhen angels fell, thair miserabil ruyne
Was never restorit: bot for our miserie,
The Son of God, Secund Persone Divyne,
In ane pure virgin tuke humanitie.
Syne for our saik great harmis suffered He,
In fasting, walking, in preiching, cauld, and heit,
And at the last ane schamefull death deit He;
Betwix twa theifis on Croce He yeild the spreit.[229]

And quhair an drop of His maist precious blude
Was recompence sufficient and conding
Ane thowsand warlds to ransoun from that wod
Infernall feind, Sathan, notwithstanding
He luifit us sa that for our ransoning,
He sched furth all the blude of His bodie,
Riven, rent, and sair wondit quhair He did hing,
Naild on the Croce on the Mont Calvery.

Et copiosa apud eum redemptio.[230]

O cruell death, be the[e] the venemous
Dragon, the Devill infirnall, lost his pray:
Be the[e] the stinkand, mirk, contageous,
Deip pit of Hell mankynd escaipit fray.
Be the[e] the port of Paradice alsway
Was patent maid unto the Heavin sa hie:
Opinnit to man and maid ane reddie way,
To gloir eternall with th'Haly Trinitie.

And yit, for all this luife incomparabill,
God askis na rewaird fra us againe
Bot luife for luife. In His command, but fabill,
Conteinit ar all haill the lawis ten:
Baith ald and new, and commandements ilk ane.
Luife bene the ledder quhilk hes bot steppis twa,
Be quhilk we may clim up to lyfe againe,
Out of this vaill of miserie and wa.

Diliges Dominum Deum tuum ex toto corde tuo,
et proximum tuum sicut teipsum: in his duobus
mandatis, etc.[231]

The first step, suithlie, of this ledder is
To luife thy God as the fontaine and well
Of luife and grace: and the secund, I wis,
To luife thy nichbour as thou luffis thy sel.
Quha tynis ane stop of thir twa gais to Hel,
Bot he repent and turne to Christe anone.
Hauld this na fabill,[232] the halie Evangell
Bears in effect thir words everie one.

Si vis ad vitam ingredi, serva mandata Dei.[233]

Thay tyne thir steps all thay quha ever did sin
In pryde, invy, in ire and lecherie,
In covetice, or ony extreme win,
Into sweirnes, or into gluttonie;
Or quha dois nocht the deids of mercie,
Gif hungrie meit and gif the naikit clayis.[234]

3475 loves 3476 (in) many 3478 exceeds 3479 condign (sufficient) 3483 without mentioning 3487 innate love 3488 forefather (Adam) 3490 into slavery 3491 miserable 3492 restored 3494 took (on) 3496 cold, heat 3497 He died 3500 condign 3501 world, mad 3502 Satan 3503 loved, ransoming 3505 sorely wounded 3508 by 3509 prey 3510 stinking, dark 3511 escaped from 3512 gate, forever 3513 made open 3514 opened, accessible 3517 in return 3518 without lie 3519 Are contained, laws 3521 ladder, only two steps 3523 vale, woe 3529 indeed 3531 loses, step, goes 3532 Unless 3536 lose 3537 envy 3538 profit (i.e. greed) 3539 sloth

225 Lyall suggests the allusion is to Ephesians 2:3–8.
226 'For God so loved the world'. John 3:16.
227 'How man was created perfectly [from nothing] in the image of God Omnipotent.'
228 i.e. as Adam fell he brought the whole human race (already immanent in his loins) with him.
229 'Between two thieves, on a Cross, He yielded up His spirit.'
230 '[For with the Lord there is mercy] and with Him is plenteous redemption.' Psalms 130:7.
231 'Love the Lord thy God with all thy heart' (Matthew 22:37) 'and [love] thy neighbour as thy self. In these two commandments [hang all the law and the Prophets]'. Matthew 22:39–40.
232 'Don't think this is just a fairy story'.
233 See l. 3473, above.
234 'Give the hungry food and the naked clothes.' For the corporal acts of mercy (the responsibility of all good Christians), see Matthew 25:35–6.

Person
Now, walloway! Thinks thou na schame to lie?
I trow the Devill a word is trew thou sayis.

Thou sayis thair is bot twa steppis to the Heavin,
Quha failyes them man backwarts fall in Hell:
I wait it is ten thowsand mylis and sevin,
Gif it be na mair, I do it upon thy sell.[235]
Schort-leggit men I se, be Bryds bell,
Will nevir cum thair, thay steppis bene sa wyde.
Gif thay be the words of the Evangell,
The spirituall men hes mister of ane gyde.

Abbot
And I beleif that cruikit men and blinde
Sall never get up upon sa hich ane ledder.
By my gude faith, I dreid to ly behinde,
Without God draw me up into ane tedder.
Quhat and I fal? Than I will break my bledder.
And I cum thair this day, the Devill speid me,
Except God make me lichter nor ane fedder,
Or send me doun gude widcok wingis to flie.

Person
Cum doun, dastart, and gang sell draiff,
I understand nocht quhat thow said.
Thy words war nather corne nor caiff,
I walde thy toung againe war laide.
Quhair thou sayis pryde is deidlie sin,
I say pryde is bot honestie:
And covetice of warldlie win
Is bot wisdome, I say for me;

Ire, hardines, and gluttonie
Is nathing ellis but lyfis fude:
The naturall sin of lecherie
Is bot trew luife: all thir ar gude.

Doctour
God and the Kirk hes givin command
That all gude Christian men refuse them.

Person
Bot, war thay sin, I understand,
We men of Kirk wald never use them.

Doctour
Brother, I pray the Trinitie
Your faith and charitie to support,
Causand yow knaw the veritie,
That ye your subjects may comfort.
To your prayers, peopill, I recommend
The rewlars of this nobill regioun:
That our Lord God His grace mot to them send,
On trespassours to mak punitioun.
Prayand to God from feinds yow defend,
And of your sins to gif yow full remissioun.
I say na mair, to God I yow commend.

Heir Diligence spyis the Freir roundand[236] *to the Prelate* [*Spiritualitie*].

Diligence
My lords, I persave that the Sprituall Stait
Be way of deid purpois to mak debait.[237]
For, be the counsall of yon flattrand freir,
Thay purpois to mak all this toun on steir.

First Licent
Traist ye that thay wilbe inobedient
To that quhilk is decreitit in Parliament?

Diligence
Thay se the Paip, with awful ordinance,
Makis weir against the michtie King of France:[238]
Richt sa thay think that prelats suld nocht sunyie
Be way of deid defend thair patrimonie.

I Licent
I pray the[e], brother, gar me understand
Quhair ever Christ possessit ane fut of land.

Diligence
Yea, that he did, father, withoutin fail,
For Christ Jesus was King of Israell.

I Licent
I grant that Christ was King abufe al Kings,
Bot he mellit never with temporall things:
As he hes plainlie done declair Him-sell,

3543 I don't believe 3545 fails 3548 Short-legged, St Bridget's 3551 need 3552 disabled 3553 high 3554 I fear I'll be left behind 3555 Unless, with, rope 3556 if, bladder 3558 lighter than a feather 3559 woodcock's 3560 go sell pigswill 3562 neither, chaff 3563 were still 3565 only 3566 profit 3568 Anger (is) strength 3569 life's food 3571 love 3578 Causing you (to) 3590 stir up the whole town 3591 Do you think 3592 decreed 3593 great power/ artillery 3595 In the same way, delay 3596 Physically to 3598 possessed, (square) foot 3601 above 3602 meddled 3603 Himself plainly declared

235 'I prove it by your example' (presumably the Doctor is a short man).
236 Whispering.
237 'Intend to put their opposition into practice.'
238 The forces of Pope Julius III fought with those of Henry II of France around Parma in 1551–2.

As thou may reid in his Halie Evangell;[239]
'Birds hes thair nests, and tods hes thair den,
Bot Christ Jesus, the Saviour of men,
In all this warld hes nocht ane penny braid
Quhair on He may repois His heavinlie head.'

DILIGENCE
And is that trew?

I LICENT
Yes, brother, be Alhallows:
Christ Jesus had na propertie bot the gallows,
And left not quhen He yeildit up the spreit
To by Himself ane simpill winding-scheit.[240]

DILIGENCE
Christs successours, I understand,
Thinks na schame to have temporall land.
Father, thay have na will, I yow assure,
In this warld to be indigent and pure.
Bot, sir, sen ye ar callit sapient,
Declair to me the caus with trew intent
Quhy that my lustie Ladie Veritie
Hes nocht bene weill treatit in this cuntrie?

BATCHELER
Forsuith, quhair prelats uses the counsall
Of beggand freirs in monie regioun,
And thay prelats with princes principall,
The veritie, but doubt, is trampit doun,
And common-weill put to confusioun.
Gif this be trew to yow I me report:
Thairfoir, my lords, mak reformatioun
Or ye depart, hairtlie I yow exhort.

Sirs, freirs wald never, I yow assure,
That ony prelats usit preiching.
And prelats tuke on them that cure,
Freirs wald get nathing for thair fleiching.
Thairfoir, I counsall yow fra hand,
Banische yon freir out of this land,
And that incontinent.

Do ye nocht sa, withoutin weir,
He will mak all this toun on steir,
I knaw his fals intent.
Yon Priores, withoutin fabill,
I think scho is nocht profitabill

For Christis regioun.
To begin reformatioun,
Mak of them deprivatioun,
This is my opinioun.

I SERGEANT
Sir, pleis ye that we twa invaid them,
And ye sall se us sone degraid them
Of cowll and chaplarie.

CORRECTIOUN
Pas on, I am richt weill content.
Syne banische them incontinent
Out of this cuntrie.

I SERGEANT
Cum on, sir freir, and be nocht fleyit,
The King, our maister, mon be obeyit,
Bot ye sall have na harme.
Gif ye wald travell fra toun to toun,
I think this hude and heavie goun
Will hald your wambe ovir warme.

FLATTERIE
Now quhat is this that thir monster meins?
I am exemptit fra kings and queens,
And fra all humane law.

II SERGEANT
Tak ye the hude and I the gown.
This limmer luiks als lyke ane lown
As any that ever I saw.

I SERGEANT
Thir freirs to chaip punitioun
Haulds them at their exemptioun,
And na man will obey:
Thay ar exempt I yow assure
Baith fra paip, kyng, and empreour,
And that maks all the pley.

3605 foxes 3607 breadth 3608 Whereon, repose 3609 by all the saints 3610 (i.e. the Cross) 3613 (i.e. the clergy) 3616 poor 3617 called wise 3622 many a region 3623 (consult) with 3624 trampled 3625 ruined 3629 never want 3630 should practise 3631 If, responsibility 3632 flattery 3636 doubt 3645 despoil 3647 cowl, scapulary (monastic surplice) 3651 afraid 3656 will keep your belly too hot 3657 intends 3663 escape 3664 Maintain that they're exempt 3668 causes all the problems

[239] What follows is a paraphrase of Luke 9:58.
[240] '[Not enough money] to buy Himself a simple winding-sheet [shroud].'

II SERGEANT
On Duimsday, quhen Christ sall say,
'Venite benedicti'[241]
The freirs will say without delay,
'Nos sumus exempti.'

Heir sall thay spuilye[242] *Flattrie of the Freirs habite.*

GUDE COUNSALL
Sir, be the Halie Trinitie,
This same is feinyeit Flattrie,
I ken him be his face.
Beleivand for to get promotioun,
He said that his name was Devotioun,
And sa begylit Your Grace.

I SERGEANT
Cum on, my ladie Priores,
We sall leir yow to dance,
And that within ane lytill space,
Ane new pavin of France.

Heir sall thay spuilye the Priores, and scho sall have ane kirtill of silk under hir habite.

Now brother, be the Masse,
By my judgement I think
This halie Priores
Is turnit in ane cowclink.

PRIORES
I gif my freinds my malisoun,
That me compellit to be ane nun,
And wald nocht let me marie.
It was my freinds greadines
That gart me be ane Priores.
Now hartlie them I warie.

Howbeit that nunnis sing nichts and dayis,
Thair hart waitis nocht quhat thair mouth sayis,
The suith I yow declair.
Makand yow intimatioun,
To Christis congregatioun,
Nunnis ar nocht necessair.

Bot I sall do the best I can,
And marie sum gude honest man,
And brew gude aill and tun.
Mariage, be my opinioun,
It is better religioun,
As to be freir or nun.

FLATTERIE
My Lords, for Gods saik, let not hang me,
Howbeit that widdiefows wald wrang me.
I can mak na debait
To win my meat at pleuch nor harrowis,
Bot I sall help to hang my marrowis,
Both Falset and Dissait.

CORRECTIOUN
Than pas thy way and greath the gallous;
Syne help for to hang up thy fallowis:
Tha gets na uther grace.

FLATTERIE
Of that office I am content,
Bot our prelates I dread repent,
Be I fleimde from thir face.

Heir sall Flatterie sit besyde his marrowis.

DISSAIT
Now, Flattrie, my auld companyeoun,
Quhat dois yon King Correctioun?
Knawis thou nocht his intent?
Declair to us of thy novellis.

FLATTERIE
Ye'ill all be hangit, I se nocht ellis,
And that incontinent.

DISSAIT
Now, walloway, will ye gar hang us?
The Devill brocht yon curst King amang us,
For mekill sturt and stryfe

FLATTERIE
I had bene put to deid amang yow,
War nocht I tuke on hand till hang yow,
And sa I saifit my lyfe.

I heir them say thay will cry doun
All freirs and nunnis in this regioun,
So far as I can feill,
Becaus thay ar nocht necessair,

3672 'We are exempt.' 3681 time 3682 pavane (a court dance) 3686 turned into a whore 3687 curse 3688 Who compelled me 3689 marry 3692 curse 3694 knows 3696 Intimating to you 3698 not necessary 3701 ale, barrel (it) 3704 Than to be a 3706 gallowsbirds 3707 I am not able 3708 food, plough, harrow 3709 fellows 3711 prepare, gallows 3716 driven 3720 news 3721 You'll, no alternative 3727 were it not that, took 3728 saved

[241] 'Come, ye blessed'. Matthew 25:34.

[242] Despoil, strip.

And als thay think thay ar contrair
To Johne the Common-weill.

Heir sal the Kings and the Temporal Stait round[243] togider.

CORRECTIOUN
With the advice of King Humanitie,
Heir I determine with rype advysement,
That all thir prelats sall deprivit be,
And be decreit of this present Parliament,
That thir thrie cunning clarks sapient,
Immediatlie thair places sall posses,
Becaus that they have bene sa negligent
Suffring the word of God for till decres.

REX
As ye have said, but dout it salbe done:
Pas to and mak this interchainging sone.

The Kings servants lays hands on the thrie Prelates and says:

WANTONNES
My Lords, we pray yaw to be patient,
For we will do the Kings commandement.

SPIRITUALITIE
I mak ane vow to God, and ye us handill,
Ye salbe curst and gragit with buik and candil:
Syne we sall pas unto the Paip and pleinyie,
And to the Devill of Hell condemne this meinye,
For quhy sic reformatioun as I weine,
Into Scotland was never hard nor seine.

Heir sall thay spuilye them[244] with silence and put thair habite on the thrie Clarks.

MERCHAND
We mervell of yow paintit sepulturis,[245]
That was sa bauld for to accept sic cuiris,
With glorious habite rydand upon your muillis,
Now men may se ye ar bot verie fuillis.

SPIRITUALITE
We say the kings war greiter fuillis nor we,
That us promovit to sa great dignitie.

ABBOT
Thair is ane thowsand in the Kirk, but doubt,
Sic fuillis as we, gif thay war weill socht out.
Now, brother, sen it may na better be,
Let us ga soup with Sensualitie.

Heir sall thay pas to Sensualitie.

SPIRITUALITIE
Madame, I pray you mak us thrie gude cheir,
We cure nocht to remaine with yow all yeir.

SENSUALITIE
Pas fra us, fuillis, be Him that hes us wrocht,
Ye ludge nocht heir becaus I knaw yow nocht.

SPIRITUALITE
Sir Covetice, will ye also misken me?
I wait richt weill ye wil baith gif and len me.
Speid hand, my freind, spair nocht to break the lockis:
Gif me ane thowsand crouns out of my box.

COVETICE
Quhairfoir, sir fuil, gif yow ane thowsand crowns?
Ga hence! Ye seime to be thrie verie lowns.

SPIRITUALITE
I se nocht els, brother, withoutin faill,
Bot this fals warld is turnit top ovir taill.
Sen all is vaine that is under the lift,
To win our meat we man mak uther schift.
With our labour except we mak debait,
I dreid full sair we want baith drink and meat.

PERSON
Gif with our labour we man us defend,
Then let us gang quhair we war never kend.

SPIRITUALITIE
I wyte thir freirs that I am thus abusit,
For by thair counsall I have bene confusit.
Thay gart me trow it suffysit, allace,
To gar them plainlie preich into my place.

3738 by decree 3739 wise 3742 decline 3744 exchange (of roles) 3747 If you manhandle us 3748 excommunicated 3749 complain 3750 company 3754 responsibilities 3755 riding, mules 3758 promoted 3760 sought 3762 sup (dine) 3763 (i.e. entertain us) 3764 We wouldn't mind remaining 3767 refuse to acknowledge 3768 give, lend (to) me 3769 Hurry 3775 heavens 3776 must, other plans 3777 unless we put ourselves to work 3778 (will) lack 3779 provide for ourselves 3780 known 3781 blame 3782 ruined 3783 made me believe it was enough 3784 in

243 Whisper.

244 i.e. the Bischop, Abbot, and Person.

245 'We are amazed at you painted [whited] sepulchres [i.e. hypocrites]'. See Matthew 23:27.

ABBOT
Allace, this reformatioun I may warie,
For I have yit twa dochters for to marie:
And thay ar baith contractit, be the Rude,
And waits nocht how to pay thair tocher-gude.

PERSON
The Devill mak cair for this unhappie chance,
For I am young, and thinks to pas to France,
And tak wages amang the men of weir,
And win my living with my sword and speir.

The Bischop, Abbot, Persone, and Priores depairts altogidder.

GUDE COUNSALL
Or ye depairt, sir, aff this regioun,
Gif Johne the Common-weill ane gay garmoun;
Becaus the Common-weill hes bene overluikit,
That is the caus that Common-weill is cruikit.
With singular profeit he hes bene sa supprysit,[246]
That he is baith cauld, naikit, and disgysit.

CORRECTIOUN
As ye have said, father, I am content.
Sergeants, gif Johne ane new abuilyement
Of sating, damais, or of the velvot fyne.
And gif him place in our Parliament syne.

Heir sal thay cleith[247] Johne the Common-weil gorgeouslie, and set him doun amang them in the Parliament.

All verteous peopill now may be rejoisit,
Sen Common-weill hes gottin ane gay garmoun,
And ignorants out of the Kirk deposit:
Devoit doctours and clarks of renoun
Now in the Kirk sall have dominioun;
And Gude Counsall with Ladie Veritie
Ar profest with our Kings Majestie.

Blist is that realme that hes ane prudent king,
Quhilk dois delyte to heir the veritie,
Punisching thame that plainlie dois maling,
Contrair the Common-weill and equitie.
Thair may na peopill have prosperitie,
Quhair ignorance hes the dominioun,
And common-weil be tirants trampit doun.

Pausa.

Now, maisters, ye sall heir, incontinent,
At great leysour in your presence proclamit
The nobill Acts of our Parliament,
Of quhilk we neid nocht for to be aschamit.
Cum heir, trumpet, and sound your warning tone,
That ever man may knaw quhat we have done.

Heir sall Diligence with the Scribe and the Trumpet pas to the pulpit and proclame the Actis.

[DILIGENCE]
The First Act: It is devysit be thir prudent Kings,
Correctioun and King Humanitie,
That thair leigis induring all thair ringis,
With the avyce of the Estaits Thrie,
Sall manfullie defend and fortifie
The Kirk of Christ and his religioun,
Without dissimulance or hypocrisie,
Under the paine of thair punitioun.

2. Als thay will that the Acts honorabill
Maid be our Prince in the last Parliament,
Becaus thay ar baith gude and profitabill,
Thay will that everie man be diligent
Them till observe with unfeinyeit intent.
Quha disobeyis inobedientlie
Be thir lawis but doubt thay sall repent,
And painis conteinit thairin sall underly.[248]

3. And als the Common-weil for til advance,
It is statute that all the temporall lands
Be set in few, efter the forme of France,
Till verteous men that labours with thair hands:
Resonabillie restrictit with sic bands
That they do service nevertheles
And to be subject ay under the wands,
That riches may with policie incres.

4. Item, this prudent Parliament hes devysit,
Gif lords halds under thair dominioun
Theifis, quhair throch puir peopil bein supprisit,
For them thay sall make answeir to the Croun,
And to the pure mak restitutioun,
Without thay put them in the judges hands,

3785 curse 3787 contracted 3788 I know not, dowry 3791 war 3794 garment 3795 neglected 3796 crooked (deformed) 3798 cold, disfigured 3800 garment 3801 satin, damask, velvet 3809 employed 3810 blessed 3812 do evil 3813 contrary to 3816 by tyrants (is) trampled 3818 leisure 3820 ashamed 3821 note 3825 subjects, throughout, reigns 3829 dissimulation 3836 Whoever 3840 is now made law 3841 feu, following the practice 3843 Reasonably, such obligation 3844 (military) service 3845 always subject to due authority 3846 increase (prosper) 3849 oppressed

[246] 'He has been brought down by the personal greed [of others]'.

[247] Clothe.

[248] 'And shall be subject to the penalties contained in those Acts.'

For thair default to suffer punitioun,
Sa that na theffis remaine within thair lands.

5. To that intent that justice sould incres,
It is concludit in this Parliament,
That into Elgin or into Innernesse,[249]
Sall be ane sute of clarks sapient,
Togidder with ane prudent Precident,
To do justice in all the norther airtis,[250]
Sa equallie without impediment,
That thay neid nocht seik justice in thir pairts.

6. With licence of the Kirks halines,
That justice may be done continuallie,
All the maters of Scotland, mair and les,
To thir twa famous saits perpetuallie
Salbe directit, becaus men seis plainlie
Thir wantoun nunnis ar na way necessair
Till Common-weill, nor yit to the glorie
Of Christs Kirk, thocht thay be fat and fair,

And als that fragill ordour feminine
Will nocht be missit in Christs religioun,
Thair rents usit till ane better fyne,
For common-weill of all this regioun,
Ilk Senature for that erectioun,[251]
For the uphalding of thair gravitie,
Sall have fyve hundreth mark of pensioun:
And also bot twa sall thair nummer be.

Into the north saxteine sall thair remaine,
Saxtein rycht sa in our maist famous toun
Of Edinburgh, to serve our Soveraine,
Chosen without partiall affectioun
Of the maist cunning clarks of this regioun;
Thair Chancellar chosen of ane famous clark,
Ane cunning man of great perfectioun,
And for his pensioun have ane thowsand mark.

7. It is devysit in this Parliament,
From this day furth na mater temporall
(Our new prelats thairto hes done consent)
Cum befoir judges consistoriall,
Quhilk hes bene sa prolixt and partiall
To the great hurt of the communitie.
Let temporall men seik judges temporall,
And splrituall men to spritualitie.

8. Na benefice beis giffin in tyme cumming
Bot to men of gude eruditioun,
Expert in the Halie Scripture and cunning,
And that they be of gude conditioun,
Of publick vices but suspitioun,[252]
And qualefiet richt prudentlie to preich
To thair awin folk, baith into land and toun,
Or ellis in famous scuillis for to teich.

9. And als, becaus of the great pluralitie
Of ignorant preists, ma then ane legioun,
Quhair throch of teicheouris the heich dignitie
Is vilipendit in ilk regioun,
Thairfoir our court hes maid provisioun
That na b[i]shops mak teichours in tyme cumming,
Except men of gude eruditioun,
And for preistheid qualefeit and cunning.

Siclyke, as ye se in the borrows toun
Ane tailyeour is nocht sufferit to remaine
Without he can mak doublet, coat, and gown,
He man gang till his prenteischip againe:
Bischops sould nocht ressave, me think certaine,
Into the Kirk except ane cunning clark.
Ane idiot preist Esay compaireth, plaine,
Till ane dum dogge that can nocht byte nor bark.[253]

10. From this day furth se na prelats pretend,
Under the paine of inobedience,
At prince or paip to purchase ane command
Againe the kow becaus it dois offence.
Till ony preist we think sufficience
Ane benefice for to serve God withal.
Twa prelacies sall na man have from thence,
Without that he be of the blude royall.

11. Item, this prudent counsall hes concludit,
Sa that our haly vickars be nocht wraith,

3855 should 3858 panel 3859 president 3866 seats (i.e. Elgin or Inverness) 3872 missed 3873 end (purpose) 3876 dignity/position 3877 a salary of 500 marks 3878 there shall be only two (colleges) 3879 sixteen (judges) 3889 have consented 3891 long-winded (complicated) 3895 shall be given in future 3900 qualified 3901 countryside 3905 teachers 3906 despised 3908 appoint 3911 Just as, burgh 3912 permitted 3914 apprenticeship 3915 admit 3921 *commendam* (extra benefice) 3922 In the hope of 3925 bishoprics

249 In Elgin (in modern Moray) or Inverness (on the Moray Firth).

250 'Northern regions'. The Act proposes to establish a second college of justice to serve northern Scotland, thus making the courts more accessible to those in the highland regions.

251 'Each member of that creation [i.e. the new northern college of justice]'.

252 'With no hint of scandal attached to them'.

253 'His watchmen are blind, they are all ignorant, they are all dumb dogs, they cannot bark, lying down, loving to slumber.' Isaiah 56:10, a favourite text among reformers with which to berate failing clergymen.

From this day furth thay salbe cleane denudit
Baith of corspresent cow, and umest claith,
To pure commons becaus it hath done skaith.
And, mairover, we think it lytill force,
Howbeit the barrouns thairto will be laith,
From thine-furth thay sall want thair hyrald hors.

12. It is decreit that in this Parliament
Ilk bischop, minister, priour, and persoun,
To the effect thay may tak better tent
To saulis under thair dominioun,
Efter the forme of thair foundatioun,
Ilk bischop, in his diosie sall remaine:
And everilk persone in his parachoun,
Teiching thair folk from vices to refraine.

13. Becaus that clarks our substance dois consume,
For bils and proces of thair prelacies,[254]
Thairfoir thair sall na money ga to Rome
From this day furth [f]or any benefice,
Bot gif it be for greit archbischopries.
As for the rest, na money gais at all
For the incressing of thair dignities,
Na mair nor did to Peter nor to Paull.

14. Considering that our preists for the maist part
Thay want the gift of chastitie, we se,
Cupido hes sa perst them throch the hart,
We grant them licence and frie libertie
That thay may have fair virgins to thair wyfis,
And sa keip matrimoniall chastitie,
And nocht in huirdome for to leid thair lyfis.

15. This Parliament richt sa hes done conclude
From this day forth our barrouns temporall
Sall na mair mix thair nobil ancient blude
With bastard bairns of Stait Spirituall:
Ilk Stait amang thair awin selfis marie sall.
Gif nobils marie with the spritualitie,
From thyne subject thay salbe, and all
Sal be degraithit of thair nobilitie,

And from amang the nobils cancellit,
Unto the tyme thay by thair libertie,
Rehabilit be the civill magistrate.
And sa sall marie the spiritualitie:
Bischops with bischops sall mak affinitie,
Abbots and priors with the priores,
As Bischop Annas in Scripture we may se
Maryit his dochter on Bischop Caiphas.[255]

Now have ye heard the Acts honorabill
Devysit in this present Parliament,
To Common-weill we think [it] agreabill.
All faithful folk sould heirof be content
Them till observe with hartlie trew intent.
I wait nane will against our Acts rebell,
Nor till our law be inobedient,
Bot Plutois band the potent prince of Hell.

Heir sall Pauper cum befoir the King and say:

PAUPER
I gif yow my braid bennesoun,
That hes givin Common-weill a goun.
I wald nocht for ane pair of plackis,
Ye had nocht maid thir nobill Actis.
I pray to God and sweit Sanct Geill
To gif yow grace to use them weill:
Wer thay weill keipit, I understand,
It war great honour to Scotland.
It had bene als gude ye had sleipit,
As to mak Acts and be nocht keipit.
Bot I beseik yow for Allhallows,
To heid Dissait and hang his fellows,
And banische Flattrie aff the toun,
For thair was never sic ane loun.
That beand done, I hauld it best
That everie man ga to his rest.

CORRECTIOUN
As thou hes said, it salbe done:
Suyith, Sergeants, hang yon swingeours sone.

Heir sal the Sergeants lous[256] the presoners out of the stocks and leid them to the gallows.

I SERGEANT
Cum heir, sir Theif, cum heir, cum heir.
Quhen war ye wont to be sa sweir?

3929 deprived 3930 (i.e. the mortuary fees) 3931 caused harm 3932 matters little 3933 loath (unhappy) 3934 henceforth, heriot horse 3935 decreed 3938 souls 3939 According to the terms 3943 wealth, use up 3947 Unless 3952 lack 3953 Cupid, pierced 3956 as 3962 marry within their own estate 3964 Thereafter, subject (to this law) 3965 degraded/deprived 3966 expelled 3968 (And are) rehabilitated/restored 3969 (i.e. among themselves) 3970 alliance 3973 to 3979 believe no one 3981 the followers of Pluto 3982 blessing 3984 fourpenny coins 3988 kept 3989 would (be) 3990 (But) it 3991 (they) be not kept 3993 behead 3996 being 3999 those villains 4001 reluctant

[254] i.e. with the costly process of formalizing their appointment to a bishopric in the Roman courts.

[255] See the York pageant of *The Conspiracy*, above.

[256] Loose.

To hunt caittell ye war ay speidie,
Thairfoir ye sall weave in ane widdie.

Thift
Man I be hangit? Allace, allace!
Is thair nane heir may get me grace?
Yit, or I die, gif me ane drink.

I Sergeant
Fy, huirsun carle. I feil ane stink.

Thift
Thocht I wald nocht that it war wittin,
Sir, in gude faith I am [beshittin]:
To wit the veritie gif ye pleis,
Louse doun my hois, put in your neis.

I Sergeant
Thou art ane limmer, I stand foird.
Slip in thy head into this coird:
For thou had never ane meiter tippit.

Thift
Allace, this is ane fellon rippit.

Pausa.

The widdifow wairdanis tuke my geir,[257]
And left me nether hors nor meir:
Nor earthlie gude that me belangit,
Now walloway, I man be hangit.

Repent your lyfis, ye plaine oppressours,
All ye misdoars and transgressours:
Or ellis gar chuse yow gude confessours,
And mak yow forde.
For gif ye tarie in this land,
And cum under Correctiouns hand,
Your grace salbe, I understand,
Ane gude scharp coird.

Adew, my bretheren common theifis,
That helpit me in my mischeffis.
Adew Grosars, Nicksons, and Bellis,[258]
Oft have we run out-thoart the fellis.
Adew Robsonis, Ha[wi]s, and Pyilis,
That in our craft bes mony wylis.
Lytils, Trumbels, and Armestrangs,
Adew all theffis that me belangs,
Tailyeours, [Erewinis], and Elwands,
Speidie of fut and wicht of hands,
The Scottis Ewisdaill and the Graimis,
I have na tyme to tell your namis;
With King Correctioun and ye be fangit,
Beleif richt weill ye wilbe hangit.

I Sergeant
Speid hand, man, with thy clitter clatter!

Thift
For Gods saik, sir, let me mak watter.
Howbeit I have bene cattel-gredie,
It schamis to pische into an widdie.

Heir sal Thift be drawin up, or his figour.[259]

II Sergeant
Cum heir, Dissait, my companyeoun;
Saw ever ane man lyker ane loun
To hing upon ane gallows?

Dissait
This is aneuch to make me mangit,
Duill fell me that I man be hangit,
Let me speik with my fallows.

I trow wan fortune brocht me heir:
Quhat mekill Feind maid me sa speidie?
Sen it was said it is sevin yeir
Than I sould weave into ane widdie.
I leirit my maisters to be gredie,
Adew, for I se na remeid:
Luke quhat it is to be evil-deidie.

II Sergeant
Now in this halter slip thy heid.

4003 swing, gallows rope 4004 Must 4007 detect 4008 known 4011 Take down my hose, nose 4013 cord 4014 more appropriate collar 4015 terrible situation 4018 belonged to me 4020 open 4021 wrongdoers 4022 make sure you have 4023 be quick about it 4026 fate 4031 across, fells 4032 Hawes, Piles 4033 wiles/tricks 4034 Littles, Armstrongs 4035 belong to me 4037 foot, strong 4038 Scots of Ewesdale, Grahams 4039 names 4040 if, caught 4042 Hurry, babble 4043 make water (i.e. urinate) 4044 greedy for cattle 4045 piss on the gallows 4050 Sorrow befall 4052 bad luck 4054 It was predicted seven years ago 4055 That 4058 (a) criminal

257 'Those gallowsbird [i.e. villainous] wardens took my stuff'.

258 Thift goes on to list the names of many of the prominent reiving (bandit) families of the border regions: the Grocers, Elwoddes ('Elwands'), and Nixons of Liddesdale, etc.

259 Effigy.

Stand still, me think ye draw aback.

DISSAIT
Allace, maister, ye hurt my crag!

II SERGEANT
It will hurt better, I woid ane plak,
Richt now, quhen ye hing on ane knag.

DISSAIT
Adew my maisters, merchant men,
I have yow servit as ye ken,
Truelie, baith air and lait.
I say to yow for conclusioun,
I dreid ye gang to confusioun,
Fra tyme ye want Dissait.

I leirit yow merchants mony ane wyle,
Upalands wyfis for to begyle
Upon ane markit-day.
And gar them trow your stuffe was gude,
Quhen it was rottin, be the Rude,
And sweir it was nocht sway.

I was ay roundand in your ear,
And leirit yow for to ban and sweir,
Quhat your geir cost in France;
Howbeit the Devill ane word was trew.
Your craft gif King Correctioun knew,
Wald turne yow to mischance.

I leirit yow wyllis many fauld,
To mix the new wyne and the auld,
That faschioun was na follie:
To sell richt deir and by gude chaip
And mix ry meill amang the saip,
And saiffrone with oyl-dolie.[260]

Forget nocht ocker, I counsall yow,
Mair than the vicker dois the kow,
Or lords thair doubill maill.
Howbeit your elwand be too skant,[261]
Or your pound wecht thrie unces want,
Think that bot lytill faill.

Adew the greit Clan Jamesone,[262]
The blude royal of Cuper toun,
I was ay to yow trew;
Baith Andersone and Patersone,
Above them all Thome Williamsone,
My absence ye will rew.

Thome Williamsone, it is your pairt
To pray for me with all your hairt,
And think upon my warks:
How I leirit yow ane gude lessoun,
For to begyle in Edinburgh toun
The Bischop and his clarks.

Ye young merchants may cry allace,
[Lucklaw, Welandis, Carruders, Dowglace,][263]
Yon curst King ye may ban.
Had I leifit bot halfe ane yeir,
I sould have leirit yow crafts perqueir,
To begyle wyfe and man.

How may ye merchants mak debait
Fra tyme ye want your man, Dissait?
For yow I mak great cair:
Without I ryse fra deid to lyfe,
I wait weill ye will never thryfe,
Farther nor the fourth air.

Heir sal Dissait be drawin up, or else his figure.

I SERGEANT
Cum heir, Falset, and mense the gallows:
Ye man hing up amang your fallows,
For your cankart conditioun.
Monie ane trew man ye have wrangit,
Thairfoir but doubt ye salbe hangit,
But mercie or remissioun.

FALSET
Allace, man I be hangit to?
Quhat mekill Devil is this ado?
How came I to this cummer?
My gude maisters, ye crafts men,
Want ye Falset full weill, I ken,

4061 neck 4062 I bet you 4063 branch 4065 served 4066 early 4069 Once you've lost 4070 trick 4071 Country 4073 goods were 4075 so 4076 always whispering 4079 (i.e. not a word) 4081 bring you 4082 manifold 4084 trick 4085 dear, buy 4086 ryemeal, soap 4088 usury (lending at interest) 4090 rent 4092 lack three ounces 4093 a small fault 4097 Patterson 4098 Another Cupar burgess 4102 works 4107 Douglas 4108 cursed 4109 lived 4112 support yourselves 4117 Father, heir (i.e. to the fourth generation) 4118 adorn 4120 corrupt 4121 wronged 4126 trouble

260 'And saffron with olive oil': i.e. adulterate expensive goods with cheap ingredients.
261 A measuring rod, supposedly an ell (*c.*45 inches) long, but actually shorter (for giving short measures).
262 The Jamesons were a prominent family in Cupar.
263 Other, lesser Cupar burgess families.

Ye will all die for hunger

Ye men of craft may cry allace,
Quhen ye want me ye want your grace:
Thairfoir put into wryte
My lessouns that I did yow leir.
Howbeit the commons eyne ye bleir,
Count ye nocht that ane myte.

Find me ane wobster that is leill,
Or ane walker that will nocht steill,
Thair craftines I ken:
Or ane millair that hes na falt,
That will nather steill meall nor malt,
Hauld them for halie men.

At our fleschers tak ye na greife,
Thocht thay blaw leane mutton and beife,
That thay seime fat and fair:
Thay think that practick bot ane mow,
Howbeit the Devill a thing it dow,
To thame I leirit that lair.

I lairit tallyeours in everie toun,
To schaip fyve quarters in ane goun,[264]
In Angus[265] and in Fyfe.
To uplands tailyeours I gave gude leife,
To steill ane sillie stump or sleife,
Unto Kittok his wyfe.

My gude maister, Andro Fortoun,[266]
Of tailyeours that may weir the croun,
For me he will be mangit.
Tailyeour Baberage, my sone and air,
I wait for me will rudlie rair,
Fra tyme he se me hangit.

The barfit deacon, Jamie Ralfe,
Quha never yit bocht kow nor calfe,
Becaus he can nocht steall.
Willie Cadyeoch will make na plead,
Howbeit his wyfe want beife and bread,
Get he gude barmie aill.

To the brousters of Cowper toun,
I leife my braid black malesoun,
Als hartlie as I may:
To make thinne aill thay think na falt,
Of mekill burne and lytill malt,
Agane the market-day.

And thay can mak, withoutin doubt,
Ane kynde of aill thay call 'Harns-out',
Wait ye how thay mak that?
Ane curtill queine, ane laidlie lurdane,
Of strang wesche scho will tak ane jurdane,
And settis in the gyle-fat.[267]

Quha drinks of that aill, man or page,
It will gar all his harnis rage.
That jurdane I may rew:
It gart my heid rin hiddie giddie,
Sirs, God nor I die in ane widdie,
Gif this taill be nocht trew.

Speir at the sowtar Geordie Sillie,
Fra tyme that he had fild his bellie,
With this unhelthsum aill.
Than all the baxters will I ban,
That mixes bread with dust and bran,
And fyne flour with beir maill.

Adew, my maisters, wrichts and maissouns,
I have neid to leir you few lessouns:
Ye knaw my craft perqueir.
Adew, blak-smythis and lorimers,
Adew, ye crafty cordiners,
That sellis the schone over deir.

Gold-smythis, fair-weill above them all,
Remember my memoriall,
With mony ane sittill cast.

4132 writing/make them holy writ **4133** teach **4134** eyes blur (i.e. trick) **4135** a trifle **4136** weaver, honest **4137** fuller, steal **4139** miller **4142** butchers **4143** inflate **4145** practice, joke **4146** avails **4147** trick **4148** tailors **4151** highland, permission **4152** leg, sleeve **4153** For **4157** son, heir **4158** angrily roar **4160** barefoot **4161** (Is one) who, bought/paid for **4163** plea **4164** beef **4165** So long as he gets frothy ale **4166** brewers **4167** leave, curse **4170** water **4171** in preparation for **4173** 'Brains out' **4174** sluttish whore, ugly rogue **4178** boy **4179** brains **4181** turn giddy **4182** may I **4184** cobbler **4185** filled **4186** unwholesome **4187** bakers, curse **4189** barley meal **4190** carpenters, stone-masons **4193** harness-makers **4194** cordwainers (leather-workers) **4195** shoes, too dearly **4198** subtle trick

264 i.e. to cut five rather than four measures from a piece of cloth when making a gown.

265 The county across the Firth of Tay to the north of Fife.

266 Lyall suggests that Andrew Fortune may have been Lindsay's own tailor. Like the other individuals named in subsequent stanzas, his identity is unknown.

267 'She'll take a chamber-pot full of strong urine and pour it in the brewing vat.'

To mix set ye nocht by twa preinis,
Fyne ducat gold with hard gudlingis,[268]
Lyke as I leirnit yow last.

Quhen I was ludgit upaland,
The schiphirds maid with me ane band,
Richt craftelie to steill:
Than did I gif ane confirmatioun,
To all the schiphirdis of this natioun,
That they sould never be leill,

And ilk ane to reset ane uther.
I knaw fals schiphirds fyftie fidder,
War thair [cawteills] kend,
How thay mak in thair conventiouns,
On montans far fra ony touns,
[God] let them never mend.

Amang crafts-men it is ane wonder,
To find ten leill amang ane hunder.
The treuth I to yow tell.
Adew, I may na langer tarie,
I man pas to the King of Farie,
Or ellis the rycht [way] to Hell.

Heir sall he luke up to his fallows hingand.[269]

Wais me for the[e], gude Common Thift,
Was never man maid ane mair honest schift
His leifing for to win.
Thair was nocht ane in all Lidsdaill
That ky mair craftelie culd staill,
Quhair thou hings on that pin.

Sathan ressave thy saull, Dissait;
Thou was to me ane faithfull mait,
And als my father brother.[270]
Duill fell the sillie merchant men,
To mak them service weill I ken,
Thaill never get sic ane uther.

Heir sall thay festin the coard[271] *to his neck with ane dum countenaunce. Thairefter he sall say:*

Gif any man list for to be my mait,
Cum follow me, for I am at the gait.
Cum follow me, all catyfe, covetous kings,
Reavers but richt of uthers realmis and rings,
Togidder with all wrangous conquerours,
And bring with yow all publick oppressours.
With Pharao, King of Egiptians,
With him in Hell salbe your recompence.
All cruell schedders of blude innocent,
Cum follow me, or ellis rin and repent.
Prelats that hes ma benefeits nor thrie,
And will nocht teich nor preiche the veritie.
Without at God in tyme thay cry for grace,
In hiddeous Hell I sall prepair thair place.
Cum follow me, all fals corruptit judges,
With Pontius Pilat I sall prepair your ludges.
All ye officials that parts men with thair wyfis,
Cum follow me, or els gang mend your lyfis;
With all fals leiders of the Constrie law,
With wanton scribs and clarks intill ane raw,
That to the puir maks mony partiall traine,
Syne *hodie ad octo* bids them cum againe.
And ye that taks rewairds at baith the hands,
Ye sall with me be bund in Baliels bands.
Cum follow me, all curst unhappie wyfis,
That with your gudemen dayly flytis and stryfis,
And quyetlie with rybalds makes repair,
And taks na cure to make ane wrangous air.
Ye sal in Hel rewairdit be, I wein,
With Jesabell of Israell the Queene.[272]
I have ane curst unhappie wyfe my sell,
Wald God scho war befoir me into Hell:
That bismair, war scho thair, withoutin doubt,
Out of Hell the Devill scho wald ding out.
Ye maryit men evin as ye luife your lyfis,
Let never preists be hamelie with your wyfis.
My wyfe, with preists sho doith me greit onricht,

4202 lodging in the country 4203 shepherds, pact 4207 honest 4208 shelter (from the law) 4209 fifty in a group 4211 if their tricks were known 4212 how they plot together 4213 mountains 4214 repent 4215 ten honest ones in a hundred 4220 Woe is 4222 to earn his living 4223 Liddisdale 4224 cows, steal 4226 Satan, receive 4227 mate (companion) 4229 sorrow befall 4231 They'll 4232 companion 4233 (i.e. about to go) 4234 villainous 4235 Bandits without rights, kingdoms 4236 wrongful 4242 benefices than 4244 unless 4247 Pilate, lodgings 4248 from 4250 interpreters 4251 scribes, all in a row 4252 poor, tricks 4253 'a week from today' 4254 from both sides 4255 bound, bonds 4256 cursed, miserable 4257 husbands, argue 4258 quietly slip away to roguish lovers 4259 don't care, illegitimate heir 4260 rewarded, believe 4263 went 4264 whore, were 4265 she'd drive the Devil out 4267 (over-) familiar 4268 injustice

268 'Don't worry two pins about mixing ducat gold [from Italian coins] with hard [Dutch] gilder [gold]'.

269 'Look up at his fellows hanging.'

270 Perhaps 'father's brother' is intended, although incestuous relationships indicative of corruption are typical among Vices.

271 'Fasten the cord.'

272 For Jezebel, see I Kings 16:31–21:23.

And maid me nine tymes cuckald on ane nicht.
Fairweil, for I am to the widdie wend,
For quhy Falset maid never ane better end.

Heir sal he be heisit up, and not his figure, and ane Craw or an Ke salbe castin up, as it war his sault.[273]

Flatterie
Have I nocht chaipit the widdie wel?
Yea, that I have, be sweit Sanct Gall,
For I had nocht bene wrangit,
Becaus I servit, be Alhallows,
Till have bene merchellit amang my fellowis,
And heich above them hangit.

I maid far ma falts nor my maits,
I begylde all the Thrie Estaits,
With my hypocrisie.
Quhen I had on my freirs hude,
All men beleifit that I was gude.
Now judge ye gif I be.

Tak me ane rackles rubiator,
Ane theif, ane tyrane, or ane tratour,
Of everie vyce the plant.
Gif him the habite of ane freir,
The wyfis will trow withoutin weir,
He be ane verie saint.

I knaw the cowle and skaplarie,
Genners mair bait nor charitie,
Thocht thay be blak or blew.
Quhat halines is thair within,
Ane wolfe cled in ane wedders skin?
Judge ye gif this be trew.

Sen I have chaipit this firie farie,
Adew, I will na langer tarie,
To cumber yow with my clatter.
Bot I will with ane humbill spreit,
Gang serve the Hermeit of Lareit,[274]
And leir him for till flatter. [*Exit.*]

Heir sal enter Foly.

Foly
Gude day, my Lords, and als God saine.
Dois na man bid gude day againe?
Quhen fuillis ar fow then ar thay faine,
Ken ye nocht me?
How call thay me, can ye nocht tell?
Now, be Him that herryit Hell,
I wait nocht how thay call my sell,
Bot gif I lie.

Diligence
Quhat brybour is this that maks sic beiris?

Foly
The Feind ressave that mouth that speirs:
Gude man, ga play you with your feiris,
With muck upon your mow.

Diligence
Fond fuill, quhair hes thou bene sa lait?

Foly
Marie, cummand throw the Schogait.[275]
Bot thair hes bene ane great debait
Betwixt me and ane sow.

The sow cryit 'guff', and I to ga,
Throw speid of fute I gat awa,
Bot in the midst of the cawsa,
I fell into ane midding.
Scho lap upon me with ane bend,
Quha ever the middings sould amend,
God send them ane mischevous end,
For that is both Gods bidding.

As I was pudlit thair, God wait,
Bot with my club I maid debait;
Ise never cum againe that gait,
I sweir yow, be Alhallows.
I wald the officiars of the toun,
That suffers sic confusioun,

4269 in 4270 going 4272 escaped 4275 deserved 4276 dealt with along with 4278 committed, crimes than 4284 libertine/fornicator 4285 tyrant 4286 source 4290 friar's surplice 4291 Engenders more trouble than 4294 wether (castrated ram) 4296 confused mess 4298 encumber (burden), chatter 4302 God's blessing 4303 in reply 4304 drunk 4308 what I'm called myself 4310 villain, noise 4312 fellows 4313 mouth 4314 idiot fool 4316 dispute 4319 away 4320 street 4321 midden (dung heap) 4322 leaped, jump 4323 clean up 4326 puddled (i.e. in the puddle) 4327 fought 4328 I'll, way 4330 officials

273 'Hoisted up [in person], and not his image, and a crow or a jackdaw shall be thrown up, as if it were his soul.'

274 The Hermit of Loreto, a shrine near Musselburgh in East Lothian.

275 Shoestreet. The Bannatyne ms has 'Bony Gate' (a street in Cupar).

That thay war harbreit with Mahown,[276]
Or hangit on ane gallows.

Fy, fy, that sic ane fair cuntrie
Sould stand sa lang but policie:
I gif them to the Devill hartlie,
That hes the wyte.
I wald the Provost wald tak in heid,
Of yon midding to make remeid,
Quhilk pat me and the sow at feid;
Quhat may I do bot flyte?

REX
Pas on, my servant Diligence,
And bring yon fuill to our presence.

DILIGENCE
That sall be done but tarying.
Foly, ye man ga to the King.

FOLY
The King, quhat kynde of thing is that?
Is yon he with the goldin hat?

DILIGENCE
Yon same is he, cum on thy way.

FOLY
Gif ye be king, God [gif] yow gude day.
I have ane plaint to make to yow.

REX
Quhom on, Folie?

FOLIE
Marie, on ane sow.
Sir, scho hes sworne that scho sall sla me,
Or ellis byte baith my balloks fra me.
Gif ye be king, be Sanct Allan,
Ye sould do justice to ilk man.
Had I nocht keipit me with my club,
The sow had drawin me in ane dub.
I heir them say thair is cum to the toun,
Ane king callit Correctioun.
I pray yow tell me, quhilk is he?

DILIGENCE
Yon with the wings; may [thou] nocht se?

FOLY
Now wallie fall that weill fairde mow!
Sir, I pray yow correct yon sow,
Quhilk with hir teith but sword or knyfe,
Had maist have reft me of my lyfe.
Gif ye will nocht mak correctioun,
Than gif me your protectioun
Of all swyne for to be skaithles,
Betuix this toun and Innernes.

DILIGENCE
Foly, hes thou ane wyfe at hame?

FOLY
Yea, that I have, God send hir schame!
I trow be this scho is neir deid:
I left ane wyfe bindand hir heid.
To schaw hir seiknes I think schame:
Scho hes sic rumbling in hir wambe,
That all the nicht my hart overcasts,
With bocking and with thunder blasts.

DILIGENCE
Peradventure scho be with bairne.

FOLY
Allace, I trow scho be forfaine.
Scho sobbit and scho fell in sown,
And than thay rubbit hir up and doun.
Scho riftit, routit, and maid sic stends,
Scho yeild and gaid at baith the ends,
Till scho had castin ane cuppill of quarts,
Syne all turnit to ane rickill of farts.
Scho blubert, bockit, and braikit still.
Hir arsse gaid evin lyke ane wind-mill.
Scho stumblit and stutterit with sic stends,
That scho recantit at baith ends.

4335 without good government 4337 blame 4338 (it) into his head 4339 a remedy 4340 put, at feud (in conflict) 4341 complain 4350 complaint 4351 Against whom? 4352 slay 4353 testicles 4356 protected myself 4357 puddle 4359 called 4362 Good luck to that well-favoured mouth 4363 punish 4364 without 4365 almost took 4368 unharmed 4369 Between, Inverness 4372 by now 4373 woman, binding 4374 reveal, it's embarrassing 4375 stomach 4377 retching 4378 Perhaps she's pregnant 4379 dead 4380 sobbed, in (a) swoon 4381 rubbed 4382 belched, bellowed, convulsions 4383 gave in, went (i.e. excreted and vomited) 4384 vomited, jugfuls 4385 stream 4386 sobbed, retched, farted 4387 went 4388 stumbled 4389 recanted (repeated the process)

[276] 'That they were harboured/living with Mahound [a corruption of the name of the Prophet Mohammed, used as the name of a devil]'.

Sik dismell drogs fra hir scho schot,
Quhill scho maid all the fluir on flot.
Of hir hurdies scho had na hauld,
Quhill who had tumed hir monyfauld.

DILIGENCE
Better bring hir to the leitches heir.

FOLIE
Trittill trattill, scho may nocht steir!
Hir verie buttoks maks sic beir,
It skars baith foill and fillie.
Scho bocks sik bagage fra hir breist,
He wants na bubbils that sittis hir neist,[277]
And ay scho cryis 'a preist, a preist!',
With ilk a quhillie lillie.[278]

DILIGENCE
Recoverit scho nocht at the last?

FOLY
Yea, bot wit ye weil scho fartit fast.
Bot quhen scho sichis my hart is sorie.

DILIGENCE
Bot drinks scho ocht?

FOLY
Ye[a], be Sanct Marie,
Ane quart at anis it will nocht tarie,
And leif the Devill a drap:
Than sic flobbage scho layis fra hir
About the wallis, God wait sic wair,
Quhen it was drunkin I gat to skair,
The lickings of the cap.

DILIGENCE
Quhat is in that creill, I pray the[e] tell.

FOLY
Marie, I have folie hats to sell.

DILIGENCE
I pray the[e], sell me ane or tway.

FOLY
Na, tarie quhill the market-day.
I will sit doun heir, be Sanct Clune,[279]
And gif my babies thair disjune.
Cum heir gude Glaiks, my dochter deir:
Thou salbe maryit within ane yeir,
Upon ane freir of Tullilum.
Na, thou art nather deaf nor dum.
Cum hidder Stult, my sone and air,
My joy thou art, baith gude and fair.
Now sall I fend yow as I may,
Thocht ye cry lyke ane ke all day.

Heir sal the barns cry 'keck' lyk ane ke, and he sal put meat into thair mouth.

DILIGENCE
Get up, Folie, but tarying,
And speid yow haistelie to the King.
Get up! Me think the carle is dum.

FOLY
Now bum-balerie, bum, bum!

DILIGENCE
I trow the trucour lyis in ane trance.
Get up, man, with ane mirrie mischance,
Or, be Sanct Dyonis of France,[280]
Ise gar the[e] want thy wallet:
Its schame to se, man, how thow lyis.

FOLY
Wa, yit agane. Now this is thryis:
The Devill wirrie me and I ryse,
Bot I sall break thy pallet

Me think my pillok will nocht ly doun:
Hauld doun your head, ye lurdon loun!

4390 Such dismal turds shot from her 4391 flooded all the floor 4392 buttocks, control 4392 Until, emptied herself completely 4394 doctors here 4395 Nonsense, cannot move 4396 (a) commotion 4397 scares, foal 4398 retches 4403 farted 4404 sighs 4405 anything 4406 (all) at once 4407 leave, drop 4408 phlegm, vomits 4410 share 4411 cop (bottle-top) 4412 basket 4413 fools-caps 4415 until 4417 breakfast 4418 glaik (a fool) 4419 married 4420 To, friar (see I. 767) 4422 *stultus*: a fool (Latin) 4425 jackdaw 4429 fool 4430 trickster 4431 merry 4433 I'll 4435 three times (you've interrupted me) 4436 curse, if 4437 head 4438 penis

277 'Whoever sits next to her lacks no bubbles [of excrement and vomit]'.

278 Either, as Happé suggests, 'With every retch she cries out for a priest', or, following Lyall, 'she calls for priests, each one with a penis'.

279 St Cluanus, a sixth-century Irish saint.

280 St Denis, patron saint of France.

Yon[281] fair las with the sating goun
Gars yow thus bek and bend.
Take thair ane neidill for your cace![282]
Now for all the hiding of your face,
Had I yow in ane quyet place,
Ye wald nocht waine to flend.

Thay bony armis thats cled in silk,
Ar evin als wantoun as any wilk;
I wald forbeir baith bread and milk
To kis thy bony lippis.
Suppois ye luke as ye war wraith,
War ye at quyet behand ane claith,
Ye wald not stick to preife my graith,
With hobling of your hippis.

[Be God, I ken yow weill annewch:
Ye ar fane, thocht ye mak it tuich.
Think ye not on into the sewch
Besyd the quarrell hoillis?[283]
Ye wan fra me baith hoiss and schone,
And gart me mak mowis to the mone,
And ay lap on your courss abone.

Diligence
Thow mon be dung with poillis!]

Suyith, harlot, haist the[e] to the King,
And let allane thy tratilling.
Lo, heir is Folie, sir, alreadie,
Ane richt sweir swingeour, be Our Ladie.

Foly
Thou art not half sa sweir thy sell,
Quhat meins this pulpit, I pray the[e] tell.

Diligence
Our new bischops hes maid ane preiching,
Bot thou heard never sic pleasant teiching:
Yon Bischop will preich throch the coast.

Foly
Than stryk ane hag into the poast,[284]
For I hard never in all my lyfe
Ane bischop cum to preich in Fyfe.
Gif bischops to be preichours leiris,
Wallaway, quhat sall word of freiris?
Gif prelats preich in brugh and land,
The sillie freirs, I understand,
Thay will get na mair meall nor malt;
Sa I dreid freirs sall die for falt.
Sen sa is that yon nobill King,
Will mak men bischops for preiching.
Quhat say ye, sirs, hauld ye nocht best
That I gang preich amang the rest?
Quhen I have preichit on my best wayis,
Then will I sell my merchandise
To my bretherin and tender maits,
That dwels amang the Thrie Estaits.
For I have heir gude chaifery,
Till any fuill that lists to by.

Heir sall Foly hing up his hattis on the pulpet and say:

God sen I had ane Doctours hude.

Rex
Quhy Folie, wald thou mak ane preiching?

Foly
Yea, that I wald, sir, be the Rude,
But eyther flattering or fleiching.

Rex
Now, brother, let us heir his teiching,
To pas our tyme and heir him raife.

Diligence
He war far meiter for the kitching,
Amang the pottis, sa Christ me saife!
Fond Foly, sall I be thy clark,
And answeir the[e] ay with 'amen'?

4440 lass, satin gown 4441 nod 4443 despite 4444 quiet 4445 wouldn't want to run away 4446 bonny arms, clad 4447 whelk 4448 give up 4449 bonny lips 4450 angry 4451 beneath the sheets 4452 hesitate to test my manhood 4453 wriggling 4454 enough 4455 pretend to be disdainful 4456 don't you remember the ditch 4457 quarry pits 4458 won, hose, shoes 4459 make faces 4460 leap, body, above 4461 driven, poles 4463 stop babbling 4465 rogue 4466 slothful 4470 throughout, region 4474 learn to be preachers 4475 shall become 4476 town and country 4478 food, ale 4479 for lack (of food) 4484 as best I can 4486 close friends 4488 merchandise 4489 for, wants to buy 4490 If only 4493 without cajoling 4495 rave 4496 more fitting, kitchen 4497 pots

281 Foly picks out a woman in the audience as the object of his bawdy advances.

282 'Here's a fine needle for your case!' For the bawdy associations of pins and pin-cases with male and female genitals, see Heywood's *Four PP*, above.

283 Foly pretends to recall a sexual encounter between himself and his stooge/victim in the audience.

284 'Then cut a notch in the post': i.e. 'make a note of it!'.

Foly
Now, at the beginning of my wark
The Feind ressave that graceles grim.

Heir sal Folie begin his sermon, as followis.

'Stultorum numerus infinitus.'[285]
Salomon, the maist sapient king,
In Israell quhan he did ring,
Thir words in effect did write:
'The number of fuillis ar infinite.'
I think na schame, sa Christ me save
To be ane fuill amang the laife,
Howbeit ane hundreth stands heir by,
Perventure als great fuillis as I.

Stultorum etc.
I have of my genelogie,
Dwelland in everie cuntrie,
Earles, duiks, kings, and empriours,
With mony guckit conquerours:
Quhilk dois in folie perseveir,
And hes done sa this many yeir.
Sum seiks to warldlie dignities,
And sum to sensuall vanities:
Quhat vails all thir vaine honours,
Nocht being sure to leife twa houris?
Sum greidie fuill dois fill ane box,
Ane uther fuill cummis and breaks the lox,
And spends that uther fuillis hes spaird,
Quhilk never thocht on them to wairde.
Sum dois as thay sould never die,
Is nocht this folie, quhat say ye?

Sapientia huius mundi stultitia est apud Deum.[286]
Becaus thair is sa many fuillis
Rydand on hors and sum on muillis:
Heir I have b[r]ocht gude chafery,
Till ony fuill that lists to by.
And speciallie for the Thrie Estaits,
Quhair I have mony tender maits:
Quhilk causit them as ye may se,
Gang backwart throw the haill cuntrie.
Gif with my merchandise ye list to mell,
Heir I have folie hattis to sell.
Quhairfoir is this hat, wald ye ken?
Marie, for insatiabill merchant men,
Quhen God hes send them abundance
Ar nocht content with sufficiance,
Bot saillis into the stormy blastis,
In winter to get greater castis:
In mony terribill great torment,
Against the Acts of Parliament.
Sum tynis thair geir, and sum ar drounde:
With this sic merchants sould be crounde.

Diligence
Quhom to schaips thou to sell that hude?
I trow to sum great man of gude.

Foly
This hude to sell richt faine I wald,
Till him that is baith auld and cald,
Reddie till pas to Hell or Heavin,
And hes fair bairns sax or seavin,
And is of age fourscoir of yeir,
And taks ane lasse to be his peir
Quhilk is nocht fourteine yeir of age,
And joynis with hir in mariage,
Geifand hir traist that scho nocht wald
Rycht haistelie mak him cuckald.
Quha maryes beand sa neir thair dead,
Set on this hat upon his head.

Diligence
Quhat hude is that, tell me, I pray the[e]?

Foly
This is ane haly hude, I say the[e].
This hude is ordanit I the[e] assure,
For sprituall fuillis that taks in cure
The saullis of great diosies,
And regiment of great abesies,
For gredines of warldlie pelfe,
Than can nocht justlie gyde them selfe.
Uthers sauls to saife it settis them weill,

4501 face 4503 wise 4508 rest 4510 Perhaps 4512 lineage 4513 Dwelling 4515 foolish 4516 persevere 4518 worldly 4520 avails 4521 live for two hours 4522 cash-box 4523 comes 4524 what, have saved 4525 to guard them 4526 as if they should 4530 Riding 4531 merchandise 4532 buy 4535 caused 4536 whole 4537 meddle 4541 sent 4543 sail 4544 profits 4547 lose, drowned 4548 this (hat), crowned 4549 To whom do you intend 4552 old, cold 4554 six or seven 4555 80 years old 4556 lass, companion 4559 Trusting her, she won't 4561 marries, being, death 4564 holy 4565 destined (with a pun on ordination) 4567 souls, diocese 4568 running 4569 greediness, profit 4570 Who, govern 4571 suits them well (ironic)

285 'The number of fools is infinite.' A version of the Vulgate Latin text of Ecclesiastes 1:15, which is translated in the Authorized Version as 'that which is wanting cannot be numbered'.

286 'For the wisdom of this world is foolishness with God.' I Corinthians 3:19.

Syne sell thair awin saullis to the Devil.
Quha ever dois sa, this I conclude,
Upon his heid set on this hude.

Diligence
Foly, is thair ony sic men
Now in the Kirk that thou can ken?
How sall I ken them?

Foly
Na keip that clois:
Ex operibus eorum cognoscetis eos.[287]
And fuillis speik of the prelacie,
It will be hauldin for herisie.

Rex
Speik on hardlie, I gif the[e] leife.

Foly
Than my remissioun is in my sleife.
Will ye leife me to speik of kings?

Rex
Yea, hardlie, speik of all kin things.

Foly
Conforming to my first narratioun,
Ye ar all fuillis, be Coks Passioun!

Diligence
Thou leis! I trow this fuill be mangit.

Foly
Gif I lie, God nor thou be hangit:
For I have heir, I to the[e] tell,
Ane nobill cap imperiell,
Quhilk is nocht ordanit bot for doings
Of empreours, of duiks, and kings.
For princelie and imperiall fuillis,
Thay sould have luggis als lang as muillis.
The pryde of princes withoutin faill,
Gars all the warld rin top ovir taill.
To win them warldlie gloir and gude,
Thay cure nocht schedding of saikles blude.
Quhat cummer have ye had in Scotland
Be our auld enemies of Ingland?
Had nocht bene the support of France,
We had bene brocht to great mischance.
Now I heir tell the Empreour
Schaippis for till be ane conquerour,
And is muifing his ordinance
Against the nobill King of France.
Bot I knaw nocht his just querrell,
That he hes for till mak battell.[288]
All the princes of Almanie,
Spaine, Flanders and Italie,
This present yeir ar in ane flocht:
Sum sall thair wages find deir bocht.
The Paip with bombard, speir, and scheild,
Hes send his armie to the feild.
Sanct Peter, Sanct Paull, nor Sanct Androw,
Raisit never sic ane oist, I trow.
Is this fraternall charitie,
Or furious folie, quhat say ye?
Thay leird nocht this at Christis scuill;
Thairfoir, I think them verie fuillis.
I think it folie, be Gods mother,
Ilk Christian prince to ding doun uther;
Becaus that this hat sould belang them,
Gang thou and part it evin amang them.
The Prophesie, withouttin weir,
[Of] Marling[289] beis compleit this yeir,
For my gudame, the Gyre Carling,
Leirnde me the Prophesie of Marling,
Quhairof I sall schaw the sentence,
Gif ye will gif me audience.

'Flan fran resurgent, simul Hispan viribus urgent,
Dani vastabunt, Vallones valla parabunt,
Sic tibi nomen in "a" mulier cacavit in olla.
Hoc epulum comedes . . . '[290]

4577 close (secret) **4579** If, bishops **4580** interpreted as **4581** boldly, permission **4582** sleeve (i.e. kept safe) **4583** permit **4584** types of **4591** only **4594** ears, mules' **4596** upside down **4598** don't worry about, innocent **4599** strife **4601** If it hadn't been for **4604** prepares **4605** moving, power/artillery **4607** quarrel **4609** Germany **4610** The Netherlands **4611** a commotion **4612** will pay dearly for their part **4613** cannon, shield **4616** Raised, host/army **4617** brotherly **4619** learned, school **4622** strike another **4623** (to) them **4624** divide **4626** is fulfilled **4627** grandmother, Hecate (the witch) **4628** Taught **4629** reveal, text/meaning

287 'By their works ye shall know them.' A version of Matthew 7:20.

288 The war between France and the Habsburg Empire was a constant feature of these years.

289 Merlin was the supposed author of many political prophecies and pseudo-prophecies.

290 A (deliberately) somewhat garbled text which burlesques the prophetic genre. Lyall suggests that it might be deciphered to read: 'Flanders and France will rise again, likewise Spain will use her strength, / The Danes will lay [you] waste, the Welsh will yield [will prepare?] the ramparts, / Such is your name in "A", the woman crapped in a can, / You dine at this feast.'

DILIGENCE
Marie, this is ane il savorit dische!

FOLY
Sa, be this prophesie plainlie appeirs,
That mortall weirs salbe amang freirs.
Thay sall nocht knaw weill in thair closters,
To quhom thay sall say thair *Pater Nosters*.[291]
Wald thay fall to and fecht with speir and sheild,
The Feind mak cuir quhilk of them win the feild!
Now of my sermon have I maid ane end.
To Gilly-mouband[292] I yow all commend,
And I yow all beseik richt hartfullie,
Pray for the saull of gude Cacaphatie,[293]
Quhilk laitlie drownit himself into Lochleavin,
That his sweit saull may be above in Heavin.

DILIGENCE
Famous peopil, hartlie I yow requyre,
This lytill sport to tak in patience.
We traist to God, and we leif ane uther yeir,
Quhair we have failit we sall do diligence,
With mair pleasure to mak yow recompence,
Becaus we have bene sum part tedious,
With mater rude, denude of eloquence,
Likewyse, perchance, to sum men odious.

[Adew, we will mak no langar tary,
Prayand to Jesu Chryst, oure Salviour,
That He, be requeist of His moder Mary,
He do preserve this famous awditour.
Withowt that grittar materis do incure:
For your plesour we sall devyse ane sport,
Plesand till every gentill creatour,
To raise your spreitis to plesour and confort.]

Now let ilk man his way avance,
Let sum ga drink and sum ga dance.
Menstrell, blaw up ane brawll of France;
Let se quha hobbils best!
For I will rin, incontinent,
To the tavern or ever I stent,
And pray to God Omnipotent,
To send yow all gude rest.

Rex sapiens aeterne Deus geitorque benigne,
Sit tibi perpetuo gloria, laus et honor.[294]

Printed at Edinburgh be
Robert Charteris
An[no] Do[mini] MDCII [1602]

4635 evil-tasting dish 4637 wars among 4638 cloisters 4640 Should 4641 Who cares who wins 4646 recently drowned 4650 if, live 4651 failed, put things right (next time) 4654 devoid 4657 saviour 4658 at the request 4659 audience 4660 greater matters, ensure 4662 Pleasing to 4663 pleasure 4666 Minstrel, a vigorous dance 4667 hobbles (dances) 4669 finish

291 During 1551 a debate arose in St Andrews over whether the *Pater Noster* could be addressed to the saints, or should be directed at God alone.

292 A contemporary Scottish court fool.

293 Another contemporary fool, whose name is a variant of 'foul speech'.

294 'Wise King, eternal God, benign Creator, / Perpetual glory, praise and honour [be to You].'

Textual Variants

YORK, *Fall of the Angels*. 8. hydande] ms hyndande. 10. Unendande] ms Une dande. 26+. s.d.] supplied Beadle. ms partially illegible. 117–19] lineation Beadle. ms gives as one line.

YORK, *Fall of Man*. (I follow Beadle's lineation except where stated.) 87. wrothe] ms wrorthe. 145. þe] ms þei.

CHESTER, *Adam and Eve*. 33. name] Lumiansky and Mills. ms man. 329. thee] Lumiansky and Mills. ms *om.*

YORK, *Joseph's Trouble*. 18. me] ms we. 162. these] Beadle. ms there. 294. forgifnesse] ms fogifnesse.

YORK, *Nativity*. 47. For] ms Fo.

WAKEFIELD, *Second Shepherd's' Play*. 57. wyndes] ms weders.

CHESTER, *Shepherds*. 299. over though] Mills. ms in thought. 409. ye] Mills. me hee. 605. her] Mills. ms him.

YORK, *Entry into Jerusalem*. Assuming a regular stanzaic pattern (never a wholly safe proceeding where medieval drama is concerned), lines may be missing after 367 and 407, although there are no gaps in the ms. 41. go] Beadle. ms *om.* 108. þam] ms hym. 160–1] Beadle assigns these lines to VI Burgensis, the ms gives them to VII Burgensis. 211. childer] Beadle. ms *om.* 228. Qwilke] ms Qwilke full. telle] ms felle. 259+. s.h. I Burgensis] Beadle. Set against l. 261 in ms. 263+. s.h. II Burgensis] Beadle gives lines 264–5 to I Burgensis, ms gives 265 to II Burgensis, leaving ascription of 264 unclear. 280. þis] Beadle. ms *om.* 286. lyste] ms lise/life. 303. I] ms *om.* 319–20. lineation in ms uncertain. Toulmin Smith suggests break after 'bolde'. 327. so may þou spye] next to l. 325 in ms (lineation Toulmin Smith). 429. hid] Beadle. ms it. 431. wille] Toulmin Smith. ms whiche. 438. fall] ms schall. 447. Mi] M added by later hand in ms. 448. halve] Beadle. ms have. 471. rewe] Beadle. ms *om.* 500. we] ms with.

YORK, *Conspiracy*. 34. thurgh] ms Thurgh thurgh. 85. tales] ms tales tales. 117–20] these lines unassigned by original scribe. Later hands have added 'Caiphas' (later deleted) and then 'Pilatus'. 128. unjust] Toulmin Smith. ms un cust. 133. þat] ms tat. 212. bar] ms by. 233. hym] ms hm. 237. þer of] ms þof. 252–4] these lines originally given to Pilate in ms, although a later hand has deleted the ascription. Beadle suggests III Doctor. 269. faythe] Toulmin Smith. ms *om.*

YORK, *Christ Before Annas and Caiaphas*. 9] lineation Beadle. line placed next to l. 7 in ms. 76–7] lines added by John Clerke. Beadle *om.* 78–82] lineation Beadle 8 lines in ms. 86. unte] Beadle ms unclear. 180+. s.h. I Miles] Beadle. unassigned in ms. s.h. III Miles] Beadle. ms I Miles. 243+. s.h. IV Miles] Toulmin Smith. ms *om.* 257. tere] ms stere. 276. we] Beadle. ms *om.* 310–11] lines at 312–13 in ms (alteration suggested by Clerke's marginalia. 354. ye] ms he.

YORK, *Christ Before Pilate I*. Lineation follows Toulmin Smith unless otherwise stated. Uxor is also referred to as 'Domina' in speech headings. I have standardized to Uxor throughout. Similarly Filius is referred to at various points as 'Primus', 'Secundus', and 'Junior' Filius. I have followed Beadle in giving all the lines to a single 'Filius'. Companies may, of course, subdivide them to provide three small parts. 49. lorde] Toulmin Smith. ms Lorde in faith. 97. Loke, nowe] Beadle. ms 'Loke which does þou, have done nowe'. 112. here is] Beadle. ms. he þis. 208–9] lineation follows ms. 295+. s.h. Pilatus] Beadle. ms *om.* 401. warre] Toulmin Smith. ms waste. 446. dede] ms dethe. 488. of] Toulmin Smith. ms also. 526+. s.h. Milites] Beadle. ms *om.* 533–4] lineation in ms. 'to dye is done / Done upponne.'

YORK, *Christ Before Herod*. 0+. Rex] ms *om.* 11. ȝae] Beadle. ends l. 10 in ms. 12. dennes] ms denne. 14–15] lineation Toulmin Smith. Reversed in ms. 24. knawes] ms knawe. 36. is] Toulmin Smith. ms as. 47, 50, 51] lineation Beadle. ms 2 lines each. 69+. s.h.] ms adds second s.h. 'I Dux' here. 112. were] Toulmin Smith. ms *om.* 190. deffis] Beadle. ms dethis. 191. Say, whare] ms repeats 'deynes þou not'. 200. This] Toulmin Smith. ms Thus. 215. þat] ms þat þat. 255–60] lineation Toulmin Smith. 260–3] lineation Beadle. 275–6] lineation Toulmin Smith. 331+. s.h. Al Chylder] Beadle. ms *om.* 369–72] lineation Toulmin Smith. 376. lang] Beadle. ms *om.*

YORK, *Christ Before Pilate II*. 15. traytoure] ms traytoures. 24. hym] ms hyn. 32ff] some lines may be missing here. 42. my] ms my my. 49. sylke] Beadle. ms *om.* 112–15] lineation Toulmin Smith. 2 lines in ms. 137+. s.h. Pilatus] Beadle. ms *om.* 145+. s.h.s [Preco] and [I Miles] Toulmin Smith. ms *om.* 155. name] Beadle. ms named. 159. his] Beadle. ms hir. 242. banners] ms barnes. 262. cantely] ms unclear Beadle suggests 'canterly', Toulmin Smith 'Cauterly'. 274. me] Toulmin Smith. ms my. 323. man] Toulmin Smith. ms nan. 438f] an entire leaf, probably containing four complete stanzas, is missing at this point. 440. fende] Beadle. ms lende. 444. gate] Toulmin Smith. ms gatis.

YORK, *Crucifixion*. 9–12] lineation Toulmin Smith. 2 lines in ms. 100+. s.h. I Miles] Beadle. ms II Miles. 118. snelly] Beadle. ms snerly/suerly. 182+ to 183+] s.h.s added in right margin of ms. 264] Two extra lines 'In welth without end / I kepe noght elles to crave' are added in the right margin in John Clerke's hand. 273. destruis] ms destruit.

YORK, *Harrowing of Hell*. 48+. s.h. Isaiah] ms Isaac. 185. What Harlot] Toulmin Smith ms *om.* 194+. s.h. I Diabolus] Beadle. ms Diabolus. 237–8] lineation Toulmin Smith. 1 line in ms.

242. neyd thowe crave!] in John Clerk's hand, replaces 'þus þe[e] I telle' in ms. 244. knave] replaces earlier 'braide' in ms. 347. dole] Toulmin Smith. ms dolee.

YORK, *Resurrection*. 158. to] Toulmin Smith. ms *om*. 186+. s.d.] main scribe has '*Tunc* [Jesus] *resurgente*', Clerk notes '*Tunc angelus cantat Resurgens*' in margin. 216+. s.h. II Maria] Beadle. ms I Maria. 245. His] ms his his. 305+. s.h. I Miles] ms III Miles.

YORK, *Last Judgement*. 85. a gaste] Beadle. ms agaste. 98. us] Toulmin Smith. ms vis. 228f] 4 lines may be missing here. 290. payns] written over penaunce in ms. 351. it] Beadle. ms *om*.

N-TOWN, *Mary Play*. 166. ȝe] ms he. 392. Lordeis grace] Meredith. ms Lorde is as gracy. 473 come] Spector. ms *om*. 879. so be] Meredith. ms be so. 1422–5] lines inserted from the interpolated N-Town Joseph's *Trouble Play* to provide continuity (I adopt Meredith's solution to the hiatus in the narrative). 1451+. s.h. Contemplacio] ms Comtemplacio. 1455. weryn] Meredith. ms weryd.

Tretis of Miraclis Pleyinge. 3. contunuely] ms contunuiely. 4. Myraclis] ms in miraclis. 8. effectuel] ms eflectuel. 31. þat ben] Davidson. ms and ben. 32. þat] ms ȝat. 41. and debatis] ms and of debatis. 74. answeryn] ms answeryng. 94. hatidest] Davidson. ms hatistde. 119. wile] ms while. 136. ȝif it] ms ȝif it it.

Play of Sacrament. *Banns*: 23. Twenty Pounds] ms xxti li. 27. hundred pounds] ms c. li. 38. new] ms nell. 58. our] ms your. 77. fro] ms fron. *Play*: 3.Hys] ms thys. 16. Surrey] Davis. ms surgery. 20. clyffys] ms chyffys. 70. Whose] ms Whoses. 78. Gold] ms godd. 87. achatys] Davis. ms Machatys. 114. Eraclea] Davis. ms graclea. 131. aver] ms sever. 148+. s.d. Aristori] ms Acrystori. 158. thy] ms they. 189. am] ms an. 202. twenty pounds] ms xxti li. 222. eresye] Davis. ms tresye. 229. Forty pounds] ms xl. li. 232. hundred] ms C. 235. hundred pounds] ms C li. 272. nyght] Davis. ms rest. 361. their] Davis ms our. 423. renne] ms reme. 431+. s.h. Masphat] ms Malspas. 434. I se] ms unclear, Davis reads 'yfe'. 435+. s.d. hand] Davis. ms sang. 451. syttyth] ms sytthyt. 470. wot] ms wotr. 477. ayleth] Davis. ms dyleth. 482. can him] Davis. ms cam I. 489. cut] Davis. ms tut. 515. wyfes] ms wyse. 557. hermes] Davis. ms hermet. 638. *sicut*] Davis. ms *similis*. 740. gert] ms gret. 760. *sacrum*] ms *scacrum convivium*. 785. amendys] ms a menyn. 844. preachers] Davis. ms creaturys. 887. Never] ms neverer.

Wisdom. 0+ s.d. enterythe] ms enteryde. 338. whom] ms whan. 373. But] Eccles. ms for. 550+. s.d. schrewde] ms screwde. 637–52] these two stanzas reversed in the ms, but the scribe has marked them 'a' and 'b' respectively to indicate the necessary change. 912+. s.d. vii] Eccles. ms vi. 946. of Hys specyall] duplicated in Macro ms. 1053. rough] ms rought. 1094. be] ms by.

Mankind. 49. Mysse-masche, dryff-draff] ms Dryff-draff, mysse-masche. 297. yowr] Eccles. ms þer. 336ff. 'wyth a colle', etc.] the repeated phrases are indicated with 'etcetera' in the ms. 443. Cristys] ms Crastys. 478. hem] ms hym. 484. qwytt] Eccles. ms qwyll. 516–17] Eccles. lines transposed in ms. 737. solace] ms solalace. 813. ys] ms ys ys. 855. I] ms he. 880. monytorye] Eccles. ms manytorge.

Everyman. 168. mad!] Pynson: made. 504. See] P: Ase.

MEDWALL, *Fulgens and Lucres*. 169. parish] Rastell: parisish. 190. help] Nelson. selp. 197–8] lineation Nelson. 'Ye is' at start of l. 198 in R. 199. forsoth] R: forseth. 220 speke] R: spede. 248. male] Nelson. R: mase. 258. yet the] Nelson. R: Yet to the. 278. intend] R: nitend. 279. To the promocyon] Nelson. R: To repromocyon. 301. wot] Nelson. R: whet. 471+. facta] Nelson. R: fctã. 540. that that] Nelson. R: that yt. 548. gentilwoman] Boas and Reed: gentilman. 564 and 578. Upon] R: wpon. 636. undertake] R: wndertake. 1018+ and 1023+. s.h. A] Nelson. R: B. 1068. forty] R: xl. 1278. he] Nelson. R: I. 1337+. s.h. Nelson. R: begins at next line. 1428. And] R: Bnd. 1450. That] Nelson. R: This. 1491. were] Nelson. R: where. 1567–70] lineation Nelson's. R prints as two lines. 1796. Tyl] R: Tyl I. 1806+. s.d.] Nelson. 1963. understode] R: wnderstonde. 2014+. s.h.] Nelson. R:B. 2103. with due] R: with my due. 2114. thryse] Nelson. R: thyrse. 2122. starve] Nelson. R: starce. 2124. scarcenes] Nelson. R: scaecenes. 2342. for] R: far. 2351. an] R: and.

SKELTON, *Magnyfycence*. 150. It is] Rastell: It it. 216. Se at] R: So at. 384–5. grotes/otes] Ramsey. Transposed in R. 435. sande] Ramsey. R: founde. 458. wolde] Dyce. R: wolbe. 597. confusyon] Dyce. R: coufusyon. 666+. s.h. Crafty Conveyaunce] Dyce. R: Cloked Colusyon. 786+. s.h. Crafty Conveyaunce] Dyce. R: Courtly Abusyon. 988. donne] Neuss. R: Don ne. 1003. Te wyt] Happé. Teuyt. 1081–2. dogge/hogge] Dyce. Transposed in R. 1143. Latin] Happé. R: Lutin. 1173. kesteryll] Dyce. R: besteryll. 1427. kay] Dyce. bay. 1494. that]. Dyce. R: the. 1553. leyre] Dyce. R: heyre. 1598. occacyon] Ramsey. Accacyon. 1612. caudell] Dyce. R: candell. 1649. Notwithstandynge] R: Notwithstanyynge. 1670. ye] Dyce. R: he. 1673. ye] Dyce. he. 1871. who] Dyce. R: why. 1945. on] Dyce. R: of. 2174. cleve] Dyce. clere. 2320+. s.h. Myschefe] Dyce. R: Magnyfycence. 2365. by] Dyce. R: to. 2461. annexyd] Dyce. R: amexyd. 2466. Faythfull] Dyce. R: Faythfully. 2508. sekernesse] Dyce. R: sekenesse. 2552. trechery] dyce. R: rechery.

Godly Queene Hester. 422. marveyle] Pickering and Hackett: maeveyle. 595. that] P&H: yt. 653. rewle] P&H. rwele. 716. wisdome] P&H: wisdnme. 717. goodes] P&H. gooddes. 743. sufferance] P&H: sufferannce. 798. woulde] P&H: wolude. 1113. inconstante] P&H: in constante. 1122. infecteth] P&H in fecteth.

HEYWOOD, *Four PP*. 8. mynde] Axton and Happé. R: myndy.

46. great] A&H. R: graet. 55. prayers] A&H. R: prayets. 56. obtayne] A&H. R: obtaye. 75. pray] R: yray. 88+. s.h. Pardoner] R: Pardonar. 119. scoffe] R: scofte. 130. reasonyng] R: sonyng. 171. honestlye] R: hostlye. 178. chaunce] A&H. R: chaunge. 217. pedler] A&H. R: pedled. 247. wyfeys] A&H. R: wyfe ys. 259. partlettes] R: parlettes. 259. bracelettes] R: barcelettes. 275. myche] A&H. R: nyche. 287. journey] R: your ney. 331. and nat] R: nat and. 357. walke] A&H. R: wake. 399. dyscharge] R: dyscharde. 397. who] A&H. R: how. 418. s.h. Palmer] A&H. R: Pardoner. 473. To hop] A&H. R: hope. 478. sure] A&H. R: sute. 486. myght] A&H. R: myghe. 503. stynketh] R: stynktth. 518. s.h. Pardoner] A&H. R: Potycary. 526. Slepers] A&H. R: sse pers. 543. devocion] R: devacion. 556. yest] A&H. R: yet. 595. dram] A&H. R: deam. 630. these] A&H. R: thefe. 856. streyght] A&H. R: streygyt. 858. named] A&H. R: maned. 887. feendes] A&H. R: frendes. 924. requyte] A&H. R: requyre. 957. hote] R: hoth. 989. trueth]. R: ttueth. 1004. great lye] A&H. R: greatlye. 1035. one . . . one] R: i . . . i. 1053. Our] R: One. 1104. never] A&H. R: nevet. 1134 syns] A&H. R: lyns. 1140. debate] R: debace. 1153. shewe] A&H. R: shewell. 1164. departed] A&H. R: depatted. 1199. beloved] R: be loved. 1201. and] R: ond. 1219. faste] A&H. R: fastt.

HEYWOOD, *Play of the Weather*. 164. woll] A&H. R; well. 244+. s.h. Mery Reporte] R: Meryreport. 260. your] A&H. R: our. 330+. s.h. Marchaunt] R: Marchaunte. 354. encreaseth] A&H. R: evereaseth. 598. or] A&H. R: of. 672. the] A&H. R: ye. 807. fell on] R: fellon. 953+. s.d.] I follow A&H in placing the marginal direction here. 981+. s.h. Mery Report] R: Meryreport. 1001+. s.h. Boy] A&H. F: Mery report. 1049+. s.h. Mery Report] R: Meryreport. 1115. lacketh] R: lackelh. 1133. debate] R: bebate.

BALE, *Johan Baptystes Preachynge*. 478. waye] Harleian: wayes.

BALE, *Three Lawes*. 89. lawes] van der Straten: lawdes. 119. dwell] S: dewell. 121. without] S: withuot. 127. Over all] Happé. S: ourall. 129. Father] Happé. S: farhet. 211. The rofe] S: Therofe. 275. fryar] S: frxar. 305. But] S: but. 401. couth] Happé. S: coughe. 648. to] S: ro. 749. Von] S: yen. 1005. see] S: so. 1215. how] S: hom. 1416. Evangelium] S: Evangeliun. 1418. your] S: yur. 1440. fall] Happé. S: sall. 1442. wyll] Happé. S: witth. 1475. voyce] Happé. S: coyse. 1519. provoke] Happé. S: pruuoke. 1671. pryme] S: pyyme. 1768. Laye] Happé. S: Olye. 1844. swarme] S: swarne. 1846. goten] Happé. S: gooten. 1982. Teache] S; Theache.

LINDSAY, *Ane Satyre of the Thrie Estaitis. Description*. 36. 26th] xxvith. 49. armes] 'lawe' deleted. ss. skayled] ms strayld. For the policy regarding variants in the play text, see headnote. *Thrie Estaitis*. 2181. her] Charteris: his.

Glossary of Common Hard Words

i/y and c/k are treated as interchangeable

agre	agree
ake	ache
als	also, as, at
amange	among
and	and, but, if
ane	a, an, one
anis	once
are, ere, or	before, since
arraie, ar(r)ay	dress, clothes, appearance
art	are
assent(e)	consent, agree(ment)
awim	own
ay	always, ever
ay-lastand	everlasting, immortal
baith	both
bale	misery, punishment, torment
ban	curse
band(e)	rope, bonds
bayne	eager, obedient, quick(ly)
be	be, by
bedene, bedyne	at once, quickly
beestys, bestes, bestys	beasts
beir	bear, carry, suffer
bel(s)chere	good sir
belyve, bylyve	quickly
beseik, beseke	beg, beseech
beshrewe, beshrowe	curse
beste	beast
betake, beteke	command
bewscher(e)	good sir
bid	order, command
bide	wait, wait for
ble	face, appearance
blisse	happiness, heaven
blissing	blessing
blist	blessed
blithe	happy, eager
blowen	spread around
bost(e)	boast
boune	eager
bowte	bought, redeemed
brand(e)	sword
braste, brest(e)	burst
brethel	wretch
briboure	villain, wretch
broll(e)	wretch
bus	must
buske	hurry
but	without
buxom, buxum(e)	obedient
caitiff(e), castiff(e)	captive, rogue, villain, wretch
care	sorrow, trouble, worry
carp(e)	say, speak, talk
certaine	certainly, surely
certes, certis, sertis	certainly
cess(e), cese, sese	cease, end
chatt	chat, talk
cheffe	chief
chorle	churl, villain
clene	pure, spotless
clepe, cleped, clepid	call, name, named
clere	beautiful, true
combered	burdened, encumbered, wretched
comely	attractive, noble
crake	boast, chatter, talk
craker, cra(i)ker	boaster
dastard	villain, wretch
dede	deed, dead
dedis	deeds
deffe, deffis	deaf, deafens
deme	judge
ding(e)	strike, knock
doth	does
dowt(e)	doubt, fear
drede	dread, fear
duill	dole, misery, suffering
eine	eyes
eke	also, increase
ellis	else, otherwise
emange	among
emel(e)	among
encres	increase, profit
entent(e)	intent, intention
es	is
ete	eat
everichoon	everyone
fadir	father
falshed	falsehood, deception
fane, fayne, feyne	eager, happy, happily
farles, ferlies	miracles, mysteries, wonderful events
faute	fault
faythely	truly
faytour, feytour(e)	liar, deceiver
fecht	fight

fend(e) (n.)	fiend, devil
feyne	feign (see also *fane*)
flitte	go, escape
fole	fool
folye	folly
fon(e)	fool, foolish
for	as, because
for quhy	because
forsuth	true, truly
forthi	therefore
forward	agreement, arrangement, bargain
fowlere	fouler
fra, fro, froo	from
fra hand	immediately
full	completely, very
ga	go
gaff(e)	gave
gang(e)	go, walk
gar, gar(r)e,	cause, make
gart(e)	caused, made
gate	way
gaude, gawd(e)	deception, trick
gedlinges	knaves, rogues
gere, geir	business, equipment, genitals
geve	give
ghost, ghostly	spirit, spiritual
gif, gyf(f)	give, if
goes, gois	go, goes
gome	fellow, man, person
gramercy	many thanks
gras	grace
grathely	properly
greffe	grief
grete	great
greve	grieve
gud(e)	good, goods/property
gyde	guide, governor
gydit	guided, governed
gyse	fashion
had I wyst . . .	had I known . . .
haif	have
hald	hold
halsed, halsyd(e)	embraced
hame	home
han	have
hard	hard, heard
harlot(te)	villain, rogue
harrow!	help!
hat	has
hefne	heaven
heir	here, heir
hem	them
hend(e)	hand
hend(e), hendely	able, ably, courtly, elegant(ly), obedient(ly)
hens	hence
her	her, their
here	hear, here, their
herte	heart
hertis	hearts
hese	his
hider, hydir	hither, here
hight	called, named
hoaw!	hey!
horeson, huirson	whore's son (son of a bitch)
howbeid	although
hyng(e)	hang
ilkane, ilkone	each one
ilke	each, every, same
ille	ill, evil
iwis(se)	indeed
jangle	chatter, prattle
juge	judge
karle	man, fellow
keip	keep
ken(ne)	know, understand, teach
knawe	know
kynd(e)	nature
kynne	kin, family, lineage
kyth(e)	country
lang(e)	long, belong
late, lattis	let
lawis	laws
lay(e)	law, authority, jurisdiction
leasings	lies
lely	loyally
lere	learn, teach
lern(e)	learn, teach
lese	lose
lete	let, hinder
leve	dear, permission
leve	believe
liff(e)	life, live
liffis	lives
likyng	pleasure
lo, loo	look
loke, lokis	look, looks
lorel(l)	deceiver, liar, rogue
losell	villain, wretch
loun	fool, villain, wretch
loute, lowte, lowtis	bow (down to), worship
luff(e), luffis	love, loves
lurdayne, lurden	villain
ly(e)	lie (untruth)

mair	more
maistrie, maistry	authority, power, sovereignty
maistries	acts of power, feats of strength
mayne	strength, power
mech(e), moch(e)	much, great, many
mede	reward, bribe
mein(ȝ)e, me(y)nye	band, company, retinue
meirthe	happiness, joy
meke, mekely	meek, meekly
mekill, mikill	great, greatly, many, much
mende	mind
mene	understand, think
menske	honour, worship
mete	food, meat
mete	appropriate, fitting
meve	move, discuss, suggest
might(e)	strength, power
mightes	acts of power, great deeds
mo	more
moche	great, much
modir	mother
mone	moon
mone	moan, (formal) complaint
mop	fool, little thing
mot(te)	may, must
myche	great, greatly, much
na	no
nede	need
nedeful	necessary
nedelyngis	necessarily
nedis	needs
nemen, nemyn	call, tell
nere	near, nearly
neven	name, speak, tell
noght(e), nought	not, nothing, nought, evil
nother	neither
nowder, nowther	neither
noy(e)	annoy, annoyance, worry, torment
nyn	nor
or	or, ere (before)
owther	either
Paip	Pope
parde	by God! (*par Deus*)
pate	head
peare, pere	peer, equal
pearles, pereles	peerless, without equal
pece, pees, pes	peace, be quiet!
pepill, pepull	people
poure	poor, power
prate	prattle, talk idly
praty	pretty, fine, cunning
prechid	preached
prest	eager, quick, ready
preve	prove
prevely	privately, secretly
puir, pure	poor, pure
pyne	pain, punishment, torment
quha	who
quhair	where
quhat	what
quhen	when
quhill	until
quhy	why
radly	quickly
read(e), rede	advice, advise, understand
renke, renkis	man, men
rennyt	runs
richt	fully, right, very
rin	run
Rod(e), Rood(e)	(Christ's) Cross
rutter	a gallant or fashionable courtier
rynne	run
sad(de)	sensible, serious, sober
saffe	safe, save (except)
saie	say, tell
salbe	shall be
sall	shall
sall(e)	hall, room
sam(e), samm(e)	together
sawe(s)	talk, teaching, wisdom, words
scho	she
se	see
sefne	seven
seg(ge)	man, say, talk
selcouth	wonderful, miraculous, miracle, mystery
sely	simple
sen	since
sene	seen
sere	many
sertis	certainly
sese, sesse	cease, end
sethen, sithen(ce)	next, since, then
setys	seats, thrones
shent(e)	destroyed, ruined, punished
sho	she
shrew(e)	villain, wretch
sic	such
sittis	sits
skape	escape
skelpe	whip
slik(e)	such

so	if, so, so long as
soche	such
som	some
sonde	control, message, voice
sone	son, soon, sun
soo	so
sooth(e), soth(e)	true, truth
sot(te)	fool, idiot
sould	should
spede	advance, prosper
stead, ste(d)de	place
steven	voice
stretis	streets
strif(f)e	trouble
sturt	trouble, contention
suld(e)	should
sweven(e)	dream
swilke	such
syn(e)	then, afterwards, next
syng(e)	sing
syns	since
þai	they
þaime, þam(e)	them
þare, þer	these
þoght(e)	thought
take/takis tent	pay attention
tempill, tempull	temple
tene	anger, pain, torment
thaime, tham	them
than	then, than
thare, ther, their	these
the(e)	you
thee	prosper/thrive
thir	these
thoghte	thought
thurgh	through
til, tyl(le)	until, to
togedir	together
tord(e)	turd
trast(e), trist(e)	trust
travayle	labour, work
trow(e), trowe(s)	believe, think
tydyngis	news, tidings
tyte, tytte	quick, quickly
tythandis	news, tidings
wa, woo	woe
walaway, welaway	alas
warande, warrant	guarantee
wark, werk, wyrk	work, act, action, deed
warks, wyrkis	acts, deeds, good deeds
warlowe	warlock, wizard
wate, wayte	wit, understand, mind
wax(e)	grow
waxis	grows
wee, whe!	exclamation of anger or surprise: wow!
weir	war
wele, welth	well, happiness, well-being
wend(e)	go, travel
wene, weyn	believe, think
werde	world
wheder	whether
whilke	which
wight, wyte	man, woman, person
wise	fashion, manner
wisse	guide, know
wist(e)	knew, known
witte, wote	wit, mind, understand(ing)
witterly	certainly
wode, wood(e)	mad
wolde	would, wish
wone, wonne, wonys	place, building(s), dwelling(s), live(s)
woo	woe, misfortune
wote, wott(e)	know, understand
wordis	words
wrayste	twist
wroghte, wrought(e)	created, done, worked
wroth(e)	angry
wynn(e)	win, happiness
xal(le)	shall
xuld(e)	should
ȝa(h), ya	yes
ȝae	yes
ȝelde	give, yield
ȝeve	give
ȝhe	you
ȝhit(t), ȝit(t)	still, yet
ȝone	yon, those
ȝong(e)	young
ȝow	you
Y	I
ya, yae	yes
yche	each
yit, yitt(te)	still, yet
yone	those